Happy Birthday, Mom
Hope you enjoy going over some of the "old times"
Love
Dick & Marian
Aug '81

THE FORTIES

Dodg

THE FORTIES

As Reported By The New York Times

Edited by
Arleen Keylin
and
Jonathan Cohen

Introduction by
Clifton Daniel

ARNO PRESS
NEW YORK • 1980

A Note to the Reader
Original copies of *The New York Times* were not available to the publisher. This volume, therefore, was created from 35mm microfilm.

Library of Congress Cataloging in Publication Data

Main entry under title:

The Forties.
"As reported by the New York times."
1. History, Modern—20th century—Sources.
I. Keylin, Arleen. II. Cohen, Jonathan. III. New York times.
D411.F64 909.82'4 80-13897
ISBN 0-405-12214-4

Book design by Stephanie Rhodes

Manufactured in the United States of America

Contents

Introduction	vii
1940	1
1941	27
1942	51
1943	75
1944	99
1945	123
1946	151
1947	175
1948	197
1949	225

Introduction

By Clifton Daniel

Those were the days — *my* days — the 1940s.

When the decade began, the second Great War of my lifetime had just started. Poland had been ravished by the Germans and Russians. Britain and France had gallantly declared war against Germany, the monster of Middle Europe. None of us knew where the war would lead us, or where and when it would ultimately end — if ever. Europe lived in a climate of fear. Personally, I was quite sure that President Roosevelt was stealthily leading the nation into war as an ally of Britain and France against our enemies, the Nazis and Italian Fascists.

By this time, I was something of a minor-league military expert. I worked for the Associated Press in a kind of pygmy Pentagon — the War and Navy buildings on Constitution Avenue in Washington. These were a string of low-slung whitewashed office buildings that were put up as "temporary" structures in the first World War. They survived three wars — including Korea — and were finally torn down five or six years ago. A garden with young trees and an artificial lake has replaced them.

All around me in 1940 there was evidence of the coming involvement of the United States and her jaunty President in the war against the Axis, then consisting of Germany and Italy. I was in Mr. Roosevelt's office, directly in front of his desk, when he announced that the United States was going to build 50,000 war planes. Fifty thousand! Unheard of! Incredible! (We subsequently built 295,957, between July 1940 and Aug. 31, 1945.)

I was in the Navy Department on that afternoon when it was disclosed that the United States was giving Britain 50 "overage" destroyers for convoy duty, in exchange for certain military bases scattered around the British Empire. The closest one to our shores was Bermuda, and it still is in operation. I watched the gradual evolution of the much more significant American policy of Lend-Lease. This was a subtle way to give the bankrupt British what they needed without requiring them to lay cash on the barrelhead, cash that they didn't have.

Finally, I went off to see the war up close. After watching the first draft number — one two eight — drawn from a glass barrel on the stage of the Labor Department auditorium in Washington, I went off to war as a correspondent, one year to the day before Pearl Harbor. I had to get my draft board's permission to leave the country. Permission was quickly granted; apparently the board thought that anybody who was fool enough to go to war without being drafted should be allowed to leave the country. Every six months, as required by law, I reported to the draft board. They never called me back to join the potato-peeling brigade.

I had what the British called "a good war." I never lacked for food, shelter, drink or the company of a good woman. Of course, I was scared half to death from time to time, but that didn't count if you were not actually killed or wounded. I was neither. I have no medals for valor, no Purple Hearts for wounds. I have my hide intact, and that is worth more to me than any bits of ribbon and brass. I *think* I would die for my country, but I'm damned glad I was not called upon to do so. I was repeatedly in range of German bombers, flying bombs (V1s) and supersonic missiles (V2s). I remember taking refuge in a Fleet Street doorway while shrapnel from the British anti-aircraft guns rattled and clanged on the sidewalk outside. But I was never hit. My nearest miss, so to speak, was when a flying bomb landed in the garden of a house in Crydon 30 minutes after I had finished lunch there.

Nineteen-forty, the year I joined up, was a semi-climactic one for both sides: The Germans overran the Low Countries, Norway and Denmark. France ignominiously fell. The British were driven off the Continent at Dunkirk, and yet won the hearts of the world by improvising the most gallant rescue-by-sea in the annals of history. Winston Churchill, the young prodigy of World War I, who lived in the political wilderness between the wars, was called back to be Prime Minister. That may have been the single most decisive political act of the war. Everybody familiarly called him "Winston," and no one in range of his voice could fail to be moved by his intensity and eloquence and the sheer magic of his rhetoric, slurred by a slight speech defect.

Cheered on by Winston and the staunch nation he led, the Royal Air Force repulsed the vaunted Luftwaffe in the Battle of Britain. The real hero of this victory was a neat little fighter plane called the Spitfire. An inspired name, and an inspired plane — not to forget inspired pilots. They were not all British; they included Poles and French, Belgians and Norwegians, and others who had smuggled themselves out of German-occupied Europe to be with their governments-in-exile in London.

Claridge's Hotel became the palace away from home for the exiled royalties of the Continent. When Queen Wilhelmina of the Netherlands was in residence during the Blitz, she would regally descend the main staircase into the lobby, wearing a warm, sensible bathrobe, carrying a blanket and wearing her hair in two braids. She made her way to the elevator that carried her to the basement — Claridge's bomb shelter.

Nineteen forty-one really signalled the end of the German military adventure in Europe, although some of us did not know it as well as the German General Staff: Hitler ordered an invasion of the Soviet Union. It had a lightning effect (due partly to Stalin's wishful belief that it was not coming). It ultimately was a colossal failure — like Napoleon's. While the titanic struggle for Russia was going on, the Japanese obligingly made up Americans' minds about entering the war: They bombed Pearl Harbor, the main American Naval base in the Pacific.

Bill King and I — two American correspondents — heard about it in the American Bar of the Savoy Hotel in London. We went around the Savoy Grill, once frequented by such notables as the Prince of Wales, Winston Churchill, Bea Lillie, Vivien Leigh and Laurence Olivier. We spread the news. There were cheers and toasts, and general delight: The Americans were in the war, and on their side!

The Forties were an age of giants, good and evil: Churchill and Hitler, Roosevelt and Stalin, and the tall, aloof, unsmiling General de Gaulle, symbol of the French Resistance. The Forties also were a climactic decade: So much history was made in such a short time, and so many political and military hostages were given to the future. In the pages that follow this introduction, you will recall, as recounted in *The New York Times,* the events of the Forties that made them so memorable.

Lou Gehrig, the handsome, gallant first baseman of the New York Yankees, died in 1941. In the midst of a great war, when millions were being slaughtered, his death might have been deemed a minor tragedy, but millions of Americans nevertheless mourned.

In 1942, the tide of victory rolled on for the Japanese in the Pacific, but the Germans for the first time were stopped dead in their tracks in Russia. A whole German army surrendered at Stalingrad. There is a memorable photograph of the dark forms of the dejected Germans trudging through the snow, on their way to surrender and Soviet prison camps. In the Libyan desert, on the doorstep of Egypt, the "Desert Fox," Field Marshal Erwin Rommel of Germany, was routed in the Battle of El Alamein by the man whom the world came to know as "Monty" — later Field Marshal Viscount Montgomery of Alamein. (His boss back at headquarters in Cairo, whom many considered a soldier superior to "Monty," received a postwar title one notch higher than his. He became Field Marshal Earl Alexander of Tunis, a handsome bloke, as the British would say.)

The tide had turned, and in America that year the most popular song was not a war song, but a sentimental ballad — Irving Berlin's *White Christmas.* Later on, at a party in London, Mr. Berlin, by request, sat down to play it. I was standing by, and I began to sing — "I'm dreaming of a white Christmas." Mr. Berlin looked up expectantly; he recognized a fellow artist. Then, disillusionment: The range of my voice was no greater than his range on the piano (he composed and played only in the key of F).

In 1943, history rushed ahead: Supplies reached Leningrad, which the Germans besieged for more than three years. (Harrison E. Salisbury wrote a heart-rending account of the siege, called *The 900 Days.* Richard Nixon later used a sentimental episode from the siege as part of a speech on Soviet television.) The Allies began to hold conferences on how the war could be brought to an end, and how the spoils of war — mainly territory — should be divided. In 1943 there were international conferences in Casablanca, Cairo and Teheran.

Meanwhile, life went on light-heartedly elsewhere. The first great musical comedy of the Broadway stage — an American approximation of light opera — opened in New York. With lyrics by Oscar Hammerstein, music by Richard Rodgers, and choreography by Agnes de Mille, it was an enchanted transformation of a folk drama by Lynn Riggs called *Green Grow the Lilacs.* Its new Broadway name was *Oklahoma,* and somewhere in the world today it is still playing. When I was in London in 1979, I saw it advertised at a theatre in the Strand.

When I was at home on leave in 1943, it was practically impossible to buy tickets for *Oklahoma.* I managed to get one — a single in the first few rows in the orchestra — for a Saturday matinee. When I sat down, I found myself directly behind Gloria Swanson, whom I happened to have met at a party the evening before. At the first intermission, I leaned over and re-introduced myself to Miss Swanson, who, in turn, introduced me to her companion for the matinee, her mother. Somehow, it had never occurred to me that movie stars had mothers, or took them to Saturday matinees.

Back in Europe in 1944, now a *New York Times* correspondent, I found the war winding down to its predictable end. In the Battle of the Bulge, the Germans made their last, desperate counter-plunge into the Allied lines in the Ardennes, and were finally brought to a halt just short of Liege. At Bastogne, in Belgium, General Anthony C. McAuliffe issued his famous rude rebuff to a German demand that he surrender. I have often been told that "Nuts" was not exactly the word the General used, but I have never known what he actually said. Whatever the word, the meaning was clear — no surrender.

The end was near. Benito Mussolini, the Italian dictator, who foolishly allied himself with Hitler, was grotesquely executed by Italian partisans and left hanging upside down at a gasoline filling station in Northern Italy. His mistress, Clara Petacci, was killed with him.

Nineteen forty-five was the climactic year: The Russians plowed into Germany. Hitler committed suicide. The war in Europe was over. The delirium in London, where I was then living, was unmatched in modern history. We poured into the streets, stopped traffic, danced and sang, and embraced each other. We turned on the lights, blacked out through the entire war, and rejoiced in our deliverance.

Before all that happened, on a quiet night in the Savoy Hotel, where *The New York Times* had its office and living quarters, a two-line urgent message from the Associated Press was laid in front of me. It said something to this effect: "President Roosevelt died today of a massive stroke in Warm Springs, Ga." I was the man in charge in London. Kathleen McLaughlin, one of the correspondents in the bureau, was standing nearby. She had recently come from Washington, and she was in a state of shock. "My God!" she said. "Harry Truman is President." It was just before 11 o'clock, the hour of the last BBC news broadcast of the evening. I told Kathleen to hurry down to the Savoy parlor, where the 11 o'clock news was turned on every night, and to report on the reaction in that tiny segment of the British public. She came back, and said women were weeping in the elevator going upstairs. (Next day, they wept in Moscow, too.) We reported what we had seen and heard and what the British government had said, and went wearily and sadly to bed. We didn't think much about President Truman, whom only Kathleen knew. We only hoped that, despite his lack of preparation, he was up to his job. As it turned out, he was.

Until he became President, nobody had ventured to tell the Vice President of the existence of the atomic bomb. Yet, within weeks, he ordered the first bomb dropped on Hiroshima, and the second on Nagasaki. These were, without doubt, among the most momentous events in human history. President Truman made the Hiroshima decision, supported by all his major political, scientific and military advisers, and then went quickly and soundly to sleep. He was not one, having made up his mind, to waste time wrestling with his conscience.

Japan surrendered, General MacArthur became the Emperor *de facto,* and the United Nations came into existence as the new and universal monitor of good behavior among the nations (the gibes and cynical laughter came later). Already in 1946, Winston Churchill, in a speech at Westminster College in Fulton, Missouri, had offered and introduced into the diplomatic lexicon, his graphic description of the "Iron Curtain" that had descended between East and West.

About this time, I left my room in the King David Hotel in Jerusalem one morning, and next door Brigadier Clayton of the British Intelligence Service in Cairo was locking his door — Brigadier

Clayton, whose years of service went back to the days of Lawrence of Arabia. Jokingly, I said, "If you are sleeping in the room next to mine, I'm going to clear out." And I did. The next evening, as I was enjoying a drink in the garden bar of Shepheard's Hotel in Cairo, where Napoleon's officers once took their ease, I was told that the King David had been blown up by the Irgun Zvai Leumi, the Jewish terrorist organization, commanded at that time by Menachem Begin, now Prime Minister of Israel. If I had been there, it would have been about the time when I was making my way to the bar for a drink before lunch. A friend of mine, Dick Mowrer, who *was* on his way to the bar, was blown out the hotel front door, with the manager. They both survived. Ninety-two people did not. They included Arab and Jewish civilians who were there on routine business with the British authorities, who had offices in a wing of the hotel. One of those who survived was Martin Charteris, a British military intelligence officer, who is now Lord Martin Charteris of Amisfield, formerly private secretary to the Queen of England.

In 1947, the cataclysms continued: India and Pakistan split apart and became independent members of the British Commonwealth. In the blood-thirsty, fratricidal process, millions were killed. The Truman Doctrine was proclaimed. It said, in effect, that the United States would not stand for a Communist conquest of Turkey and Greece. And the social transformation of the United States took a giant step forward: Jackie Robinson became the first black baseball player hired by a white major league team — the Brooklyn Dodgers.

In 1948, there was again news all over the map: The Communists took over Czechoslovakia. The State of Israel was proclaimed. Mahatma Gandhi was assassinated. The United States thwarted the Soviet blockade of Berlin with a massive airlift of food and fuel. The Marshall Plan, for the economic revival of Europe, was put into effect, with the Russians and their vassals choosing not to participate. But the really big news of the year for America was symbolized by a single photograph. It showed President Truman on the rear platform of his train, with a huge grin on his face, holding aloft a copy of the *Chicago Daily Tribune* with the front page headline that said, "Dewey Defeats Truman." Of course, Dewey didn't, and the *Tribune* went around for years with egg on its face. Lately, the *Tribune,* under new leadership, has been graciously able to laugh at itself.

The decade ended ominously with the creation of the North Atlantic Treaty Organization to confront Soviet military power in Europe; the explosion of the USSR's first atomic bomb, and the formation of the People's Republic of China — Red China. Six years later I went to Poland to witness the signing of the Warsaw Pact, Eastern Europe's counterweight to NATO, and 30 years later, I was warmly received in Peking, along with other representatives of the American Foreign Policy Association, as a guest of the People's Institute of Foreign Affairs.

Times do change, as this fascinating book will dramatically show you. It records history, not in retrospect, but as it was written when it happened.

1940

"All the News That's Fit to Print."

The New York Times.

LATE CITY EDITION
POSTSCRIPT
Cloudy, preceded by rain today, slightly colder tonight.
Temperatures Yesterday—Max., 51; Min., 44

VOL. LXXXIX...No. 30,026. Entered as Second-Class Matter, Postoffice, New York, N. Y. NEW YORK, TUESDAY, APRIL 9, 1940. P THREE CENTS NEW YORK CITY and Vicinity | FOUR CENTS Elsewhere Except in 7th and 8th Postal Zones.

GERMANS OCCUPY DENMARK, ATTACK OSLO; NORWAY THEN JOINS WAR AGAINST HITLER; CAPITAL IS REPORTED BOMBED FROM AIR

HOUSE TO CONSIDER WAGE ACT CHANGES EARLY NEXT WEEK

Leaders in Surprise Moves Also Slate Bill for Court Review of Agency Rulings

LABOR LAW ACTION LIKELY

Proponents of Amendments Expect Drive to Dispose of All Labor Legislation

House consideration next week was slated for the bill to amend the Wages and Hours Act and for the Logan-Walter bill to provide for a court review of decisions by governmental agencies. [Page 1.]

A refusal by the Supreme Court to review the Labor Board's order in the Republic Steel case sustained the reinstatement of 5,000 C. I. O. strikers with $5,000,000 back pay. [Page 20.]

The Socialist party convention, at Washington, stated in a resolution that "the interests of American working men and women will best be served by the making of an immediate peace between the C. I. O. and A. F. L." [Page 1.]

Colonel Harrington, WPA Administrator, will be questioned Thursday by the House Appropriations Subcommittee on evidence gathered by its investigators bearing on the 1941 relief outlay. [Page 20.]

The NLRB refused to relieve Mrs. Elinore M. Herrick of further responsibility in connection with the election of employes of the Consolidated Edison Company of New York after a charge of collusion with the company. [Page 20.]

Two Revision Bills Slated

By HENRY N. DORRIS

Special to THE NEW YORK TIMES.

WASHINGTON, April 8—House leaders decided today on consideration early next week of the Barden bill to amend the Wages and Hours Act, a decision which occasioned surprise in labor quarters since it had been assumed this measure would follow the Smith or Norton amendments to the National Labor Relations Act.

But this was not the only surprise, because the tentative calendar for next week also contained a place for the Logan-Walter bill providing court review of any decision of a governmental agency which has the force of law.

When these two measures are out of the way, proponents of amendments to the Wagner Act expect to win consideration of their measures. Just how they will manage this was not revealed, but it was said by one member that the procedure was for a "Bang! Bang! Bang!" program that would wipe the House calendar clean of labor legislation that has "plagued" it for more than a year.

The Barden bill has been pending since last August, when a rule was granted for its consideration. It was never considered, however, because of the "compromise" by which the lending-spending and United States Housing Authority bills—desired by the Administration —were taken up. Both of these failed to obtain consideration, but they served to crowd out the Barden bill, which primarily aims at a redefinition of the "area of production" provision of the Wages and Hours Act.

Would Remove "Ambiguities"

The amendment proposed by Representative Barden of North Carolina, a member of the House Labor Committee, proposes to remove the "ambiguities" of the "area of production" clause and the ruling subsequently made on it by the former Wages and Hours Administrator, Elmer F. Andrews.

Under that ruling processing plants located within ten miles of the area where agricultural products are grown or harvested are exempt from the provisions which require them to pay a minimum wage of thirty cents an hour or work their employes not to exceed forty-two hours per week without overtime pay of time and a half. The Barden amendment proposes

Continued on Page Twenty

The International Situation

War caught up two more countries in its clutches today as the Germans invaded Denmark and attacked Norway.

In the early morning Nazi troops crossed the southern border of Denmark, landed on Danish soil from warships and occupied the Danish capital, Copenhagen—all apparently without resistance. [Page 1.]

Almost at the same time a diplomatic dispatch to Washington announced that Norway was at war with Germany. [Page 1.] This development followed an attempt by German warships—more than 100 of which had been sighted last night moving northward in the Kattegat—to force an entry, with aerial support, into Oslo Fjord. At latest reports German troops were debarking on the Norwegian coast and had entered Narvik, Bergen and Trondheim, while the Norwegians were said to have moved their capital, which was reported bombed.

Berlin explained it was taking Denmark and Norway under its "protection" to prevent any hostile attack upon them. [Page 4.]

There had been at least one suggestion yesterday of German troop movements in Scandinavia. A Nazi transport had been torpedoed off Southern Norway with a loss of 150 out of some 300 uniformed men aboard. In the same neighborhood a large German tanker was sent to the bottom. [Page 1.]

The mining of Norwegian waters had taken Norway completely by surprise and eight German freighters were apparently in the same predicament, as they were trapped in those waters and unable to get home. With British warships patrolling the mine fields the ore traffic at Narvik was halted and it seemed likely that Swedish iron shipments would be halved. [Page 3.] Norway protested to both Britain and France against the mining, terming it "an open breach of international law" and demanding that the mines be removed. [Page 1.] London had expected the protest and discounted it. But the British were believed to be ready to go to Norway's aid against the Germans. [Page 2.]

With a loophole in the blockade apparently plugged in Scandinavia the British gave some of their attention to the Balkans; their envoys to the countries of that region began their conferences. [Page 9.] At the same time Southeastern Europe was startled by Rumania's detention of a fleet of British barges carrying dynamite, which, according to the Germans, was to have been used for blocking the Danube. British quarters insisted the explosives were to have been used only for destroying river craft in the event of a German invasion of Rumania. [Page 1.]

ROOSEVELT EFFIGY 'FRONT' GUN TARGET

Healy Also Swears Cassidy Wanted 12 in Congress Shot in Capital as Gesture

Denis A. Healy, star prosecution witness in the trial of seventeen men indicted for conspiring to overthrow the United States Government, testified yesterday in the Brooklyn Federal Court that some of the defendants had used a likeness of President Roosevelt's head as a target during rifle practice.

He swore that John F. Cassidy, a defendant who was prominent in the Christian Front, had favored "going to Washington and shooting twelve Congressmen to show that the Christian Front means business," and he testified that William Gerald Bishop, another defendant, wanted to place Major General Van Horn Mosely, U. S. A. retired, at the head of a dictatorship after overthrowing the present government.

Telling of how members of the group practiced making crude bombs out of empty beer cans, Healy said that they had discussed committing acts of sabotage here if the United States entered the war. He declared that Bishop had boasted to him of knowing who was responsible for an explosion he said had occurred on an oil tanker in the lower bay a few days earlier.

Cross-Examination Begun

Healy finished his direct testimony at 2:30 P. M. yesterday after having been on the witness stand for five hours, beginning Friday afternoon. He began at once a hammering cross-examination at the hands of defense counsel, which they estimated would last for at least two full court days in their effort to discredit his story of having posed as one of the plotters, meanwhile keeping the Federal Bureau of Investigation informed of every development.

He was forced to admit that he had lied on numerous occasions, that he had pretended to be anti-Semitic in order to "carry out my role"; that he had once approached Bishop for aid in smuggling a relative into this country from Canada, and that he had once been convicted of street fighting, for which he received a suspended sentence.

Conceding that he had testified for the government in a previous case, Healy denied that he was a "professional witness," as was charged by former Magistrate Leo J. Healy, counsel for eleven of the defendants. He said the government had arranged a leave of absence for him from the New York Central Railroad, and was paying him the same salary while he was

Continued on Page Sixteen

BRITISH EXPLOSIVES HELD BY RUMANIANS

Fleet of Barges Detained at Danube Port—Nazis Charge Plot to Block River

By The Associated Press.

BUCHAREST, Rumania, April 8—Detention of a fleet of dynamite-laden British barges, said by Germans to be designed to blow up a narrow Danube gateway and block a German supply line, today electrified Southeastern Europe with the fear war soon might spread to this quarter of the world.

Rumanian police, acting on a tip said to have been supplied by the pro-Nazi Iron Guard, halted the fleet near Giurgiu, Danube River port whence Germany ships much-needed Rumanian oil supplies. Aboard were tons of dynamite.

Germans alleged the British planned to blockade the spot in the Danube known as the Iron Gate by sinking the barges and wrecking the narrow channel where the river cuts through the Carpathian barrier between high cliffs. The Iron Gate is 280 miles up river from Giurgiu.

Official British quarters, acknowledging the barges were loaded with explosives, insisted they were to be used only for destroying Allied river craft in case of a German invasion of Rumania.

The only official British statement on the matter was a communiqué saying merely that Rumanian authorities had seized two cases of firearms which a British barge captain had neglected to declare in passing customs.

Troops Guard Gateway

The British aim was reported in Germany to be the blocking of the Iron Gate with sunken barges and blasting of the narrow artificial channel through which all river shipping must pass.

Two hundred Rumanian and Yugoslav soldiers armed with machine guns tonight were guarding the gateway where the Danube forms the boundary between Rumania and Yugoslavia. Giurgiu was turned into a military zone by the Rumanian Army, which banned all entries without special permits.

The German version of the seizure, said to have taken place Saturday, reported more than 100 British Army, Navy and Air Force men, who were to have participated in the coup, had been arrested.

Both the Rumanian Foreign Office and British quarters, however, insisted there was no basis to the German reports that Britons had been seized aboard the barges, and official London sources declined to

Continued on Page Eight

REICH SHIP IS SUNK

150 Lost Off Transport Torpedoed by British Off South Norway

ALL MEN IN UNIFORM

Large Nazi Tanker Also Sunk by Allies, but Crew Is Rescued

Special Cable to THE NEW YORK TIMES.

OSLO, Norway, April 8—A British submarine torpedoed and sank the German troop ship Rio de Janeiro today off Lillesand, on the south coast of Norway. At least 150 German soldiers are believed to have perished.

It is reported here that the German transport, formerly a freighter on the South American run, had at least 300 men aboard and that fewer than 150 are accounted for. The ship, of 5,261 tons, was out of Hamburg and was classified here as a transport because all the men aboard were in uniform.

Another large German vessel, the tanker Posidonia, was also reported torpedoed today off the south Norwegian coast, but without loss of life.

[Lloyd's Register of Shipping does not list a German tanker Posidonia. The Associated Press, in recording the report of still a third sinking, that of the German tanker Kreta, indicated that there might be some confusion over the Posidonia's case, since the Kreta, apparently to conceal her identity, had sent out the call letters of the Posidonia. Other reports said that the Posidonia used the Kreta's signals.]

The report of the torpedoing of the Rio de Janeiro received here states that the British submarine intercepted the transport off the Norwegian coast, hailed her and fired a warning shot across her bows. This was disregarded and the troopship altered her course, speeding toward land or territorial waters. The submarine then fired a torpedo.

Some Jump Overboard

With the explosion some of the Germans immediately jumped overboard. A Norwegian fishing vessel was near by and went to the rescue, taking these men out of the water.

As the transport appeared to be settling, the submarine fired a second torpedo, with terrific result. An iron bar from the ship was hurled 150 feet and struck the rescuing fishing vessel, killing three of the Germans who had been taken aboard.

The fishing vessel continued its work of rescue and was aided by other fishing craft that hurried out when an alarm was sounded along the coast. These ships took a total

Continued on Page Five

NAZIS IN NORWAY

Troops Debark at Ports —Government Leaves Oslo for Hamar

NARVIK IS OCCUPIED

Air Attacks on Capital Reported—Civilians Are to Be Evacuated

Sweden Is Mobilizing

By The United Press.

STOCKHOLM, Sweden, April 9—The Swedish radio announced today that the government had ordered general mobilization.

Wireless to THE NEW YORK TIMES.

LONDON, Tuesday, April 9—The Paris correspondent of Reuters, British news agency, reported this morning that the Oslo radio had announced that German troops had debarked in Norwegian ports at 3 A. M.

[Mrs. J. Borden Harriman, United States Minister to Norway, notified the State Department early this morning that she had been informed by the Foreign Minister that Norway considered herself at war with Germany.

[Mrs. Harriman also reported that at 5:30 A. M. Norwegian shore batteries were still engaged in battle with four invading German warships that were trying to force entry into Oslo Fjord.]

It was also announced that the Norwegian Government had left Oslo for Hamar, in Central Norway.

Reuters further reported that the Germans had occupied the cities of Bergen and Trondheim.

[The Oslo radio announced this morning that the Norwegian Government had ordered general mobilization after an all night session of the Cabinet, The Associated Press reported.]

Reuters also reported from Paris that the Oslo radio announced this morning that the Germans had occupied Narvik.

The Norwegian legation here issued the following communiqué this morning:

"The German Minister in Oslo saw the Norwegian Foreign Secretary at 4:30 o'clock this morning and demanded that Norway should be handed over to the German administration. If this was not done all resistance would be defeated. This demand was refused and hostilities have started."

LONDON, Tuesday, April 9 (AP) —A Reuters, British news agency,

Continued on Page Two

Canadian Premier to See Roosevelt Soon, Stopping Off En Route South for a Vacation

By FREDERICK T. BIRCHALL

By Telephone to THE NEW YORK TIMES.

OTTAWA, April 8—Prime Minister W. L. Mackenzie King will leave Ottawa in a few days for a short holiday in the South of the United States. On his way through Washington he will pay a visit to President Roosevelt at the White House.

This will be Mr. Mackenzie King's first visit to Washington since war was declared. There are several questions he would like to take up with Mr. Roosevelt. There are doubtless also matters the President will be glad to discuss with the Canadian Prime Minister.

While there is no information here as to the precise subjects that may figure in the conversation, some of those ripe for discussion are well known. Among these are the progress of the St. Lawrence Waterway project, continuance of the trade agreements renewed last year and the extent to which the United States can aid Canada's war effort.

As to the St. Lawrence project, it is known that both administrations are anxious to have the treaty signed with as little delay as possible so that it may be submitted to Congress in time for consideration before adjournment. Since the project again came up opposition to it has developed in both countries. It will not have easy sailing.

Among matters even more pressing are the exemption of Americans resident in Canada from the conditions affecting the ownership of foreign currency and securities and the status of American fliers who desire to come here and enlist under the Air Training Plan and for overseas service.

It has been strongly urged that Canada modify for these the oath of allegiance now required from all who join her forces, which does not automatically give them Canadian citizenship, while causing them to lose their own.

Another point of interest is Canada's desire to obtain from the United States more airplanes for use in the initial stages of the commonwealth air training plan. The present prospect is that there will be a shortage of planes until Canadian plants, now in receipt of about $40,000,000 worth of orders, can reach the stage of advanced production.

Any or all of these topics may be profitably discussed between the

Continued on Page Five

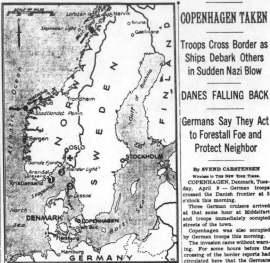

NEW THEATRE OF WAR IS OPENED

German troops invaded Denmark at 5 A. M. today. A few hours previously German warships attempted to force an entry into Oslo Fjord (cross). This action, which brought Norway into the war against the Reich, followed the sighting last night of a German armada steaming northward off Lessoe (3). Near Lillesand (1) a German troop transport was torpedoed by a British submarine and a U-boat was rumored to have been sunk. Off Faerder Light (2) one and perhaps two German tankers were sent down. The Allied mine fields off Norway are indicated by arrows.

NORWAY DECLARES WAR ON GERMANY

Washington Notified of Action by U. S. Minister at Oslo—Warships Sent There

Special to THE NEW YORK TIMES.

WASHINGTON, Tuesday, April 9—Norway is at war with Germany. This was the word received soon after 1 o'clock this morning by the State Department from Mrs. J. Borden Harriman, the American Minister at Oslo.

The startling information was received less than two hours after equally disturbing intelligence had been received of the German occupation of Denmark.

[President Roosevelt, at Hyde Park, kept in close touch with the State Department and his special train was held ready for a quick return to Washington, The United Press reported.]

The State Department announced the state of war in the following communique:

"The American Minister at Oslo, Mrs. J. Borden Harriman, telegraphed the Department tonight that the Foreign Minister had informed her that the Norwegians had fired on four German warships coming up Oslo Fjord and that Norway was at war with Germany.

In response to a request by the British Minister to Norway the American Legation at Oslo has been authorized to take over British interests in Norway in case he is forced to leave."

Envoy's Request Explained

State Department officials, in answer to queries regarding the apparently ambiguous last paragraph of Mrs. Harriman's cable, said that there could be no doubt that Norway was at war against Germany. They pointed out that the Norwegians were firing on German warships and the British envoy was considering the possibility that he might have to evacuate, although he was not certain he would need to.

[The United Press said Mrs. Harriman reported that she had taken charge of the British and French Legations.]

It was reported on usually good authority that American warships in European waters had been ordered to proceed northward so they could take part in the evacuation of American citizens in Denmark,

Continued on Page Four

ALLIED MINES BRING A PROTEST BY OSLO

Breach of International Law Charged by Koht—Sweden Takes Defense Measures

By The Associated Press.

OSLO, Norway, April 8—Foreign Minister Halvdan Koht told Parliament today that Norway had protested to Paris and London against the mining of her waters at dawn, a sudden move by which the Allies hope to cut off Germany's Swedish ore shipments through Norway's western coastal waters.

In a public statement Mr. Koht charged the Allies with an "open breach of international law" and demanded that the mines "be removed at once and that the guard by foreign warships cease." Britain was patrolling Norway's waters near the new mine fields, stating such action would be for forty-eight hours to warn away neutral vessels.

In all Scandinavia statesmen, in realization that the dreaded day had arrived bringing the European war to the north, gathered to discuss the cloudy future and await a feared retaliation from Germany.

Leaders of the Norwegian Parliament, which was called into special session, said they were behind the government's action in the crisis. A Cabinet meeting was held in Oslo, which military and naval leaders attended.

Political Leaders Meet

Leaders of all of Denmark's political parties met in Copenhagen, and in Stockholm Swedish leaders watched gravely. The Swedish Foreign Office announced there had been no violation of Swedish waters, but officials admittedly were worried.

The Oslo newspaper Arbejdarbladet, a government organ, said that "the situation is particularly grave for our country, but in such times we must keep our heads cool."

"Any tendency toward nervousness or panic would only make it worse," the paper said. "Norway naturally will protest in a most emphatic way against any closing of her waters and demand respect for international laws. But it is a ques-

Continued on Page Four

Dispatches from Europe and the Far East are subject to censorship at the source.

COPENHAGEN TAKEN

Troops Cross Border as Ships Debark Others in Sudden Nazi Blow

DANES FALLING BACK

Germans Say They Act to Forestall Foe and Protect Neighbor

By SVEND CARSTENSEN

Wireless to THE NEW YORK TIMES.

COPENHAGEN, Denmark, Tuesday, April 9 — German troops crossed the Danish frontier at 5 o'clock this morning.

Three German cruisers arrived at that same hour at Middelfart and troops immediately occupied streets of the town.

Copenhagen was also occupied by German troops this morning.

The invasion came without warning. For some hours before the crossing of the border reports had circulated here that the Germans of South Jutland were expecting German troop trains carrying 45,000 men to arrive at the town of Flensburg during the night. That German town on the border was characterized as a convenient port for shipping troops northward, and although Danish border guards had been put in the highest state of preparedness it was not thought that there would be any threat to Denmark.

This belief had been bolstered by the fact that the fleet of more than a hundred German warships that passed through the Great Belt into the Kattegat and Skagerrak yesterday and early today included troopships—and it was presumed that this fleet was on the way to Norway to retaliate against the British Navy.

More Centers Seized

Mr. Carstensen left Copenhagen after the entry of German forces and went to Kolding, where he filed the following dispatch:

Special Cable to THE NEW YORK TIMES.

KOLDING, Denmark, Tuesday, April 9—The German occupation continues here. It is reported that two ferry points on the Great Belt —Nyborg and Korsoer—have been occupied.

Troops have landed at Middelfart on a large scale. A Little Belt bridge has been reported seized and the city of Aalborg in North Jutland has been occupied.

Although there were no reports of clashes between Danish troops and the invaders today, military resistance was expected at Haderslebeen, about thirty miles north of the German border. The placing of guns and erection of barricades were reported from that town.

After leaving Copenhagen I observed from my automobile swarms of fast German planes flying over towns dropping badly printed leaflets that laid responsibility for Germany's invading Denmark and Norway to what was termed a British intention to make Scandinavia a theatre of war.

The leaflets termed Winston Churchill, Britain's First Lord of the Admiralty, "the century's greatest warmonger," who planned to police Norwegian and Danish waters against the wills of the two countries.

The statement said that, since Norway and Denmark were unable to resist effectively, Germany had resolved to act in advance of a British attack and by her own forces take over "protection" of Danish and Norwegian neutrality and "guard" the countries during the war. It was asserted that Germany did not intend to obtain bases for her fight against Britain but solely aimed at preventing Scandinavia from being a battlefield for "British expansion of the war."

According to the statement, negotiations were going on between the German and Danish Governments to make Denmark "secure" and assure that her army and navy were maintained and the Danish people's freedom respected. The country's independence, it was said, is fully secured. The procla-

Continued on Page Two

Italian colonial troops drilling. The unprepared Italian army plunged into the war in 1940.

After the Nazi invasion, Allied transport planes speeded help to the Netherlands.

1940

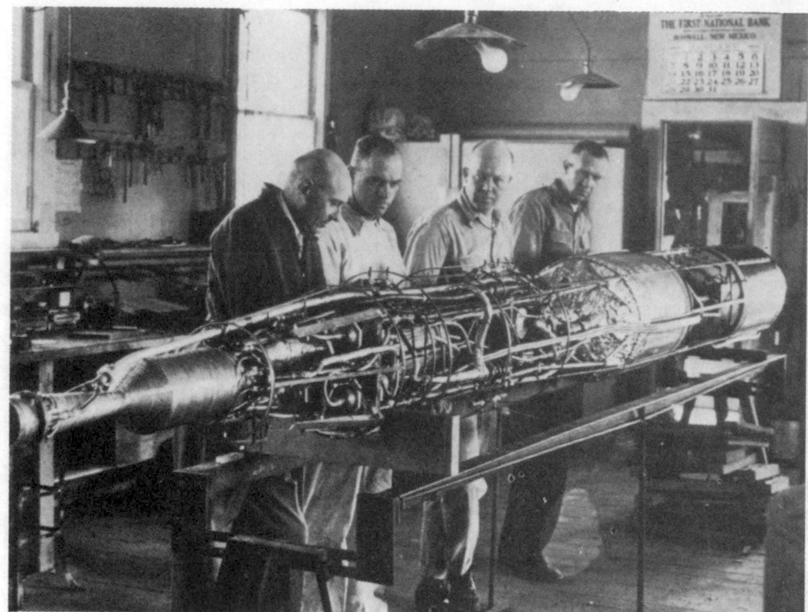

Rocketry pioneer, Robert H. Goddard with his team. Goddard was a pioneer in the field from the time that he successfully launched the first liquid-fuel rocket in 1926 until his death.

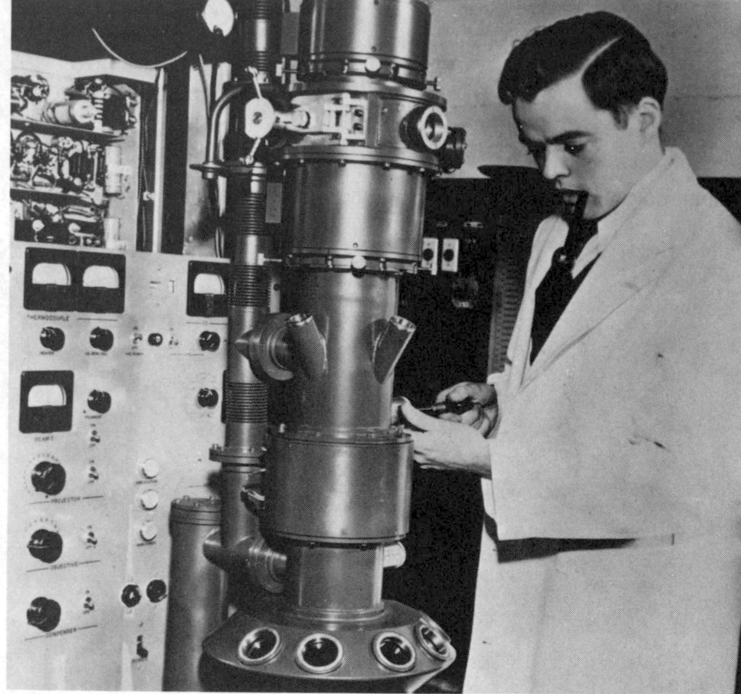

RCA inventor Dr. James Hillier working on the first commercial electron microscope in 1940. Dr. Hillier was inducted into the Inventors Hall of Fame in 1980 for his pioneering work on the electron microscope.

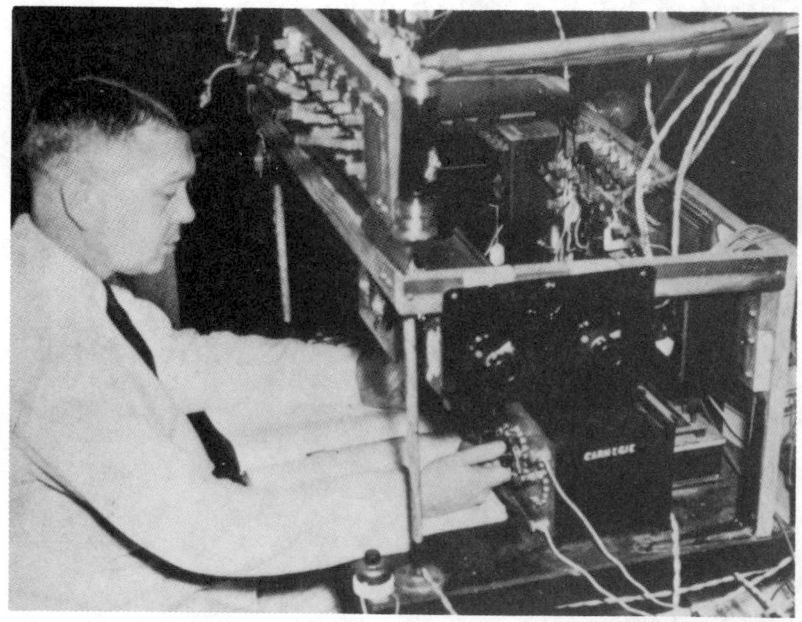

Nobel Prize winner Harold C. Urey at work on the mass spectrometer, which made the isolation of heavy isotopes possible. In 1940, he successfully separated the isotope U-235 from uranium.

"All the News That's Fit to Print."

The New York Times.

LATE CITY EDITION
POSTSCRIPT
Fair, not much change in temperature today. Tomorrow cloudy.
Temperatures Yesterday—Max. [illegible], Min. [illegible]

VOL. LXXXIX...No. 30,057. Entered as Second-Class Matter, Postoffice, New York, N. Y. NEW YORK, FRIDAY, MAY 10, 1940. THREE CENTS NEW YORK CITY and Vicinity | FOUR CENTS Elsewhere Except in 7th and 8th Postal Zones.

NAZIS INVADE HOLLAND, BELGIUM, LUXEMBOURG BY LAND AND AIR; DIKES OPENED; ALLIES RUSH AID

U.S. FREEZES CREDIT

President Acts to Guard Funds Here of Three Invaded Nations

SHIP RULING TODAY

Envoy Reports to Hull on Germany's Attacks by Air and Land

Special to THE NEW YORK TIMES.

WASHINGTON, Friday, May 10—President Roosevelt early today ordered the freezing of all credits held by Belgium, the Netherlands and Luxembourg in this country.

He called a conference for 10:30 A. M. of heads of the State, War and Navy Departments to consider pressing problems of neutrality.

The President acted swiftly after news of Germany's invasion of the three European neutral countries reached Washington and galvanized high officials into action. His order with regard to the freezing of all the invaded countries' credits and cash balances here was a counterpart of the action taken after Germany invaded Norway and Denmark.

Congress this week completed action on legislation that specifically authorizes the President by decree to freeze all such cash and credits of any belligerent. The object is to prevent these resources from falling into the hands of the invading power.

Ships to Be Considered

The President's order directed Secretary of the Treasury Henry Morgenthau Jr. to freeze all Belgian, French and Luxembourg credits before the markets open this morning.

It was announced also that the conference to be held at 10:30 will consider the question of Belgian and Netherland ships that may be in United States ports. Attorney General Robert H. Jackson also will attend this conference.

The White House, meanwhile, indicated some skepticism of the official explanation of the invasion given by German Propaganda Minister Joseph Goebbels, who was reported to have said that the Germans moved because of information that Great Britain and France intended to invade the countries involved.

"Nevertheless," said Stephen T. Early, Presidential secretary, after he had quoted the Goebbels statement, "it remains to be seen who invaded who."

It was announced that the President would remain awake throughout the night, if necessary, to receive reports and consult with officials. Sumner Welles, Under-Secretary of State, at 1:45 A. M. joined the group of State Department officials who remained on duty at the department.

Report From Ambassador

A general invasion of the three neutrals by heavy German land and air forces was reported to the State Department and Mr. Roosevelt early today by Ambassador John J. Cudahy at Brussels.

After trying vainly to re-establish telephone connection with Secretary of State Cordell Hull, over which he had relayed a "blow-by-blow" description of developments several hours earlier, the Ambassador got through the following terse message:

"German planes continue to cross the border and are bombing the airport near Brussels. It seems to be a general attack on all three countries."

A State Department press liaison officer who was relaying latest diplomatic bulletins to reporters as they came in by transatlantic telephone, dropped the cryptic remark: "As the American Ambassador spoke from Brussels, an embassy military attaché stood at his elbow."

After relaying the information to the President that the Belgian Government had ordered all hands to stand by, Ambassador Cudahy again called Secretary Hull between 10 and 11 o'clock and said he had been informed by officials in Brussels that one German and

Continued on Page Two

The International Situation

In the midst of Britain's Cabinet crisis Germany struck another powerful blow early this morning by invading the Netherlands, Belgium and Luxembourg.

After swarms of planes had engaged in air fights over Amsterdam, parachute troops, some of them clad in Netherland uniforms, descended at strategic points while planes bombed air fields. The Netherlands resisted the incursion and promptly opened the dikes that are part of her water defense system. [Page 1.]

Parachute troops likewise made surprise landings in Belgium and bombs from 100 planes blasted the Brussels airport. [Page 1.]

Appeals for help were dispatched to the Allies by the invaded countries and it was understood that machinery of assistance was being set in motion. Queen Wilhelmina in a proclamation issued at The Hague declared, "I and my government will do our duty." [Page 1.]

As in the case of Norway, Berlin explained that the German action had been taken to forestall the Allies; an announcement said that an attack on Germany had been planned through the territory of the Low Countries. What the Reich was doing, it was declared, was safeguarding the neutrality of those countries. [Page 1.]

President Roosevelt lost no time in acting on the new situation. After night conferences he ordered the freezing of credits of the three invaded countries. Further measures are to be taken today. [Page 1.]

London, meanwhile, announced that British troops had occupied Iceland to prevent a possible German seizure of that former Danish possession. [Page 1.]

Before all these happenings Neville Chamberlain had appeared to be on his way out as Prime Minister, but today it was expected the new developments might save him.

Following upon his relatively narrow escape in the House of Commons vote on Wednesday night, Mr. Chamberlain set about yesterday to see what could be done to satisfy his critics. He offered Cabinet posts to two leaders of the Labor Opposition, but they refused to serve under him. As to whether they would serve under another Conservative, they delayed their reply. If Mr. Chamberlain steps out of office, it is thought probable his place will be taken by the present Foreign Secretary, Viscount Halifax, with Winston Churchill acting as government spokesman in the Commons, from the floor of which the peer would by tradition be barred. [Page 1.]

A new offset to the Norwegian reverses was a London announcement that British submarines had attacked three German convoys and scored eleven torpedo hits, in addition to destroying two ships sailing home. [Page 6.]

Moreover, the Allies' Narvik campaign seemed to be making progress. From that far northern area it was reported that two Allied columns closing in on the railway to the port were within ten miles of each other near the Swedish border; their intention apparently was to join and drive westward along the railroad to Narvik itself, which is held by the Nazis. The Germans, in their effort to thwart the besiegers, were said to be landing parachute troops and supplying them by air. [Page 4.]

In the aftermath of the campaign in the south of the country Foreign Minister Koht disclosed that four of Norway's six divisions had been lost—killed, wounded or captured by the Nazis or interned by Sweden. [Page 6.]

Bombs Drop on Swiss Soil

By The United Press.

BERNE, Switzerland, Friday, May 10—The army staff announced today that foreign airplanes had dropped bombs in the Berne Jura Alpine district between Delemont, near the frontier, and Mount Terr, damaging a railroad.

Traffic continued over the road, the army staff said. It added that other foreign planes were flying over Swiss territory near Basle but that no details had been received.

MUSSOLINI TO LET 'ONLY FACTS' SPEAK

Press Assures Yugoslavia, but Reminds Her of Fate of Poland and Norway

By HERBERT L. MATTHEWS
By Telephone to THE NEW YORK TIMES.

ROME, May 9—The fourth anniversary of the founding of the new Italian Empire was celebrated today in an atmosphere of warlike preparation. The army was honored. Italian armed strength was glorified and the country was told by its leading commentators that the empire would soon earn that "freedom of the seas" which to Italians means domination of the Mediterranean.

Rome, like every other city in the empire, resounded today to martial music while thousands of soldiers paraded through streets from whose buildings hung innumerable flags. The great ceremony was at the Piazza Venezia this morning. Premier Mussolini awarded gold and silver medals to the kin of soldiers fallen in Fascismo's three wars in Ethiopia, Spain and Albania. Later, responding to the insistent appeal of the thousands of men massed below his balcony, he spoke very briefly, only to say that he was resuming his cloak of silence.

"May 9, 1936, was a great day in the history of the country, a day of solar victory," he said. "After my speeches, you must accustom yourself to my silence. Only facts will break it."

Small groups in the crowd thereupon began yelling "Tunisia!" and "Malta!" but the cries were not general.

At the same time this morning

Continued on Page Seven

ICELAND OCCUPIED BY BRITISH FORCE

Secret Expedition Is Justified as Thwarting Action There by Germany

By JAMES MacDONALD
Special Cable to THE NEW YORK TIMES.

LONDON, Friday, May 10—Forestalling a possible German swoop on the strategically valuable former Danish dominion of Iceland, the British have landed an expeditionary force there, it was announced this morning by the Foreign Office here.

Neither the size of the British contingent, which was sent out in the deepest secrecy, nor its place of landing was revealed in the official communiqué.

The landing of the expeditionary force was still going at an early hour this morning. Observers guessed that the landing place must be Reykjavik.

TEXT OF COMMUNIQUE

The official announcement read as follows:

Since the German seizure of Denmark it has become necessary to reckon with the possibility of a sudden German descent on Iceland.

It is clear that in the face of an attack on Iceland, even on a very small scale, the Icelandic Government would be unable to prevent their country from falling completely into German hands.

His Majesty's Government have accordingly decided to preclude this possibility which would de-

Continued on Page Three

ALLIED HELP SPED

Netherland and Belgian Appeals Answered by British and French

TACTICS ARE WATCHED

London Thinks Move an Effort to Get Bases to Attack Britain

Italians Reported Massing

By The United Press.

BUENOS AIRES, Argentina, Friday, May 10—The Madrid radio was heard broadcasting today that the British had closed the Strait of Gibraltar and that Italy was massing troops on the French frontier.

Special Cable to THE NEW YORK TIMES.

LONDON, Friday, May 10—The British Government received appeals for help early today from both the Netherlands and Belgium.

The British and French reply to the Netherland-Belgian appeals was prompt. Representatives of the respective governments here were told by 8:30 A. M. (3:30 A. M. New York time) they could expect all the help Britain could give them.

The Netherland Legation here received assurance that its country and Belgium were now regarded as Allies of Britain and France.

Within a few minutes after receipt of official news of the invasion of the Low Countries, the British Cabinet was called to 10 Downing Street and was in session with Prime Minister Neville Chamberlain.

According to information here, the Belgian Cabinet was in Brussels and Premier Hubert Pierlot conferred with King Leopold.

The German invasion of the Low Countries had been expected in London, and it must be presumed the Allies were ready for it to some extent.

Allies Visible to Planes

The biggest handicap to the British and French was in the timing of the German thrust at dawn. This prevented the Allies moving troops under cover of darkness, and since hundreds of German planes already had flown over practically all of Netherland and Belgian territory for some hours, the disposition of Allied troops and their every movement must have been known to the German High Command.

While the Netherlanders and Belgians had taken every precaution

Continued on Page Four

Chamberlain Saved by Nazi Blow In Low Countries, London Thinks

By RAYMOND DANIELL
Special Cable to THE NEW YORK TIMES.

LONDON, Friday, May 10—The first effect of the German attack on the Low Countries is expected to be that Prime Minister Chamberlain will be saved just when it looked as if he was sure to fall.

It was believed that the Labor party, which so far has refused to serve under him in a truly national government, and only yesterday rejected a formal offer to do so, will now close ranks, forget political difficulties and take any Cabinet job offered to its leaders. Furthermore, the Labor party conference, which was supposed to start at Bournemouth on Monday, now will probably be called off.

There is just a possibility that Mr. Chamberlain may quit immediately and turn his seals of office over to First Lord of the Admiralty Winston Churchill. This was a strong but unconfirmed rumor as a Cabinet meeting held this morning came to an end.

In addition, it was said that under Mr. Churchill, Alfred Duff Cooper would receive the Admiralty post, Anthony Eden the War Office and that Viscount Halifax would remain at the Foreign Office.

Until the invasion of the Low Countries was known, the consensus of political observers here had been that the end of the Chamberlain Government could not be long delayed.

The two questions uppermost were how soon it would take place and who would succeed him at No. 10 Downing Street. The betting had been that it would be sooner rather than later and that Foreign Secretary Viscount Halifax would be the next Prime Minister, with Mr. Churchill serving as his spokesman in the House of Commons, from whose floor the present Foreign Secretary, as a peer, is barred by tradition.

The troubles of the 71-year-old Prime Minister, who struggled vainly to maintain Europe's peace by appeasement and who was accused in the House of Commons of bungling the business of war-making, increased rather than diminished during the day. However, the House, despite the gravity of the internal crisis and perils abroad, decided to take its usual twelve-day Whitsuntide holiday, subject to recall in the event of major developments, which followed promptly.

Mr. Chamberlain's efforts to broaden the base of his Cabinet by

Continued on Page Five

BRUSSELS IS RAIDED

400 Reported Killed—Troops Cross Border at Four Points

PARACHUTE INVASION

Mobilization Is Ordered and Allied Aid Asked—Luxembourg Attacked

Wireless to THE NEW YORK TIMES.

BRUSSELS, Belgium, Friday, May 10—The invasion Belgium had feared since the outbreak of the European war came before dawn this morning. About a hundred German planes flew over this city and bombed the airport.

The airfield at Antwerp also was bombed. Parachute troops were landed at Hasselt in Eastern Belgium. Artillery fire was reported heard along the German and Luxembourg frontiers.

Anti-aircraft guns at the airport commenced firing with the appearance of the first invaders and kept up a steady barrage. Those in the center of the city went into action at 5:30 A. M.

Above the drone of airplane engines could be heard the staccato of machine guns. Bombs wrecked many houses in the vicinity of the airport and caused some loss of life. [Exchange Telegraph (British news agency) said 400 persons had been killed in the first raid.]

Reports from Antwerp and other parts of the country said German planes had flown constantly over since 4:30 A. M., keeping anti-aircraft batteries steadily in action.

Premier Hubert Pierlot and Foreign Minister Paul-Henri Spaak conferred with King Leopold and then called an emergency meeting of the Cabinet. The radio broadcast repeated summonses to all soldiers to join their units at once. A "state of alarm" was decreed throughout the country with the appearance of the first planes.

The Belgian radio also stated German parachute troops had fluttered down at Nivelles, less than twenty miles south of Brussels, and in Saint Trond, about thirty-five miles east of the capital. The broadcast stated that Germany had made no demarche in Brussels before the invasion.

Wireless to THE NEW YORK TIMES.

LONDON, Friday, May 10—The Germans crossed the Belgian frontier at four points this morning, according to an announcement over

Continued on Page Two

NAZIS SWOOP ON THE LOW COUNTRIES

By land and air German troops descended this morning upon the Netherlands, Belgium and Luxembourg. The principal land incursion into the Netherlands was at Roermond.

Ribbentrop Charges Allies Plotted With the Lowlands

By GEORGE AXELSSON
Wireless to THE NEW YORK TIMES.

BERLIN, Friday, May 10—Foreign Minister Joachim von Ribbentrop at 9 o'clock this morning announced that Reich forces had launched military operations against Holland, Belgium and Luxembourg to "protect their neutrality."

Earlier it was reported that German troops had occupied Maastricht, the Netherlands, and had "landed" contingents in Brussels, probably meaning parachute troops.

Herr von Ribbentrop said that Germany had received unimpeachable proof that the Allies were engineering an imminent attack through the Lowlands into the German Ruhr district wherefore the Reich had been compelled to take corresponding measures. He said the time had come for settling the final account with the "Franco-British leaders."

And thus the war to a decisive finish has at last started in the West. This was the assumption when Herr von Ribbentrop informed the world through newspaper men that the German action meant that she had decided to settle all accounts with the Allies.

"France and Britain dropped their mask," said Herr von Ribbentrop. "The alarm in the Mediterranean was a feint behind which the Allies were preparing an onslaught on German territory which the Reich could not tolerate."

The notes—handed to The Hague and Brussels simultaneously with a shorter note to the Grand Duchy of Luxembourg just prior to their invasion by Germany—accused the Lowlands with having been overwhelmingly partial toward the Allies, adding that the attitude of the press was objectionable to the Reich.

A memorandum similar in tone to that handed to Denmark and Norway last month stated:

"In the life-and-death struggle thrust upon the German people, the government does not intend to await an attack by Britain and France inactively allowing the war to be carried through Belgium and Holland onto German soil. The government, therefore, has issued orders to safeguard the neutrality of the two countries with all the military means of the Reich."

Ribbentrop Reads Statement

In eight points the memorandum outlines the German argument that Belgium and Holland had not observed the strictest neutrality upon which German respect for their territories was founded. The document accuses them with having even supported Germany's enemies in their hostile intentions. Belgium fortified exclusively her Eastern frontier against Germany, leaving the French frontier unfortified, one argument reads.

Berlin slept peacefully unaware

Continued on Page Four

HOLLAND'S QUEEN PROTESTS INVASION

Wilhelmina Vows She and the Government Will Do Duty—Bars Negotiation With Foe

By The United Press.

THE HAGUE, the Netherlands, Friday, May 10—Queen Wilhelmina said today in a statement on the German invasion of the country that "I and my government will do our duty."

The Queen, in a proclamation addressed to "my people," said

"After our country, with scrupulous conscientiousness, had observed strict neutrality during all these months, and while Holland had no other plan than to maintain strictly this attitude, Germany last night made a sudden attack on our territory without any warning.

"This was done notwithstanding a solemn promise that the neutrality of our country would be respected so long as we ourselves maintained that neutrality.

"I herewith direct a flaming protest against this unprecedented violation of good faith and violation of all that is decent in relations between cultured States.

"I and my government now will do our duty.

"Do your duty everywhere and under all circumstances. And let every one go to the post to which he has been appointed and, with the utmost vigilance and with that inner calm and serenity which comes from a clear conscience, do his work."

The Netherland general military headquarters in a communiqué said:

"Never will the High Command or government enter into negotiations with the enemy."

Dispatches from Europe and the Far East are subject to censorship at the source.

AIR FIELDS BOMBED

Nazi Parachute Troops Land at Key Centers as Flooding Starts

RIVER MAAS CROSSED

Defenders Battle Foe in Sky, Claim 6 Planes as War Is Proclaimed

First Bombing in France

Special Cable to THE NEW YORK TIMES.

PARIS, Friday, May 10—The Bron airdrome, a big airport near Lyon, was bombed by German planes today. One German aircraft was shot down. The alarm was first given at 4:25 A. M. The all-clear signal was given at 6:45 A. M.

WASHINGTON, Friday, May 10 (AP)—United States Ambassador William C. Bullitt telephoned the State Department from Paris at 4 A. M. today that the Germans had bombed a number of fortified towns in France, "such as Dunkerque and Calais."

By The United Press.

AMSTERDAM, The Netherlands, Friday, May 10—Germany invaded the Netherlands early today, land troops being preceded by widespread air attacks on airdromes and by the landing of parachute troops.

The Netherlands resisted and announced she was at war with Germany. Anti-aircraft batteries and fighter planes engaged swarms of German aircraft when they appeared simultaneously over a score of Netherland cities.

An official proclamation said:

"Since 3 A. M. German troops have crossed the Netherland frontier and German planes have tried to attack airports. Inundations are effective according to plans. The army anti-aircraft batteries were found prepared. So far as is known six German planes have been shot down."

[French, Belgian and British planes were sighted over the Netherlands this morning, a Reuters (British news agency) dispatch said in quoting the Netherland radio station at Hilversum, near Amsterdam.

German troops were first reported crossing the Netherland frontier near Roermond, eight miles north of the Belgian frontier. German planes landed troops by parachute at strategic points near Rotterdam, The Hague, Amsterdam and other large cities.

A large number of the German troops landed by parachute were said to be dressed in Netherland military uniforms.

Other Germans crossed the Maas River in rubber boats to Netherland territory. They were said to be reaching the Netherland side in "considerable numbers."

A fierce air battle raged over Amsterdam as Netherland fighter planes dived repeatedly on German bombers and troop transport planes with chattering machine guns.

Schiphol Airdrome outside Amsterdam, the nation's largest, was heavily bombed. Military authorities immediately threw a heavy guard around the airdrome in an effort to defend it against German parachute troops.

Planes identified as German Heinkels bombed Schiphol Airdrome repeatedly, loosing some thirty heavy caliber bombs on the landing field between 5:15 and 5:30 A. M.

Reports poured in of planes in great numbers over a score of Netherland cities. Netherland authorities, hurriedly organizing defense, flashed orders to the whole country to be on the alert against parachute troops.

Fifty planes were over Nijmegen, sixty miles southeast of Amsterdam on the German border.

A number of parachute troops reportedly landed at Sliedrecht, Delft and several other points. Delft is twelve and a half miles from The Hague. About 100 parachute troops

Continued on Page Three

"All the News That's Fit to Print."

The New York Times.

LATE CITY EDITION
Partly cloudy today and tomorrow with little change in temperature.
Temperatures Yesterday—Max., 63; Min., 52

Copyright, 1940, by The New York Times Company.

VOL. LXXXIX..No. 30,079. Entered as Second-Class Matter, Postoffice, New York, N. Y. NEW YORK, SATURDAY, JUNE 1, 1940. THREE CENTS NEW YORK CITY and Vicinity | FOUR CENTS Elsewhere Except in 7th and 8th Postal Zones.

75% OF B.E.F. REPORTED SAFELY OUT OF FLANDERS; ALLIES ATTACK ON SOMME, WIN ABBEVILLE AREA; ROOSEVELT WARNS WAR IMPERILS WHOLE WORLD

PLEA TO CONGRESS

President Asks Power to Call Out National Guard if Needed

BILLION MORE FUNDS

All Continents May Be Involved, Says New Defense Message

Text of the President's defense message is on Page 6.

By FELIX BELAIR JR.
Special to THE NEW YORK TIMES.

WASHINGTON, May 31—Warning today that "all continents may become involved in a world-wide war," President Roosevelt in a special message today asked Congress for "over $1,000,000,000" in supplemental appropriations for preparedness, and for specific authority to call the National Guard and Army Reserves to active duty if needed to safeguard neutrality and for the national defense.

Further enlargement of the defense forces, for which outlays of more than $3,300,000,000 are pending in Congress, were necessary, the President said, in view of the success of blitzkrieg tactics on the Flanders Front.

He did not mention Germany, but referred to the "almost incredible events of the past two weeks in the European conflict."

The message contained no analysis of the way the money would be spent, but the President said he had instructed War and Navy Department experts to appear for this purpose before Senate and House committees. Representatives of other agencies were ordered to explain Administration plans for a 1,000,000-man Army for noncombat work incident to military and naval operations.

Immediate Orders in View

War Department plans, which were not described by the President, call for placing immediate orders for 2,800 bomber and pursuit planes, 1,700 tanks, about 500 heavy artillery units and larger quantities of anti-tank and anti-aircraft guns and other weapons perfected in War and Navy Department laboratories but not yet in actual production. The airplane cannon is an example of the latter.

Meanwhile, it was apparent that President Roosevelt had continued until today his correspondence with Premier Mussolini in an effort to forestall Italy's entry into the war. White House aides refused to say whether the President sent another appeal to the Italian dictator yesterday, but said such correspondence had been on a continuing basis.

Congressional reaction to the President's message was generally favorable, but two Republican Senators attacked his request for authority to call out the National Guard and the Army Reserves. Senator Vandenberg described the proposal as "shocking," and suggested that if an emergency was imminent Congress should remain in session.

Committee Takes Up Tax Bill

While the Senate put off consideration of two big Navy bills to debate the proposed transfer of the Immigration and Naturalization Bureau of the Labor Department to the Department of Justice, the Ways and Means Committee of the House took up the taxation bill by which it is hoped to raise $656,000,000 a year to finance the unprecedented peacetime defense program.

In the executive branch, the Advisory Defense Committee was organizing its administrative machinery in an effort to realize President Roosevelt's purpose of gearing the nation's industrial capacity to full defense production at the end of six months.

President Roosevelt assigned Attorney General Jackson to cooperate with State Governors in setting up State Defense Commissions. The White House said that the Federal Government was not sponsoring such commissions, but was interested principally in avoiding conflicts in their activities.

Edsel Ford conferred with Secretary Morgenthau at the Secretary's request, and with Dr. George J. Mead, in charge of coordinating the department's aeronautical activi-

Continued on Page Six

The International Situation

On the Battle Fronts

Unofficial estimates in London last night placed the number of British Expeditionary Force troops safely removed from the Flanders pocket at three-quarters of the original forces there. The action was regarded as one of the greatest military and naval feats of all time. [Page 1.]

With the battle in the north in its final stages, the French main army and the new B. E. F. in France went resolutely ahead with their preparations to meet and checkmate the next German offensive.

French tanks pounded at the Nazi positions along the Somme, straightening the new defense line that stretches east and north from Abbeville on the Channel coast along the Somme, Aisne and Chiers Rivers to the Luxembourg border. Success was reported in all local actions. Behind the natural and man-made defenses along the French rivers was an army whose morale appeared to have been strengthened instead of broken by the reverses in Flanders. The Blitzkrieg had achieved only a half victory in four weeks of desperate fighting, it was said by the Allies, and they were now prepared to meet and repel any German attempt to overrun France and bring a quick end to the war. [All the foregoing on Page 1.]

The British Air Force continued its fight against odds in protecting the evacuation from Flanders and the Channel crossing. Between flights the young pilots of the R. A. F. calmly sipped tea at their home fields. [Page 3.]

The German High Command said the Flanders and Artois campaigns were virtually over. The three French armies in the pocket had been either captured or destroyed, a German communiqué said, with only isolated groups still offering resistance. Fog, which grounded German planes, aided the evacuation of the Allied armies from Dunkerque and the other coastal debarkation points. The completion of operations in Flanders, the High Command said, had released the German troops there "for other tasks" and the stage was set for the second phase of the war. [Page 1.]

Repercussions Elsewhere

President Roosevelt warned Congress in a special message that the war may spread to all continents and asked an additional billion dollars for Army, Navy and civilian training programs. He requested special legislation empowering him to call any part or all of the National Guard into active service, and authority to hire "dollar-a-year" men to speed defense appropriations. Congressional reaction to the new requests was generally favorable. [Page 1.]

Tension heightened in Italy as the hour of decision neared; Premier Mussolini was said to be so busy making preparations for all eventualities that he had no time to receive United States Ambassador Phillips with another message from President Roosevelt. One of the preparations made, it was reported, was negotiation of a pact with Japan for the latter country to supply Ethiopia with food and raw materials in event Italy should go to war. [Page 1.]

A Uruguayan Government investigation of fifth column activities indicated widespread Nazi penetration in South America. The estimated 3,000 Germans in that small South American nation are highly organized along Nazi lines, complete with a secret police, the investigation has revealed. The local Germans are taxed not only for the expenses of their own organization but for the Nazi party in Germany. Their organization and propaganda work has been aided by the German Legation in Montevideo, it was charged. [Page 1.]

The liner President Roosevelt arrived at Galway, Ireland, last night to bring home more than 900 Americans, warned out of the British Isles by the danger of invasion. Their baggage was carefully examined to guard against any explosion at sea that might be blamed on Britain by Germany, as was the sinking of the Athenia Sept. 3. [Page 1.] Twenty-two other vessels were en route to America from Mediterranean ports, each of them also loaded to capacity with Americans fleeing the war. [Follows Galway story.]

U. S. Cruiser Is Sent South; Uruguay Finds Nazis Plotting

Quincy Hastily Dispatched on 'Good-Will' Mission to South America—Fear of Fifth Column Is Growing

Ready to Give Aid

By FRANK L. KLUCKHOHN
Special to THE NEW YORK TIMES.

WASHINGTON, May 31—The 10,000-ton cruiser Quincy, carrying two airplanes, is rushing tonight toward the east coast of South America on what is briefly announced by the Navy to be a "good-will" cruise, but on what is reliably reported to be the special mission of aiding several Latin-American countries, if necessary, in meeting Nazi fifth column activities.

The Quincy's first stop will be Rio de Janeiro, but it is believed that the cruiser may proceed on to Montevideo, where Uruguayan officials are frankly alarmed over organized Nazi activities and where President Alfredo Baldomir has sent to Congress a bill modifying constitutional provisions dealing with freedom of assembly.

The projected cruise to Rio de Janeiro of three battleships, the New York, Texas and Arkansas, was canceled coincidentally. While no official reason for the cancellation was given, it was believed possible here that the Quincy was better suited to the needs of the situation since she is one of the Navy's later ships and extremely fast. Moreover, the battleships planned to carry midshipmen on a cruise, and the middies are not usually taken to areas where action may develop.

The Quincy was on her shakedown cruise when the Spanish Civil War started in 1936 and was immediately rushed to Spain in order

Continued on Page Five

Organization Revealed

By JOHN W. WHITE
Wireless to THE NEW YORK TIMES.

MONTEVIDEO, Uruguay, May 31—The Uruguayan investigation of fifth column activities is disclosing an almost unbelievable Nazi political penetration into South America.

Conclusive evidence has been accumulated by police raids and other investigating methods to show that the Nazi party has established a perfectly organized branch party in Uruguay known as the Uruguayan District Group of the German National Socialist Party. It is under the leadership of a "little Fuehrer" and acknowledges dependence on and allegiance to the Nazi party headquarters in Germany.

Diplomatic and other observers consider the Uruguayan Government's investigation of the utmost importance because it is uncovering the details of Nazi methods throughout Latin America.

Argentina's investigation last year showed that the Germans there had organized as the Argentine District Group Party. Newspapers in several other republics, including Chile, Colombia and Bolivia, have charged that similar organizations exist in their countries. Latin-American diplomats here are informing their governments, therefore, that the details of Nazi operations in Uruguay are indicative of what can be expected in all other South and Central American nations.

These details show the existence of a general Nazi party organiza-

Continued on Page Five

GERMANS CAPTURED

Nazi War Material Also Taken Near Abbeville in Mopping-Up Drive

ALLIES CONTROL AIR

French Planes Dropping Food to Trapped Army Battling to Coast

By The Associated Press.

PARIS, May 31—French tanks supporting a second British Expeditionary Force being formed in France pounded at the Germans along the Somme front tonight.

They mopped up the Abbeville sector and reported they had regained unbroken command south of the Somme.

The Abbeville bridgehead was taken, but the capture of the town itself—lying to the north of the river—was not claimed. It remained in No Man's Land. Hundreds of Nazi prisoners and a mass of German war material were declared seized.

In the north, where the rearguard of the Allied armies of Flanders were struggling to force a passage through the Germans—who sought to cut them off in the mountains southeast of Dunkerque—French bombers defied anti-aircraft fire and low visibility to drop food and munitions for the isolated forces.

More than twenty tons of bombs were launched by two flights of French bombers in heavy attacks on German concentrations north of the Somme and German anti-aircraft batteries and other objectives near Abbeville.

Bridgeheads Wiped Out

The tanks which led the Allied attack in the Abbeville sector were mostly of medium weight, twenty-three tons.

This apparent prelude to large-scale action on a new front—a front protecting Paris—was reported by the War Ministry spokesman along with a declaration that the flood waters spouting through locks opened by the French were holding back the German effort to smash Dunkerque, the port of exit for the retreating northern Allies.

These men were moving in retreat in a rectangle that earlier had been reported holding generally firm under the assaults of the greatest mechanized German Army ever to take the field.

Two muddy and weary divisions of the command of General René-Jacques-Adolphe Prioux—originally totaling about 30,000 men—led the march into Dunkerque, the Allied port of exit to the sea.

The Allied corridor of escape stretched from near Lille to Dunkerque.

Illustrating the cost to Germany of the massive offensive that began with the invasion of the Low Countries on May 10, the semiofficial Telefrance Agency declared that since then the Nazis had lost 500,000 men—a figure which the agency asserted "finds itself writ-

Continued on Page Two

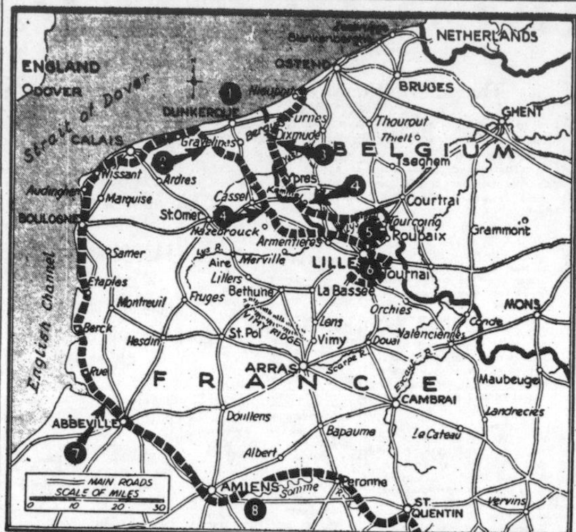

ALLIES ATTACK ON SOMME AND PUSH FLANDERS RESCUE

Large additional forces of British and French troops were embarked from Dunkerque (1) as foggy weather hampered German bombing of their retreat. The Nazis pressed against the sides of the pocket from the direction of Gravelines (2) and between Furnes and Bergues (3), but floodwaters from opened locks helped the hard-fighting withdrawing army hold them back. The Germans claimed to have wiped out a British force in the Mont Cassel area (4) and severe fighting raged between there and Mont Kemmel. The Nazis said French groups were isolated in two pockets north and south of Lille (5) and (6). The French announced the mopping up of the sector south of Abbeville (7) as French tanks pounded at the Germans along the Somme front (8).

MUSSOLINI TOO BUSY TO HEAR U. S. PLEA

Envoy Unable to Hand Him Roosevelt Note—Nation Tense With War Fever

By HERBERT L. MATTHEWS
By Telephone to THE NEW YORK TIMES.

ROME, May 31—Events seem to be approaching the grand and terrible climax for Italy.

For the first time since the tension started here, the feeling is that it is a question of days, rather than weeks; and one sign of it is that Premier Mussolini would not accept in person a message that United States Ambassador William Phillips tried yesterday to deliver to him on behalf of President Roosevelt.

The refusal was in no sense a rebuff to the United States or to Mr. Roosevelt. If it were only that there would be less anxiety about the immediate future. The reason Signor Mussolini did not receive Mr. Phillips is that there is no longer any time for such audiences.

[Italy has broken off negotiations with Britain through which the British planned to ease in behalf of Italian shipping the Allied

Continued on Page Four

'Kidnap Hitler' Prize Passes Over Deadline

Special to THE NEW YORK TIMES.

PITTSBURGH, May 31—One of those "once in a lifetime" opportunities, a chance to make $1,000,000, passed into discard at midnight, when Dr. Samuel Harden Church's offer of that sum for the kidnapping of Adolf Hitler expired.

Whether or not any one made a serious attempt to get the money is perhaps known only to Dr. Church, who refused to comment as his offer concluded, but he did admit that he would make a statement for publication Sunday.

Reporters who tried to reach the president of Carnegie Institute at his home or by phone were told by his secretary that a statement was forthcoming.

Dr. Church originally made the offer in behalf of fifty unidentified Pittsburghers, who put up $1,000,000 for the safe deliverance of Germany's leader to a League of Nations court.

FRENCH AT FRONT SEE FINAL VICTORY

War Has Shown the Germans Inferior, They Say, Despite Great Weapons

By P. J. PHILIP
Wireless to THE NEW YORK TIMES.

WITH THE FRENCH ARMIES IN THE EAST, May 31—Nothing of all the terrible things that have happened in these past three weeks since the German offensive began has shaken the amazing, one might almost say sublime, confidence with which the still intact bulk of the French Army regards the future. Coming again into this district just three weeks from the day when the first intimation of the German attack came to me and others in the shape of bombs crashing down on houses around us, it seems incredible that so much has changed.

Then the Maginot Line was an imposing barricade. The French and British Armies in the north lay behind what were believed to be the strong defenses and powerful armies of the Netherlands and Belgium and with defenses of their own. The only warfare that was going on was the Indian warfare of night skirmishing parties.

Now in these three weeks the German Army has completely overrun and conquered the Netherlands and Belgium, it has pushed through Northern France to the sea, forced,

Continued on Page Three

NEW GERMAN DRIVE NEAR, BERLIN HINTS

Push Toward Paris Expected as Flanders Battle Ends—Hitler Sees Rome Envoy

By PERCIVAL KNAUTH
Wireless to THE NEW YORK TIMES.

BERLIN, May 31—The battle in Artois and Flanders is over. The French First, Seventh and Ninth Armies engaged in these sectors, the Germans report, now are either captured or destroyed, with only isolated handfuls still offering flickering resistance in woods and villages. Between Dunkerque and Nieuport, a British rear guard is covering the evacuation of the final remnants of the British Expeditionary Force, which is escaping under cover of a thick Channel fog.

"The main bodies of the German divisions in Artois and Flanders are now free for other duties," today's communiqué of the German High Command declares. The stage is set for the second and possibly final phase of the big offensive.

At this critical hour, when Germany claims to have driven a wedge between the Allied armies, the dramatic entrance on the scene of her allied partner, Italy, is believed to be imminent. Italy's entrance in the war, in the opinion of neutral diplomatic circles here, probably will be synchronized with the launching of the second German drive.

Ribbentrop at Meeting

In his headquarters "somewhere in the West," Chancellor Hitler today received Count Dino Alfieri, the new Italian Ambassador to Germany. It was the second time that Premier Mussolini's envoy had been to the Chancellor's general headquarters, and the significance of this audience was enhanced by the fact that Joachim von Ribbentrop, German Foreign Minister, also was present.

[Authorized quarters, meanwhile, refused to confirm or deny reports that Dr. Joseph Goebbels, German Propaganda Minister, had been summoned to Herr Hitler's field headquarters from Berlin to prepare an "important announcement," according to The United Press.]

The German troops that swept

Continued on Page Four

Dispatches from Europe and the Far East are subject to censorship at the source.

Liner Roosevelt at Galway for Americans; 900 Set to Sail; Others Dash From London

Wireless to THE NEW YORK TIMES.

GALWAY, Ireland, May 31—All alight and with the United States flag prominently displayed, America's refugee ship, the President Roosevelt, arrived at the outskirts of Galway Bay at 10 o'clock tonight.

A pilot boat water tender conveying shipping officials set out from the harbor here at 9 o'clock. Police Superintendent Thomas Collins, Commander Norman Hitchcock, Naval Air Attaché of the United States in the London Embassy, and an Irish Army representative were also on the tender.

The first batch of about 900 passengers is going out by tender at noon tomorrow. The last tender is going out at midnight tomorrow night and the President Roosevelt is expected to depart for the United States at an early hour on Sunday morning.

The boom which the hotel business has experienced here as a result of the big influx of American refugees was enhanced this afternoon when 200 more arrived by special train from Dublin. But the trek of the weary and luggage-laden Americans was hastened. Since the President Roosevelt's departure is not likely to take place until Sunday, about fifty more Americans, it was stated here, are making a dash from London tonight to make the homeward trip.

In addition to the hotels, the Galway stores are reaping much extra business from the influx, and there are brisk sales on such goods as Irish linen, lace, pottery, handicrafts and souvenirs.

Stringent precautions are being taken with regard to the examination of passengers and luggage and there is a rigid exclusion of all but passenger officials from the boat, due, it was learned today, to a special request of the United States Government, with which the Irish Government is in thorough agreement. Every precaution is being taken to insure that neither undesirable persons nor property will get on the ship. The augmented

Continued on Page Two

BRITAIN HAILS MEN

Thousands More Arrive in Port to Receive a Frenzied Welcome

YACHTS, BARGES USED

Navy Praised Highly for Its Brilliant Feats in Evacuation

By HAROLD DENNY
Wireless to THE NEW YORK TIMES.

LONDON, May 31—About three-quarters of the British Expeditionary Force thus far has been evacuated from Dunkerque and brought to England, it was estimated unofficially in well-informed quarters late tonight. Military authorities would not confirm or deny this estimate, the actual figures being kept secret.

[The United Press reported that it was estimated that 75 to 80 per cent of the British Expeditionary Force and some of its Allies trapped by the Germans in Flanders had been snatched from what had appeared to be the certain annihilation of more than 500,000 men. Original estimates of the strength of the B. E. F. ranged from 300,000 to 350,000.

["At least one Belgian army corps is still fighting side by side with the Allies," the British Broadcasting Corporation said early today in a news broadcast picked up in New York by the National Broadcasting Company. The corps was said to be under the command of the former commander of the Liége district who had refused to obey King Leopold's capitulation order.]

Ragged and battle-weary British and French soldiers who fought their way out of the shambles of Northern France and Belgium continued to stream into port during the day, still dazed but happy as they hurried inland for brief leaves at home.

They were greeted with almost delirious enthusiasm by the populace as they disembarked from the motley collection of large and small boats which had ferried them across the Channel and by cheering crowds all along the railway lines.

They were welcomed not sadly as a beaten army but proudly as the heroes in one of the bravest chapters in Great Britain's military annals.

Earlier this week high army officers had expressed the fear that almost the entire British Expeditionary Force would be lost. To date a far larger number has been returned safely to England than any one had dared to hope.

The primary reason for this result is said to have been the skillful coordination with the troops by the British Navy assisted by elements of the French Navy and by the Royal Air Force in conjunction with French aviators.

Troops' Conduct Praised

The behavior of the soldiers under a pounding by a vastly superior force such as no troops ever had had to withstand before is praised without measure by commanders returning with them, who have seen much of the war. These soldiers stood their ground and retired always in perfect order under admirable discipline. So these fine battalions, among them some of the best in the British Army, were not destroyed after all, but their survivors after a rest will be able to re-form with additions and take the field again better than they were before, because now they are used to the most terrible engines the Germans can hurl against them.

Part of the B. E. F. and a considerable force of French still are holding a narrow strip of coast behind Dunkerque covering the withdrawal. This strip now is being called the "Corunna line" in memory of Sir John Moore's classic withdrawal from Spain in 1809, when his army had been placed in a similarly hopeless situation by the defection of the Spanish. French troops are in this line with the British, while more are with General Rene Prioux among those who are fighting their way to the coast.

The part played by the British fleet is so brilliant that today's returning soldiers shouted to the crowds along the beach: "Thank God for the navy" and cheered sailors on shore whenever they

Continued on Page Three

1940

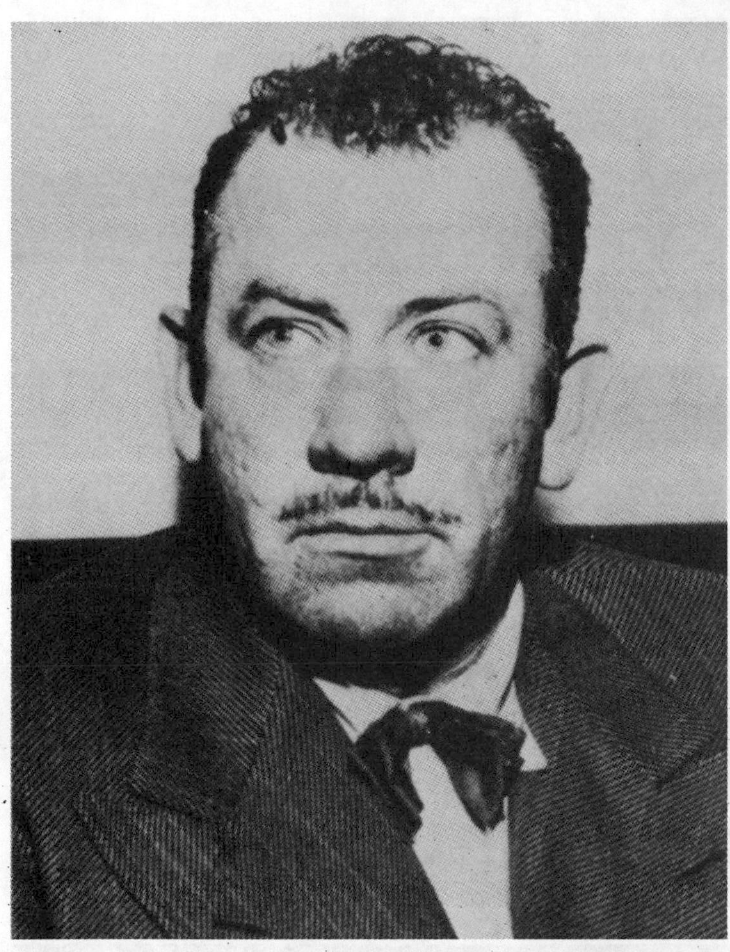

John Steinbeck's compelling novel *Grapes of Wrath* earned him the 1940 Pulitzer prize for literature.

Ernest Hemingway on a hunting trip with his close friend Gary Cooper. Hemingway insisted that Cooper play the male lead in *For Whom the Bell Tolls.*

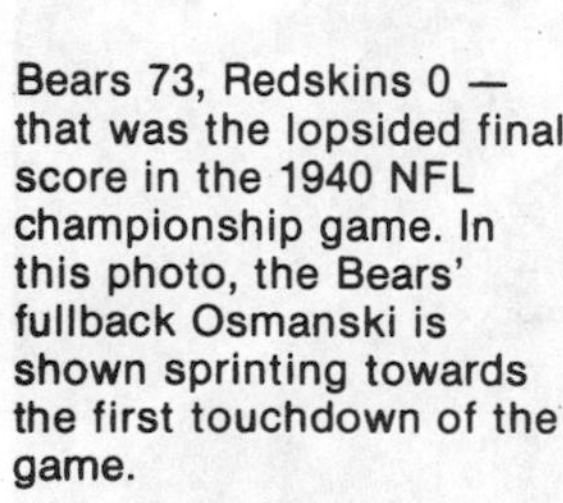

Bears 73, Redskins 0 — that was the lopsided final score in the 1940 NFL championship game. In this photo, the Bears' fullback Osmanski is shown sprinting towards the first touchdown of the game.

Duke Ellington, the legendary composer and performer, began gaining popularity.

The famed conductor Leopold Stokowski led a huge orchestra for Walt Disney's 1940 masterpiece *Fantasia*.

Tom Mix, the silent screen star, was killed in an automobile accident. He is shown here in a characteristic pose from a 1921 film.

"All the News That's Fit to Print."

The New York Times.

LATE CITY EDITION
Cloudy with showers and little change in temperature today and tomorrow.
Temperatures Yesterday—Max., 65; Min., 57

VOL. LXXXIX..No. 30,089. Entered as Second-Class Matter, Postoffice, New York, N. Y. NEW YORK, TUESDAY, JUNE 11, 1940. THREE CENTS NEW YORK CITY and Vicinity | FOUR CENTS Elsewhere Except in 7th and 8th Postal Zones.

ITALY AT WAR, READY TO ATTACK; STAB IN BACK, SAYS ROOSEVELT; GOVERNMENT HAS LEFT PARIS

NAZIS NEAR PARIS

Units Reported to Have Broken Through Lines to West of Capital

SEINE RIVER CROSSED

3 Columns Branch Out From Soissons—Enemy Held, French State

By The Associated Press.

PARIS, June 10—Marauding German tanks were reported tonight to have reached the Paris region itself as the government left the capital.

While some German armored advance guards were said to have penetrated to the environs of Paris in isolated raids through the French lines, the main front was about thirty-five miles west and northeast of the capital. Although steadily approaching, the battle's roar still could not be heard here.

[The German High Command has no knowledge that Nazi tank units have reached the Paris region, The United Press reported.]

The battle, which had been waged heretofore on familiar World War territory for the most part, swung into virgin soil as the Germans advanced west of Paris.

In the triangle bounded by Amiens on the Somme, Rouen, seventy miles west of Paris on the Seine, and Vernon, forty miles west on the Seine, the Germans redoubled their attacks, crossing the river at several points. An armored column, which crossed the Bresle last week, led the assault.

The French took their main stand west of Paris all along the Seine in an effort to prevent the Germans from effecting further passages and taking the capital from the rear.

In the central sector of the Oise Valley, directly north of Paris where the Germans had suffered tremendous losses, they held back their infantry and sent out dive bombers in an effort to break down French resistance.

They broadened their salient, however, farther east, where they had crossed the Aisne. Three columns fanned out from Soissons through La Ferte Milon and Fere en Tardenois and toward Fismes.

Hold Firm on East Flank

They were just north of Chateau-Thierry and the Marne, where they were stopped in their 1918 thrust by Americans fighting with the French.

On the east flank, where the French have been holding firm, fresh German infantry, tanks and planes battered the French lines, but with small gains.

But France, besieged on two sides by Germans driving on Paris from the north and the Italians entering the war on the south, proclaimed her grim determination to carry on the fight.

The main combats were centered in the Seine Valley to the west of Paris, with the High Command declaring that some German elements had crossed the Seine River at certain points, and in the Ourcq River Valley to the northeast of the capital.

The communiqué, however, said the "enemy is held everywhere by vigorous counter-attacks."

The French communiqué was filed from Paris, but was issued "Somewhere in France." The regular press conference of the War Office was not held this morning, as only a few attachés were in the office.

The High Command reported that the German break-through to the Seine resulted from increased pressure applied by the Nazis between the route from Amiens to Rouen and from Amiens to Vernon as far as the lower Seine.

In the other principal area of combat, east of the Oise River, German columns coming down from the region of Soissons have resumed their attack toward the Ourcq River.

The German offensive in the

Continued on Page Two

The International Situation

On the Battle Fronts

Italian guns will speak today in Europe. Italy's declaration of war against France and Britain became effective at 12:01 A. M., Rome time. Before 100,000 men and women, packed in the Piazza Venezia and near-by streets, Premier Mussolini yesterday announced his decision. It was war against "the plutocratic and reactionary democracies of the West." For the present that does not include the United States, but Rome reports that few Italians, from Signor Mussolini down, believe they will see the end of this war without having America against them.

The Italian Premier specifically excluded Turkey, Switzerland, Yugoslavia, Greece and Egypt from his military designs. Rome hoped Turkey would fail to keep her agreement to support the Allies in a Mediterranean war.

Demonstrators in Rome carried placards naming Italian objectives in the war—Tunisia, Jibuti, Corsica, Suez, Malta, Cyprus. There were reports that action against some of these places already had started. But Rome was convinced that nothing big would get under way until today. [All the foregoing, Page 1, Column 8.]

The sixth day of the Battle of France brought the German invaders still closer to Paris: at one point—south of Beauvais—they were said to be within twenty-five or thirty miles of their goal. On the French left wing the Germans crossed the Seine at several points in a dangerous advance that threatened to envelop the capital. In the center, they pushed through to the Ourcq Valley, a movement that similarly threatened to flank Reims. On the French right wing the German pressure was furiously increased; but the French said no great gains had resulted. Information from the French side was less complete than usual because the government press bureau was evacuated from Paris and had not yet established a stable headquarters. [Page 1, Column 1.]

The French Government moved, apparently to the neighborhood of Tours. An exodus of civilians from Paris got under way. [Page 1, Column 2.]

Berlin analyzed the front thus: A semicircle had been thrown around Paris, from which three wedges were being driven into the defense lines. The first, in the lower Seine Valley, succeeded in cutting off the extreme left of the French Army, which can now be pushed to the coast. The second was progressing toward the Marne from the Aisne below Soissons. The third, on the French right, had pierced the Aisne and was headed toward Reims. [Page 1, Column 5.]

London admitted the loss of the airplane carrier Glorious, two destroyers, a transport and an oil tanker—totaling 50,706 tons—in an engagement in the North Sea. King Haakon of Norway arrived in Britain with his government. Some Norwegian troops also were carried off and will continue the war on the Western Front. [Page 16, Column 3.]

Repercussions Elsewhere

President Roosevelt, in a broadcast speech, termed Italy's entry into the war a threat to the American way of life. "The hand that held the dagger has struck it into the back of its neighbor," he said. Declaring it an "obvious delusion that we of the United States can safely permit the United States to become a lone island in a world dominated by the philosophy of force," he advocated all possible material aid to the Allies. [Page 1, Column 4.]

The Canadian Parliament declared war against Italy; Prime Minister Mackenzie King denounced Premier Mussolini as "a carrion bird waiting for brave men to die." [Page 4, Column 5.]

Premier Reynaud, broadcasting to the French people after Italy's announcement, said France had won out over greater difficulties in the past. He asserted France always had been willing to negotiate Italian demands peaceably. [Page 12, Column 1.]

Berlin, jubilant over the entry of the Italians, expressed the belief that Premier Mussolini's military effort would be concentrated in the Mediterranean. It was said that no immediate Italian land attack on France was expected. [Page 5, Column 1.]

Switzerland reported much military activity, but no rumble of guns, in mountain passes between France and Italy. The Swiss were concerned about rumors that there were new German troop concentrations on the country's northern frontier. [Page 5, Column 5.]

Turkey stood ready to fulfill her engagements to the Allies under the mutual-assistance pact of last October. It was believed that the first step, once Italy made that pact operative by an aggressive move in the Mediterranean, would be the placing of Turkish ports and air fields at the disposal of the Allies. [Page 1, Column 7.]

Belgrade heard reports that the Italians had landed troops and much mechanized equipment at the Italian-owned port of Zara, which is on the Yugoslav coast, and on the Italian-owned island of Lagosta, near by. [Page 1, Column 6.]

FRENCH MINISTRIES MOVED SOUTHWARD

Tours Is Believed New Capital, but Reynaud Goes to Army —No Civilian Panic

By The Associated Press.

PARIS, June 10—The French Government left Paris tonight.

"Paul Reynaud, Premier, has gone with the armies," said a communiqué, which also declared:

"The High Command asked the Ministers to effect their withdrawal to the provinces in conformity with established dispositions. This withdrawal has been effected."

The announcement of the departure of the Ministers was made only after they were safely installed "somewhere in France" in the southern provinces.

The government transfer at General Maxime Weygand's request was approved last night at a Cabinet meeting.

Under cover of darkness the Ministers drove to their new offices

Continued on Page Ten

BRITISH NAVY GUNS HAMMER AT NAZIS

Shelling From Sea, Rushing of Troops and Planes Mark London's Share in Battle

By HAROLD DENNY
Special Cable to THE NEW YORK TIMES.

LONDON, June 10—Britain was rushing all available forces today into the battle in France, which was officially called here the "Battle of Paris and London" because of the Nazi threat to England. This reinforcement across the English Channel will continue, it was stated, "despite the imminent danger of German invasion of the United Kingdom."

The guns of British warships pounded the Germans to support Allied troops near the coast.

"Important contingents" of new troops have already gone to France, it was announced.

Even closer cooperation of the

Continued on Page Twelve

OUR HELP PLEDGED

President Offers Our Full Material Aid to Allies' Cause

AMERICA IN DANGER

Fate Hangs on Training and Arms, He Says at Charlottesville

The text of the President's speech will be found on Page 6.

By FELIX BELAIR Jr.
Special to THE NEW YORK TIMES.

CHARLOTTESVILLE, Va., June 10—"On this 10th day of June, 1940, the hand that held the dagger has struck it into the back of its neighbor." In these words tonight President Roosevelt condemned the decision of Premier Mussolini which took Italy into the war on the side of Germany.

The remark was interpolated by the President in an address at the graduation exercises of the University of Virginia here. There could be no missing the depth of his feeling, since he put into the words all the emphasis at his command.

Italy's intervention was denounced furthermore as a definite threat to the way of life and the trade and commerce of the Americas. This government, he said, would give all material aid to France and Great Britain as "opponents of force."

The Chief Executive of the United States spoke to the nation and to the world only a few hours after Premier Mussolini announced his decision to join hands with Chancellor Hitler and unleashed his fascist legions against France and Great Britain. More details were revealed by Mr. Roosevelt of his correspondence with the Italian dictator in an effort to keep Italy at peace and to prevent the spread of war to the Mediterranean basin.

"To the Regret of Humanity"

"Unfortunately—unfortunately, to the regret of all of us and to the regret of humanity—the chief of the Italian Government was unwilling to accept the procedure suggested, and he has made no counter proposal," the President said.

And a moment later:

"The Government of Italy has now chosen to preserve what it terms its freedom of action and to fulfill what it states are its promises to Germany. In so doing it has manifested disregard for the rights and security of other nations, disregard for the lives of the peoples of those nations which are directly threatened by the spread of this war, and has evidenced its unwillingness to find the means, through pacific negotiation, for the satisfaction of what it believes are its legitimate aspirations."

The President bespoke the prayers and hopes of this nation for those peoples beyond the seas who were battling for their freedom.

"In our American unity," he

Continued on Page Six

Nazi Tide Laps at Paris as Italy Joins War

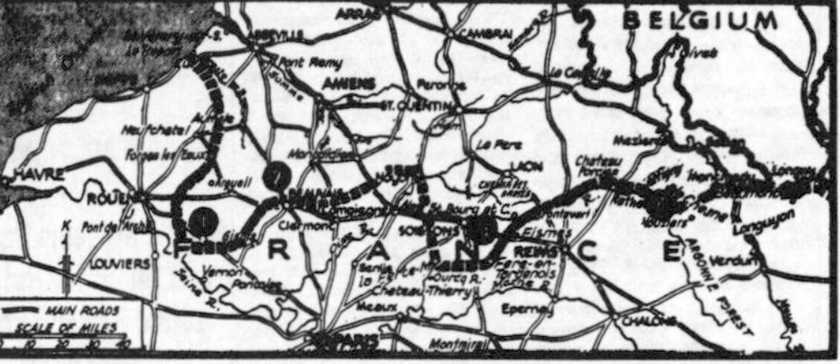

On the western end of the line the Germans pushed a wedge to the Seine southeast of Rouen (1) and struck mighty blows in the region of Beauvais (2). In the center they reached the Ourcq River below Soissons (3). To the east they crossed the Aisne at two points near Vouziers (4).

Italy's announcement of her entry into the war was accompanied by no attack anywhere. One report had Italian troops invading the French Riviera (1), but this was unsupported. Rome's troops landed at two Italian-owned points on the Yugoslav coast: Zara (2) and Lagosta (3). In Albania (4) Italian military preparations were accelerated.

NAZIS CLAIM BREAK IN SUPPLY ARTERY

Paris Cut Off From Havre by Thrust to Seine East of Rouen, Berlin Says

By C. BROOKS PETERS
Wireless to THE NEW YORK TIMES.

BERLIN, June 10—German forces in Northern France were fighting tonight to shorten the radius of a semicircle they are drawing about Paris, according to reports received here. Apparently they are attempting to drive three wedges into the remaining French territory north of the capital.

The first is on the Germans' extreme right wing, which is reported to have reached the lower Seine east of Rouen and therewith cuts off Paris from Havre. Mass tank formations, assisted by light motorized units, are claimed here to have made more than a sixty-mile ad-

Continued on Page Eleven

Three Italian Freighters Are Scuttled by Crews

By The Associated Press.

LA LINEA, Spain, Tuesday, June 11—Two Italian merchant ships, the 10,000-ton Chelina and the 2,000-ton Numbolia, were scuttled by their crews in Gibraltar waters late yesterday [Monday] when their crews heard the radio news that Italy had gone to war.

RIMOUSKI, Que., June 10 (UP)—The 3,921-ton Italian freighter Capo Noli was set afire by her crew tonight as she proceeded down the St. Lawrence, but the scuttling attempt failed.

The Marine Department said the Canadian pilot grounded the freighter near the Father Point pilot station. A naval control boat extinguished the flames.

The government salvage boat Lord Strathcona left Quebec tonight for the site with a large derrick in tow. The Capo Noli will be taken over by the Canadian Government and her crew probably will be interned.

ITALIANS REPORTED ON YUGOSLAV COAST

Said to Have Landed at Two Places Controlled by Rome—Mass on Greek Border

By The United Press.

BELGRADE, Yugoslavia, Tuesday, June 11—Large numbers of Italian troops were reported early today to have been landed along the Yugoslav coast at two Italian points as the Yugoslav Government prepared to fight in defense of its territory if necessary.

[It was reported from Berlin yesterday that Italian forces had invaded France through the Riviera, but this was denied in Rome, and German military quarters said later that they had no knowledge of any such movement.]

Reports from Split on the Adriatic coast said that large forces of Italian troops had been landed at

Continued on Page Four

TURKEY PREPARES UNDER ALLIED PACT

Partial Mobilization Expected Today—Troops Are on Move —Precautions in Balkans

By J. W. KERNICK
Special Cable to THE NEW YORK TIMES.

ISTANBUL, Turkey, June 10—Turkey, speeding her military preparations as a result of Italy's entry into the war, stood ready tonight to fulfill her obligations under her mutual-assistance agreement with Britain and France.

That accord, concluded last October, stipulates that Turkey will lend the Allies every assistance in her power in the event of hostilities in the Mediterranean as a result of aggressive action by a European power. Hence Turkish aid can be invoked as soon as the first shot is fired.

The Italian action has already resulted in the calling of several classes to the colors by the Turkish Government. It is believed that the next move will be to place ports and airfields at the disposal oi the Allies.

[The Turkish Cabinet met last night to consider the question of war or peace, The Associated Press reported, but it was believed that Turkey's entrance into the war would be by gradual steps, not immediately.]

Italy's declaration of war caused neither surprise nor excitement in Turkey. The Turks had suspected for some time and lately became certain that Premier Mussolini could not forever remain an onlooker while Chancellor Hitler marched.

Premier Mussolini's assurances that he did not intend to attack Yugoslavia, Turkey, Greece, Switz-

Continued on Page Two

Dispatches from Europe and the Far East are subject to censorship at the source.

La Guardia Warns of Strict Neutrality Here; Consuls Told to 'Adhere to Consular Duties'

Mayor La Guardia went on the air over WNYC, the city broadcasting station, yesterday afternoon with a strong plea to the million persons of Italian blood in this city to preserve strict neutrality in the face of Italy's declaration of war.

Moving with characteristic rapidity, the Mayor telephoned the city broadcasting studio in the New York City Building at the World's Fair and said he would be on the air ten minutes later. He thought over the message he wanted to deliver while driving over from the World's Fair City Hall, and was prepared to speak immediately upon his arrival. Meantime, Morris S. Novik, director of the station, had made arrangements to rebroadcast the Mayor's talk over five commercial stations at intervals later in the day.

Speaking slowly and impressively, the Mayor stated his policy that the European war must be fought on the battlefields of Europe and not on the sidewalks of New York.

Recalling his war service as an ally of the Italian forces in Italy, the Mayor said he fully realized that the Italian entry into the war on the opposite side must be as painful to others of Italian blood as it was to him. Nevertheless, he insisted that the national policy of neutrality must be observed in the city. While he pledged full protection to consular officers of various European governments in the city, the Mayor made clear that these officials must stay within the bounds of their consular duties.

The Mayor's speech follows:

This is F. H. La Guardia, Mayor of the City of New York, talking.

On Sept. 2, 1939, when the Nazi

Continued on Page Eight

DUCE GIVES SIGNAL

Announces War on the 'Plutocratic' Nations of the West

ASSURES 5 NEUTRALS

Bid Is Made to Russia, But Rome Has No Pledge of Aid

'Hostilities' Are Reported

"Hostilities were started four hours ago, Central European time," Radio Roma, the official Italirn short-wave radio, said last night at 11 o'clock Eastern daylight time in a broadcast recorded by Columbia Broadcasting System's short-wave listening station.

"The first Italian war bulletin is expected to be issued within a few hours."

At 2:18 A. M. today, however, the official British wireless said that "there have been no reports as yet of any engagements growing out of Italy's entrance into the war," Columbia's listening station reported.

By HERBERT L. MATTHEWS
By Telephone to THE NEW YORK TIMES.

ROME, Tuesday, June 11—Italy declared war on Great Britain and France yesterday afternoon, to take effect at one minute past midnight. The land, air and sea forces of the Italian Empire were already in motion.

It is a war, as Premier Benito Mussolini announced to the people from his balcony at the Palazzo Venezia at 6 in the evening, against the "plutocratic and reactionary democracies of the West." For the moment that does not include the United States, but few Italians believe that they will see the war to a finish without having the Americans against them.

Signor Mussolini expressly excluded Turkey, Switzerland, Yugoslavia, Greece and Egypt as enemies unless they attacked Italy or the Italian possessions.

Turkey provides the burning question of the day. Italians are absolutely convinced that the Turks will not move against them and will not honor their agreement with the Allies. It is hoped to confine Italian activity to France, Great Britain and the Mediterranean and to keep the Balkans tranquil. If that can be done, Italians think, the Turks will remain quiet.

Soviet Action Discounted

Russia has washed her hands of the struggle. The Italians know that any disturbance in the Balkans will immediately bring her in; but as long as the struggle is confined to the west and south the Soviet will do nothing either to hinder or help. This was told to your correspondent a few hours ago by a very authoritative source.

It was emphasized there were no agreements about furnishing material or anything else, nor any threats or promises.

The Italian Ambassador, Augusto Rosso, left in the morning for Moscow and Ivan Gorelkin, Soviet Ambassador, is coming back to Rome, thus ending a long period without such representation. The Italians were anxious to restore full diplomatic relations in this critical period, according to this writer's informant, and the Russians agreed, but without compromising themselves.

It thus appears that Premier Mussolini has embarked on this dangerous venture without really knowing what Soviet Russia will do in the long run.

President Roosevelt's speech clearly has come too late. There was nothing that the United States could do to halt this conflict, the Italians say. Whatever brake Mr. Roosevelt may have exercised was overcome by the momentum of the whole Fascist policy. Once it was set in motion, nothing could stop it.

The Italians do not believe that the United States can affect the issue, whatever it does. They are

Continued on Page Four

"All the News That's Fit to Print."

The New York Times.

LATE CITY EDITION
Partly cloudy, warmer today, followed by showers tonight. Tomorrow fair, temperature unchanged.
Temperatures Yesterday—Max., 78; Min., 65

VOL. LXXXIX...No. 30,093. Entered as Second-Class Matter, Postoffice, New York, N. Y. NEW YORK, SATURDAY, JUNE, 15, 1940. THREE CENTS NEW YORK CITY and Vicinity | FOUR CENTS Elsewhere Except in 7th and 8th Postal Zones.

GERMANS OCCUPY PARIS, PRESS ON SOUTH; CAPTURE HAVRE, ASSAULT MAGINOT LINE; FRENCH ARMY INTACT; SPAIN SEIZES TANGIER

HITLER IS DOUBTED

Roosevelt Skeptical of Pledge He Will Not Cross Atlantic

HAS RECOLLECTIONS

U. S. Doing All It Can for Allies, He Asserts of French Appeal

By FELIX BELAIR Jr.
Special to THE NEW YORK TIMES.

WASHINGTON, June 14—President Roosevelt replied today to Adolf Hitler's reported denial of territorial aspirations in the Western Hemisphere with a reference to the German Chancellor's record of broken pledges to respect the integrity of European nations over a considerable period of time.

As a part of the same answer the President said the United States was doing and would continue to do everything in its power to give aid to the Allies. He said, in effect, that Chancellor Hitler's statement in an interview that he would confine his activities to Europe was to be taken with considerable quantities of salt.

The President followed up this with an announcement of plans to mobilize American scientific genius in the interest of national defense.

"That brings recollections," the President said when asked at his press conference for his reaction to statements credited to the German Chancellor in an interview published in Hearst newspapers today. Reporters were not permitted to quote directly the rest of the President's statement, in which he said his observation might be enlarged upon with dates and nations going back over quite a period of years.

Many Rumors in Washington

Mr. Roosevelt's press conference remark was the high point of a day in which Washington was thick with rumors of the formation of a new French Cabinet without Premier Reynaud, that France would soon seek a separate peace with the Germans and that the President had been asked by France or Great Britain to propose a declaration of war against the Nazi government.

Both the White House and State Department denied that any proposal had been received from the Allied governments that the United States declare war.

Secretary Hull was asked in connection with the French situation whether the question of a declaration of war by the United States had been projected or raised in any way. He replied that so far as he knew nothing was involved beyond the sale of supplies, under terms and conditions that every one knew.

The question was asked of the Secretary of State at his press conference, which was held at 1 o'clock. Mr. Hull said the appeal Premier Reynaud made to President Roosevelt was then being decoded, that he had not seen it, but he understood it was the same that the French Premier gave by radio last night. Later the French Ambassador, Count de Saint-Quentin, said he assumed it was that or its equivalent.

Day's Other Developments

These other developments in the legislative and executive branches during the day stood out:

1. The President let it be known, by inference, that no accumulation of circumstances in the European war would alter this country's determination to arm to the teeth.

2. The House passed and sent to the Senate a bill authorizing the Reconstruction Finance Corporation to organize and lend money to corporations for plant expansion and acquisition of strategic materials for nationl defense.

3. State Department officials made no secret of their belief that France would soon undertake negotiations with Germany looking to a separate peace and that reorganization of the French Government probably would be attempted with this in mind.

4. Administration sources said legislation would be introduced next week to embargo exports of scrap iron as a measure of national defense.

5. Attorney General Jackson

Continued on Page Ten

The International Situation

On the Battle Fronts

Paris was taken over yesterday by the German war machine.

Led by dust-stained tanks, followed by motorised divisions and then by infantry, the German Army marched down the Champs Elysées. Tense, grim-faced Parisians—the few who had remained behind—stood silently on the curbs as a hostile force marched through the famous boulevards of the "City of Light" for the first time since 1871. Shops were closed and shuttered. [Page 1, Column 7.]

In Berlin there were scenes of wild rejoicing. On Chancellor Hitler's orders church bells were rung for a quarter of an hour and the Nazi flag was ordered displayed for three days. [Page 2, Column 2.]

Berlin said that the fall of Paris—described as "catastrophic" morally and economically for the French—had completed the second phase of the war. The first was the Battle of Flanders. The third, the High Command communiqué said, was pursuit and "final destruction" of all the French forces. The chief drive of this "final" phase appeared to be directed against the flank of the Maginot Line through Champagne and the Argonne Forest—famous World War battlefield of American troops. Montmédy, western anchor of the line, was reported conquered. Spearheads had driven as far east as Vitry-le François, between Paris and Nancy. Verdun was said to be threatened. On the coast Havre's fall was claimed. [Page 1, Column 8.]

Hitler's personal press representative in the field with him said that the German leader considered the fall of Paris only an incident on his road of conquest and that he was not interested in peace now. [Page 2, Column 8.]

The French High Command said it had abandoned Paris because there was no "valuable strategical reason" why it should be defended and it did not want the city devastated. The communiqué said the French Army was retreating in good order. A slackening of the German drive was reported at several points, but the heavy push in Champagne, threatening the rear of the Maginot Line, was still in progress. The armament of the line is useless against an attack from the rear. A frontal attack on the line west of the Saar was reported repulsed. [Page 1, Column 5.]

High sources in London said that Britain had agreed to accept any military or political decision the French Government might make but would fight on whatever it was. [Page 1, Column 6.] If the war is to be waged successfully, however, informed sources said, every available piece of war material in the United States must be sent to the Allies at once. [Page 1, Column 4.]

The war appeared to be developing for Italy. First reports of action on her Alpine frontier were reported in a communiqué. It was divulged for the first time, too, that the Italian fleet was at sea in force. [Page 1, Column 3.] Attacks in Africa were reported, both by the Italian air arm and by Allied troops against Libya, Eritrea and Ethiopia. Successes were claimed by the Italians in all actions. [Page 4, Column 1.]

The French Government abandoned Tours as its provisional capital and started southward, apparently for the port of Bordeaux. It was the seat of the French Government for a short time in 1914. [Page 1, Column 6.]

Repercussions Elsewhere

Spanish troops yesterday took over control of Tangier, the small internationally-policed territory in Northern Africa fronting on the Straits of Gibraltar. Madrid said the action had been taken to "guarantee its neutrality" and had been done with the full consent of the other three guarantors—Britain, France and Italy. Berlin said the consent of the Allies was given after the act. Return of Tangier has been one of the most frequently expressed territorial demands of Franco-Spain. That of British-held Gibraltar is the other. [Page 1, Column 4.] In Washington Secretary Hull said the United States would insist on its extraterritorial rights in Tangier under the treaty of 1906. [Follows the foregoing.]

"That brings up recollections," President Roosevelt said at his press conference when a purported interview with Chancellor Hitler was shown to him quoting the German leader as saying he had no aspirations in this hemisphere. The President's reference was to similar statements made about European countries. Driving ahead with the American defense program, the President announced the appointment of a scientific research commission to work with the defense advisory commission. [Page 1, Column 1.]

COLONNA PROTESTS ON ITALIAN CHARGES

Envoy Sees Hull—Inquiry Here Widened—German Agent to U. S. Warns of Reprisals

Special to THE NEW YORK TIMES.

WASHINGTON, June 14—The Italian Ambassador, Don Ascanio dei Principi Colonna, protested to Secretary of State Cordell Hull today what he considered to be an unjustified effort to foment anti-Italian feeling in the United States.

The protest was directed specifically to the charges made in New York yesterday that the Italian Consulate General there, under orders of Premier Benito Mussolini, was seeking to promote fascism in this country by ideological propaganda. He also implied there were similar activities against Italy in other American cities.

His concern was especially manifested over publication of these charges by newspapers. The fact that the New York charges were issued through Police Commissioner Valentine apparently was not mentioned. No reference was made directly to President Roosevelt's Charlottesville address denouncing Italy.

In making the protest, Prince Colonna declared that Italian consuls in this country restrict their activities to their legal functions and that Italian nationals in the United States are careful to avoid

Continued on Page Nine

ITALIANS IN CLASH ON FRENCH BORDER

Report Attack Repulsed—Fleet Action Revealed—Coast Is Shelled

By HERBERT L. MATTHEWS
By Telephone to THE NEW YORK TIMES.

ROME, June 14—The war began to develop for Italy on land, sea and air, according to this morning's communiqué, with the first activity on the Italo-French frontier and an indication that the Italian Fleet was on its way on some great mission.

The taking of Tangier by the Spaniards is considered a first-rate victory for the Axis, but, of course, the fall of Paris dominates everything else.

Among Fascisti here there is rejoicing over the fate of Paris. The newspaper Lavoro Fascista cheers in an eight-column box whose sentiments are typical.

"C'est Paris," it says. "Capitalists, Jews, Masons and snobs all over the world are in mourning. The spiritual capital of all the old civilization has fallen. Paris has fallen. Paris itself 'la ville lumière—Paris tout entier.' "

As the war shapes up, even this early, the Mediterranean seems more than ever certain to become Italy's main theatre of operations. To be sure, there was some activity for the first time yesterday on the French frontier. There were clashes by patrols and "enemy, at-

Continued on Page Four

MOROCCANS MOVE IN

Spanish Troops Take Over Zone in Which U. S. Has Rights

'GIBRALTAR' NOW CRY

Madrid Students Parade and Shout for Return of the Famous Rock

By T. J. HAMILTON
Special Cable to THE NEW YORK TIMES.

MADRID, June 14—The Spanish Government announced early this afternoon that with the object of guaranteeing "the neutrality of the international zone" in Morocco, Moroccan troops entered Tangier this morning.

It was stated officially that the action had been taken in agreement with Great Britain, France and Italy, who are other guarantors of the zone under a convention of 1903. The United States, which is also a signatory to the convention, received a copy of the announcement in a note delivered to the United States Embassy here at 11 A. M.

The text of the communiqué follows:

"With the object of guaranteeing the neutrality of the international zone and the city of Tangier, the Spanish Government has decided to take charge provisionally of the surveillance, police and public safety services of the international zone; forces of Moroccan troops entered this morning with this object.

"All existing services are assured and they continue functioning normally."

Coveted by the Spanish

Next to Gibraltar, Tangier occupies the front rank in Spanish territorial aims. In the last few days newspapers have devoted special attention to it among African territories that the French, assertedly with the connivance of the British, took away from Spain.

Although the first extra newspapers did not appear on the streets until 4 P. M., word that Tangier had been occupied spread quickly. By noon flags were appearing on houses throughout Madrid and members of the Falange youth movement were marching in uniform through the streets.

The news helped to bring an extra welcome for General Franco when he arrived late in the afternoon to open an exposition showing accomplishments of the government in rebuilding devastated regions. The press confined itself to printing the text of the government communiqué and relating the history of the international zone.

However, there were four demonstrations during the day, in which university student Falangistas predominated, all shouting, "Tangier is ours!" Some of these demonstrations passed the French and British Embassies.

British circles emphasized tonight that the occupation of Tangier had taken place with the complete agreement of Britain and France, who along with Italy and Spain were guarantors of the interna-

Continued on Page Six

FRENCH NOTE LULL

Battle Continues Along Front—At Some Points Its Violence Abates

ATTACK IS REPULSED

Nazi Losses Are Heavy in Maginot Assault—Loire Next Barrier

By G. H. ARCHAMBAULT
Wireless to THE NEW YORK TIMES.

TOURS, France, June 14—Is there any significance in the fact that although the battle continued to be waged today all along the front from the coast to the Argonne, it was notable that at certain points its violence was abating?

That question is in every mind tonight, for it may contain confirmation of the belief that the Germans have now engaged the maximum of their available forces.

The communiqué issued tonight gives little information on the day's operations, but it implies that all the retreating French forces continue to fight rear-guard actions and that at several parts of the front they have, in addition, counter-attacked the advancing Germans.

The only reference to Paris is as follows: "The prescribed withdrawal has been effected in conformity with our plans."

But if there has been a relative lull on the main line of battle the Germans were very active in front of the Maginot Line, especially west of the Saar River. Early in the morning they launched a violent attack with the now customary accompaniment of tanks and dive-bombing planes. The French claim to have thrown back the attacking force, on which they inflicted heavy losses.

Present Front Uncertain

Manifestly this attack must be considered in correlation with the fighting in the Argonne, farther to the west.

It is impossible tonight to indicate the present front even approximately. It is really one long line of pockets and salients, a situation calling for great qualities of generalship in order to preserve cohesion of the French forces.

Meanwhile, with the withdrawal of the French troops charged with the defense of Paris the first phase of the Battle of France was ended in defeat. It may be called the Battle of the Seine. The next phase may be the Battle of the Loire.

The issue was clear from the moment it was decided to declare Paris an open city and the news of withdrawal cannot have surprised many. A communiqué issued this morning from French General Headquarters explained that there were insufficient strategic reasons for defending the capital to justify risking destruction of France's very heart.

From the military point of view it is clear now that a battle for Paris would merely have immobilized troops, added to the loss of life and brought about no com-

Continued on Page Three

British Call on U. S. for Munitions at Once; French Order 120 Bombers Here for 1941

By RAYMOND DANIELL
Special Cable to THE NEW YORK TIMES

LONDON, June 14—In circles close to the government it was said today that every gun, every ounce of war materials that the United States can spare was needed urgently and needed quickly if the cause for which the Allies were fighting was not to be lost on the battlefields of France. It is not a matter of months but of weeks, even days, it was added by those in a position to know the facts, of which the ordinary people in this country only now are becoming dimly aware.

Withdrawal of the battered French armies behind their abandoned capital and contemplation of the possibility that the Government of France may be forced to withdraw from Europe to Africa, led to expressions that made increasingly apparent the extent to which the

Continued on Page Four

After the Anglo-French Purchasing Commission yesterday had announced that French purchases of war material in the United States were being stepped up, the French signed a contract at 7 P. M. for 120 "flying fortresses" to be delivered in the second and third quarters of 1941. The planes are to be built by the Consolidated Aircraft Corporation.

In an interview earlier in the day a spokesman for the Anglo-French commission said that contracts for "many millions of dollars" had been placed during the day.

Instead of curtailing purchases following the capture of Paris by the Germans, France is sending more purchasing experts, this spokesman said. In response to a question relative to the ability to pay cash for purchases, he added:

"There is no immediate end of our

Continued on Page Four

Will Fight On, British Insist, Even if the French Capitulate

London Letting Ally Make Decision on the Immediate Course as Help Is Speeded—New Nazi Peace Offensive Expected

By The United Press.

LONDON, June 14—Britain has agreed to accept any decision France may make regarding military and political policy, but if France is lost as an ally the British will fight on alone against Chancellor Hitler's war machine, it was understood tonight.

The British Government was understood to have agreed this week to any choice the French Government might make in regard to these military and political matters, which weigh more heavily with each hour of Germany's increased drive, provided the choice had the approval of Generalissimo Maxime Weygand.

Foreign observers in London today regarded the German assault against the Maginot Line, particularly the strong flanking attack south of Montmedy around Vitry-le-François, as of far greater strategic importance than yesterday's German occupation of undefended Paris. Nevertheless, the psychological importance of the fall of Paris and the effect on French morale are not underestimated.

The impression prevails in foreign embassies in London that Herr Hitler would respond affirmatively to any possible French pease overture, but would impose harsh conditions as his price for ending the war in France. These conditions, it was felt, might range from dismantling the $500,000,000 Maginot Line to the return to Germany of Alsace-Lorraine and other territorial and economic and financial concessions.

There are strong indications, however, that Herr Hitler would refuse to negotiate with Britain, since he is intent on smashing Britain's financial and industrial power.

How far Germany would be prepared to bid for a completely Nazi-dictated peace presumably would depend upon the extent of the German losses suffered in the war.

If Britain should be compelled to fight on alone without France as an ally she would be able, it is felt in British quarters, to carry on until Autumn with United States aid. The British Navy is relatively intact despite Germany's claims to the contrary. Then, it is asserted, starvation might seriously menace Germany and Italy during the Winter, impairing their military strength and the security of their home fronts.

British morale appears to be firm,

Continued on Page Five

TOURS ABANDONED AS FRENCH CAPITAL

Government Is Expected to Make Seat at Bordeaux—U. S. Move Is Awaited

By P. J. PHILIP
Wireless to THE NEW YORK TIMES.

TOURS, France, June 14—Tours has ceased to be the substitute capital of France after a brief three-day career. Premier Paul Reynaud's speech last night and other symptoms showed clearly before we went to bed that that would be so.

There were already signs of packing up again in different administrations. Sleep seemed, however, more urgent than flight, especially as we ourselves had just obtained a bed—the first we had slept in since Sunday. In that we were luckier than most, although it does seem expensive to have had only one night's sleep in a two-room apartment rented for a month. However, it permitted a proper wash and a change of linen.

And now we and everybody else are on our way again. We don't know what is happening because the information service installed here with so much trouble on Monday has opened its wings and fled with a part of the censorship service. Press Wireless is functioning for a few hours and then good-bye to Tours.

Avalanche Advancing

The morning communiqué told the story of why this should be so—in part at least. The avalanche is advancing from all sides, closing around Paris and pushing forward in Champagne. The problem is where to go to escape it.

During the day, while we are on the road, things are likely to happen that will change the whole situation. It is too much now to hope that they will change it in any way that can be counted as satisfactory.

Along the roads through here the stream of civilian and military cars has recommenced. The embassies and legations have already pulled out. Wherever we go is going to be so congested that the remnants of that camping outfit with which we started are going to be invaluable.

Only 5,000 American bombers and fighters flying across the Atlantic in response to Premier Reynaud's desperate appeal could restore to the French people their belief that they are not alone in this terrible fight. Words and promises and the complicated explanation of political circumstances will not suffice. They will serve only to break further the dying hope there is today in every French heart.

For the British all the French feeling is as if they were of the

Continued on Page Three

REICH TANKS CLANK IN CHAMPS-ELYSEES

Berlin Recounts Parade Into Paris—Third of Citizens Reported Remaining

By The United Press.

BERLIN, June 14—German tanks today clanked across the Seine bridges, past the Arc de Triomphe and down the tree-lined Champs Elysées into the heart of Paris at the head of the first cavalcade of invaders to enter the French capital in nearly seventy years.

Flanked by armored cars, the dust-stained tanks swung triumphantly into Paris from the northwest at the head of Nazi units occupying the "City of Light," German accounts of the event said.

It was the ninth recorded invasion of Paris and the first since Bismarck's legions trod the broad boulevards in 1871. The jubilant German press proclaimed the fall of Paris to be the "symbol of decision" in Chancellor Adolf Hitler's Western offensive.

[Berlin Nazis expected Adolf Hitler to visit Paris June 21, the twenty-first anniversary of Germany's acceptance of the Treaty of Versailles, an Associated Press dispatch said.]

Entry From Northwest

The advance into Paris, through the suburbs of Argenteuil and Neuilly and into the aristocratic western part of the city began early in the morning, the Germans said. It was exactly five weeks after the massive western offensive began with the German drive into the Netherlands and Belgium.

The tanks rumbled between thin lines of tense and silent Parisians, the Germans said. Reports from the French capital estimated that probably a third of the city's normal population of 2,800,000 had remained in Paris.

Behind the tanks rolled anti-tank units, still dusty and laden with evidence of the furious fighting in which they had taken part to the north.

As the long shadows of the early morning retreated, more and more Nazi contingents streamed into the capital, evacuated by French Armies hoping to save their beloved Paris from the fate of Warsaw.

Motorized infantry, riding in steel-shielded trucks mounting machine guns to command the broad streets, converged from the Seine bridges to the Place de l'Etoile.

In that hub from which radiate eleven streets stands the Arc de Triomphe and its tomb of the Unknown World War Soldier, where flickers the Eternal Flame.

German reports indicated that the parade through Paris swung around

Continued on Page Two

2 FORCES TAKE CITY

Berlin Says Industrial Losses May Be Worst Feature for French

MONTMEDY CAPTURED

Anchor of Maginot Line Lost—Nazis Report Foe Is Routed

By C. BROOKS PETERS
Wireless to THE NEW YORK TIMES.

BERLIN, June 14—Today, for the third time within the last century and a quarter, victorious German troops marched into Paris. This time, however, the legions, the clatter of whose hobnailed boots resounds throughout Paris and the entire world, are more than just German soldiers. They are the bearers of a proposed new order for Europe and perhaps the world, a major tenet of which is to destroy the old one.

With the capitulation of Paris, the Germans claim that the destruction of the remaining French forces is but a matter of "the shortest time." Well-informed quarters in Berlin put that time at two weeks at most.

For the German High Command announced today that the second phase of the western campaign has been completed successfully, the resistance of the French northern fronts has been broken and the enemy is "in full retreat along the entire front from Paris to the Maginot Line near Sedan."

Retreat Called Rout

If the statements of German military officials in Berlin are correct, this "full retreat" is really a rout. For the French, forced from their positions, have had no time to construct new ones but are being constantly harassed by German tanks, other motorized units and planes as they move southward, it is reported.

Early this morning, the Germans declare, they unleashed a frontal attack on the Maginot Line along the entire Saar front. Farther east, the fall of Montmedy, "anchor" of the Maginot Line, was claimed as well.

The extreme right wing of the German forces was not idle either. For yesterday it captured Havre, Berlin heard, and thus added approximately another hundred miles to the stretch of French coast that already is in German hands.

Advance on Cherbourg

The lower Seine, moreover, according to the High Command, was crossed on a wide front. The extreme right wing, it is believed, now is advancing on Cherbourg further to cut France off from Great Britain and provide the Germans with still another base for a future raid on the British Isles.

The front is now about 300 miles long as the crow flies, Germans declare, from Havre to the Rhine.

Although no information has been officially released here relative to the progress of the attack on the Maginot Line, it was said in usually accurately informed quarters tonight that the force of the German drive in this sector already has borne fruit and that Reich troops have broken through in several places.

Escape Held Impossible

Forces of the German left wing are reported pushing forward in a southeasterly direction in what now appears to be a plan to storm the triangle of the Maginot fortifications from several sides, while an advance west of the fortifications to Belfort—southern tip of the Maginot Line—would cut off the avenue of escape for the French troops manning the line.

This German left wing yesterday was said to have captured Vitry-le Francois and crossed the Marne-Rhine Canal, which connects that town with Strasbourg. Still farther west another tentacle of the German left wing last evening was reported to have stormed the famous Hill 304 (Dead Man's Hill) northwest of Verdun, in which sector in 1916, Germans say, they lost 80,000 men.

The southern tip of the Argonne Forest also has been reached, Germans declare.

The Meuse defenses and Verdun

Continued on Page Two

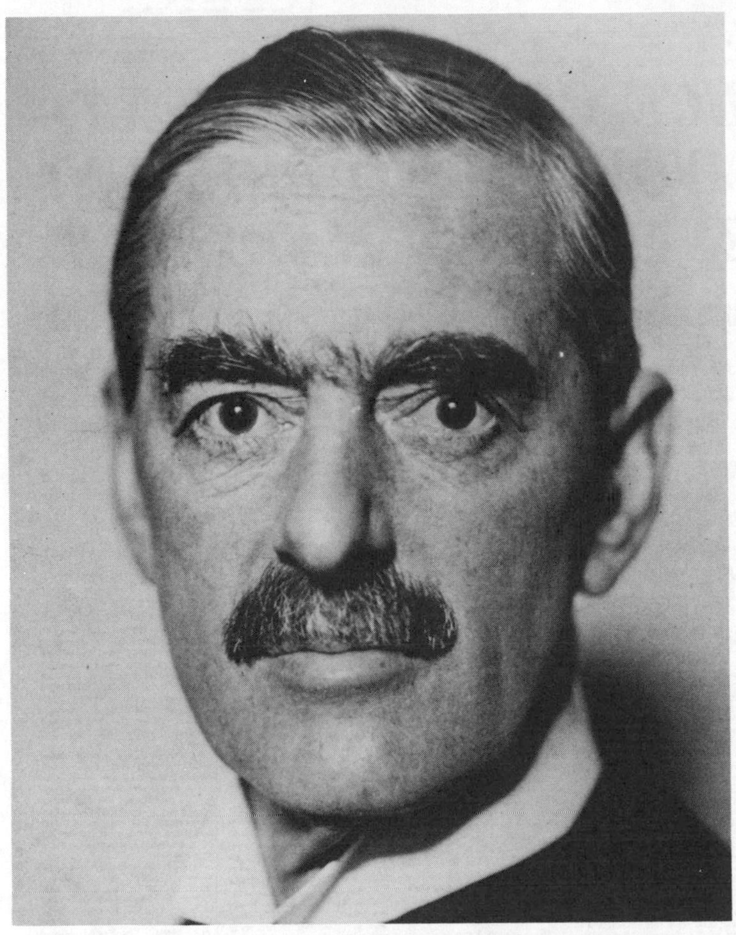

British Prime Minister Neville Chamberlain resigned on May 10.

Winston Churchill became the new Prime Minister of England and etched himself a place in history.

The French Army vainly tried to defend the Maginot Line before the German *blitzkrieg*.

A devastated London street after a German night raid during the Battle of Britain.

"All the News That's Fit to Print."

The New York Times.

LATE CITY EDITION
Cloudy today with little change in temperature. Tomorrow cloudy and slightly warmer.
Temperatures Yesterday—Max., 72; Min., 52

Section 1

NEWS INDEX, PAGE 33, THIS SECTION

VOL. LXXXIX..No. 30,101. Entered as Second-Class Matter, Postoffice, New York, N. Y. NEW YORK, SUNDAY, JUNE 23, 1940. Including Rotogravure Picture, Magazine and Book Review. TEN CENTS | TWELVE CENTS Beyond 200 Miles, Except West of Pa.—South of Md.—North of Mass.

FRENCH SIGN REICH TRUCE, ROME PACT NEXT; BRITISH BOMB KRUPP WORKS AND BREMEN; HOUSE QUICKLY PASSES 2-OCEAN NAVY BILL

REPUBLICAN FIGHT LOOMS ON WAR ISSUE AT THE CONVENTION

Dewey, Taft and Willkie Reach Philadelphia to Appeal to the Delegates

NO GROUP HAS CONTROL

Rival Candidates Make Ballot Claims—Willkie Stronger—Hoover Possibility Seen

A battle between divergent views on the war and peace issue loomed yesterday among delegates to the Republican National Convention, opening tomorrow. Messrs. Dewey, Taft and Willkie, rival candidates for the Presidential nomination, reached Philadelphia to press their campaigns. No leader or group of leaders is in a position to dominate the proceedings or the committee on resolutions. The effect of a speech by Mr. Hoover to the convention Tuesday night is expected to decide what, if any part, he will play as a Presidential nominee. [All the foregoing Page 1, Column 1.]

In press conferences Mr. Dewey declared for aid to the Allies without violating international or domestic law or entering the war; Mr. Willkie for aid to the Allies without going to war, and for reciprocal trade treaties. [Page 2, Column 1.]

The national committee approved a change in the rules under which districts which fail to show a poll of 1,000 Republicans would be deprived of representation at future conventions. Other rules changes approved would ease penalties on States which do not give a majority for the national ticket. [Page 2, Column 4.]

Drafters of the platform, split over aid to the Allies, hinted that a stand on the foreign policy plank might be left largely to the decision of the Presidential nominee. [Page 3, Column 1.]

Convention Unbossed

By JAMES A. HAGERTY
Special to THE NEW YORK TIMES.

PHILADELPHIA, June 22—The Republican National Convention, which will convene here Monday in the Municipal Auditorium, will open without a boss or even under the control of any particular group of minor bosses.

This was the indication, today, when District Attorney Thomas E. Dewey of New York, Senator Robert A. Taft of Ohio and Wendell L. Willkie, president of the Commonweath and Southern Corporation, just now regarded as the three leading candidates for the Presidential nomination, arrived in the convention city to make direct appeals to the delegates.

With no leader or group of leaders in a position to dominate either the convention or the committee on resolutions, the delegates face the prospect of a hotly contested fight for the nomination for President, and an equally bitter floor contest on the resolution on foreign relations.

Little difficulty is expected in putting through the rest of the platform which is expected to follow the recommendations of the program committee of the National Committee, headed by Dr. Glenn Frank.

Alfred M. Landon, nominee for President in 1936, who is chairman of the subcommittee on foreign relations of the committee on resolutions, continued today his efforts to get a plank that would be satisfactory both to the isolationists and to the Allies, but the formula, so far as could be learned, had not been found tonight.

Candidates Give Views

Mr. Dewey, Mr. Willkie and Senator Taft each had a press conference. Mr. Dewey declared for aid for the Allies without violating international or domestic law or getting into the war. Mr. Willkie, who was nearly mobbed by supporters in the Bellevue-Stratford Hotel, also declared for aid to the Allies without going to war and

Continued on Page Two

Major Sports Results

BASEBALL

New York's major league teams all met defeat yesterday. The Reds downed the Giants, 3—1, on Ernie Lombardi's homer with one man on base, the Pirates beat the Dodgers, 7—2, and the Tigers won from the Yankees, 3—2. Despite the setback, the Dodgers stayed in first place in the National League.

RACING

Your Chance won the $13,350 Dwyer Stakes at Aqueduct after Snow Ridge, first past the finish line, was disqualified for bumping in the stretch. Gen'l Manager was placed second and Andy K. third. The crowd of 20,520 bet $1,076,417 on the seven races, this being Aqueduct's first million-dollar day.

TRACK AND FIELD

The University of Southern California won its sixth successive National Collegiate A. A. championship in the meet at Minneapolis. The New York A. C. easily retained the metropolitan A. A. U. senior title.

(Complete Details in Section 5.)

CITY WPA TO PURGE 1,000 NAZIS, REDS

Signing of Affidavits to Be Started Tomorrow—FBI to Aid in Investigations

Without waiting for President Roosevelt to sign the new Relief Appropriations Act, Colonel F. C. Harrington, National Work Projects Commissioner, set in motion yesterday the machinery for purging the WPA rolls of Communists and Nazis by July 1.

The purge in this city will begin tomorrow, and the local administrator, Lieut. Col. Brehon B. Somervell, estimated that at least 1,000 WPA workers would lose their jobs before it was completed. All of the 101,000 persons on the rolls here, and 1,700,000 in other parts of the country, will be required to sign affidavits disavowing Communist or Nazi affiliations. The maximum penalty for false statement will be $2,000 fine and two years' imprisonment.

Colonel Somervell made clear that his office would not rely on affidavits alone in carrying out the mandate of the new law. The registration lists of the Board of Elections will be compared with the WPA payroll to turn up the names of Communists. The full facilities of the Federal Bureau of Investigation, the Police Department and the WPA's own Bureau of Investigation will be invoked as a further means of identification.

Dies Records to Be Used

Still another source of data, Colonel Somervell revealed, will be the reports and testimony gathered by the Dies committee and the record compiled in the recent trial of Fritz Kuhn, leader of the German-American Bund.

Because of "the well-known practice of Communists to deny membership in the party and to use false names in enrollment with the WPA," the administrator called upon all "responsible citizens" to make available any information they had on subversive activities among Federal relief employes. He said he expected at least 50,000 letters, and he promised that "grudge letters would be carefully sifted out from those submitting authentic information."

Although Congress did not complete action on the new Relief Act until yesterday morning, WPA officials in this city have been collecting material on Communists and Nazis on their rolls for several weeks. More than 1,000 names of persons tentatively identified as members of un-American groups are now under scrutiny, it was learned.

Under the wording of the law, Colonel Somervell said, a person does not have to be a member of the Communist party to be ineligible for WPA employment. He said he regarded Trotskyists as Communists within the meaning of the law, and indicated that other "splinter groups" would be subject to a similar interpretation. The administrator said he would function as the court of last resort in determining whether a person entertained subversive views.

The WPA purge creates a problem for municipal relief authorities.

Continued on Page Thirteen

FOR 200 NEW SHIPS

70% Increase in Fleet Authorized as Congress Recesses Till July 1

TO COST 4 BILLIONS

Chambers Enact Tax, Defense and Relief Fund Measures

Special to THE NEW YORK TIMES.

WASHINGTON, June 22—Congress took a recess at 9:10 o'clock tonight, adopting a resolution to reassemble on July 1 after the Republican National Convention at Philadelphia, and to take a similar week's recess during the Democratic National Convention at Chicago.

As a night session began to clear the decks for the recess, the House gave a dramatic flourish to a day devoted to pressing legislation by passing and sending to the Senate the "two-ocean" navy bill. No dissent was heard in the voice vote.

Within less than two hours, the House thus gave its approval to the construction of the world's mightiest navy, designed for defense of the United States and the Western Hemisphere. The Senate did not have time to act.

The "two-ocean" navy bill would authorize about 200 warships, a 70 per cent increase in the nation's fleet, or an expansion of 1,325,000 tons of combatant and auxiliary vessels to be built in the next six years at an estimated cost of $4,000,000,000.

Naval Air Force Augmented

Besides the increase in ship tonnage, the two-ocean navy measure also would increase the naval air force authorized strength from 10,000 to 15,000 planes.

It provides for $25,000,000 for "mosquito" torpedo boats, and authorizes an appropriation of $150,000,000 to expand shipbuilding facilities at government and private yards.

It provides also for the expenditure of $20,000,000 for expansion of facilities for armor plate manufacture and $50,000,000 for added facilities for construction of guns.

In calling for enactment of the bill, as recommended by Admiral Harold R. Stark, Chief of Naval Operations, Chairman Vinson of the House Naval Affairs Committee said that when the bill became law the Administration would ask for $175,000,000 for an immediate start on the program.

Mr. Vinson and Representative Maas of Minnesota, ranking minority member on the committee, led the brief debate by asserting that the United States should not depend upon the Navy of any other power for its defense.

"The time has come to realize that if the United States is to remain free and independent it must depend upon itself," Mr. Maas said. "It is foolish to risk our defense on the thin thread of a (the Panama) canal."

The Navy now has 307 ships in

Continued on Page Fourteen

$5,377,552,058 Voted For Defense This Year

By The Associated Press.

WASHINGTON, June 22—Here are the defense appropriation totals, including contract authorizations, which Congress has approved thus far this session:

*Regular Army bill..	$1,823,254,624
*Regular Navy bill..	1,492,542,750
Supplemental defense	1,768,913,908
Urgent deficiency.....	28,000,000
Emergency deficiency	252,340,776
Strategic materials (in Treasury appropriation)	12,500,000
Total	$5,377,552,058

*To which supplemental sums were added by the Senate.

There are also items intended for defense in the Civil Aeronautics Authority, Civilian Conservation Corps, WPA and the Army Civil Functions Supply Bills.

COMMITTEE LEANS TO KNOX REJECTION

But Senate Naval Group Votes to Hear Him July 1—Stimson Will Testify Next Day

By HAROLD B. HINTON
Special to THE NEW YORK TIMES.

WASHINGTON, June 22—Confirmation of Colonel Frank Knox as Secretary of the Navy probably will be opposed by the Senate Naval Affairs Committee, according to some members questioned after a stormy executive session today. If members maintain the opposition shown today, an adverse report will be made to the Senate, it was said.

The Naval and the Military Affairs committees, to which the nominations of Colonel Knox and of Henry L. Stimson as Secretary of War have been referred, will hear the nominees in person during the week of July 1, when Congress reassembles after its recess for the Republican National Convention.

There is no indication that the Military Affairs Committee will recommend rejection of Colonel Stimson, although he will probably be closely questioned by such isolationists members as Senators Reynolds and Lundeen.

The Naval Affairs Committee will give Colonel Knox a more searching examination, it was believed. Some members, it was reported, favored rejecting the nomination today, but counsel prevailed that no nominee should be disapproved without having a chance to be heard.

Senator Walsh, its chairman, announced after the meeting that Colonel Knox would be invited to appear on July 1. In other quarters it was said that eleven members attended today's meeting and that most of those who spoke were opposed to the nomination. Only Senators Hale and Barbour took no part in the discussions.

The most outspoken opponents, according to these reports, included Senators Walsh, Tydings, Smith of South Carolina, Byrd, Holt and Gillette, all Democrats. Senator Johnson of California, a Republican, also indicated his opposition. Others attending the meeting were

Continued on Page Fifteen

British Torpedo and Bomb the Scharnhorst; Submarine, Planes Waylay Nazi Battleship

By HAROLD DENNY
Special Cable to THE NEW YORK TIMES.

LONDON, June 22—The Germans' 26,000-ton battle cruiser Scharnhorst has been seriously damaged by a British submarine and airplanes off the Norwegian coast, according to reports given out tonight by the Admiralty and the Air Ministry.

The Scharnhorst was believed to be lying at bay with German destroyers and war planes clustering about her protectively, awaiting further attack by British naval units summoned by the Royal Air Force bombers.

The battle with the Scharnhorst and her escorting forces was the most important of three attacks on German and Italian naval craft reported in London.

The other incidents were the almost unbelievable exploit of the capture of an Italian submarine by a British trawler in the Gulf of Aden opposite British Somaliland and the sinking by an airplane of a German supply ship in the North Sea.

The Scharnhorst, with her sister ship the Gneisenau, the most powerful of German war vessels, had previously taken severe punishment. She was heavily pummeled in April by the British battleship Renown off Narvik, Prime Minister Winston Churchill then reported.

On June 13 she was reported here to have been badly bombed, with one—perhaps two—British bombs making direct hits on the center of the ship when she was in Trondheim Fjord.

"One of our submarines sighted the Scharnhorst soon after she left Trondheim Fjord," the day's reports said. "The battle cruiser was clearly on passage to a safe port where she could repair damage sustained when hit by at least one heavy bomb during an attack by the aircraft of the fleet arm on June 13."

This latest encounter with the Scharnhorst touched off an excep-

Continued on Page Twenty-one

ARMS PLANT IS HIT

R.A.F. Raiders Continue Assault Upon Nazis' Bases of Supply

SCORE NEAR BERLIN

Plane Factory Is Target—Germans Retaliate Along English Coast

By JAMES MacDONALD
Special Cable to THE NEW YORK TIMES.

LONDON, June 22—Royal Air Force bombers pounded the big Krupp arms works at Essen and important aircraft factories and military stores at Bremen, Kassel, Rothenburg and Goettingen and a big naval depot at Willemsoord in German-occupied Netherlands in a heavy series of air raids last night, according to the Air Ministry's communiqué today.

As against their boast of heavy damage done to the Nazis, British officials insisted that Nazi airmen had accomplished little in their retaliatory raids in this country this morning and last night.

Three persons were killed in a Suffolk town and three wounded elsewhere, it was announced. It was declared that bombs burst sporadically in "several counties on the east coast," but that most of them fell in open country, causing small damage. The German raids, it was said, were less intense than those of Tuesday and Wednesday nights. The Ministry did not state whether or not any Nazi planes were shot down, or if any defending fighter machines were lost.

All Appears Quiet

Meanwhile all appeared quiet on the British home air front tonight. There were no unwelcome noises of purring enemy motors that were picked up by the sensitive sound-detecting devices on the ground.

[Alexandria, Egypt, fought off three Italian air raids yesterday, the first of the war. British fliers attacked Tobruk, Libya, and reported hitting a large warship. Rome said bombers had destroyed a British naval base in Egypt and raided Marseille and Bizerte, Tunisia.]

Many sections of British planes are reported to have taken part in widespread raids on German objectives last night, but only one was shot down and only two are reported missing.

The plane that was shot down was one of several that subjected Willemsoord to a terrific aerial bombardment.

Almost five tons of high explosive and incendiary bombs were dropped in less than a minute. During that lightning stroke oil tanks were set afire, naval storehouses blown to rubble, two unidentified ships sunk, another badly damaged, "and German machine-gunners received a dose of their own medicine," the Air Ministry said. American built Lockheed-Hudson planes were used in that sortie.

Two Planes Missing

Many planes were engaged in the big raids over Germany. They returned with only two missing.

British raiders over Bremen directed their attack against the large Focke-Wulf airplane factory. They made direct hits with incendiary and explosive bombs in the middle of the factory buildings. Two violent explosions were seen by the British fliers after their bombs burst.

The airfield adjoining the factory was also bombed and one hangar was badly damaged, according to assertions made here.

Another section of the raiders reported that they had hit several buildings of the Krupp plant at Essen as well as railroad sidings near by. The exact extent of the damage done there, however, was not disclosed in London.

The objective at Kassel was the Fieseler aircraft factory and it was said that several bombs were seen exploding directly on the target.

Airplane hangars were damaged at Rothenberg, where also military buildings and the air field were hit. Another attacking force dropped bombs on the aircraft storage depot

Continued on Page Twenty-six

The International Situation

In Europe and Africa

An armistice between Germany and France was signed in the Forest of Compiegne yesterday at 6:50 P. M. German time (12:50 P. M. New York time). Immediately after the signing the French representatives left by a German plane, German-piloted, for Rome, where they will sign a companion document with Italy. Six hours after the signatures have been appended to the Italian armistice the order to cease fire will become effective. The terms of the armistice are still withheld; in Bordeaux they were described as "hard but honorable." London reported, without confirmation, that these were the principal provisions: (1) Occupation of France by Germany and Italy for the duration of the war with Britain; (2) surrender of all war stores; (3) surrender of all gold and foreign currency reserves; (4) delivery of coal and other raw material supplies to Germany for a fixed period. [Page 1, Column 8.]

Prime Minister Churchill said he had heard "with grief and amazement" of the French acceptance of terms that, to his mind, would mean that France and her empire would be entirely at the mercy of the dictators. He called on the French people to continue resistance. This call was reiterated by General Charles de Gaulle, former French Under-Secretary of War, who broadcast from London, calling on all French people not under Axis guns to mobilize to carry on the war. [Page 1, Column 6.]

The French negotiators arrived in Rome by plane from Compiègne. [Page 27, Column 1.]

Berlin announced that 500,000 French soldiers, encircled in Alsace-Lorraine, had surrendered, among them three army commanders. Only isolated resistance was left in that part of France. The Germans took the port of Lorient, on the southern coast of Brittany. According to Swiss reports, the French repulsed a German attack on L'Ecluse Fort, which dominates the Rhone at the Swiss border. [Page 22, Column 1.]

British bombers struck at the famous Krupp armaments works at Essen and at aircraft factories at several other points in Germany. In a raid on Willemsoord, German-held base in the Netherlands, the British said they had sunk two ships, set one afire and destroyed naval storehouses. Berlin reported that nearly 100 planes took part in Friday night's bombing of Britain. The Germans said that in recent actions they had sunk two British transports, one of 11,000 tons, the other of 32,000, the latter carrying about 5,000 men who were lost. British bombers reached the Berlin area Friday night, the Germans admitted, injuring seven persons and damaging buildings. [Page 1, Column 5.]

The British reported that the German battleship Scharnhorst, 26,000 tons, had been both torpedoed and bombed, with "considerable damage" resulting. The action took place off the Norwegian coast. A destroyer was torpedoed in the same fight, London said. The British trawler Moonstone informed the Admiralty that it had captured a large Italian submarine in the Gulf of Aden. Depth charges forced the submarine to the surface, where guns were brought into play. The Italian commander and several officers were reported killed; three officers and thirty-seven men were captured. [Page 1, Column 3.]

Three groups of Italian bombers attacked the Allied naval base at Alexandria, Egypt, early yesterday. They were driven off, the British reported, by the combined fire of both French and British naval units, and no warships were hit. Rome claimed to have sunk three enemy ships in the Mediterranean. [Page 1, Column 7.]

By the emphatic means of an official government statement, Russia denied that troops were being concentrated on the German frontier. [Page 22, Column 7.]

Developments Elsewhere

Within less than two hours, the House of Representatives adopted the "two-ocean" navy bill, which will give the United States the most powerful navy in the world—a navy 70 per cent greater than the present one. [Page 1, Column 3.]

After a stormy session of the Senate Naval Affairs Committee, it appeared in Washington that Colonel Frank Knox, Republican, would not be approved by the committee for Secretary of the Navy. Colonel Henry L. Stimson, Republican, nominated for Secretary of War, also faces hard going before the Military Affairs Committee. But confirmation of both appointments is expected when the issue gets to the floor. [Page 1, Column 4.]

In Hyde Park, where he was spending the week-end, President Roosevelt contemplated the possibility that the United States might have to shift the fleet to the Atlantic to face a superior sea power of the totalitarian nations. [Page 16, Column 1.]

GENERAL SUMMONS FRENCH TO RESIST

De Gaulle Offers to Organize Fight Abroad—Churchill Supports His Stand

By RAYMOND DANIELL
Special Cable to THE NEW YORK TIMES.

LONDON, Sunday, June 23—A broadcast to the French people by one of their own military leaders calling on them to continue the fight against Germany by every means in their power was made from here last night.

General Charles de Gaulle, assistant and adviser to Paul Reynaud when the former Premier was also War Minister, told his countrymen the proposed armistice would be not only capitulation but "submission and slavery."

[The general undertook to organize such French resistance as was possible himself and urged French fighting men and technicians everywhere to join him in the task, according to The United Press.]

General de Gaulle's arguments were reinforced early this morning by Prime Minister Winston Churchill in a statement expressing "grief and amazement" at the terms. He indicated they would transform France into an active enemy, and he too urged French-

Continued on Page Twenty-seven

ALEXANDRIA FIGHTS FIRST ITALIAN RAIDS

20 Bombs Fall in 3 Attacks—Warship Reported Fired by R. A. F. at Tobruk

By JOSEPH M. LEVY
Wireless to THE NEW YORK TIMES.

CAIRO, Egypt, June 22—Alexandria experienced its first bombing this morning when twenty bombs were dropped in three Italian air raids. Two persons were killed; twenty-three were injured.

The dead were a native woman, who was killed when bombs hit among palm trees growing in a village close to the city, and a man who was killed by a bomb that demolished four Alexandria houses. Here nineteen persons were injured.

[Another air raid warning sounded in Alexandria early today, but no planes appeared, The Associated Press reported, and the all-clear signal was given in fifteen minutes.]

Bombs were reported dropped indiscriminately on the city, harbor and native villages, the bombers flying high and dodging in their attempt to avoid anti-aircraft fire. Two Italian planes were reported badly damaged. It is not certain whether either was shot down.

Only a few bombs fell in the city.

Continued on Page Twenty-three

NAZI TERMS SIGNED

But Hostilities Persist as French Fly to Get Italy's Demands

SEVERITY PROTESTED

Huntziger Voices View at Close of 27-Hour Compiegne Parley

By GUIDO ENDERIS
Wireless to THE NEW YORK TIMES.

BERLIN, June 22—The armistice treaty between Germany and France was signed today in the forest of Compiègne at 6:50 P. M. German Summer time [12:50 P. M. New York time]. Col. Gen. Wilhelm Keitel, Chancellor Hitler's plenipotentiary, signed for Germany and General Charles Huntziger for France.

Its contents will not be made public for the present, but it is announced that the agreement does not provide for immediate cessation of hostilities. The fighting is to end six hours after the Italian Government has notified the German High Command of the signing of an armistice treaty between Italy and France.

As the latter is now believed to be a mere formality, already agreed upon by the leaders of the Axis Powers in their discussion in Munich last Tuesday, its conclusion is expected within the next forty-eight hours. The French delegation that conferred at Compiègne also will negotiate with Italy. Such procedure, it is predicted, will end the war on the Continent early in the coming week.

Scene in Car Dramatic

The French delegation returned to Compiègne from Paris at 10 A. M. and continued its deliberations throughout the day, during which it was in constant communication with the Bordeaux government. To expedite contacts, German military authorities installed a direct telephone wire connecting the armistice car with Bordeaux.

The German radio broadcast announcing the signing of the treaty closed with the words, "We thank our Fuehrer." There was a dramatic scene in the armistice car at Compiègne before the formalities were completed. General Huntziger, in a choked voice, announced that his government had ordered him to sign.

"Before carrying out my government's order," he said, "the French delegation deems it necessary to declare that in a moment when France is compelled by fate of arms to give up the fight, she has a right to expect that the coming negotiations will be dominated by a spirit that will give two great neighboring nations a chance to live and work once more. As a soldier you will well understand the onerous moment that has now come for me to sign."

After the signatures were affixed, General Keitel requested all present to rise from their seats, and then said:

"It is honorable for the victor to do honor to the vanquished. We have risen in commemoration of those who gave their blood to their countries."

Talks With Italy Speeded

The French delegation left Compiegne for Paris tonight and is expected to take up negotiations with Italy without further delay to bring the hostilities to a quick close.

With an Italian-French armistice in imminent prospect, military activities are now expected to give way to diplomatic negotiations and it is not improbable that Germany, Italy, France and possibly also Belgium will meet in conference soon in order to discuss steps for an approach to honorable peace.

Meanwhile there is no indication in German official or press utterances to suggest that Germany is not grimly determined to prosecute her war on Britain with all possible speed, and this determination has received fresh impetus through uninterrupted attacks by British bombers on German objectives.

With French Channel ports now available as German air bases, raids on English coastal points also have increased in recent days and with the final liquidation of the war in

Continued on Page Twenty-eight

"All the News That's Fit to Print."

The New York Times.

LATE CITY EDITION
Fair today, little change in temperature. Showers late tomorrow, not much change in temperature.
Temperatures Yesterday—Max., 78; Min., 54

VOL. LXXXIX No. 30,106. Entered as Second-Class Matter, Postoffice, New York, N. Y. NEW YORK, FRIDAY, JUNE 28, 1940. THREE CENTS NEW YORK CITY and Vicinity | FOUR CENTS Elsewhere Except in 7th and 8th Postal Zones.

REPUBLICANS NOMINATE WENDELL WILLKIE FOR THE PRESIDENCY ON THE 6TH BALLOT; RUMANIA GIVES UP BESSARABIA TO RUSSIA

BUKOVINA SLICED

Part of Province, Ports on Black Sea and the Danube Also Ceded

HUNGARY IS WATCHED

Carol Prepares to Resist Blow From That Nation —Will Meet Russians

By The Associated Press.

BUCHAREST, Rumania, Friday, June 28—Rumania bowed last night to a Soviet demand for great areas of her territory and moved nearly 2,000,000 men into Transylvania to meet an expected Hungarian attempt to get that province.

Despite earlier reports that Red troops already were on the march, it was disclosed late last night that Russia had agreed to hold back from the actual occupation of the ceded areas—Bessarabia and Northern Bukovina—until the last details of the cessions had been worked out. Diplomats labored at that task. It is expected to be completed today. Soviet troops then would cross the frontier.

[An authoritative diplomatic source in London said early today that Rumania had yielded to Russia on the cession of Bessarabia and Northern Bukovina and that King Carol had asked a conference with the Russians to bid for Russian aid in case of attacks by Hungary and Bulgaria, which also claim Rumanian territory, according to a dispatch to The New York Times.]

The capital was quiet. The officially censored press still was not permitted to publish a word of the Red ultimatum or of King Carol's acceptance.

The Road From Munich

Whether she fights Hungary or not, whether Bulgaria presses her own territorial claim for Southern Dobruja or lets it lie, Rumania, World War heir to Balkan supremacy, was well on the road to dismemberment. It is a road that winds from Munich, through Czecho-Slovakia and Poland to Finland and back again to France.

Apparently Germany and Italy gave their consent to Russia's latest coup. Axis Ministers were in long and earnest consultation with King Carol in his hours of deliberation and decision.

Rumania, rich in oil and grain, but poor in strategic location and useful alliances, decided she must give in to Russia—that no calling into force of her months of military preparations could alter the final result. Hence she yielded just short of a 10 o'clock deadline last night for her peaceful assent and agreed to discuss details later.

She had invoked a virtually general mobilization while the Grand Council considered Russia's demands. The council first accepted them in principle, pleaded unavailingly for time to dicker and finally capitulated.

The decision disposed only of Russia's claims. Now will come Hungary, with the reported backing of Adolf Hitler, to ask for Transylvania. Bulgaria, a friend of Russia, may seek the return of Southern Dobruja.

All told, Rumania stands to lose nearly half of her 113,884 square miles and return to Balkan obscurity—a satellite wavering between the gravitational pulls of the Axis powers in the west and the Red empire in the east.

The Reported Demands

Amid reports that Red Army planes were darkening the horizon and that Red troops, tanks and artillery were massing at her frontier, Rumania's Grand Council, under the presidency of the 46-year-old King, gave reluctant consent to demands that authoritative sources outlined as follows:

Return of Bessarabia, 17,146 square miles of fertile country, inhabited by more than 3,000,000 persons.

Cession of the northern part of Bukovina Province, but how much of Bukovina's 4,030 square miles and 911,000 inhabitants Russia wanted was not known.

Control of Rumania's big Black Sea port, Constanta, as a Red naval base.

Supervision of Galati and Braila, two Rumanian ports controlling

Continued on Page Twelve

The International Situation

Developments in Europe

Soviet Russia apparently made a bloodless attainment of her claims against Rumania yesterday. A Rumanian communiqué indicated that a Soviet ultimatum demanding two large slices of territory and concessions for Red naval forces in Black Sea ports had been accepted.

Bessarabia, once a province of Imperial Russia, and Bukovina, of the old kingdom of Austria-Hungary, were reported ceded outright, with Constanta becoming a Soviet naval base and other concessions granted in the Danubian delta ports of Galati and Braila. [All the foregoing, Page 1, Column 1.]

London heard that King Carol, after yielding to the ultimatum, sought Soviet aid against expected demands by Hungary and Bulgaria for return of their lost territories of Transylvania and Dobruja, respectively. [Page 14, Column 2.]

A well-informed Nazi source in Berlin indicated the Soviet move was within the scope of a tri-partite agreement with Germany and Italy for division of the Balkans. [Page 1, Column 3.]

In Rome, however, the Soviet grab caused undisguised surprise. Observers saw it as a contravention of the reported Axis plan to maintain the neutrality of the Balkans. It was feared that if the Russian war machine once started rolling it would not stop until the Red flag waved over the Dardanelles. [Page 13, Column 1.]

There was no official statement from Turkey, but a Turkish naval squadron moved through the Bosporus into the Black Sea, war planes patrolled the air lanes over the Dardanelles and anti-aircraft batteries went on the alert. [Page 1, Column 2.]

While London heard further reports of German troop transport concentrations in French, Belgian and Netherland ports, another British Cabinet leader—Minister of Supply Herbert Morrison—told the world by radio that Britain would hold the fort despite all odds until "the rest of the civilized world" could mobilize against the dictators. Earlier he had told the House of Commons that British war production and imports, although not satisfactory as yet, were approaching that state. [Page 1, Column 4.]

Meanwhile, Britain continued her air raids on harbors, oil refineries and airdromes in Germany and German-occupied territory. Daylight raids on refineries at Misburg and Bremen were reported especially damaging. Damage in the German raids on the East Coast Thursday night was said to have been relatively unimportant. German planes raided Britain again early today. [Page 16, Column 6.]

Repercussions Elsewhere

A proclamation controlling the movement of any foreign or American ships in domestic waters or the Panama Canal area was signed by President Roosevelt. It was believed five French ships in American ports would be affected. The President also signed the $1,768,913,000 Army-Navy Appropriation Bill. [Page 1, Column 5.]

Washington received reports from Europe that peace feelers had been put out for a settlement between Britain and Germany. These persisted despite British denials. Some indication of Germany's attitude might be revealed in an expected speech by Chancellor Hitler today, the capital believed. [Page 1, Column 4.]

A "last warning" to United States citizens in Britain to go home was issued by Ambassador Kennedy in London. He said the sailing of the liner Washington from Galway July 4 might be the last by an American ship "until after the war." [Page 16, Column 4.]

TURKISH WARSHIPS GO INTO BLACK SEA

Ankara Prepares to Defend Straits in Face of Soviet Demands on Rumania

By The Associated Press.

ANKARA, Turkey, June 27—A Turkish naval squadron steamed through the Bosporus today to the Black Sea, ready to defend the Straits against attack. [Turkey only Wednesday announced her non-participation in the European war.]

This historic guardian of the Dardanelles felt deep concern over Russia's ultimatum to Rumania demanding not only large land concessions but also naval bases on the Black Sea and Danube.

Turkish planes circled over the Straits and anti-aircraft guns were in position. Turkey's main fear was of a general move in this direction, with the Straits as the ultimate goal.

Assurance on Syria Doubted

Wireless to The New York Times.

ANKARA, Turkey, June 26 (delayed)—It was reported tonight without confirmation that Germany had assured Turkey that Italy would not be allowed to take Syria, which this country regards as its back door.

Diplomats here, however, are inclined to discredit this report. It is held significant that it should circulate just as Turkey had decided formally to announce her invocation of the escape clause in her pact with Great Britain and France.

Apart from this it is considered interesting that Syria and Lebanon are not mentioned in the Italian-French armistice terms. There is speculation as to whether this is because of German influence on Italy or because Italy does not wish to make demands on territory where a large army is established when she already has a full job with Britain in the Mediterranean.

The future of Syria is of vital interest to Turkey. As yet there is

Continued on Page Fourteen

NAZIS INSIST SOVIET ACTS UNDER ACCORD

Zones of Interest Reported to Have Been Determined by Axis and Moscow

By The United Press.

BERLIN, Friday, June 28—A tri-power agreement between Germany, Italy and Russia dividing zones of interest in Southeastern Europe opened the way for the Soviets' ultimatum against Rumania, it was stated in well-informed Nazi quarters early today.

Joseph Stalin's demands, under an ultimatum expiring at 10 o'clock last night, that Rumania surrender Bessarabia and the northern part of Bukovina Province were said to have been a direct result of this general understanding.

Germany and Italy, according to Nazi informants, agreed to recognize Russia's territorial claims as a means of making good the "injustices" of the settlements following the World War.

Chancellor Hitler and Premier Mussolini, both of whom have vital interests in Rumania and the Balkans and look to Southeastern Europe for supplies to keep their war machines going, were said to have attached conditions to the "go ahead" signal to Mr. Stalin.

The satisfaction of Russia's territorial claims must be brought about in such a manner, they were reported to have stated, as to prevent any general outbreak of war or economic disturbance in the Balkans.

Even an economic disturbance there would severely hamper Germany and Italy, it was pointed out, at a time when they are massing all their strength in preparation for a promised "knockout blow" against Britain.

This understanding with Russia regarding Southeastern Europe was understood to have been reached at a somewhat later date and in considerably "looser" form than Germany's agreement with Russia

Continued on Page Thirteen

BRITISH DIGGING IN

Speed Efforts to Make Islands a Fortress— Rise in Output Noted

NAZIS MASS A FLEET

'Hundreds' of Craft Are Assembling in Invasion Move, London Hears

By ROBERT P. POST
Special Cable to The New York Times.

LONDON, June 27—The British pushed forward today with their preparations for turning these islands into a fortress to withstand the siege and the attacks that most people here are convinced are coming.

The conception of Britain as an outpost of civilization was perhaps best summed up today by Herbert Morrison, the Minister of Supply, who followed up a fighting speech in the House of Commons with a broadcast to the United States in which he said that Britain was a strong point "which will hold on and hold out in the very jaws of the enemy while the rest of the civilized world mobilizes its resources for victory."

Earlier Mr. Morrison had given percentage figures to show how British production had been raised since the Churchill government took office. The increase in production of cruiser and infantry tanks between April and June was 115 per cent, Mr. Morrison said, and the increase in Bren gun carriers was 64 per cent. These were only indications of enormous increases that included artillery and small arms, the Minister told Parliament.

Labor Volunteers Discussed

Other indications of the speed with which Britain is moving to make this land a fortress—always with the provision that it will be a fortress from which sorties can and will be made—were also provided today. Ernest Bevin, the Minister of Labor, told the Commons he was consulting the War Office on the possibility of calling volunteer labor for construction of defenses to supplement the full-time work now being done. At the same time Mr. Bevin said that while the number of persons now being trained for skilled factory labor in government training centers was at 10,700, a new record, "we need thousands more."

Mr. Bevin appealed to any skilled fitters, machine operators and instrument makers who were not now employed and were capable of instructing others to come forward at once. The Minister said he had no women in training, but was getting ready to establish a system whereby each factory would take some.

Another facet of the plan for making Britain, uninvaded for centuries, a fortress also was discussed today. This was the question of getting women and children out. Geoffrey H. Shakespeare, Under-Secretary for Dominions, head of the scheme, told the Commons that

Continued on Page Fifteen

U. S. ACTS ON SHIPS

President to Exercise His Emergency Power Over Foreign Craft

CANAL IS INCLUDED

Bill Signed to Increase Army and Start on 68 New Warships

Special to The New York Times.

WASHINGTON, June 27—President Roosevelt today declared by proclamation the existence of a national emergency to the extent necessary to control the movement of all American and foreign shipping in United States continental waters and around the Panama Canal, and "to take full possession and control of such vessels" and remove their officers and crews.

The invocation of this war-time authority was described in a White House statement as supplementary to the proclamation last September of a "limited emergency," under which Mr. Roosevelt directed immediate expansion of the Army, Navy and Marine Corps and the Coast Guard. The President acted today under Section 1 of Title II of the Espionage Act of June 15, 1917.

Presumably subject to the proclamation were at least five French ships.

The text of the proclamation was not immediately available. Neither were the specific regulations, which the White House said were to be issued by the Treasury Department. As a result, it could not be ascertained positively that the President had proclaimed a state of national emergency beyond the language he used in the limited emergency proclamation following the outbreak of war in Europe last September.

New Defense Bill Signed

Throughout the day, plans to safeguard the security and economic welfare of the Western Hemisphere dominated White House activity. The President signed the $1,768,913,908 supplemental defense appropriation of funds to increase the Army's enlisted strength to 375,000 men, to buy 3,000 more planes and to authorize the Navy to begin the construction of sixty-eight new warships.

Before issuing the emergency proclamation, the President conferred with the Advisory Defense Commission and received a report on progress toward rapid expansion of the armed forces and for raising the output of fighting planes to a mass production basis.

With his special Cabinet committee, composed of the Secretaries of State, Treasury, Agriculture and Commerce, Mr. Roosevelt also reviewed plans for a Pan-American economic union to guard this hemisphere against totalitarian economic aggression. The plan is reported unofficially to be meeting with a cool reception from South American countries, but there was no confirmation from the White House conferees.

The text of the section of the Espionage Act under which the

Continued on Page Seven

Washington Hears of Peace Talk, But British Deny Nazi Overtures

By BERTRAM D. HULEN
Special to The New York Times.

WASHINGTON, June 27—Diplomatic circles were convinced today on the basis of confidential advices that soundings were being made in Europe for a negotiated peace between Britain and Germany, but they were far from certain that the effort would get anywhere.

The possibilities are such, however, that the attention of the diplomats was directed with more than usual interest to the speech that Chancellor Hitler is reported preparing to make tomorrow, and their immediate attention was diverted from the Russian move against Rumania.

The conviction that feelers had been put out for possible peace negotiations between the two major belligerents persisted in the face of denials from British Government spokesmen that such a move was in the wind and assertions in London that the reports were nothing more than German propaganda.

The reports have been circulated in Berlin. They also have appeared with some definiteness in Italian official quarters.

But diplomats here pointed out that, granting all this, it did not follow that the soundings would get anywhere. The possibilities, it is assumed, will be known better in a few days. It is taken for granted that if nothing comes of them the German attack on Britain will not be long delayed.

The State Department said it had no information other than dispatches that mentioned the current reports in European capitals. These reports, the department said, could not be confirmed officially. Department officials were disposed to accept at face value British declara-

Continued on Page Fifteen

THE REPUBLICAN NOMINEE
Wendell Lewis Willkie
Times Studio, 1940

Summary of the Ballots

Following are the total votes received by candidates in the balloting at the Republican convention last night:

Candidate.	First Ballot.	Second Ballot.	Third Ballot.	Fourth Ballot.	Fifth Ballot.	*Sixth Ballot.
Dewey	360	338	315	250	57	8
Taft	129	203	212	254	377	312
Willkie	105	171	259	306	429	659
Vandenberg	76	73	72	61	42	0
James	74	66	59	56	59	1
Martin	44	26	0	0	0	1
MacNider	34	34	28	26	4	3
Gannett	33	30	11	4	1	1
Bridges	28	9	1	1	0	0
Capper	18	18	0	0	0	0
Hoover	17	21	32	31	20	9
McNary	13	10	10	8	9	0
Bushfield	9	0	0	0	0	0
La Guardia	0	1	0	0	0	0

*Unofficial.

WILLKIE CREDITED FOR OWN VICTORY

Convincing Delegates of His Meeting Challenge of Day Said to Have Defeated Foes

By ARTHUR KROCK
Special to The New York Times.

MUNICIPAL AUDITORIUM, Philadelphia, Friday, June 28—The nomination of Wendell L. Willkie was a political revolution, but peaceful by contrast with others which have shaken the rest of the world. In normal times it could not possibly have happened.

The professional politicians, unaware that changed times and the impact of thunderous events have cracked the system which they long have practiced, sought to prevent the miracle by the usual methods.

These included an appeal to partisanship, because Mr. Willkie has so recently become a Republican; an attempt to match the personality of Thomas E. Dewey against him; an effort to overcome the tide with Senator Robert A. Taft, bred in the tradition and the son of a Republican President and Chief Justice, and finally one of those old-fashioned combinations which often have been successfully employed to "stop" a political intruder.

None of it worked because, as they compared the candidates put

Continued on Page Six

DEWEY WEAKENED BY PARTY RIFT HERE

His Vote in State Delegation, Smaller Than Expected, Drops to Four on the Fifth Ballot

By WARREN MOSCOW
Special to The New York Times.

MUNICIPAL AUDITORIUM, PHILADELPHIA, June 27 — Thomas E. Dewey's Presidential boom, always weak in his home State, was formally buried tonight, at exactly 11:30 P. M., when the New York delegation swung 75 of its 92 votes to Wendell Willkie on the fifth ballot. This move came after Mr. Dewey had released his delegates, at their request, relayed to him by J. Russel Sprague, the Dewey campaign manager. The prosecutor got only four votes on this roll-call.

Dewey had started off with 61 votes, fewer than expected, while Frank E. Gannett got 17; Willkie, 6; Herbert Hoover, 4; Senator Vandenberg, 1, and Joseph W. Martin Jr., 1.

Then, on the second ballot, secret as was the first, Dewey dropped to 58; Gennett got 16; Willkie, 13; Hoover, 3; Vandenberg, 1, and Mayor La Guardia, 1.

The third ballot, the first public ballot, found Dewey getting only 54 votes, and on the fourth, with Gannett releasing his votes, 6 more pledged to Dewey dropped off, and Westchester, Long Island and Brooklyn began to put the pressure

Continued on Page Four

RIVALS WORN DOWN

Willkie Garners Votes as His Opponents Free Their Delegates

MANY STATES SWITCH

Convention Adjourns in the Early Morning, Hailing Victor

By TURNER CATLEDGE
Special to The New York Times.

MUNICIPAL AUDITORIUM, Philadelphia, Friday, June 28—Wendell Lewis Willkie of New York, Indiana-born president of the Commonwealth & Southern Corporation, former Democrat who has been a foe of the New Deal, was nominated early this morning for President of the United States by the Republican party.

His nomination came on the sixth ballot of the party's twenty-second annual convention, marking one of the greatest upsets in the history of the convention system in America. A newcomer to the party, opposed by its veteran leaders, and lacking the usual organization to build up a candidate's strength, Mr. Willkie came into the picture here on the crest of a popular wave which not only did not diminish but finally asserted itself on the convention delegates themselves.

Starting out in tonight's balloting in third place, Mr. Willkie went forward in a series of thrusts until he went over on the sixth. He first eliminated Thomas E. Dewey, who came to the convention with the largest number of delegates, then Senator Taft, who was supported by many of the regular leaders. He outran a challenge which Senator Taft's smooth-operating machine was finally able to start.

Rush to Willkie Is Begun

After the middle of the sixth ballot the convention turned into a rush for the Willkie standard. Governor Bricker of Ohio, who had led Mr. Taft's largest single block of delegates on the floor, sought at that time to make the convention's vote unanimous, but Joseph W. Martin Jr., the permanent chairman, ordered the roll-call to proceed to the end. Finally, however, the ballot was made unanimous at 998, two of the 1,000 delegates being absent from the hall.

Managers of other candidates at once offered their congratulations and those of their principals. All sought to close ranks in the spirit of the enthusiasm which swept the hall and the galleries when it became apparent that Mr. Willkie had been nominated.

The main business now left to the convention is the selection of a candidate for Vice President. Mr. Willkie will be requested tomorrow to indicate his desires as to a running mate. That the second-place candidate will come from the West is practically certain, and suggestions already were being made as to the availability of Senator Charles L. McNary, Minority leader of the Senate, while some of the defeated Presidential candidates also were discussed.

Rivals to Support Willkie

After the nomination had been made unanimous, J. Russell Sprague, manager of Mr. Dewey's campaign, said the young prosecutor had asked him to express his thanks to his supporters and his assurance that he would give Mr. Willkie his whole-hearted support in the coming campaign.

David S. Ingalls, Senator Taft's campaign manager, said it had been a great fight and that Senator Taft and those who supported him would be behind Mr. Willkie, whom he acclaimed as the next President.

Governor James of Pennsylvania and Senator John Thomas of Idaho joined in making the nomination unanimous.

Former President Hoover sent his congratulations directly to the winner stressing that Mr. Willkie was the choice of a free convention and undoubtedly would move on to victory.

Mr. Willkie considered for a while going before the convention tonight and accepting the nomination, but canceled the plan because of extreme fatigue. He had been constantly on the move, with hardly three full hours of sleep a night

Continued on Page Five

Wendell L. Willkie was the Republican nominee for president. Radio was now covering every aspect of the exciting election campaign.

Eleanor Roosevelt addressing the Democratic National Convention.

Edward R. Murrow was the Columbia Broadcasting System's London war correspondent. Murrow's portrayal of the drama and tension in London stirred the heart and conscience of his American audience.

"All the News That's Fit to Print."

The New York Times.

LATE CITY EDITION

Cloudy, followed by local thunder showers and cooler this afternoon or tonight. Tomorrow fair.

Temperatures Yesterday—Max., 83; Min., 63

Copyright, 1940, by The New York Times Company.

VOL. LXXXIX...No. 30,117. Entered as Second-Class Matter, Postoffice, New York, N. Y. NEW YORK, TUESDAY, JULY 9, 1940. THREE CENTS NEW YORK CITY and Vicinity | FOUR CENTS Elsewhere Except in 7th and 8th Postal Zones.

FRANCE TO BE FASCIST STATE; LAVAL, WEYGAND IN POWER; WIDE AIR RAIDS ON GERMANY

ROOSEVELT IS TOLD FARLEY DELEGATES WILL SWING TO HIM

Massachusetts Leaders Say '95 Per Cent' of Their Group Will Climb on Bandwagon

NO RELEASE IS INDICATED

McCormack and Burke Insist They Have Had No Word From National Chairman

Special to THE NEW YORK TIMES.

WASHINGTON, July 8—President Roosevelt was assured today of virtually unanimous support of Massachusetts delegates to the Democratic National Convention previously pledged to Postmaster General James A. Farley.

After an interview with the Chief Executive yesterday, Mr. Farley said he had "full information" on the President's convention plans as well as his intentions regarding a third term in the White House.

Accompanied by Secretary Hopkins, the President returned to the capital which is still speculating upon his attitude toward renomination and, in some quarters, hopeful that he would reveal his stand before the convention opens next Monday.

The Bay State assurance was conveyed through Representative John W. McCormack, head of the delegation, and William H. Burke Jr., chairman of the State Democratic Committee, during a White House conference a few hours after Mr. Roosevelt's arrival from Hyde Park early this morning. They predicted that at least 95 per cent of the delegation would eventually climb the bandwagon for Mr. Roosevelt.

Mr. Farley announced earlier this year that his name would go before the Democratic convention. Subsequently 32½ of the 34 votes of the Massachusetts delegation were pledged to him. Yesterday, following his talk with the President, Mr. Farley refused to state whether his name would go before the convention.

Prediction for Massachusetts

With Mr. Burke agreeing, Representative McCormack said to reporters after their White House visit:

"I think I can safely say that at least 95 per cent of our votes will go for the President."

Both were quick to explain that they had pledged their support to Mr. Farley with the express reservation that the Chief Executive had first claim on their votes and they insisted that they had received no word from Mr. Farley since his interview with the President yesterday.

"We told Mr. Roosevelt that it is absolutely indispensable that he run," Mr. McCormack went on, "because he is the outstanding man in government life in the world today and the one leader of the forces of enlightenment, progress and peace in government life in the world today."

Should the President resist a draft movement at the convention, the Massachusetts delegation will go down the line for Mr. Farley, according to Mr. McCormack.

Tobin's Assignment Deferred

Another caller at the White House, Daniel J. Tobin, head of the A. F. of L. Teamsters Union, accepted a temporary appointment as administrative assistant to the President to prevent labor friction under the national defense program, the appointment to take effect after the convention.

A delegate-at-large for Indiana with the endorsement of the McNutt organization, Mr. Tobin said "that he was for Roosevelt first, last and all the time," and added:

"I told the President that I had promised to go to the convention and did not want to go and be tagged as a representative of the White House."

Then he explained that his assignment as a "trouble shooter" for the Administration on labor problems would not take effect until the national convention had ended.

Question of a Spokesman

Stephen T. Early, White House secretary, indicated that the President might have no authorized spokesman at the convention. He said that if the President had authorized Mr. Farley or any one else to speak for him at Chicago the fact had not been communicated to White House aides, but he did not deny that such action might yet be taken.

The President is understood to have urged upon the legislative leaders with whom he usually confers on Monday mornings the necessity of Congress recessing by Thursday. But, according to those present, that was his only word to them touching on the convention.

The Congressional leaders at the conference were Vice President Garner, Speaker Bankhead, Sen-

Continued on Page Fourteen

'Red' Airfield Murals Torn Down; WPA Dismisses Their Creator

Artist Refused to Swear He Was Neither Communist Nor Nazi—Somervell Inquiry May Cause Other Oustings

Because they were considered to be Communist propaganda, three of four murals painted by an artist of the WPA art project and hung in the administration building at Floyd Bennett Field, Brooklyn, were ordered removed and destroyed yesterday by Lieut. Col. Brehon B. Somervell, local administrator of the Work Projects Administration.

August Henkle, the artist, of 103-04 217th Lane, Queens Village, was dismissed from the art project. Henkle, who is 59 years old, had refused to sign an affidavit under the regulations of the WPA, in accordance with an act of Congress, requiring WPA employes to declare that they were neither Nazis nor Communists.

Colonel Somervell said that he was investigating the circumstances surrounding the painting of the murals and their display at Bennett Field. Supervisors and others who may have had to do with the matter also may face dismissal.

Removal and destruction of the two murals followed protests from members of the Women's International Aeronautic Association, the Flatbush Chamber of Commerce and the Floyd Bennett Post of the American Legion.

After the orders were issued by Colonel Somervell, a group of workmen arrived at the airfield and after reporting to Kenneth Behr, the field manager, that they had instructions to remove the murals, ripped them from the walls. The canvases, each about six feet by thirty feet, had been taped to the four walls of the rotunda of the administration building. They were torn down, rolled up into bundles and taken to WPA headquarters at 70 Columbus Avenue, Manhattan.

The particular project embracing the murals was begun three years ago.

One of the objectionable murals was removed because it had a figure resembling Joseph Stalin, Russian Communist dictator. Another was found undesirable because it displayed a red star, similar to that which graced the Russian pavilion at the World's Fair last year, painted on a United States Navy hangar. This mural contained also representations of famous American aviators, including Floyd Bennett, Colonel Charles A. Lindbergh, Wiley Post, Amelia Earhart and Roscoe Turner, and Professor Auguste Piccard, noted Belgian scientist and balloonist, together with Jimmy Collins, a radical aviator, and Joseph Rosmarin, who served in the Loyalist air force during the civil war in Spain and is a hero of American Communists.

The inclusion of Collins and Rosmarin in the mural was pointed to at WPA headquarters as "deliberate propaganda," especially "since they in no way rate the standing of the other fliers in the mural."

Also included in the group was a Soviet aviator who participated in

Continued on Page Seventeen

MARTIN WILL HEAD WILLKIE CAMPAIGN

Nominee Names Party's House Leader for New Chairman of National Committee

By JAMES C. HAGERTY

Special to THE NEW YORK TIMES.

WASHINGTON, July 8—Wendell L. Willkie has chosen Representative Joseph W. Martin Jr., House Minority Leader, to be chairman of the Republican National Committee, it was learned today after the Presidential nominee arrived in the capital to confer with Senator McNary, his running mate, and other Congressional leaders.

Although neither Mr. Willkie, who arrived by plane from New York, nor Mr. Martin would comment, pending formal announcement tomorrow after ratification by the subcommittee of the national committee, it was learned on good authority that Mr. Martin had accepted.

Mr. Willkie, who has urged the injection of "young blood" into the Republican party, has from the first wanted Representative Martin to handle his campaign, it was ascertained.

Faced with heavy Congressional duties, particularly with Congress still in session, Mr. Martin repeatedly declined the offer, but finally, upon the candidate's insistence, agreed this afternoon to accept.

After paying high tribute to Senator McNary, Mr. Willkie told newspaper reporters that he would make an announcement of his campaign organization plans tomorrow after the meeting of the subcommittee.

"The man I originally had in mind will be appointed national chairman," he said, and later admitted that his choice would be both the chairman and his campaign manager.

May Combine Two Posts

While Mr. Willkie declined to amplify his statement, it was taken as an indication that he would not carry through his proposal, which he made soon after he was nominated, to name a three-man campaign board, composed of a campaign manager, the national chairman and a personal representative.

It now appears that the first two positions will be combined into one, that of national chairman. It is not known what status the personal representative will have, but it is believed that Russell A. Davenport, former managing editor of Fortune magazine, who resigned to handle the Willkie pre-convention campaign, will be appointed.

John D. M. Hamilton, present national chairman, will play an important role in the campaign, it was learned, although to what position he will be appointed is not yet known.

Mr. Willkie's visit to Washington, his first as nominee, was marked by a series of conferences from the time he arrived at the airport until after midnight. He is scheduled to leave Washington by plane at 1 P. M. tomorrow for Colorado, where he will spend a vacation of at least two weeks.

Senator McNary and the head of

Continued on Page Thirteen

CHIEF OF U. S. FLEET MAKES SECRET TRIP TO SEE ROOSEVELT

Admiral Richardson, Flying From Hawaii, Insists His Visit Covers Routine Manoeuvres

TWO-OCEAN NAVY IS URGED

Senate Committee Reports on $4,000,000,000 Plan—Hull Redefines Monroe Doctrine

Special to THE NEW YORK TIMES.

WASHINGTON, July 8—Admiral James O. Richardson, Commander in Chief of the Fleet, arrived from Hawaii today for a visit and conference with President Roosevelt, after an unheralded flight by naval plane. He denied, after seeing the President, that any significance attached to his visit, insisting that he discussed with Mr. Roosevelt routine matters concerning the recent Pacific manoeuvres.

The admiral's unannounced visit stirred considerable speculation, despite official disavowal of any undue significance.

There was no present intention, he said, of transferring the battle fleet to the Atlantic or Caribbean from the Pacific, where it is based at Pearl Harbor. His statement was in contravention of a recent assertion by Rear Admiral William D. Leahy, retired, now Governor of Puerto Rico. Admiral Leahy had also just left the President's office when he said:

"The place for the fleet is now in the Atlantic and the Caribbean."

The President also conferred with Lieutenant Colonel Richard K. Sutherland, Chief of Staff of the Philippine military forces. The White House described the visit as "routine." Some observers professed to find more than a coincidence in the two visits and expressed the view that conditions in the Far East might have been considered.

Admiral Richardson was closeted with the President for more than an hour. When asked whether there was any plan to shift the fleet from the Pacific, he replied:

"Not that I know of. It is just that most of the ships of the fleet are now in Pearl Harbor for routine upkeep and this seemed the best time to come here to talk about routine fleet matters."

The fleet commander's statement that his visit was of routine nature was affirmed in a Navy Department announcement that he would return to his post within the week.

Navy Department Statement

The only official comment on the visit of the admiral was as follows:

"The Navy Department announced this morning that Admiral J. O. Richardson, United States Navy, Commander in Chief of the United States Fleet, arrived in Washington, D. C., yesterday to confer with officials of the Navy Department regarding routine policies for the training of the fleet.

"The custom of recalling the Commander in Chief of the United States Fleet to Washington for routine conferences is being continued.

"Admiral Richardson will return to the fleet as soon as conferences are concluded."

Soon after the Navy Department doors were opened this morning Admiral Richardson arrived at the office of Admiral Harold R. Stark, Chief of Naval Operations. Following his conference with Admiral Stark, Admiral Richardson conferred with Rear Admiral Robert L.

Continued on Page Four

STIMSON ASSAILED, PRAISED IN SENATE

Nomination Called 'Step to War,' 'Notice of Our Unity to World' in Debate

Special to THE NEW YORK TIMES.

WASHINGTON, July 8—Senate debate on the confirmation of Colonel Henry L. Stimson as Secretary of War started today with approval of the nomination conceded. Isolationist Senators, who did most of the talking, attacked the selection as "a step on the road to war" and Senator Sheppard of Texas praised it as "a notice to the world of the fundamental unity of the American people."

Senator Sheppard, chairman of the Military Affairs Committee, opened the debate, which is expected to lead to a vote tomorrow. He summarized the testimony given before the committee by Mr. Stimson and urged that the committee's 14-to-3 vote for confirmation be accepted by the Senate.

"This appointment," he said, "could not have come at a more appropriate time. The value and significance of his nomination by a Democratic President in what may prove to be one of the most tragic periods in the history of this country is that it gives notice to the world that we are standing together.

Stimson's Patriotism Praised

"Franklin D. Roosevelt, in tendering important Cabinet assignments to Henry L. Stimson and Frank Knox, members of a party not his own, in a crisis imperiling the America we know and love, has shown a steadfast and true Americanism."

Likewise, he continued, Colonel Stimson and Colonel Knox in accepting the assignments had shown a similar loyalty to American ideals.

Mr. Sheppard stated that Colonel Stimson favored "selective compulsory training and service."

"Mr. Stimson will devote himself strictly and exclusively to the duties of Secretary of War," the Texas Senator declared, adding that Mr. Stimson would oppose sending American troops abroad "unless it were absolutely necessary to protect the United States."

Senator Vandenberg, a leader among critics of the nomination, asserted that Mr. Stimson's views, if effective, would lead the United States into the European conflict without the consent of Congress.

The Michigan Senator made this charge on the basis of Colonel Stimson's advocacy, the day before he was nominated, of opening American ports to the British fleet for refueling and repairs and using American warships to convoy munitions to Britain. To this charge was added one by Senator Holt, who spoke for two hours, that Mr. Stimson had a long record of bellicosity, dating back to 1916 when he opposed President Wilson's attempts to bring peace between Germany and the Allies.

Speaking before crowded galleries, Senator Vandenberg asserted that Mr. Stimson's proposal of opening all American ports to British war vessels "would be a direct invita-

Continued on Page Four

JAPAN COMPLAINS THAT OUR MARINES INSULTED HER ARMY

Bitter Protest Is Voiced Over Arrest of Plainclothes Men in Shanghai Settlement

MANHANDLING IS CHARGED

'It's a Lie,' Declares American Commander—Attempt to Create Incident Seen

By HALLETT ABEND

Wireless to THE NEW YORK TIMES.

SHANGHAI, July 8—In the most bitterly anti-American statement officially issued from Japanese sources in Shanghai since hostilities began more than three years ago, the Japanese Army spokesman this evening, in connection with the arrest and five-hour detention of sixteen armed civilian-clad Japanese gendarmes caught in the American defense sector yesterday, charged the Fourth United States Marines with an "unfriendly act, and with insulting the honor of the Japanese gendarmes and the Japanese Army."

He declared that the stoutest protest would be filed immediately and that Japan was reserving the right to make demands upon the United States later.

Asserting that none of the apprehended gendarmes had offered the slightest resistance when arrested, the Japanese Army spokesman charged that the marines had beaten the unresisting men with rifle butts, injuring them on the hips and legs. He charged that the gendarmes were also struck in their faces and that cuts and injuries inside their mouths had occasioned profuse bleeding.

Carefully Prepared Statement

Reading a carefully prepared written statement, the Japanese Army spokesman said that the marines had apparently acted from the beginning with a view to arresting the Japanese. He charged that some of the marines, speaking the Japanese language, had asked the gendarmes, "Are you Japanese?" Upon receiving an affirmative reply, the spokesman asserted, the marines assaulted the gendarmes with the butts of their rifles.

He also declared that the marines had trained loaded rifles upon the arrested men when they were in trucks proceeding to marine headquarters. The marines, he said, struck the gendarmes later when they attempted to talk together or when they spat from their bleeding mouths.

"The arrested men were first taken to the marine rifle range," his statement said, "where they were forced to squat while the marines covered them with loaded rifles, the gendarmes being treated like condemned criminals sentenced to death. The arrested men were also struck brutally in the face when they asked permission to use the lavatory."

The writer learns from careful inquiry, subsequent to these charges, that the arrested gendarmes were first taken to marine headquarters, where they were briefly kept in a building serving as the .22-caliber range. Their leader was then permitted to telephone to the Japanese authorities, and thereafter all sixteen were taken to another compound, to the marine jail. The total time of the arrests lasted from about 10 A. M. to 3 P. M.

It is authoritatively stated by marine headquarters that most of the gendarmes did resist arrest. Moreover, as is the invariable routine

Continued on Page Two

Tempest of War Reaches British Teapots; Beverage Rationed in Advance of 'Siege'

By JAMES B. RESTON

Special Cable to THE NEW YORK TIMES.

LONDON, July 8—Lord Woolton, Minister of Foods, called on the people of Britain tonight to make that last, that supreme sacrifice. He asked them to cut down their tea drinking to two ounces, or twenty-five cups, a week.

To a country like America where they serve tea in antiseptic cloth bags, twenty-five cups of tea sounds like a generous year's ration. But not in this country. These people drink two cups of tea at every meal and lose count at tea time. They write poetry about tea kettles singing on the hob and even when they run for their air raid shelters they risk their lives fumbling in the dark for cups and saucers.

Lord Woolton did not attempt to conceal that the tea ration was a serious move. In fact, he felt obliged to go on the radio tonight to explain to the people just why it was necessary.

"I am asking you for a hard life," he said. "We are going to win this war and we are going to win it by hard fighting. To fight hard we must live hard. We must live disciplined lives—discipline; that's what I am imposing on you."

As soon as the Minister stopped broadcasting people made a rush for the nearest stores, but all were closed. The announcement had been timed for that. Lord Woolton was not taking any chances on a late evening rush for the nation's supplies.

In this, however, as in everything, the British compromised. They did not just cut a man off with twenty-five cups a week and leave him stranded. They did not put any restriction on the number of cups of tea to be sold in tea shops, for example, so that if a man has a few coppers in the afternoon he can sneak away and grab a quick one to make up for the deficiency.

Lord Woolton hopes, however, that people will not do that. He appealed to their patriotism. He put it on the basis that here was a real opportunity to do something for the country. "Drink less tea and win the war." That was his attitude.

The newspapers loyally supported him, too. They printed little tips on how to squeeze tea leaves to get

Continued on Page Nine

The International Situation

In Europe and Africa

France apparently is on the verge of becoming a totalitarian dictatorship, ruled by a triumvirate composed of Vice Premier Laval, General Weygand and Adrien Marquet, former labor leader. According to dispatches from Vichy and Berlin, Marshal Petain is to be retained as figurehead of the new State. Parliament, an advisory body only, is to be composed of an upper house appointed by the government and a lower house representing labor, service organizations, farmers and other groups, on the Italian model. Political parties are to disappear, as are labor unions. The new Constitution will be presented to Parliament today and adopted, Berlin confidently predicts, tomorrow. [Page 1, Column 8.]

The French battleship Richelieu, 35,000 tons, was reported by the British to have been kept from falling into the hands of Germany or Italy. Details were not immediately made public. The Richelieu was building when the war started; whether she had since been completed is not known. [Page 6, Column 3.]

Britain was the target for the greatest daytime air attacks she has suffered since the war started. German raiders struck at objectives ranging from the Southwest to the Northeast coasts. Eight German planes were reported shot down. British planes meanwhile raided deep in Germany. Early this morning numerous German radio stations faded out, indicating that the British bombers were busy again. [Page 1, Column 6.]

Rome reported "effective raids" on British bases at Malta and Alexandria. The Italians also claimed to have won a skirmish with British motorized units on the Libyan border. British officials in Alexandria dared the Italian fleet to "come out and fight." [Page 8, Column 3.]

The British Foods Minister put tea under the ration regulations and forbade hotels and restaurants to serve meals having both fish and meat courses. [Page 1, Column 4.]

Russia's Ambassador to Turkey left Istanbul for Moscow after having conferred with Franz von Papen, German Ambassador to Turkey. They were reported to have discussed Russia's demands on Turkey, including concessions in the Dardanelles. Foreign diplomats in Istanbul said Germany was supporting Russia. [Page 11, Column 1.]

Developments Elsewhere

The arrest of sixteen armed Japanese gendarmes, wearing civilian clothes, by United States Marines in the American defense sector of Shanghai gave rise to a controversy. A Japanese Army spokesman charged that the gendarmes had been beaten, although they had offered no resistance. Marine headquarters declared that resistance had been offered and that there had been no beatings. The incident was not important, but the attitude of the Japanese Army seemed to be. [Page 1, Column 5.]

Admiral James O. Richardson, Commander in Chief of the United States Fleet, conferred in Washington with President Roosevelt and said later that there was no present intention to move the fleet from the Pacific to the Atlantic. [Page 1, Column 4.]

Britain officially assured the United States that no blockade had been placed on Martinique, where two French warships have taken refuge. United States warships stood by at Martinique to observe developments. [Page 6, Column 4.]

In a Senate debate on the confirmation of Henry L. Stimson as Secretary of War, Senator Vandenberg said Colonel Stimson's views would, if made effective, lead the nation into war without the consent of Congress. [Page 1, Column 3.]

Prime Minister Mackenzie King of Canada revised his government to strengthen defense posts. He asked the Opposition to participate in the Administration, and he promised shortly to create a Department of National Defense for Naval Affairs. [Page 10, Column 3.]

R. A. F. UNITS STAGE SHARP RETALIATION

Bombings in Reich as Far as Berlin Are Indicated—Nazis Lose 8 Planes in Britain

By ROBERT P. POST

Special Cable to THE NEW YORK TIMES.

LONDON, Tuesday, July 9—More extensive raids into Germany by British Royal Air Force bombers were indicated early today, in retaliation for the Nazis' daily air attacks on Britain.

Blows at German bases for an invasion of England also were evident in an Air Ministry announcement of raids Sunday night and early yesterday on the harbor of Ostend, at Boulogne and deep inside the Reich.

[British radio listeners reported that stations at Berlin, Stuttgart, Cologne, Frankfort, Bremen and Hamburg went off the air just before midnight last night, indicating the approach of British raiders over those German cities, The Associated Press reported.]

This morning's communiqué said some damage to buildings near the coast had been done by Nazi bombers that came over Eastern and Southern England and Northeast Scotland during the night, but there were "very few casualties."

Nazi Glide Bombing Noted

The greatest daytime air activity over and near Britain since the war began was reported yesterday. The German attacks spread from the southwest to the northeast coast and included at least one case of glide bombing by a Nazi plane.

The Air Ministry reported that eight German planes were shot down by British defense fighters, and that little damage and a few casualties resulted from the Nazi attacks.

The most important daylight conflict took place when German bombers swooped upon a British convoy in the English Channel. All

Continued on Page Eight

HAAKON REJECTS PLEA TO ABDICATE

Norwegian King Announces in London He Will Not Bow to the German Army

Special Cable to THE NEW YORK TIMES.

LONDON, July 8—In answer to a petition from members of the German-dominated Norwegian Parliament, King Haakon tonight announced that he had refused to abdicate his throne. If the Norwegian people really wanted him to abdicate, the King said in a letter to the Presidential Board of the Storting, he would conform to their wishes, but he insisted that he would never conform to the wishes of the German Army of Occupation.

The request that Haakon abdicate was contained in a message transmitted through the Norwegian Legation in Stockholm, Sweden, to King Haakon, who fled here just before the final evacuation of the Allied troops from Norway.

The message said that since the King and his government were no longer in the country and thus were unable to perform their constitutional duties, the Presidential Board of the Storting, representatives of four political parties and the National Federation of Trade Unions had agreed with the German authorities to ask the members of the Storting to set up a new Rigsdad, or State Council, to run the affairs of the country.

Storting Would Revoke Powers

Members of the Storting would also be asked, according to this communication, to adopt resolutions revoking the powers of Premier Johan Nygaardsvold and the King until a new election could be held to end the war.

In a long, carefully worded reply to the Presidential Board, King Haakon declared that he could not cooperate with or recognise any decisions of a Parliament some of

Continued on Page Ten

3 LEADERS TO RULE

Marquet Other Member of Triumvirate Under Petain as State Head

PARLIAMENT WILL ADVISE

Laval to Present New Charter Today—Regime Expected to Be Coordinated With Axis

By The United Press.

ZURICH, July 8—France will become a totalitarian dictatorship within forty-eight hours with a government closely modeled on Italy's Fascist regime, according to dispatches from Vichy, temporary French capital, and Berlin.

A new constitution authorizing establishment of a corporative State to replace the traditional French Republic will be presented to the French Parliament tomorrow by Vice Premier Pierre Laval, who long has admired the Fascist government, it was indicated.

Dispatches from Vichy today said French leaders planned to make a "clean sweep" of the democratic constitution and that President Albert Lebrun probably would be replaced by Marshal Henri Philippe Petain with the title of "Chief of Executive Power."

These dispatches said that under Marshal Petain would be a triumvirate comprising M. Laval, General Maxime Weygand and Adrien Marquet, former labor leader.

German press dispatches datelined Vichy quoted French parliamentary circles as predicting that in a session of the National Assembly Wednesday the French Parliament would vote itself out of existence in a session lasting not more than an hour and 20 minutes.

To Abolish Party System

These reports said that members of the new French upper house would be appointed by the government, not elected, and that the new lower house would comprise representatives of labor, service organizations, farmers and the trades. The political party system would be abolished, as would be trade unions in the old sense.

Both houses, German reports said, would be mere advisory bodies to the government.

A dispatch from Vichy dated yesterday said that M. Laval explained the "constitutional reform" to a caucus of Senate members and that it was receiving "numerous adhesions." He said the new constitution aims to "give the government authority to create a new France, safeguarding the rights of labor, the family and the nation."

The Vichy dispatch said the procedure called for the Senate and the Chamber of Deputies, meeting separately, to vote approval of the sweeping change in government tomorrow. It would be submitted to the National Assembly as a whole the following day, "whereby Parliament would hand over its constitutional powers to the government in view of the reformation constitution."

A dispatch of D. N. B., official German news agency, speaking of the meeting Wednesday, said, significantly: "If the decision of the necessary number of members of both chambers, as well as the National Assembly, is lacking, a legal solution already has been provided to make delay impossible."

Government to Present Bill

D. N. B. said that after M. Laval summarizes the situation the government will present a bill expressing confidence in Marshal Petain. Then in a brief session, according to D. N. B., the government will receive full powers to draw up a constitution.

The agency said that the upper chamber of the new government would represent the interests of the professions, intellectuals and industry and would build the framework of a new corporate State. The second chamber would provide guarantees for corporations, classes and the family.

There was speculation on the possibility of a French corporative State which would fit into a Western European pattern as exemplified by Italy and Spain—both closely linked to the Reich—and into the Axis conception of a "new order" which the German press says is planned for Southeastern Europe. The recent change of Rumania into a totalitarian State closely allied with Axis policies was regarded as the cornerstone of the "new order" for the Balkans.

German diplomats also have been

Continued on Page Six

"All the News That's Fit to Print."

The New York Times.

LATE CITY EDITION
Mostly cloudy with scattered showers and not much change in temperature today and tomorrow.
Temperatures Yesterday—Max., 74; Min., 66

VOL. LXXXIX. No. 30,126. Entered as Second-Class Matter, Postoffice, New York, N. Y. NEW YORK, THURSDAY, JULY 18, 1940. THREE CENTS NEW YORK CITY and Vicinity | FOUR CENTS Elsewhere Except in 7th and 8th Postal Zones

ROOSEVELT RENOMINATED ON FIRST BALLOT; STRICT ANTI-WAR PLATFORM IS ADOPTED; NO ARMY ABROAD UNLESS U. S. IS ATTACKED

BURMA ROAD PACT AROUSES COMMONS; PEACE DEMAND MET

Japan Reported Ready to Deal With China, but Britons Call 'New Munich' Shameful

QUESTION ON U. S. EVADED

Konoye Forms a Centralized Regime in Tokyo—South Seas Drive Expected

By The United Press.

LONDON, July 17—Japan promised to attempt to reach a general peace settlement with China before Oct. 18 as part of the agreement reached today with Great Britain to close for three months the Burma supply route to China, it was learned authoritatively tonight.

British quarters reaffirmed their readiness to offer their good offices to end the long Chinese-Japanese war, provided their services were desired by the governments in Tokyo and Chungking.

Announcement in Parliament of the Anglo-Japanese agreement, forced by Japan, caused an uproar and the deal was called "shameful." It was consummated despite the declaration of Cordell Hull, American Secretary of State, that it would be considered by the United States an unwarranted obstacle to world trade.

U. S. Policy "Ambiguous"

Although the United States' continued shipments of strategic raw materials to Japan frequently has been regarded in London as making Washington's Far Eastern policy "ambiguous," it is generally believed that today's agreement probably will provoke severe criticism in the United States.

Coupled with the continuance in office of Chamberlain "appeasers," today's partial acceptance of Japan's demands is expected also to increase home dissatisfaction with the policies of the Churchill government, although the position of Prime Minister Winston Churchill himself still appears to be impregnable.

Geoffrey Mander, Liberal, who attacked the agreement, demanded sarcastically whether it was likely to be more successful than previous attempts at appeasement such as Munich. The Speaker ruled him out of order, but amid shouts of "order, order," Mr. Mander asked whether the British Government, in view of Mr. Hull's statement, was going to refuse transit to United States goods consigned to China, most of which has been going by the Burma Road.

Questions Are Evaded

"I think it rather irresponsible to make statements of that sort," replied Richard Austen Butler, Foreign Under-Secretary, whose announcement had set off the uproar.

Wilfred Roberts, who sided with Mr. Mander, asked Mr. Butler pointblank whether the United States had expressed approval or disapproval of the agreement in advance of the accord.

Mr. Butler replied evasively: "We must leave interpretation of the American statement to Americans."

Mr. Roberts said he was not satisfied and would raise the question later.

Chinese circles here bitterly compared Britain's action to the position that would arise if the United States prevented war material from reaching Britain and then offered to promote Anglo-German peace talks.

British commentators said this comparison was irrelevant because the United States was not engaged in a life-and-death struggle in the West.

Halifax Speaks in Lords

In the House of Lords, Foreign Secretary Viscount Halifax made a statement similar to that of Mr. Butler in the Commons.

Viscount Cecil of Chelwood, friend of China, cautioned the government against closing the Burma Road or putting pressure on China to make peace.

Responsible quarters here said, regarding one point of the agreement, the Japanese consular officials would not have the right to inspect and prohibit traffic through Burma but that British authorities

Continued on Page Fifteen

3 British Ports Wrecked By Nazis, Say Dutch Crew

By The Associated Press.

BOSTON, July 17—Members of the crew of the Netherland freighter Zypenberg, arriving to load scrap metal for United Kingdom ports, asserted today that Plymouth, England, and Pembroke and Cardiff, Wales, had been devastated by almost continuous raids by Nazi bombing planes and that many ships had been sunk in British harbors. [London issued a denial.]

The Zypenberg was among vessels taken over by the British Ministry of Shipping after the German invasion of the Netherlands. Officers and crew said they had had a 20 per cent wage reduction and had been forced to operate unarmed in dangerous waters.

They said that while their vessel was anchored in one British port, a Nazi bomber sank a British ship anchored close astern. Wharves in the three British ports they mentioned had been demolished, they added.

GIBRALTAR DEMAND VOICED BY FRANCO

Chief of State Gives Notice Spain Expects a Part in Post-War Settlement

By T. J. HAMILTON
Wireless to THE NEW YORK TIMES.

MADRID, July 17—General Francisco Franco told army, navy and air force officers today that "there remains for us as a duty and a national mission control of Gibraltar, expansion in Africa and continuance in the policy of unity."

Speaking at a ceremony at which he conferred Spain's highest military award, the Grand Laureate Cross of San Fernando, General Franco added that these aspirations were embodied in the will of Queen Isabella and after centuries "are still binding upon us."

The radio and press today were busy presenting Spain's claims on Morocco, the newspapers insisting that it was time that Spanish and French Morocco, each with its own Caliph, were united.

Rumors of peace negotiations here continue.

British sympathizers here get some encouragement out of the fact that the new Ambassador, Sir Samuel Hoare, was the guest of honor tonight at a dinner given by Colonel Juan Beigbeder, the Foreign Minister, even though this is a courtesy usually extended to newly arrived diplomats.

Otherwise, however, the increasing popularity of the Germans is illustrated by the reappearance of swastika flags, which had once virtually disappeared, at a majority of shops and cafes and many private homes. An interesting example

Continued on Page Ten

ARMY OF 2,000,000 A MINIMUM NEED, MARSHALL INSISTS

45 Infantry Divisions and 10 Armored Divisions Are the Objective, General Says

STIMSON HAILS BURKE BILL

Ludicrous for Any One to Oppose Compulsory Service Plan, He Tells Civilian Aides

By FRANK L. KLUCKHOHN
Special to THE NEW YORK TIMES.

WASHINGTON, July 17—A trained and fully equipped army of 2,000,000 men is the minimum necessary for adequate defense of this hemisphere, even with Navy and Air Force cooperation, General George C. Marshall, Chief of Staff, declared today in disclosing that the War Department had as its objective the formation of forty-five streamlined infantry divisions and ten armored divisions.

Both General Marshall and Secretary Stimson again urged the passage of compulsory selective service legislation in addressing a meeting today at the War Department of Civilian Aides to the Secretary of War from nine corps areas and forty-four States.

Secretary Stimson described this legislation "the very foundation stone of preparedness," and added: "Congress has appropriated billions of dollars for material to save the country, but we have not yet taken the step necessary to get the men to run the matériel."

General Marshall, in a subsequent press conference, said that Army plans were based as much on trained man power as matériel. The nine Regular Army infantry divisions and the four National Guard divisions, which it is planned to call to service as soon as Congress will authorize the step, would be fully equipped by Jan. 1, the general said, stressing that this was merely a first step toward preparedness.

"Poker With Every One Looking"

The Army could not adequately defend this hemisphere even with the 1,280,000 in the proposed Protective Mobilization Force, under all conditions, he said frankly in deploring that "we're playing poker with every one looking at our hand."

Reiterating that the entire National Guard should be called to service at least thirty days before compulsory training became effective, around Sept. 1 if possible, General Marshall held that "the greatest mistake we can make is to flood the carburetor on the first jump" in explaining that, if

Continued on Page Eight

The Only Ballot

Votes. STATES.	Farley.	Garner.	Roosevelt.	Tydings.
22—Alabama	1	..	20	1
6—Arizona	..	..	6	..
18—Arkansas	..	..	18	..
44—California	..	1	43	..
12—Colorado	..	..	12	..
16—Connecticut	..	..	16	..
6—Delaware	..	..	6	..
14—Florida	..	1½	12½	..
24—Georgia	..	..	24	..
8—Idaho	..	..	8	..
58—Illinois	..	..	58	..
28—Indiana	..	..	28	..
22—Iowa	..	..	22	..
18—Kansas	..	..	18	..
22—Kentucky	..	..	22	..
20—Louisiana	..	..	20	..
10—Maine	..	..	10	..
16—Maryland	..	..	7½	8½
34—Massachusetts	12½	..	21½	..
38—Michigan	..	..	38	..
22—Minnesota	..	..	22	..
18—Mississippi	..	..	18	..
30—Missouri	2	1½	26½	..
8—Montana	..	..	8	..
14—Nebraska	1	..	13	..
6—Nevada	4	..	2	..
8—N. Hampshire	..	..	8	..
32—New Jersey	..	..	32	..
6—New Mexico	..	..	6	..
94—New York	25	..	64½	..
26—North Carolina	..	..	26	..
8—North Dakota	..	..	8	..
52—Ohio	..	..	52	..
22—Oklahoma	..	..	22	..
10—Oregon	..	..	10	..
72—Pennsylvania	..	..	72	..
8—Rhode Island	..	..	8	..
16—South Carolina	..	..	16	..
8—South Dakota	5	..	3	..
22—Tennessee	..	..	22	..
46—Texas	..	46	..	..
8—Utah	..	..	8	..
6—Vermont	..	..	6	..
22—Virginia	3	8	5	..
16—Washington	..	..	15	..
16—West Virginia	4	..	12	..
24—Wisconsin	..	3	21	..
6—Wyoming	..	..	6	..
6—Alaska	..	..	6	..
6—D. of Columbia	..	..	6	..
6—Hawaii	..	..	6	..
6—Puerto Rico	..	..	6	..
6—Canal Zone	..	..	6	..
6—Philippine Isl.	..	..	6	..
2—Virgin Islands	..	..	2	..
Total	72	61	946	9½

The totals of the ballot prior to announcement of the official result were: Roosevelt, 946 13/30; Farley, 72 27/30; Garner, 61; Tydings, 9½; Hull, 5 2/3. Absent 3½; not voting 1.

CONFUSION RISES OVER SECOND PLACE

Some Hold Roosevelt Means to Select a Running Mate When the Time Comes

By HENRY N. DORRIS
Special to THE NEW YORK TIMES.

CHICAGO, July 17—Far from having cleared up the confused race for Vice President, the message of President Roosevelt to the convention was thought tonight to have further complicated the situation.

There was a feeling among the delegates, despite the tenor of the Presidential message, that there would be a definite White House selection of a running mate after the convention had disposed of the first place.

Nevertheless, the score or more of candidates for running mate doubled their efforts on the theory that, after all, the delegates might be allowed to choose their favorite.

One of the developments of the day was a movement among the Texas delegation to obtain Vice President Garner's consent to support Representative Rayburn of Texas, the House majority leader, who continued his activity among other delegations today.

The Texans were said to feel that Mr. Rayburn is acceptable to the President. They say that Mr. Garner is entirely out of the picture, so far as Mr. Roosevelt's acceptance is concerned.

Activity for Bankhead

There was renewed vigor among the Alabama delegation, which is instructed for Speaker Bankhead for Vice President. Since so many candidates are pressing their cases and the time is short, several delegations were reported today to have looked with favor upon Mr. Bankhead's candidacy, on the ground that he is at once a loyal supporter of the President and the symbol of traditional Democratic conservatism.

Governor Stark of Missouri, who is described by his adherents as "the perfect candidate" because of

Continued on Page Five

'STAY OUT' PLANK

Goes Slightly Beyond the Recent Pledge of the President

FOR MONROE POLICY

All Material Aid Pledged for Peoples Attacked by Aggressors

Text of the platform as adopted will be found on Page 4.

By JAMES A. HAGERTY
Special to THE NEW YORK TIMES.

CHICAGO, July 17—After a long delay due to differences of opinion among members of the committee on resolutions on the foreign relations plank, Senator Wagner of New York, chairman of the committee, presented the final draft of the platform to the Democratic convention tonight. It was adopted by a voice vote.

Controversy in the committee centered on the phrasing of the foreign relations plank, which as finally submitted was strictly noninterventionist, calling for non-participation in foreign wars and expanding the recent pledge of President Roosevelt not to send troops to fight in Europe by a definite declaration against sending the military, naval or air forces to fight in foreign lands outside of America, except in case of attack.

This strong isolation declaration was modified only by a pledge to support the Monroe Doctrine and a pledge to send "to peace-loving and liberty loving people wantonly attacked by ruthless aggressors" all material aid "consistent with law and not inconsistent with the interests of our own national self-defense."

Agreement Is Reached

Unanimous agreement by members of the resolutions committee on the final draft was reached while Senator Claude H. Pepper of Florida, who led the fight for a strong declaration for aid to Great Britain was absent. Senator Burton K. Wheeler of Montana, a leader of the anti-war group, entered the meeting room just after the agreement was reached. He pronounced the foreign relations plank satisfactory as the meeting broke up.

Secretary Hopkins said tonight:

"There is nothing on the foreign policy plank which changes by one jot or tittle the foreign policies of the President and the Secretary of State. I refer not only to the present policies, but future policies. I cannot believe that any one can mislead the American people on this point. The foreign policy of the President has the overwhelming approval of the American people."

After Senator Wagner finished reading the platform and moved for its adoption, Elmer J. Ryan of Minnesota offered an amendment to insert the declaration of the 1896 convention declaring against a third term as a violation of American tradition. The reading of the amendment was greeted with groans and jeers. There was a faint shout of ayes when Chairman Barkley asked for a vote on the amendment and then a thundering chorus of noes. The platform was then adopted with a loud shout of ayes.

Says Party Aided Democracy

The committee's report, as presented by Senator Wagner, declared that the Democratic party had labored successfully:

"1. To strengthen democracy by defensive preparedness against aggression, whether by open attack or secret infiltration;

"2. To strengthen democracy by increasing our economic efficiency and

"3. To strengthen democracy by improving the welfare of the people."

The platform endorses the leadership and statesmanship of President Roosevelt during the past seven years and declares that he has for years warned the people of the nation that our peace and security were threatened. The platform proposes to provide America "with an invincible air force, a Navy strong enough to protect all our seacoasts

Continued on Page Six

AGAIN THE DEMOCRATIC NOMINEE
Franklin Delano Roosevelt Times Studio

PLATFORM MARKED BY DOUBT ON FUTURE

Anti-War Plank and Sympathy Expressed for Victims of Attacks Reflect Uncertainties

By ANNE O'HARE McCORMICK
Special to THE NEW YORK TIMES.

CHICAGO, July 17—As finally patched up out of bitterly divergent opinions and adopted by the convention tonight, the foreign policy declaration in the Democratic platform turns out to be a plank that makes up in breadth what it lacks in thickness. It is obviously hewn to cover many points of view and to bear almost any interpretation the candidate wishes to place on it.

The isolationist Senators on the committee and their outside supporters were not able to write their own ticket, as they expected to do until today. But they received satisfaction in being permitted to dictate a strong anti-war pledge and to go much farther than the President in his recent declaration to Congress that American soldiers would never be sent to fight in "European wars" by asserting that "we will not send our Army, naval or air forces to fight in foreign lands outside of the Americas, except in case of attack."

The last phrase is typical of the leeway left to the interpreters of the platform. Its meaning depends altogether on the construction placed on "attack" and may easily be extended to mean any assault on American interests, wherever it takes place.

Roosevelt Backers Placated

On the other hand, the committee members who held out for a statement of policy more in line with the stand of the Administration which this convention seeks to keep in power were placated by the expression of sympathy and support given to the nations fighting against aggression.

Great Britain was not mentioned by name, though Senator Pepper and several members of the committee fought hard for a pledge of "aid to Britain," but the Democrats affirm that "the world's greatest democracy cannot afford heartlessly or in a spirit of appeasement"—a significant and hotly argued point—"to ignore the peace-loving and liberty-loving peoples

Continued on Page Six

NATION WILL HEAR PRESIDENT TONIGHT

Roosevelt Expected to Address Convention on Radio After Notification

Special to THE NEW YORK TIMES.

WASHINGTON, Thursday, July 18—President Roosevelt is expected to address the Democratic National Convention and the nation in a radio address tonight, following his official notification of his nomination for a third term.

The President listened for several hours to the radio broadcast of the convention proceedings into the early hours of the morning and sent out word that he would have nothing to say until formally notified of his nomination.

White House aides said that they could not confirm officially the President's reported intention to address the convention by radio, but added that he expected the notification before noon tomorrow. All indications were that he would acknowledge it before the day was out.

The President had only two callers during the day. Secretary Stephen T. Early said he "purposely kept his engagements down to the minimum in order to listen in on the radio to what happened at Chicago and to be available in case any of his key men should want to reach him over the special telephone set-up in the White House."

To all such callers over the private telephone from Chicago, Mr. Early said the President was "open and available."

Any idea among the few Democrats and Republicans left in Washington that Mr. Roosevelt would refuse renomination for a third term faded with his message to the convention Tuesday through Senator Barkley. The certainty that the President would accept a renomination was shared by the White House staff although Mr. Early answered a question by saying he was "not thinking about it just now."

Mr. Early did say, however, that he would be available to the newspaper men should the President be placed in nomination tonight. All other attempts to draw him out on the President's plan ran into a blank wall. He volunteered the information that Mr. Roosevelt

Continued on Page Six

BY 'ACCLAMATION'

Farley, Who Remained in Race, Makes the Vote Unanimous

RIVALS' POLL IS 150

Third-Term Tradition Is Upset—Garner, Tydings Stay to End

By TURNER CATLEDGE
Special to THE NEW YORK TIMES.

CHICAGO, Thursday, July 18—President Roosevelt was renominated early this morning for a third term for President of the United States by the Democratic National Convention.

The President's renomination, which climaxed a "draft" movement carried out in contravention of one of the oldest and best established traditions in American politics, came theoretically by "acclamation," but the move to nominate unanimously or by acclamation came in a dramatic surrender by Postmaster General James A. Farley and others who had stood with him against a third-term nomination.

Mr. Farley, Vice President Garner and Senator Millard E. Tydings of Maryland all had been placed in nomination in pursuance of the third-term protest. Before the move to nominate by acclamation was made by Mr. Farley more than 150 of the convention delegates had cast votes against Mr. Roosevelt, distributing them among the three named above and Secretary Cordell Hull. Governor Cooper of Tennessee explained to the convention that Mr. Hull was not and had never been a candidate.

How the Ballot Stood

The total vote before it was made unanimous was Roosevelt 946 13/30, Farley 72 27/30, Garner 61, Tydings 9½ and Hull 5 2/3.

There was but little demonstration when the convention made its momentous decision. The first thing that happened was a song led by Phil Regan, "When Irish Eyes Are Smiling," the convention's song to Mr. Farley.

Mr. Roosevelt's nomination was clinched when New York voted, giving 64½ votes for him, 25 for Farley, 1 for Secretary Hull, with 3½ missing. New York's sixty-four votes put the President over the 548 votes needed for renomination. There was no notice given by the delegates of this momentous hour. It was shortly before 1 A. M.

Senator Barkley, Permanent Chairman of the Convention, appointed a committee composed of Senators Byrnes of South Carolina, Charles F. Sawyer of Ohio and Mayor Edward F. Kelly of Chicago to notify the President of his renomination.

The convention adjourned shortly before 2 A. M. until 2 o'clock in the afternoon, when it will meet to name a candidate for Vice President.

Acceptance Held Certain

The President is counted as certain to accept the nomination, despite a statement made to the convention in his behalf that he did not desire to run again. His acceptance is expected to come in a radio message to the convention before it adjourns.

He also will be expected now to indicate his choice for Vice President from among a growing list of potential candidates. He may also take occasion in replying to the Convention "draft" to express his ideas on a platform adopted by the party and which, it is understood, did not satisfy him completely by the language of its statement against intervention by the United States in foreign wars.

The Roosevelt "draft" had been indicated from a time long before the delegates assembled in Chicago, and it moved relentlessly to its successful conclusion under the management of inner circle New Dealers, assisted by Senator James F. Byrnes of South Carolina as floor leader.

Just before the roll-call of States started for the nomination, the convention howled down a proposal of Representative Elmer J. Ryan of

Continued on Page Five

The International Situation

The Anglo-Japanese agreement, by which the Burma road to China has been closed and Japan, it is reported, has promised to seek peace with China, was attacked in the British House of Commons yesterday as a "shameful deal." [Page 1, Column 1.]

Prince Konoye, head of the one-party-government movement in Japan, named his Foreign, Navy and War Ministers. They will join him in a strong centralized government. No immediate alliance with Germany and Italy is expected from his government, but attempts at expansion southward are likely. [Page 14, Column 2.]

Sir Archibald Sinclair, British Air Minister, took advantage of a let-up in the German raids on Britain to warn his countrymen by radio that they must expect much greater bombardments from the sky than any yet experienced. He admitted Germany had air superiority. For the first time in weeks the Royal Air Force did not visit Germany Tuesday night. [Page 12, Column 1.]

The Wehrmacht, organ of the German High Command, published an article saying that vessels ready at French ports could cross the Channel to Britain in from forty minutes to four hours, that airplanes could effectively support such attacks, and that ten French points of departure, all equipped with proper defenses and with good rail connections, had been completely prepared. [Page 12, Column 3.]

Sir Stafford Cripps, Britain's new Ambassador to Moscow, recently had an interview with Joseph Stalin, it was revealed. Among matters discussed, it was understood, were some of interest to the United States. London reported that the Russian dictator had said Russia was determined to stay neutral, and that he saw no reason to fear German domination of Europe. [Page 13, Column 2.]

General Franco, chief of the Spanish Government, warned Britain in a speech that Spain expected to get Gibraltar back. This was the first official endorsement of the Gibraltar campaign carried on by students and Falangists. [Page 1, Column 2.]

An army of 2,000,000 men is the minimum for defense of this hemisphere, General Marshall, chief of staff, told a meeting at Washington of civilian aides to the Secretary of War. The War Department wants forty-five streamlined infantry divisions and ten armored divisions. [Page 1, Column 3.]

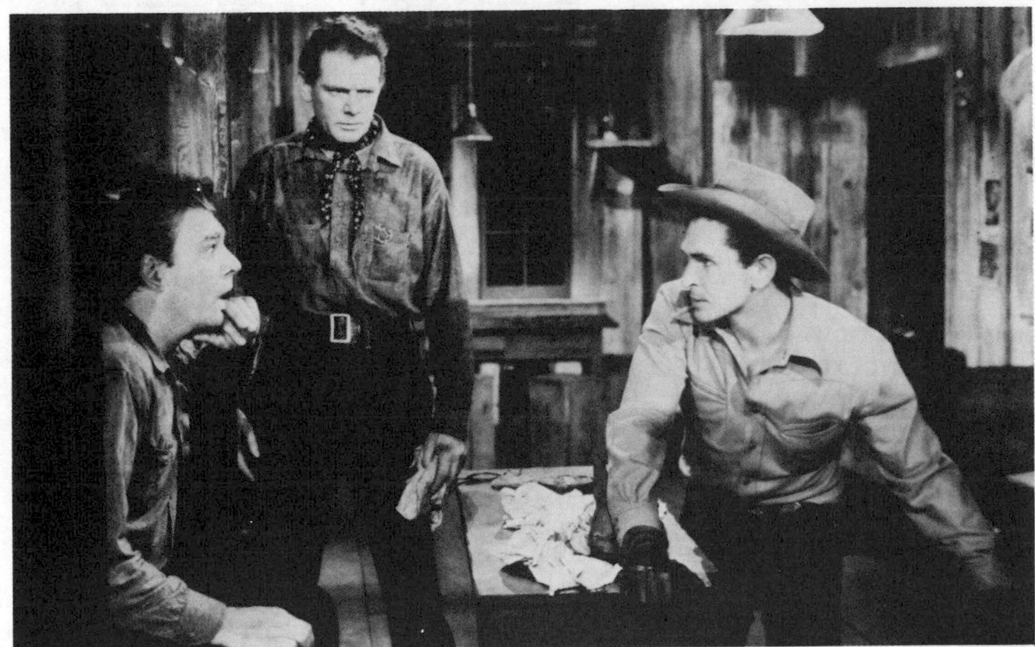

Ranch hands Bob Steele and Charles Bickford tease poor, dumb Lennie, played by Lon Chaney, Jr., in *Of Mice and Men.*

Vivien Leigh with Robert Taylor in *Waterloo Bridge.*

Walter Brennan, Gary Cooper, Irving Bacon, Barbara Stanwyck and James Gleason in the 1940 hit *Meet John Doe.*

"All the News That's Fit to Print."

The New York Times.

Copyright, 1940, by The New York Times Company.

LATE CITY EDITION
Fair and continued warm except scattered thundershowers today. Tomorrow showers, cooler.
Temperatures Yesterday—Max., 87; Min., 70

VOL. LXXXIX..No. 30,134. Entered as Second-Class Matter, Postoffice, New York, N. Y. NEW YORK, FRIDAY, JULY 26, 1940. THREE CENTS NEW YORK CITY and Vicinity | FOUR CENTS Elsewhere Except in 7th and 8th Postal Zones.

EMBARGO PUT ON OIL, SCRAP METAL IN LICENSE ORDER BY ROOSEVELT; FRENCH SHIP SUNK, 350 DROWNED

WALLACE DEFERS 'POLITICAL' MOVES TILL HE IS NOTIFIED

Campaign Steps to Be Avoided for Another Month, He Says After Talk With Roosevelt

DOUBT OVER RESIGNATION

Secretary Says He Will Decide What Is Just When He Turns to Vice Presidential Drive

By CHARLES W. HURD

Special to THE NEW YORK TIMES.

WASHINGTON, July 25—Secretary Wallace's status as a Cabinet member concerned with the disbursement of large amounts of Federal benefits coincident with his candidacy for the Vice Presidency as Mr. Roosevelt's choice for running mate was settled temporarily at the White House today by the dictum that his activities will be "nonpolitical" for at least another month.

As Secretary Wallace expressed it after a conference with the President, he and Mr. Roosevelt would not consider his activities as political until he was formally notified of his candidacy, an event scheduled for somewhere in Iowa about Aug. 20.

In other words, it was decided that the Wallace notification, obviously aimed at holding the votes of the agricultural States, should take place after Wendell L. Willkie's formal notification of his nomination by the Republicans at Elwood, Ind., on Aug. 17, and in surroundings equally close to the heart of the Middle West.

First Talk Since Convention

The first conference between the President and Mr. Wallace since the Democratic convention took place as discussion was heard in informed quarters of the possibility that Jesse Jones, Federal Loan Administrator, would succeed Secretary Wallace in the Department of Agriculture post.

There was no confirmation of this report beyond general speculative conversation, although friends of Mr. Jones also reported that he had purchased a farm near by in Virginia with the evident expectation of making his future home here. Pending a decision whether Mr. Wallace would resign, it was expected that reports of a successor would meet with official denial.

Secretary Wallace himself was reticent in talking to newspaper men about his possible resignation when the time came to turn to "political activities."

"I intend to look up all the precedents and decide what is fair and just and right for the American people," he said, speaking deliberately but smiling in the shy manner familiar to his associates.

Mr. Wallace was the first important caller received at the White House after President Roosevelt returned this morning from a three-day rest at Hyde Park. The Secretary also had just returned from a brief holiday. They were together about forty-five minutes, after which Mr. Wallace gave out the scanty details made public about their talk.

Reports Decisions Deferred

The gist of his remarks was that all decisions as to the future would await the notification ceremonies.

"We talked matters over from various angles," Secretary Wallace said, "and I have reached the conclusion that I will not be engaging in any political activity until the notification ceremony, and possibly for some little time afterward.

"The notification ceremonies will not occur before Aug. 20. As to the place, it will be some place in Iowa, but I am not sure as yet as to just the place or the date."

When a reporter reminded the Secretary that this tentative date fell soon after the scheduled Willkie ceremony, he said that there was no significance to the choice. Iowa, of course, is his home State, and the setting, along with Mr. Wallace's nomination itself, logically follows a normal political pattern.

Secretary Wallace said, in reply to a question as to when his own political activities would technically begin, that it would depend "upon when political activities begin."

"I don't interpret notification as a political activity, unless I make a rip-snorting political speech," he remarked.

Farley Successor Discussed

Mr. Wallace stated that he had "discussed very generally" with the President other political questions, including the choice of a successor to Postmaster General Farley as chairman of the Democratic National Committee, and added that they had not discussed a division of the burden of campaign speech-making.

"The question of a swing around the country will have to be a matter of future conversations," he stated.

In the meantime observers professed to see new indications that opposition to the Roosevelt candi-

Continued on Page Ten

Jar Used in '17 Drawing Available for New Draft

By The Associated Press.

PHILADELPHIA, July 25—Philadelphians wondered today whether the Compulsory Military Service Bill might bring into use again a historic glass jar on display in Independence Hall.

From it Secretary of War Newton D. Baker pulled the first World War draft names in a ceremony in Washington, July 20, 1917.

It was used again Feb. 11, 1920, to pick representatives of mothers, widows and sisters of American soldiers to receive French memorial certificates.

JOB SAFEGUARD PUT INTO TRAINING BILL

Senate Group Adds Penalties for Refusal to Re-employ Men—Measure Attacked

Special to THE NEW YORK TIMES.

WASHINGTON, July 25—The Burke-Wadsworth military service bill is scheduled to reach the floor of the Senate on Monday, Senator Sheppard, chairman of the Military Affairs Committee, announced today. The committee has virtually completed its study of the measure, adding today a last-minute amendment intended to protect the jobs of those called from private industry to the service of the flag under the selective service plan.

This amendment provides that employers refusing to re-employ men after their year's training period is completed shall be considered guilty of unfair labor practices under the National Labor Relations Act and subject to prosecution under its terms. Federal workers would be reinstated automatically to their jobs under its terms and Congress would issue a strong admonition to employers engaged in intrastate trade to take back their employes. The amendment provides that a special committee be set up in the government to enforce this part of the legislation.

While the Military Affairs Committee put the finishing touches on the bill, Senator Lee of Oklahoma pursued on the floor his drive for a measure to draft capital as well.

Norris Assails Money Draft Bill

Mr. Lee introduced a bill which would empower the President to set up a plan "for drafting the use of money according to each individual's ability to lend." The only specification regarding the plan was that it should not permit profits, high interest rates or the issuance of tax-exempt securities.

Senator Lee's proposal provoked a demand from Senator Norris of Nebraska for Congress itself to write the details of any wealth-conscripting plan and not leave them to the President.

"Does the President want this authority, and have we not stamina enough, even if he does want it, not to give it to him?" Senator Norris asked, and added:

"It is our responsibility and we should assume it and we shall have courage to do it if it is done at all. It is not fair to the President. I do not have any idea that he wants to take this responsibility. The cry against the President has been made for the last two years that he wants to be a dictator. It seems to me this bill comes pretty near to making him a dictator."

Senator Lee said that he had not discussed the bill with the President but merely introduced it to focus attention on a problem that would arise in a national emergency and to cause public thinking on it.

As the Selective Service Bill now stands it provides for the registration of all males in the country, including aliens, between the ages of 18 and 64, with those between the ages of 21 and 45 subject to selection for one year's military training at once.

Vandenberg Asks Volunteer Plan

Manoeuvring in the Senate indicated today that an attempt would be made when the bill reaches the floor next week to substitute a plan for voluntary enlistments. Senator Vandenberg practically gave notice of this in a short speech on the floor. He suggested that if one-year enlistments were offered instead of the present minimum three years enlistment period, sufficient men might be induced to enter the Army voluntarily.

"No one is denying that if expended defense personnel cannot be acquired by our traditional, voluntary, peacetime enlistment at the essential tempo, then we must proceed to the compulsory alternative," Mr. Vandenberg said.

"But I find a widespread question, which I emphatically share myself, whether the traditional, peace-time, voluntary methods of our democracy are failing; and, secondly, whether in such an event adequate effort has been made to encourage this method."

He introduced for the record three letters from citizens of three different States which raised the same question.

"After all," the Michigan Sena-

Continued on Page Ten

JOHNSON RESIGNS AS STIMSON AIDE; PATTERSON NAMED

Assistant Secretary Steps Out, With White House Attributing Change to New War Head

LIAISON POST OFFERED HIM

Judge Told of His Appointment While He Is on K. P. Duty at Plattsburg Training Camp

Special to THE NEW YORK TIMES.

WASHINGTON, July 25—Louis Johnson, assistant Secretary of War, who frequently clashed with Harry H. Woodring, former Secretary, left his office today in a resignation disclosed at the White House coincident with announcement that Robert Porter Patterson, a United States Circuit judge in New York, would succeed him at the War Department.

Mr. Johnson's letter of resignation, dated yesterday, was released while he was in San Francisco. With it, Stephen Early, White House secretary, made public a telegram of acceptance sent by President Roosevelt.

Thus the War Department now has a new executive head in the person of Secretary Henry L. Stimson and a new administrative officer.

Mr. Early also stated that the President had offered Mr. Johnson a vacant post as one of the six administrative assistants to the President to "become his eyes and ears" as "a progress reporter on the entire question of national defense." It was not indicated whether Mr. Johnson would accept, although the tone of his letter of resignation indicated that he would not.

Needs Rest, Says Johnson

The assistant secretary's letter was notable in its tribute to the Army officers "who tolerated me and my efforts for a year, and then so loyally supported me." He also wrote to the President that he was leaving yesterday "for a very necessary, if not earned, rest."

Mr. Stimson said at a press conference later in the day that his relations with Mr. Johnson had been very friendly, but he declined further comment on the resignation, although he praised the appointment of Judge Patterson.

The manner in which Judge Patterson was selected was not clear. Mr. Early told reporters that Secretary Stimson had requested the President to name Judge Patterson, in line with the traditional right of Cabinet members to name their assistants. In other equally well-informed quarters, it was indicated that, while Secretary Stimson had acquiesced gladly in the choice of Judge Patterson, the selection had been the President's rather than his own.

Judge Patterson served with distinction in the World War as a major of the 306th Infantry, being a member of the same division in which Secretary Stimson was a colonel. President Hoover appointed him a United States District Judge in 1930, and President Roosevelt promoted him to the Circuit bench in 1939.

The White House issued the following statement today:

"The President has received the following letter of resignation, dated July 24, 1940, from Louis Johnson, Assistant Secretary of War:

My dear Mr. President:

I offered by resignation as the Assistant Secretary of War immediately upon your advising me

Continued on Page Ten

U. S. Ship Off to Petsamo To Bring Back Diplomats

The United States Army transport American Legion sailed under sealed orders from the Brooklyn Army Base yesterday afternoon, and in Washington it was announced she would evacuate stranded Americans from the Arctic port of Petsamo, Finland.

Acting Secretary of State Sumner Welles told The Associated Press that Mrs. Daisy Borden Harriman, Minister to Norway, would return on the 13,736-ton transport, possibly with the Ministers to Estonia, Latvia and Lithuania, which have been absorbed by the Soviet Union. Petsamo is in the war zone and belligerent nations have been informed of the American Legion's course and destination.

The transport was to have sailed Monday, carrying troops for service in Panama and Puerto Rico, but the orders were canceled.

ARGENTINA BLOCKS TRUSTEESHIP PLAN

Reservations Deprive Project of Its Emergency Value—56 Proposals at Havana

By HAROLD B. HINTON

Special Cable to THE NEW YORK TIMES.

HAVANA, July 25—Important reservations to the United States' plan for collective trusteeship over European possessions in the Western Hemisphere in event of their threatened transfer of sovereignty were filed today by the Argentine delegation.

Dr. Leopoldo Melo, head of the delegation, offered his own proposal. He insisted that the American republics take action only on a juridical basis and even then only after consulting the population to be affected and each other.

Secretary of State Cordell Hull declined to comment, saying that he had not seen the Argentine plan. It is certain, however, that this proposal will meet with considerable opposition, as it would tend to make the trusteeship procedure inoperative in any emergency such as Secretary Hull fears may arise at any time.

The Argentine draft called attention to the position of Jamaica, a British colony, which has already gone on record that it can attend to its own affairs without Pan-American assistance. The Argentines actually have in mind, however, a possible Pan-American decision to take over, for example, the French island of Martinique on the ground that the Vichy government is controlled by Germany and that continued French administration of the island would constitute in effect a transfer of sovereignty.

Act of War Foreseen

It is believed certain that the French authorities at Martinique would resist, necessitating an act of war to accomplish actual occupation under collective trusteeship.

According to the Argentine Constitution, that country's Congress alone can declare war or countenance acts of war. Hence Dr. Melo feels unable to accept the blank check he feels Argentina is asked

Continued on Page Six

Navy Orders Give Steel Gigantic Backlog; $500,000,000 Sets Record for Bethlehem

The first 10 per cent of the expansion program of the United States Navy has increased the unfilled orders on the books of the Bethlehem Steel Corporation to nearly $500,000,000, according to figures made public by Eugene G. Grace, president, at the close of the quarterly meeting of directors yesterday. The amount is 70 per cent above the highest backlog previously reported by the company.

Backlogs at June 30 were $388,521,467, Mr. Grace announced, adding that this figure represented "purely a commercial situation," in which the national defense effort figured only slightly.

Bethlehem's share in the Navy contracts placed since July 1 amounts to between $195,000,000 and $200,000,000, he said, and increased structural steel orders for hangars and other naval and military construction and for railroad rehabilitation made necessary in the national defense program have further swelled the company's bookings.

With operations of the company for July at 99 per cent of full capacity, orders booked during the month have been at nearly 140 per cent of basic productive capacity, Mr. Grace said. Earnings were the second best for the second quarter of the year in the history of the company, and the directors ordered a common dividend of $1.25 a share, the same as three months ago, bringing 1940 distributions on the stock to $3.50 a share, compared with $1.50 paid in the whole of 1939.

In addition to the naval program, which will be tremendously expanded by the 70 per cent addition, or "Two-Ocean Navy," in process of enactment, Bethlehem expects substantial orders for the 1941 automobile season in the near future, and general business in all lines of steel production is growing. There is a substantial demand from England and other export markets, which is well in excess of the normal volume of 10 to 12 per cent of total business booked, Mr. Grace said.

Net profit for the second quarter was $10,807,318, or $3.07 a share on 2,984,994 common shares, compared with $10,891,139 in the first quar-

Continued on Page Twenty-eight

LINER IS TORPEDOED

Nazis Sink Ship Taking French Sailors Home From England

2,500 LOST ON LANCASTRIA

Cunarder With 5,300 Aboard Bombed During Evacuation of France by B. E. F.

By RAYMOND DANIELL

Special Cable to THE NEW YORK TIMES.

LONDON, July 25—Two horror stories of the war at sea were revealed publicly today in official statements.

One, less than twenty-four hours old, told how a German torpedo sent to their deaths in the English Channel 350 Frenchmen who were obeying orders from the Pétain government to return hime under the terms of the Franco-German armistice.

The other described how more than 2,500 British soldiers, women and children went down aboard the old Cunard cruise ship Lancastria to die in a blazing sea of oil, singing "There'll Always Be an England," on June 17 during the evacuation of the British Expeditionary Force from France.

The first story was told by Albert V. Alexander, First Lord of the Admiralty, this afternoon in the House of Commons. It was supplemented later by official Admiralty communiqués and more graphic tales related by some of the 950 survivors of the 6,127-ton French liner Meknes, torpedoed and sunk last night. She was manned by a crew of 100 and carried some 1,200 officers and men of the French Navy who were being repatriated.

Withheld by Censor

The other story was an old one on which the censors had been sitting so tightly ever since the Lancastria was lost more than a month ago that it was news to the British newspaper reading public when the ban on publication was lifted.

Tragic as that story was to those who had relatives listed as missing, it was overshadowed in immediate diplomatic importance by the sinking of the Meknes. She, it was said here, had sailed only yesterday from Southampton for Marseille under promises of safe conduct. She was flying the tricolor of France, which also was painted on her decks and hull, and she was showing lights from stem to stern, it was said, when she was overhauled by a small, fast surface craft that raked her decks with machine-gun fire and then sent a torpedo crashing through her sides.

Announcing what was regarded here as fresh examples of German ruthlessness and frightfulness in the conduct of the war at sea, Mr. Alexander informed the House that Germany had conceded guilt in this case by announcing in an official communiqué that one of her torpedo boats had destroyed a merchant ship in the Channel about where the Meknes sank.

Promises to Inform French

Replying to a question, Lord Privy Seal Clement Attlee assured the House that the government would use every means to make certain that the people of France were fully informed on all details of the Meknes's loss so that they might know how much faith to place in the promises of Nazi Germany.

The Meknes, Mr. Alexander informed the House, was one of several ships used in repatriating French officers and men who chose to return to France rather than continue to fight against Germany with the British Navy. The French had been notified of her departure.

Mr. Alexander said that at about 10:30 P. M. yesterday the Meknes was overhauled by a motor torpedo boat, whose commander gave the passengers and crew five minutes to take to the boats. In the interval before torpedoing the ship, the First Lord said, the torpedo boat raked her decks with machine gun fire each time the vessel tried to signal her name and mission.

A more detailed story of what happened was related tonight by survivors who landed at several British ports. Of 950 rescued by British naval forces and landed here, 120 officers and forty-one men were rushed to hospitals. Fifteen of them were severely wounded. The official Admiralty statement said there was reason to hope other survivors reached the French coast.

The captain of the torpedoed French liner declined to make a statement when he came ashore but another officer said she first was

Continued on Page Two

The International Situation

American Developments

In a sudden move President Roosevelt yesterday halted all exports of American oil and scrap metal except "under special license." Most affected will be Japan, which has recently purchased from the United States as much as 65 per cent of her oil and more than 85 per cent of her scrap metal, with which to conduct the war in China. Also affected will be the Axis powers, which, it is believed, have been receiving shipments of American oil through Spanish and Portuguese ports. [Page 1, Column 8.]

German Economics Minister Funk warned the United States to prepare to trade with a victorious Germany after the war or face a lockout of European markets. He added that the United States could never take the place of Europe in South America's economy. His statement seemed to be aimed at the nations conferring at Havana on plans for expanded intra-hemisphere trade, among other things. [Page 6, Column 2.]

In Havana itself the Argentine delegation objected to a proposal by the United States that the American republics jointly assume sovereignty over European possessions in this hemisphere in a time of crisis. Argentina suggested modifying this plan to include prior consent to such a move by the populations of the territories involved. Such an alteration, it was felt by some, would render the main plan cumbersome and inoperative in a crisis. [Page 1, column 4.]

Supporting what Lord Beaverbrook had broadcast to the British Empire, Secretary of the Treasury Morgenthau announced that the United States would do what it could to build 3,000 additional planes a month for Britain. The Secretary said the British were ready to spend "colossal sums," which would help expand this country's present plane production. [Page 9, Column 1.]

The Senate Military Affairs Committee virtually completed action on the Conscription Bill by providing for mandatory rehiring of conscripts. The bill goes to the full Senate Monday. [Page 1, Column 2.]

Assistant Secretary of War Johnson resigned and from the White House came word that he would become liaison officer between the defense program and the President. [Page 1, Column 3.]

The War in Europe

Starting next week Britain plans to extend her blockade to Spain and Portugal, thereby imposing on the whole European Continent her naval control. The United States, it was thought in London, would move to extend the combat zone and prevent all American ships and Clipper planes from entering Europe's waters or air lanes. [Page 1, column 7.]

Britain released to the public details of two ship sinkings, one a month old. In one the British cruise ship Lancastria was torpedoed while carrying men, women and children being evacuated from France, with a loss of 2,500 lives. The second occurred Wednesday night when a German torpedo boat sank the plainly marked liner Meknes returning to France with 1,200 French officers and men on their way to be repatriated. The loss of lives in this case was 350. [Page 1, Column 5.]

Again swarms of Nazi air raiders swept over the Channel and British coasts yesterday and again British fighter craft rose to meet them, shooting down twenty by day's end, according to the British Air Ministry. London claimed R. A. F. raids during the night had damaged more of Germany's aircraft factories and that these raids over the past month had made "extremely difficult" organization of the long-awaited Nazi invasion. Berlin countered with claims that its planes had bombed the great Vickers aircraft plant near London and that its torpedo boats had sunk several merchantmen. [Page 1, Column 6.]

Probably in retaliation for Rumania's pro-Axis leanings, Britain declared her support for Bulgaria's revisionist claims on Rumania. Bucharest recalled its pro-British Minister to London. Rumania, meanwhile, tightened her grip on oil properties controlled by the British and French. [Page 5, Column 4.]

Germany was said to have recognized the Breton autonomists, who demand a separate State within French territory. It was also reported that a special German Governor had been designated to administer the Province of Brittany. [Page 3, Column 6.]

R. A. F. FLIERS FIGHT HUNDREDS OF NAZIS

British Claim 20 of Enemy's Ships Were Lost in Battles Lasting All Day Long

By JAMES MacDONALD

Special Cable to THE NEW YORK TIMES.

LONDON, July 25—Hundreds of German planes fought it out with the British, sometimes at altitudes of five or six miles, and countless anti-aircraft guns roared angrily and almost continuously from dawn until late evening today as the Nazis intensified their drive to blockade this country by air attacks on its shipping and various coastal points.

The German Air Force sent over numerous squadrons that attacked shipping along the southeast and southwest coasts of England, the northeast coast of Scotland and points inland. The Germans lost twenty planes, eleven bombers and nine fighters, the British said, one being shot down by a Norwegian motor torpedo boat, another by anti-aircraft fire and the others by R. A. F. fighters. The British loss was placed at five planes.

Whether the raiders effected any serious damage to shipping or targets inland was not divulged by London officials, who decline to publish such information lest it prove valuable to the enemy.

However, the Admiralty admitted the loss of two trawlers, the 415-ton Kingston Galena and the 230-ton Rodino, as a result of German bombing attacks. It was presumed that all members of the crews of both trawlers, whose total number was not given, had gone down with the vessels. The Admiralty said their next of kin had been notified.

Continued on Page Four

BRITAIN TO EXTEND BLOCKADE TO SPAIN

Portugal Will Be Included to Bar War Supplies, Chiefly Oil, From All Europe

By The United Press.

LONDON, July 25—Great Britain will extend her blockade to Spain and Portugal next week, thereby bringing all Continental Europe within the scope of her naval control, it was stated reliably tonight.

It was believed certain that the expected British action would result in designation by the United States of a new combat zone under the Neutrality Act, thereby banning American ships and clipper planes from touching Portugal or Spain and cutting the service off from all contact with Europe.

Hugh Dalton, Minister for Economic Warfare, had been scheduled to announce extension of the blockade in Parliament today, but his statement was postponed, probably until Tuesday.

The delay was caused by administrative difficulties, authoritative quarters said, adding, however, that the British Government's policy for ruthless and complete blockade not only had been formulated but had received the Cabinet's approval.

U. S. Reported Consulted

There was evidence that the decision to extend the blockade had been reached after consultation with United States authorities and possibly with their cooperation.

According to American sources, the United States Maritime Commission, after consultation with

Continued on Page Seven

BAN AFFECTS JAPAN

U. S. Supply of Materials in Her War on China Can Be Cut Off

OIL TO SPAIN STOPPED

Holding of Tankers at Houston Blocks Axis Route—Link to British Blockade Denied

By JOHN H. CRIDER

Special to THE NEW YORK TIMES.

WASHINGTON, July 25—President Roosevelt today prohibited the export of petroleum, petroleum products and scrap metal from the United States without a specific license from the administrator of export control, Lieut. Col. Russell L. Maxwell.

The order, which added to the items placed under a virtual embargo by an initial ruling issued July 2 under the May act, was regarded as partial use of one of the most powerful economic weapons the United States could aim at Japan, which is largely dependent upon this country for iron, steel and petroleum.

It also will prevent Italy or Germany from receiving these essential war materials by way of Spain, a route that the British Government has stated was being used by the Axis powers to obtain oil and gasoline from the United States. But the amounts involved would be slight compared with exports to Japan.

Cargoes Already Held Up

It was disclosed coincidentally that the Treasury and the Maritime Commission already had acted in some instances to prevent cargoes from moving to Japan and Spain.

Information available through official sources showed that the Treasury's new Office of Ship Movements had ordered that clearance be withheld July 10 at Houston, Texas, from the tanker Aryan, scheduled to sail with cargo for Santander, Spain, and on the following day from the tanker Nevada for Bilbao, Spain.

Secretary of the Treasury Henry Morgenthau Jr. stated at his press conference that there was no relation between the London announcement that the British blockade was being extended to stop movements of American oil to Spain and the action taken by the Treasury. The dates would seem to bear this out.

At the Maritime Commission it was stated that the commission had just disapproved applications through which a Japanese firm sought to charter the American tankers Cities Service Missouri and Cities Service Kansas, and the freighter Louis Luckenbach, for shipment of 72-octane gasoline (non-aviation) to Japan. In June the commission refused to charter the same three vessels for oil shipments to Spain.

While no final conclusions as to political implications of the action would be warranted until it is observed how the government intends to exercise its licensing power, the mere act of subjecting exports of products so important to Japan to a control system was regarded as a definite step in the application of a vigorous economic policy toward Japan.

Relation to Japan Watched

For years, it was recalled, there has been talk of economic sanctions against Japan, which has used vast supplies of United States products to carry on her war in China. To some observers the day's order represented the final application of such sanctions.

From the economic standpoint the move places the United States in a strong bargaining position with Japan regarding products vital to both countries. Especially since the conquest of the Netherlands by Germany, concern has been expressed lest the Japanese might take the Netherlands East Indies, principal source of rubber and tin to this country.

With power over petroleum and scrap exports now in Executive control, the United States, it was observed, is in a position to bargain oil and scrap against rubber and tin should the Administration be so disposed.

Japan has no iron or petroleum resources of any moment. In 1939 the United States supplied 65 per cent of Japanese petroleum imports and probably in excess of 85 per cent of iron and steel scrap. Lacking iron ore, Japan takes what scrap iron and steel there is avail-

Continued on Page Seven

1940

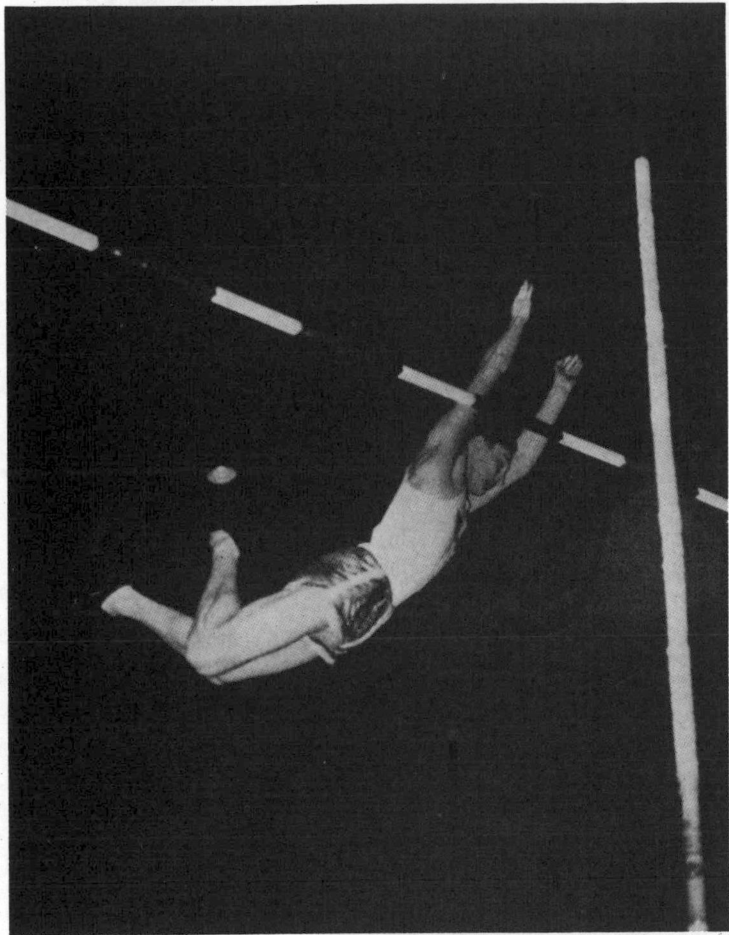

Cornelius Warmerdam, a California high school teacher, broke the pole vault record by topping 15 feet. He went on to break his own records a number of times in the 40s.

Byron "Whizzer" White, who went on to become a United States Supreme Court Justice, was football's leading yardage gainer.

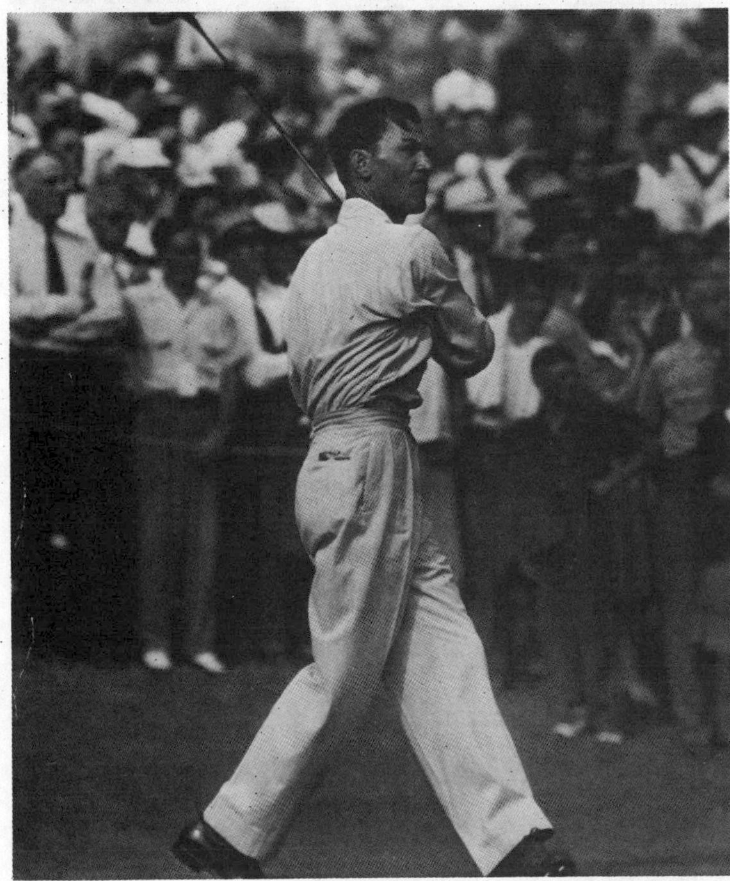

The great Ben Hogan won four tournaments, and was golf's leading money winner in 1940.

Byron Nelson broke or shattered every golf record in the book from 1936 through 1946.

"All the News That's Fit to Print."

The New York Times.

LATE CITY EDITION
Fair, with little change in temperature today and tomorrow.
Temperatures Yesterday—Max., 90; Min., 67

Copyright, 1940, by The New York Times Company.

VOL. LXXXIX..No. 30,174. Entered as Second-Class Matter, Postoffice, New York, N. Y. NEW YORK, WEDNESDAY, SEPTEMBER 4, 1940. THREE CENTS NEW YORK CITY and Vicinity | FOUR CENTS Elsewhere Except in 7th and 8th Postal Zones.

ROOSEVELT TRADES DESTROYERS FOR SEA BASES; TELLS CONGRESS HE ACTED ON OWN AUTHORITY; BRITAIN PLEDGES NEVER TO YIELD OR SINK FLEET

R.A.F. REPELS RAIDS

Fliers Turn Back Three Drives on London—Reich Perfecting Technique

PLANES REACH BERLIN

2½-Hour Alarm in City —British Hit Hard at French Coast

By JAMES B. RESTON
Special Cable to THE NEW YORK TIMES.

LONDON, Wednesday, Sept. 4—German bombers started ringing that big London doorbell early yesterday morning. They rang it again in the afternoon while Prime Minister Winston Churchill and his Ministers were commemorating the first anniversary of the war, and they kept ringing it right up till last midnight, when the third "all clear" of the day was sounded over the capital.

It was a day of fierce air battles, fought at great height in blue and silver sky all over Southeast England, and at the end, though Reich Marshal Hermann Goering's night shift was still operating all over the island, the British Air Ministry announced that twenty-five Nazi planes had been shot down to fifteen of Britain's planes. Eight British pilots were said to be safe, though it is not known whether they are in condition to fly.

[British bombing planes flew high over Berlin shortly after last midnight. Berlin spokesmen were quoted as saying that most of the Royal Air Force planes were turned back by severe anti-aircraft fire between Wittenberg and Magdeburg, but several planes escaped through the anti-aircraft barrage and reached Berlin, where they were again met with anti-aircraft fire.]

These German bombers, which have already overwhelmed five countries in the past twelve months, have now perfected a technique in attacking this vast, sprawling city, and they tried to work it again yesterday morning in the first raid.

Two Formations Meet

Just at 10 o'clock, timed to perfection, one wave of bombers approached the Thames Estuary from their bases in Belgium. Simultaneously, another formation, flying high through a light haze, came up from bases in France and met them over the Kentish coast. Altogether they were about 250 of them, and defying anti-aircraft batteries at first they started along the banks of the Thames toward London.

As they came inland, however, they met first one, then a second squadron of British fighters, who dived through Nazi fighter patrols into the bombers, broke up the formation and then attacked them singly and drove them back over the coast.

Some German bombers dropped their dynamite in Kent and Essex, but all that is said about the effect of these bombs is that they caused few casualties and little damage.

What can be said is that, if these bombers were trying to get into the heart of London to attack objectives here, they certainly failed, for while sirens were sounded everywhere in Greater London nobody in the heart of the city saw any fighting.

There was an interesting sidelight to the second mass raid of the day. At 2:45 P. M. Mr. Churchill, who somehow contrives to look more confident every day, walked into Westminster Abbey to attend the special service in commemoration of the day a year ago when Britain declared war on Germany. Alongside him walked tall, gaunt Viscount Halifax, Foreign Secretary; dapper Arthur Greenwood, Minister without portfolio; Sir Kingsley Wood, Chancellor of the Exchequer; Anthony Eden, War Secretary, and Joseph P. Kennedy, United States Ambassador to Great Britain.

They took their places in the cool church beside a great audience. At 3:50 P. M., as they were sitting there waiting for the service to start, air-raid sirens started echoing through the great cathedral.

Mr. Churchill got up, walked over to the cloisters and had a long talk with the Dean. In a few minutes he returned and took his place beside his Ministers in the chancel. It was announced that the service would proceed.

Around the city the British fight-

Continued on Page Three

The International Situation

Destroyer-War Base Deal

Completion of a deal by which the United States will transfer to Britain fifty over-age destroyers and obtain ninety-nine-year leases on eight shore and island bases stretching from Newfoundland to British Guiana was announced by President Roosevelt yesterday in a message to Congress. Coincidentally, the British Government pledged not to scuttle or surrender its fleet under any conditions. [Page 1, Column 8.]

The objective of the arrangement with Britain is to build a 4,500-mile iron fence in the Atlantic to assure this country's safety for a century, an authoritative State Department source said. To attain this, any interpretations of international law and parts of treaties in conflict must be subordinated, he said. Since this country's purpose is its defense, no well-intentioned nation can call the move a hostile act, he declared. [Page 1, Column 7.]

President Roosevelt, en route to Washington, disclosed that he looked upon the agreement as a means of keeping an enemy from the country's front door. Listing it as in some ways more important for defense than Jefferson's Louisiana purchase, he hinted there might be other similar arrangements. [Page 1, Column 6.]

The President had acted on an opinion from Attorney General Jackson, who held that the Executive had the right to negotiate the transfer without Senate consent and the constitutional power to dispose of the vessels. [Page 1, Column 5.]

Wendell L. Willkie, Republican Presidential nominee, said the country would undoubtedly approve the arrangement, but criticized Mr. Roosevelt's failure to obtain Congress's approval. [Page 1, Column 3.]

London rejoiced. A Foreign Office spokesman described the agreement as a practical method for each nation to contribute to the other's defense requirements. [Page 1, Column 4.]

Axis spokesmen did not challenge the deal's legality under neutrality laws. In Berlin it was belittled as unlikely to affect the war's outcome. It was said to be a bargain for the United States and evidence that Britain was "cracking up." In Rome it was expected the Italians would be embittered. [Page 15, Column 1.]

Developments in Congress

The House opened debate on the Selective Service Training Bill, the discussion following the lines of the Senate's deliberation. Indications were that the bill would pass by a good margin, the principal controversy centering on the question of industrial conscription. Leaders planned for final action Friday. [Page 17, Column 1.]

The Senate Finance Committee opened hearings on the excess profits tax and defense expansion amortization bill. The probability of changes in the measure increased as witnesses hit at its effects on business. [Page 10, Column 1.]

The War in Europe, Asia and Africa

German bombers hammered at Britain's airfields, harbors and naval bases, engaging the Royal Air Force in battles all over Southern England. Three raids on London were repelled. [Page 1, Column 1.]

Several R. A. F. bombers reached Berlin early today to provoke violent anti-aircraft fire after the British had loosed a powerful aerial counter-offensive in which their planes had bombed German industrial centers, the French coast and Italian power stations. [Page 3, Column 1.]

In the central Mediterranean, new type Italian bombers scored a victory, damaging a British battleship, an aircraft carrier, a cruiser and a destroyer, the Rome High Command announced. The R. A. F. again pounded Assab, port in Italian Eritrea. [Page 4, Column 6.]

Led by Tahiti, France's most important colony in Oceania, the French-protected Society Islands have voted to throw in their lot with Britain, repudiating Vichy, it was reported. [Page 6, Column 1.]

A virtual Japanese ultimatum demanding a military base and passage for troops was reported to have been rejected by French Indo-China and conflict there was believed inevitable. [Page 6, Column 3.]

In an attempted Iron Guard coup three gunmen broke through King Carol's palace guard and fired several shots into the air. Others equally vainly besieged a radio station, fought with troops. [Page 1, Column 2.]

A clash between Hungarian and Rumanian troops over the occupation of Transylvania was reported at Bucharest. [Page 4, Column 1.]

BUCHAREST CHECKS IRON GUARDS' COUP

Shots Fired in Front of Royal Palace—Handbills Call On Carol to Abdicate

By EUGEN KOVACS
Wireless to THE NEW YORK TIMES.

BUCHAREST, Rumania, Sept. 3—A group of the Iron Guards, dissatisfied with the conduct and policy of other Iron Guards who are Ministers and who participated in the Crown Council, organized and carried out several attempts tonight against different public buildings in Bucharest. All these attacks failed.

A small group consisting of three persons appeared in an automobile this evening at 8:30 before the Royal Palace and one of them fired two shots in the air. A policeman on duty in front of the gates of the palace fired at the car but failed. The man who fired the shots tried to escape, however, but was arrested, while the car disappeared.

The regular news bulletin broadcast at 10 o'clock was canceled.

A second group, consisting of young men wearing military uniforms and disguised as Iron Guards, attacked the Bucharest radio station. The guard fired and succeeded in repelling the attacking group.

At the cabin of transmission of the Central Telephone Exchange a man was found who cut off some lines so that the telephone connection with abroad was cut off for a while. At the State Railway repair works in the suburb of Grivitza an-

Continued on Page Four

WILLKIE FOR PACT, BUT HITS SECRECY

Regrets President Did Not Put Deal With Britain Before Congress and People

By JAMES A. HAGERTY
Special to THE NEW YORK TIMES.

RUSHVILLE, Ind., Sept. 3—Asked today to comment on President Roosevelt's announcement of the agreement to turn over to Great Britain fifty over-age destroyers in return for air and naval bases in British Western Hemisphere areas, Wendell L. Willkie, Republican nominee for President, declared that the country undoubtedly would approve the program, but criticized the President's failure to obtain prior approval of Congress as smacking of totalitarianism.

In a statement prepared with care and with realization that it might have important foreign repercussions, Mr. Willkie said:

"The country will undoubtedly approve of the program to add to our naval and air bases and assistance given to Great Britain. It is regrettable, however, that the President did not deem it necessary in connection with this proposal to secure the approval of Congress or permit public discussion prior to adoption.

"The people have a right to know of such important commitments prior to and not after being made. We must be extremely careful in these times when the struggle in the world is between democracy and to-

Continued on Page Fourteen

BRITISH JUBILANT

Destroyers Strengthen Their Fleet at Point of Greatest Strain

MORAL EFFECT GREAT

But Press Warns People Gesture Does Not Mean U. S. Will Enter War

By RAYMOND DANIELL
Special Cable to THE NEW YORK TIMES.

LONDON, Sept. 3—It would be impossible to overstate the jubilation in official and unofficial circles caused today by President Roosevelt's announcement that fifty United States destroyers were coming to help Great Britain in her hour of peril. They will be manned by British crews and will fly the white ensign of the Royal Navy, it is true, but they are coming, nevertheless.

It was tangible proof that American talk of giving "all aid short of war" was more than idle chatter and that this country's friends across the Atlantic, despite German propaganda and the heavy bombardment of British cities and towns, had decided there was still lots of fight left in the British lion and that it was not too late to help turn the tide against totalitarian domination of Europe.

Destroyer Losses Offset

Under the arrangement, it was pointed out by authoritative sources, the United States gained security against future aggression, while the British fleet at one stroke acquired fifty 1,200-ton destroyers as an offset to the thirty lost since the beginning of hostilities.

These destroyers are badly needed at this stage of the war with British seapower engaged in a death grapple with the German Empire. Since the French were knocked out as an ally, the whole job of protecting convoys and maintaining the lifelines of the Empire against the new enemy in the Mediterranean has fallen upon the British fleet, while the air force has concentrated chiefly on destroying the enemy's supplies and defending the homes of the people of this island, which is under repeated bombardment from the air throughout its length and breadth.

Added to this multiplication of the navy's duties has been the necessity of blockading the whole Continent of Europe while standing by to resist the very real threat of a German invasion which, as War Secretary Anthony Eden warned today, still hangs over this country.

As great as was Britain's need the material gain by today's transaction was matched in British minds by the intangible implications of most open indication yet of Anglo-American cooperation for defense against the Nazi threats.

The Times, London, will point out editorially tomorrow that such cooperation between a belligerent and a neutral is "a new departure" but one that is dictated by the necessities of modern war. The editorial goes on to say:

"The tragic fate of some of the smaller peoples of Europe might have been averted if they had not been restrained from planning for

Continued on Page Fifteen

RULING BY JACKSON

Opinion Holds Transfer by President Needs No Senate Action

AN 'EXECUTIVE' DEAL

Opponents in Congress Seek to Find Means of Obstructing It

Attorney General Jackson's opinion is printed on Page 16.

By LEWIS WOOD
Special to THE NEW YORK TIMES.

WASHINGTON, Sept. 3—President Roosevelt has unqualified power to exchange fifty over-age destroyers for British naval and air bases in the Western Hemisphere without Senate consent, in the opinion of Attorney General Jackson, made public today, but, while Mr. Jackson asserted the Executive's right to dispose of naval vessels, he again refused to sanction the legality of delivery of "mosquito boats" now under construction.

Under a World War law the Attorney General ruled that it would be entirely proper to transfer the destroyers, since these were not built "with the intent that they should enter the service of a belligerent," but turning over the uncompleted mosquito boats, he argued, would be impossible, as this would legally mean that they were intended for a belligerent.

Opponents of the British-American deal sought tonight to find means of obstruction and delay, but this seemed to hinge upon the extent to which the direct interest of a taxpayer could be proved and the general opinion here was that the adversaries were blocked from court action and could depend only upon sufficient massing of public opinion. Apparently the Administration felt legally secure.

Writing his opinion to President Roosevelt last Tuesday, Mr. Jackson went into detail as to constitutional power and especially stressed the responsibility of the Executive to use every authority for national defense at a time when "present world conditions forbid him to risk" any constitutionally avoidable delay.

"No Future Commitments"

The Attorney General conceded that the wide Presidential power over foreign relations was not unlimited, but in this case, Mr. Jackson contended, there were no promises or future commitments by the United States which would require Senate consent or, indeed, any Congressional action. The agreement provided an opportunity to establish naval and air bases for coastline defense, he maintained, but needed no appropriation of money. Thus it was unnecessary for the Senate to ratify "an opportunity that entails no obligation," he declared.

Alluding to precedents, Mr. Jackson remarked that the "proposition falls far short" of the acquisition of the Louisiana Territory by President Jefferson from a belligerent during a European war. Outside of constitutional power, he went on,

Continued on Page Sixteen

Writer on British Destroyer Sees U-Boats in Raids and One Sunk

By BRYDON TAVES

ABOARD A BRITISH DESTROYER, in the North Atlantic, Sept. 3 (UP)—Germany is shooting the works to make good the threat of total blockade of the British Isles, but after eight days aboard a little British flotilla leader I can say that hundreds of ships are entering and leaving British ports each week.

German submarine and air attacks marked my voyage. Not one day passed without action. The British crew was either manning gun and depth-charge stations to fight off a U-boat or manning anti-aircraft stations to fight attacking planes.

I saw one British merchantman take a long-range torpedo squarely amidships and sink within a half hour. The next day our destroyer evened the score.

A "tin fish," meant for us, missed by a scant thirty feet as we whipped around. Then we rocked from the concussion of our own depth charges and I saw an oil patch spread slowly over the surface, marking that U-boat's end.

The destroyer was engaged in a typical convoy job, and its duties were something between those of a conscientious sheep dog and a sister of charity leading a bunch of orphans across Times Square.

We were one destroyer and one smaller warship escorting a thirty-ship convoy spread over fifteen square miles of ocean. Watching the line of hulls stretching out behind us, I remembered what a naval officer in a convoy control room in a West coast port told me just before I sailed.

"Give me fifty over-age American destroyers," he said, "and I will

Continued on Page Four

UNITED STATES ACQUIRES DEFENSE BASTIONS

Bases at the places indicated by circled dots are being leased by Great Britain to this country for ninety-nine years. The leases for those in Newfoundland and Bermuda are in effect outright gifts; the leases for the others are in exchange for fifty over-age United States destroyers. The bases in the Caribbean area will supplement present American defense centers (black diamonds) in guarding approaches to the Panama Canal.

ROOSEVELT HAILS GAIN OF NEW BASES

Exchange of Over-Age Ships for British Leases Offers Outer Defense Line, He Says

By CHARLES HURD
Special to THE NEW YORK TIMES.

ON BOARD ROOSEVELT TRAIN, Sept. 3—President Roosevelt indicated that the chief value of the trade with Great Britain of fifty over-age destroyers for naval and air base sites in British crown colonies in the Western Hemisphere lay in the fact that this outer line of defenses would keep any enemy away from this country's front door.

For that reason, he said, his agreement with the British Government was more important for the defense of this country than anything since the Louisiana Purchase in 1803, which assured American military control over the Mississippi River.

There may be other similar negotiations, he added, but he cautioned newspaper reporters not to try to guess where they would be, listing the odds at 10 to 1 that such guesses would be wrong.

The President did not deny a suggestion made by a reporter that perhaps Greenland might be the site for another base. He merely renewed his caution against speculation.

The President's view of the agreement, which has been known to be in progress for several weeks, was given at a special press conference on his private train at the same hour that his offices in Washington sent to Congress a message that the exchange was accomplished.

A dozen newspaper reporters heard Mr. Roosevelt read the text of the message to Congress, which he completed during a trip from Hyde Park, N. Y., to Tennessee, North Carolina and West Virginia. He read the message, after laughingly telling them that there was no story. While the document, with supporting papers, was being made public in Washington at noon, he began his press conference at 11:50 A. M. Eastern time.

Mr. Roosevelt called the press conference to meet in the tiny vestibule of his private car forty-five minutes after he departed from South Charleston, W. Va., where he inspected work being done to restore to high productivity a long abandoned Navy ordnance plant built in 1917-18 to construct armor plate and shells.

Among the statements he made

Continued on Page Ten

SHIP TRADE IS HELD NOT HOSTILE ACTION

State Department Stresses Defense Phase of Exchange of Vessels for Bases

Special to THE NEW YORK TIMES.

WASHINGTON, Sept. 3—No country could consider the transfer of fifty United States destroyers to Great Britain and the obtaining by this country of naval and air bases in British New World territory as a hostile act, an informed State Department source said today.

Only a nation seeking world conquest could use this as a pretext for belligerent action, the source asserted.

The intention of this government in completing the agreement was merely to strengthen its own defenses and no other considerations were entertained, State Department officials said, in insisting that the United States had the opportunity to obtain a 4,000 or 5,0000 mile ring of steel around the eastern part of the hemisphere on terms unequaled since the Louisiana Purchase. They added that the protection would last for 100 years.

It was made clear that it was no time to consider any technical provisions which might be sought in international law by opponents of the agreement but that in these dangerous days, when the world is almost literally on fire, defense considerations must come first.

This view was expressed in answer to questions of correspondents about the Second Hague Convention of 1907, of which the United States and Germany are signatories, but Great Britain is not.

Hague 1907 Convention Is Quoted

Article VI of this convention asserts:

"The support in any manner, directly or indirectly, by a neutral power of a belligerent power, by warships, ammunition or war materials of any kind whatever, is forbidden."

Article VIII says:

"A neutral government is also bound to display the same vigilance to prevent the departure from its jurisdiction of any vessel intended to cruise, or menace in hostile operations, which had been adapted entirely or partly within the said jurisdiction for use in war."

Article XXVIII, however, states: "The provisions of this present convention do not apply except to the contracting powers and then only if all the belligerents are parties to the convention."

One could accurately visualize a

Continued on Page Sixteen

LINE OF 4,500 MILES

Two Defense Outposts Are Gifts, Congress Is Told—No Rent on Rest

FOR 50 OLD VESSELS

President Holds Move Solely Protective, 'No Threat to Any Nation'

Texts of messages on leasing of naval bases, Page 10.

By FRANK L. KLUCKHOHN
Special to THE NEW YORK TIMES.

WASHINGTON, Sept. 3—President Roosevelt informed Congress today that he had completed an arrangement by which the United States will transfer to Great Britain fifty over-age destroyers and obtain from Britain ninety-nine-year leases for sea and air bases at eight strategic continental and island points in the Western Hemisphere.

The new American defense line thus established will stretch 4,500 miles from Newfoundland to British Guiana and include other bases on the islands of Bermuda, the Bahamas, Jamaica, St. Lucia, Trinidad and Antigua.

It is intended to make difficult, if not impossible, naval and air attacks upon the United States and much of the New World. The exact sites of the bases will be determined later by the two governments.

A solemn pledge by the British Government to the United States not to scuttle or surrender the British fleet under any conditions was revealed coincidentally by the State Department's publication of correspondence between Secretary Hull and the British Ambassador, the Marquess of Lothian.

Secretary Hull was informed that it represented the "settled policy" of His Majesty's Government not to "surrender or sink" the British fleet.

Reshaping of Naval Defense

The deal, carrying with it far-flung international as well as domestic defense implications, was hailed by President Roosevelt as the most important since the Jefferson Administration completed the Louisiana Purchase in 1803.

Informed official circles contended that it assured the British Fleet as an Atlantic sea-screen for the United States and made it possible for the American Fleet to remain in the Pacific.

Some thought it might lead to an informal defensive alliance between this country and Australia similar to the arrangement recently completed administratively with Canada, although others disagreed on this point.

President Roosevelt informed Congress that the British Government had given the right to bases in Newfoundland and Bermuda as an outright gift, "generously given and gladly received," but that "the other bases mentioned have been acquired in exchange for fifty of our over-age destroyers."

Previously, the President had insisted that the destroyer and base deals were separate.

Legal Basis for Procedure

Mr. Roosevelt explained in his message that he had acted upon a legal opinion by Attorney General Jackson which held that the Chief Executive had the right to dispose of the destroyers and complete the deal without consultation with the Senate and without its approval.

The President made clear that he would not seek the Senate's endorsement by remarking that he sent his statement merely "for the information of Congress."

Chairman Walsh of the Senate Naval Affairs Committee and several other Senators publicly condemned the proposed deal as illegal under domestic and international law when it was reported in the press some weeks ago that President Roosevelt had agreed to give Britain fifty destroyers after pleas from Prime Minister Winston Churchill.

In view of Senator Walsh's stand, some Senators privately expressed the opinion that there might be an attempt to have the Naval Affairs Committee open an investigation of the whole transaction.

After the President's message was

Continued on Page Twelve

1940

W.C. Fields and his leading lady, Mae West, in *My Little Chickadee.*

Joan Fontaine, Laurence Olivier, George Sanders and Judith Anderson in the Alfred Hitchcock spine-tingler, *Rebecca.*

Cary Grant and Katharine Hepburn in *The Philadelphia Story.*

Jane Darwell, seen here with Henry Fonda, won an Academy Award for her portrayal of the mother of the migrant family in *The Grapes of Wrath.*

"All the News That's Fit to Print."

The New York Times.

LATE CITY EDITION
Showers today, cooler this afternoon and tonight. Tomorrow cloudy, temperature unchanged.
Temperatures Yesterday—Max., 75; Min., 63

Copyright, 1940, by The New York Times Company.

VOL. LXXXIX..No. 30,180. Entered as Second-Class Matter, Postoffice, New York, N. Y. NEW YORK, TUESDAY, SEPTEMBER 10, 1940. THREE CENTS

CENTER OF LONDON BATTERED BY HEAVY BOMBS; R.A.F. WREAKS HAVOC IN 3-HOUR RAID ON HAMBURG; BIG GUNS WAGE DUEL ACROSS ENGLISH CHANNEL

NAVY SIGNS ORDERS TO BUILD 201 SHIPS FOR 2-OCEAN FLEET

Department Lets Contracts Two Hours After Roosevelt Signs 5-Billion Bill

7 BATTLESHIPS TOP LIST

Giants May Be 55,000 Tons—Greatly Expanded Yards to Turn Out Armada

By LELAND C. SPEERS

Special to THE NEW YORK TIMES.

WASHINGTON, Sept. 9—The United States moved today toward realization of a two-ocean Navy designed to be the mightiest sea force in the world's history.

Within two hours after President Roosevelt signed the $5,246,000,000 Supplemental Defense Appropriation Bill, the Navy Department announced the signing of contracts with private shipbuilding yards and allocations to navy yards for the construction of 200 fighting ships and one repair vessel. Among these are seven battleships which may be of 45,000 to 55,000 tons displacement each, making them the most powerful battlecraft ever projected. The order is the largest ever placed by the Navy at one time.

The estimated cost of the new construction is $3,861,053,312, which includes the cost of armor and armament and, in the case of submarines, government-furnished machinery.

The vastness of this construction program will call for the expansion of the American shipbuilding industry to the greatest capacity in history. Thousands of skilled mechanics and other thousands of unskilled workers will be employed. New shipbuilding ways, machine shops and electrical shops will be built and every facility used in the building of ships will be expanded.

$31,653,500 for Yard Expansion

In the case of the navy yards the expansion is estimated to cost $31,653,500. The cost of increased facilities in the private yards has not been disclosed. All that is known is that it will equal the outlay of the government-owned yards and may exceed it by several millions of dollars.

The program, as approved by the President, by Secretary Knox and Admiral Stark, the Chief of Naval Operations, calls for the construction of 7 battleships, 8 aircraft carriers, 27 cruisers, 115 destroyers, 43 submarines and the one repair ship. All the battleships are to be built in navy yards, two at the New York, three at the League Island yard, Philadelphia, and two at the Norfolk Navy Yard.

The Navy Department release did not give the tonnage of the battleships, but the report on the bill by the Senate Naval Affairs Committee fixed the battleship authorization at about 385,000 tons. This tonnage, evenly divided, would mean seven ships of 55,000 tons each.

Ships in Service and Ordered

The Navy's major fighting ships now in service, building and those ordered in the contracts announced today are listed in the following table:

Type	In Service	Building	Today's Contracts	Total
Battleships	15	10	7	32
Aircraft Carriers	6	4	8	18
Cruisers	37	21	27	85
Destroyers	197	56	115	368
Submarines	103	39	43	185
Totals	358	130	200	688

The fifty over-age destroyers traded to Great Britain are not included in this table. But it includes forty-six other destroyers which have been or will be converted into mine sweepers, anti-aircraft vessels, submarine tenders, etc.

The eight aircraft carriers announced today will be built, four each, by the Newport News Shipbuilding and Dry Dock Company of Newport News, Va., and by the Bethlehem Steel Company. Each carrier will be of 25,000 tons displacement.

The twenty-seven cruisers will have a combined tonnage of about 420,000, the largest of them heavy cruisers of between 15,000 and 20,000 tons.

The 115 destroyers will be of an

Continued on Page Ten

Republicans Sweeping Maine Vote, But Brann Runs Ahead of Ticket

Brewster Gains Apparently Sure Margin for Senate While Election of Sewall for Governor Is Conceded by Democratic Rival

By The Associated Press.

PORTLAND, Me., Tuesday, Sept. 10—Maine Republicans apparently scored a clean sweep of all of the five major offices at stake as returns poured in early today from the first State election of the Presidential year.

With the tabulation past the two-thirds mark, the election of the Republican governorship nominee had been conceded and Representative Ralph O. Brewster, Republican nominee for the Senate, held an apparently insurmountable lead over former Governor Louis J. Brann, Democrat.

In the three contests for seats in the House the Republican aspirants ran far ahead.

Several heavily Democratic cities remained to be heard from, but their combined normal Democratic margins were far less than the pluralities already rolled up by the Republicans.

In 1936, Republicans retained a Senate seat by only 4,600 votes, while piling up a 37,000 majority for their Gubernatorial nominee. Two years ago the Republican Governorship margin was only 17,000.

Before midnight, Fulton J. Redman, Democratic nominee for Governor, conceded defeat by Sumner Sewall, 44-year-old World War ace who now is a banker and airline director.

Returns from 533 precincts out of 629 gave:

Brewster, 126,753; Brann, 74,930.
Sewall, 135,379; Redman, 65,778.

A drizzling rain that fell through much of yesterday kept the voting at an unusually low level, a fact at first hailed by some Democrats as a favorable sign.

Mr. Brewster asserted in his campaign that the defeat of a single major Republican candidate would be "hailed" by supporters of President Roosevelt. Mr. Brann came out strongly for a third term.

Throughout a campaign far less intense than that of 1936, Republicans generally asked for a "big victory" as a help to Willkie, while Democrats for the most part contended that the old political saying, "As Maine goes, so goes the nation," had been discredited for good in the last presidential year, when Maine went Republican in the State election but only Maine and Vermont went Republican in the national election.

The governorship contest was fought out almost entirely on State issues. Strict partly lines, guided the speeches of the Congressional

Continued on Page Sixteen

BARS PLANT RULE IN WAR PROFIT BILL

Senate Report Eases House Measure and Cuts Out Extra 10% Levy

By TURNER CATLEDGE

Special to THE NEW YORK TIMES.

WASHINGTON, Sept. 9—Under the repeated urging of the National Defense Advisory Commission, the Senate Finance Committee today struck from the Excess Profits Tax Bill, approved by the House, a Treasury-sponsored provision seeking to protect government control over disposition of new private plant facilities built for national defense beyond the period of the preparedness emergency.

Yielding to still another request of defense experts, the committee reconsidered and deleted an amendment it had written into the bill late last week, adding a 10 per cent extra tax—above the excess profits rate prescribed for all corporations—on that part of a company's excess earnings directly attributable to national defense orders.

These were two of several changes adopted by the Senate committee in its attempt to liberalize and simplify what has been called the "harsh, hodgepodge" measure sent to it by the House ten days ago. Other amendments would accomplish the following:

Raise the specific exemption of the measure—that part of a corporation's excess income which would not be taxed by the new rates on excessive earnings—from $5,000, as contained in the House bill, to $10,000, at a possible sacrifice in revenue of $19,000,000 a year.

Remove the 10 per cent profit limitation of the Merchant Marine Act from subcontractors supplying materials or finished parts for direct government contractors.

Liberalize the definition of "invested capital"—one of two bases upon which excess earnings might be calculated—by permitting a corporation to include its investments in tax-exempt government, State or municipal bonds in its "invested capital" computation, provided it agreed to report the income from these bonds and pay the regular normal income tax thereon.

Bill Now Sent to Experts

These and other changes voted by the Finance Committee in its almost wholesale rewriting of the Excess Profits Bill were turned over to drafting experts tonight, with instructions to have the measure ready to report to the Senate by Wednesday noon.

The committee members were notified by Chairman Harrison to

Continued on Page Thirteen

WILLKIE ACCLAIMS CAMPAIGN EFFORTS

Organizations of All Groups in Country Are in Good Shape on Eve of His Tour, He Says

By JAMES A. HAGERTY

Special to THE NEW YORK TIMES.

RUSHVILLE, Ind., Sept. 9—With the opening of his speaking campaign only four days away, Wendell L. Willkie said today that he knew of no let-up in the drive to elect him President of the United States.

"I think the campaign is getting along splendidly," the Republican nominee said in an interview on the porch of his Rushville home, with Samuel F. Pryor Jr., Eastern campaign director, seated beside him and nodding approval.

"From an organization standpoint everything is whipping into shape in great style. I don't think much can be done about organization for aggressive action until after Labor Day. I haven't opened my campaign yet. I will open it on Friday in Chicago, with the main opening at Coffeyville next Monday.

"The organizations of the Republican party, the Willkie clubs and the Democrats for Willkie are getting into shape very rapidly. I have heard reports from twenty-five States and I don't know of any let-up. From an organization viewpoint everything is going much better than I anticipated."

As Mr. Willkie said in his brief speech at Memorial Park on Saturday night, he has received advice from many quarters urging him to take a definite stand on various issues, but wanted to be his own master and would not take any position in which he did not believe during the campaign.

It is to his refusal to be pushed into a declaration contrary to his political beliefs, and the consequent disappointment of those urging him to make such declarations, that he attributes reports that his campaign has had a let-down.

Principal Speeches Are Ready

Mr. Willkie has devoted most of the last two days to consideration not only of the principal speeches which he will make on his Far Western trip but of forty-seven rear-platform talks.

"President Roosevelt ignores you in his speeches," a reporter said. "I wonder if you are going to ignore him in the speeches you will make."

"I have a hunch that before the campaign is over Mr. Roosevelt won't ignore me," Mr. Willkie replied.

Henry Ford called on Mr. Willkie during the forenoon. Mr. Willkie said that they had "a very pleasant chat" for about twenty minutes. Mr. Ford arrived on a special car

Continued on Page Sixteen

DRAFT CALL DELAY BARRED BY SENATE IN HOUSE BILL TEST

Clark of Missouri Is Beaten on Attempt to Bind Conferees for Fish Amendment

AGE COMPROMISE IS SEEN

House Version's 21 to 45 Left Open—Agreement Is Likely on Draft of Industry

By FREDERICK R. BARKLEY

Special to THE NEW YORK TIMES.

WASHINGTON, Sept. 9—After a two-hour debate marked by acrimonious exchanges, the Senate voted today to reject the House draft of the Burke-Wadsworth Selective Military Service Bill and to ask for a conference.

The debate turned chiefly on two motions offered by Senator Clark, of Missouri.

The first was to instruct the Senate conferees to insist on the Senate's limitation of the draft registration to men between the ages of 21 and 31 against the House bill's provision for the registration of men between 21 and 45.

The second motion by Senator Clark called on Senate conferees to accept the Fish amendment to the House bill for a sixty-day test of volunteer enlistments before the draft becomes effective.

Mr. Clark's first motion was defeated, 44 to 23, while the second went down 48 to 19, the latter vote leading both House and Senate members to agree that the Fish amendment will be eliminated. When a proposal for a similar test of volunteer enlistments was first presented in the Senate it failed of adoption by only two votes, and today's vote on the Clark proposal was thus taken to show a strong Senate shift of opinion against a further trial.

Adams Motion Defeated

Prior to adverse action on the Clark motions, the Senate defeated one by Senator Adams that it accept the House version of the legislation, a step that would have made conference action unnecessary.

There was no vocal support for this proposal except from Senator Adams himself. Some members suggested that Mr. Adams had made the motion chiefly because of reports published this morning that the prospective conferees already had agreed to oppose delay of the draft and to accede to the 21 to 45 year age range set by the House.

These reports were attributed to Representative May, chief of the House conferees. They brought from Senator Barkley, the majority leader, a statement that Mr. May had denied to him that he made any such statements, and from Senator Sheppard, chairman of the Senate conferees, a further denial that any plan of agreement had been discussed.

Senator Clark, who first brought up the reputed statements of Mr. May, agreed that they were incorrect, but added that "somebody nevertheless made a pretty good guess as to what is likely to happen."

Senator Adams said he was not fully satisfied with the House draft,

Continued on Page Fourteen

R. A. F. RETALIATES

Dock Fires Are Visible for 60 Miles After Fliers Attack Reich Port

BERLIN RAIDED ANEW

Heaviest Assault Thus Far Is Hurled at Nazis' Positions in France

By JAMES MacDONALD

Special Cable to THE NEW YORK TIMES.

LONDON, Sept. 9—British raids against Germany last night were on a big scale and included a three-hour bombardment of Hamburg and attacks on Bremen and Emden as well as on Ostend, Calais and Boulogne.

[Pilots were quoted by the Air Ministry as stating that the fires on the Hamburg wharves were visible for sixty miles, the United Press reported.]

From all of last night's raids, London officials said, thirteen planes failed to return.

[British planes raided the Berlin area early today for forty-three minutes, and afterward the Germans issued a communiqué saying that "several dwelling houses fell as a sacrifice of a willful attack," The United Press reported. Bombs fell in a suburb eight miles from the center of Berlin, it was said.]

Long-range British and German guns on both sides of the English Channel barked furiously at each other late today in a short but hot argument, which was followed by R. A. F. raids in which British bombers struck savagely at Nazi Big Berthas nested along Cap Gris Nez.

Raids on Nazi Shipping

Tonight's big gun duel and the subsequent harassing flights by the R. A. F. are believed by unofficial observers to be the direct result of heavy all-night raids on German shipping gathered in Nazi-occupied French and Belgian Channel ports.

The Dover area shook tonight when German guns, seemingly located near the Cap Gris Nez lighthouse across a narrow stretch of the Channel waters, belched their fire. Immediately afterward British guns replied.

Watchers in the Dover area saw orange tongues of flame spurting along the French coast illuminating the Cap Gris Nez lighthouse. Spirals of smoke curled upward. A few seconds later German shells thundered on this side of the Channel.

The Germans fired salvos at two-minute intervals, paused twenty minutes, and then opened up again with two, more shots. Meanwhile, the British guns blazed away in the direction of France, but officials declined to permit publication of the details of the activities of the gunners manning the coast defenses.

After the long-range guns had ceased firing, R. A. F. planes took off for France, and within a few minutes watchers in the Dover district saw lurid flashes as their bombs burst. The concussion of the bombs falling on the German gun

Continued on Page Four

The International Situation

The War in Europe and Africa

German bombers struck at the very center of London as they carried their all-out aerial warfare against Britain's capital through the third successive night. As on Sunday the raiders waited until late afternoon to launch their first attack. With dark the bombing began again in earnest. It was feared the casualty toll of 600 dead and more than 2,500 wounded in the two previous nights would be raised sharply. The Air Ministry claimed 47 German raiders shot down during the afternoon, to raise the three-day total to 161. [Page 1, Column 8.]

So far as American correspondents could see, the "little people" of London, with only their courage as a weapon, had accepted the issue Germany was attempting to make and faced their fate grimly and with morale unshaken. Their avenues of food supply and transport, communications and other public services impaired, they gave no sign of weakening in their battle of nerves with the Nazi air legions. Their faces gray from fatigue, red-eyed and sleepless, they climbed from air-raid shelters yesterday morning and went to work as usual. [Page 4, Column 3.]

Berlin said its pilots reported rapidly diminishing British resistance to their attack on London and boasted that the city was at their mercy. The R. A. F. fighter pilots appear to have been exhausted by the unrelenting assault, the Germans said. Anti-aircraft fire was reported as aimless and ineffectual. London was described by some of the pilots as a blazing sea of flame, showing through billowing clouds of smoke. The Germans gave the score as forty British planes shot down yesterday and sixteen of their own lost. [Page 1, Column 7.]

A thunderous background to the bombing of London was the roar of British and German big guns, firing at each other from opposite shores of the English Channel. The brief bombardment was followed by renewed R. A. F. attacks on the gun emplacements and German naval and army concentrations along the French coast. The British Air Ministry said its bombers had rained destruction on Germany's major port of Hamburg for three hours Sunday night, setting many fires. The Berlin area was raided early today. [Page 1, Column 5.]

While Virginio Gayda, authoritative Fascist editor, was writing in Rome that Italy had an iron grip on the Mediterranean, the Admiralty in London announced that two British submarines had sunk three Italian supply ships in that inland sea. Activity of British submarines there, the British said, was interfering with Italy's attempts to keep her Libyan army supplied. Rome reported day and night bombing raids on the British naval base at Alexandria and other military objectives in the Middle East. [Page 5, Column 1.]

Repercussions Elsewhere

The Senate, rejecting the Fish amendment to delay the draft for sixty days and a proposal to instruct its conferees to insist on the Senate age limits of 21 to 31 years, sent the Burke-Wadsworth Selective Service Bill to conference with the House. The votes on the two questions were 48 to 19 and 44 to 23, respectively. Both House and Senate members were in agreement that the Fish amendment probably would be deleted in conference, the House age limits of 21 to 45 accepted and the House "draft of industry" provision retained, in preference to the more drastic Senate amendment. [Page 1, Column 4.]

Two hours after President Roosevelt had signed the $5,246,000,000 "total defense" bill, the Navy Department announced awards of contracts for 200 warships. Their construction will give the United States a two-ocean navy more powerful than any other. Among the vessels contracted for are seven super-battleships up to 55,000 tons each, the most powerful ever designed. [Page 1, Column 1.]

The Senate Finance Committee, striving to liberalize the excess profits tax bill to speed defense plant construction, deleted the Treasury-sponsored House provision that would extend government control over the new plants beyond the period of the emergency and the House amendment that added a 10 per cent extra tax to a company's excess earnings directly attributable to national defense orders. It was hoped to have the amended bill ready for presentation by Wednesday. [Page 1, Column 2.]

Former King Carol of Rumania decided yesterday at his temporary home of exile in Lugano, Switzerland, to settle in Portugal. He will depart for Lisbon in three or four days, as soon as his bullet-pocked special train can be repaired and arrangements completed for his passage through France and Spain. [Page 6, Column 2.]

BIG BUILDINGS HIT

Anti-Aircraft Fire Fails to Deter Germans in Nine-Hour Attack

DOCKS ARE DISRUPTED

Planes Battle Above the Houses of Parliament —47 Raiders Fall

By JAMES B. RESTON

Special Cable to THE NEW YORK TIMES.

LONDON, Tuesday, Sept. 10—For the third successive night German bombers have hurled their dynamite at this capital. They rattled the foundations of the biggest buildings in Central London and caused considerable damage in many sections of the metropolitan area, but at daylight today the essential services of the city were still operating.

Returning all along the valley of the Thames at dusk yesterday after two big daylight raids, in which they were said to have lost forty-seven planes to Britain's thirteen, the German raiders droned about the sleepless city hour after monotonous hour, taking shots at whatever appeared to be likely targets.

The "all clear" was not sounded until 5:43 o'clock this morning. The Germans had been bombing for nine hours and four minutes.

Damage Is Extensive

When daylight came it appeared that this raid had caused more damage than had appeared likely in its early hours. It was also clear that primarily this was an attack against London's communications. These communications naturally are snarled this morning, but the remarkable thing about these nightmares is that in the morning, no matter what the damage in some sections, others somehow manage to keep going.

Nevertheless the metropolitan area now looks pretty grim under the gray morning sky. Dock workers, who have taken such battering in the last seventy-two hours, are moving out of battered houses. In one area far from military targets people are still trapped.

Down one busy street a street car had been overturned by one mighty explosion. Here and there a bomb had cracked a gas main and water pipes, and fire trucks and ambulances seemed to be everywhere clanging through streets.

The bombs were dropped from much greater heights than Sunday night, and for this reason the aim was often poor. It is true that some damage was done around military objectives, but the Germans also hit a maternity hospital and a children's hospital on different sides of the city; both are distant from any military objective.

[Three of London's most famous churches, one "a landmark known to every American visitor," were threatened for several hours by a fire started by bombs dropped on an extensive block of office buildings, The Associated Press reported. The same agency said that activity on London's vast docks, entrance for much of Britain's food and war supplies, had been disrupted by the raids.]

Undeterred by Gunfire

For a time the bombs came down in rapid succession. The bombers circled out from the center of the city. Anti-aircraft batteries, so far ineffective at night, bothered them scarcely at all, and they just coasted around above the balloon barrage and let two or three go all at once every ten or fifteen minutes.

Just before midnight eight big bombs dropped rapidly, as if an entire rack was being emptied, and shortly after midnight nine came down as fast as they could be counted.

Several large buildings were severely damaged in one section, and in the hour before dawn the bombing seemed to get heavier. There were reports at that time that the Germans were dropping aerial torpedoes, much heavier and more destructive than bombs, but there was no confirmation of this.

After the last few nights the people are staying in shelters now. In fact, before last night's warning sounded people appeared at many

Continued on Page Two

VICHY FOOD IMPORTS DEMANDED BY NAZIS

Levy of 58 Per Cent Upon All Supplies Reported—Many Envoys Are Forced Out

By FRANK L. KLUCKHOHN

Special to THE NEW YORK TIMES.

WASHINGTON, Sept. 9—The German Government has made a formal demand upon the French Government in Vichy for a substantial part of the food and raw materials in unoccupied France and for any such products that France may be able to import in the future, it was revealed today in reliable diplomatic reports reaching Washington. Berlin is said to be demanding 58 per cent of these products from the Pétain regime.

In view of Nazi statements that a chief objective of the new French Ambassador to this country, Gaston Henri-Haye, would be to obtain food from the United States for the relief of France, this information was expected to add a fresh obstacle to any such plans on his part.

Plane Case Unsolved

Another matter of embarrassment to Washington is the fact that the French in Martinique still maintain possession of the eighty Army and fifty Navy bombers transferred before the fall of France for use against Chancellor Hitler. The planes are still aboard a French aircraft carrier in Martinique, it was learned today, and all efforts

Continued on Page Eight

GOERING SENDS OUT WAVES OF RAIDERS

Attacking From France All Night, Germans Say They Meet Only Weak Defense

By PERCIVAL KNAUTH

Wireless to THE NEW YORK TIMES.

BERLIN, Tuesday, Sept. 10—Neither darkness nor dawn will bring London respite from the unceasing thunder and destruction by German bombers, Nazi officials asserted today.

The attack was carried out throughout the night, it was stated here, and new waves of planes roared over Britain's capital from the southeast, south and southwest after midnight. Wave on wave of them attacked at half-hour intervals, the Germans said, and as they passed more explosions shook the ground beneath them and more fires lit London's sky.

During yesterday afternoon the attack was carried out by more than 300 planes, which dropped their explosives on docks and factories that were already burning fiercely on both sides of the Thames, the German authorities said.

Returning Nazi pilots were reported to speak of an "ocean of flames" beneath them, glowing through a thick, black cloud of smoke rolling slowly to sea.

London's air defenses, it was reported, were all but silenced. There

Continued on Page Six

Bar Demands Protection of Civil Rights But Not as 'Screen' for Foes of Democracy

By LAWRENCE E. DAVIES

Special to THE NEW YORK TIMES.

PHILADELPHIA, Sept. 9—In the face of serious threats to the "American way of life," viewed as evident to "all except the willfully blind or the victims of foreign propaganda," the American Bar Association through its legislative body, the House of Delegates, today coupled a demand for preservation of "constitutional methods and procedures" with a warning against use of "alleged constitutional rights" as "a screen to hide efforts to undermine our system."

The twofold problem with respect to dealing with civil liberties in a time of emergency was set forth in a report of the association's special committee on the Bill of Rights, which received the overwhelming endorsement of the delegates.

While recognizing the necessity for restrictions during a period of crisis, the committee called for their formulation, "to the utmost practicable extent" within the "general framework of government and constitutional guarantees."

At the same time it warned that the safeguarding of free institutions "must not be permitted to imply impotence against enemies either within or without the gate."

As illustrative of the type of procedure which, in its opinion, ought to be avoided, the committee cited the House bill calling for "the deportation by name of a particular alien," Harry Bridges, West Coast labor leader.

Without expressing a view as to whether Bridges should be sent out of the country, the committee contended that the House bill, whether or not it was constitutional, was

Continued on Page Fifteen

"All the News That's Fit to Print."

The New York Times.

LATE CITY EDITION
Fair and warmer today and tomorrow.
Temperatures Yesterday—Max., 69; Min., 46

VOL. XC...No. 30,198. Entered as Second-Class Matter, Postoffice, New York, N. Y. NEW YORK, SATURDAY, SEPTEMBER 28, 1940. THREE CENTS NEW YORK CITY and Vicinity | FOUR CENTS Elsewhere Except in 7th and 8th Postal Zones.

JAPAN JOINS AXIS ALLIANCE SEEN AIMED AT U. S.; ROOSEVELT ORDERS STUDY OF THE PACT'S EFFECT; BRITISH DOWN 130 RAIDERS, BLAST NAZI BASES

REPUBLICANS MAKE 3D TERM THE ISSUE; PICK STATE SLATE

BARTON IS CHOSEN

Leaders at Convention Turn Fire on the New Deal and Roosevelt

DEWEY SEES MENACE

Keynoter Assails 'One-Man Power'—Party Hears Willkie Tonight

Text of platform and Dewey and Barton addresses, Page 8.

By WARREN MOSCOW

Special to THE NEW YORK TIMES.

WHITE PLAINS, Sept. 27—The Republican campaign in New York State was started today at the Republican State Convention here, when the party organization nominated a strong slate headed by Bruce Barton for United States Senator, heard State and national leaders unite in a stinging castigation of the New Deal and adjourned until tomorrow evening to hear Wendell L. Willkie make his bid for New York support in a speech at the Empire City race track.

The delegates to the convention heard Thomas E. Dewey, National Chairman Joseph W. Martin Jr., State Senate Leader Joe R. Hanley and Mr. Barton unite in an onslaught on the New Deal's foreign and domestic policies as menacing our safety from within and from without. They spared neither the President nor his family as they tried to drive home the meaning of the violation of the anti-third term tradition.

Members of the Ticket

The ticket, nominated without opposition, is as follows:

For United States Senator: Bruce Barton of New York.

For Judges of the Court of Appeals: Benjamin B. Cunningham of Rochester, Edmund H. Lewis of Syracuse and Albert Conway of Brooklyn.

For Representatives at Large: Messmore Kendall of Westchester and Miss Mary Donlon of Oneida and New York.

Judges Lewis and Conway, Republican and Democrat respectively, are on the bench by appointment and will get an endorsement from the Democratic State Convention on Monday.

Justice Cunningham, now a member of the Appellate Division of the Fourth Department, was picked as a compromise nominee at a conference of party leaders during a convention recess and Judges James P. Hill of Norwich and Christopher J. Heffernan of Amsterdam, who had been deadlocked in a behind-the-scenes battle, both withdrew to make way for Justice Cunningham. The latter probably will get a Democratic endorsement, in view of the fact that he was appointed to the Appellate Division by Governor Lehman and won his last election to the Supreme Court with a bi-partisan endorsement. He is a Republican.

Starts on Fighting Key

The convention started on a fighting key with Mr. Dewey's speech, in the morning, as temporary chairman, and it came to a climax with an equally strong speech by Representative Barton, selected for the nomination yesterday at the insistence of Wendell L. Willkie.

"In the next six weeks the American people must decide whether to cast away the tradition which for 150 years has stood between them and the menace of one-man power; whether they will gamble with their liberties by electing a President for the third term," Mr. Barton told

Continued on Page Eight

Tonight Will Bring End Of Daylight Saving Time

With daylight saving time ending at 2 A. M. tomorrow, most New Yorkers were expected to turn their clocks back one hour tonight before retiring—thus regaining the hour of sleep lost when the Summer time became effective on April 28.

The New York Central Railroad is adding a new train to its Chicago-to-New York fleet. To be known as the Grand Central, the train will leave Chicago at 2:30 P. M., Central Standard time, and arrive in New York at 8:30 A. M., Eastern Standard time.

The Pennsylvania Railroad and the New York, New Haven & Hartford Railroad also are providing a new train from the Pennsylvania Station to Boston and New England points. It will be called the Bay State and, starting from Philadelphia, will depart from New York at 9:45 A. M. and arrive at Boston at 2:40 P. M.

WILLKIE DEMANDS OUR SYSTEM STAND

Change of Administration Is Needed to Save Democracy, He Says in Wisconsin

By JAMES A. HAGERTY

Special to THE NEW YORK TIMES.

MADISON, Wis., Sept. 27—Wendell L. Willkie ended his 6,000-mile Western trip tonight with a speech in the Field House of the University of Wisconsin to about 15,000 persons. He was introduced by Dean Christian Christiansen of the College of Agriculture.

Mr. Willkie criticized the President for trying to enlarge the Supreme Court on the ground that some of its members were too old.

"And yet," he continued, "the President recently appointed to a most important position, Secretary of War, a man older than the age he fixed as too old to render proper judicial decisions."

The candidate also recalled that President Roosevelt had tried to "purge" members of Congress of his own party who did not agree with him, offering another instance in which the Executive tried to infringe upon the powers of the other two departments of the Federal Government.

'Must Make System Work'

He declared that the present Administration had preserved the form but not the substance of democracy and had concentrated power in the Chief Executive.

"That is the road by which every ancient and every modern democracy has died," he added.

"Do you know that in Germany there is still a Reichstag and in Italy a parliament? There is still the form of democracy, but the substance is gone.

"You must take the American system of government and make it work, with its coordinate branches, as it is, or you must admit that it is a failure. I repudiate the latter notion with all the vigor of my being.

"This American system of government can be made, and will be made, if you put another Administration into power, the most effective and most pleasant way of life."

Mr. Willkie brought laughter by saying that Thomas Jefferson, sponsor after Washington of the no-third-term tradition, was the founder of the party which President Roosevelt, "in part," now leads.

He added that every attempt so far to violate the anti-third-term tradition had been defeated, and cited that in 1928 the United States Senate adopted a resolution against the third term. Although Madison is the home of Senator Robert M. La Follette, author of that resolution, Mr. Willkie did not mention him.

On his entrance to Wisconsin, the

Continued on Page Seven

LONDON BADLY HIT

Capital and Its Suburbs Bear Brunt of Heavy German Attacks

OTHER AREAS RAIDED

Coastal Towns Pounded—600 Planes Used in Daylight Assaults

By ROBERT P. POST

Special Cable to THE NEW YORK TIMES.

LONDON, Saturday, Sept. 28—The Germans changed their recent air-raid tactics yesterday and sent over by daylight wave on wave of bombers with fighter as chaperones above.

It is estimated that at least 600 Germans crossed the coast before dark, and of these the latest figures show 130 shot down for certain. The British loss at the time of writing is put at thirty-four fighters. Fifteen of the downed British pilots are safe.

This is a preliminary count. The figures may be higher when all precincts have reported. In any case it is probable that the number of German planes that will never fly again is considerably bigger than the British announce.

From all reports on the daylight raiding, it would appear that the Germans once again were testing the British fighter defenses and paying heavily for it. Some German planes flew "cloud hopping" over London, which had five air-raids during the day. They dropped bombs that did some damage, but the worst destruction done in England before dark was on the outskirts of London and in certain coastal towns where the Germans, chased by Spitfires and Hurricanes, jettisoned their loads while trying to escape.

One of Worst Night Raids

At night the siren again wailed and the night raiders again came over to take advantage of a cloudy sky. And again the attack was directed mainly at the London area.

Several bombs crashed in the central area of London in the early morning as German planes continued to hum over the metropolis. A good many fires were started, but they were quickly extinguished.

[By early this morning, the attack had developed into one of the worst raids the capital has experienced in many nights, according to The Associated Press, with heavy bombs falling and anti-aircraft fire heaviest in the center of the city.]

But the rest of the country did not go free either by day or night. Two separate waves estimated at fifty each crossed the Dorset coast and went after the Bristol area. At night planes were reported over other towns. During the day, too, the countryside saw planes overhead. At Seven Oaks a big Junkers bomber dived to its death, narrowly missing the City Hall in High Street.

The raiders visited Northwest and Southeast England during the night, scattering explosives and incendiaries.

Big formations could be seen plainly over London during the day. In one police station a man

Continued on Page Four

New Air Defense Devices Reported Used in London

By The Associated Press.

LONDON, Sept. 27—New secret devices with which to combat night raiders were reported today in use in the London area, which last night had one of the lightest night raids in three weeks.

The devices were said to have been developed by British scientists, and observers declared there was a chance that, used together, two of the devices might make night bombing as hazardous as raiding by day.

In a gradual lifting of the curtain of censorship, British correspondents were permitted to comment upon new air-raid noises heard by Londoners in the last few nights. These were a heavy single explosion disintegrating into staccato cracks high up in the heavens, a flat roar that seems to strike a ceiling several miles up and bump its way clamorously along the top of the sky, and a muffled rattling like a "carpet slipper machine-gun."

"These queer noises are in fact caused by new types of weapons, or by well tried weapons adapted to new uses," said one observer.

R.A.F. RAKES NAZIS ON 500-MILE COAST

Pounds Invasion Fleet, Bombs Kiel Anew—Raids Gun Sites After Cross-Channel Duel

By JAMES B. RESTON

Special Cable to THE NEW YORK TIMES.

LONDON, Sept. 27—British bombers raided the German invasion fleet along 500 miles of European coast last night, bombed lines of communication deep in Nazi territory and penetrated the fortified naval base at Kiel, where the 26,000-ton German battleship Scharnhorst was said to be anchored, it was announced here today.

This afternoon, during a duel between German and British long-range guns, British bombers flew across the English Channel and attacked Nazi gun emplacements in France near Cap Gris Nez. In the artillery duel, which lasted an hour, shells fell in the Dover area, but there were no casualties and no serious damage was reported.

In the persistent night raids on Germany the British have three main objectives—to harass ships, men and supplies gathered along the coast for a possible invasion of this country, to cripple transportation and industrial production inside Germany and to carry the war to the German people. Last night's raid conformed to this general pattern, but whereas in the preceding few nights the Bomber Command centered its attention on communications and industrial plants, last night the British tried first of all to knock out the Scharnhorst.

When the first relays of bombers approached the naval basin at Kiel German guns immediately opened fire. Flying high, the raiders were able to stay out of range. They opened the attack by dropping incendiary bombs around the edge of the base and then, by the light of fires, hurled several sticks of high-explosive bombs into the basin, where two large ships were clearly seen.

An Air Ministry statement here

Continued on Page Five

Jersey Poll Books Burned, Senators Hear; Charge of Move to Block Inquiry Renewed

Special to THE NEW YORK TIMES.

WASHINGTON, Sept. 27—Poll books in Hudson County, depended upon to show padded registry, have been destroyed, according to word received today by Senator Guy M. Gillette of Iowa, chairman of the Senate committee investigating election expenditures. Similar information was conveyed to Senator Charles W. Tobey of New Hampshire, one of the subcommittee authorized to inquire into the alleged election frauds.

Senator Tobey, who caused a sensation yesterday by asserting that pressure had been exerted to stop the hearing, planned in Jersey City, renewed his charges today in the Senate. He read into the record a dispatch printed in The Newark Evening News to the effect that Representatives Edward J. Hart and Mrs. Mary T. Norton of New Jersey had exerted pressure to delay or prevent the inquiry. Mrs. Norton said that she had never approached any Senator on the subject, while Representative Hart declined to discuss the question.

Senator Gillette later exonerated both New Jersey House members from any ulterior activities. He said that Mrs. Norton had never seen him about the situation in Hudson County, while Representative Hart had asked him when the hearing would begin, but had not suggested that it be delayed or stopped.

Renewing his charges of alleged pressure, Senator Tobey, speaking in the Senate, said:

"I charged in my statement yesterday that pressure had been applied on Senators to postpone in-

Continued on Page Seven

HULL SEES NO SHIFT

Holds Accord Does Not Substantially Alter Recent Situation

DEFENSE AIDES MEET

Notables Ask President to Rush Increased Aid to Britain

By CHARLES HURD

Special to THE NEW YORK TIMES.

WASHINGTON, Sept. 27—President Roosevelt quickly directed today a sweeping search into the possibilities in the new German-Italian-Japanese alliance, but the Administration adopted an official attitude that the alliance momentarily creates little change in a situation that already existed.

Mr. Roosevelt declined to make any comment at the regular press conference in his office this morning. He merely told reporters that he had received no official notification of the conclusion of the accord.

However, while Secretary of State Cordell Hull gravely acknowledged the pact's existence at a State Department press conference, the President undertook studies involving every major branch of the government.

[A group of Americans prominent in business and political affairs called at the White House to urge that aid to Britain be increased and speeded in every form possible. They reported later that they were "enthusiastically encouraged" by the President's response, though they were unable to divulge what he said.]

Cabinet Studies Situation

A Cabinet meeting, regular scheduled for this afternoon, was devoted exclusively during a ninety-minute session to discussion of the latest developments in the foreign situation. It was preceded by a long conference in the President's office, to which were invited all the ranking officials of the War and Navy Departments.

These conferences were reported to have been concerned not only with political implications in the expanded Rome-Berlin Axis but also with economic possibilities, both from the standpoint of potential effects on American sources of commodities such as tin and rubber and a possible advancement from Oct. 16 of the effective date for the embargo on exports of scrap iron and steel, ordered yesterday.

There also was informal discussion, without conclusive decision, of a possible extension of the embargo on scrap exports to exports of pig iron and steel which currently can be sent to Japan without restriction.

It was obvious that the government's attitude was based largely on the expectation that Britain would be able to hold her line against the German attack. A collapse of Britain would create an entirely new situation.

The President's refusal to comment at his press conference came about two hours after news services had first reported the new treaty. He declined smilingly but persistently to make any statement, saying all that he had heard thus far had been a rumor, that he had nothing official. When he was asked if the news was unexpected he replied, Well, yes and no, and referred inquirers to the State Department.

Hull Expresses Official View

At the State Department, where a press conference was held soon afterward, Secretary Hull did express the viewpoint of this government in phrases which he permitted to be quoted directly.

Speaking slowly and with care and marking his words by an unusually grave countenance, he summed up the official attitude as follows:

The reported agreement of alliance does not, in the view of the government of the United States, substantially alter a situation which has existed for several years. Announcement of the alliance merely makes clear to all a relationship which has long existed in effect and to which this government has repeatedly called attention.

That such an agreement has

Continued on Page Two

The International Situation

The German-Italian-Japanese Pact

Japan yesterday formally allied herself with Germany and Italy for the task of establishing a "new order" in Europe and East Asia by signing in Berlin a mutual assistance pact, by all indications aimed at the United States.

The three bound themselves for a period of ten years to come to the aid of any one of the others attacked by a power not at present involved in the European or Chinese-Japanese conflicts. Although political commitments of the three with Soviet Russia were specifically exempted by Article V of the six-article pact, a veiled threat to Moscow was seen.

By the terms of the pact, Japan recognized German-Italian hegemony in Europe. The two dictator nations in turn recognized Japanese hegemony in the Far East, apparently leaving to her determination of the fate of British, French and Netherland possessions there. [All the foregoing Page 1, Column 8.]

The official attitude of the United States, as stated by Secretary of State Hull, was that the announcement of the alliance merely publicly confirmed a relationship already existing. President Roosevelt began a study of the pact's possible effects by conferring with the Cabinet, War, Navy and Defense Commission officials but had no public comment. Possibility of quicker invocation of the embargo on scrap steel and iron to Japan, now scheduled to go into effect Oct. 16, and its possible extension to other war materials was reported discussed. [Page 1, Column 5.] The President was visited during the day by a group of prominent Americans asking more war aid for Britain. The British Ambassador made a similar plea. [Page 2, Column 1.]

Yakichiro Suma, Japanese Foreign Office spokesman, said the alliance did not mean abandonment of Japan's attitude toward the United States and that hope still was held for a betterment of relations. Observers in Tokyo construed the formal junction with the Axis as a desperate gamble that Germany and Italy would defeat Britain before the United States was prepared to give effective aid. The benediction on the pact of Emperor Hirohito—spiritual as well as political leader of Japan—was broadcast to the nation. [Page 1, Column 7.]

Italians were surprised that Japan and not Spain proved the third party to the pact, but quickly recovered and immediately grasped its significance as a warning to the United States to keep out of the conflict. It also was accepted there as a challenge to Soviet Russia. [Page 3, Column 1.]

Information in Shanghai was that Germany was attempting to promote a rapprochement between Moscow and Tokyo, but that the Soviet had set a high price, including abrogation of most of the Portsmouth treaty, which ended the Russo-Japanese War in 1905. A Russian source in London said the pact placed the Soviet in a "dangerous and very grave" situation. [Page 1, Column 6.]

The London reaction was that the publicly announced alliance had served to clear the atmosphere, had brought Britain and the United States even closer together and had removed any brake on all possible aid to China. [Page 3, Column 8.]

The War in Europe and Africa

The Germans yesterday and last night launched the heaviest attacks in several days on London and other key cities in England. Heavy daylight raids on London and Bristol were reported turned back with a cost to the Germans by early evening of at least 130 planes against thirty-four British defenders, from which fifteen of the pilots jumped to safety. It was estimated at least 600 German planes engaged in the day raids. The day rounded out three weeks of aerial siege of the British capital. [Page 1, Column 3.]

The R. A. F. again Thursday night made devastating attacks on German invasion bases and canals, arterial highways, industrial plants and harbors in Germany proper, the Air Ministry said. The principal attack, a communiqué stated, was launched on the German naval base at Kiel, where the battle-scarred German battleship Scharnhorst is under repair. One raiding pilot said he had never seen such fires as he and his fellow fliers set there. A daylight bombing attack was made on German big gun emplacements at Cap Gris Nez after a short artillery duel with British batteries at Dover. [Page 1, Column 4.]

Both the British and Italians reported air attacks on the other's supply and military bases in Africa. Otherwise all was quiet on that front. [Page 5, Column 6.]

STALIN'S DEMANDS SAID TO BE LARGE

Reported Seeking to Cancel Many Tokyo Gains as Price of Accepting Axis Pact

By HALLETT ABEND

Wireless to THE NEW YORK TIMES.

SHANGHAI, China, Sept. 27—The immediate future of the international situation in the Far East now depends to a great extent upon what degree of understanding the Germans will be able to arrange between Japan and Russia.

It is understood that Max Stahmer, private emissary from Chancellor Hitler, having concluded the alliance satisfactorily, now is acting as go-between for Moscow and Tokyo.

[In Tokyo it was said Japan already had the assurances she required from Russia. Up to last evening, the Russian people had not been allowed to hear of the conclusion of the Axis-Japanese pact, according to The Associated Press.]

Joseph Stalin's terms as reported here, however, are extremely harsh from the Japanese viewpoint. He is said to demand first of all abrogation of the Portsmouth treaty, except that portion ceding the southern half of Sakhalin Island to Japan. This would cancel Japan's immensely valuable fishing concessions off the Siberian coast, which not only furnish an important por-

Continued on Page Four

WARNING TO U. S. IS SEEN IN TOKYO

Spokesman of Foreign Office Declines to Say Whether New Pact Affects Us Now

By HUGH BYAS

Wireless to THE NEW YORK TIMES.

TOKYO, Sept. 27—The forces driving Japan forward have finally decided to take all risks in pursuit of their Greater East Asia policy, formally allying Tokyo with Berlin and Rome. They gamble on Germany's winning the war before the United States is ready.

Any power not presently involved in the European War is menaced by their joint action if it attacks any of the contracting parties. Though no country is specified, the pact is an unmistakable warning to the United States.

The point of the document lies in Article III, which in the Foreign Office translation reads: "Japan, Germany and Italy undertake to assist one another with all political, economic and military means when one of the three contracting parties is attacked by a power not presently involved in the European War or the Sino-Japanese conflict."

Yakichiro Suma, Foreign office spokesman, declined to say whether United States assistance to Britain "short of war" would constitute an "attack" in the terms of the treaty.

Neither the word "attack" nor Greater East Asia are defined, he said. He added that Japan was not

Continued on Page Four

RUSSIA REASSURED

Accord Viewed as Threat to Soviet, in Spite of Safeguard Clause

WASHINGTON WARNED

Interference Barred With 'New Order' in Europe and Eastern Asia

Text of treaty and statements for three nations, Page 3.

By GUIDO ENDERIS

Wireless to THE NEW YORK TIMES.

BERLIN, Sept. 27—By another of those bold forays into the realm of "Blitz diplomacy" with which the world has now become familiar, the Reich's Chancellery at noon today became the birthplace of a tripartite military alliance linking Germany, Italy and Japan. Its implications seem designed to have a profound effect not only on the further course of Europe's war but more directly on the world situation in general.

It is expressly specified that the commitments assumed today shall not affect the political status existing between each of the three signatories and Soviet Russia.

Opinion in neutral diplomatic quarters tonight appears to concur on two points, one being by implication that the pact contains a veiled threat to Russia, while that to the United States is decidedly less obscure.

On the latter point advance press comment leaves no doubt, and opinions gathered in informed quarters also frankly suggest that the pact may be interpreted as being directed against "certain groups in the United States who are trying to disrupt relations between peoples and nations."

Ten-Year Pledge Given

In a highly ceremonial setting in the Chancellery's reception chamber, the German and Italian Foreign Ministers and the Japanese Ambassador pledged their respective countries for ten year to cooperation in the interest of lasting peace and to "the creation of the preconditions necessary to that new order that will promote the welfare and prosperity of their peoples."

The signing formalities occupied just about two minutes, after which Chancellor Hitler joined the scene, entering the chamber through a door opening from his private working apartments. It was the same chamber in which the German-Italian military pact was signed in 1939, but today's audience did not include the diplomatic corps. Those who witnessed the formalities comprised government officials, Nazi party leaders and representatives of the German and foreign press.

The pact negotiated today consists of a brief preamble and six articles. By its terms Japan recognizes Germany's and Italy's leadership in constituting "a new order in Europe." The Axis powers, for their part, recognize and respect Japan's priority rights in the establishment of "a new order in Eastern Asia." It was authoritatively stated that the Russian Government had been duly apprised of the impending conclusion of the three-power pact and informed that the signatory powers were in accord on this point.

Total Aid Promised

On the basis of these premises, the partners to the pact agree to support one another in fulfillment of their tasks and to throw their complete political, economic and military resources into the defense of any of the partners who may be attacked by any power not at present involved in the European war or in the Chinese-Japanese conflict.

In pronouncing his benediction on the pact after signing formalities were concluded, Foreign Minister Joachim von Ribbentrop declared: "Organized warmongers in the Jewish capitalistic democracies have succeeded in plunging Europe into a new war which was not wanted by Germany. Our fight is not directed against other peoples, but against the existence of international plotters who once before succeeded in plunging Europe into a sanguinary war."

The German Foreign Minister

Continued on Page Three

"All the News That's Fit to Print."

The New York Times.

LATE CITY EDITION
Increasing cloudiness and continued cool today. Tomorrow cloudy with occasional light rain.
Temperatures Yesterday—Max., 54; Min., 38

Copyright, 1940, by The New York Times Company.

VOL. XC. No. 30,228. Entered as Second-Class Matter, Postoffice, New York, N. Y. NEW YORK, MONDAY, OCTOBER 28, 1940. THREE CENTS NEW YORK CITY and Vicinity | FOUR CENTS Elsewhere Except in 7th and 8th Postal Zones.

ITALY INVADES GREECE, STARTING BALKAN DRIVE, AS ATHENS REJECTS A THREE-HOUR ULTIMATUM; METAXAS ASKS GREEKS TO FIGHT TO THE DEATH

ROOSEVELT TO TOUR 5 BOROUGHS TODAY, MAKING 6 SPEECHES

Due to Cross the City Line at 10 A. M. and End Busy Day With Garden Address

VISIT TO JERSEY IS FIRST

Heavy Police Guard Provided Here—Hunter Is Searched for Reported Egg Cache

New York City will get its first 1940 view of President Roosevelt today in the role of political campaigner. After a tour through near-by industrial New Jersey this morning, he will visit the five boroughs, making five brief speeches, and tonight he will talk at a mass meeting at Madison Square Garden under the auspices of the Democratic National Committee, which has hired the red and blue networks of the National Broadcasting Company from 10 to 11 P. M.

Faced with a difficult problem in protocol, the Democratic National Committee decided yesterday that President Roosevelt would make a number of stops in the city to greet local Democratic officials and others. This course was made necessary by the insistence of Democratic County leaders that they receive an opportunity to see the President and be seen with him to an extent equal to that enjoyed by Mayor La Guardia.

The original schedule called for the Mayor to meet the President at Staten Island and "accompany" him on his tour through the city. This arrangement did not sit well with the Democratic county leaders whom the Mayor has often attacked in public. Since they are the President's prime reliance in rolling up a big vote in New York City they resented any demonstration that would make it appear that the Mayor enjoyed the Presidential confidence to a greater extent than they did.

Mayor La Guardia is to ride in the Presidential car with Mr. Roosevelt and Governor Lehman on part of the tour. After the various stops to greet Democratic leaders they will replace the Mayor in the Presidential car and he will drop back and continue in another machine, it is understood.

Heavy Day Is Mapped

The President will be heavily guarded by police throughout his stay in New York. His advisers have laid out a schedule for him that will mean a most heavy day's work. According to that schedule, he is to arrive at his special train, in the Mott Haven yards of the New York Central on the Harlem River, at 5 P. M. in time to rest for the evening meeting. But police officials who 'aveled the President's route yesterday, in a final check-up of their arrangements to guard him, estimated that he would be doing well if he reached Mott Haven by 7 o'clock.

The Presidential party—police political leaders, newspaper men and camera men—will enter the city by way of the Bayonne Bridge to Staten Island. If the column is moving on schedule at that time, he should cross the city line at 10 A. M.

At 10:45 the President is to participate in ground-breaking exercises at the Brooklyn end of the Brooklyn-Battery Tunnel. At 11:45 he is to make a brief stop at Roosevelt Park, Chrystie and Canal Streets, in Manhattan. At 1 P. M. he is due at Hunter College where he will have lunch and make a speech.

At 2:45 P. M. he is to make an address at the Manhattan side of the Thirty-eighth Street Tunnel; at 3:15 P. M. he is to pause for a quick inspection of the Queens Bridge Housing Development; at 3:35 P. M. he will visit La Guardia Field, and at 4:20 P. M. make an address at Fordham University. And after that is over he will go to his train at Mott Haven. Such, at least, is the pre-arranged plan.

His arrival at Madison Square Garden is set for 9:45 P. M. Police expect a great crush of people in that area, and the order went out yesterday to close off all near-by streets at 7 o'clock, admitting only holders of tickets to the rally.

In addition to the President,

Continued on Page Eight

Willkie Promises to Place Housing on Efficient Basis

He Says Program Vitally Needed in Nation Has 'Bogged Down' and Offers 6-Point Plan—Campaigns in Midwest Today

By JAMES C. HAGERTY
Special to THE NEW YORK TIMES.

ABOARD WILLKIE SPECIAL TRAIN, Oct. 27—Charging that the New Deal's housing program had "bogged down" and was "paralyzed by a maze of red tape," Wendell L. Willkie made public today a six-point housing program which called for increasing cooperation between government and private enterprise in slum clearance and housing projects and the elimination of overlapping authority in governmental agencies dealing with the problem.

In a statement issued aboard his special campaign train bound from New York to Illinois, where he will open the final week of his campaign tomorrow, the Republican Presidential nominee held that an efficient housing program was essential. He contended, however, that there was such mismanagement of the program by the Administration that the future of housing throughout the country was seriously endangered.

He asserted that in his campaign tours across the country he had been "deeply impressed with the dilapidated appearance of the homes of millions of our people and the run-down condition of large parts of our city areas."

"It is absolutely essential to remedy these conditions, both for economic and social reasons," he added.

After assailing a "maze of red tape" in the "New Deal system generally," he declared:

"As a result of duplication and poor administration, costs have been excessive to the detriment of the home owner, tenant and general taxpayer. One of the first tasks of the next Administration should be to study and consider the housing situation as a whole."

Mr. Willkie offered his six-point program by stating that his attitude on housing could be "briefly summarized" as follows:

"1. The stimulation of slum clearance, land use planning, and housing is a government function; but the efforts of government in this direction should always supplement and stimulate private enterprise and initiative, rather than encroach upon it. As I stated in my Fortune article, before I became a candidate, government investment in slum clearance might prove to be as profitable both from the economic and social standpoints as government investments in good roads.

"2. The thirteen government agencies now dealing with housing and planning matters should be correlated, and the present conflict of functions and undue overlapping removed. Our eventual goal should be the establishment of a consolidated Federal housing agency, with sepa-

Continued on Page Nine

LEWIS IS SPURRING ACCORD WITH STEEL

He Moves to Settle Claims on Republic as Hillman Gains Points at Bethlehem

By LOUIS STARK
Special to THE NEW YORK TIMES.

WASHINGTON, Oct. 27—The Bethlehem Steel Corporation and the Republic Steel Corporation may soon sit down at a conference table with C. I. O. representatives and seek to erase the misunderstandings that have kept the steel industry in turmoil since the C. I. O.'s abortive "Little Steel" strike in 1937.

It was learned that under orders from John L. Lewis, president of the C. I. O., preliminaries are being speeded up to settle all the cases now pending against the Republic Steel Corporation, whether in the courts or before the National Labor Relations Board.

These preliminaries call for payment of several million dollars in back pay to several thousand Republic Steel employes. The basis of this payment has not yet been completed but other parts of the compact have been settled to the satisfaction of both sides.

Such a settlement would confirm the beliefs of those who say that Mr. Lewis indicated in his speech favoring Wendell L. Willkie on Friday that some arrangement had been made with Republic and possibly other large steel companies for a union contract.

Hillman Will See Grace

Sidney Hillman, labor member of the National Defense Advisory Commission, has a tentative appointment for next week with Eugene G. Grace, president of the Bethlehem Steel Corporation, to talk over the possible basis of union recognition by that company.

Considerable progress toward settling the differences between the C. I. O.'s Steel Workers Organizing Committee and the Bethlehem Steel Corporation has been made in the last fortnight. Mr. Hillman has conferred several times with James Larkin, vice president of the corporation in charge of personnel, and their talks are said to have laid the basis for Mr. Hillman to expand his ideas in a later talk with Mr. Grace.

Mr. Larkin is expected to see Mr. Hillman again this week and to clarify further the situation of the company before the Hillman-Grace meeting. This meeting with Mr. Grace was to have taken place in a few days but was postponed at the suggestion of Mr. Grace.

In the earlier conferences Mr.

Continued on Page Six

ARMS JOBS FIRST, DYKSTRA DECLARES

Production of Defense Material Has Priority Over Military Call, Says Draft Head

Special to THE NEW YORK TIMES.

WASHINGTON, Oct. 27—Assurance was given to employers, especially those engaged in defense work, tonight by Clarence A. Dykstra, Director of Selective Service, that their businesses would not be interrupted by the draft. His announcement came as plans were being completed for the drawing next Tuesday of numbers indicating the priority of call of the selected men, in ceremonies to be held in the presence of President Roosevelt, Secretary of War Stimson and other high officials.

In addressing his statement to "employers and workers alike not to become unduly anxious about occupational deferment," Dr. Dykstra laid down the following as a basic principle of deferment:

"It is a basic principle of Selective Service, at this stage of the national defense preparation, that material procurement is paramount. Therefore, where two requirements—military man power versus pro-

Continued on Page Eighteen

Kennedy Sees Roosevelt at White House; Envoy Is Silent on Arrival From London

Special to THE NEW YORK TIMES.

WASHINGTON, Oct. 27—Ambassador Joseph P. Kennedy, arriving by plane this evening on what was said to be a brief vacation from his post in London, conferred at length with President Roosevelt before the Chief Executive left by train for campaign talks in the New York area tomorrow.

After Mr. and Mrs. Kennedy had dined with the President at the White House it was said that the Ambassador would make no statement tonight, but would meet newspaper men tomorrow morning at 11 o'clock at the Waldorf-Astoria Hotel in New York.

Mr. Kennedy arrived here with Mrs. Kennedy at 6:30 o'clock tonight. He spent only a few minutes at the airport, posing for photographers before being taken to the White House in an official automobile.

Mr. Kennedy left the White House immediately after the dinner and took a plane for New York at 10:35 P. M. Mrs. Kennedy remained in Washington.

Ambassador Kennedy arrived at La Guardia Field at 12:07 o'clock this morning. As he entered his car Mr. Kennedy remarked that he had been traveling extensively for the past three days and was "glad to get home and to bed."

The Ambassador had arrived here by Atlantic Clipper at 3:07 P. M. yesterday, en route to Washington for what had been described as "consultation" with the State Department and President Roosevelt.

Mr. Kennedy looked for all the world like a man bursting with things to say, but in the interval between his arrival and his departure by plane for the capital he limited himself to these words:

"I have nothing to say until I have seen the President."

The Ambassador, long reported to be dissatisfied with his London post, ruled out all questions about whether he was resigning, whether he would campaign for the President or how the British were faring. But he promised to "talk a lot" when he had had his discussion with the President.

On the same plane was William

Continued on Page Seven

RUSH AS FAIR ENDS BRINGS OUT 537,952, ITS BIGGEST CROWD

Final Burst of Night Revelry Marks Closing Hours, but Vandalism Is Slight

SOUVENIR HUNTERS BUSY

Exhibits, Pavilions, Cafes and Amusements Are Packed as Throngs Take Last Look

By SIDNEY M. SHALETT

With a gigantic burst of energy just before the end came, the New York World's Fair, playground and haven of inspiration for nearly 45,000,000 persons since it first welcomed the public back in 1939, smashed all attendance records for both 1939 and 1940 yesterday—its last day of life.

The official ending was simple. A bugler sounded "taps" shortly after midnight, and the Fair was pronounced closed. Orderly but fun-making crowds lingered on until the early hours of morning, but the season had come to an end.

Today, Trylon and Perisphere are headed for the junk heap. Today, for the first time since the brave, new World of Tomorrow was dedicated on April 30, 1939, there is no more World's Fair.

From today on, the 1,216¼ acres, where millions laughed and played and marveled during the hectic seasons of 1939 and 1940, are but shells of vanished glory, waiting for the wrecker's hammer to clear the ground where a great people's park will rise.

Even the most optimistic Fair officials were dazed by the manner in which the unprecedented crowd began storming the Fair. Between 1 and 2 P. M. more than 100,000 customers flocked through the turnstiles. Before 4 P. M. attendance had surpassed the previous record of the 1940 season—379,268 on Sunday, June 2—and by 7 P. M. paid attendance had soared to 496,500, breaking the 1939 record of 492,446.

Yesterday's record throng reached the impressive total of 537,952 at midnight, when the entrance gates closed for the last time.

First 500,000 Day

Ironically, the last day was the first day of either 1939 or 1940 when Fair officials saw realization of their dream—the passing of the 500,000-mark in paid attendance on a single day.

Paid attendance at the Fair for the 1940 season up to Saturday midnight was 12,577,317. Yesterday's reading brought the total up to 13,115,269. Paid attendance for the 1939 season was 25,817,265.

These 1939 and 1940 New York World's Fair attendance figures compare with the Chicago Century of Progress Fair's record of 22,320,456 in 1933 and 16,306,090 in 1934, or a total of 38,626,546 for the two seasons of the Chicago Fair.

Under the eyes of 1,500 city and Fair policemen, the last visitors to

Continued on Page Ten

R. A. F. HITS REICH

Key Plants Are Ruined, Nazi Morale Hurt, British State

BERLIN RAIDED AGAIN

Liverpool and Midlands Under Attack—London Defense Effective

By RAYMOND DANIELL
Special Cable to THE NEW YORK TIMES.

LONDON, Oct. 27—Reminders to the German people that Great Britain still is fighting against the Nazi domination of Europe were spilled from British planes last night over vast areas of the Reich, including the capital itself, where factories, railroad yards and other military objectives were peppered with incendiary and explosive bombs, it was announced here.

[A Berlin air raid alarm early today was reported in news service dispatches from the Reich capital, which quoted a communiqué as saying British fliers were turned back without dropping bombs. The British Air Ministry said this morning attacks had been made on many German centers and "two invasion ports."]

Invasion ports and airports in German-occupied territory, oil tanks and refineries and industrial centers were heavily attacked as well, London heard, while across the North Sea in Norwegian waters a 2,500-ton Nazi supply ship was bombed and sunk.

These repeated attacks, the British are convinced, are beginning to have a marked effect on the German war effort and the morale of the Berlin population. This belief is based on reports which, according to the Air Ministry news service, emanated "from the most reliable neutral sources."

[Wide areas of Great Britain were bombed, Liverpool bearing the brunt of the attack, with the Midlands and London also raided.]

Large Plants Reported Hit

Officials directing the operations of British bombers found the report of the extent of the damage they had done to Berlin a source of considerable satisfaction. The big Siemens Works, which provides Germany's armed forces with much electrical equipment, is said to have been severely damaged. One-third of the Loewe factory, which makes wireless sets and other electrical equipment is reported completely destroyed.

The Allgemeine Elektricitaetsgesellschaft turbine works and the MIAG motor depot also were said to have suffered heavy damage. Two big Berlin power stations, the Berliner Electrical Works in the Charlottenburg area and the Klingenburg power house at the other side of the city, have been disorganized by repeated attacks, it was added.

Last night's raids on Germany followed a familiar pattern, but the heaviest bombs yet used by the Royal Air Force were reported dropped over the German capital.

The Brandenburg airplane engine works at Spandau, a suburb ten miles northwest of the city, were showered with fire and explosive bombs, and the Moabit power station, one of Berlin's main sources of electric supply, was heavily attacked again, it was said.

The Putlitzstrasse and Lehrter railway yards near the center of the capital were reported hit again, the raiders coming down low through thick clouds extending within 2,000 feet of the ground. The pitch darkness hampered the bombers somewhat, but the fliers said secondary explosions within the target area gave them the satisfaction of knowing they had hit something worthwhile.

Other raiders concentrated their attacks on refineries and oil storage plants in such widely separated points as Stettin on the Baltic coast, Cologne, 350 miles to the southwest, and Leuna, near Leipzig.

Planes that made a 1,300-mile round trip to Politz, near Stettin, dropped several tons of incendiaries and explosives on the Norddeutsche Hydrierwerke refineries and started fires and explosions inside the target area. In Cologne the Union Rheinische Braunkohlen plant was the objective, and a big fire was reported inside a large factory.

Direct hits were described on the Leuna refinery. Docks and shipping

Continued on Page Two

The International Situation

The Axis war drive into the Balkans started early today with an invasion of Greece by Italian troops across the Albanian border and Fascist planes reported over Athens. Greece rejected a three-hour ultimatum from Italy that expired at 6 A. M. (11 P. M. Sunday, New York time) and rallied all her forces, Premier Metaxas and King George calling upon the nation to fight for independence. Greece appealed for aid under the British guarantee to her, London announced; the reaction of Turkey, who also has a pledge to Greece, was awaited. Meanwhile, Chancellor Hitler arrived at Florence, Italy, for a conference with Premier Mussolini. [Page 1, Column 8.]

Yesterday, an official Greek communiqué described as a fabrication the Italian report of an attack by an armed Greek band on the Italian outpost at Koritza, Albania. Firing was heard from a point near that city Friday night, the communiqué said, and was reported to the Italians by a Greek officer with a request for information. A parley was arranged but never held. The Greek press said the attack might have been made by insurgent Albanians. [Page. 1, Column 7.]

Formation of a Free French War Government for the French colonies that have remained allies of Britain was announced in a broadcast from Belgian Congo by General Charles de Gaulle. He said he would be "Chief of State." "Free French" forces are reported to have attacked in Gabon, in West Africa. [Page 1, Column 6.]

With Vichy officials silent and the press gagged there was no further public conjecture in France as to what lines the agreed-on collaboration with Germany might take. An official spokesman, however, was loud in praise of German "grandeur" shown in the negotiations and resentful of British attempts to influence France's decision. Vice Premier Laval will go on the radio today to explain the agreement, it was reported. [Page 3, Column 1.]

The British Air Ministry, announcing the twenty-seventh Royal Air Force raid on Berlin, said reports from neutral sources told of severe damage done in the German capital by previous attacks. Railway, bus, subway, gas and electric services had been disrupted by the raids, the Ministry said, and many important factories damaged. One informant was said to be an American chemical engineer who had worked for a German company every one of whose twelve plants had been destroyed. The Saturday night raids hit not only Berlin but many other objectives in the Reich and the occupied countries, the Ministry said. [Page 1, Column 5.]

The Nazis kept up an almost incessant day and night attack on London, but apparently did the most damage at Liverpool and other west coast ports and in the industrial Midlands. The London attacks by fighter craft carrying only small bomb loads, did little military damage, the British said, but caused a number of casualties. The Nazi fighters, having no bomb sights, just drop their loads by guess and then run. Eight of them were reported shot down during the day. The British said they had lost six of their own craft, but that one pilot jumped to safety. [Page 2, Column 2.]

The Italian press printed photographs showing members of a German military mission at the Egyptian front. The pictures and accounts of their presence there lent credence to rumors current for some time that German bombing planes would aid the Italians when they resumed their drive toward Alexandria and the Suez Canal. [Page 3, Column 8.]

DE GAULLE FORMING FREE 'GOVERNMENT'

Proclaims Authority Over All Territory in Revolt, Calls Frenchmen to Arms

By JAMES B. RESTON
Special Cable to THE NEW YORK TIMES.

LONDON, Oct. 27.—In a broadcast proclamation from Leopoldville, in the Belgian Congo, General Charles de Gaulle announced his decision today to appoint a Council of Defense for the French Empire.

With a declaration that "a few infamous politicians were delivering up the Empire of France," General de Gaulle, who is visiting in the Congo, issued an order stating:

"As long as the French Government and the representation of the French people do not exist normally and independently of the enemy, the powers formally performed by the Chief of State and by the Council of Ministers will be exercised by the leader of the Free French forces assisted by a Council of Defense."

These new powers, General de Gaulle said, would be enforced in accordance with the laws existing in France on June 23, 1940.

This declaration is of especial interest here because of its manifest assumption that Marshal Henri Philippe Petain is ready to sell out to Chancellor Hitler. This is an assumption that is not yet accepted by the British Foreign Office.

It is pointed out in Whitehall that the official statement issued after Herr Hitler's meeting with Marshal Petain merely stated that "an agreement in principle on collaboration was reached." On the basis of this vague declaration the British are not yet ready to believe, as General de Gaulle evidently is, that the Petain government is ready to bow to Herr Hitler's terms.

British officials are carrying on tonight as if Herr Hitler were just another caller in Marshal Petain's anteroom. For example, they are even abiding by the strictest international etiquette by refusing to release the text of King George's message to Marshal Petain on the score that since it concerns the head of the French State, Marshal Petain's reply must be received before the King's message is released.

In other words, the British are

Continued on Page Three

ALBANIAN 'ATTACK' DENIED BY ATHENS

Greece Charges Italy Falsifies Border Clash—Parley Fails to Adjust Dispute

By Telephone to THE NEW YORK TIMES.

ATHENS, Greece, Oct. 27—A meeting for this afternoon between a Greek officer and an Italian military representative on the Greek-Albanian border was arranged, it was learned today, to start some kind of investigation into the incident that the Italian Stefani Agency claimed took place Friday night near Koritza, Albania, in which, according to the Italian version, an armed Greek band crossed the frontier from Greece and fired on an Albanian patrol, killing two soldiers by either gunfire or hand grenades.

However, it was learned also that the Greek officer, finding the Italian to be of inferior military rank, considered that further parley was inconsistent with his nation's dignity, and as things look tonight the affair may well have serious consequences.

So far no communiqué has been issued on the scheduled meeting and there may never be one. It is difficult to see on what grounds the two military emissaries can hope to agree because the Greek story, which the Greek Government means to stick to, says Stefani's imagination has been at work in the fabrication of an occurrence that never took place.

Not only, say the Greeks, did no armed band ever cross the frontier, but no such thing as an armed band exists in present-day Greece. Furthermore, they assert, the Greek soldiers on their side of the border heard gunfire after dark on Friday and even went so far as to make the friendly gesture of drawing the attention of the Italian soldiers opposite to this evidence of some kind of disorder. Italian officers investigated, but withheld reports on their findings from the Greeks.

The Greek press hints strongly at the possibility that these "armed bands," which the Italians insist were Greek, actually were Albanian. Reports have been current here of considerable dissatisfaction among Albanians under a rule arbitrarily imposed on them.

It is thought significant here that this particular charge about Greek

Continued on Page Three

BORDER IS CROSSED

Italians Move In From Albania—Athens Has First Raid Alarm

PREMIER IS DEFIANT

Appeal for Aid Is Sent to Britain—Attacking Force Put at 200,000

By A. C. SEDGWICK
Wireless to THE NEW YORK TIMES.

ATHENS, Greece, Monday, Oct. 28—Full mobilization went into effect at 6 o'clock this morning after an ultimatum, served at 3 o'clock, to the Greek Government by Italy had expired.

The ultimatum was refused at 6 o'clock. Hence a state of war exists or is presumed to exist between this country and Italy, as the Axis starts its Balkan drive. The nation is on a wartime footing.

Ten Divisions Attack

BELGRADE, Yugoslavia, Monday, Oct. 28 (AP)—Italy was reported today to have attacked Greece by land, sea and air, hurling at least ten divisions of 200,000 Italian troops across the Greek-Albanian frontier.

Reports from the Yugoslav frontier said troops of Greece's small army flung themselves into the path of the Fascist advance through mountain passes.

Italian warships and fighting planes were believed to have joined in the onslaught.

At the same time, British sources here declared that warships of the British Mediterranean squadron were steaming from their patrol posts to the assistance of Greece, who holds a British guarantee of aid in event of attack.

[There was no immediate confirmation of this report from London.]

Greek Minister Raoul Bibica-Rosetti declared today that a state of war existed between Italy and Greece and fighting had started at 6 A. M.

The Greek Minister said that he had learned in a telephone conversation with Athens that Italian troops pushed across the border from Albania just as a 6 A. M. Italian ultimatum expired.

Greeks Appeal for Aid

Special Cable to THE NEW YORK TIMES.

LONDON, Monday, Oct. 28—In a formal statement telling of Italy's ultimatum to Greece and the Greek rejection the British Foreign Office announced this morning that the Greek Government had "applied to His Majesty's Government for certain assistance."

The Italian ultimatum not only fulfills the terms of the British guarantee to Greece, but also fulfills the terms under which Turkey had agreed to come to the assistance of Britain in the Mediterranean. Though Turkey was theoretically obligated to enter the war when Italy attacked France, she did not do so at that time.

Since Italian troops massed on the Greek frontier, the Turks and the Greeks have been conferring and there is some reason for believing that Turkey may now decide to render some assistance to Greece.

First Air-Raid Alarm

ATHENS, Greece, Monday, Oct. 28 (UP)—Greece early today rejected an unconditional surrender ultimatum by Italy and ordered general mobilization, determined to fight to defend her territory.

Athens had an air-raid alarm at 7 A. M.—one hour after the Italian ultimatum expired. Whether this indicated an attack or merely a test alerte was not immediately known.

Urges "Fight for Honor"

ATHENS, Greece, Monday, Oct. 28 (AP)—Rejecting an Italian ultimatum calling for surrender by Greece of part of her territory, Premier John Metaxas declared today "the moment has arrived for Greece to fight for her independence and honor."

Immediately after, a decree for general mobilization was signed.

The Italian ultimatum was given to Premier Metaxas at 3 A. M. (8 P. M. Eastern standard time Sunday) and gave him three hours

Continued on Page Three

"All the News That's Fit to Print."

The New York Times.

LATE CITY EDITION
Cloudy, much colder today. Tomorrow partly cloudy and rather cold
Temperatures Yesterday—Max., 68; Min., 52

VOL. XC..No. 30,237. Entered as Second-Class Matter, Postoffice, New York, N. Y. NEW YORK, WEDNESDAY, NOVEMBER 6, 1940. THREE CENTS NEW YORK CITY and Vicinity | FOUR CENTS Elsewhere Except in 7th and 8th Postal Zones.

ROOSEVELT ELECTED PRESIDENT; CERTAIN OF 429 ELECTORAL VOTES; DEMOCRATS KEEP HOUSE CONTROL

RETAIN HOUSE GRIP

Democrats, Holding 225 Seats, Gain at Least Ten From Rivals

65 ARE NOW IN DOUBT

Latest Figures Indicate Republican Gain of 1 to 3 Senators

By TURNER CATLEDGE

Unless further complete returns today show more Republican winners in yesterday's election, the Democrats not only will have met successfully the challenge of their opponents to control the House but may actually repair some of the damage to their huge majority in the 1938 Congressional election.

The Republicans, on the other hand, may have added from one to three to their roster in the Senate, but this remains to be determined by complete reports.

Returns received up to 4 o'clock this morning indicated that the President's party had dropped only four seats to the opposition, while they had picked up at least ten now held by Republicans. This made the count 225 Democrats, 143 Republicans, one Independent Democrat and one American Labor, with sixty-five seats still in doubt.

The present House is composed of 259 Democrats, 167 Republicans, one Farmer-Laborite, two Progressives and one American Labor member, with five vacancies due to deaths and resignations.

The status of the Senatorial tabulation at that hour, with thirty-six States in contest—thirty-three for full and three for unexpired terms—showed Democrats, 18; Republicans, 7, and 11 still in doubt. This made sure that the new Senate would have at least 62 Democrats, 22 Republicans, 1 Independent, leaving the 11 in doubt. The present ratio of the Senate is 69 Democrats, 24 Republicans, 1 Progressive, 1 Independent and 1 Farmer-Laborite (Senator Shipstead of Minnesota, who ran this year as a Republican).

The Senate's lone Progressive, Senator Robert M. La Follette, trailed Fred H. Clausen, his Republican opponent, in the earlier returns from Wisconsin, but along in the morning hours he forged ahead and word from the Badger State indicated that he might pull through in the toughest fight of his career.

The four seats dropped by Democrats to Republicans were in the Eighth Oklahoma, Sixteenth New York, Fourth California and the Sixth Missouri districts. More than offsetting these were the ten picked up by the Democrats, including the First, Second and Fourth Connecticut districts and the Congressman at Large of that State; the First and Second Rhode Island districts, the Fifth and Twenty-second Pennsylvania districts and the Forty-first New York and the Sixteenth Ohio districts. The Democrats made a clean sweep of the delegations in Connecticut and Rhode Island, annexing six seats held in these two States. Perhaps the greatest upsets in the House were the defeats of Representative Phil Ferguson, Democrat, of Oklahoma by Ross Rizley, Republican, and of the Democratic Representative James Fay of the Sixteenth New York by William E. Pheiffer, Republican.

Incumbent Democrats Sticking

Incumbent Democrats were holding tenaciously to leads in most of the other contests in which they were involved and New Deal nominees were threatening sitting Republican Congressmen in a number of districts, particularly in States where the Roosevelt victory was assuming landslide proportions in the popular vote.

The Republicans had entertained no hope from the start of capturing the leadership of the Senate, but they claimed chances of picking up from five to ten new seats to add to the twenty-four they now have.

Continued on Page Two

THE VOTE FOR PRESIDENT

State.	Districts Total.	Districts Reported.	Roosevelt, Democrat.	Willkie, Republican.	Thomas, Socialist.	Electoral Vote Roosevelt.	Electoral Vote Willkie.
Alabama	2,300	1,107	140,564	21,224	....	11	..
Arizona	430	270	40,287	21,603	....	3	..
Arkansas	2,169	842	27,258	8,586	....	9	..
California	13,602	9,564	1,043,200	743,522	....	22	..
Colorado	1,610	387	43,150	54,301	....	..	..
Connecticut	169	166	412,648	358,156	....	8	..
Delaware	248	200	50,890	40,312	....	3	..
Florida	1,451	896	246,183	82,551	....	7	..
Georgia	1,720	886	196,687	39,046	....	12	..
Idaho	792	300	36,113	30,155	....	..	..
Illinois	8,378	6,017	1,514,763	1,375,092	....	29	..
Indiana	3,866	2,185	576,754	576,872	....	..	..
Iowa	2,453	1,505	358,607	276,569	....	..	..
Kansas	2,734	1,377	147,821	216,802	....	..	9
Kentucky	4,341	2,240	297,223	193,622	....	11	..
Louisiana	1,712	481	127,518	22,987	....	10	..
Maine	629	623	154,732	163,782	....	..	5
Maryland	1,331	1,194	351,224	241,447	....	8	..
Massachusetts	1,810	1,151	636,856	575,950	....	17	..
Michigan	3,630	1,349	387,245	387,738	....	..	19
Minnesota	3,696	910	258,715	216,432	....	11	..
Mississippi	1,668	635	87,180	4,179	....	9	..
Missouri	4,479	2,914	526,067	480,110	....	..	..
Montana	1,186	262	43,057	26,839	....	4	..
Nebraska	2,043	1,227	124,825	160,063	....	..	7
Nevada	260	177	15,545	11,213	....	3	..
New Hampshire	294	287	115,932	103,671	....	4	..
New Jersey	3,630	2,038	529,922	564,294*	....	16	..
New Mexico	914	413	60,998	39,300	....	3	..
New York	9,319	9,297	3,231,032	3,021,536	....	47	..
North Carolina	1,926	686	560,556	175,507	....	13	..
North Dakota	2,262	631	73,669	73,220	....	..	4
Ohio	8,675	7,722	1,465,514	1,285,750	....	26	..
Oklahoma	2,613	2,008	356,784	249,117	....	11	..
Oregon	1,663	923	89,971	89,639	....	..	..
Pennsylvania	8,113	7,132	1,912,401	1,670,032	....	36	..
Rhode Island	259	259	181,881	138,432	....	4	..
South Carolina	1,277	953	81,987	4,164	....	8	..
South Dakota	1,936	1,034	61,211	83,369	....	..	4
Tennessee	2,300	1,891	257,724	119,836	....	11	..
Texas	254	244	504,433	118,198	....	23	..
Utah	831	345	63,298	39,941	....	4	..
Vermont	246	246	64,244	78,256	....	..	3
Virginia	1,714	1,622	223,388	103,030	....	11	..
Washington	3,018	1,063	154,500	102,032	....	8	..
West Virginia	2,300	1,016	217,064	155,580	....	8	..
Wisconsin	3,038	1,782	406,095	377,717	....	12	..
Wyoming	606	490	32,889	21,765	....	..	..
						429	51

*Hudson County returns incomplete.

ROOSEVELT WINNER IN MASSACHUSETTS

Indicated Margin Is Below That of 1936—Saltonstall Ahead in a Close Race

Special to THE NEW YORK TIMES.

BOSTON, Nov. 5—President Roosevelt carried Massachusetts over Wendell Willkie in today's election. Indications tonight were that his margin would be smaller than the 174,000 by which he captured the State's 17 electoral votes four years ago.

The Democratic surge was great enough to re-elect Senator Walsh over Henry Parkman Jr. by a substantial margin and to endanger Governor Leverett Saltonstall's re-election in his contest with Attorney General Paul A. Dever.

Lieut. Gov. Cahill, State Secretary Cook, State Treasurer Hurley and State Auditor Cook apparently were re-elected, while Robert T. Bushnell seemed to have won his contest for Attorney General on the basis of returns which had been counted late tonight.

President Roosevelt was Strongest in the industrial cities outside Boston. He carried Lynn by almost 6,000 votes and New Bedford by a ratio of nearly 2 to 1. It was estimated that Roosevelt's margin in Boston would approach 100,000. He carried Somerville by 4,100 votes.

Governor Saltonstall fared much

Continued on Page Four

NEW JERSEY VOTE GOES TO PRESIDENT

Willkie Margin Cut in Normal Republican Areas—Edison and Barbour Win

By RUSSELL B. PORTER

On the basis of incomplete returns at 4 o'clock this morning, President Roosevelt appeared to have carried New Jersey with its sixteen electoral votes by a safe plurality—over Wendell Willkie—drastically reduced from 384,000 margin in 1936, and closer to his 31,000 edge in 1932.

The same returns indicated the election of Charles Edison, former Secretary of the Navy and son of the late Thomas A. Edison, the inventor, over his Republican opponent, State Senator Robert C. Hendrickson. Mr. Edison appeared to have polled more votes than the President.

United States Senator W. Warren Barbour, Republican candidate for re-election, ran far ahead of his ticket, and decisively defeated James H. R. Cromwell, former Minister to Canada and husband of Doris Duke, the tobacco heiress.

Eight hours after the polls closed at 8 P. M. there was still uncertainty over State-wide totals. Only one-half of the State's 3,631 election districts had reported their results by that time, and only a few comparatively of these were from the strong Democratic counties—Hudson, where Mayor Frank Hague of Jersey City, vice chairman of the Democratic National Committee, piled up a big Roosevelt vote, and Camden and Middlesex, where big industries with strong Roosevelt labor strength are located.

Big Vote Adds to Delay

The delay in recording the vote from these counties was caused partly by the record-breaking vote, brought out by perfect weather and unprecedentedly heavy registration, partly by the fact that voting machines are not used in these counties, and partly by the traditional withholding of the Hudson County vote until after the Republican counties have reported.

Surrogate John H. Gavin of Hudson County, spokesman for Mayor Hague, estimated early this morning, with the vote still incomplete, that Hudson would give the President and Mr. Edison a plurality of 110,000, including 60,000 in Jersey City. Mr. Cromwell was running far behind.

Four years ago Mr. Roosevelt re-

Continued on Page Twelve

The War

Leading developments yesterday in the war, accounts of which appear on Page 25—the first page of the second section, —were as follows:

1. A German pocket battleship appeared in mid-Atlantic and shelled a British convoy.

2. Prime Minister Churchill emphasized before the Commons the growing U-boat threat and said bases in Ireland were needed by Britain.

3. In the Greek-Italian hostilities Rome reported an advance in the Yanina sector, the Greeks were said to be closing in on Koritza and a Yugoslav town was bombed by Italian-type planes.

The summary headed "International Situation" also appears on Page 25.

CITY MARGIN WIDE

Lead Totals 727,254—Queens, Richmond Won by Willkie

P. R. SYSTEM UPHELD

Abolition Move Defeated by About 206,550—Simpson Is Elected

By LEO EGAN

Franklin D. Roosevelt piled up a plurality of 727,254 in New York City yesterday as voters in record-breaking numbers went to the polls under clear skies to record their choice for President. This was far short of the 1,375,396 plurality given to him in 1936, when he was a candidate for a second term.

The President carried the three most populous counties in the city but lost Queens and Richmond. Queens gave Wendell Willkie a plurality of 36,875.

Senator James M. Mead, seeking re-election on the Democratic ticket, ran slightly ahead of the President. He carried the city by 845,063, carrying all five counties.

The President's pluralities of 350,610 in Kings, 219,066 in the Bronx and 195,017 in Manhattan were much less than his supporters had counted on except in Manhattan, but they were enough to please them. The Manhattan plurality was larger than expected.

Results in Other Contests

Other features of yesterday's voting in the city were the defeat by an indicated plurality of 206,550 of the proposal to repeal the proportional representation method of selecting members of the City Council, the apparent defeat of Representative James H. Fay in the Sixteenth District, the election of Kenneth F. Simpson, New York County Republican leader, for the Congressional seat now held by Representative Bruce Barton; the election of John Cashmore and Samuel S. Leibowitz, the Democratic candidates for Borough President and County Judge, respectively, in Brooklyn, and the re-election of Representative Vito Marcantonio, outstanding Congressional foe of conscription and the Roosevelt defense program, in the Twentieth Congressional District on Manhattan's upper East Side.

The President carried all but two Assembly districts in Manhattan, losing the Fifteenth and Tenth, and all but three in King's losing the Ninth, Tenth and Twentieth. He swept all eight districts in the Bronx and lost three out of six in Queens.

In all but one borough the friends of proportional representation were able to beat down the proposal to repeal it. If the proposal had been carried the voters would have elected Councilmen next year on the basis of State Senate districts with

Continued on Page Four

Willkie Retires Refusing to Give Up; He Declines Any Statement Before Today

Grimly clinging to his avowed determination not to give up the fight, Wendell L. Willkie said at 1:30 this morning that he intended to go to bed in his suite at the Hotel Commodore, and that he would have no statement to make concerning the election until some time after he wakes up this morning.

This information, relayed from his fourteenth-floor suite to the waiting crowd of reporters in the press headquarters downstairs, was the only word that came from Mr. Willkie after he had briefly appeared before a crowd of cheering campaign workers at 12:20 A. M., to say that he was neither afraid nor disheartened, and repudiate indignantly suggestions that he should concede his defeat.

When he appeared at that time before about 1,500 faithful supporters in the Grand Ball Room of the Commodore Hotel, Mr. Willkie pleaded with them not to quit and expressed his confidence that the fight they had jointly waged would eventually be won.

His appearance before his campaign workers came after hours of seclusion in his private suite, where he repeatedly characterized the election as "a horse race" and predicted that the result would not be known definitely until some time today. Mr. Willkie appeared before the crowd of campaign workers at 12:19 A. M.

Holding up both hands to ask for silence while they gave him an ear-splitting ovation, Mr. Willkie said:

"Fellow workers: I first want to say to you that I never felt better in my life. I congratulate you in being a part of the greatest crusade of this century. And that the principles for which we have fought will prevail is as sure as that the truth will always prevail.

"And I hope that none of you are either afraid or disheartened because I am not in the slightest.

"I just wanted to come down and thank you so much for being my fellow fighters in this struggle—to

Continued on Page Five

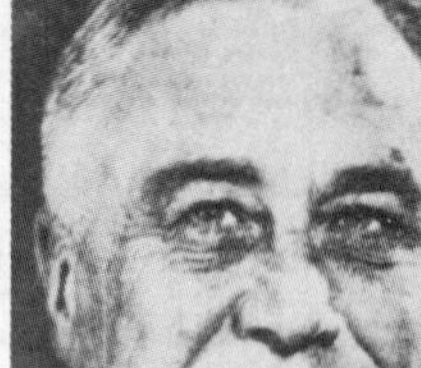

WINNERS OF PRESIDENCY AND VICE PRESIDENCY
Franklin Delano Roosevelt — Henry Agard Wallace

DEMOCRATS CARRY STATE BY 230,000

Mead, O'Day, Merritt and Desmond Join President in New York Victory Column

By JAMES A. HAGERTY

For the third time President Franklin D. Roosevelt carried his home State of New York with its forty-seven electoral votes in yesterday's election, this time by a plurality of about 230,000, over Wendell L. Willkie, his Republican opponent.

The vote in New York City with 40 election districts missing out of 4,051 gave Willkie 1,241,501 and Roosevelt 1,937,017, an actual plurality for Roosevelt of 695,516 and an indicated plurality of 700,823.

Outside New York City in 5,004 out of 5,268 election districts, the vote was Willkie 1,685,043, Roosevelt 1,219,817, an actual plurality of 465,276 for Willkie and an indicated plurality of 489,924. This gave the President an actual plurality of 230,240 on these returnst and an indicated plurality of 215,000, which may be slightly higher because of the small number of votes in the unreported districts.

Bruce Barton, Republican candi-

Continued on Page Ten

Bonfires of All Buttons Urged to Heal Bitterness

Public bonfires of all the Democratic and Republican campaign literature and buttons was suggested yesterday by William Allen White, national chairman of the Committee to Defend America by Aiding the Allies, as a means of "healing partisan bitterness and for launching a nation-wide campaign to safeguard American democracy."

Mr. White, in a statement issued last night, urged "unity mass meetings" as soon as possible after election, in a message to the representatives of the group's 717 local chapters in the forty-eight States.

The meetings should be held, he said, "not in the spirit of exaltation on the part of the victorious party but with the idea that we destroy the symbols of partisan bitterness and unite now on a national program of safeguarding American democracy."

PRESIDENT TAKES KEYSTONE STATE

Republican Chairman Concedes Pennsylvania—Guffey Ahead in Senate Race

Special to THE NEW YORK TIMES.

PHILADELPHIA, Wednesday, Nov. 6—Aided by impressive strength in the industrial areas, President Roosevelt apparently duplicated his feat of 1936 and won the thirty-six electoral votes of traditionally Republican Pennsylvania in yesterday's election.

The trend in the senatorial contest between Senator Joseph F. Guffey, Democrat, and Jay Cooke, chairman of the Philadelphia Republican Committee, was in the direction of the re-election of Mr. Guffey, who campaigned on his record of "100 per cent Roosevelt support."

The Democrats, it seemed likely, would gain an undetermined number of seats in the State's Congressional delegation, which had been Republican by nineteen to fifteen, and they appeared to have an even chance of wresting control of the State House of Representatives from the Republicans, who took it over with the election of Governor James two years ago. The Republicans were hopeful of salvaging their majority in the State Senate.

James F. Torrance, Republican State Chairman, conceded Pennsyl-

Continued on Page Four

ROOSEVELT LOOKS TO 'DIFFICULT DAYS'

But Tells Celebrators That He Will Carry On for the Country 'Just the Same'

By CHARLES HURD

Special to THE NEW YORK TIMES.

HYDE PARK, Wednesday, Nov. 6—Standing on the portico of his mother's home here, Franklin D. Roosevelt early today acknowledged his re-election with a promise to continue to be "the same Franklin Roosevelt you have known."

He made this statement to several hundred residents of Hyde Park and vicinity who formed a torch-light procession that carried out a tradition marking Democratic political victories with rallies at the old house, a parade formed by Democrats as soon as returns indicated the victory.

"We are facing difficult days in this country," Mr. Roosevelt told the throng, "but I think you will find me in the future just the same Franklin Roosevelt you have known a great many years."

The President beamed on the crowd as he leaned on the arm of his third son, Franklin Jr., in the bright light of flares set in place by motion-picture camera men.

He smiled and waved while hundreds of persons trooped through the grounds from cars parked first in the driveways and afterward on the Albany Post Road, some of them a quarter of a mile away.

President Faces His Neighbors

Behind the President were grouped about forty guests who had been entertained by Mrs. Roosevelt at supper at her cottage at Val-Kill. But the President faced a crowd in which there were no prominent politicians, no industrial leaders.

These were exclusively his neighbors, who bear to him the same relationship as the villagers bore to his father when he was a minor Democratic leader and a friend of President Cleveland.

President Roosevelt walked on to the front porch of Hyde Park house just before midnight, when he finally broke a vigil over tables on which he marked election returns behind locked doors in the dining room of his home.

The first glare of red flares was seen far off down the driveway. Ten minutes later, exactly at midnight, a town band marched into the car park in front of the house.

The President, with Franklin Jr., stood at the right side of the porch.

Continued on Page Two

BIG ELECTORAL VOTE

Large Pivotal States Swing to Democrats in East and West

POPULAR VOTE CUT

First Time in History That Third Term Is Granted President

By ARTHUR KROCK

Over an apparently huge popular minority, which under the electoral college system was not able to register its proportion of the total vote in terms of electors, President Roosevelt was chosen yesterday for a third term, the first American in history to break the tradition which began with the Republic. He carried to victory with him Henry A. Wallace to be Vice President, and continued control of the House of Representatives by the Democrats was also indicated in the returns.

But in many of the larger States so many precincts were still missing early this morning, and the contest in these States was so close, that Wendell L. Willkie, the Republican opponent, whose name Mr. Roosevelt never mentioned throughout the campaign, refused to concede defeat. He said it was a "horse race," and that the result would not be known until today. He went to bed in that frame of mind.

As the returns mounted there seemed little, however, to sustain Mr. Willkie's hope. New York, Massachusetts, Connecticut, Rhode Island, Pennsylvania, Ohio and Illinois, of the greater States, all appeared to have been carried safely by the President. The Solid South had resisted all appeals to revolt against Mr. Roosevelt's quest for a third term. The Pacific and Mountain States were following the national trend.

States for Mr. Roosevelt

States sure or probable for the President are:

Alabama, Arizona, Arkansas, California, Connecticut, Delaware, Florida, Georgia, Illinois, Kentucky, Louisiana, Maryland, Massachusetts, Missouri, Minnesota, Mississippi, Montana, Nevada, New Hampshire, New Jersey, New Mexico, New York, North Carolina, Ohio, Oklahoma, Pennsylvania, Rhode Island, South Carolina, Tennessee, Texas, Utah, Virginia, West Virginia and Wisconsin—electoral votes, 429.

States sure or probable for Mr. Willkie:

Kansas, Maine, Michigan, Nebraska, North Dakota, South Dakota, Vermont—electoral votes 51.

States doubtful or insufficiently reported:

Colorado, Idaho, Indiana, Iowa, Oregon, Washington and Wyoming—electoral votes, 51.

The Electoral Vote

Listing as doubtful nine States, including several like California, Ohio and Indiana, which seem certain to join the Democratic column, there were at 3 A. M. only 51 electoral votes in possible dispute. The President had an apparently certain total of 429, while with more or less security in Mr. Willkie's column were only 51 votes.

No shift or series of shifts could affect the electoral result and the indications were that the President's total would reach from 420 to 470.

Either figure would be much less than the nearly clean sweeps he had in 1932, when he carried forty-two States, and in 1936, when only Maine and Vermont went Republican. And unless the Far West and the Mountain States shall be shown to have given incredible majorities and late returns from the Eastern States pile up the President's votes higher than indications seem to make possible, Mr. Roosevelt's popular majority will be far less than he had against Herbert Hoover and Alf M. Landon.

It appeared early this morning that a maximum of 5,000,000 and a minimum of 2,000,000 would represent the final difference between the popular votes cast for the two major Presidential candidates. The Associated Press tabulation at 1:50 A. M. was 14,879,930 for Mr. Roose-

Continued on Page Two

"All the News That's Fit to Print."

The New York Times.

Copyright, 1940, by The New York Times Company.

LATE CITY EDITION
Partly cloudy and colder today. Tomorrow fair and slightly warmer.
Temperatures Yesterday—Max., 49; Min., 40

VOL. XC...No. 30,247. Entered as Second-Class Matter, Postoffice, New York, N. Y. NEW YORK, SATURDAY, NOVEMBER 16, 1940. THREE CENTS NEW YORK CITY and Vicinity | FOUR CENTS Elsewhere Except in 7th and 8th Postal Zones.

COVENTRY WRECKED IN WORST RAID ON ENGLAND, WITH 1,000 CASUALTIES; BRITISH SMASH BERLIN RAIL DEPOTS

ROOSEVELT NAMES DR. MILLIS TO NLRB, REPLACING MADDEN

Witt, Board Secretary, and 2 Others Quit as Shake-Up Looms in 'Leftist' Group

LEISERSON HAILS CHOICE

End of Deadlock Between Him and Smith Forecast—Madden Nominated for Claims Bench

By CHARLES HURD
Special to THE NEW YORK TIMES.

WASHINGTON, Nov. 15—President Roosevelt today appointed Dr. Harry A. Millis of Chicago to succeed J. Warren Madden, former chairman of the National Labor Relations Board. Dr. Millis, who is 67, served on the old NRA Labor Board in 1934 and 1935, prior to its reconstitution under the Wagner act.

This appointment of a man whose nomination was expected to result in considerable shuffling in the board personnel, especially its "left wing" element, was followed within a few hours by the resignation of three important aides of the board, including Nathan Witt, the secretary.

The appointment broke an impasse which has existed since Aug. 27, when Mr. Madden's term expired and his necessary retirement left the board consisting only of Dr. William Leiserson and Edwin S. Smith, whose opposing views made it impossible for them to reach agreements on many controversies before them.

Mr. Smith had voted much of the time with Chairman Madden, just as Dr. Leiserson is expected hereafter to vote generally with Dr. Millis. Dr. Leiserson called selection of Dr. Millis a "splendid appointment."

Madden Named for Court Post

Coincident with appointment of Dr. Millis, Mr. Roosevelt sent to the Senate a nomination of Mr. Madden to fill a vacancy on the United States Court of Claims, where he would receive $12,500 a year as contrasted with his former $10,000 NLRB post. Mr. Smith immediately wrote to Mr. Madden expressing regret that he had not been reappointed to the NLRB.

The appointment of Dr. Millis was expected to receive quick confirmation by the Senate.

The President, in nominating Dr. Millis, did not indicate whether he would be designated as chairman of the board, but this was the assumption in well-informed circles.

Dr. Millis is a Professor of Economics at the University of Chicago and has been acting as labor relations conciliator for the General Motors Corporation and the C. I. O. United Automobile Workers. Prior to his call to the University of Chicago he was on the faculties of Stanford University and the Universities of Arkansas and Kansas. His long experience in labor affairs includes various temporary appointments by the Federal Government. Recently he has made studies on collective bargaining for the Twentieth Century Fund.

Activities in the offices of the NLRB as a result of the appointment gave graphic indication of the changes anticipated there, as well as the division of feeling within the board.

Mr. Witt submitted his letter of resignation addressed to the board and made it public together with a somewhat longer letter to Mr. Madden, complimenting the latter's work.

Pay Tribute to Ex-Chairman

Soon after Mr. Witt took this step, Alexander B. Hawes, chief administrative examiner, and Thomas I. Emerson, associate general counsel, filed their own resignations. Both also paid tribute to Mr. Madden.

Mr. Emerson's principal work, in his five-year association with the NLRB, has been to direct the work of lawyers in the Review Section who passed upon examiners' reports. This Review Section was sharply criticized for its alleged collective lack of experience by the special House committee that studied the NLRB a year ago, and Dr. Millis was expected to overhaul its organization.

All three officials asked that their resignations be effective immediately. Mr. Hawes wrote to the board that he had served for three years under the "fearless and able chairmanship" of Mr. Madden and "I do not wish to remain with the board, now that he has not been reappointed."

Mr. Emerson publicly announced that, concerning Mr. Madden, "I have supported his policies throughout," and that it was difficult for him to see "how the members of the board could have performed a more courageous, competent and worth-while public service."

Mr. Witt's letter to the board based his resignation on failure to reappoint Mr. Madden. His person-

Continued on Page Twenty

Hull Decides to Remain In Cabinet, Friends State

Special to THE NEW YORK TIMES.

WASHINGTON, Nov. 15—Cordell Hull has reached a decision to continue as Secretary of State in the third Roosevelt administration, according to officials who said today that he has so informed friends. Mr. Hull is in Augusta, Ga., on a vacation and President Roosevelt is cruising on the Presidential yacht Potomac, consequently no comment was available from either official.

The decision turned upon the international situation, it was said. It was understood that Secretary Hull would have preferred to retire to private life. The war emergency and his familiarity with United States foreign policy for eight years induced him to remain in office, it was explained.

Mr. Hull will be the first Secretary of State to serve more than eight years. Only four have served that long, the last being Hamilton Fish, sixty-four years ago.

C. I. O. STRIKE SHUTS WAR PLANES PLANT

5,200 Vultee Workers Idle—Hillman Voices Hope for Quick Wage Accord

Special to THE NEW YORK TIMES.

LOS ANGELES, Nov. 15—Work on $80,000,000 worth of military aircraft production, described in Washington as "vital to our national defense," came to a halt today as members of the C. I. O. United Automobile Workers went on strike at the Downey plant of Vultee Aircraft, Inc., fourth largest plane producer on the West Coast.

Early this morning hundreds of pickets drew up across the huge plant's entrances. The last outgoing night shift came out with tool kits in hands. The first ingoing day shift stopped short before such picket line banners as "They Shall Not Pass!" and "Keep Out! This Means You!"

The plant, where top-speed wheels had long hummed twenty-four hours a day, was hushed and 5,200 workers found themselves idle.

Agents of the War Department, National Defense Commission and Labor Department were at work on a remedy for a situation causing the greatest interruption to date in defense production.

Secretary Perkins assigned Edward H. Fitzgerald, one of the department's veteran labor conciliators, to help Lyman Sisley, first department conciliator in the situation. Mr. Sisley has spent night and day working toward a solution since the matter was put up to him by the disputants Wednesday night.

Seek New Conversations

Upon Captain Fitzgerald's arrival from San Francisco, he and Mr. Sisley, who long have teamed together in West Coast conciliation endeavors, outlined a new peace plan which, they said, they were seeking to lay before the union leaders. The aim, it was understood, was to bring company and union negotiators around one table. Company officials said they would attend.

Company representatives charged that Vultee was being used by the union as a guinea pig for a nation-wide drive to bring all airplane manufacture under the C. I. O. banner.

The union has control only in one other West Coast airplane plant, that of North American Aviation, Inc., a much smaller establishment.

Union representatives assert that all they are after is an increase to 75 cents an hour from the present 50 cents an hour minimum wage at the Vultee plant, where they claim a large majority of the 3,800 production workers among the 5,200 total employes.

They want the rate to be retroactive to Oct. 21. They point out that they have a 75-cent minimum in local automobile manufacturing plants.

The company has offered to increase the minimum to 55 cents for three months of employment and 60 cents after six months, asserting that it takes six months to train a beginner.

Agreement on Other Points

All other points in a proposed contract between the company and the union, both sides state, have been agreed on.

Vultee is producing military planes exclusively, basic trainers for the United States Army, Vanguard pursuit planes for foreign account and a new secret type combat plane.

Highways to and from the plant were choked today with automobiles of idle workers, many bearing out-of-State license plates. Two cars, one with an Ohio license plate, were rigged up with loud-speakers to address union messages. A field kitchen with soup kettles was set up for picketers.

Police reported no disorder, but disruption of traffic. Union agents questioned persons who approached

Continued on Page Twenty

$58,000,000 TUNNEL TO QUEENS OPENED; 3,000 AT CEREMONY

Officials Praise New Unit of City's Interborough Arteries—Mrs. Harvey Cuts Tape

DRIVERS QUICK TO USE IT

Long Line Waits at Manhattan End, but a 'First' Has to Be Drafted at the Other

The $58,000,000 Queens Midtown Tunnel under the East River was opened to the public at 1:20 P. M. yesterday, nearly an hour after the close of dedicatory exercises held under lowering skies in the presence of 3,000 guests of the New York City Tunnel Authority, assembled in the traffic plaza at the Queens end of the new tube.

It was 12:36 P. M. when Council President Newbold Morris, acting in the absence of Mayor La Guardia, formally accepted the new traffic artery for the city. The acceptance came at the end of a speaking program in which city and Federal officials took part. Afterward there was a motor parade of guests through the tunnel to Manhattan and return, followed by a motorcade along the new Midtown Highway in Queens to its intersection with the Connecting Highway between Queens and Brooklyn.

At the start of the trip along the Midtown Highway that traffic artery, reached by a ramp from the Queens portal of the new tunnel, was opened to public use by Borough President George U. Harvey after Mrs. Harvey had cut a ribbon stretched across the highway.

"First" Has to Be Hunted

Not until the motor parades were over was the new tunnel ready for public use, and even then it was necessary for a police motorcyclist to scurry out into the streets of Long Island City to find a "first car" to make the crossing to Manhattan.

Harry E. Sochovit, gasoline station operator, of 585 East Sixteenth Street, Brooklyn, was the first motorist to pay a toll for use of the tunnel. It was just 1:20 P. M. when he drove his tan coupé up to a toll booth, handed over his quarter, posed for photographers and sped on toward Manhattan.

At 1:30 P. M., with a crowd of 4,000 persons watching, John Topf, a chauffeur of 26-13 Jackson Avenue, Long Island City, entered the Manhattan end of the tunnel bound for Queens, where he paid his quarter on leaving the traffic plaza. There was a long line of cars waiting to enter the Manhattan portal of the tunnel, some having arrived as early as 9 A. M. The absence of a waiting line at the Queens portal was explained by the fact that the available space was pre-empted by guests' cars taking part in the opening ceremonies and the parades that followed.

Head of Authority Presides

Alfred R. Jones, chairman of the Tunnel Authority, presided at the dedicatory exercises and introduced a group of speakers that included Senator Robert F. Wagner, Mr. Morris, Borough President Stanley M. Isaacs of Manhattan, Borough President Harvey, Maurice E. Gilmore, Regional PWA Director, and George McAneny, president of the Regional Plan Association. Jesse H. Jones, Secretary of Commerce and chairman of the Reconstruction Finance Corporation, was unable to be present but sent a telegram. John J. Carmody, PWA Administrator, was also unable to attend and sent a telegram.

Deputy Mayor Rufus E. McGahen read a letter from Mayor La Guardia voicing his regret at not being able to be present. Regret at the Mayor's absence was also expressed by Chairman Jones, who added that

Continued on Page Nineteen

Helgoland, German Ship, Reported Caught, Sunk

Shipping circles received reports yesterday that the 2,927-ton German freighter Helgoland, which fled from Barranquilla, Colombia, Oct. 28, had been cornered and sunk in the Caribbean by British warships, according to The Associated Press.

The Hamburg-American line freighter, built in 1939, was reported to be carrying pilots of Scadta, German air line in South America, when she slipped out of port at night. She was reported to have put to sea to refuel a raider attacking South Atlantic shipping.

SPAIN IMPOSES GAG ON U. S. REPORTERS

Forbids Them to Send News, Charging We Refuse to Admit Spanish Writer

By T. J. HAMILTON
Special Cable to THE NEW YORK TIMES.

MADRID, Nov. 15—The Spanish Government today forbade all representatives of American newspapers and news agencies in Spain to send out any dispatches after a time to be fixed within a day or two.

It was stated that the action was taken in reprisal for the alleged refusal of the United States to grant a visa to the recently appointed Washington correspondent of E. F. E. [the foreign service of the official Spanish news agency, E. F. E.-Cifra.] Unofficially, however, it was understood that the United States had not refused a visa to the E. F. E. correspondent, but that it was merely a matter of Spain's expecting the wheels of the State Department in Washington to grind faster than usual.

The following communiqué was issued by the Press Bureau tonight:

"It is authorized to file stories to America declaring that, since the American authorities have not permitted the entry into the United States of a representative of the E. F. E. agency and the setting up of an office of said agency in said country, The United Press and The Associated Press agencies in this country will be abandoned."

Later an official spokesman said this order would apply also to The International News Service and to the Madrid correspondents of The Chicago Tribune and THE NEW YORK TIMES.

A spokesman for the director general of the Press Bureau at first stated that American correspondents would not be permitted to file dispatches after midnight Sunday night. Later, however, the correspondents were informed that they would be notified either directly by the Press Bureau or through their embassy when the prohibition would take effect.

Weddell to Ask Information

Special to THE NEW YORK TIMES.

WASHINGTON, Nov. 15—The State Department today cabled Alexander W. Weddell, the United States Ambassador in Madrid, requesting information concerning the suspension by the Spanish Government of American newspaper and news agency correspondents and their services.

The department denied, as alleged in Madrid, that it had refused visas for correspondents of E. F. E., the official Spanish news agency, or

Continued on Page Five

R.A.F. STRIKES AGAIN

Returns to Berlin After Losing Ten Planes in Raids on Reich

HAMBURG ALSO BATTERED

Bremen Attacked and 20 Nazi Airports From Norway to Brittany Bombed

By JAMES MacDONALD
Special Cable to THE NEW YORK TIMES.

LONDON, Saturday, Nov. 16—The heavy Royal Air Force bombers that battered Berlin railroad stations and freight yards for several hours yesterday morning and Thursday night carried out only one phase of widespread raids that had for their objectives twenty-six Nazi air bases and harbors and shipping all the way from Stavanger, Norway, to Lorient, Brittany, according to an Air Ministry announcement.

[Another British raid on Berlin last night was announced by the German radio in a broadcast heard here by the National Broadcasting Company. Six raiders were reported downed as soon as they crossed the Channel, and only twelve penetrated to the Berlin area, three of them being shot down in the city and the others in the outskirts, according to The United Press, however, Berlin enjoyed a raidless night.]

London officials would not disclose the size of their fleet of night raiders, but it was believed to have been large because the attack embraced so many points and was declared to have entailed heavy bombardments, particularly of Berlin.

The Air Ministry announced the loss of ten of the British raiders, which is a greater number than usual.

Cross-Channel Gun Duel

Meanwhile freakish weather entered the war picture again. After a spell of brilliant sunshine over the Strait of Dover in the forenoon, when British and German long-range gunners had a hot argument, a southwesterly gale, which is unwelcome news for German strategists who may still be clinging to plans for the invasion of Great Britain, sprang up last night. Heavy rain clouds scudded across the sky, while the wind churned up a rough sea.

The cross-Channel shelling began just before daybreak yesterday and lasted several hours. Big shells screeched angrily in both directions, but so far as the English side of the strait is concerned there was comparatively small damage and no casualties whatever, it was said, despite the fierceness of the barrage.

The British raiders who flew to Berlin during the night had the advantage of a full moon and perfect weather, according to the Air Ministry. The first wave is said to have reached the Nazi capital two hours after dark and was followed by other waves for several hours thereafter.

The reason for bombing Berlin's various large railroad terminals and extensive freight yards, it was pointed out here, is that Berlin is the most important focal point for the railroads of Central Europe. Whatever damage is done to them would affect not only Germany herself but also her transport to the adjacent countries she has conquered.

Power Plants Bombed

Targets in Berlin included the Stettiner Station, the Schlesischer Station and Anhalter Station, the Tempelhof railroad yards and freight yards between the Potsdamer and Anhalter Stations. Other Berlin objectives were the power station in the Charlottenburg district and the Wilmersdorf power station in the heart of the German capital.

One pilot who took part in the Berlin raid said he witnessed a terrific explosion which momentarily drowned out the city's guns. He told of seeing a big building go "sky high" and several fires breaking out all around.

Hamburg suffered a British bombardment that was said to have lasted nearly an hour. The principal goal there was the Rhenania Ossag Mineral Oil Works where fifteen bomb bursts were seen, according to R. A. F. reports.

Shipping and docks at Ostend, Havre and Lorient also were raided during the early hours of the morning as well as late Thursday night, it was added. Heavy attacks

Continued on Page Two

The International Situation

The compact industrial city of Coventry, lying northwest of London in the geographical heart of England, was devastated Thursday night by an estimated 500 German planes raining incendiary and demolition bombs on it for ten and a half hours. Casualties totaled at least 1,000 persons, many of them firemen, policemen and air-raid precaution workers who went about their jobs regardless of the storm of death from the skies. The bombing was done from a high altitude, the British said, the German planes dumping their loads indiscriminately over the city, and vital manufacturing plants suffered less than churches, schools, hospitals and the homes of the workers. [Page 1, Column 8.]

The Nazis boasted that it was the "greatest attack in the history of aerial warfare" and said it had crippled British aviation production. They said the raid was in retaliation for the British attack on Munich Nov. 8 while the Brown Shirts were celebrating the seventeenth anniversary of their beer hall revolt. [Page 3, Column 2.]

They were back over England again last night, subjecting some London areas to what was described as one of the heaviest raids of the war. Many fires were started. During the day the Royal Air Force took a measure of revenge for Coventry by shooting down eighteen planes with the loss of only one of their own, the Air Ministry said. [Page 1, Column 6.]

While the Germans were over Coventry, the Royal Air Force was giving Berlin what apparently was its heaviest attack, the Air Ministry reporting that the German capital's railway yards and stations—nerve center of the transportation system of Central Europe—were heavily and effectively attacked under perfect weather conditions. Seven stations also were reported hit. Berlin said the raid was the heaviest of the war. Another attack was in progress last night. Hamburg, the German base at Stavanger in Norway, and twenty-six Nazi airdromes were other objectives of the British pilots. [Page 1, Column 5.]

The Greeks continued to drive the Italian invaders before them all along the front, reports from Athens said, shock troops advancing to within a few miles of Koritza, and the defenders of Yanina, in the southwest, driving toward the border to threaten the Albanian port of Porto Edda. The Italians were reported in disorderly retreat in the latter area, where they previously had made their greatest advance into Greece. The land actions were supported by British and Greek bomber and fighter planes, harassing the Italian rear and attacking the ports through which reinforcements and supplies from Italy must come. [Page 1, Column 7.]

The Yugoslav border city of Bitolj was bombed again by three unidentified planes, the fourth time its neutrality had been invaded since the start of the Grecian campaign. The first bombing was Nov. 5, when three planes, unofficially identified as Italian, dropped bombs on the city, killing nineteen persons and wounding many others. Belgrade already was tense with reports of German troop concentrations along the Yugoslav-Rumanian border and the continued evacuation of German nationals from Greece. [Page 4, Column 5.]

That some new Axis military move was imminent seemed apparent with the announcement in Berlin and Rome of a conference at Innsbruck, Austria, of General Field Marshal Wilhelm Keitel, Chief of the German High Command, and Marshal Pietro Badoglio of Italy. The official Germany agency said it was a natural development, military action always following political action. The probability that what they discussed was a German-Italian attack on Gibraltar was seen in some quarters, who read that significance into the trip to Paris and Berlin of Spain's Foreign Minister, Ramon Serrano Suner. [Page 4, Col. 1.]

A Spanish ban on United States reporters was interpreted by some observers as another indication of impending military action against Gibraltar. The Spanish explanation of the order was that it was in retaliation for the refusal of Washington to grant a visa to a correspondent for the official Spanish news agency, EFE, or to allow it to operate in this country. State Department officials in Washington denied that any such refusal had been made. Not even an application has been made, they said. [Page 1, Column 4.]

The United States, however, did follow Britain in protesting to Spain against seizure of the former international zone of Tangier in Africa, which is on the Atlantic side of the Strait of Gibraltar and control of which would aid any attack on that British fortress. [Page 5, Column 1.]

BOMBING OF LONDON HEAVIEST IN MONTH

200 Planes Raid Capital, 80 in One Formation—Damage Is Reported Widespread

By The United Press.

LONDON, Saturday, Nov. 16—More than 200 German raiders, taking advantage of a full moon, a cloudless sky and a slight haze, last night and early today gave London its heaviest and most protracted pounding in a month.

Large formations of as many as eighty Nazi planes swept the capital and maintained a Blitzkrieg intensity for several hours after midnight and then dwindled to the customary parade of nuisance raiders until dawn. [The "all clear" sounded shortly before 7 A. M., according to The Associated Press.]

Two of the night raiders were reported to have been shot down.

Bombs damaged two hospitals. Incendiaries penetrated the dispensary of one hospital but were doused quickly by the staff before the flames reached medical supplies, some of an explosive nature. At the second hospital, two explosives landed on the grounds but did not cause any casualties.

Scores of Fires Started

LONDON, Saturday, Nov. 16 (AP)—German raiders during the night have started scores of fires, leveled apartment houses and buried civilians in the wreckage.

One whole block of apartments caved in, and the casualties were believed to be heavy. Sweating rescuers toiled in the ruins amid falling anti-aircraft shrapnel and bomb explosions. Firemen working their

Continued on Page Three

700 ITALIANS TAKEN AS GREEKS PUSH ON

Drive Is Aimed at Cutting Off Fascisti in South Albania—Koritza Again Bombed

By C. L. SULZBERGER
By Telephone to THE NEW YORK TIMES.

ATHENS, Greece, Nov. 15—Slashing its way further into Albania, the Greek Army completed its second day of full-fledged offensive action tonight by capturing 700 more Italian soldiers and forcing enemy units to retreat on at least two sectors.

Major encounters are obviously occurring, and once again the military communiqué refers to intensive infantry, artillery and aerial action. Three Italian planes were shot down and two Greek aircraft failed to return to their bases, it was said.

The Greek drive is aimed in two directions. The forces on the Epirus and the Pindus fronts are seeking to cut off Italian troops in Southern Albania. These units were heavily concentrated between Porto Edda and Konispolis when the war started. They launched the original attack, the impetus of which carried them considerably south of the Kalamas River.

Having cleaned up the Pindus sector and eliminated the remaining Italian outposts around Mount Smolika, the Greek Army is pushing down the Albanian side of Mount Grammos, north of Koritza, and fighting through Albania westward in the direction of Porto Edda.

This action is supported by another push from the region of Kalpaki and the march north by the units stationed near the Kalamas

Continued on Page Four

'REVENGE' BY NAZIS

Industrial City Bombed All Night in 'Reply' to R.A.F. Raid on Munich

CATHEDRAL IS DESTROYED

Homes and Shops Bear Brunt of Mass Assault—Military Damage Is Minimized

By RAYMOND DANIELL
Special Cable to THE NEW YORK TIMES.

LONDON, Nov. 15—Daybreak today unveiled scenes of devastation wrought in another night of widespread air raids, but there was nothing to match the bruised and battered face of Coventry, a little Midlands city that was the victim of one of the worst bombardments from the air since the Wright brothers presented wings to mankind.

There the Nazi bombers accomplished what they tried to do to this capital in the early days of the Battle of London, by using as big a force of sky marauders against that compact city of 250,000 as they used against London with its 8,000,000 inhabitants. The tons of bombs they dropped caused at least 1,000 casualties, wrecked countless homes and destroyed the lovely fourteenth-century St. Michael's Cathedral, one of the finest examples of perpendicular architecture left in these islands.

To accomplish the full purpose of the assault, which the Germans said was intended as revenge for the Royal Air Force bombing of Munich while Reichsfuehrer Hitler was speaking there last Friday, Nazi raiders made repeated feints against London to keep the defenders busy while the main body of attackers roared over Midlands industrial centers and concentrated the fury of their bombings on Coventry.

Debris Marks Cathedral Site

Visitors to Coventry today found a scene of devastation where the cathedral once stood. The blackened arches and window faces of fretted stone, for all their disfigurement, still retained traces of their stately grace. But blocks of masonry, heavy pieces of church furniture and plaques commemorating the lives of famous men merged in the common dust heaped up between the teetering walls.

Elsewhere in the city other buildings had been severely damaged. Throughout the day business men and shopkeepers salvaged what remained of their possessions by grubbing among shattered timber and piled-up bricks. Some shopkeepers were doing business on the sidewalks. On roads leading away from the city could be seen a pitiful parade of refugees who were trying to reach billets in the countryside before black-out time.

Coventry lies in the very heart of England, almost equidistant, about ninety miles, from four great ports—Liverpool, Bristol, London and Hull. An industrial center specializing in the manufacture of motor cars and cycles, Coventry is an important cog in Britain's war machine.

But it was not Coventry's factories that took the worst punishment from the raiders, but human life, little homes, churches and hospitals—as it has been everywhere in Britain since the Nazis, forced to fly high above barrage balloons and anti-aircraft guns, began their concentrated bombings.

Scenes of Damage Everywhere

It was impossible today to stroll through many of the streets of the ancient city, where Lady Godiva is said to have made her famous ride, without seeing tragic evidence of the hell loosed from the skies through the night, when bombs crashed at intervals of one or two minutes.

Coventry is now like a city that has been wrecked by an earthquake and swept by fire. Its people looked dazed today as they poked about the ruins of their homes and surveyed the wreckage of the downtown business section, and they laughed bitterly at the chalked mottoes of defiance to Hitler scrawled on pavements and buildings.

The local authorities lost no time in starting to repair the damage and in caring for the injured, homeless and hungry. Herbert Morrison, the Minister of Home Security, was on the scene directing relief operations. Orders were issued for the release of stores of emergency food if necessary, and shopkeepers and wholesalers who normally compete against one another cooperated to assure the distribution of essential supplies.

There was much to be done. Tele-

Continued on Page Three

Hoover Urges Aid to 5 Little Democracies; Says Famine and Disease Peril War Victims

Special to THE NEW YORK TIMES.

POUGHKEEPSIE, N. Y., Nov. 15—Former President Herbert Hoover in an address at Vassar College tonight renewed his plea for international assistance to the conquered nations of Europe, with a warning that famine and its accompanying epidemic diseases would reach an acute stage there this Winter or next Spring.

Mr. Hoover named specifically "the five little democracies" of Finland, Norway, Holland, Belgium and Central Poland, and asserted that the United States had a moral responsibility toward these nations, all of which, he said, "sacrificed and fought against overwhelming odds to maintain freedom and their democratic ideals."

"I am not making any proposals as to the French, although they are indeed suffering, because of the present obscurity of their food and political situation," he added.

Reiterating his proposal for a lifting of the British blockade to permit the passage of shiploads of food to be distributed under German guarantees and neutral control, Mr. Hoover emphasized the increased urgency of the situation since he first advanced the program three months ago.

"The people of Brussels are already on a ration of seven ounces of bread a day," he pointed out. "Typhus already rages in Warsaw. Holland is killing its animals for lack of feed."

Though lives and "infinite suffering" still could be saved, Mr. Hoover asserted, no time should be lost in the effort, for three months would be required to set up the necessary organization.

At the same time he discussed arguments that Germany would then

Continued on Page Seven

1941

"All the News That's Fit to Print."

The New York Times.

LATE CITY EDITION
Fair, slightly colder today. Tomorrow fair, little change in temperature.
Temperatures Yesterday—Max., 42; Min., 32

Copyright, 1941, by The New York Times Company.

VOL. XC...No. 30,368. Entered as Second-Class Matter, Postoffice, New York, N. Y. NEW YORK, WEDNESDAY, MARCH 12, 1941. THREE CENTS NEW YORK CITY and Vicinity

PRESIDENT SIGNS, STARTS WAR AID; TO ASK $7,000,000,000 FUND TODAY; BRITISH SEA LOSSES RISE SHARPLY

BUS STRIKERS FIRM AS 20 DAY PASSES; MAYOR HINTS HOPE

Indicates He May See C. I. O. Leader Today—Throngs Tax Subways in Rush Hours

24-HOUR OFFER EXPIRES

Lines Won't Extend Proposal to Negotiate on Old Contract —Union Replies to Charges

The strike of the 3,500 employes of the Fifth Avenue Coach Company and the New York City Omnibus Corporation, called at 5 A. M. on Monday by the Transport Workers Union, C. I. O. affiliate, remained 100 per cent effective last night with all of the companies' 1,300 buses still idle in picketed garages and their 900,000 daily riders compelled to depend, for the second successive day, on subways and other substitute facilities.

There was one faint ray of hope of a settlement, however, as Mayor La Guardia, leaving his office at City Hall at 6:30 P. M., hinted that he might confer today with Allan S. Haywood, C. I. O. National Director of Organization.

The Mayor threw out this hint after he had conferred with John A. Ritchie, board chairman of the two companies, and Boykin C. Wright, their counsel. Mr. Ritchie and Mr. Wright came to City Hall soon after 5 P. M. to meet the Mayor, who had just returned from a trip to Washington, where he appeared before a Congressional committee on military affairs.

Mayor Makes Statement

Following the afternoon meeting at City Hall, the Mayor made the following statement:

"In response to my announcement that I would be here at 5 o'clock ready to receive either or both sides, and I expressed the hope that both sides would be here, Mr. Ritchie and Mr. Wright came here. The other side did not.

"I cannot settle an agreement with one side only. I just can't understand this attitude, and I repeat that this is a matter which concerns the welfare of the City of New York and again announce that I am ready to aid in bringing about restoration of service and a settlement of any dispute which may exist either by direct negotiation—I am assured of this by the employers—mediation or arbitration."

The Mayor revealed that he had talked to Mr. Haywood by phone in Washington. He indicated that the C. I. O. leader might come to New York today and that the two of them might confer at City Hall.

Set for Long Strike

Former Councilman Michael J. Quill, international head of the union, and other officers of the organization, at a mass meeting of 3,000 of the striking employes and 1,500 other union men employed on city-operated transit lines, declared that the union was prepared for a long strike, if necessary.

"The strike will go on from day to day, week to week, or even month to month, until victory is won, Mr. Quill declared. Other speakers, who joined with Mr. Quill in urging the men to stand firm, were Austin Hogan, president of the New York local; John Santo, international secretary-treasurer; Harry Sacher, counsel, and Matthias Kearns, general organizer of bus workers.

While the mass meeting was in progress the companies issued a statement declaring that their offer to resume negotiations on the basis of an extension of the old contracts that expired Feb. 28 had been withdrawn. This offer was made Monday after Mr. Ritchie and Mr. Wright had conferred with the Mayor at City Hall.

"That twenty-four-hour period has now expired," the statement declared. "Not having heard further from the Mayor as to this, it is not our intention to extend the twenty-four-hour period."

During the mass meeting of the striking employes telegrams from many labor organizations endorsing the strike were read by union leaders. Later in the day the executive board of the Greater New York Industrial Council, an organization of 300 C. I. O. unions with a claimed membership of 600,000 workers, adopted resolutions pledging full support of the strike and deploring "the fact that the Mayor has chosen to support the companies in the dispute."

Reply to Companies

The union distributed to its members and to the public handbills replying to arguments advanced by the companies in paid advertisements published in newspapers. These handbills charged the companies with responsibility for the strike and the attendant inconvenience to the riding public.

The total immobilization of the 1,300 buses operated by the two

Continued on Page Thirteen

Cabs Flock to Manhattan As Strike Yields Bonanza

There was no lack of taxis in Manhattan yesterday despite the bus strike and the downpour of rain, as nearly all of New York's 13,838 cabs, it seemed, crowded into the borough to pick up fares. About half of them were empty.

The cabbies made a holiday of it on Fifth Avenue, literally taking up all the space from curb to curb. The machines sped almost bumper to bumper up and down the avenue, and the traffic policemen let them have the right of way.

Cruising cabs are not ordinarily permitted on Fifth Avenue, but yesterday and for the duration of the strike they will be a "necessary evil" traffic, as one patrolman put it.

COAL MINERS SEEK $1-A-DAY PAY RISE

200 Days' Work a Year Among Demands Read by Lewis to Bituminous Parley

A blanket increase of $1 a day for all regular classifications of inside and outside day men, with corresponding increases for piece workers, was the demand presented by the United Mine Workers in behalf of 450,000 soft-coal miners before the Appalachian joint conference of miners and operators that convened at the Hotel Biltmore yesterday to negotiate a new agreement for the industry. The present agreement, negotiated two years ago, expires April 1.

Represented in the conference are operators from eight States of the Appalachian region where wage and working conditions determine standards in all bituminous regions throughout the country.

Contrary to expectations, the union's demands did not include the 6-hour day and 30-hour week, but called for a minimum guarantee of 200 days work a year, two-week vacations with pay and rigid safeguards against accidents enforceable by the organization.

Lewis Reads Demands

The demands were presented in a formal statement read by John L. Lewis, president of the United Mine Workers and former president of the C. I. O. This was followed by his first public address since his radio campaign speech in support of Wendell L. Willkie for the Presidency.

Backing Mr. Lewis in the wage negotiations was the union's policy committee of 150, consisting of executive officers of the union's national and district organizations, members of the international executive board and the scale committee. Mr. Lewis was attended among others by Philip Murray, vice president of the United Mine Workers and president of the C. I. O., and Thomas Kennedy, secretary-treasurer of the U. M. W.

Mr. Murray's presence served to emphasize the relation between the negotiations in the soft coal industry and the situation in steel arising from the demands presented recently by Mr. Murray to leading steel companies. The steel situation is expected to reach a crisis at about the time when the soft coal agreement expires. The close affinity of coal and steel and their bearing on national defense lent a prime importance to the demands presented yesterday by Mr. Lewis.

While the operators characterized these demands as "formidable," the impression prevailing in U. M. W. circles was that an agreement would be reached without a stoppage in the industry. Neither Ezra Van Horn, executive vice president of the Ohio Coal Association, who was elected president of the joint conference, nor Charles O'Neill, head of the United Eastern Coal Corporation, press spokesman for the operators, would comment on the union's demands. The operators will meet today to consider the proposals and will make their reply at an open session of the conference in the Biltmore tomorrow morning.

Government a Partner

The union's wage demands make the government a partner in the negotiations in so far as any increase in operating costs for the owners would have to be considered by the Bituminous Coal Commission under the Guffey Coal Stabilization act in any price readjustments that the commission might find it necessary to make. It was believed likely that President Roosevelt would intervene in the event of an impasse in the negotiations, as the government intervened to break the deadlock between the miners and operators two years ago after a stoppage of six weeks. At that time the main issue was establishment of a tight union shop in the soft coal industry. In this the union was victorious.

It was Mr Lewis's contention yesterday that the wage increases demanded would add a maximum of only 17 cents a ton to the price of soft coal, based on figures obtained from records of the Bituminous Coal Commission. He was certain this increase could be borne by the industry out of present and pro-

Continued on Page Eleven

BALDWIN ELECTED TO SEAT IN HOUSE BY MARGIN OF 6,562

Republican Polls 23,252 Votes Against 16,690 for Alfange and 3,985 for Connolly

WILLKIE HAILS VICTORY

Calls It 'Forward Step Toward Unity' as Winner Gives Him and Policies Chief Credit

City Councilman Joseph Clark Baldwin was chosen yesterday at a special election to serve as Representative in Congress from the Seventeenth (Silk Stocking) district. He succeeds the late Kenneth F. Simpson, also a Republican, who died after less than a month in office.

Dean A. Alfange, the Democratic candidate, conceded defeat a little after 7 P. M. when returns indicated that he would lose by about 6,000 votes. Eugene P. Connolly, American Labor party candidate, the only one of the three to campaign in opposition to the aid-to-Britain policy and the defense program, was out of the running.

The final vote, with no election districts missing, was:

Baldwin, R.	23,252
Alfange, D.	16,690
Connolly, A. L.	3,985

The results were described by Mr. Baldwin and by Wendell L. Willkie, one of his principal backers, to whom Mr. Baldwin gave chief credit, as a victory for national unity on foreign policy. In a statement issued at Baldwin headquarters Mr. Willkie said the vote also indicated that the doctrine of isolationism was losing ground.

Statement by Willkie

Mr. Willkie's statement follows:

"I am greatly gratified by the election of Joseph Clark Baldwin. He will ably represent his district in Congress. The issues were larger, however, than even Joseph Baldwin's fine capacity for public service. The result is a great forward step toward unity in our country's foreign policy and likewise for competence in the administration of our defense program and sanity in our domestic policies. The people of the Seventeenth District of New York have gone clearly on record in favor of full and immediate aid to the democracies of the world in their struggle against totalitarianism.

"The election also indicates that the doctrine of isolationism is rapidly losing favor with American voters. In a very few years that doctrine will be only a memory in both the Republican and Democratic parties."

After thanking his campaign workers Mr. Baldwin made a radio speech over Station WMCA and then paid a visit to Mrs. Helen Porter Simpson, widow of his predecessor.

"I am gratified and proud at the result of this election," he told his campaign workers. "Gratified that the district which I had served for so many years has expressed its continued confidence in me and proud and pleased that we can face our enemies abroad with further proof of the unity that exists in the democracy on its foreign policy to aid all other democracies in their struggle against aggression.

"There is no doubt about the fact that the splendid support I have received from many people but particularly from Wendell Willkie, who is leading the fight in our party for national unity on foreign policy, contributed largely to my success."

Thomas J. Curran, Republican county leader, in a statement telephoned from St. Catherine's Hospital, Brooklyn, where he is confined with a fractured hip, said the re-

Continued on Page Fourteen

British Reported Landing Troops at Greek Ports

By The United Press.

BELGRADE, Wednesday, March 12—Unconfirmed reports reached diplomatic circles here early today that a big British expeditionary force from North Africa was being landed at Piraeus, the port of Athens, for action on the Greek front.

It also was reported that British transports were about to land troops at Salonika, key Greek port at the top of the Aegean Sea, barely sixty miles from where German mechanized forces are massed along the Bulgarian-Greek Macedonian border.

Diplomats in Belgrade heard, without any direct confirmation, that forty British military transports arrived yesterday at Piraeus and began unloading troops.

The British expeditionary force, it was said, was drawn from General Sir Archibald Wavell's Army of the Nile in Egypt and Libya after the shattering of Marshal Rodolfo Graziani's Italian North African forces.

ITALIAN TROOPSHIP IS SUNK BY BRITISH

Laden Transport Is Torpedoed in Mediterranean—Tripoli Bases Suffer in Raids

Special Cable to THE NEW YORK TIMES.

LONDON, March 11—The Admiralty announced tonight that a British submarine had torpedoed and sunk a heavily laden Italian troop transport of the Sicilia class, 9,646 tons.

[A Sicilia of this tonnage is listed in Lloyd's Register as an Italian passenger vessel that was under German registry as the Coblenz until 1935. She was built in 1923 in Bremen. There is no reference to a Sicilia "class."]

The communiqué does not specify the whereabouts of the sinking or the name of the submarine. It says however, that the sinking has been confirmed by the British Commander in Chief in the Mediterranean.

Raids on Tripoli Pressed

CAIRO, Egypt, March 11 (AP)—The Royal Air Force announced tonight that it had made heavy overnight raids on Tripoli and airdromes in Tripolitania last night and early today, destroying two enemy aircraft on the ground, damaging others and setting off a large fire and loud explosions.

Air raiders again bombed the Suez Canal area today, but caused no damage, the Egyptian Government reported.

[The Germans say that traffic through the Suez Canal has been paralyzed by ships sunk in the channel by previous air attacks.]

"An air-raid warning was sounded early this morning in the Suez Canal area, in the course of which a few bombs were dropped," the Egyptian Ministry of the Interior announced. "No damage or casualties resulted."

Malta Attacked Again

CAIRO, Egypt, March 11 (UP)—Axis aircraft attacked Malta yesterday, but there were no R. A. F. casualties, today's R. A. F. communiqué said. Enemy aircraft also approached Port Said and Ismailia.

Continued on Page Four

WEEK'S SINKINGS, 29

Tonnage Total 148,038 Nearly Double Average During February

BATTLE OF ATLANTIC IS ON

Admiralty Says Spring Drive Has Begun—Former U. S. Destroyers Active

By ROBERT P. POST

Special Cable to THE NEW YORK TIMES.

LONDON, March 11—A grim footnote was written to the signature of the lease-lend bill today when the Admiralty announced that shipping losses for the week ended March 2 were the third highest than for any week of the war.

During the week for which the figures were published today twenty-nine ships were sunk with a total tonnage of 148,038, twenty of them being British, of 102,871 tons; eight allied, of 42,970 tons, and one neutral, of 2,197 tons.

The only two worse weeks were one in October last year and one in September of the same year, when the losses were 215,000 tons and 176,000 tons respectively.

The average weekly figure since the war began, excluding Dunkerque, has been 63,342 tons.

It is true that these figures are about half of what the Germans and Italians claim. It is true that they include losses from a big convoy which the Germans caught during that week. It is probably also true that the progress of the battle for the Atlantic should not be judged by one week alone and that the February shipping losses still totaled only 300,000, or less than that for last November and the five preceding months.

Yet there are a lot of "buts." The days are getting longer, the seas are getting smoother and the German attack on shipping—Reichsfuehrer Hitler's boasted first Spring activity—apparently is being speeded up.

Atlantic Battle Started

Even while British news agencies are pouring out soothing qualification of the losses and talking of vague, new methods of defense and reminding readers that the more submarines, the more targets, they also are reminding the public that they will probably have to face as bad, or worse in the future. If, as the British seem to think, the Battle of the Atlantic has started, then the Germans seem to be doing pretty well.

It is not the farthest cry from these figures reflecting sudden death by torpedo or bomb, or slower death in the freezing waters of the North Sea, to a quiet office in Washington where the lease-lend bill was signed today. For it is a firm British belief that, firstly, they are only fighting the battle of Britain for the purpose of keeping open sea lanes, the most important of which lead to Canada and the United States, from where that which is lent or leased must come. Secondly, that they cannot win that battle without United States help. There is some doubt as to whether Britain can feed herself and still transport her war supplies in her own bottoms. She may have to ask the United States to provide convoys for them. One thing is almost definitely certain. Britain cannot beat the combined menace of plane, submarine and raider unless she gets more warships from the United States.

More Destroyers Expected

The British are correspondingly pleased with reports that the first move after the bill has become law will be transference of many more destroyers and escort vessels. But even here there is more the United States can do than turn over ships as was done with the first fifty now forming the Town class of destroyers which are most active.

There is hardly a British convoy in which you will not find one. But the British want even more. It took some time to fit those destroyers for heavy duty work in the North Sea and with the special devices necessary for the modern submarine hunter and aircraft carrier. The British, their own shipyards overburdened with building and repairs, would like to see these ships entirely fixed up for the job they will have to do—except possibly for the mounting of special anti-aircraft guns—then sent over in little batches as soon as can be done.

Incidentally, the British—or many of those in a position to know—would like to see them manned by United States sailors. For the supply of trained seamen is getting

Continued on Page Ten

Strike Is Called at Jersey Aluminum Plant Working 7 Days a Week on Defense Orders

Special to THE NEW YORK TIMES.

EDGEWATER, N. J., Wednesday, March 12—Three thousand workers at the sheet mill of the Aluminum Company of America here were called out on strike early this morning by the executive committee of the Aluminum Workers of America, Local 15, a C. I. O. affiliate.

The men were asked to quit work in the plant, which has been working day and night solely on defense orders, after the executive committee returned from Pittsburgh, where conferences were held with company officials. The committee had been authorized on Friday by the workers to call a strike whenever it was deemed necessary.

The first announcement of the strike call came from the Edgewater police at 1:40 A. M. They said they did not know how effective the walkout was. Should the sheet mill suspend operations, it was said, the whole plant would have to discontinue work.

Although no union or company officials were reached after the police announced the walkout, it was said that the union had requested an increase of ten cents an hour for workers and time and a half for overtime. These request were endorsed by a vote of 1,641 to 65 on Friday, when the workers gave the executive committee the right to call a strike.

The company recently began construction of an eight-story building to help fill the defense orders for the government. Many plant parts are made at the present plant.

The C. I. O. union was made the collective bargaining agent at the plant about a year and a half ago following an election that was contested by an A. F. of L. union.

Members of the Edgewater Police Department were sent to the plant. At 3 o'clock this morning they had received no report of any disorder there.

The International Situation

WEDNESDAY, MARCH 12, 1941

President Roosevelt signed the lease-lend bill yesterday afternoon after the House had passed it with the Senate amendments by a vote of 317 to 71. Then he started on the way to Britain and Greece war materials from the stores of the United States Army and Navy. Further, he went to work on a request to be sent to Congress today for the immediate appropriation of $7,000,000,000 to put into highest gear the gigantic effort in behalf of the democracies. During his busy day, the President also discussed industrial production with Bernard M. Baruch, chairman of the War Industries Board of the last war, and had other conferences with officials intimately associated with the defense program and with Congressional leaders. [Page 1, Column 8.]

American planes will reach Britain in time for the expected Nazi Spring drive, Sir Archibald Sinclair, British Air Secretary, told the Commons. He depicted "fleets of airplanes" crossing the ocean and challenged Adolf Hitler to produce a secret weapon to meet this ever-swelling swarm of planes. In giving hitherto undisclosed war figures, he said that Britain had destroyed 4,250 German planes and 1,100 Italian planes, and had lost fewer than 1,800 of her own. [Page 5, Column 5.]

Nazi air raiders, meanwhile, were active over many parts of Britain, but chiefly in the industrial Midlands and at a northwest town, which was bombed for hours last night by wave after wave of German planes. The Portsmouth naval base was bombed for six hours Monday night with many casualties and the loss of seven German planes, it was announced. [Page 2, Column 2.]

R. A. F. bombing planes struck another heavy blow at Cologne, the German transportation center, where fires were started in factories and the famous Hohenzollern bridge approaches hit and set ablaze. Invasion ports and airdromes in Northern France were visited. [Page 2, Column 6.]

In the warfare at sea there was every indication that the threatened "Blitz" campaign was on. London announced the sinking by the Axis in the week ended March 2 of twenty-nine ships totaling 148,038 tons, almost twice the average weekly tonnage losses in February. [Page 1, Column 5.]

With the Thai-Indo-Chinese border settlement concluded [Page 10, Column 2, with map], Japanese Foreign Minister Matsuoka announced he would depart tonight from Tokyo for Moscow and the Axis capitals. Although his trip was viewed in Tokyo as an evil omen for the democracies, it was suggested Japan was unlikely to take any violent steps until she saw how the Axis Spring drive was going. [Page 6, Column 4.]

Both Berlin and Rome saw in Mr. Matsuoka's journey at this time special significance in the light of the passage of the lease-lend bill. In Berlin it was termed an answer to the action of the United States Congress. [Page 6, Column 5.]

An unsuccessful attempt was made to assassinate in an Istanbul hotel George W. Rendel, departing British Minister to Bulgaria. Two powerful bombs that had been placed in the luggage of the Legation party, apparently on the train that had taken them from Sofia, exploded in the lobby of the hotel, killing six persons and wounding others, including members of the British party. The Minister was uninjured. [Page 1, Column 6.]

Turkish sources reported that the Soviet Foreign Commissar had assured the Turkish envoy in Moscow that Russia would not attack Turkey if she entered the war. The Turks heard of more Nazi troop movements into Bulgaria and were considering plans for evacuating Istanbul. [Page 8, Column 2; Map, Page 8.]

The Yugoslav Government has been confronted with an internal crisis and Regent Prince Paul has called an emergency meeting of the Crown Council for today. A rising sentiment against Yugoslavia's yielding to German demands threatens to overthrow the present government. [Page 8, Column 3.]

Italian resistance in Ethiopia appeared to be on the verge of collapsing as British forces closed in on all invasion points and opened up a new front near the Sudanese border. [Page 7, Column 1; Map, Page 7.] The British Admiralty announced that a submarine had torpedoed a heavily laden Italian troopship. Both British and Axis planes were active on the North African front from Tripoli to the Suez Canal. [Page 1, Column 4.]

BRITISH DIPLOMATS BOMBED IN TURKEY

Blast in Istanbul Hotel Is Believed Aimed at Envoy From Sofia—6 Killed

By G. E. R. GEDYE

Wireless to THE NEW YORK TIMES.

ISTANBUL, Turkey, March 11—Explosion of an infernal machine in the entrance hall of the British-occupied Hotel Pera Palace here within a few minutes of the arrival at 9:15 o'clock tonight of George W. Rendel, British Minister to Bulgaria, and his party of sixty-seven, killed or injured twenty-three persons.

[Six persons, all Turks, were killed, according to The United Press. After ten persons of unidentified nationality had been questioned by Turkish police, the authorities announced that it was "almost certain" that the bombs had been planted in Sofia in luggage accompanying the British mission.]

Seven of the injured were Britons, two of them being diplomats from Sofia and two others attached to the British diplomatic mission in Turkey.

This correspondent visited the hotel shortly after the bombing occurred and just after the dead and injured had been removed. The entire ground floor wall was blown out. The street was littered with fragments of the great plate glass windows, bits of window casements, broken chairs, tables, trunks and suitcases that had been blown into the street.

The explosion occurred while the first members of the British Minister's party were registering their names in the hotel lobby. Mr. Rendel himself was not in the lobby and was not hurt.

It is believed that the bomb was

Continued on Page Nine

URGES U. S. CHARTER FOR CORPORATIONS

O'Mahoney Statement at Final TNEC Session Says We Need an Economic Constitution

Special to THE NEW YORK TIMES.

WASHINGTON, March 11—The economic demobilization which the United States will face at the end of the national defense effort can be cushioned only by "a national economic constitution which shall abolish the economic uncertainties which seem to threaten even our political system," said Senator O'Mahoney of Wyoming today in closing the public sessions of the Temporary National Economic Committee, of which he is chairman.

After nearly three years of work, he stated, the committee has only to complete its task. For his part, he recommended that the report include the following steps:

1. National charters for national corporations which transact business on a national scale in order that they may have a definite and a free place in our economy, and local business may be differentiated and protected from national business.

2. The effective and thorough enforcement of the anti-trust laws to maintain competition and to prevent all combinations and agreements that destroy business.

3. The encouragement of new business and small enterprise by revision of the tax laws for the purpose of encouraging new employment and new industry.

4. A national conference called by Congress of representatives of business, labor, agriculture and consumers to concentrate public thought and action on the objectives on which there is general agreement instead of, as now, on

Continued on Page Fifteen

FINAL STEP SWIFT

White House Is Waiting When the House Votes Bill, 317 to 71

MATERIALS MOVED AT ONCE

Kind of Assistance Sent First Is Not Revealed—Greece Is Sharing and China May

By TURNER CATLEDGE

Special to THE NEW YORK TIMES.

WASHINGTON, March 11—President Roosevelt signed the history-making lease-lend bill at 3:50 P. M. today immediately after receiving it from the Capitol, where the House completed action by accepting the Senate amendments by a vote of 317 to 71.

Five minutes after the bill was signed the President approved a list of undisclosed quantities of war materials to be transferred at once from the American Army and Navy to the British and the Greeks, to bolster these powers in their life-and-death struggle with the Axis. Most of these first materials, the nature of which the President guarded, will go to Great Britain.

Having thus promptly set the machinery in motion toward making the United States "the arsenal of democracy," Mr. Roosevelt began work on a request to be sent to Congress tomorrow for an immediate appropriation of $7,000,000,000 with which to press the lease-lend effort to the fullest possible extent under the new law. This, he intimated, would be likely to include help to China as well as to Great Britain and Greece, and to all other nations which later may find themselves under threat of the Berlin-Rome-Tokyo alliance.

The President apparently paid no attention to threats of "isolation" Senators to continue their opposition in an appeal to the country. Proposals for a campaign "to keep the United States out of war" were reported to have been discussed at a meeting of opponents of the lease-lend bill at the Capitol today.

Plan to Speed Appropriations

Another Congressional fight may be expected when the $7,000,000,000 appropriation comes up. The President announced he would send his request to Capitol Hill tomorrow in a letter to Speaker Rayburn.

In first disclosing the proposal to a group of Congressional leaders early in the day he suggested that a subcommittee of the Appropriations Committee of each house be set up to keep in touch with him on progress.

A short time after this conference, but more as a coincidence than as a result, the move in the House for an independent committee of nine members to investigate and keep a continuing check on defense operations apparently blew up. The House voted, 252 to 112, to table a resolution offered by Representative Cox of Georgia, authorizing such procedure.

In the midst of the rapid-fire moves incident to final enactment and signature of the lease-lend bill, the President took time to consider plans for the further speeding up of industrial production. It was understood to have talked over various proposals with Bernard M. Baruch, chairman of the War Industries Board of the first World War, at a luncheon conference at his desk. Relations between the President and Mr. Baruch are becoming almost weekly affairs.

Mr. Baruch is known to hold that a much more extensive industrial mobilization than yet undertaken must be put into force if the production job imposed upon this country is to be carried out successfully. He favors a revision of the priorities set-up of the Office of Production Management, as well as some sort of ceiling to guard the program against runaway prices. He is reported, moreover, to be urging the President to simplify the present rambling defense set-up under a single head, with greater authority.

Plans a Radio Talk Soon

Tightening up of the defense production mechanism all along the line is understood to be definitely among the President's plans. He may disclose some of his intentions in a radio "fireside chat" which he plans tentatively to deliver soon.

The President not only declined to reveal any of the items on the list of immediately transferable materials, but would not disclose the dollar-value, although he said that a calculation had been made on the basis of original costs. He gave assurances that details would be re-

Continued on Page Three

As a result of the Lend-Lease Act, the United States sent military and civilian equipment to its allies.

Hideki Tojo was Japan's Prime Minister during World War II.

After visiting Mussolini in Italy, Generallisimo Francisco Franco met with Marshall Pétain in Montpellier, France.

1941

Orson Welles as Charles Foster Kane, gubernatorial candidate, in the 1941 classic, *Citizen Kane.*

Cary Grant and Joan Fontaine in *Suspicion.*

The Maltese Falcon starred Humphrey Bogart, Peter Lorre, Mary Astor and Sydney Greenstreet.

"All the News That's Fit to Print."

The New York Times.

LATE CITY EDITION
Occasional rain, little change in temperature today. Tomorrow partly cloudy, continued cool.
Temperatures Yesterday—Max., 47; Min., 40

Section 1

NEWS INDEX, PAGE 51, THIS SECTION

VOL. XC No. 30,388.
Entered as Second-Class Matter, Postoffice, New York, N. Y.
NEW YORK, SUNDAY, APRIL 6, 1941.
Including Rotogravure Picture, Magazine and Book Review
TEN CENTS New York City and Vicinity

GERMANS INVADE YUGOSLAVIA AND GREECE; HITLER ORDERS WAR, BLAMING THE BRITISH; MOSCOW SIGNS AMITY PACT WITH BELGRADE

U. S. STEEL STRIKE IS CALLED BY C. I. O., EFFECTIVE TUESDAY

Murray Says Wage Talks Failed and Plans Picketing in Tie-Up Involving 261,000 Men

ROOSEVELT MAY STEP IN

President Is Reported to Have Summoned C. I. O. Chief in Move to Bar Walkout

By The Associated Press.

PITTSBURGH, April 5 — The C. I. O. Steel Workers Organizing Committee tonight ordered its members in all steel mills of the giant United States Steel Corporation, employing about 261,000 wage-earners, to stop work at midnight next Tuesday.

The union said that negotiations for a wage increase and other benefits had collapsed.

Philip Murray, C. I. O. president and chairman of the Steel Workers Organizing Committee, telegraphed instructions to local union units of the corporation to establish c-ntinuous picket lines at all plant gates.

[The United Press reported from Pittsburgh last night it had learned authoritatively that President Roosevelt, concerned over the threatened stoppage, had invited Mr. Murray to a White House conference tomorrow or Tuesday.]

The company produces more than one-third of America's steel, an amount exceeding all of that made in England. It hold millions of dollars in defense contracts.

Mr. Murray termed the cessation of work a "lockout" rather than a strike, asserting that the company had rejected his suggestion to continue negotiations, which began March 20, another week, with any agreement to be retroactive to April 1. The company was said to be willing to make the agreement retroactive only to April 8.

The sudden development, threatening to spread the nation's strike area to the vital steel industry, came during an interim of wage negotiations, which still are scheduled tc be resumed Monday at 10 A. M.

Mr. Murray called in 100 local union leaders today for conference. It was the third such meeting since the union made known its nine-point demands, which included a wage increase of 10 cents an hour, a closed shop, check-off of union dues by the company, liberalized vacations and establishment of seniority rights.

The company's minimum pay, established in 1937, is 62½ cents an hour, with the average pay of wage-earners about 87 cents an hour. This contract expired April 1 and was extended to April 8.

The company's original counter-offer of a 2½ cents an hour wage rise was rejected by Mr. Murray. Tonight it was learned this offer had been raised to five cents an hour but again was refused by the union. The company contended it made but $60,000,000 of its $102,000,000 profit last year in its steel plants. The other profits came from coal, cement shipping and other subsidiaries. The company has insisted it cannot increase wages without increasing the price of steel. The Government has firmly refused to sanction any such price advance.

In his instructions to local unions, Mr. Murray said:

"The Carnegie-Illinois Steel Company has either rejected entirely or submitted unsatisfactory counter proposals with respect to each of the points offered by the S. W. O. C. in its program.

"The S. W. O. C. will attempt to arrive at an agreement with the companies involved to provide for the continuance at work of the necessary maintenance men during the suspension of operations. Further instructions regarding this situation will be forwarded to you by wire.

"Peaceful picket lines shall be established at all plant gates and maintained at all times during the cessation of work. There should be no violence or other unlawful acts on the part of members or representatives of the S. W. O. C."

No comment was forthcoming from the company on the development.

Continued on Page Forty-one

The International Situation

SUNDAY, APRIL 6, 1941

Germany's armies this morning launched a vast attack upon Yugoslavia and Greece. The move was announced over the Berlin radio in an order of the day from Reichsfuehrer Hitler, read by Propoganda Minister Goebbels; it denounced "the Belgrade government of intrigue" and said German troops would not lay down their arms until "this band of ruffians" and every last Briton had been eliminated from Southeastern Europe. [Page 1, Column 8.]

As Belgrade's first air raid was reported, it was believed the principal Nazi attacks had been launched from Bulgaria, one across Southern Yugoslavia and another southward toward Salonika. Bulgaria's army was said to have an active role, but Hungary's was believed inactive for the present. The Yugoslavs were expected to fight a rear-guard delaying action until they reached their strong natural defense positions. The Belgrade Government had planned to evacuate the capital, going to some southern point. The United States Minister was reported remaining in Belgrade. [Page 1, Column 5.]

With dramatic suddenness Yugoslavia and Soviet Russia signed a five-year non-aggression and friendship pact providing that if either signatory became the victim of aggression by a third State the other would maintain a policy of "strictest friendship." The pact will take effect immediately and the articles of ratification will be exchanged in Belgrade "at the earliest possible moment." [Page 1, Column 4.]

On the African front, British Headquarters in Cairo reported that an Axis advance east of Bengazi, Libya, "has been successfully held and the situation is well in hand." Empire forces in Ethiopia crossed the Awash River, to a point only eighty miles from Addis Ababa, while other units driving down on the capital from Eritrea captured Adowa and Adigrat. [Page 1, Column 6; Map, Page 7.]

The British Air Ministry augmented early brief accounts of the R. A. F. attack on Brest Friday night and early Saturday by stating that the 26,000-ton German battleships Gneisenau and Scharnhorst had been "very, very lucky" if they had escaped serious damage from new and powerful British bombs. R. A. F. aircraft, it was said, had dived to 1,000 feet to unleash their missiles on the Nazi raiders and had fired oil stores and warehouses near by, while other British planes dropped bombs on Rotterdam and the Ruhr. [Page 9, Column 1.]

The sharp British blow at the two German raiders coincided with a Berlin claim that 718,000 tons of British and Allied shipping had been sunk during March by German surface craft, U-boats, mines and airplanes. A German auxiliary cruiser operating "overseas" was said to have sunk the British auxiliary cruiser Voltaire of 13,255 tons. Moreover, Berlin said, U-boats in two days had sunk eighteen ships, totaling 106,000 tons, in a British convoy. [Page 13, Column 1.]

President Roosevelt's hint that he might soon lift combat-zone restrictions on the Red Sea to permit passage of American ships with war supplies for Britain aroused considerable interest in Washington. Senator George, chairman of the Senate Foreign Relations Committee, was said to feel that such action would necessitate Congressional amendment of the Neutrality Act; other members of Congress were believed to hold the President already had power to do this through provisions of the Lease-Lend Law. [Page 21, Column 1.]

Uruguay formally seized two Italian and two Danish ships in her harbors and placed the crews, comprising 119 men, under the direction of the Italian and Danish consuls, respectively. Many of the Danish seamen were reported to have expressed pleasure over the seizures and to have exhibited pro-British emblems. [Page 19, Column 1.]

TREATY NOW VALID

Moscow Discloses That Pledge of Friendship Was Made Yesterday

PEACE IS TERMED AIM

Strictest Neutrality Is Provided—Accord Is Hailed in London

By The Associated Press.

MOSCOW, Sunday, April 6—Soviet Russia and Yugoslavia have signed a treaty of friendship and non-aggression after several days of negotiation, Tass, Soviet official news agency, announced early today.

The agency said the pact had been signed yesterday by the Russian Premier and Foreign Commissar, Vyacheslaff M. Molotoff, and Milan Gavrilovitch, former Yugoslav Cabinet Minister and Yugoslavia's representative in Moscow.

The treaty declared that Russia and Yugoslavia were "inspired by the friendship existing between the countries and convinced that the preservation of peace forms their common interest" and hence had decided to conclude the pact.

The treaty was for five years.

Its first article provided neither country would attack the other and that each would respect the sovereign rights and territorial integrity of the other.

It provided that, in case of aggression against one of the countries by a third power, the other would observe a policy of friendly relations with the country attacked.

TEXT OF THE TREATY

MOSCOW, Sunday, April 6 (UP)—Tass News Agency gave out today the text of the treaty between the Soviets and Yugoslavia, as follows:

A treaty on friendship and non-aggression between the Union of Soviet Socialist Republics and the Kingdom of Yugoslavia.

The Presidium of the Supreme Soviet U. S. S. R. and His Majesty the King of Yugoslavia, inspired by friendship existing between the two countries and convinced that preservation of peace forms their common interest, decided to conclude a treaty on friendship and non-aggression and appointed for this purpose their representatives:

Presidium of the Supreme Soviet U. S. S. R.—Vyacheslaff M. Molotoff, chairman of the Council of Peoples Commissars and Peoples Commissar of Foreign Affairs; His Majesty the King of Yugoslavia—Milan Gavrilovitch, Envoy Extraordinary and Minister Plenipotentiary of Yugoslavia, Bozhin Simich and Colonel Dragutin Savich, which representatives, after exchanging their credentials found in proper form and due order, agreed on the following:

ARTICLE I

The two contracting parties mutually undertake to desist from

Continued on Page Twenty-five

YUGOSLAVIA FIGHTS

Belgrade Has Air Raid as Armies Resist, Berne Hears

DRIVE FROM BULGARIA

Greeks Announce Nazi Attack—Stukas Clear Path, Germans Say

By RAY BROCK

Wireless to The New York Times.

BELGRADE, Yugoslavia, Sunday, April 6—At 3:25 o'clock this morning the air-raid sirens in Belgrade sounded an alarm. For the Yugoslavs it was the first indication that the nation was at war.

An hour later, at 4:32, two Yugoslav fighter planes appeared over the city, flying in an easterly direction. They came from the Zemun airdrome. Two more fighter planes appeared a short time later.

[At this point wireless connections with Belgrade were cut.]

Greeks Announce Attack

The Greek High Command announced in a communiqué broadcast from Athens that since 5:15 A. M., Athens time, the German troops had been attacking Greek troops on the Bulgarian border, the Columbia Broadcasting System announced this morning. No further details were in the communiqué as it was received here.

The German Propaganda Ministry announced in a broadcast from Berlin, according to CBS, that swarms of German planes, including Stuka dive bombers, were "pouncing like hornets" on Greek and Yugoslav airdromes and railways in an effort to cripple the resistance to the invading German armies. The Nazi Propaganda Ministry also asserted that the planes were clearing a path for tanks and infantry, and that parachute troops were landing at strategic points within the Greek-Yugoslav defenses. There was no confirmation of these claims, however.

Belgrade Has Second Alarm

By Telephone to The New York Times.

BERNE, Switzerland, Sunday, April 6—The Belgrade correspondent of The New York Times reported at 5:30 o'clock this morning that naturally he had heard of the situation, but that "you wouldn't know the difference." Aside from two air-raid alarms in the capital early this morning, no incident had yet occurred. Reports as to the exact location of the fighting were very scant.

On the Greek frontier the invasion doubtlessly came from Bulgaria through the Struma Valley with a secondary attack down the Vardar Valley. This latter attack, however, would entail driving across the southeastern border of Yugoslavia—the Third Army region based on Skoplje under General Ilija Brasitch.

For some time before the Yugoslav crisis began to take on even faintly menacing tones, the Yugoslav High Command had been re-

Continued on Page Twenty-four

Hitler's Order of the Day

Adolf Hitler's declaration that Germany was at war with Yugoslavia was read over the Berlin radio early today by Propaganda Minister Joseph Goebbels. As heard by the National Broadcasting Company's station in New York and translated from the German, it read:

In the name of the Fuehrer, Adolf Hitler, I am reading the following order of the day to the German Army of the East:

Berlin, April 6, 1941.

Soldiers of the Southeast Front:

Since early this morning the German people are at war with the Belgrade government of intrigue. We shall only lay down arms when this band of ruffians has been definitely and most emphatically eliminated, and the last Briton has left this part of the European Continent, and that these misled people realize that they must thank Britain for this situation, they must thank England, the greatest warmonger of all time.

The German people can enter into this new struggle with the inner satisfaction that its leaders have done everything to bring about a peaceful settlement.

We pray to God that He may lead our soldiers on the path and bless them as hitherto.

In accordance with the policy of letting others fight for her, as she did in the case of Poland, Britain again tried to involve Germany in the struggle in which Britain hoped that she would finish off the German people once and for all, to win the war, and if possible to destroy the entire German Army.

In a few weeks long ago the German soldiers on the Eastern Front, Poland, swept aside this instrument of British policy. On April 9, 1940, Britain again attempted to reach its goal by a thrust on the German north flank, the thrust at Norway.

In an unforgettable struggle the German soldiers in Norway eliminated the British within a period of a few weeks.

What the world did not deem possible the German people have achieved. Again, only a few weeks later, Churchill thought the moment right to make a renewed thrust through the British Allies, France and Belgium, into the German region of the Ruhr. The victorious hour of our soldiers on the West Front began.

It is already war history how the German Armies defeated the legions of capitalism and plutocracy. After forty-five days this campaign in the West was equally and emphatically terminated.

Then Churchill concentrated the strength of his Empire

Continued on Page Twenty-six

NAZI TROOPS MARCH

Goebbels Reads Order to Germans to Rid Europe of All Britons

QUICK BLOW PLEDGED

Greece Told She Invited It—U. S. Is Said to Share Blame

By DANIEL T. BRIGHAM

By Telephone to The New York Times.

BERNE, Switzerland, Sunday, April 6—At 5 o'clock this morning German forces attacked Yugoslavia and Greece in the long-awaited culmination of the Balkan war of nerves.

The news broke on the world with startling suddenness when a German radio station announcer with a triumphant blast this morning introduced Dr. Joseph Goebbels, Minister of Propaganda, who then read Reichsfuehrer Hitler's order of the day to "my forces in Southeast Europe."

"Since dawn this morning," said Dr. Goebbels, "the German Reich has been at war with Yugoslavia and Greece."

It was indicated that the friendship pact signed between Yugoslavia and Russia yesterday was one of the factors of which Germany complained. This was another version of the Nazi charges of "aggressive encirclement of Germany," which have been used since Herr Hitler's advent to power.

Yugoslav Arming Held Cause

Another source of grievance, it would seem, was Belgrade's mobilization, a point that Herr Hitler mentioned in his order of the day as one of the chief reasons for the attack.

Immediately after Dr. Goebbels's broadcast, telephone communications to the eastward from this city—and south to Rome—were cut off.

[United States and British encouragement to the Yugoslavs in their resistance to German demands was also cited as grounds for Germany's attack, according to The Associated Press. Alleged American offers of material aid were also quoted.]

The German Army was told it would not lay down its arms until the "ruffians" and "plotters" in Belgrade had been deposed and the last Briton driven out of this territory.

Friendship for Greeks

German soldiers have been fighting in Greece since dawn today, the proclamation stated. It was indicated that the battle in Greece was not directed against the population but only against the "world enemy," Great Britain, who had dispatched troops there for an attack against the interests of the Reich.

Germany, Herr Hitler was quoted as saying, does not consider herself at war with Greece and will not molest any Greek who does not take up arms against the German Army, but any who lends his support to the British will be crushed.

"Soldiers of the Southeast Front," the Reichfuehrer proclaimed, "your hour has now come."

He then told these troops that they must emulate their comrades in Poland, Scandinavia, the Lowlands and France. He added that the general mobilization in Yugoslavia was considered by the Reich as final proof that Britain had mixed into the internal affairs of Yugoslavia and would lead that country into hostile acts against Germany.

Yugoslav Provocation Charged

BERLIN, Sunday, April 6 (AP)—The German radio, in broadcasting Reichsfuehrer Hitler's order to the German Army, quoted him as saying Germany was unable longer to endure the Yugoslav attitude. The Reich was said to be reacting to the mistreatment, "attacks and murdering" of Germans in the Serb Kingdom.

The order said the greatest patience had been exercised by Germany respecting Yugoslavia and Greece, but that now the moment for action had arrived.

It was said that Herr Hitler had frequently called attention to the dangers in the Southeast.

Now, it was said, Germany was

Continued on Page Twenty-six

COAL TIE-UP ENDED IN 65% OF THE MINES

Southern Operators Hold Out but Contract for Rest Will Be Signed Tomorrow

Yielding to pressure from the Federal Government, representatives of 65 per cent of the nation's soft-coal producers agreed yesterday to sign a new contract with the United Mine Workers tomorrow. At least 300,000 miners are expected to return to work Tuesday or Wednesday, ending a week's stoppage that threatened to cut off vital fuel supplies for defense industries.

Dr. John R. Steelman, director of the United States Conciliation Service, who succeeded in breaking the four-week deadlock between the C. I. O. union and the operators, predicted that virtually all the mines would be open within a week. Other government officials said they believed the settlement in the soft-coal fields would provide a key to peaceful adjustment of employer-union differences in steel and anthracite, thus removing two additional threats of delay in the defense program and insuring uninterrupted work for 1,000,000 men.

Thirteen associations of Southern bituminous operators were the sole holdouts against the tentative accord effected by Dr. Steelman, and there were indications that their ranks were beginning to crumble. Union officials said scattered companies in the Southern States had indicated their intention of signing with the John L. Lewis organization, whether or not their associations went along. The union relied on the pressure of competition to bring the others into line in a few days.

Under the terms of the proposed contract the United Mine Workers will win its full demand for a basic wage of $7 a day. This represents an increase of $1 over the rate previously in effect in the North and $1.40 over the Southern rate. The union's insistence on abolition of

Continued on Page Thirty-three

KNUDSEN ASSAILS RADICALS IN LABOR

Charges They Hamper Output for Defense—Cooperation by All Vital, He Warns

Text of Mr. Knudsen's address appears on Page 40.

Asserting that the most serious thing about the strike in the Allis-Chalmers plant in Milwaukee was not the time lost in the production of defense materials but the fact that it showed that "radical" labor leaders could tell the State and Federal Governments "where to get off," William S. Knudsen last night proposed a program for dealing with labor difficulties that he said would eliminate 90 per cent of the strikes.

The director-general of the Office of Production Management, who spoke at the Army Order of the Military Order of the World War at the Hotel Waldorf-Astoria, said that the labor situation during the last month had grown worse and warned that the epidemic of strikes must be stopped or the effort for defense and aid to Great Britain, Greece and Yugoslavia would fail.

Interrupted by applause when he started to discuss the labor situation, Mr. Knudsen declared that time was the all-important element in America's defense program and declared that if the nation could put on a "little steam" in production during the eighty-nine days remaining before the Fourth of July "we might save a lot of blood later on."

"I do not believe that legislation against strikes is necessary or enforceable," Mr. Knudsen said, "but I do believe that during the emergency period a definite procedure should be followed in order that strikes may be held to a minimum.

"For instance, I believe that strike votes should be taken under the supervision of the Labor Department. I believe a certain mini-

Continued on Page Forty

New Army Marches in Rain Here; Nation Joins in Military Tribute

By HANSON W. BALDWIN

The new Army of the United States paraded down the Fifth Avenues of many cities yesterday in an unprecedented week-end celebration of Army Day.

Veterans of past wars marched with youngsters who may become veterans of a future war, as the muffled beats of drumheads dampened by the rain epitomized the somber attitude with which thousands of spectators in many cities viewed their marching men. Not since 1917 and another war has the nation so taken the Army—now truly a national army—to itself with quiet, restrained pride.

For the music of the bands was but a faint echo in people's minds of the growing thunder of Europe's guns, and the serious attitude of the onlookers was matched in New York, Washington and other Eastern cities by the weather. The skies were a sullen gray and the peaks of New York's skyscrapers were veiled in mist as the Army marched and drumheads burst and slickers poured off torrents of the rain.

The New York parade along upper Fifth Avenue, which had been expected to be the greatest Army Day event in the city's history, lost considerably in volume but gained in solemnity because of the weather. Not many more than half of the expected 30,000 marchers participated, and the sparse, umbrellaed crowd that watched could not have numbered at its peak more than 30,000 to 40,000. The crowd dwindled at times during the two-hour parade to less than half that number. The weather, too, turned the march-past into a real test of soldiering, particularly for 4,500 men of the Forty-fourth Division from Fort Dix, N. J., who had negotiated seventy-eight miles of roads slick with rain in motor convoys to participate in the parade.

Mayor La Guardia, huddled be-

Continued on Page Forty-two

BRITISH HALT DRIVE IN LIBYA, GET ADOWA

Axis Checked East of Bengazi—South Africans Within 80 Miles of Addis Ababa

Wireless to The New York Times.

CAIRO, Egypt, April 5—The British announced today that their forces in Libya had halted the advance of German and Italian armored units somewhere east of Bengazi. The situation here after the recapture of that port by the Axis was said to be "well in hand."

At the same time the swift progress of the British Imperial forces in East Africa resulted in the capture of Adowa [and of near-by Adigrat, according to The Associated Press] while South African troops in Ethiopia crossed the Awash River and struck to within eighty miles of Addis Ababa.

[Massawa, the Red Sea port toward which the British armies of East Africa are racing, was reported to have defied a British demand for surrender, according to an Associated Press dispatch from Khartum.]

South African Advance

After the British in the last two days took the two most easily defendable areas in East Africa, Italian resistance appeared to be crumbling fast. The South African troops, who have marched all the way from Italian Somaliland now are moving westward along the Jibuti railway. After a brisk but brief battle at the crossing of the Awash, this column is pushing through the African hill country toward the higher rolling grassland plateau around Addis Ababa.

It is said the South Africans averaged a twenty-five-mile advance every day in the last two months.

North of the capital, combined British and Indian forces are pursuing the fleeing Italians toward Dessye through difficult mountainous terrain. Between Asmara and Adowa they advanced with only slight skirmishing at many points that might have become other Cherens had Italian morale been good.

The occupation of Adowa again frees the battle site where in 1896 Ethiopia's Emperor Menelik routed the Italians, killing 6,000 and capturing 4,000, thus preserving his nation's independence until 1935. The town itself has a population of 6,000.

Despite the lightness of the fighting in this area, advancing British forces surprised and captured a battalion of Italian infantry. Italians are running southward, apparently almost wholly disorganized, throwing away their arms and surrendering on the slightest excuse,

Continued on Page Seven

NAZI UNITS CROWD YUGOSLAV BORDERS

Some Are Reported in Albania, Many in Southern Hungary—German Plane Downed

By C. L. SULZBERGER

By Telephone to The New York Times.

BELGRADE, Yugoslavia, April 5—The German military encirclement of Yugoslavia was nearing completion tonight as eight new divisions reportedly jammed the Hungarian roads, a powerful armored unit concentrated at Bela Crkva, on the Rumanian frontier one and a half hours' drive from Belgrade, and the first Nazi troops entered Albania.

British information sources reported from Bucharest and Budapest that the invasion of Southeastern Yugoslavia by the German Army of the Struma was ready to begin at any moment.

It is only worth noting that most of the more pessimistic predictions emanate from German-controlled countries, such as Hungary, Rumania and Bulgaria, or from the Croat capital of Zagreb, which is the center of the small but active German-inspired Fascist movement.

The facts of the situation are clear. Once more the normal peasant life of Hungary has been thrown into turmoil by the huge disruption caused by the passage of German Armies, and eight separate divisions were said to have been sighted. The motorized units on three points of the Hungarian southern frontier—Mohacs, Szeged and Nagy Kanizsa—were increased, as were the concentration in the Rumanian Banat.

An absolutely reliable source said German soldiers were known to have arrived in Albania—the debarkation point coming as somewhat of a surprise and indicating the probability that airplane transport was employed. Four Tyrolean mountain divisions have entered Italy in the last four days.

The government ordered the closing of all frontiers this morning. Outerbridge Horsey, secretary of the United States Legation in Budapest, who is coming here by train for emergency work, was stopped at the Hungarian frontier and the legation here is trying to facilitate his transport now by automobile.

All Danube traffic on the Yugoslav stretch of the river has now been halted. A German Messerschmitt plane was shot down yesterday while cruising over Maribor and it crashed at Ptuj.

Circulation through the country save with special military permit has been halted. All cars are being stopped by the police and are being requisitioned unless they have special passes. A new War Press Bureau has been established. At the same time Yugoslav technical con-

Continued on Page Twenty-five

"All the News That's Fit to Print."

The New York Times.

LATE CITY EDITION
Mostly cloudy and mild today. Tomorrow scattered showers and mild.
Temperatures Yesterday—Max.,58; Min.,37

Copyright, 1941, by The New York Times Company.

VOL. XC...No. 30,396. Entered as Second-Class Matter, Postoffice, New York, N. Y. NEW YORK, MONDAY, APRIL 14, 1941. THREE CENTS NEW YORK CITY and Vicinity

RUSSIA AND JAPAN SIGN A NEUTRALITY TREATY; GERMANS CAPTURE BARDIA, PUSH INTO EGYPT; YUGOSLAVS COUNTERATTACK, GREEKS HOLD FIRM

WAR CASTS GLOOM OVER EASTER'S JOY IN MOST OF WORLD

Shocks of Conflict Mingle With Prayers for Peace in Much of Christendom

GREAT TURNOUT IN NATION

Churches and Fashion Parades Attract Throngs—Roosevelt at Service in Capital

While the civilized world alternately reeled under new shocks and grasped at glimmerings of hope on Easter yesterday—as black an Easter as mankind has known in modern times—all Christendom soberly celebrated the hallowed day of the resurrection of Jesus Christ.

It was Easter in New York, where thousands arose at dawn to worship at the cross and where 300,000 persons—the largest crowd in at least twenty years—overflowed from the broad sidewalks of Fifth Avenue to form a brilliant, moving carpet of fashion that could not be duplicated in any part of the world today.

It was Easter for desperately fighting British expeditionary forces, who hurled back panzer units in the shadow of Mount Olympus. It also was Easter in defeated France, where Marshal Henri Philippe Pétain and his people had foremost in their thoughts the hundreds of thousands of prisoners still held by the Nazis.

Perhaps the most sorrowful of all Easter notes came from the Vatican City, where Pope Pius XII, weighed down by emotion, broadcast his Easter message to the world. To the hushed crowds that gathered at the Vatican the Pope could bring no hope of any early attainment of a "just peace." Apparently fearful that poison gas may be brought into the conflict, he humbly begged that the belligerent nations refrain from using "still more homicidal instruments," and he pleaded for kindness for the prisoners of war and the dazed citizens of occupied countries.

No Peace in the Holy Land

In Jerusalem, profoundly impressive ceremonies took place on the ground made sacred by the tradition of Christ's resurrection nineteen centuries ago. "Christ is risen—He is risen, indeed!" the faithful told one another—and the words were echoed throughout Christendom. But there was no peace in the Holy Land, either, for everywhere there were khaki-clad British soldiers—constant reminders that even the land of the Prince of Peace is under threat today.

In Dublin, where twenty-five years ago Easter week saw the outbreak of the bloody Irish rebellion, Prime Minister Eamon De Valera somberly watched marching troops and warned his people that they must stand ever ready to resist attack.

In the capital of the United States President Roosevelt went to Easter services and heard his minister deliver a prayer that "peace with righteousness and justice may be established for the sake of all mankind." As the President listened with bowed head, the minister asked that the United States be led into doing "whatever is right" to re-establish righteousness in the world.

Vice President Wallace at Arlington Cemetery placed a cross of lilies on the Tomb of the Unknown Soldier—the Unknown Soldier of the first World War.

Cars Shunted from 5th Ave.

Yet, while elsewhere in the world husbands and fathers were herded into concentration camps, and wives, mothers and children knew the pinch of hunger, in America the people were not resigned to gloom. Throughout the breadth of the land the leaders and the plain citizens, the rich and the poor, momentarily forgetting the headlines, put on their finery in traditional American custom and paraded on the main streets of their cities and towns.

New York's Easter parade was spectacular. Shortly after noon, police were forced to rope off motor traffic between Fiftieth and Fifty-third Streets. Immediately, the huge crowds bubbled from the sidewalks and flowed into the street. Rich raiment of every hue and fa-

Continued on Page Twelve

300,000 Paraders Jam Fifth Ave.; Brilliant Pageant Ties Up Traffic

Mild Day Turns Street Into Huge Showcase of Styles—Cars Barred in One Area as Throngs Overflow Sidewalks

By KATHLEEN McLAUGHLIN

For New York, it was an epic Easter. Almost alone among the proudest boulevards of the world's greatest cities, Fifth Avenue marked as usual yesterday the surge and flow of multitudes celebrating the rebirth symbolized by the feast of the Resurrection.

Circumstances that produced this pageant were characteristic of 1941. Surface serenity was there, the deeply spiritual atmosphere, the seasonal blaze of color. But it had also disturbing undertones—implicit in the thin trickle of khaki and naval uniforms through the crowds; the frequent, crisp British phrases of pink-cheeked children; the spatter of French and less familiar foreign tongues; the officers' insignia, epaulets, and peaked caps, and the spread wings of the American eagle, each now a fashion motif.

Combined with the impetus of the war crisis, to which clergymen pointed for explanation of the densely packed pews in every midtown place of worship, was the moderate temperature, which, aided by a somewhat grudging sun, lured forth the teeming throngs to saunter much more leisurely than of recent years, when a brisk Easter promenade was not the exception but the rule. Fur coats and mittens, for years a badge of paraders, for once could be shed, and Spring suits stepped forth smartly, untroubled by a persistent breeze.

No such Easter morning jam has been experienced on the thoroughfare in the last twenty-two years, on the word of Deputy Inspector Valentine W. Corell, in charge of the special detachment of 225 police detailed to the upper Fifth Avenue sector. Inspector Corell took up his work as a rookie on guard at St. Patrick's Cathedral just twenty-seven years ago on Easter Sunday, and has not missed a survey of the annual traffic since.

At its peak, shortly after the noon hour, he estimated that there were 300,000 persons inching along the sidewalks and curbstones between Forty-sixth and Sixtieth Streets. This outpouring, especially from the pontifical high mass at St.

Continued on Page Thirteen

POPE PIUS ASKS BAN ON WORSE WEAPONS

Broadcast Believed to Have Referred to Gas—Calls for Imitation of Martyrs

The text of the Pope's Easter message appears on Page 3

By CAMILLE M. CIANFARRA
By Telephone to THE NEW YORK TIMES.

ROME, April 13—In an Easter message broadcast to the Catholic world from his private library in the Vatican the Pope today appealed to all belligerents to abstain from using "still more homicidal instruments."

Although no one knows what type of arms he had in mind, the Pope made clear that the appeal sprang from his desire to alleviate the sufferings of the civilian population, which, he said, are often exposed to greater and more widespread perils of war than soldiers in the line of battle.

Vatican circles suggest that the Pope might have been referring to the use of poison gas. Except for this, nearly every other weapon that was used in the World War has already been tried. The Pope, they said, could not have meant large-scale bombings or mechanized warfare because both have been outstanding features of this war since its beginning. In support of this interpretation they pointed to the phrasing of the appeal which came soon after expressions of grave concern for the fate of noncombatants.

Asks Regard for Civilians

"May all the belligerents," said the Pope, "who also have human hearts molded by mothers' love, show the same feeling of charity for the sufferings of civilian populations, for defenseless women and children, for the sick and the aged, all of whom are often exposed to greater and more widespread perils of war than those faced by soldiers of the front!

"We beseech the belligerent powers to abstain until the very end from the use of still more homicidal instruments of warfare; for the introduction of such weapons inevitably results in their retaliatory use, often with greater violence and cruelty by the enemy.

"If already we must lament the fact that the limits of legitimate warfare have been repeatedly exceeded, would not a more widespread use of increasingly barbarous offensive weapons soon transform the war into an unspeakable horror?"

That the Pope felt it necessary to make this appeal was regarded as highly significant in Catholic quarters, since it is an established fact that the Vatican, because of its manifold sources, is always extremely well informed.

In the words that followed the Pope thanked the Catholics of the entire world for the fervent response to his invitation to prayer

Continued on Page Three

ALARMED CONGRESS TO RUSH SHIP BILL

No Opposition to Purchase of Immobilized Foreign Craft Is Apparent as Recess Ends

By JAMES B. RESTON
Special to THE NEW YORK TIMES.

WASHINGTON, April 13—Alarmed by Germany's success in Africa and the Balkans and apprehensive about the implications of the new Russo-Japanese nonaggression pact, members of Congress ended a ten-day Easter recess tonight with predictions that a new effort will be made to rush all pending national defense legislation through both houses.

After a hurried roll-call tomorrow, when, despite the general apprehension about the war, the main event in the capital will still be the opening baseball game between the Washington Senators and the New York Yankees, both houses will get down to work Tuesday with special investigations of the national defense effort.

On Thursday President Roosevelt's request for authorization to purchase foreign ships immobilized in American ports will be studied in committee. Administration leaders expect this to be hurried to the floor of the House and probably passed early next week. There is a possibility that it will get to the floor of the House on Friday.

No Opposition in Sight

Even opposition Representatives showed no inclination to oppose the President's desire to supplement the United States merchant fleet with the foreign-owned vessels now in American ports. It is recognized in Republican quarters that unless new tonnage is added to the United States merchant fleet the Administration will not be able to import the 19,000,000 tons of raw materials needed for the 1941 national defense program. They also realize that by adding foreign-owned ships to the United States merchant marine the Administration is likely to delay the requisition of privately owned American ships.

Allied reverses in Libya and the Balkans have at the same time evidently induced members on all sides of the House to do everything possible to help the Administration increase production. There are still deep cleavages about what should be done with the war material once it is produced but very little opposition to producing it as rapidly as possible.

Despite the improvement in both production and labor relations recently, some members of both houses are still dissatisfied with the defense program. The House Military Affairs Committee, which has been investigating this situation for weeks, will reopen its inquiry Tuesday, when either Donald Nelson, purchasing director for the Office of Production Management, or J. B. Matthews, chief investigator of the

Continued on Page Fourteen

SERBS SLOW NAZIS

Yugoslavs in Offensive at Five Points Report Gaining Territory

LONDON IS HEARTENED

More Germans Said to Be Needed to Avoid War of Position

By DANIEL T. BRIGHAM
By Telephone to THE NEW YORK TIMES.

BERNE, Switzerland, April 13—While little of a concrete nature developed in the Yugoslav situation during the last twenty-four hours, the Yugoslavs' resistance is stiffening and at several points they have taken the offensive.

Their tardiness in reacting to the undeclared war that commenced shortly after 5 o'clock in the morning one week ago has been largely due to the incompleteness of their preparations.

In the Morava Valley between Nish and Kragujevac, Yugoslav forces, supported by their own planes and the British air force, are successfully harassing German columns that have advanced so far that their lines are in danger of being cut. In this sector a medium Yugoslav force drove the Germans back from Kragujevac, which the Germans said they captured yesterday. About twenty miles farther south at Prokuplje the enemy was surrounded and many prisoners captured when the town fell.

Big Hungarian Losses Seen

Fighting rear guard actions against the Hungarian forces, the Yugoslavs are taking a heavy toll for every foot of ground the Hungarians are taking. Yugoslav losses in this area are reported to be very small in men and matériel, whereas German sources report that aerial bombardment of the Hungarian lines of communication is known from reconnaissance to be heavy.

As seen from here the German forces, after capitalizing on the fear value of their tremendous motorized columns for one whole week, are now forced to permit the Yugoslavs to open the second phase of the conflict. This phase, which may last another week, will consist mainly of guerrilla warfare, with German lines being menaced everywhere.

At the end of this second phase, unless Germany pours in much more man power and matériel than she appears to be prepared to do now, the German troops will be obliged to accept engagement on a fixed front. A war of position in the mountainous Drina region would be very costly for the attackers. Even if they succeed in forcing the issue the results cannot be considered conclusive. It is one thing to conquer the komitajis' territory; it is another to conquer the komitaji.

LONDON, April 13 (UP)—An authoritative British statement said the Yugoslavs, fighting in do-or-die units, had hurled the Germans back and recovered lost territory in five

Continued on Page Four

NILE ARMY RETIRES

Holds Fast in Tobruk, but Axis Forces Go Around Port

CLASH NEAR SOLUM

Reinforcements Rushed by the British—Nazi Losses Put High

Wireless to THE NEW YORK TIMES.

CAIRO, Egypt, April 13—Axis mechanized columns swept past British forces in the Tobruk area yesterday and have now occupied Bardia, seventy miles farther along the coast, it was announced here today. Following this news came reports that British reinforcements had been going steadily to the western desert for the last few days and that the situation in that respect was considerably better than last week.

It was said here that the British forces in the Tobruk area are not surrounded as Axis announcements claim and that it is still possible for British mechanized columns to establish contact across the desert. It is believed the German mechanized units are getting fuel supplies by air, but only in relatively small quantities.

Well-informed quarters here said the fighting was proceeding in the neighborhood of the Egyptian frontier port of Solum, but it was not established whether German forces had yet crossed the Egyptian border. In skirmishes at El Adem and El Gazala the Germans were reported repulsed.

[In Berlin it was assumed that the Axis forces were continuing their advance into Egypt. In Rome it was predicted that the swift offensive would push as far as possible toward Alexandria.]

Evacuation Not Explained

The British forces had previously evacuated Bardia, which is surrounded by Italian fortifications much like those at Tobruk. The reason for the evacuation was not revealed here. Although the German forward units are understood to be light, the movement of the present battle is so rapid it is difficult to ascertain the exact strength of the enemy.

The strength of the British garrison at Tobruk has not been revealed, but if it is large it would appear that the Germans are in considerable danger of having their communications cut.

The advancing Germans are said to have suffered fairly heavy casualties. According to information reaching here, all the British forces are still intact.

The patriot movement is reported to be growing rapidly in Ethiopia and the Italians in many cases are said to be asking protection from the natives. British forces are advancing northward from Addis Ababa, but the columns moving southward toward Gondar and

Continued on Page Two

Danish Legation Backs Defiance Of Copenhagen by Minister Here

Special to THE NEW YORK TIMES.

WASHINGTON, April 13—Danish Minister Henrik de Kauffmann, although officially recalled by the German-controlled Copenhagen government, has the complete support of the staff of the legation in his defiance of the order, a spokesman at the legation said tonight.

All members of the legation and Danish consular officers throughout the United States will back Mr. de Kauffmann's agreement with the United States to permit this country to protect Greenland during the European war.

Einar Blechinberg, counselor of the legation, who was put in charge by the Danish Foreign Office in its message to Mr. de Kauffmann relieving him of his duties, supports the Minister's attitude completely, the spokesman said.

Mr. de Kauffmann, who is supported by the State Department, which will continue to recognize him as the Danish Minister, attempted today to see the Secretary of State but was unable to reach him. He expects to see Mr. Hull tomorrow.

The Minister said that he had prepared a report to submit to Mr. Hull. This report, he said, embodies the statements he gave to the press that the action of the Danish Foreign Office was taken under duress from the Nazis and that he has no intention of obeying the orders or of returning to Denmark.

"I came to this country to represent a free and democratic Denmark," Mr. de Kauffmann told reporters, "and I will continue to do so. I will not accept any orders emanating directly or indirectly from Germany."

The Danish Minister negotiated the agreement which allows this country to establish military bases in Greenland. He signed the agreement on behalf of King Christian X of Denmark, and before taking the step obtained the approval of the two royal governors of the island colony.

While both Berlin and Copenhagen have called the agreement illegal and contrary to international law, Mr. de Kauffmann and the United States recognize in it no deviation from the historic policy of

Continued on Page Fourteen

The International Situation

MONDAY, APRIL 14, 1941

A new confusing element was added to the pattern of international affairs yesterday when Moscow announced the signing of a neutrality pact between Russia and Japan, guaranteeing each from attack in the rear should either be "the object of military activity on the part of one or several powers." The accord guaranteed as well the territorial integrity of Japanese-dominated Manchukuo and the Russian-dominated Mongolian People's Republic. [Page 1, Column 8; Map Page 8.]

Each of the major capitals interpreted the news of the treaty differently.

In Tokyo Premier Konoye said it would help "secure the peace of greater East Asia." [Page 10, Column 1.]

Washington officials declined to comment prior to official consultation, but it was generally believed that the pact had been signed by Moscow under German instigation. Though it will ostensibly free Japan's hands in the Far East, it was pointed out, it will also free Russia's hands for any eventuality in the Balkans or Near East, where Germany is advancing. [Page 1, Column 7.]

London emphasized that no mention of cessation of Russian aid to China had been included in the accord and responsible quarters held that the new treaty apparently nullified the Axis proviso of Japanese aid should Germany become involved in hostilities with Russia. [Page 10, Column 5.]

Berlin and Rome acclaimed the accord and termed it a direct menace to Anglo-American interests in the Pacific. [Page 8, Column 3.]

It became evident, meanwhile, that the German drive into Greece and Southern Yugoslavia was slowing, and in some sectors had stopped.

Scattered reports from Yugoslavia indicated that Yugoslav guerrilla tactics, and pressure in the Skoplje zone, had disrupted German supply lines and halted the drive down through Bitolj Pass against the Allied line in Greece. [Page 1, Column 4; Map, Page 4.]

Repeated German mechanized attacks against both flanks of the Allied line across Greece throughout the day were reported hurled back with losses to the attackers. The Royal Air Force and Allied aircraft were said to be doing heroic service in smashing and disrupting tenuous German supply lines. [Page 3, Column 1.]

The German Government announced the occupation of Belgrade by Reich forces one week after the opening of the invasion, bringing to thirteen the number of European capitals placed under Nazi domination since 1936. The capture of 12,000 Yugoslav troops, including twenty-two generals and 200 officers, in the Zagreb area was also reported. [Page 1, Column 6.]

The Axis armored divisions driving along the Mediterranean coast in Libya were said to have swept around a strong British garrison in Tobruk, to have taken undefended Bardia, seventy miles to the east, and to have reached Solum, eleven miles within Egypt, where, British circles in Cairo said, fierce fighting is in progress. Axis reports said the Tobruk garrison was "trapped." [Page 1, Column 5; Map, Page 2.]

Dispatches reaching Stockholm said forces from a British "torpedo boat" that had put into an unidentified port in Northern Norway had destroyed harbor works with the assistance of local anti-Nazi Norwegians. [Page 7, Column 3.]

Strong Royal Air Force night attacks on the Nazi-held bases of Brest and Lorient and on the airfield at Merignac were reported in London. German air activity over Britain was slight. [Page 7, Column 1.]

Pope Pius, in an Easter broadcast from the Vatican, appealed to the belligerents to refrain from the use of "still more deadly weapons." Observers familiar with the Vatican's wide sources of information feared that the Pope's message applied to an impending use of gas. [Page 1, Column 2.]

REICH NOW CLAIMS FALL OF BELGRADE

22 Yugoslav Generals and 100 Cannon Reported Taken in Fighting Near Zagreb

By C. BROOKS PETERS
By Telephone to THE NEW YORK TIMES.

BERLIN, April 13—German troops of the motorized group under the command of Col. Gen. Paul von Kleist began the occupation of Belgrade at 6:30 this morning, the High Command announced in a special communiqué.

There was not a single mention in today's communiqué of what, if any, military actions have been carried out by the German forces on the Greek front. The High Command reported merely that on the night of April 11 to 12 German bombers in an attack on the roads of Salamis sank an enemy vessel of 4,000 tons and hit four other "large" ships. Two storage tanks, one power plant and one mill in the harbor of Piraeus were "successfully" attacked, the German report continued, and one Hurricane was shot down.

On the same evening the German High Command declared other German bombers set fuel oil storage depots at the airport of Venezia on the island of Malta aflame.

Today, just one week after commencement of hostilities in the Balkans, the German armies operating in the Yugoslav Kingdom appeared from reports here to be rapidly completing the conquest of that country. Belgrade was captured early this morning by an attack from the south. Yesterday afternoon, however, the Germans declare, a small group of men under the command of Captain von Klingenberg, all from the "Reich" Division of the Elite Guards, forced their way across the Danube and into the city from the north and raised the German flag on the German Legation there.

In the process of cleaning up op-

Continued on Page Six

CAPITAL RESERVES JUDGMENT ON PACT

U. S. Relations With Soviet Are More Likely to Be Affected Now Than Those With Japan

By BERTRAM D. HULEN
Special to THE NEW YORK TIMES.

WASHINGTON, April 13—The announcement of the conclusion of the Soviet-Japanese pact today threw confusion into a situation that had already become black in consequence of the German military achievements in the Balkans last week, but some slight comfort was found in the fact that the pact did not go farther than it did.

Officials frankly declared that at first blush the agreement did not look pleasant. However, they did not regard it as a bombshell. They did interpret it as a diplomatic defeat for Moscow.

Undoubtedly, it was remarked, those who have been hoping that Russia might swing away from the Axis will be disappointed, but on its face the pact was considered important primarily as a political gesture and because of its psychological effects.

From the practical standpoint the most important feature was considered the Soviet recognition of Japan's suzerainty over Manchukuo. Not only is this the first time that such recognition has been accorded by other than an Axis power but the equivalent Japanese recognition of Russia's position in Outer Mongolia was interpreted as signifying that Moscow and Tokyo had agreed to partition North China for their own advantage.

From this standpoint, the pact was viewed as a blow to China. Whether it means that Japan will now feel free to move southward in the Pacific was considered far less certain.

The State Department received no official details or reports concerning the pact today and for that reason refrained from making any

Continued on Page Eight

ACCORD IN MOSCOW

Integrity of Manchukuo and Inner Mongolia Pledged by Both

PACT FOR FIVE YEARS

Matsuoka Rewarded on Second Visit—Stalin Sees Him Leave

Text of the Soviet-Japanese Pact and declaration, Page 8.

By The Associated Press.

MOSCOW, April 13—Soviet Russia and Japan, frequently opposed powers in the Far East, joined today in a neutrality pact.

In a four-point accord, each agreed to remain neutral throughout any period during which either of the signatories was the "object of military action on the part of one or several powers."

Each undertakes to respect the "territorial inviolability" of the other.

The pact, so it says, "guarantees peaceful and friendly relations" between the two powers.

The character of the pact was emphasized in an accompanying joint declaration pledging the Soviets to respect the territorial integrity of Japan's puppet State, Manchukuo, something to which the Soviet never before has agreed. Equally the subject of comment was Japan's parallel pledge to respect the status of the Moscow-dominated Outer Mongolian People's Republic.

Effective for Five Years

The pact is effective for five years and is renewable for an additional five-year term unless one side denounces it a year before expiration of the first period.

It is to be ratified as quickly as possible and the formal exchange of ratification documents is to take place in Tokyo.

The document was signed by Japan's touring Foreign Minister, Yosuke Matsuoka, and the Soviet Premier and Foreign Commissar, Vyacheslaff M. Molotoff, at the Kremlin at 2:30 P. M.

It was announced on the Moscow radio at 5 P. M., and Mr. Matsuoka, who had spent nearly a week in Moscow in secret negotiations, took the Trans-Siberian express for Tokyo fifty-five minutes later.

Joseph Stalin personally saw him off at the train, a high compliment to Mr. Matsuoka.

Mr. Matsuoka, for whom the pact was a signal triumph, arrived here March 23 for a one-day stay on his journey for Axis conferences in Berlin and Rome, where he saw Adolf Hitler and Benito Mussolini.

He saw Mr. Molotoff then in the presence of Mr. Stalin.

Conferences With Molotoff

Returning from Berlin and Rome last Monday, he saw Mr. Molotoff four more times, including one conference of three and a half hours, and another conference yesterday in which Mr. Stalin again engaged.

German Ambassador Count Friedrich Werner von der Schulenburg and Slovak Minister Franz Tiso left tonight for consultations with their governments in Berlin and Bratislava.

Slovakia is a part of the German-protected Czecho-Slovakia, of which Hungary also got a slice in Carpatho-Ukraine.

While Russia was putting the seals to her non aggression pact in the East, the official press gave prominent display to a Foreign Office communiqué reproving Hungary for invading a Slav nation, Yugoslavia.

"Considered especially significant" was the Foreign Office's reference to Hungary's own national minorities and the danger to Hungary should she become involved in trouble.

[Carpatho-Ukraine is largely inhabited by a people kindred to Russia's Ukrainians.]

The rebuke to Hungary was similar but more outspoken than the one administered to Bulgaria six weeks ago for permitting German troops to enter the country.

The papers also gave an extensive account of a broadcast by the Yugoslav Premier, General Dusan Simovitch, in which he was reported to

Continued on Page Eight

1941

Bud Abbott and Lou Costello in *Buck Privates.*

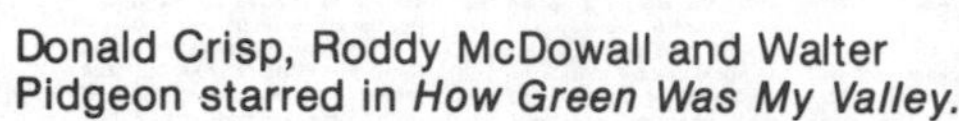

Donald Crisp, Roddy McDowall and Walter Pidgeon starred in *How Green Was My Valley.*

Gary Cooper and Joan Leslie in *Sergeant York.*

"All the News That's Fit to Print."

The New York Times.

LATE CITY EDITION
Fair and continued cool today and tomorrow.
Temperatures Yesterday—Max., 65; Min., 46

VOL. XC..No. 30,424. Entered as Second-Class Matter, Postoffice, New York, N. Y. NEW YORK, MONDAY, MAY 12, 1941. THREE CENTS NEW YORK CITY and Vicinity

BOMBS WRECK COMMONS CHAMBER, UNROOF ABBEY, HIT BRITISH MUSEUM; R.A.F. BLASTS HAMBURG AND BERLIN

POLICE WILL HEM COAST SHIPYARDS TO MEET PICKETS

Strong Forces Take Posts Today as 1,900 Machinists Try to Clamp Strike on 11 Plants

UNION LEADERS PROTEST

Admiral Denies Asking Guard, but Says Navy Will Act on Orders From Washington

Heavy police guards were assigned to shipbuilding plants in San Francisco and Oakland in preparation for the establishment this morning of picket lines by 1,900 striking A. F. of L. and C. I. O. machinists. [Page 1.]

A strike by the United Automobile Workers, C. I. O., at sixty-one General Motors plants was deferred until Thursday by a vote of union officials at Detroit after the union's negotiating committee had reported on mediation efforts at Washington. The decision permits resumption of mediation tomorrow. [Page 10.]

A survey by The United Press showed that twenty-four strikes involving 40,000 men chiefly engaged in production of defense material were still in force. Some were declared in early March and April. [Page 10.]

Coast Shipyards Guarded

By FOSTER HAILEY
Special to THE NEW YORK TIMES.

SAN FRANCISCO, May 11—More than 500 San Francisco police were ordered to strike duty tomorrow as 1,900 striking machinists of the American Federation of Labor and the Congress of Industrial Organizations prepared to throw picket lines around eleven shipbuilding plants in the Bay area to implement a strike called at midnight Friday. Similar precautions were being taken in Oakland, where six of the plants are located.

Leaders of the strikers protested that there was no necessity for the police concentrations, which were said to be even more elaborate than any in force during the general strike of 1934. Harry Hook and E. F. Dillon, business agents for Local 68 of the A. F. of L. machinists, said that their orders to their men were to allow any one to pass through picket lines who wanted to work.

"We machinists believe our work is so important that it won't make any difference if the other 18,000 men who are not on strike do report for work," Mr. Hook said. "However, we do not expect them to violate the picket line. Out here on the West Coast a picket line always has been sacred to union men and we do not expect the other crafts to violate ours."

Responsibility for Police Call

Frank Fox, spokesman for the Bay Area Shipbuilders' Negotiating Committee, said he understood that the large police guard had been asked by naval authorities, because the plants are engaged solely on contracts from the Navy and the Maritime Commission. But Rear Admiral John Wills Greenslade, commandant of the Twelfth Naval District, said:

"We have made no request as yet on the Mayors (of San Francisco and Oakland). The shipbuilders have notified the Mayors of the situation and their anticipation. We will take action when we see fit after a conference with Washington. Washington is directing the situation here."

Police Chief Charles Dullea of San Francisco said that he had been in communication with Admiral Greenslade and that the shipbuilders had talked to Mayor Rossi, but that he had taken the police action of his own volition. No specific request was made by either party, he added.

Hour-Wage Terms at Issue

The strike is in protest against the terms of a coastwise master agreement for the shipbuilding industry which was negotiated by the A. F. of L., the Department of Labor, representatives of the Office of Production Management and the shipbuilders.

This agreement provides for a basic hourly wage of $1.12 as compared with the strikers' demand for $1.15 and the $1 an hour wage under the old contract which expired April 1.

The new agreement, however, provides only time and a half for overtime work, as against the strikers' demand for double time, which they had for several years under the old agreement.

The 1,200 striking A. F. of L. machinists contend that their local autonomy was violated in the signing of an agreement to which they had never subscribed and which their members had overwhelmingly

Continued on Page Ten

Winant, With Sand Bucket, Doused Many Fire Bombs

By The United Press.

LONDON, May 11—John G. Winant, American Ambassador who long since has graduated from the tenderfoot stage as a "Blitzee," went through last night's bombings armed with a bucket of sand, with which he doused incendiaries dropped in his neighborhood.

He helped an assistant and military attachés remove clothing from his home, which appeared to be endangered by a hit next door.

CONVOY SHOWDOWN LIKELY THIS WEEK

Tobey Says He Will Press for Senate Test—Roosevelt May Clarify Stand Wednesday

Special to THE NEW YORK TIMES.

WASHINGTON, May 11—A showdown this week on the question of United States naval vessels convoying lease-lend aid to Britain is expected by many members of Congress.

Wednesday may be the day when such a turn will be reached, for then the Senate will probably get the bill which would permit the President to acquire foreign ships now lying idle in United States ports. And on that day the President is scheduled to make an address before the Pan American Union here.

Many Administration supporters believe that Mr. Roosevelt will make this speech an occasion for clarifying his views on the convoy question and perhaps on other points of foreign policy.

While it was thought that the President's illness might prevent the talk, this belief is being dissipated as he continues to improve.

Today Representative George H. Tinkham, Republican of Massachusetts, challenged Mr. Roosevelt to ask Congress for a declaration of war and "abide by the decision of Congress on this issue."

The ship-seizure bill will be considered tomorrow by the Senate Commerce Committee. Senator Josiah W. Bailey of North Carolina, chairman of the committee, has said that he hopes to report it to the Senate by Wednesday in the form that it passed the House.

Tobey Expected to Stand Pat

Several amendments are planned by opponents of the sweeping authority the bill would give the President as it was passed by the lower chamber. Chief of these, of course, is the amendment planned by Senator Charles W. Tobey, Republican of New Hampshire, who is a leader of the fight against convoys.

Mr. Tobey, whose anti-convoy resolution was defeated in committee, wishes to attach it to the ship-seizure bill. Other amendments anticipated include one to provide that the ships could only be used in American waters or outside the combat areas. Another would forbid the turning of either Italian or German ships over to the British.

Some supporters of the Tobey resolution are now trying to persuade him not to submit it as an amendment. Senator Gerald P. Nye, Republican of North Dakota, said that its defeat was indicated and that he thought President Roosevelt "would take its defeat as a signal to go ahead with convoys." But it was believed that Mr. Tobey would stand pat on his intentions.

The President's address Wednesday, it is predicted, will be one of his most important since the war began. It will be broadcast throughout this country and will be translated into foreign languages for transmission by short wave to other lands.

Tinkham Calls for Statement

Mr. Tinkham's statement challenging Mr. Roosevelt was, in part, as follows:

"The time has come when the American people are entitled to have from the President a truthful and unequivocal statement of his own position and his own intent. He should either deny and repudiate these covert declarations of war by those around him, or else he should avow them and be prepared to face the American people with the greatest betrayal of trust in the history of our Republic; for let it be remembered that the American people have had no wish or will to enter into war in Europe or in Asia, and that the President sought reelection to a third term in office, in violation of a most precious American tradition, upon the promise and pledge that he would keep this country out of war. He has repeatedly attempted to justify his warlike actions with the specious and deceitful plea that they were intended to keep this country at peace."

Meanwhile, another showdown was nearing. This is on demands in Congress that $1,000,000,000 be trimmed from government nondefense expenditures on the grounds that the $3,600,000,000 defense revenue program would be made easier if economies are made in nondefense expenses.

It was learned that Speaker Sam

Continued on Page Four

CONVOYING OPPOSED BY HOOVER, URGING MORE AID TO BRITISH

Use of Navy Seen Leading to War, Dictatorship Here and Eventual Bankruptcy

LACK OF UNITY IS CITED

Also Unpreparedness, Which He Says Would Divert the Materiel England Needs

Text of Mr. Hoover's address appears on Page 4.

Warning the American people that the use of our Navy to guard shipments of war matériel will make certain our entry into a war that may drag on for years and lead to dictatorship and bankruptcy here, Herbert Hoover suggested, instead, last night that the United States should increase the share of its own production going to Great Britain, regardless of its own preparedness.

Mr. Hoover, speaking over the Red Network of the National Broadcasting Company, said that the urgent needs of Great Britain today are bomber and fighter planes to guard her sea lanes and ports; merchant ships to make good her war losses; minor naval vessels to guard them, and tanks, munitions and food. He implied that the United States should make available these "tools of war" but should allow the British to man them.

The United States is not prepared to go to war today and a large majority of its people are opposed to any action that might get it into war, the former President declared.

Our Entry Curb on British Aid

He contended that American entry into the war in the near future inevitably would decrease the amount of help available to Britain, by forcing us to retain for our own defenses a large part of our production of planes, ships and guns.

"Is it not clear that we will give less tools to Britain if we join in the war?" he argued. "The solution is not for us to go to war but to give her every tool that will really aid her regardless of our own preparedness. There are risks in this course, but it is the least perilous road we can now take. This solution will not please extremists on either side. Common sense and stark truth rarely do. And I am convinced that here lies the road to national unity that is so essential to America at this time."

Mr. Hoover contended that the United States could take the risk of reducing its own share of its production in the present crisis because "the potential might of this nation is the strongest thing in this whole world," and because in case of necessity the United States could always raise and equip an army of as many millions of men as it might need.

"The defense of America is not dependent upon any other nation, for America cannot be defeated," the former President said with solemn emphasis.

Represents No Group, He Says

Mr. Hoover spoke with evident emotion, making more numerous minor changes of phraseology than is his custom. Early in his speech he interjected a disclaimer that he was speaking as the representative of any party or group or committee, and he added that he would endeavor to speak with respect for the opinions of those who differed with him.

Great Britain's most critical period is right now, during the next

Continued on Page Four

Indian Tribe Still at War With Reich, Berlin Finds

By The Associated Press.

BERLIN, May 11—The German press discovered today that "part of America" is formally at war with Germany.

The Tuscarora Indian tribe of New York State, part of the Iroquois group, formally declared war on Germany in 1917 as "independent people," the press said, because it did not consider itself included in the United States' declaration of war.

But the Tuscaroras "never offered to smoke the peace pipe with a German representative" during peace negotiations and therefore still are at war, the press said.

NAZIS LOOT SERBIA; AMERICANS SUFFER

Soldiers Steal Valuables of British Diplomats—Trucks Take Heavy Items

By RAY BROCK
By Telephone to THE NEW YORK TIMES.

BUDAPEST, Hungary, May 11—The German Army of Occupation in Serbia is conducting a systematic campaign of looting and confiscation and unauthorized seizure of homes and property belonging to Serbians and foreigners, including Americans.

Homes, apartments and villas throughout Belgrade and in scores of resorts in Northern and Central Serbia and in Bosnia have been sacked by Germans down to the last stick of furniture, the last shred of clothing, the last potato and the last loaf of bread.

American Legation seals affixed to the doors of British property—under American protection since the German invasion April 6—have been ignored almost completely. The Belgrade apartments of British diplomats, including those of Armine Dew, the British first secretary, and Peter Garron, the second secretary, were seized by the first German officers to enter Belgrade. All clothing, wines, liquor, foodstuffs, cigars and cigarettes were loaded into officers' automobiles and taken away. German officers are occupying the apartment today.

German officers stole the automobile of Shems Arif Hardin, the Turkish Embassy's first secretary, from its parking place before the embassy. The car—a small Fiat—was clearly marked "CD" (Corps Diplomatique) and was unmistakably the property of a Turkish diplomat.

Americans Keep Their Cars

The German officers vainly tried to "requisition" the automobiles of American diplomats. They attempted to force Mrs. James Bonbright, wife of the American Legation's second secretary, to get out of her coupe and turn it over to a German captain. Mrs. Bonbright refused, and, after having been forced to drive to the German command post to discuss the matter, convinced the Germans that she was determined to retain her automobile at all costs, whereupon she drove it home.

This correspondent lost luggage, clothing, files and other property in his hotel and in the home of the United States Minister, both of which were destroyed in the Sunday

Continued on Page Eight

Mutual Chain Signs Contract With ASCAP; Society's Music Will Return to Air Tomorrow

By JACK GOULD
Special to THE NEW YORK TIMES.

ST. LOUIS, May 11—Music of the American Society of Composers, Authors and Publishers, which has been off the major chains since Jan. 1, will be returned on Tuesday evening to the national network of the Mutual Broadcasting System.

An agreement between ASCAP officials and directors of Mutual was announced tonight after network officials had worked through last night and today to have the society's catalogue of 1,250,000 songs on the air during the convention here of the National Association of Broadcasters. The session begins tomorrow.

In breaking the united front of the broadcasting industry against ASCAP, Mutual reversed its stand of yesterday, when the chain's affiliates blocked any conclusive action on a contract with the society, and threw the N. A. B. delegates into a turmoil. An acrimonious debate was assured for Wednesday, when the music issue will be discussed on the convention floor.

The N. A. B. administration, the Columbia Broadcasting System and the National Broadcasting Company had opposed signing of a contract with ASCAP now because they felt better terms could be won after the Federal consent decree accepted recently by the society becomes effective the first week in June.

The consensus of the delegates was that Mutual's action would force NBC and Columbia to hasten negotiations to avoid being put at a competitive disadvantage.

Edward Klauber, executive vice president of Columbia, said tonight, however, that his chain would continue negotiations with ASCAP until "better terms" than those provided in the Mutual pact were won.

Niles Trammel, NBC president, insisted that signing of the contract by Mutual would not hasten his company's negotiations with the society. He said that NBC would wait until it had gained "the best terms possible."

Neville Miller, N. A. B. president, declined to comment.

Edwin C. Mills, chairman of the

Continued on Page Twelve

REICH PORT SEARED

100 British Planes Raze Docks, Factories With New Big Bombs

BERLIN 'OBJECTIVES' HIT

Offensive Units Battle Nazi Fighters and Down Four—Fire Enemy Oil Stores

By JAMES MacDONALD
Special Cable to THE NEW YORK TIMES.

LONDON, Monday, May 12—Royal Air Force bombers hit at Berlin over Saturday night at the same time German raiders were conducting their terrific onslaught against London.

Directing major offensive efforts against Nazi war objectives, however, the British made their fiercest air attack that night on the port, shipyards and industrial sections of Hamburg.

Late last night the German broadcasting station that announces itself as Deutschlandsender, and which is apparently the most important station in the Reich, suddenly went off the air.

A brief official statement early today said the R. A. F. had again bombed Hamburg heavily during the night. Other Northern German coastal centers, including Bremen, were also under British air attack, it was stated.

Biggest Bombs Used on Hamburg

Concerning the Saturday night attack on the Reich capital, Air Ministry officials did not go beyond the statement that "objectives in Berlin" were bombed. The Ministry's communiqué said the attack was by "smaller forces" than those that blasted Hamburg.

The R. A. F. dropped many of its biggest bombs and the new, very powerful explosives on the major German port in the second destructive attack there in a week.

R. A. F. bombing planes also attacked Bremen, Emden, Rotterdam and La Pallice, France, the site of important docks and oil storage tanks near La Rochelle. Oil stores and a refinery at La Pallice were fired, officials said, and dock buildings damaged.

Other British bombers raked the skies for hundreds of miles over the North Sea. They damaged a German naval vessel and attacked Nazi shipping off the Netherlands and Danish coasts.

From the Saturday night offensives, seven R. A. F. planes failed to return, according to the official statements. The British attack planes shot down four Nazi machines and damaged—probably destroyed—several others that tried to intercept them.

"It was not only a night of formidable bombing, but also of marked success against enemy fighters which the enemy put up to help their ground defenses," the Air Ministry report commented.

Moon Aids in Blasting of Hamburg

Aided by the full moon that clearly lighted ground targets the big forces of British bombers battered Hamburg with heavy loads of high explosive and incendiary bombs, creating big fires through the industrial and docks areas.

Industrial plants with their smokestacks definitely silhouetted in the moonlight proved what the Air Ministry described as "easy targets for our bomb aimers."

Strings of bombs burst across freight yards and along railroad tracks at the port. The Nazi submarine construction area also was bombed. In one Hamburg district the R. A. F. pilots said they started fires of such magnitude they appeared beyond control.

"The night was so clear, when one of our heavy bombs left the plane, I could see it going down for 1,000 feet," a bomb-aimer related.

"Then came the most amazing sight I have ever seen. The flash of the bomb burst was like a great flaming red ball half a mile wide. Even at the height where we were flying we felt a kick from the blast.

"Everything inside the ball seemed to be burning and crumbling, and the docks all around were lighted up. A large block of buildings was caught in the flames, and a few minutes later there was a shattering explosion.

"When another heavy bomb whizzed down, other members of our crew reported that all the anti-aircraft guns and searchlights in a wide radius halted all activity."

While over Germany one R. A. F. bomber, captained by a New Zealander who was making his first raid, was attacked by a Junkers 88

Continued on Page Two

The International Situation

MONDAY, MAY 12, 1941

A pall of smoke hung over London yesterday after German bombers in hundreds had bombed the British capital from Saturday dusk till dawn the next morning. With the coming of day Londoners learned that Westminster Abbey and Westminster Hall, the chamber of the House of Commons, the Egyptian wing of the British Museum and Big Ben, renowned clock landmark of London, had all been hit and damaged by the rain of Nazi missiles. Virtually no section of the metropolis was left unscarred. Last night London had three short alarms but no serious attack was reported. [Page 1, Column 8; Map, Page 2.]

Berlin announced that hundreds of German bombers had rained at least 100,000 incendiary and explosive bombs on London during their Saturday night attack. A reason for the intensity of recent German raids on British ports and cities was suggested in the published opinion of a high German Air Force commander that "total air warfare" was accomplished when the energy centers of the enemy were destroyed and when the enemy's will to resist was paralyzed, so that occupation could be accomplished "more or less" without fighting. [Page 1, Column 6.]

The German blow on London was reported matched in part by an armada of 100 British bombers that dealt Hamburg an attack that was acknowledged, even in Berlin, to have caused unusually heavy damages and casualties. British air units last night again bombed Hamburg and other Reich ports. As the Hamburg raid was going on Saturday night other R. A. F. bombers hit at Berlin, Bremen, Emden, Rotterdam and La Pallice in Nazi-occupied France; others harried shipping along the Continental coast. London announced that seven planes had failed to return. [Page 1, Column 5.]

Moscow entered the Iraqi picture with an announcement that it was prepared to recognize the pro-Axis regime of that country. On the other hand, Cairo heard that both King Ibn Saud of Saudi Arabia and the Premier of Iran had turned deaf ears to pleas by the pro-Axis Premier of Iraq for aid. The belief spread in Turkey that, barring a sudden German move, Britain would have control of the situation in Iraq within ten days. An R. A. F. attack on Iraqi garrisons at Mosul was reported. An Iraqi communiqué said British troops had been repulsed at Rutbah, on the Mosul pipe line, but latest reports from Cairo declared the British had captured Rutbah. [Page 1, Column 7.]

The German Army of occupation in Serbia was reported systematically looting and pillaging the homes of Serbs and foreigners, including United States citizens. German troops were said to be seizing every article of value from residences, apartments and villas. All automobiles were reported seized and it was declared that the German High Command had demanded the right to station Nazi troops even in the homes of United States diplomatic officials. [Page 1, Column 4.]

Many members of Congress were reported in Washington to be expecting a showdown on the question of convoying United States war matériel to Britain when the ship-seizure bill came before the Senate this week. President Roosevelt's speech before the Pan-American Union Wednesday night was expected to contain a momentous declaration of the future policy of the United States in regard to the war. [Page 1, Column 2.]

One leading opinion on the present course of United States policy was expressed by former President Hoover, who said in a broadcast that convoying would inevitably lead to war and that the United States was not prepared to enter the war at present. Mr. Hoover proposed that the United States stay out of the conflict and devote its energies to producing for Britain the vast quantities of matériel that, he said, she so urgently needs. [Page 1, Column 3.]

NAZI RAIDING PACE SUGGESTS INVASION

Rising Tempo Hints at Aim to Destroy 'Energy Centers' as Prelude to Landings

By C. BROOKS PETERS
By Telephone to THE NEW YORK TIMES.

BERLIN, May 11—Indications of the recent past suggest that aerial attacks of the German air force on the British Isles are getting into higher gear. Although with the advance into Spring the nights become shorter and the duration of the attacks appears thus to be increasingly curtailed, the flying weather and therewith the ease of attack appear to become correspondingly better.

With bases all along the occupied Channel coast immediately opposite London and the southern English coast, the Germans obviously enjoy a strategic advantage in the exchange of air raids, and this is furthered by their numerical superiority in planes. However, whether their advantages in these respects can prove decisive only time will demonstrate. But it is interesting to recall the recent remarks of General Field Marshal Albert Kesselring, chief of German Air Fleet II.

Discussing Douhet's theory of total air warfare, Marshal Kesselring declared:

"I consider total air warfare as having fulfilled its objective when the energy centers of a land have been destroyed and the will to resistance of a people paralyzed so that an occupation can take place more or less without fighting or when the threat of occupation breaks the last opposition of a people."

The German air force was officially reported today to have carried out a large-scale "reprisal" attack on London last night. Several hundred German planes participated in the raid, which lasted almost six hours, the official news agency declared. "Many tons" of explosive and incendiary bombs were dropped on the British capital.

Announcing the raid, the German

Continued on Page Two

SOVIET RECOGNIZES NEW IRAQI REGIME

Accepts Proposal of Baghdad—Iran and Saudi Arabia Rebuff Plea for Aid

By The United Press.

MOSCOW, Monday, May 12—Russia has accepted a proposal by the government of Iraq for establishment of diplomatic relations between the countries, the official Tass news agency announced today.

The agency said the offer was tendered through the Soviet Ambassador in Ankara on May 3.

[On May 1 a fresh contingent of British troops landed at Basra. On May 2 the Iraqis were reported to have opened fire on the British garrison at the Habbania air base west of Baghdad.]

"At the end of 1940 the Iraqi Government, through the medium of its Minister in Turkey, repeatedly proposed to the Government of the U. S. S. R. the establishment of diplomatic relations between the U. S. S. R. and Iraq," the Tass statement said.

[According to recent dispatches, the Iraqi Minister in Ankara is a brother of Premier Rashid Ali Beg Gailani.]

"In so doing the Iraqi Government expressed the wish that simultaneously with the establishment of diplomatic relations the Soviet Government should publish a declaration on the recognition of independence of the Arabian countries, including Iraq.

"The Government of the U.S.S.R., entertaining a positive attitude toward the proposal on the establishment of diplomatic relations between the U.S.S.R. and Iraq, did not consider it possible, however, to make this conditional on the publication of any declaration.

"A reply in this sense was given at that time to the Iraqi Government, in consequence of which negotiations were interrupted.

"On May 3, 1941, the Iraqi Government, through the medium of the Soviet Ambassador in Ankara, again proposed the establishment of diplomatic relations between the

Continued on Page Six

LONDON IS HARD HIT

Westminster Is Scene of Destruction—Heart of Empire a Target

FAMOUS HALL IS DAMAGED

Deanery Burns—Kings' Tombs and Poets' Corner Are Safe—Big Ben Is Blackened

By ROBERT P. POST
Special Cable to THE NEW YORK TIMES.

LONDON, Monday, May 12—The sun rose red over London yesterday after one of the worst air raids that London had experienced.

Weary and drawn after a night of horror and fire—a night that even women living alone spent in putting out incendiaries—London began to make a preliminary reckoning of what had happened.

Westminster Abbey, heart and center of the Empire, where every King except Edward V and Edward VIII had been crowned, gapes open to the sky. The Commons Chamber in the Houses of Parliament, where so much political history has been written, got a direct hit. It is completely destroyed and must be rebuilt. Westminster Hall, where Charles I stood his trial, where Warren Hastings was tried and where Gladstone and George V lay in state, was also hit. Its roof, perhaps one of the noblest in architecture, was burned and damaged but still survives.

British Museum Hit

Incendiaries showered down on the British Museum, seriously damaged the Egyptian section and did some damage to the famous library, one of the greatest in the world. However, all the most important treasures of the museum were moved to safety soon after the war broke out. That was the official damage as released by the censor. But there was untold other damage, too. Five hospitals were hit, one of them a children's hospital, and there were casualties in three of them. Besides Westminster Abbey, other churches, one of them one of the most rare and historical in London, were gutted and destroyed. And mile after mile of houses and shops of poor and rich alike were blasted, burned or damaged.

It is not perhaps important to the historian that little shops have been blasted or that a street of little homes has been destroyed; but it is vital to men who own and work in those shops and live in those houses.

But Londoners recovering from this raid—and though it was bad it is too early yet to say that it was one of the worst in history—felt a savage satisfaction when they read in their papers or heard on their radios that thirty-three raiders had been shot down, four by anti-aircraft fire and twenty-nine by fighters.

It was good news and it would probably have been better news if all the speculation had been told, because it is probable that many more Nazi planes were damaged or brought down. Some speculations go far beyond the official figure and in any case it was a very fair percentage of the total raiders over England.

Quiet Night Passed

Last night and this morning there were no further raids. There was a short alert early in the evening but the all clear came very shortly thereafter. Later there were two other warnings, but there was only the distant rumble of gunfire and reports were to the effect that no concentrated raid had developed in any part of the country, though planes were reported at various places.

Early today it was reported that seven Nazi planes had been shot down during the night. Three were hit by anti-aircraft fire and four by night fighters.

A joint communiqué by the Air Ministry and the Ministry of Home Security this morning said that enemy aerial activity during the night was widespread, but that damage was not heavy anywhere. Bombs were dropped in many places, however, but nowhere were the attacks concentrated.

Apparently there was a certain amount of daylight activity yesterday. Large formations of enemy bombers came over the Channel, but they were met and broken up by the British before they could get inland, except in scattered instan-

Continued on Page Two

"All the News That's Fit to Print."

The New York Times.

LATE CITY EDITION
Fair and continued cool today and tomorrow.
Temperatures Yesterday—Max., 62; Min., 49

VOL. XC..No. 30,425. Entered as Second-Class Matter, Postoffice, New York, N. Y. NEW YORK, TUESDAY, MAY 13, 1941. THREE CENTS NEW YORK CITY and Vicinity

HESS, DESERTING HITLER, FLIES TO SCOTLAND; BERLIN REPORTED HIM MISSING AND INSANE; DARLAN MEETS HITLER; R. A. F. POUNDS PORTS

COAST SHIPYARDS SHUT BY PICKETS; RETURN REJECTED

Navy and Maritime Work Stops as Other Crafts Refuse to Pass Heavy Lines

POLICE STAY IN RESERVE

Union Leaders Declare Fight to Finish as Meeting Votes Against Lapsing Strike

By FOSTER HAILEY
Special to THE NEW YORK TIMES.

SAN FRANCISCO, May 12—A request from the Office of Production Management that striking machinists in eleven shipbuilding yards in the San Francisco Bay area return to work pending an attempt to settle their wage and hour demands in conference was unanimously rejected today by a mass meeting of those of the strikers affiliated with the American Federation of Labor.

Picket lines around the eleven plants, established by the 1,200 A. F. of L. machinists and the 700 who belong to the Congress of Industrial Organizations, brought a complete halt to operations as 15,000 to 18,000 other workers who are not on strike refused to pass through the machinists' picket lines.

The strike was called Friday midnight by Local 68 of the A. F. of L. and Lodge 1304 of the C. I. O. The latter is affiliated with the Steel Workers Organizing Committee, headed by Philip Murray, president of the C. I. O. The walkout is in protest against hourly wage and overtime provisions of a master contract for the whole coast signed April 23 in Seattle by representatives of labor, the OPM and the shipbuilders.

Reason for Refusal to Return

The request to go back to work pending a conference came from Joseph Keenan, A. F. of L. representative of the OPM. It was presented to a mass meeting of about 1,000 members of Local 68 by its business agents, E. F. Dillon and Harry Hook, who later said:

"Our members took the position, and passed a resolution to the effect, that inasmuch as we've never been able to get an agreement out of Bethlehem in the past twenty-two years, we don't feel any good purpose would be served by sending the men back to work before an agreement is reached now.

"We feel it would only prolong the controversy and probably result in a repetition of what we are going through now."

Although Bethlehem Shipbuilding, a division of Bethlehem Steel, is only one of the eleven plants involved in the strike, it is by far the largest, employing about 900 of the 1,200 A. F. of L. machinists who are on strike, and it is considered the bellwether of the group.

Out to Compel Settlement

"We intend to tell Mr. Keenan, if he telephones us from Chicago, the attitude of the strikers," Mr. Dillon said. "When he made the request yesterday he said he would call back today. (He had not called up to late tonight.)

"We would be glad to have a representative of the OPM on the ground here to go into a thorough analysis of the situation.

"As things stand now, the strike will continue in effect until we are able to make some agreement with Bethlehem and the rest."

No formal action was taken by the C. I. O. machinists, since the request was not directed to them, but pickets handed out leaflets signed by J. P. Smith, business agent of Lodge 1304, asserting that "hard-won conditions must be preserved and employers, under a smoke screen of national defense, are not going to destroy them." The C. I. O. was not represented in the negotiations for the master contract.

In a joint statement, Mr. Dillon and Mr. Hook said that the machinists, because of the "friendly attitude and fine spirit of the other metal trades organizations," intend to see to it "that all such metal trades men that respected our picket lines will be returned to their jobs without discrimination" and on a basis satisfactory to them.

Apprised of the strikers' position, Frank H. Fox, chairman of the Bay Area Shipbuilders Negotiating Committee and authorized spokesmen

Continued on Page Sixteen

'Peace' Pickets Routed At White House Gates

Special to THE NEW YORK TIMES.

WASHINGTON, May 12—One soldier and one Marine tonight broke up a line of eight pickets marching in front of the White House who represented the American Peace Mobilization. This organization has been charged with being a Communist Front group.

At the hour all Washington theatres were letting out, police emergency cars and motorcyclists roared through downtown Washington to the White House. The two assaulters were arrested and one picketeer was removed to Emergency Hospital where he was reported slightly injured. The picketing continued.

Tonight's fracas followed one at 3 A. M. when a larger group of soldiers and Marines attacked the pickets, tore up their placards and warned them they would be back if the picketing continued. In an earlier assault the policemen did not interfere. Tonight the assailants were seized and one was charged with simple assault. The police then closed and manned the White House gates for the night.

ROOSEVELT TO TALK TO NATION MAY 27

'Fireside Chat' Two Weeks From Today Is Substituted for Address Tomorrow

By FRANK L. KLUCKHOHN
Special to THE NEW YORK TIMES.

WASHINGTON, May 12—President Roosevelt will make a "fireside chat" to the nation May 27, but will not make his scheduled speech before the Pan American Union Wednesday night, it was announced at the White House today.

This change in plans was interpreted generally to mean that the President has in mind no important announcement on American foreign policy for two weeks and that, at least for this period, he does not contemplate any new type of aid for Britain.

The Executive seldom makes fireside chats except upon important matters, however, and his talk on the 27th is generally expected to present an outline of the current position of the United States as he sees it and the future steps that should be taken.

Mr. Roosevelt completed his seventh day in bed because of illness today, and his widely publicized speech was canceled to give him time to recover fully, according to official statements.

Stephen T. Early, White House Secretary, emphasized, however, that the President had never intended his talk before the Pan American Union to be of "world-shaking" importance.

Pressure on President

In informed circles it was understood that the Executive did not intend to be pushed into any important statement and that he considered the present time poor for any announcement of vital importance.

Speaking of the canceled Wednesday address, Mr. Early said:

"So, despite reports from abroad, there will be no world-shaking pronouncement from President Roosevelt Wednesday night, as this office has stated right along."

Three Cabinet officers, Secretaries Henry L. Stimson, Frank Knox and Claude Wickard, have urged use of the American Navy to protect shipment of war supplies to Great Britain, their speeches generally being interpreted as an appeal for escort of convoys by the American Navy. Other individuals or groups publicly have urged the Executive to go so far as ask for a declaration of war. Pressure has come from all sides on these controversial questions and others.

The decision to cancel Wednesday night's speech was revealed through White House announcement of a resolution adopted by the Board of Governors of the Pan American Union.

Diplomats Ask Postponement

"The Ambassadors, Ministers and chargés d'affaires of the republics of Latin America," the resolution said, "realizing that President Roosevelt has recently been indisposed and in view of the fact that the reception to be tendered him would involve strain upon him, take the liberty of suggesting that the reception be postponed until such time as President Roosevelt may

Continued on Page Eight

HAMBURG HIT HARD

Miles of Docks Fired in British Bombing a Second Night

BREMEN LIKE TARGET

U-Boat Yards and War Plants of Reich Bases Kept Under Attack

By DAVID ANDERSON
Special Cable to THE NEW YORK TIMES.

LONDON, Tuesday, May 13—Nine miles of docks along the River Elbe at Hamburg were set ablaze with heavy British bombs and thousands of incendiaries over Sunday night when the Royal Air Force followed up its attack of the previous night with another vigorous raid on German war ports.

The Hamburg docks were "threaded and crossed with fire, continuing the destruction and disorganization of vital parts of this great seaport," the British Air Ministry reported.

Bremen, the Reich's second port in the size of its war activities, was attacked also with what R. A. F. officials moderately termed a "heavyweight of high-explosive and incendiary bombs."

Shipbuilding yards and especially the plants of the two ports where Germany has built most of her U-boat fleet were blasted.

Previous Havoc Extended

Explosives hammered down on industrial works in both cities, the Air Ministry stated, and vast fires were started to continue the havoc of previous attacks.

Last night "objectives" at the great German industrial center of Mannheim, also a frequent target for the British, were attacked by R. A. F. bombers, a brief official report early today said.

Sunday night attacks were made by the R. A. F. on a number of other targets in the Reich, including Emden again, and the docks of Rotterdam were also bombed.

Four aircraft of the Bomber Command were missing from all these operations, British officials said.

The Coastal Command carried out Sunday night attacks on docks at the Netherland port of Ijmuiden, and on the Nazi seaplane bases on the island of Texel without loss.

The attacks seemed to mark a definite stepping-up of the R. A. F. offensive, as officials of the Bomber Command, in giving some detail of the operations, said the objective was to strike Hamburg again before that city could "recover from the impact of the attacks made Saturday night."

Weather Right for Bomb-Aimers

Fine weather and the brilliant moonlight enabled the British pilots to pick their spot with relative ease over "the vast expanse of docks which was the particular focus" of this raid, it was stated.

An R. A. F. flier's account of the Bremen attack said:

"It was not so cold as when we visited Bremen three nights before, but there was the same bright sky. All the way over there were patches of cloud which looked like stepping

Continued on Page Six

Russians See Advantage In R.A.F. Planes' Big Load

By The Canadian Press.

LONDON, May 12—Increased bomb loads carried by Royal Air Force bombers "partly offset" the German advantage of having air bases close to Britain, Red Star, organ of the Soviet Army, said in an article quoted today by the British Broadcasting Corporation.

The article commented on "the tremendous load of bombs that now can be carried by a single British machine."

In a review of war developments, the newspaper observed that "the hardest blows delivered by the German Air Force in recent weeks have been aimed at British ports and centers of shipbuilding" and also that "the experience of the last war proved that British and United States industry made up for sinkings by U-boats."

PAPEN SEES HITLER, RETURNS TO TURKEY

Envoy Is Expected to Reveal Nazi Plans for Near East—Soviet Move Studied

The following dispatch was received by direct voice broadcast through the Ankara wireless station last night. C. L. Sulzberger prefaced the broadcast in this way:

"The following direct broadcast from Ankara to THE NEW YORK TIMES, New York City, contains news dispatches for THE TIMES. These are exclusive property of the New York Times Company. Dispatches follow."

By C. L. SULZBERGER
Special Broadcast to THE NEW YORK TIMES.

ANKARA, Turkey, May 12—Franz von Papen, the German Ambassador, came back to his post today aboard a large camouflaged Junkers troop transport plane, following a series of last-minute conferences with Reichsfuehrer Hitler at the latter's Obersalzburg retreat.

The Ambassador, who was accompanied by his wife and daughter, was met at the Ankara Airport by the diplomatic representatives of the countries that have signed the tripartite accord. He appeared in excellent spirits and conferred for several minutes with the Italian Ambassador.

Herr von Papen has been expected back almost daily for the better part of the last fortnight and the fact that he continually delayed his return and then at the last minute had a long personal conversation with Herr Hitler is regarded as significant.

Events are shaping up rapidly in the Middle East, and the only hand that now remains to be disclosed fully is that of Germany. Russia has abandoned her disinterest in this area by according full diplomatic recognition to the bellicose Rashid Ali Beg Gailani government of Iraq.

Britain, already engaged in extensive military operations in Iraq, has

Continued on Page Two

Bodies of Brewster and Wife Found In Plane Wreckage in Alleghenies

The bodies of Benjamin Brewster, New York investment broker, and his wife, the former Leonie de Bary Lyon, who disappeared Friday on a projected flight from Roosevelt Field to Warren, Ohio, were found last night in the charred wreckage of their plane on a rugged mountain top forty miles north of Harrisburg.

The discovery was made after several pilots reported they had seen the badly damaged wreck nestled in tree branches on Shade Mountain near Beavertown.

The report that the bodies had been found was telephoned to Private Charles Hicklin of the Pennsylvania Motor Police by Private John Zeigler, one of a party sent out from the barracks at Selinsgrove.

The bodies were taken in charge by Dr. Charles W. Strand, coroner of Snyder County, who will remove them to Middleburg as soon as permission is received from members of the Brewster family.

Late last night positive identification was made by Whitney Stone, vice president of the Stone & Webster Company, a brother-in-law of Mr. Brewster. In a telephone conversation with his sister, Mrs. Edward C. Brewster, Mr. Stone said the plane crashed against the side of a 1,500-foot mountain and then exploded. A reward of $1,000 had been offered by Mr. Stone to the person locating the plane.

The Brewsters' plane was a radio-equipped black and green Beechcraft with a Wright motor. Mr. Brewster was a prominent sportsman pilot and had more than 1,000 flying hours to his credit.

The tangled, charred wreckage was sighted at about 5 P. M. (daylight saving time) by two private pilots from Philadelphia, who were among more than seventy who searched the mountain area by air. They reported having circled the scene and sighted a twisted wing lying near by. The wing, they said, apparently had escaped the flames, and its black and green striping could be seen clearly. These fliers,

Continued on Page Nineteen

ADMIRAL HAS TALK

Berlin Says Ribbentrop Was Present—Place Is Not Disclosed

VICHY PRESS TENSE

U. S. Attitude Is Cause of Worry—Leahy May Protest Attacks

By The Associated Press.

BERLIN, Tuesday, May 13—Reichsfuehrer Hitler has received the French Vice Premier, Admiral François Darlan, in the presence of German Foreign Minister Joachim von Ribbentrop, it was officially announced early today.

The communiqué announcing the meeting did not say where or when it took place.

The announcement said:

"The Fuehrer, in the presence of the Reichsminister of Foreign Affairs, received the vice president of the French Ministerial Council, Admiral Darlan.

Hitler-Stalin Talk Forecast

VICHY, France, May 12 (AP)—Separate meetings of Reichsfuehrer Hitler with Premier Joseph Stalin and Premier Mussolini were considered in diplomatic circles here tonight as likely to result from the current political moves over Europe.

The object of the meetings, these circles said, probably would be complete economic if not military organization of the Axis-dominated Continent.

Observers listed the current shake-up of Spain's civil and military organization and Vice Premier Admiral François Darlan's negotiations with the Germans as indicators of forthcoming conferences of Herr Hitler and Mr. Stalin and Signor Mussolini.

U. S. Gives Press Concern

By G. H. ARCHAMBAULT
Wireless to THE NEW YORK TIMES.

VICHY, France, May 12—For the time being it is not possible to separate the two hemispheres in any discussion here of the world situation. That the situation is tense and is likely to remain so, at least until President Roosevelt has spoken, is admitted.

In every newspaper as well as in every conversation the United States and what it may or may not do is a recurrent topic.

There are some here who surmise that it may have been mentioned in Paris during the visit there of Vice Premier Admiral François Darlan, who is expected back in Vichy tomorrow to report to Marshal Henri Philippe Pétain, who himself returned this morning after a few days' rest in his Riviera estate.

A semi-official commentary declared today that the Marshal has expressed his satisfaction to the Admiral with the progress of his negotiations hitherto.

It is understood that another Admiral—William D. Leahy, the United States Ambassador—may also see Marshal Pétain in the near future for one of their periodical conversations on food supplies and cognate subjects.

To Stick to Collaboration

While there is complete official silence regarding the negotiations with Germany, as also regarding the United States, the Inter-France News Service, now situated in Vichy, which circulates editorials "for free reproduction by any newspaper," advanced the following arguments:

"Should war occur between the United States and Germany and should it be prolonged, the political reasons which led France to follow the road of collaboration would be reinforced by even more decisive practical reasons. For war between the United States and the Axis would immediately create a European solidarity that would be stronger than any sentimental factor.

"An American blockade, which would necessarily be extended to all our coasts, will develop the notion of a common interest among the peoples of old Europe, since from Brest to Koenigsberg and from Narvik [Norway] to Cadiz [Spain] we should be compelled to do without meat from Argentina and coffee from Brazil, to dispense with cotton from the United States and oil from Mexico. The French

Continued on Page Five

Nazis Allege 'Hallucinations'; Silent on Glasgow Arrival

Arrest of Hess's Aides Ordered Since Hitler Forbade Him to Fly—Letter He Left Said to Show Disordered Mind

By Telephone to THE NEW YORK TIMES.

BERLIN, May 12—Authoritative quarters in Berlin refused to comment late tonight on a British statement that Rudolf Hess, 47-year-old deputy leader of the National Socialist party and Reichsfuehrer Hitler's personal representative, had bailed out of a Messerschmitt plane near Glasgow, Scotland, and was in the hands of the British authorities. Earlier in the evening the Germans had officially reported Herr Hess to be missing.

The man who, on Sept. 1, 1939, was designated by Herr Hitler as his second choice, next to Reich Marshal Hermann Goering, in the line of succession for leadership of the German State, was last heard of in Augsburg, in Bavaria, on Saturday. He was reported to have taken an airplane there for an unknown destination in violation of Herr Hitler's orders prohibiting him from flying because of physical disability.

THE GERMAN STATEMENT

The news of the mysterious disappearance of Herr Hess was released, forty-eight hours after he had been reported missing, in the following communiqué:

Rudolf Hess has met with an accident.

Party Comrade Hess, who because of a disease that for a year has progressively worsened has been categorically forbidden by the Fuehrer to continue his flying activities, recently found means in violation of this command to come into possession of an airplane.

On Saturday, May 10, about 6 P. M., Party Comrade Hess took off from Augsburg for a flight from which until today he has not yet returned. A letter that he left behind unfortunately indicated, by its incoherence, symptoms of a mental derangement that permits the inference that Comrade Hess became the victim of hallucinations.

The Fuehrer immediately ordered the arrest of the adjutants of Party Comrade Hess, who alone knew of these flights and, knowing of their prohibition by the Fuehrer, did not prevent or immediately report them.

Under the circumstances, the National Socialist movement must regretfully assume that Comrade Hess has crashed or met with an accident somewhere on his flight.

Herr Hess last spoke in public in an official capacity on May 1 as the representative of Herr Hitler at the Labor Day demonstration of the party in Augsburg, where he addressed the congress of the Reich Labor Chamber.

Herr Hess, who also was a member of the German Cabinet as Minister Without Portfolio, was born in Alexandria, Egypt, on April 26, 1894. He became identified with the party in 1921, and in recognition of his services Herr Hitler appointed him as private secretary, a post that he held from 1925 until 1932, when he received more responsible positions in the party organization.

Despite his position as deputy

Continued on Page Four

The International Situation

TUESDAY, MAY 13, 1941

A laconic announcement from 10 Downing Street gave to an astounded world last night the news that Rudolf Hess, deputy leader of the Nazi party in Germany and the third most powerful figure in the Reich, had landed by parachute in Scotland and was in safe custody in a Glasgow hospital suffering from a broken ankle. The official statement gave no direct explanation for the dramatic development, but it was presumed that the man who was named at the outset of the war by Adolf Hitler as his second in succession had deliberately fled Germany.

Herr Hess flew to Scotland in a Messerschmitt 110, a plane incapable of carrying sufficient fuel for his return to Germany. The plane crashed Saturday night on the Duke of Hamilton's estate. The flier established his identity in the hospital, and the Foreign Office dispatched an attaché to interview him there. [All the foregoing, Page 1, Column 8.]

Berlin issued a communiqué earlier in the day stating that Herr Hess, apparently suffering from "hallucinations" induced by a long-standing ailment, had taken off by plane from Augsburg Saturday evening against the express orders of Herr Hitler and was "missing" and presumably had "met with an accident." It was announced that Herr Hess's adjutants had been ordered arrested. [Page 1, Column 6.]

Hundreds of German bombers flew over South England and the Midlands Sunday night, attacking airdromes and other objectives, and causing destruction over widespread areas. Nine Nazi planes were shot down. A Berlin statement that forty-five British airfields were attacked was contradicted by the British, who said the military damage was "not considerable." Few raiders were reported over Britain last night. [Page 6, Column 1.]

Over Sunday night the R. A. F. was sending wave after wave of bombers against German ports, particularly Hamburg and Bremen. Nine miles of docks and shipyards on the River Elbe were laced with fires from British incendiaries, and attacks were made on Emden, Rotterdam and Ijmuiden. Last night British planes again bombed Mannheim. [Page 1, Column 3.]

The return to Ankara of German Ambassador von Papen from an extended visit to Berlin gave rise to a belief that Germany would propose a far-reaching economic treaty to all but isolated Turkey. Ankara also looked for an early meeting between the Ambassador and the Iraqi Defense Minister, who has been visiting Ankara. [Page 1, Column 4.]

The situation in Iraq was described by the British as now "stabilized." R. A. F. planes harried remnants of Iraqi forces, and British mechanized forces completed the occupation of Rutbah, a vital point on the oil pipe line and site of an airplane base. [Page 2, Column 6.]

The British forces in Ethiopia tightened their pincer around Alagi, the last Italian stronghold on the Asmara-Dessye road. The Italian garrison at Gondar was said to be virtually isolated. In North Africa, the Admiralty announced, British warships bombarded Bengazi Saturday night, but Rome asserted the British vessels had been routed after having suffered direct hits. [Page 3, Column 4.]

Reichsfuehrer Hitler received Admiral Darlan, the French Vice Premier, in the presence of German Foreign Minister von Ribbentrop at an undisclosed place, it was announced in Berlin. The role that the United States might play in world events was believed in Vichy to loom large in any discussion of European affairs that might be going on. "Collaborationist" sources predicted a "European solidarity" in the event the United States engaged in war with Germany. [Page 1, Column 5.]

In Washington the ship-seizure bill sponsored by the Administration passed its first test in the Senate when the Commerce Committee reported it favorably by a vote of eleven to four, thus making it possible to bring the measure to the floor later this week. The committee defeated an attempt to prevent transfer to a belligerent of any of the ships that might be seized. [Page 7, Column 1.]

President Roosevelt's scheduled speech before the Pan American Union tomorrow night has been canceled, but he will make a fireside chat to the nation on May 27, in which it is expected that he will deal with the position of the nation in the international situation and the future steps that should be taken. [Page 1, Column 2.]

BRITISH ASTOUNDED

Hitler's Deputy Is in Hospital After Bailing Out of War Plane

HAS A BROKEN ANKLE

London Believes Hess's Flight May Portend a New Purge in Reich

By ROBERT P. POST
Special Cable to THE NEW YORK TIMES.

LONDON, Tuesday, May 13—Rudolf Hess, deputy leader of the German Nazi party and the third-ranking personage in the German State, parachuted to earth in Scotland on Saturday night and is now a prisoner of war.

That may sound like something from a mystery thriller by Oppenheim. But in sober truth, 10 Downing Street issued a communiqué last night that is probably the strangest and most dramatic document ever to come from the official home of a British Prime Minister.

THE BRITISH STATEMENT

This statement said:

Rudolf Hess, the Deputy Fuehrer of Germany and party leader of the National Socialist party, has landed in Scotland in the following circumstances:

On the night of Saturday, the tenth, a Messerschmitt 110 was reported by our patrols to have crossed the coast of Scotland and to be flying in the direction of Glasgow. Since a Messerschmitt 110 would not have fuel to return to Germany, this report was at first disbelieved.

Later on a Messerschmitt 110 crashed near Glasgow with its guns unloaded. Shortly afterward a German officer who had bailed out was found with his parachute in the neighborhood, suffering from a broken ankle.

He was taken to a hospital in Glasgow, where he at first gave his name as Horn, but later on he declared that he was Rudolf Hess.

He brought with him various photographs of himself at different ages, apparently in order to establish his identity.

These photographs were deemed to be photographs of Hess by several people who knew him personally. Accordingly, an officer of the Foreign Office closely acquainted with Hess before the war has been sent up by airplane to see him in the hospital.

Identified by Official

Ivone A. Kirkpatrick, who used to be first secretary in the British Embassy in Berlin, was the official sent to Scotland, and the Ministry of Information announced early this morning that Herr Hess's identification had been definitely established.

Earlier the Germans had announced that Herr Hess, who was outranked only by Reichsfuehrer Hitler and Reich Marshal Hermann Goering in the Nazi hierarchy, had been suffering from hallucinations and had violated Herr Hitler's orders in taking the plane.

It was just before nightfall Saturday that Herr Hess was found by a Scottish farm worker; he was groaning in agony, with his parachute wrapped around him. He was taken first to a little two-roomed cottage and then was turned over to the military authorities. This morning he was in a military hospital somewhere near Glasgow.

That is the bare outline of the facts as they are known so far. What do they mean? The Germans have already announced that Herr Hess's "adjutants" have been arrested. The British are inclined to believe that there may be another purge in Germany—a purge similar to the one following the arrest of Captain Ernst Roehm, who was also one of Herr Hitler's closest collaborators, on June 30, 1934.

But from this distance it is almost impossible to say what this development means as far as Germany is concerned. One can record only what the British believe it means. One Briton told the writer that "this is the first 'break' we have had since the war started."

Alfred Duff Cooper, the Minister of Information, himself acted as messenger boy to take the British

Continued on Page Four

1941

1941 marked the first major league season for Stan Musial. The St. Louis star was one of baseball's greatest hitters for two decades.

Joe Louis knocked out challenger Billy Conn in the 13th round of their first bout.

Whirlaway, ridden by Eddie Arcaro, won the Triple Crown in 1941. One of the greatest horses of all time, and one of the greatest jockeys.

"All the News That's Fit to Print."

The New York Times.

LATE CITY EDITION
Partly cloudy and continued warm today and tomorrow.
Temperatures Yesterday—Max., 91; Min., 75

Section 1

NEWS INDEX, PAGE 35, THIS SECTION

Copyright, 1941, by The New York Times Company.

VOL. XC..No. 30,465. Entered as Second-Class Matter, Postoffice, New York, N. Y. NEW YORK, SUNDAY, JUNE 22, 1941. Including Rotogravure Picture, Magazine and Book Sections TEN CENTS New York City and Vicinity

HITLER BEGINS WAR ON RUSSIA, WITH ARMIES ON MARCH FROM ARCTIC TO THE BLACK SEA; DAMASCUS FALLS; U.S. OUSTS ROME CONSULS

MUST GO BY JULY 15

Ban on Italians Like Order to German Representatives

U. S. DENIES SPYING

Envoys Told to Protest Axis Charges—Nazis Get 'Moor' Text

By BERTRAM D. HULEN
Special to THE NEW YORK TIMES.

WASHINGTON, June 21—The Italian Embassy was directed by the State Department in a note published today to close all its consular offices and other agencies in this country having connections with the Italian Government by July 15. This was the reply to the Italian demand for the closing of all American Consulates in Italy.

At the same time Sumner Welles, Under-Secretary of State, announced that he had sent to Dr. Hans Thomsen, the German Chargé d'Affaires, the text of President Roosevelt's message to Congress yesterday denouncing the sinking of the American freighter Robin Moor in the South Atlantic on May 21.

This message, which accused Germany of being an international outlaw, engaging in piracy and attempting to intimidate the United States by the sinking and to drive American commerce from the seas, contained notice that this country would not yield before such measures and stated that compensation would be sought for the sinking.

It was transmitted "for the information" of the German Government, but constituted in effect a note of protest. A further communication will be sent asking damages when a final determination has been reached of the extent of damages that should be sought.

Will Deny Improper Acts

In addition, the State Department instructed the American Embassies in Berlin and Rome to inform the respective governments that the United States objects to all allegations of improper acts by American consular officials in those countries and to complete arrangements for the withdrawal of the consular officials and their staffs by July 15, the limit set by the German and Italian Governments.

The Axis governments had charged that the American Consuls had spied for the British. No reply has been made by the State Department to the German protests against the order closing Nazi consulates in this country, but the protest will be rejected. The United States alleged subversive activities as the reason for the demand for them to be closed by July 10.

The notes to the German and Italian Embassies were sent by messenger last night. However, no direct charge of improper activities was made against the Italian consuls in the note Mr. Welles sent to Don Ascanio dei principi Colonna, the Italian Ambassador. He merely stated that the continued functioning of Italian consular establishments within United States territory "would serve no desirable purpose."

In addition, the closing of Italian agencies having connections with the Rome government was requested. The Italian Embassy, as in the earlier case of the German Embassy, was exempted, but the closing of the office of the Italian Commercial Counselor in New York was demanded, along with the consulates.

Welles Note to Colonna

The note from Mr. Welles to Prince Colonna follows:

June 20, 1941

His Excellency
Don Ascanio dei principi Colonna
Royal Italian Ambassador
Excellency:

I have the honor to inform Your Excellency that the President has directed me to request that the Italian Government promptly close all Italian consular establishments within United States territory and remove therefrom all Italian consular of-

Continued on Page Two

Hope Dims for Submarine; Diver Balked at 370 Feet

Knox Believes All 33 Are Dead on the O-9 and Expects Rites at Scene for Navy 'Heroes'—Pressure Halts Descent

By RUSSELL PORTER
Special to THE NEW YORK TIMES.

PORTSMOUTH, N. H., June 21—As hope faded rapidly for the crew of the Submarine O-9, which failed to rise after submerging yesterday morning twenty-four miles east of this city, it became known tonight that the Navy might be unable to complete its salvage operations, and might be compelled to leave the bodies entombed where they lie—440 feet below the surface of the Atlantic.

This theory was based upon the assumption that the two officers and thirty-one men must already be given up as lost, but that assumption has become stronger with every new development since the submarine was reported missing.

Last night cork insulation from the interior of the hull was picked up, showing that at least part of the submarine had collapsed, and early today, after fourteen hours of dragging, grapnels located an object believed to be the sunken craft. Since then no signals from the O-9 have been received on the sensitive sound-detection devices on the salvage ships in response to their repeated messages.

The view that the O-9's fate was sealed was strengthened this afternoon when reporters and photographers, visiting the scene in a Navy press boat, saw one of the Navy's most experienced divers fail in an attempt to reach the O-9 after descending 370 feet, or within seventy feet of where the Navy believes it has located the submarine with grapnel lines.

The diver, George Crocker, 30 years old, of Seattle, asked to be hauled up when he became convinced that he was not getting enough air pressure from his life lines of helium-oxygen mixture to overcome the increasing sea pressure as he went lower and lower.

A message from the Falcon said: "Diver descended 370 feet. Had difficulty in breathing. Brought to surface. Will continue attempts by varying diving techniques."

On the salvage ship the dive was called "the most dangerous in submarine history." It was pointed out that no one had ever made a successful "working" dive at 440 feet and that any diver who went down so far, where he would have to grope his way in complete darkness under terrific sea pressure, 195.8 pounds to the square inch, could do so only at extreme risk to his life.

Colonel Frank Knox, Secretary of the Navy, returning tonight on

Continued on Page Thirty

ARMY ASKS GUARD BE KEPT IN SERVICE

Recommends Congress Act to Hold State Troops, Reserve Officers Indefinitely

By HALLETT ABEND
Special to THE NEW YORK TIMES.

WASHINGTON, June 21—Members of the National Guard and Reserve Officers Corps will be kept in active service beyond the single year planned when they were called, if a recommendation made today by the War Department is approved by President Roosevelt and Congress.

Instead of a return to civilian life, starting Sept. 15, their terms of service in uniform may be extended indefinitely, or at least until the Army selectees have been sufficiently trained in ample numbers to permit the Guardsmen to be demobilized. The recommendation to the President does not specify any limit to the proposed extension of service.

At present there are 289,800 National Guardsmen, including their 21,800 officers, on active duty with the Federal Army. They were inducted into service in increments beginning Sept. 15 of last year. Some went into uniform as late as March of this year. Their terms of service, at time of induction, were limited to twelve months, which may not be extended except by act of Congress.

341,300 Would Be Affected

In addition to the National Guardsmen, who comprise eighteen divisions and one cavalry brigade now on active service, the government has called up 51,500 Reserve officers under the same terms, making collectively 341,300 officers and men who would be affected.

Today's War Department recommendation to the President that steps be taken to retain in the service these Guardsmen and Reserve officers was taken, according to the official announcement, because "the War Department has been flooded with queries from the field" as to whether or not the specified one-year limit of service would hold good or be changed.

"These queries are to be expected," continues the announcement, "because whatever the decision, there are many adjustments which the citizen-soldier must make in his affairs."

As yet no decision has been reached in the War Department whether or not to seek authority to retain selectees in the Army beyond the one-year training period specified in the Selective Service Act, but presumably such a step

Continued on Page Nineteen

NAVY MAY REPLACE SHIPYARD STRIKERS

Weighs Putting Own Machinists to Work to End Long Tie-Up in San Francisco

By The Associated Press.

SAN FRANCISCO, June 21—Striking A. F. L. machinists in a $300,000,000 defense program have come to a showdown with the United States Navy and their own international officers.

Reliable reports, not officially denied, indicated that the Navy might install its own machinists in the huge Bethlehem shipyards Monday if the local union did not heed the order of its international president to call off the strike by that time.

The same reports indicated that the Army also might be on hand

Continued on Page Twenty-eight

R. A. F. BLASTS FOE

Bags 26 Nazi Planes in Record Day Raids on Invasion Coast

GERMANY IS BOMBED

British on 11th Straight Night Offensive Into Western Reich

Special Cable to THE NEW YORK TIMES.

LONDON, Sunday, June 22—Twenty-six Nazi fighter planes were destroyed in daylight yesterday by Royal Air Force fliers on their fifth straight day of raiding the Germans' invasion coast and air bases in Northern France.

Twice before dark, waves of R. A. F. warcraft—reportedly numbering at least 150 planes each—swept over the Channel in offensive operations.

Bombers attacked the Nazi's airdromes on each occasion while strong forces of fighters blasted the way for the big planes through formations of German defense fighters. While the major raids were going on, other strong R. A. F. units patrolled over the French coast and battled Messerschmitts.

Attack Goes On; Big Bombs Used

Last night and early this morning the R. A. F. was still attacking the invasion coast, using some of the latest type of high-powered bombs.

Explosions rolled across the Channel like peals of thunder, shaking the ground and rocking buildings for miles along the Kentish coast, observers there reported.

A night curtain of fog hung over the Strait of Dover and little could be seen of the raids. The latest British attacks were apparently being made in the Boulogne area, where some of the heaviest daylight bombing was carried out.

Meanwhile R. A. F. bomber forces were again attacking Western Germany, officials here said briefly early today. The attacks marked the eleventh consecutive night in which the British have bombed industrial centers and war bases in the Reich.

Two Nazi bombers were shot down during the night in small scattered enemy raids on the east and southeast coasts of England. A few German bombs were reported dropped there; there were no accounts of casualties or damage.

The R. A. F. coastal patrol squadrons reported destroying at least two enemy planes and one Nazi

Continued on Page Eighteen

The International Situation

SUNDAY, JUNE 22, 1941

At 5:30 o'clock this morning, Berlin time, two statements were read over the German radio that constituted a declaration of war upon the Soviet Union by Germany. A proclamation of Adolf Hitler, read by Propaganda Minister Goebbels, said that Russia, with Britain and the United States, had sought to "throttle" Germany and that he had therefore decided to put the fate of the German people in the hands of the army. A statement by Foreign Minister von Ribbentrop contained the actual declaration of war. The Finns and the Rumanians were mentioned as allies. Berlin reported subsequently that troops were on the march in East Prussia. [Page 1, Column 8; with map.]

Yesterday was a good day for British arms.

In the Syrian campaign Damascus was occupied. The British announced its capture and Vichy reported its evacuation to avoid street fighting and destruction of the city. Another British force was pushing nearer Beirut, supported by the fleet and the air arm, while a third column was moving toward Tadmur. [Page 1, Column 5; Map on Page 12.]

No less encouraging to the British was a victory much closer to home in the largest British daylight air attack of the war. In a sweep two waves of 150 planes each pounded the French Channel coast, going particularly for airdromes, and engaged German air defenses. The British reported downing twenty-six Nazi planes in these attacks for a loss of five of their own. Late last night the British were continuing their attacks across the Channel. [Page 1, Column 4; Map, Page 18.]

The Libyan theatre was quiet, but British pressure in East Africa was indicated by a protest from Vichy against what was declared to be a virtual ultimatum from General Wavell to French Somaliland to join the Free French or suffer an intensified blockade. London confirmed the representations of General Wavell. [Page 14, Column 1.]

Washington continued the accelerated pace of its anti-Axis diplomatic offensive. The Italian Embassy was instructed to close the forty-nine Italian consulates and seven agencies in this country before July 15. President Roosevelt's message to Congress on the Robin Moor was handed to the German Embassy while the State Department instructed the United States embassies in Berlin and Rome to inform those governments that the United States objected categorically to any allegations of improper acts by United States consuls. [Page 1, Column 1.]

Italian consular circles here were silent concerning the Washington order, but Italian anti-Fascist quarters expressed jubilation. [Page 3, Column 1.]

SYRIAN CITY TAKEN

French Withdraw After a Hard Fight—British Closer to Beirut

TADMUR PUSH IS ON

Allied Planes Harassing Vichy Troops, Whose Defense Falters

By C. L. SULZBERGER
By Telephone to THE NEW YORK TIMES.

ANKARA, Turkey, June 21—French troops evacuated the city of Damascus today after a persistent bombardment by British artillery and withdrew to new positions outside the Syrian capital, according to official advices from Beirut. Early in the afternoon it was learned that the Allied vanguard was already beginning to enter the city. This evening the British reported complete occupation.

The Damascus airport at Mezze has been taken by Indian detachments of the Allied forces and one of the key points east of Damascus has been surrounded by Druz tribesmen fighting on the side of the British.

The Beirut radio announced tonight that a British motorized column pushing westward from Iraq was now heading toward Tadmur. The British column, it was said, has been bombed constantly by the French Air Force, which has just been reorganized and reinforced by French squadrons coming from North Africa. Some German planes also were said to have arrived in Syria.

Advance in High Gear

It is clear that the Allied advance is beginning to move into high gear. Unconfirmed reports that the British forces have reached Beirut indicate that it may also fall soon. Beirut's fate depends largely on whether the British will call in their superior naval forces to shell the city proper. So far this has been avoided in order to keep damage and casualties at a minimum.

[A dispatch from Cairo said that Australian forces had been progressing toward Beirut for two days and had passed Ras Damour.]

The Allies, convinced of the seriousness of the French resistance, evidently have begun to fight this undeclared war in earnest and intend to get it over with fast at any cost. The main center of French resistance in the east has been Damascus, and the capture of the city is of great importance.

The Allied counter-move to the French attack in the south, which developed earlier in the week, is now proceeding with dispatch in the Merdjayoun district. The fortress of Merdjayoun is in Allied hands and it is obvious that the region is being rapidly cleared, since the coastal advance is dependent to a large degree on a corrollary advance in the center.

Considerable concentrations of French artillery had been brought up around Damascus. The French dug in and placed batteries in many of the villas and gardens in the outer sections of the city. These batteries were slowly picked off by British gunners with Royal Air Force support, but the principal British effort was artillery shelling. The British sought to avoid excess damage by aerial bombardment, which is less accurate than artillery fire.

Tadmur Believed in Peril

The French admission that a British column is pressing toward Tadmur would seem to indicate that perhaps the town is endangered. Several days ago reliable sources here reported the existence of the column, but this was steadfastly denied by Beirut.

While there have been new reports that the trouble for the British in Iraq is far from over, the fact that they are able to spare considerable forces from there would indicate that everything is under control. It is known that British forces also are working westward along the North Syrian frontier toward Aleppo, but the exact strength of these units is not known here.

British military circles admit that the Syrian adventure can no longer

Continued on Page Twelve

FINLAND
NORWAY
SWEDEN
Gulf of Bothnia
LENINGRAD
ESTONIA
GOTLAND
DENMARK
LATVIA
MOSCOW
BALTIC SEA
LITHUANIA
EAST PRUSSIA
WHITE RUSSIA
MINSK
BERLIN
Warsaw
SOVIET RUSSIA
Brest Litovsk
POLAND
KIEV
GERMANY
Lwow
UKRAINE
CZECHOSLOVAKIA
Dniester R.
AUSTRIA
HUNGARY
Odessa
RUMANIA
Bucharest
Constanta
YUGOSLAVIA
BLACK SEA
ADRIATIC SEA
BULGARIA
ITALY
ALBANIA
GREECE
Istanbul
TURKEY

WHERE GERMAN ARMIES MARCH ON RUSSIA

Shown on the map is the western frontier of the Soviet Union, a battle line of more than 2,000 miles. Berlin indicated an attack from Norway to Rumania.

The Hitler Proclamation

The text of Adolf Hitler's proclamation, as recorded here by Columbia Broadcasting System, follows:

It was a difficult step for me to send my Minister to Moscow in order to attend to work against the policy of encirclement of Britain.

I hoped that at last it would be possible to put away tension.

Germany never intended to occupy Lithuania. The defeat of Poland induced me to again address a peace offer to the Allies. This was declined because Britain was still hoping to bring about European coalition.

That is why Cripps [Sir Stafford Cripps, British Ambassador] was sent to Moscow. He was commissioned under all circumstances to come to an agreement with Moscow. Russia always put out the lying statement that she was protecting these countries [evidently Lithuania, Estonia and Latvia, the Baltic States].

The penetration of Russia into Rumania and the Greek liaison with England threatened to place new, large areas into the war. Rumania, however, believed she was able to accede to Russia only if she received guarantees from Germany and Italy for the remainder of the country. With a heavy heart, I did this, for if Germany gives guarantees, she will fulfill them. We are neither Englishmen nor Jews.

I asked Molotoff [Soviet Foreign Commissar V. M. Molotoff] to come to Berlin, and he asked for a clarification of the situation. He asked, "Is the guarantee for Rumania directed also against Russia?"

I replied, "Against every one."

And Russia never informed us that she had even more far-reaching intentions against Rumania.

Molotoff asked further, "Is Germany prepared not to assist Finland, who was again threatening Russia?"

My reply was that Germany has no political interests in Finland, but another attack on Finland could not be tolerated, especially as we do not believe that Finland is threatening Russia.

Molotoff's third question was, "Is Germany agreeable that Russia give guarantees to Bulgaria?"

My reply was that Bulgaria is a sovereign State and I did not know that Bulgaria needed guarantees. Molotoff said Russia needed a passage through the Dardanelles and demanded bases in the Bosporus.

A few days later she [Russia] concluded the well known friendship agreement which was to incite the Serbs against Germany. Moscow demanded the mobilization of the Serbian Army.

When I still was silent, the men in the Kremlin went one step further. Russia offered to deliver war material against Germany. This was at the same time that I advised Matsuoka [Japanese Foreign Minister Yosuke Matsuoka] to bring about a lessening of the tension with Russia.

Serbian officers flew to Russia, where they were received as allies. Victory of the Axis in the Balkans at first foiled the plan to involve Germany in a long war and then, together with England and with the hope of American supplies, to throttle Germany.

Now the moment has come when I can no longer look at this development. Waiting would be a crime against Germany.

For weeks the Russians have been committing frontier violations. Russian planes have been crossing the frontier again and again to prove that they are the masters. On the night of June 17 and again on June 18 there was large patrol activity.

The march of the German Armies has no precedent. Together with the Finns we stand from Narvik to the Carpathians. At the Danube and on the shores of the Black Sea under Antonescu [Rumanian Dictator Ion Antonescu], German and Rumanian soldiers are united.

The task is to safeguard Europe and thus save all.

I have therefore today decided to give the fate of the German people and the Reich and of Europe again into the hands of our soldiers.

BAD FAITH CHARGED

Goebbels Reads Attack on Soviet—Ribbentrop Announces War

BALTIC MADE ISSUE

Finns and Rumanians Are Called Allies in Plan of Assault

Statement by von Ribbentrop [is] printed on Page 6.

By C. BROOKS PETERS
By Telephone to THE NEW YORK TIMES.

BERLIN, Sunday, June 22—As dawn broke over Europe today the legions of National Socialist Germany began their long-rumored invasion of Communist Soviet Russia. The non-aggression and amity pact between the two countries, signed in August, 1939, forgotten, the German attack began along a tremendous front, extending from the Arctic regions to the Black Sea. Marching with the forces of Germany are also the troops of Finland and Rumania.

Adolf Hitler, in a proclamation to the German people read over a national hook-up by Propaganda Minister Dr. Joseph Goebbels at 5:30 this morning, termed the military action begun this morning the largest in the history of the world. It was necessary, he added, because in spite of his unceasing efforts to preserve peace in this area it had definitely been proved that Russia was in a coalition with England to ruin Germany by prolonging the war.

Saw Stalemate in West

Herr Hitler, in his proclamation as reported here, made one vitally interesting statement, namely, that the supreme German military command did not feel itself able to force a decisive victory in the West—apparently on the British Isles—when large Russian troop concentrations were on the Reich's borders in the East.

The Russian troop concentrations in the East began in August, 1940, Herr Hitler asserted. "Thus, there occurred the effect intended by the Soviet-British cooperation," he added, "namely, the binding of such powerful German forces in the East that a radical conclusion of the war in the West, particularly as regards aircraft, could no longer be vouched for by the German High Command.

[The German radio announced early today that documentary proof would shortly be given of a secret British-Russian alliance, made behind Germany's back.]

Designed "to Save Reich"

The German action, Herr Hitler explained to his fellow-National Socialists, is designed to save the Reich and with it all Europe from the machinations of the Jewish-Anglo-Saxon warmongers.

The German Foreign Minister, Joachim von Ribbentrop, followed Dr. Goebbels on the air with a declaration of the Reich Government read before the foreign correspondents in the Foreign Office. Herr von Ribbentrop said he received V. G. Dekanosoff, the Russian Ambassador, this morning and informed him that in spite of the Russian-German non-aggression pact of Aug. 23, 1939, and an amity pact of Sept. 28, 1939, Russia had betrayed the trust that the Reich had placed in her.

"Contrary to all engagements which they had undertaken and in absolute contradition to their solemn declarations, the Soviet Union had turned against Germany," the Reich note asserted. "They have first not only continued, but even since the outbreak of war intensified their subversive activities against Germany in Europe. They have second, in a continually increasing measure, developed their foreign policy in a tendency hostile to Germany, and they have third massed their entire forces on the German frontier ready for action."

The Soviet Government, it was charged, had violated its treaties

Continued on Page Seven

"All the News That's Fit to Print."

The New York Times.

LATE CITY EDITION
Showers and local thunderstorms today, cooler tonight. Tomorrow fair, moderate temperature.
Temperatures Yesterday—Max., 79; Min., 70

VOL. XC..No. 30,481. Entered as Second-Class Matter, Postoffice, New York, N. Y.

NEW YORK, TUESDAY, JULY 8, 1941. THREE CENTS NEW YORK CITY and Vicinity

U. S. OCCUPIES ICELAND TO THWART NAZI PERIL, NAVY TO CLEAR SEA THAT FAR FOR BRITISH AID; RUSSIANS REPEL DRIVES, GERMANS TAKE CERNAUTI

J. L. LEWIS ASSAILS ROOSEVELT'S USE OF ARMY IN STRIKE

Miners' Chief Also Denounces Hillman's Part in Effort to Settle Soft Coal Dispute

ATTACK STIRS C. I. O. IRE

Potofsky, Acting A.C.W. Head, Accuses Lewis of Playing Politics in National Crisis

By W. H. LAWRENCE
Special to THE NEW YORK TIMES.

WASHINGTON, July 7—A sharp attack by John L. Lewis on President Roosevelt's Administration and Sidney Hillman, OPM associate director general, today brought from Jacob Potofsky, acting president of Mr. Hillman's union, the Amalgamated Clothing Workers, a charge that Mr. Lewis was "playing politics" in the national emergency and creating disunity within the C. I. O.

The clash between Mr. Lewis and Mr. Potofsky took place at a closed meeting of about 250 C. I. O. leaders, but enough details were revealed by participants so that it stood out as the highlight of the conference summoned by Philip Murray, C. I. O. president, to mobilize influence against "all pending bills in Congress which curtail in any way the rights of labor, such as the May and Connally bills, the Vinson bill and the Ball bill."

Mr. Lewis was reported to have been most vigorous in his denunciation of the President and Mr. Hillman for utilizing the Army to break the U. A. W.-C. I. O. strike at the Inglewood, Calif., plant of North American Aviation, Inc., and to have expressed renewed dissatisfaction with the National Defense Mediation Board.

Lewis Cites Coal Dispute

He charged Mr. Hillman with responsibility for certification of the soft coal strike to the Mediation Board, a step opposed by Mr. Lewis. The miners' president pointed out to the delegates that the United Mine Workers Union in negotiating the final contract with Southern bituminous operators yesterday had accepted only those Mediation Board recommendations favorable to them, and had disregarded the Mediation Board suggestions which were unfavorable to the U. M. W.

Recalling his own opposition to President Roosevelt's re-election for a third term, Mr. Lewis was said to have spoken so critically of C. I. O. unions which support Administration labor policy and Mr. Hillman that Mr. Potofsky regarded his speech as a virtual invitation for the clothing workers' union to get out of the C. I. O.

When Mr. Potofsky arose to speak his voice was raised so high that it was clearly audible outside the meeting room. He pledged anew the loyalty of the A. C. W. to the C. I. O. and said that the clothing workers union, like the mine workers union, would fight vigorously against compulsory arbitration.

But Mr. Lewis was "playing politics," Mr. Potofsky continued, and in his anger against President Roosevelt and Mr. Hillman seemed to be inviting the Amalgamated to leave the C. I. O., which it had helped to found and to which it had made large contributions of men and money.

Potofsky Points to C. I. O. Gains

Mr. Hillman and the Roosevelt Administration needed no defense, Mr. Potofsky said. The record of labor's gains was clear and in recent months, while Mr. Hillman had been exerting considerable influence on labor policy, the C. I. O. had made some of its greatest gains, including the Ford Motor Company contract and the abolition of Bethlehem Steel Company's

Continued on Page Twelve

The International Situation

TUESDAY, JULY 8, 1941

President Roosevelt informed Congress yesterday that United States bluejackets and marines had occupied Iceland. This step was taken, the President explained, to forestall possible German occupation and thus reduce the threat to shipping in the North Atlantic, as well as to insure the delivery of American goods to Britain. Equally important was the announcement that the United States Navy had been instructed to assure safe communications between Iceland and this country. The dispatch of troops was made upon Iceland's invitation and was surrounded with agreed restrictions to assure that it should involve no impairment of Iceland's present or future sovereignty. [Page 1, Column 8.]

Possibility that soldiers might be added to the occupying force was seen in the suggestion that Congress would be asked immediately to amend the Selective Service Act to permit the retention of trainees beyond a period of one year, and to allow their use anywhere that proved necessary. [Page 2, Column 2.]

Congressional reaction to the announcement was predominantly favorable. Even some of the anti-interventionist members declared their support of the move if it were on a purely defensive basis. [Page 1, Columns 6 and 7.]

Britain cheered. The Foreign Office called the announcement "a most significant event" and observed that British troops would be released for duty elsewhere. They will be withdrawn by stages. The additional safeguarding of Atlantic sea lanes was not overlooked. [Page 1, Column 7.]

On the Nazi-Soviet battlefront there appeared to be little significant change. Even Berlin admitted that the Russians were putting up a desperate defense and Moscow said all lines were holding their own or doing better than that.

On three fronts, indeed, the Russian reports said, the Nazis have been thrown back on the defensive. In the Baltic region, in what the Soviet called the first major battle of the campaign, the tide was said to have turned in Russia's favor. In the Minsk area German thrusts near Lepel were said to have been contained. The northern prong of the attack on the Ukraine, striking at Novograd Volynsk, was declared to be stopped. Far to the south, the evacuation of Cernauti was acknowledged, but the lines were said to be holding. [Page 1, Column 4; Map, Page 4.]

German reports were not entirely at variance with this picture. German troops were said to be "battling toward the Dnieper" in the central zone, and some units were said to have pierced the "Stalin Line." An advance was reported in the south, after the repulse of a heavy counterattack and the capture of Cernauti. Air activity was again stressed, with Berlin putting the losses at 204 Russian and ten German planes. [Page 5, Column 1.]

While the British continued their advance in Syria on three principal cities, Beirut, Aleppo and Homs [Page 7, Column 1], they struck a new blow in the Mediterranean with a sharp air raid on Palermo, Sicily. Shipping in the port was the chief target, and damage to five vessels was reported. Cruisers were machine-gunned and "confusion and alarm" were observed. Docks and shipping were also raided at Bengazi in Libya, while German planes raided Alexandria. [Page 6, Column 2.]

Ships were also attacked, and six disabled, in a very heavy daylight assault on the Continent by the Royal Air Force. Factories and airfields in Northern France were the chief targets, but a convoy was fired on off the Netherland coast. Big day raids were made between Sunday and Monday night blows in the Reich. Berlin acknowledged heavy attacks from Thursday to Sunday but put the plane losses at eighty-three British to nine German. [Page 1, Column 5.]

The Argentine Foreign Minister took immediate steps to solve the border crisis between Peru and Ecuador. He sought to associate Brazil and the United States in an offer of good offices. Acting Secretary of State Welles hinted at possible foreign instigation of the clash by speaking of the desire to "fish in muddy waters." [Page 10, Column 2.]

BALTIC BATTLE ON

Germans Reported Held or Thrown Back in All Sectors But One

INVADER AT DNIESTER

Advances in Bessarabia—Claims More Stabs Into Stalin Line

By DANIEL T. BRIGHAM
By Telephone to THE NEW YORK TIMES.

BERNE, Switzerland, Tuesday, July 8—The first major battle in the Russo-German conflict, on the northern Baltic front in an area where Russian counter-offensives reportedly have forced the Germans to take the defensive, continued yesterday in the Russians' favor, according to reports received here. The Russians, it was said, were pounding German lines of communication with aerial bombing and artillery shelling.

[Today's Red Army communiqué reported that the Germans had been thrown back or held at a standstill in all but one of the major fighting sectors. It was acknowledged that in the Bessarabian region German forces had reached the Dniester River east of Cernauti.

[The Germans reported unofficially that they had pierced the Stalin Line in "several places" and indicated that Reich forces were heading toward the Russian city of Kiev, capital of the Ukraine. The High Command announced the capture of Cernauti. The most intense resistance by the Russians was admitted all along the wide front.]

Dvina River Line Held

Farther south, in the area between Polotsk and Lepel, the Red Army was reported to have contained strong attacks by fresh German forces and to have prevented the Germans from crossing the Dvina River or extending a bridgehead beyond the Berezina-Dvina Canal behind Lepel. A German column that had penetrated southward toward the Minsk-Smolensk road was encircled and destroyed, the Russians stated.

Intense fighting continued in the Lepel area, with the Germans apparently trying there, after having failed at Borisov, to force the Russian positions and form a northern arm for a pincers movement encircling the Minsk forces.

At Bobruisk, where the Germans hope to hinge the southern arm of that pincers, wave after wave of attacking German tanks was annihilated by Russian artillery fire, according to Russian accounts. The Russians also asserted that machine-gunners firing from fixed positions on the eastern bank

Continued on Page Four

UNITED STATES EXTENDS ITS DEFENSE FRONT FARTHER EAST

President Roosevelt disclosed yesterday that American naval forces had landed on Iceland (top of map) at the invitation of the Reykjavik government. He also announced that troops had gone to new United States bases on Trinidad, off the north coast of South America, and in nearby British Guiana to forestall any Nazi "pincers movement" against the Western Hemisphere.

NAVY FORCES LAND

Roosevelt Holds Move, on Reykjavik's Bid, Bars Triple Threat

AIR SQUADRONS SENT

British to Quit Island—U. S. Forces Also Go to Trinidad and Guiana

The texts of the messages on the Iceland occupation, Page 3.

By FRANK L. KLUCKHOHN
Special to THE NEW YORK TIMES.

WASHINGTON, July 7—United States naval forces today occupied Iceland, in the German blockade zone, at the invitation of the island's government, President Roosevelt informed Congress.

The step was taken to forestall German occupation of the island, with a consequent threat to North America and Atlantic shipping, and to assure delivery of United States munitions to Britain, the President told Congress in a special message. Bluejackets and marines were the advance body of United States forces that will supplement, and eventually replace, British forces on this strategic Atlantic base.

Coincidentally the Chief Executive instructed the United States Navy to assure safe communications between Iceland, lying less than 700 miles from Scotland and about 900 from German-occupied Norway, and the United States. American ships carrying war supplies as far as Iceland, which is not in a domestically fixed combat zone, thus will be protected.

Threat by Germany

Germany has threatened to sink ships entering Icelandic waters. On Feb. 10 the Nazis announced that they had machine-gunned the airport of Reykjavik, capital of Iceland. Today's move, which met with an initially favorable reception in Congress, even from non-interventionists, was regarded, therefore, as one of the most portentous taken by this country since the European war started.

As part of swift action undertaken while the main German war effort was being directed against the Soviet Union, the President revealed, "substantial" United States forces also have been transported to bases at Trinidad, near the Panama Canal, and British Guiana, farther south, "in order to forestall any pincers movement undertaken by Germany against the Western Hemisphere." These bases were acquired from the British in the deal for fifty United States destroyers.

"The United States cannot permit the occupation by Germany of strategic outposts in the Atlantic to be used as air or naval bases for eventual attack against the Western Hemisphere," the President said to Congress in a blunt explanation of his action. "We have no desire to see any change in the present sovereignty of these regions.

"Assurance that such outposts in our defense frontier remain in friendly hands is the very foundation of our national security and of the national security of every one of the independent nations of the New World."

Silence on Other Bases

Whether this was a hint that eventually the Cape Verdes, the Azores and Dakar on the African coast might have to be occupied could not be ascertained. The President mentioned these places in his most recent fireside chat as potential bases for use against the New World.

Complete secrecy was maintained today by the White House as well as by the Navy, the State Department and other interested departments as to what naval units had arrived in Iceland. All that Navy officials would say was that only

Continued on Page Three

R. A. F. DAY RAIDERS INCREASE IN POWER

Two Big Sweeps Over France Follow Brest-to-Ruhr Attacks—Blows Kept Up in Night

By JAMES MacDONALD
Special Cable to THE NEW YORK TIMES.

LONDON, Tuesday, July 8—The Royal Air Force maintained its seemingly tireless offensive against the Nazis during the last thirty hours, spreading havoc among enemy shipping and at more than a dozen places in Germany and German-occupied territory.

Once again British air operations were on a large scale in daylight yesterday, with great numbers of R. A. F. planes, both bombers and fighters, engaged in two offensive sweeps over Northern France, after extended raids over Sunday night.

Continuing its battering of the occupied territory, the R. A. F. flew over the Channel in bright moonlight early today to attack targets in the region of Calais and Boulogne.

After two hours British bombers were still pressing the offensive in spite of a fierce barrage put up by the German anti-aircraft guns. The noise of bursting bombs and shells

Continued on Page Six

Most in Congress Approve, A Few Critical of Method

By TURNER CATLEDGE
Special to THE NEW YORK TIMES.

WASHINGTON, July 7—Occupation of Iceland by United States armed forces as a step in the defense of the United States and the Western Hemisphere was approved quite generally in Congress upon the disclosure by President Roosevelt of the fait accompli today. Some of the leading non-interventionists could see "persuasive" reasons for the move as a defense measure, but they insisted upon assurances that it was not calculated to ease the United States further toward open participation in the European war.

Some expressed the fear that it was in the line of fulfillment of the recent assertion of Secretary of the Navy Frank Knox that the time had come for the American Navy to help to clear the seas of the German menace, while a few questioned the right or advisability of the President acting without the consent of Congress.

Supporters of the President's foreign policy and Administration followers in general praised the act and the President's explanation in the highest terms. A number of Congressional leaders had given their approval already at a White House conference last night.

Non-Interventionists Concur

But the approving attitude of some of the non-interventionists, although reserved to a degree, was considered as the most significant reaction of all. Some observers saw in it an indication of the sobering effect of "action" as distinguished from "talk" and a suggestion of the quality of unity that could be expected when the government has made a concrete move or commitment.

The non-interventionists' position was perhaps best epitomized by the remark of Senator Arthur H. Vandenberg, Republican, of Michigan, after he had heard the President's message and accompanying documents read in the Senate.

"As presented by the President in his message, a very persuasive case can be made for the occupation of Iceland for purely defense purposes," Senator Vandenberg said. "The chief anxiety will come from the fact that the occupation is preceded by the unrepudiated statement of Secretary Knox—I repeat, the 'unrepudiated' statement—which might indicate the use of Iceland for totally different and totally unacceptable purposes."

The attitude of the non-interventionist leader, Senator Burton K. Wheeler, Democrat, of Montana,

Continued on Page Two

BRITISH 'WELCOME' U. S. OCCUPATION

Our Move in Iceland Hailed in London as 'Big News'—Dilemma for Nazis Seen

By ROBERT P. POST
Special Cable to THE NEW YORK TIMES.

LONDON, July 7—The official announcement that the United States had landed naval forces in Iceland and would replace the British defenders of that island was characterized here tonight as "big news, welcome news" and as "one of the most important events for some time past."

British officials were careful not to say anything about the United States action beyond pointing out that it was a step taken to guard the Western Hemisphere and that it underlined the realization of the United States that the entire Atlantic was part of its own danger area.

There is, of course, a second aspect to be considered. The British have had a large, well-equipped force in Iceland for more than a year now. Since the United States step means that eventually the United States will have taken over the complete defense of Iceland, it follows that this British force will be released for use elsewhere. In other words, as the United States takes over responsibility at this vital post in the West, the British will be able to use their troops for equally vital work in the East. With Russia and Germany locked in conflict, British ability to dispose more and more troops becomes more vital.

Furthermore, United States occupation of Iceland brings the United States closer to the European war. Iceland is an important naval base and an even more important base for the air forces doing convoy work in the Atlantic, and unless the Germans want war with the United States it would

Continued on Page Four

JOINT TAX RETURN MAY BE ABANDONED

Ways and Means Group Gets Flood of Protests Over the $323,000,000 Revenue Plan

Special to THE NEW YORK TIMES.

WASHINGTON, July 7—The Ways and Means Committee was disclosed today to be considering removal from the defense tax bill of the proposal to require married couples to file joint returns.

One member said privately that the committee had met much opposition to this proposal, and that it, together with the 10 per cent added excess profits tax on corporations, probably would precipitate heated fights on the floors of both House and Senate.

In addition to protests from citizens regarding the tax, the committee was said to have run into difficulties in phrasing the bill to provide an equitable basis for payment of the tax liability. Several members have called the requirement unconstitutional, since the Supreme Court several years ago ruled, in an appeal from a Wisconsin law, that the State had no right to measure the tax on one person's property or income by reference to the property or income of another.

Justice Stone, now Chief Justice, joined Justices Holmes and Brandeis in a dissent to that decision. The minority held that a State had the right to go back to the old common law to tax, the old common law being that the property of the wife belonged to the husband and that the husband was responsible for her debts.

Justice Roberts, who delivered the majority opinion in that case,

Continued on Page Eleven

NEW GROUP TO SEEK NON-DEFENSE CUTS

Dr. H. M. Wriston of Brown University Heads Committee to Curb Government Costs

Special to THE NEW YORK TIMES.

PROVIDENCE, R. I., July 7—Henry M. Wriston, president of Brown University, announced today the formation of a nation-wide citizen committee to work for a reduction of nonessential and non-defense expenditures of Federal, State and local governments. The group, under the chairmanship of Dr. Wriston, will be known as the Citizens Emergency Committee on Nondefense Expenditures. It will open headquarters in Washington. The committee will be representative of all elements in American life—the consumer, business, agriculture, labor, women's groups and church organizations—and will include residents of all forty-eight states.

Among citizens, economists, tax authorities and college presidents from thirty-two States who have joined the committee are Louis J. Taber, master, National Grange, Columbus; Mark S. Matthews, retiring president, United States Junior Chamber of Commerce; Robert L. Flowers, president, Duke University; Robert I. Gannon, president Fordham University; Roy G. Blakey, Professor of Economics, University of Minnesota; Olin Glenn Saxon, Professor of Business Administration, Yale University; F. H. Stinchfield, former president American Bar Association, Minneapolis; Tom K. Smith, president Boatmen's National Bank, St. Louis; Thomas S. Gates, president

Continued on Page Ten

Girl Golfers in Shorts Upset Troops' Morale; Gen. Lear, a Witness, to Discipline His Men

By The Associated Press.

MEMPHIS, Tenn., July 7—Some 1,200 tired soldiers slept at Municipal Airport tonight, with the tentative prospect of a warm hike at least part of the 150 miles back to Camp Robinson, Ark., tomorrow, punishment for saluting a group of girl golfers in shorts too gayly and at the wrong time.

After retracing their way from Camp Robinson to Memphis on orders from Lieut. Gen. Ben Lear, commander of the Second Army, who saw the incident, the soldiers were stationed at the airport, given provisions for forty-eight hours and told to await further instructions.

A report they would be required to leave their vehicles and walk at least part of the way back to camp was making the rounds. Officials would not confirm or deny the report.

General Lear was golfing on a Memphis course yesterday as the troops rolled by. Several girls clad in shorts also were playing and many of the soldiers whistled and called to them, setting off a noisy demonstration.

One of the soldiers yelled "fore," at a man in civilian clothes, General Lear himself, who was playing the course. When the general stopped the transport to remonstrate with the officers, another shouted, "Hey, buddy, don't you want a caddy?"

Army sources said General Lear considered the troops' conduct "a severe breach of discipline" and immediately stopped the column, remonstrated with the officers and directed that the convoy be allowed to continue to Camp Robinson and then be sent back here at once.

The battalion's officers and non-commissioned officers were on the carpet before General Lear to-

Continued on Page Twelve

Gene Autry (center) had an Oklahoma town named for him. The people of Berwyn changed their town's name in a tribute to the western movie star.

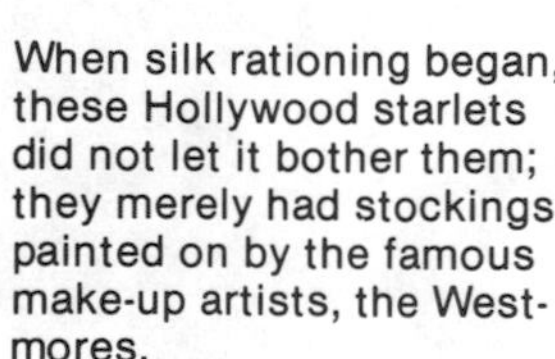
When silk rationing began, these Hollywood starlets did not let it bother them; they merely had stockings painted on by the famous make-up artists, the Westmores.

1941

President Roosevelt and Prime Minister Churchill singing hymns aboard the *Prince of Wales*.

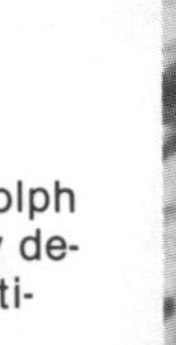

In the Reichstag, Adolph Hitler impassionately denounced Britain's anti-German policy.

"All the News That's Fit to Print."

The New York Times.

LATE CITY EDITION
Cloudy and somewhat warmer today with occasional showers. Tomorrow showers, moderately warm.
Temperatures Yesterday—Max., 76; Min., 56

VOL. XC...No. 30,519. Entered as Second-Class Matter, Postoffice, New York, N. Y. NEW YORK, FRIDAY, AUGUST 15, 1941. THREE CENTS NEW YORK CITY and Vicinity

ROOSEVELT, CHURCHILL DRAFT 8 PEACE AIMS, PLEDGING DESTRUCTION OF NAZI TYRANNY; JOINT STEPS BELIEVED CHARTED AT PARLEY

TREASURY WEIGHS INCREASED RATE OF SECURITY TAX

Doubled Levy and Broader Base Are Considered as Curb on Inflation, Says Morgenthau

DISMISSAL PLAN IS URGED

It Would 'Cushion' Workers in Defense After Arming Ends —House to Get Projects

By JOHN MacCORMAC
Special to THE NEW YORK TIMES.

WASHINGTON, Aug. 14—Secretary Morgenthau stated today that the Treasury was studying the question of higher social security taxes on a broader basis and the supplementing of them by a "dismissal" wage with a view to preventing inflation now and providing a cushion against post-war dislocation.

He said that he had intended to suggest such a plan to the House Banking and Currency Committee if that body had not postponed his appearance from today to Sept. 15.

Mr. Morgenthau explained that the Treasury had considered various means of controlling inflation, including the restriction of installment buying and fixing of prices which already have been decided on, the diminution of consumer purchasing power by the sale of defense bonds and higher taxes, and lastly an increase in social security contributions.

Bank Reserves Under Scrutiny

He hinted that still another method of restricting credit might ultimately be tried, admitting that excess bank reserves required "careful watching." This was the first intimation from Treasury circles that the proposals of the Federal Reserve Board in January for increased powers to increase bank reserve requirements might have merit.

What the Treasury contemplates, it was explained, is an increase not in unemployment contributions but in the Social Security old-age benefit tax of 1 per cent on employer and employe. In the last fiscal year this realized $690,000,000.

According to the original act it was to have been increased to 1½ per cent in 1940-41-42, to 2 per cent in 1943, to 2½ per cent in 1946-47-48 and to 3 per cent after 1949. Because of the recession in 1938, however, Secretary Morgenthau and Marriner S. Eccles, Governor of the Federal Reserve Board, recommended that it be kept at 1 per cent to prevent deflation.

Effect of Tax Rise Is Told

If the tax were increased to 2 per cent it would mean, as a result of the increase in payrolls brought about by defense activity, that at least $1,500,000,000 would be withdrawn this year from purchasing power.

Since the Treasury contemplates broadening the scope of the act to bring in agricultural, domestic and other workers not now covered, the amount would be greater. An increase to 3 per cent would be a $2,500,000,000 bulwark against inflation.

Addition of a "dismissal tax" equivalent to three months' pay for every worker when the war ends would increase still more substantially the amount to be levied and thus to be withdrawn from consumer purchasing power, it was said.

Mr. Morgenthau said that the Treasury was studying the whole question of Social Security rather than enforced savings.

"I also think," he said, "we should move in the direction of what some people call 'a separation wage.' A certain percentage can be set toward which employer and employe contribute and build up

Continued on Page Nine

Defense Plant Cost Is $3,549,770,000

By The Associated Press.

WASHINGTON, Aug. 14—New industrial plants and expansions to existing ones authorized since the beginning of the defense program number 2,082, government statisticians estimated today, and their cost will aggregate $3,549,770,000.

The government is committed to plant financing totaling $2,720,936,000, and private financing will amount to $828,834,000. For the most part the financing by private sources has been limited to the smaller projects.

U. A. W. BARS REDS FROM UNION POSTS

Ban on Nazis, Fascists and Communists Is Voted After Bitter Debate in Buffalo

By LOUIS STARK
Special to THE NEW YORK TIMES.

BUFFALO, Aug. 14—After two and a half hours of turbulent debate, the United Automobile Workers-C. I. O. convention tonight adopted a strong declaration amending the constitution to bar from office members of Communist, Fascist or Nazi organizations.

Opponents of the proposal who insisted on a roll call vote found that they had been beaten by 1,950 to 920, according to an unofficial tabulation.

The report which was adopted, referred to as a "super-minority" report, offered by Harvey Kitzman of Racine, Wis., went farther than the majority report, which would have banned from office supporters "of any organization whose loyalty is to a foreign government." The latter report did not mention Communists, Nazis or Fascists by name.

Opponents of the resolution which was adopted urged its defeat because it would be a sign of support for Philip Murray and John L. Lewis, respectively president and ex-president of the C. I. O., and would show that the delegates were

Continued on Page Thirty-six

NAZIS GAIN IN SOUTH

Seize Iron Ore Center—See Ukraine Army in Hopeless Trap

SOVIET ADMITS LOSS

Yields 2 Defense Bases, but Says Germans Pay 'Terrible Price'

By C. BROOKS PETERS
By Telephone to THE NEW YORK TIMES.

BERLIN, Aug. 14—In a special communiqué issued from Reichsfuehrer Hitler's field headquarters somewhere on the Eastern Front the Germans declared this evening that the defense of the Western Ukraine by the Russian armed forces was facing complete collapse.

German, Rumanian, Hungarian and Italian troops were said to be in relentless pursuit of the Soviet armies, pushing them southward between the Dniester and Dnieper Rivers toward the Black Sea. Odessa was reported to be encircled by Rumanian troops and Nikolaev, after Odessa the most important Ukrainian port, beleaguered from east and west by German and Hungarian units.

[The Russians acknowledged that they had abandoned Pervomaisk and Kirovograd, important towns in the defense of Odessa. It appeared that the Ukraine army's escape across the Dnieper had become doubtful. Moscow, however, denied that Odessa was encircled and reported the drives toward Leningrad checked. The Soviet press listed more than thirty Nazi divisions as having been wiped out or badly smashed.]

In the drive toward the lower regions of the Dnieper German motorized forces were officially reported to have occupied the Krivoy Rog iron ore area, which supplies the important Donets basic industrial sector east of the Dnieper.

Continued on Page Eight

HISTORIC MEETING AT SEA BETWEEN MR. ROOSEVELT AND MR. CHURCHILL
The President and the Prime Minister on the deck of H. M. S. Prince of Wales after church services last Sunday
Associated Press Wirephoto

International Situation

FRIDAY, AUGUST 15, 1941

Out of an unprecedented series of secret conferences between the President of the United States and the Prime Minister of Britain somewhere on the Atlantic, with American naval planes circling overhead, there emerged yesterday a joint declaration of peace aims, indications of new steps to speed up material aid to Britain and Russia and the probability that an understanding had been reached for fuller Anglo-American cooperation in dealing with the Far East, France and other storm centers throughout the world.

The joint declaration evolved at the dramatic meeting, which was attended by the Army, Navy and Air chiefs of both nations, consisted of an eight-point program founded on "the final destruction of the Nazi tyranny." On the of the points stated that aggressor and potential aggressor nations must be completely disarmed pending the establishment of a "permanent system of general security." [All the foregoing, Page 1, Column 8.]

London quarters saw greater significance in the fact that the meeting was held and in its undisclosed decisions than in the eight-point program, which, however, won approval. It was assumed that the discussions centered on matters more pressing than peace aims. [Page 1, Column 4.]

One of the participants in the conferences, Lord Beaverbrook, Britain's Minister of Supply, arrived in Washington by plane to arrange for shipment of tanks, planes and foodstuffs in "the largest possible" quantities. [Page 4, Column 1.] His arrival heightened expectations in the capital that the Administration would move quickly to increase aid to all the nations resisting aggression. Predictions were made that the President would seek from $7,000,000,000 to $10,000,000,000 more for the lease-lend program. Congressional reaction to the conferences was overwhelmingly favorable. [Page 1, Column 7.]

In Berlin an official spokesman pooh-poohed the meeting as a "propaganda bluff," and official circles described the eight-point program as an "unhappy" reminder of President Wilson's fourteen points. [Page 5, Column 1.] The Italian reaction was largely one of relief that the conferences had not produced a more drastic move. [Page 5, Column 6.] In Tokyo authorized sources said the eight points "contained nothing new" and, besides, were "now too late." [Page 3, Column 1.]

In the Russo-German war a special Berlin communiqué reported that the complete collapse of Russian forces in the Western Ukraine had been sealed by deep thrusts behind their lines. The communiqué declared that Odessa and Nikolaev, another port near by, were encircled. The capture of the Krivoy Rog iron ore area, which was said to produce 61 per cent of Russia's ore output, also was announced. [Page 1, Column 3; Map, Page 2.]

A Soviet communiqué admitted that Russian troops had been forced to abandon two key points in the area guarding Odessa and Nikolaev, about 100 miles above the Black Sea coast. [Page 8, Column 2.]

LONDON EXPECTS MORE FROM TALKS

Britons Believe Discussion of War Aid, Still Secret, Will Prove Important

By ROBERT P. POST
Wireless to THE NEW YORK TIMES.

LONDON, Aug. 14—The fact that Prime Minister Winston Churchill and President Roosevelt have met is regarded in Great Britain as far more important than anything that was announced as the outcome of their meeting.

The British took full note of the eight-point peace program the two statesmen released after their three-day meeting at sea, but it would have pleased most Britons far more if a little less had been said in the vaguest terms.

In fact, some quarters felt a sort of shiver when they compared the eight-point Roosevelt-Churchill program with President Wilson's fourteen points. At least, some persons said, Mr. Wilson had fourteen points instead of eight and some of them suggested specific changes.

But the measure of disappointment apparent in London tonight can perhaps be best judged in the light of what the statement left unsaid rather than what it said. Leaving out the entire question of statement as to the future it would appear obvious that the important fact is that Mr. Roosevelt and his chief military and diplomatic advisers conferred with Mr. Churchill and his heads of staff.

There are few persons in these islands who think that Mr. Churchill at great personal risk and inconvenience crossed the Atlantic to consult with Mr. Roosevelt on such statement as "their countries seek no aggrandizement, territorial or other." Mr. Churchill made the trip at President Roosevelt's personal request. But even at that request he would hardly have made the trip just to produce a set of war aims such as Lord Privy Seal Clement R. Attlee announced today.

Therefore, it is generally agreed here that the real purpose of the conference was how and where the United States and Britain could best work together to defeat Germany.

That statement implies that the two men discussed military plans, including not only the future of Iceland but the possible seizure of other bases by the United States.

It implies discussion of the whole question of United States supplies to Britain. If any proof of this is

Continued on Page Four

The Official Statement

By The United Press.

WASHINGTON, Aug. 14—The text of the official statement on the Roosevelt-Churchill meeting follows:

The President of the United States and the Prime Minister, Mr. Churchill, representing His Majesty's Government in the United Kingdom, have met at sea.

They have been accompanied by officials of their two governments, including high ranking officers of their military, naval and air services.

The whole problem of the supply of munitions of war, as provided by the Lease-Lend Act, for the armed forces of the United States and for those countries actively engaged in resisting aggression has been further examined.

Lord Beaverbrook, the Minister of Supply of the British Government, has joined in these conferences. He is going to proceed to Washington to discuss further details with appropriate officials of the United States Government. These conferences will also cover the supply problems of the Soviet Union.

The President and the Prime Minister have had several conferences. They have considered the dangers to world civilization arising from the policies of military domination by conquest upon which the Hitlerite government of Germany and other governments associated therewith have embarked, and have made clear the steps which their countries are respectively taking for their safety in the face of these dangers.

They have agreed upon the following joint declaration:

The President of the United States of America and the Prime Minister, Mr. Churchill, representing His Majesty's Government in the United Kingdom, being met together, deem it right to make known certain common principles in the national policies of their respective countries on which they base their hopes for a better future for the world.

FIRST, their countries seek no aggrandizement, territorial or other;

SECOND, they desire to see no territorial changes that do not accord with the freely expressed wishes of the peoples concerned;

THIRD, they respect the right of all peoples to choose the form of government under which they will live; and they wish to see sovereign rights and self-government restored to those who have been forcibly deprived of them;

FOURTH, they will endeavor, with due respect for their existing obligations, to further the enjoyment by all States, great or small, victor or vanquished, of access, on equal terms, to the trade and to the raw materials of the world which are needed for their economic prosperity;

FIFTH, they desire to bring about the fullest collaboration between all nations in the economic field with the object of securing, for all, improved labor standards, economic adjustment and social security;

SIXTH, after the final destruction of the Nazi tyranny, they hope to see established a peace which will afford to all nations the means of dwelling in safety within their own boundaries, and which will afford assurance that all the men in all the lands may live out their lives in freedom from fear and want;

SEVENTH, such a peace should enable all men to traverse the high seas and oceans without hindrance;

EIGHTH, they believe that all of the nations of the world, for realistic as well as spiritual reasons, must come to the abandonment of the use of force. Since no future peace can be maintained if land, sea or air armaments continue to be employed by nations which threaten, or may threaten, aggression outside of their frontiers, they believe, pending the establishment of a wider and permanent system of general security, that the disarmament of such nations is essential. They will likewise aid and encourage all other practicable measures which will lighten for peace-loving peoples the crushing burden of armaments.

FRANKLIN D. ROOSEVELT.
WINSTON S. CHURCHILL.

ANOTHER AID BILL IS SEEN IN CAPITAL

Reaction to Roosevelt-Churchill Parley Is Largely Favorable —Some Criticism Sharp

By TURNER CATLEDGE
Special to THE NEW YORK TIMES.

WASHINGTON, Aug. 14—Expectations of new moves by the United States Government to enlarge and accelerate material aid to Great Britain, Russia and China and other countries that may later resist the aggressions of the Axis powers sprang high in Washington today following disclosure of the Roosevelt-Churchill meeting at sea.

They were heightened even further by the arrival early this afternoon of Lord Beaverbrook, the British Minister of Supply, who flew here directly from the Roosevelt-Churchill conference with a view to discussing expansion of material aid with American officials. He announced at a press conference that he had come to the United States to get tanks, airplanes and foods in quantities as large as the United States could supply, adding that Britain was able now to use all the equipment she could get.

Predictions that the Administration would soon request a new lease-lend appropriation of $7,000,000,000 to $10,000,000,000 were heard immediately at the Capitol, where the Roosevelt-Churchill statement caused practical legislators to look more to what it forecast for the immediate future than to the post-war aims outlined therein.

Reaction to the statement was overwhelmingly favorable among those who expressed themselves despite the expected criticism from opponents of the President's foreign policy. Among these, however, there was a question whether to accept the discussions of President Roosevelt and Prime Minister Winston Churchill as in reality a "peace offensive" on the part of the democracies or to brand them as another step toward active participation by the United States in the war.

There was considerable reluctance among members of Congress to discuss the sea meeting at all until more details concerning its setting and purpose had been disclosed; also there was an undertone of disappointment, which spread through various groups, that the President had not taken Congress and the people more into his confidence in this latest stroke of diplomacy.

One of the most outspoken critics

Continued on Page Three

TALKS HELD AT SEA

Closer War Cooperation to Doom Aggressors Pledged by Leaders

SOVIET AID INCLUDED

Disarmament of Axis Is Envisaged in a World Freed From Want

By FRANK L. KLUCKHOHN
Special to THE NEW YORK TIMES.

WASHINGTON, Aug. 14—A joint declaration of eight bases for world peace to follow "final destruction of the Nazi tyranny" was made public through Washington and London today in the names of President Roosevelt and Prime Minister Winston Churchill after a series of historic and dramatic conferences between the two leaders somewhere on the Atlantic.

The chiefs of the United States and British Governments insisted that aggressor and potential aggressor nations must be completely disarmed and they made clear that there would be closer Anglo-American cooperation in the war effort, at least as far as the production and distribution of modern sinews of war, including those to be provided to the Soviet Union, were concerned.

Mr. Roosevelt and Mr. Churchill held out for all peoples, including those of the nations that are now aggressors, an equal part in a better world after the elimination or defeat of Reichsfuehrer Hitler. This would have its base in opportunity to work in peace and justice and in the right of all peoples to have access to raw materials through lowering of trade barriers. The declaration indicated that there was to be no harsh retribution for the common people in Axis countries.

Further Statements Expected

This statement was expected by official Washington to be followed by further declarations and actions setting forth definitive Anglo-American policies concerning the Far East, France and other key regions and making clearer the exact extent and form of Anglo-American collaboration.

The President and the Prime Minister were assisted at their conferences, presumably held with due ceremony, by "high-ranking" army, navy and air officers of both countries. It would cause surprise in official circles if military situations and problems in all parts of the world had not been canvassed and decisions taken.

The Roosevelt-Churchill statement was silent regarding such matters, however, and Secretary of State Cordell Hull refrained in his press conference today from direct answers to questions on what decisions, if any, had been taken on the prosecution of the war and whether the United States would play a more belligerent part.

Hitlerite Peril Studied

The only hint on this subject was an assertion in the declaration that the President and the Prime Minister "in several" meetings had "considered the dangers to world civilization arising from the policies of military domination by conquest upon which the Hitlerite government of Germany and other governments associated therewith have embarked, and have made clear the steps which their countries are respectively taking for their safety in the face of these dangers."

That the conferences, from which the veil of secrecy was only partly torn, would result in action was indicated by the arrival in Washington today of Lord Beaverbrook, British Minister of Supply, who took part in the Roosevelt-Churchill talks and who, the joint statement said, will confer with United States officials on the "whole problem of the supply of munitions of war."

President Roosevelt is expected

Continued on Page Two

"All the News That's Fit to Print."

The New York Times.

LATE CITY EDITION
Mostly clear and continued cool today. Tomorrow fair and slightly warmer.
Temperatures Yesterday—Max., 73; Min., 63

VOL. XC...No. 30,547. Entered as Second-Class Matter, Postoffice, New York, N. Y. NEW YORK, FRIDAY, SEPTEMBER 12, 1941. THREE CENTS NEW YORK CITY and Vicinity

ROOSEVELT ORDERS NAVY TO SHOOT FIRST IF AXIS RAIDERS ENTER OUR DEFENSE ZONES; PATROL TO PROTECT BRITISH SHIPS ALSO

SENATORS DENY ANY OIL SHORTAGE EXISTS IN EAST

Inquiry Reports to the Senate 'Over-Enthusiasm' of Ickes's Office Aroused Alarm

END OF CURBS IS URGED

But Consumers Are Asked to Save Fuel—R. K. Davies Insists Situation Is Acute

By JOHN H. CRIDER
Special to THE NEW YORK TIMES.

WASHINGTON, Sept. 11—The special Senate committee investigating the reports of a gasoline shortage on the Eastern seaboard reported today that not only was there no shortage but that "had an adequate analysis been made by those to whom the responsibility of coordination was delegated the confusion of the past few months might have been avoided."

The report to the Senate, signed by all the five committee members, was described by its authors as hastily prepared and merely preliminary, subject to a final report.

In answer to the report, Ralph K. Davies, acting petroleum coordinator, issued a statement reasserting what he has been telling the committee for weeks—namely, that there was a shortage and that "we are far from being in a condition warranting complacency."

To the extent that the committee recommended a voluntary fuel conservation program on the part of the public it endorsed Mr. Davies's demand for consumption economies, but it added that "present restrictions should be lifted."

Gasoline consumers on the Eastern seaboard are now subject to an over-all 10 per cent reduction in supply of gasoline, which means an actual 15 per cent cut for private motorists from the July level of supply.

Shortage of Petroleum Is Denied

"Our conclusions may best be summed up," the committee said, "by stating that there is no shortage of petroleum products nor a shortage, as of this date, of transportation facilities, but that the whole frightening picture, from the standpoint of the coordinator's office, seems to lie in the fact that the shortage, which has excited the activity of the coordinator, is really 'a shortage' in a large surplus which is desired.

"Paradoxical as it sounds, the shortage, as we see it, is a shortage of surplus and not a shortage of products or a lack of facilities to transport them."

In criticizing the handling of the gasoline situation by Federal officials, the Senate committee, headed by Senator Maloney of Connecticut, stated that it believed "unnecessary alarm was created."

However, the committee unanimously rejected the view of anti-Administration Senators who said that the shortage was conjured up in order to create a war spirit on the Eastern seaboard.

"The committee is unanimously of the opinion," the report stated, "that charges made that 'the shortage' situation was magnified by a desire to create 'a war scare' are without foundation."

It found that "unnecessary alarm" was caused "by over-enthusiasm on the part of those charged with the direction of the petroleum situation."

Recent Confusion Is Scored

"The committee has no desire to assume credit for its small effort, nor to criticize those charged with the coordinating effort, but feels duty bound to make the observation that had an adequate analysis been made by those to whom the responsibility of coordination was delegated the confusion of the past

Continued on Page Thirteen

The International Situation

FRIDAY, SEPTEMBER 12, 1941

President Roosevelt warned Germany and Italy last night that their warships would meet the fire of United States naval and air forces if they were sighted within the waters "the protection of which is necessary for American defense." In his most outspoken declaration since the war began, the President asserted that American patroling vessels and planes would protect ships of every flag engaged in commerce in defense waters. The United States, he declared, will keep open the line of commerce in those waters "no matter what it costs."

Reviewing attacks on American naval and merchant shipping and incidents of German intrigue in South America, Mr. Roosevelt accused Germany of a systematic drive to get absolute control of the seas and to set up "bridgeheads" for attack in the Western Hemisphere. He declared there would be no "shooting war" unless Germany continued to seek it. [All the foregoing, Page 1, Column 8.]

Prime Minister Churchill, in a bitter exchange with Parliament's only Communist member over charges that a Cabinet member was sabotaging aid to Russia, revealed in the Commons that hundreds of British fighting planes already were being sent to the Soviet Union. [Page 6, Column 3.]

On the Eastern fighting line, the Russians pressed their counter-offensive in the central sector, throwing the Germans back twelve miles at some points along a 400-mile front running northward from Gomel, according to Moscow. Northwest of Smolensk, it was reported, the Russians recrossed the Dvina River. Soviet counter-attacks were reported at Leningrad and Kiev, whose defenses held firmly. [Page 1, Column 4; Map, Page 8.]

German sources declared that the Russians had advanced to within forty-five miles of Smolensk, and a propaganda company report said they had been shelling that city with long-range guns. Otherwise, spokesmen dealt mostly in threats and promises. They said that two months of fighting weather remained before Winter sets in and that offensive action would be undertaken even after the snow fell. [Page 8, Column 1.]

In the diplomatic phase of the war, Soviet Foreign Commissar Molotoff formally charged that Bulgaria—an Axis junior partner since March—was serving as a full-fledged base for Axis attack against Russia. Mr. Molotoff's statement declared Bulgaria was prepared to join in these attacks and hinted strongly that the Bulgarian Government could expect trouble from Russia. [Page 10, Column 3, with Map.]

Behind the German lines, a brooding quiet lay over Norway as the German commander commuted a death sentence to life imprisonment and the Quisling regime ordered the Boy Scouts and several cultural organizations disbanded under the state of civil siege. New incidents of resistance were expected momentarily. [Page 9, Column 1.] In both zones of France, special courts handed down numerous prison sentences for Communist agitation ranging from the playing of "The Internationale" to the distribution of tracts. A policeman was shot while arresting a Communist. [Page 12, Column 6.]

A R. A. F. bombing mission, on a 1,200-mile round trip that crossed the Alps, struck at Turin and other industrial areas Wednesday night in the heaviest raid of the war upon Northern Italy and the first attack there since January. The bombers, including four-motored machines, left many fires burning. [Page 1, Columns 4 and 5.]

Japan appeared to be leaning farther away from the Axis and closer to a settlement with the United States as Emperor Hirohito took over direct command of a new defense set-up in a drastic military reorganization. This move was viewed by some observers as tending to check military domination of Japan's policies. [Page 1, Column 3.]

DAVIES IS WINNER IN APPEALS COURT

His Right to Place on Ballot in Primary Race Is Upheld by Vote of 5 to 2

By WARREN MOSCOW
Special to THE NEW YORK TIMES.

ALBANY, Sept. 11—The Court of Appeals, at the end of an eleven-hour session devoted entirely to election cases, decided tonight by a 5-to-2 vote that the name of John R. Davies shall stay on the ballot for the Republican Mayoralty nomination in the primary election next Tuesday.

The court's decision means that Mayor La Guardia will have the opposition for the Republican nomination that his supporters had sought to avert by seeking invalidation of the Davies nominating petitions. They won the first round when Supreme Court Justice Ferdinand Pecora decided that the Davies petitions were "saturated with fraud." Next, the Appellate Division of the First Department reversed Justice Pecora, and tonight the State's highest court upheld the Appellate Division.

The court was unanimous in upholding the Appellate Division on two points, but on a third point Chief Judge Irving Lehman and Associate Judge Edward R. Finch dissented. It had been made clear during the argument in the court today that reversal of the Appellate Division on any of the three principal points would have meant the loss of the case for the Davies supporters, since the margin of "valid" petitions, as described by the Appellate Division, was slender.

In political circles, and among the political leaders and lawyers who thronged the court room to-

Continued on Page Forty-four

HIROHITO DIRECTS NEW ARMY SET-UP

Creation of a General Defense Office Held Curb on Military —Press Mild on U. S.

By OTTO D. TOLISCHUS
Wireless to THE NEW YORK TIMES.

TOKYO, Friday, Sept. 12—The War Office announced yesterday the creation of a new General Defense Headquarters under direct command of the Emperor, which will be responsible for the defense of Japan proper, Korea, Formosa and Sakhalin.

This step and the circumstances surrounding it aroused attention both in political and diplomatic quarters and precipitated numerous speculations as to its significance. According to the press and the government radio, the new headquarters was created "to complete arrangements for the defense of national territories in view of the growing tension in East Asia."

The new arrangement places all military forces in the national territories, which are often prone to pursue their own policies, under direct command of the Emperor, whose authority cannot be challenged. And since the civilian government, which is now less than ever dependent upon Parliament, is likewise working under the authority of the Emperor, the new set-up would tend to consolidate and unify the supreme leadership of the nation in the hands of the Emperor himself, thereby giving added authority to policies receiving imperial sanction.

On the other hand, taken in connection with the national "ready-for-war structure," propagated lately in place of the previous "high-degree defense state," it sug-

Continued on Page Six

RUSSIANS DRIVE ON

Report Retaking a Town Far West of Smolensk on Central Front

ARCTIC FIGHT RAGES

Drive Toward Frontier Claimed—Leningrad Heavily Bombed

By CYRUS L. SULZBERGER
Wireless to THE NEW YORK TIMES.

MOSCOW, Sept. 11—Spreading the scope of their persistent counter-attacks in the central sector, Russian troops have crossed the Western Dvina River, retaking the small town of Starina, have repulsed a German thrust northeast of Nevel, presumably aimed at checking the mounting force of the Soviet initiative, and in other salients of the increasingly active front between the regions of Gomel and Velikiye Luki have pushed back the German lines as much as twelve miles, it was reported here today.

[Berlin acknowledged that German units had been pushed back from their nearest approach to Moscow, but predicted important decisions "in the next eight weeks"—that is, before severe Winter weather. Nazi reports from Leningrad merely referred to heavy bombing of the city. The midnight Moscow communiqué said Russian troops were engaged in stubborn battles along the entire front.]

The fulcrum of the Red Army attacks still appears to be in the region southeast of Smolensk where, according to the latest information from Yelnya, Soviet troops are advancing at a rate averaging nearly ten miles daily in the wake of the retreating Germans, who apparently have been unable to reorganize since the reported smashing of eight of their divisions a week ago.

Fighting in White Russia

Marshal Semyon Timoshenko would appear to be launching a growing series of jabs at the weakening Nazi center. As far west as the Polesian district of White Russia [around Pinsk], fierce fighting is reported to be developing where the Germans, bitterly contesting the widening area of the Russians' attack, struck back at the confluence of two rivers [possibly the Dnieper and the Pripet], but were stopped by Soviet defenses, including aircraft, artillery and river gunboats, which blew up a bridge and sank many barges.

A strong tank force commanded by General Yeremenko, a famous Soviet hero, which previously had recrossed the "N" River and advanced six miles, now is said to have gone on more than ten miles farther, recapturing ten villages

Continued on Page Eight

WILLKIE APPLAUDS

Calls on All Americans to Back President in Firm Policy

NYE DENOUNCES PLEA

But Democratic Leaders Welcome the Words of the Executive

Special to THE NEW YORK TIMES.

WASHINGTON, Sept. 11—Wendell L. Willkie, Republican candidate for President in 1940, called upon all Americans today to rally to the support of President Roosevelt in the policy enunciated in his radio address. Mr. Willkie declared that, while no man could say that the naval action ordered by the President "will involve us in war, any thoughtful person knows that if the President were less firm, disastrous war would be inevitable."

Mr. Willkie listened to the speech in his hotel room. With him were Bernard M. Baruch, 1918 chairman of the War Industries Board, and Associate Justice James F. Byrnes, who was one of Mr. Roosevelt's leaders in the Senate until his appointment to the Supreme Court.

"The President spoke as he should have spoken," Mr. Willkie said. "He could not yield on such a fundamental right. This is the time for all Americans to rally to his support. I hope Hitler understands that, whatever may be the divergent views in the United States on other questions, the people of the United States are united in their support of the President in this crisis.

"If Hitler acts on any other assumption because of the voice of an insignificant few in America, he will do so to his sorrow. No man can say whether this will involve the United States in war, but any thoughtful person knows that if the President were less firm, disastrous war would be inevitable."

Capital Comment Is Split

By The Associated Press.

WASHINGTON, Sept. 11—Capital reaction to President Roosevelt's address tonight ranged from the assertion of Senator McCarran that it was "nothing short of an unauthorized declaration of war" to a statement of Senator Thomas of Utah that "driving pirates off or out of the seas is not war."

Senator Nye said:

"Clearly, we are going to have convoys irrespective of law and irrespective of President Roosevelt's own promises and assurances. This means definitely that we are nearer to a shooting war by Presidential proclamation. The President declares in effect that we shall defend our rights on such

Continued on Page Four

Big R.A.F. Bombers Pound Turin; Italy Raided in North and South

Special Cable to THE NEW YORK TIMES.

LONDON, Friday, Sept. 12—The junior Axis partner, Italy, came in for a pounding by the Royal Air Force over Wednesday night when the new British four-engined bombers switched their offensive from industrial targets in Germany to those at Turin. The Royal Italian Arsenal and other factories and railways there were heavily bombed.

The attack—the most powerful yet made against Italy and from which four R. A. F. planes were reported missing—came seven months after the last attack by planes from Britain against the Fascist homeland, which was the night of Jan. 12.

The raid was the first time the R. A. F.'s heaviest bombers have made the 1,200-mile round trip that includes a double crossing of the Alps; and the attack on Turin was carried out, reports from Italy indicated, while other R. A. F. bombers of the Middle East Command were striking from the south, hitting Messina, Sicily, for the second night in succession.

[The R. A. F. Command at Cairo yesterday reported raids on Palermo, Sicily, on Monday night and on Messina Tuesday night.]

The R. A. F. made offensive sweeps over occupied Netherland, Belgian and French regions during yesterday.

Spitfires shot up Nazi airfields in the afternoon without meeting any opposition.

Late last night R. A. F. bombers could be heard roaring out over the Strait of Dover. Heavy explosions rumbled across the sea from the direction of Boulogne, the vi-

Continued on Page Seven

PUTS NAVY 'AT THE READY'
President Roosevelt speaking last night
Associated Press Wirephoto

The President's Speech

Following is the text of President Roosevelt's address last night as transcribed by THE NEW YORK TIMES:

My Fellow-Americans:

The Navy Department of the United States has reported to me that on the morning of Sept. 4 the United States destroyer Greer, proceeding in full daylight toward Iceland, had reached a point southeast of Greenland. She was carrying American mail to Iceland. She was flying the American flag. Her identity as an American ship was unmistakable.

She was then and there attacked by a submarine. Germany admits that it was a German submarine. The submarine deliberately fired a torpedo at the Greer, followed later by another torpedo attack. In spite of what Hitler's propaganda bureau has invented, and in spite of what any American obstructionist organization may prefer to believe, I tell you the blunt fact that the German submarine fired first upon this American destroyer without warning, and with deliberate design to sink her.

Our destroyer, at the time, was in waters which the Government of the United States had declared to be waters of self-defense, surrounding outposts of American protection in the Atlantic.

In the north of the Atlantic, outposts have been established by us in Iceland, in Greenland, in Labrador and in Newfoundland. Through these waters there pass many ships of many flags. They bear food and other supplies to civilians; and they bear matériel of war, for which the people of the United States are spending billions of dollars, and which, by Congressional action, they have declared to be essential for the defense of our own land.

Destroyer's Mission Called Legitimate

The United States destroyer, when attacked, was proceeding on a legitimate mission.

If the destroyer was visible to the submarine when the torpedo was fired, then the attack was a deliberate attempt by the Nazis to sink a clearly identified American warship.

On the other hand, if the submarine was beneath the surface of the sea and, with the aid of its listening devices, fired in the direction of the sound of the American destroyer without even taking the trouble to learn its identity, as the official German communiqué would indicate, then the attack was even more outrageous. For it indicates a policy of indiscriminate violence against any vessel sailing the seas, belligerent or non-belligerent.

This was piracy, piracy legally and morally. It was not the first nor the last act of piracy which the Nazi government has committed against the American flag in this war, for attack has followed attack.

A few months ago an American-flag merchant ship, the Robin Moor, was sunk by a Nazi submarine in the middle of the South Atlantic, under circumstances violating long-established international law and violating every principle of humanity. The passengers and the crew were forced into open boats hundreds of miles from land, in direct violation of international agreements signed by nearly all nations, including the government of Germany. No apology, no allegation of mistake, no offer of reparations has come from the Nazi government.

In July, 1941, nearly two months ago, an American battleship in North American waters was followed by a submarine which for a long time sought to manoeuvre itself into a position of attack upon the battleship. The periscope of the submarine was clearly seen. No British or American submarines were within hundreds of miles of this spot at the time, so the nationality of the submarine is clear.

Five days ago a United States Navy ship on patrol picked up three survivors of an American-owned ship operating under the flag of our sister republic of Panama, the S.S. Sessa.

On Aug. 17 she had been first torpedoed without warning, and then shelled, near Greenland, while carrying civilian supplies to

Continued on Page Four

WAR UP TO HITLER

President Says We Can No Longer Stand By as Nazis Imperil Sea

ACTION 'AT ONCE'

Attacks and Plots Are Linked to Design to Conquer Americas

By FRANK L. KLUCKHOHN
Special to THE NEW YORK TIMES.

WASHINGTON, Sept. 11—President Roosevelt has ordered the Navy to destroy on sight any German or Italian submarines or raiders entering waters "the protection of which is necessary for American defense." Not only shall American shipping be thus protected, but British and Allied shipping as well.

In a radio address tonight to the American people and the world, amid circumstances reminiscent of Woodrow Wilson's Sussex note preceding American entry into the World War, the President solemnly warned the people that Germany sought absolute control and domination of the seas as a step to conquest of the Western Hemisphere.

"No matter what it costs," he said, "we will keep open the line of legitimate commerce in these defense waters."

Asserting that this country must protect the freedom of the seas, he gravely stated:

"There will be no shooting war unless Germany continues to seek it."

But American warships and planes, he said, will no longer wait until Axis submarines or raiders strike their deadly blow first.

"Very Simply and Clearly"

"Let this warning be clear," the President stated. "From now on, if German or Italian vessels of war enter the waters, the protection of which is necessary for American defense, they do so at their own peril.

"Upon our naval and air patrol—now operating in large number over a vast expanse of the Atlantic Ocean—falls the duty of maintaining the American policy of freedom of the seas—now.

"That means, very simply and clearly, that our patrolling vessels and planes will protect all merchant ships—not only American ships but ships of any flag—engaged in commerce in defense waters. They will protect them from submarines; they will protect them from surface raiders.

"The orders which I have given as Commander in Chief of the United States Army and Navy are to carry out that policy—at once."

In listing attacks on American shipping and in dealing with the Greer incident the President repeated that the destroyer was attacked in broad daylight southeast of Greenland while carrying mail to Iceland. She was flying the American flag and "her identity as an American ship was unmistakable."

"I tell you the blunt fact," he said, "that the German submarine fired first upon this American destroyer without warning and with deliberate design to sink her."

Says It Is Time for Us to Stand

The President spoke from the diplomatic reception room in the center of the ground floor of the Executive Mansion. The address was broadcast over all major chains, and, through rebroadcasts in fourteen languages, to the world.

The challenge was flung down to Nazi Germany, the President said, because the time for defense is "now."

"Hitler already is seeking to establish 'footholds and bridgeheads' in the New World through 'conspiracy' after 'conspiracy.'

"The Nazi danger to our Western world has long ceased to be a mere possibility," he said.

The time has come, he empha-

Continued on Page Two

1941

Certainly one of baseball's greatest all-around players, "Joltin' Joe" DiMaggio is usually remembered for his 56-game hitting streak.

Ted Williams is the last baseball player to have batted .400. His average reached a sensational .406 on September 28, 1941.

Baseball's famed "Iron Man"—Lou Gehrig. The greatest first-baseman the game ever saw sadly passed away at the age of 37.

Clark Gable and Rosalind Russell in *They Met in Bombay.*

Marlene Dietrich in *The Flame of New Orleans.*

Bette Davis in the opening scene of *The Letter.*

"All the News That's Fit to Print."

The New York Times.

LATE CITY EDITION
Cloudy, cooler preceded by rain today, colder tonight. Tomorrow fair and somewhat colder.
Temperatures Yesterday—Max., 61; Min., 56

VOL. XCI...No. 30,603. Entered as Second-Class Matter, Postoffice, New York, N. Y. NEW YORK, FRIDAY, NOVEMBER 7, 1941. THREE CENTS NEW YORK CITY and Vicinity

U. S. LENDS $1,000,000,000 TO RUSSIA; STALIN FORECASTS SECOND FRONT; ROOSEVELT ASKS FULL WAR EFFORT

BIOFF, BROWNE GUILTY; FACING 30-YEAR TERMS

Racketeers of Stage Union Are Convicted in $1,200,000 Extortion From Movies

COURT COMMENDS JURORS

Verdict Reached in 2 Hours—Each Is Liable to $30,000 Fine Next Wednesday

George E. Browne and Willie Bioff, Chicago hoodlums who won control of the 125,000 members of the International Alliance of Theatrical Stage Employes, were found guilty in Federal court yesterday of violating the anti-racketeering statute on three counts. They had used their positions as leaders of the big American Federation of Labor union to extort $1,200,000 from the movie industry in the biggest shakedown known, according to evidence presented by United States Attorney Mathias F. Correa.

Both defendants were taken to jail and Judge John C. Knox will fix sentence Wednesday, when a penalty of thirty years in prison, with fines up to $30,000, may be imposed on each defendant.

The jury's verdict, reached after two hours' deliberation, seemed to surprise nobody. Browne's flushed, heavy face worked for a moment and there were tears in his eyes. Bioff, always the more self-contained of the two, stroked the old scar on his chin absently, but remained as calm as ever.

Judge Praises Jurors

Judge Knox seemed to have expected a verdict of guilty and he commended the jurors for the time and attention they had given the case. Then he declared:

"If these racketeers, these Chicago hoodlums, can get to a place where they can cast their shadows over the lives of 125,000 American workers and their families it constitutes, in my mind, gentlemen, a national scandal. I'm quite certain your verdict will let fresh air into a lot of homes in this country. Certainly that is something that is eminently desirable.

"Now, I don't believe that there is a firmer believer in labor unions than myself. But all labor will doubtless be glad to have the unions purged of such individuals as these. If union labor is to endure it must rid itself of men who stand ready to sell out labor when it suits their purposes."

Judge Knox had given the case to the jury at 3:47 P. M. after Martin Conboy had summed up the defense for Browne, Mr. Correa had delivered the government's summation of the evidence and the court had read a charge lasting barely forty-five minutes. At 5:45 the twelve jurors, all men, announced that they had reached a verdict and a quarter of an hour later Judge Knox was on the bench ready to receive it. He rejected formal motions for dismissal of the verdict by defense counsel and remanded Bioff and Browne, both of whom had been at liberty under bonds of $50,000 each, to the custody of the marshal.

Reject Bids for Freedom

In convicting both Browne and Bioff the jurors rejected several possible theories, offered both by defense counsel and the court, that might have justified the freeing of both men. Judge Knox, in giving them the technical legal information required, told them they could not convict Browne if they found that he had done no more than extort money from local New York theatre operators.

This comment referred to $40,000 collected by Browne from Charles C. Moskowitz, Loew's theatres executive, and another $150,000 put up by the same group. Those were collateral issues and were admitted in evidence only to throw light on Bioff's testimony that Browne knew nothing of the major shakedown.

Judge Knox also told the jury that if it found that the movie producers had paid more than a million dollars to the two union men for the purpose of getting them to refrain from performing their rightful services to their union membership no crime could be charged against them. This situation had been hinted at by defense counsel.

Another defense contention, sup-

Continued on Page Fourteen

FOUND GUILTY

Willie Bioff
The New York Times

George E. Browne
Associated Press

HOUSE GROUP COLD TO ANY NEW TAXES

Action on Morgenthau Proposal Is 'Temporarily Deferred'—Price Control Put First

By HENRY N. DORRIS
Special to THE NEW YORK TIMES.

WASHINGTON, Nov. 6—The House Ways and Means Committee decided today to defer "temporarily" consideration of Secretary Morgenthau's "suggestion" for a new tax bill, and thus apparently shelved for this session of Congress any probability of enactment of legislation for new levies for revenue or anti-inflationary purposes.

Going beyond a statement that action on a new tax measure would not be considered at this

Continued on Page Fifteen

CRIME OUTBREAK IN HARLEM SPURS DRIVE BY POLICE

Mayor Admits 'Bad Situation' in Area After 2 Killings—Guard Is Increased

YOUTH SEEN RUNNING WILD

Boy Hoodlums Called the Chief Offenders in Wave of Terror, Especially in Parks

Following the fatal stabbing of a 15-year-old white boy by three Negro children last Saturday within ten blocks of Mayor La Guardia's home and the discovery of the body of a murdered man in Morningside Park yesterday morning, the Mayor said recent crimes in lower Harlem represented "a bad situation" but promised that the additional police assigned to the area would soon clear up the condition.

The Mayor said the flareup of serious crimes had been receiving police attention for some time prior to the stabbing of James O'Connell, 15, at Fifth Avenue and Ninety-ninth Street last Saturday. After the O'Connell boy died of his stab wounds, three youngsters, two 16 and the third 12 years old, were arrested on suspicion of homicide and are being held without bail for a hearing on Nov. 19. The police reported that the youngsters had intended to rob the O'Connell boy but fled when his older brother James, 18, ran to help him.

Mayor Responds to Protests

When the Mayor was asked at City Hall yesterday for his reaction to the protests sent to him by uptown civic groups he said:

"The matter has received attention for some time. The fact that arrests were made indicates that. The situation is indeed a bad one. What makes it all the more difficult is that the crimes are committed by young hoodlums in their teens, from 12 to 16 years. Many of the cases have been broken, and the majority were more youngsters.

"I personally took charge of one case and eight or ten boys were arrested; two aided in getting the evidence, and one was as young as 8 years of age. Of the whole gang, only one or two were old enough to be taken to a criminal court. The rest went to Children's Court.

"I have ordered strong reinforcements of police in that locality and am sure the condition will soon be corrected."

Individual policemen assigned to Harlem have often complained to newspaper men in the district that they were hampered in doing their

Continued on Page Fifteen

The International Situation

FRIDAY, NOVEMBER 7, 1941

Russia will get $1,000,000,000 of lease-lend aid from the United States as the result of a pledge by President Roosevelt to Premier Stalin in a cordial exchange of letters made public yesterday by the State Department. In accepting the loan, which will finance purchase of military equipment, munitions and raw materials and will bear no interest, Mr. Stalin promised repayment over a ten-year period beginning five years after the end of the war. [Page 1, Column 8.]

In an international broadcast on the eve of the Russian Revolution's twenty-fourth anniversary, Mr. Stalin declared that Russia's setbacks were only temporary, that a second front would be created soon and that the "inevitable doom" of the Hitlerite forces would be brought about by "the coalition of Great Britain, the U.S.S.R. and the United States of America." He put German casualties at 4,500,000 and Russian at 1,748,000. He vowed that the invaders would be destroyed "to the last man." [Page 1, Column 5.]

The Soviet Premier named as a new Ambassador to the United States Maxim Litvinoff, former Foreign Commissar who was shelved with his policy of collective security when Russia made her pact with Germany. The choice was seen in Washington as bolstering Russia's cause here. [Page 1, Columns 6 and 7.]

Another development pointing to help for Russia came in a Finnish radio announcement that "military operations are drawing to a close as far as our country is concerned." [Page 1, Column 4.]

Russia gained hope from the trend of battle, too. Soviet sources reported breaches in the German lines at several points before Moscow as Russian counter-attacks gained ground. The defenders apparently held the initiative in the Donets Basin. [Page 1, Column 7; Map, Page 2.]

Unofficial Berlin reports told of the capture of Tula, southern anchor of the Moscow defenses. The High Command, silent on the Moscow fighting, said that German forces had crushed the defenses east of Sevastopol in Crimea and had broken through to the peninsula's southeast coast on a broad front. [Page 3, Column 1.]

A rare concession of the possibility of German defeat appeared in an article by Dr. Joseph Goebbels, Reich Propaganda Minister, who told the German people that they would face an "inferno" dwarfing past hardships if they lost. [Page 1, Columns 5 and 6.]

Like Premier Stalin, President Roosevelt broadcast a speech to the world. He told the International Labor Organization that Americans must work "three shifts a day" for the defeat of Hitler. With Japanese-American relations at a critical stage, he called China's invaders "barbarians." [Page 1, Columns 6 and 7.]

In Tokyo the Foreign Office's press mouthpiece warned that Japan might strike next at the Burma Road to cut off American supplies to China unless the United States came to terms with Tokyo's special envoy. [Page 8, Column 3.] The Foreign Office protested the sinking of the Japanese liner Kehi Maru by a floating "Russian mine." [Page 8, Column 2.]

British End Closure Of 'Invasion' Coast

Special Cable to THE NEW YORK TIMES.

LONDON, Friday, Nov. 7—Visitors will be permitted, beginning today, to travel in the east coastal areas from The Wash to the Thames, formerly a restricted defense area.

The ban has likewise been lifted on the southeastern region from Littlehampton to Hastings. It was stressed that these changes were of a temporary nature and would end Feb. 15.

The towns opened to visitors include Worthing, Brighton, Eastbourne, Southend, Clacton, Felixstowe, Lowestoft, Yarmouth and Cromer.

FINNS' RADIO SEES END OF WAR NEAR

Fixing of New Frontier Must Await Final Peace, Asserts Helsinki Broadcaster

By The Associated Press.

HELSINKI, Finland, Nov. 6—"Military operations are drawing to a close, as far as our country is concerned," the Finnish radio announced tonight.

"Even though war goes on between great powers," the announcer added, "Finland will not carry on any longer than is necessary for her own safety and defense, although it is realized that our frontiers cannot finally be determined until the coming peace conference."

Finland already has reconquered substantially all the territory she lost to Russia in the Winter war of 1939-40.

Earlier, the Finnish news agency issued a denial of reports abroad that Finland had received Russia's peace terms Aug. 18. [Secretary of State Cordell Hull said on Nov. 3 that he had told Finnish Minister Hjalmar Procope that the United States had learned Russia was prepared to discuss peace with territorial compensation for Finland.]

The United States' demand Monday that Finland get out of the war beside Germany against Russia or forfeit American friendship drew yesterday from the newspaper Sanomat the observation that the United States was thus seeking to open the Murmansk railroad to British and American supplies and to release the Russian forces engaged by the Finns.

Helsinki Denies Disorder

A Finnish spokesman yesterday denied reports of demonstrations in Helsinki and clashes of crowds and police. [The British Broadcasting Corporation reported that twenty-one persons were arrested after a strong anti-German demonstration and that the Socialist Minister of Trade, Vaino A. Tanner, was asked by his party to withdraw support from the Cabinet because of the continuing war.]

For almost two months there have been reports of imminent peace in Finland. On Sept. 14 Mr. Tanner broadcast to the nation that Finland was Germany's ally "only by accident and will not continue the war any longer than Finnish interests demand." He asserted that Finland never would make a separate peace with Soviet Russia but that the country had "good hopes of peace in the near future." He said that the Finns "are no party to a great war."

"It is for us an entirely defense war," he went on, "a defensive war with the aid of which we desire to secure our frontiers and a lasting peace. Whatever is needed to assure this must be done, but there our task ends."

Washington Expects Reply
Special to THE NEW YORK TIMES.

WASHINGTON, Nov. 6—Reports received here today indicated that the reply of the Finnish Government to the suggestion of the United States that Finland cease fighting Russia would be made by the end of this week. It is understood to be under preparation in Helsinki, with some questions still under discussion.

It has never been expected that the reply even if adverse, would cause any immediate alteration in the relations of the two countries.

PREMIER CONFIDENT

He Says Nazis Will Be Annihilated With U. S. and British Help

LISTS REICH CASUALTIES

Stalin Puts Them at 4,500,000, Soviet's at 1,748,000—Talks of Aim of Hess Flight

The text of Stalin's speech will be found on Page 4.

By DANIEL T. BRIGHAM
By Telephone to THE NEW YORK TIMES.

BERNE, Switzerland, Nov. 6—Addressing the Moscow Soviet on the twenty-fourth anniversary of the October Revolution in an atmosphere electric with suspense, Premier Joseph Stalin of the Soviet Union this evening for fifty-two minutes told his audience in a speech broadcast to the world that since Germany wanted a war of extermination she "will get that war."

"From now on the task of the peoples of the U.S.S.R.," he said, "the task of the fighters, the commanders and the political instructors of our Army and Navy will be the extermination to the last man of all Germans who have penetrated the territory of our native land in the role of invaders. There will be no mercy to them!

"Death to those who, having lost all human semblance long ago, sank to the level of wild beasts * * * who have doomed themselves to inevitable perdition."

Predicts a Second Front

While launching this scathing denunciation of the brutal atrocities that he said had been committed upon women and children and the aged by the invading Nazi hordes, Premier Stalin twice appealed to the British to form a second front, "without which the Germans feel secure in their rear, but the appearance of which—and it undoubtedly will not be long in coming—will considerably relieve the situation of our armies."

While he admitted the Germans had overrun great areas of the Soviet Union, Mr. Stalin put Nazi casualties in killed, wounded and prisoners at 4,500,000. He said the Soviet casualties totaled 1,748,000, with the breakdown of that figure as follows—350,000 killed, 378,000 missing and 1,020,000 wounded.

Mr. Stalin said the "inevitable perdition" of the Hitlerites was foreordained not merely by their "moral degradation" but by "three more fundamental factors." These he listed as the collapse of the German rear through unrest among the peoples of the occupied nations of Europe; internal dissension in Germany, where, he said, "a profound change had occurred among the German people," and, finally, "the coalition of the U. S. S. R., Great Britain and the United States of America."

The Soviet Premier described the smoldering condition of the subjugated European peoples as a "volcano ready to erupt and bury the Hitlerite adventurers." He derided the notion that Herr Hitler

Continued on Page Four

Stalin Appoints Litvinoff Ambassador to Washington

Veteran's Restoration to Favor Held to Reflect Importance Attached by Soviet Regime to American Aid in the War

By The Associated Press.

KUIBYSHEV, Russia, Nov. 6—The Soviet Government announced today the appointment of Maxim Litvinoff to be Ambassador to the United States.

The announcement said that the Washington government had given its agreement to the selection of Mr. Litvinoff, who, as Foreign Commissar, journeyed to the United States in 1933 for the negotiations that led to American recognition of the Soviet Union.

Mr. Litvinoff succeeds Constantine A. Oumansky, who is now in Kuibyshev and will join the management of Tass, the official Soviet news agency.

Special to THE NEW YORK TIMES.

WASHINGTON, Nov. 6—The designation of Maxim Litvinoff as Soviet Ambassador to the United States is accepted here as meaning that Premier Joseph Stalin has de-

Continued on Page Five

Maxim Litvinoff
The New York Times

Labor and Industry Warned By President to End Strikes

By FRANK L. KLUCKHOHN
Special to THE NEW YORK TIMES.

WASHINGTON, Nov. 6—President Roosevelt today called for Americans "to stay on the job and get things made" warning that the United States stood at the crossroads and faces domination if its people were not prepared to make full sacrifices right now. Addressing the delegates of the International Labor Organization from thirty-five countries gathered in the East Room of the White House, Mr. Roosevelt said there are still some among us—"thank God, they are but few—both industrialists and labor leaders, who place personal advantage above the welfare of the nation."

The text of the President's speech is printed on Page 10.

"The American people," he added, "have made an unlimited commitment that there shall be a free world. And against that commitment no individual and no group shall prevail."

Industrial grievances could be entrusted to the machinery established for collective bargaining, he said in his denunciation of those "misguided" industrialists and labor leaders who put "their little victories over one another above triumph against Hitlerism."

"The choice we have to make is this," he said. "Shall we make our full sacrifice now, produce to the limit, deliver our products today and every day to the battlefields of the world? Or shall we remain satisfied with our present rate of armament output, postponing the day of real sacrifice—as did the French—until it is too late?

"The first is the choice of realism, realism in terms of three shifts a day; the fullest use of every vital machine every minute of every day and every night; realism in terms of staying on the job and getting things made."

Declaring that the whole Western Hemisphere has been marked on a Nazi timetable of world domination, the President warned that

Continued on Page Ten

Goebbels Warns Reich of 'Inferno' If She Loses the 'Hard War' Ahead

By Telephone to THE NEW YORK TIMES.

BERLIN, Nov. 6—The German people must resign itself to a "hard and relentless" war, and if this war is lost it will face an "inferno beside which all past hardships will pale."

In those terms Dr. Joseph Goebbels, the leading Nazi propagandist, will paint the German future in an article to be published in Berlin next week.

Banishing once and for all the notion of a quick and comfortable victory, which prevailed among the German masses a year ago and enjoyed nourishment in the utterances of leading publicists, Dr. Goebbels's essay will demand "a gigantic expense of national strength from which no one can be spared" for the continuation of hostilities.

The article will appear Friday in the German weekly Reich, and is already the subject of comment by well-informed German circles, who apply to it such superlatives as the "most realistic" and the "most sober" outline of German prospects to be written here since the beginning of the war.

The title will be "When or How?" and the text will take the form of a debate as to whether it is more important to the German people to consider the duration of the war or the manner in which it

Continued on Page Two

RUSSIANS GAINING AROUND MOSCOW

Report General Progress as They Push Attacks—Nazis Tell of Crimean Advance

By Telephone to THE NEW YORK TIMES.

BERNE, Switzerland, Friday, Nov. 7—With the Germans' fifth major drive against Moscow's defenses hammered to a standstill, the Russians reported today that their developing counter-operations were pushing the Nazis back northwest and southwest of the capital.

Fierce counter-attacks throughout yesterday in the Maloyaroslavets region, sixty-five miles southwest of Moscow, broke up four separate German efforts to reform and attack, and in each one the Russians threw the Nazis back for further territorial losses, according to an authoritative Soviet broadcaster.

[The German High Command claimed that the defense of Sevastopol in Crimea had been broken and that Nazi troops were pouring down to the Black Sea coast between Theodosia and Yalta through a widened breach in the Yaila Mountains. Unofficial reports in Berlin said that Tula, 110 miles south of Moscow, was in German hands. Official sources remained silent on the Moscow front.]

After having consolidated their positions the Russians were reported to be holding a line "at some points" more than seven miles ahead of their original positions. The recapture of four strategically important wooded heights west of Zarusa, on the Oka River seventy miles south of Moscow, was said to have endangered the German lines to the north to such an extent that the Germans "voluntarily" started a further withdrawal. Fearing a trap, the Russians remained in their positions and kept the enemy liner under an intensive artillery bombardment.

At Volokolamsk, sixty-five miles northwest of Moscow, further attacks to the north drove the Nazis back across the Lama River along further "important" lengths of the

Continued on Page Two

SOVIET GETS CREDIT

Roosevelt Pledges Help to Stalin With Grant of Lease-Lend Fund

LOAN WITHOUT INTEREST

Ten-Year Repayment Provided—President Also Assures Kalinin of Our Concern

By BERTRAM D. HULEN
Special to THE NEW YORK TIMES.

WASHINGTON, Nov. 6—Lease-lend aid in the amount of $1,000,000,000 was pledged to Soviet Russia by President Roosevelt through an exchange of letters with Premier Joseph Stalin that was made public by the State Department without comment late today.

The loan will be used for military equipment, munitions and raw materials and will bear no interest. It is to be repaid over a period of ten years beginning five years after the close of the war. In the meantime the United States plans to acquire essential materials from Russia and charge their cost against the lease-lend aid bill.

Coupled with the pledge, which was made by President Roosevelt on Oct. 30 and accepted by Mr. Stalin on Nov. 4, went words of encouragement to Russia from Mr. Roosevelt and denunciation by the Soviet Premier of "bloodthirsty Hitlerism."

Material Aid to Be Speeded

The President also sent a message of encouragement to President Mikhail I. Kalinin, assuring him of a desire to do everything possible in this "critical hour."

In his letter to Mr. Stalin, President Roosevelt announced approval of what the United States delegation had done at the tripartite supply conference in Moscow in the way of promising military equipment and munitions, and said he had ordered the delivery of raw materials to Russia to be expedited.

The President praised Russia's handling of the Moscow conference and declared "we will carry out to the limit all the implications thereof." He also suggested that Mr. Stalin communicate directly with him at any time, an offer that the Soviet Premier welcomed.

In his reply, Mr. Stalin accepted the offer of the loan "with sincere gratitude." He said it was "unusually substantial aid in its [his government's] difficult and great struggle against our common enemy, bloodthirsty Hitlerism." He promised to expedite in every possible way the supplying of "available" raw materials and goods required by the United States.

The United States particularly buys from Russia furs, manganese ore, magnesite, potash, apatite, phosphate rock and asbestos. Russia needs most from the United States tanks and planes, but there is said to be virtually no limit to the extent of materials she could use.

LETTER TO KALININ

The text of President Roosevelt's message to President Kalinin follows:

Nov. 7, 1941.

His Excellency, Mikhail Kalinin,
President, All Union Central Executive Committee,
Kuibyshev, U.S.S.R.

Upon the national anniversary of the Union of the Soviet Socialist Republics I wish to extend to you my felicitations and sincere good wishes for the well-being of the people of your country and to tell you how enheartening the valiant and determined resistance of the army and people of the Soviet Union to the attacks of the invader is to the people of the United States and to all forces which abhor aggression. I am confident that the sacrifices and sufferings of those who have the courage to struggle against aggression will not have been in vain.

I wish to assure you of the desire of the government and people of the United States to do

Continued on Page Thirteen

"All the News That's Fit to Print."

The New York Times.

LATE CITY EDITION
Increasing cloudiness with rising temperature today. Tomorrow cloudy, somewhat colder.
Temperatures Yesterday—Max., 34; Min., 25

VOL. XCI No. 30,634. Entered as Second-Class Matter, Postoffice, New York, N. Y. NEW YORK, MONDAY, DECEMBER 8, 1941. THREE CENTS NEW YORK CITY and Vicinity

JAPAN WARS ON U. S. AND BRITAIN; MAKES SUDDEN ATTACK ON HAWAII; HEAVY FIGHTING AT SEA REPORTED

CONGRESS DECIDED

Roosevelt Will Address It Today and Find It Ready to Vote War

CONFERENCE IS HELD

Legislative Leaders and Cabinet in Sober White House Talk

By C. P. TRUSSELL
Special to THE NEW YORK TIMES.

WASHINGTON, Dec. 7—President Roosevelt will address a joint session of Congress tomorrow and will find the membership in a mood to vote any steps he asks in connection with the developments in the Pacific.

The President will appear personally at 12:30 P. M. Whether he would call for a flat declaration of war again Japan was left unannounced tonight. But leaders of Congress, shocked and angered by the Japanese attacks, were talking of a declaration of war on not only Japan but on the entire Axis.

The plans for action tomorrow were made tonight in a White House conference at which the President, surrounded by his Cabinet and by Congressional leaders of both parties, went through reports, some official, some unconfirmed, of the continued assaults of the Japanese upon American Pacific outposts.

Meet Far Into Night

The conference lasted until after 11 o'clock and at its close an official statement was issued. This said that the President had reviewed for his conferees the latest advices from the Pacific and declared:

"It should be emphasized that the message to Congress has not yet been written and its tenor will, of course, depend on further information received between 11 o'clock tonight and noon tomorrow. Further news is coming in all the time."

Congressional leaders asserted as they left the White House that they did not know what the President would say tomorrow.

"Will the President ask for a declaration of war?" Speaker Rayburn was asked.

"He didn't say," answered the Speaker.

Asked whether Congress would support a declaration of war, Mr. Rayburn observed:

"I think that is one thing on which there would be unity."

Politics Declared Dropped

"There is no politics here," said Representative Joseph W. Martin Jr., Minority House Leader. "There is only one party when it comes to the integrity and honor of the country."

"The Republicans," said Senator Charles L. McNary of Oregon, the Senate minority leader, "will all go along, in my opinion, with whatever is done."

Unless international developments and plans changed overnight, it was indicated, the Presidential recommendations would be directed for the present, at least, at Japan only. This was asserted authoritatively in the face of widespread expectation that any

Continued on Page Six

NEWS BULLETINS

are broadcast by The New York Times every hour on the hour over Station WMCA—570 on the dial.

WEEKDAYS
8 a. m. through 11 p. m.
SUNDAYS
9 a.m., 1 p.m., 5 p.m., 11 p.m.

TOKYO ACTS FIRST

Declaration Follows Air and Sea Attacks on U. S. and Britain

TOGO CALLS ENVOYS

After Fighting Is On, Grew Gets Japan's Reply to Hull Note of Nov. 26

By The Associated Press.

TOKYO, Monday, Dec. 8—Japan went to war against the United States and Britain today with air and sea attacks against Hawaii, followed by a formal declaration of hostilities.

Japanese Imperial headquarters announced at 6 A. M. [4 P. M. Sunday, Eastern standard time] that a state of war existed among these nations in the Western Pacific, as of dawn.

Soon afterward, Domei, the Japanese official news agency, announced that "naval operations are progressing off Hawaii, with at least one Japanese aircraft carrier in action against Pearl Harbor," the American naval base in the islands.

Japanese bombers were declared to have raided Honolulu at 7:35 A. M., Hawaii time [1:05 Sunday, Eastern standard time].

Premier-War Minister General Hideki Tojo held a twenty-minute Cabinet session at his official residence at 7 A. M.

Soon afterward it was announced that both the United States Ambassador, Joseph C. Grew, and the British Ambassador, Sir Robert Leslie Craigie, had been summoned by Foreign Minister Shigenori Togo.

The Foreign Minister, Domei said, handed to Mr. Grew the Japanese Government's formal reply to the note sent to Japan by United States Secretary of State Cordell Hull on Nov. 26.

[In the course of the diplomatic negotiations leading up to yesterday's events, the Domei agency had stated that Japan could not accept the premises of Mr. Hull's note.]

Sir Robert was summoned by

Continued on Page Five

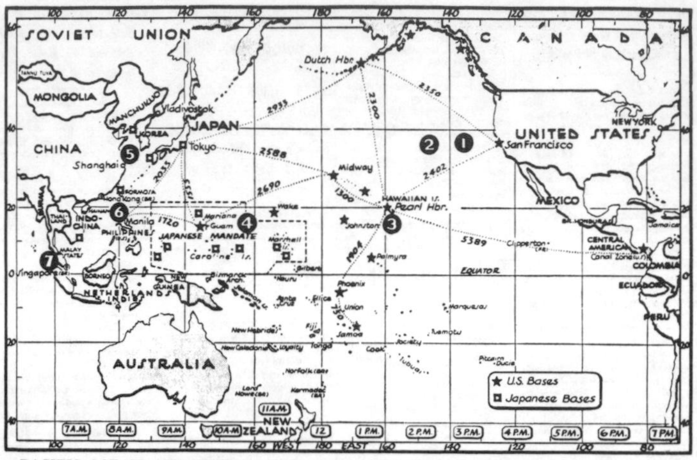

PACIFIC OCEAN: THEATRE OF WAR INVOLVING UNITED STATES AND ITS ALLIES

Shortly after the outbreak of hostilities an American ship sent a distress call from (1) and a United States Army transport carrying lumber was torpedoed at (2). The most important action was at Hawaii (3), where Japanese planes bombed the great Pearl Harbor base. Also attacked was Guam (4). From Manila (6) United States bombers roared northward, while some parts of the Philippines were raided, as was Hong Kong, to the northwest. At Shanghai (5) a British gunboat was sunk and an American gunboat seized. To the south, in the Malaya area (7), the British bombed Japanese ships, Tokyo forces attempted landings on British territory and Singapore underwent an air raid. Distances between key Pacific points are shown on the map in statute miles.

JAPANESE FORCE LANDS IN MALAYA

First Attempt Is Repulsed—Singapore Is Bombed and Thailand Invaded

By The Associated Press.

SINGAPORE, Monday, Dec. 8—The Japanese landed in Northern Malaya, 300 miles north of Singapore, today and bombed this great British naval stronghold, causing small loss of life among civilians and property damage.

About 300 Japanese troops landed on the east coast of Malaya and began filtering through jungle-fringed swamps and rice fields toward Kota Bahru airdrome, which is ten miles from the northern terminus of a railroad leading to Singapore.

An official report from the

Continued on Page Two

Tokyo Bombers Strike Hard At Our Main Bases on Oahu

By The United Press.

HONOLULU, Dec. 7—War broke with lightning suddenness in the Pacific today when waves of Japanese bombers attacked Hawaii this morning and the United States Fleet struck back with a thunder of big naval rifles. Japanese bombers, including four-engined dive bombers and torpedo-carrying planes, blasted at Pearl Harbor, the great United States naval base, the city of Honolulu and several outlying American military bases on the Island of Oahu. There were casualties of unstated number.

[The United States battleship Oklahoma was set afire by the Japanese attackers, according to a National Broadcasting Company observer, who also reported in a broadcast yesterday that two other ships in Pearl Harbor were attacked.

[The Japanese news agency, Domei, reported that the battleship Oklahoma had been sunk at Pearl Harbor, according to a United Press dispatch from Shanghai.

[Governor Joseph B. Poindexter of Hawaii talked with President Roosevelt late yesterday afternoon, saying that a second wave of Japanese bombers was just coming over, and the Gov-

Continued on Page Thirteen

ENTIRE CITY PUT ON WAR FOOTING

Japanese Rounded Up by FBI, Sent to Ellis Island—Vital Services Are Guarded

The metropolitan district reacted swiftly yesterday to the Japanese attack in the Pacific. All large communities in the area, including New York City, Newark, Jersey City, Bayonne and Paterson, went on immediate war footing.

One of the first steps taken here last night was a round-up of Japanese nationals by special agents of the Federal Bureau of Investigation, reinforced by squads of city detectives acting under FBI supervision. More than 100 FBI men, fully armed, were assigned to the detail.

The prisoners were sent to Ellis Island, where they will be held pending action at Washington. It was indicated hundreds would be detained.

Earlier Mayor La Guardia had convened his Emergency Board and directed that Japanese nationals be confined to their homes pending decision as to their status and had their clubs and other meeting places closed and put under police guard.

A police sergeant and five policemen immediately went to the Japanese Consulate at 630 Fifth Avenue in Rockefeller Center where the Consul General, Morito Morishima, and his staff were preparing to leave, and posted a guard there. The Consul General and his staff were escorted to their homes when they left. They were not to move about the city without police in attendance.

Rear Admiral Adolphus Andrews, commander of the North Atlantic Squadron, told reporters at a conference in the Federal

Continued on Page Three

HULL DENOUNCES TOKYO 'INFAMY'

Brands Japan 'Fraudulent' in Preparing Attack While Carrying On Parleys

Texts of Secretary Hull's note and Japan's reply, Page 10.

By BERTRAM D. HULEN
Special to THE NEW YORK TIMES.

WASHINGTON, Dec. 7—Japan was accused by Secretary of State Cordell Hull today of making a "treacherous and utterly unprovoked attack" upon the United States and of having been "infamously false and fraudulent" by preparing for the attack while conducting diplomatic negotiations with the professed desire of maintaining peace.

But even before he knew of the attack, Mr. Hull had vehemently brought the diplomatic negotiations to a virtual end with an outburst against Admiral Kichisaburo Nomura, the Japanese Ambassador, and Saburo Kurusu, special envoy, because of the insulting character of the reply they deliv-

Continued on Page Eleven

The International Situation

MONDAY, DEC. 8, 1941

Yesterday morning Japan attacked the United States at several points in the Pacific. President Roosevelt ordered United States forces into action and a declaration of war is expected this morning. [Page 1, Columns 7 and 8.] Tokyo made its declaration as of this morning against both the United States and Britain. [Page 1, Column 2.] The first Japanese assault was directed at Pearl Harbor Naval base in Hawaii. Many casualties and severe damage resulted. [Page 1, Columns 4 and 5; Map, Page 13.] United States Army aircraft took off from the Philippines this morning and some points in the Archipelago were bombed. [Page 8, Column 2.] Singapore and Hong Kong were bombed and a Japanese landing in Northern Malaya and a move on Thailand were reported. [Page 1, Column 3.] In Shanghai, Japanese marines occupied the waterfront; a British gunboat was sunk, a United States gunboat seized. [Page 9, Column 1.]

Factional lines dissolved as an angered Congress prepared to meet this morning. [Page 1, Column 1.] Secretary of State Hull accused Japan of having made a "treacherous and utterly unprovoked attack" after having been "infamously false and fraudulent." [Page 1, Column 6.] He released the text of diplomatic exchanges with Japan [Page 10], while the President gave out the text of his fruitless appeal to the Japanese Emperor. [Page 12.] The White House was the hub of Washington activity and news bulletins were released there. [Page 12, Column 3.]

The Federal Bureau of Investigation was ordered to begin a round-up of some Japanese in this country. [Page 6, Column 8.] As New York City went on a war footing and public precautions were taken, the FBI began the detention of Japanese nationals. [Page 1, Column 4.]

The unification of the country under the impact of the attack was swift. [Page 6, Column 6.] Formerly conspicuous isolationists indicated full support for the war effort. [Page 6, Column 4.]

Prime Minister Churchill notified Tokyo that a state of war existed. [Page 4, Column 1.] Declarations were made last night or early today by Australia, Canada [Page 14 Column 1], the Netherlands Indies [Page 7, Column 2] and Costa Rica. [Page 15, Column 1.]

Libya was the scene of a renewed tank battle and the Tobruk corridor was reported again clear of Axis forces. [Page 20, Column 2, with map.] On the Moscow front the German line was broken at two places, said Soviet sources. [Page 17, Column 2.]

Lewis Wins Captive Mine Fight; Arbitrators Grant Union Shop

The three-man arbitration board appointed by President Roosevelt to arbitrate the union shop dispute in the captive coal mines last night reversed the decision of the National Defense Mediation Board and ruled that all workers in the captive mines should be required to join John L. Lewis's United Mine Workers as a condition of employment.

The decision was made by a two to one vote, with Benjamin F. Fairless, president of the United States Steel Corporation, dissenting. Dr. John R. Steelman, who took a leave of absence from his post as director of the United States Conciliation Service to serve as chairman of the arbitration panel, and Mr. Lewis voted in favor of extension to the captive mines of the union shop provision of the standard Appalachian agreement.

Despite his dissent, Mr. Fairless promised that the coal mining subsidiaries of United States Steel would put the ruling into effect. All eight steel companies operating captive mines had given formal assurances before the decision was reached that they would accept it as binding.

The arbitration award ended a dispute in which Mr. Lewis had repeatedly defied the President by calling strikes that menaced the production of steel and that had had its repercussions in the enactment by the House of the Smith anti-strike bill.

In explaining his vote for the union shop, Dr. Steelman pointed out that 95 per cent of the 53,000 captive miners had voluntarily assumed membership in Mr. Lewis's C. I. O. union and that 99.5 per cent of all the miners in the nation were now members of the union.

Since the bulk of the industry, including many owners of captive mines, was already operating under the union shop, it could not be argued that the United Mine Workers was endeavoring to take

Continued on Page Forty-three

GUAM BOMBED; ARMY SHIP IS SUNK

U. S. Fliers Head North From Manila—Battleship Oklahoma Set Afire by Torpedo Planes at Honolulu

104 SOLDIERS KILLED AT FIELD IN HAWAII

President Fears 'Very Heavy Losses' on Oahu—Churchill Notifies Japan That a State of War Exists

By FRANK L. KLUCKHOHN
Special to THE NEW YORK TIMES.

WASHINGTON, Monday, Dec. 8—Sudden and unexpected attacks on Pearl Harbor, Honolulu, and other United States possessions in the Pacific early yesterday by the Japanese air force and navy plunged the United States and Japan into active war.

The initial attack in Hawaii, apparently launched by torpedo-carrying bombers and submarines, caused widespread damage and death. It was quickly followed by others. There were unconfirmed reports that German raiders participated in the attacks.

Guam also was assaulted from the air, as were Davao, on the island of Mindanao, and Camp John Hay, in Northern Luzon, both in the Philippines. Lieut. Gen. Douglas MacArthur, commanding the United States Army of the Far East, reported there was little damage, however.

[Japanese parachute troops had been landed in the Philippines and native Japanese had seized some communities, Royal Arch Gunnison said in a broadcast from Manila today to WOR-Mutual. He reported without detail that "in the naval war the ABCD fleets under American command appeared to be successful" against Japanese invasions.]

Japanese submarines, ranging out over the Pacific, sank an American transport carrying lumber 1,300 miles from San Francisco, and distress signals were heard from a freighter 700 miles from that city.

The War Department reported that 104 soldiers died and 300 were wounded as a result of the attack on Hickam Field, Hawaii. The National Broadcasting Company reported from Honolulu that the battleship Oklahoma was afire. [Domei, Japanese news agency, reported the Oklahoma sunk.]

Nation Placed on Full War Basis

The news of these surprise attacks fell like a bombshell on Washington. President Roosevelt immediately ordered the country and the Army and Navy onto a full war footing. He arranged at a White House conference last night to address a joint session of Congress at noon today, presumably to ask for declaration of a formal state of war.

This was disclosed after a long special Cabinet meeting, which was joined later by Congressional leaders. These leaders predicted "action" within a day.

After leaving the White House conference Attorney General Francis Biddle said that "a resolution" would be introduced in Congress tomorrow. He would not amplify or affirm that it would be for a declaration of war

Congress probably will "act" within the day, and he will call the Senate Foreign Relations Committee for this purpose, Chairman Tom Connally announced.

[A United Press dispatch from London this morning said that Prime Minister Churchill had notified Japan that a state of war existed.]

As the reports of heavy fighting flashed into the White House, London reported semi-officially that the British Empire would carry out Prime Minister Winston Churchill's pledge to give the United States full support in case of hostilities with Japan. The President and Mr. Churchill talked by transatlantic telephone.

This was followed by a statement in London from the Netherland Government in Exile that it considered a state of war to exist between the Netherlands and Japan. Canada, Australia and Costa Rica took similar action.

Landing Made in Malaya

A Singapore communiqué disclosed that Japanese troops had landed in Northern Malaya and that Singapore had been bombed.

The President told those at last night's White House meeting that "doubtless very heavy losses" were sustained by the Navy and also by the Army on the island of Oahu [Honolulu]. It was impossible to obtain confirmation or denial of reports that the battleships Oklahoma and West Virginia had been damaged or sunk at Pearl Harbor, together with six or seven destroyers, and that 350 United States airplanes had been caught on the ground.

The White House took over control of the bulletins, and the Navy Department, therefore, said it could not discuss the matter or answer any questions how the Japanese were able to penetrate the Hawaiian defenses or appear without previous knowledge of their presence in those waters.

Administration circles forecast that the United States soon might be involved in a world-wide war, with Germany supporting Japan, an Axis partner. The German official radio tonight attacked the United States and supported Japan.

Axis diplomats here expressed complete surprise that the Japanese had attacked. But the impression gained from their attitude was that they believed it represented a victory for the Nazi attempt to divert lease-lend aid from Britain, which has been

Continued on Page Four

1941

Dismayed servicemen looked on as smoke and flames billowed upward during the aerial attack on Pearl Harbor.

The battleship U.S.S. Arizona burns furiously.

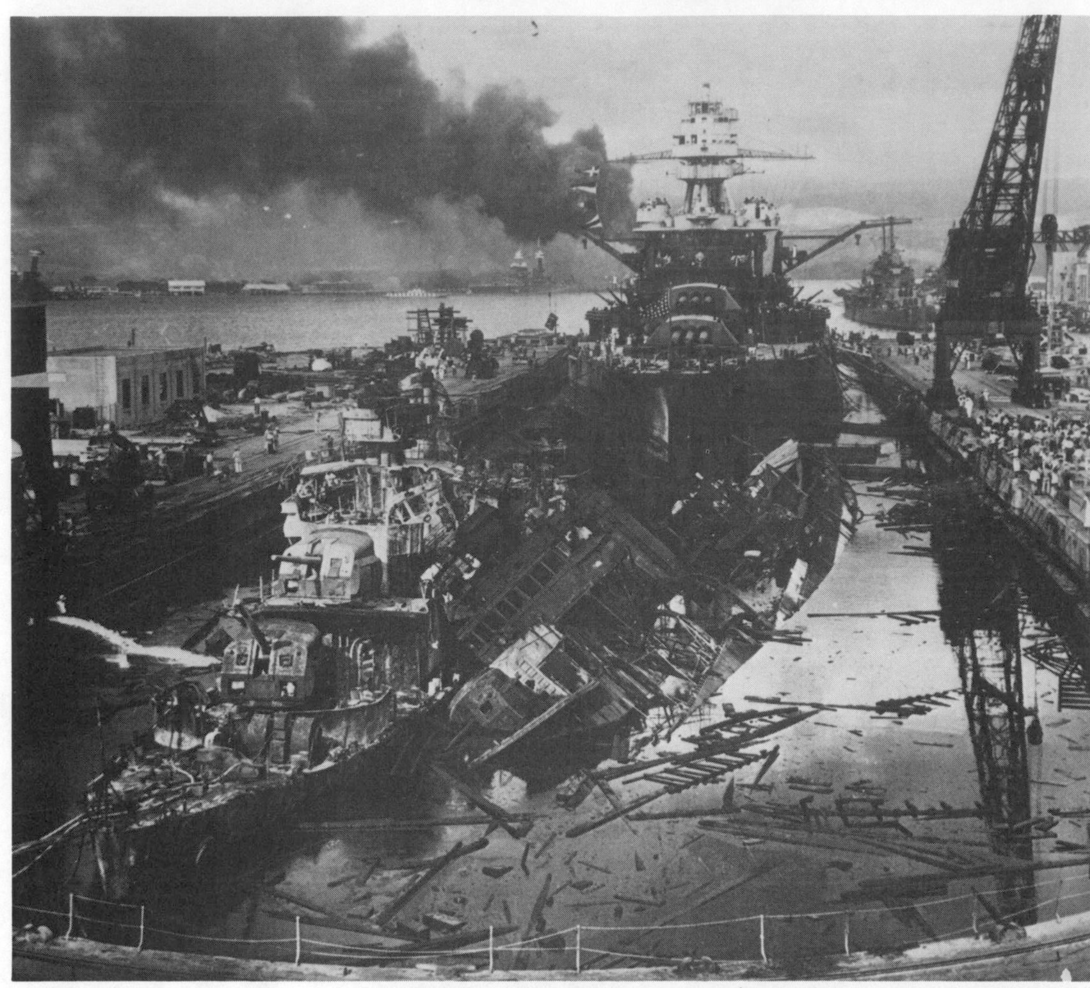

Aftermath of the Japanese attack on Pearl Harbor.

Immediately after the attack on Pearl Harbor, the United States mobilized 11,600,000 men and sent soldiers, sailors and airmen all over the world; there were many tearful goodbyes.

"All the News That's Fit to Print."

The New York Times.

LATE CITY EDITION
Cloudy followed by clearing and colder today. Tomorrow fair and moderately cold.
Temperatures Yesterday—Max., 44; Min., 25

VOL. XCI. No. 30,635. Entered as Second-Class Matter, Postoffice, New York, N. Y. NEW YORK, TUESDAY, DECEMBER 9, 1941. THREE CENTS NEW YORK CITY and Vicinity

U. S. DECLARES WAR, PACIFIC BATTLE WIDENS; MANILA AREA BOMBED; 1,500 DEAD IN HAWAII; HOSTILE PLANES SIGHTED AT SAN FRANCISCO

TURN BACK TO SEA

Two Formations Neared City on Radio Beams, Then Went Astray

ALARM IS WIDESPREAD

Whole Coast Has a Nervous Night—Many Cities Blacked Out

By LAWRENCE E. DAVIES
Special to THE NEW YORK TIMES.

SAN FRANCISCO, Dec. 8—Two formations of "many planes," described as undoubtedly enemy aircraft, flew over the San Francisco Bay area tonight, it was announced officially by Brig. Gen. William O. Ryan, commander of the Fourth Interceptor Command, after a progressive blackout had blotted out naval and military establishments and whole cities along the Pacific Coast.

Conflicting reports spread, contributing to the "war of nerves," as the sirens wailed and broadcasting were silenced.

After another spokesman, through an error, had declared the blackout to be an air raid test, General Ryan said at the Presidio that it was no test but "the real thing."

The ships were detected first about 100 miles at sea, he said. In two formations they headed for the Monterey Peninsula, about eighty miles south of this city, and for San Francisco Bay itself.

Radio detectors plotted their course, bringing one formation in just north of the Golden Gate and the other to a point near Fort Barry, at the south end of the Golden Gate Bridge.

Planes Turn Back to Sea

After flying northward for some distance the planes turned south to a point thirty-five or forty miles down the peninsula section below San Francisco. Apparently trying to orient themselves, they flew about a while longer and then headed southwest to sea, General Ryan said.

The commanding officer, whose station is at Riverside and who said he just "happened" to be at the Presidio tonight, declared that the planes followed radio beams to these shores. When radio stations on the West Coast were silenced as part of the blackout the enemy craft apparently were not sure of their position.

No American planes were sent to the attack, he said, because "you don't send planes up unless you know what the enemy is doing and where he is going and you don't send planes up in the dark unless you know what you are doing."

Although there was no official explanation for the absence of anti-aircraft fire, it was indicated that the planes were hardly close enough for effective use of the guns.

Plane Carriers Rumored

Although General Ryan had no information, he said, as to the presence of enemy aircraft carriers hovering off the Pacific Coast, rumors of their presence had been broadcast during the day and this, it was acknowledged, would be the logical explanation for the appearance of the planes.

Lieut. Gen. John L. Dewitt,

Continued on Page Twenty-eight

Philippines Pounded All Day As Raiders Strike at Troops

Air Base Near Capital Among Targets Hit by Japanese—Landing on Lubang With Aid of Fifth Columnists Reported

By H. FORD WILKINS
Wireless to THE NEW YORK TIMES.

MANILA, Tuesday, Dec. 9—After a day of widespread aerial attacks throughout the Philippines, Japanese bombers swept in over Manila Bay early this morning and attacked Nichols Field, the United States Army air base on the outskirts of this capital, and simultaneously reports were received of a Japanese landing on Lubang Island, off the northwestern tip of Mindoro.

This morning's attack, which began shortly after 3 o'clock, was the first in the Manila area. The damage was believed to have been slight, but some casualties were reported. [A National Broadcasting Company correspondent reported that an official statement issued in Manila after the raid said: "In the raid on Nichols Field, which was conducted by approximately ten Japanese bombers, one hangar was damaged and one officers' quarters was burned. The casualty list consists of one soldier killed and twelve wounded—all Americans."]

The reported landing on Lubang, sixty miles southwest of Manila, was not officially confirmed, but the reports received credence here. [Other unconfirmed reports, relayed by the Columbia Broadcasting System, told of landings in the Davao region, on the southern island of Mindanao.]

The Manila area's first experience with bombs was a climax to a day and night of tension and activity. The explosions could be

Continued on Page Nine

1 BATTLESHIP LOST

Capsized in Pearl Harbor, Destroyer Is Blown Up, Other Ships Hurt

FLEET NOW IS FIGHTING

Aid Rushed to Hawaii—Some Congressmen Sharply Critical

By CHARLES HURD
Special to THE NEW YORK TIMES.

WASHINGTON, Dec. 8—The Battle of the Pacific spread tonight over a 5,000-mile "front" from Hawaii to the Philippines while a badly battered United States Fleet fought back at Japanese sea and air forces that launched severe attacks yesterday afternoon.

Tonight the Japanese were reported to be launching their main attack at the Philippines, particularly at Palawan, the greatest natural harbor in the archipelago. That attack was preceded today, according to reports from Manila, by an onslaught against the United States military air fields there, which put these out of commission for the time being and set fire to storage tanks containing vital gasoline for air operations.

The Japanese Sunday attack on Hawaii was reported in informed quarters to have been launched from the mandated islands, rather than from Japan proper, and aircraft carriers apparently approached undetected within 250 or 300 miles of Pearl Harbor.

3,000 Casualties on Oahu

The White House announced officially that the attack on the Island of Oahu, site of Honolulu and the Pearl Harbor naval base, probably has cost about 1,500 lives and resulted in an equal number of wounded persons.

To the toll of lives announced for this region, and undisclosed casualties in the Philippines and at other points, was added official word that one "old battleship" had capsized in Pearl Harbor, a destroyer had exploded and that several other

Continued on Page Four

The President signs the declaration of war — Associated Press Wirephotos

UNITY IN CONGRESS

Only One Negative Vote as President Calls to War and Victory

ROUNDS OF CHEERS

Miss Rankin's Is Sole 'No' as Both Houses Act in Quick Time

By FRANK L. KLUCKHOHN
Special to THE NEW YORK TIMES.

WASHINGTON, Dec. 8—The United States today formally declared war on Japan. Congress, with only one dissenting vote, approved the resolution in the record time of 33 minutes after President Roosevelt denounced Japanese aggression in ringing tones. He personally delivered his message to a joint session of the Senate and House. At 4:10 P. M. he affixed his signature to the resolution.

There was no debate like that between April 2, 1917, when President Wilson requested war against Germany, and April 6, when a declaration of war was approved by Congress.

President Roosevelt spoke only 6 minutes and 30 seconds today compared with Woodrow Wilson's 29 minutes and 34 seconds.

The vote today against Japan was 82 to 0 in the Senate and 388 to 1 in the House. The lone vote against the resolution in the House was that of Miss Jeanette Rankin, Republican, of Montana. Her "No" was greeted with boos and hisses. In 1917 she voted against the resolution for war against Germany.

The President did not mention either Germany or Italy in his request. Early this evening a statement was issued at the White House, however, accusing Germany of doing everything possible to push Japan into the war. The objective, the official statement proclaimed, was to cut off American lend-lease aid to Germany's European enemies, and a pledge was made that this aid would continue "100 per cent."

A Sudden and Deliberate Attack

President Roosevelt's brief and decisive words were addressed to the assembled representatives of the basic organizations of American democracy—the Senate, the House, the Cabinet and the Supreme Court.

"America was suddenly and deliberately attacked by naval and air forces of the Empire of Japan," he said. "We will gain the inevitable triumph, so help us God."

Thunderous cheers greeted the Chief Executive and Commander in Chief throughout the address. This was particularly pronounced when he declared that Americans "will remember the character of the onslaught against us," a day, he remarked, which will live in infamy.

"This form of treachery shall never endanger us again," he declared amid cheers. "The American people in their righteous might will win through to absolute victory."

Then, to the accompaniment of a

Continued on Page Five

PLANES GUARD CITY FROM AIR ATTACKS

Army Interceptors Join the Navy Patrols—Anti-Aircraft Apparatus Set Up Here

While long lines of men of fighting age waited impatiently outside of every Army, Navy and Marine Corps recruiting office in the city yesterday, representatives of the city, State and Federal Governments went ahead with the grim business of making New York City ready for war.

Beginning at dawn yesterday Army fighting planes took off at regular intervals from Mitchel Field to maintain, in conjunction with a Navy patrol, a constant fighting force in the air, so there could be no repetition here of the surprise in Hawaii. At the same time the First Interceptor Command called to active duty 40,000 volunteer civilian aircraft spotters at 1,300 posts scattered through thirteen eastern coastal States and the District of Columbia.

Anti-Aircraft Guns Set Up

The Sixty-second Coast Artillery of Fort Totten, Bayside, Queens, set up anti-aircraft apparatus at vantage points around the city. One base was in Prospect Park, Brooklyn.

Air raid wardens went on duty at midnight in every part of the city, as a result of a series of conferences among Police and Fire Department officers and representatives of the Board of Education and the Department of Housing, at which it was agreed that air raid warnings would be broadcast by the blowing of the sirens of all police radio cars and emergency trucks and all Fire Department apparatus.

Alternating long and short blasts of the sirens will be sounded from the moment the Army notifies the Police and Fire Departments of the approach of an enemy and will be continued throughout the duration of the raid. The all-clear signal will be given by a series of short blasts from the sirens, it was agreed.

Teachers to Be Warned

The Police and Fire Departments, with their network of communications reaching into every neighborhood in the city, also undertook to advise the 800 public schools of an impending raid when the alarm is sounded, so the teachers can shepherd their pupils to their homes in accordance with plans already made.

Precautions against sabotage of bridges, tunnels, railroads, reservoirs, dams, power plants and other points of key importance throughout the city also were discussed at conferences of high police officials with Commissioner

Continued on Page Twenty-six

MALAYA THWARTS PUSH BY JAPANESE

Thailand Capitulates and Is Seen Virtually in Axis—Two Raids on Singapore

By F. TILLMAN DURDIN
Wireless to THE NEW YORK TIMES.

SINGAPORE, Dec. 8—The Japanese in the first eighteen hours of their attack on the Malaya peninsula have forced Thailand to capitulate, but do not now appear to have achieved any appreciable success in an invasion of British Malaya.

There was an air raid on Singapore this morning. Prai, on the mainland opposite Georgetown, more commonly known as Penang from the name of the island on which it is located, was also bombed, but damage was said to be slight.

[Bombs again started dropping on Singapore at 4 A. M. today, The Associated Press reported.]

Continued on Page Ten

The International Situation

TUESDAY, DECEMBER 9, 1941

The United States yesterday made a formal declaration of war on Japan after President Roosevelt had addressed a joint session of Congress. [Page 1, Column 8.] The Senate approved by unanimous vote [Page 6, Column 1] while one woman in the House of Representatives dissented. [Page 6, Column 4.]

In the national effort the Supply, Priorities and Allocations Board mapped expanding production [Page 36, Column 1], leaders of organized labor pledged support [Page 36, Column 4], and Mayor La Guardia issued a proclamation giving air raid defense instructions [Page 34, Column 1.]

In San Francisco two formations of enemy aircraft were sighted over the city, which was blacked out. [Page 1, Column 1.]

White House announcements indicated that the battle of the Pacific was raging with the United States still on the defensive. [Page 1. Column 4; Map, Page 4.] There were extensive air attacks in the Philippines [Page 1, Columns 2 and 3; Map, Page 9], raids on Hong Kong [Page 11, Column 1] and a Tokyo report that both Guam and Wake had been put under the Japanese flag. [Page 12, Column 1; with map.] The British were mopping up on a Japanese landing party in Malaya, but Thailand had yielded. [Page 1, Column 3; Map, Page 10.]

The small detachment of United States Marines at Tientsin and Peiping was disarmed and detained by the Japanese and they closed the United States Consulate in Shanghai [Page 3, Column 1.] Imperial Headquarters in Tokyo made sweeping claims of victory in the battle of the Pacific, listing great damage to the United States forces. [Page 1, Column 5.]

In London, Prime Minister Churchill announced Britain's declaration of war to Parliament and made a stirring address to the world. [Page 14, Column 1.]

The American nations began to line up behind the United States. A conference will be held, but seven countries have already declared war on Japan, two have broken diplomatic relations and several others are preparing to act. [Page 22, Column 3.] China decided to declare war not merely on Japan but on Germany and Italy as well. [Page 9, Column 4.] The various European governments in exile also supported the United States. [Page 18, Column 1.] Russia's position is obscure. [Page 2, Column 2.]

The United States accused Germany of having egged Japan on; said lease-lend aid would continue. [Page 1, Column 6.]

Berlin gave out word that Winter had stopped the Germans short of Moscow and that the capture of the Russian capital had been put off until Spring. [Page 1, Column 7.]

In Libya, the Axis armored forces were attacked from three directions by the British and what was expected to be a major engagement was eventually merely a rearguard action. [Page 24, Column 3.]

LARGE U. S. LOSSES CLAIMED BY JAPAN

Tokyo Lists 2 Battleships, 1 Mine-Sweeper Sunk, 4 Capital Ships, 4 Cruisers Damaged

TOKYO, Tuesday, Dec. 9 (From Official Broadcasts, Distributed by The Associated Press)—Japanese Imperial Headquarters announced last night the sinking of two United States battleships and a mine-sweeper, severe damage to four other American capital ships and four cruisers and the destruction of about 100 American planes in Japan's surprise blows at Hawaii, the Philippines and Guam.

The official news agency, Domei, quickly interpreted "these magnificent early gains" as giving Japan naval mastery over the United States in the Pacific, and said that any force that the United States could muster now "would be regarded as utterly inadequate to accomplish any successful outcome in an encounter with the thus-far-intact Japanese fleet."

In addition, "many enemy merchant ships were captured" in the Pacific, it was announced, and the communiqué listed an unconfirmed report that a Japanese submarine had sunk an American aircraft carrier off Honolulu.

"No Japanese ships were lost during the fighting," it added.

Domei said today it was "understood that Japanese forces had destroyed more than 300 American planes, including 200 in dogfights and on the ground in Hawaii. The others, it said, were "believed" destroyed in the Philippines. Of the total, the news agency said, thirty were Fortress planes and thirty long-range bombers.

Japanese newspapers identified the two American battleships declared sunk Sunday at Pearl Harbor, Hawaii, as the 31,800-ton West Virginia, and the 29,000-ton Oklahoma. [An Italian broadcast, however, quoted Domei as listing the Oklahoma and the 33,100-ton Pennsylvania as lost. In Berlin, D. N. B. said in a Tokyo dispatch that an American transport ship carrying 350 men had been sunk off Manila.]

Japanese planes were reported to have again attacked the Philippines and British Hong Kong yesterday, inflicting "heavy damage" in a follow-up of the raids launched Sunday. "Twelve out of fourteen enemy planes on the ground were

Continued on Page Thirteen

The President's Message

Following is the text of President Roosevelt's war message to Congress, as recorded by THE NEW YORK TIMES *from a broadcast:*

Mr. Vice President, Mr. Speaker, members of the Senate and the House of Representatives:

Yesterday, Dec. 7, 1941—a date which will live in infamy—the United States of America was suddenly and deliberately attacked by ,. .'·l and air forces of the empire of Japan.

The United States was at peace with that nation, and, at the solicitation of Japan, was still in conversation with its government and its Emperor looking toward the maintenance of peace in the Pacific.

Indeed, one hour after Japanese air squadrons had commenced bombing in the American island of Oahu the Japanese Ambassador to the United States and his colleague delivered to our Secretary of State a formal reply to a recent American message. And, while this reply stated that it seemed useless to continue the existing diplomatic negotiations, it contained no threat or hint of war or of armed attack.

Attack Deliberately Planned

It will be recorded that the distance of Hawaii from Japan makes it obvious that the attack was deliberately planned many days or even weeks ago. During the intervening time the Japanese Government has deliberately sought to deceive the United States by false statements and expressions of hope for continued peace.

The attack yesterday on the Hawaiian Islands has caused severe damage to American naval and military forces. I regret to tell you that very many American lives have been lost. In

Continued on Page Six

U. S. TO CONTINUE AID TO BRITAIN

White House Charges Nazis Sought Pacific War, but Will Fail to Gain Ends

Special to THE NEW YORK TIMES.

WASHINGTON, Dec. 8—A statement accusing Germany of having done everything in her power "to push Japan into the war" was issued this evening at the White House.

The statement declared that Germany's objective was "to put an end to the lease-lend program," which has aided the European enemies of Germany, including Britain and Russia and their allies and Turkey. It added that this program would continue "in full operation" and that the German attempt to end lease-lend shipments was "100 per cent" mistaken.

This statement took full cognizance of the belief in diplomatic circles here that Germany would carry out its pledges to Japan, its Axis ally, by declaring war on the United States and that Italy would

Continued on Page Seventeen

NAZIS GIVE UP IDEA OF MOSCOW IN 1941

Winter Forces Abandonment of Big Drives in North Till Spring, Berlin Says

By The Associated Press.

BERLIN, Dec. 8—Winter has stopped the Germans short of Moscow and the capture of the Soviet capital is not expected this year, a military spokesman declared tonight.

[A surprise Russian attack on Eastern Crimea from the Caucasus was revealed in a Moscow broadcast. A counter-attack from Sevastopol also was reported. The Soviet claimed important progress around Taganrog and on Moscow's defense lines.]

It seemed likely from the spokesman's statement that until Spring there could be no further major German offensive except along the extreme southern front. This word reduced the Russian campaign to secondary interest for the Germans for the first time, and attention focused instead on Ja-

Continued on Page Twenty-five

President to Talk On Radio Tonight

By The Associated Press.

WASHINGTON, Dec. 8—President Roosevelt will make a radio address to the nation tomorrow night at 10 P. M., Eastern standard time, at which time the White House said he would make "a more complete documentation" of the Japanese attack than has yet been possible.

Stephen Early, Presidential secretary, announced that the Chief Executive would speak for half an hour and that the address would be carried by all networks.

Mr. Roosevelt began dictating the speech tonight in his White House study.

NEWS BULLETINS

Please do not telephone The New York Times for war news. Every hour on the hour news bulletins are broadcast over Station WMCA—570 on the dial.

WEEKDAYS
8 a. m. through 11 p. m.
SUNDAYS
9 a.m., 1 p.m., 5 p.m., 11 p.m.

"All the News That's Fit to Print."

The New York Times.

LATE CITY EDITION
Fair, slowly rising temperature today. Tomorrow cloudy, moderately cold, occasional snow.
Temperatures Yesterday—Max., 34; Min., 24

VOL. XCI..No. 30,688. Entered as Second-Class Matter, Postoffice, New York, N. Y. NEW YORK, FRIDAY, DECEMBER 12, 1941. THREE CENTS NEW YORK CITY and Vicinity

U.S. NOW AT WAR WITH GERMANY AND ITALY; JAPANESE CHECKED IN ALL LAND FIGHTING; 3 OF THEIR SHIPS SUNK, 2D BATTLESHIP HIT

BLOCKED IN LUZON

But Japanese Put Small Force Ashore in South of Philippine Island

SABOTEURS ARE HELD

Some in Manila Seized for Spreading Rumor About City Water

By H. FORD WILKINS
Wireless to THE NEW YORK TIMES.

MANILA, Friday, Dec. 12—The United States Army Far East headquarters announced today that a small Japanese invasion force was reported to have pushed ashore at Legaspi, Southern Luzon, and "the enemy has improved his strength in Northern Luzon," where, however, the situation remains unchanged materially. The announcement added that the report of the Legaspi landing was still unconfirmed and there were no details.

[Small forces of Japanese apparently have been landed at Legaspi, it was said officially three hours after the morning communiqué had said merely that the Legaspi development had not yet been confirmed, a United Press dispatch from Manila said.]

There was no further indication of the progress of the sea war. The office of Admiral Thomas C. Hart, commander in chief of the United States Asiatic Fleet, remained silent.

One Japanese plane was shot down by an American fighter near Bancayan, in the mountain mining district.

2,000 Families Are Moved

Manila took further emergency measures to evacuate portions of the old walled city. The Red Cross supervised the removal of 2,000 families, loading them into buses and trucks and taking them to safety zones considerably removed from the city. Identification cards were issued and checked as the evacuees lined up for removal.

With Lieut. Gen. Douglas MacArthur's United States Far Eastern forces fully in control of the North Luzon invasion threat and his air force sufficiently active to disperse Japanese raiders headed for Manila, his intelligence service turned yesterday to mopping up fifth columnists.

Their latest trick was to circulate rumors that the city water supply had been poisoned. Army, city and government officials quickly scotched the rumors with assurances and proof that nothing whatever was wrong with the water supply. Several persons were arrested, including air-raid wardens, on a city-wide house-to-house campaign warning the people against "impure water."

Several persons entered hospitals asserting that they had been poisoned, but examination disclosed that nothing was wrong with them but upset stomachs and fear. Elaborate analysis proved that the water they drank was not contaminated.

The official communiqué asserting that mopping-up operations were progressing heightened the morale of the nation, suddenly plunged into total war and its first taste of conflict in forty years.

The sinking of a United States Army transport in Manila Bay, as announced by Tokyo, was denied officially here yesterday.

Interned Japanese, numbering around 2,000, were revealed to be extremely uncomfortable under the threat of bombs from Japanese planes, recognizing that bombs do not distinguish nationalities.

Legaspi Move Discounted

MANILA, Friday, Dec. 12 (U.P.)—The small Japanese landings at Legaspi, a port of about 36,000

Continued on Page Eight

Line-Up of World War II

THE ALLIES

Australia	Haiti
†Belgium	*Honduras
Canada	Netherlands
China	Indies
Costa Rica	New Zealand
Cuba	Nicaragua
†Czecho-Slovakia	†Norway
Dominican Republic	*Panama
	†Poland
*El Salvador	South Africa
Free France	Soviet Union
Great Britain	United States
†Greece	†Yugoslavia
Guatemala	

THE AXIS

Finland	Japan
Germany	Manchukuo
Hungary	Rumania
Italy	Slovakia

*Have declared war on Japan only.
†At war only with Germany, Italy and their European allies.

CITY CALM AND GRIM AS THE WAR WIDENS

Loyalty and a Determination to Win Are Evident in Every Class and National Group

The people of New York City received the news that we are at war with Germany and Italy as well as Japan with profound calm and a quiet, stern determination to see it through, no matter how long it takes. Patriotism and loyalty were the spontaneous order of the day in every household, every business office, every factory, every school and every institution. The whole city rallied in support of the war.

All over the city the Stars and Stripes flew proudly from public and private buildings, and those in charge of Army, Navy, Coast Guard and civilian defense organizations swung promptly and forcefully into action to protect the city

Continued on Page Twenty-one

U. S. FLIERS SCORE

Bombs Send Battleship, Cruiser and Destroyer to the Bottom

MARINES KEEP WAKE

Small Force Fights Off Foe Despite Loss of Some of Planes

By CHARLES HURD
Special to THE NEW YORK TIMES.

WASHINGTON, Dec. 11—A Japanese battleship, a cruiser and a destroyer have been sunk in the Pacific and a second battleship badly damaged by bomb hits, the United States forces announced in communiqués today recording their first major victories in the warfare that began last Sunday with surprise Japanese attacks.

Damage to the second battleship was revealed tonight in a Navy communiqué, which said a man-of-war of the Kongo class had been hit by Navy patrol planes off the coast of Luzon. This was "the second battleship to be bombed effectively by United States forces," the communiqué asserted.

The battleship sunk, also of the Kongo class, was believed to have been the 29,330-ton Haruna. She went down after having been set afire by aerial bombardment north of Luzon. She had been supporting an attack in which the Japanese effected a landing at Aparri, a remote village on the northern Philippine coast, separated from Manila by mountains and forests.

The cruiser, unidentified except that it was of the light class, and the destroyer were sunk also by fliers who took off from Wake

Continued on Page Six

The International Situation

FRIDAY, DECEMBER 12, 1941

The United States declared war yesterday on Germany and Italy. Congress acted swiftly without a dissenting vote. [Page 1, Column 8.] Then, without debate, it passed a bill to permit the use of all United States land forces anywhere in the world. [Page 1, Column 7.]

This action coincided with good news from the Pacific. Washington announced the sinking of a Japanese battleship, a cruiser and a destroyer and reported severe damage to a second battleship by bomb hits. [Page 1, Column 3, Map, Page 6.]

The American declaration came within a few hours after Germany and Italy had declared war on the United States. The Reich's declaration was made in a diplomatic note and in a Reichstag address by Adolf Hitler. [Page 4, Column 1.] Benito Mussolini proclaimed Italy's declaration. [Page 4, Column 5.]

In London, where news of America's full entry into the world war brought predictions of an Allied grand strategy [Page 13, Column 5], Prime Minister Churchill declared that the Allies would win ultimately at any cost. [Page 1, Column 4.] Mexico broke off relations with Germany and Italy, while ten other Latin-American nations declared war on those countries or prepared to take that step. [Page 9, Column 1.]

The Soviet radio asserted that any Axis hopes for a separate peace with Russia were in vain. The radio declared that Russia was determined to fight alongside the United States and Britain until the Allies won. [Page 19, Column 1.]

In all of yesterday's land fighting, Japan was checked. In the Philippines, attempts to win a firm foothold on Luzon appeared smashed, except for a landing of parachutists at an airport 180 miles northeast of Manila and another small landing on the southeastern coast of the island. [Page 1, Column 1; Map, Page 2.] The British reported a slow-down of Japanese attacks in Malaya. [Page 13, Column 1.] While British forces fought off new assaults on Hong Kong, a two-day Chinese offensive to relieve pressure there was reported to have inflicted 15,000 casualties. [Page 11, Column 1, with map.]

Tokyo claimed the destruction of an American destroyer, a submarine and eighty-one planes, in addition to the capture of 350 Americans on Guam. [Page 8, Column 5.] With the commander of Britain's Far Eastern Fleet among 595 men still missing in the sinking of the Prince of Wales and the Repulse, the British named a new commander. [Page 14, Column 3.]

Amid debate in Washington over a proposed investigation of what happened at Pearl Harbor Sunday [Page 10, Column 1], Secretary of the Navy Knox arrived in Honolulu, presumably to seek first-hand information on that attack. [Page 1, Columns 5 and 6.]

President Roosevelt called upon industrial and labor representatives to meet next week and reach a voluntary agreement to end labor disputes for the duration. [Page 29, Column 2.] It was revealed also that the Administration was considering the registration of all men between the ages of 18 and 65 for military and civilian service. [Page 34, Column 1.]

On the European fighting front the Russians reported further gains against German forces. [Page 18, Column 3.] The Berlin radio revealed that the Nazis had replaced their commander on the Moscow front. [Page 19, Column 3.] In Libya, the main Axis forces were still withdrawing westward, Cairo announced. [Page 17, Column 1.]

Left: The President set his signature to the act against Germany. Center: He checked the time with Senator Tom Connally. Right: After that he placed the United States officially at war with Italy.
Associated Press Wirephotos

AXIS TO GET LESSON, CHURCHILL WARNS

He Announces Replacement of Libyan General—Upholds Phillips's Judgment

Text of Mr. Churchill's speech will be found on Page 16.

By CRAIG THOMPSON
Special Cable to THE NEW YORK TIMES.

LONDON, Dec. 11—Prime Minister Winston Churchill delivered a review of the war in the Pacific, North Africa, Russia and the Atlantic today that contained a compound of gloom and of optimism, but he ended with this ringing declaration:

"Just handfuls and cliques of wicked men and their military or party organizations have been able to bring these hideous evils upon mankind. It would indeed bring shame upon our generation if we did not teach them a lesson which will not be forgotten in the records of a thousand years."

Precedes Declarations

He spoke to the House of Commons before the Axis war declarations and the United States' reply.

Mr. Churchill gave hitherto unpublished details about the sinkings of the Prince of Wales and the Repulse, which made plain that the British had lost the use of airdromes on the Malay Peninsula and that the ships had had to rely solely on their anti-aircraft guns for protection against the attacking planes. In so doing he stoutly defended the judgment whereby Vice Admiral Sir Tom S. V. Phillips, who appeared tonight to have been lost, undertook an attack on Japanese transports that resulted in the sinkings of the warships.

Mr. Churchill announced that Lieut. Gen. Sir Alan Gordon Cunningham had been replaced in Libya by Major Gen. Neil Methuen Ritchie, adding that General Cunningham "has been reported by medical authorities to be suffering from serious overstrain and was granted sick leave."

General Ritchie, the new commander of the Eighth Army, is 44 years old. His was one of three "young-men" appointments to the General Staff that were made last June. In the last war he was commissioned a second lieutenant in the Black Watch at the age of seventeen and was a captain when he was twenty. He fought in France, Mesopotamia and Palestine, and received the Distinguished Service Order and the Military Cross.

Mr. Churchill gave an indication of the size of British and Allied losses in merchantmen in the Battle of the Atlantic for November that would, from his statement, appear to have been no greater than 100,000 tons. This would be a

Continued on Page Seventeen

Our Declaration of War

Special to THE NEW YORK TIMES.

WASHINGTON, Dec. 11—Following are the texts of the documents wherein the President asked a war declaration against Germany and Italy, and Congress acted:

The President's Message

To the Congress of the United States:

On the morning of Dec. 11 the Government of Germany, pursuing its course of world conquest, declared war against the United States.

The long-known and the long-expected has thus taken place. The forces endeavoring to enslave the entire world now are moving toward this hemisphere.

Never before has there been a greater challenge to life, liberty and civilization.

Delay invites great danger. Rapid and united effort by all of the peoples of the world who are determined to remain free will insure a world victory of the forces of justice and of righteousness over the forces of savagery and of barbarism.

Italy also has declared war against the United States.

I therefore request the Congress to recognize a state of war between the United States and Germany, and between the United States and Italy.

FRANKLIN D. ROOSEVELT.

The War Resolution

Declaring that a state of war exists between the Government of Germany and the government and the people of the United States and making provision to prosecute the same.

Whereas the Government of Germany has formally declared war against the government and the people of the United States of America:

Therefore, be it

Resolved by the Senate and House of Representatives of the United States of America in Congress assembled, that the state of war between the United States and the Government of Germany which has thus been thrust upon the United States is hereby formally declared; and the President is hereby authorized and directed to employ the entire naval and military forces of the United States and the resources of the government to carry on war against the Government of Germany; and, to bring the conflict to a successful termination, all of the resources of the country are hereby pledged by the Congress of the United States.

(An identic resolution regarding Italy was adopted)

Secretary Knox Visits Honolulu; Bases There Were Raided 5 Times

Special to THE NEW YORK TIMES.

WASHINGTON, Dec. 11—The Navy Department announced tonight that Secretary Frank Knox had arrived in Honolulu this afternoon.

There was no previous announcement that he had left for Hawaii, nor was there any intimation of the specific purpose of his visit.

WASHINGTON, Dec. 11 (U.P.)—Delegate Samuel W. King of Hawaii disclosed tonight after a telephone conversation with Governor Joseph B. Poindexter that twenty Japanese planes were shot down during the Sunday raid on Pearl Harbor.

Mr. King said the information was authorized for release in Hawaii by Lieut. Gen. Walter C. Short and that Mr. Poindexter was permitted to make the disclosure by transpacific radio-telephone.

Mr. Poindexter told Mr. King that "civilian morale is 100 per cent throughout the territory.

"Civilian defense measures are working without a hitch," he added.

HONOLULU, Dec. 11 (U.P.)—In addition to two deadly attacks on the United States naval base at Pearl Harbor last Sunday, Japanese bombers followed with a third attack later that day and with a fourth Monday morning, it is possible to disclose today for the first time.

Censorship permits a cautious description of the attack. A few seconds after the first bombers came over, with the rising sun insignia of Japan on their wings, defending anti-aircraft batteries sent up a heavy barrage.

Within a few minutes heavy clouds of black smoke began rolling up from Pearl Harbor, fourteen miles from Honolulu.

Planes roared in over the harbor, dropping bombs on navy centers and ships. Torpedo planes splashed

Continued on Page Eleven

CONGRESS KILLS BAN ON AN A. E. F.

Swift Action Without Debate—Service Terms Are Extended to Six Months After War

Special to THE NEW YORK TIMES.

WASHINGTON, Dec. 11—Congress swiftly eliminated prohibitions against American expeditionary forces today and continued terms of enlistment or induction to a date six months after hostilities end. Acting without debate, the two houses dropped the A. E. F. ban by removing restrictions in the Selective Service Act on the use of troops outside the Western Hemisphere.

The Senate Appropriations Committee, meanwhile, added an undetermined sum to the $8,246,000,000 third supplemental national defense appropriation bill as passed by the House. This change was said to have raised the bill's total above $10,500,000,000.

A ranking member of the committee was unable to say tonight what the exact amount of the bill was, but he said he was "satisfied it is above $10,500,000,000." He added that the amendments approved by the committee were mostly for new items, regarded as emergency ones by the Army and the Navy and Coast Guard. If approved, the measure would set a record for the size of a single appropriation bill.

Fund for Army Pay Specified

Among the amendments approved by the committee was one setting at $314,000,000 the supplemental item for pay of the Army, but immediately following it was a proviso that this amount should not be taken to mean the limit if the Army inducted or enlisted thousands of new personnel. If this took place, under the amendment practical authority would be granted for pay of the personnel under Congressional promise to pass deficiency bills to whatever extent was necessary.

Some $390,000,000 was added to the bill for military air construction. The Signal Corps also received a sizable increase for construction and equipment, while to the Navy were granted increases of many millions for landing fields, yards and docks. The Coast Guard received $4,750,000 for extraordinary expenses and $8,743,000 for new equipment.

The Army Chief of Staff received $125,000,000 as an emergency fund, to be accounted for to Congress every three months, and various sums were voted for additions to forts and posts within the United States.

The measure changing the Selective Service Act regarding the tenure of service and the extent of service came on the heels of action by both houses in declaring war on Germany and Italy, follow-

Continued on Page Thirty-four

WAR OPENED ON US

Congress Acts Quickly as President Meets Hitler Challenge

A GRIM UNANIMITY

Message Warns Nation Foes Aim to Enslave This Hemisphere

By FRANK L. KLUCKHOHN
Special to THE NEW YORK TIMES.

WASHINGTON, Dec. 11—The United States declared war today on Germany and Italy, Japan's Axis partners. This nation acted swiftly after Germany formally declared war on us and Italy followed the German lead. Thus, President Roosevelt told Congress in his message, the long-known and the long-expected has taken place.

"The forces endeavoring to enslave the entire world now are moving toward this hemisphere," he said.

"Never before has there been a greater challenge to life, liberty and civilization."

Delay, the President said, invites great danger. But he added:

"Rapid and united effort by all of the peoples of the world who are determined to remain free will insure a world victory of the forces of justice and righteousness over the forces of savagery and barbarism."

For the first time in its history the United States finds itself at war against powers in both the Atlantic and the Pacific.

Quick and Unanimous Answer

Congress acted not only rapidly but without a dissenting vote to meet the Axis challenge. Within two and three-quarters hours after the reading of Mr. Roosevelt's message was started in the Senate and House at 12:26 P. M., the President had signed the declarations against Germany and Italy. Seventy-two hours previously the Japanese attack on Hawaii had brought about the declaration of war against the other Axis partner.

Congress also quickly completed legislation to allow selectees and National Guardsmen to serve outside the Western Hemisphere and set the term of service in the nation's forces until six months after the termination of the war.

In the Senate the vote was 88 to 0 for war against Germany and 90 to 0 for war against Italy. The vote in the House was 393 to 0 for war against Germany and 399 to 0 for war against Italy. The larger Congressional vote against Italy was attributable to the fact that some members reached the floor too late to vote on the declaration against Germany.

In the House, Miss Jeannette Rankin, Republican, of Montana, who cast the lone dissenting vote on Monday against declaring war on Japan, today voted a non-committal "present" with regard to Germany and Italy.

Ignoring Hitler's declarations before the Reichstag today regarding American policy, and Mussolini's to a crowd before the Palazzo di Venezia in Rome, Congress adopted identical resolutions against Germany and Italy. It merely noted that their governments had thrust war upon the United States.

Grim Mood in Congress

Congress acted in a grim mood, but without excitement. Not only on the floors of the Senate and House, but in the galleries the grim mood prevailed. President Roosevelt, busy at the White House directing the battle and production effort as Commander in Chief, did not appear to read his message, as he did when war was declared upon Japan.

There was a deeply solemn undernote as the members assembled at noon. Senator Walsh, chairman of the Senate Naval Affairs Committee, had announced that the

Continued on Page Five

1942

"All the News That's Fit to Print."

The New York Times.

LATE CITY EDITION
Warmer today.
Temperatures Yesterday—Max., 35; Min., 16

Copyright, 1942, by The New York Times Company.

VOL. XCI. No. 30,698. Entered as Second-Class Matter, Postoffice, New York, N. Y. NEW YORK, TUESDAY, FEBRUARY 10, 1942. THREE CENTS NEW YORK CITY and Vicinity

FIRE-SWEPT NORMANDIE KEELS OVER AT PIER; 1 DEAD, 128 HURT; BLAZE TERMED ACCIDENT; ENEMY NEARER SINGAPORE; BATAVIA RAIDED

HOUSE CUTS 'FRILLS,' PASSES OCD BILL WITHOUT ROLL-CALL

$100,000,000 Measure, Shorn of Funds for Art and Dancers, Is Sent to the Senate

FULL INQUIRY IS PROMISED

Critics Assured of Hearing, While Mrs. Roosevelt Offers to Testify

By C. P. TRUSSELL
Special to THE NEW YORK TIMES.

WASHINGTON, Feb. 9—Still revolting against dancers' arts and other so-called frills as parts of the national civilian defense program, the House of Representatives today stood formally and finally behind the restrictions it imposed tentatively last Friday upon the use of the $100,000,000 it was appropriating for the OCD.

So decisive was the voice vote that retained in the money measure an amendment prohibiting expenditures for instructions in physical fitness by dancers, fan dancers, street or theater shows that no member was forced to go on the record. The revolt, the oral edict disclosed, had spread deeply into Administration strongholds.

Although both majority and minority leaders had summoned all absentees back to town for a threatened roll-call showdown, the roll was not called on this highly controverted issue. The House seemed much relieved.

Donald Duck Voted Out

However, the House went on record to reach beyond the OCD and the quarrel which has involved Mrs. Eleanor Roosevelt, assistant director of OCD; Miss Mayris Chaney, her dancer protégée, and Melvyn Douglas, movie star, and condemned the Treasury Department for what it viewed as a "frill" or a "furbelow."

By a roll-call vote of 259 to 112, the House refused to reimburse the Treasury for the $80,000 it already has paid out for a movie cartoon, now showing to the public, in which Donald Duck capers to boost the morale of the wartime taxpayer.

The House battle was as heated as that which was suspended on Friday, through abrupt adjournment, supposedly for a week-end cooling-off period. The interval, instead, appeared to have been only a period of preparation for further battle.

Through the afternoon the chamber echoed with charge and counter charge, most of them of a highly personal character, and with freshly coined war cries such as "Billions for defense, but not one cent for frivolities" and "Not a buck for Donald Duck."

First Lady Criticized

Mrs. Roosevelt figured largely in the debate, directly and by somewhat pointed indirection. Repeatedly, however, she received high praise for patriotism and perseverance as well as criticism for her activities in the OCD.

At one point of the debate, only the back stage intercession of House leaders prevented the voicing of a suggestion from the floor, by a Democrat and member of the Appropriations Committee, that she resign her assistant directorate of OCD "and take her friends with her."

However, the House was told by leaders who fought the restrictive amendments, that the action regarding OCD physical fitness and theatrical activities was "entirely meaningless." Not a dime of the $100,000,000 being appropriated, said Representative Woodrum of Virginia, could be used, any way, to pay Miss Chaney or Mr. Douglas.

Foes of frills in civilian defense refused to concede that the result was meaningless.

"The intention of the amendment," said Representative Leland M. Ford, of California, its sponsor, "was to establish a principle here to show that we are not in favor of that type of boondoggling, and to see that in the future these funds were not spent for any such purposes."

This principle, he held, had been set Friday and confirmed today.

But, Representative Cannon, of Missouri, chairman of the Appropriations Committee, protested that the fight on OCD activities had been waged by giving emphasis to the appointment to high posts in the OCD of only a few persons.

"Five per cent of all shells," he

Continued on Page Thirteen

Gen. Pershing's Son In Army as Private

Francis Warren Pershing, only son of General John J. Pershing, Commander in Chief of the A. E. F. during the World War, has enlisted in the Army as a private, it was disclosed here yesterday at the Army Building, 39 Whitehall Street.

Private Pershing, who was a broker with offices in 120 Broadway, enlisted on Feb. 4 and requested that recruiting authorities give out no publicity. He is married and has a son, 1 year old.

Private Pershing was inducted at Fort Dix, N. J., and then was sent to his present station at Fort Belvoir, Va. As a soldier in a Citizens Military Training Camp at Fort Snelling, Minn., in 1926, he was named the "best first-year soldier" of 2,000 men.

KERN SCOLDS MAYOR AT OUSTER HEARING

His and Sayre's Suspension Stands, Morton's Is Lifted—La Guardia in Gentle Mood

Paul J. Kern, president of the Civil Service Commission, and Wallace S. Sayre, commission member, remained under suspension in removal proceedings yesterday after a ninety-minute public hearing in City Hall at which Mayor La Guardia absolved Ferdinand Q. Morton, third member of the three-man agency, of all charges against him.

Mr. Morton, a Negro, told the Mayor he was ill at home when the Civil Service Commission issued a statement last Thursday which Mayor La Guardia construed as an attack on Corporation Counsel William C. Chanler. He added that he had had nothing to do with the commission's decision to file action against Mr. Chanler in an effort to compel him to represent the commission in litigation over the retention of four employes of the City Register's office.

On the basis of that explanation, the Mayor lifted Mr. Morton's suspension and ordered him back to work.

Adopting a mild paternal tone toward the six-foot-two, 33-year-old official who has been his protégé for twelve years, Mayor La Guardia addressed Mr. Kern as "Paul" throughout the hearing. The Mayor's attitude was like that of a father who believed punishment was in order, but disliked the idea of administering it.

Mr. Kern, in contrast, was stiff-backed and more than once reproached the Mayor for surrounding himself with "fawning sycophants" in preference to old friends

Continued on Page Fifteen

BRITISH FALL BACK

Japanese Dive-Bombers and Big Guns Pound Singapore Defenders

TANKS LAND, TOKYO SAYS

British Fighter Planes Battle Invaders, Who Claim Airport and Tell of Fires on Island

By The Associated Press.

SINGAPORE, Tuesday, Feb. 10—Under extreme pressure by Japanese invasion forces, British troops have executed a further withdrawal on Singapore Island, it was announced officially last night.

A communiqué from British headquarters said the withdrawal had been forced yesterday afternoon under the weight of Japanese dive-bombing and artillery bombardment and the menace of infiltrating ground forces.

Thus the first invaders ever to set foot upon this outpost of empire in the 123 years of its existence widened the foothold they established on a ten-mile stretch of the northwestern part of the island late Sunday night and yesterday morning. The struggle surged through thick mangrove swamps and rubber plantations.

[Tokyo broadcasts reported that Japanese tank units had been landed on Singapore Island and that the important Tenga airdrome, ten miles northwest of Singapore City, had been captured.]

The latest blow to the British fortunes came after it had seemed that the defenders had absorbed the first shock and were in a good position.

British headquarters issued the following communiqué at 10 o'clock last night:

"Strong enemy attacks which have developed from the landing on the west coast have been supplemented by dive-bombing and machine-gunning from the air throughout the day and by heavy enemy artillery bombardment. As a result of this pressure and enemy infiltration there has been some further

Continued on Page Two

The former French liner Normandie, officially the U. S. S. Lafayette, burning at her pier at the foot of West Forty-eighth Street yesterday. This photograph was taken with a long-range telephoto lens camera from Jersey side of Hudson.
The New York Times (by Eckenberg)

12-HOUR FIGHT VAIN

Water-Logged Vessel Is Turned Over by Tide After Disastrous Fire

HAD BEEN ABANDONED

Ship Was Being Fitted Out as a Navy Auxiliary—Smoke Haze Covers Midtown

A blaze attributed to the sparks from a workman's oxy-acetylene torch led at 2:35 o'clock this morning to the keeling over at her West Forty-eighth Street pier of the former superliner Normandie, recently taken over by the United States Government and renamed the U. S. S. Lafayette.

The fire broke out shortly after 2:30 yesterday afternoon and was believed under control before 8. During the interval at least 128 men—sailors, Coast Guardsmen and civilians—had been injured, and one of the civilians died in Roosevelt Hospital at 6:50 P. M.

Yet, shortly before 3 o'clock this morning, with the stricken giant lying on her side in fifty to sixty feet of water and mud, the flames leaped again—primarily from a point beyond the rear funnel. One of the fireboats that had loitered near by eased in, a stream of water under high pressure arched through the darkness, and within an hour the new blaze seemed quenched.

Although the original fire was largely restricted to the three upper decks, and did damage considered as slight considering the size of the ship, fighting it involved pouring aboard an enormous quantity of water. This led to the list, which had reached a safe 16 degrees by 10 P. M., according to naval officials under Rear Admiral Adolphus R. Andrews, Third District commandant.

Loudspeaker Blares Warning

But, somehow, things got worse from then on. At 12:20 A. M., the loudspeaker in Pier 88, where the 83,423-ton former queen of the French Line had disembarked thousands of passengers, began to blare ominously:

"Admiral Andrews has ordered all hands to leave the ship . . . The Admiral has ordered all hands to leave the ship . . . The Admiral has ordered all hands to abandon the Normandie. . . ."

At 1 A. M., the Third Naval District issued a brief statement somewhat qualifying the broadcast announcement. It said:

"The Admiral has ordered all hands off the ship as a safety precaution. It does not mean that the ship has been abandoned [in the usual sense] or hope given up but no one can be certain what the reaction of the ship will be to the flood tide."

Meanwhile observers at the darkened pier saw seamen from the United States Receiving Station at Pier 92, a few blocks north, standing by with small ropes at the shipside. A spokesman said these were for last-minute rescues of any one who might be stranded aboard. Two small gangways crashed as the ship's tilt slowly increased toward an estimated 25 degrees.

Tugboats Are Withdrawn

Tugboats that had been nosing the ship toward the vertical were withdrawn as the list increased. Admiral Andrews, in his car parked at the stringpiece just opposite the oblique perpendicular of the ship's famous uprearing bow, commented tersely on the broadcast order:

"The men have been ordered to evacuate the ship by reason of a dangerous list."

Asked directly if he thought she might topple, he shook his head non-committally.

Then, a little past 2 this morning, the increasing sag was reflected in clattering sounds from the upper decks, as articles began to topple toward the deep-dipping rail.

Tense watchers gasped, hoping the bottom mud would retain its precarious grasp on the keel. But at 2:35, quietly, with very little

Continued on Page Seven

U. S. WARNS VICHY OF POSSIBLE BREAK

Learns War Materials Were Sent to Rommel, While Indo-China Bargains With Japan

By JAMES B. RESTON
Special to THE NEW YORK TIMES.

WASHINGTON, Feb. 9—A crisis is impending in the relations between the United States and Vichy France. Increasing evidence of collaboration between the Vichy Government and the Axis has led the State Department to review, though not yet to reverse, its policy of limited cooperation with the administration of Marshal Henri Philippe Pétain, it was learned tonight.

The immediate cause of this crisis is a report that Marshal Pétain has allowed the Germans to use French ships to supply the Axis forces in Libya and that his representatives in Indo-China are now negotiating with the Japanese to turn over the French ships there for action against the United Nations in Malaysia.

The negotiations with the Japanese are now being carried on by Admiral Jean Decoux, Vichy's Governor General of French Indo-China, whose public statements recently have been exceedingly favorable to the Axis. These negotiations are already in an advanced stage, and there is reason for stating that the United States will make it clear that the transfer of these ships to the Japanese will be interpreted as an unfriendly act that may result in a completely new United States policy toward Vichy France.

Embassy Denies Knowledge

The French Embassy in Washington disclaimed any knowledge tonight of the transfer of French ships either to the Germans or to the Japanese, but Viscount Halifax, the British Ambassador, took an entirely different story to the State Department this evening.

The precise amount of merchant tonnage in Indo-China is not known, but it is described in reliable quarters here as considerable. In addition, one French cruiser and a number of smaller warships are said to be under Admiral Decoux's control.

Lord Halifax placed before Sumner Welles, Under-Secretary of State, detailed evidence that French ships carried French war materials from French North Africa to Field Marshal Erwin Rommel for the

Continued on Page Five

Survivors Tell How Spark Caused Normandie Disaster

A clear account of the fire that damaged the liner Normandie at her pier yesterday came from the lips of sooty and blistered survivors as doctors and nurses worked over them in city hospitals. Pieced together these brief accounts cover the start of the fire, tell its quick spread, and how more than 2,000 men tried in vain to stop it; how, eventually, all reached the pier alive, though many were injured and one died later.

Charles T. Collins, 18 years old, of 63 DeSales Place in Brooklyn, an ironworker, brought into Roosevelt Hospital to be treated for burns on the head and on the right hand, said he saw the fire start.

"I was working on a chain gang," Collins said. "We had chains around some pillars and eased them down when they were cut through. Two men were operating an acetylene torch. About thirty or forty men were working in the room, and there were bales and bales of mattresses.

"A spark hit one of the bales, and the fire began. We yelled for the fire watch and Leroy Rose, who was in our chain, and I tried to beat out the fire with our hands. Rose's clothes caught fire, and I carried him out. The smoke and heat were terrific."

Charles Florence, 22, a seaman in the Coast Guard, whose home is at 107 Fane Court, Brooklyn, was

Continued on Page Eight

ALBANY HITS MAYOR ON CITY GUARD PLAN

Gen. Brown Tells La Guardia State Law Forbids 'Little Private Armies'

By WARREN MOSCOW
Special to THE NEW YORK TIMES.

ALBANY, Feb. 9—The State Administration today publicly rebuked Mayor La Guardia for his announced intention of establishing a regiment of volunteers in New York City to be known as the City Guard. The Mayor made known his intention to set up the guard in a radio address on Sunday. In the same broadcast he said he would quit his post this week as Federal Director of the Office of Civilian Defense.

Adjt. Gen. Ames T. Brown sent to the Mayor a telegram, the text of which was made public here, and in which he told Mr. La Guardia that the military law of the State bars the setting up of "little private armies" by municipalities. Further, he told the Mayor also that he had the power to accomplish the same end by different means, including "the power to organize an auxiliary police force as recommended by the United States Director of Civilian Defense."

Lehman Approval Sensed

The telegram was sent by Brig. Gen. Brown, but it is almost certain that it was sent with the full knowledge of the Governor, since it has been known for weeks that the conduct of civilian defense in New York City has been a source of worry to Mr. Lehman, as well as to the State's legislative leaders.

This development may serve to bring to a head a move which has now been hanging fire for at least ten days, namely, an appeal to the President of the United States to end the Executive Order which divides New York City from New York State for defense purposes. A resolution putting the Legislature on record in favor of such a move has been drafted by the Senate Democrats, and it was scheduled to get bipartisan backing, with

Continued on Page Fourteen

CAPITAL OF INDIES HAS ITS FIRST RAID

Japanese Attack Two Airports and Center of City—Harbor Defense Repels Enemy

By F. TILLMAN DURDIN
By Telephone to THE NEW YORK TIMES.

BATAVIA, Netherlands Indies, Tuesday, Feb. 10—Batavia, the capital of the Netherlands Indies, was attacked by Japanese planes yesterday for the first time. The attack was carried out by eight fighter planes that swept in at a low altitude and machine-gunned two airdromes in the suburbs of the capital. Military planes were damaged, and at one field two passenger planes were splattered with bullets. One enemy plane was shot down and another probably was destroyed.

Coming just after noon, the raid upset the normal trend of life in Batavia to a considerable extent. Batavia's citizens, warned by sirens that probably are the most blood-curdling yet brought into action, carried gas masks as they trooped to shelters. A new precaution against bomb blasts was in evidence. This is a chunk of rubber that is held between the teeth to keep the mouth open. Attached to

Continued on Page Four

The War Summarized

TUESDAY, FEBRUARY 10, 1942

British forces fought bitterly yesterday on a ten-mile front in west Singapore Island to destroy the Japanese bridgehead that threatens the United Nations' hold on one of the most strategically vital positions in the world, but last night a withdrawal was acknowledged. A Tokyo broadcast said the Japanese had captured Tenga airdrome, ten miles northwest of Singapore City. All over the island British positions were assaulted by dive bombers. [1:3; map, P. 2.]

In the Netherlands Indies Japanese planes machine-gunned two airports near Batavia and streets of that city, but were driven away from the harbor area. There was some damage to grounded aircraft, but no bombs were dropped. On Borneo Japanese patrols were reported pushing southward toward Banjermassin, a port only 300 miles across the water from Surabaya. [1:7; maps, P. 4.]

In London the Ministry of Information announced a Pacific Council would meet there today, with Australia, Great Britain, the Netherlands and New Zealand represented. [6:3.]

From the Philippines General Douglas MacArthur reported repeated Japanese assaults in the past two days had been repulsed everywhere and that fire from the forts at the entrance to Manila Bay had silenced some Japanese batteries. [3:1.]

In Burma the Japanese were still being held in check along the Salween River front. The one hundred and first aerial combat victory for the American volunteer fliers was reported. Japanese plane losses in Burma were estimated to total 220. [4:1.]

Moscow reported Soviet troops had broken through extensive German land mine fields in the Donets Basin, brought heavy losses to the Germans before Sevastopol, taken eighteen more villages on the central front and entered the outskirts of besieged Rzhev. The Germans claimed to have fought their way back to the outskirts of Mozhaisk, fifty-seven miles southwest of Moscow. [10:1.]

In Libya the Axis advance had apparently halted, and the British sent out patrols southwest of El Gazala and fought an engagement twelve miles west of there. Alexandria was bombed for the first time in five months, and the British bombed the German naval base at Salamis, Greece. [5:1.]

United States relations with Vichy were under great strain because of reports that the Pétain regime had turned over shipping to the Germans to aid their African campaign and was considering similar aid to the Japanese in Indo-China. [1:4.]

The former French liner Normandie, now the United States naval auxiliary Lafayette, upset after being swept by fire at her pier in New York. The blaze was attributed to accident, not sabotage. [1:8.]

In Washington President Roosevelt sent a $26,740,000,000 Army and Maritime Commission appropriation request to Congress [3:4] and nominated Admiral William Standley, former chief of naval operations, as Ambassador to Russia. [6:4.]

Dewey Planning to Run Again For Governor, Leaders Declare

Special to THE NEW YORK TIMES.

ALBANY, Feb. 9—Reports reaching Republicans here is that Thomas E. Dewey has definitely stated to party leaders his intention of running for Governor again this year. Mr. Dewey disclosed his plans to a small group of party leaders in response to a question from them, it was reported.

The question came up as a result of rumors, without foundation, that Mr. Dewey was thinking of not making the race. Since the leaders of the State organization were committed to his candidacy, and would have to get another candidate if the rumors were true, a group put the question up to the former District Attorney directly and got his pledge that under no circumstances would he change his mind.

The net result of the conference, which took place some time ago, has been increased activity in Mr. Dewey's behalf on the part of the Republican State Committee. One example has been the publicity, sent out through the State, concerning Mr. Dewey's Lincoln Day speech before the National Republican Club in New York on Thursday.

The publicity, bearing the imprint of the National Republican Club, has been mailed out in envelopes of the Republican State Committee and contains complimentary references to Mr. Dewey. Speaking of the dinner, one of the releases said:

"The extraordinary interest in this year's affair stems from the fact that Thomas E. Dewey, New York's former District Attorney who set a precedent in metropolitan politics by arranging to turn over his office to a nonpartisan successor, is the principal speaker.

"In addition, the occasion will mark Mr. Dewey's first important public appearance since he concluded a nationally applauded program of cleansing New York of countless bands of public, official, labor and political racketeers."

"All the News That's Fit to Print."

The New York Times.

LATE CITY EDITION
Rain and warmer today.
Temperatures Yesterday—Max., 35; Min., 28

VOL. XCI..No. 30,703. Entered as Second-Class Matter, Postoffice, New York, N. Y. NEW YORK, MONDAY, FEBRUARY 16, 1942. THREE CENTS NEW YORK CITY and Vicinity

SINGAPORE SURRENDERS UNCONDITIONALLY; CHURCHILL ASKS UNITY IN HOUR OF DEFEAT; FOE POURS INTO SUMATRA, STRIKES IN BURMA

78% REGISTERED HERE ON FIRST DAY OF THE THIRD DRAFT

Estimates Place Those Enrolled at 468,000, With 7,020,000 Listed in the Nation

ROLLS TO CLOSE TONIGHT

20-44 Age Group Brings Out Many Middle-Aged Men Who Are Nationally Known

List of registration places will be found on Page 13.

The third registration under the Selective Service Act went into full swing yesterday, particularly in cities, and when the books closed for the day at 9 P. M., indications were that perhaps 7,020,000 men in the United States and 468,000 in New York City had been written into the record of the nation's man-power.

Exact figures, in accordance with an Army announcement ten days ago, will not be made public. But reasonably accurate estimates were made possible by the statement of Colonel Arthur V. McDermott, director of the New York City draft system, that about 78 per cent of those required to register this time had done so by closing time last night.

It has been generally believed that the current "T" or father-and-son draft would affect 9,000,000 men throughout the country and 600,000 within the five boroughs. The assumption that the local turnout would apply on a percentage basis from coast to coast seemed reasonable because of the sleety weather here; which some officials felt would mean that if the percentage differed elsewhere, it would be greater, but surely not less.

Every Class Is Tapped

Regardless of figures, the third draft, like the first two, tapped every stratum of American life. Applying to the 20-44-year age group, but not including those who signed up on either Oct. 16, 1940 or July 1, 1941, it dipped into the large group of men in early middle life that includes some of the nation's best known names in all fields of endeavor.

Many of them may not register until today — when registration centers will be open from 7 A. M. to 9 P. M. throughout the land. But today will be the last chance, and by tonight the roll of potential draftees will have been expanded to take in the following, including several who appeared yesterday:

Former Colonel Charles A. Lindbergh, 40 years old on Feb. 4; former District Attorney Thomas E. Dewey and his successor, Frank S. Hogan, both 39; Acting Governor Charles Poletti, 38; Council President Newbold Morris, 40; John Barbirolli, conductor, 42; Controller Joseph D. McGoldrick, 40; President R. M. Hutchins of the University of Chicago, 43, and Carl Hubbell, veteran baseball pitcher, 39.

Celebrated entertainers, writers, business men, educators and scientists also were on the list.

But the drama of the father-son draft lay not in the "big names" involved so much as in its bridging of two generations; and its reaching out to touch thousands of Americans whose national and racial backgrounds were as diffuse as their idiosyncrasies and their incomes.

Fathers literally appeared with sons, and in at least one case, a father was registrar while the son was registrant. Veterans who bore the scars of World War I appeared, ready to join the list of potential eligibles for World War II; a good example was Andrew W. Knebel of Addison, N. Y., State com-

Continued on Page Three

Australia Arrests Aliens Along Coast

By The Associated Press.

BRISBANE, Australia, Monday, Feb. 16—Hundreds of enemy aliens, mostly Italian sugar-field workers, were arrested in a wide-spread round-up Friday night and Saturday in North Queensland. The sugar belt lies along the coast where Japanese could land in an attempted invasion.

A special barred and guarded train is taking the aliens southward for internment at Townsville. The Italians had been boasting, according to newspapers, that "the Japanese won't touch us." Many had hidden firearms.

SYDNEY, Australia, Feb. 15 (From Australian broadcast recorded by The United Press in New York)—The government completed plans today for the registration of all male aliens tomorrow and Tuesday.

HEATING WITH GAS CURTAILED BY WPB

New York Is Among Seventeen States Named in Order to Supply War Industries

Special to THE NEW YORK TIMES.

WASHINGTON, Feb. 15—Curtailment in the consumption of natural and mixed natural and manufactured gas was ordered by the War Production Board today to assure adequate supplies for war production activities.

Curtailment is necessary, the board said, because of increased gas requirements for both war purposes and civilian use, coupled with the scarcity of materials that would be required if existing systems were expanded.

One of increased war production uses of natural gas will be the program to manufacture 400,000 tons of synthetic rubber, the major part of which will be made from butadiene, which is produced from natural gas.

Part of the WPB's order becomes effective on March 1 and applies to seventeen States, including New York and the District of Columbia "where the need for curtailment is greater." Other parts

Continued on Page Ten

PREMIER IS SOMBER

Calls Singapore Military Disaster, but He Warns Against Weakness

ACCLAIMS U. S. ENTRY

Lists It as Dream 'Come to Pass'—Gives Russia as Example in Peril

The text of Mr. Churchill's address is on Page 6.

By ROBERT P. POST

Wireless to THE NEW YORK TIMES.

LONDON, Feb. 15—The entrance of the United States into the war is a fact that cannot be compared with anything else "in the whole world," Prime Minister Churchill said in a world broadcast tonight.

When he surveyed the power of the United States and its resources and felt that they were now in it "with the British Commonwealth of Nations, all together, however long it lasts, till death or victory," Mr. Churchill said that this was the first and greatest event he had to report to the British people.

"That is what I have dreamed of, aimed at and worked for and now it has come to pass," Mr. Churchill said.

But at the same time he balanced the good of the latest war developments—in which he included the efforts of Russia—against the heavy and grave events elsewhere. And frankly telling the people throughout the world that he spoke "under the shadow of a heavy and far-reaching military defeat," the loss of Singapore, Mr. Churchill went on to call for a spirit of unity and new exertions in this dark hour.

Adverse news "of many misfortunes and gnawing anxieties lie before us," Mr. Churchill said, but from that very fact he invoked a new spirit of toughness from the people who march against the Axis.

Perhaps with reference to the widespread spirit of uneasiness that has covered this country and

Continued on Page Six

The War Summarized

MONDAY, FEBRUARY 16, 1942

Japan became the master of Singapore yesterday. At Rangoon, back door to China, civilian evacuation went on. Japanese troops were invading Southern Sumatra, stepping stone to Java. In London Winston Churchill warned the British people to remain united behind their government, but expressed no word of optimism regarding the immediate future in the Far Eastern war theatre.

Prime Minister Churchill announced the fall of Singapore a few hours after the Tokyo radio had announced that hostilities ceased. The British Army, according to the Tokyo report, surrendered unconditionally. The surrender came one week after the Japanese had started to storm the island. [1:8; map, p. 4.] Official Washington called the fall of Singapore the darkest moment of the war. [1:7.]

The British Prime Minister's broadcast drew Britain's attention to Russian firmness in supporting the government in the hour of peril and emphasized the great importance of American entry into the war. [1:3].

The invaders that landed in Southern Sumatra apparently intended to drive on the Palembang oil center. Netherland bombers attacked Japanese transports and scored hits. Fewer than 100 of 700 Japanese parachutists who had landed in the Palembang zone Saturday escaped, according to Batavia; the Tokyo radio claimed, however, that the parachutists had occupied several important positions. [1:5-6; map, p. 2.]

In Burma the Japanese were developing drives from two directions toward Thaton, on the Martaban - Rangoon Railway. Landing parties were moving inland from the seacoast above Martaban and the Japanese were moving out from their Salween River bridgehead up the river at Paan. Protected by American fighter planes, British bombers attacked enemy supply dumps at Paan and Martaban. [1:4; map, p. 2.]

General MacArthur's report from the Philippines indicated that the Japanese were advancing preparations for another full-fledged offensive against his Bataan positions. Enemy front-line forces, which had suffered heavy casualties, were being relieved by fresh troops. [1:5.]

Germany was reported to be drawing on her "Spring offensive" reserves for the campaign in Russia, but without, as yet, halting the Russian advance. Moscow said Soviet columns at one point were about seventy-five miles from the former Polish frontier. [8:2.]

British and Australian pilots flying planes made in the United States smashed a formation of thirty of the Axis' dive-bombers and fighters in Libya near El Gazala. Twenty of the enemy planes were shot down. In the Mediterranean, submarines sank two Axis supply ships and probably a third. A fourth ship was set afire by British bombers. On land the Germans seemed to be attempting to flank the British lines before Tobruk. [7:1]

SINGAPORE SURRENDERS: WHERE TERMS WERE SET AND 2 SIGNATORIES

The Ford Motor Company plant where commanding officers of British and Japanese armies conferred

Associated Press

Lieut. Gen. Tomoyuki Yamashita

Lieut. Gen. Arthur E. Percival

2-WAY BURMA DRIVE AIMS AT RAIL TOWN

Japanese Strike for Thaton on Line to Rangoon—R. A. F. Bombs Supplies

By The Associated Press.

RANGOON, Burma, Feb. 15—Japanese forces struck from two directions tonight at Thaton, forty miles northwest of Martaban on the Rangoon railroad, and the battle for the east coast of the Gulf of Martaban neared its climax.

The invaders are attacking from seaside landing points above captured Martaban as well as from a deep salient thrust from their Salween River bridgehead at Paan, unofficial reports said.

The Army communiqué merely said:

"There were no further attacks on the Salween front but reports indicate the enemy is preparing for an attack in the area of Duyinzaik-Thaton."

British bombers, accompanied by American fighters, heavily bombed enemy supply dumps at Paan and Martaban and swept wide over enemy-occupied territory on reconnaissance flights. Canadians piloted two of the Blenheim bombers that blasted and machine-gunned a Japanese troop camp at Martaban and river craft and motor vehicles.

The Blenheims flew with a fighter screen of American and British fighters and pressed home two heavy attacks yesterday. Some defense fire was encountered but all Allied planes returned safely.

The Japanese have established bridgeheads over the Salween at Paan and Martaban and it was there that the British bombers concentrated.

The front flared into battle today; twenty-four hours after bombers had thinned the enemy lines so

Continued on Page Two

Ships Land Foe in Sumatra; Dutch Blow Up Oil Property

By F. TILLMAN DURDIN

By Telephone to THE NEW YORK TIMES.

BATAVIA, Netherlands Indies, Monday, Feb. 16—The Japanese, having opened their drive on Sumatra with a parachute attack Saturday on the Palembang oil region, continued their campaign yesterday with a large-scale landing of troops from ships on the coast about sixty miles from Palembang. The landing was made in an area of marshes and mangrove swamps along the muddy banks of the Musi River, which leads to Palembang.

The Indies defense forces in the Palembang region have started the destruction of one of the world's greatest oil fields, together with refineries and other installations. The Japanese parachute-troop attack on Saturday, made in an attempt to forestall the destruction, has failed, and it was announced in Batavia yesterday that the wrecking of all "vital points" in the vicinity of Palembang began Saturday night.

The destruction of the Palembang oil fields, stores and machinery will represent a loss of properties worth more than $100,000,000. However, it is a move that will ultimately be a major contribution to the fight against the Japanese. It denies to the enemy more than 50 per cent of the oil production of the Netherlands Indies.

Enemy Aim Frustrated

Nearly all the other oil-producing areas of the Indies already have been destroyed and thus the main aim of the Japanese attack on Indonesia—to obtain oil quickly—has been frustrated.

The Netherlanders reported that nearly all the Japanese parachute troops who landed Saturday, in the vicinity of the refineries of the Socony-Vacuum and Netherland companies, had been accounted for. Of an estimated 700 soldiers

Continued on Page Two

M'ARTHUR EXPECTS BIG ENEMY ATTACK

Reports Japanese Regrouping on Bataan for a Resumption of Their Offensive

By C. BROOKS PETERS

Special to THE NEW YORK TIMES.

WASHINGTON, Feb. 15—General Douglas MacArthur reported from his Philippine stronghold on the Island of Luzon today that enemy preparations for the long-anticipated all-out Japanese offensive against the American and Filipino positions in the Battle of Bataan were visibly under way. He suggested that the attack was imminent.

General MacArthur said that the enemy was regrouping his forces. The evident objective of such a regrouping, he added, would be "a resumption of the offensive."

Now that the mighty British bastion of the East, Singapore, has fallen, the Bataan front remains the only theatre of the war in which the Japanese have been unable to advance almost at will and achieve their objectives.

It may be that, regardless of the sacrifices in men and equipment that a devastating assault would cost, the enemy will consider an overpowering attack justified to

Continued on Page Four

Bataan 'One-Man Army' Kills 116 On Raids Behind Japanese Lines

By CLARK LEE

Associated Press Correspondent

ON THE BATAAN PENINSULA, Feb. 13 (Delayed)—Captain Arthur W. Wermuth of Chicago, who has killed 116 Japanese and captured many more, is America's No. 1 one-man army to his fellow-officers of the Fifty-seventh Filipino Scout Regiment.

He "absolutely accounted" for at least 116 Japanese with his 45-caliber tommy-gun and Garand rifle, his fighting companions said today. He has won the silver star for gallantry, the Distinguished Service Cross for extraordinary heroism, and the Purple Heart with two clasps.

Thrice wounded, he spent more than two weeks in January more behind the Japanese lines than in the American line. He has led so many scouting raids he has lost count. His actions have forestalled many enemy attacks and prepared the way for American counter-attacks.

I finally located him today, just out of the hospital and on his way to battle. At dinner, I got part of his story and other officers gave me the rest.

Captain Wermuth, who is from Chicago, fights the war as he played football for Northwestern Military Academy at Lake Geneva, Wis.—fearlessly and for keeps. This 190-pounder with a Van Dyke beard is at home in the Bataan Mountains, where he has spent many years. He knew life in the open before he saw Bataan. His

Continued on Page Four

WASHINGTON SEES DIRE BLOW IN EAST

Sumatra Is Expected to Fall, Cutting Off Allies' Main Oil Supply in the Indies

By JAMES B. RESTON

Special to THE NEW YORK TIMES.

WASHINGTON, Feb. 15—The considered judgment of responsible officials in Washington is that the fall of Singapore marks the darkest moment of the war for the United Nations. Even the anticipation of the event and the rhetoric of Winston Churchill did not minimize the feeling that this blow may be decisive in the Southwest Pacific and may vitally affect the outcome of the conflict in China and the Middle East.

If there was any confidence in the fate of Sumatra, with its rich oil fields and coast line bordering the Malacca Strait, the feeling here would not be so pessimistic, but it is virtually conceded that Sumatra, too, must inevitably fall, cutting the United Nations off from their main supply of oil in the Southwest Pacific and leaving the Japanese free passage into the Indian Ocean, from where they can raid the Allied supply lines to China, Suez and the Persian Gulf.

The only bright spot in this dreary picture is some indication that more United States aircraft have arrived in Java, though deliveries to the Netherlands Indies from the United States are only about one-quarter of what the Dutch have ordered. The number of aircraft involved in these recent deliveries cannot be disclosed, but there is reason to believe that enough were landed to give the Dutch some chance of sending a few planes into the air against the invaders.

Also, there was confidence among United Nations' representatives here that the battle of production will bring the tools of war

Continued on Page Five

BRITISH CAPITULATE

Troops to Keep Order Until Foe Completes Occupation of Base

3 DRIVES HEM CITY

Tokyo Claims Toll of 32 Allied Vessels South of Singapore

By JAMES MacDONALD

Special Cable to THE NEW YORK TIMES.

LONDON, Feb. 15—Singapore has fallen.

The long dreaded news that the key British base of the Pacific and Indian Oceans would be captured by the Japanese—a major reverse clearly foreseen many days ago—was announced tonight by Winston Churchill, a few hours after dispatches from Vichy and Tokyo reported that Lieut. Gen. Arthur E. Percival's forces had surrendered unconditionally at 3:30 P. M. today British daylight saving time [9:50 P. M. Sunday Singapore time and 10:30 A. M. Eastern war time].

London officials naturally declined to disclose what plans had been made or were perhaps in the making for establishing a naval base elsewhere to meet the grave emergency arising from the loss of Singapore. They could not or would not divulge how many Imperial troops were taken prisoner or how many got away.

Commanders Meet

According to the official Tokyo announcement, fighting ceased along the entire front three hours after a meeting between General Percival and the Japanese Commander in Chief, Lieut. Gen. Tomoyuki Yamashita, in the Ford motor plant at the foot of Timah Hill, where the documents of surrender were signed. The terms were not disclosed here, but a Japanese Domei Agency dispatch late tonight said that under the capitulation up to 1,000 armed British soldiers would remain in Singapore City to maintain order until the Japanese Army completed occupation.

Similar terms, it is recalled, were contained in the surrender of Hong Kong on Christmas Day.

The Tokyo radio said the Japanese had constantly kept pouring in fresh troops to make up for losses from the fierce resistance of British Imperial troops.

In the final battle, three Japanese columns were said to have advanced on the city. Yesterday the central column completed occupation of the water reservoirs and a part of this column reached the northern outskirts of the city on a six-mile front. Another column bypassed the reservoirs, crossed the Kalang River and cut the road from Singapore to the civil airport. The third column reached Alexandria Road in the western part of the city.

Some Resisting, Tokyo Says

[Japanese units left the main island in barges and seized Blakang Mati, the island opposite Keppel Harbor, thereby gaining control of the sea approach to Singapore from the south, according to a Tokyo broadcast recorded by The United Press.

[Japanese troops entered Singapore City today under the terms of the surrender by the British, but a Domei dispatch said some of the defending forces and "other hostile elements" still were resisting, another Tokyo broadcast heard by The United Press stated.]

The Berlin radio, quoting the Japanese newspaper Asahi, said the largest part of the British and Australian forces "obviously" left Singapore Friday for Sumatra.

Unofficial reports reached London late tonight that 2,000 persons

Continued on Page Four

"All the News That's Fit to Print."

The New York Times.

LATE CITY EDITION
Mild and windy today.
Temperatures Yesterday—Max., 49; Min., 37

VOL. XCI—No. 30,734. Entered as Second-Class Matter, Postoffice, New York, N. Y. NEW YORK, WEDNESDAY, MARCH 18, 1942. THREE CENTS NEW YORK CITY and Vicinity

M'ARTHUR IN AUSTRALIA AS ALLIED COMMANDER; MOVE HAILED AS FORESHADOWING TURN OF TIDE; THIRD NATIONAL ARMY DRAFT BEGINS IN CAPITAL

PRESIDENT WARNS AGAINST RUSHING ANTI-STRIKES LAW

No Problem Exists at Present and Things Are Going Along Pretty Well, He Cautions

HE EXPLAINS 40-HOUR ACT

But Bill to Ban It Is Pushed to Hearings in House—Senate Also Swept by Debate

By W. H. LAWRENCE
Special to THE NEW YORK TIMES.

WASHINGTON, March 17 — President Roosevelt, at the moment when Congressional sentiment for anti-strike legislation became accentuated, stated today that there was no strike problem at the present moment and cautioned against rushing labor legislation to enactment when things were going along pretty well.

Congress, Mr. Roosevelt told his press conference this afternoon, could not pass a law that would make a man turn out more work. That, he observed, was up to the enthusiasm of the individual. More parades, band playing and flag waving, he suggested, would stir up enthusiasm more than restrictive law.

Organized labor, meanwhile, reported that the President was in agreement that the performance of labor was "exceptional, and, of course, satisfactory." It was agreed, spokesmen said, that voluntary action on the part of labor to yield its right to strike was a more satisfactory answer to the production problem than resort to legislation such as has been presented to the House in the last twenty-four hours.

Action Demanded in Congress

On Capitol Hill, however, steps toward legislative action persisted.

On the House side plans were made to go ahead with almost immediate hearings on a bill which would suspend the forty-hour week for the duration, would freeze open and closed shop conditions, and also clamp ceilings upon industry's profits on war contracts. Demands for Congressional action, which centered in the House yesterday, swept across the Capitol today to the Senate, where, for more than four hours, they displaced other thought and business.

Mr. Roosevelt told the press conference that he favors continuance of time-and-a-half pay for work over forty hours a week, but revealed that he had called upon the "combined Labor War Board," composed of six representatives of the American Federation of Labor and Congress of Industrial Organizations, to give up union contract rules which require double pay for work on Sundays. William Green, president of the A. F. of L., and Philip Murray, president of the C. I. O., and other representatives of both labor organizations visited the White House a few hours before the press conference.

Advocating continuous operation of plants to speed up the production of war materials, the President in his press conference remarks urged plant management to adopt a staggered shift system under which workers would receive double pay only if they worked seven consecutive days.

Says Law Is Misunderstood

Decrying "an amazing state of public misinformation," which he blamed in part upon the newspapers and irresponsible speeches in Congress, the President told of receiving a letter from a professional economist, who drew the conclusion that Japan would not have declared war and the United States would not have lost the Philippines or the Dutch East Indies if 30,000,000 man-days had not been lost by strikes in the first twenty-one months of the defense program.

The President said, with a smile,

Continued on Page Twenty

Gen. Homma Suicide Confirmed by Chilean

By The United Press.

SANTIAGO, Chile, March 17 —The suicide of General Masaharu Homma, commander of the Japanese forces in the Philippines, as reported by General Douglas MacArthur, was confirmed today by Carlos Barry, a Chilean journalist stranded in Japan, in a report to his newspaper, the Chileno.

Señor Barry and five other Chilean newspaper men, guests of the Japanese Government on a visit to Japan and Manchuria, were on their way home on a Japanese steamer when the Japanese bombed Pearl Harbor. Their ship turned about and landed them again at Yokohama. They now await passage on a vessel returning exchanged Western Hemisphere diplomats.

50% AIRPLANE RISE REPORTED BY NELSON

He Warns Three-Month Gain Is Not Enough—K. T. Keller Asked to Head Output

Text of Mr. Nelson's address is printed on Page 18.

Special to THE NEW YORK TIMES.

WASHINGTON, March 17—Plane production has been stepped up 50 per cent since Pearl Harbor, Donald M. Nelson, chairman of the War Production Board, said tonight in a radio address. He warned, however, that there was no reason for complacency, because the country was nowhere near its goals.

"We need more and forever more of these weapons and we need them now," he said. "We have got to realize the value of time."

It was learned tonight that K. T. Keller, president of the Chrysler Corporation, had been strongly urged by the War Production Board to direct the agency's airplane production program and to effect "short cuts" which will make possible the production of a greater

Continued on Page Eighteen

3,485 FIRST NUMBER

All Night Is Required for Drawing That Affects 9,000,000 Men

USE IN NAVY IS URGED

Hershey Also Suggests Assigning Some Labor for War Projects

List of the draft numbers drawn is on Pages 12, 13 and 14.

Secretary of War Stimson drew the first number—3,485—from the famous goldfish bowl in Washington at 6:05 o'clock last night to begin America's third draft lottery in seventeen months, although its first in wartime since 1918.

The drawing continued throughout the night. By 6 A. M. 6,000 of the 7,000 numbers had been listed and it was expected that the lottery would be completed by 8 o'clock.

Green capsules containing the serial numbers of those who registered last month, drawn in this St. Patrick's Day lottery, gave to 9,000,000 men between 20 and 44 years of age the green light to go ahead in the tasks to which they may be assigned in total war against Hitler and the Japanese. Green cards will be used in Selective Service headquarters to record the order of their liability to military service.

In a brief introductory address Brig. Gen. Lewis B. Hershey, Director of Selective Service, urged conscription of men for the Navy as well as the Army and suggested that at least on some war projects labor also should be "selected."

The No. 1 boy of the draft in New York City, just as on the two previous occasions, was a Chinese —Chin Fong Ho, a 20-year-old waiter born in China, now living in New York's Chinatown and

Continued on Page Fifteen

M'ARTHURMEN: ON THE ALERT EN ROUTE TO AUSTRALIA

Gun crew manning a mobile anti-aircraft gun on one of the transports—the fighters and the gun are now on the island-continent
The New York Times (official U. S. Navy)

The War Summarized

WEDNESDAY, MARCH 18, 1942

General Douglas MacArthur assumed command of the United Nations forces in Australia and the Southwest Pacific yesterday at a moment when both sides in the war were evidently devoting themselves principally to preparations for offensives later in the Spring. Only in Russia was there heavy action, with Soviet forces pounding furiously at the Staraya Russa sector and at Kharkov.

Washington announced that General MacArthur had already arrived in Australia by order of President Roosevelt. He has assumed command by request of the Australian Government. His command will include the Philippines, where he has been succeeded by Major Gen. Wainwright. Although the President announced that General MacArthur's withdrawal did not mean the Philippines were to be abandoned, the Japanese yesterday staged their first assault since March 8 on the Bataan defense line. They were sharply repulsed. [1:8.]

At the United States Army Headquarters in Australia it was disclosed that two Army planes had been used for General MacArthur's flight and that they had passed through areas of the most intense Japanese activity. The greatest secrecy was observed, and not even Premier Curtin of Australia was informed until the flight had been completed. [1:5-6.]

High officials of the government in Washington and Congressional leaders were unanimous in praising Mr. Roosevelt's decision to send General MacArthur to Australia. [4:4.]

In Britain General MacArthur's appointment was hailed as a demonstration of the coordination existing between the Empire and the United States. [4:1.]

Australians called the selection the best news since the outbreak of the war in the Far East. [1:7.]

In Burma Chinese troops on the Allied left flank routed Japanese-officered Thai troops. [8:1; with map.]

During a British parliamentary debate the assertion was made that the thirteen United Nations naval ships destroyed off Java had had to oppose a force of ninety-nine Japanese war vessels. [8:5.]

A possible new development in the European sphere was foreshadowed by a German order closing all Norway's ports from North Cape to Aalesund. The order suggested that German troop and naval movements of some importance were being screened. [1:4; map, P. 9.]

The Soviet reports indicated that the Germans were being forced back northwest and west of Kharkov in fierce hand-to-hand fighting. Advance units appeared to have broken through the surrounding fortifications at one point and to be engaged in a house-to-house battle. [7:1.]

Germany's increasing grip on French North Africa was demonstrated by a Vichy order for the internment of all Britons between the ages of 18 and 50 living on the coast of Morocco. [9:1.]

The sinking of three and possibly four vessels in our Atlantic waters was disclosed, including one Uruguayan ship. Uruguay promptly seized the German ship Tacoma, lying in Montevideo harbor. [1:5.] In Santiago, Chile, anti-Axis rioting broke out because of the sinking last Friday off New York of the Chilean ship Tolten. [17:1.]

NAZIS CLOSE PORTS OF NORTH NORWAY

Reported Adding to Forces—British Say Tirpitz Eluded Torpedo-Plane Attack

By The Associated Press.

LONDON, March 17—All Norway's ports from North Cape to Aalesund had been closed by the Germans today, presumably to screen stealthy marshaling of German military and naval forces that indicated that those far-northern waters were about to become a newly active major war theatre.

Speaking just after a disclosure that the mighty German battleship Tirpitz "appears to have avoided" a recent British torpedo-plane attack off Narvik, and thus even now is presumably loose upon the high seas, a responsible London informant speculated that the Germans were preparing attempts to isolate Russia's Arctic ports, cut her supply lines from her allies or even move against United States-garrisoned and British-garrisoned Iceland.

Another View Suggested

Another informant, who is in constant communication with the Norwegians, suggested a second possible interpretation—that the Germans were worried about the possibilities of United Nations response to Russian calls for the opening of a second front.

And in that connection he declared that Norway was seething against the Germans.

Among the day's accumulating incidents that pointed to major action in the north, the sharpest and most alarming in British eyes was the news that the Tirpitz had not been run to cover.

The British source who said that the Tirpitz "appears to have avoided" attacks in the vicinity of Narvik March 9 added that he had "no information" about her present whereabouts. After the torpedo-plane attack, he said, the Tirpitz retired to the coast under a smoke screen and was lost there among the fjords.

When the attack on the Tirpitz was made, he continued, she probably was within cover of fighter protection, but "the attacks were pressed home under rather difficult weather conditions."

He said that the Tirpitz and the German 10,000-ton cruiser Prinz Eugen had been located in a fjord near Trondheim before the Tirpitz had sailed, that the Prinz Eugen had been torpedoed on the passage to Trondheim, and that thus the three ships that made a dash recently through the English Channel—the Prinz Eugen and the Ger-

Continued on Page Nine

MacArthur Party in 2 Planes Soars Over Japanese Fronts

By BYRON DARNTON
Wireless to THE NEW YORK TIMES.

UNITED STATES ARMY HEADQUARTERS, in Australia, Wednesday, March 18—General Douglas MacArthur flew over some of the hottest fighting areas in the Southwestern Pacific on his journey of more than 2,000 miles from the Philippines to assume supreme command of the United Nations' forces in this area, it was revealed this morning when news of the general's arrival with his family and staff was made public.

Two United States Army planes were used for the journey. General MacArthur has not yet arrived at headquarters, although he is in Australia and has assumed command. Some of his officers are here, and they are in the best of health. It is understood that General MacArthur and his family are resting after their journey, but that he will arrive at headquarters soon. He is tired.

It was officially disclosed that the appointment of General MacArthur had been made with the "most enthusiastic" approval of Australia. American correspondents here have heard repeatedly from Australian civilians and soldiers the question, "Why don't you send us MacArthur?"

Details of the general's journey have not yet been fully revealed, but it was explained that the long flight had taken the party over the areas of the heaviest recent Japanese activity. Whether the planes used by the MacArthur party had been dispatched from Australia for that purpose or already were in the Philippines was not disclosed. But the feat demonstrates that communications exist between the

Continued on Page Five

URUGUAYAN VESSEL, TWO OTHERS SUNK

Nation Seizes German Ship in Retaliation—Fourth Craft Feared Lost in Bahamas

The sinking of at least three, and possibly four, ships by Axis submarines operating off our Atlantic coast was disclosed yesterday. The victims were a medium-sized merchant ship of United States registry, a 5,785-ton Uruguayan vessel, an unidentified vessel from which fifty-seven survivors were landed in Nassau, and possibly a large United States tanker reported sunk in the Bahamas.

Most important from the standpoint of international relations was the Uruguayan ship Montevideo, which was sent to the bottom with seventeen of her crew off Jeremie, Haiti. Her loss brought the number of South American republics that have suffered submarine sinkings to three. Four Brazilian ships have been torpedoed and on Monday the sinking of the Chilean freighter Tolten was announced.

In swift retaliation the Uruguayan Government seized the 8,268-ton German ship Tacoma, which had been interned in Uruguayan waters ever since the destruction of the pocket battleship Graf Spee in December, 1939.

Uruguay, which had already broken off relations with the Axis powers, ordered the suspension of further sailings of her ships until arrangements could be made to safeguard them. It was expected, according to The Associated Press, that the government would arm them. In view of the public indignation caused by the announcement of the sinking, the Uruguayan Government placed guards over the property of Axis nationals.

Previously 200 rioting students had stoned a toy shop operated by a Spaniard believed to be a member of the pro-Fascist Falangists and called for the imprisoning of a Uruguayan nationalist leader.

Foreign Minister Alberto Guani,

Continued on Page Seventeen

PLEASED AUSTRALIA GREETS A 'FIGHTER'

MacArthur Warmly Welcomed —British Expect That Policy of Defense Will End

By The Associated Press.

MELBOURNE, Australia, Wednesday, March 18 — General Douglas MacArthur's arrival to assume the United Nations command in the Southwestern Pacific was hailed jubilantly by the Australian press today as the most important and most welcome move thus far in the defense of this Commonwealth.

"It will be regarded as the best single piece of news since the outbreak of the Pacific war," said one editorial. "His gallant stand in the Philippines has fired the imagination of Australians, who love a fighter, and his command of Australians in addition to American troops will be an inspiration to the fighting forces."

[In London it was suggested that the appointment of General MacArthur, which was highly approved, meant that the United Nations intended to substitute offense for defense in the Far East.]

The selection of so high a United States officer for the important post, it was pointed out, gives emphasis to the statement by Secretary of War Henry L. Stimson that "considerable" American forces are here.

"It is also an indication," the newspaper added, "of President Roosevelt's realization of how important is the Southwest Pacific in this global war and of what aid the

Continued on Page Five

Bill for Women's Auxiliary Corps Of 150,000 Passed by the House

By NONA BALDWIN
Special to THE NEW YORK TIMES.

WASHINGTON, March 17—The House passed today a bill creating a volunteer Women's Army Auxiliary Corps, whose members, by taking over duties now performed behind the lines by enlisted men, would release many men for combat duty. The roll-call vote was 249 to 86.

The bill, sponsored by Representative Edith Nourse Rogers of Massachussets, was passed with two amendments, the major one limiting the strength of the corps to 150,000. The other permits Army nurses to enroll in the corps.

The bulk of the four-hour discussion on the measure revolved around the extent to which Army discipline and military law would apply to members of the WAAC. Reading Section 2 of the Articles of War, Chairman May of the Committee on Military Affairs expressed the opinion that members of the WAAC would be subject to court-martial.

The issue was raised by Representative Nichols of Oklahoma in proposing an amendment to entitle members of the corps to the same compensation, pensions and disability claims that are extended to soldiers. The amendment was rejected by a standing vote of 70 to 30, but his contention that, under the

Continued on Page Twenty-one

GENERAL FLIES OUT

Wife, Child Accompany Him on Trip From Philippine Post

ORDER BY PRESIDENT

Roosevelt Asserts All Americans Back It—Expect Action Now

By CHARLES HURD
Special to THE NEW YORK TIMES.

WASHINGTON, March 17 — General Douglas MacArthur today became Supreme Commander of the United Nations forces in the Southwestern Pacific.

This dramatic shift of command and promotion for the dashing officer who has held the Japanese at bay on the Island of Luzon for three months and ten days was announced by the War Department simultaneously with his arrival in Australia. Traveling by plane, he arrived with his staff and his wife and child.

A few hours after announcement of the action, President Roosevelt told a press conference that he was "sure that every American" agreed with his decision to take General MacArthur out of the Philippines.

He recognized, he said, that Axis propaganda agents would see in this move abandonment of the Philippines, but this is not the case. General MacArthur will command everything, including sea and air forces, east of Singapore in the Southwestern Pacific, the President added, and will be more useful in Australia than on Bataan Peninsula.

President's Statement

Finally, the President authorized quotation of the following statement:

"I know that every man and woman in the United States admires with me General MacArthur's determination to fight to the finish with his men in the Philippines. But I also know that every man and woman is in agreement that all important decisions must be made with a view toward the successful termination of the war. Knowing this, I am sure that every American, if faced individually with the question as to where General MacArthur could best serve his country, could come to only one answer."

[Lieut. Gen. George H. Brett, United States Army, is Deputy Supreme Commander of the United Nations Forces in the Southwest Pacific and is in command of all the United Nations air forces in the region, according to a United Press dispatch from Melbourne, Australia.]

No move made by the United States Government since the war began has had a more vivid or optimistic reaction than this one. Officials in and out of Congress rushed to commend the action, and reports from New York indicated that the Stock Exchange immediately registered higher prices.

In the reaction manifested here were two indicated causes for optimism. One was the feeling that General MacArthur was equal to the task of stemming the Japanese advance southward, in view of his record in the Philippines, and of planning future offensive operations. The other was a belief that perhaps he had not been assigned to the High Command until United Nations intelligence officers felt that there was a good chance of changing the tide of battle.

On Washington's Birthday

In any event, he landed somewhere in Australia not long after the arrival of heavy United States air and ground forces, sent to augment the Australian troops. The action, in which Australia endorsed the choice of General MacArthur, has been a closely guarded secret since Feb. 22, when President Roosevelt ordered General

Continued on Page Three

Chiang Kai-shek unwittingly became an ally of the United States after the U.S. declared war on Japan—the common enemy. He is shown here with Mme. Chiang who, in 1942, became the first private citizen to address the United States' Congress.

Churchill and Roosevelt leaving a Washington, D.C., church. Churchill had come to the United States for conferences.

Eleanor Roosevelt giving good wishes to servicemen headed for the front.

"All the News That's Fit to Print."

The New York Times.

LATE CITY EDITION
Slightly cooler today.
Temperatures Yesterday—Max., 65; Min., 44

Copyright, 1942, by The New York Times Company.

VOL. XCI No. 30,765. Entered as Second-Class Matter, Postoffice, New York, N. Y. NEW YORK, SATURDAY, APRIL 18, 1942. THREE CENTS NEW YORK CITY and Vicinity

JAPAN REPORTS TOKYO, YOKOHAMA BOMBED BY 'ENEMY PLANES' IN DAYLIGHT; CLAIMS 9; BIG RAIDS OVER FRANCE; LEAHY IS RECALLED

FARM LEADERS ASK CONGRESS TO CURB LEWIS DAIRY DRIVE

House Group Is Told He Aims at Control of Nation's Food and Imperils War Program

RACKET LAW AID IS SOUGHT

Action Is Urged to Put Unions Under Trust Act—Vinson Labor Measure Hits Snag

By C. P. TRUSSELL
Special to THE NEW YORK TIMES.

WASHINGTON, April 17—Congressional attention to proposals for suspension of the forty-hour week, freezing of open and closed shop conditions and related war labor issues were turned sharply today to the unionization of the farmer, a fast-spreading movement that brought leaders of agricultural organizations before a House Judiciary subcommittee in mass protest.

Declaring that the "Food for Freedom" program faced danger if John L. Lewis's new Dairy Farmers' Union and other active groups attained their organizational objectives, witnesses urged the enactment of legislation that would put labor unions under the anti-racketeering law of 1934, and subject them to prosecution under anti-trust statutes.

"If Lewis succeeds in his organizational program," W. P. Davis, manager of the New England Milk Producers Association, told the subcommittee, "it will give him power to paralyze the food supply of the nation."

The Lewis union, an affiliate of his United Mine Workers, is driving now for a closed shop for New York City that would reach from the producer on the farm, through the handler and processor and to home deliveries in the city. In the Flint (Michigan) area, where it started, it claims about 85 per cent unionization.

Remedial Bills Considered

There are three bills before the subcommittee, all designed to give the Federal courts jurisdiction in cases involving work stoppage for non-labor purposes and to tighten up statutes dealing with interference of interstate commerce by violence, threats, coercion or intimidation. Sponsoring the measures are Representative Monroney of Oklahoma, Walter of Pennsylvania and Hobbs of Alabama, all Democrats.

As this hearing progressed the forty-hour week legislation sponsored by Representatives Vinson of Georgia and Smith of Virginia ran into a snag before the House Committee on Naval Affairs, which Mr. Vinson heads. Only a tie vote of

Continued on Page Nine

No Convoys Lost As Blimps Guard

By The United Press.

MOFFETT FIELD, Sunnyvale, Calif., April 17—Rear Admiral John Wills Greenslade said today that the Navy's use of blimps for convoy protection and submarine patrol has been so effective that "to date on both coasts no convoy has been successfully attacked while under lighter-than-air convoy."

Admiral Greenslade spoke at the formal commissioning of the Moffett Field air base as a naval air station, to serve as operating headquarters for blimps being used in coastal patrol.

STATE SENATE BARS REAPPORTIONMENT

Legislative and Congressional Redistricting Both Beaten—Republicans Cold to Change

By WARREN MOSCOW
Special to THE NEW YORK TIMES.

ALBANY, April 17—Both Legislative and Congressional reapportionment legislation met defeat in the Senate today, thus ending for some time plans for a more even distribution, according to population, of representation in the Legislature and in Congress. There is little likelihood that either measure will be brought up again in the present session.

Arguments as to constitutionality, equity and necessity dominated two hours of debate, but the effect lay in matters not mentioned, such as the feeling among up-State Republicans that the urban areas would control their party as well as the Legislature; the hesitancy to vote to unseat a friend, if the legislator himself were not affected; fear of loss of Republican control of the Assembly in a bad year and similar intangibles. This is not new or unusual, since Tammany blocked a legislative reapportionment in 1935, when the Democrats controlled both houses, because it would have lost its dominant position in relation to the other Democratic counties.

All of this was reflected in the

Continued on Page Sixteen

WAR PRODUCTION OF ALLIES EXCEEDS AXIS, NELSON SAYS

WPB Chief Predicts That by End of Year We Can Overcome Foes' Accumulated Reserve

BUT WARNS OF LETDOWN

MacLeish Chides Editors for Failing to 'Police' Spread of 'Defeatist Propaganda'

The United States is "over the hump" on war production, Donald M. Nelson, chairman of the War Production Board, declared at the annual dinner last night of the American Society of Newspaper Editors in the Hotel Waldorf-Astoria.

"We can see daylight ahead in our whole war production effort," he added.

Combined production of the United States, Russia and England, he asserted, today is much greater than that of the Axis nations, and by the end of the year, he said, "it is safe to predict" that we shall have overcome the accumulated reserve built up by Japan since 1930 and by Germany since 1933.

From then on, he promised, we shall "have our enemies at an increasing disadvantage."

Nearly 500 members and guests of the society received Mr. Nelson's address with enthusiastic applause. He was introduced as a man who is doing a "whale of a job" by Dwight Marvin of The Troy (N. Y.) Record, retiring president of the society, who announced that last night's was the largest dinner ever held by the society. Editors attended from all parts of the country.

Chinese Envoy a Speaker

Dr. Hu Shih, Chinese Ambassador at Washington, also addressed the gathering. He said that China, like the United States, is "fighting a war to preserve a peaceful way of life against a militaristic Japanese dictatorship." Another speak-

Continued on Page Thirteen

ENVOY SUMMONED

Roosevelt Directs Him to Report on Outlook Facing France

EMBASSY TO REMAIN

Diplomatic Tie Is Kept—Laval Still Trying to Form Cabinet

By BERTRAM D. HULEN
Special to THE NEW YORK TIMES.

WASHINGTON, April 17—Admiral William D. Leahy, the United States Ambassador to France, was directed by President Roosevelt today to return to this country in view of the return to power of Pierre Laval.

The announcement was made by Sumner Welles, acting Secretary of State. The technical reason given was that Admiral Leahy's return was ordered for consultation, which means that if events should turn more favorably in the future, he would be in a position to return to his post.

But it amounts at the present juncture to a recall because of the turn of affairs in France. Whether that will have its effect on the French people and result in internal political pressure against the retention of M. Laval in power, or increased German pressure on France for all-out collaboration with the Axis, is a question that it is assumed will soon be answered.

Laval's Domination Cited

Mr. Welles, in making the announcement, said Admiral Leahy had been requested to return immediately for consultation in view of the events of the last few days in France and in view of information received that the new government of France is composed of elements dominated by M. Laval and all that implies. A more complete statement of American policy may be forthcoming soon.

[In Vichy, Pierre Laval was reported to be having difficulty in forming a Cabinet. After the resignation of the Darlan Cabinet, the French Government was informed that Admiral Leahy had been called to Washington.]

Admiral Leahy will not leave immediately because Mrs. Leahy is recovering from an operation performed a week ago and is not yet in condition to travel. Mr. Welles said this would delay their departure for at least a brief period. According to Vichy reports, this may be two or three weeks.

The United States Embassy staff and consuls, under present plans, will remain in France after Admiral Leahy leaves. They will be under the direction of S. Pinkney Tuck, counselor of the Vichy embassy, as chargé d'affaires. They would have had to leave with the Ambassador had the United States action been extended to a severance of diplomatic relations.

As matters now stand, the plan has been abandoned, or is being held in abeyance indefinitely, of sending limited quantities of food, clothing and essential economic supplies to French North Africa from the United States, as well as food and clothing for children in France.

Henry-Haye Rebuffed

Mr. Welles disclosed at his press conference that he had refused yesterday to receive from Ambassador Gaston Henry-Haye the French rejection of his note of April 13 because this had been submitted for approval to German authorities before being transmitted here.

In his note of April 13 Mr. Welles rejected a Vichy protest over the establishment of an American consulate general at Free French Brazzaville, in Equatorial Africa, without consulting Vichy. The French rejection charged that the note of Mr. Welles was "injurious," not "insulting," as first reported.

Mr. Welles said he told the

Continued on Page Two

FLYING GENERAL IS DECORATED

Brig. Gen. Ralph Royce, who hopped 4,000 miles to bomb Japanese bases in the Philippines, receives the Distinguished Service Cross from Major Gen. Rush Lincoln, somewhere in Australia. Lieut. Col. J. H. Davies, who was on the flight, is at the right. He, too, won the D. S. C. This picture was radioed from Australia to San Francisco. Associated Press Wirephoto

DAMAGE IS 'LIGHT'

Japanese Say Raiders Hit Schools, Hospitals, Not War Objectives

THEIR PUBLIC 'ANGRY'

No Confirmation of the Tokyo Radio Report Is Given in Washington

By The Associated Press.

SAN FRANCISCO, April 17—The Tokyo radio announced tonight that "enemy bombers" had attacked Tokyo, the Columbia Broadcasting System's listening station reported. The Tokyo broadcast said:

"Enemy bombers appeared over Tokyo for the first time in the current war, inflicting damage on schools and hospitals. The raid occurred shortly past noon on Saturday [Tokyo time].

"Invading planes failed to cause any damage on military establishments, although casualties in the schools and hospitals were as yet unknown.

"This inhuman attack on these cultural establishments and on residential districts is causing widespread indignation among the populace."

Communiqué Claims Planes

"It is confirmed that three enemy aircraft were shot down when hostile planes attacked the Tokyo-Tosame region this afternoon for the first time since the war [started]," said a communiqué issued by Japanese Imperial Headquarters. "The enemy planes approached from several directions." Later another Tokyo radio broadcast reported that nine of the raiders had been shot down.

This later broadcast said that none of the hostile planes had penetrated to the heart of the city. It was said that they had released "a few bombs on the outskirts" and that "Japanese interceptor planes immediately took chase."

The Columbia Broadcasting System said the first announcement of the bombing was in an English-language broadcast. The announcement was repeated a few minutes later in a Japanese-language broadcast, which injected a new angle that "the enemy planes did not attempt to hit military establishments."

Raid "Just After Noon"

The Japanese-language broadcast said:

"Just after noon on the 18th the first enemy planes appeared over the city of Tokyo. A number of bombs were dropped. The enemy planes did not attempt to hit military establishments and only inflicted damage on grammar schools, hospitals and cultural establishments.

"These planes were repulsed by a heavy barrage from our defense guns.

"The previous training of the Tokyo populace for air raid defense was put into immediate practice. I wish to reveal that our losses were exceedingly light."

Tokyo Radio Interrupts Itself

TOKYO, Saturday, April 18 (From Japanese broadcast recorded by The United Press in San Francisco)—Enemy airplanes bombed Tokyo today, it was announced officially.

The Tokyo radio, in giving the announcement, interrupted another program "to give you this flash." The announcement said:

"Enemy bombers appeared over Tokyo for the first time since the outbreak of the current war of Greater East Asia. The bombing inflicted telling damages on schools and hospitals."

Yokohama Also Reported Hit

BERLIN, Saturday, April 18 (From German broadcasts recorded by The Associated Press)—

Continued on Page Three

600 R. A. F. Planes Attack; Reich City Bombed in Day

Wireless to THE NEW YORK TIMES.

LONDON, Saturday, April 18—For the sixth successive day—and using an increased number of planes, estimated at more than 600 fighters and fast bombers during the day—the Royal Air Force continued its large-scale offensive sweeps over Northern France yesterday. The day-long attacks followed a night in which the big planes of the Bomber Command rained huge missiles on the docks at Havre again, on the Nazis' submarine base at Lorient, France, and on German stations in the Netherlands.

With the continually growing intensity of the R. A. F. raids, the Air Ministry made public an estimate that the Germans were now being forced to keep an army of 1,500,000 men tied up in defensive positions along the coast of Western Europe.

To add to the British operations, heavy bombers of the R. A. F. went out during the last hours of daylight and blasted an important factory at Augsburg, Southern Germany, the Air Ministry announced early today.

Augsburg, about thirty-five miles northwest of Munich, is an important aircraft manufacturing center for the Germans and is also the site of a large chemical works.

The raid meant a round-trip flight over 1,000 miles of enemy country, and the target was one of the most

Continued on Page Five

STIMSON PLEDGES EARLY OFFENSIVE

Army Is 'Pretty Near' Striking Stage, He Says—Belittles Confusion on MacArthur

Special to THE NEW YORK TIMES.

WASHINGTON, April 17—The American Army is "getting pretty near to the stage of being ready for an offensive," and will take that offensive "at the earliest practicable moment," Secretary of War Henry L. Stimson said at a press conference today.

[A War Department communiqué issued by Mr. Stimson yesterday said that an estimated 25,000 civilians and 35,000 United States and Filipino combatant troops and sixteen generals were now presumably in Japanese hands as a result of the fall of Bataan. A communiqué on the latest military action said that three Japanese batteries had been silenced by the Manila Bay forts and that "fierce fighting" was going on in Panay Island, which the Japanese invaded Thursday.]

Mr. Stimson described as "a tempest in a teapot" recent reports that General Douglas MacArthur had been unable to appoint a staff for his new command because he never had received an official directive delineating the extent of his authority in the Southwest Pacific.

The geographical boundaries of General MacArthur's command are a military secret, Mr. Stimson declared. None the less, he added, General MacArthur's command closely approximates that which the United Nations gave General Sir Archibald P. Wavell in much the same area.

"The practical coordination of effort and its strategic direction," Mr. Stimson stated, "is a matter for General MacArthur and General MacArthur alone."

Mr. Stimson's assertion that an

Continued on Page Seven

BRITISH BLOW UP BURMA OIL WELLS

Defenders Abandon Magwe but Fight to Protect Chinese Flank North of Toungoo

By CRAIG THOMPSON
Wireless to THE NEW YORK TIMES.

LONDON, April 17—Destruction of the oil fields at Yenangyaung—most important of Burmese producing centers with an output of 1,000,000 gallons daily—was reported here today as the British fell back to north of Magwe, twenty miles south of Yenangyaung.

Communiqués and other information received here show the Japanese have not yet reached the oil fields, but their destruction indicates that the British forces plan to continue their retreat. Meanwhile the Chinese were fighting above Myohla about thirty miles north of Toungoo.

[The Burma oil fields were the last source of supply for the United Nations in the Pacific and Eastern Indian Ocean area. The United Press said it would require from six months to a year for the Japanese to recondition and operate the wells destroyed. Six thousand of 8,000 wells are said to have been blast-

Continued on Page Four

War News Summarized

SATURDAY, APRIL 18, 1942

Bombs fell on Tokyo in daylight today, it was announced by Japanese Imperial Headquarters. The Tokyo radio said that "enemy planes" had inflicted "telling damage" on "schools and hospitals" without causing damage to military establishments. Another broadcast said that nine of the raiders had been brought down. No confirmation of the attack came from any United Nations source. [1:8.]

Secretary of War Stimson disclosed that the United States Army was "getting pretty near to the stage of being ready for an offensive." He said the offensive would be taken at the earliest possible moment. [1:5.]

On the Far East's crucial Burma front the British abandoned Magwe, gateway to the Yenangyaung oil fields, and applied the scorched-earth policy to oil wells that produce 1,000,000 gallons a day. They retreated slowly under severe pressure. [1:7; map, P. 4.]

In the Philippines, the War Department announced, 35,000 combatant troops were in Japanese hands on Bataan Peninsula, together with several thousand non-combatant and supply troops and about 25,000 civilians. Sixteen of the captives were generals. [4:5.]

On the diplomatic front, President Roosevelt ordered Ambassador Leahy to return from Vichy in a swift aftermath to a French Cabinet resignation that left the ultra-collaborationist Pierre Laval to form a new government.

Admiral Leahy's virtual recall was officially described as a return for consultation—a loophole that would enable him to take up his post again if events should change for the better. Of this there seemed little likelihood. Acting Secretary of State Welles accused Vichy of having submitted one of its diplomatic notes for German approval. [1:4.]

M. Laval had not yet completed his Cabinet late last night, after a day of conferences. Under the developing new governmental set-up, Admiral Darlan, retiring Vice Premier, remained head of France's land, sea and air forces through a political device apparently designed to allay American qualms about the French Fleet. [2:2.]

France's coast reverberated for the sixth consecutive day to the crash of British bombs as more than 600 planes engaged in sweeps against German targets. The day's operations, following night raids on enemy airdromes and a U-boat base, included the longest daylight raid yet reported—an assault on a plant at Augsburg, Germany, thirty-five miles short of Munich. [1:5-6.]

On Europe's land front, the Russians were advancing against strong resistance in the area of Demidov, forty miles northwest of Smolensk, the Moscow radio reported. [6:2.]

An Italian communiqué reported a futile British attempt to land troops on an island south of Crete—an attempt of which the British said they knew nothing. The Italians also told of the sinking of a British submarine, while London announced the sinking of a large Italian transport. [5:5.]

'No. 1 Bank Robber' Is Seized in Jersey

Special to THE NEW YORK TIMES.

NEWARK, N. J., April 17—Agents of the Federal Bureau of Investigation swarmed into a tavern in Long Branch, N. J., last night and arrested Ralph Greco, 35 years old, of Hoboken, who was described by Federal authorities as the "No. 1 bank robber fugitive" of the nation.

Greco, who had boasted that he would never be taken alive, surrendered meekly when the agents caught up with him in Wilson's bar after a three-year search, it was announced this afternoon by E. E. Conroy, in charge of the Newark office of the F. B. I. Unarmed, he was seated with his wife and a group of friends. The prisoner, owner of a long police record, is held in connection with the theft of $76,000 last August from the First Stroudsburg (Pa.) National Bank and of $11,500 from the First National Bank of Suffield, Conn., in 1938.

Writer Tells of Philippine Escape And Stay at Secret U. S. Air Base

By NAT FLOYD
Wireless to THE NEW YORK TIMES.

SOMEWHERE IN AUSTRALIA, April 17—After watching America's planes going and coming on secret fields during our initial offensive blow at the Japanese deep in the Philippines I was permitted to make the long hop to Australia in the plane that carried Brig. Gen. Ralph Royce, the commander of the flight.

I had become acquainted with the athletic, hard-hitting General during his stay at the air fields, which I had reached almost a month earlier after a series of dashes from island to island. I shall never forget the uplift of morale when the long-expected planes came sailing in and settled on those fields.

During the succeeding days and nights the temporary operating headquarters was a busy place. General Royce and his officers were continually planning raids and dispatching planes upon their distant missions in large and small groups. In the afternoon General Royce would eat and rest briefly while awaiting the return of the planes.

He sat deep in a comfortable chair. I thought he would take a needed siesta, but a few minutes later when he heard a Flying Fortress land he sat up and said:

"I know how I am going to spend the afternoon. I'm going to take that plane out and bomb * * *"

He started briskly toward the field, but he turned back later after he had met the pilot, who told him a Japanese missile had caused enough damage to require several hours for repairs.

Later in the day I talked with the co-pilot of one of the B-25s [medium bombers], who was en-

Continued on Page Four

"All the News That's Fit to Print."

The New York Times.

LATE CITY EDITION
Mild today.
Temperatures Yesterday—Max., 74; Min., 52

Copyright, 1942, by The New York Times Company.

VOL. XCI..No. 30,783. Entered as Second-Class Matter, Postoffice, New York, N. Y. NEW YORK, WEDNESDAY, MAY 6, 1942. THREE CENTS NEW YORK CITY and Vicinity

CORREGIDOR SURRENDERS UNDER LAND ATTACK AFTER WITHSTANDING 300 RAIDS FROM THE AIR; BRITISH HIT MADAGASCAR BASE; VICHY RESISTS

CHARGE ACCOUNTS ARE DUE IN 40 DAYS AS INFLATION CURB

Reserve Board's Regulation, in Effect Today, Is First Check on Such Retail Customers

Bringing retail charge accounts under control for the first time and ruling that installment purchases must be liquidated in twelve months the Federal Reserve Board promulgated yesterday amendment No. 4 to its consumer credit regulation W, carrying into effect the seventh point in President Roosevelt's anti-inflation program.

Under the amendment, which is effective today, charge account customers of retail stores will be required to speed up their payments to complete them within forty days after the end of the month in which purchase is made. If this is not done the account will be transferred to an installment basis requiring liquidation within six months and no further charge account purchases will be permissible until the items in default are paid for.

The amendment also tightened substantially the earlier restrictions on installment sales and broadened the scope of the merchandise covered to forty-six listed classifications, including almost every item used in the American home, and clothing and jewelry as well. The down payment was generally raised to 33 1/3 per cent and the payment period to twelve months.

Explains Aim of Rules

Allan Sproul, president of the Federal Reserve Bank of New York, in announcing the amendment here, said:

"As amended, the regulation is extended to cover a comprehensive list of durable and semi-durable goods for civilian consumption and contemplates that the volume of outstanding consumer credit, already substantially diminished, will be further contracted in keeping with the government's purpose to prevent the rapid bidding up of prices.

"The purpose of this revision is to help make effective the last point in the seven-point program which the President set forth in his special message to Congress of April 27, 1942, as follows: 'To keep the cost of living from spiraling upward, we must discourage credit and installment buying, and encourage the paying off of debts, mortgages and other obligations; for this promotes savings, retards excessive buying and adds to the amount available to the creditors for the purchase of war bonds.'"

With respect to charge accounts, the regulation, in effect and depending upon the date of the purchase, provides for a forty to a seventy day payment period, similar to that in effect in Canada. The average period for payment of

Continued on Page Fourteen

Nazis' War Industry Spurs Plane Output

By Telephone to The New York Times.

BERNE, Switzerland, May 5—German war industry has been ordered to devote all its attention henceforth to turning out airplanes, even to the detriment of tanks and other matériel. This news from Berlin tonight confirms indications reaching foreign circles here that mastery of the air is the paramount consideration for the moment.

Figures declared to be trustworthy indicate that the peak of plane production in the Reich was reached in June, 1941, when 3,300 were turned out. Now it has fallen to between 2,700 and 2,800. Italy's contribution does not exceed 700 machines a month.

It is understood the Germans' estimate of their opponents' production is: United States, 3,300 planes a month; Britain, 2,400; Russia, 2,600 to 2,900. But the Nazis can draw upon considerable reserves.

WPB CUTS GASOLINE 50 PER CENT IN EAST

Non-Essential Users May Be Down to 5 Gallons a Week After May 16 Order

By The Associated Press.

WASHINGTON, May 5—Gasoline consumption in the East will be slashed 50 per cent below normal starting May 16, the War Production Board said tonight. This means that many of the area's 10,000,000 motorists probably will have to get along with as little as five or six gallons a week.

The reduction will become effective the day the seaboard area begins using ration cards.

[In New York motorists will register for gasoline rationing next Tuesday, Wednesday and Thursday. Rationing will begin on May 15.]

While the overall curtailment will be one-half, informed sources explained that it would amount to about a 60 per cent cut for non-essential users of automobiles, since necessary vehicles will continue to receive their full requirements of fuel.

Action Recommended by Ickes

The WPB action, taken on recommendation of Harold L. Ickes, petroleum coordinator, came shortly after Joseph B. Eastman, defense transportation director, declared "every owner of a motor vehicle in public or private service should realize that he holds this vehicle in trust for the national war effort and that it should be used only for purposes of necessity."

This statement of Mr. Eastman's applied to the whole country, not merely to the East.

Simultaneously with the gasoline order, WPB directed that de-

Continued on Page Thirteen

BRONX GRAND JURY CLEARS EVERYONE IN THE FLYNN CASE

County Is 'Singularly Free of Fraud and Corruption,' Presentment Says

The Bronx County grand jury that has been hearing evidence on the paving with city materials and labor of a courtyard on the Lake Mahopac estate of Edward J. Flynn, chairman of the Democratic National Committee, as well as other irregularities in the Bronx, handed up a seventeen-page presentment yesterday, finding that Bronx County is "singularly free of fraud and corruption," but that many irregularities are prevalent.

The grand jury declared that after hearing all the evidence submitted, it did not find that the facts warranted the indictment of any one.

Work on Flynn Estate Reviewed

In discussing the work done on the Flynn estate on Nov. 14, 15, 17 and 18 of last year, the presentment said city employes had been transported to the estate from the city by city-owned station wagons and that the work had consisted of laying 8,000 second-hand granite blocks.

The city employes, the presentment said, were paid in full for their services; 8,000 blocks were returned to the city and the gasoline and oil issued to the city station wagons for the Mahopac trip were returned in full. The cost of trucking the blocks by private concerns was paid by Mr. Flynn. The courtyard was only part of a general alteration on the estate, with the total job to cost more than $30,000.

The evidence adduced, it continued, showed that Mr. Flynn had never expressed any desire that the work be done under city auspices or by city employes and without expense to him, but that the job would be done by a private contractor and paid for by Mr. Flynn. The work done by city employes was under the supervision of Robert L. Moran, Bronx Commissioner of Public Works.

Paul J. Kern, deposed president of the Civil Service Commission, who conducted an investigation in the paving job while still in office, was severely rebuked by the grand jury for hampering the investigation conducted by William B. Herlands, Commissioner of Investigation.

No Conspiracy Found

"In respect to the second phase of the investigation," the presentment said, "the alleged conspiracy between Mayor La Guardia, Mr. Flynn and Commissioner Herlands to suppress the Kern investigation, the charge was entirely without foundation and we feel that it never would have been made but for the fact that Mr. Kern is greatly influenced by what he terms 'his intuition.'"

Mr. Kern had charged that Mayor La Guardia was trying to suppress his investigation in Mr. Flynn's behalf, and that in return Mr. Flynn was to obtain for the Mayor the Democratic nomination for United States Senator.

The grand jurors found that the records of the Department of Highways and Sewers under Commissioner Moran were in a "deplorable condition." They said they believed Borough President James J. Lyons when he testified that he was ignorant of the Mahopac paving job, and "we strongly condemn this ignorance." Commissioner Moran, they said, was Mr. Lyons's appointee and the Borough President could not avoid responsibility for the manner in which any subordinate conducted a department.

The Grand Jury's Presentment

In its presentment the grand jury said:

"The subject matter of our investigation resolved itself, naturally, into three phases; 1, the Maho-

Continued on Page Twenty-eight

Direct Hit on Tirpitz By British Reported

By Telephone to The New York Times.

STOCKHOLM, Sweden, May 5—British Royal Air Force bombs scored a direct hit on the battleship Tirpitz when she was in Kiel harbor prior to her transfer to her present anchorage at Trondheim, Norway, according to an eyewitness account by a Swedish seaman published in Ny Dag. The observer also reported a great change of morale among German civilians.

"Although the British attacks on Kiel were usually made from a great height, sometimes from 20,000 feet," he is quoted as saying, "the bombs hit their targets with astonishing precision. Thus in every bombing the biggest wharf in Kiel was regularly set ablaze, and on one occasion a British bomber scored a direct hit on the Tirpitz."

FOE ENTERS CHINA ACROSS BURMA LINE

Advance Units Over Border While Main Columns Wait—Planes Aid British Retreat

By DAVID ANDERSON

Wireless to The New York Times.

LONDON, May 5—The Japanese have entered Yunnan Province in China via the Burma Road, it was announced today. Their vanguards reached the suburbs of Wangting, which is on a small river dividing Burma and China, and Chungking said the Japanese were being engaged by Chinese troops in the hills. The main enemy column was waiting within Burma at Chukok, near by.

The invading force must have made a detour around the Chinese fighting at Kutkai because the battle there was reported still going on. Other Chinese units were believed holding out north of Mandalay on the banks of the Irrawaddy River. British soldiers were continuing their slow retreat west of Mandalay.

"At times their [the Japanese]

Continued on Page Four

BRITISH ADVANCING

Landing Force Reported Within Four Miles of Madagascar Base

'CHUTISTS ARE USED

Warships and Aircraft Make Frontal Assault to Help Troops

By RAYMOND DANIELL

Wireless to The New York Times.

LONDON, May 5—Small units of British Commandos and regular troops won a bridgehead at Courier Bay in the action against Madagascar and were reported tonight to be fighting their way across a ten-mile-wide isthmus toward the important naval base of Diego Suarez.

[A London dispatch of The Associated Press quoted Vichy reports that waves of British parachutists had been landed at the outset of a double attack in which warships and squadrons of aircraft made a frontal thrust from the sea timed to coincide with the overland assault on the rear of the base by British light armored units landed at Courier Bay.

[The Associated Press said that, according to advices released by Vichy sources, the British occupying forces had reached Andrakaka, four miles from Diego Suarez. The French estimated that the attacking forces numbered 20,000 and the French and native defenders about 7,000.]

There were only sketchy accounts of the battle for the big French island, which lies athwart vital United Nations supply routes. However, a joint Admiralty-War Office communiqué issued this afternoon clearly indicated that opposition had been offered by the Vichy French garrison. The capture of a defending battery was reported.

A communiqué issued late to-

Continued on Page Two

JAPANESE FINALLY TAKE CORREGIDOR

MARIVELES MT. — BATAAN — MANILA BAY — Lamao — Cabcaben — Mariveles — COCHINOS PT. — Boca Chico — CORREGIDOR I. Ft. Mills — LA MONJA I. — CABALLO I. Ft. Hughes — CHINA SEA — Boca Grande — EL FRAILE I. Ft. Drum — Ternate — CARABAO I. Ft. Frank — CAVITE — LIMIT PT. — Patungan — 0 5 10 Miles — MAY 6, 1942

Japanese forces attacking from the Bataan Peninsula have forced the surrender of Corregidor and other United States island fortresses at the entrance to Manila Bay.

Laval Protests 'Aggression' But Won't Seek U. S. Break

By LANSING WARREN

By Telephone to The New York Times.

VICHY, France, May 5—Replying to the American note expressing approbation of the British occupation of Madagascar, Pierre Laval as Chief of the French Government and Foreign Minister, tonight protested the move as an aggression. He rejected as inadmissible the "pretension of the Government of the United States to forbid France to defend her territory when attacked," and declared that he leaves "to President Roosevelt the share of responsibility that may fall to him in consequence of this aggression."

[In Washington, Secretary Hull made it clear that there would be no deviation from the approval of the British action at Madagascar. After a White House session, Pacific War Council members praised the move.]

M. Laval, in handing his note to the American Chargé d'Affaires, S. Pinckney Tuck, recalled the long record of friendship between France and the United States and added:

"You were present at my recent interview with your Ambassador, Admiral Leahy, and I wish again to repeat to you what I said to him, that no definitive gesture leading to a break will be initiated by France."

Indicates Grave Situation

M. Laval read his reply to the assembled French and foreign press in a salon of the Hotel du Parc, and completed it with comments that indicated the full seriousness for French-American relations because the United States for the first time was directly involved in diplomatic controversy with France.

Following is the text of the note as read to the correspondents by M. Laval:

In replying to the note handed in today by the Chargé d'Affaires of the United States of America, the French Government raises the most energetic protest against the aggression of which Madagascar has just been the object on the part of British forces.

It notes the assurance given that Madagascar will be returned to France some day.

It rejects as inadmissible the pretension of the Government of the United States to forbid France to defend her territory when attacked.

The French Government is the sole judge of the obligations imposed by its honor. In that manner, the defenders of Madagascar have understood correctly their duties. They have not hesitated, despite their numerical inferiority, to carry out their duties according to the most noble tradition of the French Army.

England so often since the Armistice has manifested hostility to France and the aggression

Continued on Page Two

RED ARMY ATTACKS KEY GERMAN BASES

Timoshenko Smashes at Kursk, Kharkov and Taganrog to Forestall Nazi Drive

By The Associated Press.

MOSCOW, May 5—Stealing the jump on Reichsfuehrer Hitler, hundreds of thousands of Russian soldiers, tanks and planes smashed head-on today at three key German bases from which it was believed the Nazi leader was planning his Spring or Summer drive.

Under command of Marshal Semyon Timoshenko, the first Russian general to turn back the German military machine with the recapture of Rostov last November, the Red Army struck at Kharkov, Kursk and Taganrog in the strongest Nazi-held section of the long battle line.

Action was also stepped-up in the northern sectors, particularly the hard-fought Kalinin area northwest of Moscow. The army newspaper Red Star said the Germans were

Continued on Page Ten

OTHER FORTS FALL

American Soldiers Had Held Out in Spite of Supply Shortage

COURAGE IS PRAISED

Roosevelt Views Their Example as Guarantee of Final Victory

By The Associated Press.

AT UNITED NATIONS HEADQUARTERS, Australia, Wednesday, May 6—The American fortress of Corregidor and the other fortified islands in the entrance to Manila Bay surrendered today, it was officially announced here.

Besides the rock that is Corregidor, the United States forts that had held out were Fort Hughes, Fort Drum and Fort Frank.

The end came in the second day of the final Japanese assault, launched at midnight Tuesday, Manila time, with landings from Bataan Peninsula after Corregidor had been pounded again and again by Japanese big guns and aerial bombs. Corregidor alone had had 300 air raids since Dec. 29, when thirty-five Japanese bombers attacked for three hours.

A spokesman for General Douglas MacArthur, who led the brilliant defense of Bataan and the forts at the mouth of Manila Bay until ordered to Australia, made this announcement:

"General Wainwright has surrendered Corregidor and the other fortified islands in Manila Harbor."

There were believed to be about 7,000 men and women altogether on Corregidor and the other fortified islands. Besides the original garrisons, there was a naval detachment consisting originally of some 3,500 Marines and bluejackets who were removed to Corregidor when fighting ceased April 9 on Bataan Peninsula. A group of Army nurses also reached Corregidor.

Troops Half-Starved

By CHARLES HURD

Special to The New York Times.

WASHINGTON, May 5—The fortified island of Corregidor in Manila Bay, last bastion of the American defenders of the Philippine Island, Luzon, was fighting a landing attack by Japanese troops today.

The issue of the fighting was not known in Washington at 8 P. M., when the War Department issued a communiqué, but two factors indicated grave concern over the outcome of a contest in which the defenders are outnumbered,

Continued on Page Five

War News Summarized

WEDNESDAY, MAY 6, 1942

Corregidor, the island fortress at the entrance to Manila Bay, was surrendered to the Japanese after a furious assault. The British were engaged in breaking French resistance to their landing in Madagascar. Japanese forces reached and crossed the Burma-China frontier. Other war fronts were largely unchanged.

The surrender of Corregidor and other island bases was announced by United Nations Headquarters in Australia, following an earlier Washington communiqué stating that the Japanese had started landing operations. The defenders were reported to be short of both food and ammunition. [1:8.]

British landing forces on Madagascar were reported to be within four miles of the Diego Suarez naval base at the northern extremity of the island. The French garrison was resisting, but Vichy reported that some 20,000 British had landed or were preparing to land. London said the Commandos had encountered little resistance. [1:5; map, P. 2.]

The Vichy regime ordered the garrison at Madagascar to resist. Pierre Laval in a note to the United States Government rejected Washington's warning against French belligerent action, but he insisted his government would not be the first to take measures to break relations with the United States. Admiral Darlan, chief of the Vichy military forces, expressed extreme bitterness toward Britain. [1:6-7.]

Secretary of State Hull indicated clearly at his press conference that the United States would adhere to a policy of full support of British occupation of Madagascar. [3:1.]

Meanwhile, Japanese forces in Burma had reached the Chinese frontier in the Burma Road sector and had penetrated a slight distance into China. A battle was raging on the frontier, and the Japanese had been halted, according to Chungking. United States bombers from India attacked successfully Mingaladon airport north of Rangoon. The Japanese said their planes had set on fire the Chinese city of Yungchang, 120 miles inside China in Yunnan Province. [1:4, map, P. 4.]

Chungking said that Chinese guerrillas in Eastern China had raided fifteen Japanese-occupied cities during the past two weeks and destroyed power plants and communications. [6:3, with map.]

The United Nations Australian Headquarters announced successful air attacks on Lae, New Guinea, and Rabaul, New Britain. A Japanese air attack on Port Moresby was repulsed. [4:4.]

On the other side of the world, London announced Royal Air Force attacks on the Skoda munitions plant in Czechoslovakia and factories at Stuttgart in Southwestern Germany. The Germans raided points on the British south coast. [10:2.]

The story was heard in London that a group of German generals had informed Adolf Hitler that if the campaign in Russia this year should fail, they would seek to abolish the National Socialist system. [8:4-5.]

Moscow reported an offensive in the south against German-held Kharkov, Kursk and Taganrog. [1:7.]

Washington disclosed the sinking of three more merchant vessels off the United States east coast. [5:1.]

Mrs. Rosenberg in 2 Federal Jobs While Making $22,500 on the Side

By LOUIS STARK

Special to The New York Times.

WASHINGTON, May 5 — Some members of the House Appropriations Committee asserted today that they were determined to write into all future supply bills a provision prohibiting Federal administrative officials from accepting employment outside the government. This came following the disclosure at a closed meeting of an appropriations subcommittee today that Mrs. Anna M. Rosenberg of New York, regional director of the Social Security Board, receives a large income from private industry and also draws pay from another agency.

Mrs. Rosenberg's Social Security Board post pays $7,500 on a full time basis. Besides this Federal position she revealed to the subcommittee today that she received $20,000 a year for part time work as public and labor relations consultant to the Macy-Bamberger stores in New York and Newark, and $2,500 a year for similar services performed for I. Miller, New York shoe dealer.

In addition, Mrs. Rosenberg is a consultant on the staff of Nelson Rockefeller, coordinator of American Affairs. For this service she receives $6,000 a year. Her total earnings therefore are $36,000 a year, $13,500 paid by two government agencies and $22,500 by industry.

Arthur J. Altmeyer, chairman of the Social Security Board, who accompanied Mrs. Rosenberg to the committee meeting today, revealed that when the regional directorship was offered to her six years ago Mrs. Rosenberg made it a condition that she be permitted to continue her work as labor consultant for private concerns. Correspond-

Continued on Page Twenty-eight

G. M. Defies WLB on Double Pay; Hearing Will Take Up Issue Today

Special to The New York Times.

DETROIT, Mich., May 5—On the eve of the start of negotiations before a panel of the National War Labor Board between the General Motors Corporation and the United Automobile Workers, C. I. O., C. E. Wilson, president of the corporation, revealed today that it had defied the board on the issue of double-time pay for Sunday and holiday work.

The disclosure came in the release by Mr. Wilson of the texts of exchanges of correspondence among the corporation, the board and the union. The correspondence dated from April 27. It included a copy of the order by the board to Mr. Wilson May 1 that double-time pay for Sunday work be continued by the company to May 18.

In reply to the order, the releases by Mr. Wilson showed, H. W. Anderson, vice president of General Motors, sent the board on May 2 a telegram which said that "we protest and do not agree to comply with your directive order."

The hearings before the NWLB panel are scheduled to open in Washington tomorrow morning. They aim at a renewal of the union contract which expired April 28. The contract has been continued in effect except for a stipulation by General Motors April 27 that "pending a final adjustment," double time "will not be paid for Sunday and holiday work." It has been agreed that when a new agreement is reached all its terms will be retroactive to April 28.

Walter P. Reuther, director of the General Motors division of the union, has made known that the union wished to have the Washington hearing open to the public, including the press. Mr. Wilson, in a telegram to the board today,

Continued on Page Fourteen

"All the News That's Fit to Print."

The New York Times.

LATE CITY EDITION
Mild today.
Temperatures Yesterday—Max., 66; Min., 53

Copyright, 1942, by The New York Times Company.

VOL. XCI..No. 30,786. Entered as Second-Class Matter, Postoffice, New York, N. Y. NEW YORK, SATURDAY, MAY 9, 1942. THREE CENTS NEW YORK CITY and Vicinity

JAPANESE REPULSED IN GREAT PACIFIC BATTLE, WITH 17 TO 22 OF THEIR SHIPS SUNK OR CRIPPLED; ENEMY IN FLIGHT, PURSUED BY ALLIED WARSHIPS

BASIC 'GAS' RATION TWO TO 3 GALLONS A WEEK, SAYS OPA

This Quota Will Be Given for Nonessential Autos, With No Limit on Bus, Taxi, Truck

DOCTORS, ETC., UNCURBED

Three to Five Gallons a Week Allowed for Persons Who Drive to Their Jobs

By THOMAS J. HAMILTON
Special to THE NEW YORK TIMES.

WASHINGTON, May 8—Motorists of the Eastern seaboard States doing nonessential driving will receive between two and three gallons of gasoline a week, probably about two, under gasoline rationing starting May 15, Leon Henderson, Price Administrator, stated today.

Drivers who have to use their cars to get to work will receive higher allotments according to the distance they have to go, Mr. Henderson said. For the seven-week period between the beginning of rationing on May 15 and the start of a permanent system on July 1, these motorists will be classified for allotments as follows:

B-1 will receive 11 units, or 22 gallons, for the seven weeks; B-2, 15 units, or 30 gallons; B-3, 19 units, or 38 gallons.

No restrictions will be placed on operators of trucks, buses and other commercial vehicles; physicians or other civilians performing essential duties, who will buy gasoline on the "honor system." Mr. Henderson hoped that it would not be necessary to have local boards do "police work" to see to it that the regulations were not abused.

Rationing under the permanent system will be even more severe than the quotas disclosed today, the Price Administrator indicated.

Areas in 3 States Exempted

Mr. Henderson, however, did offer one scrap of comfort: thanks to improvement in their transportation situation, all of West Virginia, most of Pennsylvania west of Harrisburg and a section of Western New York will be removed from the rationed area under an order to be issued shortly by Secretary Ickes, the Petroleum Coordinator.

Starting May 15, about one-third of the 9,500,000 or 10,000,000 motorists in the Atlantic seaboard States, classified as Group A, will receive the basic two to three gallons a week for "non-essential" automobiles, Mr. Henderson estimated in testimony before a House Interstate Commerce subcommittee.

Pressed to explain why the reduction will be so drastic, he exclaimed that such a motorist "will be getting a damned sight more than he's entitled to in view of the situation."

Several committee members questioned Mr. Henderson about con-

Continued on Page Twenty-eight

Cars Made 'Trucks' To Evade Rationing

Many New Jersey automobile owners are seeking to evade gasoline rationing limitations by changing the listing of their cars from passenger to commercial classifications, William J. Culver, secretary of the Jersey City Rationing Board, said yesterday.

Trucks, clearly recognizable as such, do not require rationing cards to get fuel, and owners of other trucks, not clearly recognizable as such, can get cards entitling them to unlimited quantities.

Mr. Culver predicted that the ruse would not work. School teachers who issue the rationing cards have been instructed to challenge the right of commercial car owners to an unlimited card where the registry classification has been changed.

So far as could be learned there has been no similar shift in registry in New York.

German Cardinal Indicts Nazi 'War on Christianity'

Faulhaber Reports to Vatican That Regime 'Blackmails' Believers and Uses Spies to Put Pressure on the Clergy

By DANIEL T. BRIGHAM
By Telephone to THE NEW YORK TIMES.

BERNE, Switzerland, May 8—Michael Cardinal von Faulhaber, militant leader of the religious opposition in the Reich, has just sent an eleven-point indictment of the church situation in Germany to the Holy See. Intimations from Vatican sources received here tonight indicate that the Vatican Secretariat of State is taking a serious view of the situation.

As outlined in reports trickling through Italian censorship, Cardinal von Faulhaber's statement of the situation is as follows:

1. A "veritable war against Christianity" is being waged in Germany. This, he intimates, has contributed largely to present "spiritual unrest" in the Reich, which is translated into "manifestations against the regime" that are catalogued by the authorities as "machinations of foreign Judeo-Communistic elements." There is a noticeable "armistice" between the Catholic and Protestant Churches in the Reich, to their mutual benefit.

2. The church continues to be treated with mistrust by the regime, which maintains an elaborate system of "anti-Christian espionage" in the principal religious centers. This system attempts to prevent the reading of "certain episcopal documents" from the pulpits by the simple process of ordering the arrest of Bishops or priests prior to their issuance: if the document is not read the ecclesiastic is released; if it is read, sometimes he is not.

3. Moral "blackmail" is being applied to faithful Catholics with reminders that "less faithful attendance at church means keeping your job." This "blackmail," says Cardinal von Faulhaber, also is applied to the church itself, which is called on for proportionately greater sacrifices in money and property than the "unbelieving in-

Continued on Page Five

DRAFT 'SCREEN TEST' ASSAILED STRONGLY

Officials and Army Officers Denounce Cursory Tests Before Induction

By MEYER BERGER

Army officers, Selective Service officials, Local Board members and other responsible citizens interested in Selective Service procedure yesterday added their emphatic protests to the common outcry against "screen test" or cursory examination methods of accepting registrants for military duty.

They unanimously concurred with popular demand that Washington put an end at once to this system of medical examination because it works cruel and unnecessary hardship, because it has more than doubled rejections and because it not only has failed to accelerate delivery of recruits but also has retarded it.

Selective Service officials, high Army authorities and prominent civilians already have begged Washington either to restore the previous Selective Service system, which worked perfectly, or to accept suggestions on possible changes that will end the cruelty, hardship and embarrassment the "screen test" has created. This was confirmed in authoritative sources yesterday.

300 Out of 1,000 Rejected

"Probably more than 1,000 men were delivered at Governors Island today for physical examination because their local boards, acting on the 'screen test' system, passed them through unless they were obviously blind, halt or lame," one officer said. "By tonight three hundred or more out of that draft will be returning home.

"Most of these three hundred will have no jobs because they have resigned. Some will have sold their cars, their homes, or will have given away their clothing and other possessions. Some will have sb-leased their apartments. Some will have jettisoned their shops in forced sale.

"Many will have been wept over in farewell parades, will have gone through emotional partings with their wives, mothers, sweethearts and families, or with the people with whom they had worked for years in shop or office. They will go home—or sneak home—dejected and bitter, all because of 'screen test' method."

Under the previous system registrants were examined at local boards, a Selective Service man pointed out, and had thirty days

Continued on Page Six

SHIPYARD BOWS TO EDICT ON UNION

'Maintenance of Membership' Accepted Despite Objection to Policy of NWLB

Despite a continuing belief in the unsoundness of any contract provision requiring workers to belong to a union as a condition of employment, the Federal Shipbuilding and Dry Dock Company, a subsidiary of the United States Steel Corporation, agreed last night to abide by a National War Labor Board decision directing it to grant the Industrial Union of Marine and Shipbuilding Workers, C. I. O., a "maintenance of membership" clause at the company's shipyard at Kearny, N. J.

L. H. Korndorff, president of the company, which allowed its plant to be commandeered by the government last August rather than comply with a similar ruling of the

Continued on Page Twenty-three

CHINESE WIN FIGHT

Foe Said to Be Checked in Yunnan, but Tokyo Alleges Advance

CLAIMS BHAMO FALL

London Concedes Akyab Occupation, but Denies Invasion of India

By CRAIG THOMPSON
Wireless to THE NEW YORK TIMES.

LONDON, May 8—Japanese forces today continued fighting along the Burma Road in Yunnan, with imperial headquarters in Tokyo claiming that Lungling, fifty miles inside the border, had been occupied, but Chungking reports said the Chinese forces were counter-attacking at Chefang, twenty miles from the border.

Tokyo also claimed the occupation of Bhamo, but this was not confirmed by any United Nations source. Bhamo, at the head of navigation on the Irrawaddy, is 345 airline miles from Kunming and the Burma terminus of the last important supply route into Free China. It is fifty miles south of Myitkyina, terminus of a railway from Mandalay, along which the Japanese previously were reported advancing.

The Japanese claim of occupation of Akyab, near the border of India, was confirmed today, but there was no confirmation—nor any reports from Tokyo—of the broadcast of the German-controlled Paris radio that Japanese troops had penetrated into India. The British flatly denied the report.

United States air forces carried out their fifth heavy raid in eight days on Rangoon.

In Chungking reports of the fighting in Yunnan it was said the Chinese forces had inflicted losses of 1,000 men and possibly more on the invaders in checking them at Chefang. The Japanese had split in two directions in an attempt to encircle the Chinese, and Chungking said the encircling arm northward was nipped off completely, causing the loss of 1,000 Japanese, while the southward arm was repulsed with heavy losses.

The effect remains to be seen of the continued bombing of Ran-

Continued on Page Three

War News Summarized

SATURDAY, MAY 9, 1942

United States and allied naval and air forces have repulsed a Japanese fleet, bringing to a "temporary" halt the vast five-day engagement northeast of Australia in the Coral Sea, it was announced today at General Douglas MacArthur's headquarters.

By official accounts, the latest Japanese losses consisted of the sinking of an aircraft carrier, a heavy cruiser and an auxiliary vessel and damage to an additional aircraft carrier and heavy cruiser. Thus the official figures of enemy losses reached eleven vessels sunk and six damaged. Unofficial reports put the total toll of the enemy at eighteen ships sunk and four damaged and said American losses had been comparatively light. A Navy communiqué, describing our losses as "not fully known," declared no credence should be given to Japanese claims, which included the sinking of two United States aircraft carriers and a battleship and damage to two British warships. The British issued a flat denial. [1:8; map, P. 2.]

Before the engagement ended Prime Minister Curtin had warned the Australian people that invasion might be "an actuality at any hour." [3:1.]

The Japanese invaders of Burma stood stymied at the high mark of their penetration into China's Yunnan Province, the Chinese announced, reporting the killing or isolation of 2,000 enemy troops. Tokyo, however, claimed a gain of thirty miles in Yunnan, as well as the capture of Bhamo, in Upper Burma, terminus of the last important completed supply route into Free China. American bombers set fires in Rangoon in their third raid of the week. [1:4.]

At the other side of the Indian Ocean, strong British reinforcements were being sent to the Madagascar naval base to convert it into an Allied bastion. Ceylon also was reinforced. [1:5; map P. 3.]

In Europe, R. A. F. bomber squadrons that included American fliers scored hits on eight of twelve heavily escorted German supply ships off the Netherland coast. The R. A. F. raided Germany last night after a bad-weather interruption. [4:8.]

Britain's Secretary for Air, Sir Archibald Sinclair, predicted that the attack would be pressed this Summer to destroy the German air force and lay the groundwork for an invasion of Europe. [1:7.]

On the northern sector of Germany's Eastern Front the Russians reported the repulse of three German columns that had made some headway on the Karelian Isthmus. [4:1.]

Within Germany opposition increased from a militant religious leader, Cardinal von Faulhaber, who accused the Reich of a "war against Christianity" in an eleven-point indictment forwarded to the Vatican. [1:2-3.]

UNSPOKEN THOUGHT: THE GANG SEEMS TO BE DOING ALL RIGHT

Service men following yesterday's battle bulletins of The New York Times
The New York Times

CEYLON REINFORCED, WITH MADAGASCAR

Americans Reported Landed on Island Off Africa—British Ready to Protect India

By The United Press.

LONDON, May 8—Britain poured strong reinforcements today into the newly-occupied Diego Suarez naval base on Madagascar and into the Island of Ceylon, off Southern India, tightening the United Nations grip on a 2,100-mile line dominating the vital western half of the Japanese-menaced Indian Ocean.

[The London Daily Mail published yesterday a dispatch from Madrid saying that, "according to reports from Vichy," United States and South African troops were "pouring into Diego Suarez," an Associated Press dispatch from London reported.]

Britain has reinforced Ceylon with African troops and is now ready to protect India, it was announced here.

"Troops include Africans from Kenya, Zanzibar, Northern Rhodesia, Uganda and Nyasaland," the official statement said. "Most of them are already seasoned troops, experienced in fighting in the Ethiopian campaign. They include all manner of fighting units."

Large detachments of South African troops, along with masses of artillery and planes, were being landed on Northern Madagascar. Vichy dispatches indicated that little or no damage had been done to the Diego Suarez port and arsenal in the forty-eight-hour battle in which British land, sea and air forces beat down French resistance.

British Optimistic

By RAYMOND DANIELL
Wireless to THE NEW YORK TIMES.

LONDON, May 8—The British today expressed satisfaction that the capitulation of Diego Suarez, principal harbor in Madagascar, had come so quickly because it was felt that wounds to local French pride would heal more quickly. There appears to be some basis for the hope that, the defenders having offered resistance as ordered by Vichy and having been overcome by superior force, a basis for an understanding may be found between the Madagascar French and the British, who have taken possession for the duration to keep the Japanese from doing so permanently.

Although Prime Minister Winston Churchill in announcing the surrender of Diego Suarez and

Continued on Page Three

Marblehead's Voyage Home An Epic of Heroism, Tragedy

From a Staff Correspondent

AN EAST COAST PORT, May 8—This is the story of the ship that was "bombed to hell" and of the men who brought her back across 13,500 miles of open water. Her skipper, Captain Arthur G. Robinson, told it today in the cabin of the ship he had saved, as the U. S. S. Marblehead, 7,050-ton light cruiser, lay moored to the bollards of an East Coast port safe after three months of peril rarely equaled in the history of the sea.

He told it simply and without benefit of dramatics as newspaper men crowded around the cabin table and as the ship's officers, to whom the captain gave a general accolade of merit and heroism, filled out a tale of heroic tragedy and grim endurance.

About three months to a day after she was bombed by Japanese planes in Macassar Strait off Borneo, the Marblehead, still taking water, steamed slowly into an East Coast port, her dead long since buried, her wounded hospitalized, her visible scars of war patched and painted, but her 'tween decks a shambles, and the struggle it had been to save her written in the lined faces of her crew.

She was a "ghost ship," a ship written off by the Japanese as sunk; a ship, indeed, that at moments was all but gone, but that was kept afloat by the will of her crew, and a bucket brigade. Yesterday her story came out as she lay, home from the sea, surrounded by other fighting ships—veterans of deep water and those yet to be covered with the salt rime of the open ocean.

It was a story punctuated by riveting hammers and the hiss of cutting torches as workmen wasted no time in repairing the Marblehead for the battles yet to come.

"I was on the bridge," Captain

Continued on Page Twenty-eight

AIR WAR ON REICH CALLED A 'PRELUDE'

Sinclair and Eden in Britain Say R. A. F. Is Paving Way for Invasion of Europe

By ROBERT P. POST
Wireless to THE NEW YORK TIMES.

LONDON, May 8—Two British Cabinet members, Sir Archibald Sinclair, Secretary for Air, and Foreign Secretary Anthony Eden, joined today in indicating that the present British air attack against the Germans was the forerunner of an eventual United Nations invasion of the Continent.

The present severe bombings by the Royal Air Force in the Reich are only a foretaste of what is to come in the air war, said Sir Archibald in a speech at Birmingham. Details of the coming "Anglo-American offensive in Germany must remain secret," he remarked.

"But there is reason to believe it will be tremendous when it develops, even bigger than anything which the British are doing now," he went on. "What its effect will be on German production and morale of course is something that only time can test."

He predicted "a terrible Summer

Continued on Page Four

Bulkeley Sure We 'Can Lick Them' If Odds Are but 5 to 1 Against Us

Lieutenant John D. Bulkeley, who returned yesterday to his family in Long Island City after having made the mosquito boat a symbol of lightning-quick destruction to the Japanese, said he would like to be left alone for a few days with the wife and 19-months-old daughter he had not seen since last August, to say nothing of the son born in his absence and "mom's cooking."

Today, however, he is to receive the plaudits of his home borough at a noon reception at the Queens Borough Hall in Kew Gardens, where Borough President James A. Burke is to hand to him a scroll proclaiming him Queens' own No. 1 hero. Then there will be a luncheon at the Forest Hills Inn, with the lieutenant and his wife as the guests of honor.

And neighbors, who hung out flags and sent flowers for the hero's homecoming to the fifty-six-family apartment house in which the Bulkeleys have their home at 45-42 Forty-first Street, started at once to plan a community party to be held next week for the tired, family-hungry naval officer.

Of the three companions who had arrived with Lieutenant Bulkeley in San Francisco on Thursday on a ten-day leave, Lieutenant

Continued on Page Four

FLEET IS SMASHED

Allies Said to Have Added 2 Carriers, Big Cruiser, 6 Destroyers to Bag

LAND PLANES SCORE

Fight Over 'Temporarily,' Our Blows to Continue —U. S. Losses 'Light'

By The United Press.

AT UNITED NATIONS HEADQUARTERS, Australia, Saturday, May 9—The titanic air and naval battle between United Nations and Japanese forces, raging since Monday over thousands of miles of the Coral Sea off Northeastern Australia, has "temporarily ceased" and the "enemy has been repulsed," it was announced today.

"Our attacks will continue," said a communiqué issued by the headquarters of General Douglas MacArthur.

[A report from an advanced United Nations base gave the Japanese losses as eighteen warships sunk and four damaged, according to a Reuter dispatch from Sydney, Australia. These included the certain destruction of two aircraft carriers, one heavy cruiser and six destroyers in addition to the losses previously reported officially. The latest official tabulation, however, stood at eleven Japanese ships sunk and six damaged.]

United Nations losses were said to have been "comparatively light."

[The remnants of the battered Japanese force were said to be fleeing northward with United States and British naval units in hot pursuit, The Associated Press reported from United Nations Headquarters.]

MacArthur Praises Forces

General MacArthur, in issuing the most cheering news for the democracies since he arrived in Australia from Bataan on March 17 to assume supreme command of the Southwest Pacific area, paid high tribute to the men who had fought the mightiest sea battle of the war.

"They handled themselves with marked skill and fought with admirable courage and tenacity," the communiqué said.

The communiqué began with the news that the battle had "temporarily ceased." Then it went on to tell how the Japanese move had represented continued efforts to extend enemy "aggressive conquests" toward the south and southeast. That phrase strengthened the belief that the Japanese might have been aiming at the Free French island of New Caledonia, garrisoned by United States troops and lying athwart the supply line east of Australia, or that they might even have contemplated invading Australia.

The Japanese, the communiqué said, made their first efforts for the new aggression by seeking to expand their air bases along the arc of "invasion islands" along the fringe of Northern Australia.

Foe's Plans Disrupted

"But our air force consistently and effectively attacked Japanese air fields during the past six weeks, dislocating Japanese plans through destruction of installations and aircraft," the communiqué declared.

United States Flying Fortresses and other bombers played a major part in that part of the campaign, blasting Japanese bases day after day at Rabaul, on New Britain Island, and at Lae and Salamaua, on New Guinea.

United Nations reconnaissance planes, swooping low over the Japanese-held bases to the north, "revealed a gradual building up of Japanese naval and transport elements for a coordinated attack by combined forces, which was initiated several days ago," the communiqué said, adding that "our naval forces then attacked in interception."

A part of the Japanese fleet was

Continued on Page Two

Tim Holt and Agnes Moorehead starred in Orson Welles' *The Magnificent Ambersons.*

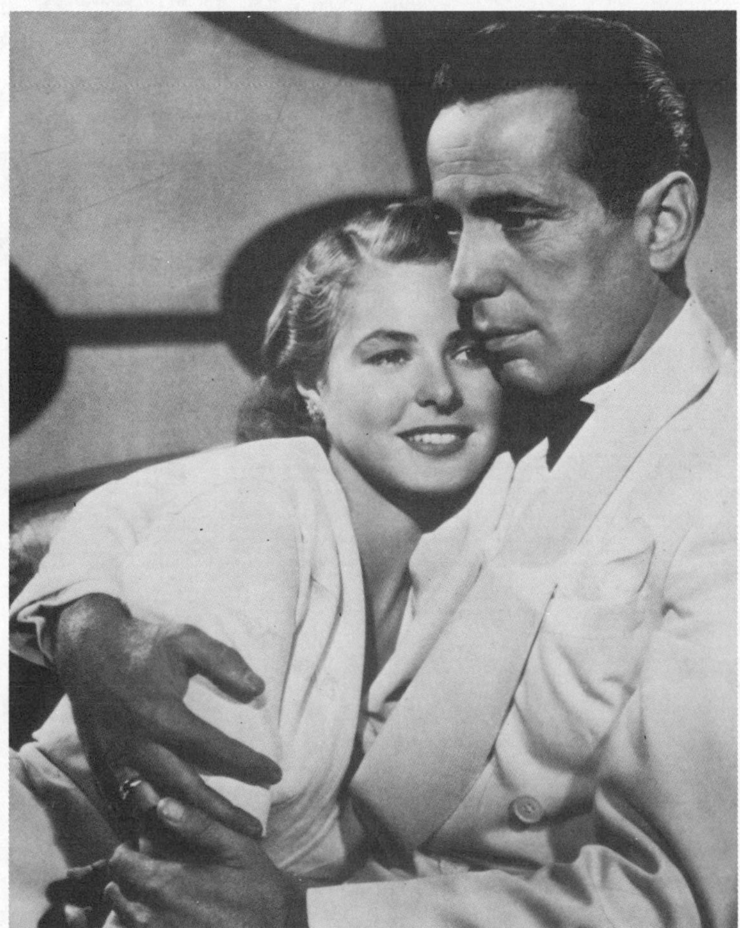

The stars of the film classic, *Casablanca:* Humphrey Bogart and Ingrid Bergman.

Mrs. Miniver starred Greer Garson.

"All the News That's Fit to Print."

The New York Times.

LATE CITY EDITION
Moderate temperature today.
Temperatures Yesterday—Max., 80; Min., 63

Copyright, 1942, by The New York Times Company.

VOL. XCI..No. 30,809. Entered as Second-Class Matter, Postoffice, New York, N. Y. NEW YORK, MONDAY, JUNE 1, 1942. THREE CENTS NEW YORK CITY and Vicinity

1,000 BRITISH BOMBERS SET COLOGNE ON FIRE; USE 3,000 TONS OF EXPLOSIVES IN RECORD RAID; GERMANS ARE HURLED BACK IN BID FOR TOBRUK

NEAR 'MIRACULOUS,' IS MAYOR'S RETORT TO ARMY ON DIMOUT

'Good Job Is Being Done,' He Insists, Taking Issue With Report of Air Survey

HE INVITES AN INSPECTION

Westchester, Other Sections Say They Are Observing Regulations Strictly

Great progress has been made in dimming out the lights of New York City, Mayor La Guardia declared yesterday in his weekly radio broadcast over WNYC, the municipal radio station. He maintained that considering the extent and population of the city and its normal illumination the success of the dimout "borders on the miraculous."

Mayor La Guardia took issue with the report released Saturday by Major Gen. T. A. Terry, commanding the Second Corps Area, which characterized the observance of dimout regulations throughout the metropolitan area as "in general disappointing." He stoutly maintained that the dimout "has been very successful" and he invited an inspection of Broadway or any other thoroughfare of the city.

"Oh yes, I read the papers this morning," the Mayor said. "I read the report and I am quite certain that Major Gen. Terry regrets the characterization and the description in that report as much as I do. I say I am sure that Major Gen. Terry regrets it, because he told me so this morning."

Says "Good Job Is Being Done"

Mayor La Guardia contended that "if you will strip the report of its characterizations and descriptions, using diamonds very profusely, it will be seen that a good job is being done."

The Mayor announced that arrangements had been made to dim-out the Lewisohn Stadium at City College for the usual Summer season of symphony concerts and that the series would start this year on June 17.

When General Terry was informed of the Mayor's remarks about the Army report, he merely said:

"The city, so far as I know, is cooperating splendidly in the dim-out effort, but it is a big job and it has quite a way to go."

Persons familiar with General Terry's struggle to reduce the sky glow over the metropolitan area explained that the report was meant to be helpful and not to be critical, and that the difference between the general and the Mayor was simply a difference of opinion as to literary style. The Mayor did not like the way the report was written, they said, but the general did. They denied that the general had expressed regret at the language of the report; they said he had merely expressed regret that the Mayor didn't like it.

Colonel Frederick L. Devereux, chief director of civilian protection of Westchester County, made a personal inspection yesterday to make sure that Westchester communities obeyed the blackout regu-

Continued on Page Eight

If in Doubt, Put It Out

Army officials are still perturbed over many "flagrant" instances of non-compliance with the dimout regulations and are continuing their efforts to educate citizens to the vital importance of extinguishing all unnecessary lights and shielding all those that are necessary.

Pointing out that the massed effect of countless thousands of lights in New York City and its surrounding area is to create a sky glow that silhouettes ships for enemy submarines far at sea, they are endeavoring to drive home to the public the slogan of the Second Corps Area: "If in doubt, put it out."

Swedish Ship Brings 908 From War Zone

The Swedish-American liner Drottningholm, bringing 908 citizens of the United States and other American republics from the war zones in Europe, arrived in the Narrows at 7 o'clock last evening and anchored to wait until this morning. According to the Navy Department, she will dock at 8 A. M. today at Pier F, Jersey City.

Her passenger list includes many diplomats and consular officials with their families, war correspondents from Africa, Egypt, Italy and other countries in Europe and the East.

G. Hilmer Lundbeck, managing director of the Swedish-American Line, who will meet the Drottningholm at the pier, said the ship would leave again on June 3 or 4 for Lisbon and make a return trip to New York bringing back more American citizens.

DECEPTION IS LAID TO STANDARD OIL

Arnold in New Complaint Says Firm Misled Senators on Buna Rubber and Plane Gasoline

By C. P. TRUSSELL

Special to The New York Times.

WASHINGTON, May 31—The Standard Oil Company of New Jersey "covered up" and "distorted facts" in its rebuttal to charges that the company's cartel arrangement with I. G. Farbenindustrie of Germany had hampered the development of synthetic rubber in the United States, Thurman Arnold, assistant attorney general, asserted today.

The head of the Anti-Trust Division of the Department of Justice accused the company of similar misrepresentations about the effect of the cartel on aviation gasoline for the United States and about the company's sale of gasoline to Axis airlines and negotiations with Matsui, a Japanese firm, before the war.

Mr. Arnold will present tomor-

Continued on Page Seven

NAZIS HELD IN LIBYA

British Hammer Enemy by Land and Air With Hint at Offensive

R. A. F. RAIDS FURIOUS

Rommel Force Reported in Trap Facing Flight or Annihilation

By JOSEPH M. LEVY

Wireless to The New York Times.

WITH BRITISH FORCES in the Western Desert, May 31—After four days of miscalculated Blitzkrieg, Field Marshal Erwin Rommel and his Axis armored forces, together with reinforcements that he had rushed through gaps forced in mine fields in a vain effort to solve his supply problem, were making a last attempt today to achieve their original objective—Tobruk.

As the British Eighth Army continued to batter the enemy in the fighting in Eastern Libya, it seemed most probable that the British commander, Lieut. Gen. Neil Methuen Ritchie, would turn from the defensive to the offensive.

Credit for the decisive turn in the battle goes jointly to the Royal Air Force, which cut the German supply columns to pieces, and to the British armored forces, which, with the help of United States-built tanks, attacked the Axis armored elements.

Enemy Gets Panicky

Although the German moves, in the main, were orderly, around Harmat, about eighteen miles northeast of Bir Hacheim, the Nazis were so bewildered that they destroyed or abandoned thirty-five of their own tanks, while at a few other points they showed similar signs of nervousness.

Magnificent fighting by the British and the Free French, coupled with the ceaseless attacks by the R. A. F. that previously had blocked the German bid for Tobruk, turned the enemy westward. Thus, for all their efforts the Ger-

Continued on Page Seven

War News Summarized

MONDAY, JUNE 1, 1942

Britain's Air Force subjected Cologne, Germany's third city, early yesterday to the heaviest single air raid ever undertaken, while the situation on the world battle fronts changed little, though there was heavy fighting in Libya.

A thousand or more bombers participated in the great raid on Cologne and in all 1,250 planes took part in the operation. Some 3,000 tons of bombs were dropped on the city in ninety minutes, according to the British, and returning pilots said they had seen a cloud of smoke 15,000 feet high rising above Cologne. The smoke remained visible as far as the Netherland coast, 135 miles away. Forty-four British planes failed to return. [1:8; map, P. 2.]

Pilots who gave a more detailed picture of the raid said that they had left Cologne a sea of flame. One of the returning pilots said that seven-eighths of Cologne had been set afire. [1:7.]

The great assault involved elaborate planning. At least thirteen different types of planes were used. They took off from sixty different airfields and had to go in over the objective at six-second intervals. [1:6.]

The German High Command granted that the British had done "great damage" to Cologne in the "terror raid," but alleged that it was mostly in residential sections. German broadcasts also claimed that only seventy British planes had taken part and that the figure given by the British was fantastic. [3:1.]

The Prague radio announced that eighteen more Czechs had been executed, raising to eighty-one the total since the attack on Reinhard Heydrich, the notorious deputy chief of the Gestapo. Herr Heydrich was believed to be near death. [4:1.]

Vichy reported that two policemen had been killed and three others wounded in a food riot in Paris. [1:5.]

British forces in Libya were battering at the Axis troops making a last attempt to get at their objective, Tobruk. The battle appeared to have taken a decisive turn in favor of the British. [1:3; map, P. 7.]

The Russians claimed to have taken important enemy lines on the Kalinin front northwest of Moscow. Only local encounters were reported from the Kharkov front. [1:4.]

United Nations Headquarters, Australia, announced that three Japanese midget submarines probably had been destroyed during a wholly unsuccessful Japanese mass submarine attack on Sydney harbor. [1:5-6.]

Chungking announced attacks on eight Japanese positions in Anhwei Province some 200 miles west of Shanghai. The Japanese were making a new landing on the coast of Chekiang Province and pressing their attack in that region. [6:3-4.] The Chinese military attaché at Washington urged the United Nations to strike quickly at Japan from air bases in the Chinese coastal region now threatened by the Japanese. [6:2.]

The United States Navy released the news of the sinking of three United States merchant vessels in the Caribbean and one Norwegian vessel in the Gulf of Mexico. [6:7.]

TEA AFTER THE GREATEST AIR RAID IN HISTORY

A warming cup from an American-donated canteen is welcomed by Canadian bombers

Associated Press Radiophoto, passed yesterday by British censor

NAZIS' LINES SEIZED IN KALININ FIGHTING

Red Army Takes the Initiative After Repelling Heavy Blows —Izyum Barrier Holds

By RALPH PARKER

Wireless to The New York Times.

MOSCOW, May 31—While fighting on the Kharkov front subsides, action on other fronts is characterized by reconnaissance in considerable force by both sides. This reconnaissance, when challenged by one side or the other, leads to sharp and bitter fighting.

Action of this sort has developed on the largest scale on what the Russians still call the Kalinin front, although Red Army troops are fighting far from the city of Kalinin itself. Kalinin Province is large, stretching from the Latvian border to a point east of Moscow.

The army newspaper Red Star reports that several days ago the Germans showed considerable activity in several sectors of this front, starting frequent attacks after having accumulated heavy forces. The failure of these local attacks seems to have discouraged them from persisting and their activities have decreased. But in several areas the Russians now have taken the initiative and have captured lines described as highly favorable for future action.

[A Russian communiqué said, according to The Associated Press, that Soviet forces had seized important lines after three days spent in repulsing German counter-attacks. The Germans left 1,100 dead or wounded on the field, it was added.]

Von Leeb Forces Routed

It also is reported that two battalions of the German 254th Division, which is part of General Field Marshal Wilhelm Ritter von Leeb's army on the Leningrad front, were routed in an attempt to advance through swampy country. Russian artillery checked German tanks using a road, but German flanking movements through swamps made some progress until the enemy forces were trapped. The Germans fled after severe hand-to-hand fighting with Russian grenadiers. The Russians are constantly improving their positions on this front, Red Star says.

On the Kharkov front the Russian river barrier in the Izyum-Barvenkova sector, southeast of Kharkov, was firmly held against new German attempts to cross it. Reports reaching Moscow from the

Continued on Page Five

3 Midget Submarines Raid Sydney; All Believed Sunk

By The United Press.

MELBOURNE, Australia, Monday, June 1—Three Japanese midget submarines penetrated the great harbor at Sydney, Australia's largest city, last night, but they were believed to have been destroyed after they had damaged one small vessel, it was announced today.

The raid, first threat to this part of Australia, was thought to indicate the presence of at least a small Japanese naval force off the southeastern—and most populous—section of the country. Midget submarines, which have only a short range, operate from a mother ship and it was felt that such a vessel hardly would travel unescorted.

The first submarine was sighted moving slowly along the main harbor channel, its periscope and upper conning tower exposed. It passed close to a harbor ferry loaded with passengers. Depth charges, released by naval vessels soon afterward, rocked waterfront buildings, and gunfire echoed across the harbor.

Announcement of the raid by the two-man submarines—of the type used in the attack on Pearl Harbor last Dec. 7—was made in a special communiqué issued by General Douglas MacArthur's headquarters.

"The enemy's attack was completely unsuccessful," the communiqué said. "Damage was confined to one small harbor vessel of no military value."

One of the submarines was believed to have been destroyed by

Continued on Page Six

2 POLICEMEN SLAIN IN PARIS FOOD RIOT

More Wounded in Bitter Clash —Gang Raids Shop, Throws Goods to Waiting Queue

By LANSING WARREN

By Telephone to The New York Times.

VICHY, France, May 31—Crowds mobbed a food store in Paris today and in the clash that followed two policemen were killed and three wounded. A considerable number of other persons were injured.

The trouble started when persons inside the store began looting supplies and throwing foodstuffs and canned goods from the windows to those who were waiting in the food lines outside. The police were called and met with armed resistance from the rioters.

Arrests were made after the riot, showing, according to the police, that the incident had been organized by "Communist agitators." Those accused will be brought before the special court-martial.

The store where the clash took place is located on the left bank of the river, on the Rue de Seine.

In another quarter of Paris youths of a political organization during the night overturned the statue of Edward VII. The statue to the founder of the Entente Cordiale was located in the small

Continued on Page Four

FINE TIMING USED IN R. A. F. ASSAULT

Coordination at Home Fields Sends a Plane Over Reich City Every 6 Seconds

Wireless to The New York Times.

LONDON, May 31—A vast amount of intricate planning and preparation preceded last night's attack on Cologne by more than 1,000 bombers. The operation, the first in which all Royal Air Force commands were concerned in one night's activity, called for perfect timing and perfect coordination. At least thirteen different types of aircraft were used—the greatest assortment ever engaged together.

More than 1,000 bombers had to be got into the air from scores of fields in a very short space of time at exactly regulated intervals. Each plane had to have a bomb load appropriate to its type and suitable for the part it was to play in the great raid.

The nicest timing was required of the "intruder" squadrons, whose task it was to keep German fighters busy while the bombers slipped through the defenses and attacked the objectives. Another bit of fine timing was required to arrange the bombers' arrival so that they would be coming in from all direc-

Continued on Page Three

COLOGNE 'INFERNO' ASTONISHES PILOTS

Defenses Overwhelmed, British Fliers Say—Germans on Air Describe Horrors

By The United Press.

LONDON, May 31—Seven-eighths of Cologne, a city the size of Boston, was in flames, an inferno "almost too gigantic to be real," when the history-making raid was over last night, pilots who took part in it said tonight.

"When we got there, I almost felt like leaving and trying to find another target. It didn't seem possible to do more damage than had already been done," Wing Commander Johnny Fauquier, Canadian pilot officer, related.

"Cologne was just a sea of flames," said Squadron Leader Len Frazer of Winnipeg, one of the more than 1,000 Canadian airmen who had a hand in the epic raid.

"I saw London burning during the Battle of Britain, and it was nothing compared with Cologne," Pilot Officer H. J. M. Lacelle of Toronto, gunner in the tail of a Canadian bomber, contributed.

Their reports were typical of the thousands being sifted tonight and compiled into a record of the mightiest piece of destruction ever devised by man.

Defenses Overwhelmed

The lurid sky over Cologne for ninety minutes was as busy as Piccadilly Circus as the great Lancasters and Halifaxes, Stirlings and Manchesters, streaked in at the rate of one every six seconds to unload their total cargo of steel-cased death.

Before the overwhelmed and bewildered German defenses could focus on one plane, it was zooming away and another was on its tail. The Royal Air Force plan of supersaturating the enemy's target field was described as an absolute success. German fighter planes were there, but not enough to interfere seriously with the attack.

"It was almost too gigantic to be real," said the pilot of one Halifax. "But it was real enough when we got there. Below us in every part of the city buildings were ablaze. Here and there you could see their outlines, but mostly it was just one long stretch of fire.

"It was strange to see the flames reflected on our aircraft. It looked at times as if we were on fire ourselves, with the red glow dancing up and down our wings."

"I could identify every type of

Continued on Page Three

A 90-MINUTE RAID

R. A. F. Causes Havoc in the Rhine City—Nazis Admit 'Great Damage'

COST IS 44 PLANES

250 Extra Aircraft Hit Foe's Bases—Attack a Start, Says Churchill

By RAYMOND DANIELL

Wireless to The New York Times.

LONDON, Monday, June 1—More than 1,000 British bombers dumped 3,000 tons of high explosive bombs Saturday night on Cologne and elsewhere in the Rhineland and in the Ruhr.

"Cologne was the main objective," the Air Ministry said, and British officials asserted the raid was the biggest air attack in the history of warfare.

Prime Minister Winston Churchill, congratulating Air Marshal A. T. Harris, chief of the Bomber Command of the Royal Air Force, who planned and directed the devastating attack on one of Germany's largest and industrially most important cities, described it as "a herald of what Germany will receive city by city from now on."

Losses Relatively Slight

It was indeed the heaviest blow the R. A. F. has delivered yet in its promised air offensive against the Nazis, and it will not be long now before the American Air Force joins the British. The shadow that two years ago was no bigger than a man's hand has grown to a huge cloud threatening the whole Reich.

Forty-four British planes failed to return to their bases from the Saturday night operations, which included heavy attacks on Nazi coastal bases and airfields and fighter action against enemy interception.

This was the largest number of planes the British have ever lost in one raid, but it was still little more than 4 per cent of all the planes that were used.

That the losses for an assault upon a German city defended, as Cologne was, by 120 searchlights and at least 500 anti-aircraft guns and big Nazi night fighter forces, were not heavier was due largely to new tactics used by the R. A. F.

Tactics Counter Nazi Defenses

The bombers went in over their target at the rate of one every six seconds to distract and confuse the searchlight operators and the German gun crews and prevent their concentrating long on any single plane.

At the same time at least 250 other planes were drawn from every command of the R. A. F. and swarmed over the Nazi airports, from which enemy fighters might have been drawn to intercept the Cologne attackers.

[The Germans claimed to have shot down forty-seven British planes, thirty-six over Cologne and eleven near the coast. Berlin, while reporting "great damage" at Cologne, tried to discount the size of the raid by saying only seventy R. A. F. bombers were over the city. At the same time, Nazi officials talked of "reprisals."

[British bombers were over Western Germany again last night, according to a Berlin broadcast recorded by The Associated Press early today.]

Offensive Goes on During Day

Saturday night's supreme effort by no means exhausted the R. A. F. In daylight yesterday British fighters made several sweeps over Nazi-occupied France and Belgium. They shot down four Nazi fighters and lost eight of their own planes.

Off the Netherland coast British planes set afire and sunk a German armed trawler and two other vessels were driven aground, ac-

Continued on Page Two

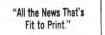

"All the News That's Fit to Print."

NEWS INDEX, PAGE 43, THIS SECTION

The New York Times.

Copyright, 1942, by The New York Times Company.

LATE CITY EDITION
Warm followed by thunder showers in the early evening today.
Temperatures Yesterday—Max., 81; Min., 67

Section 1

VOL. XCI. No. 30,815. Entered as Second-Class Matter, Postoffice, New York, N. Y. NEW YORK, SUNDAY, JUNE 7, 1942. Including Magazine and Book Sections. TEN CENTS New York City and Vicinity

2, PERHAPS 3, JAPANESE CARRIERS SUNK WITH ALL THEIR PLANES, NIMITZ REPORTS; 3 BATTLESHIPS, 8 OTHER WARSHIPS DAMAGED

1,000 AIDES OF OPA FIND BOOTLEGGING OF 'GAS' WIDESPREAD

Women After a Tour Report Sales by Many Stations Without Punching Cards

VISITS MADE TO 5,000 HERE

Philadelphia and Newark Also Covered—Violators Face Ban on Supplies

Hundreds of filling stations throughout the New York City, Newark and Philadelphia metropolitan areas were caught selling gasoline to motorists without ration cards yesterday in the first large-scale enforcement round-up by the Office of Price Administration.

One thousand volunteer investigators, many of them women members of nationally and internationally known patriotic service organizations, who had been carefully coached for their task by OPA lawyers, were mobilized for the survey.

Some women who were instructed to report to local OPA headquarters in the Empire State Building at 9:30 A. M. said they had no inkling of their mission. They said they only knew that they had been asked not to wear uniforms and to remove any stickers or other marks of identification from their cars. One young woman was reported to have objected to her task but had gone through with it.

Mobilized for what Walter Gellhorn, local regional attorney for the OPA, described as "the first large-scale use of a civilian auxiliary staff by OPA in connection with its enforcement work," the investigators in a few hours' tour found widespread violations.

Result Here Is Withheld

While Mr. Gellhorn would venture no estimate of the percentage of violations in the New York City area, the Philadelphia round-up revealed 13 violations out of 103 filling stations visited. Some 5,000 stations were covered in the New York investigation and if the same proportion prevails, the OPA offices will be swamped by filling station operators responding to appearance notices they will begin to receive tomorrow.

Over the week-end an analysis of the reports of the investigators is being made to determine the filling-station operators who will be required to appear. Those found guilty face suspension of deliveries for thirty days or longer.

Shortly before Mr. Gellhorn announced the preliminary results of the investigation, the Red Cross in New York explained that any of its members who might have taken part did so merely as individuals acting of their own volition.

"Acting with the concurrence of

Continued on Page Thirty

If in Doubt, Put It Out

The dimout is improving, but it still is not rigorous enough to prevent the sky glow that silhouettes ships along the coast and makes them easy targets for lurking submarines.

Civilian lighting experts cooperating with Army officials of the Second Corps Area repeated to the Army yesterday their statement that a glow from the land need be only two and one-half times as bright as the normal glow over the sea to silhouette a ship.

So far, Army officials pointed out, the best test made has revealed a ten-to-one glow, and, even since the dimout, on some occasions the glow from the shore has measured 100 times brighter than the sea glow.

Accordingly, Major Gen. T. A. Terry's headquarters repeated for civilian benefit the slogan of the Second Corps Area: "If in doubt, put it out."

Major Sports Results

HORSE RACING

Mrs. Payne Whitney's Shut Out, winner of the Kentucky Derby, again defeated Alsab in the seventy-fourth running of the Belmont Stakes yesterday. The 2-to-5 favorite was beaten by three lengths at the end of the mile and a half. A crowd of 29,812 saw the Belmont Park program, from which war relief benefited by an estimated $130,000.

BASEBALL

Pitcher Red Ruffing scored his 250th major league victory when the Yankees downed the Indians, 3-0. Joe Gordon drove in all the runs with a first-inning double. The Dodgers defeated the Cubs, 2-0, Curt Davis gaining his eighth pitching success of the campaign.

TRACK AND FIELD

Don Burnham of Dartmouth beat Leslie MacMitchell by inches in the mile run at the Metropolitan A. A. U. games. Greg Rice broke the American record for three miles.

GOLF

Mike Turnesa and Willie Goggin, with 209s, tied for first in the metropolitan qualifying round for the Hale America tourney. Mrs. Reinert Torgerson beat Mrs. Charles Whitehead, 4 and 2, in the women's metropolitan final.

(Complete Details in Section 5.)

ACCUSES AGENCIES OF DRAFT ABUSES

Tydings Asks Restudy of the Deferment of One Thousand Government Workers

Special to THE NEW YORK TIMES.

WASHINGTON, June 6—Charging abuses by some government agencies of their privilege of obtaining draft deferments for essential officials and employes, the Tydings committee, investigating conditions within the executive branch, will call upon the Selective Service System to restudy the cases of about 1,000 Federal workers under 25 years of age who have been excused from call to military duty.

This would mean a re-checking on one out of every six deferments granted to date outside the War and Navy Departments.

Senator Tydings said the committee will recommend that re-examinations be made, especially in the cases of three men 21 years of age, forty-two in the 21-year age group, 162 who are 22 and 228 who are 23.

"The committee, the Senator added, was considering a resurvey of the departments and agencies and the holding of public hearings on deferment cases, in order that the people may learn just how a young man of 21 years of age can become so expert as to be deferred from the draft because a major govern-

Continued on Page Thirty-four

GOVERNORSHIP PACT IS HINTED AS FARLEY VISITS WHITE HOUSE

President Said to Be Receptive to Bennett Nomination if State Party Wants It

VARIOUS NAMES DISCUSSED

State Chairman Noncommittal After Conference—Fish Is a 'Casual' Subject

By FRANK L. KLUCKHOHN
Special to THE NEW YORK TIMES.

WASHINGTON, June 6—An agreement with regard to the New York Governorship race was said to have been reached today by President Roosevelt and James A. Farley, State Democratic chairman and former Postmaster General, at a White House luncheon conference.

While Mr. Farley would only say on leaving that John J. Bennett Jr., State Attorney General, and a number of others were discussed, it was reported in political circles here that the President would not oppose Mr. Bennett's nomination for Governor if it appeared that the State organization wanted him. It had been reported that Mr. Farley favored Mr. Bennett's nomination, but that the President was opposed to it.

It was the first personal meeting between the President and Mr. Farley since April, 1941, and Mr. Farley told reporters that "we had a nice chat about a lot of things."

Survey of Views Reported

Reports in political circles here had been to the effect that some weeks ago the President sounded New York Democratic politicians on the question of the candidate to succeed Governor Herbert Lehman, who has announced that he will not run for another term and is slated to accept a high Federal post. According to these reports, Mr. Roosevelt was surprised to find that many organization leaders already were pledged to Mr. Bennett and decided then to confer with Mr. Farley.

As Mr. Farley left the White House he was asked:

"Did Mr. Bennett's name come up?"

"Yes, Mr. Bennett's name was mentioned and a number of other names were discussed," Mr. Farley answered.

"As chairman of the State committee," he added, "I don't think it would be good judgment to talk about individuals. I am satisfied there will be no difficulty so far as the Democratic nominee in New York State is concerned and that the Democratic nominee will be the next Governor."

Mr. Farley said that the name of Hamilton Fish had come up in a casual way at the conference, but denied that the projected plan

Continued on Page Thirty-seven

City Honors 15 British, U. S. Heroes With Parade and Rally Tomorrow

Fighting men right from British and American fronts, heroes of the sweeping raids of the R. A. F. over Germany, of Pearl Harbor, the Philippines, and naval combat in the Java Sea, of Commando raids on Norway and occupied France and air operations over Libya will be hailed by New York City tomorrow.

New York's welcome to the fifteen war heroes will start with their landing at Battery Park at 11:30 A. M., and include a parade up Broadway, a reception at City Hall by Mayor La Guardia and many notables, a parade up Seventh Avenue and outdoor appearance at the Duffy Statue in Times Square, Forty-seventh Street and Broadway, and a great evening mass meeting at Madison Square Garden, at which each of the fighting men will tell the story of his experiences. There will be no charge for the Madison Square Garden rally.

The names of the ten British and five American fliers, naval officers and Commandos were made public yesterday with brief descriptions of their acts of heroism.

After two days in New York City they will go as a group on a tour of twenty other cities. The tour is sponsored by the Treasury Department and expenses in the various cities will be paid by local committees of citizens. The war activities committee of the motion-picture industry is in charge of arrangements here.

The men will arrive at the Battery in three patrol boats that will bring them from the seaplane base

Continued on Page Thirty-four

U. S. and Britain Get All Dutch Shipping

By The United Press.

LONDON, June 6—All ships under the Netherland flag were requisitioned today for the United States and Britain. The ships will be held under charter to the British War Transport Ministry until six months after the war.

Netherland officials emphasized that the action did not mean that the government had taken ownership of the fleet, but merely would control its use until after the war, when the ships would be returned to their owners.

Before the fall of Java the Netherland merchant fleet totaled about 2,750,000 tons and it is believed that most of the fleet still is afloat. Last March Britain and the United States already were operating 1,250,000 tons of it. This would mean that the new decree, effective as of June 1, would place about 1,500,000 additional tons at the disposal of the two governments.

HULL WARNS FINNS ON HELPING HITLER

Hints We May Declare War if Fight Against Soviet Widens —Nazis Massing in North

Special to THE NEW YORK TIMES.

WASHINGTON, June 6—Secretary of State Cordell Hull said today that the United States was watching closely to ascertain whether the personal visit of Adolf Hitler to Finland would lead to a greater degree of Finnish cooperation against the United Nations. This was widely interpreted in diplomatic circles to imply that this country was prepared to declare war against Finland if that Baltic country took further military steps against Soviet Russia.

Congress, acting upon the request of President Roosevelt, this week approved declarations of war against Hungary, Bulgaria and Rumania. These three countries had declared war first on the United States, while Finland has not. Britain is at war with Finland and a United States declaration might affect Finland's post-war status.

Hitler Called Desperate

Mr. Hull emphasized, in a statement given out in reply to inquiries, according to the State Department, that the Reichsfuehrer's visit constituted a "desperate attempt" to induce Finland to make further contributions to the Axis military campaign.

Reports from Stockholm indicated that reinforcements of German planes, troops and supplies were moving up to the Finnish front on the Karelian Isthmus north of Leningrad and along the frontier north of Lake Ladoga.

[Stockholm dispatches said advices from Helsinki predicted an Axis offensive against Leningrad and the Murmansk railroad within forty-eight hours, according to The United Press. The Moscow radio announced that ten German vessels, nine of them transports, had been sunk by Soviet bombers in attacks on three convoys and a Nazi naval base in the Baltic area.]

A Finnish spokesman said yesterday that his country would follow "an independent course," and the Secretary of State asserted that this meant the Finns were "balking" at Herr Hitler's pressure. Because of traditional Finnish-American friendship and because Russia had invaded Finland before the current struggle, this government has been loath to break off diplomatic relations or go to war with Finland.

Mr. Hull's statement, which some diplomats thought fitted in with Soviet-American negotiations in Washington, follows:

The Secretary of State, in reply to inquiries from the press

Continued on Page Five

AXIS IN LIBYA HIT

British Attack Salient Held by Foe and Dent Nazi Line

HEAVY FIGHTING ON

South Africans' Sortie in El Gazala Region Takes Prisoners

By JOSEPH M. LEVY
Special Cable to THE NEW YORK TIMES.

CAIRO, Egypt, June 6—Attacking at night, perhaps to avoid the blistering heat of the desert by day, British and Indian infantry supported by tanks moved forward in Libya late Thursday and early yesterday against the German salient west of Knightsbridge and succeeded in denting the German defenses.

The Germans resisted vigorously, however, and heavy fighting continued all day yesterday and was still going on.

Armored forces are again bearing the brunt of the battle, which is so fluid and changing in character that it is difficult to assess positive results. It is clear, nevertheless, that German forces remain east of the British mine fields that stretch from El Gazala to Bir Hacheim.

British Score Advances

During the night attack British forces knifed from the north on the right flank of the German advanced positions. Although the British did not succeed in clipping off that Nazi spearhead they made definite advances. The Allied stroke stirred up the entire area, which had been comparatively quiet during several days of sandstorms, and precipitated fighting on a scale not seen since the first days of the Axis offensive.

On the northern sector South African forces operating from El Gazala attacked Italian-held strong points and took about 150 prisoners.

In the south, around Bir Hacheim, the enemy was inactive, apparently having had, for the time

Continued on Page Ten

British Pictures of Cologne Show 8 Square Miles Razed

Cameras Reveal Six Great Gaps Defining Stricken Zones—Industrial Plants Hit Are Named—Cathedral Intact

By RAYMOND DANIELL
Special Cable to THE NEW YORK TIMES.

LONDON, June 6—Flying cameras of the Royal Air Force have brought back indisputable proof that the May 30 raid by more than 1,000 British bombers wrecked at least 5,000 acres, or about eight square miles, of Cologne.

It is only by comparing the latest photographs with earlier ones that the damage done in the raid a week ago can be distinguished from that of the 106 raids that preceded it, but with the aid of experts it is possible to pick out sections where even the efficient Nazis have not had time to tidy up the wreckage.

It was not until yesterday—six days after the crippling ninety-minute raid on the Reich's third largest city—that reconnaissance planes were able to get clear pictures of the ancient Rhenish cathedral city because until then smoke and clouds obscured the ground. Even then it was necessary to take great risks and to fly very low to get those which the writer saw today showing the famous old cathedral near the railroad station apparently intact among acres of destruction. Patches on the prints showed where fires were still smoldering.

It takes experts to interpret what the camera records and their examination is not complete and probably will not be until after the week-end. However, a preliminary examination convinced them that in addition to isolated points, the damage caused by the thousands of tons of explosives and incendiaries dropped created six great gaps, one of which stretches to within 100 yards of the famous cathedral.

There are three big areas due

Continued on Page Twenty-two

R. A. F. Bombs Ruhr Centers; Pounds at Nazis in France

By JAMES MacDONALD
Special Cable to THE NEW YORK TIMES.

LONDON, June 6—Rounding out a week of steady, large-scale attacks by the Royal Air Force on Germany and German-occupied territory, a strong force of British bombers unloaded a thunderous weight of explosives on industrial centers of the Ruhr Valley last night. Just after dawn "many squadrons" of R. A. F. fighters and bombers took up great offensive sweeps over Northern France that continued through the day, the Air Ministry reported.

Hundreds of British planes were engaged on the daylight attacks. They were chiefly concentrated in bombing and shooting up Nazi transportation lines, encampments and air bases in the area around Havre, Abbeville and Berck and on the Cherbourg Peninsula.

[Another R. A. F. attack on Nazi positions in the Boulogne-Cap Gris Nez area was made early today, while British coastal guns fired across the Channel,

Continued on Page Twenty-one

GESTAPO'S INQUIRY STRANGELY EASED

Writer Believes an Influential German Curbed the Secret Police in Berlin Prison

The following is the fifth of a series of articles by a correspondent of THE NEW YORK TIMES who was captured in Libya six months ago and has just returned to this country.

By HAROLD DENNY

There was something very peculiar about my treatment by the Gestapo, which I do not understand to this day. The fact that the Gestapo sent fairly important officials to escort me from the Italian border to Berlin and the fact that I was lodged in the de luxe prison in central Gestapo headquarters would imply that they considered me an important prisoner.

The nature of their questions indicated that I had deeply offended the Nazi regime by some of my writings and that they were, or at least had been, considering bringing serious charges against me. I felt during much of my imprisonment in Berlin that I was in great danger.

After my liberation, just before leaving Europe for the United States, I learned from a diplomatic acquaintance who had confidential information that I had been lucky to escape with my life. All this sounds melodramatic, but in rampant dictatorships things happen to ordinary people that make the fancies of an E. Phillips Oppenheim seem pallid.

Yet I was treated throughout with meticulous courtesy. My examiners, for instance, never omitted the "Mister" in addressing me, even when they were driving the hardest. And at one point, on the most trying day of questioning, they really had me on the ropes, and they must have known it. Yet at that very point they slackened their attack and neglected to press home their advantage.

I left that exhausting session feeling that some influential person had intervened in my behalf.

Continued on Page Thirty-five

War News Summarized

SUNDAY, JUNE 7, 1942

Exactly six months after her attack on Hawaii, Japan found herself threatened today with a great naval disaster as the hard-hit task force that had been sent to Midway Island waters attempted to escape from United States naval and air forces. In general the Axis was not doing too well, and Marshal Rommel was apparently in increasing difficulties in Libya.

Admiral Nimitz reported that two and perhaps three Japanese carriers had been sunk with all their planes in the battle west of Midway. One or two additional carriers were damaged. Also damaged were three battleships, one seriously; four cruisers, two of them seriously, and three transports. Admiral Nimitz said the battle was continuing. [1:8; map, P. 2.]

Chinese reports from the Chekiang front claimed that the Japanese attack on Chuhsien had been repulsed once again. The Japanese reported that the city had fallen. There was hard fighting on various other fronts in China. [3:2-3.]

From Australia came the announcement that United Nations planes had sunk two more Japanese submarines in the Southwestern Pacific, raising to seven the week's toll of enemy undersea raiders there. [2:2.]

Moscow announced that nine German transports and at least one other vessel had been sunk by Soviet bombers of the Baltic Fleet. The Germans were believed to be reinforcing the northern fronts through the Baltic. Activity on the main battle fronts was limited, but the Germans reported heavy artillery and air bombardment of Sevastopol in the Crimea. [4:1.]

Britain's Eighth Army in Libya, making use of its aerial superiority, ended the lull in the desert battle by launching a drive that dented the German positions west of Knightsbridge. [1:5; map, P. 10.]

On the European air front the British, after a night assault on the Ruhr, the third of the week, made a heavy daylight sweep over Northern France that was followed by a night attack on the French Channel coast. [1:6-7.]

Aerial photographs of Cologne taken six days after the 1,000-plane raid there revealed that eight square miles of the city had been wrecked, and that at least three important industrial plants had been practically destroyed. [1:6-7; map, P. 22.]

In an address in England, Ambassador Winant of the United States called for a great offensive against poverty and social evils after the war to prevent a reappearance of such systems as fascism. [17:2.]

Secretary of State Hull said that Adolf Hitler's visit to Finland had been a "desperate attempt" to win closer Finnish-German cooperation. If this should result, it was believed in Washington, the United States might declare war on Finland. [1:4.]

SEA FIGHT GOES ON

Momentous U. S. Victory in Midway Battle Is in View, Admiral Says

4 CRUISERS ARE HIT

3 Japanese Transports Damaged—American Carrier Is Struck

By ROBERT TRUMBULL
Special Cable to THE NEW YORK TIMES.

PEARL HARBOR, June 6—Admiral Chester W. Nimitz, Commander in Chief of the United States Pacific Fleet, announced today that two or three Japanese aircraft carriers had been destroyed and that "a momentous victory is in the making" in the great battle on the Midway Island sea front.

The admiral, who said in a communiqué that "Pearl Harbor has now been partially avenged," also announced that the United States forces had damaged one or two other carriers, as well as three battleships, four cruisers and three transports of the enemy invasion fleet that failed in its assault on Midway, which never got beyond the stage of aerial preparation.

TEXT OF COMMUNIQUE

Admiral Nimitz's communiqué, the third he has issued since the battle got under way on Thursday, follows:

> Through the skill and devotion to duty of their armed forces of all branches in the Midway area, our citizens can now rejoice that a momentous victory is in the making.
>
> It was on a Sunday just six months ago that the Japanese made their peacetime attack on our fleet and Army activities in Oahu. At that time they created heavy damage, it is true, but their act aroused the grim determination of our citizenry to avenge such treachery, and it raised, not lowered, the morale of our fighting men.
>
> Pearl Harbor has now been partially avenged. Vengeance will not be complete until Japanese sea power has been reduced to impotence. We have made substantial progress in that direction. Perhaps we will be forgiven if we claim we are about midway to our objective.
>
> The battle is not over. All returns have not yet been received. It is with full confidence, however, that for this phase of the action the following enemy losses are claimed:
>
> Two or three carriers and all their aircraft destroyed, in addition to one or two carriers badly damaged and most of their aircraft lost.
>
> Three battleships damaged, at least one badly.
>
> Four cruisers damaged, two heavily.
>
> Three transports damaged.
>
> It is possible that some of these wounded ships will not be able to reach their bases.
>
> One of our carriers was hit and some planes were lost. Our personnel casualties were light.
>
> This is the balance sheet that the Army, Navy and Marine

Continued on Page Two

'Midway' Spurs Pun By Admiral Nimitz

By The Associated Press.

PEARL HARBOR, June 6—In the midst of recounting the details of one of the greatest naval battles in history, Admiral Chester W. Nimitz, Commander in Chief of the United States Pacific Fleet, found a spot for a smile.

In his third communiqué on the continuing battle off Midway Island, the admiral said:

"Perhaps we will be forgiven if we claim we are about midway to our objective."

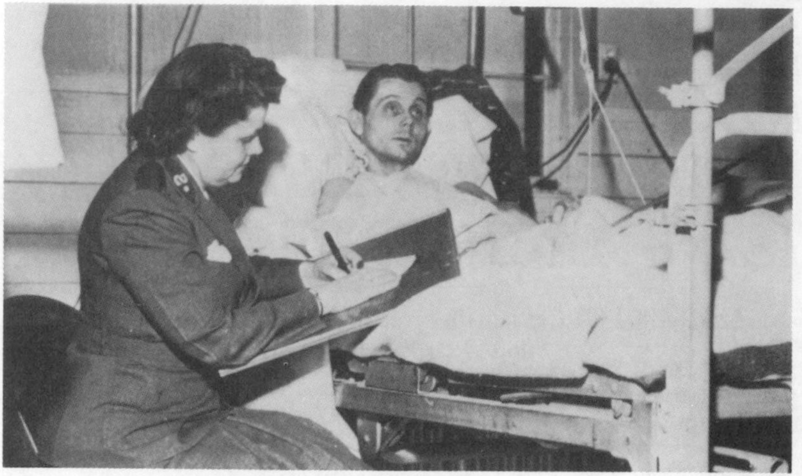

Salvation Army "lassies" gave of themselves generously for the benefit of GIs at home and abroad.

Bob Hope, Frances Langford, Tony Romano and Jerry Colonna performed many times for countless GIs near most battlefronts of the war.

Spike Jones and his "City Slickers" band popularized the anti-Hitler song *Der Führer's Face*.

Civilians in Santa Barbara, California, inspect damage after shelling by enemy submarines. They countered by setting up a volunteer defense corps, 24-hour "spotter" crews, air-raid alert systems, first-aid classes and increased fire protection.

"All the News That's Fit to Print."

The New York Times.

LATE CITY EDITION
Little change in temperature today.
Temperatures Yesterday—Max., 85; Min., 69

VOL. XCI..No. 30,830. Entered as Second-Class Matter, Postoffice, New York, N. Y. NEW YORK, MONDAY, JUNE 22, 1942. THREE CENTS NEW YORK CITY and Vicinity

TOBRUK FALLS, AXIS CLAIMS 25,000 PRISONERS; GERMANS DRIVE WEDGE INTO SEVASTOPOL LINES; JAPANESE ASHORE ON KISKA IN THE ALEUTIANS

'GAS' DROUGHT CUTS HOLIDAY PLEASURE AS CITY SWELTERS

New Yorkers Stay at Home or Drive Only to Suburbs—Many Avoid Main Roads

CROWDS AT SOME RESORTS

Others Are Hard Hit as Travel Is Spotty—Humidity Soars and Mercury Reaches 84°

New Yorkers, afflicted with the first sweltering Sunday of the season under the gasoline shortage, stayed at home yesterday, sitting on the sidewalks or in penthouse or roof gardens, or went to near-by parks and beaches. Pleasure driving was only half of normal, by and large, and the resorts, particularly the distant ones, bore the brunt of the decline. Relatives and friends in the suburbs apparently had many visitors.

The heat was not record-breaking. Temperatures rose from a low of 69 degrees at 5:45 A. M. to a high of 84 degrees at 5:30 P. M. The humidity, however, remained at 75 per cent, which the Weather Bureau said was extremely high for such high temperatures. In the morning two-tenths of an inch of rain fell and skies were overcast long after, accounting for many of the stay-at-homes in the city.

Brooklyn's first heat prostration of the season was reported last night when John Chambers, 45 years old, of 244 West End Avenue, Coney Island, collapsed as he was walking in Flatbush Avenue near East Twenty-sixth Street, Brooklyn. He was removed to Coney Island Hospital, where his condition was described as fair.

Motoring Is Spotty

The drop in pleasure driving, although marked as far as resorts were concerned, and severe if parkway use was an accurate indication, did not fully reflect the gasoline supply situation. With many stations dry, traffic on the George Washington Bridge was reported normal for a Sunday, through the Holland Tunnel a third off, and over other bridge and tunnel exits the reduction was not significant.

Yet on the Westchester parkways motor traffic was 30 per cent of normal and on the Long Island parkways about 60 per cent of normal. Police traffic experts believed that this reflected the spotty character of the gasoline shortage, which was acute in Westchester and near-by Long Island and some sections of New Jersey, but not serious in others.

Those who had gasoline in their tanks apparently went pleasure driving in spite of the appeals to save gasoline, but avoided the parkways and resorts, where they would be conspicuous. Many, the traffic experts thought, must have gone to visit friends and relatives

Continued on Page Nine

If in Doubt, Put It Out

Carelessness remains the greatest enemy of the Army's dimout regulations, it was said yesterday by civilian lighting experts who have been working with the Army on ways of cutting down the nightly illumination over the city that is used by enemy submarines in spotting shipping off our coast.

Windows and doors thoughtlessly opened for relief from the heat continue to loose light rays that help build up the sky glow over the metropolitan area, these experts said. They urged that whenever a window or door is opened for this purpose, it should be properly shaded or screened to prevent direct rays of light from emerging. These and other precautions should be placed in effect by one hour after sundown, which is at 8:31 P. M. tonight.

Meanwhile, the Army adjures all citizens: "If in doubt, put it out."

Peter of Yugoslavia Reaches Washington

Special to THE NEW YORK TIMES.

WASHINGTON, June 21—King Peter of Yugoslavia arrived here by airplane today. He was accompanied by M. Nincitch, the Yugoslav Foreign Minister.

They will discuss with President Roosevelt and other officials their country's continued opposition to the Axis. One of their objectives, it is understood, will be to obtain lease-lend aid for the guerrilla forces resisting the Nazis in Yugoslavia.

The King and his entourage will spend tonight at Blair House and will leave tomorrow to spend a few days in the country. He is traveling incognito until Wednesday, when he will return to Washington to begin the official program of his visit to the United States.

DIMOUT 'FAILURE' IS LAID TO MAYOR

Defense Council Members Say He Has Not Ordered Police to Enforce Army Rules

Charges that Mayor La Guardia has failed to give the Police Department orders to enforce the Army's dimout regulations, but has endeavored unsuccessfully to get the Army to modify its specifications, were advanced yesterday by two members of the executive board of the Lower West Side Defense Council, acting as a special committee in behalf of the council.

Howard Mulligan, a lawyer, of 103 Waverly Place, and J. B. C. Woods of 38 Perry Street, made public copies of a letter they had sent to the Mayor charging that conditions in their area were "deplorable." Mr. Mulligan explained that he and Mr. Woods had been authorized to take this action at a meeting at the council's headquarters, 27 Barrow Street, last Tuesday evening.

"Nightly, men are dying and ships are being sunk by the enemy off our coast because you, sir, prefer not to carry out the Army's orders," the letter charged.

In his weekly radio broadcast on June 7 Mayor La Guardia an-

Continued on Page Thirteen

RED ARMY RETIRES

Paris Radio Says Nazi Troops Have Reached Town of Sevastopol

AXIS LOSSES SEVERE

Placed at 7 Divisions—Germans Repelled on Kharkov Front

By RALPH PARKER
Wireless to THE NEW YORK TIMES.

MOSCOW, Monday, June 22—The Russian High Command acknowledges in its communiqué this morning that the Germans have succeeded, at a high cost in lives lost, in driving a wedge into the defenses of Sevastopol. But the bulletin also reports the repulse of numerous severe German assaults on the Sevastopol front.

[The German-controlled Paris radio said today that German troops had reached the town of Sevastopol after breaking through the Russian inner defense lines, The United Press reported from London. German sappers smashed their way through the final defense line outside the town with flame throwers, the Paris broadcast claimed.]

[The Germans reported the Red Army forces on the Kharkov front, where fighting on any considerable scale appears to be confined to one narrow sector, are said to have achieved an important success. After two enemy regiments had crossed a river barrier and advanced on the eastern bank, the Russians struck back, driving the Germans into and across the river. The Russians themselves then crossed the river and captured points on the western bank.

Press reports yesterday indicated that the Germans were continuing to pour troops into the Sevastopol fighting and that the situation there was grave. These reports said that waves of German and Rumanian infantry, attacking Russian lines in the southern sector of the Crimean base's defenses while planes dive-bombed Soviet artillery positions, had

Continued on Page Five

NEW LANDING MADE

Japanese Cruiser Is Hit in Army Air Blow at Kiska's Harbor

TRANSPORT IS SUNK

U. S. Fliers See Enemy's Temporary Buildings on Aleutian Isle

By C. BROOKS PETERS
Special to THE NEW YORK TIMES.

WASHINGTON, June 21—The Japanese forces that have been operating in the western Aleutian Islands since June 3 have succeeded in occupying Kiska, 650 miles west of Dutch Harbor, strategic American operations base, the Navy Department announced today.

Enemy occupation of Attu, westernmost island of the American chain and some 275 miles northwest of Kiska, was acknowledged in a Navy announcement on June 12.

Flying conditions in the Aleutian region—in which "foul weather and fog" are the general rule, the Navy reported recently—were sufficiently satisfactory in the last few days to permit "some restricted air operations against Kiska," today's Navy communiqué asserted.

Long-range Army aircraft attacked a small force of Japanese ships in Kiska's harbor and reported hits on a cruiser, the Navy announced. An enemy transport was sunk.

Tents of Japanese Seen

The American planes that finally were able to penetrate to the remote island of Kiska, where until the Japanese occupation the United States Navy maintained a weather station, observed that the enemy had set up tents and "minor temporary structures on land."

The communiqué added that operations in that area continued to be restricted "by considerations of weather and great distances."

Last Monday the Navy Department reported that Army and Navy planes were continuing air assaults "against the Japanese forces which recently were reported to have landed on western islands of the Aleutian group." At that time the Navy asserted that at least three Japanese cruisers, one destroyer, one gunboat and one transport had been damaged, "some of them severely," by air attacks.

Since the announcement on June 12 of the occupation of Attu naval circles in Washington have minimized the seriousness of Japanese landings in the western Aleutians, characterizing them as having been inspired primarily by a desire "to save face" after the defeat administered by American Army and Navy forces in the Coral Sea and off Midway Island.

Supply Problem Difficult

Military experts here have stated that supply would be a major problem for any enemy forces that endeavored to establish themselves in the Aleutians. The distance from bases in Japanese territory to the Aleutian Islands is so great, these circles have contended, that aerial transport is not feasible, particularly in view of the uncertain weather conditions. Therefore, supplies must be transported by surface craft, which are constantly exposed to attack by American submarines.

There is, however, a possibility that in the Rat Island group, of which Kiska is one island, the Japanese could conceal submarine mother ships and perhaps even small aircraft carriers, the experts here said. Submarines from such bases might prove effective should Japan attack Russia, they added.

But for the most part, according to the opinion conveyed to reporters in Washington by military circles, the enemy will have to be

Continued on Page Four

War News Summarized

MONDAY, JUNE 22, 1942

Tobruk fell yesterday, and the resultant threat to Egypt and the British position in the Eastern Mediterranean changed the war picture drastically, while the Russians acknowledged a significant German advance at Sevastopol, though at the cost of heavy enemy losses.

Tobruk fell to a smashing blow delivered by waves of German tanks according to London reports. The Germans claimed that 25,000 prisoners had been taken. In London the opinion prevailed that there had not been time to lay minefields around Tobruk before the Axis attack. [1:8.]

Military observers in London referred to the fall of Tobruk as an "incontestable disaster." The Germans were believed to have obtained a large quantity of stores. General Rommel was expected to drive on Suez. [2:2.]

British bombers attacked Emden, German submarine base, for the second successive night, airfields in the Netherlands and enemy shipping off the Netherland coast. Heavy air attacks were also made on the French and Belgian coasts. [1:5.]

Moscow granted that the defenders of Sevastopol had been forced to fall back as the enemy forced a wedge in their lines, but declared that the action had crippled five German and two Rumanian divisions. Sharp activity was reported in the Kharkov and Leningrad sectors. [1:3.]

President Kalinin of the Soviet Union, in a review of a year of war, stated that the Germans no longer were capable of a general offensive. [5:5; map, P. 5.]

Lord Beaverbrook, addressing a "Salute to Russia" meeting in Britain, again urged the United Nations to open a second front. He asserted that the British Army was now sufficiently prepared. [3:1.]

Chungking reported that the Japanese had been halted in Kiangsi and had lost 1,300 troops in Honan. The Minister of War asserted that the Japanese soon would be so bogged down in China that they would not be able to attack Russia with full strength. [4:1.]

The United States Navy announced that Japanese forces in the Aleutians had succeeded in occupying the island of Kiska, 650 miles west of Dutch Harbor. Bomb hits were made on a Japanese cruiser and a Japanese transport was sunk. [1:4; map, P. 4.]

Colonel J. L. Ralston, Canadian Defense Minister, disclosed that a government telegraph station at Estevan Point, Vancouver Island, had been shelled by a submarine Saturday night, but no damage was done. [1:5-6.]

As President Roosevelt and Prime Minister Churchill continued their conversations yesterday Washington reported that the fall of Tobruk and Russian withdrawals at Sevastopol had checked "second front speculation." Concern was being shown over the necessity for holding the present front in Egypt. [1:7.]

ROMMEL'S FORCES TAKE IMPORTANT PORT IN LIBYA

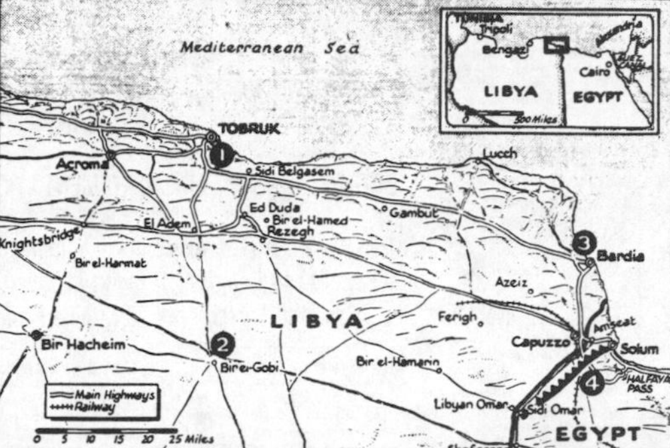

Tobruk (1) has been overwhelmed and captured with its garrison by the Axis, which also claimed the capture of Bir el-Gobi (2) and the minor port of Bardia (3). There were indications that the Germans were working their way from Bardia southward to Capuzzo for an assault across the border into Egypt. Here they will find defenses between Solum and Sidi Omar (4).

Vancouver Island Shelled; Northwest Coast Dims Out

By P. J. PHILIP
Special to THE NEW YORK TIMES.

OTTAWA, June 21—Estevan Point on Vancouver Island was shelled by an enemy submarine at 10:35 o'clock, Pacific time, last night (1:35 A. M., Sunday, Eastern war time), Colonel J. L. Ralston, the Defense Minister, announced here today. The submarine was presumed to be Japanese.

The enemy's objective was the government wireless and telegraph station there. No damage was done, said a report from Lieut. Gen. Kenneth Stuart, Canadian Chief of Staff and acting Commander in Chief of the West Corps defenses.

[Coastal dimouts in the States of Washington and Oregon were put into effect last night, following the shelling of Estevan Point, which is about 125 miles north of the United States border.]

There is an airfield near Estevan Point, but no report has come through as to whether action was taken against the attacking submarine.

The attack was the first against Canadian soil in the history of Canada as a Dominion. Last month two ships were torpedoed and sunk in the Gulf of St. Lawrence.

The Defense Minister's announcement said:

"The Commander in Chief, West Coast defenses, reported that the Dominion Government telegraph station at Estevan Point, Vancouver Island, was shelled by a submarine at 10:35 P. M. (Pacific time) on Saturday night. No damage resulted."

Estevan Point lies halfway along the western shore of Vancouver Island, about 150 miles northwest of Victoria. Its only importance seems to be the estab-

Continued on Page Four

R. A. F. PAYS EMDEN 2D VISIT IN 2 NIGHTS

Also Hammers Other Targets in Northwest Reich—Hits Ship Off Dutch Coast

By JAMES MacDONALD
Wireless to THE NEW YORK TIMES.

LONDON, June 21—A large number of British bombers hammered Emden, Germany, last night for the second night in succession and also other objectives in Northwest Germany and air bases in the Netherlands.

At the same time American-built Hudson planes of the Coastal Command, ever on the lookout for enemy shipping, searched waters off the Netherland coast, where a Canadian flying crew dropped two bombs on a medium-sized cargo vessel.

The communiqué announcing these operations did not divulge the number of planes engaged, but said the raids cost the Royal Air Force six bombers and one Coastal Command plane. The R. A. F. losses were increased today when one fighter plane failed to return home from a daylight attack on Dunkerque.

[The Berlin radio went off the air at 1:50 A. M. today, a possible sign that British bombers were again over Germany, The United Press reported from London.

[German planes dropped bombs early today in a sharp attack on the south coast of England, The Associated Press reported. Two of the raiders were shot down and two more Nazi planes destroyed over Europe.]

As in the case of the R. A. F. raids on Emden late Friday night and early yesterday morning, the Air Ministry did not go into details about the targets for the night or indicate the extent of damage.

While patrolling along the Netherland coast during the night Coastal Command fliers caught up with an enemy convoy of three ships. The rear gunner on a Canadian-manned plane said on his return to his base that he saw two bombs hit one vessel amidship, hurling debris high in the air in the resulting explosions. Whether the vessel sank was not determined. What became of her two companion ships was not learned here.

Although the sky was clear, there was less daylight activity to-

Continued on Page Five

NEWS PUTS DAMPER ON CHURCHILL VISIT

But Washington Sees Mid-East Crisis as Incidental in His Planning With Roosevelt

By JAMES B. RESTON
Special to THE NEW YORK TIMES.

WASHINGTON, June 21—Washington was in a sober and realistic mood tonight. The fall of Tobruk and the situation of the Russians at Sevastopol have put a damper on the unrestrained second-front speculation that has surrounded the Roosevelt-Churchill talks. The chief immediate concern was viewed as the holding of the second front the United Nations now have in Egypt, rather than opening up new fronts on the European Continent.

The President and Mr. Churchill continued their talks during the day, and the chiefs of staff of the United States and Britain, General George C. Marshall and General Sir Alan Brooke, who came to the United States with Mr. Churchill, continued their exchange of information and their planning for the future.

The plain and simple truth about these important discussions is that only a few persons know what has gone on since Mr. Churchill arrived, and they are not telling what they know.

The purpose of the conversations is much less complicated, dramatic and urgent than one would tend to deduce from the secrecy with which they have been surrounded.

It is undoubtedly true, as Stephen Early, White House secretary, has said, that they are dealing with the future plans of the

Continued on Pag. Eight

'Never a Dull Moment' at Midway, Reporter Watching Battle Found

The following account of the Battle of Midway is by a correspondent of THE NEW YORK TIMES *who was aboard one of the United States warships.*

By FOSTER HAILEY
Special to THE NEW YORK TIMES.

WITH THE PACIFIC FLEET, at Sea, June 4 (Delayed)—Today is the day. Mark it on your calendar in red ink, Thursday, June 4. It may be the one on which the tide definitely turned in the battle of the Pacific.

This morning at dawn the Japanese launched planes from a strong striking force northwest of Midway. We are in a position to strike them on the flank. If our planes can only get to their carriers before the Japanese planes attacking Midway car return, the result may be a naval disaster for the Japanese.

White water is curling away from the clipper bows of the cruisers and the big carriers, whose escort we are, as we drive on at high speed with the destroyers ahead and on the flanks. It is a relief for the nerves when the first alarm is sounded. It turns out to be false, but the activity has eased the tension.

There is another spurt of activity as another air contact is reported, but it turns out to be a big patrol plane from Midway that joins the force to act as an anti-submarine guard.

"Midway was attacked at 8:48 A. M.," our Admiral and Chief of Staff says crisply when an inquiry on the situation is made.

"We should be in launching distance soon."

The dawn was a gloomy one, but now the clouds are breaking up.

Continued on Page Four

NAZIS NEAR EGYPT

British Are on Border as Rommel Presses On After Victory

PORT'S LOSS SERIOUS

Plan for a Second Front Seen Upset by Need to Hold New Line

By DAVID ANDERSON
Special Cable to THE NEW YORK TIMES.

LONDON, June 21—A smashing blow delivered yesterday by waves of German tanks, heavily supported from the air, crushed the defenses of Tobruk in Libya. The War Office tonight confirmed the loss of the town, already claimed by the enemy, who said 25,000 prisoners, including "several generals" had been captured.

The story of what happened, as given by both German and Italian sources, appears to cover the battle fairly fully, but the accuracy of these reports cannot be checked at present. Briefly, it can be said Field Marshal Erwin Rommel's armored units that had passed Tobruk in pursuit of the British Eighth Army did so to make certain whether the British showed any signs of preparing a counter-attack.

When the German Marshal was satisfied this was not the case he reversed his forces, bringing back tanks against Tobruk from the south, driving from the vicinity of Ed Duda, and did this fiercely with every ounce of power at his command. At the same time the Luftwaffe began intensive bombing of Tobruk's defenses. Within a matter of hours the battle was over.

Tobruk Long in Battle

Tobruk must have been softer in its last moments than during the many other attacks it beat off during the last seventeen months since it was captured from the Italians on Jan 22, 1941. It has been on the fringe of the Libyan battlefield for some weeks with inevitable strain as strategy wavered between one of concentration of strength there and one of evacuation.

Despite the presence of a large garrison when Tobruk fell it is believed there was not time to lay minefields on its perimeter or otherwise strengthen its defenses to face an immediate storming.

A Cairo communiqué, released here at noon today, paved the way for the worst. It read:

"Yesterday the enemy attacked the perimeter of Tobruk in great strength. In spite of most determined resistance by our forces the enemy succeeded in penetrating the defenses and in occupying a considerable area inside them."

Twelve strong points in the defenses were taken by the first wave of enemy tanks, according to Berlin. This made a wedge two and a half miles wide, and German sources state the British defenders then realized that further resistance was useless.

Bombers Blast Defenses

But they had other reasons for weighing most seriously the advantages of carrying on the fight. The Germans said today that "numerous bombers' ceaseless attack wrought great destruction in the fortifications and other military works of the port and town."

It was not long after noon yesterday when large formations of German bombers swooped down on a group of four anti-aircraft batteries, all of which were silenced, it was reported by Berlin. Still more of the Luftwaffe's heavy aircraft, laden with high explosives, cruised over a column of twenty tanks, setting many of them ablaze.

Finally, the German radio said, "About 2 P. M. another great attack was made on Tobruk, which lasted three hours without interruption and caused numerous fires.

Continued on Page Two

"All the News That's Fit to Print."

NEWS INDEX, PAGE 35. THIS SECTION

The New York Times.

LATE CITY EDITION

Somewhat warmer today.

Temperatures Yesterday—Max., 70; Min., 61

Section 1

VOL. XCI—No. 30,836. Entered as Second-Class Matter, Postoffice, New York, N. Y. NEW YORK, SUNDAY, JUNE 28, 1942. Including Magazine and Book Sections. TEN CENTS New York City and Vicinity

FBI SEIZES 8 SABOTEURS LANDED BY U-BOATS HERE AND IN FLORIDA TO BLOW UP WAR PLANTS; ALLIES PLEDGE MOVES TO RELIEVE RUSSIANS

PRICE OF GASOLINE GOES UP 2½ CENTS IN EAST TOMORROW

OPA Also Orders Increase of 2 Cents on Oils, Including Four of the Fuel Types

LACK OF SUBSIDY DECRIED

Henderson Calls Higher Costs Unfair to Public—Wider Ration Area Expected

Special to THE NEW YORK TIMES.

WASHINGTON, June 27—Gasoline will cost Eastern motorists 2½ cents a gallon more beginning Monday.

Increases of 2 cents a gallon, effective at the same time, also were ordered by the Office of Price Administration today for range oil, kerosene, tractor fuel, distillate Diesel fuel oils, gashouse oils and Nos. 1, 2, 3 and 4 fuel oils. Residual fuel oils are not affected.

The increases, third allowed by the OPA on gasoline and other oils since the beginning of the year, were made necessary, Leon Henderson, Price Administrator, said, by increased costs of moving petroleum to the East Coast by means other than tanker.

Word came also that when permanent gasoline rationing goes into effect in the East July 22 the boundaries of the affected area will in all probability be extended to include the ninety-three counties in Western New York, Pennsylvania, West Virginia, Maryland and Virginia which have been exempt to date.

OPC Approval Reported

According to reports here tonight, the Office of Petroleum Coordinator favors such an extension, and it is said to have gained favor with the Office of Price Administration because of a view that the problem of rationing administration would be greatly simplified by having the area bounded by State lines.

The plan would carry rationing to Buffalo and other important cities which have been exempt.

The ninety-three counties were exempted when emergency rationing became effective May 15, because the Office of Petroleum Coordination found that they had sufficient supplies of gasoline to take care of demand. Officials warned at that time, however, that the exemption might be only temporary.

In a special statement accompanying his announcement of the price increases on gasoline and other oils, Mr. Henderson declared that it was unfair to make Eastern consumers shoulder the expense of moving gasoline by means other than by tanker, but that for the time there was nothing that could be done about it in the absence of arrangements for subsidies.

"The Office of Price Administration," he said, "is keenly aware of the inequity of making consumers of petroleum products bear the entire cost of the submarine warfare

Continued on Page Twenty-eight

If in Doubt, Put It Out

The outdoor weenie roast and the beach fire are out for the duration, civilian defense offficials said yesterday as a reminder for picnickers. Sings, story-telling and hayrides are among the outdoor pastimes in which groups of people can join after dark without adding to the sky glow that helps enemy submarines find our ships. Vacationists are learning that a darkened circle is just as conducive to sociability as a blazing fire that shoots sparks into the skies.

All dimout regulations go into effect one hour after sunset. Tonight the sun sets at 8:32 o'clock. Don't take a chance with any outdoor light. Play safe and remember the Army's admonition: "If in doubt, put it out."

Major Sports Results

RACING

Whirlaway won the Brooklyn Handicap by two lengths from Swing and Sway on Aqueduct's closing day, which netted a minimum of $100,000 for Army-Navy relief. Warren Wright's thoroughbred thereby boosted his earnings to $404,486, only $33,244 less than Seabiscuit's all-time record.

BASEBALL

The Reds upset the Dodgers, 3—1, on Pinch-hitter Ray Lamanno's three-run homer with two out in the ninth. The Giants defeated the Pirates, 5—2, behind Bob Carpenter. At Chicago, Joe DiMaggio and Buddy Hassett led the Yankees to a 7-3 triumph over the White Sox.

GOLF

Frank Tatum Jr. of Stanford captured the N. C. A. A. golf title by downing Manuel De La Torre of Northwestern, 5 and 4, at South Bend. Vincent Raskopf vanquished Olin P. Boone, 2 up, in Long Island junior final at Cherry Valley. Miss Betty Jameson of San Antonio won the women's Western open at Chicago.

(Complete Details in Section 5.)

WILLKIE DEMANDS 'MEN OF FORESIGHT'

Backing Baldwin for Post in Connecticut, He Says Party Must Have Such Leaders

By JAMES C. HAGERTY

Special to THE NEW YORK TIMES.

WESTPORT, Conn., June 27—Wendell L. Willkie, speaking here this afternoon at a luncheon meeting sponsored by the Fairfield County Republican Women's Association, threw the full weight of his position as titular leader of the Republican party behind the candidacy of Raymond E. Baldwin as the party's nominee for Governor of Connecticut.

In supporting Mr. Baldwin, who served as Governor from 1938 to 1940 and who acted as one of the Willkie floor managers at the 1940 Republican National Convention, the former Republican Presidential candidate declared that he favored Mr. Baldwin because he represented the type of leadership so urgently needed in the Republican party. He said that his action was

Continued on Page Thirty-one

ROMMEL PUSHES ON

Enemy Units in Egypt Slow Down 15 Miles From Matruh

BRITISH HARRY FOE

Two-Week Halt in Axis Supplies to Bengazi Reported Forced

By DAVID ANDERSON

Special Cable to THE NEW YORK TIMES.

LONDON, June 27—General Field Marshal Erwin Rommel's Axis war machine was reported tonight to be slowly rolling toward a standstill in front of the British line that extends from Matruh, Egypt, to a point some forty miles inland.

Cairo gives little sign of knowing when or where the enemy will strike, but has issued reports of heavy aerial activity against advancing German supply columns and of delaying actions fought by British mechanized units.

The latest definite information from Cairo is that Marshal Rommel's forces are about fifteen miles from Matruh and apparently are tending to bear somewhat in the direction of the seacoast.

Opinion in London

Prudent observers here believed tonight that it would be safer to assume that the pace of the invasion of Egypt had slowed down of its own accord than to indulge in wishful thinking that the enemy had been checked.

[The Associated Press reported from Cairo that the British Eighth Army stood reinforced at full strength against a powerful Axis striking force, and, in a dispatch from Alexandria, said it had been learned unofficially that, with British submarines blasting away at Axis supply vessels, not a single enemy convoy had reached Bengazi, Libya, in the past fortnight.]

Speculation concerning the anticipated battle has not yet entirely ruled out the possibility that Marshal Rommel may risk the great gamble of attempting to swing southward of the Qattara Depression.

Fierce running fights have been going on along the tracks of the

Continued on Page Six

REPORT ON PARLEYS

Roosevelt and Churchill Say Germans Will Be Diverted by Push

STATEMENT HOPEFUL

Cuts in Shipping Losses, Blows at Japan, Help for China Projected

By W. H. LAWRENCE

Special to THE NEW YORK TIMES.

WASHINGTON, June 27—Coming operations by the military forces of the United Nations "will divert German strength from the attack on Russia," it was announced today by President Roosevelt and Prime Minister Churchill in a final communiqué on their week-long series of conferences in which the offensive strategy of the war was mapped.

For obvious reasons, the two leaders offered no more enlightenment on the methods they had agreed upon to carry out a previous British-Soviet-American understanding on the "urgent tasks of creating a second front in Europe in 1942."

They left the leaders of Germany and Italy with only a guess as to when, where and how the operations would be begun that would require the diversion of Axis man power now pressing against the Soviet armies on the eastern front.

Churchill Left Thursday

The second-front declaration, purposely vague, was the high point of the joint statement issued simultaneously at 11:30 A. M. here and in London after Prime Minister Churchill had arrived safely home by airplane from the United States, which he left secretly Thursday night.

Other major strategy decisions indicated by the joint statement were:

New plans for using the naval forces of the United Nations to reduce the toll of merchant shipping were made. In recent months losses have outstripped ship building.

Measures against Japan have been prepared.

New methods to relieve sorely pressed China will be undertaken.

Statement Is Optimistic

The Roosevelt-Churchill statement was optimistic. They reviewed the circumstances of their meeting in August, 1941, when the Atlantic Charter was drawn at sea before the United States entered the war, and again in late December, 1941, after the attack on Pearl Harbor. They declared their belief that "the over-all picture is more favorable to victory than it was either in August or December of last year."

But they warned against complacency. The task ahead, they said, must not be underrated and the conferences here have been conducted "with the full knowledge of the power and resourcefulness of the enemy."

Nowhere in the statement did the two leaders mention the sharp British reverses in the North African campaign, which took place while Mr. Churchill was en route here and during his stay in this country. These have aroused considerable criticism of the Prime Minister in Britain, but Mr. Churchill assured a Congressional delegation on Thursday that Egypt would be held and he minimized the advances of the Axis armies led by General Field Marshal Erwin Rommel.

Big Production Stressed

Mr. Roosevelt and Mr. Churchill said that their survey of the production of munitions of all kinds disclosed "an optimistic picture" on the whole, and that the arsenals of the two countries were approaching maximum production "on schedule." This was borne out by the President's special production report yesterday, which dis-

Continued on Page Two

War News Summarized

SUNDAY, JUNE 28, 1942

In New York last night J. Edgar Hoover announced the arrest of eight Nazi saboteurs, who were landed from submarines on Long Island and the Florida coast with TNT, maps, $150,000 in cash and instructions for blowing up such objectives as Hell Gate Bridge, the Aluminum Company of America, vital rail terminals and major war plants. [1:8.]

President Roosevelt and Prime Minister Churchill issued yesterday a joint statement asserting that the military forces of the United Nations would engage in operations that would divert German strength from the attack on Russia. The statement indicated decisions had been reached calculated to lower the submarine toll of shipping and to expedite aid to China. It was issued after the safe arrival of Prime Minister Churchill in Britain. [1:4.]

The Prime Minister returned to face political difficulties arising from the defeat in Libya, but it was still indicated that there was no serious challenge to his leadership. [2:2.]

A large vanguard of the United States Army Air Forces has been established in the British Isles and is making preparations to engage soon in mass attacks on Germany, coordinated with those of the Royal Air Force, according to London reports. Friday night there were a number of British attacks on German-occupied regions, and the Germans attacked fairly severely the city of Norwich. [1:7.]

Moscow granted that Soviet troops were being slowly pushed back in portions of the Kharkov front but said that the Germans were making no rapid advances and had gained no immediate military advantage except the capture of Kupyansk. The Sevastopol front was holding under the same sort of heavy German pressure. [1:5.]

Cairo announced that the main Axis forces were only fifteen miles west of Matruh, major British base on the Egyptian coast. A big battle seemed imminent and may have begun. [1:3; map, P. 6.]

British submarines were reported to have attacked many Axis supply vessels in the Mediterranean, and it was said in Alexandria that not an enemy convoy had reached Bengazi in the past two weeks. [6:5.]

The Chinese admitted the loss of Lishui, last of three major air bases in the Eastern Kiangsi-Chekiang area from which Japan could be bombed. The Japanese recapture of Kweiki on the Hangchow-Nanchang railway also was acknowledged. [12:3, with map.]

At Atlanta, Ga., it was disclosed that the first major expeditionary force of the United States Marine Corps had landed at a South Pacific base with a formidable arsenal of modern equipment. [1:5-6.]

EXPLOSIVES HIDDEN BY NAZI SABOTEURS ON FLORIDA BEACH

Four boxes containing TNT which was to have been used to destroy war plants

The New York Times (FBI)

First Major Marine A. E. F. Reaches South Pacific Port

By The Associated Press.

ATLANTA, June 27—This war's first major expeditionary force of United States marines has landed at a South Pacific port apparently equipped for offensive landing in that theatre of war. The far-off arrival of "transports swarming with marines" was revealed here today by Major Meigs O. Frost, Southern public relations chief for the Marine Corps.

Accompanying the announcement that the convoy carried the Marines' biggest overseas contingent of the war was the first story to be released as written by one of the Marines' own war correspondents assigned to combat forces.

The story told merely of the human side of life aboard the transports during the voyage from an unrevealed American port to the undisclosed destination, but contained clear implications of the job ahead of the task force.

With a number of Southern leathernecks known to have been included, first official advice regarding the force was relayed here from Washington by Brig. Gen. Robert L. Denig, Marine Headquarters Public Relations Director, in line with an effort to bring Marine news close to home.

The anonymous sergeant correspondent related how some of the Marines enjoyed the tropical nights by sleeping in Higgins landing boats aboard their ships.

The sergeant's story recorded no attacks on the convoy.

Recalling blacked-out nights, band concerts and swing sessions, the sergeant decided that the trip was far from dull and "living conditions aboard ship weren't as bad as anticipated."

"Most popular place aboard ship was the soda fountain, where Marines and sailors relaxed on cokes and ice cream.

"The chaplain's library was pop-

Continued on Page Eleven

RED ARMY CHECKING NAZI UKRAINE PUSH

Axis 'Fist' Kept From Spreading Out Beyond Kupyansk—Sevastopol Gain Slow

By RALPH PARKER

Wireless to THE NEW YORK TIMES.

MOSCOW, June 27—Though yielding ground slowly in fierce rear-guard fighting, Marshal Semyon Timoshenko has prevented the Germans from taking immediate or spectacular advantage of the capture of Kupyansk.

Russian dispatches from the southwestern front describe the fighting as of exceptional fierceness, but though it is apparent that General Field Marshal Fedor von Bock is trying to widen the battle front, the stubbornness of the Russian defense in depth has prevented his powerful armored force, attacking in a narrow sector, from ripping open the Russian lines and causing confusion.

The "fist" that struck is, as it were, still clenched, with its tanks and motorized infantry bunched together, though after the capture of Kupyansk it probably was the German plan to thrust probing fingers into various sectors of the Russian resistance.

[The midnight Soviet communiqué said Sevastopol's defenders had repulsed more attacks that cost the Axis heavily, while on the other fronts there were no significant changes. Berlin reported that a new Russian attempt to land at Kerch had been frustrated and said additional positions had been captured at Sevastopol.]

At Sevastopol yesterday a dangerous German wedge was driven into the northeastern sector. Though the pressure now is heavy on all fronts as new German regiments hastily brought from other fronts come into line, Col. Gen. Fritz Erich von Mannstein's gains are measured in yards. Small groups of shock troops succeeded in skirting through in the southern sector, where three enemy divisions now are believed to be operating, but these in no way represent any general advance and are vigorously engaged in hand-to-hand combat.

Much of the fighting now is described as a close-quarter struggle in trenches and gun emplacements, and here the Red Army men and

Continued on Page Nineteen

U. S. AIR ACTIVITIES IN BRITAIN RUSHED

Increasing Forces Arrive to Join From Own Bases in Offensive Against Nazis

Special Cable to THE NEW YORK TIMES.

LONDON, June 27—With preparations of the British Royal Air Force about complete for continuing—or rather, doubling in power—its attacks against Germany, such as that on Thursday night, which left still-smoking ruins at Bremen, authoritative sources here directed attention today to the important part predicted for the United States Army Air Forces in the offensive over Europe.

A great deal has been said about the arrival of tens of thousands of American soldiers in the British Isles; but little or nothing has been permitted to be published hitherto about the large number of United States Air Forces personnel now reaching here.

These American airmen have been taking over flying fields in the United Kingdom, studying the operational systems of the R. A. F. and working on plans for close coordination with the British.

The preparations indicated the establishment of United States air bases in Britain from which American units would bomb Germany in joint operations with the R. A. F.

[The R. A. F. bombed Germany again last night and a Berlin broadcast heard at London said Bremen had been attacked once more, according to a United Press dispatch.]

The time is rapidly approaching when the Liberators, Flying Fortresses and other giant United States bombers will be augmenting the R. A. F.'s Stirlings, Halifaxes,

Continued on Page Fifteen

Japan Bombed With 20-Cent Sight; Arnold Gives D. F. C. to 23 Raiders

By C. BROOKS PETERS

Special to THE NEW YORK TIMES.

WASHINGTON, June 27—The American B-25 bombers that carried out the daring surprise attack on Tokyo and other Japanese objectives last April 18 were equipped with improvised bombsights that cost about 20 cents each.

This and other interesting details of the aerial assault carried out by a force under the command of Brig. Gen. James H. Doolittle were revealed by the War Department today as the Distinguished Flying Cross was pinned on twenty-three members of the Army Air Forces who participated in the raid.

Because the raid on Japan was planned as a low-altitude operation, "with the planes' wings barely skimming the treetops as they flew toward their objective," it seemed inevitable that some of the planes might fall into Japanese hands (not one did, however), which would have given the enemy an opportunity to become familiar with the Norden bombsight.

But low-altitude bombing does not, in the Army's opinion, require the extreme accuracy of the Norden bombsights and they were not used in the planes participating in the attack. Major Charles R. Greening, armament officer of the squadron and one of the officers decorated today, improvised the 20-cent bombsights.

Five Japanese cities were marked for bombing in the April 18 raid: Tokyo, Yokohama, Nagoya, Kobe and Osaka. Objectives were tank, armament and aircraft

Continued on Page Eighteen

INVADERS CONFESS

Had TNT to Blast Key Factories, Railroads and City Water System

USED RUBBER BOATS

Carried $150,000 Cash—All Had Lived in U. S.—Face Death Penalty

By WILL LISSNER

Two groups of saboteurs, highly trained by direction of the German High Command at a special school for sabotage near Berlin, carrying cases of powerful explosives and nearly $150,000 in cash, were landed on the Long Island and the Florida coasts from submarines in the last fortnight with orders to blow up certain key plants and to cause panics in large cities, it was disclosed last night.

Despite their training the two gangs of four men each fell afoul of special agents of the Federal Bureau of Investigation almost immediately and the arrest of all eight was announced last evening by J. Edgar Hoover, director of the Bureau. They were in custody within a month after they had shipped on their expedition out of a submarine base on the French coast.

Mr. Hoover reported the arrests to President Roosevelt and released full biographies of the men, which showed that they were former waiters, machinists and German-American Bund agitators, long resident here and fluent in English, who were repatriated by the German Embassies in the United States and Mexico to be recruited for the sabotage school.

Carried List of Objectives

In the possession of the men was a list of special assignments of industrial plants they were to sabotage and department stores in which they were to create panics. The plants were the following:

Aluminum Corporation of America, Alcoa, Tenn.

Aluminum Corporation of America, Massena, N. Y.

Aluminum Corporation of America, East St. Louis, Ill.

Aluminum Corporation of America, Cryolite (aluminum base) plant, Philadelphia.

Chesapeake & Ohio Railroad (around industrial areas.)

Pennsylvania Railroad (at Newark, N. J.)

Hell Gate Bridge (railroad bridge from Astoria, Queens, to the Bronx.)

Canals and locks of the Ohio River from Cincinnati to St. Louis. (St. Louis, contrary to German geography, is not connected with the Ohio River.)

Specified department stores and

Continued on Page Thirty

Spy Crew Escaped From a Coast Guard

A story was told in Amagansett, L. I., last night that purported to give details of the landing of the sabotage crew there. According to this version, when the gang had finished burying its cases of equipment on the beach, the saboteurs were discovered by a young Coast Guardsman on shore patrol. He challenged them and the spies attempted to bribe him with some of their large store of money. He spurned the bribe and they fled.

Unable to round the men up single-handed, the Coast Guardsman ran back to his station, gave the alarm and called out patrols. The Army sent a detail to the scene and, together with the Coast Guard, the Army men searched the area, but the saboteurs had made good their escape, temporarily.

"All the News That's Fit to Print."

NEWS INDEX, PAGE 55, THIS SECTION

The New York Times.

Copyright, 1942, by The New York Times Company.

LATE CITY EDITION
Warmer today.
Temperatures Yesterday—Max., 65; Min., 51
Sunrise, 6:54 A. M.; Sunset, 6:35 P. M.

Section 1

VOL. XCII. No. 30,934. Entered as Second-Class Matter, Postoffice, New York, N. Y. NEW YORK, SUNDAY, OCTOBER 4, 1942. Including Magazine and Book Sections. TEN CENTS New York City and Vicinity

ROOSEVELT FREEZES WAGES, RENTS, FARM PRICES; NAMES JUSTICE BYRNES ECONOMIC DIRECTOR; U. S. TROOPS MOVE OUT TO A NEW ALEUTIAN BASE

CITY SPEEDS SCRAP ON ITS WAY TO WAR; PROFITEERS SUFFER

Bids to Be Opened Wednesday on 33,729,000 Pounds Piled Up in the Queens Drive

PRICE CUT BY $10 A TON

Burke Says His Collection Forced It Down and Spread Panic Among Gougers

While seventy city trucks were still adding their loads to the Queens household scrap pile—which surpassed all expectations by reaching 33,729,000 pounds—the Department of Purchase moved quickly yesterday to start part of the vast collection of metal on its way to the war fronts.

The size of the Queens collection, according to Mr. Burke, has forced the price of scrap iron down from $15 a ton to $5.

"Would-be profiteers are now in a state of panic and are trying to unload the stuff which they had been holding for a higher price," he said.

Mayor La Guardia disclosed that 135 proposals were mailed out by Commissioner Albert Pleydell to the waste industry trade in the city listing for sale 14,255 gross tons of the scrap collected Friday. Because sorting of the scrap, piled up at five receiving depots, will be a big part of the job of preparing the metals for the mills, every bidder will have to indicate how long it will take him to remove the material.

Quick Delivery Stressed

A special clause in the proposal describes the scrap as a war contribution of the people of Queens and emphasizes that its delivery to the smelting or processing plants must be effected in the shortest possible time. Bids will be opened Wednesday at 11 A. M. in the Municipal Building.

The 14,255 gross tons of 2,240 pounds each tell only part of the story of how the patriotic enthusiasm of the people of Queens caused Borough President James A. Burke to double his original estimate. This was that the official collection would show ten pounds of metal for every man, woman and child, but then they put so much material on the sidewalks that it took two days to

Continued on Page Forty-two

U. S. to Pay to Get Out the Heavy Scrap

Park Commissioner Robert Moses, appointed by Mayor La Guardia as coordinator for the collection of heavy scrap metal in the current newspaper drive, made the following statement yesterday:

"Large tonnage of heavy scrap metal is needed immediately in order to keep our country's steel mills running. Household scrap is being collected, but this alone will be entirely insufficient. The United States Government, through its agent, War Materials, Inc., will remove at its own expense fixed installations of obsolete ferrous machinery, heating plants, pumps, compressors, hoists and other heavy ferrous equipment and repair damage to property caused by such removal.

"Operators of industrial plants having ferrous machinery and equipment of three or more tons, who will consent to its removal as scrap metal by War Materials, Inc., should notify Commissioner Moses, Arsenal, Central Park, stating location, estimated ferrous tonnage, nature of installation and owner's requirements for removal.

"Act now."

Russians Smashing Ahead; Shaposhnikoff in Command

Red Army Seizes Vital Positions in Flank Counter-Offensive, Retakes Stalingrad Streets, but Yields Suburb in North

By The Associated Press.

MOSCOW, Sunday, Oct. 4—Resurgent Soviet counter-drives inside Stalingrad and northwest and south of the Volga city broke German offensive power and regained position after position, the Russians announced today, but in one sector north of the city the Nazis hammered their way into a populated place.

[The Germans confined their Stalingrad reports to general terms, saying strong Soviet relief attacks north and south of the city had failed, but claimed "complete success" in fighting southeast of Leningrad with the destruction of seven encircled Russian divisions.]

In the vast and confused battle, now in its forty-third day, in which cannon thundered on all sides of the city and bombs crashed among the stones of shattered masonry, German and Russian salients were

Continued on Page Twenty-nine

Stalin Gives Supreme Authority to Military Aide, Ex-Czarist Strategist of Soviet Defense, in Move to Defeat Germans

By DANIEL T. BRIGHAM

Special Cable to THE NEW YORK TIMES.

BERNE, Switzerland, Oct. 3—In a significant move to halt the German war machine storming the western front, Premier Joseph Stalin late this afternoon relinquished the post of People's Commissar for Defense and nominal Commander in Chief of the Russian Armies to his military adviser, Marshal Boris Mikhailovitch Shaposhnikoff, Chief of the General Staff since November, 1941, whom he simultaneously named as Commander in Chief of the Red Army and Air Force and a member of the Central Committee of the Communist party.

This unification of command of all sectors in the hands of a professional soldier instead of a politician was announced in a special Tass communiqué broadcast up to

Continued on Page Twenty-nine

Fliers Tell How Fortresses Downed 13 Nazi Fighters

By The United Press.

A UNITED STATES ARMY AIR FORCES BASE, Somewhere in England, Oct. 3—American flying men told today how a formation of six Flying Fortresses fought off thirty-five crack German fighter planes over France yesterday, destroying a record-breaking total of thirteen—and possibly twelve more—in a ten-minute duel at 25,000 feet. It was probably the biggest bag of fighters ever scored by a bombing formation.

The Flying Fortresses fired all their guns simultaneously to break up the German attack without the aid of fighter-plane escort.

The American planes had just dropped a bombload "right on the spot" at the St. Omer airfield when they were attacked by German fighters and anti-aircraft fire. The German fighters attacked from every direction, but concentrated on trying to hit the Flying Fortresses from below.

Sergeant Beryl Cundick of Mid-

Continued on Page Thirteen

ALLIES REACH EFOGI IN NEW GUINEA PUSH

Advance Six Miles More Up Trail—3 Japanese Cruisers Believed Hit in Solomons

By The Associated Press.

AT UNITED NATIONS HEADQUARTERS, Australia, Sunday, Oct. 4—Scrambling in aggressive pursuit of the Japanese along the upward trail of the Owen Stanley Range, Australian bush soldiers scored a six-mile advance up a precipitous 1,200-foot ridge and have reached Efogi, only seven miles from the entrance to the gap through the mountain backbone, it was announced today.

Punctuating this reversal of Japanese fortunes, in which the enemy has been thrust backward twenty miles from his farthest advance upon Port Moresby in New Guinea during a week-long Australian offensive, Allied torpedo bombers lashed out at a naval concentration surprised at anchor in the Solomons and probably registered close-range hits upon three cruisers and two merchant ships, said a communiqué from General Douglas MacArthur's headquarters.

The torpedo plane raid was made at dawn at Buin, on the southwest tip of Bougainville Island in the Northern Solomons, the communiqué said, and although hits were believed scored, the visibility was too poor to determine the results definitely.

Action burst about the ears of the Japanese in yet a third sector, too, at Mubo, twelve miles south of Salamaua on the New Guinea northeast coast. There Allied outpost forces conducted a daring raid on Japanese positions, killing and wounding at least twenty-five of the enemy.

Perhaps stronger than has been suspected, Allied forces in this quarter have carried out numerous irritating stabs in the very back yard of Japanese-occupied parts of New Guinea.

Allied fighters and bombers pounded hard up and down the

Continued on Page Three

BIG CONVOY IS SENT

U. S. Army Forces Land in Andreanof Islands, Closer to Kiska

MEET NO OPPOSITION

New Fields Send Planes Against the Japanese —Transport Hit

By BERTRAM D. HULEN

Special to THE NEW YORK TIMES.

WASHINGTON, Oct. 3—Positions in the Andreanof group of islands in the Aleutians have been occupied, without opposition, by American Army troops with naval support, the Navy announced today. The movement took place "recently," and Army aircraft, including Flying Fortresses and pursuit planes, now are operating from airfields in the islands, it was stated.

The exact place of the occupation was not announced, but the westernmost island of the Andreanof group is only 125 miles east of Kiska, the main base held by the Japanese in the Aleutians. The easternmost of the group is 365 miles from Kiska and 245 miles from Dutch Harbor, the main American base in the Aleutians.

[An Associated Press correspondent, in a dispatch sent from an island occupied by the Army, said that the convoy that carried the United States forces probably was the largest American convoy ever to sail the North Pacific. It included heavy naval craft, several large transports packed with troops and supplies, and many smaller vessels.]

It is expected that American operations against the Japanese positions can now be conducted with greater facility. Although no details were given concerning the size of the forces at the new vantage point, the operation was obviously a significant step in the direction of increasing pressure on Kiska.

Ever since the Japanese established themselves at Kiska, American planes, surface warships and submarines have been carrying out attacks, and today's Navy com-

Continued on Page Eleven

War News Summarized

SUNDAY, OCTOBER 4, 1942

United States forces were disclosed yesterday to have pushed westward in the Aleutians, while the war still centered in the huge seesaw battle at Stalingrad, where the Russians continued to show strength.

Army units supported by naval craft have occupied the Andreanof group of islands in the Aleutian chain between Dutch Harbor and Japanese-held Kiska, according to a Navy Department announcement. A second attack on an apparently abandoned enemy cargo ship northwest of Kiska and the setting afire of an enemy transport in the habor at Kiska also were revealed. [1:4; map P. 11.]

A dispatch from the Aleutians indicated that the convoy was large and fully equipped. [10:1.]

General MacArthur's headquarters announced that United Nations troops had reached Efogi in their advance against the Japanese in the Owen Stanley range north of Port Moresby. [1:2; map, P. 3.]

In Chungking Wendell L. Willkie told the Chinese he regarded offensive action in the Asiatic battle zones as important as the opening of a European front. [6:1.]

Moscow reported that the Soviet offensive northwest of Stalingrad continued to make headway, but acknowledged loss of a populated place north of the city, while claiming the recapture of positions south of the city previously lost. Berlin reported seven Russian divisions had been destroyed near Lake Ladoga outside Leningrad and 12,370 prisoners taken. [1:2.]

Joseph Stalin announced the surrender of his posts as Commissar for Defense and nominal Commander in Chief to his military adviser, Marshal Boris Shaposhnikoff. [1:3.]

In Berlin Marshal Rommel told the press that "the gates to Egypt" were in Axis hands and promised that his troops would hold their ground. He acknowledged that conditions in the desert were "very difficult." [26:2.]

Britain's Air Ministry announced a strong bombing attack on the Rhineland during the night. Seven planes were lost. Krefeld, textile and heavy industrial city, was the center of the raid. [12:2, with map.]

United States Flying Fortress pilots disclosed after a bombing of St. Omer airfield in Northern France that a record-breaking total of thirteen and possibly twelve more German fighter planes had been shot down in a ten-minute air duel. [1:2-3.]

Deportation of 6,000 persons from Paris, a round-up of several thousand more hostages and the arrest of seventeen alleged British secret agents were reported in connection with spreading evidence of French unrest. [25:1.]

NEW FOOD CEILINGS

Henderson Adds Peaks to Cover Virtually the Entire Field

SOME CUTS SLATED

Order in Few Days Will Place Curbs on All Rents in Country

By FREDERICK R. BARKLEY

Special to THE NEW YORK TIMES.

WASHINGTON, Oct. 3—Acting promptly in compliance with a directive by President Roosevelt under the new price control legislation which became law yesterday, Leon Henderson, Federal Price Administrator, today placed emergency price ceilings, effective Monday, on virtually all food items hitherto exempt from price control.

He also announced that within a few days he would issue an order placing under current rent control procedures all dwelling units in the nation, urban and rural, which were not subject to control under the earlier law, which regulates rents in 190 defense rental areas with an aggregate population of about 50,000,000.

With rent control "ultimately" extended to the entire country, the Office of Price Administration said, it would apply for the first time in Greater New York, Boston, Cincinnati, St. Paul, Minneapolis, Fort Worth, Dallas, Los Angeles and other heavily populated centers.

Five-Day Peak Set as Guide

The emergency food ceilings will freeze at the highest levels of the last five days—Sept. 28 through Oct. 2—the prices charged by individual food retailers, wholesalers and processors. The ceilings will cover prices for butter, cheese, evaporated and condensed milk, eggs, poultry, flour, dry onions, potatoes, fresh and canned citrus fruits and juices, dry edible beans, corn meal and mutton.

The only important foodstuffs exempt from price control for the time being, the OPA pointed out, would be fresh fruits and vegetables (other than potatoes, dry onions and citrus fruits) and fresh fish and peanuts, all of a highly seasonal character and therefore held very difficult of price-ceiling control.

The OPA cited that when the present general maximum price regulation was issued last Spring about 40 per cent of the average family's food budget was excluded from control because the law contained special exemptions or provisions for prices of farm products.

Those conditions, which led President Roosevelt to demand remedial legislation to keep the price level from getting completely out of control, produced the new law, which, Mr. Henderson said, had now permitted extension of the controls to about 90 per cent of the average family food budget.

Conferences Scheduled

Mr. Henderson announced that work would begin immediately to translate into permanent OPA regulations the sixty-day emergency ceilings set today. In keeping with OPA practice, he added, conferences would be held with the growers, processors, wholesalers and rétail sellers of the various food products affected.

For example, the citrus industry will be called into consultation concerning differentials on grades and varieties.

"The action completed by Congress and swiftly confirmed by the President's signature is of most vital importance to every man, woman and child in this country," Mr. Henderson stated. "As I have said before, we have tried to hold down the cost of living with wholly inadequate weapons. The Congress and the President have now in-

Continued on Page Forty-six

HEADS NATION'S ECONOMIC STABILIZATION

Associate Supreme Court Justice James F. Byrnes entering the White House yesterday to confer with President Roosevelt.

Associated Press Wirephoto

CHRYSLER'S 90,000 WIN WLB PAY RISE

Board Allows a 4-Cent Hourly Increase. Which Will Total $7.488,000 for a Year

By The Associated Press.

WASHINGTON, Oct. 3—The War Labor Board today allowed a wage increase of four cents an hour to 90,000 Chrysler Corporation employes who had sought a 12½-cent raise. The decision also set forth a definition of "pay inequalities" significant in connection with the discretionary duties imposed on the board under President Roosevelt's new anti-inflation order.

The increase amounts to $7,488,000 a year. The board's decision was reached more than a week ago but was not made public until after the President issued an executive order stabilizing wages at Sept. 15 levels except where gross inequities exist.

Dr. George W. Taylor, vice

Continued on Page Forty-six

FREE WAGE PACTS BARRED BY ORDER

Management and Unions Lose Right to Work Out Contracts Without Federal Assent

By W. H. LAWRENCE

Special to THE NEW YORK TIMES.

WASHINGTON, Oct. 3—The labor sections of President Roosevelt's economic control order today removed, for the first time in American history, the freedom of employers and trade unions to negotiate wage contracts without recourse to government.

The order, in general, overruled the protests of the American Federation of Labor and the Congress of Industrial Organizations in that it set up a dictator in the person of James F. Byrnes and gave him the power to veto wage advances ordered by the National War Labor Board if either the board or Leon Henderson, Federal Price Administrator, felt that the pay rise would

Continued on Page Forty-five

Major Sports Yesterday

WORLD SERIES

Behind left-handed Ernie White, the Cardinals shut out the Yankees, 2 to 0, to gain a 2-1 lead in games. With 69,123 spectators at the Yankee Stadium, the defending champions were blanked in baseball's Autumn classic for the first time since 1926, which was also the last series in which the Yankees lost two straight. Spud Chandler held St. Louis to three singles in eight innings, but was lifted for a pinch-hitter when trailing, 1—0.

HORSE RACING

Whirlaway won the Jockey Club Gold Cup by three-quarters of a length from Alsab at Belmont Park and boosted his record earnings total to $511,486. In the $77,090 Futurity, Occupation beat Askmenow by five lengths, with Count Fleet third.

FOOTBALL

Tennessee crushed Fordham, but Columbia easily defeated Maine. Penn beat Harvard while Williams upset Princeton. Notre Dame was another upset victim. Scores of leading games:

Alabama 21	Miss. State ... 6	Nebraska 26	Iowa State 0
Amherst 27	Springfield ... 19	No. Carolina . 18	So. Carolina .. 6
Army 14	Lafayette 0	Northw'n 3	Texas 0
Auburn 27	Tulane 13	Ohio State 32	Indiana 21
Boston Coll. .. 33	West Va. 0	Oregon St. ... 13	California ... 8
Bowdoin 18	Wesleyan 0	Penn. 19	Harvard 7
Brown 28	Rhode Island . 0	Penn State ... 14	Bucknell 7
Colgate 18	Cornell 6	Pittsburgh ... 20	S. M. U. 7
Columbia 34	Maine 2	Rice 27	La. State 14
Dartmouth ... 58	Miami (O.) ... 7	Santa Clara . 14	Stanford 6
Duquesne 25	Holy Cross ... 0	Tennessee ... 40	Fordham 14
Georgia 40	Furman 7	T. C. U. 13	Arkansas ... 6
Ga. Tech 13	Notre Dame .. 6	Tulsa 23	Oklahoma ... 0
Great Lakes .. 25	Iowa 0	Vanderbilt .. 26	Purdue 0
Illinois 67	Butler 0	Wake Forest . 20	Duke 7
Iowa Pre-Fl. .. 7	Minnesota ... 6	Washington .. 0	So. Calif. 0
Manhattan ... 27	Muhlenberg .. 7	Wash. State .. 7	Oregon 0
Michigan 20	Mich. State ... 0	Williams 19	Princeton 7
Missouri 26	Colorado 13	Wisconsin ... 35	Marquette ... 7
Navy 35	Virginia 0	Yale 33	Lehigh 6

(Complete Details of These and Other Sports Events in Section 5.)

NEW ERA ORDERED

Justice Gets Full Rule Over Purchasing Power and Costs of Living

SALARIES UNDER CURB

'Congress Has Done Its Part to Stabilize Costs,' President Says

The text of the President's order freezing costs, Page 45.

By C. P. TRUSSELL

Special to THE NEW YORK TIMES

WASHINGTON, Oct. 3—President Roosevelt appointed Associate Justice James F. Byrnes of the Supreme Court today to be Director of Economic Stabilization, clothed him with sweeping authority to control civilian purchasing power, created a board to help him coordinate and command the war upon inflationary living costs, and ordered the immediate stabilization of farm prices, urban and rural rents, wages and salaries paid in industry.

Justice Byrnes resigned his court post to assume the task in which he is charged with formulating and developing, with Presidential approval, a comprehensive national policy covering not only prices, pay and rentals, but profits, rationing, government subsidies and all related matters.

On White House order, Leon Henderson, Price Administrator, put sixty-day emergency ceilings, effective Monday, over the prices of sufficient foods to increase from 60 to 90 per cent the OPA control over the commodities which go into the household market basket.

President Acts Quickly

Acting twenty-nine days before the November date set only last night by the Congress, President Roosevelt put the statutory directives of Congress into motion before noon today, stating:

"The Congress has done its part in helping substantially to stabilize the cost of living. The new legislation removes the exemption of certain foods, agricultural commodities and related products from the price controls of the Emergency Price Control Act, with the result that I have today taken action to stabilize 90 per cent of the country's food bill.

"It leaves the parity principle unimpaired. It reaffirms the powers of the Executive over wages and salaries. It establishes a floor for wages and for farm prices.

"I am certain that from now on this substantial stabilization of the cost of living will assist greatly in bringing the war to a successful conclusion, will make the transition to peace conditions easier after the war and will receive the wholehearted approval of farmers, workers and housewives in every part of the country."

Favorable Reaction in Congress

The President's prompt and decisive action and his selection of Justice Byrnes, a former member, first of the House and later of the Senate, as the head of civilian economy received a favorable reaction in Congress.

Representative McCormack, House Majority Leader, expressed belief that the President had chosen "the best-equipped man in the nation" for the post. Representative Martin, the Minority Leader, called upon Mr. Byrnes and the administrative agencies he would direct to act "quickly, decisively and completely" to halt inflation.

For the new director the President established an Office of Economic Stabilization to function as a part of the Office of Emergency Management, and to advise and consult him the President created an economic stabilization board, of which Mr. Byrnes is chairman. This

Continued on Page Forty-four

"All the News That's Fit to Print."

The New York Times.

LATE CITY EDITION
Slowly rising temperatures today; gentle to moderate winds.
Temperatures Yesterday—Max.,50; Min.,37
Sunrise, 7:30 A. M.; Sunset, 5:40 P. M.

VOL. XCII..No. 30,966. Entered as Second-Class Matter, Postoffice, New York, N. Y. NEW YORK, THURSDAY, NOVEMBER 5, 1942. THREE CENTS IN NEW YORK CITY

ROMMEL IN FULL RETREAT, TANKS, GUNS SMASHED, GENERAL KILLED, ANOTHER AND 9,000 PRISONERS; REPUBLICANS IMPERIL CONTROL OF CONGRESS

MARGIN IS NARROW

Democrats Get Nominal 220 to Rule House—G. O. P. Gains 43

NINE SENATE UPSETS

So Majority's Lead in the Upper House Is Below Twenty

By W. H. LAWRENCE

Mounting Republican gains—43 in the House of Representatives and nine in the Senate on the basis of still incomplete returns—imperiled the Roosevelt Administration's control of Congress, although the Democratic party remained nominally in the majority in both houses.

As each tabulation of the vote in Tuesday's election revealed new inroads yesterday on Democratic strength which surprised even the most optimistic Republican chieftains or pre-election prophets, the New Deal majority in the House and Senate was reduced to the lowest level since President Roosevelt took office in 1933. Frequent combinations of Republicans and conservative Democrats appeared a probable block to Presidential proposals, especially on domestic issues.

The flood of Republican ballots in the first wartime election in twenty-four years was interpreted generally as a reflection of the voters' dissatisfaction with the conduct of the war, both at home and abroad, but in no sense was it regarded as any manifestation of a desire to slacken the war pace or the preparations which must be made at home for victory.

Dewey to the Forefront

Thomas E. Dewey's 590,000-vote plurality in the race for Governor of New York led in the Republican sweep across the country, and placed Mr. Dewey in a leading position in speculation over the 1944 Presidential nominee, along with three other re-elected Governors—John W. Bricker of Ohio, Harold E. Stassen of Minnesota, and Leverett E. Saltonstall of Massachusetts, all of whom won third terms. There was a net gain of three Republican Governors, with some contests still in doubt.

But the most impressive gains were in Congress, which has been under attack consistently by both President Roosevelt and his critics for alleged failure to play its full role in the prosecution of the war.

Early this morning the indicated make-up of the new Congress which will convene on Jan. 3, as compared with the present Congress, was:

SENATE

	New.	Present.
Democrats	56	65
Republicans	38	29
Progressive	1	1
Independent	0	1
In doubt	1	0

HOUSE

	New.	Present.
Democrats	220	256
Republicans	208	165
American Labor Party	1	1
Progressives	2	3
Farmer-Labor	1	1
Independent Democrat	0	1
In doubt	3	*8

*Vacancies.

Notable New Dealers Lose

Notable was the caliber of men whom the Administration lost, especially in the Senate. Gone from the new Congress will be such New Deal stalwarts as these:

Senator George W. Norris, 81-year-old Independent and dean of Congress, who ran a poor second in a three-way race, losing to a Republican, Kenneth Wherry, despite the backing of President Roosevelt.

Senator Prentiss M. Brown, Democrat, of Michigan, leader in the anti-inflation fight, defeated by racket-busting Circuit Judge Homer Ferguson, a Republican.

Senator Josh Lee, Democrat and sponsor of prohibition for

Continued on Page Thirty

Dewey Maps Drastic Change In the Set-Up of State Rule

All 18 Departments of Government Will Be 'Streamlined' Under His Regime—Tax Reforms Pledged by New Governor

By WARREN MOSCOW

Assumption of control of the State government by the Republicans through the election of their entire State ticket and strengthened legislative majorities carries with it complete authority over eighteen State departments as well as a number of special divisions and bureaus set up within these departments, particularly the executive department.

It carries with it some 300 exempt State jobs, for which a patronage rush is certain to develop, as well as power to set up the State government in a form difficult for the Democrats to change, even if they regained power at the next State election.

The latter is particularly important, because laws passed at the next two sessions of the Legislature can be changed only, if partisanship is followed, by a Legislature and a Governor of the same political party. The Democrats have enjoyed control of the Legislature in only one of the twenty years they held the Governorship, making the passage of laws of necessity a matter of compromise between the Governor and the Legislature.

That sweeping changes are in the wind was indicated definitely by Governor-elect Thomas E. Dewey yesterday in his first press conference, when he pledged himself to a "streamlining" of the State government. Since the eighteen departments are required by the Constitution, the streamlining would apparently chiefly affect bureaus and statutory commissions, so far as form is concerned.

For example, the Public Service Commission, the Transit Commission, the State Liquor Authority, the Parole Board, the State Racing Commission and others, such as the State Labor Relations Board, all are headed by men holding of-

Continued on Page Thirty-one

MEN AND MACHINES FOUND STILL IDLE

C. I. O. Witnesses Tell Senate Committee of Flaws Noted in Use of Manpower

By LOUIS STARK

Special to THE NEW YORK TIMES.

WASHINGTON, Nov. 4—Witnesses representing unions in the automotive, steel, shipbuilding, metal mining and communications industries told a Senate Labor and Education subcommittee today that the manpower problem was in a critical state because some plants and cities had large pools of idle, skilled labor while many plants overloaded with war contracts had idle machines.

Some plants are hoarding skilled workmen and others are not using them at their top skills, according to the witnesses, who also referred to what they felt was a lack of properly integrated training programs and centralization of the manpower effort.

James Wishart, research director of the United Automobile Workers, C. I. O., declared that for the first time in its history the automobile industry was facing the threat of a labor shortage. Some 170,000 more workers will be required in Detroit by next June, he said, but the city can no longer absorb 20,000 workers a month because its transportation system is at the breakdown point and houses for the existing working population are simply not available.

"The chaos which now threatens

Continued on Page Nineteen

DRAFT CURB FOUGHT AS THREAT TO ARMY

Foes of O'Daniel Plan to Train Boys a Year at Home Warn It Might Cripple Divisions

By CHARLES HURD

Special to THE NEW YORK TIMES.

WASHINGTON, Nov. 4—Arguments are being advanced in some Congressional circles that incorporation into the draft measure of the amendment by Senator O'Daniel to require that youths of 18 and 19 years who may be drafted should receive a full year of training in the United States might establish a principle which would result in the loss of the war.

Some observers have hazarded the opinion that if the measure goes to the President with the one-year training restriction, Mr. Roosevelt may feel impelled to veto it.

It is possible now to state some of the basic reasons for opposition to the O'Daniel amendment, which sponsors of the 'teen-age draft proposal felt could not be used in debate prior to the election because of the fear that they would cause too much confusion between military necessities and political issues.

Some leaders in the fight against the O'Daniel amendment expressed the wish that Secretary Stimson or some high spokesman for the War Department give a statement of these reasons. But Mr. Stimson declined on the ground that the War Department, having stated its desire to have the 18-19-year-old

Continued on Page Sixteen

POLETTI DEFEATED

Finally Loses by 17,230 With 161 Up-State Districts Missing

MERRITT RE-ELECTED

Representative at Large Is Only Democrat to Escape Sweep

By JAMES A. HAGERTY

The overwhelming victory of Thomas E. Dewey, Republican nominee for Governor, in Tuesday's election, carrying with it the election of all other Republican candidates for State office and increases in the Republican majorities in both houses of the Legislature, will give the Republicans complete control of the State government on Jan. 1 and will then end twenty years of Democratic control of its executive department.

Mr. Dewey defeated Attorney General John J. Bennett, Democrat, by a plurality of 611,022, with fifty-three election districts, all up-State, missing. He carried the State outside New York City by 695,583 and held Mr. Bennett to a plurality of 84,561 in New York City. The total vote in the State, with fifty-three districts missing, was Dewey 2,115,916, Bennett 1,504,894 and Dean Alfange, American Labor party candidate, 400,389.

Dewey Wins Clear Majority

With the Communist, Socialist and Industrial Government candidates for Governor polling an aggregate vote of not more than 80,000 and with the Labor party vote approximately 400,000, Mr. Dewey's election was by a majority. This is believed by his supporters to increase his availability as a candidate for the Republican nomination for President in 1944.

The one Republican State-wide candidate to be defeated was Dr. Charles Muzzicato, nominee for Representative at Large. His running mate, Miss Winifred C. Stanley, was elected along with Representative Matthew J. Merritt, Democratic candidate with Mrs. Flora D. Johnson for these two offices.

Returns with ninety-two up-State election districts missing

Continued on Page Twenty

AT CLOSE QUARTERS IN THE DESERT WARFARE

Advancing British troops take cover behind a knocked-out Nazi tank to dodge a German shell

Associated Press Radiophoto, passed yesterday by British censor

RUSSIANS BEAT OFF FIERCE NAZI BLOWS

Parry Stalingrad Onslaughts, Hold Line Below Nalchik, Gain on Other Fronts

By The Associated Press.

MOSCOW, Thursday, Nov. 5—The Red Army held its ground in Stalingrad and the Central Caucasus yesterday and scored successes on the Black Sea front and northwest of Stalingrad, a Soviet communiqué said today.

[A brief German communiqué claimed no new gains in Russia, but reported continued heavy fighting on the two Caucasus fronts and mopping-up operations in Stalingrad.]

The Germans continued to hurl masses of tanks into the battle on the Nalchik Plains, at the foot of the 18,000-foot Caucasus Mountains, and in the rubble-strewn streets of Stalingrad, but the Russians repulsed all attacks, inflicting heavy losses.

On the two other major fronts—northwest of Stalingrad and in the Black Sea area—the Red Army continued to hold the initiative and

Continued on Page Eight

Italians in One Sector Ask Truce to Bury Their Dead

A truce has been asked by the Italians in one sector of the blazing Egyptian battlefront to permit them to bury their dead, according to dispatches from Cairo yesterday. The request was addressed to the British command, said a Reuter news agency dispatch received in London.

This news came while the Axis radio, in broadcasts heard by The Associated Press and The United Press in both London and New York, acknowledged British gains and admitted British superiority in infantry and armored strength.

Berlin, in a message sent out by the Transocean News Agency, said that the British advance had been accomplished by an infantry attack, supported by tanks, after the repulse of a previous unsupported thrust. The agency explained however, that the Axis troops had adopted a defense in depth, minimizing the British ground gains.

In London, meanwhile, it was announced that the Vichy Government had begun to transfer to the Axis thirty-five Allied merchantmen held in French Mediterranean ports. This disclosure contrasted with the Nazi-controlled Vichy radio's broadcast of reports from La Linea, Spain, of a heavy concentration of British warships at Gibraltar, together with several merchantmen carrying large contingents of American troops. Supplementing this report, D. N. B., the official German news agency, asserted that the British aircraft carriers Furious and Argus, as well as another carrier of an unknown type, had arrived at Gibraltar within the past few days. With the carriers, D. N. B. said, were six cruisers, an auxiliary cruiser, sixteen destroyers and four submarines.

In addition, twenty-six freighters and twelve oil tankers were reported in the convoy. D. N. B. added that developments were being followed by official German quarters with "great interest."

The news of the Italian request

Continued on Page Five

U. S. FORCE OF 7,000 ARRIVES IN EGYPT

Not a Man Lost or an Enemy Sighted on the Voyage From This Country

Special Cable to THE NEW YORK TIMES.

CAIRO, Egypt, Nov. 4—About 7,000 American troops, the largest single contingent yet to be sent, has arrived safely at an Egyptian port, but the simultaneous arrival of 175 United States Army nurses had a greater impact on the country, which is accustomed to the sight of American military men.

Perhaps because the ship was so well equipped to handle hospitalization, the entire shipload came through almost without illness, the most serious instances being four cases of appendicitis. The troopship also arrived with exactly the same number it started with, although stops were made twice en route. Convoy experts say this is rare.

The 7,000 men represent almost every branch of the United States Army, including the air force and medical, signal, postal and quartermaster units. They were under the command on shipboard of Colonel John E. Baird. Now they will be distributed among various existing Middle East agencies, which include the bomber and fighter commands, repair depots for tanks and planes, the Air Service Ferry

Continued on Page Two

War News Summarized

THURSDAY, NOVEMBER 5, 1942

News from all fronts was cheering yesterday, with the war situation dominated by a severe defeat suffered by the Axis in Africa.

Marshal Erwin Rommel's forces in Egypt were declared in a Cairo communiqué to be in full retreat. Nine thousand prisoners had been taken, including General Ritter von Thoma, commander of the Africa Corps, and other high officers. The death of Marshal Rommel's second in command, General von Stumme, was announced. Enemy casualties were said to be exceptionally high. The Axis was also said to have lost 600 planes, 260 tanks, 270 guns and 50,000 tons of supply-laden shipping. United Nations air units were pounding the retreating enemy columns. [1:8; map, P. 2.]

From Cairo it was reported that the Italians had asked for an armistice in one sector to bury their dead. [1:6-7.]

United States fliers participated fully in the offensive. All classes of planes bombed and strafed the enemy. Flying Fortresses destroyed two Axis merchant ships, smashed half of an important jetty and fired fuel installations during Monday's raid on Tobruk. [3:5.]

It was disclosed that 7,000 American troops had arrived safely in the Middle East from United States east coast ports. They consisted chiefly of contingents for the ground crews of the air forces, tank mechanics and other back-of-the-lines units. [1:7.]

Vichy was reported to be collaborating in a new move to help the now hard-pressed Axis forces in Africa. Britain's Ministry of Economic Warfare announced that thirty-five merchant vessels interned in French ports were in the process of being handed over to the Germans and Italians. Three had already been sent to Genoa. [4:5.]

Moscow announced that the Red Army had held firm in the Central Caucasus region beyond Nalchik and at Stalingrad, and had made additional gains near the Black Sea coast and just northwest of Stalingrad. Soviet positions in Stalingrad were again heavily assaulted. [1:5.]

The Soviet Government has appointed a commission to investigate and assess reparation for damage done by the Germans to life and property in Russia. [10:1.]

Japanese troops in New Guinea were still retreating toward their coastal base at Buna, with Australian infantry in pursuit. [12:3.] A Navy Department communiqué on action in the Solomon Islands disclosed that American forces had been advancing westward on Guadalcanal Tuesday and that twenty machine guns and two small artillery pieces had been captured. [1:6-7.]

Mayor Runs Afoul of Mrs. Epstein In City Hall, Gets Sharp Scolding

Mayor La Guardia had an unexpected and somewhat embarrassing meeting at City Hall yesterday afternoon with Mrs. Ethel Epstein, whom he dismissed as his labor secretary last Monday.

Mrs. Epstein had gone to City Hall to say good-bye to her associates there. She was talking to a group of girl secretaries just outside the Mayor's office when the Mayor emerged, apparently unaware that she was in the building. Mrs. Epstein's version of the ensuing conversation follows:

Mayor: Hello, Eddie dear.

Mrs. Epstein: Hello, I don't know what to call you.

Mayor: Wait a minute, Eddie. I want to see you. Stay around.

Mrs. Epstein: I'm sorry, I can't wait. If you want to see me, you see me right here. I'd like to know—why did you fire me?

Mayor: I had a bigger job in mind for you, but you spoiled it by giving out my letter to the newspapers.

Mrs. Epstein: Just give me one reason why you fired me. Why didn't you call me down here, instead of sending a letter? You didn't have the guts to tell me.

Mayor: You should not have criticized my administration in the radio speech you made Monday night. You said my first term was my best. No, Eddie, it wasn't. This is my best administration.

Mrs. Epstein: You are causing an open scandal by your failure to provide an agency where city employes can present their grievances.

Mayor: Oh, Eddie—how can you be so unfair?

Continued on Page Twenty-nine

U. S. Forces on Guadalcanal Win Some Enemy Positions on West

Special to THE NEW YORK TIMES.

WASHINGTON, Nov. 4—The United States forces on Guadalcanal Island continued their advance against the Japanese westward of our position as recently as the morning of Tuesday (Solomons date), the Navy reported in a communiqué issued tonight.

At the same time it was noted that there had been no report of activity by the reinforcements of Japanese reported yesterday as having been landed on the east flank of the American positions on the night of Monday-Tuesday.

The American troops in their advance, it was stated, captured twenty enemy machine guns and two small artillery pieces. The Navy announcement said that only "small gains" were made, as the attacking forces plunged through jungle country, closely supported by Army and Navy bombers and fighters, which presumably blasted Japanese entrenched positions with bombs and strafed whatever enemy forces were in sight.

Nevertheless, continuance of the attack indicated that the American troops, who seized the initiative on Sunday, not only controlled the situation in the immediate vicinity of their position on the north shore of Guadalcanal but were getting supplies ample for the needs of an offensive operation.

Tonight's communiqué, while brief, indicated that the American forces, including both Marines and Army troops, apparently had mastered by three months of bitter experience the type of jungle war-

Continued on Page Twelve

BRITISH SWEEP ON

Foe Loses 600 Planes, 260 Tanks, 270 Guns, 50,000 Ship Tons

AIR BLOWS CONTINUE

Casualties Suffered by the Enemy Are Termed 'Exceptionally High'

By JAMES MacDONALD

Special Cable to THE NEW YORK TIMES.

LONDON, Nov. 4—The Axis forces in Egypt were in "full retreat" tonight, with the British Eighth Army in hot pursuit, in which it was aided by Allied air forces, according to a special joint communiqué reaching London late tonight from Cairo.

Their strong advance positions having finally crumbled under relentless hammering by infantrymen and ceaseless pounding by artillery and attacks by United States, British, Dominion and other Allied airmen, General Field Marshal Erwin Rommel's forces appeared to be almost completely routed only twelve days after the present struggle began. The communiqué said that the enemy had suffered big losses.

More Than 9,000 Prisoners

More than 9,000 Axis troops have been captured, among whom the most important prize is General Ritter von Thoma, commander of the German Africa Corps. General von Stumme, senior general, said to have been in command during Marshal Rommel's recent trip to Germany, is known to have been killed. A number of other high-ranking German and Italian officers have been captured. Moreover, enemy losses in killed and wounded have been "exceptionally high."

Although full details regarding the amount of booty taken by the Eighth Army are still lacking, the communiqué said that at least 270 guns had been destroyed or captured and that 260 German and Italian tanks had been destroyed.

The big tank battle between the opposing forces reached the full pitch of its fury yesterday.

In the twelve days since the Allied offensive began, Allied air forces have destroyed or damaged more than 300 enemy planes in air combats and have destroyed or put out of action a similar number on the ground during raids on Marshal Rommel's rear positions.

At the same time naval and air forces have sunk 50,000 tons and have damaged almost the same amount of enemy shipping taking supplies across the Mediterranean to the Axis forces in North Africa.

The only mention of losses on the Allied side is that those of the air forces have been "light."

Narrow Road of Retreat

At present the retreating German and Italian armies must follow a narrow course that will keep them so tightly compressed that air attacks could be made with devastating effect.

Observers here expect that such attacks will be made by the Allied airmen, who have kept up almost ceaseless blows day and night, not only on Marshal Rommel's forward area but also on his airfields and ammunition and storage dumps in the rear.

It is about 300 airline miles from El Alamein to Tobruk, and roughly 550 to Bengazi, but how far forward of those places Marshal Rommel has made preparations against the eventuality of the present Allied drive is not known here.

There is a possibility that he will at least attempt stands at Ma'aten Bagush and Matruh, since there are field fortifications in both those areas. Beyond Matruh the

Continued on Page Five

1942

John Barrymore, whose 1922 portrayal of *Hamlet* set a record for Shakespearean performances, died.

Carole Lombard, the wonderful comedienne loved by all America, perished in a plane crash while on a War Bond-selling tour.

Hedy Lamarr flashes the "V" sign while promoting the sale of War Bonds.

A scene from the film biography of George M. Cohan, *Yankee Doodle Dandy,* with Jeanne and James Cagney, Joan Leslie, Walter Huston and Rosemary De Camp.

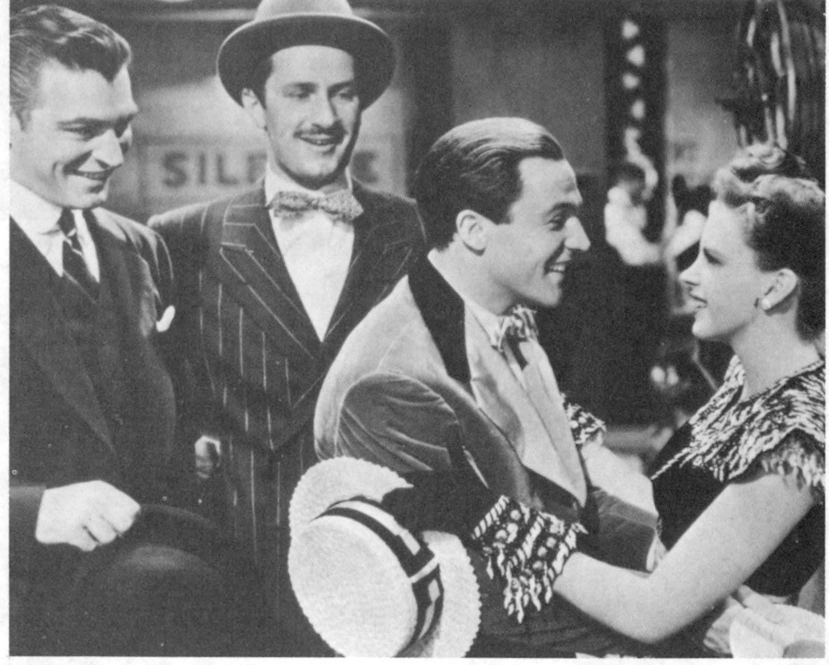

Gene Kelly and Judy Garland starred in Busby Berkeley's *For Me and My Gal.*

Dorothy Lamour, Bing Crosby, Bob Hope and Donna Drake in *The Road to Morocco.*

"All the News That's Fit to Print."

NEWS INDEX, PAGE 55, THIS SECTION

The New York Times.

Copyright, 1942, by The New York Times Company.

LATE CITY EDITION
Continued cool today with light winds.
Temperatures Yesterday—Max., 57; Min., 45
Sunrise, 7:34 A. M.; Sunset, 5:48 P. M.

Section 1

VOL. XCII—No. 30,969. Entered as Second-Class Matter, Postoffice, New York, N. Y. NEW YORK, SUNDAY, NOVEMBER 8, 1942. Including Magazine and Book Sections. TEN CENTS New York City and Vicinity

AMERICAN FORCES LAND IN FRENCH AFRICA; BRITISH NAVAL, AIR UNITS ASSISTING THEM; EFFECTIVE SECOND FRONT, ROOSEVELT SAYS

U.S. DRIVES ON BUNA

American Troops Flown to Area Closing In on Big Japanese Base

PAPUA IS OVERRUN

All Except Beachhead of Buna-Gona Seized in New Guinea Push

By The Associated Press.

AT UNITED NATIONS HEADQUARTERS, Australia, Sunday, Nov. 8—American combat troops are in action near Buna, vital Japanese base on the north New Guinea coast, General Douglas MacArthur disclosed today.

Simultaneously, General MacArthur disclosed that the Allies have occupied Goodenough Island to the northeast of New Guinea, off Collingwood Bay, in an obvious flanking movement.

[American Army troops on Guadalcanal advanced on Friday (Solomons time) in the area to the west of Henderson airfield, the Navy reported yesterday. They crossed the Malimbui River a few miles south of Koli Point, where the Japanese recently landed reinforcements, but met little opposition.]

It was from Buna, in midsummer, that the Japanese began a drive across tortuous trails of the Owen Stanley Mountains which carried to within thirty-two miles of Port Moresby, Allied base on the south coast, before it was stalled. Late in September the Allies began encircling and infiltration movements which rolled the Japanese back and yesterday's communiqué had mentioned bitter fighting at Oivi, which is fifty-five miles south of Buna.

Japanese Resist at Oisi

"American ground troops in force, transported by air from Australia during the last month, have penetrated Central and Northern Papua to the vicinity of Buna," a communiqué stated.

"The Allied forces now control all of Papua except the beach head in the Buna-Gona area."

The surprising development came as a thrust around the eastern end of New Guinea from Milne Bay where Japanese troops landed in July only to be pinned against the sea and slain or forced to their ships.

"Units from Milne Bay," the communiqué said, "have now completed clearing remnants of hostile forces from the islands to the north and have occupied adjacent strategic points."

While this disclosure was being made, Australian ground forces still were meeting fierce resistance at Oivi where the retreating Japanese are making a stand. Today's communiqué said the Australians maintained constant pressure and were resorting to their hitherto successful tactics of local encircling movements in efforts to dislodge the defenders.

The Allied air force continued to support the overland drive with strafing attacks on the Japanese troops.

Island Attacked Oct. 22

AT UNITED NATIONS HEADQUARTERS, Australia, Sunday, Nov. 8 (UP)—The announcement of sweeping Allied gains in New Guinea came as a surprise to observers here, although an Australian offensive through mountainous central New Guinea had been making steady progress toward the north coast for the past five weeks.

[Delayed dispatches from Harold Guard, United Press staff correspondent in New Guinea, revealed that the Americans had

Continued on Page Forty-five

LEADS IN AFRICA

Lieut. Gen. Dwight Eisenhower
Associated Press

R. A. F. ROCKS GENOA; U. S. RAID ON BREST

Bombers From Britain Pound North Italy 2 Nights in Row —Hit Nazis on Coast

Special Cable to THE NEW YORK TIMES.

LONDON, Sunday, Nov. 8—Bombers from Britain struck a heavy blow at Northern Italy over Friday night, blasting the port of Genoa again in support of the Eighth Army's battling of the Nazis and Italians in the African desert.

Again last night the Royal Air Force sent its big bombers over Northern Italy, British officials reported briefly early today. The announcement meant that the R. A. F. from here was seeing to it that the Axis forces in Africa got no help from home.

American heavy bombers, both Flying Fortresses and Liberators, escorted by Allied fighters, carried out a smashing attack on the docks and U-boat pens at Brest in occupied France yesterday afternoon, United States Army headquarters here announced.

Bombs were seen to strike the targets at Brest. The communiqué stressed that sharp Nazi anti-aircraft fire and enemy fighter opposition were encountered over the coast of Brittany.

The Brest raiders shot down four Nazi fighters. All the United States bombers returned, but one Allied fighter was lost.

The R. A. F.'s fighter squadrons

Continued on Page Twenty-one

NAZIS NEAR LIBYA

British Drive Out to Bar New Stand by Enemy or Reinforcements

FOE BOMBED ALL NIGHT

Pursuers Reported to Be Within 40 Miles of Halfaya Pass

By The United Press.

CAIRO, Egypt, Nov. 7—The British Eighth Army under Lieut. Gen. Bernard L. Montgomery hurled armored forces, motorized infantry and swarms of planes tonight at the remnants of German General Field Marshal Erwin Rommel's once-proud Afrika Korps—possibly only 25,000 out of an original 140,000—now trying to brace for a stand at Halfaya [Hellfire] Pass on the Libyan frontier, 240 miles west of the Alamein battleground.

The main body of the British forces was reported to be well west of Matruh, 110 miles west of El Alamein, and advance striking forces were believed to be as far as 200 miles west of El Alamein, or close to the Egyptian-Libyan frontier, 240 miles west of El Alamein.

How many men Marshal Rommel had left in the Halfaya area could not be established. Already 20,000 prisoners have been counted in British hands. Marshal Rommel's desert casualties were estimated at approximately 20,000 more. In addition, 75,000 Italian troops had been left far behind the swirling battleground, ready to surrender when the British could find time and men to round them up.

Marshal Rommel entered the battle with a maximum of 140,000 troops in the forward area. It was doubted whether he had more than one or two divisions left to attempt another stand at Halfaya unless he had been able to rush large reinforcements from the rear.

It appeared possible tonight that the Axis forces might not even attempt to stand at Halfaya, but would, instead, continue their headlong flight as deeply as possible into Libya in an effort to open a gap between themselves and the Eighth Army.

Such a manoeuvre, however, may already be doomed to failure. General Montgomery has ordered that every attempt be made to cut off Marshal Rommel's retreat. It was believed that he might have sent a hard-hitting, fast-moving

Continued on Page Four

SHOCK TROOPS LEAD

Simultaneous Landings Made Before Dawn at Numerous Points

PLANES GUARD SKIES

An Armada Pours Men on the Beaches—Early Actions Satisfactory

By WES GALLAGHER
Associated Press Correspondent

ALLIED HEADQUARTERS IN NORTH AFRICA, Sunday, Nov. 8—American soldiers, marines and sailors from one of the greatest armadas ever put into a single military operation swarmed ashore today on the Vichy-controlled North Africa shore before dawn, striking to break Hitler's hold on the Mediterranean.

[Reports reaching Allied headquarters in North Africa today disclosed that successful landings had been made by American assault parties on beaches of North Africa near two main objectives outlined in operational plans, an Associated Press dispatch stated.

[British forces reported attemping a landing at Algiers after a bombardment were said by the Vichy radio to have been "beaten off."]

Tall, decisive Lieut. Gen. Dwight D. (Ike) Eisenhower, supreme commander of the huge forces involved in the operation, worked throughout the night directing the first great American blow at the Axis.

Included in the forces were crack combat troops, Rangers (airborne units) and the cream of America's airmen.

British naval and air force units supported the American landing forces, who were preceded by a snowstorm of leaflets and a radio barrage promising the French that the United States had no intention of seizing French possessions and only sought to prevent Axis infiltration.

It undoubtedly was the longest over-water military operation ever attempted, with hundreds of ships in great convoys coming thousands of miles under the protection of British and American sea and air might.

I came on one of these big convoys.

Fighting-fit American soldiers

Continued on Page Five

WHERE THE UNITED STATES PREPARES FOR NEW FRONT

As the survivors of Marshal Rommel's beaten German legions fled westward toward the Libyan border (1), powerful American land, sea and air forces landed behind them at various places in Vichy France's colonies along the Mediterranean (2) and on the shores of the Atlantic, apparently in Morocco (3). British naval and aerial units are assisting them. There was no indication of military action against Vichy's possessions on the western bulge of the Atlantic (4). A large and comprehensive map of the African and Mediterranean theatre of war will be found on Page 1 of Section 4 of this issue of THE TIMES. However, Section 4 had gone to press before the announcement last night of the landing of American troops.

LANDING PLAN KEPT SECRET BY WRITERS

Americans Selected for Duty, Bureaus Sworn to Silence—Eisenhower Slipt Away

By RAYMOND DANIELL
Special Cable to THE NEW YORK TIMES.

LONDON, Sunday, Nov. 8—For weeks American newspaper men have been the custodians of one of war's biggest secrets. It was not an easy secret to keep because through all that time they had to improvise excuses for the absence of a large number of the members of their London staffs to conceal the fact that they had gone with the expeditionary forces.

Most London offices of Amer-

Continued on Page Fourteen

President's Statement

Special to THE NEW YORK TIMES.

WASHINGTON, Nov. 7—President Roosevelt's statement announcing the opening of a second front in French North and West Africa follows:

In order to forestall an invasion of Africa by Germany and Italy, which, if successful, would constitute a direct threat to America across the comparatively narrow sea from Western Africa, a powerful American force equipped with adequate weapons of modern warfare and under American command is today landing on the Mediterranean and Atlantic coasts of the French colonies in Africa.

The landing of this American Army is being assisted by the British Navy and air forces, and it will, in the immediate future, be reinforced by a considerable number of divisions of the British Army.

This combined Allied force, under American command, in conjunction with the British campaign in Egypt is designed to prevent an occupation by the Axis armies of any part of Northern or Western Africa and to deny to the aggressor nations a starting point from which to launch an attack against the Atlantic coast of the Americas.

In addition, it provides an effective second-front assistance to our heroic allies in Russia.

The French Government and the French people have been informed of the purpose of this expedition and have been assured that the Allies seek no territory and have no intention of interfering with friendly French authorities in Africa.

The government of France and the people of France and the French possessions have been requested to cooperate with and assist the American expedition in its effort to repel the German and Italian international criminals, and by so doing to liberate France and the French Empire from the Axis yoke.

This expedition will develop into a major effort by the Allied Nations and there is every expectation that it will be successful in repelling the planned German and Italian invasion of Africa and prove the first historic step to the liberation and restoration of France.

U. S. MEETS 'THREAT'

Big Expeditions Invade North and West Africa to Forestall Axis

EISENHOWER AT HEAD

President Urges French to Help, Calls Move Aid to Russia

Roosevelt's appeal to French people and Eisenhower's message to North Africans, Pg. 8.

By C. P. TRUSSELL
Special to THE NEW YORK TIMES.

WASHINGTON, Nov. 7—Powerful American forces, supported by British naval and air forces, landed simultaneously tonight at numerous points on the Mediterranean and Atlantic coasts of French North Africa, forestalling an anticipated invasion of Africa by Germany and Italy and launching effective second-front assistance to Russia, President Roosevelt announced tonight.

Lieut. Gen. Dwight D. Eisenhower is in command.

The President made the announcement even as the American forces, equipped with adequate weapons of modern warfare, he emphasized, were making the landings.

President Speaks to France

Soon he was speaking direct to the French Government and the French people by short-wave radio and in their own tongue, giving assurances that the Allies seek no territory and have no intention of interfering with friendly French, official or civilian. He called upon them to cooperate in repelling "the German and Italian international criminals."

By doing so, he said, they could help liberate France and the French Empire.

[United States and British planes dropped leaflets in France and French Africa containing messages to the people from President Roosevelt and General Eisenhower, London reported.]

General Eisenhower himself, the White House let it be known, also spoke by radio to the French people, explaining the purposes of the invasions.

His proclamation, delivered while the American troops were making their landings, gave specific directions to French land, sea and air forces in North Africa as to how they could avoid misunderstanding and prevent action against them by a system of signals. This is a military operation, General Eisen-

Continued on Page Three

Major Sports Yesterday

FOOTBALL

Making both touchdowns in the second half, Notre Dame defeated Army before 75,142 spectators at the Yankee Stadium. With a scoring pass in the first period and several goal-line stands, Navy thrilled 74,000 fans at Philadelphia by upsetting Penn. Both Fordham and Columbia lost free-scoring contests here and the Big Three—Princeton, Yale and Harvard—all went down to defeat. Iowa toppled hitherto unbeaten Wisconsin. Scores of leading games:

Winner	Score	Loser	Score	Winner	Score	Loser	Score
Alabama	29	So. Carolina	0	Miss. State	7	Tulane	0
Amherst	35	Trinity	6	Missouri	26	Nebraska	6
Boston Coll.	28	Temple	0	Moravian	32	C. C. N. Y.	0
Brown	20	Holy Cross	14	Navy	7	Penn.	0
Colgate	35	Columbia	26	Notre Dame	13	Army	0
Cornell	13	Yale	0	Ohio State	59	Pittsburgh	19
Dartmouth	19	Princeton	7	Oklahoma	76	Kan. State	0
Duke	42	Maryland	0	Oregon	14	U. C. L. A.	7
Duquesne	7	St. Mary's	7	Penn State	18	Syracuse	13
Georgia	75	Florida	0	Rice	40	Arkansas	9
Ga. Pre-Fl.	41	Auburn	14	So. Calif.	21	California	7
Ga. Tech	47	Kentucky	7	Stanford	20	Washington	7
Great Lakes	42	Purdue	0	Texas	20	Baylor	0
Illinois	14	Northwestern	7	Tex. A. & M.	27	S. M. U.	20
Indiana	7	Minnesota	0	Texas Tech	13	T. C. U.	6
Iowa	6	Wisconsin	0	Vanderbilt	19	Mississippi	0
La. State	26	Fordham	13	Wash. State	25	Mich. State	13
Michigan	35	Harvard	7	Williams	31	Wesleyan	6

HORSE RACING

Good Morning won the Florence Nightingale Purse by half a length from Too Timely on the war-relief program before 22,099 racegoers who bet $1,550,089 at Belmont Park. Aonbarr defeated Riverland by a neck in the Grayson Handicap at Pimlico.

HOCKEY

The New York Rangers downed the Montreal Canadiens, 4—3, in the overtime opening game at Madison Square Garden.

(Complete Details of These and Other Sports Events in Section 5.)

War News Summarized

SUNDAY, NOVEMBER 8, 1942

The White House announced last night that powerful American forces were landing on the Atlantic and Mediterranean coasts of French North Africa to forestall a German invasion. The announcement stated that the landing was to prevent the creation of an Axis threat to the Atlantic coast of the Americas across the narrow sea in Western Africa. France has been assured that the Allies seek no territory. [1:8.]

American correspondents with the African expeditionary force told of simultaneous landings by the United States troops at many points hundreds of miles apart. [1:4.]

Britain's Eighth Army continued its pursuit in North Africa of Marshal Rommel's shattered army. Twenty thousand prisoners had been taken, according to Cairo. British columns were said to be 200 miles west of El Alamein, close to the Libyan border. [1:3; map, P. 4.]

London announced that British heavy bombers had launched a "concentrated and effective" attack on Genoa Friday night and again raided Northern Italy last night. United States bombers attacked the U-boat base at Brest, France, and other planes from Britain pounded Nazi targets from the Netherlands to the Bay of Biscay. [1:2; map, P. 21.]

Moscow reported that the Soviet armies held on all fronts and killed some 1,800 of the enemy on the Stalingrad and Caucasus fronts. The German advances in the Nalchik region had apparently been halted. [38:4-5.]

General Douglas MacArthur's headquarters announced that American troops in force had been transported by air to New Guinea and had penetrated to the vicinity of Buna, Japanese base on the north coast. [1:1; map, P. 45.]

The United States Navy announced that Army forces on Guadalcanal Island in the Solomons had attacked Japanese troops to the east of the airfield Nov. 6 and had encountered little opposition. Announcement was also made that at least 5,188 Japanese had been killed in land fighting on Tulagi and Guadalcanal since the United States occupation Aug. 7. [46:1 with map.]

United States bombers attacked successfully the docks at Rangoon, Burma, and returned to their bases in India. [46:8.]

Blow to Knock Italy Out of the War Called Goal of American Invasion

Special Cable to THE NEW YORK TIMES.

LONDON, Sunday, Nov. 8—Allied Army, Navy and air forces commanded by Lieut. Gen. Dwight D. Eisenhower, commander of all American forces in the European theatre, have struck a powerful blow to free the Mediterranean from Axis control and knock Italy out of the war. That, in the opinion of military observers here, is the meaning of the movement of United States forces that now become part of the gigantic pincers with which it is expected that the last vestiges of the German and Italian forces in North Africa will be annihilated.

The movement now under way called for the finest timing. It was essential that, before that huge armada of whose presence at Gibraltar the Nazis were aware got under way, Britain's Eighth Army in Egypt should break through Marshal Erwin Rommel's defenses and start the westward push that is fast becoming a rout. Now United States soldiers swarming ashore at many points in French North Africa are closing Marshal Rommel's back door.

The first stage of the battle just beginning will be a struggle for the control of roads, railways and airfields in Algeria and the neighboring colony of Tunisia. Once the control of these has been won, Allied reinforcements and supplies will be able to dispense with the long journey around the Cape of Good Hope that has been one of

Continued on Page Thirteen

Petain Says Vichy Will 'Defend' Lands

By The Associated Press.

LONDON, Sunday, Nov. 8—The Vichy radio said today that Marshal Henri Philippe Petain had sent President Roosevelt a message expressing his "astonishment and sadness" at learning of "the aggression of your troops against North Africa."

Marshal Pétain said that the reasons given by the President for the landings failed to justify them and added:

"France and its honor are involved. We are attacked and we will defend ourselves."

The Vichy government issued a communiqué opening with an "appeal to Frenchmen not to allow yourselves to be swayed by foreign broadcasts."

"All the News That's Fit to Print."

The New York Times.

LATE CITY EDITION
Much colder today with diminishing winds.
Temperatures Yesterday—Max., 65; Min., 50
Sunrise, 7:28 A. M.; Sunset, 5:46 P. M.

VOL. XCII. No. 30,972. Entered as Second-Class Matter, Postoffice, New York, N. Y. NEW YORK, WEDNESDAY, NOVEMBER 11, 1942. THREE CENTS IN NEW YORK CITY

HITLER TO TAKE OVER ALL FRANCE AND CORSICA; OUR TROOPS IN ORAN, SPEEDING TOWARD LIBYA, TANKS IN CASABLANCA; ROOSEVELT TELLS PLANS

ALLIES IN ACCORD

President Reveals Stalin Was Informed of Plan by Churchill

'NOW IT CAN BE TOLD'

How Decision on Second Front Move Was Made Is Described

By W. H. LAWRENCE
Special to THE NEW YORK TIMES.

WASHINGTON, Nov. 10—Declaring that a second front has to be tailor-made and custom-built and cannot be purchased ready made in a department store, President Roosevelt gave his press conference today a detailed account of the months of planning that preceded the French North African expedition and the limiting factors that made impossible a large-scale Allied offensive across the English Channel before the middle of 1943.

In excellent humor, Mr. Roosevelt leaned back in his chair, puffing on a cigarette and described tersely how Prime Minister Winston Churchill and he had decided on the African offensive as early as the end of June, but had to take it on the chin in silence when ignorant outsiders, who could not have been cognizant of the fact, were demanding something—a second front—that had already been decided upon by the two governments after consultation with their principal fighting allies.

Chronology of Planning

The President's chronology of offensive planning, with the first decision to attack across the English Channel being changed to an expedition into French North Africa, cleared up a major change in language relating to a second front from the June 12 joint communiqué issued by Mr. Roosevelt and Vyacheslaff M. Molotoff, Soviet Foreign Commissar, and the June 27 joint statement of the President and Prime Minister Churchill.

On June 12, when the President and Commissar Molotoff said that the United States and Russia had reached a full understanding on the "urgent tasks of creating a second front in Europe in 1942," a final decision to abandon the Channel offensive in favor of the North African attack had not yet been made, it appeared from the President's recital.

But on June 27, when the President and Prime Minister said simply that coming operations by the military forces of the United Nations would "divert German strength from the attack on Russia," this government and Great Britain already were in agreement on shifting the offensive to North Africa.

The final decisions on the North African move, including the points of attack, the number of men to be employed and the problems of transport and naval protection, were settled toward the end of July at the London conferences of the Prime Minister and British military and naval leaders with General George C. Marshall, Army Chief of Staff; Admiral Ernest J. King, Commander in Chief of the United States Fleet and Chief of Naval Operations, and Harry L. Hopkins, personal representative of the President. The actual date of attack was decided by the end of August, he said.

As the President explained it, in response to a request for a "now it can be told story," the inception of the offensive action in which the American and British armies are engaged in North Africa goes back to about two weeks after Pearl Harbor, when the President invited Prime Minister Churchill and his joint staff to come to Washington just before Christmas. The time had come, he said,

Continued on Page Seven

Thanksgiving Feast Is Set for Army

Here is the menu, announced yesterday by the War Department, for the Thanksgiving dinner on Nov. 26 to be served to American soldiers in all parts of the world as well as in the United States:

Fruit Cup
Roast Turkey — Dressing and
Cranberry Sauce — Giblet Gravy
Mashed Potatoes
Corn — Peas
Stuffed Celery — Tomato Salad
Assorted Pickles
Bread — Butter
Pumpkin Pie
Apples — Grapes
Coffee
Candies — Nuts

MANPOWER DRAFT OPPOSED IN REPORT

Management and Labor in WMC Policy Group Join in Backing Voluntary Plan

The war manpower report is printed on Page 21.

Special to THE NEW YORK TIMES.

WASHINGTON, Nov. 10—A Management-Labor Policy Committee, unanimously opposing enactment of a national war service act for the conscription of labor at this time, has submitted a broad-scale voluntary program designed to eliminate serious manpower problems which now threaten successful prosecution of the war, it was announced today.

After the White House had made public the report submitted Friday, President Roosevelt told his press conference that, while he had been giving considerable study to the recommendations, he had not yet decided whether to put any of them in effect. He said there was no immediate emergency which would require executive action or a request for legislation at once, but added that the problem would grow increasingly serious in the months ahead and that something would be done in a few weeks.

In response to a question, the President said he had not yet decided whether to shift the Selective Service system, which handles the drafting of men for the Army, from its present independent status to the War Manpower Commission, which was one of the recommendations of the Management-Labor Policy Committee.

Major Policy Changes Proposed

Warning that "major weaknesses exist in the present approach to the over-all manpower situation, weaknesses that require immediate attention and correction, and which, if not corrected, will seriously impede the war effort," the committee suggested these major changes in governmental policy if an industrial and military force of 62,500,000 men

Continued on Page Twenty-one

ORAN BATTLE BRIEF

500 Miles of Africa's Coastline Now in Hands of Allies

PLANES, SHIPS HELP

New Assault Southeast of Algiers Reported by Paris Radio

By The Associated Press.

LONDON, Nov. 10 — United States expeditionary armies wiped out effective resistance along 500 miles of Africa's Western Mediterranean coast today with the conquest of Oran, Algeria's second city, and a German report said that the Bey of Tunis had granted President Roosevelt's request for the passage of American troops to Libya.

[In Washington, President Roosevelt said yesterday that he had received no reply to his message to the Bey of Tunis.]

On the Atlantic coast, the resistance of Casablanca, the chief city of Morocco, was fast crumbling under all-out naval and air assault by United States Rear Admiral Henry K. Hewitt's heavy warships and dive-bombers as American armored columns infiltrated the city's eastern suburbs with tanks.

Rabat, the normal seat of French power in Morocco, on the coast above Casablanca, evidently was isolated and evacuated by the Vichy commander, General Charles Nogues.

Broad Victory Seen Near

Hence it appeared that in a matter of hours the United States armies commanded by Lieut. Gen. Dwight D. Eisenhower would be in effective control of all French North Africa, save for Eastern Algeria and Tunisia.

[Yves Chatel, Governor General of Algeria, has moved his headquarters to Constantine, in the east, and reassumed his administration there, the Vichy radio announced last night, according to The Associated Press in New York.

[In London The United Press recorded a Paris broadcast saying that American forces were advancing from Algiers in the direction of Bou Saada, 120 miles southeast.]

American contingents evidently were well on their way to Libya, either through Tunisia or around it. The report of the Bey's acquiescence was received with some reserve here lest it be merely an attempt to justify the movement of Axis troops into Tunisia.

Time and time again today Vichy's radio insisted that "all is calm" in Eastern and Central Algeria and Tunisia. Some broadcasts, however, reported fighting at Blida, twenty-five miles inland from Algiers.

Official Allied Headquarters as

Continued on Page Four

AMERICAN OPERATIONS IN AFRICA PROCEED SMOOTHLY

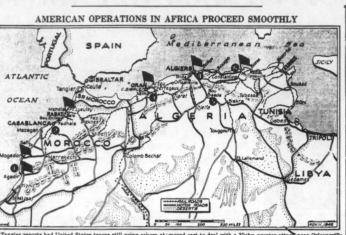

Tangier reports had United States troops still going ashore at Agadir and Mogador (1). The principal, almost the only, center of resistance was at Casablanca (2), where the United States Navy largely subdued Vichy naval opposition and three American tank columns were said to have smashed into the outskirts. Oran (3) fell to an American pincers manoeuvre and one occupying force moved east to deal with a Vichy counter-attack near Orleansville. Land operations had ceased at captured Algiers (4), but there was some resistance at Blida, to the south. From Algiers the Americans were reported to have struck southeastward toward Bou Saada (5), and from Philippeville (6) they were said to be moving eastward in the direction of the frontier of Tunisia.

CHURCHILL CREDITS PLAN TO PRESIDENT

His Own Role That of 'Active and Ardent Lieutenant' in African 'Second Front'

The text of Mr. Churchill's address is on Page 4.

By RAYMOND DANIELL
Wireless to THE NEW YORK TIMES.

LONDON, Nov. 10—The first public utterance by Prime Minister Winston Churchill since General Sir Bernard L. Montgomery's victory in Egypt and the landing of Lieut. Gen. Dwight D. Eisenhower's American Army in French Colonial Africa was made today at Mansion House. It was a renunciation of any Allied territorial aims, a pledge that France should rise again, and a flat declaration that the sole purpose of the Allied landings in Morocco and Algeria was

Continued on Page Four

Tanks Batter Casablanca; Battleship Afire in Harbor

By The United Press.

LONDON, Nov. 10—Vichy broadcasts recorded here reported today that three United States tank columns had crashed into Casablanca, Morocco, and that the city was under heavy attack by superior American forces and was being bombarded violently. Governor General Charles Nogues of Morocco has fled from Rabat to the interior, the radio added.

The broadcasts said that "our troops still are holding out east of Casablanca," while coastal artillery and field guns were resisting vigorously.

Three tank columns closed in on Casablanca, the French said, and swarmed into its outskirts.

A Tangiers dispatch revealed that Fighting French forces were in action at Casablanca against the Vichy troops. It said the Fighting French were battling in the old part of the city, where they were encircled. Americans held the Casablanca reservoir, enabling them to cut off the city's water

Continued on Page Eight

NEW ALLIED FLEET REPORTED MASSING

Concentration of Warships and Transports Noted in Gibraltar Harbor

By The Associated Press.

LONDON, Nov. 10 — Reports from France tonight said another powerful fleet of United Nations warships and a great number of merchantmen were gathering at Gibraltar, while throughout European waters and in the Atlantic naval activities were reported on a vast scale.

Reports from the Continent said some of the vessels of that portion of the French fleet stationed at Toulon had slipped off into the Mediterranean. There was speculation as to whether they were heading for the vicinity of Bizerte, Tunisia, through which American land forces proposed to advance on what is left of General Field Marshal Erwin Rommel's force in Libya.

The German High Command made an unsupported announce-

Continued on Page Six

HITLER, MUSSOLINI, LAVAL IN A PARLEY

Rome Reported Scene of Talks—Duce Said to Ask Nazis for Aid in Crisis

By DANIEL T. BRIGHAM
By Telephone to THE NEW YORK TIMES.

BERNE, Switzerland, Nov. 10—Negotiations for an alliance of Germany, France and Italy against the United Nations were reported under way "somewhere in Europe" tonight.

Most indications pointed to the scene as Rome, although Balkan speculation suggested Munich and other sources hinted at Salzburg. The Brenner Pass, in view of the reported presence of Adolf Hitler and Pierre Laval, Vichy Chief of Government, with their suites at the conferences, is not regarded as sufficiently equipped to house such a parley.

The negotiations and discussions of the future agreement are understood to be in the hands of Herr Hitler, who is accompanied by Reich Marshal Hermann Goering and General Field Marshal Wilhelm Keitel, for the Germans. M. Laval is attended only by his envoy to the Vatican, Leon Berard, and Premier Mussolini is being advised by General Ugo Cavallero, on the military side, and Count Ciano, Italian Foreign Minister.

Asked at his usual press conference for foreign newspaper men today for confirmation on denials of the reports of such a gathering

Continued on Page Ten

War News Summarized

WEDNESDAY, NOVEMBER 11, 1942

The Paris radio reported early today that Adolf Hitler had ordered his army to march into unoccupied France "to repel a possible American or British landing." In a letter to Marshal Pétain, Hitler said that he wished "as far as possible, in collaboration with the French Army, to protect the African possessions of European powers." [1:8.]

United States forces eliminated major resistance along the greater part of the Mediterranean coast of French North Africa yesterday with the fall of Oran. [1:3.]

General Eisenhower, Allied commander in North Africa, told correspondents that he expected the fall of Oran would be the signal for the cessation of organized resistance in the French colonies. [7:1.]

United States troops supported by tanks were reported to have entered the outskirts of Casablanca, Morocco, and a British broadcast said that all resistance of the Vichy naval forces at Casablanca had ceased. An Allied headquarters communiqué disclosed that the new French battleship, Jean Bart, was out of action and burning in the harbor. [1:5-6.]

There were reports that a United States column had struck out eastward in Algeria in the direction of Tunisia. President Roosevelt said that no reply had been received to his notification to the Bey of Tunis that United States troops would be sent through the protectorate. [2:2.]

Vichy reported that another powerful Allied convoy had reached Gibraltar. Berlin announced destruction of two Allied cruisers and a transport by Axis submarines and planes. London told of the torpedoing of an Italian cruiser off the north coast of Sicily. [1:6.]

Berne heard that Adolf Hitler, Benito Mussolini and Pierre Laval were in conference "somewhere in Europe." [1:7.]

President Roosevelt disclosed that the decision to open a North African front this year had been made last Summer after it had been decided that it would be impossible to open an effective second front in the northern portion of the European continent this year. [1:1.]

Prime Minister Churchill said that the landings in Africa were the prelude to a new front against Hitler and declared that the plan had been devised by President Roosevelt. [1:4.]

Action on the Egyptian-Libyan front was limited to minor rear-guard activity at Sidi Barrani and Solum. The enemy's position was apparently becoming increasingly catastrophic. [3:2.]

Soviet troops registered some small successes at Stalingrad and near Tuapse on the Black Sea. German assaults were repulsed. [13:1.]

Darlan in U. S. Hands at Algiers; Petain 'Commands' Vichy's Forces

By DAVID ANDERSON
Wireless to THE NEW YORK TIMES.

LONDON, Nov. 10—Admiral François Darlan, chief of Vichy's armed forces, is now in Allied hands at Algiers "being entertained by one of our American generals with the respect and dignity due an officer of his rank," London headquarters of the Allied force announced tonight. No detail was given as to how and when Admiral Darlan got into his present situation.

Ever since his presence in French North Africa was confirmed soon after American operations began—he had gone ostensibly for a check-up on Vichy's defenses—it was suspected here that Admiral Darlan might permit himself to be caught or might voluntarily walk into General Dwight D. Eisenhower's camp.

Admiral Darlan has never been one to carry resistance to extremes, especially when there is something to gain by following the opposite course. He has long been known for his marked dislike of the British, however, and that has been given as an explanation of many of his actions at Vichy.

Many observers here feel that Admiral Darlan would not be able to re-establish his fortunes just by joining the United Nations, as did General Henri Giraud. The admiral is considered too unreliable.

LONDON, Nov. 10 (AP)—With Admiral Darlan definitely a prisoner of General Eisenhower at Algiers, old Marshal Henri Philippe Pétain, stubbornly repeating his order for resistance, took over the disorganized and melancholy defense of all

Continued on Page Four

East Faces Gasoline Ration Slash And Possible 5% Fuel Oil Cut

By CHARLES E. EGAN
Special to THE NEW YORK TIMES.

WASHINGTON, Nov. 10—Faced with increasing difficulties in maintaining petroleum supplies on the East Coast, the government plans a further slash in the amount of gasoline to be allowed civilian motorists in this area.

Suggestions to cut the fuel-oil allowance to householders have been studied but, according to reports, there is strong opposition to any substantial cut, on the ground that the health hazards created by reducing allowable home temperatures below 65 degrees are too great to justify more than a slight decrease.

A formal announcement on both these proposals is expected later in the week from the War Production Board.

Official concern over the difficulties in transporting petroleum to the Atlantic Coast area, where gasoline rationing is in effect, was evident in many quarters here today. Shipments by railroad tank car, which have exceeded 800,000 barrels a day in some weeks, declined to 753,594 barrels a day last week, and averaged 759,233 the week before. This fact was called to the attention of the WPB at its regular weekly meeting today, along with a request that it authorize a reduction in gasoline rations.

Although no official announcement of the WPB's action was made, one report was that the board had actually approved a proposed slash of one-fourth in the gasoline allowance to be given "A" card holders in the seventeen Eastern States.

In addition, it was stated, the

Continued on Page Eleven

LETTER TO PETAIN

Hitler Says Occupation of Whole Country Is Made Necessary

HE SOLICITS ACCORD

Versailles to Be Seat of Puppet Regime Under Nazi Soldiery

By The United Press.

LONDON, Wednesday, Nov. 11—Adolf Hitler has ordered German troops to occupy the remainder of France and the Mediterranean island of Corsica, 300 miles north of the coast of Africa, to counter the United States invasion of French possessions in Northern Africa, the Paris radio announced today.

The Paris radio said Hitler announced his decision was to "prevent further British-American aggression against French territory."

[A wireless dispatch to THE NEW YORK TIMES this morning from Berne, Switzerland, said five German divisions entered the Northern Doubs Valley as the Nazis began the occupation of all of France.]

A letter from Hitler to Marshal Henri Philippe Pétain, read by an official German Army spokesman over the Paris station, announced that Hitler had decided to lift armistice restrictions forcing the French Government to be located in the previously-unoccupied zone of France.

[The French Government will be moved from Vichy to Versailles, said a Paris broadcast recorded by The Associated Press.]

"I have given orders to the German Army to advance through the unoccupied zone to take up positions in order to safeguard the zone against Anglo-American attack," said Hitler's announcement to the French people.

The United States and Britain, after various attempts to carry the war into Europe, "now have proceeded to attack the territories of the French Empire, thereby threatening Corsica as well as the south coast of France," Hitler said.

HITLER LETTER TO PETAIN

LONDON, Nov. 11 (AP)—German troops were reported speeding through unoccupied France today toward a Mediterranean area at which Adolf Hitler said American and British troops proposed landings as a sequel to the American coup in North Africa.

A Paris broadcast quoted Hitler as saying "we have known for twenty-four hours" that Allied attacks were planned upon the French fleet, Corsica and the French mainland coast. He said British and American strategists had "regard to the weakness of the French forces in those parts."

"In these circumstances," Hitler said, "I felt compelled to order the German Army immediately to march through the unoccupied zone—and this is now being done—and to march to the point aimed at by the Anglo-American landing troops."

The letter from Hitler to Marshal Pétain said:

"We have known for twenty-four hours that it is the intention of our enemies to direct the next attack against Corsica, which island they will occupy, and against the south of France."

"I have given this (order) with one single aim, and that is to repel an American and British landing."

"I have given the order to the troops to look after the interests of France," Hitler's letter went on. "The German Government desires as far as possible in collaboration with the French army to protect

Continued on Page Six

After the Tenaru River battle on Guadalcanal.

A German tank commander surrendering to a British infantryman during one of the many battles for North Africa.

1942

The 1942 Packard *Clipper*—
a classic automobile.

Bing Crosby's rendition of Irving Berlin's *White Christmas* swept the airwaves. It is still the most popular song of all time, in terms of number of recordings sold.

One of America's greatest tragedies occured when fire swept the overcrowded Cocoanut Grove nightclub in Boston. Nearly 500 people were killed.

America's railroads carried civilians and soldiers in record numbers during the war. The busy scene here is in Washington, D.C.'s, Union Station.

Victory Gardens sprang up all over the country—even on downtown street corners. This garden is just one block from the bustling traffic on New Orleans' Canal Street.

"All the News That's Fit to Print."

The New York Times.

LATE CITY EDITION
Continued warm and fresh winds today.
Temperatures Yesterday—Max., 57; Min., 34
Sunrise, 7:46 A. M.; Sunset, 4:37 P. M.

Copyright, 1942, by The New York Times Company.

VOL. XCII No. 30,978. Entered as Second-Class Matter, Postoffice, New York, N. Y. NEW YORK, TUESDAY, NOVEMBER 17, 1942. THREE CENTS IN NEW YORK CITY

U.S. SMASHES JAPANESE FLEET IN SOLOMONS; SINKS 23 SHIPS, DAMAGES 7 IN 3-DAY BATTLE; ALLIES FIGHT WAY TOWARD TUNISIAN BASE

WILLKIE DEMANDS FRANK DISCUSSION OF OUR WAR AIMS

Says if We Fight in Silence We Will Win 'Nothing but Blood and Ashes'

POLICY ON VICHY ASSAILED

Churchill's 'We Mean to Hold Our Own' Is Criticized at Herald Tribune Forum

The text of Mr. Willkie's address is on Page 20.

Wendell L. Willkie in a plea for early agreement between ourselves and all our Allies on the aims of this war, declared last night in a speech at The New York Herald Tribune's eleventh Forum on Current Problems at the Waldorf-Astoria that the need for basic agreement "among the Allied peoples themselves" obligated "every one of us" to speak out, to exchange ideas "freely and frankly" at home and across the oceans.

Mr. Willkie asked whether Americans must keep quiet about American collaboration with Vichy, or while Winston Churchill, whom he did not name, "has in the last few days seemingly defended the old imperialistic order and declared to a shocked world, 'We mean to hold our own.'" He asserted that there can be no hope of agreement unless the American people and the British people know what the other is thinking.

Speaks of "Tortuous Policies"

"It is the utmost folly—it is just short of suicide—to take the position," he declared, "that citizens of any country should hold their tongues for fear of causing distress to the immediate and sometimes tortuous policies of their leaders."

Even if war leaders apparently agree upon principles, when they come to the peace tables they make their own interpretation of their previous declarations, he warned. Political internationalism alone will not accomplish the Four Freedoms, for they must rest on economic internationalism forged by the people of the world into actuality, he said.

When the Malayan Peninsula and the islands of the Southeast Pacific, the principal source of the rubber supply of the world, are reconquered by the Allies, "shall we return them to their previous status, where their defense was courageous but inadequate and their peoples undeveloped under governmental custody of some one nation," or shall they be wards of the United Nations with their basic commodities freely available to the world, he asked.

Plea for Sacrifice Cheered

The 1940 Republican candidate for President, recently returned from a tour of the global war fronts, addressed an audience of several thousand persons that frequently had been moved to wartime fervor by the fighting speeches of other speakers.

The delegates from more than forty States listened to his loud applause their hearty approval when James F. Byrnes, Director of Economic Stabilization, and Claude R. Wickard, Secretary of Agriculture, asserted that we "must tighten our belts" and accept sacrifices as cheerfully as the men on the battle fronts; and when Henry J. Kaiser, West Coast industrialist, challenged the theory that a post-war depression is inevitable and held that the "astronomical cost of this war may well be justified by the nation's discovery of its 'amazing potential.'"

The delegates were loud in their applause when William M. Jeffers, National Rubber Director, asserted that after the war "America never again will depend upon any

Continued on Page Twenty

Montgomery's Vice Is Churchill's Virtue

By The Associated Press.

LONDON, Nov. 16—General Sir Bernard L. Montgomery, commander of the victorious British Eighth Army in Africa, who will be 55 years old tomorrow, told Prime Minister Churchill before he was appointed to the command: "I don't smoke, I don't drink and I am 100 per cent fit."

Military circles say Mr. Churchill replied: "I smoke, I drink and I am 200 per cent fit." He will be 68 years old Nov. 30.

Lady Montgomery, the general's 78-year-old mother, telegraphed birthday greetings to him today and said: "I am tempted to address it 'Tripoli.'"

TRANSIT MEN TO GET $1,000,000 PAY RISE

Mayor Denies Fare Increase Is Planned—Union Wants WLB to Rule in Dispute

Mayor La Guardia said yesterday that the Board of Transportation would probably announce a million-dollar wage increase for the 32,000 employes of the unified city transit system within ten days, but denied that the transit fare would go up as a result.

Asked about a published report that the city was contemplating a fare of $7\frac{1}{2}$ cents to meet the pay increase and other costs, the Mayor said:

"I don't think that any reliable source of information can justify this conclusion at this time. There is no official source for any such speculation."

Calls Adjustment Necessary

On the wage increase itself, the Mayor said:

"There is an adjustment of working conditions being studied. It is difficult for any one not familiar with the intricacies of the many classifications to understand the problem.

"There should be an adjustment costing us about $1,000,000 in addition to the $7,000,000 we gave last year. It should be made clear that neither the Mayor nor the Board of Transportation can enter into a newspaper controversy. We have been trying patiently to ignore misstatements of fact that have been made."

The Mayor said the city had granted $6,054,000 in straight salary increases last year, adding that another $1,000,000 had been spent to make the adjustment possible.

Douglas MacMahon, president of the New York local of the Transport Workers Union, was quick last night to express the dissatisfaction of the union men with the Mayor's offer.

"The million dollars of which the Mayor speaks falls far short of immediate requirements for the 32,000 employes of the transit system," he said. "A million dollars a year would mean an increase of about 60 cents a week, which of

Continued on Page Fifteen

FRENCH JOINING U.S.

Local Garrisons Put Up Delaying Resistance to Axis at Tunis

LANDINGS HARASSED

Time, Space and Speed Called Vital Factors in Africa Struggle

Special Cable to The New York Times.

LONDON, Nov. 16—British and American troops in Tunisia, under British Lieut. Gen. Kenneth A. N. Anderson, were reported today to be fighting fiercely against an enemy screening force that stood between them and the battle line where French garrisons are carrying on delaying actions against Italian and German forces arriving by air and sea in the French protectorate.

The main line of the struggle between the Axis and the French, on whose resistance the Allies rely considerably, was outside Tunis, the capital, forty-five miles southeast of Bizerte, the vital Mediterranean naval base that is the goal of the Allied drive.

[A small French garrison has joined the British First Army's advance forces in Tunisia, Allied Headquarters in North Africa reported, according to The Associated Press.

[British forces advancing westward in Libya occupied the landing ground at Martuba, near Derna, while Allied planes strafed traffic of the fleeing Axis army between Agedabia and El Agheila.]

Reichsfuehrer Hitler seems to have decided that he has a chance to hold Bizerte against the advancing Allied army. The French garrisons there have turned back his first thrust, but the outcome of the battle developing in that part of North Africa depends on three dimensional factors: time, space and the velocity of sea-borne and airborne troops against those traveling along roads harassed from the air.

The great decisive battle of this phase of the campaign to force the Nazi citadel of Europe seems likely to be fought out on the shores of Tunisia around Bizerte and Tunis, where the preliminary skirmishes are now being fought. This sequel to the "Battle of the Bulge" that was fought in France on land in the early Summer of 1940 may become known as the "Battle of the Triangle," which will be fought in the air over the Sicilian narrows.

The strong points of this battlefield are held by the Axis. They are airfields in Tunisia, Sicily and Sardinia that control the narrowest parts of the Mediterranean. The Allies' aim now is to knock out part of this triangle by driving the Axis troops out of Tunisia. Most of the drama in the war news

Continued on Page Six

NIMITZ IS ELATED

Believes Japanese May Have Lost 20,000 to 40,000 Men

A 'DECISIVE' BATTLE

Enemy Reported to Have Had No Carriers in Force Engaged

By ROBERT TRUMBULL

By Telephone to The New York Times.

PEARL HARBOR, Hawaii, Nov. 16—The Japanese came down to Guadalcanal with the intention of ousting the American forces that are holding Henderson Field there, and to do that job they brought all the forces they could muster.

This time the Americans under the fighting command of Vice Admiral William F. Halsey Jr. went out to meet the enemy for a decisive slugging match.

The result, Admiral Chester W. Nimitz, Commander in Chief of the United States Pacific Fleet, said in a communiqué today, was that the Japanese transport force was "almost annihilated" in two night battles last Friday and Saturday and yesterday (Guadalcanal time).

In a press conference following the issuance of his communiqué, Admiral Nimitz indicated that this night victory surpassed anything of the kind that the United States Navy had done before in its history.

Battles Believed Short

The two battles, Admiral Nimitz said, must have been very short, each a matter of minutes, and they were fought at extremely close range.

In those minutes, he said, the United States eliminated the immediate danger to our hold on Guadalcanal, so that now we can begin the reinforcement, consolidation and onward offensive to which the admiral referred in an interview several weeks ago.

In two ways these battles have particular significance.

First, in sinking eight transports that were moving in to reinforce the Japanese on Guadalcanal, the United States Navy accounted for a considerable body of enemy land forces, Admiral Nimitz estimating conservatively that the

Continued on Page Six

ENEMY 'COMPLETELY FRUSTRATED' IN SOLOMON ISLANDS

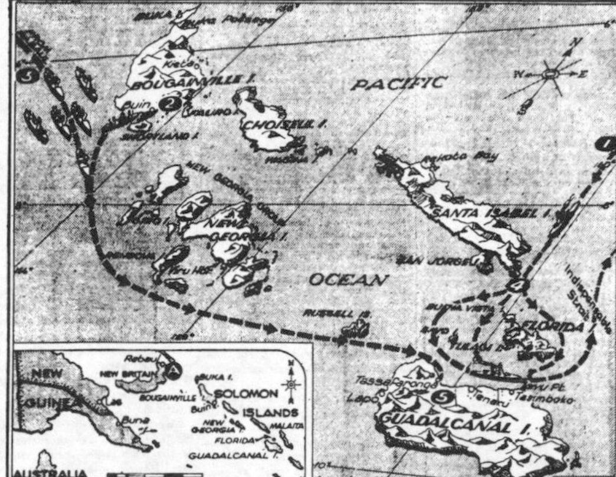

As a prelude to the battle for Guadalcanal Japanese naval forces were sighted approaching the island from the north (1) on Nov. 10, while other warships and transports moved in from Buin (2) and Rabaul (3 and A on inset). In the early morning of Nov. 13 the enemy naval forces reached the Guadalcanal area in three groups (4), were engaged by our surface units at close range and were compelled to retire northward. Late that afternoon twelve transports from Bougainville (2) were sighted on their way to Guadalcanal. Japanese warships shelled the island after midnight and then American planes went to work on the transports; eight were sunk and the remaining four continued on their way, but were found beached at Tassafaronga (5) on Nov. 15 and were there destroyed by our forces. As all the Japanese withdrew northward the score stood: 23 Japanese ships sunk, 7 damaged; 8 American ships sunk, damage undisclosed.

RED ARMY SCORES IN LENINGRAD ZONE

Captures and Holds Volkhov Point—German Wedges in Stalingrad Smashed

By The United Press.

MOSCOW, Tuesday, Nov. 17—The defenders of Stalingrad have smashed German wedges and resealed their lines after a two-day battle in which more than 1,500 enemy troops were killed or wounded, the Soviet High Command announced today.

The Red Army wiped out another 1,500 Nazi officers and men in beating off all enemy attempts to recapture a strategically important village on the Volkhov front, below Leningrad, which the

Continued on Page Thirteen

MacArthur at Buna Front Leads Assault on Japanese

By The United Press.

AT UNITED NATIONS HEADQUARTERS, Australia, Tuesday, Nov. 17—General Douglas MacArthur and his air and ground force commanders have gone into the New Guinea jungles to lead American and Australian troops who are pressing fast from two directions on the Japanese coastal base of Buna and driving the enemy into a narrowing trap, it was announced here today.

Establishing field headquarters in a fighting zone for the first time since he was with his American and Filipino troops in the defense of Bataan last Winter, General MacArthur was accompanied by Lieut. Gen. George C. Kenney, American commander of the Allied air forces in the Southwest Pacific Command, and Lieut. Gen. Sir Thomas Blamey, Australian chief of the ground forces.

The day's communiqué here announced that General MacArthur's Flying Fortresses hit the Japanese another hard blow yesterday in the Northern Solomons, damaging a destroyer and a transport.

The attack was made against the enemy's Buin-Faisi naval anchorage 360 miles northwest of Guadalcanal, near which United States naval forces have scored a smashing victory. It was the sixth attack on the Northern Solomons since last week and ran the Allied total in this period to fourteen Japanese ships put out of action or damaged.

Regarding New Guinea, the communiqué indicated that the

Continued on Page Five

CALLAGHAN KILLED LEADING IN BATTLE

Admiral's Cruiser Had Sunk Two Warships Before Her End in the Solomons

By Telephone to The New York Times.

PEARL HARBOR, Hawaii, Nov. 16—Rear Admiral Daniel J. Callaghan, whose death in the Solomon Islands naval engagement was announced by the Navy Department today, died in the midst of battle—victorious battle, in which Admiral Callaghan's cruiser sank an enemy cruiser and a destroyer in lightning salvos, then courageously engaged a Japanese battleship. It was in this latter phase of the fight that Admiral Callaghan was killed on his bridge.

Admiral Callaghan was commander of a task force which attacked a concentration of Japanese battleships, cruisers and destroyers screening a large group of enemy transports attempting to land

Continued on Page Three

FOE'S NAVY ROUTED

Our Losses Are Only 2 Light Cruisers and 6 Destroyers Sunk

WE SINK BATTLESHIP

5 Cruisers Also in Toll—Japanese, Confused, Fire on Each Other

By CHARLES HURD

Special to The New York Times.

WASHINGTON, Nov. 16—United States naval forces in the Solomons overwhelmingly defeated a formidable Japanese force, destroying twenty-three warships and transports, including one battleship and five cruisers, in a three-day series of actions that ended yesterday (Solomons date), the Navy Department reported today.

Our losses in this fighting—the Navy stated without reservation that all known ones had been included—were listed as two light cruisers and six destroyers sunk.

The Navy announcement further stated that a Japanese battleship and six destroyers had been damaged. There was no announcement of damage suffered by American warships because this is information that would be of great value to the enemy.

Planes Not Dominant

Air power played an important role in the victory, the Navy stated, but it was not the dominant factor as in the battles of the Coral Sea and Midway Island. The bulk of the destruction was accomplished by gun crews of American warships who outfought the enemy in slashing engagements of the traditional sort.

Navy spokesmen who supplemented the factual announcement contained in the communiqué said that this action should not be considered a decisive and conclusive victory, assuring our domination of the Pacific. It was apparent, however, that the naval victory had cleared away one critical threat hanging over our land forces on New Guinea and in the Solomons.

This was the largest surface engagement yet fought in the Pacific and possibly set a record for the war.

The running battle occurred after victories by our ground and air forces in the battle area of the southwestern Pacific had forced the Japanese to attempt to counterattack in force to relieve their own soldiers. For that reason, the American command, operating through Admiral Halsey and General Douglas MacArthur, whose army bombers have collaborated in every sea engagement for months past, could lay their plans to meet the

Continued on Page Four

Battle in Solomons Likened to Jutland

Armchair naval strategists began a debate last night over whether the rout of the Japanese fleet in the Solomons surpassed the Battle of Jutland in 1916 as a major naval engagement.

Jutland bottled up the German High Seas fleet in Helgoland Bight, led the German crews to mutiny when they were ordered to sea and resulted in the fleet's surrender. It was too early to predict the effect of the rout on the Japanese fleet.

The Germans lost eleven ships at Jutland, the British fourteen, a total of twenty-five. The Japanese lost twenty-three in the Solomons and the United States eight, according to the first announcement, a total of thirty-one. Of the twenty-five lost at Jutland, all were warships while of the thirty-one lost in the Solomons, eight were troop ships and four were cargo ships.

At Jutland 252 ships were involved, the Solomons total is not known.

De Gaullists Bar a Darlan Deal; Seek U. S. Reassurance on Status

By RAYMOND DANIELL

Special Cable to The New York Times.

LONDON, Nov. 16—The British Government and people and Fighting French headquarters, while ready enough to cheer the military achievements of the troops under Lieut. Gen. Dwight D. Eisenhower, Commander in Chief of the Allied forces in French North Africa, are somewhat disturbed by the political developments that have followed in their wake.

That is not to say that Fighting French headquarters or the people who ride the underground, buses and trams to work are not aware of the military problems General Eisenhower faces as he digs in in Algeria and Morocco and faces east to Tunisia, but they would all like to be assured that what is happening in French colonial Africa is dictated by the emergency of the moment and not reflective of the long-term policy of Washington.

By long-term policy they mean anything beyond the requirements of the military situation.

Followers of General Charles de Gaulle, the leader of the Fighting French, are so disturbed at the turn of events that they were constrained tonight to issue a statement declaring that they could not accept arrangements that would establish a "Vichy regime in Africa."

Today General de Gaulle lunched

Continued on Page Eight

War News Summarized

TUESDAY, NOVEMBER 17, 1942

United States naval forces have destroyed twenty-three Japanese warships and transports, including a battleship and five cruisers, in a successful three-day defense of Guadalcanal and Tulagi in the Solomons, according to a Navy Department communiqué. In addition, one Japanese battleship and six destroyers were damaged. Two United States light cruisers and six destroyers were sunk during the battle. [1:8.]

Rear Admiral D. J. Callaghan, former naval aide to President Roosevelt, was killed during the battle. [1:7.]

Admiral Chester W. Nimitz, Commander in Chief of the Pacific Fleet, estimated that the Japanese had lost 20,000 to 40,000 men in the "decisive" engagement. [1:4.]

Tokyo claimed a great victory for its naval forces and presented a list of alleged heavy American losses. [5:1.]

United Nations Headquarters in Australia announced that General MacArthur had taken the field to direct the assault on the Japanese base at Buna, in Northeastern New Guinea. [1:6-7.]

Moscow reported that the Germans had lost another 1,500 killed in assaults at Stalingrad and that the Red Army had made a slight gain in the Nalchik region, in the Caucasus. Capture of a strategically important locality on the Volkhov front, southeast of Leningrad, was announced. [1:5.]

British and United States forces were reported to be engaged in heavy fighting with an Axis screening force in Tunisia, while the French fought Axis troops outside of the city of Tunis. The situation at Bizerte was not clear. The enemy said that the Axis hoped to hold that city. [1:3; map, P. 6.]

Fighting French Headquarters in London disclosed that General de Gaulle and his associates did not intend to deal with Admiral Darlan. The Vichy radio carried a declaration, allegedly by Marshal Pétain, outlawing Admiral Darlan. [1:2-3.]

British forces in Libya were moving beyond Martuba, while Marshal Rommel's troops appeared to be speeding toward the narrow passage farther west at El Agheila. [7:1.]

British bombers again raided Genoa successfully while United States fighter planes launched low-level attacks on German military installations in Northern France and the Low Countries. [10:1.]

Wendell Willkie criticized both Prime Minister Churchill's recent declaration of Britain's intention to hold her imperial possessions and United States dealings with Vichy France. [1:1.]

Nazis in France Reported Seizing Two Spanish Republican Leaders

By The Associated Press.

According to a Berlin broadcast yesterday that was recorded by The Associated Press, German troops occupying Southern France arrested Francisco Largo Caballero and Santiago Casares Quiroga, Spanish Republican leaders, and yesterday turned them over to the Nationalist Government of Generalissimo Francisco Franco.

"Both were arrested shortly after entry of German and Italian troops into hitherto unoccupied French territory and handed over to Spanish authorities at the frontier on Monday for court-martial," the D. N. B., German official news agency, dispatch from Madrid was quoted as saying.

The report added that the Spanish authorities had not yet officially announced the seizure of the two men, nor had the Spanish press contained any reference to the affair.

"Informed quarters here [Madrid] regard it as fairly certain that the two notorious Reds will be sentenced to death," the German report added.

Señor Largo Caballero and Señor Casares Quiroga served the Spanish Republican Government both as Premiers and War Ministers in the losing fight against Generalissimo Franco's Nationalists.

The two men escaped to France when the Nationalist revolution, aided at first surreptitiously and then openly by Italy and Germany, triumphed.

"All the News That's Fit to Print."

The New York Times.

LATE CITY EDITION
Rain and moderately cool today
Temperatures Yesterday—Max., 56; Min., 40
Sunrise, 7:14 A. M.; Sunset, 5:32 P. M.

VOL. XCII...No. 30,986. Entered as Second-Class Matter, Postoffice, New York, N. Y. NEW YORK, WEDNESDAY, NOVEMBER 25, 1942. THREE CENTS IN NEW YORK CITY

NAZIS' GRIP ON STALINGRAD BROKEN; 15,000 SLAIN AS SOVIET PUSH GAINS; BRISK FIGHTING SPREADS IN TUNISIA

EXTORTION CHARGED BY MAYOR IN ROW OVER STIRRUP PUMPS

Herlands Says Effort Was Made to 'Shake Down' a Dealer by Promise to 'Fix' Council

REPORT HELD 'RECKLESS'

Solomon, Ex-Deputy Controller, Modell, La Guardia Critic, Deny the Accusations

Mayor La Guardia and William B. Herlands, Commissioner of Investigation, charged yesterday that an attempt had been made to "shake down" a stirrup-pump distributor on the claim that a proposed local law could be killed by the City Council as the result of "influence."

The Mayor said that he learned of the "crude and brazen attempt of a shakedown" from Commissioner Herlands on Saturday and that it was for this reason that he announced on Sunday his plans to have the city sell stirrup pumps directly to consumers.

Copies of Mr. Herlands' official report supplying details of the alleged extortion attempt were given yesterday afternoon to District Attorney Frank S. Hogan and to the grievance committee of the Association of the Bar of the City of New York.

Modell Called "Contact Man"

Named as principals in the Herlands' report were:

Henry Modell, president of Modell's, a sporting goods and uniform store at 198 Broadway, described as "the contact man."

Milton Solomon, an attorney with offices at 165 Broadway, former Deputy City Controller and one-time Democratic candidate for President of the Board of Aldermen, listed as the "alleged fixer."

Maurice Holt, owner of the Triangle Appliance Corporation of 11 West Forty-second Street, which is said to have a stirrup pump distribution monopoly. Although he appeared cast in the role of victim, the report indicated he went through with the deal on the advice of the Department of Investigation.

"Stated baldly, this is the case of a lawyer trying to obtain a large sum of money from a business man by assuring him that he, the lawyer, had the 'influence' to 'kill' certain legislation which was objectionable to said businessman," Commissioner Herlands' report said.

"Outrageous," Says Solomon

Mr. Solomon described the charges as "outrageous" and "reckless" when informed of the contents of the report at his home, 9 Prospect Park West, Brooklyn, last night.

Mr. Modell declared that the accusations were "a dastardly lie" and a "red herring," and declared that he would not allow the Mayor "to get away with it." On Sunday Mr. Modell had assailed the Mayor for putting the city into the pump-selling business, declaring this municipal venture to be unfair competition with business men who were selling the equipment at retail at a small profit.

Councilman Walter R. Hart, chairman of the City Council Defense Committee, declared that he was surprised and astounded by the charges. The report quoted Mr. Solomon as boasting to Mr. Holt that Mr. Hart was his "man" and could kill the pending bill.

According to Commissioner Herlands's report, Mr. Holt was disturbed over the prospect of enactment of a local law sponsored by Councilman Hugh Quinn, Queens Democrat. This measure, still pending before the Council, eliminates stirrup pumps from the list of fire fighting weapons that building owners or tenants must have under the Air Raid Law. As the law now stands they may be used as an alternative to rubber hose under certain conditions.

Mayor Charges Shakedown

"When I made my statement Sunday announcing my decision to give the consumers the benefit of direct sale of stirrup pumps as provided by the Office of Civilian Defense, I did so because it was the only way to put an end to the crude and brazen attempt at a shakedown," the Mayor told reporters yesterday afternoon after he had conferred with Commissioner Herlands.

"I received Saturday a report from the Commissioner of Investigation. That report was given to District Attorney Hogan this after-

Continued on Page Thirty

Two Thanksgivings For Pacific Troops

Wireless to THE NEW YORK TIMES.

WELLINGTON, N. Z., Nov. 24—There will be two Thanksgiving Days this year—one on the western side of the International Date Line as well as that on the American side.

For the first time, Thanksgiving Day will be nationally celebrated in the Antipodes wherever United States troops are now stationed. In the Fiji and Samoan Islands it may cause a headache. The date line bisects these islands and forces in American Samoa will mark the continental American day, but in Fiji it will be a day earlier if Americans are there.

WAR POWERS BILL STRIKES NEW SNAG

House Group Considers Repeal of Income Curb, Calling It Invasion of Rights

Special to THE NEW YORK TIMES.

WASHINGTON, Nov. 24—New manifestations against "government by bureaucracy" became plain in Congress today, leaving the future of the Third War Powers Bill in doubt and suggesting that moves were afoot for application of brakes to administrative authorities when the new session begins in January.

Only a technicality prevented what was viewed as an almost certain insertion into the powers-granting measure by the Ways and Means Committee of a provision which would nullify by statute President Roosevelt's recent executive order limiting annual salaries to $25,000 net.

Sponsors of the proposed "repealer" said they had sufficient committee votes in sight to write it into the bill, if Representative Doughton, the chairman, had not ruled it not germane, and thus out of order. Further attempts will be made, it was asserted, when and if the legislation reaches the Senate, if not before.

During two executive sessions, lasting most of the day, the Ways and Means body dealt with protests by members against Executive Department interpretations of limitations written into previously enacted power-giving legislation by the Congress, it was reported later.

No Decision as to Hearings

The salary limiting order, it was brought out, was only one of many administrative actions drawing the fire of members as allegedly having gone beyond the intent of Congress in the carrying out of its directives.

The Ways and Means Committee refused to write the $25,000 limitation into the tax bill when the proposal was made specifically. Mr. Roosevelt acted under a clause in the anti-inflation price and wage control bill.

At the end of the day no decision had been reached even as to the holding of hearings on the modified draft of the powers program, which was approved unanimously by a subcommittee Saturday after the committee had rejected the Administration's sweeping draft. Doubt was expressed by members that the legislation could get through both the House and Senate before Congress adjourned.

Committee members insisted, however, that further hearings should be held before any bill was reported, and a decision on this phase may be made tomorrow. They maintained further, that

Continued on Page Thirteen

PRESIDENT WARNS PRODUCTION CHIEFS TO RECONCILE AIMS

If They Can't Agree He Will Put Them in Foodless Room Until They Reach Solution

NEW CONTROL PLAN DENIED

WPB-Armed Services Dispute on Aircraft Brushed Aside at Press Conference

By W. H. LAWRENCE
Special to THE NEW YORK TIMES.

WASHINGTON, Nov. 24—With reports current in the capital of a growing crisis within the Administration on the issue of civilian versus military control of the country's economy, President Roosevelt today brushed aside questions as to whether the War Production Board or the armed forces have the final authority on war production problems.

While Washington speculated about a possible Presidential move to break the stalemate between the civilian and military leaders, now manifested in a quarrel over a new master production set-up, the Chief Executive, at his press conference, said that WPB, Army and Navy officials are supposed to agree, and, when they do not, he will lock them in a room and tell them they will get no food until they come out with an agreement.

Denying reports that he was working on plans for a new one-man control of production, supply, manpower and related wartime problems, the President said that, on the whole, the present system is working very well.

WPB Circles Apprehensive

The President's optimism was not shared in well informed WPB circles, which apprehensively heard reports that the Army was attempting to take control of manpower and looked upon the aircraft stalemate as the first challenge to Donald M. Nelson's authority to take back powers over production which he himself delegated to the Army and Navy last March. The WPB official said, half seriously and half jokingly, that he feared "quasi-martial law" was ahead for the country.

Persons familiar with the views of the armed services denied, however, that there was any challenge to Mr. Nelson in the dispute revolving around the creation of a new aircraft production committee, representing the Army and Navy and headed by Charles E. Wilson, former president of the General Electric Corporation. These persons, expressing the highest admiration for Mr. Wilson's production abilities, were confident of a compromise solution which would give influence in aircraft matters to Lieut. Gen. William S. Knudsen, former OPM head and now War Department Production Director, and would eliminate Harold E. Talbott, of WPB from the committee.

While the aircraft production fight may be settled amicably without a definite test of authority, there was no doubt in informed quarters, where production authorities have been discussed with the civilian and military leaders, that there is a conflict between the services and Mr. Nelson over how much authority he should exercise over such matters as production scheduling.

The armed services feel that WPB should give its major atten-

Continued on Page Twelve

ALLIES' GAIN SLOW

Attack of Axis Armored Unit Broken Up by Chutist Forces

MORE CLASHES IN SOUTH

New Landings Reported at Sfax and Gabes as U. S. Planes Shoot Up Troop Train

By RAYMOND DANIELL
Special Cable to THE NEW YORK TIMES.

LONDON, Nov. 24—Sharp fighting took place today in several sectors of Tunisia, where the Allied forces are advancing on Axis-held Tunis, the capital, and Bizerte, the vital naval base. There has been no major clash yet, however, although air activity is increasing as the opposing forces manoeuvre for positions.

The official Allied communiqués continued to be as uninformative as the Axis radios were misleading. However, the communiqués contained enough information to indicate that the Allies were advancing on a broad front while the Axis continued its hasty preparations to make the Tunis-Bizerte corner a sort of Tobruk.

Tonight's communiqué from headquarters, mentioning "local engagements" of Allied forward units, gave few details. Continued activity was reported from the southern sector, where French patrols are operating. A unit of Allied paratroopers repulsed an enemy mechanized column, taking prisoners, according to the communiqué. Unofficial sources reported that British troops advancing eastward along the coastal road had engaged in several minor brushes with enemy patrols.

Four enemy aircraft were shot down by British and American fighters, which also attacked an enemy troop train near Gabès, while heavy bombers raided Bizerte and Tunis. All the bombers and fighters returned safely to their bases, the communiqué said.

[The Vichy radio said that the Axis had landed large troop formations on the Tunisian east coast at Sfax and Gabès, far below Bizerte and Tunis. The Associated Press reported from London. Another Associated Press dispatch, from Allied Headquarters in North Africa, said that British troops had driven back a German advance screen in Northern Tunisia while the

Continued on Page Six

U. S. BOMBERS SCORE BULL'S-EYE IN TRIPOLI HARBOR

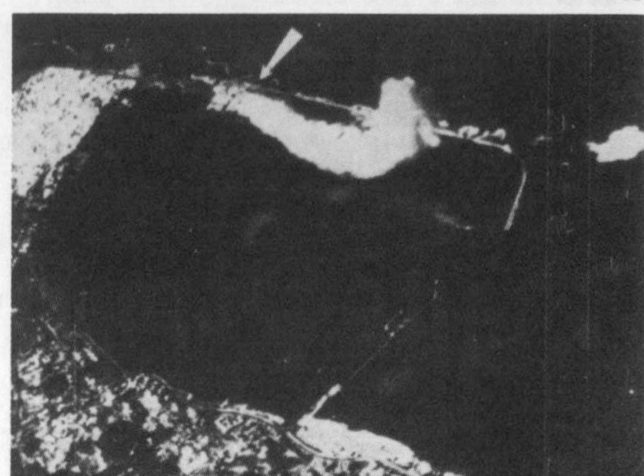

Smoke (arrow) marks direct blast on the Spanish Mole during a raid on the Libyan port
Associated Press Radiophoto (U. S. Army Air Forces)

12,000 MORE TAKEN

Russians Smash Ahead, Capture Many Places in Multiple Drive

HELP REACHES VOLGA CITY

Column Arrives From North—Three Divisions With Generals Among Forces Encircled

By The Associated Press.

MOSCOW, Wednesday, Nov. 25—The three-month-old Nazi grip on Stalingrad was weakening today after a swiftly advancing Red Army had killed 15,000 more Germans yesterday and captured 12,000, including three divisional generals, in a great Winter offensive rolling so fast that some Nazi units were cut down from behind in panicky retreat.

Russian official announcements raised the toll of Nazis to 77,000 dead or captured, not counting huge numbers of wounded who apparently are freezing to death on the frozen steppes, as did other German units last Winter in the rout from Moscow.

The Red Army's effort to encircle the entire Nazi army stalemated before Stalingrad, estimated at 300,000, clearly was gaining in power. Two communiqués told of vast stocks of war equipment falling to the Soviet tide, of at least one enemy airdrome being seized so swiftly that scores of German planes were unable to take to the air.

Stalingrad Defenders Gain

Inside Stalingrad the Russians in frontal assaults also were gaining against Nazi detachments whose rear communications had been slashed by Russian flanking armies sweeping across the Don River far to the west.

[The German High Command admitted the gravity of the situation by acknowledging the penetration of Nazi defenses southwest of Stalingrad. But it said "countermeasures" were under way and reported "savage battles" in the Don bend region. The London Express quoted a Stockholm report that the Germans had "begun to pull out of Stalingrad."]

The midnight Soviet communiqué said 900 Germans were killed and dozens of enemy blockhouses occupied in a slow but steady advance inside Stalingrad, while in the Caucasus Red Army units cut down additional hundreds of Nazis in successful stands in the Nalchik and Tuapse sectors.

This bulletin added some details to the striking Russian successes above and below Stalingrad and inside the Don River bend, as announced in a special communiqué. One Red Army unit captured a Nazi airdrome so swiftly, it said, that forty-two enemy planes did not have time to take to the air. Twenty-five of these planes were destroyed and the seventeen others were captured intact.

In some sectors there was evident Axis demoralization, because hundreds of fleeing Germans were being struck down from behind as

Continued on Page Eight

BRITISH PUSH FOE TOWARD AGHEILA

Take Oasis Far to Southeast as Axis Forces Continue Retreat Across Libya

Special Cable to THE NEW YORK TIMES.

CAIRO, Egypt, Nov. 24—If there is to be a battle at El Agheila it is likely to begin soon, for the German rear guard is moving southwestward from Agedabia toward there, putting up only enough of a fight to keep from being overrun.

Agedabia is now in British hands. The need for consolidation and building of supply services is undoubtedly a greater factor in determining the British rate of advance in that area now than are any efforts of the weak rear guard screens.

The Germans have few tanks left and not too many guns. But they must cast the die one way or the other soon. They must either rush back to Tripoli or fight desperately at El Agheila.

It is regarded as a question whether the present members of the German Africa Corps will be anxious to fight a hopeless battle

Continued on Page Six

Nazis Retreat, Some in Panic, Leaving Rumanians in Lurch

By RALPH PARKER
Wireless to THE NEW YORK TIMES.

MOSCOW, Nov. 24—While the Red Army's two-barbed thrust was plunging deeper into the enemy's flanks, Stalingrad's defenders grasped the initiative and, exactly three months after the city was first assaulted, began to clear the Germans systematically from fortresses and cellars.

Continuing their gradual advance last night, the Russians took blockhouses by storm and broke resistance in both the northern factory and southern regions of the impregnable city.

On the Don steppes, on the western slopes of the Ergeni Hills and southwestward along the main highway and railroad toward the Kuban, the counter-offensive is maintaining its tempo and proceeding according to a careful strategic plan to undermine the entire position of the German armies in the south. This is a reward, the newspaper Izvestia asserts, for the heroic resistance of the Red Army, the skillful training of its commanders and other tireless work in the rear.

Russia's allies, too, had a share in it, the paper adds, for the Germans' strategic difficulties were aggravated by the Allies' operations in Africa and the threatening prospect of a continental invasion. It is understood that British and American-built tanks are being used in the present offensive.

No attempt is made to minimize the stern tasks ahead of the Red Army on the Don-Volga front. The Germans' resilience and power in defensive fighting are known from bitter experience, reserves are being accumulated hastily to meet the Red Army's advance and time is reducing the advantages gained by the element of surprise—prisoners' testimony agree that the

Continued on Page Eight

GUADALCANAL FOES CUT OFF, KNOX SAYS

Secretary Asserts Enemy Can Not Send In Aid—Nimitz Denies Naval Battle

By CHARLES HURD
Special to THE NEW YORK TIMES.

WASHINGTON, Nov. 24—The Navy believes it has closed the routes by which the Japanese may reinforce their garrisons on Guadalcanal Island, Secretary of the Navy Frank Knox said today. This result was credited to the naval victory recently won by American sea forces against "seemingly hopeless odds" in the waters around the Solomon Islands.

[Admiral Chester W. Nimitz, Commander in Chief of the Pacific Fleet, said yesterday that, so far as he knew, there was no naval action going on in the Solomons area such as had been reported by the Japanese radio Monday night.]

Secretary Knox expressed the belief that our own soldiers and marines now face a straitened enemy, while further dispatches from Guadalcanal reported that the Americans there were extending

Continued on Page Four

War News Summarized

WEDNESDAY, NOVEMBER 25, 1942

Adolf Hitler's forces in the Stalingrad salient of the eastern front appeared to be on the verge of total disaster yesterday. The situation on the African fronts was little changed and activity in the Pacific war theatre was limited.

West of Stalingrad the Russian Army was reported to be advancing on a 200-mile front and to have penetrated as deep as twenty-five miles into enemy-held territory, while other Soviet troops drove down into the city from the north through the encircling German lines. Another 15,000 German soldiers were reported killed and 12,000 more taken prisoner. [1:8.]

Berlin acknowledged that the Russians had penetrated the German defensive line in the Don bend region. [8:2.]

Rumanian troops, fighting with the Germans in the region, were said to be surrendering in masses and apparently the Germans were retreating and leaving them to their fate. [1:6-7.]

It still seemed doubtful that Marshal Rommel's forces in Libya would give battle at El Agheila. The Axis rear guard was approaching El Agheila rapidly and was offering little opposition. [1:5.]

Sharp clashes took place in Tunisia between Axis forces and Allied troops advancing out of Algeria, but battle had not yet been joined and the Germans and Italians continued to strengthen their positions around Bizerte and Tunis. [1:4; map, P. 6.]

In London a Labor member of Parliament asserted that Prime Minister Churchill had suppressed a broadcast scheduled by the chief of the Fighting French, General de Gaulle, after Foreign Secretary Anthony Eden had approved it. A charge that "reactionary tendencies" were gaining the upper hand was raised in connection with the incident. [6:1.]

The Polish Government in Exile announced that the German Gestapo Chief, Heinrich Himmler, had ordered half the Jews in Poland killed by the end of this year in preparation for the eventual slaughter of all Jews in the country. [10:1.]

Secretary of the Navy Knox told reporters that Japanese reinforcements had not been landed recently on Guadalcanal and that the island could probably be kept isolated from further Japanese infiltration. United States troops advanced farther west of Henderson Field. [1:7.] The situation of the Japanese defending Buna in Northeastern New Guinea remained desperate. [3:1.]

United States bombers based on India raided the railway installations at Mandalay, Burma, again Sunday and reported that the previous raid last Friday had been very effective. [4:1.]

Valtin Arrested for Deportation; Board Cites 'Wavering Loyalties'

Special to THE NEW YORK TIMES.

WASHINGTON, Nov. 24—Jan Valtin, author of "Out of the Night," was arrested today in Bethel, Conn., on a warrant issued by the Immigration and Naturalization Service and held for deportation to Germany. The arrest was announced here soon afterward by Attorney General Biddle.

Valtin, who is 37 years old and whose real name is Richard Julius Herman Krebs, had been the subject of extended hearings before the Board of Immigration Appeals. The deportation order is not expected to be carried out until after the war, and Valtin probably will be interned meanwhile.

The board found that Krebs entered this country illegally after once having been arrested and deported and after committing a crime involving moral turpitude, in this case perjury. Technically, the board unanimously voted to order the deportation after first denying an application for suspension of deportation proceedings on the ground that Krebs had not been "a person of good moral character for the past five years, as required by law, and that he was otherwise deportable."

Within the last five years, the board asserted, Krebs "has been considered an agent of Nazi Germany."

The board minced no words in ordering the deportation. Unanimously, said Thomas G. Finucane, chairman, the members found the author's life "so marked with violence, intrigue and treachery that it would be difficult, if not wholly unwarranted, to conclude

Continued on Page Fifteen

Chicago Trio Get Death Penalty For Treason, Wives Prison Terms

Special to THE NEW YORK TIMES.

CHICAGO, Nov. 24—Three German-Americans who aided and sheltered Herbert Hans Haupt, executed Nazi saboteur and spy, were sentenced to death for treason today by Federal Judge William J. Campbell "as a timely and solemn warning to all who would attempt the smallest act of sabotage." Their wives, who were convicted of the same crimes, were ordered to prison for twenty-five years and fined $10,000 each.

"The sentence must serve notice upon the enemy that the cunningly devised scheme for the use of American citizens of German birth as pawns in the game of sabotage and espionage in this country is doomed to failure," the judge asserted.

The men are Hans Max Haupt, father of Herbert, who was captured with seven other saboteurs after they had landed in June from German submarines on the Long Island and Florida coasts; Walter Wilhelm Froehling, uncle of Herbert, and Otto Walter Wergin, close friend of the Haupts and Froehlings. Their wives are Erna Emma Haupt, Lucille Froehling and Kate Martha Wergin. All had been convicted by a jury of eight women and four men on Nov. 14.

Judge Campbell set Jan. 22 as the execution day, but the defense filed an appeal this afternoon, and Paul A. F. Warnholtz, chief counsel, said he would fight the sentences to the Supreme Court.

If the death sentences are sustained the three men will be executed at either the Cook County jail in Chicago or at the States-

Continued on Page Fifteen

Daladier and Others Seen in Nazi Hands

Wireless to THE NEW YORK TIMES.

ON THE SPANISH FRONTIER, Nov. 24—France's former leaders who had been held at the Pourtalet prison in the Pyrenees, including former Premiers Paul Reynaud, Edouard Daladier and Léon Blum and General Maurice Gustav Gamelin, are reported to have been moved to Bordeaux in the last forty-eight hours to be sent to Germany, according to a statement here today by a Frenchman who has just crossed the frontier.

The informant said the dossiers for the Riom war-guilt trials had been demanded by the German Ministry of Justice for study and that Vichy officials had surrendered them to the Germans.

1943

1943

Eleanor Roosevelt visiting troops in the South Pacific.

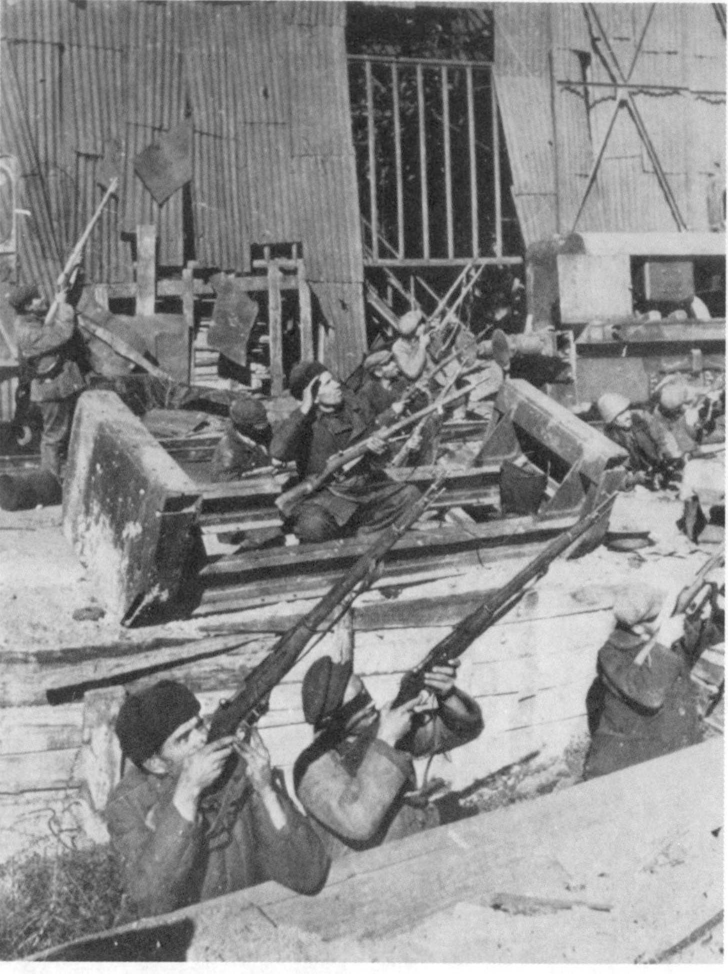
A Russian workers' battalion defending themselves against a Nazi attack.

President Roosevelt and Prime Minister Churchill at the Casablanca Conference in early 1943.

"All the News That's Fit to Print."

The New York Times.

LATE CITY EDITION
Occasional rain today; freezing rain and colder tonight.
Temperatures Yesterday—Max.,39; Min.,33
Sunrise, 8:17 A. M.; Sunset, 5:07 P. M.

VOL. XCII..No. 31,041. Entered as Second-Class Matter, Postoffice, New York, N. Y. NEW YORK, TUESDAY, JANUARY 19, 1943. THREE CENTS IN NEW YORK CITY

RUSSIANS BREAK LENINGRAD SIEGE; BRITISH RAID BERLIN FOR 2D NIGHT; DRIVE 30 MILES NEARER TO TRIPOLI

A. M. A. LOSES FIGHT IN SUPREME COURT ON A HEALTH PLAN

Its Conviction Under Anti-Trust Law in Cooperative Case Unanimously Upheld

'TRADE' QUESTION AVOIDED

Refusal of Defendants to Let Doctors and Hospitals Aid Business Is Called Issue

By LEWIS WOOD
Special to THE NEW YORK TIMES.

WASHINGTON, Jan. 18—Ruling unanimously, the Supreme Court upheld today the conviction of the American Medical Association and the District of Columbia Medical Society, local affiliate, for violating the Sherman Anti-Trust Law by conspiring to block the activities of Group Health, Inc., a government employe cooperative.

Justice Roberts wrote the opinion approved by all the present eight members of the high court except Justices Murphy and Jackson, who did not participate since the case came under their purview when Attorneys General.

The court left undecided the question whether a physician's practice is "trade," in the meaning of the Sherman law. Justice Roberts based his decision on the conclusion that the association and the society conspired to restrain Group Health, which he said was operating within "the sphere of business."

He refused to hold the medical societies immune from prosecution. They alleged that their dispute with Group Health was covered by the Clayton and Norris-La Guardia acts.

Whereas lower court decisions were filled with details of alleged unfair practices by organized medicine against Group Health, the Roberts opinion did not discuss these activities. It merely reiterated part of the testimony given in lower courts and discussed the legal procedure of those tribunals. Mr. Roberts closed his discussion with the words, "The judgments are affirmed."

Group Health Is Described

Group Health, around which the four-year dispute revolved, was described by Justice Roberts as "a nonprofit corporation organized by government employes to provide medical care and hospitalization on a risk-sharing prepayment basis." Physicians were employed on "a full-time salary basis" and hospital facilities were sought for treatment of members and their families.

"This plan was contrary to the code of ethics of the petitioners," said Justice Roberts, referring to the medical societies.

"The indictment," he went on, "charges that, to prevent Group Health from carrying out its objects, the defendants conspired to coerce practicing physicians, members of the petitioners, from accepting employment under Group Health, to restrain practicing physicians, members of the petitioners, from consulting with Group Health's doctors who might desire to consult with them, and to restrain hospitals in and about the city of Washington from affording facilities for the care of patients of Group Health's physicians."

The controversy arose in December, 1938, when the medical associations and twenty-one physicians of Washington and Chicago were indicted as participants in an unlawful combination and conspiracy to restrain trade. Also indicted were the Washington Academy of Surgery and the Harris County (Houston, Texas) Medical Society.

A Federal district court threw out the case on the ground that medical practice was not "trade" under the Sherman act. The local Circuit Court of Appeals reversed that decision and ordered trial of the suit.

Early Defendants Are Cleared

Some of the defendants were acquitted by order of the court and others were found not guilty. The association was fined $2,500 and the society $1,500.

The conviction was sustained by the Circuit Court of Appeals and has been approved by the Supreme Court. Through intervening procedure the number of defendants was stripped to the association and the society.

"Much argument has been addressed to the question whether a physician's practice of his profession constitutes trade under Sec-

Continued on Page Thirteen

Age of Enlistment Cut by Army to 17

By The Associated Press.

BOSTON, Jan. 18—Authorization for the enlistment of 17-year-old qualified American citizens in the Army reserves—to be called into service within six months after they reach their eighteenth birthdays—was announced today by Major Gen. Sherman Miles of the First Service Command.

General Miles declared that the new Army policy permitted youths, who are physically fit, to enlist either in the Army Enlisted Reserve Corps, unassigned, or—if they qualify—to enlist as aviation cadets in the Air Corps Enlisted Reserve. They must, however, have the written consent of their parents.

Army recruiting officials said that this change marked the first time within a generation that the Army has permitted the actual enlistment of boys before they reach the age of 18.

OPA BEGINS ARRESTS TO CUT MEAT PRICES

14 Wholesale Plants and 29 Persons in Them Accused of Black Market Practices

Opening a drive that officials predicted would result in reducing the retail price of meat for consumers, the regional office of the Office of Price Administration began the prosecution yesterday of fourteen beef wholesalers and small packers and twenty-nine of their officers and employes in this city, Newark, Philadelphia and Pittsburgh.

Warrants were issued here yesterday for seven companies and seventeen persons affiliated with them. In Newark warrants were issued for four companies and five individuals, and in Pittsburgh for two companies with as many individuals. In Philadelphia, where the procedure was varied slightly, informations were filed against one company and five individuals.

This action was only the beginning of the OPA drive, according to Sylvan L. Joseph, regional OPA administrator, who promised that more could be expected soon. He said the prosecutions were the initial results from the questioning of more than a thousand retail butchers in the regional area by OPA enforcement attorneys and agents in the last two weeks.

Ending of Black Market Is Aim

"These arrests are the opening of a campaign by which we hope to break up the black market which has developed on an extensive scale and has resulted in exorbitant prices to the public for its meat," Mr. Joseph said. "The public itself, despite the fact that complaints against butchers might be considered inadvisable because they would so antagonize the butchers and thus cut off supplies to the consumer, had registered numerous complaints with our office and with the district office."

When the questioning of the retail butchers began many of them readily admitted taking part in price ceiling evasions, according to the investigators, but pleaded that they had been forced to comply with the illegal demands of wholesalers in order to obtain beef. They said they had feared to complain to the OPA lest their sources

Continued on Page Fifteen

COAL STRIKE GOES TO THE PRESIDENT; QUICK END IS SEEN

Case Taken 'Under Advisement' After WLB Delegation Makes Visit to White House

MEN SPLIT IN NEW VOTES

Demands Increase in Congress for Anti-Strike Laws—Halt Called Near Treason

By W. H. LAWRENCE
Special to THE NEW YORK TIMES.

WASHINGTON, Jan. 18—A prediction that the unauthorized strike of Pennsylvania anthracite coal miners "will be all over by Wednesday" was voiced tonight by a well-informed authority after the National War Labor Board had referred the walkout to President Roosevelt for action.

Seven members of the NWLB informed Marvin H. McIntyre, Presidential secretary, that their efforts to get the striking miners back to work had failed. Mr. McIntyre referred the dispute to the President, who, the White House said tonight, had the case "under advisement."

The WLB did not make public its recommendations, if any, but it was indicated that the President would make a public appeal, as President and Commander in Chief in time of war, before taking any drastic action, such as seizure of the mines or the dispatch of Federal troops to protect a back-to-work movement.

Action Linked to Men's Decision

Some action by the President was expected possibly tomorrow and certainly within a very few days if the strike is not ended by the men themselves. The men are on strike in protest against an increase of 50 cents a month in union dues.

The person who forecast the ending of the walkout by Wednesday pointed to indications which developed today that the men would drop the strike. He cited word that the South Wilkes-Barre local of the United Mine Workers, which started the strike action, had decided to return to work in a vote taken this afternoon before the case went to the President.

He reported word of similar action by other locals. It was predicted that more striking locals would follow the lead thus set.

The WLB group at the White House was led by William H. Davis, board chairman. It talked with Mr. McIntyre and James F. Byrnes, Economic Stabilization Director. Other members of the delegation were Dr. George W. Taylor, vice chairman; Wayne L. Morse, public member; Van A. Bittner, C. I. O. representative; Robert Watt, A. F. of L. representative, and Cyrus S. Ching and George Mead, employer representatives.

Denunciation in Congress

Demands increased in Congress today for enactment of anti-strike legislation.

Representative Ramspeck of Georgia, ranking member of the House Labor Committee, declared that "the government should take whatever action is necessary to open and operate the coal mines."

Representative Andresen, Minnesota Republican, asserted that the coal strike bordered on treason and called on the Justice Department

Continued on Page Twelve

Nazi Chutist Steals An Auto in London

Special Cable to THE NEW YORK TIMES.

LONDON, Jan. 18—After a successful parachute landing, a crewman of a German bomber shot down during this morning's raid on London coolly stole a motor car.

Whatever his intentions, he did not get far, as two policemen, checking up on cars, stopped him.

DEMOCRATS NAME WALKER CHAIRMAN

National Committee Accuses Flynn's Foes of 'Treasonable Plot' Against President

Special to THE NEW YORK TIMES.

CHICAGO, Jan. 18—Postmaster General Frank C. Walker was unanimously elected today to succeed Edward J. Flynn as Chairman of the Democratic National Committee at a meeting marked by denunciation of opposition in the Senate to confirmation of Mr. Flynn as Minister to Australia.

A telegram was received from President Roosevelt attesting his friendship for the retiring chairman and commending his services to the committee and the party.

In a speech of acceptance broadcast nationally tonight, Mr. Walker voiced his championship of the two-party system. It was viewed as his answer to some leaders of his party who have contended that politics should be adjourned for the duration of the war.

Mr. Roosevelt's telegram was read by Edwin W. Pauley, secretary of the committee, in the midst of the attacks on the anti-Flynn bloc in the Senate, which was characterized in resolutions as "a dastardly, treasonable plot to hamper the Commander in Chief by seeking to destroy confidence in the President."

Unity of Nation Stressed

Noting that the committee was meeting "to receive the resignation of its chairman and to elect his successor," the President's telegram continued:

"I am sure that all members join me in expression of gratitude to

Continued on Page Sixteen

22 BOMBERS LOST

R. A. F. Meets Stiff Nazi Fighter Defense Over Reich Capital

MORE BIG FIRES STARTED

London Has Another Attack as Swiss Alarms Indicate Continued British Blows

Special Cable to THE NEW YORK TIMES.

LONDON, Tuesday, Jan. 19—For the second night in succession Berlin on Sunday night was lighted by flashes and rocked by the explosions of two and four-ton bombs loosed by a "strong force" of British heavy bombers.

In contrast to cloudy conditions that prevailed over Germany on Saturday night, the Royal Air Force bombers had to fly the best part of the way to Berlin and back in bright moonlight.

With Nazi night fighters out in force, the raid cost the R. A. F. twenty-two planes. Pilots and crews reported many aerial battles to and from the target area, in which at least one German fighter was sent crashing to earth.

When the bombers arrived over the Reich capital they found some clouds and, through heavy German anti-aircraft fire, made their runs.

"Great Load" of Bombs Dropped

"A great load of bombs was dropped and by the end of the attack large fires were burning," said the Air Ministry's report.

[An R. A. F. strength of 400 to 500 bombers was used against Berlin on Sunday night and hundreds of the biggest high explosives and probably 100,000 incendiaries were loosed on the Reich capital, according to press service dispatches from London.

[Air raid alarms lasting about an hour around midnight were reported in Zurich and Basle, Switzerland, last night, indicating that the R. A. F. might be attacking Northern Italy or Southwest Germany.]

While the R. A. F.'s big planes were on the Berlin trip British fighters on intruder patrol throughout the night attacked

Continued on Page Five

RUSSIANS SMASH SEVENTEEN-MONTH BLOCKADE

Jan. 19, 1943

A junction of Soviet troops from immediately around Leningrad and others from the Volkhov front to the east cleared a railway running east and ended the siege of the former capital. The troops from the west crossed the Neva River and the combined forces occupied Schluesselburg, Marino, Moskovsk Dubrovka and other points. A map of the entire Russian front is on Page 3.

SOVIET GAINS GROW

Eight Miles of Nazi Lines Smashed in Break of Leningrad Ring

DRIVE IS NEARER KHARKOV

Russians Cross Donets Below Kamensk on Way to Rostov —Push On in Caucasus

By The Associated Press.

MOSCOW, Jan. 18—The historic siege that Leningrad, Russia's second largest city, has undergone for seventeen months was broken today by a Red Army offensive south of Lake Ladoga that shattered the German ring around the city, it was announced officially tonight.

The ancient fortress city of Schluesselburg, on Lake Ladoga east of Leningrad, where the Germans closed their ring in August, 1941, was recaptured by Russian forces under Marshals Gregory Zhukoff and Klementi Voroshiloff, the communiqué said.

This news was greeted with rejoicing throughout the country as other Russian troops operating in Southern Russia steadily smashed ahead toward Kharkov, in the Ukraine; Rostov, at the mouth of the Don River, and the Maikop oil fields in the Caucasus.

Moscow residents hearing the announcement shouted with joy and hugged each other. Workers in Russian arms factories, toiling day and night to supply the armies engaged in seven great offensives on the snow-swept plains and swamps, heard the news over loudspeakers and kept on working.

The Russians battered their way through almost nine miles of tremendous German fortifications and crossed the Neva River to end Leningrad's blockade. In a week of bitter fighting, the Russians announced, the Germans left 13,000 dead on the battlefield and four German divisions and remnants of other detachments were routed. More than 1,260 prisoners were taken.

Zhukoff Promoted for His Work

Marshal Zhukoff, the hero who led the Red Army that rolled back the Germans from the gates of Moscow last Winter, has received his present rank for his work at Leningrad. Marshal Voroshiloff commanded Leningrad's hard-fighting garrison during the first months of the city's siege, when the Germans threw hundreds of thousands of men against the strategic city, but failed to crack it.

Leningrad is a vital lever in the defense of Northwestern Russia because of its proximity to the Gulf of Finland and the Baltic States. Ever since its envelopment the Germans had repeatedly maintained that it was doomed.

Further striking Russian victories were announced from the Voronezh, Stalingrad, middle Don and Caucasian fronts.

The Fourth Italian Army Corps was reported to have been smashed as the Russians fought their way into Kamensk, eighty-five miles above Rostov. The Red Army spilled across the Donets River in this area, and Likhaya, about fifteen miles south of Kamensk on the important railway to Rostov, apparently was its next goal.

Red Army Crosses Manych River

In the Caucasus the Russians crossed the Manych River to capture Divnoe, the railhead for a line running westward to the Rostov-Baku railway. Farther south the Russians captured Cherkessk, on the way west from Pyatigorsk toward the Maikop oil fields.

At all these points the latest successes meant not only the occupation of vitally important points but also the breaking of the main German defense lines, opening the way for further advances.

In some sectors the Axis troops were reported to be in hasty flight. German troops re-formed at every possible point where the terrain offered some defense advantages, only to be sent fleeing again by the massed weight of Soviet tanks,

Continued on Page Three

Allied Planes Smite Rommel As 8th Army Gains in Libya

By GRANT PARR
Special Cable to THE NEW YORK TIMES.

CAIRO, Egypt, Jan. 18—Following up rapidly the retreating German Africa Corps, General Sir Bernard L. Montgomery's British Eighth Army has made another thirty-mile advance in Libya, and last evening had reached a line about seventy-five miles beyond the Axis' old Wadi Zemzem positions and within 100 miles of Tripoli. Points occupied formed a front more than sixty miles wide, running west and slightly south of Tauorga, which adjoins the coastal marshes twenty-five miles south of Misurata.

The center of the line was Bir Dufan, where formerly there was a German airdrome, and farther west the front ran through Beni Ulid. If this British front continues to roll forward in the same direction it appears destined to envelop the coast where it bends westward between Misurata and Homs and to cover the hill country south of Tripoli as well. It is this hill country that now offers almost the sole barrier between the Eighth Army and Tripoli.

Allies in Fierce Air Attacks

Allied air forces found the retreating Germans crowding on to narrow tracks as they reached rougher terrain farther north. On the prime targets thus presented fighter-bombers launched their fiercest attack since the break-through at El Alamein, Egypt. Trucks were blown up, fires were started and troops were strafed. Damage and casualties were heavy.

Artillery fire and mines sown in awkward places were about the best the Germans could offer as a means of trying to hamper the Eighth Army's drive, and the British had more difficulty with the rough terrain over which they had to advance. But the British were secure from enemy air attack and made steady progress.

Saturday night the Germans halted on a line about forty-five miles northwest of Wadi Zemzem, occupying positions in a wadi [dry water-course] called Sofeggin. But the next morning the Nazis resumed their withdrawal. The evident weakness of the Africa Corps

Continued on Page Six

SUPER-FUEL PLANT PUT IN OPERATION

Unit Opened in Jersey to Turn Out Large Quantities of 100 Octane Gasoline

By WILLIAM L. LAURENCE
Special to THE NEW YORK TIMES.

BAYWAY, N. J., Jan. 18—The Standard Oil Company of New Jersey today put in full operation a giant new catalytic cracking plant for producing large quantities of 100-octane gasoline, the superfuel that tests have shown will convert our fighters and bombers into superplanes far beyond the powers of our enemies to match.

The plant was dedicated to the service of the country by Ralph W. Gallagher, recently elected president of the Standard Oil Company, in the presence of representatives of the Army and Navy, members of the crew of the lost aircraft carrier Hornet, Standard Oil employes and officials and invited guests.

The Bayway plant, strategically situated both for war and peacetime uses, is the first to be built in the vital Eastern seaboard region. Two other plants using the same process are in operation, one in Louisiana and one in Texas. Thirty-three of these units are scheduled for operation in this country in the near future, giving our armed forces the equivalent of one of the most efficient and destructive "secret weapons" ever devised.

The amount that the new unit will produce is a military secret, but an indication of what its possession means for speeding the day

Continued on Page Seven

War News Summarized

TUESDAY, JANUARY 19, 1943

Axis forces continued to lose ground in both Russia and Libya, as reports on the R. A. F. raids upon Berlin indicated they had been on an unprecedented scale for the distance involved.

Moscow announced that the seventeen-month siege of Leningrad had been broken in a seven-day offensive by Russian troops, resulting in the capture of Schluesselburg and Sinyavino and the opening of a corridor from the east into the city. The capture of the railway station of Kamensk, eighty-five miles north of Rostov, was also announced, and the Soviet claimed 22,000 Hungarians, 7,000 Italians and 2,000 Germans as prisoners on the Voronezh front. Further advances were reported on the upper Donets front and the lower Don and Caucasus front. [1:8.]

Britain's Air Ministry announced that large fires had been left burning in Berlin Sunday night. Hundreds of bombs weighing 8,000 pounds and probably 100,000 incendiaries were dropped in this second successive raid on the Reich capital. The Germans lost ten planes in two raids Sunday night over London and the British lost twenty-two big bombers over Berlin. [1:5.]

Prime Minister Per Albin Hansson warned Sweden of a possible attack. He told Parliament in Stockholm that false orders might be issued and urged every Swede to help repulse the enemy if the country should be invaded. [3:1.]

Britain's Eighth Army advanced to within 100 miles of Tripoli on a broad front, stretching deep into the desert. Allied planes pounded incessantly the retreating Axis columns. [1:6-7; map, P. 6.]

In Tunisia British and United States planes continued attacks on enemy communications. The Twelfth United States Army Air Force released figures showing that in air combat it had maintained a superiority of two to one. [6:5.]

British submarines torpedoed and shelled three enemy supply ships in the Mediterranean, sinking them or putting them out of action. Surface forces accounted for two other enemy supply vessels and damaged an escort ship. [6:7.]

The return of Marcel Peyrouton, one-time Vichy Minister and opponent of Pierre Laval, to North Africa and other developments were reported to indicate that the Imperial Council was prepared to make changes in the North African administration. [6:1.]

United States bombers carried out a successful series of three raids over Burma during the week-end. Royal Air Force planes were also active, particularly about Rathedaung, north of Akyab. [8:3.]

Bombers operating from Guadalcanal made five sweeps in two days over various Japanese bases in the area, concentrating on the Buin and Shortland districts. [10:3.]

Allied troops in New Guinea were reported to have captured Sananada Point and village and a bomber destroyed an 8,000-ton Japanese vessel in the Bismarck Sea. [9:1.]

Allies Held on Italian Submarine Escape in Blast by British Plane

Special Cable to THE NEW YORK TIMES.

CAIRO, Egypt, Jan. 18—American airmen and British fliers and army men are safe in Allied territory instead of prisoners of the Axis because a British bomber sank an Italian submarine aboard which they were being transported.

The Americans included men of a Flying Fortress that had been forced down during a raid on Tripoli.

The British and American prisoners forced their way out of the submarine's conning tower while the submarine was being attacked. When a British destroyer came up they were found swimming.

A depth charge blew the submarine, which had been sighted in the Mediterranean by an aircraft operating from Malta, almost out of the water.

"It was terrific," said the Flying Fortress observer, who had been on the submarine. "We were locked in the forward torpedo compartment with some Italian soldiers as guards. A few Italian sailors were there too. I was lying on a bunk when suddenly there was an ear-splitting crash and the lights went out. I found myself on the floor and the next minute there were two enormous bangs. The Italian soldiers were already on the floor, being seasick, and the sailors walked over them to get to the conning tower.

"They went through the hatch from our compartment and locked it. We were down there in the dark with no life jackets."

By that time the motors had stopped and the submarine was rolling heavily in big seas. Water was trickling into the compartment and there was a loud hissing noise, which, it was learned later, had merely been the submarine blowing out its tanks.

"We heard a rattling noise and

Continued on Page Seven

Slash of 40% Is Ordered in Fuel Oil Used Industrially Except in Heating

Special to THE NEW YORK TIMES.

WASHINGTON, Jan. 18—In the first curtailment order affecting commercial, industrial and governmental users of fuel oil for non-heating purposes, Harold L. Ickes, Petroleum Administrator for War, and John Hamm, acting price administrator, issued a joint regulation today requiring a 40 per cent cut in consumption of such oil for the first quarter of this year, by all but an exempted list of users.

The order does not affect home-owners and other consumers burning fuel oil for heating space and hot water, or for domestic cooking and lighting.

Those specifically exempted are commercial, industrial and governmental users burning less than 9,000 gallons of fuel oil in a quarter-year for other than space-heating purposes, and a list of essential war production and civilian industries.

Included in the list of users exempted from the order are public communication services, including newspapers, radio, telephone and telegraph systems; hospitals; transportation services; water supply and sanitation systems; food preservation and packing plants; and industrial plants making various materials essential in the war effort.

The new order, applying in the seventeen East Coast States and District of Columbia, will remain in effect until April 1. Whether it will be renewed and the allotments readjusted will depend on conditions prevailing then, officials said.

Government spokesmen were vague as to the amount of oil to be saved by the new restrictions. They indicated that exact figures on consumption for non-heating purposes were not as complete as

Continued on Page Twelve

"All the News That's Fit to Print."

The New York Times.

LATE CITY EDITION
Continued moderately cold and windy today.
Temperatures Yesterday—Max., 48; Min., 30
Sunrise, 8:13 A. M.; Sunset, 6:06 P. M.

Copyright, 1943, by The New York Times Company.

VOL. XCII..No. 31,049. Entered as Second-Class Matter, Postoffice, New York, N. Y. NEW YORK, WEDNESDAY, JANUARY 27, 1943. THREE CENTS IN NEW YORK CITY

ROOSEVELT, CHURCHILL MAP 1943 WAR STRATEGY AT TEN-DAY CONFERENCE HELD IN CASABLANCA; GIRAUD AND DE GAULLE, PRESENT, AGREE ON AIMS

15,000 QUIT WORK IN DRESS PAY ROW; PEACE MOVES START

85,000 in 2,000 Shops Here Due to Be Out This Week Unless U. S. Calls Halt

STEELMAN AIDE ARRIVES

But Need for WLB Action Is Seen—Mayor Asks OPA to Modify Price Order

Between 15,000 and 20,000 dressmakers, members of the International Ladies Garment Workers Union, quit their jobs yesterday in what the union called a "spontaneous" stoppage to enforce demands for wage readjustments after the breakdown of negotiations with employers on Monday. No war production is involved.

Both employers and union spokesmen predicted that all 85,000 workers in the industry, affecting 2,000 shops in New York City and vicinity, would be tied up by the end of the week if the stoppage was not arrested. Spokesmen for five employer associations charged the stoppage was in violation of the current agreement in the industry, which does not expire until Jan. 31, 1944.

While David Dubinsky, president of the I. L. G. W. U., reaffirmed the union's willingness to abide by arbitration or to call off the stoppage if the War Labor Board assumes jurisdiction in the controversy, efforts to settle the dispute were begun by the United States Conciliation Service and Mayor La Guardia.

Complaint Filed Against Union

Upon complaint filed with Harry Uviller, impartial chairman of the dress industry, charging violation of contract by the union, Mr. Uviller will confer with employer and union representatives in his office at 1440 Broadway this morning. He, too, however, expressed the belief that the dispute could be settled through action by the War Labor Board.

Involved in the controversy is the declaration by Mr. Dubinsky that the union would oppose the application of the War Labor Board's Little Steel formula in the dress stoppage on the ground that it had been voided by the rise in the cost of living. Acceptance of the union's position would invalidate for all industries subject to President Roosevelt's wage stabilization order the board's criterion of measuring the justification of wage increases on the basis of living costs as they stood in May, 1942.

The position taken by the employers in the dress industry is that while they are cognizant of the justice of the union's demand for a wage equalization because of the rise in living costs, they are unable to grant it as long as prices remain frozen under OPA order.

Mayor Seeks OPA Order Change

Efforts to bring about modification of the OPA order were being pressed by Mayor La Guardia yesterday, as Bernard J. Forman, Federal conciliator, acting on instructions of Dr. John R. Steelman, director of the United States Conciliation Service, arrived in the city and met representatives of the employers and the union. Both employers and union officials were of the opinion that Mr. Forman's intervention was not likely to succeed and that Dr. Steelman would have to ask Frances Perkins, Secretary of Labor, to certify the dispute to the War Labor Board.

After conferring yesterday afternoon at City Hall with George A. Sloan, city Commissioner of Commerce, Mr. La Guardia disclosed that he had recommended to Prentiss Brown, OPA administrator in Washington, that OPA order 287, which fixes maximum prices for the dress industry, be modified. In

Continued on Page Eighteen

Rationalizing of Industry Undertaken in War Drive

WPB Officials Outline Steps Purposing to Make Entire Lines of Enterprise Act as a Single Manufacturer

By The Associated Press.

WASHINGTON, Jan. 26—A far-reaching plan to "rationalize" a vast segment of American industry—to end duplication of effort and other practices described as wasteful—is in the final stages of consideration in the War Production Board, high officials disclosed tonight.

The aim, the officials said, was to increase war production, but they predicted that in peace years the plan would mean more goods for consumers at cheaper prices.

These officials, who prefer to remain unidentified at this time, said the immediate objective was to solve the crucial problem of "components"—the valves, engines, heat exchangers, instruments and other bottleneck items for which many of the "must" war production programs are competing.

The net result, if carried through as contemplated, would be to make an entire industry function as a single manufacturer, ending what is termed the "wasteful" use of critical machines, equipment, manpower and transportation.

Inefficiency results when each of several companies in an industry is making a score of different objects, it was explained. The WPB idea is that total output can be increased if each company is concentrated on a few products. Similarly, the effort will be made to get rid of the waste motion involved when several companies are making several versions of the same product.

WPB intends to attack the problem, it was disclosed, by going direct to industry, bringing leaders from each industry to Washington—probably as WPB employes on a "without compensation" basis—

Continued on Page Fifteen

E. J. FLYNN QUITS PARTY COMMITTEE

Move Apparently Spells Favorable Vote by Senate Group on His Nomination

By W. H. LAWRENCE
Special to The New York Times.

WASHINGTON, Jan. 26—Edward J. Flynn resigned today as a Democratic National Committeeman from New York and this step apparently cleared the way for a close but favorable vote by the Senate Foreign Relations Committee on his nomination to be Minister to Australia.

The resignation was announced by Frank C. Walker, who succeeded Mr. Flynn as chairman of the national committee.

The Senate Foreign Relations Committee will meet in executive session tomorrow morning to vote on recommending Mr. Flynn's nomination. While most observers believed that he would win approval by a very slender margin, opponents were still hopeful that they could deadlock the committee by a tie vote in the absence of favorable proxy from Senator Glass of Virginia, who is ill at his Lynchburg home.

Senate to Vote Monday

The Senate itself will consider the nomination on Monday and a vigorous floor fight is expected.

Mr. Flynn's resignation of all party political positions assured him the vote of Senator Clark of Missouri, who had made this action the price of his support and who had told Democratic leaders that if it were not forthcoming he and Senator Hatch of New Mexico would wage an intensive campaign among Senate Democrats to block Mr. Flynn's confirmation.

Although Mr. Flynn had said when he quit as national chairman that he would retain his committee membership, administration leaders felt that they needed the support of Senators Clark and Hatch and persuaded the New Yorker to reconsider this decision, although it meant, in all probability, that the New York place on the national committee would go to James A. Farley, who now is counted among the anti-New Dealers and an opponent of any effort to win a fourth term for the President.

If Mr. Farley doesn't take the job himself, he is expected to dictate the selection of Mr. Flynn's successor by the New York Democratic Committee.

"With full appreciation of his great services both as chairman and New York National Committeeman, I feel the exercise of his duties in the post to which the President has appointed him and the implied absence from the

Continued on Page Forty-two

250 SLAIN RESISTING NAZIS IN MARSEILLE

Seventy Women Victims of the Fighting as 40,000 Are Ousted From Port Area

By MILTON BRACKER
Special Cable to The New York Times.

LONDON, Jan. 26—One hundred and eighty men and seventy women have been shot in connection with the round-up of what the Germans term "subversive elements" and evacuation of the Old Harbor area of Marseille, according to Swiss reports.

The occupation authorities have reiterated their warning that whoever enters the forbidden area, now under a state of siege, will be executed.

Although naturally more concerned with the return of General Charles de Gaulle from his conference, Fighting French circles in London have closely followed reports from France's greatest seaport, hitherto not regarded as a

Continued on Page Ten

NAZI RING IS CUT UP

Only 12,000 of Foe Left in Stalingrad Force—'Liquidation' Near

RAIL LINES CLEARED

Red Army's Offensives Increase in Violence, Berlin Reports

By The Associated Press.

LONDON, Jan. 26—Russian troops have killed or captured all but 12,000 German troops of the huge forces trapped at Stalingrad and have freed the three main railways radiating westward for the continuing offensive that has carried the Red Army forward 245 miles, Moscow announced tonight in a special communiqué recorded by the Soviet monitor here.

[Soviet troops have entered Stalingrad from the west through the former Nazi seige lines, said a Moscow broadcast recorded by The United Press at London early today.]

Since Jan. 10, the Russians said, they have killed more than 40,000 Germans and captured 28,000, leaving 12,000 split there in two pockets yet to be liquidated.

Two Groups Isolated

"We have not yet liquidated two small enemy groups, separated and isolated from each other, totaling in all no more than 12,000 men, one to the north of Stalingrad and the other nearer to the central part of the town," the communiqué continued. "Both these groups are doomed and their liquidation is only a question of two or three days."

[The Germans said their remaining troops in Stalingrad were concentrated in a narrow space and were continuing their "heroic resistance" under the command of their generals. The Soviet onslaught on large parts of the front were said to have increased in violence.]

Twenty-two Nazi divisions of some 220,000 men had been reported encircled in the Don-Volga pocket before Stalingrad after the Russians began their November offensives above and below the Volga River city.

The Russians threw a cordon

Continued on Page Twelve

War News Summarized

WEDNESDAY, JANUARY 27, 1943

President Roosevelt and Prime Minister Churchill, together with their joint chiefs of staff and other military and civil officials, have concluded a ten-day conference at Casablanca, Morocco, in which a general program of military strategy for 1943 was worked out. The President disclosed that the United Nations would be satisfied with nothing short of the enemy's unconditional surrender. He said the objectives for the year would be to maintain and extend the initiative won late in 1942, to dispatch all possible aid to Russia and to give assistance to the Chinese armies. General Giraud and General de Gaulle met during the conference and reached an agreement to cooperate in the prosecution of the war. [1:8.]

Washington believed that the conference would result in a continuing planned offensive on all fronts and observers were struck by the fact that the aim to win an unconditional surrender of the enemy excluded the possibility of a negotiated peace. [1:5.]

Other dispatches concerning the conference appear on Pages 1 to 8.

United States troops supported by other units broke through a pass northwest of Kairouan in Tunisia and recaptured considerable territory seized by the Germans in a recent clash. Britain's Eighth Army captured Ez Zauia, thirty miles west of Tripoli. [9:1, with map.]

A report was heard in London that the Germans had killed 250 French inhabitants of Marseille, including seventy women, during resistance to their effort to clear the Old Harbor district. Some 40,000 persons were moved out of the area, according to the Vichy radio. [1:3.]

A Soviet special communiqué announced that the Russians had killed or captured all but 12,000 of the Axis soldiers trapped at Stalingrad. Three main railway lines leading out of the city were reported freed. [1:4.] Reports from Berlin reaching Switzerland indicated that the force trapped at Stalingrad had been written off. [12:1.]

President Ryti of Finland, in closing the session of Parliament, expressed the hope that friendly relations would be restored with the United States. [12:4.]

From Australia came a protest by Prime Minister Curtin in an Australia Day broadcast. He said that the Pacific area was too important to be left to a force of "caretakers." [13:2.]

A large force of Japanese planes approaching Guadalcanal was driven off by United States planes and four Zeros were shot down without loss to the Americans. United States ground forces consolidated their position at Kokumbona village. [13:4.]

CAPITAL SEES PLAN

Offensive With Common Strategy Is Viewed by Washington as Key

FRENCH UNION A GAIN

Bar Upon a 'Negotiated Peace' Cited as Blow to Hopes of Axis

By HAROLD CALLENDER
Special to The New York Times.

WASHINGTON, Jan. 26—The meeting at Casablanca of President Franklin D. Roosevelt and Prime Minister Winston Churchill was regarded in official circles here as a council of war designed to clear the way for Allied unity and a common strategy on all fronts, and to plan a continuing offensive whose object is, not the negotiated peace for which the Axis has at times angled and may angle again, but "unconditional surrender" of the enemy. It was the first time this phrase had been used in an official definition of the war aims of the United Nations.

As an expression of the common strategy that is being worked out, it was expected by many that a war council of the "big four"—Britain, Russia, China and the United States—would emerge, and that the mutual aid and coordinated purposes of the United Nations would receive increasing emphasis in the form of more inclusive consultations on all major aspects of the war and on the distribution of the sinews of war in the future.

This was the interpretation placed by observers here tonight upon those words of the official announcement concerning efforts to include Premier Joseph Stalin and Generalissimo Chiang Kai-shek in the dramatic meeting on the coast of Morocco, which symbolized the growing offensive power of the Allies on the southern margin of the European war theatre and the alignment of the bulk of the French Empire on the side of the United Nations.

Parley Essentially Military

It was emphasized in official circles here that the gathering at Casablanca was essentially military, as indicated by the presence there of the highest American and British strategists of the navies, armies and air forces, including the commanders of the North African operations, and that the major preoccupation was the winning of the war rather than political issues, save as they directly affected the grand strategy of the Allied coalition.

Tonight's announcement from Casablanca cleared up some of the mystery that has surrounded the proceedings since Jan. 9, when the press was informed by the Office of Censorship that President Roosevelt was going on a trip and the attention of correspondents was drawn to the code of voluntary censorship, which forbids publication of any hints or speculation about the President's movements.

In the seventeen-day interval of silence that followed, private guesses had placed the President at numerous widely separated spots all the way from Alaska to Moscow. One rumor was that he had gone to London; others had him at intervening points; but most guesses were warm in that they pointed to the coast of Africa as the probable place of his rendezvous with Mr. Churchill and the leaders of the Allied fighting services.

Rumor About Stalin

Some expected that Mr. Stalin and the Chinese Generalissimo would turn up at the appointed meeting place to personify, with the American and British leaders, the over-all unity lately discussed.

It was generally assumed that, wherever the meeting, the question of union of the French forces on a military rather than a political basis and the formulation of

Continued on Page Two

President Pays Surprise Visit To U. S. Troops in Morocco

Roosevelt Reviews Soldiers at Base Outside Casablanca—Visits Graves of Americans Who Fell During Landings

By WALTER LOGAN
United Press Correspondent

CASABLANCA, French Morocco, Jan. 21 (Delayed)—President Roosevelt inspected American troops in French Morocco today, surprising them by his presence and leaving their faces wreathed in smiles.

The President reviewed the troops from a jeep driven by Staff Sergeant Oran Lass of Kansas City, Mo., who was the proudest soldier in the United States Army but maintained an air of impeccable dignity throughout.

In the jeep with the President were Lieut. Gen. Mark Clark, Commander of the United States Fifth Army; Charles Fredericks, the President's personal bodyguard, and the general officer

Continued on Page Five

HONORED BY PRESIDENT

Brig. Gen. William H. Wilbur, who received from Mr. Roosevelt in Africa the Congressional Medal of Honor. Associated Press Wirephoto

[Story on Page 5]

The Official Communique

By The Associated Press.

CASABLANCA, French Morocco, Jan. 26—Following is the text of the official communiqué on the conference of President Roosevelt and Prime Minister Churchill:

The President of the United States and the Prime Minister of Great Britain have been in conference near Casablanca since Jan. 14.

They were accompanied by the combined Chiefs of Staff of the two countries; namely,

FOR THE UNITED STATES:

General George C. Marshall, Chief of Staff of the United States Army; Admiral Ernest J. King, Commander in Chief of the United States Navy; Lieut. Gen. H. H. Arnold, commanding the United States Army Air Forces, and

FOR GREAT BRITAIN:

Admiral of the Fleet Sir Dudley Pound, First Sea Lord; General Sir Alan Brooke, Chief of the Imperial General Staff, and Air Chief Marshal Sir Charles Portal, Chief of the Air Staff.

These were assisted by:

Lieut. Gen. B. B. Somervell, Commanding General of the Services of Supply, United States Army; Field Marshal Sir John Dill, head of the British Joint Staff Mission in Washington; Vice Admiral Lord Louis Mountbatten, Chief of Combined Operations; Lieut. Gen. Sir Hastings Ismay, Chief of Staff to the Office of the Minister of Defense, together with a number of staff officers of both countries.

They have received visits from Mr. Murphy [Robert Murphy, United States Minister in French North Africa] and Mr. Macmillan [Harold Macmillan, British Resident Minister for Allied Headquarters in North Africa]; from Lieut. Gen. Dwight D. Eisenhower, Commander in Chief of the Allied Expeditionary Force in North Africa; from Admiral of the Fleet Sir Andrew Cunningham, naval commander of the Allied Expeditionary Force in North Africa; from Major Gen. Carl Spaatz, air commander of the Allied Expeditionary Force in North Africa; from Lieut. Gen. Mark W. Clark, United States Army [commander of the United States Fifth Army in Tunisia], and, from Middle East Headquarters, from General Sir Harold Alexander, Air Chief Marshal Sir Arthur Tedder and Lieut. Gen. F. M. Andrews, United States Army.

The President was accompanied by Harry Hopkins [chairman of the British-American Munitions Assignment Board] and was joined by W. Averell Harriman [United States defense expediter in England].

With the Prime Minister was Lord Leathers, British Minister of War Transport.

For ten days the combined staffs have been in constant session, meeting two or three times a day and recording progress at intervals to the President and Prime Minister.

The entire field of the war was surveyed theatre by theatre throughout the world, and all resources were marshaled for a more intense prosecution of the war by sea, land, and air.

Nothing like this prolonged discussion between two allies has ever taken place before. Complete agreement was reached between the leaders of the two countries and their respective staffs upon war plans and enterprises to be undertaken during the campaigns of 1943 against Germany, Italy and Japan with a view to drawing the utmost advantage from the markedly favorable turn of events at the close of 1942.

Premier Stalin was cordially invited to meet the President and Prime Minister, in which case the meeting would have been held very much farther to the east. He was unable to leave Russia at this time on account of the great offensive which he himself, as Commander in Chief, is directing.

The President and Prime Minister realized up to the full the enormous weight of the war which Russia is successfully bearing along her whole land front, and their prime object has been to draw as much weight as possible off the Russian armies by engaging the enemy as heavily as possible at the best selected points.

Premier Stalin has been fully informed of the military proposals.

The President and Prime Minister have been in communication with Generalissimo Chiang Kai-shek. They have apprised him of the measures which they are undertaking to assist him in China's magnificent and unrelaxing struggle for the common cause.

The occasion of the meeting between the President and Prime Minister made it opportune to invite General Giraud [General Henri Honoré Giraud, High Commissioner of French Africa] to confer with the Combined Chiefs of Staff and to arrange for a meeting between him and General de Gaulle [General Charles de Gaulle, Fighting French Commander]. The two generals have been in close consultation.

The President and Prime Minister and their combined staffs, having completed their plans for the offensive campaigns of 1943, have now separated in order to put them into active and concerted execution.

LEADERS GO BY AIR

Aim at 'Unconditional Surrender' by Axis, President Says

MILITARY AIDES TALK

French Chiefs Declare Groups Will Unite to Liberate Nation

By DREW MIDDLETON
Special Cable to The New York Times.

CASABLANCA, French Morocco, Jan. 24 (Delayed)—President Roosevelt and Prime Minister Churchill today concluded a momentous ten-day conference in which they planned Allied offensives of 1943 aimed at what the President called the "unconditional surrender" of the Axis powers.

The President flew 5,000 miles across the Atlantic with his Chiefs of Staff to confer with Mr. Churchill and British military, naval and air chieftains in a sun-splashed villa within sound of Atlantic breakers. Every phase of the global war was discussed in conferences lasting from morning until midnight. Both war leaders emphasized that the conference was wholly successful and that complete agreement had been reached on great military enterprises to be undertaken by the United Nations this year.

General Henri Honoré Giraud, High Commissioner for French North Africa, and General Charles de Gaulle, leader of Fighting France, met at the conference and found themselves in accord on the primary task of liberating France from German domination. President Roosevelt predicted that French soldiers, sailors and airmen would fight beside the Allied armies in the liberation of France.

Stalin Kept Informed

The President and Mr. Churchill expressed regret for Premier Joseph Stalin's inability to leave the Russian offensive, which he is directing personally, but emphasized that all results of the conferences had been reported to the Soviet leader. [Generalissimo Chiang Kai-shek was similarly advised, The Associated Press reported.]

Assurance of future world peace will come only as a result of the total elimination of German and Japanese war power, the President declared. He borrowed a phrase from General Grant's famous letter to the Confederate commander at Forts Donelson and Henry—"unconditional surrender"—to describe the only terms on which the United Nations would accept the conclusion of the war.

He emphasized, however, that

Continued on Page Six

Trondheim Blasts Heard in Sweden

By The United Press.

STOCKHOLM, Sweden, Jan. 26—Residents of the Swedish frontier area tonight reported having heard thunderous explosions throughout the day from the direction of Trondheim on the Norwegian coast.

[Trondheim Fjord, reputed still the berth of important German warships, including the battleship Tirpitz, extends inland from Trondheim to within thirty miles of the Swedish border.]

The explosions were described as of an intensity comparable with those of last Spring when British planes bombed the Trondheim area.

Border district residents at first thought the explosions were from gunfire, but later thought it more likely an air raid was under way, advices reaching here said.

However, no planes were visible and the explosions resounded steadily from 10:30 A. M. to 5 P. M. except for brief intervals—an unusually long period for an air attack.

Robert Walker and Keenan Wynn in a scene from *See Here, Private Hargrove.*

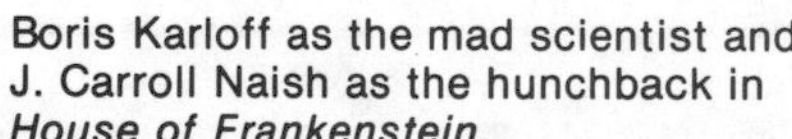

Boris Karloff as the mad scientist and J. Carroll Naish as the hunchback in *House of Frankenstein.*

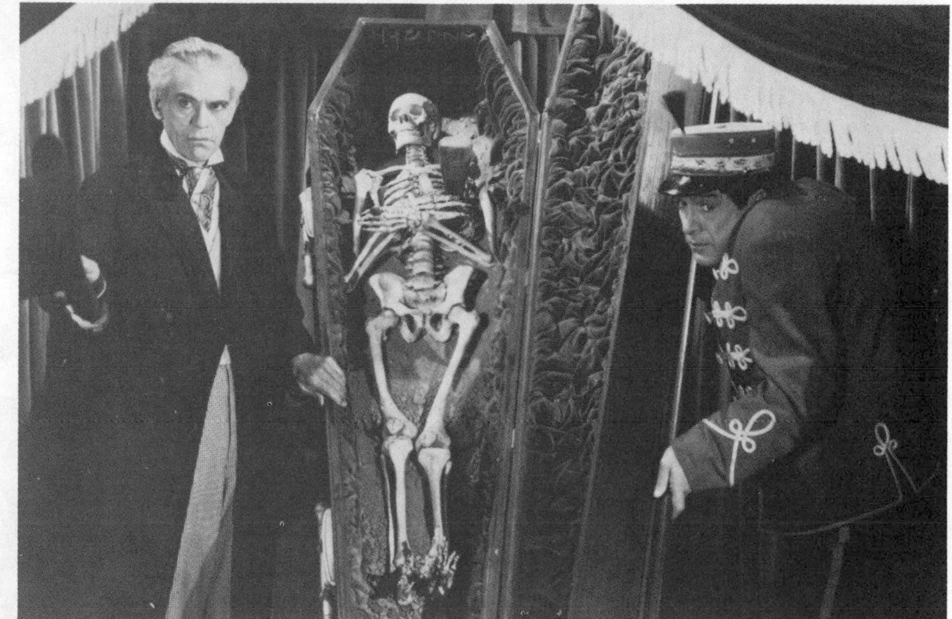

Barry Fitzgerald, Risë Stevens and Bing Crosby in the classic *Going My Way.*

An Office of Price Administration poster urging Americans to use their ration stamps.

Riots broke out in many U.S. cities in the summer of 1943. In industrial Detroit, race-riots left 34 dead and over 700 injured; riots also occured in eastern and western cities.

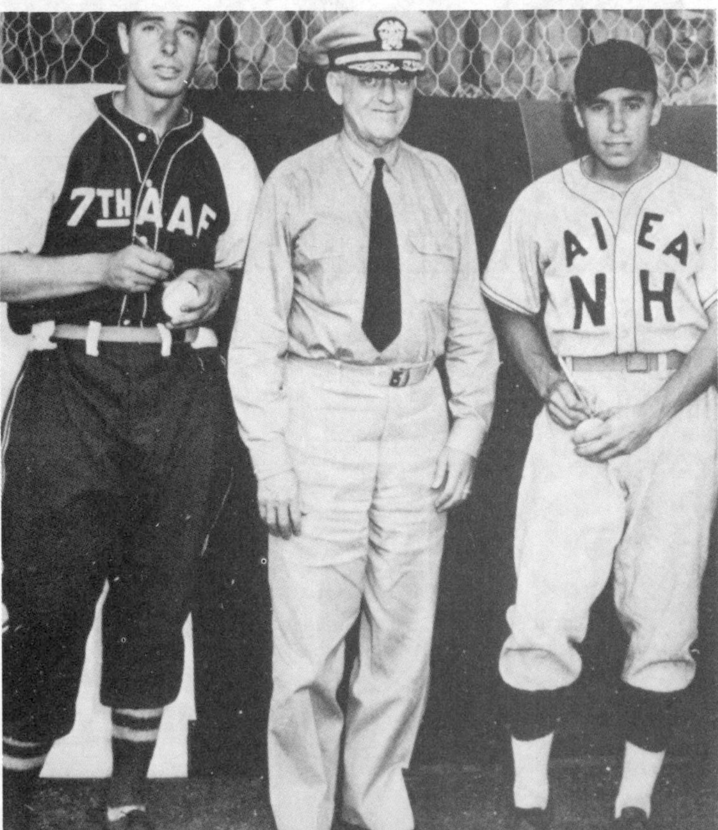

Professional sports suffered as many athletes were drafted or enlisted. In this photo, Joe DiMaggio (left) and Pee Wee Reese (right) are suited up for an armed forces game.

Joe Louis, the World Heavyweight Champion, enlisted in the army and promoted the war effort in this poster.

"All the News That's Fit to Print."

The New York Times.

LATE CITY EDITION
Somewhat warmer today with light winds.
Temperatures Yesterday—Max.,53; Min.,34
Sunrise, 6:28 A. M.; Sunset, 7:26 P. M.

Copyright, 1943, by The New York Times Company.

VOL. XCII..No. 31,121. Entered as Second-Class Matter, Postoffice, New York, N. Y. NEW YORK, FRIDAY, APRIL 9, 1943. THREE CENTS IN NEW YORK CITY

ROOSEVELT ORDER FREEZES WAGES AND PRICES AND BARS SHIFTING OF JOBS FOR HIGHER PAY; TUNISIA DRIVES GAIN; JAPANESE LOSE 37 PLANES

AXIS PUSHED BACK

8th Army Moves 15 Miles and Is 25 From U. S. Maknassy Force

FIRST ARMY ATTACKS

Gains in North—Allies Ready 'to Exact Price,' Says Eisenhower

By FRANK L. KLUCKHOHN

Wireless to THE NEW YORK TIMES.

ALLIED HEADQUARTERS IN NORTH AFRICA, April 8—As Britain's First Army pushed the German columns some miles back from the vital road between Beja and Medjez-el-Bab, the shortest route to Tunis and Bizerte, the Eighth Army and Allied Air Force forced the Afrika Corps fifteen miles northward toward Sfax.

[This advance placed the Eighth Army beyond Cekhira, on the coast, and, as The Associated Press noted, only twenty-five miles from a junction with the American column driving toward the sea in the Mezzouna sector.]

Thus the Germans and their Italian satellites were attacked in the north and south, and Field Marshal General Erwin Rommel, with his flank to the sea and a dubious line of mountains protecting his other side, was seeking to extricate himself from an exceedingly difficult but by no means hopeless position.

But General Dwight D. Eisenhower declared that the Allied naval forces, as well as the Army and Air Force, were in a position "to exact the full price" from the Axis forces in Tunisia.

Allied Airmen Pound Rommel

By midafternoon today it was disclosed at headquarters that the Eighth Army had advanced at least fifteen miles north of its position at the start of the latest break-through, and Marshal Rommel, with that long, precarious mountain range to protect, pushed toward Sfax. His forces were pounded by planes working in relays and there appeared sound grounds for the optimism expressed by General Eisenhower.

Although bitter rear guard action was being fought, the Eighth Army continued to pick up prisoners and abandoned matériel. The air force punished the retreating forces, setting tanks and equipment on fire.

While the movement on the northern front was less dramatic and obviously preparatory, it nevertheless was one of the major features of the campaign, if not the most important, since it takes no military genius to know that the final action, from whatever direction it comes, must center around Tunis and Bizerte.

In his drive in the north following his Kasserine pass failure against the Americans in February, Col. Gen. Dietloff von Arnim not

Continued on Page Three

THE GRASP OF VICTORY IN NORTH AFRICA

General Dwight D. Eisenhower (right), Allied chief in the theatre, and General Sir Bernard L. Montgomery, commander of the British Eighth Army, meet on the Tunisian front after the latter had smashed the Mareth Line.

The New York Times Radiophoto, passed yesterday by British censor

YANK MET TOMMY WITH BACK SLAPS

Motorized American and 8th Army Units Joined Gleefully on the Gafsa-Gabes Road

By C. L. SULZBERGER

Wireless to THE NEW YORK TIMES.

WITH THE SECOND UNITED STATES CORPS, in Tunisia, April 7 (Delayed)—Two Army sergeants, one a thin Devonshire boy named William Brown and one a slight young man named Joseph Randall of State Center, Iowa, stopped on the Gafsa-Gabès highway at midafternoon today, shook hands and slapped each other on the back.

In that fashion General Sir Bernard L. Montgomery's brilliant Eighth Army and the American northwest African Expeditionary Corps brought to a conclusion their tremendous march toward each other, the former starting from the borders of the Nile Valley and the latter rolling from Atlantic beaches on the coast of Western Morocco.

No words of their historic meeting were recorded. Forty-five minutes later the main bodies met and swung north on the enemy's heels.

The first contact was between a handful of members of both forces who had driven peaceably toward each other only a few hours after the Germans and Italians had has-

Continued on Page Four

CITY TOLD IT CAN CUT BUDGET $27,655,232

Two Groups Submit Detailed Proposals—$50,000 Offered for Study of Savings

Specific recommendations for reducing Mayor La Guardia's executive budget of $753,071,123 for 1943-44 by amounts ranging from $19,965,059 to $27,655,232 were submitted to the Board of Estimate yesterday at the first of its two public hearings on the document.

The $19,965,059 cut was recommended by the Citizens Budget Commission, which declared that its adoption would leave the real estate tax rate at its present level of $2.79 per $100 of assessed valuation and remove the danger of a record rate of $2.94 or $2.95 proposed by the Mayor.

The $27,655,232 reduction was put forward by the Commerce and Industry Association of New York, which said it would not only remove danger of a tax rate rise but would mean a substantial reduction in the present rate.

Both organizations submitted detailed schedules showing how expenses could be reduced and revenues increased. Both indicated that increased revenues would be available, on the theory that Controller Joseph D. McGoldrick's estimates of general fund revenues and the

Continued on Page Forty-two

GUADALCANAL RAID

U. S. Breaks Up Attack on Ships by 98 of Foe—7 Planes Lost

OUR BOMBERS ACTIVE

Wreck a Flying Boat and Hit Japanese Bases in the Solomons

By SIDNEY SHALETT

Special to THE NEW YORK TIMES.

WASHINGTON, April 8—United States fighter planes have scored a smashing victory over the Japanese at Guadalcanal, shooting down thirty-seven of an attacking force of ninety-eight planes, with a loss of seven American craft, the Navy announced today in a communiqué that told of the greatest aerial battle in the Solomons since last Winter.

Only scanty details of the great battle were revealed. Whether it was a complete American victory was not disclosed by the Navy Department, for the communiqué told nothing of the results of the apparently determined Japanese raid, which was directed against United States shipping in the vicinity of Guadalcanal Island.

The aerial battle took place yesterday, South Pacific time. The make-up of the defending forces was not revealed, but it was indicated by the identification of the American planes lost that both Army and Navy fighters participated. Further details are expected from the Navy when, in its opinion, the facts may be disclosed without giving information to the enemy.

Four Raids by Our Fliers

The previous day there was a light raid on Guadalcanal that did little damage, while four punishing raids were made by our own fliers, in which six enemy strongholds in the Solomons area were struck and damaged.

The Japanese air armada that set out to destroy American shipping near Guadalcanal, now the American bastion in the Japanese-dominated South Pacific area, was composed of fifty bombers, escorted by forty-eight Zero fighters. It was not disclosed how many American fighters rose to engage

Continued on Page Six

ORDER IS ACCLAIMED

Aims of President Win Approval Among Both Parties in Congress

LABOR IS SURPRISED

Its Chiefs Stress Cost of Living—Farm Concern Is on Wage Freezing

Special to THE NEW YORK TIMES.

WASHINGTON, April 8—President Roosevelt's "hold-the-line" order tonight against inflation was received with general approval on Capitol Hill and in official circles, but representatives of organized labor preferred in the main not to comment until they had studied the order and the message which accompanied it.

Labor spokesmen were taken by surprise, but while they would not comment officially, they said that the move appeared to be in the direction of coping with wages, prices and living costs at the same time.

The order found favor in all quarters of Congress but the farm group, which recently won passage of the Bankhead bill and of the Pace bill in the House which would require the inclusion of farm wages in calculation of parity, gave approval with reservations.

Question of Farm Labor

Representative Pace of Georgia thought the President's order would be a fine thing if its wage-freezing features applied to farm labor.

"Unless the order applies to farm wages I don't see how the farmer can continue to produce at present prices," he said. "If it does apply, the House should be congratulated on passing the so-called Pace bill."

Senator Vandenberg, veteran Michigan Republican, said that "the order sounds very satisfactory," and added:

"I would welcome any positive action which the President is now taking. I am sure he will have no trouble with Congress if he sets the right example."

None of the legislative leaders reached for comment had been able to examine the President's order,

Continued on Page Thirteen

President on Inflation

By The Associated Press.

WASHINGTON, April 8—Following is the statement on inflation issued today by President Roosevelt:

The Executive Order I have signed today is a hold-the-line order.

To hold the line we cannot tolerate further increases in prices affecting the cost of living or further increases in general wage or salary rates except where clearly necessary to correct substandard living conditions. The only way to hold the line is to stop trying to find justifications for not holding it here or not holding it there.

No one straw may break a camel's back, but there is always a last straw. We cannot afford to take further chances in relaxing the line. We already have taken too many.

On the price front the directions in the order are clear and specific.

All items affecting the cost of living are to be brought under control. No further price increases are to be sanctioned unless imperatively required by law. Adjustments in the price relationships between different commodities will be permitted if such adjustments can be made without increasing the general cost of living.

But any further inducements to maintain or increase production must not be allowed to disturb the present price levels; such further inducements, whether they take the form of support prices or subsidies, must not be allowed to increase prices to consumers. Of course, the extent to which subsidies and other payments may be used to help keep down the cost of living will depend on Congressional authorization.

Some prices affecting the cost of living are already above the levels of Sept. 15, 1942. All of these cannot be rolled back. But some of these can and should be rolled back. The order directs the reduction of all prices which are excessively high, inequitable or unfair. The Stabilization Act was not intended to be used as a

Continued on Page Thirteen

ACTS ON INFLATION

President Bars Rises Above Steel Level to 'Hold the Line'

FAVORS HIGHER TAXES

Congress Is Urged to Act to Siphon Away Buying Power

The text of the President's order will be found on Page 14.

By W. H. LAWRENCE

Special to THE NEW YORK TIMES.

WASHINGTON, April 8—President Roosevelt strengthened the anti-inflation program today with a sweeping executive order forbidding wage increases above the level of the "Little Steel" formula and restricting future price rises to the minimum extent required by law.

To implement what he called a "hold-the-line order," the President authorized Paul V. McNutt, War Manpower Commission chairman, to issue regulations which would prevent employes from shifting to a job at a higher rate of pay unless the change would aid in the prosecution of the war.

He called upon Congress to impose higher taxes in order to reduce and hold in check excess purchasing power and to pass no new legislation which would require further price increases.

Warns on "Further Chances"

"The only way to hold the line is to stop trying to find justifications for not holding it here or not holding it there," the President said in an accompanying statement. "No one straw may break a camel's back, but there is always a last straw. We cannot afford to take further chances in relaxing the line. We already have taken too many."

The order appeared certain to bring a showdown between the Administration and John L. Lewis, president of the United Mine Workers of America, who is demanding a $2-a-day wage increase for 450,000 bituminous coal miners and 90,000 anthracite coal miners.

On wages, the President specifically directed the National War Labor Board, the Commissioner of Internal Revenue and other agencies administering wage or salary controls "to authorize no further increases in wages or salaries except such as are clearly necessary to correct substandards of living" and except in accordance with the "Little Steel" formula, which limits general wage rises to a total of 15 per cent since Jan. 1, 1941, in order to compensate for increased living costs between January, 1941, and May, 1942.

Merit Increases Permitted

The wage control agencies also will be permitted, under general policies laid down by James F. Byrnes, Economic Stabilization Director, to authorize "reasonable adjustments of wages and salaries in case of promotions, reclassifications, merit increases, incentive wages or the like, provided that such adjustments do not increase the level of production costs appreciably or furnish the basis either to increase prices or to resist otherwise justifiable reduction in prices."

Bituminous miners would be entitled to no general increase under the "Little Steel" formula, and anthracite miners would be entitled to only a small general rise.

Late tonight the full War Labor Board met and, after studying the President's order, sent this telegram to all regional boards, commissions and other agencies to which authority has been delegated by the agency:

"First, continue to prepare as heretofore all your cases.

"Secondly, approve no further

Continued on Page Fourteen

Senate Votes Land Army Bill; 40 Millions for Mobile Corps

By C. P. TRUSSELL

Special to THE NEW YORK TIMES.

WASHINGTON, April 8—The Senate farm group, in another showing of strength today, pushed through a bill to set up a mobile and migratory land army, composed largely of imported Mexican and Bahaman workers, to relieve agricultural manpower shortages.

Under the measure, which goes to conference with a somewhat similar bill approved by the House, the program would be under the direction of Chester C. Davis, the Food Administrator. Mr. Davis, debate brought out, is "vigorously opposed" to some phases of the legislation, which would take the transportation and care of migratory workers from the Farm Security Administration and put the Department of Agriculture's Extension Service in charge in the States.

While the legislation emphasizes the mobility of the projected land force and large-scale movements of farm workers to critical labor shortage areas, it provides specifically that no worker may be transported from his home county without consent in writing from the county extension agent.

To obtain a transfer from his base county to another area for farm work, if the county agent refused permission, a worker would have to appeal to the food administrator for a certification that he was needed elsewhere.

This brought protests from Senators from Western States, where shortages of farm labor are acute and where much dependence had been put upon the migration of experienced hands from the south, where cotton workers, in particular, are tied at that work only a few months out of the year.

It was indicated that seasonal

Continued on Page Eleven

COAL PLEA TO WLB DESPITE STEELMAN

Southern Operators' Action Is Scored by Conciliator—Board Takes Up Case Today

The Southern Coal Producers Association, representing soft coal operators employing 135,000 of the nation's 450,000 bituminous miners, appealed to the War Labor Board in Washington yesterday to intervene in the wage dispute with the United Mine Workers on the ground that "the parties are in complete and irreconcilable disagreement on all major issues" and that "a continuance of collective bargaining offers no hope of success."

The appeal of the Southern operators was addressed to William H. Davis, chairman of the WLB, over the head of Dr. John R. Steelman, director of the United States Conciliation Service and President Roosevelt's representative in the wage negotiations, who has been trying since March 29 to move the operators and miners to an agreement.

While the Northern operators, employing 175,000 men, refrained

Continued on Page Thirteen

War News Summarized

FRIDAY, APRIL 9, 1943

The British First Army in Northern Tunisia advanced five miles yesterday, pushing the Germans back several miles from the road between Beja and Medjez-el-Bab. The Eighth Army, meanwhile, drove fifteen more miles up the coast from Wadi el Akarit, putting it beyond the port of Cekhira. Enemy counterattacks were repelled. The British were reported to be only twenty-five miles from American troops driving ahead in the Mezzouna sector. [1:1; map, P. 3.]

A dispatch from the northern sector declared that General Anderson had employed the heaviest artillery barrage so far in the campaign before the infantry drove ahead at dawn. [3:1.]

A correspondent with the Second United States Army Corps wrote that the junction of British and American forces on the Gafsa-Gabès road had been effected by two sergeants who met on the highway in the afternoon and shook hands. [1:2.]

Secretary of War Stimson told reporters that to all practical purposes the two German armies in Tunisia were now one and would "presumably" fight to the end under one command. [3:6.]

The Royal Air Force resumed the aerial offensive in Europe with a raid last night on the industrial Ruhr region. [7:1.]

The Soviet midnight communiqué reported no important changes along the eastern front. It indicated that the Germans had shifted their main pressure on the Donets front to the Balakleya sector after vain and costly attempts to break through near Izyum. [5:1.]

The Japanese made one of their biggest attempts to destroy our shipping near Guadalcanal, sending out a force of ninety-eight planes. Intercepting American planes, however, shot down thirty-seven of the raiders at a cost of seven aircraft. Our bombers continued to pound enemy bases in the Solomons. [1:4; map, P. 6.]

A wildcat strike of dock workers in Sydney, Australia, has resulted in American and Australian soldiers' having to unload ships in that port. [10:3.]

It was indicated in Washington that French political unity might be postponed until the Axis has been driven from Africa. A dispatch from Algiers said that General Eisenhower's letter to General de Gaulle, which resulted in postponement of the latter's trip, had expressed the opinion that there should be no political crisis behind the fighting front. [4:4.]

Foreign Secretary Eden reported to the House of Commons on his trip to the United States and Canada. He was loudly applauded when he revealed he had invited Secretary of State Hull to visit Britain. [4:1.]

Find Maps of Sweden In Transit to Reich

By The Associated Press.

STOCKHOLM, Sweden, April 8—The Swedish Foreign Office announced tonight that maps of Sweden and Norway, which it described "as extraordinarily detailed," had been confiscated from a freight car bound across Sweden from Finland to Germany.

All goods in the car were removed by Swedish authorities, the announcement said, and a complete investigation has been ordered by the Foreign Office.

Discovery of the maps came on the eve of the anniversary of Germany's invasion of Norway three years ago and in the midst of a controversy over shipments of German goods and soldiers through Sweden between Germany, Norway and Finland.

MacArthur Marks Fall of Bataan By New Vow to Retake Philippines

By The United Press.

ALLIED HEADQUARTERS IN AUSTRALIA, Friday, April 9—General Douglas MacArthur commemorated the anniversary of the fall of Bataan today in a statement that revealed his bitterness over successive disappointments and his unswerving hope that he may lead a conquering army back to the lost Philippines.

He said that at Bataan the American flag had been spat upon, that American and Filipino men and women were in prisons and that 16,000,000 Filipino people who had trusted their fate to America were enslaved.

"I was the leader of that lost cause," he said, "and from the bottom of my stricken heart I pray that a merciful God may not delay too long their redemption, that the day of salvation be not so far removed that they perish, that it be not again too late."

It was the first time General MacArthur had mentioned the name Bataan publicly in the 364 days since last April 10, the day after 35,000 United States and Philippine troops surrendered, when he said in a penciled note:

"No army has ever done so much with so little."

People here believe that had MacArthur known what was fated to happen in the year since Bataan he would never have left the Philippines. He thought he was coming to organize an immediate offensive; he even hoped that the Army

Continued on Page Nine.

Army Won't Take La Guardia Now; Needed as Mayor, Stimson Says

Special to THE NEW YORK TIMES.

WASHINGTON, April 8—There will be no Army commission, "at least for the present," for Mayor La Guardia, Secretary Stimson stated today in his press conference.

Before reporters could ask about it, Mr. Stimson offered a prepared statement which disposed of rumors current for several weeks.

"Mayor La Guardia visited me last Tuesday to offer personally and patriotically his services to the War Department," the Secretary said.

"It was my view that in his present office as Mayor of New York he is rendering directly to that city, and indirectly to the entire nation, an example of such usefulness that it is very difficult now to find any place in the Army where he could be equally useful.

"After talking it over with him on Tuesday, we decided to leave the matter open for the present, the Mayor assuring me that he would always be available for service."

The talk about the Mayor's possible Army service began with the passage of a bill by the New York Legislature permitting him to take leave of office to enter the Army.

There were reports that the Mayor was in line for a brigadier generalship and was slated to serve as an administrator with occupation forces.

Mayor La Guardia declined to comment on Secretary Stimson's statement.

Women by the thousands took jobs formerly performed by men only.

Jack Benny entertaining servicemen on the home front.

"All the News That's Fit to Print."

The New York Times.

LATE CITY EDITION
Near freezing in early morning; later, slowly rising temperature.
Temperatures Yesterday—Max., 53; Min., 39
Sunrise, 5:56 A. M.; Sunset, 7:52 P. M.

Section 1

NEWS INDEX, PAGE 47, THIS SECTION

VOL. XCII..No. 31,144. Entered as Second-Class Matter, Postoffice, New York, N. Y. NEW YORK, SUNDAY, MAY 2, 1943. Including Magazine and Book Sections. TEN CENTS New York City and Vicinity

ROOSEVELT SEIZES ALL STRUCK COAL MINES; TROOPS TO GUARD RETURNING MEN, IF NEEDED; COLLIERIES ARE CLOSED; LEWIS REMAINS SILENT

AMERICANS PUSH ON

Take 2 Hills in Northern Tunisia as They Pace Allies' Advance

BRITISH GAIN, LOSE

New Attack Opened on Coast by 8th Army, Berlin Declares

By FRANK L. KLUCKHOHN
Wireless to THE NEW YORK TIMES.

ALLIED HEADQUARTERS IN NORTH AFRICA, May 1—Seasoned New Yorkers, veterans of many Tunisian battles, drove up the steep sides of Hill 523, one of the key heights essential to the control of the valley leading to Mateur, thirteen miles northeast on the road to Bizerte, and captured it in bitter bayonet fighting, it was officially reported today.

Coincidentally, other American troops, despite odds that favored a determined enemy holding such a position, battled up to the northern slopes of Hill 609—Djebel Tahent, thirteen miles southwest of Mateur—where the precipices of the 2,000-foot elevation are wall-like in their steepness. Whether Hill 609, just north of Hill 523, had been completely taken was not ascertainable. Some reports from the front said that it had been, but a headquarters spokesman would say only that the northern slope had been taken. Advances were made yesterday along the southern and western slopes.

[A later Associated Press dispatch said that the final capture of the hill had been announced officially.

[A London broadcast heard by The United Press quoted the Berlin radio last night as saying that the British Eighth Army had started an offensive in the coastal area of Tunisia, north of Enfidaville, but that it had been repulsed. An Italian communiqué announced that the Eighth Army had opened up a "particularly intense and prolonged" artillery barrage, The Associated Press said. Such a bombardment, the customary prelude to a full-scale attack, was not mentioned by other sources.]

Major Gains Americans'

Despite the heavy losses in the fighting to date and the fact that even well-trained men in perfect physical trim are exhausted by the time that they have struggled up such crevassed and twisted obstacles, the Americans were determined to keep pounding ahead. Theirs were the chief important gains registered yesterday along the whole 125-mile front.

Americans and Moroccan goumiers, at one point of the multi-pronged advance in the northern seacoast sector, made progress in the area seven miles west of Garaet [Lake] Achkel, near Bizerte, and neared the key peak of Djebel Hazemat, fourteen miles northwest of Mateur. The British, despite ferocious enemy counter-attacks, advanced slightly toward Tebourba on the northern road between Medjez-el-Bab and Tunis. On the Eighth Army's front small advances were registered amid other steep hills.

The Germans were losing men without counting the cost. But the Allies were pounding with unrelenting power and with confidence that they would eventually crunch the ribs of the enemy's defenses by sheer strength and courage, even though these ribs might go one by one rather than all together.

As the United States infantry plowed through the tortuous mine fields under mortar fire and advanced in groups up the hills, the American artillery continued to pump shells into Mateur, the key point of the enemy's communica-

Continued on Page Twenty-six

CAPTURED CREW OF U-BOAT LANDED ON U. S. SOIL

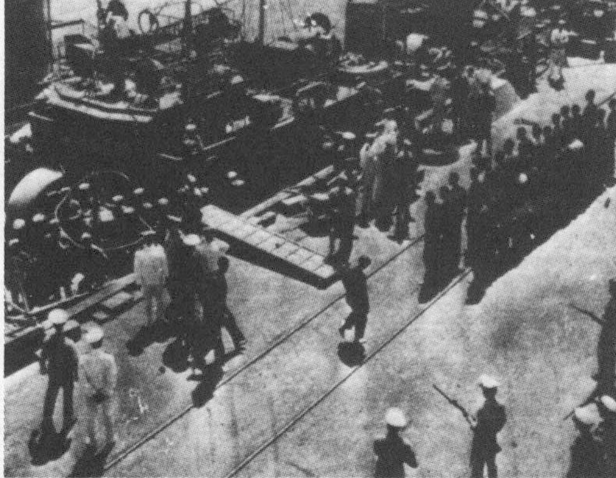

Thirty-three survivors of the Nazi submarine sunk by the Coast Guard patrol craft Icarus off the Carolinas are lined up after being brought ashore from the vessel at the Charleston, S. C., Navy Yard. Captain Lieutenant Hellmut Rathke stands beside his men in the front row at the extreme right. His executive officer and a sailor (left center) approach the formation under a marine guard. The New York Times (U. S. Navy)

CUTTER GETS U-BOAT AND 33 OF ITS CREW

Marauder Sunk Off Carolina Coast and Captain Seized by Coast Guard Craft

By The Associated Press.

WASHINGTON, May 1—A Coast Guard cutter sank a German U-boat off the Carolina coast several months ago, the Navy reported today, and captured thirty-three members of the crew, including the commanding officer. This was the first time the Navy has announced the capture of prisoners from a German submarine.

Another officer and thirty-one enlisted men made up the group captured. The prisoners were taken to Charleston, S. C., and presumably now are being held in a United States prison camp, although the Navy did not comment on their present disposition. [One of the prisoners died of bullet wounds and was brought ashore for burial, Commander Maurice D. Jester reported in Miami.]

Destruction of the U-boat and the capture of the prisoners was achieved by the 165-foot cutter Icarus, which used depth charges to force the submarine to the surface and then raked its deck with gunfire. Immediately afterward the undersea raider began to sink and members of its crew who had sought to man a deck gun jumped into the sea.

Those were the men picked up

Continued on Page Thirty-four

Allies, by Air and Sea, Sink 16 Ships in Mediterranean

Wireless to THE NEW YORK TIMES.

ALLIED HEADQUARTERS IN NORTH AFRICA, May 1—Slashing through a protective umbrella of enemy aircraft, Allied planes sank at least a half dozen enemy ships bearing men and supplies to Tunisia yesterday. One of the ships sunk was a destroyer. An Italian light cruiser was left in flames as bomb-hits were scored on eight vessels.

[In London, the Admiralty announced that ten more enemy ships had been sunk in the Mediterranean by British submarines.]

As the Allied pilots again "ran wild" yesterday despite the Germans' frantic efforts to halt them, one of the most amazing single feats of the campaign was recorded when Flight Sergeant A. B. Browning of the Royal Air Force, flying a lone plane, shot down five Junkers transports in little more than five minutes.

It was United States bombers bearing the name of General Billy Mitchell—who once was ridiculed for insisting that planes could sink warships—that sighted the cruiser while patrolling over the Cap Bon area off Northeastern Tunisia, and dived in to attack. Bombs crashed in a line along the ship, hitting near her vulnerable superstructure, her bow and her stern guns. Even as the pilots pulled quickly away, fire broke out and clouds of black-and-white smoke rose from the vessel. The fliers reported that she seemed to be in a sinking condition.

As the Mitchells flew off, six Messerschmitts that had been un-

Continued on Page Twenty-seven

Major Sports Yesterday

HORSE RACING

Mrs. John D. Hertz's Count Fleet, the 2-5 favorite, won the Kentucky Derby by three lengths at Churchill Downs. Blue Swords was second, six lengths before Slide Rule. Despite restrictions on travel to Louisville that had caused this to be dubbed the "street-car" Derby, about 60,000 persons attended. With Johnny Longden up, Count Fleet took the lead heading out of the clubhouse turn and stayed in front to earn $60,725. The ailing Ocean Wave, considered Count Fleet's most dangerous rival, was one of two withdrawals. At Pimlico, Riverland broke the track record to capture the Dixie Handicap by half a length from Attention. Overdrawn took the Jamaica Handicap for the third straight year, leading Doublrab by half a length. With 27,608 racegoers present, the wagering at Jamaica totaled $1,934,863.

BASEBALL

With Bobo Newsom pitching a one-hit shut-out in the second game, the Dodgers took a double-header from the Giants, 9—2 and 3—0, at the Polo Grounds. Three home runs, by Arky Vaughan and Dolph Camilli in the first contest and by Dixie Walker in the second, highlighted the Brooklyn attack. At Washington, the Yankees beat the Senators in the eleventh inning, 9—7, on Rollie Hemsley's double, a wind-blown pop fly that was lost in the sun.

ROWING

Harvard's varsity crew nipped Navy in the last five strokes of the Adams Cup race on the Schuylkill at Philadelphia to capture the trophy for the sixth year in a row. Cornell, an added starter, was third. Columbia defeated Rutgers by two-thirds of a length, fighting off the Scarlet's strong closing bid on the Harlem.

(Complete Details of These and Other Sports Events in Section 3.)

CALLS ON OWNERS

Secretary Tells Mine Operators to Prepare to Open the Pits

WARNS ON TROOP USE

He Also Asks Eastman to Bar Unnecessary Railroad Travel

Special to THE NEW YORK TIMES.

WASHINGTON, May 1—Secretary Ickes took over the country's bituminous and anthracite mines today upon authorization of President Roosevelt. He immediately mobilized all government agencies in an effort to have the mines reopened as soon as possible and to assure a steady supply of coal to the war industries which may be imperiled by the cessation of work by 450,000 bituminous and 80,000 anthracite miners.

The Solid Fuels Administrator quickly enrolled all operators and managers of the 3,400 soft-coal mines and the several hundred hard-coal workings as government employes.

Would Curb Rail Travel

He followed this action by calling upon Joseph B. Eastman, chief of the Office of Defense Transportation, to eliminate at once all nonessential railroad travel for the duration of the emergency.

In his letter he explained that pending resumption of normal production the limited coal supplies must be conserved in every way possible "lest we soon see the complete stopping of work in many plants throughout the country now turning out munitions and essential civilian products."

The coal chief also was reported to be ready to ask Donald M. Nelson, chief of the War Production Board, to declare a national dim-out for the conservation of coal.

The grant of authority by the President was exceedingly broad and apparently gave the Secretary authority to go into any coal yard and take whatever coal was necessary to divert it for use in war plants and industry generally.

Mr. Ickes's first action was to send a telegram to the 3,400 bitum-

Continued on Page Thirty-seven

ESSEN IS POUNDED; U.S. FLIERS ATTACK

R.A.F. Blow at Krupps Costs 13 Planes—10,000 Tons of Bombs Hit Germany in April

By JAMES MacDONALD
Wireless to THE NEW YORK TIMES.

LONDON, May 1—Winding up what is believed to have been the greatest month of aerial bombing in history—with nearly 10,000 tons of high explosives and incendiaries loosed on targets inside Germany and additional tons on objectives in Nazi-occupied territories and Italy during April—the Royal Air Force pounded Essen, site of the big Krupp armament works, again last night. The R. A. F. had last attacked Essen on April 3.

The Air Ministry described the raid on the vast 800-acre Krupp plant, as was the case with all other recent night attacks in Germany, as "heavy." Thirteen British bombers were lost there and over other targets in the Ruhr.

Several squadrons of heavy bombers, believed by observers to be the Liberators or Flying Fortresses of the United States Eighth Air Force were seen swarming out over the southern coast of England

Continued on Page Nineteen

Japan's 'Punishment' Given Allied Group

The Japanese Domei Agency reported last night in an English-language transmission that "appropriate punishment" had been meted out by the Japanese to twenty-five United States Army and Navy officers and men and seven British sailors who were said to have revealed their identities after having been interned until recently as civilians in the Philippines.

The Domei broadcast, as recorded by the Federal Communications Commission, quoted the Tokyo newspaper Mainichi as reporting that the men had been transferred to a war prisoners' camp from the Santo Tomas internment camp in the Philippines after they had made their "confessions." The "punishment" given them was not stated.

Anthracite Mines Closed; 80,000 Standing By Lewis

Hard-Coal Miners Join Bituminous Strike, Quietly Await Word From Union—Prepared to Ignore Roosevelt

By WALTER W. RUCH
Special to THE NEW YORK TIMES.

WILKES-BARRE, Pa., May 1—The entire anthracite field in Eastern Pennsylvania was made idle today by a walkout of about 80,000 miners who remained unmoved by the announcement that the Federal Government had taken control of the mines which they quit last midnight at the expiration of their contract.

Not a shovel of coal was turned in the hard coal region, forming a rough triangle bounded by Scranton, Shamokin and Pottsville, and it was obvious that the miners were looking toward New York rather than Washington for the cue to return to work.

Although the miners were looking forward to President Roosevelt's radio address tomorrow night, their leaders who were available for comment declared that nothing he could say would induce the men to resume operations Monday morning.

The only thing that could persuade the men to return, these leaders said, would be word from New York that a new contract had been signed or that the old one had been extended, with wage provisions retroactive to April 30.

There was no disorder in the hard coal field during the day. The men simply failed to appear for work, many of them turning up later on the street corners instead in their Sunday best to discuss the action they had taken.

Spokesmen at the union headquarters in the three hard coal districts of the United Mine Workers of America reported this morning

Continued on Page Thirty-eight

Lewis, at Crisis of Career, Refuses to Tell His Plans

By JOSEPH SHAPLEN

John L. Lewis and other leaders of the United Mine Workers of America spent most of the day and evening yesterday pondering their next move in the union's general stoppage of the bituminous and anthracite coal industries, which appeared to be fairly complete, as President Roosevelt seized control of mines throughout the United States.

Mr. Lewis, who on occasion uses the English language with force and dexterity, had "nothing to say" as he faced the most crucial problem of his career: to ask the 480,000 miners who quit work yesterday to return to the pits, as requested by the President, or to advise them to continue defiance of the government.

That request will be repeated by the President when he speaks on the radio at 10 o'clock tonight.

Indications were that no answer would be forthcoming from the United Mine Workers before tomorrow, when additional thousands may fail to report for work. It was apparent that Mr. Lewis and his associates would await what happened in the mine fields and such

Continued on Page Thirty-nine

War News Summarized

SUNDAY, MAY 2, 1943

American soldiers from New York, in a determined bayonet charge, have captured the vital Hill 523 blocking the way to Mateur in Tunisia. Other United States soldiers fought their way up the steep sides of Hill 609 to the north and were reported to have seized the 2,000-foot crest. Still other Americans, fighting with French Goumiers, moved along a route farther north toward Djebel Hazemat, west of Lake Achkel.

The British First Army beat off heavy Axis counter-attacks in most sectors and edged forward in the Tebourba area, while the Eighth Army was reported by Berlin to have broken the comparative lull in the coastal area by resuming its offensive around Enfidaville. The Nazis, ignoring heavy losses inflicted by artillery and aerial pounding, were fighting stubbornly. [All the foregoing 1:1; map P. 26.]

British and American fliers punched holes in a heavy air umbrella the Axis had spread over the Mediterranean. At least half a dozen ships, including a destroyer, were sunk and an Italian cruiser was left blazing. British submarines sank ten more Axis vessels, while one British Beaufighter attacked five Junkers-52 transport planes and shot down all in a brief engagement. [1:3-4; map P. 27.]

The R. A. F. pounded Essen, site of the Krupp works, and other points in the Ruhr Friday night; thirteen bombers failed to return. London announced that since the war began 10,000 tons of bombs had fallen on Essen, the heaviest load ever loosed on a single city. R. A. F. fighters yesterday made sweeps over the Continent and United States bombers were reported raiding the coast. Berlin claimed to have downed eight American planes. [1:4.]

Moscow said the Red Army had destroyed forty enemy batteries and twenty-four planes in repelling Axis counter-attacks in the northwest Caucasus but did not confirm German reports of a Soviet offensive in the North. [12:1.]

The Coast Guard cutter Icarus sank a U-boat off the Carolina coast, the Navy announced, and captured the commander, another officer and thirty-one members of the crew. The raider was forced to the surface by depth bombs and then raked by machine-gun fire. [1:2.]

Army command changes announced by Tokyo were interpreted to indicate a strengthening of the Japanese air force and to forecast increased air activity. [29:2.]

Vice Admiral John H. Hoover, commanding the Tenth Naval District, declared the United States Navy would keep open communications with Martinique in the West Indies. [11:1.]

NEW OFFICE IN WPB TO AID CONSUMER

Civilian Requirements Headed by Whiteside Takes Over Some Ickes-Jeffers Powers

Special to THE NEW YORK TIMES.

WASHINGTON, May 1—An administrative order setting up the Office of Civilian Requirements within the War Production Board, and clothing it with power necessary to provide civilians with all essential goods and services except food, housing and transportation, was issued today by Chairman Donald Nelson. The Office of Civilian Requirements will succeed the Office of Civilian Supply under Joseph Weiner and will be headed by Arthur D. Whiteside, president of Dun & Bradstreet, Inc.

The new office will have every power that its predecessor enjoyed, plus authority over coal, oil, rubber and utilities. In other words, it will take over from Secretary Ickes, Petroleum Coordinator, and from the Rubber Director, William M.

Continued on Page Forty

ICKES IN CONTROL

President Orders Him to Run Mines in Interests of 'Nation at War'

NEW PLEA TO MINERS

They Will Not Balk War Effort, Executive Says—Radio Talk Tonight

The texts of Roosevelt and Ickes orders are on Page 37.

By LOUIS STARK
Special to THE NEW YORK TIMES.

WASHINGTON, May 1—President Roosevelt today ordered Secretary Ickes, as Solid Fuels Administrator for War, to take over all the bituminous and anthracite properties because "the national interest is in grave peril as a result of almost complete cessation of operations of 450,000 soft-coal and 80,000 hard-coal miners."

Secretary Ickes complied immediately, taking over 3,400 bituminous properties, and the hard-coal workings as well, and ordering the flag of the United States to fly from all tipples.

Acting swiftly and firmly, the President, by executive order based on his constitutional powers and his authority as Chief Executive and Commander in Chief of the Army and Navy, directed the Secretary of War to give protection to those who might wish to work, if this were requested by Secretary Ickes.

In a public statement the President called upon all miners "who may have abandoned their work to return immediately to the mines and work for their government."

Stresses the Country's Need

"Their country needs their services as much as those of the members of the armed forces," he declared. "I am confident that they do not wish to retard the war effort; that they are as patriotic as any other Americans and that they will promptly answer this call to perform this essential war service."

The President announced that he would "talk over the radio to the miners of the nation" at 10 P. M. tomorrow. His address will be carried on all networks.

Mr. Roosevelt's action today was based upon the continued refusal of John L. Lewis, president of the United Mine Workers, and his associates to submit their dispute with the Appalachian operators to the determination of the WLB.

The miners have maintained for many weeks that the board would not give them an unprejudiced

Continued on Page Thirty-six

Early Shortage of Meat for Army As Result of OPA Rules Predicted

Representative Walter Ploeser of the House Small Business Committee advised the members of the New York Council of Wholesale Meat Dealers yesterday that they would have to "slug it out" with the Office of Price Administration Meat Section if they expected to continue in existence.

Addressing a luncheon meeting of the council at the Hotel New Yorker, Representative Ploeser, a Missouri Republican, declared that "a stubborn impasse" already had developed in the meat section.

Moreover, Mr. Ploeser warned that "the OPA has got to wake up to the fact that within two or three months it will be telling the Army and the Navy that they can't get meats" because of the paralyzing effects of OPA regulations.

Meanwhile, the City Department of Markets, by direction of Mayor La Guardia, began the sale of 600,000 pounds of California potatoes obtained from the firm of Tassini & Salisch. The first consignment placed on sale at two pounds for 15 cents was snapped up in a quarter of an hour. Dealers in the public markets were supplied with 500 pounds each as a start, and their stocks will be replenished tomorrow as more potatoes are received.

Max Mencher, secretary of the Department of Markets, announcing that additional shipments were expected today, said the department expected to meet the shortage "without very much trouble."

Spokesmen for the packing industry and for government agencies supervising meat supplies here reported that the meat shortage was about the same as last week, but that it was expected to become somewhat worse this week.

Patsy D'Agostino, president of

Continued on Page Forty

"All the News That's Fit to Print."

The New York Times.

LATE CITY EDITION
Slowly rising temperatures today with moderate to fresh winds.
Temperatures Yesterday—Max., 66; Min., 48
Sunrise, 5:43 A. M.; Sunset, 8:06 P. M.

VOL. XCII..No. 31,155. Entered as Second-Class Matter, Postoffice, New York, N. Y. NEW YORK, THURSDAY, MAY 13, 1943. THREE CENTS IN NEW YORK CITY

TUNISIAN RESISTANCE ENDS IN ROUT OF GERMANS; GEN. VON ARNIM AND 150,000 MEN CAPTURED; PACIFIC BELIEVED ROOSEVELT-CHURCHILL TOPIC

BYRNES RESTORES WLB PAY CONTROL, MODIFYING ORDER

He Saves the Agency's Life by Permitting Rises if Costs and Prices Are Held

LABOR AND BOARD PLEASED

Former Leans to Compromise, and Resignations Are No Longer Called Likely

By LOUIS STARK
Special to THE NEW YORK TIMES.

WASHINGTON, May 12—James F. Byrnes, Director of Economic Stabilization, preserved the judicial character of the National War Labor Board today and saved it from threatened dissolution by restoring its authority to make wage adjustments "to aid in the prosecution of the war or correct gross inequities," provided such adjustments did not increase prices or increase production costs.

By modifying the "rigid" nature of the "hold-the-line" executive order of April 8, which had limited wage adjustments to the Little Steel formula, and to correct substandards of living, Mr. Byrnes diminished the likelihood of labor resignations from the WLB.

Labor spokesmen were pleased with the directive clarifying the hold-the-line order, feeling it to be a compromise for their complete program, which had included scrapping the Little Steel formula. This formula was reaffirmed by Mr. Byrnes.

Board Calls Order a Victory

The order met with the complete approval of the public members of the WLB and was regarded by them as a victory in so far as it met with their minimum demands upon Mr. Byrnes.

"The directive order makes it possible for the WLB to perform its part in helping the Director of Economic Stabilization to hold the line against inflation," said Wayne L. Morse, public member.

The situation now presented by the Byrnes order will be on the agenda of the meeting to be held by the executive board of the Congress of Industrial Organizations in Cleveland on Friday. The executive council of the American Federation of Labor will take up the wage policy at its meeting in this city on Monday.

Until the interpretation of Executive Order No. 9328 was announced this evening, informed labor sources had indicated that the meetings of these two organizations probably would result in resignations by the labor members, making the board's collapse inevitable.

Coal Wage Rise is Unlikely

In his directive Mr. Byrnes did not go as far as the board had requested by restoring to it the authority to make wage adjustments to correct "inequalities." This power had been removed from the board by the executive order of April 8.

A wage increase for coal miners under the directive is considered an extremely remote possibility, since it calls for Mr. Byrnes to approve wage adjustments which might increase price ceilings or resist other justifiable reductions in price ceilings.

In a statement summarizing the directive Mr. Byrnes said that it reaffirmed the Little Steel formula, made clear "the authority of the board to make wage adjustments under the authority contained in the order, provided such adjustments are within the existing price structure and within existing levels of production costs," and made clear "that any wage adjustments which may furnish the basis either to increase price ceilings or increase production costs cannot become effective until approved by the director."

The decision to make the changes

Continued on Page Twelve

Bulletin of Victory

By The Associated Press.

ALLIED HEADQUARTERS IN NORTH AFRICA, May 12—The text of a special communiqué tonight announcing the end of the Tunisian campaign follows:

Organized resistance, except by isolated pockets of the enemy, has ceased.

General von Arnim, commander of the Axis forces in Tunisia, has been captured.

It is estimated that the total of prisoners captured since May 5 is about 150,000.

Vast quantities of guns and war material of all kinds have been captured, including guns and aircraft in a serviceable condition.

OPA SPEEDING DRIVE ON FOOD VIOLATORS

Federal Grand Juries to Take Up Cases in 2 Boroughs—New Meat Ceilings Fixed

Federal grand juries are being convened in Brooklyn and Manhattan to investigate price-gouging in poultry and other foods, it was disclosed yesterday after six wholesale poultry concerns and thirteen of their officers had been arraigned before United States Commissioner Edward E. Fay in Brooklyn and held in $1,000 bail each for grand jury action.

Each of the defendants pleaded not guilty to complaints filed by the Office of Price Administration alleging that they sold poultry to retailers above ceiling prices. The complaints were signed by Albert I. Schmalholz, enforcement officer of OPA.

The convening of the grand juries is part of a new integrated drive being conducted by the OPA in cooperation with city and State officials to wipe out black markets in foodstuffs that have been disorganizing legitimate trade and illegally boosting the cost of living.

Meat Ceilings Announced

As part of the same campaign, cents-per-pound ceilings for all beef, lamb and mutton sold at retail through independent stores and chains and supermarkets were announced by the OPA. Similar cents-per-pound ceilings for smoked meats are to be announced today. Both sets of ceilings become effective next Monday.

The OPA also continued yesterday its campaign against smaller dealers who flout ceiling prices, obtaining convictions in five cases through various magistrates courts under a recent resolution of the State War Council that gave OPA regulations in effect April 28 the effect of State law. At several of the hearings it was indicated that one of the main goals of the OPA in prosecuting this type of violator is to force the disclosure of their supply source if they assert they have to pay wholesalers and jobbers prices above ceiling levels.

Continued on Page Fourteen

INDIA STAFF HERE

Wavell's Presence Seen as Hint of Early Action Against Japanese

STALIN TALKS SOUGHT

Conferees May Try Again to See Him Before Invading Europe

By W. H. LAWRENCE
Special to THE NEW YORK TIMES.

WASHINGTON, May 12—President Roosevelt and Prime Minister Winston Churchill began today their intensive global war conferences, both separately and with their key military, naval and air leaders. The scant circumstantial evidence available in the capital was interpreted as indicating that considerable attention was being given to new offensive moves against the Japanese.

A White House announcement concerning a small portion of the Prime Minister's large staff spurred the talk of Far Eastern offensives. It disclosed the presence in Washington of the three top British commanders in the India-Burma theatre—Field Marshal Sir Archibald Percival Wavell, Commander in Chief in India; Admiral Sir James Somerville, commander of British forces in the Bay of Bengal, and Air Marshal Sir Richard Peirse, Commander in Chief of the Air Forces in India.

U. S. Leaders Available

American commanders from that theatre who are here for war conferences are Lieut. Gen. Joseph W. Stilwell, who has charge of American forces in China, India and Burma, and Major Gen. Claire L. Chennault, leader of China's famous "Flying Tigers," who now heads the American Air Forces in China.

The revelation of these names, plus the report that the President's invitation to come here had been sent to the Prime Minister shortly after word had been received of the execution in Tokyo of some of the American fliers who bombed Japan, loosed a flood of rumors in the capital. However, there was not one word of official information concerning the military subjects under discussion.

There were two kinds of reports about the possibility of Far Eastern offensives. One was that they might be undertaken during the breathing spell following conclusion of the Allied campaign in North Africa and prior to an invasion of Europe. The other was that Prime Minister Churchill was fearful of any important diversion of Allied strength to the Pacific theatre until Adolf Hitler had been eliminated.

The prevailing opinion was that the time and place for the European invasion had been set at the Casablanca conference last January. There were, however, sug-

Continued on Page Seven

UNITED NATIONS GAIN CONTROL OF WHOLE NORTH AFRICAN COAST

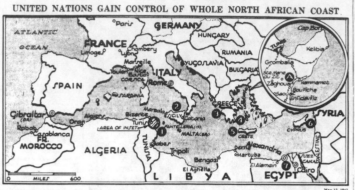

May 13, 1943

With the triumph in Tunisia, which was clinched by a junction of French and British forces near Ste. Marie du Zit (A on inset), the Axis was dislodged from its last foothold in Africa and observers scanned the Mediterranean for signs of the next Allied step. One possible sign was the aerial pounding of Pantelleria (1), another was the continuance of raids on Sicily (2). Greece came into the picture with air attacks on shipping off the west coast (3) and in the Aegean Sea (4) and with word that the Germans had held anti-invasion manoeuvres on Crete (5). Farther east an American division was reported bolstering the strength of Cyprus (6). In Cairo (7), whence came news of the arrival of a South African armored divisior. in the Levant, British leaders conferred.

WPB RULES PLANTS AMPLE TO BEAT AXIS

Orders Halt on New War Facilities and Tools, to Increase Guns, Tanks

By JOHN MacCORMAC
Special to THE NEW YORK TIMES

WASHINGTON, May 12—The United States now has all the plant and machine tools it needs to beat the Axis, and as a result $5,000,000,000 to $5,500,000,000 worth of contracts for the construction of new war facilities will be re-examined by the War Production Board with a view to their cancellation.

This announcement by the WPB today was accompanied by a statement emphasizing that the cancellation and conversion would result not in a lessened but in an increased production of war material, since the labor and materials released by it would go to making more munitions instead of more facilities.

The effect of the decision will be to stop work on some new facilities now under construction; to curtail others which are already producing

Continued on Page Forty-two

Marsala 'Wiped Off the Map'; Planes Leave Catania Aflame

By The United Press.

ALLIED HEADQUARTERS IN NORTH AFRICA, May 12—Almost 400 Allied planes hammered Sicily yesterday for the third straight day, leaving a trail of fiery destruction in the ports of Marsala and Catania, while other aerial forces smashed at the Island of Pantelleria.

[Returning airmen said that the onslaught on Marsala by 200 Flying Fortresses, Marauders and Mitchells and 100 fighters had virtually wiped out the port.]

About fifty American heavy bombers of the Middle East Command, protected by British fighter escort, dropped more than 125 tons of bombs on Catania. The Marsala raid, returning fliers said, caused more damage than the 400-plane raid Sunday on Palermo.

Fifteen enemy planes were shot down over Marsala, on the west coast of Sicily, while only one Allied plane was lost. Direct hits were scored on the harbor, railroad yards, warehouses and seaplane base. Fires visible for 100 miles were set. The air force revealed that six motor barges had been half sunk or seriously damaged; four "E" boats probably sunk and numerous small craft sunk.

In addition, thousands of leaf-

Continued on Page Three

4 TO 10 U-BOATS SUNK IN A CONVOY BATTLE

Most of Freighters Safe After Eight-Day Fight in Atlantic, British Admiralty Says

By The Associated Press.

LONDON, May 12—Allied escort ships and planes fighting a fierce, eight-day running battle against a pack of as many as twenty-five Axis submarines attacking an Atlantic convoy recently sank four and perhaps ten of the U-boats, the Admiralty announced today.

It was the greatest success against submarines thus far reported by the Admiralty.

The battle against the savage thrusts of the undersea vessels took place intermittently for eight days and nights late in April and early in May. The "convoy suffered some damage but the majority of the merchantmen reached port in safety," the communiqué declared.

"First reports state that in the course of these actions four U-boats are known to have been destroyed, four very probably were destroyed and two others were probably destroyed," it added.

One of the British cutters in the battle was the Sennen, the former U. S. S. Champlain, completed in 1929 and one of the ships trans-

Continued on Page Seven

PRISONERS FLOCK TO BRITISH FORCES

Mere Approach of Armor Acts Like Magnet on Soldiers of Vanquished Axis

By DREW MIDDLETON
Wireless to THE NEW YORK TIMES.

TUNIS, May 11 (Delayed)—Moving with a speed that surpassed that of the Germans in Belgium three years ago today, British tanks and infantry penetrated to the northern tip of Cap Bon and to the Gulf of Hammamet and, with the help of the Royal Navy and Allied Air Forces, completely cut off the remaining Axis forces in Tunisia.

The Allied ground forces have already gathered in about 110,000 prisoners, of whom 35,000 were taken by the Second United States Corps and 20,000 by the British Eighth Army. The remainder were rounded up by troops of the British First Army, whose Fourth Infantry Division reached the end of Cap Bon, while the Sixth Armored Division struck south at Hammamet.

Promoted on Point of Capture

Prisoners are coming in in wholesale lots. It is not uncommon for an entire German battalion or company to hoist the white flag and march into the British lines. The enemy, usually so serious about the war, added a touch of comedy to the defeat today by wholesale promotions, insuring better treatment and rates of pay for those promoted.

While the First Army continued its mopping-up operations, which ended any German pretenses of making a second Dunkerque or Bataan out of the wreckage of the

Continued on Page Four

War News Summarized

THURSDAY, MAY 13, 1943

The war in Tunisia is over. A special communiqué from Allied headquarters yesterday read: "Organized resistance except by isolated pockets of the enemy has ceased." The capture of General von Arnim, Axis Commander in Chief, and 150,000 prisoners since May 5 was also announced. Vast quantities of matériel and planes were seized.

The Americans and French took 37,998 prisoners in the Bizerte zone, and around Zaghouan the French captured 25,000 more. A total of twelve generals were among the prisoners. Since the African war started 400,000 prisoners have been taken. [All the foregoing, 1:8.]

General von Arnim was captured with the remnants of his troops on the Cap Bon Peninsula. He had led the Axis forces in Tunisia since Marshal Rommel returned to Germany. [1:6-7.]

A correspondent describing the end of the resistance on the Cap Bon Peninsula said: "In some ways it is a terrifying sight to see the army that once was the terror of Europe dissolve into little clusters of dirty, tired men eager to gain the shelter of prison cages." [1:7.]

The end of land fighting served to accentuate the increased tempo of the air war over the Mediterranean. Marsala, on the west coast of Sicily, was virtually wiped out, while the whole dock area of Catania on the east coast was set afire. The island of Pantellieria was also bombed again. [1:5-6.]

As the Middle East took on the aspect of an active theatre of war with the arrival of veteran British units, the first evacuées from the Calabrian "toe" of Italy reached Switzerland. Military jurisdiction in Italy was extended as far north as Naples. [3:1.]

The British Admiralty reported an eight-day running battle with a U-boat pack in the North Atlantic that at one time numbered twenty-five. While there was some damage to the convoy, four U-boats were destroyed, four others "very probably" and two more "probably." [1:6.]

In Russia the Red Air Force continued its attack on Nazi communications and Soviet artillery demolished Axis defenses around Novorossiisk. [9:2.]

Prime Minister Churchill and President Roosevelt were believed paying considerable attention to Japan in their conference at the White House. The presence of Field Marshal Sir Archibald Wavell and others from the India-Burma theatre emphasized the war in the East. The attitude of Russia was also under discussion, it was said. [1:3] President Benes of Czechoslovakia, who will visit Moscow soon, arrived and was a guest at the White House. [7:1]

Stoessel Falls to Stage and Dies Conducting at Arts Academy Fete

Albert Stoessel, noted conductor and violinist, collapsed and died a few minutes later on the auditorium stage of the American Academy of Arts and Letters yesterday afternoon as he was conducting an orchestra at the annual ceremonial of the academy and the National Institute of Arts and Letters.

The incident, witnessed by a distinguished audience, brought to an end a program in which the academy and institute bestowed awards on Carl Milles, the sculptor; the late Stephen Vincent Benét, and ten others for their work in art, literature and music.

Elmer Davis, director of the Office of War Information, had just finished an address on "The Survival of European Culture." The next event on the program was a rendering of Robert Nathan's ballad poem, "Dunkirk," put to music by Walter Damrosch.

Mr. Stoessel was directing fifteen members of the New York Philharmonic-Symphony Orchestra and Hugh Thompson, the soloist, in this composition, when he suddenly slumped to the floor. Mr. Damrosch, president of the academy and a close friend of Mr. Stoessel, was seated a few feet away.

The program came to an abrupt end, and members of the academy seated on the stage quickly carried the conductor to an adjoining room. Recipients of the awards and other guests on the stage immediately filed off. Most of the 500 persons present thought Mr. Stoessel had fainted. The ballad poem was next to the last number on the

Continued on Page Fifteen

Von Arnim Is Biggest Prize of All In Allies' Bag of Dozen Generals

Wireless to THE NEW YORK TIMES.

ALLIED HEADQUARTERS IN NORTH AFRICA, May 12—Col. Gen. Dietloff von Arnim, the commander of all German troops in North Africa for several months, has been captured, it was officially announced tonight.

In the past few days twelve generals have been captured. The latest to be added to the list were Major Gen. Graf von Sponeck, commander of the famous Ninetieth Light Division, and Major Gen. von Broich, commanding the Tenth Armored Division, which fought at Dieppe last Summer and throughout the campaign here.

[The French reported the capture of two other German generals, The Associated Press said. One was a Major Gen. Yelich, who had taken over command of the Italian Superba Division and other Italian remnants, and the other, Major Gen. Pfeiffer, commanded a group bearing his own name.]

General von Arnim, who succeeded Lieut. Gen. Walther Nehring in command in Northern Tunisia in January and took over the entire command when Field Marshal General Erwin Rommel returned to Europe this Spring, is perhaps the most important German prisoner to be taken by the Allies since Rudolf Hess. He is of an old Prussian military family.

It is interesting to speculate whether the Germans sacrificed him to save Marshal Rommel, although the latter apparently had been ill. The German radio appar-

Continued on Page Five

AFRICAN WAR OVER

110,000 of Captive Total Believed German—Booty Is Huge

FEW STILL RESISTING

British and French Draw Ring Tighter Around Pocket in South

By FRANK L. KLUCKHOHN
Wireless to THE NEW YORK TIMES.

ALLIED HEADQUARTERS IN NORTH AFRICA, May 12—The war in Africa is over, it was officially announced tonight.

Col. Gen. Dietloff von Arnim, the Prussian Commander in Chief of the Axis forces in North Africa, has been captured by the British, apparently on Cap Bon. In all, 150,000 prisoners are believed to have been taken since May 5, when the final assaults on Tunis and Bizerte began. Twelve generals have been captured.

[Of the 150,000 captives, it was estimated that some 110,000 were Germans and the remainder Italians, The United Press said.]

This brings to 400,000 the total of Axis prisoners taken since the North African campaign began two years ago. Eleven German and twenty-six Italian divisions have been destroyed in this period.

End Is Sudden

The end came with dramatic suddenness when German tanks, being battered to pieces in the middle of the entrance to Cap Bon and north of Enfidaville, where six French and British divisions were closing in on the remnants of the Africa Corps, decided to surrender. British First Army tanks had swung south to take Bou Ficha and then swept farther.

When Major Gen. Graf von Sponeck approached Lieut. Gen. Sir Bernard Freyberg for peace terms somewhere north of Enfidaville, the New Zealand commander said two words: "Unconditional surrender."

General von Sponeck announced that he would fight to his last bullet. Then, that Prussian point of military honor having been satisfied by fire from British guns heavier than his own, he surrendered.

That the end would come within a few hours was apparent by noon today, after British tanks, with infantry hanging on their sides, had toured the coast roads of what might have been the strong fortress of Cap Bon in virtual joyrides. Every time a tank pointed its gun, hordes of prisoners came in to give up. Moreover, the Germans and Italians had begun surrendering en masse to the French commanded by General Mathenet.

The French, defeated in 1940, received the surrender of 25,000 Axis soldiers, including two German major generals. The Americans announced today that they had taken 37,998 prisoners, of whom 33,498 were Germans.

Reichsfuehrer Hitler's disastrous

Continued on Page Three

Churchill on Radio At 3 P. M. Tomorrow

By The Associated Press.

LONDON, Thursday, May 13—Prime Minister Winston Churchill will broadcast to the British people from Washington at 9 P. M. Friday [3 P. M. Eastern War Time], it was announced officially today by the British Broadcasting Corporation.

In the address, his first to the British nation since March 21, the Prime Minister is expected to recount briefly the gigantic success of the Allied North African campaign, and possibly hint at the subject of the Washington talks and where the next phases of the campaign are coming.

Ingrid Bergman with Gary Cooper in the screen version of Ernest Hemingway's novel *For Whom the Bell Tolls.*

Paul Lukas, Bette Davis and Beulah Bondi in *Watch on the Rhine.* Lukas won an Academy Award for his role in the film.

Henry Fonda and Henry Morgan in *The Ox-Bow Incident.*

Stalin, Roosevelt and Churchill attended the Teheran Conference in 1943.

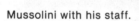

Mussolini with his staff.

Sprawled bodies on the beach of Tarawa were mute testimony to the fierce battle that took place there.

"All the News That's Fit to Print."

The New York Times.

LATE CITY EDITION
Showers, warm and humid today; moderate winds.
Temperatures Yesterday—Max., 79; Min., 66
Sunrise, 5:38 A. M.; Sunset, 8:30 P. M.

Copyright, 1943, by The New York Times Company.

VOL. XCII..No. 31,213. Entered as Second-Class Matter, Postoffice, New York, N. Y. NEW YORK, SATURDAY, JULY 10, 1943. THREE CENTS IN NEW YORK CITY

ALLIED TROOPS START INVASION OF SICILY; NAVAL ESCORTS BOMBARD SHORE DEFENSES; LANDINGS PRECEDED BY SEVERE AIR ATTACK

ROOSEVELT VOICES DOUBT ON MAKING LEWIS OBEY WLB

He Asks at Press Conference How to Force Someone to Sign Against His Will

ORDER TO WARD IS CITED

He Declares He Could Take Property but Probably Could Not Seize Union

By SAMUEL B. BLEDSOE

Special to THE NEW YORK TIMES.

WASHINGTON, July 9—President Roosevelt indicated today that he had no intention of taking action to force John L. Lewis, head of the United Mine Workers, to obey the War Labor Board's directive that he sign an agreement with the bituminous mine operators.

Asked at his press conference whether he intended to reaffirm the board's order in the mine union case, the President said that, after all, the order was that of a quasi-judicial body and spoke for itself. He asked what action he could take—send a little polite note on pink paper and say, "Dear Mr. Lewis, I hope you will sign the contract"?

Pressed to say what he would do if Mr. Lewis did not sign, the President inquired in turn what the reporter would do and got the reply, "I don't know. I'm not President." The President then commented upon the difficulty of forcing some one to sign something against his will.

Montgomery Ward Case Cited

A reporter reminded that Sewell Avery, head of Montgomery Ward & Co., had been directed by the President to sign a wage agreement which provided for a maintenance of membership clause and check-off of union dues after the company had defied a WLB order.

President Roosevelt said that, although he did not want to take over Montgomery Ward, he had authority to do so, but doubted that he had similar authority to take over the mine union.

Asked if he felt he needed some sanction of law to deal with recalcitrant miners, Mr. Roosevelt replied that there was Section 4 of the Smith-Connally Anti-Strike Act and the first seven sections of the bill. He suggested that these sections be examined.

War Labor Board officials refused to be quoted on Mr. Roosevelt's statements. They said they still were hoping that the President intended to crack down on Mr. Lewis, but they also disclosed that they feared the board had been left high and dry.

Interpretation of WLB Order

They said that while the directive of June 18 did not specifically order Mr. Lewis to sign an agreement with the operators, such action clearly was implied by the directive. Although the matter had been put up to President Roosevelt, there was no indication, they stated, that the President had asked Mr. Lewis to obey the directive and no indication that he intended to do so.

One official declared that the real issue in the Lewis case was whether an individual, or pressure group, could continue in wartime to defy a Government directive intended to further prosecution of the war.

If President Roosevelt does not intend to take further action in the Lewis case, but continues to operate the mines under the direction of Secretary Ickes, some officials here declared, a good deal will be heard about the differences in handling a situation when an employer defies the WLB and when a union defies it.

Obedience by Ward Forced

Acting as "Commander in Chief in time of war," the President issued the order to Montgomery Ward & Co. last December. The company had objected strenuously to the maintenance-of-membership

Continued on Page Seven

Cripps Bids Workers Back New Air Phase

By Wireless to THE NEW YORK TIMES.

LONDON, July 9—Appealing for maximum production and the cessation of absenteeism and strikes among aircraft workers, Sir Stafford Cripps, Minister of Aircraft Production, declared in a radio broadcast tonight that this country has entered a new and more intensive phase of the war "and almost at any moment there may be a great intensification" of the present offensive.

He asked the workers to support this offensive to their utmost.

"An assault upon the Axis powers in Europe and the Far East," Sir Stafford said, "entails dislodging them from occupied territories. That will be a costly task. Our casualties will inevitably be heavy but we can help to keep down those losses."

PRESIDENT BARS DATA FOR INQUIRY

On His Order Army, Navy, Budget Bureau Deny Radio Committee's Request

By WINIFRED MALLON

Special to THE NEW YORK TIMES.

WASHINGTON, July 9—Acting on the order of President Roosevelt, the War and Navy Departments refused today to transmit information requested by the House committee investigating the Federal Communications Commission.

Their reply stated that production of documents and testimony of witnesses relative to the proposed executive order transferring to the War and Navy Departments the radio intelligence activities of the commission had been forbidden by the President as "contrary to the public interest."

In a letter to the committee, James V. Forrestal, Under-Secretary of the Navy, wrote:

"The President of the United States authorized me to inform the committee that he, the President, refuses to allow the documents described in your letter to be delivered to the committee, as such delivery would be incompatible with the public interest.

"I must decline to permit the appearance of naval officers, active or inactive, before your committee, as such appearance would be incompatible with the public interest."

A letter to the same effect was received from Robert P. Patterson, Under-Secretary of War.

On similar ground Harold D. Smith, Director of the Budget, declined to testify at today's hearing of the committee and refused to deliver Budget Bureau data.

James Lawrence Fly, chairman of the FCC, appearing as chairman of the Board of War Communications, also declined to answer questions, declaring himself bound

Continued on Page Seven

RUSSIANS STIFFEN

Red Army Repels Heavy Attacks in Orel and Kursk Sectors

AXIS LOSSES SOAR

Both Sides State Fight Grows in Intensity—Nazis Win 'Inches'

By The Associated Press.

LONDON, Saturday, July 10—The Russian armies of the center bloodily beat off savage German attacks all along the Orel and Kursk fronts yesterday, held their own in the Belgorod sector to the south, and destroyed 193 Nazi tanks and 94 planes in the great battle of attrition, the Soviet command announced early today.

The German dead, in two battle areas specifically mentioned, were nearly 5,000 for the day, Moscow declared in the regular midnight communiqué recorded here by the Soviet monitor, thus bringing to about 40,000 the total German casualties for five days of violent action.

German losses in matériel also were rising to tremendous proportions:

Yesterday's destruction raised to 2,036 the number of enemy tanks thus far listed as knocked out, and to 904 the number of Nazi planes smashed since the beginning of the offensive.

In the Orel-Kursk sector, said the bulletin, the Nazis after four days of heavy losses had "gained no success" and had been forced to shift the weight of attack to other areas, reinforcing their "battered troops" by nine infantry divisions and one tank division.

Twenty Attacks Beaten Back

A score or more of German attacks were beaten off—thirteen of them in a single area of action—and fighting at times was hand-to-hand.

Fifteen hundred Nazis were wiped out in these actions, said the Soviet command, as was most of a German battalion in a near-by action.

About Belgorod—scene of four previous German penetrations against which the Russians had battered all day—no further Nazi progress was reported, although it was declared the invaders were "bringing into battle all their reserves, striving at any cost to achieve success."

In the Belgorod sector 2,000 Germans were killed during the day. But it was in the Kursk-Orel sector where the supreme Nazi efforts were being made.

The Germans themselves, in a long broadcast propaganda report, spoke of "ferocious fighting" south of Orel, where Nazi troops "could gain ground only inch by inch."

Further German advances—

Continued on Page Four

MUNDA HAMMERED

Planes, Warships, Guns Batter Japanese at New Georgia Base

GROUND PUSH GAINS

Enemy's Counter-Blows to Ward Off Assault Are Declared Weak

By TILLMAN DURDIN

By Wireless to THE NEW YORK TIMES.

ALLIED HEADQUARTERS FOR THE SOUTHWEST PACIFIC, Saturday, July 10—American planes unloosed the most terrific aerial attack yet made on Japanese positions on New Georgia Island yesterday. More than a hundred bombers escorted by fighters pounded Munda and the Bairoko Harbor areas early in the morning. At the same time United States destroyers shelled Munda.

Seventy tons of bombs, including two thousand-pounders, were used to blast the camp areas, supply dumps and anti-aircraft positions. The biggest group of bombers concentrated on the area between Munda Point and the Lamberti coconut plantation, where part of the main Japanese defenses around the Munda airdrome are located.

While dive bombers and level bombers were circling and hurling their bombs in this area American artillery from across Blanche Channel on Rendova shelled Japanese anti-aircraft sites. Other groups of bombers pounded the Japanese at Bairoko harbor, port across the peninsula from Munda and Enogai inlet, three miles north of Bairoko Harbor.

Heavy Damage Done

There is every reason to believe that the combined aerial, naval and land artillery bombardment of yesterday morning heavily damaged the Japanese defenses. It was one of the most devastating artillery and air attacks ever made in the Pacific on a land target. The destroyers shelled the base before dawn.

Forty-five Japanese fighters attempted to intervene in the battle for Munda early yesterday afternoon. They appeared over Rendova Island, where they were intercepted by patrolling American fighters. Four were shot down in the

Continued on Page Five

ISLAND OF SICILY IS INVADED BY ALLIED FORCES

General Eisenhower announced that his troops had debarked at various points on Sicily early today. The landings were preceded by furious air assaults and warships accompanying the transports shelled the coastal defenses. Troops got ashore at the western tip of the island (cross), according to the Algiers radio. Strong forces of tanks were reported being used. The invasion had been preceded by heavy bombings of a variety of targets (bomb devices).

SEVERAL LANDINGS

American, British and Canadian Troops Carry Out the Attack

A 'LIBERATION' START

But Eisenhower Urges French Be Calm Till Their Hour Strikes

By DREW MIDDLETON

By Wireless to THE NEW YORK TIMES.

ALLIED HEADQUARTERS IN NORTH AFRICA, Saturday, July 10—Allied infantry landed at a number of places on the rocky Sicilian coast under a canopy of naval gunfire early this morning as the long-awaited invasion began.

Gen. Dwight D. Eisenhower, Allied Commander in Chief, speaking to the people of metropolitan France, called the attack "the first page in the liberation of the European Continent," and promised "there will be others."

Allied headquarters announced the invasion in the following communiqué:

Allied forces under command of General Eisenhower began landing operations on Sicily early this morning.

The landings were preceded by Allied air attack.

Allied naval forces escorted the assault forces and bombarded the coast defenses during the assault.

[The Algiers radio, in an English-language broadcast to North America at 12:40 A. M. today, said that Allied forces had landed on the rocky western tip of Sicily, 260 miles from Rome. The broadcast was recorded by United States Government monitors.

[The broadcast said the landings were made in good weather, with German and Italian air forces providing "fierce" opposition. In anticipation of the assault, the island's Italian-German defenders blew up harbor installations, the broadcast said.]

"Softened Up" By Air Attack

A heavy attack was carried on by planes of the Northwest Africa Air Force and the Middle East Air Command for nearly two weeks, reaching blitz proportions in the last week, when a round-the-clock assault blasted Axis air bases and communication centers with hundreds of tons of bombs. This came to a furious climax yesterday and last night.

The Allied naval force that escorted the invading troops pounded the formidable defenses of Sicily with salvos of shells while infantrymen, their bayonets twinkling in the starlight raced ashore from landing crafts. Many tanks were landed.

Sicily, largest island in the Mediterranean, has a population of just under 4,000,000 persons and has been strongly fortified, especially along the southern coast, since 1939. The coasts are heavily mined and beaches are covered by batteries of artillery that fire from hills.

French Urged to Be Calm

General Eisenhower's announcement to the French people, which was sent by radio, asked them to remain calm and not to expose themselves to reprisals through "present rash actions."

Many of the troops involved in the invasion of Sicily are veterans of the Tunisian campaign.

Military men here expect very heavy fighting. The Germans are known to have reinforced the island comparatively recently, and despite the prolonged aerial bombardment strong fortifications remain to be overcome.

Many military objectives were hit by American and British bombers during the two weeks' attack on the island. The main weight of the bombing at night was directed against the airfields, particularly

Continued on Page Two

PRESIDENT PARRIES FRENCH BIAS QUERY

There Is No France Now, He Explains—Giraud Wins Arms for 300,000

By HAROLD CALLENDER

Special to THE NEW YORK TIMES.

WASHINGTON, July 9—Commenting upon the accusation that the United States was interfering in French affairs, President Roosevelt at his press conference today said that 95 per cent of the French people were still under the German heel and that there was no France now.

When a correspondent remarked that, at any rate, there was a French committee, and asked whether this Government would recognize it, the President said that question had not arisen.

Regarding the visit here of General Giraud, who is also Commander in Chief of the French forces in North and West Africa, Mr. Roosevelt said merely that at lunch yes-

Continued on Page Four

RAF Pounds Cologne Again In 1,000-Ton 'Repeat' Attack

By FREDERICK GRAHAM

By Cable to THE NEW YORK TIMES.

LONDON, July 9—Cologne, which was the first city to feel the weight of a 1,000-plane raid in the British attack of May 30, 1942, was plastered again last night by the Royal Air Force with more than 1,000 tons of bombs. The raid was the 119th of the war on the Rhine city, and it was described by officials here as effecting "a crushing setback to the German attempts to revive the skeletonized industrial life of the town."

Despite an intense Nazi anti-aircraft barrage and severe icing conditions and electrical storms, the heavy British and Canadian bombers pressed home an "effectively concentrated" attack at a cost of only eight planes, the Air Ministry reported.

[British heavy bombers raided Germany again last night, said a brief London announcement early today, reported by The Associated Press.

[RAF fighters and light bombers raided northern France in force by daylight yesterday and attacked German shipping along the coast. The Eighth Air Force, it was said, had fighters punished Nazi traffic.

[Nazi raiders attacked the London area yesterday afternoon, two of the about ten attackers being shot down. Bombs caused casualties in the suburbs. In a southeast English town an enemy raider landed a bomb in a movie theatre filled with children and at least twelve persons were reported killed and injured.]

Authoritative comment on the

Continued on Page Three

BOMBS TORE SICILY BEFORE INVASION

Allied Fliers Ripped Airfields, Communications and Plants in Week-Long Blitz

By Wireless to THE NEW YORK TIMES.

ALLIED HEADQUARTERS IN NORTH AFRICA, July 9—Swarms of Allied bombers maintained their round-the-clock pounding of Axis air bases in Sicily, and formations of fighter bombers, including new A-36's, which are also fitted as dive-bombers, hammered transport, communications and industrial plants on the besieged island yesterday as the great Allied aerial offensive centered on Sicily for the sixth straight day.

The new A-36 fighter-bomber, which was developed from North American's P-51 Mustang fighter, is the newest "plane of all work." It is used as both a dive and glide bomber and takes part in strafing missions as well. The Mustang is supposed to be the world's most effective fighter under 15,000 feet.

Continued on Page Two

War News Summarized

SATURDAY, JULY 10, 1943

American, British and Canadian troops landed early this morning on Sicily, the last-stepping stone to Italy. While the size of the invasion force was not known, the War Department said naval forces had escorted the invasion troops and bombarded Sicilian coast defenses. The enemy is believed to have between eleven and thirteen divisions on the rugged island, of which nine or ten are Italian and the rest German.

As the Allies struck, General Eisenhower broadcast an appeal to the French people warning them against rash actions that would bring upon them reprisals from the Nazis. He urged them to listen to Allied broadcasts. "When the hour of action strikes," he declared, "we will let you know." [All the foregoing, 1:8.]

The invasion came on the heels of six consecutive days of powerful Allied air assaults on Sicily, during which air bases, communications centers and industrial plants had been pounded almost incessantly. During the last day twenty-one enemy planes had been destroyed and a quarter of a million pounds of bombs had been dropped on Catania alone. [1:7.]

The German offensive along the Orel-Kursk-Belgorod front increased in fury yesterday as the Nazis threw ten more divisions against the Russians near Belgorod. But the Russians said their forces were holding at all points and had destroyed another 193 tanks and ninety-four planes and had slain 5,000 men. In the four days since the Germans opened their drive the Russians claim to have killed 40,000 men and knocked out 2,036 tanks and 904 planes. [1:3.]

Germany, too, was blasted as the RAF inflicted another powerful blow on Cologne. Making their 119th raid on the Ruhr city, the fliers lost only eight bombers as they dropped more than a thousand tons of bombs in what was termed "a crushing setback to German attempts to revive the skeletonized industrial life" of Cologne. [1:6-7.]

More than 100 Allied bombers joined warships and artillery in launching the strongest barrage to date against the Japanese base of Munda. The Japanese sent forty-five Zeros over Rendova Island, but they were dispersed and four were destroyed. The enemy also tried, with small success, a dive-bombing attack on our base at Nassau Bay, New Guinea. [1:4; map, P. 5.]

A joint American-British announcement said that Allied and neutral shipping losses from U-boat attacks during June were the smallest since the United States entered the war. [1:6-7.]

Son-in-Law Held in Oakes' Murder; Bahaman Police Cite Fingerprints

By The United Press.

NASSAU, Bahamas, July 9—Alfred de Marigny, 36, was booked at the police station here tonight on a charge of killing his father-in-law, the multimillionaire British baronet, Sir Harry Oakes.

A formal charge of murder was placed against the bearded accused, who denied any connection with the slaying.

Sir Harry was known to have been unhappy over the marriage of his eldest daughter, Nancy, then 17 years old, to M. de Marigny at New York in May, 1942. It was the second marriage for the Count, who had been divorced in Miami, Fla., in 1937.

He was arrested at 6 o'clock tonight by Lieut. Col. R. A. Lindop and Major Embert Pemberton of the Nassau constabulary.

Capt. E. W. Melchen of the Miami Police Department, summoned by airplane to aid in the investigation after Sir Harry's body was found on a bed that had been set afire Thursday morning, said the arrest and charge were based on "hair analysis, fingerprints and interrogation."

Attorney General Eric Hallinan reported that Sir Harry had been bludgeoned to death. There were four severe head wounds, he said, as well as burns on the body.

Officers believed an electric fan had blown out the flames before they had destroyed the bed.

The charge against Count de Marigny came as a sensational climax to the death of Sir Harry, one of the world's richest men, with a fortune unofficially estimated to be as great as $200,000,000.

Until the announcement came, details of the slaying had been

Continued on Page Twenty-six

June Losses to U-Boats Lowest Since We Entered the Conflict

Special to THE NEW YORK TIMES.

WASHINGTON, July 9—Intimations that the United Nations have been winning the war against the submarine were confirmed by a joint statement issued today by the British and United States Governments.

June losses of Allied and neutral ships by submarine attack, said the report, were the lowest since this country entered the war, sinkings of Axis submarines were substantial, and the main transatlantic convoys were now proceeding practically unmolested.

The statement was as follows:

1. In June the losses of Allied and neutral merchant ships from submarine attacks were the lowest since the United States entered the war. The losses from all forms of enemy action were the second lowest recorded since the war between Britain and Germany began.

2. The number of targets offered to the anti-submarine vessels and aircraft of the United Nations was not as great in June as previously, but the sinkings of Axis submarines were substantial and satisfactory.

3. The heavy toll taken of the U-boats in May showed its effect in June in that the main transatlantic convoys were practically unmolested, and the U-boat attacks on our shipping were in widely separated areas. However, every opportunity was taken of attacking U-boats leaving and returning to their bases on the west coast of France.

4. The merchant shipping ton-

Continued on Page Three

"All the News That's Fit to Print."

The New York Times.

LATE CITY EDITION
Moderately warm today, with gentle winds.
Temperatures Yesterday—Max., 85; Min., 70
Sunrise, 5:46 A. M.; Sunset, 8:18 P. M.

VOL. XCII..No. 31,229. Entered as Second-Class Matter, Postoffice, New York, N. Y. NEW YORK, MONDAY, JULY 26, 1943. THREE CENTS IN NEW YORK CITY

MUSSOLINI OUSTED WITH FASCIST CABINET; BADOGLIO, HIS FOE, MADE PREMIER BY KING; SHIFT BELIEVED FIRST STEP TOWARD PEACE

PEACE INITIATIVE URGED BY WALLACE ON AMERICA NOW

For 'Common Man' He Asks Full Production, Employment and Security

WITH DEMOCRACY FOR ALL

Vice President, at Detroit, Accuses 'Fascists' of Trying to Undermine Roosevelt

The text of Mr. Wallace's address is on Page 10.

By The United Press.

DETROIT, July 25—Vice President Henry A. Wallace called upon America today to take the initiative now and plan a war-proof post-war world pledged to enlightenment of all peoples, "full production and full employment" and cooperation with other nations to enforce international justice and security.

Urging America to heed a destiny "that calls us to world leadership," he assailed "small but powerful groups which put money and power first and people last" and declared that "nothing will prevail against the common man's peace in a common man's world."

A crowd of 20,000, composed predominantly of workers, filled the center grandstand at the State fairgrounds track to hear Mr. Wallace's thirty-minute address, "America tomorrow," which was also broadcast by radio.

"Defeatists" for "Good Old Days"

The Vice President deviated from his prepared address to voice indirectly the charge he made yesterday that "certain American Fascists" had turned against the present Administration because President Roosevelt "stopped Washington from being a way station on the way to Wall Street."

He asserted that "defeatists who talk about going back to the good old days of Americanism (after the war) mean the time when there was plenty for the few and scarcity for the many."

Then, departing from his text, he raised his right arm and said:

"Or the days when Washington was only a way station in the suburbs of Wall Street."

Mr. Wallace was introduced by R. J. Thomas, president of the United Automobile Workers, CIO, as "the architect and crusader for a new world."

It was Mr. Wallace's first address since President Roosevelt abolished the Board of Economic Warfare, which Mr. Wallace had headed, to end a public quarrel between the Vice President and Secretary of Commerce Jesse Jones over war buying policies.

Roosevelt Foes Denounced

Indicating no rift in his relations with the President, Wallace assailed persons sniping at the Chief Executive while he is engaged in prosecuting the war.

He charged that powerful money-minded groups—"some call them isolationists, some reactionaries and others American Fascists"—seek to destroy Mr. Roosevelt's domestic achievements of the past ten years by capitalizing on his preoccupation with the war.

"I have known the President intimately for ten years and in the final showdown he has always put human rights first," he said. "Sooner or later the machinations of these small but powerful groups which put money and power first and people last will inevitably be exposed to the public eye."

He inveighed against those who oppose post-war planning now to hold to the realities of the past or cling to the present without thought of the future.

"Both opinions," he said, "are fighting delaying actions against our destiny in the peace—a destiny

Continued on Page Ten

Cheers Halt Games As Duce Strikes Out

The thousands of baseball spectators at parks where the Mussolini incident was announced yesterday roared and jumped up from their seats. Games were halted as happy men and women thronged the aisles and shouted the news to each other.

At the Yankee Stadium, where 36,779 had suffered with the Yankees as the New Yorkers lost the first game of a double-header to the White Sox, baseball momentarily ceased to exist when the news of the resignation came through the loudspeakers in the sixth inning of the second contest. The rest of the announcement, to the effect that King Victor Emmanuel had taken over, was lost in the tumultuous reaction.

A similar circumstance was reported in Pittsburgh, where 30,309 onlookers saw the Pirates sweep a double-header from the Brooklyn Dodgers.

NORTH JERSEY OPA DROPS DRIVING BAN

Maze of Rulings, Plus Vacation Permits, Is Too Confusing—Inspectors Tired of Abuse

Enforcement of the "pleasure driving" ban in northern New Jersey broke down completely yesterday with Office of Price Administration officials in that area frankly admitting that they were making no effort to enforce the restriction. New Jersey highways leading from bridge and tunnel exits that had been more or less deserted since initiation of the "pleasure ban" were heavily burdened yesterday with motorists blandly disregarding the ban and inspectors conspicuous by their absence.

OPA inspectors indicated that they were "throwing up the sponge" because they found themselves entangled in a maze of conflicting rulings from Washington and by local ration boards. In addition they are tired of being sneeringly referred to as "Gestapo agents, sneaks and snoopers" by drivers they stop for questioning.

No Inspectors on Roads

"It is true there were no inspectors on the highways today," Nathan L. Jacobs, chief OPA enforcement attorney in the northern New Jersey area, said. "We have discovered that ration boards have issued so many vacation permits that it is a waste of time to stop cars."

While other OPA officials refused to be quoted it was generally conceded that no effort was being made to enforce the "pleasure ban."

"We are continuing to the best of our ability to enforce the law," an inspector declared. "However, the maze of conflicting rulings

Continued on Page Thirty-two

RUSSIANS PUSH ON

Drive 2½ Miles Closer to Orel and Take 30 More Villages

NAZI STAND STIFFER

Enemy Counter-Attacks Desperately to Hold Escape Corridor

By The Associated Press.

LONDON, Monday, July 26—The great Russian counter-offensive battering upon Orel from three directions engulfed thirty more populated places and swept forward two and a half to five and a half miles yesterday, Moscow announced in a special communiqué. Complete encirclement of the great Nazi base appeared only a matter of time.

Red Army columns driving down behind Orel have cut to within seven miles or so of the Bryansk railway feeding supplies and reinforcements into the stronghold.

The Russians are steadily narrowing the fifty-mile escape corridor held open by the half-encircled Germans, for another Soviet column is pushing up from the south to the west of the city.

Beating down severe German counter-attacks, the Red Army slogged on to capture the important railroad station of Glazunovka and the populated places of Poponov, Chizhovka and Narykovo on the western bank of the Oka River northeast of Orel, said the communiqué, broadcast by Moscow and recorded by the Soviet monitor.

Other villages included among the thirty reported captured yesterday were Rybnitsa, Gremyache, Zakharovka, Lebedikha, Voronets, Verkhneye Sagino and Nizhneye Sagino.

South, in the Belgorod area, there were scouting engagements and "fighting of local importance," while scouts increased their activities in the battle areas on the Donets front still farther south, it added.

Advance on Three Sides

The regular midnight communiqué said the Red Army had advanced on the north, east and south sides of Orel, knocking out twenty-eight tanks, killing 2,840 Germans, taking prisoners and capturing an important height on the south side of the city.

Several populated places were captured east and south of Orel, the announcement added. In several places the Germans mounted strong counter-attacks.

In other sectors, the communiqué said, twenty-one more German tanks were destroyed and over 800 Germans killed.

A previous special announcement of the Soviet command had declared that the German wedge, nine by twenty-two miles, that had been driven into Russian lines at

Continued on Page Eight

LONDON IS CAUTIOUS

Evidence of Crack in the Rome-Berlin Axis Is Viewed With Joy

BADOGLIO 'WAR HERO'

Britons See Possibility of His Being 'Front' for Fascist Deal

By RAYMOND DANIELL
By Cable to The New York Times.

LONDON, Monday, July 26—London's first reaction to the news that Benito Mussolini had stepped down as head of the Fascist Government of Italy was that it left the military situation unchanged.

It was seen as the first tangible evidence of a crack in the Rome-Berlin Axis. But emphasis was put on the point that, whatever internal troubles led Signor Mussolini to get out in favor of Marshal Pietro Badoglio on the eve of his sixtieth birthday after twenty years of dictatorship over Italy, King Victor Emmanuel's proclamation made it clear that for the moment at least Italy intended to carry on the fight.

The possibility that the dramatic shift in leadership by Italy might be the forerunner of an attempt to sue for a separate peace was not overlooked, however.

For a long time it has been suspected here that, when things got too tough for the Fascists or the Nazis in the Reich, they would try to save their necks by elevating someone they believed acceptable to the United Nations as front man to arrange a soft armistice.

Not Trusted by Britain

Marshal Badoglio, 73-year-old Italian Army Chief, who has been regarded as a critic of Mussolini and as a bogus friend of Britain, is one of those men. Count Dino Grandi, a former Ambassador to London, is another.

But the fact that Victor Emmanuel chose his old friend, Marshal Badoglio, who rallied Italy in World War I after the Caporetto disaster, instead of Count Grandi, is susceptible to two interpretations.

The first, taking the proclamations of the Italian King and his new Premier at their face value, is

Continued on Page Five

ONE IS OUT, THE OTHER IN

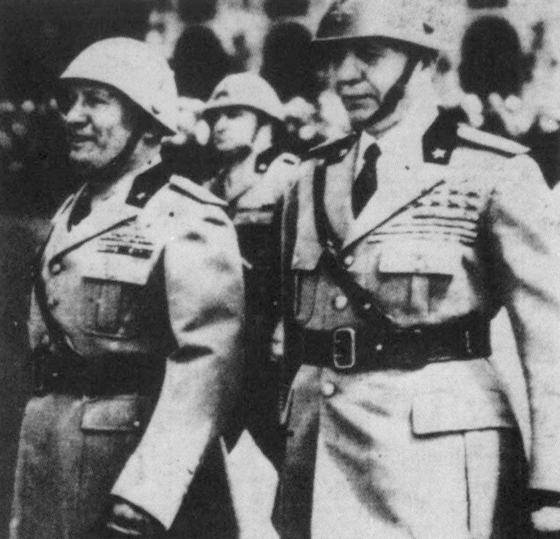

Benito Mussolini and his successor as Premier, Marshal Pietro Badoglio — Associated Press

British Eighth Army Opens New Drive to Take Catania

By DREW MIDDLETON
By Wireless to The New York Times.

ALLIED HEADQUARTERS IN NORTH AFRICA, July 25—Routed in the west by the hard-hitting American Seventh Army, the battered Axis forces are retreating across the north central sector of Sicily today to the sanctuary of the Germans' new "Etna line." The southern and southwestern faces of this line are already being hammered by the British Eighth Army, which is inflicting dreadful casualties on the stubborn German defenders of the position. The Canadian forces, striking northward and northeastward on the Eighth Army's left flank, are making good progress. [The Canadians have driven a wedge well into the enemy's lines, the United Press said.]

After two weeks of smashing success unequaled by any other American Army in this war, the Seventh Army is wheeling east-

Continued on Page Three

BERLIN RADIO SEES MUSSOLINI AS 'ILL'

First Nazi Comment Arrives Five Hours Late—Official Statement Lacking

LONDON, Monday, July 26 (AP)—The Berlin radio in its first comment on the Mussolini resignation—made almost five hours after Rome's first announcement—quoted the Italian-Stefani news agency as saying that the change of Italian Government was believed to have been owing to the Premier's health. Premier Mussolini "has been ill for some time," Berlin said.

Official Comment Lacking

By Telephone to The New York Times.

BERNE, Switzerland, Monday, July 26—Official quarters in Berlin were still out of telephonic touch with Berne at an early hour Monday morning, and authoritative reaction to the resignation of Signor Mussolini and his Cabinet

Continued on Page Two

ITALY SEEN MAKING FIRST PEACE STEP

Observers in Washington Look for Similar Action by Axis Satellites in Balkans

By HAROLD CALLENDER
Special to The New York Times.

WASHINGTON, July 25—The transfer of power in Italy from Premier Mussolini to Marshal Pietro Badoglio was interpreted by military and diplomatic observers tonight as a first step toward an Italian appeal for peace. They thought that this would be quickly followed by similar appeals from Hungary, Rumania and Bulgaria, which might seek favorable terms by acting swiftly.

The immediate consequences, military men thought, would be an Allied occupation of Italy, especially the air bases in the north near the German border, and the surrender of the Italian Army, Navy and air fleet.

In diplomatic circles it was predicted that Marshal Badoglio would seek a negotiated peace, but it was assumed that the unconditional surrender doctrine would be applied in the qualified form given to it by the recent statement to Italians by President Roosevelt and Prime Minister Churchill. This implied generous treatment for Italy once the fascist regime had disappeared.

It has been authoritatively indicated here that the Allied Govern-

Continued on Page Six

ARRESTS REPORTED

Berne Hears the Fascist Leaders Are Being Held in Homes

'PEACE' CRY IN ROME

Nazis in Milan Said to Have Fired on Mob of Demonstrators

By DANIEL T. BRIGHAM
By Telephone to The New York Times.

BERNE, Switzerland, July 25—King Victor Emmanuel announced to Italy tonight that he had accepted the "resignations" of Premier Benito Mussolini and his entire Cabinet. He ordered Marshal Pietro Badoglio to form a military government "to continue the conduct of the war."

The announcement was made in a proclamation that was broadcast to the people of Italy from Rome at 11 P. M. Rome time. The Rome radio then signed off for twenty minutes, resuming its broadcast at 11:20 to carry a proclamation by Marshal Badoglio. Before giving this, however, the announcer said:

"With the fall of Mussolini and his band, Italy has taken the first step toward peace. Finished is the shame of fascism! Long live peace! Long live the King!"

Badoglio Says He'll Fight

Marshal Badoglio's proclamation was then read. It appealed to the nation for "calm" in this hour of trial, saying:

"Italians! On the demand of His Majesty the King-Emperor, I have assumed the military government of the country with full powers. The war will continue. Italy, bruised, her provinces invaded, and her cities ruined, will retain her faith in her given word, jealous of her ancient traditions.

"We must tighten our ranks behind the King-Emperor, the living image of the country, who stands as an example for all today. The task I have been charged with is clear and precise. It will be executed scrupulously, and whoever believes he can interrupt the normal progress of events or whoever seeks to disturb internal order will be struck down without mercy.

"Long live Italy! Long live the King! PIETRO BADOGLIO."

For the first time in twenty-one years the Italian radio signed off a nation-wide program by playing only the royal march. "Giovinezza," the fascist anthem, like fascism, is dead.

[Field Marshal General Albert Kesselring, German Commander in Chief in Italy, and Hans-Georg Viktor von Mackensen, the Ger-

Continued on Page Three

Mayor Expects Italy To Surrender Soon

Mayor Fiorello H. La Guardia declared yesterday afternoon that in view of the dismissal of Premier Benito Mussolini he expected the complete capitulation of Italy within a few days.

His statement follows:

"I anticipate the complete capitulation of Italy within the next few days. Of course to me it's a source of great satisfaction that Mussolini has been finally discovered. He will go down in history as the betrayer of Italy.

"If there is one amusing sidelight to this whole thing, that is the cheap, gutter politicians in this country who catered to Mussolini when they thought he was going strong. I had to fight that very tendency in 1929 and 1933.

"In so far as Italy is concerned, she is out of the war.

"We must now prepare to meet the situation, as the Nazis will consolidate their lines. The Office of War Information is now free to release the appeal that I made to the King several months ago."

Mayor Sees Slight Hope for Meat; Warns City Will Boycott $1 Eggs

Although the meat supply for New York City looks better for the coming week, there is no assurance that the civilian population will get it, Mayor Fiorello H. La Guardia warned yesterday in his weekly radio broadcast. He said the black market would continue until there was proper identification of meat, tracing it from the slaughterhouse to the retailer.

The outlook is serious on eggs, the Mayor said, with prices at present as high as 66 cents a dozen for jumbos, 62 cents for extra large and 60 cents for large. He said the news that the price ceilings of eggs would go up about a cent a week was "disturbing" and that some persons were predicting egg prices would reach $1 a dozen before winter.

"I hope not," he declared. "Now I just want to serve notice on everybody that if eggs continue to increase in price much higher and before it arrives at the dollar a dozen, we in New York will adjust ourselves to substitutes for eggs. I hope that will not be necessary, but I am not in a position now to say that New York City will take a-dollar-a-dozen eggs without protest."

Mayor La Guardia expressed disappointment that the Office of Price Administration and the Food Distribution Administration had not yet taken final action on his proposal to cut the ration point values of pork products and eliminate some of them from rationing entirely, which, he said, would have relieved the meat situation.

"Our Government is paying millions of dollars in subsidies to

Continued on Page Thirty-two

War News Summarized

MONDAY, JULY 26, 1943

The Fascists surrendered their control over Italy yesterday when Premier Mussolini quit. He presented his own resignation and those of his Cabinet to King Victor Emmanuel, who immediately accepted them and named Marshal Badoglio as Prime Minister. Thus, after twenty years of complete power, Mussolini became the first Axis dictator to have run his course.

The King gave the news to the world when a proclamation signed by him was broadcast to the Italian people, saying that Marshal Badoglio would form a military government to continue the conduct of the war. The Rome radio announcer declared the development was the first step toward peace, but the Marshal said the war would go on.

The Italian people immediately demonstrated in the streets, looking for Blackshirts. A report from Milan said German troops had fired on demonstrators. [All the foregoing 1:8.]

While London welcomed the first sign of a crack in the Rome-Berlin Axis, observers were not too greatly impressed. They saw in it an effort to make the best peace terms by putting an anti-Fascist at the head of the Italian Government. They also saw an attempt by the Italian King to save his crown. [1:4.]

The Italian political upheaval served to overshadow what was one of the most active days on the military fronts. Allied troops in Sicily were pressing the Axis defenders into a small triangle, with Messina as the apex. [1:5-6; map P. 2.] Flying Fortresses flew 1,500 miles without meeting any opposition to blast the north Italian rail junction at Bologna, while other planes concentrated on southern Italian communications. [3:1.]

British and American air forces struck their heaviest blows against Germany. The RAF rocked Hamburg Saturday night with 2,500 tons of bombs. Yesterday Flying Fortresses hit that port again and pounded Kiel and other centers. The RAF's big bombers raided Germany again last night. [1:6-7.]

The Red Army captured another thirty villages, halted incessant German counter-attacks and virtually encircled the enemy base at Orel. [1:3.]

The Fourteenth United States Air Force in China beat off four waves of more than 100 planes when the Japanese attacked advanced American bases in Hunan Province. Forty-four enemy planes were destroyed or damaged; damage to the air bases was slight. [9:4.]

More than 200 Allied planes gave the beleagured Japanese base at Munda, in the Solomons, its heaviest bombing of the South Pacific war. [9:1.]

Biggest RAF-U. S. Raids on Reich Blast Hamburg, Hit Baltic Cities

By The United Press.

LONDON, Monday, July 26—United States heavy bombers struck deep and hard into Germany by daylight yesterday, hammering aircraft factories at the Baltic port of Warnemuende and showering hundreds of high explosives into the smoking ruins of Hamburg, gutted by the British Royal Air Force's night bombers twelve hours earlier in the greatest bombing assault of the war.

At the same time, other American heavies struck in force at the great German shipyards in Kiel and raided the Baltic industrial center of Wustrow, twenty-five miles west of Rostock.

The attack marked the biggest around-the-clock aerial assaults yet made by the American-British bombing teams. The raid on Warnemuende, seaport for the big manufacturing center of Rostock, was the deepest penetration of Germany yet made by the United States Eighth Air Force.

The RAF's night bombers in fifty blazing minutes blasted Hamburg with 2,300 tons of explosive and incendiary bombs, a far greater weight of bombs than ever before had been dropped in a single operation. [The British Air Ministry gives its figures in tons of 2,240 pounds; at 2,000 pounds to the ton, the RAF blasted Hamburg with 2,576 tons of bombs.]

RAF heavy bombers returned to the assault on Germany during last night. British officials reported early today. Channel coast watchers reported that a ninety-minute procession of heavy bombers flew

Continued on Page Seven

Chiang Kai-shek attended the Cairo Conference with Roosevelt and Churchill in 1943. His relations with the West were marked by perpetual tensions.

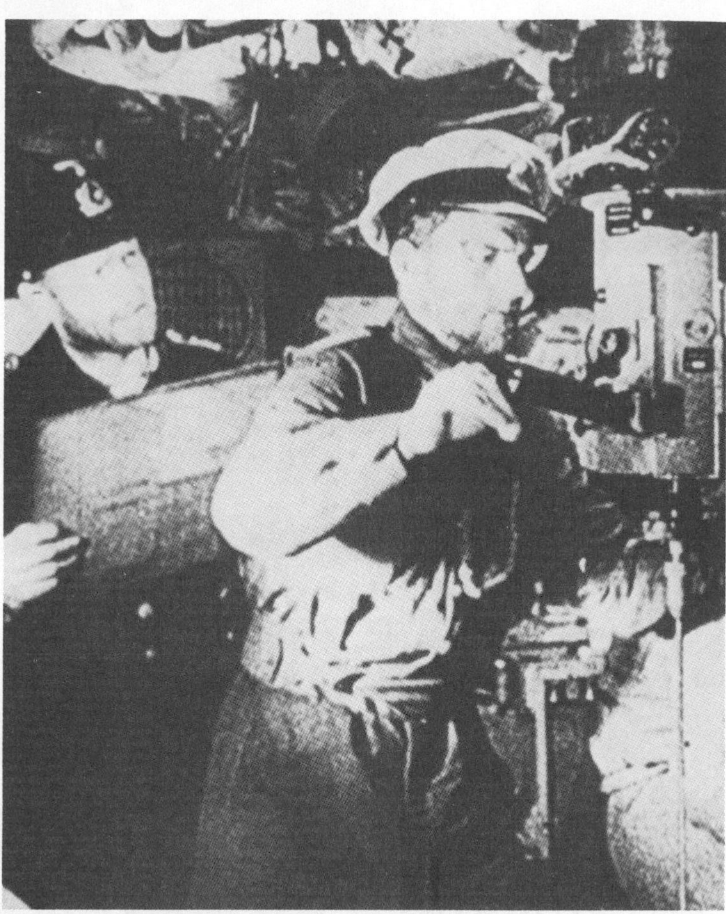

This frame from a captured film shows a German U-Boat attacking a convoy.

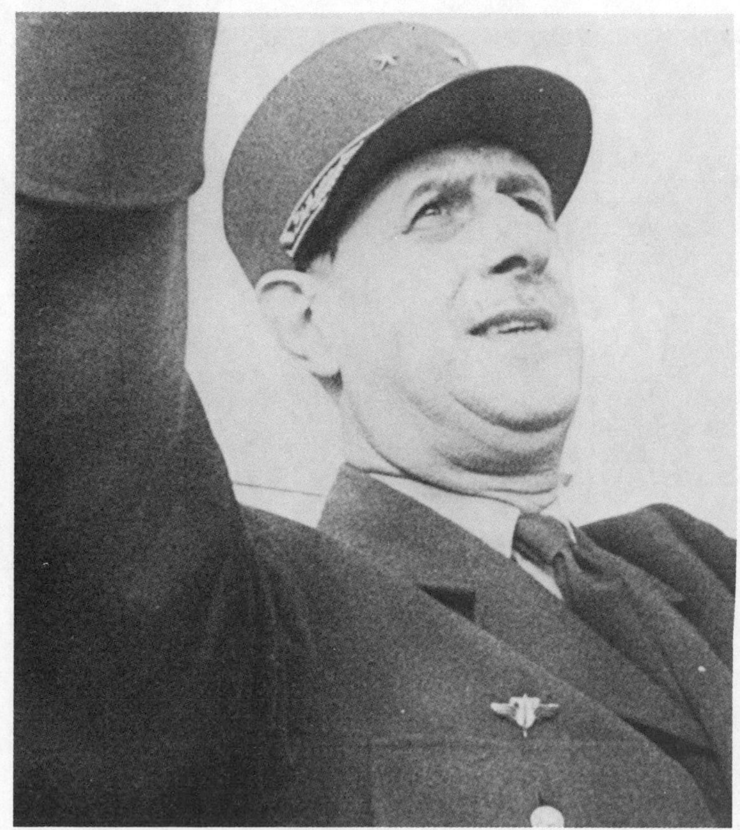

General Charles de Gaulle of France.

American hysteria led to the "relocation" of over 100,000 Japanese-Americans on the West Coast, but, by 1943, Niseis were allowed to enlist. In this photo, Mrs. Hisako Tanouye, who had six sons in the service, is being honored at a Gold Star Mothers banquet in a Wyoming relocation camp.

Jane Russell starred in the controversial film *The Outlaw.*

James Craig and Margaret O'Brien starred in *Journey for Margaret.*

"All the News That's Fit to Print."

The New York Times.

LATE CITY EDITION
Continued moderately cool today; moderate winds.
Temperatures Yesterday—Max., 74; Min., 67
Sunrise, 6:29 A. M.; Sunset, 7:17 P. M.

Copyright, 1943, by The New York Times Company.

VOL. XCII..No. 31,274. Entered as Second-Class Matter, Postoffice, New York, N. Y. NEW YORK, THURSDAY, SEPTEMBER 9, 1943. THREE CENTS IN NEW YORK CITY

ITALY SURRENDERS, WILL RESIST GERMANS; ALLIED FORCES LAND IN THE NAPLES AREA; RUSSIANS IN STALINO, CLEAR DONETS BASIN

SOVIET TIDE RISES

Swift Red Army Blows Capture Key City, Free Rich Region

DRIVE NEARS DNIEPER

More Rail Hubs Fall—Thrust Toward Kiev Also Extended

By The United Press.

LONDON, Thursday, Sept. 9—The Red Army recaptured Stalino, Russia's twelfth city, yesterday and freed the Donets Basin, which before the war produced more steel than Japan and Italy combined, in a great surge that took it to Grishino, ninety miles east of Dniepropetrovsk on the lower Dnieper River.

While the armies of Gen. Rodion Y. Malinovsky and Gen. Fedor Tolbukhin drove the enemy from the rich Donets Basin, crowded with coal mines and factories, the army of Gen. Konstantin Rokossovsky drove to a point ninety six miles northeast of Kiev by capturing Borzna, twenty-three miles west of Bakhmach.

Bakhmach and Romni, forty-two miles to the southeast, were surrounded on three sides, a Moscow radio bulletin reported, and thus the Bakhmach-Kremenchug railroad was cut. The roads leading from Bakhmach to Kursk and Gomel had been cut previously and only the lines to Kiev and Odessa remained open.

Picked Troops Take Stalino

Red Army shock troops, picked from the sixteen infantry divisions that had driven the Germans through city after city in six days of tireless fighting, took Stalino by storm.

The Russian communiqué said the Red Army troops drove in on Stalino throughout Tuesday night and yesterday morning. They fought through the suburbs and then stormed the city from north and south, routing the enemy in a street-by-street fight and capturing a great store of spoils.

Twenty-five miles northwest of Stalino the Russians took Krasnoarmeiskoye, a big railroad junction controlling two of four rail roads leading west from the basin.

In all the Russians took, in addition to Stalino, a city of 462,000 persons, more than 150 towns in the Donbas alone, twenty of them important, in gains of up to twelve and a half miles. During their Donbas offensive the Russians took twelve towns of more than 50,000 persons each.

The Germans at Krasnoarmeiskoye were so swiftly beaten that the Russians took nineteen planes and several loaded railroad trains.

March on Kiev Gains

On the Kiev front, the Russians took more than sixty towns in advances of up to twelve and a half miles. Their capture of Borzna in that area meant that the battle for the Dnieper River line had started. An advance of twenty-three miles to Nezhin would cut the only remaining German supply line east of the river. The Russians had already advanced 101 miles in nine days from Rylsk, half the distance to Kiev.

More than 1,000 Germans were killed at Borzna, and 1,000 were killed in another sector.

South of Bryansk the Russians advanced up to six miles to take several villages. They were reported only twenty miles south of Bryansk. The Soviet communiqué, recorded from the Moscow radio, reported that the Russians were advancing west of the Navlya railroad junction in this area, driving the Germans through dense forests.

West and southwest of Kharkov nearly four miles were gained in some sectors and about 1,200 Germans were killed.

The Germans were first to ad-

Continued on Page Twenty-two

New Fascist Regime Set Up, Nazis Report

By Cable to THE NEW YORK TIMES.

LONDON, Thursday, Sept. 9—The German radio announced early today that a "National Fascist government has been set up in Italy and functions in the name of Benito Mussolini."

The announcement, called a "proclamation by the National Fascist Government of Italy," said "this Badoglio betrayal will not be perpetrated. The National Fascist Government will punish traitors pitilessly."

The broadcast, in Italian, said nothing about the whereabouts of Mussolini, who has been reported under arrest. It was preceded by the playing of "Giovinezza," the Fascist anthem.

FOE'S MARCUS LOSS 80%, NIMITZ SAYS

U. S. Carrier Planes Alone Hit at Japanese Isle—Hell Cat Fighter Excels in Test

By ROBERT TRUMBULL

By Telephone to THE NEW YORK TIMES.

PEARL HARBOR, Sept. 8—Admiral Chester W. Nimitz, Commander in Chief of the Pacific Fleet, issued today a communiqué that gave the first details of the raid on Marcus Island Sept. 1. Coincidentally three naval air officers who participated in the action gave an interview covering all phases of the raid, which they said destroyed a surprisingly well-fortified Japanese air base.

Action Consisted of Bombing

Admiral Nimitz's communiqué said that a United States Pacific Fleet task force under command of Rear Admiral Charles A. Pownall attacked the little island, 1,185 miles southeast of Tokyo, at dawn Sept. 1. The air officers revealed that the action consisted entirely of bombing and strafing by carrier-borne aircraft.

They said that the new Grumman F6F Hellcat fighter was employed in combat for the first time in the

Continued on Page Twenty-two

IN HEART OF ITALY

American 7th Army Is Reported in Van of Naples Operation

MORE POINTS NAMED

Landings Rumored at Genoa, Pizzo, Gaeta and Leghorn

By Wireless to THE NEW YORK TIMES.

ALLIED HEADQUARTERS IN NORTH AFRICA, Thursday, Sept. 9—The Allies have carried the land campaign against the Nazis in Italy to the vicinity of Naples in new operations announced within twelve hours of the disclosure by Gen. Dwight D. Eisenhower that the Italian armed forces had unconditionally surrendered.

The news was announced here a few minutes past 6:30 A. M. in the following thirteen words:

"Further operations have started on the Italian mainland in the vicinity of Naples."

In the absence of the slightest expansion of the communiqué, no details are available as to the forces participating. The single fact remained that the attack had been pressed near Italy's southern metropolis and port, second only to Genoa, in what obviously was a major amphibious thrust.

Naples is a city of more than 700,000 population—nearer 1,000,000 if the suburbs are included. The assault was launched eighty-three years and two days after Garibaldi entered the city alone in a dramatic liberation gesture, which culminated in the unification of the country ten years later.

Although there is no indication just how near the city itself the landing or landings were carried out, it is plain that Naples is the objective of the sea-borne invaders.

[This dispatch did not indicate the make-up of the landing parties. A Tunis radio broadcast

Continued on Page Four

U. S. SOLDIERS IN LONDON CHEER THE NEWS

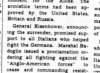

Americans in front of the Red Cross Washington Club in the British capital when the news of Italy's surrender was announced.

Associated Press Radiophoto, passed yesterday by censor

GEN. EISENHOWER ANNOUNCES ARMISTICE

Capitulation Acceptable to U. S., Britain and Russia Is Confirmed in Speech by Badoglio

TERMS SIGNED ON DAY OF INVASION

Disclosure Withheld by Both Sides Until Moment Most Favorable for the Allies—Italians Exhorted to Aid United Nations

By MILTON BRACKER

By Wireless to THE NEW YORK TIMES.

ALLIED HEADQUARTERS IN NORTH AFRICA, Sept. 8—Italy has surrendered her armed forces unconditionally and all hostilities between the soldiers of the United Nations and those of the weakest of the three Axis partners ceased as of 16:30 Greenwich Mean Time today [12:30 P. M., Eastern War Time].

At that time, Gen. Dwight D. Eisenhower announced here over the United Nations radio that a secret military armistice had been signed in Sicily on the afternoon of Friday, Sept. 3, by his representative and one sent by Premier Pietro Badoglio. That was the day when, at 4:50 A. M., British and Canadian troops crossed the Strait of Messina and landed on the Italian mainland to open a campaign in which, up to yesterday, they had occupied about sixty miles of the Calabrian coast from the Petrace River in the north to Bova Marina in the south.

The complete collapse of Italian military resistance in no way suggested that the Germans would not defend Italy with all the strength at their command. But the capitulation, in undisclosed terms that were acceptable to the United States, the United Kingdom and the Union of Soviet Socialist Republics, came exactly forty days after the downfall of Benito Mussolini, the dictator who, by playing jackal to Adolf Hitler, led his country to the catastrophic mistake of declaring war on France three years and three months ago this Friday.

Negotiations Begun Several Weeks Ago

The negotiations leading to the armistice were opened by the war-weary and bomb-battered nation a few weeks ago, it was revealed today, and a preliminary meeting was arranged and held in an unnamed neutral country.

The Italians who had approached the British and American authorities were bluntly told that the terms remained what they had been: unconditional surrender. They agreed, and the document was signed five days ago. But it was agreed to hold back the announcement and its effective date until the moment most favorable to the Allies.

That moment came today, when the Allied Commander in Chief, in a historic broadcast, announced the armistice. He concluded with the reminder that all Italians who aided in the ejection of the Germans from Italy would have the support and assistance of the United Nations.

One hour and fifteen minutes after the General's voice had gone out over the air, Marshal Badoglio faced a microphone in Rome and confirmed the armistice. He concluded with the promise that the Italian forces would oppose attacks "from any other quarter," although they were laying down the arms that they had taken up against the Anglo-American armies.

Military Aspect Emphasized

Although it was emphasized that the armistice was a strictly military instrument, "signed by soldiers," it was disclosed that it contained a clause binding Italy to comply with political, economic and financial conditions to be imposed at the Allies' discretion.

[It was believed that the armistice conditions were substantially the same as those imposed on France in 1940, which allowed the Germans to use all strategic French ports and military bases to wage war against Britain, The United Press reported.]

Immediately after the announcement of the armistice, the Allies made two appeals—one to the Italian people and one to the Italian Fleet—urging them to rally to a cause that was, in effect, the liberation of their own country. The appeal to the people was disseminated by radio and air-borne leaflet, while that to the Navy was broadcast by Admiral Sir Andrew Browne Cunningham, the Allies' Mediterranean naval commander.

The Italian people, particularly transport, railroad and dock workers, were asked not to give the slightest aid to the Germans. The men who man Italian ships received specific instructions how to bring their vessels into the protection of the United Nations.

Although the fear was proved unjustified by Marshal Badoglio's broadcast, the Allies had taken no chances of a German move to forestall his giving the news to the people. As a safeguard, they had obtained from the Italians an agreement to leave one senior military representative behind when the others returned to Rome. This man is now in Sicily and presumably, had Marshal Badoglio not gone on the air, his representative would have broadcast the decision to the Italian public.

As a further earnest of good faith, Marshal Badoglio had arranged to send the text of the proclamation that he made this evening to Allied Headquarters here. He kept his word.

1,181 Days at War and Losses

Italy quit the war after 1,181 days, during which she steadily lost territory and prestige. Last May 7, with the fall of Tunis and Bizerte, the last Italian soldier in North Africa was doomed. Since then, Sicily, part of Metropolitan Italy, was occupied in thirty-eight days.

The Italians endured two raids on military targets in Rome

Continued on Page Three

Announcements of the Surrender

By Broadcast to THE NEW YORK TIMES.

ALLIED HEADQUARTERS IN NORTH AFRICA, Sept. 8 — The texts of the proclamations by Gen. Dwight D. Eisenhower and Premier Pietro Badoglio follow:

By GENERAL EISENHOWER

This is Gen. Dwight D. Eisenhower, Commander in Chief of the Allied Forces.

The Italian Government has surrendered its armed forces unconditionally. As Allied Commander in Chief, I have granted a military armistice, the terms of which have been approved by the Governments of the United Kingdom, the United States and the Union of Soviet Socialist Republics. Thus I am acting in the interest of the United Nations.

The Italian Government has bound itself to abide by these terms without reservation. The armistice was signed by my representative and the representative of Marshal Badoglio and it becomes effective this instant.

Hostilities between the armed forces of the United Nations and those of Italy terminate at once. All Italians who now act to help eject the German aggressor from Italian soil will have the assistance and the support of the United Nations.

By PREMIER BADOGLIO

The Italian Government, recognizing the impossibility of continuing the unequal struggle against the overwhelming power of the enemy, with the object of avoiding further and more grievous harm to the nation, has requested an armistice from General Eisenhower, Commander in Chief of the Anglo-American Allied forces. This request has been granted. The Italian forces will therefore cease all acts of hostility against the Anglo-American forces wherever they may be met. They will, however, oppose attack from any other quarter.

CITY 'JUMPS GUN' IN WAR BOND DRIVE

Rallies, Sales Begin on Vast Scale—State Savings Banks Will Invest $600,000,000

As President Roosevelt and Secretary of the Treasury Henry J. Morgenthau Jr. opened the Third War Loan Drive for $15,000,000,000 last night over the radio, it was announced here that in the campaign to raise the State's quota of $4,709,000,000 the mutual savings banks in the State would buy $600,000,000 in Government bonds. The United States Steel Corporation and its subsidiaries will buy $100,000,000 in Government securities, with parts of the total allocated to districts where the corporation operates.

Restive to get its drive under way, New York City held preliminary rallies yesterday as Army convoys took into the five boroughs Navy gunners who had been rescued at sea. The largest meetings were held in Times Square and on the steps of the Sub-Treasury Building at Wall and Broad Streets.

Burgess Hails Italy's Surrender

The thousands assembled in the streets for these two gatherings cheered wildly as speakers announced the capitulation of Italy. Ticker tape, confetti and torn paper were thrown from the windows of buildings where workers in the financial community were listening to the rally.

The unconditional surrender of Italy is "bullish news" and will be a great help in the bond drive, W. Randolph Burgess, chairman of the War Finance Committee for New York State, said later in the

Continued on Page Sixteen

President Hails Victory But Warns of Real Foes

By JOHN H. CRIDER

Special to THE NEW YORK TIMES.

WASHINGTON, Sept. 8—President Roosevelt hailed the surrender of Italy tonight as "a great victory for the United Nations" and also "a great victory for the Italian people" against "their real enemies, the Nazis," but cautioned against over-optimism. Addressing the nation on the opening of the Third War Bond drive, the President said "the time for celebration is not yet" and added that "our ultimate objectives in this war continue to be Berlin and Tokyo."

Toward the middle of his speech the President interpolated three words which gave basis to reports that Allied armies already were on the move again in the Mediterranean when he spoke of troops in landing barges moving up to enemy coasts "at this moment."

"This war does not and must not stop for one single instant," he declared. "Your fighting men know that. Those of them who are moving forward through jungles against lurking Japs—those who are landing at this moment in barges moving through the dawn up the strange enemy coasts—those who are diving their bombs down on the target at roof-top level at this moment—every one of these men knows that this war is a full-time job and that it will

Continued on Page Seventeen

Germans Charge Betrayal by Italy In Plot With Russian Government

By GEORGE AXELSSON

By Wireless to THE NEW YORK TIMES.

STOCKHOLM, Sweden, Sept. 8—Berlin's newspapers branded Italy's capitulation as cowardly treachery last night. The German press abounds in scatching denunciation of Premier Pietro Badoglio and King Victor Emmanuel, as well as the Italian people.

"Mussolini was too great a person for a nation like that," a German official said. This is the second time that Victor Emmanuel has broken his word, the newspapers say, because the King "left Germany in the lurch" in 1915 when he joined the Allies.

Forgetting its praise of the Italians during the heyday of their pact, Berlin now condemns the Italians as third-rate individuals. "The cowardly perfidy of Badoglio caps the crime," one paper said, "by being committed in collusion with the Soviet Government, which is treason not only against Italy and Germany but also against all Europe."

Berlin added that the Germans had no intention of giving up their entrenchments in Italy, where they hoped to offer efficient resistance. Italy, since last night, is German-occupied territory to the extent that the Germans have been able to gain a firm footing there. In the Italian provinces occupied by the Germans, Berlin boasts fascism will be revived even if "we leave it to the Italians in those provinces to organize themselves along fascist lines.

Official circles are reviving accusations of broken words of honor

Continued on Page Nine

War News Summarized

THURSDAY, SEPTEMBER 9, 1943

Italy has surrendered unconditionally, and all hostilities between that country and the United Nations ceased yesterday. An armistice was signed last Friday, the same day that Italy was invaded, but the victors reserved the right to withhold announcement until the most favorable moment for the Allies. The armistice terms had been approved by the United States, Britain and Russia.

General Eisenhower, announcing the surrender, promised support to all Italians who helped fight the Germans. Marshal Badoglio issued a proclamation ordering all fighting against the "Anglo-American forces" to cease and commanding resistance to "attacks from any other quarter."

Allied radios and planes carried messages urging the Italians to take vengeance on their "German oppressors" and to prevent trains, ships and trucks from carrying German troops or supplies. [All the foregoing, 1:8; map, P.3.]

Landings in the Naples area followed only a few hours after the surrender announcement and it was believed the Allies were attempting to cut off German troops in southern Italy. The American Seventh Army was reported among the invading forces. [1:3; map, P. 4.] Earlier, the Italian Navy and merchant marine had been urged to take their ships to designated points and to scuttle the vessels as a last resort to keep them from the Germans. [7:4.]

Wild demonstrations of joy were reported from all over Italy, but in the north they gave way to sober realization of continued danger when the Germans occupied Milan and other cities and imposed martial law. [3:1.] No official comment came from Berlin, but the German radio, after withholding the news for hours, was furious at the "treachery." [1:5-6.]

Germany's Balkan satellites were so shaken by the Italian surrender that Bulgaria, Rumania and Hungary were reported ready to follow Italy out of the war. [10:3.]

President Roosevelt, in a radio address last night, termed the surrender a great victory for the Italian people as well as for the United Nations. But he warned: "The time for celebration is not yet. Our ultimate objectives in this war continue to be Berlin and Tokyo." [1:5-6.]

The actual fighting in Italy was of a minor nature. Land forces advanced on both coasts. [3:6.] Airfields were hit by Allied bombers and the Rome radio reported heavy raids on suburbs of the city. [4:1.]

With one Axis partner out of the war, the two others continued to be hit hard. The Red Army captured Stalino and cleared the Germans out of the Donets Basin. [1:1; map, P. 22.] Allied bombers from Britain struck enemy airfields in France and Belgium [23:2], while down in New Guinea Japanese troops were providing weak opposition as the Allies closed in on Lae. [22:1.]

The naval task force that raided Marcus Island Sept. 1 destroyed 80 per cent of the Japanese military installations. We lost three planes. [1:2.]

"All the News That's Fit to Print."

The New York Times.

LATE CITY EDITION
Scattered showers in morning; cooler in evening.
Temperatures Yesterday—Max., 60; Min., 41
Sunrise, 7:36 A. M.; Sunset, 6:03 P. M.

Copyright, 1943, by The New York Times Company.

VOL. XCIII..No. 31,328. Entered as Second-Class Matter, Postoffice, New York, N. Y. NEW YORK, TUESDAY, NOVEMBER 2, 1943. THREE CENTS NEW YORK CITY

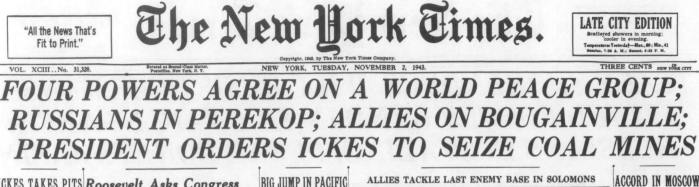

FOUR POWERS AGREE ON A WORLD PEACE GROUP; RUSSIANS IN PEREKOP; ALLIES ON BOUGAINVILLE; PRESIDENT ORDERS ICKES TO SEIZE COAL MINES

ICKES TAKES PITS

Roosevelt Tells Miners 'Enemy Does Not Wait,' Demands Return

HE OFFERS CONTRACT

Officials Here Move to Stretch City's Falling Supplies of Coal

By LOUIS STARK
Special to THE NEW YORK TIMES.

WASHINGTON, Nov. 1—President Roosevelt, as Commander in Chief of the Armed Forces, tonight ordered Secretary of the Interior Harold L. Ickes to take immediate possession of the coal mines as a result of the fourth war strike of 530,000 bituminous and anthracite mine workers. The strike began last midnight.

Carrying out his pledge of "decisive action to see that coal is mined," the President, in a statement supplementing his executive order, called upon "every miner to return to work without a day's delay" and said that he expected all to be back in the pits Wednesday.

"Coal must be mined," the President declared. "The enemy does not wait."

He told the miners that the Government was offering them a "fair contract" and "they have no right in wartime to refuse to work under it."

To assure peaceful operation of the mines, the President authorized the use of troops if necessary. His executive order provided that, if requested by Mr. Ickes, the Secretary of War "shall take such action, if any, as he may deem necessary or desirable to provide protection" to all persons who wish to work and protection to mines.

Secretary Ickes, who is also solid fuels coordinator, complying at once with the seizure order, took possession of the more than 3,000 coal mines for the second time since May 1.

Delay Is Forestalled

The President acted several hours after the United Mine Workers policy committee, convened by John L. Lewis, union president, had met here and adjourned to hear a report at 4 P. M. tomorrow from a subcommittee of twenty-eight.

Under the subcommittee arrangement the report would have been discussed tomorrow and Wednesday, with action Wednesday. This would have meant that if the union ordered the strikers back to work, they would not, under the most favorable circumstances, have begun to return until Friday. Even so, it was not felt that the response would have been 100 per cent, and it was estimated that probably most of the week's production of 12,000,000 tons would have been lost.

[Federal and anthracite spokesmen considered ways to stretch New York's coal supply, estimated to last two or three normal days. A half-ton limit for individuals and ten days' use for multiple dwellings were suggested. The City Markets Department, meanwhile, began action to suspend the license of a major distributor accused of selling a non-combustible product as coal.]

Ickes to Do the Bargaining

Changing the terms of the procedure when the Government took over the mines the first time, President Roosevelt, voicing appreciation of the desire of the miners to work under a contract, granted to Secretary Ickes authority to make collective bargaining agreements. Such agreements, he stipulated, shall be made "in accordance with the opinion of the National War Labor Board in the matter of Illinois Coal Operators Association and United Mine Workers of America of Oct. 26, 1943, and with such further directives as may be given by the WLB."

Mr. Lewis and his associates are now expected to confer with Secretary Ickes on a new contract to replace the one which expired April 1.

Secretary Ickes, who has ordered the American flag to fly over the

Continued on Page Sixteen

Roosevelt Asks Congress To Keep Food Subsidies

Proper Way to Keep Nation Fed, Hold Down Prices and Bar Inflation, He Says in His Longest Message to Congress

By SAMUEL B. BLEDSOE
Special to THE NEW YORK TIMES.

WASHINGTON, Nov. 1—President Roosevelt, in his longest message to Congress, today stoutly defended the use of food subsidies and left little doubt that he would veto any bill which sought to prevent use of them.

While he did not mention the measure by name, the President apparently aimed much of his 10,000-word message on the food and related situations at the pending bill to extend the life of the Commodity Credit Corporation beyond Dec. 31. This bill, as it was reported from the House Banking and Currency Committee, would prohibit after Dec. 31 the paying of subsidies to hold down food costs. The President vetoed an anti-subsidy bill last summer and the House upheld him.

Mr. Roosevelt said the support price program for farmers, coupled with subsidy programs "to meet special farming costs without raising prices to consumers, is an essential part of winning the war."

"The subsidies that are used," he said, "cannot properly be called producer subsidies or consumer subsidies. They are war subsidies. The costs which they cover are war costs."

Food subsidies in 1943, the message said, would cost about $800,000,000, but their use "has saved the Government and consumers billions of dollars."

According to comment by Congressmen, those who opposed subsidies before the message opposed them after it had been read in both houses to a scattering of Senators and Representatives. Speaker Ray-

Continued on Page Twenty-one

The President's message to Congress, Pages 20 and 21.

Court Unanimously Upholds The Verdict Clearing Aurelio

By FRANK S. ADAMS

By unanimous decision of the four justices who were sitting, the Appellate Division confirmed yesterday the report of Official Referee Charles B. Sears and dismissed the disbarment proceeding against former Magistrate Thomas A. Aurelio, whose name will appear on the voting machines in Manhattan and the Bronx today as the nominee of the Democratic and Republican parties for the Supreme Court.

The text of Referee's findings in the Aurelio case on Page 18.

The decision was handed down at 12:20 P. M. by Justices Alfred H. Townley, Edward J. Glennon, Edward S. Dore and Joseph M. Callahan. Presiding Justice Francis Martin was unable to participate because he is in St. Luke's Hospital recuperating from an emergency appendectomy. The remaining members of the court, Justices Irwin Untermyer and Albert Cohn, disqualified themselves because they are candidates for re-election today.

The court, in a one-sentence opinion, accepted the reasons set forth by Mr. Sears in his 7,000-word report recommending against the disbarment of Mr. Aurelio. The opinion merely said: "Motion to confirm the report of the referee granted and the proceedings dismissed for the reasons stated in the report of the referee."

According to the normal procedure, the petitioner in the disbarment proceeding, the Association of the Bar of the City of New York, has the right of appeal from the Appellate Division's ruling to the Court of Appeals in Albany, if it can obtain the permission of the Appellate Division. If the Appellate Division should refuse permission, it also has the right to appeal that refusal to the Court of Appeals.

There was no indication, however, whether the bar association would seek to take advantage of

Continued on Page Eighteen

NEW YORK ELECTION WATCHED BY NATION

Lieutenant Governorship Fight Today Seen as Barometer for Presidential Vote

By JAMES A. HAGERTY

With fewer than 4,000,000 voters scheduled to go to the polls today in this State to determine whether Senator Joe R. Hanley, Republican nominee, or Lieut. Gen. William N. Haskell, retired, Democratic and American Labor party, will be elected Lieutenant Governor, campaigning for these and local candidates continued until midnight.

Because of implications that may be drawn from the result, this contest in President Roosevelt's home State has aroused nationwide interest. The election of General Haskell would indicate that the President's policies, both foreign and domestic, had the approval of a majority of New York voters and that if the President, as expected, should be a candidate for re-election, he would have little difficulty in winning New York's 47 electoral votes.

The election of Senator Hanley, particularly if his majority should

Continued on Page Nineteen

4-Cent Letter Postage Put in Bill; No Credit for Excise Taxes Paid

Special to THE NEW YORK TIMES.

WASHINGTON, Nov. 1—The Ways and Means Committee today pushed the yield of the new tax bill up to an estimated $2,183,000,000 as it neared the end of work on the revenue raising sections of the measure.

Estimated revenue of $140,000,000 was added when the committee voted not to allow taxpayers to deduct Federal excise taxes paid by them in computing their returns.

The committee also voted to raise the rate on first class, out-of-town mail to 4 cents an ounce, but reconsidered its previous approval of 10 cents an ounce on air mail, and fixed the rate at 8 cents, as compared to the present 6 cents.

Newspapers and church and religious papers were exempted from increases previously voted on second class postage.

The tax on admissions was set at 2 cents for each 10 cents, instead of the previously agreed upon 3 cents for each 10 cents. The existing rate is 1 cent.

All the new increases in excise rates were made terminable six months after the war emergency ends.

The rates of 5 cents a pound on tires made from natural rubber and 9 cents a pound on tubes were extended to tires and tubes made from synthetic rubber.

The committee agreed to allow depletion percentages of 15 per cent on flake graphite and vermiculite.

BIG JUMP IN PACIFIC

Americans Surprise Foe, Seize Bay on Largest Solomons Island

RABAUL IS IMPERILED

MacArthur Challenges the Japanese Fleet to Come Out and Fight

By FRANK L. KLUCKHOHN
By Wireless to THE NEW YORK TIMES.

GUADALCANAL, Tuesday, Nov. 2—Green-clad United States Marines swarmed ashore from landing craft early yesterday against fortified Japanese positions at Empress Augusta Bay on the west side of Bougainville Island in the biggest single Allied landing in this theatre.

They quickly had the situation "well in hand" and within an hour had established themselves between the two main Japanese forces on the island, which are estimated to total at least 30,000 men.

With American naval vessels standing proudly off after a deafening hour-long bombardment, with white columns of water from Japanese bombs spouting in the bay and with American naval Avenger planes strafing the beaches ahead, the landing craft bearing crack United States fighting men wound their way to shore.

[A spokesman at Allied South Pacific headquarters was quoted by The Associated Press as saying the Japanese planes that tried vainly to interrupt the landing were from Rabaul as all the enemy's Bougainville and Buka fields had been put out of operation by Allied bombings.]

The Avengers twice raced over the beaches, where crashing shells already had ground up the enemy's trenches and gun positions when the landing craft, coming from big transports out at sea, neared their destination.

Then the landing craft fanned out along the shore in movement of sharp precision and the Marines raced through the waves, and across the beaches.

So impressed apparently were Japanese reconnaissance pilots observing not only this but the American naval dispositions through the north Solomons area that a Japanese cruiser force, approaching

Continued on Page Six

ALLIES TACKLE LAST ENEMY BASE IN SOLOMONS

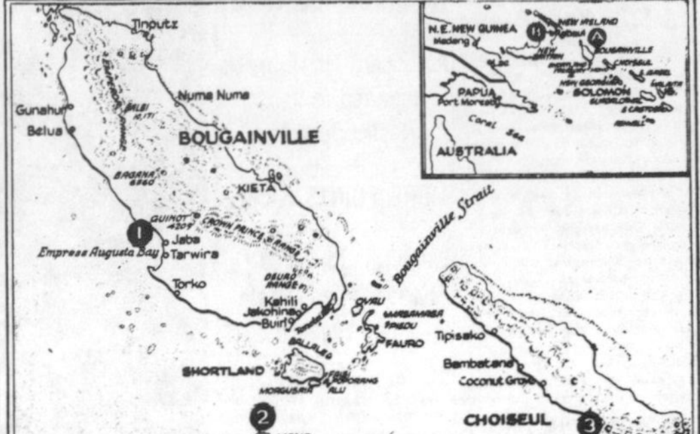

Meeting little opposition, Allied forces seized and occupied Empress Augusta Bay (1) on Bougainville Island, thus by-passing the Japanese base at Buin, on the island's southern tip, and those in the Shortland Islands, to the south. The move also put the Allies behind the enemy on Mono Island (2), where he is being pinned to the northern coast. A grip on Bougainville, which is also shown at (A) on the inset, will put the Allies within striking distance of the Rabaul stronghold (B). In southwestern Choiseul (3) General MacArthur's paratroops were advancing.

2 ARMIES IN ITALY GAIN DESPITE MUD

Triple Road Junction of Teano Falls as Allies Increase Threat to Isernia

By MILTON BRACKER
By Wireless to THE NEW YORK TIMES.

ALGIERS, Nov. 1—As rain swept the entire Italian front, the Allied Fifth and Eighth Armies pressed indomitably forward through mud yesterday to increase their threats to Isernia and Venafro. Further advances in the center of the line ranged up to four miles.

The junction town of Teano finally fell to Lieut. Gen. Mark W. Clark's army, and the Eighth Army, rushing up south of the central highway to Isernia, captured Cantalupo. An American unit under General Clark also thrust to Valle Agricola, three and a half miles above Ailano, and the Eighth Army seized Macchiagodena and Frosolone. The Fifth Army's gains were most significant in the triangle formed by Ailano, Piedimonte d'Alife and Valle Agricola,

Continued on Page Four

War News Summarized

TUESDAY, NOVEMBER 2, 1943

The four leading powers of the United Nations agreed at Moscow to fight their common enemies to submission on terms of unconditional surrender and to continue to act in unison as a guarantee of world peace.

The official communiqué on the results of the Anglo-American-Soviet conferences revealed that China had also been represented at some of the twelve meetings. The four powers agreed to carry their collaboration and cooperation beyond the period of hostilities and laid down principles for a "broad system of international cooperation and security" that would include "all other peace-loving nations, great and small."

Great Britain, Russia and the United States set up machinery for "the closest military cooperation"; created a European Advisory Commission to sit in London to study and make recommendations on continental problems; provided for continuing tripartite discussions; created an Italian Advisory Council with the French Committee of National Liberation as a member, and calling for later participation by Greece and Yugoslavia; guaranteed the restoration of Austrian independence and laid down the principle that German war criminals, military and civilian alike, would be taken back to "the countries in which their abominable crimes were committed" for trial under the laws of those countries. [All the foregoing 1:8.]

Secretary of State Cordell Hull and British Foreign Secretary Anthony Eden told a press conference in Moscow that the accomplishments of the conference had exceeded the most optimistic hopes. Mr. Hull, stressing the interdependence of Russia and the United States, denounced isolationism as futile. [1:7.]

The Russian Army went on to capture Perekop and smash through to Armyansk, cutting off the Germans in the Crimea from retreat by land. The enemy was suffering great losses in men and equipment. [1:6-7; map P. 8.]

At least forty German divisions were faced with destruction along the lower reaches of the Dnieper, and the Germans may be so disastrously routed they may have to sue for peace, a London source declared. [8:1.]

Allied armies in Italy pushed forward through rain and mud to capture Cantalupo on the road to Isernia and the important junction of Teano. [1:5; map P. 2]. Bombers struck a railroad bridge near Cannes, in France, communications around Rome and the Albanian airfield at Tirana. [4:2.]

Another combined sea, air and land operation in the Solomons resulted in the capture of Empress Augusta Bay, half way up the Bougainville coast. This landing put the Allies behind the Japanese positions at Buin and in the Shortlands. [1:4.]

Germans Caught in Crimea; Red Army Near Black Sea

By The Associated Press.

LONDON, Tuesday, Nov. 2—The Red Army trapped tens of thousands of Germans in the Crimea yesterday by cutting the Perekop Isthmus, and Moscow announced early today that one fleeing enemy group above the peninsula had been surrounded, losing 2,000 killed and 6,000 captured in a continuing battle of annihilation.

Nearly 5,000 Germans also were killed and scores of tanks, guns and trucks were captured or destroyed in fresh Russian gains inside the Dnieper River bend, Moscow said, as the Red Army reached the lower Dnieper River, four miles east of the Kakhovka crossing, in its pursuit of demoralized German troops, thousands of whom have perished on the Nogais Steppe. [The capture of Lyubimovka placed the Russians just west of the marshes that line the Dnieper at this point and marks the Red Army's southernmost hold on the river.]

In sealing off the Crimea the Russians stormed and captured Perekop, on the isthmus of that name, and smashed five miles farther south on the narrow land bridge that crosses into the Crimea proper. [The Red Army communiqué said it had captured Armyansk, south of Perekop.]

Kakhovka in Steel Jaws

Other units racing westward above the Crimea converged on the Kakhovka and Nikopol crossings of the lower Dnieper River in an effort to cross that stream and join two other Russian armies inside the Dnieper bend, where fresh Red Army gains also were made.

[The capture of Chernenka, twelve miles southeast of Kakhovka, meant the Nazi garrison there was flanked both east and south. Chernenka is thirty-three miles east of Kherson, representing the point of greatest Russian penetration toward that

Continued on Page Eight

U. S. ISOLATIONISTS CENSURED BY HULL

Stresses in Moscow They Did Not Prevent War—Says Soviet Leaders Scorn Doctrine

By Cable to THE NEW YORK TIMES.

MOSCOW, Nov. 1—At press conferences last night Secretary of State Cordell Hull and Foreign Secretary Anthony Eden both made it clear the Moscow meetings had accomplished far more than the most optimistic had predicted before it began. Mr. Eden spoke off the record but Mr. Hull permitted attribution of his remarks without direct quotation.

Looking well and cheerful despite the twelve lengthy sessions Mr. Hull gave reporters a long background talk on the steps that led to the war and, finally, to international cooperation to defeat the Axis and then to preserve peace.

He thought the conference had laid the foundation for cooperation of the United States, Russia, Britain and China on a basis of broad, sound, mutually advantageous policies and that now there was no way to stop a sound, healthy concept of the post-war world.

He expressed the belief that since the cooperation was founded on trust and confidence and was to mutual advantage there would be a

Continued on Page Fourteen

City Glows Again as Dimout Ends, But Far Less Brightly Than of Old

Times Square's incandescent tiara, hidden in the dimout chest for the last eighteen months, burst into about 40 per cent of its pre-war brilliance last night, as lighting restrictions were eased. It wore all its jewels except the giant spectaculars.

From twilight through 10 P. M. marquees and store and hotel signs blinked, quivered and chased their tails as they had before Pearl Harbor. Unmasked traffic lights loomed inordinately large to eyes unaccustomed to their full power.

Motor traffic moved with old-time assurance, though few drivers had removed the paint or shielding from the upper parts of the lamps. Pedestrians unconsciously took up a brisker pace and forms and features were bathed in the old, familiar glow.

Shopkeepers made the most of the change. Many, indeed, were quite brash. Though sternly warned not to increase window wattage, many did, and the sidewalks, which had been sunk in gloom these many months, cast effulgence on the endless pedestrian parade.

Still deep in gloom, however, were all city parks and tree-filled squares. Central Park was one great zone of darkness; so, too, were Union Square, Madison Square and Washington Square.

Commissioner Patrick Quilty of the Department of Water Supply, Gas and Electricity promised speedy replacement of low-wattage lamps in street lights. He said that by tonight Park, Fifth, Sixth, Seventh and Eighth Avenues and

Continued on Page Five

ACCORD IN MOSCOW

3 Conferees Fix Steps to 'Shorten War'—China Joins Peace Pledge

ATROCITY TRIALS SET

Germans to Be Returned to Crime Scenes—Free Austria Envisaged

Documents signed in Moscow and joint communiqué, Page 14.

By W. H. LAWRENCE
By Cable to THE NEW YORK TIMES.

MOSCOW, Nov. 1—Cordell Hull, United States Secretary of State; Anthony Eden, British Foreign Secretary, and Vyacheslaff M. Molotoff, Soviet Foreign Commissar, announced tonight that their Governments had agreed to closer collaboration in the conduct of the war and pledged the creation of an international organization to maintain future world peace and security—a declaration to which China adhered as an original signatory.

The communiqué announcing the end of the Moscow conference said the Foreign Ministers had discussed frankly and exhaustively "measures to be taken to shorten the war against Germany and her satellites in Europe."

The conference decided upon practical steps to organize for victory on the basis of unconditional surrender and to keep the peace once it was achieved.

Simultaneously President Roosevelt, Premier Joseph Stalin and Prime Minister Churchill published a joint statement declaring that German officers and men and Nazi party members who were responsible for, or who had consented to, atrocities, massacres and executions in the occupied territories would be sent back to the countries "in which their abominable deeds were done in order that they may be judged and punished according to the laws of those liberated countries which will be created therein."

Hope for a Free Austria

Separately, Messrs. Hull, Eden and Molotoff signed an agreement expressing hope for the re-establishment of a free, independent Austria, which was the first free country to become a victim of Adolf Hitler's aggression.

It warned Austrians that the victors' generosity would be tempered by the extent of their participation on Hitler's side and by their own contribution to their own liberation.

To improve machinery for war and post-war collaboration, Russia, the United States and Britain agreed to establish in London a European Advisory Commission that will make plans and recommendations to the three Governments on multifarious subjects arising in Europe as the war develops. These three will be the only

Continued on Page Seven

King Must Abdicate, Badoglio Declares

By The Associated Press.

SOMEWHERE IN SOUTHERN ITALY, Nov. 1—Premier Pietro Badoglio told King Victor Emmanuel today that he could not form a representative Government while the King remained in power.

Thus Marshal Badoglio, who had just returned after an air tour of southern Italy, including Naples, where he conferred with political leaders, handed the King his gravest problem in the forty-three years of his reign—whether to abdicate or to allow Italy to tear herself apart in political strife.

While the National Liberation Front prefers a republic, Count Carlo Sforza and other leaders let it be known that they would not oppose a regency for the Prince of Naples, the 6-year-old son of Crown Prince Humbert. They told Marshal Badoglio, however, that the regent would have to be selected with care and that they would decline to consider Prince

U.S. Marines moving through muddy terrain on the island of Bougainville, during their advance towards Rabaul.

Marine artillerymen loading their 75mm howitzer in battle, on Cape Gloucester.

1943

Frank Sinatra

"All the News That's Fit to Print."

The New York Times.

LATE CITY EDITION
Showers in forenoon; clear in afternoon; fair at night.
Temperatures Yesterday—Max.,50; Min.,35
Sunrise, 8:06 A. M.; Sunset, 8:29 P. M.

Copyright, 1943, by The New York Times Company.

VOL. XCIII...No. 31,363. Entered as Second-Class Matter, Postoffice, New York, N. Y. NEW YORK, TUESDAY, DECEMBER 7, 1943. THREE CENTS IN NEW YORK CITY

'BIG 3' CHARTS TRIPLE BLOWS TO HUMBLE REICH AND AGREES ON A PEACE TO ELIMINATE TYRANNY; CARRIERS ATTACK MARSHALLS; 5TH ARMY GAINS

MAYOR PORTRAYED AS SCHOOL RULER BY OUSTED OFFICIAL

Kuper, Former Law Adviser to Board, Tells NEA Inquiry Appointments Were Blocked

SEES MORALE IMPAIRED

Fear of Having Funds Held Up Kept the Members From Asserting Rights, He Says

Charges that Mayor La Guardia has interfered with the city school system, causing educational officials to bow to his will and robbing the Board of Education of its independence by threatening to withhold funds, were made at the National Education Association school inquiry, which began public hearings here yesterday.

A behind-the-scenes version of how the board operates, and of the role of the Mayor in deciding matters of school policy, was presented by Theodore Fred Kuper, law secretary of the board for eleven years until he was dismissed recently by order of the Mayor. Mr. Kuper took the witness stand at 10 A. M. and did not complete his testimony until the hearing adjourned late in the afternoon.

Hearing in Bar Building

Held in the trial room of the Bar Association Building, 42 West Forty-fourth Street, the open sessions are the culmination of three months of investigation and study by the National Education Association's panel of educators appointed to determine the charges of City Hall interference with school issues.

Dr. Ernest E. Cole, former New York State Commissioner of Education, who is acting as counsel for the inquiry, is conducting the hearings. Members of the panel include Dr. Orville C. Pratt, past president of the NEA and superintendent emeritus of schools at Spokane, Wash.; Dr. Ernest O. Melby, chancellor of the University of Montana; Miss Mabel Studebaker, president of the NEA's department of classroom teachers, and Dr. Donald DuShane, past president of the NEA and secretary of its commission for the defense of democracy through education.

Representatives of various school, civic and parents' groups appeared at the opening session. The investigation was requested by the New York High School Teachers Association and the Kindergarten-6B Teachers Association, two of the city's largest educational bodies. Mrs. Johanna M. Lindlof, president of the kindergarten group and former Board of Education member, sat through the entire session; she is to take the stand this morning.

Testimony by Kuper

Mr. Kuper marshaled a parade of statements and figures to support his contention that Mayor La Guardia interfered with local school independence and "frightened" board officials into submission. He cited incidents to illustrate the many points he raised. Members of the panel or Dr. Cole interrupted frequently to ask questions.

As a result of the Mayor's control over the school board 100 appointments to clerical and administrative positions, for which funds were provided in the budget, have been blocked, Mr. Kuper declared. This has resulted in decreased efficiency as well as a lowering of morale among the employes, he testified.

Important administrative positions, which the board sought to fill and for which money was present in the budget, remain vacant because the city Budget Director does not give the necessary certificates, it was brought out. One instance was cited in which the Superintendent of Plant Operation and Maintenance requested a supervising custodian; the position was approved by the Board of Education, but it took 404 days before the Mayor gave his consent.

"Bear in mind that the Board of Education has the inherent legal power and, in my opinion, the duty to fill these positions," Mr. Kuper

Continued on Page Twenty

Stalin Says U. S. Aid Saved the Allies

By Cable to THE NEW YORK TIMES.

CAIRO, Egypt, Dec. 6—The greatest tribute possibly ever paid American industrial production came from Premier Stalin during the Teheran talks.

In a toast at a dinner party the Soviet Premier said:

"Without American machines the United Nations never could have won the war."

He should know.

It is understood Premier Stalin said Russia was manufacturing 3,000 planes monthly against 3,500 British and 10,000 American.

FROZEN FOOD SPACE IS TO BE EXPANDED

Warehouses Here Are to Add Million Cubic Feet—Row Brews Over U. S. Hoards

By JEFFERSON G. BELL

Major warehouse interests of New York City disclosed yesterday that they already had taken steps to expand freezer capacity at least 1,000,000 cubic feet. This move is part of a program to ease storage, transportation and other problems caused by the Federal Government's vast hoard of food.

The Government stockpiles have so taxed the capacity of warehouses, notably freezer space, that the Office of Defense Transportation last week appealed for help to the War Food Administration and the Office of Price Administration.

The refrigeration expansion program was revealed by local WFA and warehouse spokesmen as chilly relations between national WFA and OPA on one side and ODT on the other threatened to develop into an interdepartmental row over charges that foods needed by civilians are being allowed to deteriorate or spoil because of improper warehousing.

Release of Supplies Suggested

In view of the explanation by warehouse interests here that they could not increase their freezer capacity sooner than sixty to ninety days, food-trade circles were unable to see what would be the solution of warehouse congestion unless supplies were released.

When Joseph B. Eastman, director of the Office of Defense Transportation, confirmed last week reports that he had asked WFA and OPA to take steps to ease the congestion of freezer facilities, he disclosed that he had received a letter promising "immediate" action. Neither Mr. Eastman nor any member of the ODT staff was reached yesterday for comment on the disclosure that plans for freezer expansion here held no promise of relief for another two or three months.

The local office of the Food Distribution Administration, WFA, 150 Broadway, disclosed that a survey of storage facilities here had showed that New York City warehouses are operating at 89 per cent of capacity.

"When we are operating at 90 to 95 per cent of capacity," explained

Continued on Page Twenty-three

BATTLING IN ITALY

3 More Camino Peaks Are Taken Despite Fierce Resistance

COUNTER-BLOW FAILS

Germans Beaten Back at Venafro—Eighth Army at Moro River

By MILTON BRACKER
By Wireless to THE NEW YORK TIMES.

ALGIERS, Dec. 6—The battle of the mountains continued yesterday in Italy as Lieut. Gen. Mark W. Clark's Fifth Army wrested three more peaks of the Mount Camino group from the Germans, who are putting up a fanatic battle for every inch of the rocky ground.

The slow and tortuous envelopment of the numberless ridges and peaks proceeded in an epic of difficult fighting in which the individual soldier had to combine the technique of the jungle fighter with that of the mountain goat. More rain tended to retard the four-day-old offensive as German gunfire swept the slopes and crevices from deeply dug-in positions. But the British and American infantry ground steadily forward and mopped up the isolated resistance strong points by-passed by the Allies' spearheads.

There is at least one ridge that our forces have pressed beyond and flanked without being able to silence the German fire from its crest. The entire tone of the struggle is one of a fierce will to resist. Despite severe losses, the German Tenth Army is setting a standard of savage defensive fighting that its opponents will never forget.

[American artillery has begun shelling Cassino, The United Press reported.]

Counter-Attack Repulsed

In the Venafro sector of the Fifth Army's front, above the Via Casilina, the Germans flung in another sharp counter-attack against American units. As they have done several times before, the Americans hurled back the attack, leaving the positions in this sector about the same.

On the British Eighth Army's front, too, the Germans poured in reinforcements as the battles for Orsogna and Guardiagrele raged unabated. Both points remained in the enemy's hands.

The Eighth Army has, in general, pressed nearer to the Moro River from San Vito Chietino, however, and, at Casone, some four miles inland, three miles above Lanciano and 1,000 yards from the Moro's south bank, the Allies' infantry and tanks crushed several advanced German machine-gun posts in their drive to the bank.

The Eighth Army captured at least one German tank that proved to be without question a flame-thrower. This settled the dispute that began here on Nov. 29, when a flame-throwing tank was first

Continued on Page Sixteen

THE LEADERS OF THE 'BIG THREE' MEET IN TEHERAN

Marshal Stalin, President Roosevelt and Prime Minister Churchill on the porch of the Russian Embassy
The New York Times (U. S. Twelfth Air Force)

HEAVY TASK FORCES STRIKE IN PACIFIC

Blow at the Marshall Islands Comes as Allies Step Up Air Drive Against New Britain

By GEORGE F. HORNE
By Telephone to THE NEW YORK TIMES.

PEARL HARBOR, Dec. 6—Strong carrier task forces and heavy Navy bombers have attacked a number of bases in the Japanese-held Marshall Islands in the last few days, indicating a new development in the central Pacific offensive, which was touched off by our invasion of the Gilbert Islands.

[In the southwest Pacific, Allied fliers struck with increasing violence against invasion-menaced New Britain Island, on which lies Rabaul, main Japanese base in that war theatre. Our airmen poured 155

Continued on Page Seventeen

New Cairo Talks Reported To Get Turkey to Join War

By JAMES B. RESTON
By Wireless to THE NEW YORK TIMES.

LONDON, Dec. 6—The conversations that Prime Minister Churchill and, presumably, President Roosevelt had with President Ismet Inonu of Turkey in Cairo after the Teheran parleys have led to considerable speculation about the possibility of Turkey's entering the war. The background of these conversations would seem to justify this speculation. The question for Turkey, as an ally of Britain, now seems to be not whether but when and how she will help the Allies. This, it is presumed, is the question being discussed by Messrs. Churchill and Inonu.

[Reports that Messrs. Churchill, Roosevelt and Inonu were conferring in Africa have come from enemy and neutral sources.]

The basis of these conversations is the Anglo-French-Turkish treaty of alliance of Oct. 19, 1939. Article II stated: "In the event of an act of aggression by a European power

Continued on Page Seven

UKRAINE RAILWAY IS CUT BY RUSSIANS

Huge German Forces Are Split —Red Army Is Only 23 Miles From Kirovograd

By The Associated Press.

LONDON, Tuesday, Dec. 7—Russian troops smashed the enemy's Smela-Znamenka line in the central Ukraine yesterday, splitting huge German forces guarding those vital junctions on railways leading to Rumania and putting the Red Army within twenty-three miles of the Axis bastion of Kirovograd.

A Moscow communiqué and a midnight supplement announced the capture of Taybulevo, eight miles northwest of Znamenka on the double-track railway leading to Smela, and the fall of Alexsandriya, twenty miles east of Znamenka. Twenty other towns and villages were swept up, said the bulletin, recorded by the Soviet monitor from a Moscow broadcast.

[The crossing of the Znamenka-Smela line probably took place in the Krasnoselye-Taybulevo sector. Each village is two miles from the railroad line and represents the farthest penetration in yesterday's advance.

Continued on Page Twelve

WASHINGTON HAILS UNITY AT TEHERAN

Hull Stresses 'Concerting' of Plans to Crush Axis Forces—Congress Leaders Pleased

By BERTRAM D. HULEN
Special to THE NEW YORK TIMES.

WASHINGTON, Dec. 6—Opinion in the executive branch of the Government concerning both the Teheran and the Cairo conferences was set forth by Secretary of State Cordell Hull today in a statement declaring that the concerted plans adopted "will undoubtedly result in making effective to the fullest extent the fighting strength of all of the United Nations."

Opinion in general in the capital was that the communiqué issued on the Teheran conference showed that the three Chiefs of Government, President Roosevelt, Prime Minister Churchill and Premier Stalin, had had a meeting of minds and had reached detailed decisions for destroying the German Army, even though the declaration, perhaps significantly, did not use the phrase "unconditional surrender."

All in all, the announcement gave grounds for encouragement at a time when America is entering the third year of the war.

Way Open for Small Nations

It was of first importance that the three leaders had met, it was felt. And in meeting they had agreed to cooperate in the war and in the peace, and to invite the collaboration of small nations.

There were conjectures as to whether this collaboration might include the German people, if they sought it as a chastened people free of nazism and militarism.

Military details, obviously, could not be revealed, it was realized, but

Continued on Page Eleven

ATTACK PLANS SET

Dates Fixed for Land Drives From the East, West and South

IRAN TO BE FREED

Allied Leaders Say 'No Power on Earth' Can Balk Our Victory

The texts of the three-power declarations appear on Page 4.

By C. L. SULZBERGER
By Cable to THE NEW YORK TIMES.

CAIRO, Egypt, Dec. 6—Final concord on a campaign to destroy the German military power by land, sea and air and to erect an enduring peace in which all nations, both great and small, shall participate, was agreed upon in the momentous Teheran meeting between President Roosevelt, Premier Stalin and Prime Minister Churchill.

Simultaneously, the three leaders, as a sign of their faith in each other and as proof of the validity of their intentions toward little nations, guaranteed the post-war independence, sovereignty and territorial integrity of Iran.

These Allied agreements were announced to the world today in two joint declarations signed in order by President Roosevelt [the only titular Chief of State among the three], Premier Stalin and Prime Minister Churchill. They were issued in Teheran Dec. 1 after a long final sitting of the leaders and their innermost circles of advisers in the magnificent Soviet Embassy where President Roosevelt lived as a guest.

3-Pronged Attack Pledged

Their military promises can be summed up accordingly: the three powers will work together throughout the war; their military staffs have concerted plans for the destruction of German forces; these staffs have reached a "complete agreement as to the scope and timing of operations which will be undertaken from the east, west and south."

Guarantees satisfactory to the three chiefs now exist that the final victory will rest with the United Nations. "No power on earth can prevent our destroying the German armies by land, their U-boats by sea and their warplants from the air," says one of the joint declarations. "Our attacks will be relentless and increasing."

Seal Doom of Hitler

Thus in four days of deliberation in the romantic Iranian capital the "Big Three" laid the second half of the plans for ending the global war and establishing lasting peace for the benefit of all in its ruins. The Asiatic talks in North Africa between Mr. Roosevelt, Mr. Churchill and Generalissimo Chiang Kai-shek already had laid the program for accelerating the defeat of Japan and for building up a new Asia.

Now European talks of exactly the same length have rounded off the final plans for smashing Hitler which obviously must precede the destruction of Japan in the over-all scheme of the Allied grand strategy planners. Britain and America have clearly coordinated their ultimate schedule for the invasion of Europe from several points from the west and south with a program for new Russian offensives against the Reich.

It may be assumed that once the fulfillment of these plans comes about and Moscow's long plea for a second front are entirely answered that the Soviet Union might conceivably alter its present neutral attitude toward Japan. This certainly was discussed at Teheran but the outcome of these discussions is not known.

It would seem a fair assumption from a complete survey of both the present wartime and future post-war problems indicated in the latest declarations that the three powers must now have agreed on

Continued on Page Four

War News Summarized

TUESDAY, DECEMBER 7, 1943

President Roosevelt, Premier Stalin and Prime Minister Churchill announced to the world yesterday that "no power on earth can prevent our destroying the German armies by land, their U-boats by sea and their war plants from the air."

The three leaders, in a declaration dated Teheran, Dec. 1, said they had "reached complete agreement as to the scope and timing of operations which will be undertaken from the east, west and south."

"We came here with hope and determination," the three men said. "We leave here friends in fact, in spirit and in purpose." One of the purposes is to "work together in the peace" that will follow the war. All countries, large and small, were invited into "a world family of democratic nations" pledged to eliminate tyranny, oppression and intolerance and to "banish the scourge and terror of war for many generations."

In a second declaration the conferees pledged the independence and territorial integrity of Iran as a token of their determination to protect small nations. [All the foregoing 1:8; map P. 5.]

The meetings were held in the Soviet Embassy at Teheran about a round table ten feet in diameter. It was the first time Mr. Roosevelt had ever met Premier Stalin and the first time the latter had left his country since 1909. [3:1.]

A third international meeting was reported to have followed in North Africa, where, it was said, Mr. Roosevelt and Mr. Churchill conferred with President Inonu of Turkey regarding his country's entrance into the war. [1:5-6.]

The military plans laid at Teheran were expected to be in full effect by March or April of next year, when invasion from Britain would follow the Russian winter drive and an all-out aerial offensive against Germany. [1:6-7.]

Secretary of State Hull declared that the fighting strength of the United Nations could now become fully effective [1:7] and London opinion held that the Teheran announcement was designed to conceal more than was revealed. [9:2.] The people of Moscow were delighted that agreement on timing all blows against Germany had ended the "second-front" issue. [10:1.]

Allied troops continued to make progress on all fronts. Both the Eighth and Fifth Armies in Italy pushed forward against bitter opposition, reaching the Moro River and bringing Cassino under artillery fire. [1:3; map, P. 16.] The Red Army, smashing southwest of Kremenchug, was only four miles from Znamenka as it cut the Smela-Znamenka rail line. [1:6; map, P. 12.]

In the Pacific 155 tons of bombs were showered on Cape Gloucester as the assault on the western end of New Britain was maintained. [17:2-3.] A strong American carrier force attacked Japanese positions in the Marshall Islands [1:4] and United States submarines sent eleven more enemy ships to the bottom. [16:6.]

2d Brooklyn Jury Scores Mayor For Failing to Hire Enough Police

Already under censure by the August grand jury in Kings County for alleged failure to suppress crime in the Bedford-Stuyvesant section of Brooklyn, the administration of Mayor La Guardia was accused yesterday by the holdover July grand jury of inadequately policing the entire borough.

"We charge," the July panel declared in a presentment to County Judge Franklin Taylor, "that the present administration over a long period of years has utterly failed to take adequate measures to promptly fill the vacancies regularly occurring in the department, and also to provide additional patrolmen during this time."

At the same time County Judge Nathan R. Sobel was charging the December grand jury and pointing out, for the guidance of the August panel, that its presentment was faulty in that it had the effect of "indicting" an entire people for the crimes of a very few and "stirring up resentment, hatred and fear."

The August panel reconvened yesterday, continuing its inquiry into what it declares to be widespread and unchecked lawlessness in Brooklyn's "Little Harlem." It heard the testimony of several witnesses, then adjourned without disclosing when it would meet again.

In its presentment the July grand jury, whose term had been extended to permit it to investigate police protection in the city's most populous borough, attributed the critical police situation to the "short-sighted, improvident policies of this administration," which it said "have in large part contributed to the development of a situ-

Continued on Page Twenty

First Quarter of 1944 Likely to See Fruition of the Teheran Strategy

By DREW MIDDLETON
By Cable to THE NEW YORK TIMES.

LONDON, Dec. 6—Military plans for the defeat of the Wehrmacht drawn at Teheran, Iran, by President Roosevelt, Prime Minister Churchill and Premier Stalin, will probably be fully activated in the first three months of 1944.

During that period the strategic aerial offensive against Germany will assume its maximum proportions, the winter offensive of the Red Army should have brought it to the Dniester in the south and into Poland in the north and the Anglo-American invasion of northern Europe from Britain will be ready to start, with the tactical air forces already operating against the defenses in Western Europe and the lateral communications on which those defenses rely.

One of the first tangible results of the Teheran conference should be the arrival of Gen. George C. Marshall, United States Army Chief of Staff, in Britain to take up his position as Commander in Chief of all Allied invasion forces.

Once the invasion leader is settled into his job it is considered likely that the long-awaited announcement of the formation of an Allied Tactical Air Force and the names of its commanders and the appointment of American and British commanders to lead Allied Army groups involved in the invasion, will follow.

It may well be that the southern Europe front, now represented by a slow, painful advance in Italy may

Continued on Page Five

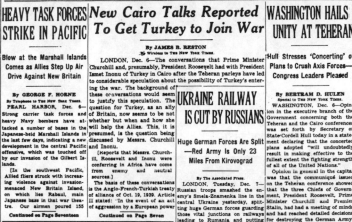

1943

Errol Flynn (right) was acquitted of the charge of rape. The plaintiff, Peggy Satterlee, is seen standing behind him.

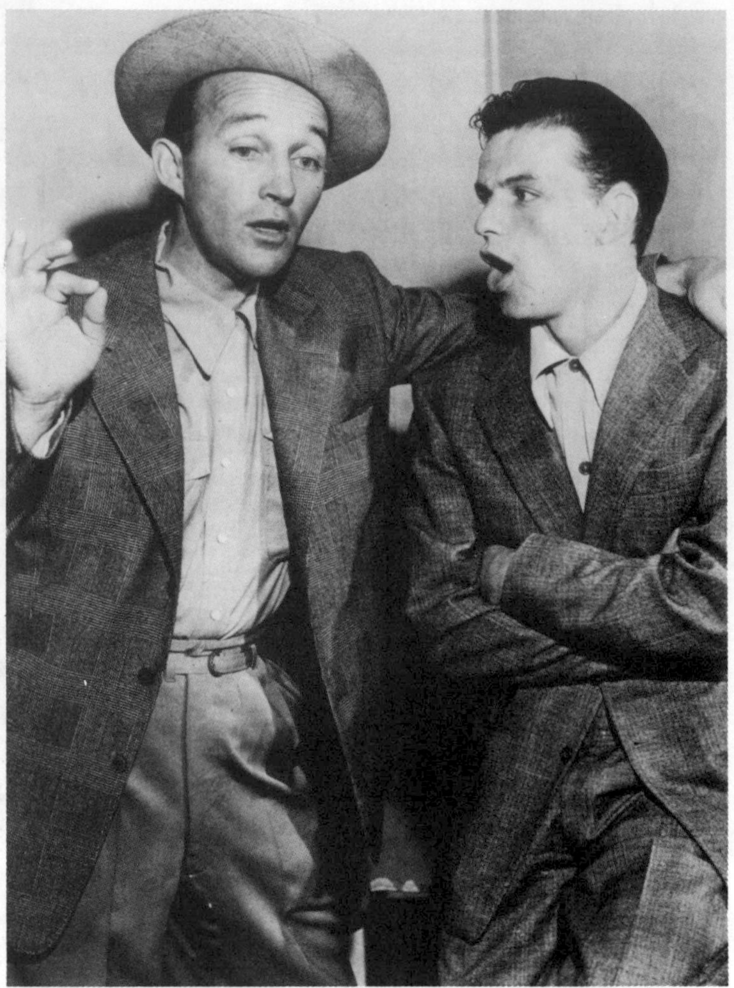

Bing Crosby and Frank Sinatra surely made beautiful music.

Bud Abbott and Lou Costello were very popular on radio, and later on TV as well.

Garry Moore and Jimmy Durante appeared together on a 1943 radio show.

"All the News That's Fit to Print."

The New York Times.

LATE CITY EDITION
Cloudy and warmer today; fresh winds.
Temperatures Yesterday—Max., 30; Min., 9
Sunrise, 8:18 A. M.; Sunset, 5:34 P. M.

VOL. XCIII..No. 31,381. Entered as Second-Class Matter, Postoffice, New York, N. Y.
Copyright, 1943, by The New York Times Company.
NEW YORK, SATURDAY, DECEMBER 25, 1943.
THREE CENTS IN NEW YORK CITY

EISENHOWER NAMED COMMANDER FOR INVASION; 3,000 PLANES SMASH FRENCH COAST; BERLIN HIT; ROOSEVELT PROMISES NATION A DURABLE PEACE

STRIKE CALLED OFF BY 230,000 IN TRAIN AND ENGINE UNIONS

But Non-Operating Men Meet Carriers and Reject Offer Made for Overtime Pay

GIVE BYRNES NO ANSWER

He Says Agreement Must Meet Requirements Set Forth in the Stabilization Program

By LOUIS STARK
Special to THE NEW YORK TIMES.

WASHINGTON, Dec. 24—The Brotherhood of Locomotive Engineers and the Brotherhood of Railroad Trainmen today canceled notices for a strike of their 230,000 members on Dec. 30 in view of President Roosevelt's offer and their acceptance of arbitration by the Chief Executive.

The conductors, firemen and switchmen's unions, also members of the "Big Five" operating and transportation brotherhoods, representing more than 120,000 employes, have rejected arbitration by the President and have not called off the strike of their members set for Dec. 30.

The other major development today in the railroad wage situation was a three-hour conference in the office of James F. Byrnes, chief of the Office of War Mobilization, participated in by committees of the railroads and of spokesmen for the fifteen non-operating unions, whose 1,100,000 members are scheduled to strike on Dec. 30.

At this meeting it was reported that the non-operating unions asked for a wage increase of 6 cents an hour as compensation for overtime after forty hours. These employes receive overtime after forty-eight hours of service. The carriers are reported to have offered 4 cents an hour for overtime, but it is understood that this was rejected by the unions.

Insists on Negotiations

B. M. Jewell, chief negotiator for the unions, is said to have been pressed by Mr. Byrnes for a reply to the President's demand that the non-operating employes permit him to act as sole and final arbiter in their dispute with the carriers.

The union leader is said to have replied with some asperity that the President last night gave the unions until Monday to reply to the arbitration proposal, and that in the meantime they had obtained from the President authority to proceed and seek an agreement with the carriers, whose committees were headed by Jacob Aronson, vice president of the New York Central Railroad.

The offer of 4 cents an hour for overtime was understood to be above the 4 to 10 cents an hour sliding scale wage increase recommended in the non-operating unions' case by an emergency board, convened after Frank M. Vinson, the Economic Stabilization Director, had rejected the 8 cents an hour proposal of a previous emergency board.

Byrnes' Statement

The conference in Mr. Byrnes' office, which was attended for a short time by Mr. Vinson, ended at 5:30 P. M. and the following statement was issued on Mr. Byrnes' behalf:

"The representatives of the carriers and the non-operating brotherhoods met in the conference room of the Office of War Mobilization.

"The representatives of the carriers were not present at the conference the President held with the representatives of the brotherhoods yesterday afternoon. Justice Byrnes advised the carriers' representatives that the President desired to know whether they would object to his arbitrating the differences between the carriers and the non-operating brotherhoods.

"The representatives of the carriers stated that they were entirely willing to agree that the President should arbitrate the differences just as they had agreed in

Continued on Page Twenty-six

17 Perish as Fire Sweeps 42d Street Lodging House

Scores Hurt in 'Bowery-Type' Building Disaster, Worst of Its Kind Here in Years—Many Trapped Asleep

Sixteen bodies had been removed last night from a five-story brick structure at 437-439 West Forty-second Street, between Ninth and Tenth Avenues, the four upper floors of which were occupied by a "Bowery-type" lodging house, after one of the city's worst fires in years virtually had consumed the entire interior.

A seventeenth victim died at 7:15 P. M. in Roosevelt Hospital, to which most of the score of injured were removed.

The actual loss of life probably never will be known. With most of the victims burned beyond recognition and in many cases nothing remaining but bones, the task of counting the dead and identifying them was proving almost impossible. Authorities, after checking for hours, could not even determine how many persons were in the building at the time of the fire. They were faced with the fact that the lodging house had beds in three-foot by six cubicles, separated by flimsy plywood partitions, and in hall-like dormitories "accommodating" 248 persons. It was said the beds were well filled with restaurant and other night workers.

The fire, believed to have smoldered for three hours, started at 2 P. M. as if set by a hundred torches. Trapped in their sleep many were burned to death in their "cells," rooms so tiny that a lodger had literally to crawl into bed through a special door on a central vertical hinge that folded to permit entry.

The victims groped through con-

Continued on Page Twenty-six

WLB PEACE OFFER WIRED STEEL UNION

Davis Tells Murray Retroactivity Can Be Reconsidered Within Wage Formula

Special to THE NEW YORK TIMES.

WASHINGTON, Dec. 24—William H. Davis, chairman of the War Labor Board, telegraphed today to Philip Murray, president of the CIO United Steel Workers, that if labor members of the board desired to reconsider their vote on the retroactive pay issue "the public members will favor such reconsideration."

But, while he indicated that a retroactive basis might be approved within the framework of the present ("Little Steel") wage stabilization formula, Mr. Davis stated in his message that the public members could not now determine "any question of retroactivity that might come up in any future change in the wage stabilization policy."

Presuming that any such future change would be applied to "all wage-earners," he wrote that retroactivity in general or in particular cases might be decided when and if the change is made.

[A production stoppage was reported early this morning by The Associated Press with the expiration of contracts at midnight covering 35,000 employes at the Republic Steel Corporation and Youngstown Sheet and Tube Company. At these plants in Youngstown and in Cleveland picketing began.]

"Misunderstanding" Deplored

Mr. Davis' telegram said:

"You are quoted as saying that the proposal of the public members of the War Labor Board as to retroactivity in the steel negotiations violates principles enunciated by the board in the recent cases affecting hundreds of thousands of workers, that the proposal of the

Continued on Page Twenty-six

CITY AN OPEN HOUSE FOR WARTIME YULE

Heart-Warming Parties for Service Men and Women Are Chief Among Festivities

New York was far from a big, cold, gray city as it ushered in its third wartime Christmas last night with heart-warming church services, gay parties, gifts for the ill and unfortunate, and messages of good-will that brought cheer to its teeming millions and to the men and women visitors in the services.

It will not be a white Christmas, according to the weather man, but it will be cold.

Tens of thousands of visitors, many of them members of the families of service men, were in the city for the week-end. Railroads, doing a peak business, were handicapped by the bitter cold in the surrounding country. Virtually every train to and from the city was loaded to capacity, with standees in the aisles. Because of the cold, many trains were late.

Grand Central Terminal and the Pennsylvania Station were packed. Policemen kept the crowds moving. Buses and bus terminals throughout the city did a land-office business, too.

Stores Experience Let-Up

Only in the stores did Christmas Eve bring a let-up. While business was brisk, the real crush had subsided and only last-minute shoppers were on hand.

The churches of all faiths welcomed the Holy Day with midnight services, offering prayers for a victorious peace. There were many men in uniform at masses, carol services and communion.

Virtually every Roman Catholic church celebrated a midnight mass by permission of Archbishop Francis J. Spellman. Episcopal churches celebrated communion, while many churches of other faiths held can-

Continued on Page Nine

Biggest of War Plants Will Make Army Bomber Engines at Chicago

By The United Press.

CHICAGO, Dec. 24—The country's largest war plant, a series of structures sprawling over 500 acres of land, was ready today to turn out an unending stream of engines for Army bombing planes.

The giant inland plant on Chicago's South Side was built by the Dodge division of the Chrysler Corporation. Willow Run could be set down in the main building with enough room left to lay out twenty baseball diamonds.

There are nineteen buildings in the plant, all ready for production. The main building, the machining-assembly unit, covers eighty-two acres.

The plant has fourteen cafeterias and kitchens, butcher shops and bakeries to feed employes.

A parking lot a mile and a quarter long will accommodate 14,000 automobiles. The interplant communication system has 500 miles of telephone lines. Utility services are sufficient for a city of 75,000 population.

Officials revealed that the machine shops had been turning out parts for 2,200-horsepower, eighteen-cylinder Wright engines.

The plant, already called "Hitler's headache," will employ more than 25,000 persons when it enters mass production.

Prior to the completion of the Chicago plant, the bomber factory owned by the Government and operated by Henry Ford at Willow Run, twenty-five miles from Detroit, was called the largest war production unit in the world. It covers two square miles.

RECORD AIR BLOW

'Forts,' Liberators and Medium Bombers Rock 'Special' Targets

ALL CRAFT RETURN

RAF Pounds the German Capital With 1,120 Tons Before Dawn

By DAVID ANDERSON
By Cable to THE NEW YORK TIMES.

LONDON, Dec. 24—The greatest number of American heavy bombers ever to take off from Britain attacked "special military installations" of the Germans along the coast of northern France today as part of record operations of probably 3,000 Allied warplanes across the Channel.

Before dawn hundreds of the most powerful bombers of the Royal Air Force struck Berlin again with more than 1,120 tons of high explosives and fire missiles.

Several features of this two-fisted battering by the Allied air forces on the eve of Christmas made the day a memorable one for the enemy, even taking into account the Anglo-American achievements of recent weeks.

Headquarters of the United States Eighth Air Force announced that 1,300 planes handled by American crews took part in the daylight missions.

An even greater number of RAF, Dominion and Allied planes were out. Every one of the bombers and fighters of the joint forces returned to its base, according to a communiqué issued by headquarters of the United States Army here and the British Air Ministry.

Included in the American force were the largest formations of Flying Fortresses and Liberators ever sent into the air. Since an estimated 750 United States "heavies" at one time have attacked targets in western Germany within the past month, the day's operations entailed the use of close to, if not exceeding, 800 four-motored bombers.

The most concentrated attacks were carried out in the Pas-de-Ca-

Continued on Page Three

TO KEEP IT BY ARMS

President Says 4 Nations Agree on This for as Long as Necessary

'COST MAY BE HIGH'

German Might Must End, He Says on Air, Warning 'Japs' of Bad News

The text of the President's address appears on Page 8.

By JOHN H. CRIDER
Special to THE NEW YORK TIMES.

HYDE PARK, N. Y., Dec. 24—President Roosevelt promised the country and the world this Christmas Eve that they could look for insured peace with "certainty," even though "the cost may be high and the time long," and said that the United States, Great Britain, Soviet Russia and China were agreed to use force to maintain that peace "for as long as it may be necessary."

Speaking from the study in the Franklin D. Roosevelt Library, one of his favorite rendezvous, with his family gathered informally around him, the President gave his first comprehensive report on his recent conferences in the Middle East over the most extensive broadcast facilities ever set up in this country.

For the first time the President tempered his "unconditional surrender" ultimatum of Casablanca by stating that the United Nations did not want to enslave the German people but wanted them to have "a normal chance to develop in peace as useful and respectable members of the European family."

Here appeared to be one of the great achievements of the conference at Teheran—a united view by the Allies in Europe on what kind of a post-war Germany they would look for, which closes the gulf which appeared to exist between the Anglo-American "unconditional surrender" demand, and the more hopeful outlook for the future which the Russians have been

Continued on Page Eight

War News Summarized

SATURDAY, DECEMBER 25, 1943

President Roosevelt proudly announced to the world yesterday the appointment of General Dwight D. Eisenhower as supreme commander of the Anglo-American invasion forces—a selection, he said, that was made at the Teheran conference, where every point concerning the impending east-west-south attack on Germany had been decided.

It was announced from London that General Wilson would succeed General Eisenhower as commander of the Allied forces in the Mediterranean theatre; that General Montgomery would be chief of British Army units under General Eisenhower; that General Alexander would head the Allied forces in Italy, and that General Spaatz would be American Air Force commander against Germany. [All the foregoing, 1:8.]

Peace is certain, but the cost of bringing it about will be high and the realization may be distant, President Roosevelt declared during the Christmas Eve broadcast from his Hyde Park home. He said the United Nations had no desire to enslave the German people but wanted them to develop as respectable members of the European family. As for Japan, he said that empire is being enveloped in a band of steel and there is plenty of bad news for the Japanese in the offing. [1:5.]

Speaking from the German-surrounded Vatican, Pope Pius XII made a plea for a just peace and declared that a normal measure of power and the employment of force were needed to achieve it, but he decried any harsh imposition supported by arms alone. [1:6-7.]

An estimated 3,000 American and British planes of virtually all types—the greatest concentration in air history—bombed the Pas-de-Calais area of France, where, it is believed, the Germans have implanted rocket guns. In this, the fifth straight assault on these targets, the American Eighth Air Force sent 1,300 planes, a record number for any single operation. All Allied planes returned. The attack followed a Royal Air Force blow at Berlin, reportedly hitting the southeast industrial area near Tempelhof. [1:4, map P. 3.]

The fortified town of Gorodok, seventeen miles from Vitebsk and on the Vitebsk-Nevel railroad, was successfully stormed by the Russian Army, which drove ahead to capture sixty other places. Southwest of Zhlobin, in southern White Russia, large German tank and infantry attacks were beaten back. [1:7, map, P. 5.]

The British Eighth Army captured Vezzani, three miles southwest of the Adriatic port of Ortona, where fighting continued in the streets. There was little activity except for patrol thrusts on the Fifth Army front, because of deep mud. Medium Allied bombers struck at the Riviera coast, hitting bridges, railroads and viaducts. [1:6-7.]

Cape Gloucester, which seems to be shaping up as another possible invasion point on New Britain Island, was hit by 300 more tons of Allied aerial bombs, bringing the total tonnage dropped since Dec. 1 to 2,500. [6:1.]

The Navy announced that the United States submarine Grayling was presumably lost with her complement of sixty-five men. [6:2.]

NEW INVASION COMMANDER IN CHIEF

Gen. Dwight D. Eisenhower
The New York Times, 1943

Pope Prays for Just Peace Kept by Wise Use of Force

By The Associated Press.

LONDON, Dec. 24—Praying that this may be the last war Christmas and that a truly Christian peace may be celebrated in the coming year, Pope Pius XII today called for the world's responsible leaders to check the instincts of hate and vengeance and give rise to "the resplendent dawn of a new spirit of world union."

The text of the Pope's address appears on Page 10.

Raising his voice to a vibrant ring in outlining "the principles for a peace program," the Pontiff called for a "normal measure of power," sanctions and "the employment of force" to achieve and maintain peace, but warned that true peace "can never be a harsh imposition supported by arms" alone.

"An hour like the present—so full of possibilities for vast beneficent progress no less than for fatal defects and blunders—has perhaps never been seen in the history of mankind," said the Holy Father, who spoke on Christmas Eve from the bayonet-circled Vatican, where he has been isolated except by radio since the Germans occupied Rome in September.

The 35-minute address was delivered on the radio in Italian, but an official English language translation later was made available.

Juridical Basis for Peace

"A true peace is not the mathematical result of a proportion of forces, but in its last and deepest meaning is a moral and juridical process," said the Pope, speaking from what he called the "abysmal ruins of this terrible war."

"It (peace) is not, in fact, achieved without the employment of force, and its very existence

Continued on Page Ten

RED ARMY TAKES KEY TO VITEBSK

Gorodok, 17 Miles From Goal, Falls After Russian Feint Outwits Nazi Defense

By The Associated Press.

LONDON, Saturday, Dec. 25—The Russian Baltic Army cracked a model German defense-in-depth line and captured the heavily fortified lake town of Gorodok, seventeen miles north of Vitebsk yesterday, sweeping on over 2,000 German dead in a continuing offensive to take sixty more towns and hamlets, Moscow announced early today.

Resuming their drive after a two-day slow-down, the Russians swept to within fifteen miles of the Vitebsk-Polotsk rail line, an important east-west supply artery for the Germans, as they advanced southward along the Nevel-Vitebsk railroad.

In another fighting area to the south—southwest of Zhlobin—the

Continued on Page Five

8th Army Wins Town Near Ortona; Americans Take a Hill, Lose One

By MILTON BRACKER
By Wireless to THE NEW YORK TIMES.

ALGIERS, Dec. 24—The Allied armies in Italy kept up pressure all along the line yesterday despite the imminence of Christmas, but were unable quite to complete the capture of Ortona or accomplish substantial gains on the Tyrrhenian half of the front.

Although Canadian units of Gen. Sir Bernard L. Montgomery's Eighth Army had driven back the last German defenders of Ortona to the northwest corner of the shell-blasted and tank-razed town, the defenders kept returning fire and apparently intended to deprive the Allies of the full use of the most important port immediately below Pescara as long as possible.

Evidence of the toll the Germans have been paying for their desperate defense of the area was the discovery of a new cemetery at the crossroads just southwest of Ortona with at least 100 German graves.

The Eighth Army did manage to wrest from the enemy another village three miles southwest of Ortona and a mile beyond the Ortona-Orsogna road. It was Vezzani, which is three and a half miles from the coast and, like Ortona, just about twelve from Pescara. Other units of General Montgomery's veteran army have also penetrated to the outskirts of Villa Grande, a mile northeast of Vezzani on a secondary road paralleling the coast.

On the Fifth Army front the

Continued on Page Three

GENERAL IS SHIFTED

Choice of 'Big 3' Parley, He Has Montgomery as British Field Leader

WILSON IS SUCCESSOR

Mid-East Head Honored—Spaatz to Direct U. S. Air Strategy

Special to THE NEW YORK TIMES.

HYDE PARK, N. Y., Dec. 24—President Roosevelt announced today the appointment of Gen. Dwight D. Eisenhower to lead the invasion of Europe from the north and west, and from London came word that Gen. Sir Bernard L. Montgomery of North African fame would head the British troops under General Eisenhower to form a proved and hard-hitting team to lead the assault on Adolf Hitler's "Fortress Europe."

The President's announcement of General Eisenhower's selection at the recent Teheran conference to lead the main attack against Germany also set to rest the old rumors regarding the probable appointment of Gen. George C. Marshall, Army Chief of Staff, to that post.

The President, in his radio report today on the recent conferences at Teheran and Cairo, also named Lieut. Gen. Carl A. Spaatz as commander of "the entire American strategic bombing force operating against Germany."

This was taken to mean that while General Eisenhower will confine his command to the mass attack on Europe from the north and west, General Spaatz' command over all American strategic bombardment of Germany extends to operations against Germany from all neighboring bases.

Quashes Marshall Rumors

The President gave a vivid picture in his radio report of complete agreement between Prime Minister Churchill, Premier Stalin and himself regarding a detailed program for the annihilation of Germany by land and air from all directions.

He also paid high tribute to General Marshall, presumably to set old rumors at rest. Some persons have argued that the position to be occupied by General Eisenhower is of greatest importance, but the official decision now revealed seems to give credence to the opinion that the most important position in the Army is that of Chief of Staff, just as Washington is the only place from which the whole global operation can be commanded.

"To the members of our armed forces, to their wives, mothers and fathers, I want to affirm the great faith and confidence that we have in General Marshall and Admiral King (Chief of Naval Operations), who direct all of our armed might throughout the world," the President declared.

Their Military Genius Stressed

"Upon them," he said, "falls the responsibility of planning the strategy; of determining where and when to fight. Both of these men have already gained high places in American history; places which will record in that history many evidences of their military genius that cannot be published today."

The announcement from London told not only of General Montgomery's appointment to head the British invasion forces under General Eisenhower but also of Gen. Sir Henry Maitland Wilson's appointment to replace General Eisenhower as commander of the Mediterranean Theatre and Gen. Sir Harold R. L. G. Alexander's appointment to command all Allied forces in Italy.

The Teheran military decision announced by the President proved as much as anything else that the American handling of the invasion of North Africa and of Italy had deeply impressed the United States allies. Those invasions may now be regarded as the testing phase of the main European invasion, since the American officers identi-

Continued on Page Two

"All the News That's Fit to Print."

The New York Times.

LATE CITY EDITION
Cloudy and mild with moderate winds today; colder tonight.
Temperatures Yesterday—Max.,51; Min.,37
Sunrise, 8:19 A. M.; Sunset, 3:56 P. M.

Copyright, 1943, by The New York Times Company.

VOL. XCIII..No. 31,384. Entered as Second-Class Matter, Postoffice, New York, N. Y. NEW YORK, TUESDAY, DECEMBER 28, 1943. THREE CENTS NEW YORK CITY

ARMY SEIZES RAILROADS ON PRESIDENT'S ORDER; PAY RISE TO 2 UNIONS; STEEL MEN ORDERED BACK; MARINES GAIN IN NEW LANDINGS IN NEW BRITAIN

ISLAND TIP GRIPPED

Americans Push on Cape Gloucester Air Strip From 2 Beachheads

LOSSES ARE LIGHT

Navy Guns and Bombers Pave Way—Foe Loses 61 Planes to Our 7

By Wireless to THE NEW YORK TIMES.

ADVANCED ALLIED HEADQUARTERS IN NEW GUINEA, Dec. 27—United States Marines, many of them heroes of Guadalcanal, have landed at two points around Cape Gloucester, New Britain, and occupied Long Island, at the entrance to Vitiaz Strait, following a cruiser and destroyer bombardment and a blasting by 300 tons of aerial bombs.

The Japanese, hurling in their reserve air power in a desperate attempt to block a movement giving the Allies a hold in western New Britain near Rabaul, lost sixty-one planes—thirty-six bombers and twenty-five fighters—against a loss of seven American planes.

[The Marines have pushed inland from their beachheads established in the invasion of Cape Gloucester, Gen. Douglas MacArthur announced, according to The Associated Press.]

One American ship was lost and others sustained minor damage from near misses, but our firm hold on the beachheads was unbroken.

Admiral William F. Halsey's South Pacific Air Forces bombed Rabaul, New Britain, and Kavieng, New Ireland, in conjunction with the movement, so as to help neutralize enemy air power.

The movement, under the command of Gen. Douglas MacArthur and Lieut. Gen. Walter Krueger, with Rear Admiral Daniel Barbey commanding the task force, and Maj. Gen. W. H. Rupertus the landing force, was most difficult, since it was necessary to "round the corner" of New Britain into supposed enemy waters.

Both American and Australian naval vessels participated in the action. How the enemy will react from Truk to the growing threat to Rabaul remains to be seen.

Air Strip Under Fire

ADVANCED ALLIED HEADQUARTERS IN NEW GUINEA, Tuesday, Dec. 28 (AP)—American marines have pushed inland from their beachheads established in the invasion of Cape Gloucester, New Britain, Gen. Douglas MacArthur announced today.

The battle-hardened Leathernecks, veterans of Guadalcanal, who made the beachheads east and west of the cape, on the northwest tip of this vital Japanese defense island, have established the first Allied hold on the inside of the gigantic "C" formed by curving New Britain and New Ireland Island.

Moving with but little opposition into the jungle hinterland of Cape Gloucester, the marines put the enemy air strip there and Borgen Bay to the east under artillery fire.

The principal Japanese opposition was encountered at Target Hill, which had been heavily pounded by Allied planes as the invasion got under way. Light and medium tanks were thrown into the advance here.

The landings were made in coordinated land, sea and air operations east and west of Cape Gloucester, which had been pulverized by some 3,500 tons of bombs since Dec. 1.

Several enemy counter-attacks in the air, directed at the beachheads and at shipping from which large forces were pouring ashore, were crushed.

The additional occupation of New Britain, the second within a fortnight, strengthens the Allied hold on the western end of the island, General MacArthur said, and "presages growing command of Bismarck Sea approaches."

One landing was made just north of Silimati Point on Borgen Bay

Continued on Page Five

AMERICANS TAKE NEW BITE INTO PACIFIC ISLAND

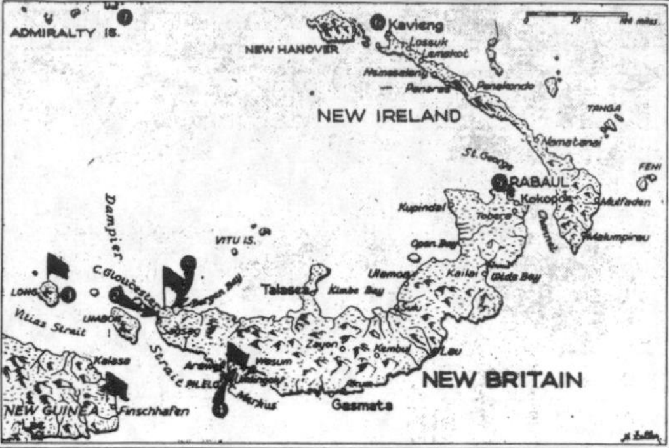

Marines made two landings around Cape Gloucester. The principal operation was conducted on the western shore of Borgen Bay (1) and a subsidiary one took place west of the cape (2). Simultaneously, marines occupied Long Island (3), dominating Vitiaz Strait. The landings at Cape Gloucester give the Americans a second foothold on New Britain—the first is in the Arawe area (4), where our troops were reported today to have repulsed attacks. The footholds threaten enemy lines to Rabaul (5) and, according to General MacArthur, soon will put Kavieng (6) and the Admiralty Islands (7) within reach of our land-based air power.

Marines Hit Shore Cheering In Cape Gloucester Attack

By FRANK L. KLUCKHOHN

By Wireless to THE NEW YORK TIMES.

WITH U. S. MARINES ON NEW BRITAIN, Dec. 26 (Delayed)—The thin line of green-clad men that has been creeping up the ridge of Target Hill has reached the top, planted a mortar and opened fire beyond. We can see this with our field glasses: It is noon and snipers' bullets are zinging near us, but we have taken the controlling hill.

The marines, many of them heroes of Guadalcanal, are finally ashore at Cape Gloucester and "round the corner" of New Britain, in one of the biggest landings of the Pacific war.

Already, several miles away, our artillery is pounding the vital Cape Gloucester air strip which soon will be in our hands, giving us control of the air over Rabaul.

Into the blinding, suffocating pall of black smoke from the booming guns of our big ships and the heavy bombs of our planes, the hard-bitten, youthful veterans moved in cheering to deliver another smashing blow at the already trembling Japanese arch protecting the key Truk base.

At 7:45 A. M. Christmas Day at home, they leaped waist deep into the surging, tepid water on three beaches and then hit the lush, spongy, jungle shore.

A mighty naval and aerial bombardment had sheered the palm trees, we found, and forced the Japanese to abandon their thick-roofed blockhouses right on the beach. But the truth is that Gen. Douglas MacArthur had outguessed the Japanese again by sending his forces ashore at the one area in the whole of much-bombed and heavily garrisoned Cape Gloucester where the reefs and shoals had made the enemy believe we could not land.

But the American Navy, venturing boldly into "enemy-dominated waters," achieved the impossible in

Continued on Page Five

EISENHOWER SURE OF VICTORY IN 1944

Allies' Triumph in Europe Near, He Says, Invoking All-Out Aid From Home Front

By MILTON BRACKER

By Wireless to THE NEW YORK TIMES.

ALGIERS, Dec. 27—Gen. Dwight D. Eisenhower, who is about to assume the most important command in American military history as leader of the Allied invasion forces from the west, predicted confidently at his farewell press conference here today that the Allies would win the European war in 1944.

"The only thing needed for us to win the European war in 1944," he added presently, "is for every man and woman all the way from the front line to the remotest hamlet of our two countries [the United States and England] to do his or her full duty."

As for his own share in the gigantic task, the conqueror of Tunisia, Sicily and southern Italy went on:

"My own and personal job immediately, of course, will be to do what we have done here. That is to weld the directing team together in such way that no real friction ever develops, that people

Continued on Page Three

Tedder Named Eisenhower Aide; Briton Called Top Air Tactician

By FREDERICK GRAHAM

By Cable to THE NEW YORK TIMES.

LONDON, Tuesday, Dec. 28—Air Chief Marshal Sir Arthur Tedder, who furnished and directed the air warfare lightning that as much as any other single thing made possible Gen. Sir Bernard L. Montgomery's drive from El Alamein to Italy, was named deputy supreme commander, under Gen. Dwight D. Eisenhower, of the Allies' invasion force in an announcement issued today from 10 Downing Street.

The appointment of Marshal Tedder, a wiry, pipe-smoking little Scot who not only defeated the Luftwaffe on the wing and on the ground, but helped keep Field Marshal Gen. Erwin Rommel's ground army on the run across the top of Africa, was most significant because it is the first time the Allies had given so high a place in so important a task to an air commander.

In the same announcement from 10 Downing Street it was made public that Gen. Sir Bernard Paget had been named commander in chief in the Middle East under Gen. Sir Henry Maitland Wilson, supreme Allied commander in the Mediterranean theatre. General Paget is an infantryman. He assumed command of the home forces on Christmas Day in 1941 and had a part in training the many men who will invade the Continent.

A graduate of the Royal Naval Staff College and Imperial Defense College, General Paget, who is 55

Continued on Page Three

CONVOY UNHARMED IN ARCTIC BATTLE

Nazis, in Losing Scharnhorst, Did Only Minor Damage to Two British Warships

By Cable to THE NEW YORK TIMES.

LONDON, Dec. 27—In the Arctic Sea battle in which the German battleship Scharnhorst was sunk last evening the Allied convoy escorted by the British Home Fleet units that sent the Nazi vessel down, was untouched and only two British warships received "minor damage," the Admiralty announced tonight.

"It is not yet possible to give a detailed account of the action in which the German battleship Scharnhorst was sunk," the Admiralty said. "It can, however, be stated that the convoy was unmolested and only minor damage was sustained by two of His Majesty's ships."

This statement contradicted German official accounts asserting

Continued on Page Three

RUSSIANS DRIVE ON

Smash to Within 18 Miles of Zhitomir West of Kiev

VITEBSK LINE IS CUT

Germans Say 500,000 Men, 1,000 Tanks Are in Ukraine Push

By The United Press.

LONDON, Tuesday, Dec. 28—Russian troops, expanding their winter offensive on two fronts, smashed fourteen miles through the tottering German lines west of Kiev yesterday to move within eighteen miles of the Zhitomir railway junction, while in White Russia they tightened a siege arc around Vitebsk by cutting the Vitebsk-Polotsk railroad.

Gen. Nikolai F. Vatutin's First Ukraine Army, estimated by the Germans to have 500,000 men and 1,000 tanks, killed more than 4,000 Germans and destroyed or captured fifty-five tanks in tank and infantry battles as it captured more than 100 towns and villages for a five-day total of 250 in drives toward German railway lines in the central Ukraine.

In all of yesterday's fighting more than 6,600 Germans were killed and eighty-three tanks destroyed or captured on three fronts, where nearly 1,000,000 Russian troops were in action.

Gain 14 Miles in 24 Hours

Moscow's broadcast communiqués announced that General Vatutin's men, advancing west and southwest along a twenty-mile front, captured the town of Ivnitsa, eighteen miles southeast of Zhitomir for a gain of fourteen miles northwestward from Verbov in twenty-four hours. At the southern end of that front they swept into Vcheraishe twenty-four miles east of the Berdichev railway junction and 135 miles northeast of the prewar Rumanian border.

Using the Fastov junction, thirty miles southwest of Kiev, as a base, General Vatutin's men are driving northwest to Zhitomir along the Fastov-Zhitomir railroad and southwest toward Berdichev and the near-by junction of Kazatin along the Kiev-Zhmerinka railroad.

Continued on Page Two

War News Summarized

TUESDAY, DECEMBER 28, 1943

United States Marines under Maj. Gen. William H. Rupertus swarmed on to the western end of New Britain Sunday and established beachheads on either side of Cape Gloucester. One landing place was north of Silimati Point, on Borgen Bay, and the other was on Dampier Strait, west of Cape Gloucester. Long Island, at the northwest entrance to Vitiaz Strait separating New Britain from New Guinea, was also occupied.

The landings were accomplished with "practically no loss, either in ships, planes or men," General MacArthur reported. But the Japanese lost at least sixty-one planes in a delayed attack on the beachheads. Yesterday the marines pushed inland, occupying Target Hill and bringing the Cape Gloucester airfield under artillery fire. [All the foregoing 1:1.]

Marines, cheering as they went ashore, quickly reached the top of Target Hill and laid down a mortar barrage. [1:2-3.]

Russian forces west of Kiev gained fourteen miles and captured more than 100 places as they drove toward Zhitomir. They were only eighteen miles from that city and threatened the strategic railway between Zhitomir and Berdichev. In the Vitebsk area the Red Army cut the railroad to Polotsk. [1:5; map, P. 2.]

Heavy rains continued to dog the Allied soldiers in Italy, but Indian troops of the Eighth Army captured Villa Grande, and the Fifth Army took two more important hills around Mount Sammucro. [3:6.]

General Eisenhower predicted at his final press conference in Algiers that the Allies would win the war in Europe in 1944 if everyone at home as well as at the front did his full duty. Every available ship, plane and man will be let loose on Germany at the proper time, he added. [1:2.]

Air Chief Marshal Sir Arthur Tedder, head of the Allied air forces in the Mediterranean, was named General Eisenhower's deputy commander for the invasion from Britain. [1:2-3.]

Details of the battle in which the German battleship Scharnhorst was sunk were still lacking, but the British announced that the convoy had gone through unmolested and that two of their warships had suffered minor damage. [1:4.]

Recognition of the new regime in Bolivia has been deferred by the United States until all the American republics lined up against the Axis can consult together. [7:1.]

Secretary of War Stimson took over the nation's railroads at 7 o'clock last night, one hour after President Roosevelt had signed an order designed to halt the strike called for Thursday. Mr. Roosevelt said he had to act promptly to assure "the successful prosecution of the war" and pointed out that any strike would be a strike against the Government. Earlier the nonoperating unions had accepted the President's arbitration offer. [1:8.] President Murray of the CIO called off the steel strike after the WLB reversed its "retroactive pay" ruling. [1:6-7.]

WLB Reverses Pay Ruling Under Roosevelt Steel Plan

Board Lifts Its Ban on Retroactive Wage Adjustments Sought by Union—Murray Calls Off the Tie-Up

By C. P. TRUSSELL

Special to THE NEW YORK TIMES.

WASHINGTON, Dec. 27 — With 170,000 workers remaining away from their posts at vital steel producing centers in seven States in the face of President Roosevelt's urgent appeal for continued uninterrupted production pending the writing of new contracts, the labor members of the National War Labor Board reversed an eight-to-four vote of the board of Dec. 22 which, in its effect, would have denied retroactive wage readjustments under the formula demanded by the unions.

Thus, by another vote of 8 to 4, the board concurred in the proposal of the President, in his Sunday night communications to the steel workers and management, that any wage changes made according to settlement procedures under the no-strike agreement and existing law and executive order be computed and applied retroactively to the dates of expiration of the old contracts.

The reversal was started by the labor members, headed by John Brophy, after Philip Murray, president of the United Steel Workers of America, CIO, had taken measures to get or keep about 350,000 workers, covered by contracts which expired Christmas Eve, on their jobs. At the special night session of the WLB, called for 7 o'clock, Mr. Brophy read into the record a telegram which Mr. Murray had dispatched four hours earlier to the directors and representatives of the international union.

The Murray message said:

"In accordance with telegram of the President of the United States addressed me yesterday, I am directing you to urge upon the members of your organization the need of continuing uninterrupted the production of steel and steel products essential to the war needs of our nation. This is in conform-

Continued on Page Ten

Rail Job Bias Case Certified To President by the FEPC

Special to THE NEW YORK TIMES.

WASHINGTON, Dec. 27—The President's Committee on Fair Employment Practice called on President Roosevelt today to enforce its orders for sixteen Southeastern railroads and seven unions to cease discrimination in the employment and promotion of Negroes. Three of the unions and the carriers have defied the committee's authority to issue such orders.

Representative Howard W. Smith, Democrat, of Virginia, announced that he had started an investigation to determine whether the committee had gone beyond its authority in ordering war industries and unions in a number of instances to cease discrimination against employes because of race, creed, color or national origin.

Case Reviewed by Ross

In announcing that the committee was certifying the railroad jobs case to President Roosevelt, Chairman Malcolm Ross told a press conference that the Brotherhood of Firemen and Enginemen, the International Association of Machinists and the Order of Railway Conductors had challenged the authority of the committee to proceed against them, while the other four unions had ignored the committee's order, issued Nov. 30, which gave the railroads and the unions thirty days to cease discriminatory practices.

On Dec. 13 the Southeastern railroads, in a joint reply to the order, refused to comply on grounds that the committee had no constitutional or legal authority to act. Six other railroads did not join in defying the committee, and Mr. Ross said that conversations between them and the committee were proceeding in an effort at settlement of the issues involved in the order.

The possibility of executive

Continued on Page Eight

COAL DEALERS SEE 'TRAGIC' SITUATION

Must Get Relief in 2 Weeks, They Assert—Unable to Fill 300 City-Certified Orders

By JEFFERSON G. BELL

The full implications of New York City's desperate coal shortage became evident yesterday, when dealers reported their inability to supply coal covered by 300 applications for emergency deliveries certified by the Department of Health. Last week Mayor La Guardia described the coal shortage as "very bad."

Only the mild weather in this area saved widespread suffering, according to dealers, who declared that the situation would become "tragic" within two weeks unless more coal is routed here by the Solid Fuel Administration, headed by Secretary Harold L. Ickes.

The Department of Health reported that it had received in the twenty-four hours ending at 4 P.M. yesterday 1,262 complaints of "no heat," of which 121 had been forwarded to coal dealers for emergency deliveries.

Dealers reported that they no longer were able to give priority to

Continued on Page Thirty-four

'Emergency' to Be Declared Jan. 1 To Give Firemen More Work, Pay

Fire Commissioner Patrick Walsh disclosed yesterday that he would declare a state of emergency in the Fire Department, effective at 12.01 A. M., Jan. 1, under which firemen will be required to work three extra eight-hour tours every twenty days and thus qualify for a $420 annual cost-of-living bonus.

"We've got to do it," he declared. "We're running short of men. We have to protect the city, and we can't protect the city without declaring an emergency."

Scarcely an hour earlier Police Commissioner Lewis J. Valentine said there would be no action, at least until Jan. 13, on a proposal for an identical cost-of-living bonus and longer working hours for men in his department.

He revealed that he had under consideration two plans for stepping up working hours and would reach no decision until after scheduled meetings of the Patrolmen's Benevolent Association on Jan. 11 and the board of trustees of the Police Pension Fund on Jan. 13.

These statements from the commissioners came after the two men had been in conference with Mayor La Guardia earlier in the day. Before they disclosed their plans a note was sent by newspaper men to the Mayor asking if an emergency would be declared. In reply he scrawled across the note: "Gedult," a Yiddish corruption of the German word meaning "patience."

Later, when confronted with the varying program of his commissioners as he prepared to leave City Hall, he was again terse and

Continued on Page Eleven

WAR IS PUT FIRST

Roosevelt Says He Must Make Sure Troops Get Goods Without Halt

MORE UNIONS YIELD

But Action Is Offset as 3 Keep Strike Plan—Somervell at Helm

Texts of the statements on the rail situation, Page 8.

By LOUIS STARK

Special to THE NEW YORK TIMES.

WASHINGTON, Dec. 27—President Roosevelt ordered Secretary of War Henry L. Stimson at 6 P. M. today to take over all railroads in the continental United States at 7 P. M., despite assurances at 5 P. M. that the fifteen nonoperating unions were canceling their notices for a strike Dec. 30 and were ready to have him arbitrate the amount they were to receive for overtime pay.

The President, however, declared that he could not wait "until the last moment to take action to see that the supplies to our fighting men are not interrupted."

He said that he was taking over the railroads because the nonoperating employes, numbering 1,100,000, did not agree with the carriers "upon the scope of the issues to be arbitrated by the President." Strike orders of three operating brotherhoods, the firemen, conductors and switchmen, were still in force.

Lieut. Gen. Brehon B. Somervell, commanding the Army Service Forces, was designated by Secretary Stimson to take over the railroads in conformity with the Presidential order.

Operating Chief Named

Directly responsible for operating the roads under General Somervell will be Maj. Gen. C. P. Gross, Chief of Transportation, Army Service Forces.

Mr. Stimson also announced that the Army officials would have the advice of Martin W. Clement, president of the Pennsylvania Railroad, as well as the staff of the Association of American Railroads.

An offer to act as labor consultants is being made by Mr. Stimson to A. F. Whitney, president of the Brotherhood of Railroad Trainmen, and Alvanley Johnston, president of the Brotherhood of Locomotive Engineers. These two brotherhoods accepted President Roosevelt's wage arbitration offer last week and canceled their strike orders.

The President's arbitration award was announced today. It granted to the trainmen and engineers 5 cents an hour for work in excess of forty hours a week, or in lieu of claims for expenses while away from home.

Increase Is 9 Cents an Hour

Added to the 4 cents an hour previously awarded to the operating unions by a Presidential board, the President's award makes a total wage increase of 9 cents an hour, which gives to the trainmen and engineers increases aggregating $81,000,000 a year.

The President also ruled that these two unions were entitled to a vacation of one week a year with pay at the basic hourly rate of employment. The wage increases, according to the Presidential announcement, shall remain in effect until the end of the war.

Seizure of the railroads appeared to have been averted when the fifteen nonoperating unions sent a letter to the President advising him they were ready to abandon their repeated refusal to accept a sliding scale of wage increases of 4 to 10 cents an hour and were willing to have him arbitrate what they were entitled to for overtime after forty hours a week.

The President had stated on June 16 at a press conference and had repeated several times that there was no justification for railroad workers not being paid time and a half after forty hours.

The heads of the brotherhoods of firemen, conductors and switchmen, who rejected the Presidential

Continued on Page Nine

1944

1944

During the fighting for the island of Saipan, a Navy corpsman administers blood plasma to a wounded Marine while another waits for treatment.

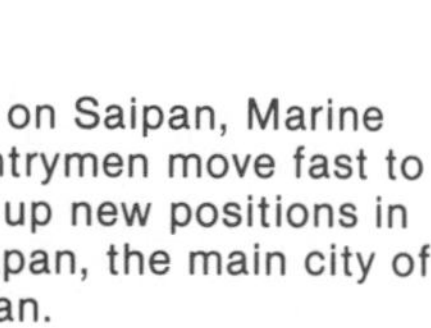

Also on Saipan, Marine infantrymen move fast to take up new positions in Garapan, the main city of Saipan.

"All the News That's Fit to Print."

The New York Times.

LATE CITY EDITION
Cloudy and mild with occasional rain today.
Temperatures Yesterday—Max., 61; Min., 34
Sunrise, 8:11 A. M.; Sunset, 6:07 P. M.

Copyright, 1944, by The New York Times Company.

VOL. XCIII..No. 31,415. Entered as Second-Class Matter, Postoffice, New York, N. Y. NEW YORK, FRIDAY, JANUARY 28, 1944. THREE CENTS IN NEW YORK CITY

5,200 AMERICANS, MANY MORE FILIPINOS DIE OF STARVATION, TORTURE AFTER BATAAN; ALLIES REPEL CRACK NAZI UNITS NEAR ROME

REPUBLICANS BACK VOTE BILL CHANGES AMID WARM DEBATE

Ball Measure Offered Senate Would Allow State Control Where Laws Conform

PARTISANSHIP BOILS OVER

Holman Call for Amendment to Bar Roosevelt From Race Assailed by Democrats

By C. P. TRUSSELL
Special to THE NEW YORK TIMES.

WASHINGTON, Jan. 27—With consideration of service men's voting procedure developing into spirited and at times bitter fourth-term debate in the wake of President Roosevelt's message to Congress yesterday, a compromise proposal was offered in the Senate today by Senator Joseph H. Ball, Republican, of Minnesota, under which the proposed Federal ballot would prevail to the extent that the States failed to meet specifications.

The measure gained immediate support in some Senate quarters, and brought evident encouragement of leaders of the fight against the pending Green-Lucas bill. Previously it had appeared that either an offer or acceptance of compromise was farthest from the Senatorial minds. Partisanship, boiling over from the first outbreaks that occurred with the receipt of the President's message, came boldly to the front again.

Boos from one section of the visitors' galleries and applause from another drew an admonition from Senator Hattie W. Caraway of Arkansas, who was presiding.

Would Bar a Fourth Term

Senator Rufus C. Holman, Republican, of Oregon, presented an amendment which would bar President Roosevelt as a candidate for a fourth term if he accepted the authority granted by the pending bill.

"It seems to me that the difficulty centers around the fact that the Commander in Chief of the Army is himself a candidate for the Presidency," Senator Holman said. "If he would eliminate himself from the advantageous or unfair position, I think debate on the pending bill would cease."

Senator Abe Murdock, Democrat, of Utah, in the course of a reply referred to Harrison E. Spangler, chairman of the Republican National Committee.

"I think it is the prayer in his heart and the prayer in the heart of every other good old stand-pat Republican in the United States today, and has been ever since 1932," he said, "that Franklin D. Roosevelt would eliminate himself from politics and give them at least a shadow of a chance to bring in the G. O. P. again.

"But I say to them today that in my opinion the American people, certainly the great mass of them, want Franklin Delano Roosevelt to continue as President of the United States, notwithstanding the prayer of Mr. Spangler. The American people still want Roosevelt to go on until unconditional surrender is brought about in Germany and Japan."

Senator Arthur H. Vandenberg, Republican, of Michigan, cut in: "I was wondering what connection there could be between this and the pending service men's voting legislation?"

"I admit," Mr. Murdock replied, "that there is not much connection."

"I thought there was not any," Mr. Vandenberg retorted, "but the Senator makes me begin to think that perhaps there is a connection."

Taft and Bridges Attacked

Senator Murdock blamed the Republicans, particularly Senators Robert A. Taft of Ohio and Styles Bridges of New Hampshire, who participated in yesterday's debate following receipt of the White House message, for injecting the President's name.

"Why can't we as Senators leave Roosevelt in the White House?" he asked. "Why can we not ignore the fact that under the Constitution he must continue as Commander in Chief of the armed forces until some other President succeeds him, and expedite action on the service men's vote?"

Senator Scott W. Lucas of Illinois, co-author of the Green-Lucas bill, interjected:

"The individual who raised all the hullabaloo about the fourth term was the senior Senator from Ohio (Mr. Taft). It was brought in in a most ignominious and blunt way by the Senator from Ohio, and the Senator from New Hampshire saw fit to question me with one

Continued on Page Ten

Sewer Masons Rob 'Safe' Paris Bank

By Telephone to THE NEW YORK TIMES.

BERNE, Switzerland, Jan. 27—Two Parisian masons have been arrested near Meaux outside of the French capital for "achieving the impossible" in robbing the vaults of the French National Bank in Paris of 25,000,000 francs in thousand-franc banknotes, according to an official statement issued tonight. Most of the stolen money was recovered.

Employed on repair work in a sewer in the neighborhood of the vaults, one of the men discovered he could remove some iron bars blocking one of the drains leading to the room in which freshly printed banknotes were stored. Investigating further, he discovered that the job of removing the money would need some assistance, so he enlisted the aid of his foreman.

When the new vaults were inaugurated in 1934 newspaper reporters who were shown some of the booby traps protecting France's wealth were told it was a "physical impossibility" to penetrate the vaults without encountering immediate death. But someone forgot a sewer pipe.

W. T. DEWART DIES; PRESIDENT OF SUN

Leader in Newspaper Field Here Succumbs at 68—Was Seriously Ill 3 Weeks

William T. Dewart, president and a principal owner of The Sun, long a leader in the newspaper publishing business, died at 8:30 o'clock last night at his home at 660 Park Avenue. He was 68 years old.

Mr. Dewart, who had been general manager of the newspaper since 1903, when he succeeded Erman J. Ridgway as chief executive of the far-flung interests of the late Frank A. Munsey, merchant, banker and publisher, had been in ill health for some time, but had been seriously ill only three weeks.

After Mr. Munsey's death in 1925 Mr. Dewart disclosed that it had been the late publisher's plan, during the last year of his life, to have his associates in the management of his newspapers, which included The New York Telegram as well as The Sun, to join him in the ownership of the properties.

Purchase Made in 1926

Mr. Dewart purchased The Sun in 1926, acting in behalf of himself and several associates in the conduct of the newspaper, from the residuary legatee under Mr. Munsey's will, the Metropolitan Museum of Art. The consideration was announced as $13,000,000, certain other properties being included in the sale, and arrangements were made to mutualize the ownership and to pay the museum in stated installments.

The Telegram was included in the group, but was disposed of in February, 1927, to the Scripps-Howard interests and later became The World-Telegram, merging with The Evening World. Mr. Dewart explained the sale by saying that "the growth of The Sun demands, so far as my newspaper interests are concerned, that I devote my time to one newspaper." He added that a similar system of mutualization applied to the Scripps-Howard papers.

Mr. Dewart had a varied business career before he joined the Munsey interests. He was of Scottish origin, his ancestors coming from Duart Castle, Isle of Mull, a Maclean Clan stronghold. His mother, whose maiden name was Jessie

Continued on Page Eighteen

A. E. F. OF 5 MILLION

Two-Thirds of the Army Will Be Abroad Jan. 1, Stimson Declares

MANY CAMPS TO CLOSE

Soldiers at Home a Year Will Be Examined for Overseas in Change to the Offensive

Special to THE NEW YORK TIMES.

WASHINGTON, Jan. 27—Two-thirds of the American Army representing a fighting force of 5,000,000 to 6,000,000 men will be overseas by Jan. 1, Secretary Stimson announced today.

The plan of the authorities, the Secretary of War told a press conference, involved a shift of personnel from the defensive to the offensive, from the continental United States to the world's battlefronts.

Mr. Stimson did not mention specific numbers, but latest data had set a goal of 7,700,000 men for the Army.

Under the new program the enlisted personnel in the United States will be carefully reviewed for physically fit, well-trained troops. The best men will be sent overseas and their places here taken by civilians, new recruits, members of the Women's Army Corps and soldiers who did not meet physical standards for duty abroad.

In addition, thousands of commissioned officers more than 38 years of age who are no longer needed by the Army will revert to inactive duty. Many of the training camps, Army posts and stations will be discontinued and put on "a caretaker basis."

Many Camps on Stand-By Basis

Secretary Stimson said that he had no idea how many enlisted men, officers or Army camps would be affected. The change, he stated, came as "an inevitable situation when you have a rapid expansion" of the Army, such as came when the war machine was being built up hurriedly.

Already the Army has put many of its training camps on a stand-by basis or announced that this would be done. About seventy Air Force establishments have been relinquished, and the ground forces have likewise closed some of their training centers.

Announcement of the new program means the end of the principal part of the training program and a concentration on the all-out offensive phase.

"The readjustments were dictated generally by the progressive shift of Army operations from the defensive to the offensive and by the growth of air power," Mr. Stimson remarked. "As of Dec. 31, 1943, approximately one-third of the Army's strength was overseas. By the end of this year it is contemplated that two-thirds of the Army will be overseas."

As the Army overseas movement became accelerated, activities at the home establishments would be curtailed "with sharp reductions in administrative and overhead personnel," he stated. With the Army no longer needing all of its existing troop-housing

Continued on Page Five

OPA Raises Meat 1 to 2 Points, Cuts Canned Vegetables 2 to 4

Special to THE NEW YORK TIMES.

WASHINGTON, Jan. 27—Point values for all twelve of the major canned vegetables are reduced two to four points, and in some cases more, in a new schedule for rationed foods, effective Sunday and expiring March 4, which the Office of Price Administration announced today. At the same time there are to be advances of one to two points on beef, lamb and veal, while pork, excepting loins, will be unchanged.

Butter stays at the January level of sixteen points a pound, but cheese gets a higher ration "cost."

Four canned fruit items are increased in point value and an equal number decreased.

In announcing the February schedule for processed foods, Chester Bowles, Price Administrator, said that "our food needs are as great this year as last" and that there was no justification for a "ration holiday" on tinned vegetables as canners had urged as a means of clearing stocks carried over from the previous pack.

Civilians, said Mr. Bowles, were receiving an allocation of 228,000,000 cases of canned foods from the 1943-44 production, slightly less than the 1942-43 allocation and substantially less than the 1941-42 civilian supply of 321,400,000 cases.

Canners retorted that Mr. Bowles failed to differentiate between canned fruit supplies, which are short, and canned vegetables in making his over-all statement as to allocations. They said also that

Continued on Page Twelve

Japanese Threaten To Sink Mercy Ships

Japan "is ready to take adequate measures in retaliation" against the "Anglo-American sinking of Japanese hospital ships," the Berlin radio said yesterday, quoting Mamoru Shigemitsu, Japanese Foreign Minister.

The German radio, as heard by NBC, said Shigemitsu had told the Diet that "Japan has protested many times against the Anglo-American sinking of Japanese hospital ships and so far no satisfactory answer has been given. Therefore Japan is now ready to take adequate measures in retaliation."

U. S. WILL DEVELOP OIL OF NEAR EAST

Government and Private Funds to Build Record Network of Lines to Mediterranean

By J. H. CARMICAL

With the United States Government actively participating, the biggest single development in the history of the oil industry is contemplated for the Middle East, it became known yesterday. Involving the construction of a network of pipe lines from the Persian Gulf area to Mediterranean ports and the erection of several new refineries, the cost is reckoned at several hundred millions of dollars and it is expected that from eighteen months to two years will be required for its completion.

The objective of the development is to increase the amount of oil available to the European area. Because of the time expected to elapse before its completion, although construction will start as soon as possible, it is considered more or less as a project for increasing the oil supply in the post-war period. With several private companies already holding the concessions, it will be a venture in which both private and Government capital will be used. Since other interests have laid the groundwork for this development, it is expected that the necessary funds for the expansion will be furnished almost entirely by the United States Government.

The project also would involve the establishment by the United States Government of a new policy in the development of foreign oil resources. Previously all such operations have been left to private capital. However, last July the United States Government formed the Petroleum Reserves Corporation to engage in the production of oil abroad. Harold L. Ickes, Secretary of the Interior, is president of the new company and several members of the Cabinet are directors.

U. S. Companies Hold Concessions

The oil exploitation in the Middle East really started after the close of the first World War. To obtain a source of oil for its navy, the British Government acquired a controlling interest in the Anglo-Iranian Oil Company, which held an oil concession in Iran. Then a group composed of United States, British, Netherlands and French interests obtained the important concession in Iraq. In recent years, the Standard Oil Company of California, the Texas Company and the Gulf Oil Corporation have acquired concessions in Saudi Arabia, the Island of Bahrein and Kuwait.

In just what manner these properties will be shuffled so that the Petroleum Reserves Corporation will obtain an interest was not made clear. So far its participation includes only the financing of the construction of a high-octane gasoline plant at Bahrein. However, for months the PRC has been attempting to purchase a 40 per cent interest from the United States companies in their concessions in Saudi Arabia, Kuwait and the Island of Bahrein. On Thursday a special meeting of the directors of PRC was held to consider new proposals for the acquisition of an interest in these concessions.

Companies owned jointly by Standard of California and the Texas Company hold the concessions on the Island of Bahrein and

Continued on Page Twelve

5TH ARMY FANS OUT

Routs Hermann Goering Tank Division Unit Near Littoria to the East

VELLETRI REPORTED TAKEN

Town Is 18 Miles From Rome —French Advance in Battle Raging on Main Front

By MILTON BRACKER
By Wireless to THE NEW YORK TIMES.

ALGIERS, Jan. 27—In the low coastal plain southwest of the Fascist-built town of Littoria, administrative center for the Pontine Marshes, British and American forces fanning out from the invasion beaches around Anzio and Nettuno have fought and won the first important battle since the landing five days ago.

It was a local action—not involving the main body of German troops—but those involved were members of the Hermann Goering Panzer Division, last identified on the Fifth Army front around the Garigliano River. [British troops repulsed four German attacks with Mark VI and Tiger tanks, front dispatches said. Three enemy tanks were destroyed in fighting in heavy rain and sleet.]

Thus the process whereby Field Marshal Gen. Albert Kesselring hopes to withdraw units from the south to stave off the dangerous Allied threat to his vital communication lines has obviously begun and German tactics in connection with Lieut. Gen. Mark W. Clark's amphibious operation appear today slightly less mysterious.

[The Rome radio asserted that German troops had recaptured the town of Borgo Piave, two miles northwest of Littoria and four miles from the Appian Way. The Allies had not announced the capture of Borgo Piave.

[The roar of Allied artillery is plainly heard in all parts of Rome, a correspondent in the capital reported to a Swedish newspaper yesterday.]

Bombers Shoot Up Cavalry

One aspect of the Germans' south-north shift involved an attempt to move fifty horsed artillery vehicles up the lower Liri Valley toward Ceprano. Allied light bombers caught the column near Pontecorvo, nine miles from Cassino, and riddled eight caissons with flying steel.

But it was believed that it was only a single battle group of the Goering Division that traded shots

Continued on Page Two

Red Army Expands Front Plunging Toward Estonia

Russians Sweep Westward on 23-Mile-Wide Front—Tosno and Volosovo Taken—324 Guns Boom Record Salute

By W. H. LAWRENCE
By Wireless to THE NEW YORK TIMES.

MOSCOW, Friday, Jan. 28—The swiftly advancing Red Army yesterday captured the important rail junctions of Volosovo and Tosno and completely cleared the Germans from the section of the main Moscow-Leningrad railway between Tosno and Lubyan. Last night in Leningrad 324 artillery guns thundered twenty-four times—a record—as a salute for the complete liberation of the city from the German blockade and the enemy's artillery bombardment.

In a general straightening of the line west of Leningrad, the Red Army yesterday pushed its positions toward the Estonian border—forty miles away—from Volosovo to Jakornovo in the north. The earlier zigzag line now has become an unbroken line twenty-three miles long.

The special order of the day by the Leningrad High Command was announced as the result of twelve tense battles in which the Germans had been driven back from thirty-eight to sixty-three miles along the whole front. More than 700 inhabited settlements were liberated in the two-week-old drive.

"The city of Leningrad has been completely liberated from the enemy blockade and from the barbaric artillery shelling of the enemy" was joyful news for the Russians and bad news for the Germans and Finns.

Volosovo is twenty-six miles southwest of Krasnogvardeisk, which was taken Tuesday night, and is the terminus of the spur railway leading from Mshinskaya, on the Krasnogvardeisk-Luga-Pskov railway.

By clearing the important nineteen-mile rail section between Tosno and Lubyan and driving to the very suburbs of Lubyan itself, the Red Army reduced the stretch of Moscow-Leningrad rail track in German hands to approximately

Continued on Page Four

Allies Below Rome Hold Initiative, Says Alexander

By C. L. SULZBERGER
By Wireless to THE NEW YORK TIMES.

ABOARD A BRITISH WARSHIP, Jan. 26 (Delayed)—The Fifth Army forces who have established themselves firmly on the Anzio-Nettuno beachhead south of Rome are now in position to take the initiative, Gen. Sir Harold R. L. G. Alexander told this correspondent following a tour of the area.

"Everything is very encouraging," said the Allied commander of the Central Mediterranean who, together with Lieut. Gen. Mark W. Clark, planned the operations. "We have not only seized the initial beachhead but have built up our forces.

"Everything is going wonderfully."

Sitting in an easy chair in his cabin, the energetic, youthful-appearing general had been intermittently chatting with a senior American staff officer and reading a German book to polish up on his knowledge of the enemy's language.

Gently shutting the book and reaching for a cigarette, the mild-mannered Alexander declared "every credit should be given to

Continued on Page Three

War News Summarized

FRIDAY, JANUARY 28, 1944

The wanton murder by torture of American and Filipino soldiers captured by the Japanese at Bataan and Corregidor was told in a detailed statement issued jointly by the Army and Navy last night. The report, based on testimony by Americans who escaped, described a form of savagery without parallel in modern times. In one Japanese camp 2,200 Americans died within two months. [1:8.]

Units of the famed Hermann Goering Panzer Division, last known to have been operating on the main Fifth Army front in Italy, clashed with British-American forces southwest of Littoria and lost the first battle. The invasion troops have fanned out farther from their beachheads at Anzio and Nettuno. Fierce battles continued along the Garigliano-Cassino line to the east, while the Navy shelled the Appian Way around Formia to prevent movement of German troops westward. [1:5, map P. 2]

With Leningrad formally proclaimed free from German pressure, the Red armies in that area moved to within forty miles of the Estonian border with the capture of Volosovo, and to the east took the Moscow-Leningrad railroad junction of Tosno. Other spearheads west of Novgorod reached a point two miles from the Leningrad-Vitebsk railway, one of the last two remaining north-south lines left to the Germans. [1:6-7, map P. 4.]

While the RAF bombed Berlin again last night, the French invasion coast was hammered from the air for the fifth straight day, along with targets in the Low Countries, including steel mills at Ijmuiden, the Netherlands. In the Nazi raid on England last Friday, fourteen of the ninety German planes were shot down. [4:2.]

President Ramirez of Argentina warned the Axis against intimidation and announced the freezing of his merchant fleet. Meanwhile a Cabinet crisis was reported. [8:2.]

It was declared in Washington that the February supply of Caribbean oil to Spain had been cut off, while in London charges were made in the House of Commons that Spanish seamen were being recruited for German U-boat service and threats were made to stop British oil to Spain. [1:7.]

In the heaviest attack yet made against the Japanese shipping bases in the Admiralty Islands, northwest of Rabaul, New Britain, American heavy bombers blasted installations with 120 tons of bombs. [7:1; map, P. 7.]

A reshuffling of Army personnel that will place five to six million fighting men overseas by the end of the year was announced by Secretary Stimson. Many of the officers over 38 will be placed on the inactive list, he said. [1:3.]

U. S. SAID TO CUT OFF OIL GOING TO SPAIN

Caribbean Loadings Reported Stopped Because of Ties to Germany

By The Associated Press.

WASHINGTON, Jan. 27—The United States has suspended oil shipments from the Caribbean area to Spain for February, it was learned on excellent authority tonight.

The step is understood to be part of a general reconsideration by this Government of Spain's position with regard to the war.

Spain has received a limited amount of fuel oil and gasoline from the Caribbean area, virtually her only source of supply. The quotas supply most essential needs but make it virtually impossible for Spain to gather any reserves.

Matters involved in the reconsideration of Spain's position regarding the war include her failure to release Italian ships interned in her ports, failure to control German agents operating on her territory and failure to reduce exports of war materials to Germany.

Credit Granted to Germany

The climactic step on Spain's part was the negotiation recently of an agreement with Germany providing 400,000,000 pesetas credit to the Germans. The credit was accorded as payment for debts incurred during the Spanish civil war.

This was a severe blow at Allied efforts to reduce strategic German imports, since during the past six months Germany has received very little from Spain because of Germany's lack of pesetas.

The most important material the Germans import from Spain is wolfram, ore from which tungsten is derived. The Allies have adequate supplies but have made vigorous efforts to prevent German acquisition of the vital metal, used to make armor-piercing steel.

The American action follows British protests to Madrid over activities of German spies and saboteurs alleged to be operating on Spanish territory, especially near Gibraltar.

Spain's oil supplies for next month were withheld by this Government's cancellation of loading dates at Caribbean ports for February. Spain had been receiv-

Continued on Page Eight

HORROR TALE BARED

3 Survivors Say Thirst Sent Men Crazy on 'March of Death'

AMERICANS BURIED ALIVE

Men Worked to Death—All 'Boiled' in Sun—12,000 Kept Without Food 7 Days

Text of the Army-Navy report on atrocities is on Page 6.

By LEWIS WOOD
Special to THE NEW YORK TIMES.

WASHINGTON, Jan. 27—Stories of how the Japanese barbarously tortured and cold-bloodedly starved to death and mercilessly murdered more than 5,200 American and many times that number of Filipino soldiers captured on Bataan and Corregidor were disclosed in official reports made public jointly by the Army and Navy tonight.

The ghastly recital revealed beatings, allowing parched men to drink only from a carabao wallow, crowding them into barbed-wire bullpens and horsewhipping some who picked up comrades who had collapsed from the terrible heat.

In one instance 12,000 men were jammed into a space 100 yards square and compelled to stand on a concrete floor for seven days without food and with a spigot that took a twelve-hour wait to reach as the only source of water.

Prisoners Become "Skeletons"

Prisoners in one camp shrank from 200 down to 90 pounds; they "had no buttocks, they were human skeletons."

When, on a "march of death" from Bataan to the prison camps, through sickening dust and blazing heat, an American colonel sought some Japanese Army salmon for his starving men, "a Japanese officer picked up a can and hit the colonel in the face, cutting his cheek wide open."

Two American Army officers and a Navy officer who tried to escape were beaten, stripped to their shorts, taken out on the road in full view of the camp, their hands tied behind them and pulled up by ropes from an overhead purchase, so that they had to remain standing but bent forward to ease the pressure on their arms. Constantly the Japanese beat these men with a two-by-four scantling and compelled Filipinos, too, to beat the Americans.

These were only a few of the examples of the inhuman tactics of the Japanese. These and others were taken from sworn statements made by three officers who escaped from the Philippines April 4, 1943, after nearly a year in Japanese captivity.

The reports were made by Comdr. Melvyn H. McCoy, USN, of Indianapolis; Lieut. Col. S. M. Mellnik, Coast Artillery Corps, of Dunmore, Pa., and Lieut. Col. (then Capt.) William E. Dyess, Air Corps, of Albany, Tex.

Report Only What They Saw

No hearsay whatever was included in the shocking stories related by the American officers. They told only what they had endured and what they had actually seen. Their statements, it was said, have been verified from other sources.

After he had made his statement to the War Department, Colonel Dyess, 23 years old, was killed last Dec. 21 when his fighter plane crashed at Burbank, Calif., as he was preparing to return to meet his torturers again. Colonel Mellnik is now attached to the staff of Gen. Douglas MacArthur, while Commander McCoy is on duty in the United States.

According to these three Americans, "several times as many" American prisoners of war have died chiefly from starvation, forced hard labor and general brutality as the Japanese have acknowledged. They reported the death of 2,200 American prisoners at Camp O'Donnell in April and May, 1942, and said that some 3,000 had died at the Cabanatuan Camp up to the close of October, 1942. Even more Filipinos perished

Continued on Page Six

"All the News That's Fit to Print."

The New York Times.

LATE CITY EDITION
Fair and continued cold today; winds slowly diminishing.
Temperatures Yesterday—Max., 37; Min., 17
Sunrise, 5:07 A. M.; Sunset, 4:13 P. M.

VOL. XCIII..No. 31,420. Entered as Second-Class Matter, Postoffice, New York, N. Y.

NEW YORK, WEDNESDAY, FEBRUARY 2, 1944. THREE CENTS NEW YORK CITY

U. S. FORCE WINS BEACHES ON MARSHALLS ATOLL; BATTLES RAGE ON FIRST JAPANESE SOIL INVADED; ALLIES ATTACK BELOW ROME; RUSSIANS ADVANCE

ROLL-CALL RECORD ON SOLDIERS' VOTE REFUSED BY HOUSE

180 Republicans, 52 Democrats Opposed—146 Democrats, 11 Republicans for It

A 'STATE RIGHTS' VICTORY

President Says People Need to Know How Members Stand—Senate Test Likely Today

By C. P. TRUSSELL
Special to THE NEW YORK TIMES.

WASHINGTON, Feb. 1—The House by a vote of 233 to 160 refused today to subject itself to the "stand-up-and-be-counted" showdown between Federal and State ballot plans for the armed forces as President Roosevelt urged in his recent message to Congress.

On the question of forcing a roll-call test on the Worley Federal ballot bill, endorsed by the Administration, in direct competition with the "States' rights" (Eastland-Rankin) measure, the House divided as follows:

For a roll-call test: 146 Democrats, 11 Republicans, 2 Progressives and 1 American-Laborite.

Against a roll-call test: 180 Republicans, 52 Democrats and 1 Farmer-Laborite.

Vote Is on Committee Rule

While the vote was construed as an expression of attitude on the Worley bill, as against the Eastland-Rankin bill, the question upon which the issue was joined was a parliamentary one.

The Eastland-Rankin bill had been taken to the floor under a rule of the Rules Committee which did not assure a record vote on the Worley bill. To amend this rule the House was required to defeat a motion to close consideration and debate at the end of an hour's debate. Instead the motion carried and the rule was adopted. Thus the roll-call was blocked.

Fifty of the fifty-two Democrats who helped block the roll-call were from Southern States. Five were from Alabama, three from Arkansas, nine from Georgia, one from Kentucky, six from Louisiana, seven from Mississippi, the solid vote of the delegation; two from North Carolina, one from Oklahoma, three from South Carolina, one from Tennessee, eight from Texas and four from Virginia. The others were Representatives Slaughter of Missouri and Jellicott of California.

The eleven Republicans voting to assure the roll-call vote were Representatives Andrews, Kearney, Mruk and Taylor of New York; Anderson and Welsh of California, Bender of Ohio, Burdick of North Dakota, Gale of Minnesota, La Follette of Indiana and Wolverton of New Jersey.

President's Remark on Test

President Roosevelt, when told of the House's action at his press conference soon after the vote was taken, observed that roll-calls were a part of representative government, and said that he could not cast an intelligent vote in an election without knowing how his Congressman voted.

The House having made the first voting decision in the controversy, the Senate, after six hours of heated debate over constitutional phases of the issue and the President's charge that the "States' rights" bill passed by the Senate was a "fraud," as well as the delay in test voting in Congress, agreed to vote not later than noon tomorrow on the Overton amendment to the Green-Lucas Federal ballot bill.

This amendment would prescribe that while the Federal ballot might be used, State and local election officials would determine the validity of the votes cast in accordance with State law. The principal effect would be to repeal provisions of the existing soldier voting law which suspend requirements for personal registration and payment of poll taxes and, to an undetermined extent, invalidate the Federal ballot.

Members of the "States' rights"

Continued on Page Twelve

Public Told to Delay '44 Tax Estimates

Taxpayers are being advised not to file their estimates of 1944 income with their tax returns for 1943, because Washington legislation is expected to affect the rates on 1944 income. Internal revenue officials in New York City believe Congress will authorize a delay of at least thirty days for the declarations.

"We are trying to discourage taxpayers from filing their declarations of estimated 1944 income until we get the new forms," one internal revenue official said. He indicated that the new legislation could not be made effective before March 1 and that April 15 was regarded as a logical date for the necessary extension.

RISE IN CITY RENTS FOUGHT BY MAYOR

He Urges OPA 'Unqualifiedly' to Reject Landlords' Plea for 10% Blanket Increase

By LEE E. COOPER

Mayor La Guardia has asked the Office of Price Administration to reject "unqualifiedly" the petition of New York City landlords for a blanket increase of at least 10 per cent in housing rents, it became known last night.

In a 10,000-word memorandum filed with the OPA "as Mayor and on behalf of the tenants residing in the City of New York," Mr. La Guardia replied in detail to each of the objections to the rent ceiling regulations voiced by property owners in their plea for an increase, and called an upward adjustment of charges for living quarters here "unjustified and unwarranted."

He charged that the petitioners had "only one real aim—to impair the successful administration of rent control in New York."

The Mayor's brief challenges as "false and fantastic" the estimates of the petitioning groups that there were upward of 79,000 habitable apartment units available for rent in the five boroughs on Oct. 8, 1943.

He cited figures and surveys, including many by the Real Estate Board of New York, to support his contention that New York owners have been enjoying the "best rental market in almost two decades," disputed the argument that there had been a general increase in realty taxes and in scathing tone answered the statistics regarding foreclosures and depressed conditions in the realty market.

The Mayor's memorandum was tinged with sarcasm also in his answer to the plea that higher operating costs of buildings justified a rent rise. He expressed the view that the increase in apartment occupancy alone had "entirely or at least substantially offset any increase in building maintenance costs," while many building owners at the same time, he charged, were employing fewer workers and curtailing service. Although there has been a rise in fuel costs, he added, "thousands of tenants have

Continued on Page Fifteen

TWIN GAINS IN ITALY

British 16 Miles Below Rome After Cutting Coastal Railway

CISTERNA IS MENACED

Americans Half Mile From Town—Allies on Lower Front Gain

By MILTON BRACKER
By Wireless to THE NEW YORK TIMES.

ALGIERS, Feb. 1—Smashing ahead against furious resistance, American troops have driven into the suburbs of Cisterna, the most vital choke-point in the German supply system below Rome.

There the Appian Way and the main coastal railway intersect. Through the town enormous quantities of supplies have passed to the German forces on the lower front.

[The Americans were only a half-mile from Cisterna proper, according to The United Press.]

British units farther west have eased the Americans' task by driving three miles beyond Aprilia along the road from Anzio, cutting the railroad at the Campoleone station ten miles above Cisterna and hammering into the outskirts of Campoleone proper, one mile beyond.

But, while the Allies appear to be about to sever the electrified trackage at two points and the historic highway at one, the Germans have finally brought down reinforcements from north of Rome. Thus, although the British and American penetrations threaten the flank of the German defense line along five miles of the railway between the Campoleone station and Cisterna, the Allies must be prepared to meet a thrust from the north on their own exposed left flank.

No Factor of Surprise

The probability of new German pressure from the north has long been expected and in no way gives the Germans the advantage of surprise. But how large a force the enemy has been able to divert to the south and whether he can build it up to constitute a grave menace are not known.

Offsetting factors are the continuing Allied air offensive against all the supply routes leading to Rome, which militates against further troop movement, and the fine weather around the beachheads, which is permitting the Allies to expand on an even more solid foundation.

The battlefield is still wedge-shaped. Its point is at the Anzio-Nettuno area and its rim extends between Campoleone and Cisterna. At the outskirts of the former village the British are barely sixteen miles from Rome, while the Americans clamping down on Cisterna are twenty-six miles from the capital. The ten-mile stretch between, along which the Germans have built their defenses, is within easy range of light artillery. Continued naval bombardments between the beachhead and Formia throttled

Continued on Page Eight

$103,889,600 in War Bonds Sold At Rally on Stock Exchange Floor

After being "told" by the marines—specifically Lieut. Gen. Alexander A. Vandegrift, commandant of the Marine Corps—Wall Street yesterday "told" it to Hitler and Hirohito by subscribing for $103,889,600 in bonds of the Fourth War Loan.

General Vandegrift, addressing 2,000 brokers and employes at a rally on the floor of the New York Stock Exchange, Wall and Broad Streets, declared the quick success of the drive would be "equal to a major victory on the battlefield—and it will not cost a single drop of blood."

Emil Schram, president of the Exchange, announced the day's total, which brought the aggregate of both purchases and sales made by members of the Exchange in 322 cities and forty-six States to $501,000,000 in the current drive.

Another large subscription announced yesterday was $55,000,000 by the Mutual Life Insurance Company of New York. Lewis W. Douglas, president, said it was the company's way of celebrating its 101st birthday. The Mutual Life's Government bond holdings have increased by $310,344,000 since Pearl Harbor, he said.

Huge sales were recorded in city, State and nation yesterday, the first day on which the books were opened in the drive for corporate subscriptions. At the same time sales of E-bonds, the type favored by the small investor, continued to soar as they have since

Continued on Page Fourteen

MARSHALL ISLANDS BASE WHERE WE HAVE ESTABLISHED BEACHHEADS

The Japanese airfield on Roi (left). Coral strip connects it with Namur (right), on which the enemy has a roadway.

Associated Press Wirephoto (U. S. Navy)

BERLIN'S BLOT-OUT PUT NEARER BY RAF

10,000 Tons of Bombs Loosed in January on City—Sunday's Blow Fired Plant Areas

By DREW MIDDLETON
By Cable to THE NEW YORK TIMES.

LONDON, Feb. 1—The city of Berlin, until lately the heart of Hitler's great military empire, is dying under the British bombing assault, which in January devoted about 10,000 tons of missiles to the destruction of the Reich capital in six great assaults.

[During daylight RAF Coastal Command planes attacked German shipping off Norway, sinking a mine-sweeper, setting a cargo ship afire and shooting up an escort vessel.

[Telephone contact between Stockholm and Berlin was broken early Tuesday night, but was re-established at 11:45 P. M. and Swedish correspondents in the Reich capital gave no indication that there had been a new at-

Continued on Page Seven

Soviet Republics Get Right To Own Armies and Envoys

By W. H. LAWRENCE
By Wireless to THE NEW YORK TIMES.

MOSCOW, Feb. 1—The Supreme Soviet late tonight unanimously approved a proposal by Foreign Commissar Vyacheslaff M. Molotoff for major changes in the Soviet constitutional system under which each of the sixteen constituent republics will form its own army formations and have separate diplomatic representation abroad.

[The text of Mr. Molotoff's statement appears on page 10.]

In less than four hours of debate, including the forty-three-minute opening address by Mr. Molotoff, both chambers approved the constitutional changes by a show of hands without having the full text read to them. They had copies of the proposal in their desks but they waived the reading of it.

On the motion of President Mikhail I. Kalinin, the Supreme Soviet also elected Nikolai Shevrnik as first Vice President of the Presidium of the U.S.S.R. and then adjourned sine die.

While Premier Joseph Stalin looked on from a back-row seat on the platform, Mr. Molotoff gave a general outline of the Government's new plan which, he said, resulted

Continued on Page Ten

KINGISEPP IS TAKEN IN RED ARMY SWEEP

Entry of Estonia Is Indicated as Three-Way Drive Squeezes the Germans in Pocket

By The United Press.

LONDON, Wednesday, Feb. 2—Gen. Leonid A. Govoroff's Leningrad army captured the German stronghold of Kingisepp yesterday after brief street battles, while his advanced spearheads pushed on toward Estonia along a ten-mile front, reaching to within less than a mile of the border at the town of Keikino. [The western edge of Keikino is only 300 yards from the border.]

The Red Army was nearing the border on a front northwest of Kingisepp and it was probable that some units might have crossed into the Baltic State.

More than fifty towns and settlements were captured yesterday—the eve of the first anniversary of the German defeat at Stalingrad—by General Govoroff's army, which concentrated its overall offensive in three directions along a sixty-five-mile front curving down from the Gulf of Finland to within thirty-three miles north-

Continued on Page Eleven

FLEET CONFIDENT ON WAY TO ATOLL

Fight Tougher Than Tarawa Seen but Men Were Sure Marshalls Would Fall

By ROBERT TRUMBULL
By Wireless to THE NEW YORK TIMES.

ABOARD A FLAGSHIP APPROACHING KWAJALEIN ATOLL, Jan. 30 (Delayed)—A large part of the American Navy, constituting the most powerful sea force ever assembled, is converging from north and south today on Kwajalein Atoll in the Japanese mandated Marshall Islands. We have already attacked with planes and naval gunfire, and tomorrow we land our troops.

Today a number of battleships, including our newest and largest, opened fire on Kwajalein's principal shore installations.

For the first time we are invading a part of the Japanese empire and in so doing we are exposing ourselves to possible strong aerial and submarine opposition and natural hazards of which we have little knowledge. We are in waters now that have been the cruising area of the Japanese fleet exclusively for many years. We would like very much to meet that fleet here and now.

Tomorrow the Fourth Marine Division and the Seventh Army Division comprising an amphibious force under command of Rear Admiral Richmond Kelly Turner will make the most audacious attack attempted by the United States in this war.

We expect Kwajalein to be tougher than Tarawa. We know we will lose many men on the beaches. We expect Japanese dive bombers and submarines to sink

Continued on Page Four

War News Summarized

WEDNESDAY, FEBRUARY 2, 1944

American marines and soldiers set foot for the first time in this war on Japanese territory and established beachheads near Roi and Kwajalein Islands in the Marshalls. Under the cover of hundreds of planes and the guns of battleships, cruisers and smaller craft, the American forces were beating down strong opposition with apparently moderate casualties.

The Seventh Infantry Division landed near Kwajalein and the Fourth Marine Division near Roi, both in the Kwajalein Atoll. The combined air forces pounded Maloelap, Wotje, Mili, Jaluit and Eniwetok and Wake Island in addition to Kwajalein. [All the foregoing 1:8, map P. 2.]

A large part of our Navy sailed confidently into a ring of Japanese air and submarine bases to hammer the Marshalls and protect the landing forces. [1:7.] Tokyo papers said an American victory there would be a "regrettable loss." [3:5.]

In the Southwest Pacific and in Burma the Japanese were also under heavy attack. At Rabaul, New Britain, they lost at least twenty-three planes and it was revealed that an Allied post had been established within Netherland New Guinea. [3:1, with map.] American-trained Chinese troops advanced five miles in two days in the Hukawng Valley in Burma. [7:5.]

President Roosevelt answered Japanese propaganda by saying our troops were in India not for political but for military purposes—"to assure the defeat of Japan." [4:2.] He repeated assurance that the individuals responsible for atrocities against prisoners would be tracked down and brought to justice. [5:5.]

The Fifth Army fighting on the beachhead below Rome had reached the outskirts of Campoleone and Cisterna, threatening to close a pincers around the Germans, who were said to be rushing reinforcements from northern Italy. [1:3; map P. 8.] American fliers hit the enemy's refueling airfields at Klagenfurt, Austria, and Aviano and Udine; the RAF struck Trieste. [8:1.]

Russian troops captured Kingisepp and moved to within a few hundred yards of the Estonian border. More than ninety places were recaptured in gains on many fronts. [1:6; map P. 11.]

Moscow presented a sudden, new development when the Supreme Soviet unanimously approved proposals of Foreign Commissar Molotoff changing the constitutional system whereby the sixteen constituent republics would have their own army formations and their own diplomatic corps. This would tend to give Russia sixteen votes at the peace conference. [1:5-6.] A writer in the Soviet newspaper Izvestia said the Vatican's policy was "pro-fascist in character." [1:6-7.]

Izvestia Calls Pope Pro-Fascist; Says Catholics Are Disillusioned

By The United Press.

MOSCOW, Feb. 1—The Government newspaper Izvestia asserted today that Vatican foreign policy had disillusioned Catholics throughout the world and "earned the hatred and contempt of the Italian masses for supporting fascism."

Endorsing a report issued on Jan. 15 by the Foreign Policy Association, New York, which said that a rising tide of anti-clericalism might be expected in Italy, the Soviet organ said the Vatican pledged its support to Italian fascism following conclusion of the Lateran treaty in February, 1929, "but the Vatican's support for fascism wasn't limited solely to Italy. It approved many acts of aggression by fascism although the true meaning of these aggressions was no secret.

"The Vatican is now suffering the consequences of its endorsement of the Italian conquest of Abyssinia and is now reaping the fruits of the débâcle of the Italian African empire."

Reviewing Vatican foreign policy before and during the present war, Izvestia said "the disgraceful role the Vatican played in Hitler's and Mussolini's Spanish adventure is widely known. The Vatican emerged in the role of a supporter of armed intervention."

It said Generalissimo Francisco Franco of totalitarian Spain was a "Vatican pet" and that Generalissimo Franco's Spain was the "image of the clerical States of post-war Europe" which the Vati-

Continued on Page Eleven

GRIP ON KWAJALEIN

Marine and Infantry Units Strike, Shielded by Record Armada

LOSSES ARE MODERATE

Our Forces as Close to Japan as Foe Was to U. S. at Pearl Harbor

By GEORGE F. HORNE
By Telephone to THE NEW YORK TIMES.

PEARL HARBOR, Feb. 1—Tremendous American amphibious forces have invaded the Marshall Islands and established beachheads in bitter fighting on islands of the Kwajalein Atoll.

Admiral Chester W. Nimitz, Commander in Chief of the Pacific Fleet and of the Pacific Ocean Areas, announced this morning what most of the world had surmised: that United States fighting strength was being pitted on Japanese soil for the first time in what must be considered a decisive battle in the war of the Pacific.

Protected by fire power overshadowing anything we had concentrated against the fierce warriors who dreamt of dictating peace terms in the White House, well-trained forces, both marines and Army infantrymen now skilled in amphibious operations, stormed ashore yesterday morning in daylight.

As they went in at fighting pitch and armed with the best weapons ingenuity can provide, carrier aircraft and surface forces bombarded and raked near-by atolls to blanket the enemy.

The assault forces landed on unidentified islands in the vicinity of Roi and Kwajalein, both in the Kwajalein Atoll.

Strong opposition has been encountered, but first reports from the area, necessarily meager, are in an optimistic tone. The first stages of the operation appear to have opened successfully.

[Besides Kwajalein and Roi, the landing forces had as an objective a third Japanese base, Namur Island.

[A Japanese Imperial Headquarters announcement recorded from the Tokyo radio by CBS said Army and Navy garrisons had counter-attacked and that "furious fighting is now in progress."]

Admiral Nimitz's communiqué stated that "initial information indicates that our casualties are moderate."

Spruance Again in Command

Vice Admiral Raymond A. Spruance, who directed the successful Gilberts invasion only ten weeks ago, again is in command.

Roi Island is in the northern

Continued on Page Three

We Lose 22 Planes, Save All but 6 Men

By The United Press.

WASHINGTON, Feb. 1—The Navy revealed tonight that twenty-two Corsair fighter planes from a twenty-three-plane marine squadron were lost in a severe storm last Friday while on a "routine flight" between the American-held Gilbert and Ellice Islands.

All but six of the pilots have been rescued. The body of one was also recovered.

One of the twenty-two planes made a crash landing in the Ellice Islands, but the other twenty-one, so far as is known, were forced down at sea.

The Navy said search operations were started immediately after the one plane had arrived safely at the Ellice Island base.

The next of kin of the dead pilot and the five still missing have been notified.

Loss of the planes was revealed in a Pacific Fleet headquarters announcement released here and at Pearl Harbor.

In 1944, the U.S. flag was first placed on Guam by these two U.S. Marines.

Marines advancing on Majuro in the Marshall Islands.

Two Japanese soldiers surrender to Marines during the battle of the Marshalls.

"All the News That's Fit to Print"

The New York Times.

LATE CITY EDITION

Partly cloudy, slightly warmer today; gentle to moderate winds.

Temperatures Yesterday—Max., 63; Min., 55
Sunrise, 5:26 A. M.; Sunset, 8:22 P. M.

Copyright, 1944, by The New York Times Company.

VOL. XCIII. No. 31,544. | Entered as Second-Class Matter, Postoffice, New York, N. Y. | NEW YORK, MONDAY, JUNE 5, 1944. | THREE CENTS NEW YORK CITY

ROME CAPTURED INTACT BY THE 5TH ARMY AFTER FIERCE BATTLE THROUGH SUBURBS; NAZIS MOVE NORTHWEST; AIR WAR RAGES ON

TRANSIT MEN BALK AT MAYOR'S INQUIRY INTO OUTSIDE JOBS

Demand for Sworn Statements Covering Family Earnings Evokes Union Protest

RESENTMENT WIDESPREAD

Many Department Heads Cold Toward Policy and Some Authorize Dual Work

By PAUL CROWELL

Widespread resentment among city employes against Mayor La Guardia's crusade to keep them from holding outside jobs on their own time was intensified yesterday. It became known that Investigation Commissioner Edgar Bromberger, by direction of the Mayor, had asked the 35,000 employes of the unified transit system to make sworn answers to forty questions concerning their own employment and that of all working members of their families.

The Transport Workers Union and other organizations representing city transit workers already have registered informal protests and are considering formal action. It was reported that the TWU was prepared to ask its members receiving such questionnaires from Commissioner Bromberger's office to turn them over to the union.

The questionnaire, of a type said to have been sent to employes of other city agencies, asks the transit worker to give full details about his own job, any job his wife may have outside, any job his children may be filling. Full details concerning pay rates on all such jobs are demanded. The workers are asked also how they obtained outside jobs, whether they paid anyone to get them and whether they are making payments to anyone in connection with outside jobs.

Board Members Dislike Policy

The regulations of the Board of Transportation do not forbid the holding of outside jobs and individual members of the board were known to feel that so long as employes were punctual and efficient in their tasks their outside activities were their own affair. Despite this feeling, however, the board is prepared to carry out the policy laid down by the Mayor. An informal survey of other city agencies conducted last week indicated that most of their heads held about the same attitude, but felt that the Mayor's policy must be carried out if he insisted upon it.

The Mayor's insistence that city employes, regardless of departmental rules forego such activities, led him recently to demand that charges be brought against an electrical engineer employed by the Board of Transportation who was teaching one night a week at City College, receiving $12 for each night's work. An exchange of views between the Mayor and the Board of Transportation resulted in a decision to let the employe continue teaching until the end of the current term, with the understanding that he would not resume teaching in the fall.

The electrical engineer, who is a graduate of one of the country's leading technical schools, was certified by the Board of Transportation, after investigation, to be efficient, painstaking and punctual, and the Mayor was told that his outside work made him a better city servant, while the small additional income was a welcome addition to his modest salary. It was also pointed out to the Mayor that there was nothing in the board's rules or the law to bar the outside work. The Mayor is reported to have replied that the man must keep one job or the other, but could not hold both.

Outside work by employes is a live issue in the Board of Transportation, where it is estimated that at least 10 per cent of the 35,000 transit workers have extra work to increase family income.

Resentment against the Mayor's

Continued on Page 11

Laval Tries to Shift Funds to Argentina

Pierre Laval, chief of the Vichy government, recently tried to transfer $50,000 from Spain to Argentina, the Brazzaville radio said yesterday in a broadcast recorded at the Columbia Broadcasting System's short-wave listening station.

"A Madrid bank revealed to the Spanish authorities that a deposit of $50,000 had been made with them for transfer to an Argentinian bank," the French radio said. "An inquiry was opened, and the person behind the depositor was discovered: He is Pierre Laval."

The same broadcast reported: "Germans in France have been buying gold at very high prices. Among the German agents arrested by French police for illegal traffic in gold was one who identified himself in order to be freed. He told the police commissioner that he was the director of a bank in a small German town. Because of his age, he had not been drafted into active military service, but his competence in financial matters made possible his being used in this work, in which he had been engaged since 1940."

JOHNSTON IN RUSSIA SCOFFS AT U. S. REDS

Business Leader Also Praises Soviet 'Capitalism'—Calls Ideologies Bridgeable

By The United Press.

MOSCOW, June 4—With straight-from-the-shoulder frankness, Eric Johnston, president of the United States Chamber of Commerce, told 100 Soviet trade leaders yesterday that a gulf separated the economies of the United States and Russia, but that bridges of practical cooperation could be thrown across that gulf.

Mr. Johnston advocated extensive post-war trade and visits between American business and "Soviet capitalists" as one bridge, but said that "each of our countries should be allowed to pursue its own unique economic experiment unimpeded by the other."

Bluntly, he told the Russians that Americans "were most private-minded and most individual-minded and, make no mistake, we are determined to remain so and even become more so."

Mr. Johnston, who arrived in Russia last week, was luncheon guest of A. I. Mikoyan, Soviet Foreign Trade Commissar, at Spiridonovka House. At the table sat Soviet trade experts, members of the Soviet Foreign Office, United States Ambassador W. Averell Harriman and Soviet military men.

At first the Russians appeared nonplussed by Mr. Johnston's bluntness, but later they burst into gales of mirth at his sallies at American Communists and Marxians.

"I shall try to show you my admiration for your heroic deeds and

Continued on Page 6

FOE 'EXPLAINS' STEP

Hitler Ordered Troops Out to Save Rome, Germans Assert

ENEMY PLEA BARED

Kesselring Made Last-Minute Renewal of Open-City Offer

By The Associated Press.

LONDON, June 4—The Germans announced tonight in a special communiqué—broadcast after the Allies had liberated Rome—the withdrawal of German troops to the northwest of the city and said that the Allies had received a plan whereby Rome would have been regarded as an "open city."

The open-city proposals were said to have been advanced at 11 P. M. on Saturday, less than twenty-four hours before Rome changed hands. The first word from Adolf Hitler's headquarters in several days asserted that the fight in Italy would continue and that measures were being taken "to force final victory for Germany and her allies." The communiqué said:

"As the front line, in the course of the present fighting in Italy, was gradually approaching nearer and nearer to the city of Rome, there was danger that Rome, one of the oldest cultural centers of the world, would be directly involved in the present fighting. Hitler has ordered the withdrawal of German troops to the northwest of Rome to prevent the destruction of Rome.

"The struggle in Italy will be continued with unshakable determination to break the enemy attacks and to force final victory for Germany and her allies. The necessary measures for an eventual German victory are being taken in close collaboration with fascist Italy and other allied powers.

"The year of invasion will bring Germany's enemies an annihilating defeat at the most decisive moment."

Kesselring's Proposals Listed

Field Marshal Gen. Albert Kesselring, the German commander in Italy, sent the Allies proposals that Rome be regarded as an open city, a special announcement from Hitler's headquarters said. The statement was broadcast by the German radio and was received only after a dispatch filed from Rome had announced the crushing of the last German resistance units within the city. The broadcast said:

"The German High Command announced that the supreme commander of German troops in Italy, Field Marshal Kesselring, had submitted proposals to the Vatican with the request that they should be conveyed to the Anglo-American High Command. The proposals confirmed the recognition of Rome

Continued on Page 4

THE FIRST OF EUROPE'S WAR CAPITALS TO FALL TO THE ALLIES

The sign tells the troops they have entered Rome.

The New York Times (U. S. Signal Corps Radiotelephoto)

AMERICANS IN FIRST

U. S. Armor Spearheads Thrust Through Last Defenses of Rome

FINAL BATTLE BITTER

Fifth and Eighth Armies Rush On Beyond City in Pursuit of Foe

By The United Press.

NAPLES, June 4—The Fifth Army captured Rome tonight, liberating for the first time a German-enslaved European capital. German rear guards were fleeing in disorganized retreat to the northwest.

Except for the railway yards, smashed by the Allies' bombs, the city is 95 per cent intact United Press correspondents reported, after their arrival in the city.

Late tonight, the British Eighth Army, rushing into Rome from the southeast along the Via Casilina, was reported to be joining the Fifth Army in close pursuit of the hard-pressed enemy remnants, under orders to destroy them to a man if possible. Only enough troops to maintain order and ferret out any German snipers or suicide nests were to be left in Rome as the Allies' main armies pounded on without pausing to celebrate their greatest triumph, coming 270 days after the start of the Italian campaign.

[The Allies battled German rear guards to the edge of the ancient Forum, The Associated Press reported. A force from the old Anzio beachhead completed the mopping up of German forces at 9:15 P. M. by knocking out an enemy scout car in front of the Bank of Italy, almost within the shadow of Trajan's Column.]

Final Stand at Rome's Gates

At the very gates of Rome, the Germans had made a final stand but Lieut. Gen. Mark W. Clark, after having waited three hours for the enemy troops to withdraw in accordance with their own declaration of Rome as an open city, ordered a violent anti-tank barrage. Then masses of Fifth Army men and weapons crashed into the city and began mopping up enemy snipers and a few tanks and mobile guns trying to cover the retreat.

More of the enemy survivors of the Allies' whirlwind offensive were streaming in congested retreat to the northwest at the mercy of the Allies' planes, which, during the day, destroyed or damaged 600 enemy trucks and other vehicles. The Germans' jammed traffic columns stretched fifty-five miles to Lake Bolsena.

Direct radio contact with American correspondents in Rome was established tonight. A United Press reporter said that the main entry into the city had been made along the Via Casilina, which passes through the Porta Maggiore at the southeastern edge of the city. Other Allied troops were reported to have fought their way through the Ostiense freight yards, just south of St. Paul Gate, the main entrance to the city from due south and only one and one-quarter miles from the Venice Palace.

The entry into Rome came with dramatic suddenness after the Al-

Continued on Page 3

U. S. 'HEAVIES' BOMB IN FRANCE ALL DAY

Attack Boulogne Area Twice, Rip Rail, Air Targets Near Paris—Genoa Blasted

By JAMES MacDONALD

By Cable to The New York Times

LONDON, Monday, June 5—Continuing to pave the way for the Allied invasion of the Continent hundreds of Allied bombers and fighters from Britain scorched a 200-mile stretch of the French coast yesterday and penetrated inland.

Three separate missions were carried out by the Flying Fortresses and Liberators of the United States Eighth Air Force with fighter escort over northwestern France. They met little Luftwaffe opposition; the enemy flak ranged from moderate to heavy.

In the morning and again in the afternoon strong formations of the

Continued on Page 5

Road to Rome Hard Fought, Yet Crowded With Civilians

By MILTON BRACKER

By Wireless to The New York Times.

IN THE OUTSKIRTS OF ROME, June 4—The Fifth Army's entry into the suburbs of Rome was made along Highway 6—the Via Casilina—which runs into Rome at Centocelle, a suburb test known for its airport. But the advance did not mean a simple triumphal procession into the heart of Rome. It meant going in in careful infantry columns along the sides of the road. Most of the men had their bayonets fixed and they wore deadly earnest expressions because two wrecked Sherman tanks along the approaches told what had happened to other Americans earlier today.

Just before 4 P. M., a huge column of smoke billowed up from the southwest corner of the city, indicating a demolition. At the same time, a mine went off with a terrible burst beyond the farthest of the two tanks, and it tore an Italian woman to pieces. As the afternoon wore on, the sniping

Continued on Page 4

CONQUERORS' GOAL REACHED BY ALLIES

Fifth and Eighth Armies Drive Up From South on Rome in a Historic Campaign

By HERBERT L. MATTHEWS

By Wireless to The New York Times.

ROME, June 4—The Allies' troops fought their way into Rome this morning and at nightfall they were still fighting on the outer edges, which the Germans were defending despite all their protestations about considering Rome an open city. Other large German units faced entrapment south of Highway 6 unless they could be pulled back across the Tiber or through Rome.

But Rome has been reached—the goal of conquerors throughout the ages, though none was ever before able to make the almost impossible south-north campaign. What Hannibal did not dare to do, the Allies' generals accomplished, but at such a cost in blood, matériel and time that it will probably never again be attempted.

All roads from all over the world led to Rome today as a United

Continued on Page 3

CITY'S FALL FOCUSES POLITICAL CHANGES

Victor Emmanuel's Promise to Retire Recalled—Badoglio Cabinet May Step Down

Special to The New York Times.

WASHINGTON, June 4—Pending receipt of final details of the fall of Rome, most Government leaders tonight refrained from direct comment. It was felt that the first official reaction to the Allied victory would come from President Roosevelt in the radio address that the White House announced he would make tomorrow night.

Interest in the news of the capture of the Italian capital centered not so much in the military victory as in the probable political consequences, particularly those stemming from King Victor Emmanuel's recent statement that he planned to retire as Italy's ruler as soon as Rome fell to the Allies.

The King announced April 12 that he intended to turn Italy's affairs over to Crown Prince Humbert, and said the transfer of power would take place "on the day on which the Allied troops entered Rome."

Even more important than this move are the effects the change may have on the future of the Italian Government now headed by Marshal Pietro Badoglio. Developments, it was said, will be watched closely not only as to other high appointments to be made after Prince Humbert takes over control but also as to any alterations in the structure of the Italian Government.

While the diplomatic and politi-

Continued on Page 4

War News Summarized

MONDAY, JUNE 5, 1944

Rome was liberated from the Nazi-Fascist aggressors last night. The first European capital to be wrested from the enemy came under full Allied control when a force that had fought its way up from the old Anzio beachhead knocked out a German scout car in the center of the city. There was fierce fighting with enemy rear-guard detachments at the outskirts of Rome before the city was liberated.

Fifth Army units and the vanguard of the Eighth Army, which entered the Eternal City later, were sent in hot pursuit of the fleeing Germans. Rome was found to be 95 per cent intact, with destruction centered in the railroad yards. [All the foregoing 1:8; maps P. 2.]

German artillery and snipers held off the Allied advance between the airport at Centocello and the city limits. Civilians, obviously happy over the departure of the Nazis, remained calm as United Nations troops moved in. [1:5-6.]

Hitler's headquarters announced after the Fifth Army had entered the city that the Germans had withdrawn to new lines northwest of Rome. Shortly before the city fell they dispatched a proposal that Rome be declared an open city. [1:3.]

Capture of Rome, according to military observers in London, made it much more likely that the main objective of the offensive—destruction of the German Tenth and Fourteenth armies—would be accomplished, with possible enemy losses reaching up to 100,000. [3:1.]

The AMG, following closely upon the victorious Allied forces, was fully prepared to undertake the gigantic task of feeding some 2,000,000 civilians. Vast stocks of food have been accumulated for distribution. [1:6-7.]

Washington withheld official comment until President Roosevelt's radio address tonight, but the capital was interested in how soon King Victor Emmanuel would fulfill his promise to retire when Rome had fallen to the Allies. [1:7.]

American heavy bombers from Britain smashed three times at enemy installations in France yesterday as the air invasion continued unabated against little enemy opposition. Italian-based aircraft struck rail lines on the French-Italian border. [1:4.]

United States troops resumed the offensive against the three airfields on Biak Island off New Guinea. Thirty Japanese planes were shot down in widespread fights from Biak to Truk. [8:2.] Continued improvement in Allied positions was reported from Burma [8:3] although in China the Japanese made some gains toward Changsha while losing ground in other sectors. [8:4-5.]

Eric Johnston, president of the United States Chamber of Commerce, told 100 Soviet trade leaders at a Moscow luncheon that the way to bridge the economic gulf separating American and Russian economies lay in closer knowledge and greater mutual respect. [1:2.]

Enraged Bull Kills 2 Brothers, Gores Neighbor on Long Island

Special to The New York Times.

BABYLON, L. I., June 4—Two dairy farmers, brothers, were found this morning gored and trampled to death on the Ames Farm in North Babylon, victims of their Guernsey bull, which had run wild and scattered their herd of thirty cows over near-by roads. A neighbor, trying to round up the scattered herd, was gored in the groin by the infuriated animal.

State troopers were forced to shoot and kill the belligerent bull.

The victims were George W. Ames, 41 years old, and his brother, James Hawley Ames, 35, who operated the Ames Farm on Phelps Lane, North Babylon. So far as is known no one saw the unequal encounter that cost them their lives. Their bodies were discovered, lying about 100 feet apart, several hundred yards from the cow barn.

The first intimation that anything was amiss came with complaints to the State Police in North Babylon that the Ames cows were wandering off the pasture and on the near-by Phelps Lane and Belmont Road. Two State troopers were sent to the farm and succeeded in getting most of the cows back into the pasture along with the bull. They put in a call for two additional troopers to round up the remainder of the herd.

Their suspicions aroused by the fact that the milk delivery truck, fully loaded, was standing in its place although it usually left on its rural route at 8 A. M., the troopers made their way to the farmhouse. There they found Mrs. Kathleen Ames, mother of the two men, and her daughter, Jane L. Ames, a school teacher.

A search of the farm was begun and Trooper Anthony Cherry came

Continued on Page 30

AMG Will Rush Food for Rome, Teeming With 750,000 Refugees

By HAROLD CALLENDER

By Wireless to The New York Times.

ALGIERS, June 4—The fall of Rome will add about 2,000,000 persons to those whom the Allies have assumed responsibility of feeding, Allied authorities estimated today. But the Allied Military Government, now operating under the Allied Control Commission, has long prepared for the task and is believed to be ready.

The normal population of the Italian capital is estimated to have been swollen by 750,000 refugees from Naples and other places.

Allied authorities have stocks of wheat, canned milk and dehydrated vegetables ready to send to Rome quickly with the cooperation of the Fifth and Eighth Armies regarding transport by trucks.

At Anzio landing facilities have been built since the establishment of the bridgehead, and ships can be unloaded at Gaeta.

In the plans already made Rome has been divided into regions for the distribution of foodstuffs by Italian and Allied personnel under the authority of the commission. An emergency system has been prepared to provide strict control over the black market, which otherwise might absorb the local produce destined to go into the Allied pool for distribution on a ration basis to the masses who cannot afford the black market.

Capt. Matthias F. Correa, former United States Attorney for the Southern District of New York, has a staff of investigators, including 150 Guardia di Finanza, ready to combat the black market

Continued on Page 4

President to Talk On Rome Tonight

By The United Press.

WASHINGTON, June 4—A fifteen-minute radio address will be made by President Roosevelt to the nation tomorrow night on the liberation of Rome, the White House announced tonight.

Mr. Roosevelt will speak from 8:30 to 8:45 P. M.

The President's message will be broadcast over all major networks.

1944

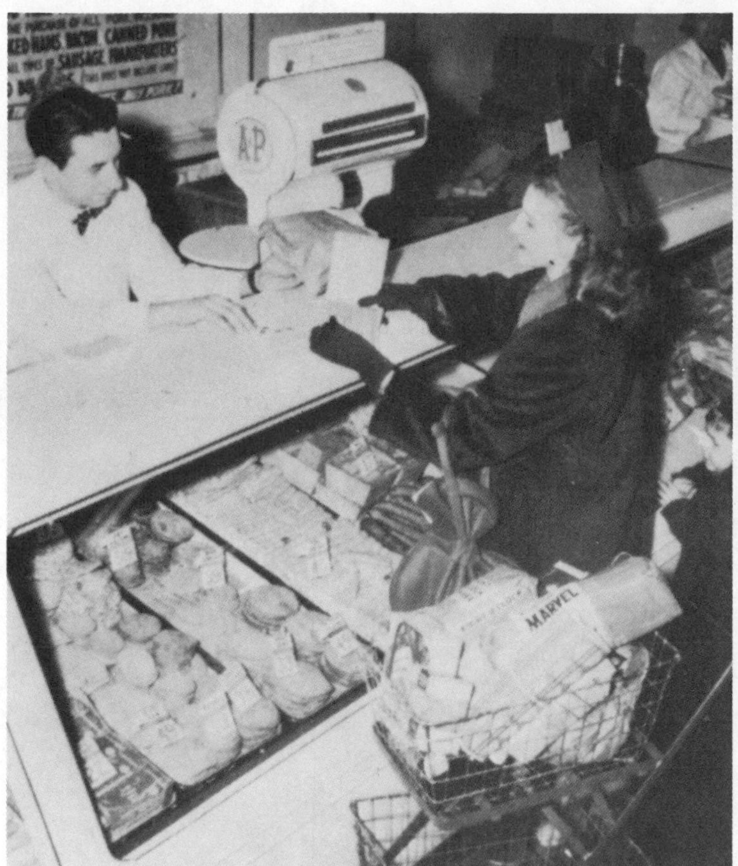

Meat was rationed, and counting coupons became an everyday occurrence.

That war can have positive effects was evidenced by the discovery of new drugs. Streptomycin was one of the first of the new "wonder drugs."

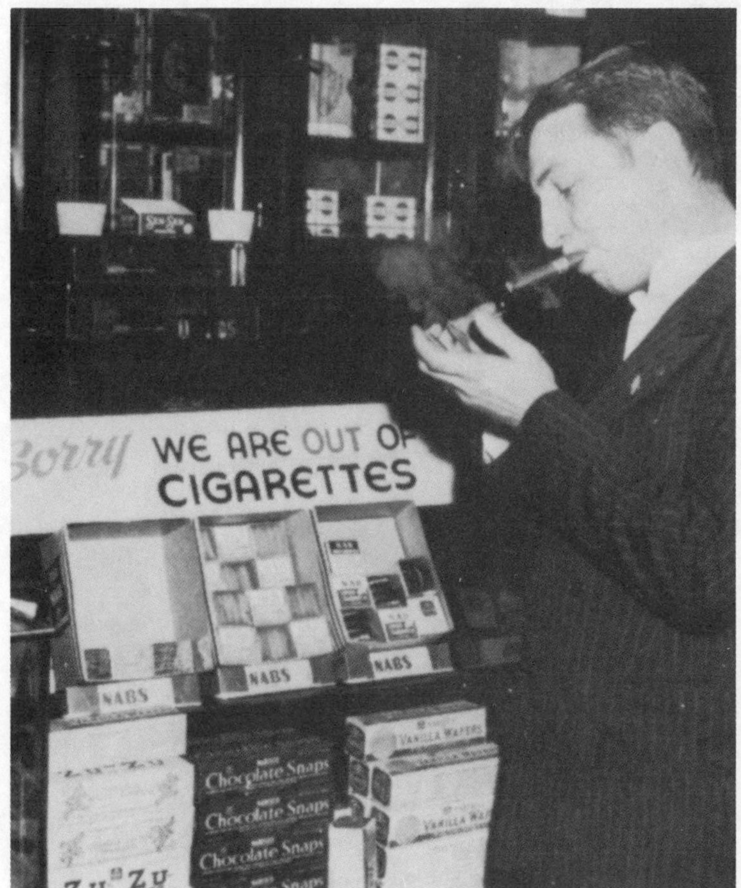

More and more stores were out of popular cigarette brands; some frustrated smokers took up cigars and pipes.

Vitamins became big business as their mass production enabled mass distribution.

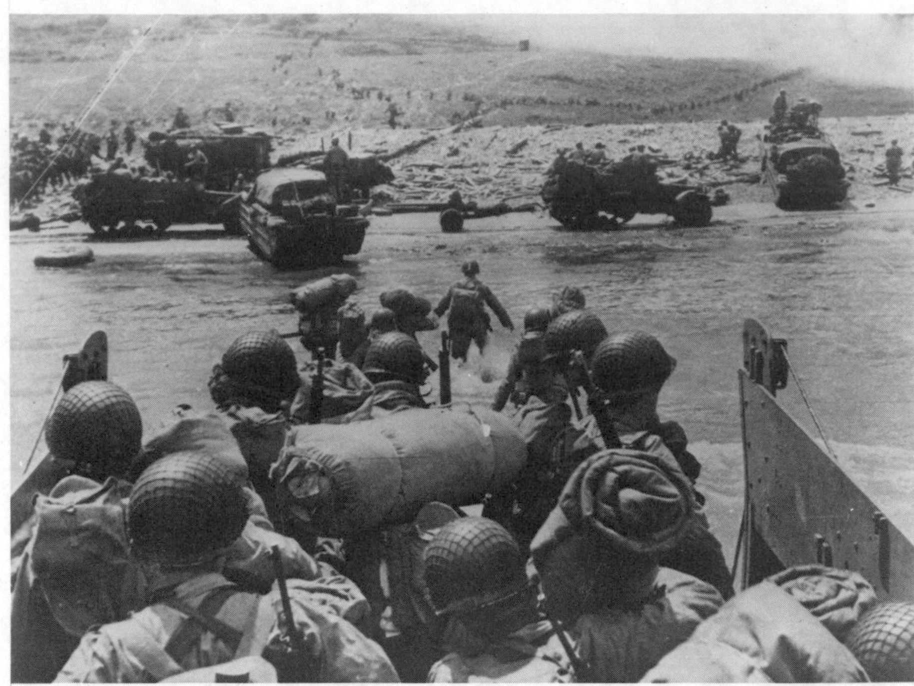

American assault troops land on the Northern coast of France on D-Day.

Gliders being towed to the Normandy coast on D-Day.

A Nazi shell explodes on the beach at Anzio, narrowly missing an amphibious duck carrying supplies from cargo ships anchored offshore.

"All the News That's Fit to Print"

The New York Times.

6 A. M. EXTRA

Partly cloudy and warmer today; moderate to fresh winds.
Temperatures Yesterday—Max., 67; Min., 51
Sunrise, 5:25 A. M.; Sunset, 8:24 P. M.

VOL. XCIII..No. 31,545. Entered as Second-Class Matter, Postoffice, New York, N. Y. NEW YORK, TUESDAY, JUNE 6, 1944. THREE CENTS NEW YORK CITY

ALLIED ARMIES LAND IN FRANCE IN THE HAVRE-CHERBOURG AREA; GREAT INVASION IS UNDER WAY

ROOSEVELT SPEAKS

Says Rome's Fall Marks 'One Up and Two to Go' Among Axis Capitals

WARNS WAY IS HARD

Asks World to Give the Italians a Chance for Recovery

The text of President Roosevelt's address is on Page 5.

By CHARLES HURD

Special to The New York Times.

WASHINGTON, June 5—President Roosevelt hailed tonight the capture of Rome, first of the three major Axis capitals to fall, as a great achievement on the road toward total conquest of the Axis. Rome, he said, marked "one up and two to go."

The President spoke for a quarter-hour on the radio, as had been announced yesterday, but his speech was notable for its lack of heroics. It was in no sense a speech of triumph, but rather a tribute to the United Nations forces and leadership that drove the Germans from Rome.

With this tribute he combined a solemn warning that much greater fighting lies ahead before the Axis is defeated, as well as high tributes to the Italian people, whom he again welcomed as a people into the family of nations opposed to the Axis.

"Italy should go on," Mr. Roosevelt said, "as a great mother nation, contributing to the culture and the progress and the good-will of mankind, developing her special talents in the arts, crafts, and sciences, and preserving her historic and cultural heritage for the benefit of all peoples.

"We want and expect the help of the future Italy toward lasting peace. All the other nations opposed to fascism and nazism ought to help to give Italy a chance."

Shrines Should Live, He Says

President Roosevelt saw considerable significance in the fact that Rome should be the first Axis capital to fall. He remarked its shrines, "visible symbols of the faith and determination of the early saints and martyrs that Christianity should live and become universal," and added that "it will be a source of deep satisfaction that the freedom of the Pope and of Vatican City is assured by the armies of the United Nations."

There is significance, too, he added, in the fact that Rome was liberated by a composite force of soldiers from many nations.

Reviewing the military picture, the President pointed out that "it would be unwise to inflate in our own minds the military importance of the capture of Rome." He cautioned his auditors that while the Germans have retreated "thousands of miles" across Africa and back through Italy "they have suffered heavy losses, but not great enough yet to cause collapse."

"Therefore," he added, "the victory still lies some distance ahead. That distance will be covered in due time—have no fear of that. But it will be tough and it will be costly."

Turning to the relief problem in the newly liberated portion of Italy, Mr. Roosevelt noted that some persons thought of the financial cost, but he maintained that the work would pay dividends "by eliminating fascism" and any future desire by Italians to "start another war of aggression." Relief has been planned, he added, but transport demands are so great that "improvement must be gradual."

He warned Italy that it "cannot grow in stature by seeking to build up a great militaristic empire."

Continued on Page 5

Conferees Accept Cabaret Tax Cut

By The Associated Press.

WASHINGTON, June 5—A House-Senate conference committee agreed today to cut back the cabaret tax from 30 to 20 per cent, but eliminated a provision exempting service men and women from the levy.

The group decided to put the national debt limit at $260,000,000,000 as originally requested by the Administration.

The action is subject to House and Senate votes. The conferees met informally today, but members said that the decisions probably would stand as their final recommendation.

The House, at the insistence of a group of Republicans, passed a bill raising the debt ceiling only from $210,000,000,000 to $240,000,000,000. The Senate then put the figure at $260,000,000,000 and attached a rider reducing the cabaret tax from 30 to 20 per cent and exempting men and women in uniform from paying the tax on their checks.

Some tax experts argued that this exemption would make administration of the excise on night clubs impossible.

FEDERAL LAW HELD RULING INSURANCE

Supreme Court, 4-3, Decides Business Is Interstate and Subject to Trust Act

Special to The New York Times.

WASHINGTON, June 5—The Supreme Court, by a four-to-three decision today, held that the insurance companies of the country, with assets of $37,000,000,000 and annual premium collections in excess of $6,000,000,000, are in interstate commerce and thus subject to the Sherman Anti-Trust Law.

The decision upset precedents which began with a contrary decision by the court more than seventy-five years ago and have been reaffirmed repeatedly since the adoption of the anti-trust law in 1890.

The majority decision, written

Continued on Page 13

PURSUIT IN ITALY

Allies Pass Rome, Cross Tiber as Foe Quits Bank Below City

PLANES JOIN IN CHASE

1,200 Vehicles Wrecked —Eighth Army Battles Into More Towns

By The Associated Press.

ROME, June 5—The Allies' armor and motorized infantry roared through Rome today without pausing, crossed the Tiber River and proceeded with the grim task of destroying two battered German armies fleeing to the north.

Fighter-bombers spearheaded the pursuit, jamming the escape highways with burning enemy transport and littering the fields with dead and wounded Germans. The enemy was tired, disorganized and bewildered by the slashing assault, which in twenty-five days had inflicted a major catastrophe on the Germans and liberated Rome almost without damage.

Railway Yards Bombed

Five hundred American heavy bombers blasted railway yards at five points in northern Italy between Venice and Rimini along which the Germans might attempt to move reinforcements and equipment to bolster their beaten armies. Hour after hour, the Allies' planes swept down on highways leading northward and tore the fleeing enemy apart. Twelve hundred combat vehicles were destroyed from dawn to dark yesterday, and hundreds more today. Farther north, medium bombers smashed bridges and rail facilities.

[The Germans have abandoned the entire left bank of the Tiber from Ostia, at its mouth, to Rome, according to a Vichy broadcast quoted by The Associated Press.

[The Germans are already entrenched in mountain positions

Continued on Page 2

War News Summarized

TUESDAY, JUNE 6, 1944

The invasion of western Europe began this morning.

General Eisenhower, in his first communiqué from Supreme Headquarters, Allied Expeditionary Force, issued at 3:30 A. M., said that "Allied naval forces supported by strong air forces began landing Allied armies this morning on the northern coast of France."

The assault was made by British, American and Canadian troops who, under command of Gen. Sir Bernard L. Montgomery, landed in Normandy. London gave no further details but earlier Berlin had broadcast that parachute troops had landed on the Normandy Peninsula near Cherbourg and that invasion forces were pouring from landing craft under cover of warships near Havre. Dunkerque and Calais were being heavily bombed, the Germans said.

Later announcements from Berlin said that there was fighting between Caen and Trouville and that shock troops had swung into action to halt the invasion. [All the foregoing, 1:8.]

General Eisenhower, in an order of the day to each member of the "great crusade," told his men the enemy would fight savagely and added: "We will accept nothing less than full victory. Good luck." In a broadcast to the "Peoples of Western Europe," he said the day would come when he would need their full help. A special word to France added that Frenchmen would rule the country. [1:6-7.] Almost simultaneously it was announced that General de Gaulle had arrived in London. [6:2.]

The liberation of Rome in no way slowed the Allied pursuit of the tired and disorganized German armies in Italy yesterday. Armored and motorized units sped across the Tiber River to press hard upon the retreating enemy's heels. Five hundred heavy bombers joined with lighter aircraft to smash rail and road routes leading to northern Italy and to add to the foe's demoralization. The Eighth Army, despite heavy opposition, especially northeast of Valmontone, captured a number of strategic towns. [1:3; map P. 2.]

General Clark said that parts of the two German armies had been smashed. He doubted the ability of the German Fourteenth to put up effective opposition and declared that the Tenth had taken a bad beating. [3:1.]

King Victor Emmanuel fulfilled his promise and turned over all authority to his son, Crown Prince Humbert. [1:5-6.]

President Roosevelt warned the people of the United States in a radio talk last night not to over-emphasize the military significance of the liberation of Rome. "Germany has not yet been driven to surrender," he said. "Victory still lies some distance ahead. * * * It will be tough and it will be costly." The President appealed to the world to give Italy a chance to contribute her share to a lasting peace. [1:1.]

In the Pacific theatre Americans were converging on the Biak airfields. Allied planes sank one and damaged two Japanese destroyers and shot down at least eighteen aircraft. [8:1.]

FIRST ALLIED LANDING MADE ON SHORES OF WESTERN EUROPE

June 6, 1944

General Eisenhower's armies invaded northern France this morning. While the landing points were not specified, the Germans said that troops had gone ashore near Havre and that fighting raged at Caen (1). The enemy also said that parachutists had descended at the northern tip of the Normandy Peninsula (2) and heavy bombing had been visited on Calais and Dunkerque (3).

POPE GIVES THANKS ROME WAS SPARED

Voices Appreciation to Both Belligerents in Message to Throng at St. Peter's

By Wireless to The New York Times.

VATICAN CITY, June 5—Pope Pius XII appeared on the balcony of St. Peter's at 6 P. M. today to thank God that Rome had been spared from the ravages of war while before him in the densely packed square of St. Peter's and the new broad Via Della Conciliazione tens of thousands of Romans cheered themselves hoarse.

It was the third time today that the Pontiff had showed himself to cheering crowds, as he had appeared twice at a window of his office this morning. But this was a solemn, sacred occasion and no one knowing anything about Pius XII can doubt the fervor of his thankfulness that Rome had been saved.

The Pontiff seemed strong and well and his voice carried far, though it was difficult to hear every word he said because of the crowd.

"We must give thanks to God for the favors we have received," said the Pope. "Rome has been spared. This day will go down in the annals of Rome."

He went on to say he hoped that Italians would be worthy of the grace shown them and put aside hatred and all personal vendettas. He then thanked both belligerents—the Allies and Germany—for having left Rome intact.

After a prayer of thankfulness to the Blessed Virgin and Saints Peter and Paul, guardians of Rome, the Pontiff gave his blessing, "urbe et orbis," as the immense crowd knelt before him.

[The Associated Press estimated the crowd was between 250,000 and 500,000.]

The world has changed for Rome but the Vatican goes on imperturbably as it has through so many other conquests in centuries gone by. It is neutral in fact and spirit. The Pope and all high officials went about their daily routine today as in the past. Except for the tanks and armored cars running along the street in front of St. Peter's one could never know what had happened today.

Continued on Page 5

Italy's Monarch Yields Rule To Son, but Retains Throne

By The Associated Press.

NAPLES, June 5—Victor Emmanuel III stepped aside as King of Italy today, as he previously had said he would do upon the liberation of Rome, and handed to his 39-year-old son, Crown Prince Humbert, all "royal prerogatives." Italian political pressure had been brought to bear against him since the occupation of Naples.

In a decree signed by himself and countersigned by Premier Pietro Badoglio, head of the Italian Liberation Government, the King named his son Lieutenant General of the Realm. The monarch, however, retained his title as head of the House of Savoy and remains as King without power.

[The first act of the Council of Ministers after the transfer of royal powers was a formal denunciation of the 1940 armistice treaty inflicted on France, The United Press said.]

Victor Emmanuel, who became King July 29, 1900, had announced last April 12 his "irrevocable" decision to withdraw from public life "on the day on which Allied troops enter Rome."

Little more than a figurehead since Benito Mussolini assumed the dictatorship of Italy, Victor Emmanuel had won a reputation in the first years of his reign as a sympathetic monarch, interested in his people and their problems.

Prince Humbert, tall and erect, opposed fascism in Italy at the start, but later made a truce with Mussolini. In effect, Humbert becomes the King's regent.

TEXT OF ROYAL DECREE

The King's withdrawal decree:

I, Victor Emmanuel III, by the grace of God and by the will of the nation King of Italy, in collaboration with the President of the Council of Ministers and with the agreement of the Council, have ordered and order as follows:

My beloved son, Humbert of Savoy, Prince of Piedmont, is nominated our Lieutenant General. In collaboration with responsible Ministers he will in our name superintend all matters of administration and exercise all royal prerogatives without exception, signing royal decrees which will be countersigned and authenticated in the usual way.

We order all concerned to observe this decree and to see that it is observed as the law of the State.

Given at Ravello June 5, 1944.
VICTOR EMMANUEL.
(Countersigned) PIETRO BADOGLIO.

The withdrawal was presented to

Continued on Page 4

ALLIED WARNING FLASHED TO COAST

People Told to Clear Area 22 Miles Inland as Soon as Instructions Are Given

By Cable to The New York Times.

LONDON, Tuesday, June 6—The British Broadcasting Corporation began its 8 A. M. news bulletin this morning with quotations from a Supreme Headquarters' "urgent warning" to inhabitants of the enemy-occupied countries living near the coast.

Gen. Dwight D. Eisenhower has directed that whenever possible in France a warning shall be given to towns in which certain targets will be intensively bombed.

This warning, the broadcast said,

Continued on Page B

PARADE OF PLANES CARRIES INVADERS

Witness Says First 'Chutists Met Only Light Fire When They Landed in France

The first eyewitness account of the Allies' invasion of Europe was given in a pool broadcast from London this morning by Wright Bryan of the National Broadcasting Company, who accompanied the airborne troops in their landings.

His account said the first spearhead of Allied forces landed by parachute in northern France in the first hour of D-day.

"In the navigator's dome in the flight deck of a C-47, I rode across the English Channel with the first group of planes from the United States Ninth Air Force Troop Carrier Command to take our fighting men into Europe," Mr. Bryan said.

He added that just before he left French soil for the return trip he saw seventeen American paratroopers, led by a lieutenant colonel, jump with their arms, ammunition and equipment into German-occupied France."

He declared that his group at the head of the leading wing was met with "only scattering small

Continued on Page B

Eisenhower Instructs Europeans; Gives Battle Order to His Armies

Following are the texts of a statement by Gen. Dwight D. Eisenhower broadcast to the people of western Europe and his Order of the Day to the Allied Expeditionary Force as recorded by The New York Times and the Columbia Broadcasting System:

People of western Europe! A landing was made this morning on the coast of France by troops of the Allied Expeditionary Force. This landing is part of the concerted United Nations plan for the liberation of Europe, made in conjunction with our great Russian Allies. I have this message for all of you. Although the initial assault may not have been made in your own country, the hour of your liberation is approaching.

All patriots, men and women, young and old, have a part to play in the achievement of final victory. To members of resistance movements, whether led by national or outside leaders, I say: "Follow the instructions you have received." To patriots who are not members of organized resistance groups I say, "continue your passive resistance, but do not needlessly endanger your lives until I give you the signal to rise and strike the enemy. The day will come when I shall need your united strength. Until that day, I call on you for the hard task of discipline and restraint."

Citizens of France! I am proud to have again under my command the gallant forces of France. Fighting beside their Allies, they will play a worthy part in the liberation of their

Continued on Page 3

EISENHOWER ACTS

U. S., British, Canadian Troops Backed by Sea, Air Forces

MONTGOMERY LEADS

Nazis Say Their Shock Units Are Battling Our Parachutists

Communique No. 1 On Allied Invasion

By Broadcast to The New York Times.

LONDON, Tuesday, June 6—The Supreme Headquarters of the Allied Expeditionary Force issued this communiqué this morning:

"Under the command of General Eisenhower, Allied naval forces, supported by strong air forces, began landing Allied armies this morning on the northern coast of France."

By RAYMOND DANIELL

By Cable to The New York Times.

SUPREME HEADQUARTERS ALLIED EXPEDITIONARY FORCES, Tuesday, June 6—The invasion of Europe from the west has begun.

In the gray light of a summer dawn Gen. Dwight D. Eisenhower threw his great Anglo-American force into action today for the liberation of the Continent. The spearhead of attack was an Army group commanded by Gen. Sir Bernard L. Montgomery and comprising troops of the United States, Britain and Canada.

General Eisenhower's first communiqué was terse and calculated to give little information to the enemy. It said merely that "Allied naval forces supported by strong air forces began landing Allied armies this morning on the northern coast of France."

After the first communiqué was released it was announced that the Allied landing was in Normandy.

Caen Battle Reported

German broadcasts, beginning at 6:30 A. M., London time, [12:30 A. M. Eastern war time] gave first word of the assault. [The Associated Press said General Eisenhower, for the sake of surprise, deliberately let the Germans have the "first word."]

The German DNB agency said the Allied invasion operations began with the landing of airborne troops in the area of the mouth of the Seine River.

[Berlin said the "center of gravity" of the fierce fighting was at Caen, thirty miles southwest of Havre and sixty-five miles southeast of Cherbourg, The Associated Press reported. Caen is ten miles inland from the sea, at the base of the seventy-five-mile-wide Normandy Peninsula, and fighting there might indicate the Allies' seizing of a beachhead.

[DNB said in a broadcast just before 10 A. M. (4 A. M. Eastern war time) that the Anglo-American troops had been reinforced at dawn at the mouth of the Seine River in the Havre area.]

[An Allied correspondent broadcasting from Supreme Headquarters, according to the Columbia Broadcasting System, said this morning that "German tanks are moving up

Continued on Page A
Following Page 8

"All the News That's Fit to Print"

The New York Times.

LATE CITY EDITION
POSTSCRIPT
Partly cloudy and warmer today
Temperatures Yesterday—Max., 67; Min., 57
Sunrise, 5:23 A. M.; Sunset, 8:29 P. M.

VOL. XCIII—No. 31,555. Entered as Second-Class Matter, Postoffice, New York, N. Y. NEW YORK, FRIDAY, JUNE 16, 1944. THREE CENTS IN NEW YORK CITY

OUR SUPERFORTS BOMB CITIES IN JAPAN; AMERICAN FORCES LANDING IN MARIANAS; ALLIES GAIN ON CHERBOURG PENINSULA

NAZI ROADS IN PERIL

Americans Are Nearing Two Vital Points on Cherbourg Neck

GERMAN TANKS LOSE

British Gain in Caen Sector—Battleship Shells Le Havre

5 A. M. Communique

By The United Press.

SUPREME HEADQUARTERS, Allied Expeditionary Force, Friday, June 16—Allied forces on the Cherbourg peninsula have made further progress west of Pont l'Abbé, seventeen miles from the west coast, a communiqué said today.

No major change has been made in any sector, the communiqué 21 said.

All attempts by the Germans to seize the initiative have been frustrated and their counterattacks have been repelled.

At midnight Thursday, it was learned American troops were six miles from La Haye du Puits, where western communications along the peninsula narrow to a junction before running on southward.

By DREW MIDDLETON
By Cable to The New York Times.

SUPREME HEADQUARTERS, Allied Expeditionary Force, Friday, June 16—Americans, supported by tanks, are advancing on a front of ten miles across the neck of the Cherbourg Peninsula, threatening La Haye du Puits and St. Sauveur-Le Vicomte, two of the most important links in the enemy's chain of communications with Cherbourg.

Late yesterday Allied patrols were reported fighting in Pretot, four miles northeast of La Haye, and at Reigneville, only three miles northeast of St. Sauveur-Le Vicomte, after the occupation of Baupte, nine and a half miles east of La Haye and five miles west of Carentan. Baupte was occupied yesterday morning as the Allied American offensive to cut off the great Norman port developed swiftly.

The Allied line in this area is now only about seven miles from the main enemy supply network on the western side of the peninsula.

Quinéville, on the east coast of the peninsula, four and a half miles northeast of Montebourg, has also been captured and the American right now is firmly anchored on the sea.

No Major Fight in Quadrilateral

Although there were still a number of sharp skirmishes in the quadrilateral of Balleroy, Tilly-sur-Seulles, Villers-Bocage and Caumont, neither side launched a major attack yesterday. German armored divisions suffered "substantial" tank casualties in Wednesday's fighting, which culminated in a "very heavy" assault in the Villers-Bocage area in which eight Panther and nine Tiger tanks were destroyed by British tanks and anti-tank guns. British veterans, including men of a once famous division in the Troarn area, were slowly pushing forward southwest of Troarn in the face of bitter enemy resistance.

Hundreds of airplane engines sounded reveille over the front at dawn yesterday as the United States Ninth Air Force and the British Second Tactical Air Force launched large-scale operations in support of the ground forces. Fighter-bombers and fighters skimmed over Allied tanks and troops to harry German troop concentrations, tanks, convoys and supply dumps in the battle area.

The flow of enemy reinforcements to the fighting zone was seriously hampered by Marauders and Havocs, which bombed bridges at Conde-sur-Noireau, St. Lô, Lessay, Chartres, Coltainville and a road junction at Argentan.

The Navy's part in the cam-

Continued on Page 6

President Outlines U. S. Plan For World Security Union

Four Major Powers Would Have Permanent Place in Elected Council—All Would Keep Forces to Halt War

By CHARLES HURD
Special to The New York Times.

WASHINGTON, June 15—President Roosevelt advanced a plan today for post-war international security calling for the formation of "a fully representative organization" of peace-loving countries. It would elect a smaller council on which the four major United Nations would be constantly represented with a "suitable" number of smaller countries. An international court of justice would be set up.

"The purpose of the organization," the President's statement said, "would be to maintain peace and security and to assist the creation, through international co-operations of conditions of stability and well-being necessary for peaceful and friendly relations among nations."

Of course, he said, the plan will become possible only when our present enemies are defeated "and effective arrangements are made to prevent them from making war again."

Mr. Roosevelt suggested no formal name for the proposed organization and made no recommendations as to the details of establishing it. He said, however, that "we are not thinking" of a super-state with its own armies and police forces. Instead "we are seeking" effective arrangements through which the nations would maintain adequate forces to prevent war and make impossible deliberate preparations for war and, when necessary, to have such forces available for joint action.

At first glance the plan, in the skeleton outline by the President, rested on about the same basis as the League of Nations; that is, an

Continued on Page 12

SAIPAN IS STORMED

Americans Fight Way Inland on Base Vital to Japan's Defense

BATTLING IN TOWN

Navy's Fire Covers Leap to Marianas, 1,465 Miles From Tokyo

By GEORGE F. HORNE
By Telephone to The New York Times.

PACIFIC FLEET HEADQUARTERS, June 15—American troops who fought their way ashore on Saipan Island in the Marianas Islands on Wednesday have firmly established their beachheads and are making good progress in an advance inland against heavy opposition, Admiral Chester W. Nimitz said in a communiqué tonight.

The enemy is fighting bitterly and has attempted several counterattacks with tanks, but they have been broken up by our troops with the support of aircraft and warships lying offshore. Thus the most important battle fought so far in the Pacific offensive, now reaching to within 1,465 statute miles of Tokyo and a threat to the Japanese homeland itself, was going well for the invaders.

Tonight's communiqué was the second of the day issued by Admiral Nimitz. The first confirmed previous Japanese reports that Saipan was being invaded.

Defenses Well Organized

Tonight the Commander in Chief of the Pacific Fleet told of the advance inland. He said that in general the fighting was heavy and the defenses well organized.

We have captured Agingan Point, on the southwestern extremity of the big island, he said, and troops have forced their way into the town of Charan-Kanoa, where brisk fighting was still going on. Charan-Kanoa is the center of Saipan's big sugar refining industry and has a number of mills.

Between Charan-Kanoa, the first Japanese community to witness an engagement between land forces of the United States and Japan, and Agingan Point, a distance of about two miles, stretches a flat beachland and trees. Outside is a reef.

Our control of the air over Saipan and possibly over other Mari-

Continued on Page 3

STUNNING BLOWS STRIKE FOE IN PACIFIC ARENA

Introducing a new weapon for this global war, the United States sent Superfortresses from Asiatic bases to rain explosives on Japan (1). Tokyo said several cities on the island of Kyushu had been hit (detailed map Page 2). Earlier, American amphibious forces stormed ashore on Saipan Island (2) in the Marianas group, outpost of Japan itself (detailed map Page 3). From General MacArthur's command long-range planes struck at the bases of Yap (3) and Truk (4).

DE GAULLE NAMES NORMANDY AGENT

Appointing of Commissioner While on Beachhead Visit Presents Poser to Allies

By E. C. DANIEL
By Wireless to The New York Times.

LONDON, June 15—Without waiting for an agreement with the United States and Great Britain on the civil administration of France, Gen. Charles de Gaulle has already installed a Commissioner for Civil Affairs in Normandy.

This action, which became known today upon the general's return from his visit to France, apparently was taken without consulting Allied military or political authorities.

At first glance the functions of this Commissioner would seem to duplicate those of the civil affairs section which the Allied Supreme Command has organized to administer liberated areas in the rear of the advancing armies.

However, if the United States and Britain do not take umbrage at General de Gaulle's haste in in-

Continued on Page 7

ALLIED TIDE IN ITALY ENGULFS ORVIETO

8th and 5th Armies Break New German Line, Win Narni, Aquila, Many Other Places

By The Associated Press.

ROME, June 15 — Bursting through another line of defenses hastily thrown up by the retreating Germans beyond Rome, Allied forces have captured the large Italian towns of Orvieto, Aquila and Narni in a general advance and were fighting tonight in the outskirts of the important industrial and communications center of Terni, forty-five miles north of the capital.

American troops moving up the Tyrrhenian coast captured Magliano and threatened Bengodi, only fourteen miles from Grosseto, after having seized vast quantities of Nazi food supplies at Orbetello. They had entirely cleared lateral highway 74, running inland from the coast past the northern shore of Lake Bolsena.

Eighth Army columns, now carrying the brunt of the inland advance, fought their way into Orvi-

Continued on Page 9

Invasion and Other War News Summarized

FRIDAY, JUNE 16, 1944

Japan felt the force of two mighty American blows, while her Axis partner was being steadily pushed back on the fields of Normandy.

The new B-29 Superfortresses made their initial major bow with a sudden heavy assault on the island of Kyushu, part of the Japanese home territory. It was the first time bombs had fallen on Japan itself since General Doolittle's Shangri-la sweep more than two years ago. The only details disclosed by Washington were that the B-29's had "probably" operated from bases in China and were from a new Twentieth Air Force.

This force, under direct command of General Arnold and supervision of the Joint Chiefs of Staffs, will be used as an aerial battle fleet, or major task force, in future operations. [All the foregoing 1:8.]

Tokyo's version of the attack said that Yawata, site of the Imperial Steel Works, the communications center of Moji and the suburbs of Kokura, all near Shimonoseki, had been hit. The Japanese asserted two Superfortresses and five other American planes had been shot down. [1:6-7; map P. 2.]

The B-29 flies so high and so fast that it appears to ground defenders as a small gnat with a vapor trail. It carries the heaviest bomb load of any plane in the world. [4:2-8.]

While Japan was bearing this blow at home it was announced that American amphibious forces had stormed ashore on the strategic island of Saipan in the Marianas. A four-day battering by ships and planes preceded the first assault on Wednesday. Strong forces have landed and are battling fierce enemy opposition. A late communiqué said beachheads had been secured and our troops were advancing inland. [1:4; map P. 3.]

Tokyo reported early today that an American task force had attacked the Bonin Islands, midway between Japan and Saipan, and that hostile planes had attacked Korea. [Box 1:8.]

Southwest Pacific planes kept the enemy occupied by dumping 180 tons of bombs on Truk in the heaviest attack yet made on that island by General MacArthur's fliers. Yap and other neighboring places were also hit. [3:8.]

In Burma airborne Chindits launched a sudden attack on Mogaung, supporting base for Myitkyina, but along the Shweli River the Japanese recaptured Hsiangta and threatened to win back Lungling. [4:1.]

The invasion of Normandy showed steady progress yesterday. Americans advancing on a ten-mile front across the neck of the Cherbourg Peninsula menaced La Haye. Baupte and Quineville were captured and the Germans suffered heavy tank losses in strong counter-attacks in the Caumont-Tilly sector. Battleships and cruisers poured shells into enemy positions and Le Havre. [1:1; map P. 6.]

More than 7,000 Allied aircraft gave close support to the ground troops. The E-boat base at Le Havre was heavily bombed, and on Wednesday night the RAF struck again at the German synthetic oil center of Gelsenkirchen in the Ruhr. [5:1.]

General de Gaulle, described by his headquarters as "President of the Provisional Government of the French Republic," before returning from the beachhead installed a Commissioner for Civil Affairs in Normandy without consulting Allied military or political leaders. [1:2.]

In Italy, too, the Germans were being pushed back. The Allies smashed through another defense line to take Orvieto, Aquila and Narni, and to come within eighty miles of Florence. [1:3; map P. 9.] The Red Army continued to beat down strong Finnish resistance and was only thirty-three miles from Viborg and twenty-six from Koivisto. [1:7; map P 8.]

President Roosevelt made public an outline of his plan for post-war security. He suggested an organization of all peace-loving countries, a smaller council on which the four major powers and small nations would be represented and an international court of justice. "We are not thinking of a super-state with its own police forces," he said, but of peace by agreement. [1:2-3.]

PETRILLO IS ORDERED TO END RECORDS BAN

WLB Tells Union, Companies to Agree on Royalty Plan—Musicians' Head Defiant

By LOUIS STARK
Special to The New York Times.

WASHINGTON, June 15—The War Labor Board ordered the American Federation of Musicians today to end the ban which it put on production of phonograph recordings on Aug. 1, 1942.

In its directive, the board also provided that the transcription companies should set up machinery for the payment of royalties on records, reversing a panel recommendation which opposed payments.

Although the board did not specifically order the payment of royalties into the union unemployment fund, as had been requested, it provided that the money be held in escrow. The board did not fix the amount of these payments but proposed that the parties agree on this detail by direct conference. Failure to agree, the board stated, would result in arbitration by the board itself.

The industry members who, with the public members, made up the eight-man majority, favored the seven-point program proposed by the public spokesmen reluctantly lest a worse compromise be the alternative, it was stated.

The four labor members dissented. They did not state their reasons but it was reported that they sided with Mr. Petrillo, who had asserted that the ban was not really a strike, that the WLB had no jurisdiction of the case and that the dispute did not affect war production.

The companies involved in the case were the National Broadcasting Company, radio recording division; the Columbia Recording Corporation, and the RCA Victor division of the Radio Corporation of America.

The board held that contracts for royalty payments to the union made by a group of companies led by Decca Recordings did not require board approval since the funds set up did not involve a wage increase and thus did not require board approval under the wage stabilization program.

The union announced that it had signed agreements with more than eighty companies and it withdrew

Continued on Page 20

Tokyo Tries to Belittle Raid; Claims Two Superfortresses

By The United Press.

SAN FRANCISCO, June 15—The official Japanese radio announced today that American warplanes, including B-29 Superfortresses, had bombed Yawata, home of the great Imperial Steel Works; Moji, a communications center, and Kokura in northern Kyushu Island of the Japanese homeland Friday morning, June 16 (Japanese time).

The broadcast, recorded by United Press, admitted the attacking planes had started "two or three fires," but claimed they were "extinguished immediately."

Late news broadcasts from Tokyo continued to minimize the effects of the raid, claiming that damage was "limited" to "two or three light industrial shops."

The attacking force took off from a China air base and flew "by way of Antung, situated on the Manchukuo-Chosen border," Tokyo claimed, adding that the presence of the B-29's "came as no surprise."

The Japanese claimed their intercepting planes had shot down six of the attacking American aircraft. Two of these, said the Japanese announcement, were B-29 Superfortresses.

The Tokyo radio also reported that the railway line between Orio and Hasaka had been "slightly damaged" in the raid. The Japanese broadcast said the rail line "was repaired at once * * * and traffic service has been resumed without any hitch."

Moji is the site of the Mitsui

Continued on Page 2

RED ARMY EXPANDS WEDGE IN FINLAND

Breach Widened to 46 Miles With Spearhead Thrusting Closer to Viborg

By The United Press.

LONDON, Friday, June 16—Red Army forces have widened their breach in the Finnish lines across the Karelian Isthmus to more than forty-six miles and have pushed to within thirty-three miles of Viborg by capturing the heavily fortified town of Kanneljaervi, near the Leningrad-Helsinki Railroad, Moscow announced last night.

The Moscow bulletin announced that Gen. Leonid A. Govoroff's Leningrad Army, in the six days it has been on the offensive, had smashed through two powerful Finnish defense belts, advanced a total of almost twenty-five miles and widened its break-through to

Continued on Page 8

Bond Purchases by Armed Forces Help City to Raise 8.7% of E Quota

New York City fighting men purchased war bonds aggregating $4,641,751 in value between June 1 and June 10, it was announced yesterday by Nevil Ford, chairman of the War Finance Committee for New York, who said that their action has helped to lift the city's total sale of E bonds in the Fifth War Loan drive to $19,785,345, or 8.7 per cent of its E bond quota of $227,526,600.

"This striking evidence of double-action patriotism by our men and women in the armed forces should give every citizen something to think about," Mr. Ford declared. "Not only are they offering their lives—something that we are not asked to do—but they are also allotting large sums from their service pay to help speed the day of victory.

"If anyone, after reading today's headlines, still needs to be prodded in order to do his full share in raising the largest War Loan quotas ever asked of our city and State, let him think this over."

Sales of all types of issues to individual purchasers in New York City soared to a total of $48,984,276 through the close of business on Wednesday, according to Mr. Ford. Single day sales totaling $15,400,000 on Wednesday to individual purchases in New York State brought the Fifth War Loan total for the State to $69,000,000.

The State-wide total sales of E bonds have risen to $33,500,000, or 9.1 per cent of the State's quota of $367,000,000 in this category. It was explained that the daily totals of E bond sales for the city and State are one day behind those of the sales of other types to individual investors because of the amount of work involved in processing sales from the great num-

Continued on Page 10

B-29'S MAKE DEBUT

Tokyo Reports Assaults on Industrial Heart of Kyushu Island

20TH AAF CREATED

New Command Will Be the Air Equivalent of a Naval Task Force

Details of new Superfortress bomber plane are on Page 4.

By SIDNEY SHALETT
Special to The New York Times.

WASHINGTON, June 15—The air war against the heart of the Japanese Empire has begun, the War Department announced this afternoon. B-29 Superfortresses of the new Twentieth Air Force, which is part of a new "super-air force" under the personal command of Gen. H. H. Arnold, bombed Japan today, a special communiqué revealed.

There are three epochal factors in the announcement:

First, that the monster B-29, half again as big as the Flying Fortress, is in operation.

Second, that the type of aerial attrition that reduced Germany to the stage where an invasion of Europe could be launched has commenced against Japan proper.

Third, that, in creating the Twentieth Air Force, a special organization that is not subject to the jurisdiction of any theatre commander, the Joint Chiefs of Staff have set up what virtually amounts to a separate air force.

Tokyo Road Shortened

The importance of this new phase of the Pacific war was emphasized by statements from Gen. George C. Marshall, Chief of Staff, who termed it the beginning of "a new type of offensive against our enemy"; from General Arnold, commanding general of the AAF, who declared it was "the fruition of years of planning for truly global warfare," and Secretary of War Henry L. Stimson, who asserted that the action had "shortened our road to Tokyo."

The history-making communiqué was confined to the following bare statement, personally handed out by Maj. Gen. Alexander D. Surles, War Department Director of Public Relations, at 1:39 o'clock this afternoon:

"B-29 Superfortresses of the United States Army Air Forces Twentieth Bomber Command bombed Japan today."

No details of where we struck the enemy, or how hard we hit, were revealed, although it was understood that the War Department would release this information as quickly as it felt the story might be told without imperiling security.

Representative Joe Starnes of Alabama, member of the Military Subcommittee of the Appropriations Committee, told the House that Tokyo was the target, and that a "heavy task force" of B-29's had "successfully" bombed

Continued on Page 4

Air Attack on Korea Reported by Tokyo

By The Associated Press.

The Japanese Domei agency said early today in a broadcast reported by Federal Communications Commission monitors that several "enemy" planes had raided Korea, Asiatic mainland area immediately opposite Japan.

The broadcast, transmitted to occupied East Asia areas, said the planes had hit in southern Korea. It quoted an announcement issued by the Japanese Army in Keijo (Seoul) that "we suffered no losses."

A Tokyo broadcast said later an "enemy task force" had attacked the Bonin Islands southeast of the Japanese mainland Thursday afternoon. This group stands midway between Japan and the Marianas, where American forces have effected a landing.

"All the News That's Fit to Print"

The New York Times.

LATE CITY EDITION
Partly cloudy with moderate winds today.
Temperatures Yesterday—Max., 80; Min., 68
Sunrise, 5:42 A. M.; Sunset, 8:22 P. M.

Copyright, 1944, by The New York Times Company.

VOL. XCIII..No. 31,590. Entered as Second-Class Matter, Postoffice, New York, N. Y. NEW YORK, FRIDAY, JULY 21, 1944. THREE CENTS IN NEW YORK CITY

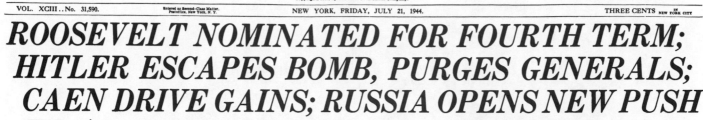

ROOSEVELT NOMINATED FOR FOURTH TERM; HITLER ESCAPES BOMB, PURGES GENERALS; CAEN DRIVE GAINS; RUSSIA OPENS NEW PUSH

FUEHRER 'BRUISED'

Bomb Wounds 13 Staff Officers, One Fatally—Assassin Is Dead

'USURPERS' BLAMED

Hitler Names New Chief of Staff—Himmler to Rule Home Front

Texts of Hitler, Doenitz and Goering speeches, Page 3.

By JOSEPH SHAPLEN

Adolf Hitler had a narrow escape from death by assassination at his secret headquarters, the Berlin radio reported yesterday, and a few hours later in a radio broadcast to the German people he blamed an "officers' clique" for the attempt to kill him. His address disclosed a movement in the armed forces to overthrow him and his regime. He announced that a purge of the conspirators was under way.

Thirteen members of his military staff were injured, one fatally and two seriously, by a bomb set off at an undisclosed place while many of his highest advisers were assembled around him. The man who played the role of assassin, Hitler said, was Colonel Count von Stauffenberg, one of his collaborators, who stood only six feet away from him as he hurled the bomb. Von Stauffenberg is dead, Hitler announced.

Waiting to see Hitler before the assassination attempt was Benito Mussolini. Reich Marshal Hermann Goering, who rushed to Hitler's side, was in the immediate vicinity. Hitler escaped with singes and bruises.

Army Clique Blamed

While Dr. Joseph Goebbels and Nazi radio propagandists at first tried to put the blame for the attempt to kill the Fuehrer upon the Allies, Hitler himself exploded the bombshell by announcing that the culprits were a group of German Army officers. He thus confirmed reports of a serious rift between the Nazi High Command and German military elements.

In his broadcast, recorded by the Federal Communications Commission, Hitler told the German people: "If I address you today I am doing so for two reasons: first, so that you shall hear my voice and know that I personally am unhurt and well, and, second, so that you shall hear the details about a crime that has no equal in German history.

"An extremely small clique of ambitious, unscrupulous and at the same time foolish, criminally stupid officers hatched a plot to re-

Continued on Page 3

Nazi-Army Rift Is Revealed In Gravest Reich War Crisis

'Usurpers' Who Hatched Plot Not Named—Accused of Being Officer Group Wanting to Repeat the 1918 'Stab in the Back'

By RAYMOND DANIELL

By Cable to THE NEW YORK TIMES.

LONDON, July 20—Broadcasting so that the German people could hear his voice and know that he was unhurt after the attempt to assassinate him, Chancellor Adolf Hitler confirmed tonight all rumors and suspicions of disaffection and unrest in the Reich.

Heinrich Himmler, the Fuehrer said, has been made commander in chief of the home army to "create order once and for all." Hitler also ordered that no "military authority, no leader of any unit, no private in the field" was to obey any orders emanating from "usurpers" who were seeking peace.

He left the identity of those usurpers something of a mystery, for he referred to them as "a small group that emerged in Germany, just as in Italy, in the belief that they could repeat the 1918 stab in the back." Later he said they had "no bond with or nothing in common with the Wehrmacht, and, above all, none with the German people."

It is clear that a real crisis has arisen in the Reich and it remains to be seen whether the Nazis have chosen the wisest way to deal with it. A purge is as likely to widen the schism as not, and the German people, with their traditional respect for their officer class, may feel that if the Nazis choose war, and the old officers favor peace, the time may have come to question the infallibility of the Fuehrer.

The announcement left open to speculation the question of not only who was behind the assassination attempt but, even more interesting, the question of who in Germany was in position to make the attempt.

That Germany is going through

Continued on Page 5

Admiral and General Told To Form New Tokyo Regime

Gen. Kuniaki Koiso, a member of the same Kwantung Army group to which former Premier Gen. Hideki Tojo belongs, arrived in Tokyo from Korea yesterday to participate with Admiral Mitsumasa Yonai in the formation of a new "critical decisive wartime" Cabinet by "command" of Emperor Hirohito, it was disclosed in Japanese broadcasts and press dispatches reported to the Office of War Information by the Federal Communications Commission.

General Koiso, Governor General of Korea, and Admiral Yonai, a former Premier and member of the Supreme War Council, were summoned as "senior leaders of the army and navy," the Japanese Domei agency said. Each is 64 years old.

Meanwhile, the Domei agency, in a wireless dispatch to the controlled East Asia press warned its bureaus to be "on the alert" for new developments, presumably regarding an announcement of the new Cabinet's membership.

"Competent political observers expect that the new Cabinet will be formed swiftly," Domei said. Another Japanese account predicted that the new Government would be formed by "Friday morning at the latest."

Co-Premiership Doubted

Koiso and Yonai were designated to form a new Government after Emperor Hirohito had called in Marquis Koichi Kido, Lord Keeper of the Privy Seal, to sound out Japan's "elder statesmen" for candidates to serve as the nucleus for what Domei termed a "more powerful Cabinet."

In a continuation of the "elder statesman" system of choosing Cabinet leaders, Kido then called a caucus of former Premiers. After this meeting, the following an-

Continued on Page 3

ALLIES STORM ARNO ON A 25-MILE FRONT

Americans, in Hot Pursuit of Bewildered Germans, Plunge to Town 12 Miles From Pisa

By The Associated Press.

ROME, July 20—American troops battered their way across the Arno River Valley on a 25-mile front between Pisa and Florence today as German forces, bewildered by the sudden breakthrough, retreated across the Arno into the mountain defenses of their Gothic Line.

Lieut. Gen. Mark W. Clark's doughboys held complete control of hill masses overlooking the Arno from the south, and American artillery raked the entire valley in search of German rear-guard units protecting the withdrawal of the main body of enemy forces to the north of the stream.

German resistance was confined almost entirely to these small groups armed with automatic weapons—tactics similar to those that delayed the entry of General Clark's troops into Rome an entire day. One American column was firmly established on the south bank of the Arno at Pontedera, twelve miles inland from Pisa.

An Allied spokesman said Ger-

Continued on Page 5

Nazi Party Clashes With Army Reported

BERNE, Switzerland, July 20 (UP)—Skirmishes took place in various parts of Germany today between Nazi party members, led by SS [Elite Guard] Troopers, and groups of the regular army, according to unconfirmed reports reaching here tonight.

Conferences of the Nazi party organization were held in all principal cities of the Reich this evening, and members were asked to reaffirm their loyalty to the party and to Adolf Hitler, according to reliable information.

Zurich reported that responsible quarters there had information that a subversive movement was under way in various parts of the Reich.

By Wireless to THE NEW YORK TIMES.

BERNE, Friday, July 21—There were unconfirmed reports at the Swiss-German frontier shortly after 1 o'clock this morning that some shooting had occurred on the other side of the line, but whether or not it indicated mutiny could not yet be ascertained.

Allies Report Belgian Uprising Comparable to French Sabotage

By Wireless to THE NEW YORK TIMES.

SUPREME HEADQUARTERS, Allied Expeditionary Force, July 20—Belgium's extensive and complicated network of rail and road communications was reported in a special Allied communiqué today to have been "largely disrupted" as the result of the "highly satisfactory" operations of the Belgian underground. The communiqué was the first from Supreme Headquarters to mention the Belgian resistance movement that has been declared by Belgian authorities to be a formal military organization the same as the French Forces of the Interior.

Reporting that Belgian operations "throughout the entire country" had "contributed substantially to the delaying movement of enemy reinforcements to the battle areas," the communiqué also said that French forces had detained a Panzer division moving toward Normandy for thirty hours and had wrecked twenty-six strategic bridges between June 24 and July 6.

Eighty Germans were killed and 300 wounded in the attack on the Panzer division, said the communiqué, which also confirmed an earlier French report that patriots had destroyed a train carrying flying bombs in eastern France.

From July 4 to 15, the communiqué said, the French forces continued operations "in face of violent German attacks," defeating or eluding the Germans in every case.

In addition, the French slowed traffic on the "whole railway sys-

Continued on Page 4

BRITISH PUSH SOUTH

Take Troarn Rail Depot While Second Column Captures Bourguebus

ENEMY SLOWS DRIVE

Strong Anti-Tank Belt Checks Smash Toward Plains Before Paris

By DREW MIDDLETON

By Cable to THE NEW YORK TIMES.

SUPREME HEADQUARTERS, Allied Expeditionary Force, Friday, July 21—Tanks and infantry of the British Second Army, battling stubborn German rearguards at Troarn and St. André-sur-Orne, yesterday, widened the eleven-mile front south and east of Caen that Lieut. Gen. Miles C. Dempsey's troops have punched out in three days of audacious and arduous fighting.

Strong German anti-tank positions northwest of Vimont slowed down the advance to the southeast toward Vimont, momentarily at least. However, British artillery and infantry were assaulting these positions last night as the second stage of the great trial of strength with the Seventh German Army opened.

British Positions Solid

Bourguebus, five and a quarter miles southeast of Caen, was the most important of a dozen towns and villages taken by the British in the twenty-four hours ended at midnight last night. It is almost in the center of an arc extending from the Orne west of St. André to the railroad station at Caen, which marks the area in which the Second Army is solidly established.

Farther to the south, southeast and east, in front of the main positions, British tanks were operating against the German lines, seek-

Continued on Page 4

LWOW IS MENACED

Red Army Near Polish City—New Wedge Is Driven From Kovel

GRIP ON BUG WIDENS

Foe's Supply Lines Cut—Dvinsk Rail Link Slashed on West

By W. H. LAWRENCE

By Wireless to THE NEW YORK TIMES.

MOSCOW, Friday, July 21—Revealing another terrific Red Army offensive, Marshal Joseph Stalin announced last night that forces led by Marshal Konstantin K. Rokossovsky, after three days' fighting in the Kovel sector, had driven a wedge thirty-one miles deep on a 123-mile front, pushing the Germans back to the western Bug River.

He disclosed, also, that Marshal Ivan S. Koneff's First Ukrainian Army had captured Rawa Ruska, an important rail junction, severing the most direct supply and retreat route for the Germans' outflanked Lwow garrison.

These new triumphs over the battered, reeling German Army at the southern end of the eastern front were celebrated in Moscow at 10 and 11 P. M. by two salutes of twenty salvos each from 224 guns—demonstrations that brought hundreds of thousands of Muscovites into the streets.

The first salute was directed to Marshal Rokossovsky in tribute to the drive of his forces from Kovel through the strongly fortified German defense line, which culminated in reaching the western Bug at C[illegible]in and in the capture of more than 400 inhabited points. Opalin, on the eastern side of the Bug, is less than fifteen miles from Chelm on the road to Lublin.

Other forces under Marshal Kon-

Continued on Page 6

War News Summarized

FRIDAY, JULY 21, 1944

An almost successful attempt on Hitler's life and Emperor Hirohito's command to two jingo war lords to form a new Japanese Cabinet pushed actual battlefield developments into the background yesterday.

Hitler was conferring at his secret headquarters with the staff of the German High Command, Berlin said, when Col. Count von Stauffenberg, one of his collaborators, threw a bomb at the Fuehrer. Although the assassin was only six feet away Hitler escaped with bruises and burns. One of the thirteen staff officers was killed and two others were seriously injured.

Shortly after the explosion Hitler informed the German people of what had happened, blaming an "officers' clique" that wished to bring about a revolt. He immediately placed Gestapo Chief Himmler in absolute command within the Reich, said the "criminal elements" would be ruthlessly exterminated and indicated grave concern by warning all soldiers and civilians not to obey orders unless they had been confirmed. He also named Col. Gen. Guderian Chief of Staff, replacing Field Marshal Gen. Keitel. [All the foregoing 1:1.]

In Japan, Admiral Mitsumasa Yonai, Premier during the tense days of early 1940, and his then Overseas Minister and later Governor General of Korea, Gen. Kuniaki Koiso, were commissioned to form a "critical decisive wartime" Cabinet. Both men are militarists and expansionists of the Tojo type. [1:2-3.]

Allied statesmen saw in both developments evidence of crisis in the enemy camps. London observers believed that Hitler's order for a new purge indicated clearly that unrest within Germany was general [1:2-3], while former Ambassador Grew and Secretary of State Hull in Washington expressed the prevalent opinion that Tokyo had at last admitted the gravity of the military situation. They warned, however, against expecting a Japanese collapse. [3:6.]

On the actual war fronts Allied gains were reported everywhere. The British Second Army in France was widening its eleven-mile bulge south and east of Caen and trying to force Field Marshal Rommel into a decisive tank battle. Americans advanced in the St. Lô area and crossed the River Ay to a depth of 300 yards in the Lessay sector. [1:4, map P. 2.] The resistance movement that has proved so effective in France has spread into Belgium. [1:2-3.]

Although torrential rains slowed Allied progress in Italy the Fifth Army reached the Arno River along a twenty-five-mile front above Leghorn and was close to Pisa. [1:3.]

Overhead some 2,000 planes from Britain and nearly 1,000 from Italy teamed in a coordinated attack on aircraft plants, ball-bearing factories, airfields and other targets in southeast Germany. It was one of the war's most concentrated blows. [5:1.]

The Russians scored the most impressive gains in a new offensive in the Kovel area. The Red Army reached the western Bug River on a wide front after driving as deep as thirty-one miles on a 123-mile line in three days. Another advance brought Soviet troops to within five miles of Lwow and a flanking thrust cut the main German supply and escape railroad. [1:5; map P. 6.]

Action in the Pacific was on a lesser scale. American planes blasted Guam with 721 tons of bombs in two days. [7:5.] Chinese troops were attacking the Japanese from within Hengyang and from outside the Hunan city [7:1] while along the Burma front other Chinese routed an enemy relief force trying to reach Pingka. [6:6.]

AGAIN NAMED FOR PRESIDENCY

Franklin Delano Roosevelt

Associated Press, 1944

Roosevelt's Acceptance

Following is the text of President Roosevelt's acceptance speech from a Pacific Coast naval base, as recorded and transcribed by THE NEW YORK TIMES:

Mr. Chairman, ladies and gentlemen of the convention, my friends:

I have already indicated to you why I accept the nomination that you have offered me, in spite of my desire to retire to the quiet of private life.

You in this convention are aware of what I have sought to gain for the nation, and you have asked me to continue.

It seems wholly likely that within the next four years our armed forces, and those of our Allies, will have gained a complete victory over Germany and Japan, sooner or later, and that the world once more will be at peace, under a system, we hope, that will prevent a new world war. In any event, whenever that time comes new hands will then have full opportunity to realize the ideals which we seek.

In the last three elections the people of the United States have transcended party affiliation. Not only Democrats but also forward-looking Republicans and millions of

Continued on Page 8

PRESIDENT FAVORS TRUMAN, DOUGLAS

Would Take Either as Running Mate, Letter to Hannegan Says—Battle Gets Hotter

By JAMES A. HAGERTY

Special to THE NEW YORK TIMES.

CHICAGO, July 20—In an attempt to bolster the waning strength of Senator Harry S. Truman of Missouri for the nomination for Vice President, Robert E. Hannegan, Democratic national chairman, made public tonight the letter written to him by President Roosevelt, saying that either Senator Truman or William O. Douglas, justice of the United States Supreme Court, would be satisfactory to him as a running mate and would add strength to the ticket.

Mr. Hannegan said he had not made the letter public earlier because he considered it necessary to obtain the consent of the sender before releasing a personal letter for publication. He said he had talked today with President Roosevelt by telephone and had received such consent.

The letter, which was written on White House stationery and dated July 19, 1944, was as follows:

"Dear Bob:

"You have written me about Harry Truman and Bill Douglas. I should, of course, be very glad to run with either of them and believe that either one of them would bring real strength to the ticket.

"Always sincerely,

"FRANKLIN D. ROOSEVELT."

The letter was addressed to

Continued on Page 10

ARMS USE TO KEEP PEACE IS PLEDGED

Platform Backs World Role on Sovereignty Basis—Opposes Racial Vote Ban

Text of the Democratic platform is on Page 12.

By CHARLES E. EGAN

Special to THE NEW YORK TIMES.

CHICAGO, July 20—A platform calling for the participation of this country with the United Nations in a world organization, empowered to use armed force when necessary to preserve international peace, was adopted by the Democratic convention tonight.

It committed the party to support a program to have the United States join in "the establishment of an international organization based on the principle of the sovereign equality of all peace-loving states, open to membership by all such states, large and small, for the prevention of aggression and the maintenance of international peace and security."

Embodied also in the platform was a plank stating that racial and religious minorities "have the right to live, develop and vote equally with all citizens and share the rights that are guaranteed by our Constitution."

The platform, of 1,500 words, carried expressions in favor of the opening of Palestine to unrestricted Jewish immigration and

Continued on Page 12

VOTE IS 1,086 TO 90

Byrd Gets 89, Farley One—President on Radio Accepts

STANDS ON RECORD

Says 'Experience,' Not 'Immaturity,' Will Win War, Peace and Jobs

Wallace and Barkley texts, Page 10; Jackson's, Page 11.

By TURNER CATLEDGE

Special to THE NEW YORK TIMES.

CHICAGO, July 20—Franklin Delano Roosevelt of New York was nominated today for a fourth term as President of the United States by a noisy, irritable Democratic convention, meeting in the same hall where he was chosen for his first term in 1932 and for a third in 1940.

A few hours later, speaking to the convention directly by radio from his train at a Pacific Coast naval base, he accepted the nomination and opened his re-election bid on the note of "experience" versus "immaturity."

Mr. Roosevelt asserted that he considered the convention's action as a call upon him to serve. He said it was up to the American people in the November election to decide whether plans already made and men already serving to achieve victory and make America and the world a better place in which to live were to be continued or supplanted by an administration with no program but to oppose.

His Three-Point Program

He presented a three-point program—to win the war, to secure the peace with force if necessary, and to build an economy with full employment and a high standard of living—as a promise of himself and the party which had called him again to lead.

In this election, he said, the people would not consider "glowing words or platform pledges," but would decide on the record made in the war and in "domestic achievements."

The President said he was too busy, and the emergency too serious, to permit him to engage in an active campaign for re-election.

But he added that he should "feel free" to report to the American people from time to time on the progress of their efforts and to "correct misstatements of fact" which might be made by the Republican opposition.

He disclosed that he was on the West Coast now in pursuance of his "constitutional duties" in connection with the war.

Roar of Cheering for Speech

The President's words came strong and magic-like through the loud speaker system—just as it did in his acceptance speech at his third-term nomination in this hall four years ago.

At the end the crowd in the arena and galleries broke into uproarious cheering. People were still shouting in a deafening roar when adjournment was moved. They attempted to shout down the motion.

The motion was carried, however, and the convention recessed at 10:55 o'clock until 11:30 tomorrow morning when it will reassemble to settle the Vice Presidential nomination.

The renomination of the President went through swiftly.

Mr. Roosevelt received 1,086 votes on the first roll call. Senator Harry F. Byrd, who was not a candidate, received 89, and James A. Farley, former chairman of the Democratic National Committee, who would not let his name go before the convention, received one from his home State of New York.

A telegram notifying the President of his nomination was dispatched to him immediately by Senator Samuel D. Jackson, Per-

Continued on Page 9

U.S. Marines taking cover on the honeycombed island of Pelelieu.

Men of the U.S. Army using flame-throwers on a Japanese blockhouse as troops invade Kwajalein Island.

"All the News That's Fit to Print"

The New York Times.

LATE CITY EDITION
Clear with light to moderate winds today.
Temperatures Yesterday—Max.,76; Min.,66
Sunrise, 5:43 A. M.; Sunset, 8:21 P. M.

Copyright, 1944, by The New York Times Company.

VOL. XCIII..No. 31,591. Entered as Second-Class Matter, Postoffice, New York, N. Y. NEW YORK, SATURDAY, JULY 22, 1944. THREE CENTS NEW YORK CITY

NAZIS BLOCK PLOT TO SEIZE GOVERNMENT; AMERICANS LAND ON GUAM, PUSH INLAND; TRUMAN NOMINATED FOR VICE PRESIDENCY

2D BALLOT DECIDES

Wallace, Leading 429½ to 319½ on First, Is Crushed 1,100 to 66

BREAK BY MARYLAND

Real Fight Ends With Big Shift by Illinois—Ready, Says Senator

By TURNER CATLEDGE
Special to THE NEW YORK TIMES.

CHICAGO, July 21—Senator Harry S. Truman of Missouri was nominated tonight as the Democratic candidate for Vice President in the fifth and final session of the twenty-eighth national convention of the party.

He appeared immediately before the cheering delegates massed in the arena of the great hall to accept his "responsibility" as a running mate in President Roosevelt's bid for a fourth term in the White House.

Directly following the nomination, support of the ticket was pledged by Vice President Henry A. Wallace, James A. Farley, former National Chairman, and Sidney Hillman, head of the CIO Political Action Committee, which had supported Mr. Wallace.

Mr. Truman's victory, which was also an overwhelming defeat for the renomination hopes of Vice President Wallace, came on the second ballot. The official announcement of the tally clerks gave the Missouri Senator 1,100 votes to 66 for Mr. Wallace and 4 for Associate Justice William O. Douglas.

[A tabulation of this ballot by The Associated Press from official records of the convention gave: Truman 1,031, Wallace 105. Other votes in the compilation were: Governor Cooper of Tennessee, 26; Senator Barkley of Kentucky, 6; Justice Douglas, 4 and Paul V. McNutt, 1.]

Truman Speaks to Throng

Mr. Truman, who rose from comparative political obscurity in Kansas City to win the second highest honor of his party, was sitting on the platform eating a sandwich when the result was announced.

Pulled up to the microphone by Senator Samuel D. Jackson of Indiana, permanent chairman of the convention, Senator Truman responded to the demands from the crowd for a word.

"You don't know how very much I appreciate the very great honor which has come to the State of Missouri," he said in a halting, shy manner. "It is also a great responsibility which I am perfectly willing to assume.

"Nine years and five months ago I came to the Senate. I expect to continue the efforts I have made there to help shorten the war and to win the peace under the great leader, Franklin D. Roosevelt.

"I don't know what else I can say, except that I accept this great honor with all humility. I thank you."

It was the shortest speech of the day and was appreciatively applauded by a crowd that literally had become surfeited with oratory. A moment later the convention passed into history on a motion by Governor Herbert O'Conor of Maryland to adjourn sine die.

"This convention has completed the business for which it was assembled, to nominate the next President and Vice President of the United States," he said.

Swing Led by Maryland

Senator Truman, President Roosevelt's second choice for place, ran through to win the nomination after having trailed Vice President Wallace on the first ballot by 110 votes.

On the opening roll-call Mr. Wallace received 429½ ballots and Mr. Truman 319½, with the remainder scattered among fourteen other candidates who had been named in nominating speeches or

Continued on Page 8

ROOSEVELT'S RUNNING MATE

Harry S. Truman Blackstone, 1944

Monetary Parley Agrees On Terms of World Bank

By RUSSELL PORTER
Special to THE NEW YORK TIMES.

BRETTON WOODS, N. H., July 21—The United Nations Monetary and Financial Conference reached an agreement today on a plan for an $8,800,000,000 International Bank of Reconstruction and Development to guarantee post-war international investments. The total capital of the world bank is the same as the aggregate of the international monetary fund to stabilize currencies which was accepted last week. Thus two vital parts of the post-war program to try to insure world peace and prosperity have been accepted, with some reservations, by all the forty-four United and Associated Nations participating in the conference, subject to the approval of the Congress of the United States and the executive and legislative branches of other Governments.

In order to reach an agreement, the United States delegation had to abandon its position that the subscriptions to the bank, which represent each country's risks in guaranteeing international loans, should be the same as the quotas in the fund, which represent a country's rights to acquire foreign exchange with which to buy goods in the world market.

However, it is the opinion of the United States delegation, after receiving the advice of its four members of Congress, two Republicans and two Democrats, and its one banker member, Edward E. Brown, president of the First National Bank of Chicago, that the fund and bank agreements have been

Continued on Page 28

BIG CITY BOSSES WON OVER HILLMAN

Two Presidential Letters Had Important Influence on Convention Strategy

By JAMES A. HAGERTY
Special to THE NEW YORK TIMES.

CHICAGO, July 21—Somewhat belatedly, leaders of the Democratic organizations in a score and a half of States, headed by big city bosses, Edward J. Flynn and Frank V. Kelly of New York, Mayor Edward J. Kelly of Chicago, Mayor Frank Hague of Jersey City and Robert E. Hannegan, national chairman, of St. Louis, brought about the nomination of Senator Harry S. Truman of Missouri for Vice President by the Democratic National Convention.

By the nomination the Democratic politicians won a victory over Sidney Hillman, chairman of the Congress of Industrial Organizations Political Action Committee, who stuck to Vice President Henry A. Wallace to the last and whose influence had been sufficient

Continued on Page 10

Farley Pledges Roosevelt Backing, Accepting Decision of Convention

Special to THE NEW YORK TIMES.

CHICAGO, July 21—James A. Farley, former Democratic national chairman and former Postmaster General, announced tonight that he would support President Roosevelt for re-election despite his opposition to a fourth term.

"I have been opposed on principle to a third or fourth Presidential term," Mr. Farley said in a statement, which he released just after the nomination of Senator Truman for Vice President. "For that reason, I voted for the nomination of Senator Harry F. Byrd of Virginia for President.

"Having participated in the proceedings of the convention, I accept its decision and will support the party nominees."

Mr. Farley declined to amplify his statement. He resigned recently as chairman of the New York State Democratic Committee and is not expected to take an active part in the campaign.

Mr. Farley, who was of great help to Mr. Roosevelt in the latter's first nomination for President and in his first and second campaigns for election, broke with the Chief Executive during the latter part of Mr. Roosevelt's second term.

Secretary of the New York State Democratic Committee in 1928, when Mr. Roosevelt was first elected Governor of New York, Mr. Farley was promoted to State chairman and managed Mr. Roosevelt's campaign for re-election as Governor in 1930. Mr. Roosevelt's plurality of 730,000 at that elec-

Continued on Page 9

RUSSIANS RACE ON

Bug River Is Crossed Again on Wide Front Due East of Lublin

LWOW BATTLE BEGUN

Brest-Litovsk Railway to Chelm Cut—Ostrov Is Captured in North

By W. H. LAWRENCE
By Cable to THE NEW YORK TIMES.

MOSCOW, Saturday, July 22—The Soviet battle for the liberation of Poland began in earnest yesterday as the Red Army smashed across the Bug River from Lyuboml on a thirty-seven-mile front and advanced up to nine miles beyond the west bank. In that operation the railroad between Chelm and Brest-Litovsk was severed.

Other Red Army forces moved closer to Lwow and to Brest-Litovsk, and the Soviet High Command announced that Soviet troops had captured 570 inhabited points on both the northernmost and the southernmost sections of the front.

At the northern end of the front, troops of the Third Baltic Front executed an outflanking maneuver and captured the important enemy stronghold and communications hub of Ostrov—a victory that Moscow celebrated with a salute of twelve salvos from 124 guns.

Although the capture of Ostrov won the salute, from a military and strategic point of view the biggest news was the crossing of the Bug west of Lyuboml by Marshal Konstantin K. Rokssovsky's First White Russian Army and the nine-mile advance beyond it, which sent his troops streaming toward Lublin and Warsaw.

In the sector southwest of Brody, where four or five German divisions are encircled, Marshal Ivan S. Koneff's First Ukrainian Army continued the process of extermination, capturing 2,000 more prisoners and 100 artillery pieces. The

Continued on Page 5

BEACHHEADS SET UP

Americans Invade Guam After Mighty U.S. Blow From Sea and Air

OPPOSITION IS LIGHT

Resistance Increases as Japanese Are Pushed Toward Inland Hills

By GEORGE F. HORNE
By Telephone to THE NEW YORK TIMES.

PEARL HARBOR, July 21—United States assault troops and sea forces began yesterday the long awaited invasion of the big island of Guam and have established good beachheads against light opposition, although resistance increased in some sectors as the Americans drove inland.

[Front dispatches reported that the landings were made on either side of Port Apra, The Associated Press said. From the shore areas, where Japanese defenses had been blown to pieces, the invaders drove swiftly toward a range of hills in the interior.]

They stormed ashore after enemy defenses received their seventeenth straight day of heavy attack from the air. All this week, up to the time of the landings, surface units of the Fifth Fleet had battered the island with tons of steel. They continued yesterday, covering the marines and Army assault troops making the invasion. A terrific rain of 627 tons of bombs and 147 rockets was unloosed by our planes in the day preceding the landings.

Admiral Chester W. Nimitz, Commander in Chief of the Pacific Fleet and Pacific Ocean areas, announced the landings at 1:30 o'clock this morning.

Japanese Are Weakened

With Saipan securely in our hands, the tremendous Pacific forces have turned, as was expected, to carry retribution to the Japanese where their strongly armed and confident forces poured ashore

Continued on Page 7

War News Summarized

SATURDAY, JULY 22, 1944

The few facts seeping through the tight German censorship yesterday indicated that the anti-Hitler revolt was still alive and that a purge of anti-Nazi leaders was still under way. German army officers who attempted to take Hitler's life simultaneously tried to take over the government offices in Berlin, the German radio said. The same source declared the revolt had been mercilessly suppressed and that Propaganda Minister Goebbels had frustrated the attempt to seize the Government offices. A Stockholm report said two German divisions had revolted Wednesday in East Prussia, while another dispatch from Switzerland relayed unconfirmed reports of a revolt among German naval units at Kiel and Stettin. [1:8.]

Secretary of State Hull attributed the unrest in Germany and the attack on Hitler to a spreading realization in the Reich of impending defeat. He cautioned, however, against overoptimism on an early end of the war in Europe. [3:2-3.]

Red Army forces blasted a thirty-seven-mile-wide hole in Hitler's much-publicized "East Wall" defenses along the Bug River and are threatening to crumble the whole German defense structure guarding Warsaw, now only eighty-two miles away. Other Russian troops seized Ostrov, the last Nazi fortress before the Latvian border on the direct route to Riga. The Red Army was increasing its threat to the imperiled strongholds of Lwow, Brest-Litovsk, Kaunas and Dvinsk by the hour, as beaten German armies fell back everywhere along an almost continuous 800-mile front from Finland to the Carpathian foothills. [1:4; map P. 5.]

Allied troops in Normandy slugged through rain and mud to cement positions below Caen to a depth of five miles. Canadians seized St. André-sur-Orne and St. Martin-de-Fontenay near Caen as the enemy gave ground slowly. American forces increased their pressure on Périers after winning a foothold on the road from St. Lô to Périers. [1:6-7; map P. 3.]

The two-way aerial offensive from Britain and Italy continued for the fourth consecutive day as nearly 3,000 American bombers and fighters pounded a dozen German targets. [4:1.] Ground troops in Italy pierced strong German Arno River defenses, forcing the water barrier into the mountain fringes of the "Gothic Line" in at least one place. [1:7.]

Striking at Japan's inner defense zone, American assault troops landed on Guam Island, first American territory seized by the Japanese, early Thursday and have established good beachheads. Admiral Nimitz reported that additional troops were landing against light initial Japanese resistance, and that casualties were moderate. A terrific naval and aerial bombardment of the strategic island, 1,565 miles southeast of Tokyo, softened up the enemy defense before our landings. As our troops moved inland the Japanese put up stiffened resistance in some sectors. [1:5; map P. 7.]

In China fierce fighting raged around Hengyang for the twenty-sixth day as relief forces attacking Japanese troops who have besieged that major junction on the Canton-Hankow railroad drove deeper into the enemy lines. [6:1.]

Drive South of Caen Stalls As Rain Floods Battle Area

British Forced to Withdraw Armored Units—Canadians Beat Off Fierce German Counter-Attacks in Mud and Mists

By DREW MIDDLETON
By Cable to THE NEW YORK TIMES.

SUPREME HEADQUARTERS, Allied Expeditionary Force, Saturday, July 22—British and Canadian infantrymen, their uniforms muddy and sodden after thirty-six hours of heavy rains, were fighting a grim, bloody battle for Verriers and St. Martin-de-Fontenay on the British Second Army sector south of Caen last night, but the remainder of the Allied front in Normandy was quiet save for the measured pounding of cannon and mortars.

The offensive launched by the Second Army Tuesday morning with such high hopes had stalled, frustrated as much by the thick doughlike mud that covered the roads and fields as by the lethal fire of German anti-tank positions around Vimont. These positions now must be rooted out by infantry and artillery, under adverse conditions for the attackers, while British armored divisions follow the example of German Panzer units and retire from the battlefield until the stage has been set for a great armored battle for the road to Paris.

The gains registered yesterday were all on the western flank of the Second Army's salient along the east bank of the Orne River. Canadians were fighting German infantrymen for Etavaux and St. André-sur-Orne in conditions reminiscent of World War I.

At St. Martin-de Fontenay, half a mile south of St. André-sur-Orne, the Canadians took the village and then stood off a heavy German counter-attack supported by tanks. When the counter-attack was over the Canadians went forward to find German dead lying thick on the muddy ground. The enemy casualties were "satisfactory," a report from the front said.

There was mud and mist everywhere and little knots of men were fighting silently with bayonets in a dank, dripping world where gun flashes were the only light.

The weather, which has favored the enemy since D-day, has imposed a stalemate on the operations in this sector, although farther west British infantrymen

Continued on Page 3

British Label Hitler Attack Rivals' Bid for False Peace

By Cable to THE NEW YORK TIMES.

LONDON, July 21—Although the news from Germany is taken as an indication of a grave crisis within the Reich, there is no disposition here to regard it as a ground for hoping for an early termination of hostilities. As The Times of London will say tomorrow, when the enemy "wavers," that is the time for throwing in reserves, not for relaxing.

It is strongly felt here that Adolf Hitler's rivals, far from being converts to the Allied cause, are merely another brand of champions of militarism who merely believe themselves better able to rescue the Reich from disaster than the present Nazi leaders.

Their game, it was said, is to supplant Hitler so as to try to make peace on terms that would preserve the Wehrmacht for another war under more favorable conditions. Therefore, it is recognized by the people as well as officials that even had the officers' coup succeeded, peace would still be a long way off.

Generals Reach Conclusion

"Unconditional surrender" is still an Allied condition of an armistice, and there is little conviction here that even the generals who would like to rid their country of Hitler would accept that without continuing the struggle in the hope of getting better terms later.

However, this evidence of a rift in the façade of German unity is recognized as important evidence that at least some German military leaders have reached the conclusion that the Nazi direction of the war has brought Germany to a

Continued on Page 3

U. S. PATROLS STAB ACROSS ARNO RIVER

Pierce Mountain Fringes of Gothic Line While British Thrust Nearer Florence

By The United Press.

ROME, July 21—American Fifth Army combat patrols pierced strong German Arno River defenses today, forcing the river into the mountain fringes of the Gothic Line in at least one point, while artillery blasted German installations north of the river from captured high points on the south bank.

The Americans took advantage of improved weather to roll up scattered German resistance groups south of the river, while on the coast German guns of all calibers hammered the battered port of Leghorn from advantageous positions on Mount Pisano, northeast of Pisa.

This height, on which the Germans have installed many field guns, anti-aircraft batteries, machine guns and pillboxes, affords

Continued on Page 5

Invaders Find Defenses of Guam Blown to Shreds by Our Attacks

By JOHN R. HENRY
Of International News Service
For the Combined Allied Press

ABOARD A FLAGSHIP AT GUAM, July 21 (Guam Time)—A liberation force of Third Amphibious Corps marines and Army troops thundered ashore at Guam today with the destructive blast of a Pacific typhoon.

The Leathernecks spearheaded two separate beachhead assaults, storming across coral-studded shorelines in the wake of a 17-day sea and air bombardment that reached a stupefying crescendo as landing craft churned into remnants of the Japanese coast defenses.

Casualties were described as "light" for United States forces. The Japanese dead were uncounted.

At nightfall Maj. Gen. Roy Geiger's Third Amphibious Corps troops dug in on perimeters between Adlup and Asan, a point north of Orote Peninsula, and from the shattered town of Agat to Bangi Point, south of the rocky finger of land.

The northern beachhead, where the terrain was most rugged, stretched in an arc several thousand yards. The southern force shoved inland and established its own substantial beachhead. General Geiger is a marine aviator and veteran South Pacific commander.

So effective had been the preparatory barrages that troops flowed ashore with negligible initial resistance and in record time.

Despite sprinkling enemy fire

Continued on Page 7

HITLER HUNTS FOES

Thousands of Officers Reported Arrested in Purge of Army

MUTINY IS RUMORED

Sailors at Kiel, Stettin and Troops in East Said to Revolt

By RAYMOND DANIELL
By Cable to THE NEW YORK TIMES.

LONDON, Saturday, July 22—Although reports from Berlin insist that the plot of army officers to overthrow the Nazi regime and seize power themselves has been suppressed and its instigators liquidated, the isolation of the Reich from the rest of the world continues and it is apparent that counter-measures are being pressed.

[A Swiss report to The United Press said it was understood that German naval units had revolted at Kiel and Stettin. Stockholm dispatches said 5,500 German officers had been arrested throughout Germany and that there had been disorders in eastern Germany and East Prussia.]

Everything suggests that the plot that had its climax in the attempt to assassinate Adolf Hitler was deep and well laid, with far-reaching ramifications. On evidence supplied by the highest Nazi authorities it is known that the plotters, who included Col. Gen. Ludwig Beck, who was dismissed as Chief of Staff by Hitler in November, 1938, attempted to kill Hitler and bring off a coup d'état.

The scheme apparently succeeded to the point where the conspirators were able to issue orders in conflict with the plans of Hitler and other Nazi leaders.

Leaders Revealed Troubles

The extent of the disaffection seemingly caused such consternation in the Nazi camp that Hitler, Reichmarshal Hermann Goering and Grand Admiral Karl Doenitz felt impelled in the small hours yesterday morning to try to set things straight by urgent appeals, even though their action involved disclosure to a hostile world that a rift had developed between some high army officers and the Nazi party on the best way to save Germany from destruction.

There is no evidence to show that the challenge to Hitler's leadership and domination of the Nazi party has spread to the civilian population but Transocean, German news agency, revealed that certain "precautionary measures" had been taken in the center of Berlin.

Alfred Rosenberg, Nazi party "philosopher," writing in a special edition of the Voelkischer Beobachter yesterday morning, called the attempt on Hitler's life the opening of hostilities on a "fifth front."

Some additional light on what happened in the Reich in those crucial hours preceding Hitler's broadcast was provided last night from Berlin. According to the official story, provided for soldiers in the field, a clique that was connected with "an enemy power" had obtained control of "certain means of communications" through a subordinate officer.

Major Informed Goebbels

Through these channels, it was said, orders were sent to Major Remer, commandant of a battalion of the Berlin guard, telling him Hitler was dead, that disorders had been reported in the Reich and that the Wehrmacht had taken over the government. Major Remer was directed to occupy with his force the administrative headquarters at Berlin, which he did.

But then, according to this account, Major Remer immediately communicated with Propaganda Minister Joseph Goebbels, head of the Berlin municipal administration, who convinced him that he had been obeying faked orders. The fact that "traitors" had laid hands on certain communications systems brought about yesterday

Continued on Page 2

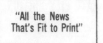

"All the News That's Fit to Print"

The New York Times.

LATE CITY EDITION
Showers, ending before noon; clearing, cooler later today.
Temperatures Yesterday—Max., 86; Min., 69
Sunrise, 6:14 A. M.; Sunset, 7:41 P. M.

VOL. XCIII. No. 31,624. Entered as Second-Class Matter, Postoffice, New York, N. Y. NEW YORK, THURSDAY, AUGUST 24, 1944. THREE CENTS IN NEW YORK CITY

PARIS IS FREED; RUMANIA QUITS; MARSEILLE AND GRENOBLE WON; GERMAN FLIGHT NEARS A ROUT

BREAK IN BALKANS

King Proclaims Nation's Surrender and Wish to Help Allies

NAZIS IN AREA FIGHT

New Bucharest Regime Asks United Nations Aid Against Hungary

By DANIEL T. BRIGHAM
By Telephone to THE NEW YORK TIMES.

BERNE, Switzerland, Aug. 23—In a brief proclamation to the Rumanian people broadcast from Bucharest at 9:25 o'clock this evening, King Michael of Rumania ordered his armed forces to cease fire against the forces of the Allies, saying he had accepted their terms of unconditional surrender in the name of the nation.

The youthful King called on the nation to take up the fight immediately by the side of the Soviet forces on Rumanian soil against their common enemy, Germany.

Dramatic and apparently sudden as was the entire announcement the Germans were obviously forewarned, for when the home broadcast service at Bucharest interrupted its regular transmission at 9:24 P. M., within thirty seconds the two powerful Bucharest transmitters were shrouded by interference from a battery of German jammers of all varieties.

[Moscow, which broadcast the Rumanian surrender—beaming it especially to Germany—soon after the Bucharest announcement, reported later in the night that German troops were fighting Rumanian forces that were withdrawing from the Red Army front.

Bulgaria Expected to Quit

[Bulgaria's withdrawal from the war was believed to be imminent, according to reports from Cairo, which said the Allies were insisting on the return of territory seized in the war.]

King Michael, who had until recently been virtually a prisoner of the Gestapo, has overthrown the pro-Nazi dictatorship, ousting the Premier and Commander in Chief, Marshal Ion Antonescu. [The Berne radio, heard by Columbia Broadcasting System, said early Thursday that Antonescu had fled to Germany.]

He named as Chief of Government and Marshal of Rumania the master of his military household, Gen. Constantin Sanatescu. He announced a new Cabinet that constituted a Government of national union.

The new Cabinet includes Peasant party leader Juliu Maniu, as Minister of State Without Portfolio, and the leader of the Liberal party, Dinu Bratianu, in a similar post.

[Lucretiu Patrascanu, a Rumanian Communist party leader, and Constantin Petrescu, a Socialist leader, were also named Ministers of State, said a Bucharest broadcast recorded by the Federal Communications Commission.]

War With Hungary Evident

The new Rumanian Government is made up of a wide grouping of forces from the liberal, independent center to the extreme left.

King Michael's proclamation announced the denunciation by Rumania of the Treaty of Vienna of Aug. 30, 1940, by which the Nazis gave Transylvania to Hungary. It made it plain that Rumania is now at war with Hungary to recover Transylvania and seeks Allied backing in that effort.

A new Rumanian General Staff, as well as the country's political leaders, met at the King's palace,

Continued on Page 11

President Tells Delegates 'Four of Us' Can Keep Peace

Staying Friends and Meeting Often May Mean Generations Without War, He Says —Washington Studies U. S. Plan

By JAMES B. RESTON
Special to THE NEW YORK TIMES.

WASHINGTON, Aug. 23—President Roosevelt told delegates to the Washington Conversations on International Organization today that if the United States, Soviet Russia and Great Britain could maintain their new and close friendship and spread that friendship around the world "we may have a peaceful period for our grandchildren to grow up in."

Speaking informally to the delegates at the White House during a recess in their labors to draft an effective security league, Mr. Roosevelt seemed to emphasize the special responsibility of the great powers in maintaining peace, by the use of force if necessary.

"We have got to make not merely a peace but a peace that will last," the President said, "and a peace in which the larger nations will work absolutely in unison in preventing war by force. But the four of us have to be friends, conferring all the time on the basis of getting to know each other."

Although no representative of China was present, the President's reference to "the four of us" was interpreted as an indication that when Mr. Roosevelt thinks of "the great powers" he counts China as one of those nations.

It was a remarkable fact, Mr. Roosevelt said, that the great powers had attained such unanimity during the war, and he added that the hope of the future lay in the ability of the nations to perpetuate that unity for a long time to come.

"The prisoners of 17, 18, 20 that

Continued on Page 13

The text of the President's remarks is on Page 13.

RED ARMY SPEEDS DEEP INTO RUMANIA

Bendery and Akkerman Taken —Polish Plane Center Falls —Russians Near Tartu

By The Associated Press.

LONDON, Thursday, Aug. 24—The two-fisted Soviet offensive that knocked Rumania out of the war roared through its fourth day yesterday, capturing Vaslui, 140 miles northeast of the Ploesti oil center, and toppling the two big Bessarabian bastions of Bendery and Akkerman on the west bank of the Dniester, besides more than 400 other towns.

Disregarding developments on the political front, at least for the present, the Second and Third Ukrainian Armies deepened to as much as sixty miles the holes they have ripped in the German-Rumanian defenses and advanced within 167 miles of the capital city of Bucharest.

Rumania still was garrisoned with thousands of German troops, and the Russians were likely to continue their lightning campaign to clear the Nazis entirely out of the country, regardless of what the Rumanian troops chose to do.

While this campaign was bearing its first great fruits in Rumanian surrender, the First Ukrainian Army of Marshal Ivan S. Koneff in southern Poland lashed out westward and seized the city of Debica, a large aircraft industry center and communications point sixty-four miles east of Cracow and nineteen miles east of Tarnow, next

Continued on Page 10

47 RAILROADS SUED AS WESTERN TRUST

J. P. Morgan & Co., Kuhn-Loeb and Two Associations Accused of Conspiracy

By LEWIS WOOD
Special to THE NEW YORK TIMES.

WASHINGTON, Aug. 23—In a civil suit filed at Lincoln, Neb., today major railroad interests of the United States were accused by the Federal Government of violating the Sherman Anti-Trust Act by collusive rate-fixing and discouraging improvements in service and equipment in the western part of the country.

The Department of Justice made these charges against the American Association of Railroads, its officers and directors; the Western Association of Railway Executives; J. P. Morgan & Co., Inc.; Kuhn, Loeb & Co.; forty-seven railroads and their chief executives, and thirty-one other individuals.

Attorney General Francis Biddle, now on the Pacific Coast, announced the action here through Wendell Berge, assistant Attorney General, in charge of anti-trust prosecutions.

In a forty-page complaint, the Government charged that a "combination of private financial, industrial and railroad interests have acted collusively to maintain non-competitive rates for transportation and to prevent and retard improvements in the services and facilities of railroads for the western part of the United States. (They) have retarded and suppressed the development and growth of the

Continued on Page 20

Willkie Would Empower President To Use U. S. Forces to Keep Peace

By LEO EGAN

In a series of talks in the last week and a half with Republican Senators and Representatives who have sought his views with respect to the international conference at Dumbarton Oaks, Wendell L. Willkie, it was learned yesterday, has been urging Republican support for the proposal to give the President power to use the military forces of the United States, without the prior approval of Congress, in fulfillment of American obligations to any international organization set up to preserve peace.

Mr. Willkie's advice on this score has been coupled with two other suggestions as to Republican policy: 1. That the party insist that the organic structure of an international security organization be established and American participation therein approved at once, without waiting for the treaties formally ending the present conflict; and, 2, that it insist upon the fullest possible information and discussion of all proposals considered at the Dumbarton Oaks Conference and that it take the lead in developing a body of public opinion within the United States favorable to American participation in international peace machinery.

As to the form that an international security organization should take, Mr. Willkie's views, as con-

Continued on Page 13

FRENCH TAKE PORT

Pockets of Resistance Are Being Cleared Up in Marseille

ARMY JUNCTION SEEN

American Dash Inland Said to Have Carried to Annecy, Near Border

By The Associated Press.

ROME, Aug. 23—Marseille, France's second city and greatest seaport, fell to the swift onslaught of French infantry and armor today as American forces swept 140 miles inland from the Mediterranean and were within less than 240 miles of a junction with Gen. Dwight D. Eisenhower's legions below liberated Paris.

Only eight days after the landings in southern France the inspired Poilus battered their way into the heart of Marseille against slight resistance and tonight were cleaning out pockets of last-ditch defenders.

The unexpectedly easy capture of the great port assures the Seventh Army an adequate flow of supplies and reinforcements for speedy continuation of the thrust toward northern France. Prior to the city's fall, other French troops had cut the last escape route for the German garrison along the coast to the west.

Toulon Still Holding Out

The encircled and doomed German force in Toulon, big naval base twenty-seven miles east of Marseille, still was holding out tonight, but French troops had fought their way within a few hundred yards of the docks.

[Confirmed reports in Berne said American troops had entered Annecy, less than eighteen miles from the Swiss frontier. Radio France at Algiers said Allied patrols had reached Avig-

Continued on Page 6

HAILING THE LIBERATION OF PARIS

Lily Pons leads the gathering in Rockefeller Plaza in singing "The Marseillaise"
The New York Times

GRIMNESS TINGES JOY OF FRENCH HERE

Concern for Kin and Thoughts of Tasks Ahead Mingle With Jubilation Over Paris

By MEYER BERGER

The French in New York City celebrated the liberation of Paris yesterday with impressive restraint. They sang "La Marseillaise" while ticker tape and handmade confetti danced above them in the sun, but hearts were still weighed down by worry over kin from whom they have not heard for years.

A few left the streets for quiet French churches to thank God for

Continued on Page 5

French Armored Division Sent Into Paris by Bradley

The following dispatch by a representative of the Columbia Broadcasting System, the first American correspondent to enter Paris, was cabled to London and broadcast from there.

By CHARLES COLLINGWOOD

PARIS, Aug. 23—The French Second Armored Division entered Paris today after the Parisians had risen as one man to beat down the German troops who had garrisoned the city.

It was the people of Paris who really won back their city. It all happened with fantastic suddenness.

The American Army was occupied with the drive through Evreux to the mouth of the Seine, after which it planned to invest Paris. But yesterday a Frenchman burst into Lieut. Gen. Omar N. Bradley's headquarters. He was the chief of the French Forces of the Interior in Paris and he had a staggering, incredible story to tell.

He said that he had concluded an armistice with the German forces in Paris. The people of Paris had risen and he had cornered the Germans that the German commander had requested an armistice. He wanted to withdraw troops from the road blocks west and south of Paris, where they had been facing the Americans, and pass them through the city.

The armistice was to expire at noon today.

This news caused a sensation in General Bradley's headquarters because, although we had known that rioting had been going on in Paris since Saturday, we had not known that things had gone so far that obviously the French had given the Germans a terrific beating.

The whole operation was geared to the complete encirclement of the

Continued on Page 5

ENEMY FLEES 'KILL' BY ALLIES AT SEINE

Americans Drive North, British Near Le Havre—3d Army Rolls Toward Troyes

By DREW MIDDLETON
By Cable to THE NEW YORK TIMES.

SUPREME HEADQUARTERS, Allied Expeditionary Force, Thursday, Aug. 24—The last German army south of the Seine River and west of Paris is being destroyed.

The American forces thrusting along the south bank of the Seine have taken Evreux and smashed on more than seven miles, while the British and Canadian troops on the left and center of the Allies' line are hammering the Germans back into a pocket south of Le Havre and Rouen. Two hundred miles to the east, the American column at the nose of the Third Army's salient is rolling eastward toward Troyes, on the road to Germany, in a bold operation that threatens to cut off all southern France from reinforcement from Germany.

It is estimated that almost 90,-

Continued on Page 4

War News Summarized

THURSDAY, AUGUST 24, 1944

Germany sustained a double blow yesterday when the citizens of Paris threw out the invaders and Rumania deserted the Axis to join with the United Nations.

The liberation of the French capital came after four days of hard fighting. Some 50,000 French resistance troops, supported by large bodies of unarmed civilians, had risen on signal from underground leaders. The Paris police, who had previously gone on strike, seized strategic centers. Generals Eisenhower and Patton kept their men from entering the city while the French people went about the job of creating another Bastille Day. [1:8; map, P. 2.]

King Michael proclaimed the immediate end of the war for Rumania as an Axis satellite and the joining of his country with the Allies against Germany. He ousted the Antonescu dictatorship, said armistice terms had been accepted and formed a new Government to conclude peace with the United Nations immediately. [1:1.]

Bulgaria was expected soon to follow Rumania out of the war. The Allies were reported to have demanded Bulgaria's evacuation of all territory seized in Yugoslavia and Greece and withdrawal to pre-war boundaries. [10:1.] Prime Minister Churchill planned with officials of the Greek Government in Exile that country's future military activities. [10:5.] Nothing was heard from Hungary or Finland.

Meanwhile Allied armies continued to roll through France. Marseille and Grenoble were liberated, most of Toulon had been taken, Lyon was threatened and American troops were reported in Annecy, less than twenty miles from the Swiss frontier. [1:4; map P. 6.] In northern France the Germans south of the Seine were being rapidly destroyed and herded into a pocket south of Le Havre and Rouen. The American Third Army was nearing Troyes. [1:7; map P. 4.]

Italian-based Allied planes smashed the Vienna area for the second straight day, meeting heavy opposition. Medium bombers flew deep into France to attack targets around Lyon. [8:4.]

Russian successes were reported from all fronts. The Red Army was only four miles from Tartu and eight miles from Lomzha. In the Rumanian sector they brought both points of a great pincers to within thirty-five miles of closing. [1:2, map P. 10.]

The only victory Berlin could announce was the heaviest dawn barrage of flying bombs yet to strike England. [9:1.]

Allied bombers in the Pacific virtually wiped out a Japanese convoy off the Bonins and struck Davao, in the Philippines. [1:6-7.] The Japanese Premier warned his people that the United States was planning an invasion of the home islands. [11:1.]

President Roosevelt told delegates to the Dumbarton Oaks conference that "we have got to make a peace that will last" so that "we may have a peaceful period for our grandchildren to grow up in." [1:2-3.] Wendell Willkie has urged Republicans to support the State Department's proposal to permit the use of American military forces without prior approval of Congress and to approve a security organization at once, apart from the peace treaties. [1:2-3.]

U. S. Bombers Set Davao Aflame In Stepped-Up Philippines Blow

By The Associated Press.

GENERAL HEADQUARTERS, Southwest Pacific, Thursday, Aug. 24—Striking into the southern Philippines for the tenth time in two weeks United States Navy Liberators touched off towering fires at Davao and sank a small Japanese freighter northeast of Mindanao, headquarters reported today.

Five other enemy vessels, one a destroyer tender, were hit in raids ranging from Celebes, south of Mindanao, to Palau in the Caroline Islands north of New Guinea.

[On Wednesday Pearl Harbor reported the sinking of two Japanese cargo ships caught in a convoy by Navy bombers near Chichi, in the Bonin Islands.]

Air patrols bombed Palau Monday night, setting fires and explosions, and returned Tuesday to attack the destroyer tender and leave it dead in the water. Two enemy fighters ineffectively attempted interception, the only aerial interference reported in the raids listed today.

Near Celebes, patrol planes sank or badly damaged a small freighter and three coastal vessels on Tuesday.

In the ten raids in the southern Philippines announced since Aug. 7, the planes have bombed Davao airdromes and waterfront four times and have sunk three ships and damaged five.

Continuing aerial assaults

Continued on Page 11

PARISIANS ROUT FOE

50,000 FFI Troops With Civilians' Aid Battle Germans 4 Days

POLICE HELP REBELS

Turn Ile de la Cite Into Fortress—Casualties Among People High

By RAYMOND DANIELL
By Cable to THE NEW YORK TIMES.

LONDON, Aug. 23—Paris is free again and, because of that, the rest of the world can breathe a little more freely. In a manner befitting a capital with the history and tradition of Paris, its own citizens rose and threw off the tyrant's yoke as soon as their own troops and the Allies' armies of liberation had given them the opportunity to challenge their conquerors on equal terms.

In leaving it to the French themselves to announce that the swastika had been lowered and the Tricolor had been raised over their own gracious and lovely capital, the Allies were following a policy that was both strategically and politically sound.

Gen. Dwight D. Eisenhower's columns were able to continue their eastward sweep unimpeded by the need for pausing to mop up, and France, which was knocked out of the war more than four years ago, was able to stand before the world on her own feet again.

Armored Division Enters

The French Second Armored Division, which fought its way across the African desert under Maj. Gen. Jacques LeClerc, seems to have been the first Allied force to enter Paris. It went in after the local leader of the FFI had concluded an armistice with the Germans, it was said.

But before many more hours have passed, the Arc de Triomphe at the head of Champs-Elysées will be the scene of yet another pageant in the panoply of history, when the tread of victorious armies will mark the close of more than four years in which the City of Light had been the outpost of the jack-booted forces of darkness.

Paris, which began to weep but not to cringe on June 14, 1940, when the German heel first echoed in the boulevards, will laugh and sing again to welcome an army of repatriates and of aliens who come not to conquer but to insure the newly won freedom.

Koenig Announces Liberation

Maj. Gen. Joseph Pierre Koenig, commander of the French Forces of the Interior, informed the world that the French people had at last chased the Germans out of their beloved capital. He gave some of the details. But the full story of what happened in Paris between Aug. 19 and today is a saga that will have to be written by many men over a long period before the whole story is told.

Tonight, however—seventy-seven days after D-day—the world can rejoice without asking the whys and wherefores, for Paris is free again. "The Marseillaise" again is sung there, the Tricolor flies there again and the German tide is on the ebb in western Europe.

Until the newspaper correspondents now in Paris or waiting on the outskirts to get there can write their stories and transmit them, General Koenig's terse official statement will have to suffice.

A general insurrection, he said, began four days ago, when, in response to the orders of the underground leaders and the self-styled Provisional Government of France for a general uprising against the Germans, 50,000 members of the FFI armed and supported by "several hundred thousand unarmed

Continued on Page 3

After the liberation of Paris, American troops marched in the victory parade. They soon resumed fighting in the nearby countryside.

The city of Caen after it was freed in one of the most bitter and destructive battles of the entire war.

Soldier and civilian drink to freedom.

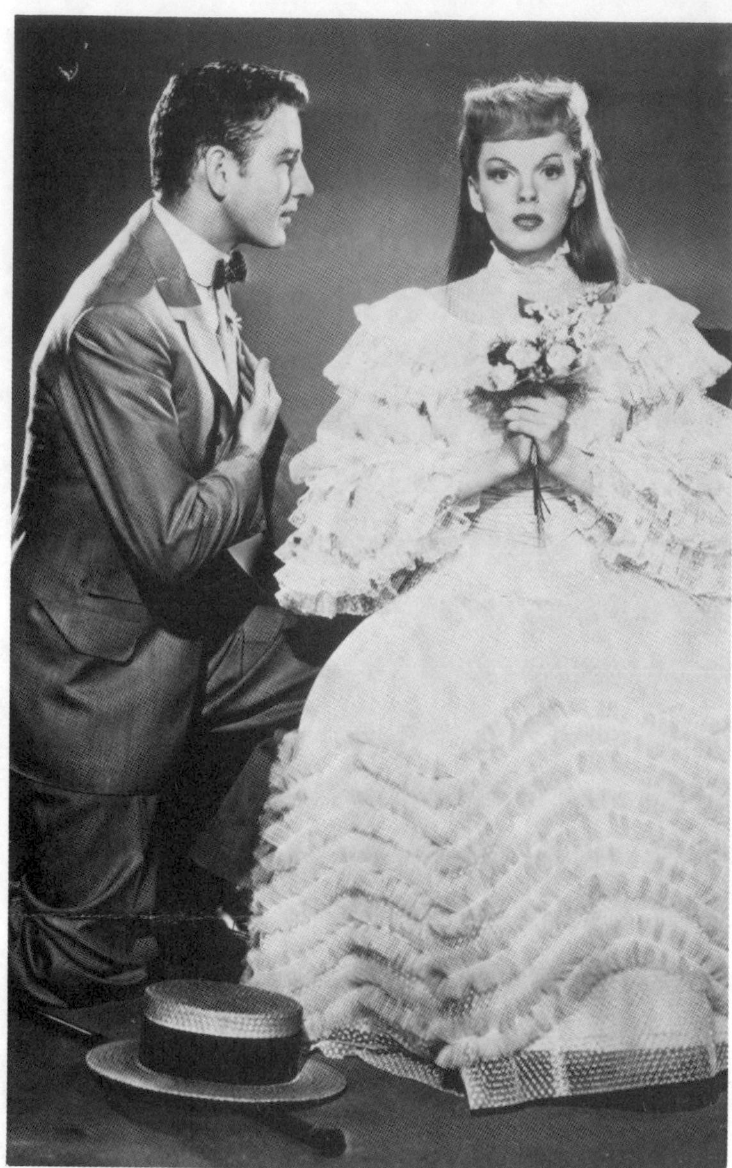

Judy Garland with the boy-next-door Tom Drake in *Meet Me in St. Louis.*

1944's *White Cliffs of Dover* starred Irene Dunne and Alan Marshal.

"All the News That's Fit to Print"

The New York Times.

LATE CITY EDITION
Partly cloudy with gentle to moderate winds today.
Temperatures Yesterday—Max.,76; Min.,58
Sunrise, 6:49 A. M.; Sunset, 6:44 P. M.

VOL. XCIV...No. 31,659. Entered as Second-Class Matter, Postoffice, New York, N. Y. NEW YORK, THURSDAY, SEPTEMBER 28, 1944. THREE CENTS IN NEW YORK CITY

ARNHEM POCKET GIVEN UP, 2,000 GET OUT; GERMANS BEGIN QUITTING WEST HOLLAND; DRIVE FOR RIGA GAINS; ALLIES IN ALBANIA

BYRNES DEMANDS PRICES, PAY CURBS TILL FINAL VICTORY

Controls Must Not Be Relaxed Until Danger of Inflation Is Past, He Declares

ASKS RECONVERSION PLAN

We Should Mobilize for Peace on a World Scale, He Tells National Press Club

By C. P. TRUSSELL
Special to THE NEW YORK TIMES.

WASHINGTON, Sept. 27—James F. Byrnes, director of War Mobilization, said in a radio address before the National Press Club today that the task after the war would not be industrial and economic demobilization but mobilization for peace. This, he emphasized, would mean a moving forward, rather than backward, not only for the maintenance and elevation of living standards in this country, but overseas as well. He contended that we could not attain peace and prosperity for ourselves alone.

"It will be tomorrow's accomplishments on the home front," he said, "which will, in no small measure, determine America's contribution to a better world at home and abroad."

At the same time, he warned, the Government must keep its controls on prices, wages and rationing until after the defeat of Germany and until total victory is achieved over Japan.

"Rear guard actions have been fought against the attacks of groups that are powerful while we are fighting a war," he said, "but, on the whole, the 'line has been held' and the Government should continue to hold it until the dangers of inflation are passed."

The relationship between wages and prices must continue to be kept stabilized, he added.

"If we do not preserve a stable economy," Mr. Byrnes warned, "post-war deflation will ruin all our plans for post-war prosperity."

Mr. Byrnes talked in terms of summation of what had been done to swing into force a production for war larger than the combined production of all other countries and three times that of our enemies, while "holding the line" against inflation, and of the job that lay ahead for readjustments when hostilities cease.

While it was not necessarily a final report on his stewardship as Director of War Mobilization, his audience, which included a score of top-ranking executive, military and naval officials, were aware that, months ago, he had given notice that he did not intend to head the new Office of War Mobilization and Reconversion which is to be set up under the Industrial Reconversion Bill now awaiting the President's signature.

Road to Victory Still "Hard"

While the roads to Berlin and Tokyo remain "long, hard and bloody," and while rationing and wage controls would remain at home indefinitely, Mr. Byrnes said, the problems of post-war reconversion must be faced now. These problems, he brought out, involve not only this country but our Allies. He gave an example.

"When on V-E (Victory in Europe) day the War Department reduces its requirements 40 per cent because thereafter there will be a war on only one front," he said, "it must then be determined whether there should be a corresponding reduction in the munitions of war we produce and through lend-lease furnish to our Allies. The seriousness of the problem is apparent when you realize that our lend-lease expenditures for all purposes for the first six months of this year amounted to $5,794,000,000.

"The problem, however, involves not only dollars, but the extent to which we and our Allies should change from war production to civilian production and what our respective contributions to the war against Japan should be. This can be determined only by the heads of governments."

Mr. Byrnes looked beyond V-E day to V-J (victory over Japan) day which from the point of view of reconversion, he asserted, would present more serious problems in industry and domestic and world trade and travel.

These problems, he contended, could not be solved on a purely domestic basis.

"In the past," he said, "much of the world commerce was transported by other nations, like Great Britain and Norway, where ships

Continued on Page 22, Column 6

Admiralties Linked To Marianas by Air

By The Associated Press.

WASHINGTON, Sept. 27—An air transport link between the Marianas and Admiralty Islands in the Pacific—over the heart of the Japanese-held Carolines—has been established by the United States Seventh Air Force and has been used to transport passengers and high-priority freight.

A statement from the War Department said today that four C-47 sky-train transports had made a 2,000-mile pioneer flight late in August and that since then other flights had been made. The new route links the forward areas of the central and southwest Pacific theatres.

The pioneer flight was led by Major Thomas B. Bramlett of Roanoke, Ala. One-fourth of the 2,000-mile round trip had to be made on instruments because of adverse weather.

WALLACE ASKS ALL TO STUDY AND VOTE

Bids Cramp Ship Workers to Do 'Hard-Boiled' Thinking, Then Back Roosevelt or Dewey

By WALTER W. RUCH
Special to THE NEW YORK TIMES.

PHILADELPHIA, Sept. 27—Vice President Wallace urged organized labor in an address at Cramps shipyard today to support the candidacy of President Roosevelt in the interest of post-war jobs, but only if "hard-boiled" thinking led the workingman to the same conclusion. He was speaking under the auspices of the Political Action Committee of the CIO. He said that he was convinced that the worker stood to gain more through the re-election of President Roosevelt, but he added:

"If you are convinced that the Republican party is best equipped for reconversion to insure jobs, by all means be sure you are registered and vote for Governor Dewey."

About 3,500 members of the Industrial Union of Marine and Shipbuilding Workers, CIO, heard his talk during their luncheon hour.

"Think the Thing Through"

"Think the thing through and be perfectly hard-boiled about it," Mr. Wallace told the workers, to whom he spoke for seven minutes.

The Vice President told the men that in his opinion "under President Roosevelt's background, experience, heart and imagination, you will be more likely to get jobs under Roosevelt and the Democratic party than under the Republican party."

For the country as a whole, Mr. Wallace said, the choice was between "the party that puts dollars ahead of men and the party that puts men ahead of dollars."

PAC workers said afterward they were disappointed with Mr. Wallace's remarks, one saying that "he had a perfect audience, waiting to cheer, but he never gave them a chance."

From the shipyards Mr. Wallace went to a hotel, where, speaking under the auspices of the Democratic City Committee, he deplored the fact that some persons thought "a little unemployment would be a good thing."

"I sense that there is some of this feeling right here in Philadelphia," he said. "There are those who would like to be able to insert an ad in the paper and have twenty-five or thirty applicants for the job. There are ladies who would like such a condition when they are looking for a maid. Fortunately, this is not the feeling of all.

"We have to choose between full employment at high wages and abundant cheap labor and a lot of unemployment."

Continued on Page 16, Column 3

ADRIATIC PORT WON

Commandos Annihilate Himara Garrison—Americans Land

YUGOSLAV ISLES INVADED

Berlin Reports Fighting Along 400-Mile Coastal Stretch—100,000 Patriots Aid

By The United Press.

ROME, Sept. 27—Allied forces have invaded Albania and the Adriatic Islands of Yugoslavia on a wide front, it was announced today, in what was believed to be the opening blow of a gigantic pincers drive against Germany's crumbling Balkan empire in coordination with the Red Army to the east and northeast.

Airborne and seaborne troops of the newly formed Land Forces of the Adriatic, in the eighth major invasion of the European war, made the first big penetration of the Balkans by the western Allies. Berlin said that fighting was in progress along a 400-mile front on the Albanian and Yugoslav coasts.

[A broadcast from Rome by a Columbia Broadcasting System correspondent said that the Allies were "past the raid stage and the landings in Albania undoubtedly will be followed by others at various points around the Balkan peninsula."]

Although headquarters drew a curtain of secrecy around the operation—which, a naval communiqué said, started eleven days ago—it appeared that the main blow was directed against Albania, which Italy seized on April 7, 1939. It was revealed, however, that the force was composed mainly of British Commandos, with a very few Americans participating. A small number of Yugoslavs were included to serve as interpreters, liaison officers and guides.

Albanian Garrison Destroyed

Headquarters announced that the German garrison at Himara, in southwestern Albania just above the Greek island of Corfu, had already been destroyed and that as a result the Germans had had to abandon the Albanian coastal road and send supplies to other coastal garrisons by small ships through the Allied-dominated Adriatic. At Himara the Allies stood only 200 miles southwest of the Red Army in Bulgaria and were in a position to knife 145 miles eastward to the Aegean coast of Greece and lop off a force estimated at five German divisions.

Early advices indicated that the invasion was on a big scale, in contrast with the long series of harassing stabs by the Commando-like forces of the Adriatic Army during the four months since its inception, and that it was aimed at closing the gap between the Adriatic, the Yugoslav Partisans and the Red Army massed on the Bulgarian-Yugoslav border.

Headquarters did not announce which of the many Yugoslav islands had been invaded, but a Partisan communiqué said that Partisans, cooperating with the Allies, had occupied the Island of Pag, at the northern end of the Adriatic, thirty miles below Fiume.

Continued on Page 9, Column 3

RUSSIANS CLOSE IN

Tighten Arc on Latvian City in Three-Way Push Past Barriers

ALSO DRIVE INTO HUNGARY

Budapest Reports Ten-Mile Penetration—Battle for East Prussia Is Renewed

By The Associated Press.

LONDON, Thursday, Sept. 28—Breaking through the lake and river barriers to Riga, the Russians drove within twenty-three miles north of the Latvian capital yesterday and tightened their ring to thirty-five and thirty-one miles east and southeast, capturing more than 200 communities from the German defenders, who were throwing in their last desperate reserves.

The Russians were silent on German accounts that credited them with a ten-mile penetration of Hungary from the Arad area of Rumania, but early today a supplement to their regular communiqué supported German assertions that a new offensive was in the making against East Prussia.

Southwest of Marijampole, in the Suwalki triangle that Adolf Hitler annexed to East Prussia in 1939, Russian detachments dislodged the Germans from a front line of trenches and seized two fortified heights, then beat off three counter-attacks with heavy losses to the enemy, the Soviet statement said.

Offensive Swings Southward

The German radio said a series of sharp attacks had been launched against the East Prussian fortifications from the east.

This offensive—though the Russians have not dignified it with that name as yet—appeared timed with the Red Army's racing descent on Riga and the breaking up of the German positions in the Baltic States, which heretofore have constituted a flanking threat to any Russian drive against East Prussia.

The Russian bulletin mentioned only one other front, that in southern Poland, where another half-dozen mountain villages were taken, and the Polish-Czechoslovak

Continued on Page 8, Column 3

A PARATROOPER LANDS HEAD FIRST IN HOLLAND

Coming down in a field behind the German lines during the operations of the First Allied Airborne Army.

The New York Times (U. S. Signal Corps Radiotelephoto)

FIFTH ARMY FIGHTS TO REGAIN HEIGHTS

Fierce Battles Continue Below Bologna—Eighth Army Now 7 Miles Above Rimini

By The United Press.

ROME, Sept. 27 — American troops of the Fifth Army battled today to regain mountain positions from which heavily reinforced German units forced them to retreat in a savage attack, while British Eighth Army forces on the Adriatic coast reached a point more than seven miles north of Rimini and approached an important Po Valley highway junction eight miles northwest of the coast.

Reports reaching Rome through the Italian underground said that the Germans had flooded part of Ferrara Province, northeast of Bo-

Continued on Page 6, Column 4

Arnhem Troops Undaunted After Escape From a 'Hell'

By ALAN WOOD
Of The London Daily Express
For the Combined Allied Press.

WITH THE ARNHEM AIRBORNE FORCE, Tuesday, Sept. 26 (Delayed)—This is the end. The most tragic and glorious battle of the war is over, and the survivors of this British airborne force can sleep soundly for the first time in eight days and nights.

We split up into little groups, ten to twenty strong, and setting out along different routes at two-minute intervals simply walked through the German lines in the dark.

The first party was to set off at 10 P. M., and our group was to leave at 10:04 P. M. Little packets of sulfanilamide and morphia were passed around. We tore up blankets and wrapped them around our boots to muffle the sound of our feet, and chose the password "John Bull." If we became separated, each man was to make his way by compass due south until he reached the river.

Links Party Together

Our major is an old hand. He led the way and linked our party together by getting everyone to hold the tail on the parachutist's smock of the man in front of him, so that our infiltrating column had an absurd resemblance to some children's game.

Orders came to us yesterday to break out from our forest citadel west of Arnhem across the Rhine and join up with the British Second Army on the south bank. Our commander decided against a concerted assault on the Germans around us.

Cheeky patrols went out ahead of us, tying bits of white parachute tape to the trees to mark our way. To prevent the Germans from realizing what was happen-

Continued on Page 4, Column 2

By RICHARD D. McMILLAN
United Press Correspondent

WITH THE BRITISH ARMY Before Arnhem, the Netherlands, Sept. 26 (Delayed)—The men of the British First Airborne Division came back, what was left of them, during the night from their Arnhem bridgehead, limping, hungry and fighting utter exhaustion to keep on their feet.

This brave band of British parachutists had carved out a perilous bridgehead around Arnhem, north of the Lek River, and defended it for nine terrible days and nights with their guns, their bayonets and their fighting hearts.

They were ferried across to the British lines in the dark before dawn today, under a furious barrage by German guns that they had defied, by two regiments—one British, one Polish—who got them across the Lek River in assault boats. The tragic passage continued from 11 P. M. until daylight. At dawn German gunfire cut off further escape and the remainder of the men were left, perforce, to their fate. [Allied Supreme Headquarters said that additional survivors were rescued Tuesday night.]

The Worst Hell on Earth

I watched the cavalcade come back from what a sergeant described as "the kind of hell I never dreamed could exist on earth." Survivors told me the story as their comrades passed endlessly by, many on stretchers, many wrapped in blankets, some hobbling on sticks, a welling tide of broken but stanch-hearted men.

They had taken everything the Germans could give from giant gunfire to flame throwers that burned men to death in screaming agony from Sunday, Sept. 17, to

Continued on Page 4, Column 5

6,000 LEFT BEHIND

1,200 Wounded Among Them—Germans Are Reinforcing Arnhem

DEMPSEY PLANS ATTACK

British General Is Grouping Forces South of the City—Patton's Men Assault Fort

By E. C. DANIEL
By Cable to THE NEW YORK TIMES.

SUPREME HEADQUARTERS, Allied Expeditionary Force, Thursday, Sept. 28—The Germans have boastfully written an end to a new epic in British military history, the gallant but forlorn stand of the First Airborne Division at Arnhem, but drawing no confidence from this fortuitous triumph they have begun to haul tens of thousands of men out of the western Netherlands.

These German troops funneling through a twenty-five-mile gap between Arnhem and the fabled Ijsselmeer will be used to buttress the northern gateway to the Rhineland and Westphalia against a threat that they see burgeoning along the British salient through the Netherlands.

Two thousand hollow-eyed heroes survived the ill fortunes of the airborne division landed north of the Lek River on Sunday, Sept. 17, in an attempt to seize a bridge or bridgehead at Arnhem across the last great water barrier guarding the vast plain eastward to Berlin. By the savage light of flaming houses these 2,000 filtered through the German ring around their hilltop camp three miles west of Arnhem Monday night.

"Operation Berlin" Is Name

They traveled in Indian file in groups of ten to twenty, their footfalls deadened by strips of blanket around their shoes, their routes marked by strips of parachute tape hung on trees by advance scouts. They chose "John Bull," symbol of a dogged breed of fighting men, as their password, and "Operation Berlin" as the code name for their escape plan.

They left 1,200 wounded to the care of the Germans, with some British doctors to assist them, and made their way to the shore of the Lek, where assault boats carried them back to the British Second Army's lines and sleep.

Some of the reinforcements from the Second Army and the Polish parachute regiment that had ferried the river to assist them also returned.

Besides the 1,200 wounded, possibly as many as 4,800 men killed or taken prisoner were left behind. Estimates of the division's original strength yesterday ran from 6,000 to 8,000.

"The ambitious attempt * * * to open the northern gateway to Germany has failed," the German High Command declared yesterday. The words were hardly on the air before Capt. Ludwig Sertorius, German military commentator, was describing a concentration of Lieut. Gen. Sir Miles C. Dempsey's forces for a thrust against this same gateway, and the Berlin military spokesman was reporting that the British were regrouping throughout the whole Eindhoven-Nijmegen area leading up to the Arnhem crossing.

Germans Reinforce Arnhem

The Wehrmacht's reaction to this peril was manifold. A dispatch from Nijmegen reported that more than 100,000 Germans in the western Netherlands — here the estimate is scaled down to as low as 70,000 — were trying to withdraw to the northwest, being unable to break through the corridor driven north to the Lek River at Arnhem and now being hourly thickened and hardened.

German reinforcements continued to move into Arnhem. Along the Lek from Rhenen eastward pick and shovel brigades were fortifying the river bank. While tank attacks on the Allied supply corridor had ceased, the Germans did

Continued on Page 3, Column 2

Dewey Drops Sedate Campaign, Strikes Out at New Dealers, Reds

By The Associated Press.

EN ROUTE WITH DEWEY TO ALBANY, Sept. 27—The October phase of the Presidential campaign was being notched up today as Governor Dewey sat back "between rounds" to survey the results of his 6,700-mile trip to the Pacific Coast and back.

While emphasizing that he would not join his opponent in his descent to "mud slinging," the Governor has developed an obvious relish in his last few rear-platform appearances for attacking such New Deal figures as Secretaries Ickes and Perkins and Harry Hopkins.

The response was always wild cheering, which brought a grin to the candidate's face.

The trip now drawing to a close started out sedately with platform appearances confined to handshaking and autograph-signing.

Unlike Wendell L. Willkie in 1940, Mr. Dewey planned to speak only to big political rallies where his carefully chosen words could be broadcast throughout the country.

But as the train crossed the country and complaints began coming in from the smaller stops, the Governor started making little talks to those who came to see him. Mostly they were excerpts from the major speeches he had delivered in Philadelphia and Louisville.

The station talks began growing

Continued on Page 16, Column 2

War News Summarized

THURSDAY, SEPTEMBER 28, 1944

Two withdrawals were reported yesterday on the Netherland front: the safe retirement from the Arnhem area to the south bank of the Lek of survivors of the British First Airborne Division and the retreat of thousands of Germans through a twenty-five mile gap between Arnhem and the Ijsselmeer toward the Rhineland. The enemy evidently fears a strong attack against the northern end of the Siegfried Line by the British Second Army.

Some 2,000 survivors of the original force of 8,000 Arnhem sky troops made their way to safety; 1,200 of their wounded comrades were left to be picked up by the enemy.

The United States Third Army delivered combined land and air blows at the fortifications defending Metz. The troops captured a bridge leading to Fort Driant and the fliers destroyed at least 25 per cent of the main and subsidiary fortifications. There was little change in the Aachen area. At the southern end of the line the Seventh Army was attacking north and east of Epinal. [All the foregoing 1:8; map P. 2.]

The airborne troops broke out of the "hell" of the Arnhem pocket in small groups during a rainy night without arousing the suspicions of the Germans. They were ferried across the Lek in assault boats. During the nine days and nights in which they had faced flame throwers and tanks they killed between 10,000 and 15,000 Germans. [1:6-7.]

Strong forces of British and American bombers maintained the assault on rail and industrial targets in the Reich. Cologne, Ludwigshafen, Mainz, Frankfort on the Main and Karlsruhe were hit. [3:1.]

Russian troops swept through Latvia to reach the Gulf of Riga on a wide front and to drive within twenty-three miles of Riga itself. The Estonian island of Vormsi was captured. Budapest said the Red Army had taken two Hungarian towns. [1:4.]

Albania has been invaded by the new Allied Land Forces of the Adriatic in conjunction with the seizure of a large number of southern Dalmatian islands. [1:3; map P. 8.]

In Italy the Fifth Army was battling to regain heights below Bologna lost in German counter-attacks. The Eighth Army cleared the south bank of the Rubicon. [1:5.]

Australian-based planes flew more than 3,000 miles to deliver the first blow at the Batavia area of Java. Only a mountain and a small pocket of land on Peleliu remained in Japanese hands. [13:1.] Not a single Superfortress in a force of more than 100 was lost in the attack on enemy targets in Manchuria. Army officials called this a "remarkable record." [13:5.] Japanese drives on Kweilin in China spread to new directions as they gained speed. [14:1, with map.]

Leading Government officials agreed that the surface of Japan's capacity to resist had barely been scratched and warned that the enemy in the Pacific had sufficient resources to fight on for years. [13:4.]

Yesterday was the fourth anniversary of the Berlin-Rome-Tokyo Axis. What was left of it "celebrated" on a note of desperation. [9:1.]

Ship Shortage to Keep in Europe Men Not Needed to Beat Japan

Foreseeing a transportation shortage that will prevent the prompt return of service men from Europe after Germany is defeated, the War Department is planning the establishment of vocational training courses to be given abroad to soldiers who can be spared from the war with Japan and the policing of Germany, Col. Lawrence Westbrook, assistant director of the department's planning division, disclosed yesterday.

The educational courses, he said in an address before an industrial relations conference of the American Management Association at the Hotel Pennsylvania, "will likely be supplemented by organized travel tours to places of historical interest in the countries concerned, for those who are interested."

The shift in the war after the defeat of Germany, Colonel Westbrook explained, will make it "necessary to use most of our shipping for a considerable time to get troops and supplies to the Pacific-Asiatic theatre." Consequently, he added, "it should not be expected that those in Europe who can be spared from the war with Japan and from the policing job abroad will be able to get home in large numbers." He expressed the hope that industry would consider this when making re-employment plans.

"The department," he continued, "has been planning for more than

Continued on Page 13, Column 1

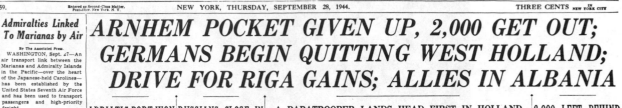

Mickey Rooney with Lyn and Lee Wilde in the title roles of *Andy Hardy's Blonde Trouble.*

Donald Crisp and Elizabeth Taylor in *National Velvet.*

Frederic March in the title role of *The Adventures of Mark Twain.*

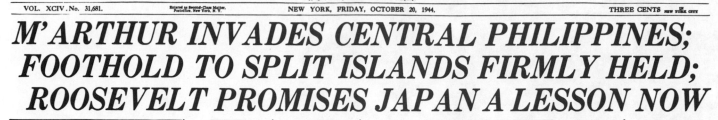

"All the News That's Fit to Print"

The New York Times.

LATE CITY EDITION
Cloudy with fresh to strong winds; rain tonight.
Temperatures Yesterday—Max.,67; Min.,53
Sunrise, 7:13 A. M.; Sunset, 6:09 P. M.

VOL. XCIV..No. 31,681. Entered as Second-Class Matter, Postoffice, New York, N. Y. NEW YORK, FRIDAY, OCTOBER 20, 1944. THREE CENTS IN NEW YORK CITY

M'ARTHUR INVADES CENTRAL PHILIPPINES; FOOTHOLD TO SPLIT ISLANDS FIRMLY HELD; ROOSEVELT PROMISES JAPAN A LESSON NOW

10,000 POLICE READY TO GUARD ITINERARY OF PRESIDENT HERE

He Will Arrive in Brooklyn, Then in an Open Car Tour Three Other Boroughs

TO ATTEND WAGNER RALLY

Trip Will Be Made Tomorrow Preceding Foreign Policy Talk, Rain or Shine

Police Commissioner Lewis J. Valentine yesterday canceled all police leaves for Saturday and recalled all officers of the rank of captain or higher from vacations for that day to provide a police guard for President Roosevelt's campaign tour of the city that will be adequate for all emergencies. It was estimated that the Commissioner's actions will make a force of 10,000 policemen, including detectives, available for the President's protection during his stay in the city.

Robert E. Hannegan, Democratic National Chairman, released yesterday the itinerary for the President's trip and said that the tour will be made rain or shine. The President is planning to make the tour in an open car, he added.

Laughing aside a question as to whether Mayor La Guardia was taking over direction of the campaign, that had been prompted by the Mayor's supervision of the arrangements for the President's tour, Mr. Hannegan said that Mr. La Guardia "has been cooperating with us in arranging plans for visits here to this city of which he is the Mayor."

Not Solely a Health Tour

The Democratic chairman denied that the tour was arranged to prove that the President's health was good, but he conceded that it might serve that purpose.

"After the people have seen him they can make up their own minds as to his vigor and health," he explained. "The people will have a chance to see him as the correspondents do twice a week."

The President's itinerary, as released by Mr. Hannegan, provides for his arrival at the Brooklyn Army Base Terminal in the Bay Ridge section of Brooklyn. From there the President will go to the New York Navy Yard in Brooklyn via Fifty-eighth Street, Fourth Avenue, Ashland Place, Navy Street and Flushing Avenue, entering the yard through the Cumberland Street gate.

Upon leaving the Navy Yard the White House party will drive along Cumberland Street, Park Avenue, Tillary Street, Washington Street, Fulton Street and Bedford Avenue to Ebbets Field, where the President is scheduled to greet Senator Robert F. Wagner at about 10:30 A. M. This is the only time announced for a stop on the entire tour.

Wagner to Join Party

Senator Wagner is joining the Presidential party at Ebbets Field and will ride with the President for the rest of the trip. Leaving the ball park, the President will go to the United States Naval Training School, Women's Reserve (Hunter College), in the Bronx, via Bedford Avenue, Empire Boulevard, Washington Avenue, Classon Avenue, Eastern Parkway, Pitkin Avenue, Pennsylvania Avenue and Interboro Parkway to Queens.

Leaving the Interboro Parkway at Metropolitan Avenue, the President and his group will cross Queens by way of Union Turnpike, Queens Boulevard, Thirty-ninth Street, Steinway Street and Astoria Boulevard north to the Triborough Bridge.

Arriving in the Bronx on the Triborough Bridge, the President will follow Bruckner Boulevard, 138th Street, St. Ann's Avenue, 149th Street, Prospect Avenue, Boston Road, Southern Boulevard, East Tremont Avenue, Washington Avenue, Fordham Road, University Avenue, Kingsbridge Road, Reservoir Avenue and Goulden Avenue

Continued on Page 13, Column 5

Moscow Is Paying For Petsamo Mines

Special to The New York Times.

OTTAWA, Oct. 19—The Government of the Soviet Union has agreed to pay 20,000,000 United States dollars to the Government of Canada for the interests in the nickel mines in the Petsamo district of Finland, owned by the International Nickel Company of Canada and its subsidiary, the Mond Nickel Company of the United Kingdom.

Announcement of the agreement, which was signed in Moscow by the British and Canadian Ambassadors, was made this evening by Prime Minister W. L. Mackenzie King. The Petsamo district was ceded to the Soviet Union by Finland under the armistice agreement of Sept. 19.

Payment will be made during six years in equal installments.

HURRICANE LASHES CAROLINA COASTS

Charleston Is Dark as Storm Roars Northward — Florida Citrus Growers Lose Millions

By The United Press.

CHARLESTON, S. C., Oct. 19—A tropical hurricane which caused damage to Florida's rich citrus crop estimated in the millions, and at least twenty-five deaths since boiling up in the Caribbean more than a week ago, lashed at this shipbuilding and naval center tonight, plunging the city into darkness through power failure.

At 8:30 P. M., the Weather Bureau said the center of the disturbance was in the Atlantic off Parris Island, site of the big marine boot training camp, but already gale winds of 55 to 60 miles an hour were sweeping this city.

Waves were pounding over the seawall at the Battery, and low parts of the old city were expected to be flooded.

[Little damage and no casualties were reported by The Associated Press from the hurricane's progress over the Carolines. Power was restored at Charleston at 1 A. M. High water caused slight damage at the Battery. Florence, S. C., and Southport, N. C., had forty to sixty-five-mile winds.]

Because of the power failure, The News and Courier was unable to publish tomorrow's editions.

Florida Citrus Crop Is Hard Hit

JACKSONVILLE, Fla., Oct. 19 (AP)—The hurricane swept northward tonight along the South Atlantic Coast after crossing Florida, causing two deaths in Miami and estimated damage of $20,000,000 to the citrus crop.

The Weather Bureau said the storm probably would reach a point off Cape Hatteras, N. C., early Friday and pass out to sea.

Relatively little damage occurred at Jacksonville, which had its worst blow since 1928, but nearly fifty beach houses were destroyed by wind and tides at Fer-

Continued on Page 32, Column 2

ALLIES NEAR VENLO

British Troops, Our Tanks Push Foe Back Upon Meuse in Holland

AACHEN MOSTLY WON

Canadians Speed Drive to Chase the Germans From Antwerp Area

By CLIFTON DANIEL
By Wireless to The New York Times.

SUPREME HEADQUARTERS, Allied Expeditionary Force, Oct. 19—Parallel columns of British and American tanks, driving through incessant rain and soggy Netherland fields, closed in today toward Venlo, on the great bend of the Meuse River thirty miles east of Eindhoven, and major junction of the main railway from the Ruhr and Rhineland industrial areas to Eindhoven. At the nearest point the Allied forces fighting under Lieut. Gen. Sir Miles C. Dempsey's command were within eleven miles of Venlo in a drive south and east of Venray.

The gains here, as elsewhere on the Western Front, were limited by persistently unfavorable weather. Canadian Army troops, pressing west against the shrinking perimeter of the German pocket on the south shore of the Schelde estuary, approached to within 2,000 yards today of the center of the pocket at Oostburg [near Waterlandkerkje, The Canadian Press reported]. British tactical aircraft gave close support to the advance.

American First Army troops were working in the streets of Aachen. Outside Aachen today the Germans were thrown out of pillboxes that they had occupied during the night in the Haaren area, northeast of the city. A German counter-attack there gained ground this afternoon, but Americans struck back and recaptured the lost yardage.

German Armor Attacked

Generally bad weather curtailed air operations, but American Thunderbolts, operating beyond Lieut. Gen. George S. Patton's Third Army front, hit railway rolling stock at Kaiserslautern and made an accurate attack on a concentration of German tanks east of Luneville, fifteen miles southeast of Nancy.

A German counter-blow against the British Second Army advance toward the Meuse was made today from the vicinity of the village of Overbroek, just southeast of Venray. It was contained, and the Allied forces now hold a line roughly along a secondary road from Overbroek to the southwest. The American part of this Allied force was working through swamp lands south of Venray along the railway from Eindhoven and Deurne to Venlo. About 750 prisoners were taken in this area yesterday, 150 of them by the Americans.

Fighting against the French

Continued on Page 3, Column 3

EAST PRUSSIA IS HIT

Huge Red Army Blow Takes German Town, Berlin Reports

DANZIG SECOND GOAL

Soviet Pincers Feared—Debrecen's Defenses Crack in Hungary

By The United Press.

LONDON, Friday, Oct. 20—The Red Army has invaded East Prussia, capturing at least one German town in "one of the war's bloodiest struggles," Berlin said last night, while Moscow reported that other Soviet forces had cracked the German defense line south of Debrecen, Hungary's third city, and seized more than 11,000 prisoners.

Using more than 500 tanks to spearhead single thrusts, Russian troops captured the German frontier station of Eydtkau, half a mile inside the eastern border of the Junkers stronghold, and pushed across German soil toward the great East Prussian rail hub of Insterburg, thirty-eight miles to the west, Berlin said.

German broadcasts, stressing the gravity of the "mammoth" Russian offensive and speaking of a "grand assault" by "monstrous" Soviet forces, said the deepest penetration of German soil was made west of Eydtkau as the Russians drove past the town to within striking distance of the strategic rail junction of Stallupoenen.

Moscow Remains Silent

While the German radio gave a day-long picture of German troops fighting desperately against an avalanche of men and material and yielding only blood-stained ground, Moscow remained silent on the battle that reportedly has been raging for three days.

At the same time German commentators told of a grandiose Soviet plan apparently aimed at throwing a steel ring around East Prussia's 14,000 square miles. While Red Army forces attacked East Prussia's eastern borders on a fifty-mile front between the frontier station of Schirwindt and the former Polish city of Suwalki, annexed to Adolf Hitler's Greater Reich, Berlin said Soviet forces

Continued on Page 6, Column 4

GENERAL M'ARTHUR FULFILLS A GALLANT VOW

Oct. 20, 1944

The return to the Philippines began at Leyte Gulf (1). Tokyo said the Americans had first invaded Suluan Island (shown in detail on inset). General MacArthur announced the capture of Tacloban in northern Leyte Island, a landing near Cabalian at the southern tip and occupation of the whole eastern side of the island. Bombings were reported at Davao (2), Cotabato (3), Zamboanga (4), Cebu (5), the much-bombed area of Clark Field and Manila (6) and Aparri (7).

2 POLISH FACTIONS NEARER TO ACCORD

Parley Suspends Temporarily, but London Spokesman Is Frankly Optimistic

By The Associated Press.

MOSCOW, Oct. 19—Leaders of the Soviet-sponsored Polish Committee of National Liberation have reached a tentative understanding with Premier Stanislaw Mikolajczyk of the London Government in Exile, and a spokesman for M. Mikolajczyk's delegation said:

"We expect it will be only a matter of weeks before both Polish

Continued on Page 6, Column 2

'We'll Strangle' War Lords, Roosevelt Statement Says

Special to The New York Times.

WASHINGTON, Friday, Oct. 20—The White House declared in a statement early today that American troops had landed in the Philippines to redeem the pledge made for our return on the surrender of Corregidor and that we would press on to bring about the utter defeat of Japan. Coincident with this announcement President Roosevelt sent a message of congratulations to Gen. Douglas MacArthur, telling him that the whole American nation exulted that the day had come when he had returned to the Philippines and said:

"You have the nation's gratitude and the nation's prayers for success as you and your men fight your way back to Bataan."

[The texts of the President's statement and messages are on Page 11.]

In another message to Admiral Chester W. Nimitz and Admiral William F. Halsey, the President told of the pride with which "the magnificent sweep" of the fleet into enemy waters had been observed and praised them for their "fine cooperation" with General MacArthur.

In still another message President Roosevelt informed President Osmena of the Philippine Government that when the Japanese had

Continued on Page 11, Column 5

OUR PACIFIC FORCES KEYED FOR BIG TASK

Marvels of Land-Sea Warfare Performed by Hard-Hitting Precision Machine

By LINDESAY PARROTT
By Wireless to The New York Times.

ADVANCED HEADQUARTERS IN THE SOUTHWEST PACIFIC, Oct. 19—What has at last become one of the most elaborate and best trained military precision machines in the world and one that is perhaps unique in the history of warfare was built up for the long, hard push into the Philippines under the leadership of Gen. Douglas MacArthur.

Veterans of the early fighting

Continued on Page 10, Column 3

War News Summarized

FRIDAY, OCTOBER 20, 1944

General MacArthur, at the head of the United States Sixth Army and Australian units, has landed in the Philippines.

The east shore of Leyte Island has been seized and supplies and heavy equipment are pouring onto the beachheads, he reported today. The landings were made under the guns of the United States Third and Fifth Fleets, an Australian squadron and an umbrella of carrier planes, the RAF and the Far Eastern Air Forces.

The Leyte area is the hardest part of the Philippines to defend; guerrillas there have continually harassed the Japanese occupation troops. It is about 450 miles from Manila, but represents an advance of 600 miles from Morotai and 2,500 miles from Milne Bay, from which General MacArthur started the drive back up the Pacific sixteen months ago.

Meanwhile, Admiral Halsey sent some of his carrier planes over the Manila area to pin down the enemy and wreck more than 100 aircraft. [All the foregoing 1:8; maps, Pages 1 and 10.]

President Roosevelt, calling the landing just a stepping-stone to Japan, radioed General MacArthur: "The whole American nation today exults at the news that the gallant men under your command have landed on Philippine soil." [1:6-7.]

During the past year a task force of unprecedented power has been built up in the Pacific for the reconquest of the Philippines. [1:7.]

Far to the west Allied carrier planes and naval guns battered the Nicobar Islands in the Indian Ocean, Tokyo said [9:5.] and in Burma Tiddim was recaptured by the British. [11:1.]

Foul weather hampered activity on Europe's Western Front. Nevertheless, British and American armor closed in on Venlo, rail junction for the Ruhr and Rhineland, and the Netherland town of Breskens on the Schelde estuary seemed about to fall to the Canadians. [1:3; map, P. 2.] The battle for Aachen was rapidly drawing to a close against diminishing resistance. [3:1.]

In Italy the Eighth Army bridged the Pisciatello River and captured two towns near Cesena. The Fifth Army took important heights near Bologna and on the west coast. [5:2-3.]

The Red Army, according to Berlin, has invaded East Prussia, capturing the frontier station of Eidtkau and pushing on six miles to threaten Stallupoenen. Moscow was silent on this front, reporting successes only in Latvia, Transylvania and near Debrecen, Hungary, now nearly encircled. [1:4; map, P. 6.]

A tentative understanding was reported reached in Moscow between the contending Polish factions. Premier Mikolajczyk will return to London to obtain his Cabinet's approval. The Lublin Committee was optimistic. [1:5.]

Dewey Backs State Department In Warning Nazis Over Murder

By WARREN MOSCOW
Special to The New York Times.

ALBANY, Oct. 19—Before leaving tonight for a major address in Pittsburgh tomorrow, Governor Dewey issued a statement approving the State Department's warning to Germany against acts of terrorism and extermination of victims of Nazi aggression still held in German concentration camps.

Mr. Dewey declared that the information that the Nazis were making threats to exterminate victims still alive in occupied countries came to this country "from unquestionably reliable sources."

His statement read:

"Information comes to this country from unquestionably reliable sources that the Nazis, trapped and knowing that they are faced with inevitable defeat, are now resorting to the known gangster terror device of threatening to exterminate their very victims—Poles, Jews and other non-German nationals—now imprisoned by them in their horrible concentration camps in parts of Poland and other countries still occupied by the Nazis.

"The civilized world is now in a position in unmistakable terms to warn the Nazis—military commanders, members of the German Government, their aiders, abettors and supporters—that certain and inevitable justice awaits them for these brutal and wanton murders if their schemes should be carried out.

"I am happy to note that our State Department has issued a

Continued on Page 18, Column 4

Kaiser Presents to the President 'Specific Pattern' for Reconversion

By C. P. TRUSSELL
Special to The New York Times.

WASHINGTON, Oct. 19—Henry J. Kaiser, industrialist, put before President Roosevelt today "an immediate specific pattern" for industrial reconversion to peacetime production which he and other manufacturers could begin to carry into operation "right away."

On leaving the White House, Mr. Kaiser reported that the President was "tremendously impressed," adding: "I am convinced that he believes that this pattern of aiding industry is an important step to assure now the transition to full employment in peacetime."

Under the pattern, Mr. Kaiser and other manufacturers, whom he declined to identify, would begin at once to take over war plants which have completed their contracts and are going out of business. The Kaiser group would then transfer to these plants the contracts and machine tools which are preventing reconversion to civilian production in other plants by using floor space required for peacetime production machinery.

Some manufacturers, Mr. Kaiser said, are willing to remain in war production and to take over the partly completed contracts and the machinery which handicaps the transition sought by those desiring to return to civilian manufacture as soon as possible without interfering with the war program.

To insure full-scale production for war, Mr. Kaiser emphasized, the projected reconversion pattern would have to operate gradually. However, he added, the program

Continued on Page 27, Column 1

BEACHHEADS WON

Americans Seize East Coast of Leyte Isle, Are Widening Hold

TACLOBAN CAPTURED

Casualties Are Reported Small in Mighty Blow by Air and Sea

By The Associated Press.

GENERAL MACARTHUR'S HEADQUARTERS in the Philippines, Friday, Oct. 20 (Army radio pool broadcast)—American invasion of the Philippines was officially proclaimed today by Gen. Douglas MacArthur.

Two years and six months after he took sad leave of the islands and relinquished them to Japanese invaders, vowing "I shall return," he announced that his Navy and air-covered ground forces had landed in the archipelago.

[Japanese broadcasts, beginning some twenty-four hours previously, had listed at least three landings, all in the central sector where the invaders would be in position to split the archipelago's 150,000 defenders in half.]

General MacArthur, aboard a warship, went along with the huge convoy from New Guinea, and within four hours after his forces landed began making plans to go ashore.

East Coast Seized

The special communiqué text, in part, follows:

"In a major amphibious operation we have seized the eastern coast of Leyte Island in the Philippines, 600 miles north of Morotai and 2,500 miles from Milne Bay from whence our offensive started nearly sixteen months ago.

"The landing in the Visayas is midway between Luzon and Mindanao and at one stroke splits into two Japanese forces in the Philippines. The enemy expected the attack on Mindanao.

"Tacloban was secured with small casualties. The landing was preceded by heavy air and naval bombardment which was devastating in effect. Our grounds troops are already extending their hold."

General MacArthur said supplies were rolling ashore.

225,000 of Foe in Isles

Among participants in the action were the Sixth United States Army, Navy forces of the Seventh United States Fleet, the Third United States Fleet and the Far Eastern Air Force.

The landings pitted the invaders against Japanese Philippine defenders, estimated at 225,000 under command of Field Marshal Juichi Terauchi.

[The Japanese exulted exactly four days ago that their alleged naval-air victories off Formosa had set back "the impending invasion of the Philippines by at least two months." It turned out that they didn't score any naval-air victories either.]

Eyewitness accounts from the scene reported the American Navy and airforce were on hand in such mammoth strength that the Japanese Navy was nowhere in sight and the Japanese air force, knocked out at all airfields in the Philip-

Continued on Page 10, Column 1

Fleeing Toward Foe, Halsey Tells Nimitz

By The United Press.

PEARL HARBOR, Oct. 19—Admiral Chester W. Nimitz, Commander in Chief of the Pacific Fleet, said today:

"I have received from Admiral Halsey the comforting assurance that he is now retiring toward the enemy following the salvage of all the Third Fleet ships recently reported sunk by radio Tokyo."

Tito of Yugoslavia in a hide-out with partisans in 1944.

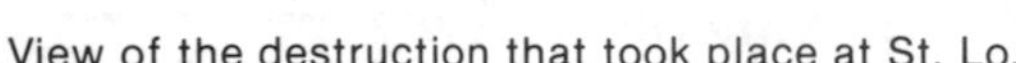

View of the destruction that took place at St. Lo.

American and British commanders and their staffs planned the final moves of the war when they met in Quebec in 1944.

"All the News That's Fit to Print"

The New York Times.

LATE CITY EDITION
Sunny, cool and windy; fair and becoming cooler tonight.
Temperatures Yesterday—Max., 63; Min., 51
Sunrise, 7:19 A. M.; Sunset, 6:01 P. M.

Copyright, 1944, by The New York Times Company.

VOL. XCIV..No. 31,687. Entered as Second-Class Matter, Postoffice, New York, N. Y. NEW YORK, THURSDAY, OCTOBER 26, 1944. THREE CENTS IN NEW YORK CITY

U. S. DEFEATS JAPANESE NAVY; ALL FOE'S SHIPS IN ONE FLEET HIT; MANY SUNK; BATTLE CONTINUES

SPECIAL PRIVILEGE SOLD BY NEW DEAL, DEWEY CHARGES

Says Roosevelt Backs Plan for 1,000 to Put '$1,000 on the Line' to Aid Campaign

PARTY LETTER IS QUOTED

Governor Declares in Chicago Administration Lacks 'Honesty' to Solve Post-War Problems

The text of Mr. Dewey's speech will be found on Page 13.

By ALEXANDER FEINBERG
Special to THE NEW YORK TIMES.

CHICAGO, Oct. 25—Governor Dewey declared tonight that "for $1,000 laid on the line to finance the fourth-term drive, this Administration boldly offers for sale 'special privilege.'" which includes the "assisting in the formulation of Administration policies."

Attacking the "rudimentary honesty" of the New Deal, Mr. Dewey, in a major campaign address preceding the appearance of President Roosevelt here Saturday, charged that the Chief Executive himself was the sponsor of the fund raising idea.

The Chicago Stadium, which accommodates 25,000 persons, was packed to capacity, with several thousand others clamoring to obtain admittance. Gov. Dwight H. Green of Illinois presented Mr. Dewey, who was received with tumultuous acclaim. He kept pointing to the microphone to still the demonstration, but it was just short of five minutes before he could begin his speech.

Governor Dewey said that the fund raising plan was disclosed in a letter signed by H. L. McAlister and Sam J. Watkins, State finance chairman, and written on the letterhead of the National Democratic Campaign Headquarters, Little Rock, Ark.

Dewey Quotes Letter

Mr. Dewey quoted the letter as follows:

"This is an invitation to you to join the One Thousand Club.

"The idea of such a club originated at a recent conference at the White House between the President, Robert E. Hannegan, chairman of the Democratic National Committee, and Edwin W. Pauley, treasurer of the committee. At this meeting the President commented:

" 'I think it would be a good idea to have a list of one thousand persons banded together from all over the United States to act as a liaison to see that facts relating to the public interest are presented factually to the President and members of Congress.'

"Members of this organization undoubtedly will be granted special privilege by party leaders. These members will be called into conference from time to time to discuss matters of national importance and to assist in the formulation of Administration policies.

"To be eligible for membership in the One Thousand Club will require a contribution of $1,000 to the National Democratic campaign fund."

Mr. Dewey declared that "there in crude, unblushing words is the ultimate expression of New Deal policies," adding:

"And the sponsor of this idea is frankly stated in that letter to be the President himself. The man who holds the highest office within the gift of the American people at a conference in the White House sponsors an idea to sell 'special privilege' and a voice 'in the formulation of Administration policies' for one thousand dollars on the barrelhead."

The Governor said that New

Continued on Page 13, Column 1

No Extra Gasoline For Trip to Polls

By The Associated Press.

WASHINGTON, Oct. 25—Chester Bowles, OPA head, in a letter to Senator Davis, Republican, of Pennsylvania today stated that the OPA could not allow extra gasoline rations for private automobiles to take voters to the polls if other means of transportation are available.

Pennsylvania has no absentee voting law and Senator Davis contended that many persons from his State working elsewhere would be unable to return to cast their ballots unless they received extra gas rations.

"A special ration may be granted to carry persons to and from the polls for the purpose of voting in public elections (including primary elections), provided reasonably adequate alternative means of transportation are not available," Mr. Bowles wrote.

Where no other form of transportation is available those wishing to use cars for voting may apply to their local ration boards on special forms which the boards have available.

WAGNER ACCLAIMS PARTY FARM POLICY

He Says That Dewey Is Vague on Agriculture—Calls His Platform 'Double Talk'

By CLAYTON P. KNOWLES
Special to THE NEW YORK TIMES.

SYRACUSE, N. Y., Oct. 25—The farm plank in the Republican platform offers nothing but "double talk" and Governor Dewey, rather than clarifying the issue, puts forward proposals "as vague and airy as a wisp of smoke," Senator Robert F. Wagner declared tonight as he carried his campaign for re-election into this city in the heart of the farm area.

"Mr. Dewey ridicules the so-called aphabetical agencies," he declared. "But how could low-interest loans have been provided without the Farm Mortgage Corporation? How could farm prices have been supported without the Agricultural Adjustment Administration? How could the number of farms with central electric service have been multiplied three times without the Rural Electrification Administration?

"These programs are not perfect. They need to be improved, but they are solid, they can be seen, they can be felt. When Mr. Dewey talks about the farmer, what he proposes is as vague and airy as a wisp of smoke."

His address, broadcast over a State-wide hook-up by the Columbia Broadcasting System, said that Governor Dewey's Commissioner of Agriculture last spring set minimum milk prices "far above

Continued on Page 12, Column 4

PRESIDENT ELATED

Gives News From Halsey That Foe Is 'Defeated, Damaged, Routed'

TEST IS ON, KING SAYS

Practically All Japanese Fleet in the Battle, Admiral Believes

By LEWIS WOOD
Special to THE NEW YORK TIMES.

WASHINGTON, Oct. 25—President Roosevelt exultantly announced late today the receipt of a report from Admiral William F. Halsey saying that the Japanese Navy in the Philippine area had been "defeated, seriously damaged and routed" by our forces.

Two hours earlier Admiral Ernest J. King, Commander in Chief of the United States Fleet and Chief of Naval Operations, had disclosed that virtually all of the long elusive Japanese Fleet had been engaged at last in the furious sea battle of the Philippines.

These two startling revelations, exciting Washington as nothing has done since the European invasions, were taken here to mean that the vaunted Japanese naval power had been seriously crippled and the road to Tokyo made much easier. At last, it was presumed, the principal part of Japanese naval strength had been nettled out of hiding and then decisively beaten.

Announcement Is Dramatic

The circumstances of the President's statement were thrilling. When only a half dozen newsmen remained in the White House press room at 5:20 P. M., Press Secretary Stephen T. Early appeared at the door.

"Come quick," he cried, slapping his palms together for emphasis.

Rushing to the President's oval-shaped office, the reporters found him seated at his desk, smiling broadly. Obviously he had been interrupted in his late afternoon dictation. Before him lay scattered papers, but directly in front of him was a single sheet of paper, inscribed apparently with his own handwriting.

He had, said the President beamingly, a "real flash," just telephoned to him by Admiral William D. Leahy, Chief of Staff to the President as Commander in Chief of the Army and Navy. Picking up the paper, Mr. Roosevelt slowly and distinctly read:

"The President received today a report from Admiral Halsey that the Japanese Navy in the Philippine area has been defeated, seriously damaged and routed by the United States Navy in that area."

For a moment there was a pause. No one said a word.

Continued on Page 3, Column 3

SEA POWER OF LAND OF THE RISING SUN SHATTERED IN BATTLE

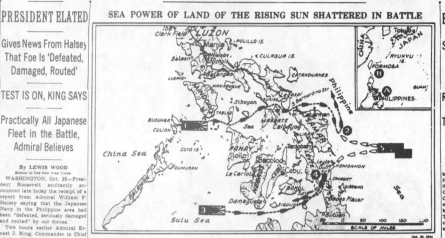

Piecing together the statements of Admiral Nimitz and General MacArthur gives this picture of the battle around the Philippines: One Japanese force, including four battleships, ten cruisers and thirteen destroyers, first sighted south of Mindoro (1) steamed east, across the Sibuyan Sea, through San Bernardino Strait and down the coast of Samar (2), where Admiral Kinkaid's combined force (5) attacked it and forced it to retire northward with perhaps ten ships damaged. It was apparently in this action that the American light carrier Princeton was sunk. A second enemy force, first sighted southwest of Negros (3), included two battleships, one or two cruisers and four destroyers. It moved east across the Sulu Sea and through Surigao Strait (4). Admiral Kinkaid attacked this group and it lost one battleship and several cruisers and destroyers; the rest of the force retreated west through the strait. This whole battle scene is at (A) on the inset. A third Japanese force was engaged southeast of Formosa (B).

ALLIES CUT UP FOE IN WEST HOLLAND

British Hammer Germans in One Area of 's Hertogenbosch—Canadians Tighten Traps

By CLIFTON DANIEL
By Wireless to THE NEW YORK TIMES.

SUPREME HEADQUARTERS, Allied Expeditionary Force, Oct. 25—The Germans were rapidly losing their grip tonight on their strongholds between the North Sea and the British Second Army's salient in the Netherlands.

British forces converging from three sides drove them out of all

Continued on Page 7, Column 2

'17 Hours of Hell' Raised In Sea Battle Off Leyte

By RALPH TEATSORTH
United Press Correspondent

ABOARD ADMIRAL KINKAID'S FLAGSHIP, off the Philippines, Thursday, Oct. 26—The Tokyo Express rammed into the American Navy Limited today. The pride of Japan was wrecked so badly it may never make another long run. It was the day our Navy had dreamed about for considerably more than a year.

It was seventeen hours of concentrated hell and the most amazing thing about the battle was that our Pacific Flight Carrier Force—which nobody thought could deliver such a terrific punch—held off the bulk of the Japanese fleet all day and had it on the run all afternoon.

When evening came and most of

Continued on Page 4, Column 7

AIR PLANT IN JAPAN SMASHED BY B-29'S

Omura Target Is 'Perfectly Patterned,' Pilots Say—Foe Lists 100 Planes in Attack

Special to THE NEW YORK TIMES.

WASHINGTON, Oct. 25—While the remnants of the demoralized Japanese Fleet were fleeing from Admiral William F. Halsey's forces in Philippine waters, United States Army Superfortresses today were carrying the war another step closer to the heart of Japan by carrying out a successful mission against the key aircraft assembly plant at Omura on the island of Kyushu.

Twentieth Air Force Headquarters here announced that a medium-sized task force of the mammoth bombers, operating from Twen-

Continued on Page 4, Column 4

AMERICANS MAKE BIG LEYTE JUMPS

Troops Push Westward on Isle—Southern Coast of Samar to the North Now Held

By The United Press.

ADVANCED HEADQUARTERS ON LEYTE, Thursday, Oct. 26—American dismounted cavalry troops have invaded Samar, third largest of the Philippines and last island barrier on the road to Luzon and Manila, while forces fighting on Leyte have punched nine miles inland to seize the key road junction of Burauen.

Gen. Douglas MacArthur also announced in a special communiqué that Field Marshal Count Juichi Terauchi's Japanese defenders of the northern Leyte front were "disintegrating" under the American hammer blows.

The three-mile American advance that occupied Burauen, southern terminus of an inland highway, split the Japanese lines in northern Leyte and threw the enemy back toward the hills, where Filipino guerrillas were reported in action.

The new American triumphs pushed our lines nine miles inland and raised to thirty-one the number of towns and villages captured. Six airfields also have been seized.

The invasion of Samar, with an

Continued on Page 4, Column 5

BATTLESHIP IS SUNK

Seventh Fleet Smashes Two Japanese Forces Converging on Leyte

REMNANTS IN FLIGHT

They Are Hotly Pursued—Third Enemy Force Is Hit Off Formosa

The Imperial Japanese Fleet has been brought to battle. It is suffering a crushing defeat. Two of its divisions have been routed. One has been almost destroyed. Contact has been made with the main force southeast of Formosa by Admiral William F. Halsey's Third Fleet. That engagement is continuing, said the last communiqué.

Two strong Japanese naval forces converged on Leyte Gulf through the San Bernardino Strait in the Philippines to the north and the Surigao Strait to the south. Vice Admiral Thomas C. Kinkaid's Seventh Fleet smashed these two forces and put the remnants to flight after sinking or heavily damaging every ship in the southern enemy force.

One big Japanese carrier has been sunk. Two more have been heavily damaged and undoubtedly are out of action. One Japanese battleship of the Yamasiro class has been sunk. At least four others have been heavily damaged. Several enemy cruisers and destroyers have been sunk. Many others have been hit, both by bombs and torpedoes.

Enemy Defeated and Routed

The only announced American loss is the converted cruiser-carrier Princeton sunk. Other escort carriers were damaged by fire from one of the enemy battleship forces.

Gen. Douglas MacArthur reported triumphantly that "the Japanese Navy has suffered its most crushing defeat of the war." Admiral Ernest J. King, in Washington, said that "practically all" of the Japanese fleet was engaged and that he was confident of the outcome. President Roosevelt called a special press conference to announce receipt of a message from Admiral William F. Halsey reporting that the enemy has been "defeated, seriously damaged and routed."

Pending official word from Pearl Harbor, it appeared the greatest surface and naval air action in the history of naval warfare was being fought and won by the Pacific Fleet, the greatest naval force that ever went down to the sea.

Fate of Leyte Decided

SEVENTH FLEET HEADQUARTERS, Philippines, Thursday, Oct. 26 (UP)—Japan lost the first, and possibly the decisive, round in an all-out battle to halt on the Philippines line the American advance toward her home islands.

This occurred early yesterday morning when Admiral Kinkaid's outnumbered fleet battered and put to rout Japanese battle forces converging on Leyte Gulf.

Complete results are lacking as the action is continuing, with planes from Admiral Kinkaid's hurt but still fighting carrier force hitting the surviving enemy warships as they are retiring. [General MacArthur said the Japanese force that came through Surigao Strait fled back through it to the west and the other was in flight in a northerly direction.]

[Gordon Walker in a Mutual broadcast from the Philippines said "a Navy spokesman here claimed that practically every

Continued on Page 3, Column 2

War News Summarized

THURSDAY, OCTOBER 26, 1944

The Japanese Navy came out to fight in the waters off the Philippines and was severely mauled. One force of four battleships, ten cruisers and thirteen destroyers moved up south of Mindoro into the Sibuyan Sea. Every battleship and at least one cruiser was hit. This flotilla rounded Samar and fled north. We lost an escort carrier. A second force of two battleships, two cruisers and four destroyers came into the Sulu Sea from southwest of Negros Island. After all the ships had been hit it turned tail and retreated. A third force, this one with carriers, came down from home waters and the battle was still going on. Most of the engagements were fought from the air and the enemy suffered heavily in plane losses. Our light carrier Princeton was hit and its magazine subsequently exploded. Most of the crew were saved. The Third Pacific Fleet took on the enemy carrier force and the Seventh turned back the two others. [All the foregoing 1:8.]

President Roosevelt, in an impromptu press conference, said that Admiral Halsey, commanding the Third Fleet, had just reported that the Japanese Navy had been "defeated, seriously damaged and routed." Earlier Admiral King had said that almost the entire enemy naval strength was involved in the Philippines battle. Fighting covered an area 600 miles north and south and 250 east and west. Navy officials were elated and felt the whole course of the war might be speeded. [1:3.]

On Leyte American troops had pushed twenty miles north of Tacloban and nine miles inland from Dulag. Additional landings on the northern part of Leyte and the southern part of Samar won control of San Juanico Strait, which separates them. [1:7; map P. 2.]

Superfortresses delivered a smashing assault on Japan's key aircraft plant at Omura on the island of Kyushu. One B-29 was missing. [1:6.]

German positions in the Belgium-Netherland pocket were becoming increasingly untenable as Canadian and British troops drew closer and menaced the enemy retreat line. [1:4; map P. 7.] More than 2,200 American and British bombers lashed rail and oil targets in the Reich. Six bombers and one of a great fighter escort were missing. [9:1.]

Russian forces captured the German port and U-boat base of Kirkenes in Norway and thirty other Norwegian villages. [1:6-7; map P. 11.] To the south the Red Army renewed its drive on Warsaw, gained more ground in East Prussia and liberated all of Transylvania by capturing Satu-Mare and Carei. [12:1, with map.]

Mount Belmonte, guarding the southern approaches to Bologna, was captured by Americans of the Fifth Army in Italy. The British Eighth Army gained three miles in the Adriatic sector. A German withdrawal was indicated. [10:7.]

The United Nations have resumed diplomatic relations with Italy, the first former enemy state to receive recognition. [1:2-3.]

U. S. and Britain Recognize Italy; Action Is First With an Ex-Enemy

By BERTRAM D. HULEN
Special to THE NEW YORK TIMES.

WASHINGTON, Oct. 25—Diplomatic relations with Italy were resumed by the Allies tonight.

Recognition is being accorded by the United States, the other American republics in the United Nations and Britain. The Soviet Union had previously extended recognition to the Government of Premier Ivanoe Bonomi.

Our action was announced by Edward R. Stettinius Jr., acting Secretary of State, who said that Alexander C. Kirk, who has been serving as our diplomatic representative in Rome with the personal rank of Ambassador, would now be accredited to the Italian Government with the rank of Ambassador.

It is expected that Italy will now send an Ambassador here. The appointment of Count Carlos Sforza, long a friend of the United States, to the post, has been forecast since it became evident that recognition would not long be delayed.

Announcement of the recognition has been made at London and is expected at the Latin-American capitals, except for Buenos Aires. Argentina never severed relations with Italy, although she did with Germany and Japan.

The announcement by Mr. Stettinius follows:

"After consultation with the other American republics, as provided in the Resolutions of Rio de

Continued on Page 10, Column 5

Russians Invade North Norway; Take Kirkenes in Wide Advance

By W. H. LAWRENCE
By Wireless to THE NEW YORK TIMES.

MOSCOW, Oct. 25—Entering their ninth country in less than seven months, Red Army forces smashed across the Norwegian frontier today and liberated the Barents Sea port of Kirkenes and thirty other Norwegian villages just fifty-four months and twenty-one days after the beginning of Adolf Hitler's treacherous invasion of the Scandinavian country.

This new expedition of Russian troops outside the Soviet Union was announced by Premier Joseph Stalin in a special order of the day and was saluted by Moscow's massed guns and highlighted in tonight's communiqué.

The Soviet Union's Norwegian campaign brings Allied armies back on the soil of that restless country for the first time since June 15, 1941, when the British had to withdraw their poorly equipped forces in the face of numerically superior German forces.

[On its European front the Red Army reopened the battle for Warsaw by outflanking the Polish capital on the north, drove farther into East Prussia against desperate resistance and completed the liberation of Transylvania.]

It would be wrong to assume from this dash across the Norwegian frontier at its northernmost point that the liberation of

Continued on Page 11, Column 4

Aside from the rationing of materials, the war also had other effects on fashion. This crepe blouse was adapted from the popular "Eisenhower jacket."

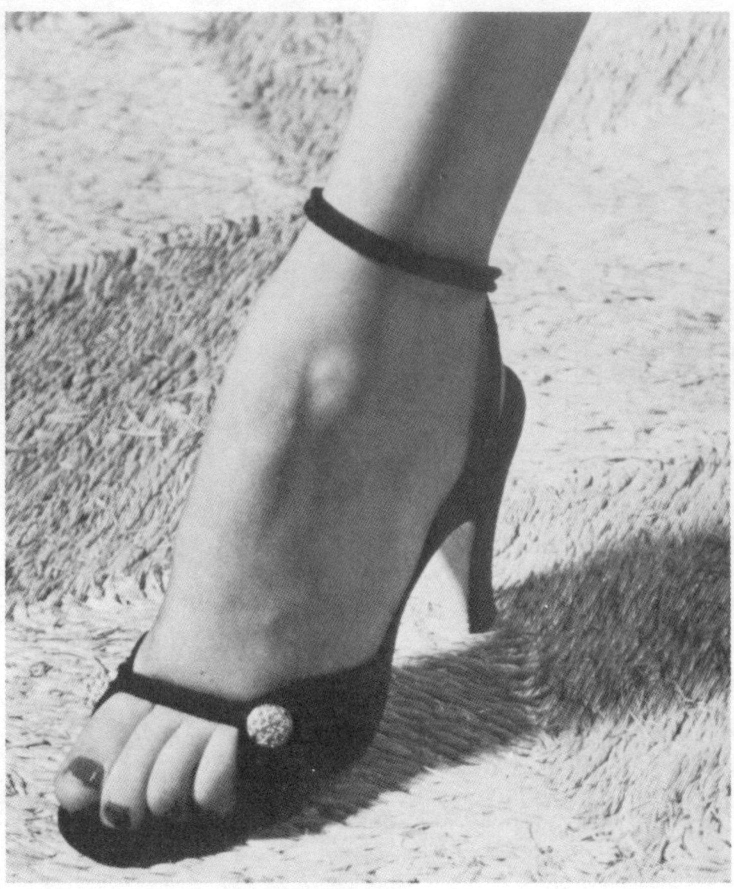

Eye-catching accessories were very popular.

Glenn Miller and his orchestra. The great band leader was killed in a plane crash, while serving as Director of the U.S.A.F. band.

"All the News That's Fit to Print"

The New York Times.

LATE CITY EDITION
POSTSCRIPT
Considerable cloudiness and milder today; moderate winds
Temperatures Yesterday—Max., 51; Min., 37

Copyright, 1944, by The New York Times Company.

VOL. XCIV. No. 31,700. Entered as Second-Class Matter, Postoffice, New York, N. Y. NEW YORK, WEDNESDAY, NOVEMBER 8, 1944. THREE CENTS IN NEW YORK CITY

ROOSEVELT WINS FOURTH TERM; RECORD POPULAR VOTE IS CLOSE; DEMOCRATS GAIN IN THE HOUSE

2-DAY LUZON BLOWS SMASH 440 PLANES, 30 JAPANESE SHIPS

Halsey's Fliers Destroy 249 Aircraft, Sink Four Vessels in Sunday Sweep

MANILA FIELDS RAVAGED

Ports and Installations Hit Hard—Enemy Lines to Leyte Defenders Are Strained

By GEORGE HORNE
By Telephone to THE NEW YORK TIMES.

PEARL HARBOR, Nov. 7—Admiral William F. Halsey's Third Fleet carriers spread death and damage over southern Luzon Island in the Philippines for the second successive day on Sunday, sinking another five ships and destroying 249 additional enemy aircraft.

It was a major air strike, apparently an all-out effort to annihilate the Japanese air forces supporting enemy counter-attacks on Leyte, where American military leaders have reported the campaign nearing its final stages.

Over the two days, according to Admiral Chester W. Nimitz's communiqué today, the enemy has lost 440 aircraft, 327 of which were caught and destroyed on the ground and 113 shot down in the air. The principal plane concentrations were found on seven fields in the Manila network. They were Nichols, Clark, Nielson, Lipa, Tarlac, Bambam and Mabalacat.

[The two-day toll of enemy ships sunk or damaged was about thirty.]

Unable to Rise in Strength

As the widespread attacks continue, the enemy air opposition is becoming steadily weaker, as is evidenced by the fact that on the second day all but a few of the lost enemy aircraft were caught on the ground, unable to get into the air.

Terrific damage is being inflicted on port facilities and ground installations in and around Manila harbor. In addition to ships sunk and planes destroyed, many air and surface craft were listed as damaged. Reports on the action were still of a preliminary nature and there was no count of our own losses.

Admiral Nimitz said three oil storage areas were left blazing at the northern section of Clark Field and at the northeast of the field a tremendous explosion was observed, followed by fire. North of Malvar a railroad engine and five tank cars were blown up.

Five Ships Sunk at Manila

In the harbor of Manila the fighters, torpedo planes and dive-bombers sank three cargo ships and an oil tanker, probably sank a destroyer and damaged two destroyers, two destroyer escorts, a trawler and several cargo ships. Fourteen cargo ships were damaged during the two-day attack, in which wave after wave of American planes swept in from the sea to wipe out available enemy strength that might be used to bolster the hard-pressed Japanese forces on Leyte.

Meanwhile the steady attacks on the Bonins and Kuriles are continuing. On Sunday a Liberator of the Eleventh Army Air Force, flying hundreds of miles from our Aleutian bases, hit three small transports off Onnekotan Island in the Kuriles and other Liberators flying with it concentrated on land targets of the island base.

Seven enemy fighters fought the big bombers in a running battle, and guns from three Liberators brought down one and probably destroyed another. Two Liberators were damaged.

Otomari and Tori Island, also in the Kuriles, were attacked.

Seventh Air Force Liberators

Continued on Page 19, Column 2

War News Summarized

WEDNESDAY, NOVEMBER 8, 1944

Japanese Lose 440 Planes

Japanese air power in the Philippines received a staggering blow on Saturday and Sunday when Third Fleet carrier planes destroyed 440 enemy aircraft in the Manila and southern Luzon areas. Nearly thirty ships, including a number of wartraft, were also destroyed or damaged. Our fliers reaped their greatest harvest at seven airfields where they wiped out 327 planes on the ground. Port and ground installations suffered terrific damage. Reports were still incomplete and our own losses were not known. [1:1.]

Battle Joined on Leyte

American troops on Leyte were battling elements of four Japanese divisions in the hills north of Ormoc and repulsed three heavy attacks, inflicting great loss on the enemy. The area of Valencia, north of Ormoc, was under American artillery fire. [19:1, with map.]

Tokyo Sees B-29's

The jittery Japanese reported more Superfortresses on reconnaissance flights over Tokyo and surrounding territory. They also said that the Bonins and Volcanos had been bombed. [19:2.] In China the enemy scored by driving to within twenty miles of Liuchow, but in Burma the British captured Kennedy Peak and threatened Fort White and Paletwa. [21:1.]

Grim Fight Below Aachen

The United States First Army fought its way back into the streets of Vossenack in some of the bitterest fighting of the war.

Luzon fields pounded from air

Three German counter-attacks from Schmidt were repulsed. The Sixth Army Group made important advances in the Vosges Mountains and in the Netherlands Allied troops were mopping up the liberated areas. [19:8, with map.]

Soviet Drive Forecast

Behind the lull on Russia's fighting fronts the Red Army was reported to be preparing for a great new offensive. [19:4.] The Athens radio announced the the Greek Government had ordered dissolution of the guerrilla bands Edes and Elas. [19:5.]

Robot Blows at U. S. 'Possible'

A joint Army-Navy statement said that it was "entirely possible" for flying bombs to reach the United States from Europe, but gave no indication such an attack was expected. [19:6-7.]

FISH IS DEFEATED; CLARE LUCE WINS

Congress Veteran Concedes Bennet's Victory—Close Finish in Connecticut

Special to THE NEW YORK TIMES.

NEWBURGH, N. Y., Wednesday, Nov. 8—Representative Hamilton Fish, for twelve terms a Republican member of the House and a leading isolationist and critic of President Roosevelt's foreign policy, conceded his defeat by Augustus W. Bennet just before 1 o'clock this morning.

"From reports I have received to date, it looks like I have lost the district by a 5,000 vote majority," he said.

"It looks as if the Republicans have lost the House, and if that is so, as much as I regret it, I have no great desire to continue to serve as a minority member, which I have for the last fourteen years in an uphill fight."

Mr. Bennet, in a victory statement, paid tribute to those who had supported him from all parties, "including the much-abused Political Action Committee." He hailed his election as the result of the citizens' determination "to eliminate Ham Fish from Congress."

Factors in the Result

Heavy Republican defections to Mr. Bennet in Orange County and strong support for Mr. Fish's opponent in the parts of the district in Rockland, Sullivan and Delaware counties sent the Republican nominee down to defeat in the bitterest Congressional election in this part of the State in years.

Complete returns from Orange County gave Fish 35,126 votes to 27,371 for Bennet, a majority for Fish of 7,755. This indicated that Mr. Bennet's majority for the whole Twenty-ninth Congressional District would be about 5,600.

Complete returns from Rockland County gave Bennet 19,706 votes to 12,323 for Fish, a majority of 7,383.

In Sullivan County, with twenty-four election districts missing, including those where Mr. Bennet was expected to run strongest, the vote was Fish 3,877, Bennet 3,776.

Continued on Page 2, Column 7

ROOSEVELT VICTORY CLAIMED IN JERSEY

Hague Spokesmen Also Say Wene Will Win—Constitution Revision Is Rejected

Despite greatly reduced pluralities in Hudson County, Democratic stronghold of New Jersey, lieutenants of Mayor Frank Hague of Jersey City, Democratic boss of the State, predicted shortly before 4 A. M. today that the State's sixteen electoral votes would be delivered to President Roosevelt, largely by virtue of an estimated plurality of 75,000 votes in Hudson. In 1940 Mr. Roosevelt carried the county by a plurality of 100,877.

Mayor Hague's spokesman also predicted victory for the party nominee for the United States Senate, Representative Elmer H. Wene, although by a close vote, and rejection of the proposed revised State Constitution by a substantial margin.

Mr. Hague himself left headquarters in Jersey City early today without making any statement.

The Jersey City predictions were made despite the fact that eight of the twelve wards in the city had not reported returns up to that hour, but the estimates on the fate of charter revision appeared to be borne out by Statewide returns. At 4 A. M., with 1,311 of the State's 3,657 election districts missing, the vote for rejection was 480,503 to 361,686 for approval.

At the same hour Mr. Dewey was leading Roosevelt by a vote of 481,677 to 456,275, with 1,819 districts missing, and H. Alexander Smith, Mr. Wene's Republican opponent, was leading the Democratic nominee by a vote of 562,261 to 503,763, on the basis of returns from 2,226 districts.

Five Hudson Communities Bolt

The apparent failure of the Hague machine earlier to deliver the expected large Democratic plurality in the county had caused some political observers to place the State in the doubtful class.

Continued on Page 9, Column 4

GET 11 TO 20 SEATS

Victories Blast Hopes of Rivals to Control the House

SENATE UNCHANGED

Democrats Have 180 in House, Republicans 155, 98 in Doubt

By TURNER CATLEDGE

Democratic gains of from eleven to twenty seats in the House and a possible new place or two in the already one-sided Senate, appeared on returns received up to 5 A. M. today to have followed in the wake of yesterday's fourth-term landslide for President Roosevelt.

Republican hopes of controlling the House appeared to have been blasted beyond any possibility of realization and what in the earlier count seemed to portend a G. O. P. gain in the Senate began to fade with the later returns.

These same reports showed the defeat of Representative Hamilton Fish, Republican, of New York, one of the most controversial figures in the lower house; the possible defeat of Senator John A. Danaher, Republican, of Connecticut; a victory for Mrs. Clare Luce, Republican, in a close race in the Fourth Connecticut Congressional District; a trend in the early count against Senator Gerald P. Nye, Republican "isolationist" of North Dakota, and a neck-and-neck contest in which Senator James J. Davis, Republican, of Pennsylvania, was trailing his Democratic opponent, Representative Francis J. Myers, by a slight margin.

Leading Senators Re-elected

These returns also revealed the re-election of Senator Alben W. Barkley, Democrat, Majority Leader, in Kentucky; of Senator Scott Lucas, Democrat, in Illinois; of Senator Robert A. Taft, Republican, in Ohio; of Senator Millard Tydings, Democrat, in Maryland, and numerous other sitting Senators, both Democratic and Republican.

With 98 House seats still in doubt, the Democrats had clinched 180 seats in the House of Representatives of the Seventy-ninth Congress; the Republicans were certain of at least 155; the American Labor party of 1 and the Progressives of 1.

Seventeen Senate places were still awaiting the decision of the final count, but the Democrats were certain of 49, or an actual majority. The Republicans appeared certain of thirty-one and the Progressives of one.

With the latest returns received the Democrats had garnered a net

Continued on Page 2, Column 5

ELECTED TO PRESIDENCY AND VICE PRESIDENCY

Franklin D. Roosevelt

Harry S. Truman

ROOSEVELT STRONG IN WAR VOTE TALLY

Partial Count of Ballots of Armed Forces Increases President's Majority

By CHARLES GRUTZNER Jr.

The majority given to President Roosevelt by civilian voters who went to the polls throughout the nation yesterday was increased by the count of war ballots marked, some of them as long as two months ago, by members of the armed forces in camps here and in far-flung theatres of operations.

The decisiveness of the President's victory over Governor Dewey removed the possibility that the outcome of the election might hinge on the soldier vote in some of the eleven States that delayed counting their war ballots, but partial returns from States that counted their war ballots yesterday made it clear that the support of the men and women in the armed forces would be a strong factor in building up the final majority of their Commander in Chief.

A breakdown of the vote into civilian and war ballots was slow in coming in from nearly all of the thirty-seven States that counted their soldier vote yesterday, because election officials were concerned chiefly with transmitting

Continued on Page 4, Column 2

New York for Roosevelt; Wagner Re-elected Senator

By JAMES A. HAGERTY

For the sixth consecutive time, four times as a candidate for President and twice as a candidate for Governor, President Roosevelt carried his home State of New York in yesterday's election and won its forty-seven electoral votes. With 3,609 of the 3,700 election districts in New York City and with 4,978 of the 5,421 election districts outside New York City reporting, President Roosevelt had an actual lead over Governor Dewey, his Republican opponent, of 300,831 and a plurality of about 283,000 for the President in the State was indicated.

Returns from 3,609 election districts out of 3,700 in New York City gave Dewey 1,240,216, Roosevelt 1,966,539. This is an actual plurality of 726,273 and an indicated plurality of 743,700 for Roosevelt.

Returns from 4,978 election districts out of 5,421 outside New York City gave Dewey 1,585,771, Roosevelt 1,160,329. This is an actual plurality of 425,442 and an indicated plurality of 460,785 for Dewey.

Re-elected in the sweep for the President was United States Senator Robert F. Wagner who defeated Secretary of State Thomas J. Curran by a plurality probably greater than that for Mr. Roosevelt. Also elected was Associate Judge of the Court of Appeals, Marvin R. Dye, who defeated John Van Voorhis, Republican. The President, Senator Harry S. Truman, candidate for Vice President, Senator Wagner and Mr. Dye, all Democrats, also were nominees of the American Labor and Liberal parties.

Returns from 3,566 election districts of the 3,700 in New York City gave Curran 1,183,020, Wagner 1,957,026. This is an actual plurality of 774,006, and an indicated plurality of 802,900 for Wagner.

Returns from 4,797 of 5,421 election districts outside of New York City gave Curran 1,468,985, Wagner 1,086,736. This is an actual plurality of 382,249, and an indicated plurality of 433,680 for Curran.

Both Houses of the State Legislature remain Republican. Among the greatest upsets in the State was the defeat of former Mayor Rolland B. Marvin of Syracuse, Republican candidate for State Senator in the Forty-third Senatorial District, by Richard P. Byrne, Democratic and American Labor party nominee. On incomplete returns, Senator John J. Dunnigan, Democratic leader of the

Continued on Page 6, Column 4

DEWEY STATEMENT ADMITS HIS DEFEAT

Candidate Concedes Loss of Election at 3:12 A. M. and Congratulates Victor

Gov. Thomas E. Dewey, Republican candidate for President, conceded defeat at 3:12 o'clock this morning.

His statement was made at Republican National Headquarters in the Hotel Roosevelt, where both he and Herbert Brownell Jr., chairman of the National Committee, earlier had refused comment on the growing indication of a lopsided electrical college vote for his Democratic opponent, President Franklin D. Roosevelt.

Mr. Dewey said:

It is clear that Mr. Roosevelt has been re-elected for a fourth term, and every good American will whole-heartedly accept the will of the people.

I extend to President Roosevelt my hearty congratulations and my earnest hope that his next term will see speedy victory in the war, the establishment of lasting peace and the restoration of tranquillity among our peoples.

I am deeply grateful for the confidence expressed by so many million Americans for their labors in the campaign.

The Republican party emerges from the election revitalized and a great force for the good of the country and for the preservation of free government in America.

I am confident that all Americans will join me in a devout hope that in the years ahead Divine Providence will guide and protect the President of the United States.

President Roosevelt, from his Hyde Park home, acknowledged, at 3:28 o'clock this morning Gov-

Continued on Page 3, Column 2

Roosevelt Leads as Davis Trails, In Mounting Pennsylvania Count

Special to THE NEW YORK TIMES.

PHILADELPHIA, Wednesday, Nov. 8—On the basis of partial returns from all but three of the sixty-seven counties in Pennsylvania, it appeared early that President Roosevelt for the third successive time had captured the State's electoral votes.

Swept on the Roosevelt wave, it appeared, was Representative Francis J. Myers in his race to unseat James J. Davis, 71-year-old Republican Senator who was elected first in 1932 and re-elected six years ago.

Whether the Roosevelt impetus would be sufficient to sweep into office the Democratic candidates for the five State offices remained in doubt. Reports in these instances, lagging far behind the count on the two top contests, were inconclusive.

With 6,012 of 8,202 precincts reporting, President Roosevelt was leading Governor Dewey, 1,282,392, to 1,238,986. Among the returns were all the 1,338 precincts in this city where the President gained a lead of 117,000.

The returns showed that once again the soft coal miners in western Pennsylvania and the anthracite miners in the East repudiated John L. Lewis, president of the United Mine Workers of America, by turning in thumping pluralities for Mr. Roosevelt.

On the other hand, with less than half the precincts reporting and Governor Dewey reducing the President's lead, Republican leaders were hoping that late returns and a fair share of the soldier vote, to be counted on Nov. 22 would mean victory for the party in the State.

Although the President seemed

Continued on Page 8, Column 4

DEWEY CONCEDES

His Action Comes as Roosevelt Leads in 33 States

BIG ELECTORAL VOTE

Late Returns in Seesaw Battles May Push Total Beyond 400

By ARTHUR KROCK

Franklin Delano Roosevelt, who broke more than a century-old tradition in 1940 when he was elected to a third term as President, made another political record yesterday when he was chosen for a fourth term by a heavy electoral but much narrower popular majority over Thomas E. Dewey, Governor of New York.

3:15 A. M. Governor Dewey conceded Mr. Roosevelt's re-election, sending his best wishes by radio, to which the President quickly responded with an appreciative telegram.

Early this morning Mr. Roosevelt was leading in mounting returns in thirty-three States with a total of 391 electoral votes and in half a dozen more a trend was developing that could increase this figure to more than 400. Governor Dewey was ahead in fifteen States with 140 electoral votes, but some were see-sawing away from him and back again. Typical of these were Wisconsin, where he overtook the President's lead about 2 A. M.; Nevada where Mr. Roosevelt passed him at about the same time, and Missouri.

In the contests for seats in Congress, the Democrats had shown gains of 11 to 20 in the House of Representatives, assuring that party's continued control of this branch. In the Senate the net of losses and gains appeared to be an addition of one Republican to the Senate, which would give that party twenty-eight members—far short of the forty-nine necessary to a majority. A surprise was the indicated defeat of the veteran Pennsylvania Republican, Senator James J. Davis.

Mrs. Luce's Opponent Concedes

The Congressional races were featured by a mass Democratic attempt, in which the President and Vice President Henry A. Wallace personally participated, to unseat Representative Clare Boothe Luce of Connecticut. But shortly after 3 A. M., following a night in which the lead had swung back and forth, her election was conceded by her opponent, Miss Margaret Connors. Some hours before, to his neighbors at Hyde Park, the President had expressed rejoicing over Mrs. Luce's "defeat." Her success is the vitriol in the Democratic honey.

Despite the great general victories by the Democrats, the popular vote will evidently show a huge minority protest against a fourth term for the President. Tabulations by the press associations indicated that the disparity between the ballots cast for the two candidates will be so small that a change of several hundred thousand votes in the key States, distributed in a certain way, would have reversed the electoral majority. At 4:40 A. M. The Associated Press reported 16,387,999 for Mr. Roosevelt and 14,235,051 for Mr. Dewey from more than one-third of the country's election districts. This ratio, if carried through, would leave only about 3,000,000 votes between the candidates.

One of the most interesting struggles for the Presidency was that in Wisconsin, where Mr. Dewey took an early lead, lost it and regained it again. Wisconsin is the State where the late Wendell L. Willkie made his stand for renomination, posing the issue of

Continued on Page 2, Column 2

"All the News That's Fit to Print"

The New York Times.

LATE CITY EDITION
Cloudy with scattered mixed snow and rain showers today.
Temperatures Yesterday—Max., 47; Min., 32
Sunrise, 7:13 A. M.; Sunset, 5:31 P. M.

VOL. XCIV..No. 31,716. Entered as Second-Class Matter, Postoffice, New York, N. Y. NEW YORK, FRIDAY, NOVEMBER 24, 1944. THREE CENTS IN NEW YORK CITY

B-29'S FROM SAIPAN BOMB TOKYO BY DAY; OPEN NEW DRIVE TO KNOCK OUT INDUSTRY; FRENCH TANKS SMASH INTO STRASBOURG

TELEPHONE STRIKE SUDDENLY ENDED BY UNION CHIEFS

Operators in Detroit, Washington and Ohio Cities Are Urged to Return to Work

SETTLEMENT LEFT TO WLB

Pollock Expects Fair Decision by Board Which Had Sent Dispute to White House

By JOSEPH A. LOFTUS
Special to The New York Times.

WASHINGTON, Nov. 23—Officers of the Ohio Federation of Telephone Workers suddenly called off tonight a week-old strike of Dayton operators and urged an ending of sympathy walkouts in the other Ohio cities as well as in Washington and Detroit.

Robert Pollock, president of the Ohio Federation, expressed in a statement the union officers' confidence in a prompt and fair determination of the dispute by the War Labor Board, which earlier had formally referred the controversy to the White House.

Washington telephone union leaders, who quickly responded yesterday to the "assistance" appeals of the Ohio strikers, were just as prompt in concurring in ending the walkout.

Some 2,000 Detroit operators who walked out this morning in sympathy with the Ohioans called off their strike, and Chicago telephone workers who had voted to strike decided to stay on the job.

N. P. Feinsinger, an alternate public member of the WLB, announced the Ohio union's action after a forty-minute meeting with Mr. Pollock and other officers of the union.

Seizure Was Discussed

While that conference was in progress, top White House advisers were reported to have been conferring on the advisability of taking possession of the affected exchanges. Seizure is a necessary preliminary to enforcement of the criminal provisions of the War Labor Disputes Act.

In midafternoon, the WLB announced that it had referred the dispute to Fred M. Vinson, Economic Stabilization Director. In an accompanying statement, William H. Davis, WLB chairman, said:

"The attitude of the union officials was in complete disregard of the national no-strike policy. The strike was a clear violation of the War Labor Disputes Act. Their conduct before the board constituted a pitiful failure to assume the obligations of responsible union leadership in time of war."

Mr. Feinsinger said that the WLB had exerted no pressure since the hearing yesterday at which the telephone union leaders rejected a back-to-work order and appeals to recommend that their members end the strike.

Saying that he believed the strike was called off because the union leaders were impressed that "the Government meant business and that seizure was imminent," Mr. Feinsinger pointed out that in the event of Federal operation of the affected exchanges the pre-strike working terms and conditions would be continued.

Government officials, studying reports on the effectiveness of the strike, were not inclined to be precipitous in recommending seizure of the properties. Sympathetic strike action was under consideration in New York, western Pennsylvania and elsewhere, but was rejected in Indiana and Connecticut.

Mr. Pollock's statement, which was released by Mr. Feinsinger, said, "As president of the Ohio Federation of Telephone Workers, I urge the immediate termination of the strike now in progress at the Dayton branch of the Ohio Bell Telephone Company and request that sympathy strikes called by sister locals affiliated with the

Continued on Page 17, Column 2

Eisenhower, Hailing Men, Urges Us All to Buy Bonds

Tells Nation on Radio Troops Are Forging On by Courage and Suffering but They Need 'Myriads' of Supplies

By The Associated Press.

WASHINGTON, Nov. 23—Gen. Dwight D. Eisenhower said today that his soldiers are making daily headway by courage and suffering but they need "myriads of shells and tires and guns and blankets and planes."

The man commanding the gigantic Western Front offensive against Germany appealed personally to the American people to oversubscribe the Sixth War Loan drive and "transform the money quickly into vital fighting equipment."

It was General Eisenhower's second urgent appeal to buy war bonds. He made it in a talk prepared for a broadcast from his European headquarters. The text of the statement also was released by the Treasury Department.

Mud, cold, bullets and minefields can't stop the millions of American boys from pushing the enemy back if they are plentifully supplied and supported from the homeland, the general declared.

The equipment is needed "now," he said. And the soldiers must get it "from the money you lend the Government."

He said the American fighting men are "entitled to the constant assurance of your understanding, of your resolution and of your unflagging zeal."

Reports from all sections of the country showed that Thanksgiving was a "big day" in the sixth war loan, the Treasury said tonight.

"Thanksgiving should help and not hamper the drive," said Ted R. Gamble, national war finance director, after hearing news of intense and unexpected activity in the fourteen-billion-dollar cam-

Continued on Page 9, Column 2

Churchill Hails U. S. Forces As Strongest in the World

By CLIFTON DANIEL
By Wireless to The New York Times.

LONDON, Nov. 23—Prime Minister Winston Churchill, making an unexpected appearance at a Thanksgiving Day ceremony held by the British in honor of their American allies, acclaimed the United States tonight as "the greatest military, naval and air power in the world."

In a brief speech before an audience of five thousand at Albert Hall the Prime Minister said there had never been "more justification, more compulsive need than now" for thanksgiving by the British and the American people.

"When we see," he said "that in three or four years the United States has in sober fact become the greatest military, naval and air power in the world—that I say to you in this time of war is itself a subject for profound thanksgiving."

Another reason for giving thanks, he continued, is that "we are moving forward surely, steadily, irresistibly, and perhaps with God's aid, swiftly toward victorious peace."

Remarking that "it is a British and American Thanksgiving that we may celebrate today," Mr. Churchill concluded:

"There is a greater Thanksgiving Day which still shines ahead, which beckons the bold and loyal and warm-hearted, and that is when this union of action which has been forced upon us by wars against tyranny, which we have maintained during those dark and fearful days, shall become a lasting union of sympathy and feeling and loyalty and hope between all the British and American peoples wherever they may dwell. Then, indeed, there will be a day of thanksgiving and one wherein all the world will share."

The Prime Minister spoke at a ceremony of tribute to the United States in music, prose and verse. His appearance had not been an-

Continued on Page 14, Column 2

EISENHOWER ACTS IN CIGARETTE SNARL

Orders Court-Martial of Those Selling Packages at $2.75 Each in Paris Area

By Wireless to The New York Times.

SUPREME HEADQUARTERS, Allied Expeditionary Force, Nov. 23—Gen. Dwight D. Eisenhower expressed personal interest today in the cigarette problem which has bedeviled American forces and ordered military police to crack down on illegal sales, which in Paris have reached such an extent that one can buy a package of American cigarettes in any bar for the standard price of 135 francs ($2.75).

Violators of this command will be court-martialed, General Eisenhower's statement to the press said. The communications zone, which has been handling—or mishandling—the tobacco problem, soon will announce the distribution of five packs of cigarettes each week for combat troops and two packages for troops in rear areas through post exchanges.

Troops living on "C" or "K" rations automatically get four cigarettes at each meal, or a total of twelve a day.

No cigarettes, pipe tobacco or

Continued on Page 10, Column 1

Men on Battlefronts Get Turkey And Trimmings Where Possible

The third wartime Thanksgiving was celebrated yesterday by the armed forces on the far-flung battlefront overseas and by Americans here with prayers and expressions of hope and confidence in a speedy victory in all theatres of war.

Around the world the day was observed in various ways. The fighting forces on the European front observed a dismal Thanksgiving as they pressed forward into Germany in bitter fighting under gray and dripping skies.

In Leyte in the Philippines American troops sat down or stood up to a traditional dinner of turkey and fixings. It was raining hard there too, as the soldiers received ammunition with their portions of the holiday dinner.

In China, India, Alaska and other parts of the world where American troops are stationed, at naval bases and aboard ships, the armed forces got turkey, if possible, or other holiday foods to make the day different from the rest.

Americans celebrated in the Cathedral of Reims, in France, at the embassy in Moscow, under air-raid alarms in Chungking, with canned turkey in India and an illegal peacock or two in Burma.

In a broadcast to the United States, Gen. Dwight D. Eisenhower asked all Americans to over subscribe the Sixth War Loan and to transform the money quickly into fighting equipment, which, he said, "is urgently needed now."

"There is just one way to gain

Continued on Page 14, Column 4

RHINE CITY FALLING

American Infantry Battle in Strasbourg—Patton Near Saarbruecken

GREAT RETREAT SEEN

Enemy Draws Back From Luxembourg to South —Ferocious in North

By DREW MIDDLETON
By Wireless to The New York Times.

SUPREME HEADQUARTERS, Allied Expeditionary Force, Nov. 23—Strasbourg, a city that means as much to the Germans as would Concord, Mass., to Americans under similar circumstances, has been reached by French tanks of the American Seventh Army, and the Germans, leaving pathetically weak rear guards behind them, are retreating on the front from the Luxembourg frontier south to Mulhouse.

[A United Press dispatch from the Sixth Army Group front, dated Friday, said French armor of the American Fifteenth Corps held the western part of Strasbourg and that battles had been raging in the streets through the night around the Strasbourg Cathedral.]

The German Army is in retreat, if not in rout, in this sector, but it is fighting with great stubbornness and skill in the sector along the Cologne Plain, where, despite Homeric fighting by doughboys and Tommies, Allied gains are measured in hundreds of yards, while in the blood-soaked Huertgen Forest to the south advances by Lieut. Gen. Courtney H. Hodges' doughboys of the American First Army are counted from tree to tree.

Little Resistance Outside City

Two of the most rapid advances of the day were made on the southern half of the front. Tanks of Brig. Gen. Jacques-Philippe Leclerq's French Second Armored Division, fighting in the Fifteenth Corps of the American Seventh Army, fought their way into the outskirts of Strasbourg against resistance so light as to be nonexistent along most of the route.

This swift exploitation of the German withdrawal in the southern sector was equaled by the precise advance of the Twelfth Corps of the United States Third Army toward Saarbruecken against

Continued on Page 4, Column 1

OUR GIANT BOMBERS VISIT JAPANESE CAPITAL

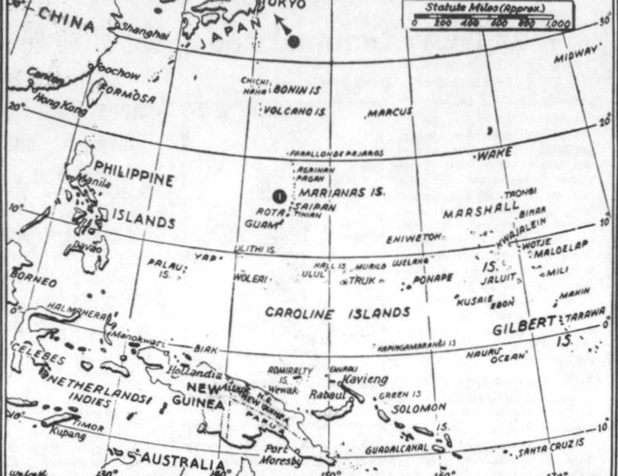

Taking off from newly conquered bases on Saipan Island in the Marianas (1), a large force of Superfortresses roared northward to Tokyo (2), where they blasted the city's industries.

FRENCH MASS MEN FOR RHINE CROSSING

Opening Salvos of Artillery Battle for Loerrach Gate to Southern Reich Fired

By DANIEL T. BRIGHAM
By Wireless to The New York Times.

AT THE ALSATIAN FRONTIER, Nov. 23 — Advance formations of Maj. Gen. Jean de Lattre de Tassigny's French First Army are tonight crouching less than two miles north of the Swiss-Alsatian frontier outside Basle for what promises to be one of the heaviest battles yet fought in the Belfort gap. At stake are the possession of southern Alsace, the Loerrach gateway over the Rhine to Baden, the Black Forest and the heights of Mappach controlling the "Verdun of Alsace," the German-held fortress of Istein, whose guns sweep the entire area from here to the Vosges.

On their part the French from first-hand observation show no inclination toward premature action.

On its part the German SS garrison holding the Huningue bridge-

Continued on Page 3, Column 3

B-29's Fill Air at Saipan As They Leave to Hit Tokyo

By The Associated Press.

SAIPAN, the Marianas, Friday, Nov. 24—The United States launched a mighty aerial weapon—the brand-new Twenty-first Bomber Command of the Twentieth Army Air Force—straight at the heart of Japan today. A great task force of B-29 Superfortresses thundered into the dawn at breath-taking one-minute intervals from this island, which five months ago belonged to Japan.

The giant planes dog-legged in the sky to form patterns of nine or twelve as they headed northwestward toward the most heavily guarded target in the Far East—Tokyo itself, some 1,500 miles from this base.

Leading the entire formation was 38-year-old Brig. Gen. Emmett O'Donnel of Jamaica, Queens, former West Point football coach.

The B-29 fliers took off knowing the enemy was alerted by recent practice missions against Truk and the Bonin Islands and by photographic reconnaissance over Tokyo.

But they expected to surprise the Japanese rudely from the standpoint of the impressive scale of this initial major combat mission, engineered under the watchful eye of the new organization's brilliant youngish commander—Brig. Gen. Haywood S. Hansell Jr., of San Antonio, Tex.

A photo reconnaissance B-29, which photographed Tokyo Nov. 1 and several times since then, discovered the Japanese capital was ringed by elaborate airfields, packed with planes. The entire Yokonama area, adjacent to the sprawling capital, bristles with anti-aircraft guns, which put up a most intense barrage.

On the photo plane's third trip to Tokyo a number of days ago, 100 Japanese fighters rose but failed to attack.

Earlier, smaller formations of

Continued on Page 12, Column 5

LEYTE LINE TURNED AS LIMON IS SEIZED

Entire Defense of Enemy Threatened—Japanese First Division Is Destroyed

By The Associated Press.

ADVANCED HEADQUARTERS, on Leyte, Friday, Nov. 24—Rain-soaked American infantrymen have captured the Japanese bastion of Limon and have driven 1,600 yards south in a sudden upsurge of a battle that has virtually destroyed the enemy's First Division.

Headquarters reported today that the Thirty-second Infantry Division had plunged through shell-battered Limon Wednesday, in the biggest advance in more than two weeks.

The entire Yamashita Line, upon which the Japanese depend to hold Leyte Island, is in danger of being rolled up, the communiqué said.

As heavy rains continued to lash the battlefront, the American infantrymen drove through the mountain village to the near-by Leyte River.

Later headquarters announced that Lightning fighter planes sank five small freighters and probably

Continued on Page 12, Column 2

War News Summarized

FRIDAY, NOVEMBER 24, 1944

Tokyo was bombed for the second time when Superfortresses from Saipan bases, 1,500 miles away, attacked industrial targets in the enemy capital by daylight. In announcing the mission, conducted by the newly established Twenty-first Bomber Command, Gen. H. H. Arnold in Washington said it marked a new extension of the range of American air power. [1:8; with map.]

In the Philippines, American troops scored their biggest gains in two weeks of bitter fighting on Leyte Island by crushing the Japanese at Limon and smashing through to the Leyte River. The enemy's First Division was "practically destroyed" in the drive which now threatens to roll up the whole Yamashita Line, the main Japanese defense zone on Leyte. [1:7; map P. 12.]

General Wedemeyer predicted that a large American Army would be fighting in China. He also reported that Generalissimo Chiang had accepted the general concept of a plan for the disposition of Chinese troops for more effective opposition to the Japanese invasion. [13:4.]

The Chinese drive to reopen a land supply route to China made further progress, with troops advancing from fallen Mangshih on the old Burma Road to within three miles of Chefang. Meanwhile, the Japanese claimed that their offensive in southern China was unchecked and that they had captured Chinchengkiang, about 120 miles from Kweiyang, in Kweichow Province. [13:1.]

In a swift exploitation of the German retreat on the lower end of the western front, French tank units stabbed into Strasbourg, ancient Alsatian city just west of the Rhine. In marked contrast to the weak resistance offered by enemy rear guards from the Luxembourg frontier south to Mulhouse, there was bitter fighting, with violent German counter-attacks in the sector before Cologne. There, Allied gains were measured in yards and, in the Huertgen Forest, they were made tree by tree. The American Third Army was ten miles from Saarbruecken. [1:4; maps P. 4.]

The Red Army invaded the southeastern borders of Slovakia, while maintaining its steady pressure on enemy lines before Budapest. A Berlin report said the Russians had landed on the large island of Csepel in the Danube in front of the Hungarian capital. Moscow said the rail junction of Cop in Czechoslovakia had fallen to other Russian columns. Enemy troops on the Estonian island of Oesel had been further compressed. [6:1; with map.]

Canada Drafts Men for Europe; Policy Shift Intensifies Crisis

By P. J. PHILIP
Special to The New York Times.

OTTAWA, Nov. 23—Applying its existing powers, the Canadian Government today issued an order-in-council making 16,000 drafted men immediately available as reinforcements for the Canadian Army overseas. This sensational departure from the principle of voluntary enlistment for overseas service came only twenty-four hours after Prime Minister W. L. Mackenzie King, in explaining the reasons for Col. J. L. Ralston's resignation as Defense Minister, had seemed to convey to Parliament the impression that there would be no change of policy.

The Prime Minister also gave notice that at the end of the debate he will ask for a vote of confidence in the following terms: "That this House will aid the Government in its policy of maintaining a vigorous war."

[Meantime, the Canadian Press reported that it had been announced officially at the Quebec offices of Air Minister C. G. Power early Thursday night that the Air Minister had resigned "because he is opposed to conscription for overseas service." Mr. Power represents Quebec South in the House of Commons.]

The announcement of Government policy on conscription followed a long Cabinet meeting last

Continued on Page 34, Column 2

INDUSTRY BLASTED

Japanese Capital 'Hurt by 'Sizable Force' From New Base

A STEP TO INVASION

Arnold Pledges Blows to Destroy the Fighting Power of Foe

By The Associated Press.

WASHINGTON, Friday, Nov. 24 — Tokyo was attacked today by Superfortresses in a daylight mission launched from bases in the Marianas Islands.

The War Department announced that "a sizable task force of B-29 aircraft of the Twentieth Air Force today attacked industrial targets in Tokyo."

The mission was conducted by the newly established Twenty-first Bomber Command operating from bases on Saipan, approximately 1,500 miles to the south and east.

THE ARMY'S ANNOUNCEMENT

The War Department statement:

A sizable task force of B-29 aircraft of the Twentieth Air Force today attacked industrial targets in Tokyo, Gen. H. H. Arnold, in his capacity as commanding general of the Twentieth Air Force, announced at the War Department.

The mission was a daylight operation by the newly established Twenty-first Bomber Command, under command of Brig. Gen. H. S. Hansell Jr., from bases on Saipan.

A communiqué covering this operation will be issued when further details are available.

[Matsuwa Island, in the Kuriles, was bombarded Tuesday by a Pacific Fleet task force, which started large fires and set off explosions among enemy defense installations, Admiral Chester W. Nimitz announced.]

More than two years have elapsed between the first and second bombings of the enemy capital. The first attack was made by sixteen medium bombers launched from the deck of the carrier Hornet on April 18, 1942. That flight was commanded by the then Lieut. Col. James A. Doolittle, now a lieutenant general and commander of the Eighth Air Force in Europe.

The civilized world was disturbed later by reports that some of the fliers who participated in the first attack had been executed by the Japanese.

The work of building the airfields in the Marianas was started at almost the moment the last organized enemy resistance ceased in those islands, now held by the United States. Saipan was secured on July 8 and Guam a few weeks later.

The Twenty-first Bomber Command was activated on March 8 this year and started training at

Continued on Page 10, Column 3

Voroshiloff Seen In Far East Post

By The Associated Press.

LONDON, Nov. 23—The German-controlled Budapest radio said tonight it had learned "from reliable sources" that Russia's Marshal Klementy E. Voroshiloff had been appointed "Commander in Chief in the Far East and has probably already taken up his new post."

It was announced yesterday in Moscow that Marshal Voroshiloff had been relieved by Premier Joseph Stalin of his duties as a member of the Soviet State Committee of Defense.

The Berlin radio gave out the same report and quoted a Wilhelmstrasse spokesman as saying: "If Stalin decided to send such an important man as Voroshiloff to the Far East some definite developments might be expected there."

1945

1945

Vice President Harry S. Truman plays the piano for an approving Lauren Bacall at the National Press Club in Washington, D.C.

"All the News That's Fit to Print"

The New York Times.

LATE CITY EDITION
Increasing cloudiness with moderate winds today.
Temperatures Yesterday—Max., 46; Min., 29
Sunrise today, 7:53 A. M.; Sunset, 6:58 P. M.

Copyright, 1945, by The New York Times Company.

VOL. XCIV...No. 31,797. Entered as Second-Class Matter, Postoffice, New York, N. Y. NEW YORK, TUESDAY, FEBRUARY 13, 1945. THREE CENTS IN NEW YORK CITY

BIG 3 DOOM NAZISM AND REICH MILITARISM; AGREE ON FREED LANDS AND OAKS VOTING; CONVOKE UNITED NATIONS IN U. S. APRIL 25

IVES ASSAILS FOES OF ANTI-RACE BILLS AS DISFAVOR RISES

But Demand for Immediate Vote by CIO Head Is Unlikely to Head Off Opposition

PRESS FOR PUBLIC HEARING

Legislators Confident of Aid From Minorities—Chamber Attack Called 'Degrading'

The text of the statement by Assemblyman Ives, Page 18.

Special to THE NEW YORK TIMES.

ALBANY, Feb. 12—Irving M. Ives, Republican leader of the Assembly, and Louis Hollander, president of the State Congress of Industrial Organizations, struck back tonight at critics of the Ives-Quinn anti-discrimination bills.

In a statement defending the proposal to set up a five-man commission with power to eradicate discrimination in employment on racial or religious grounds, Mr. Ives sought to set at rest a strong feeling that it would have the effect of increasing rather than eliminating interracial frictions.

Meanwhile, opposition to the measure continued to grow. It was believed that neither Mr. Ives' statement nor Mr. Hollander's appeal to pass the Ives-Quinn proposals "at once and without any crippling amendments" appear likely to head off that opposition.

Pressure for Public Hearing

In the Senate, where the bill remains in the Finance Committee, there is very strong pressure for a public hearing. Senator Elmer F. Quinn, Democratic leader of the Senate and co-sponsor with Mr. Ives of the legislation, described the pressure for a hearing as "terrific."

Mr. Quinn said that he had been besieged in New York over the week-end by representatives of employment agencies who want an opportunity to present amendments to the bill. But supporters of the measure are opposed to granting further hearings.

Advocates of the legislation also believe that only a few legislators will dare to vote against the measure in view of the strong demand for its passage from CIO unions, Negro and other minority groups.

Some Republican strategists are viewing the proposal as an opportunity to regain the favor of minority groups. Democratic leaders in turn are cracking the whip to obtain a solid Democratic vote in favor of the legislation in both Senate and Assembly.

Governor Dewey has avoided taking any stand on the measure, but he has gone on record in his annual message in favor of the enactment of bills along the lines of the Ives-Quinn proposal to put "our State in the forefront of the nation in the handling of that vital issue."

Mr. Hollander in his appeal for strong CIO pressure in favor of immediate enactment of the legislation characterized the attack on the bill made in New York by the State Chamber of Commerce as "degrading and un-American."

Calls Statement Outrageous

"In this outrageous statement," Mr. Hollander continued, "the Chamber of Commerce, representing the most reactionary forces in our State, has the gall to threaten us with possible race riots, pogroms and other evils. This sinister attempt at blackmailing the Legislature into throwing out the Ives-Quinn bill must be repudiated in the sharpest fashion possible."

Assemblyman Wilson C. van Duzer, Republican, of Orange County, joined Senator Frederic Bontecou, Republican, of Dutchess County, and Assemblyman William Stuart, Republican, of Steuben County, in demanding further hearings before the Ives-Quinn bills are put to a vote.

Opposition forces were receiving some encouragement from the

Continued on Page 18, Column 2

WPB Takes Charge Of Match Output

By The Associated Press.

WASHINGTON, Feb. 12—The War Production Board took control today over production and distribution of matches, to assure, it said, the meeting of military requirements and preventing maldistribution of civilian supplies.

The allocation of matches will be controlled at the producer level.

Production of matches this year is expected to total 460,000,000,000 as compared with an average pre-war level of 480,000,000,000. The reduced production is attributed to the labor shortage.

Military requirements will take about a third of the 1945 output, including the entire production of strike-on-box matches and about 35 per cent of the book matches.

Civilians will find it more difficult to obtain strike-on-box and book matches, but the WPB said that the supply of strike-anywhere, or kitchen, matches would be adequate if there were no hoarding.

BIG 3 AGREEMENT LAUDED BY HOOVER

'Strong Foundation' for New World, He Says—Austin Asks Bipartisan Planning

Before 1,000 persons high in the leadership of the Republican party, former President Herbert Hoover, long a spokesman for an important section of his party, gave an enthusiastic endorsement last night to the agreement reached by President Roosevelt, Marshal Joseph Stalin and Prime Minister Winston Churchill at the Big Three conference in the Crimea.

Called upon for an impromptu speech at the fifty-ninth annual Lincoln Day dinner of the National Republican Club at the Hotel Waldorf-Astoria, Mr. Hoover said he believed the agreement provided "a strong foundation" for the reconstruction of the post-war world. He said:

"On the radio this evening there was announced news of tremendous importance to the whole world. That is the agreement reached in the Black Sea area.

"I believe it comprises a strong foundation on which to rebuild the world.

"If the agreement's promises and ideals which are expressed shall be carried out, it will open a great hope to the world.

"It is fitting that it should have been issued to the world on the birthday of Abraham Lincoln."

As Mr. Hoover resumed his seat after his brief remarks, there was applause from every section of the audience.

Senator Warren R. Austin of Vermont, another speaker at the gathering, joined Mr. Hoover in hailing the Crimea agreement as a constructive step toward peace.

Continued on Page 2, Column 3

CLEVE, PRUEM FALL

Allies Capture Two Key Westwall Positions in North and Center

OPPOSITION IS LIGHT

Germans Draft Women for Volkssturm—New Clashes Reported

By CLIFTON DANIEL

By Wireless to THE NEW YORK TIMES.

SUPREME HEADQUARTERS, Allied Expeditionary Force, Feb. 12—With surprising dispatch, Allied troops broke the Germans' hold on key centers of two sectors of the Western Front today, evicting all except a few snipers from Cleve, at the northern end of the line, and from Pruem, in the center.

British and Canadian forces quickly mopped up the Siegfried fortress town of Cleve and also pressed through the full length of the Reichswald (Reich Forest) to its eastern edge.

Gen. H. D. G. Crerar's forces also were converging on Goch, a German position southeast of the Cleve in the north. One force had captured Hau, seven miles north of Goch, while another unit was at Kessel, four miles northwest.

[Due west of Goch, General Crerar's forces also cleared Gennep, another fortified town in that area, press services reported.]

Patton Sets Up New Threat

At the same time Lieut. Gen. George S. Patton's American Third Army fought to merge two of its bridgeheads across the Sauer River, twenty-five miles south of Pruem, into a solid six-mile front that would present a new threat to the road and rail network west of Bonn and Coblenz, of which Pruem was one important hub.

[As the two important Westwall strong points of Cleve and Pruem fell, Germany conscripted all women from 16 to 60 years of age for service in the Volkssturm, while reports from Sweden, Switzerland and Moscow told of mounting unrest and new clashes inside Germany, press services said.]

While the slow but ominous encroachments of the Allies' pent-up strength continued, the Germans were apparently hoping to flood out the Allies' armies, which they repeatedly have reported were ready to attack. A German communiqué today said the flooding of the Roer River Valley had forced the Allies to abandon positions in many sectors and to abandon preparations for an attack.

A natural flooding already made operations extremely difficult on the northern flank of the Canadian First Army's advance around Cleve and there were further reports today of explosions along the

Continued on Page 12, Column 5

THE BIG THREE MEETING AGAIN TO MAKE PLANS FOR THE WORLD

Prime Minister Churchill, President Roosevelt and Marshal Stalin on the grounds of Livadia Palace

The New York Times (British Official Radiophoto)

MANILA TRAP SHUT; LUZON IS CROSSED

U. S. Forces Unite to Squeeze Capital as Armored Push East Reaches Coast

By GEORGE E. JONES

By Wireless to THE NEW YORK TIMES.

MANILA, Tuesday, Feb. 13—A broad front of American troops embracing three divisions now confronts the stubbornly resisting Japanese garrison in Manila, and there is reason to believe that the drive to complete seizure of the Orient's fourth largest city has now been accelerated.

The First Cavalry Division vet-

Continued on Page 16, Column 3

Red Army Is at Bober River After 16-Mile Gain in Silesia

By The United Press.

LONDON, Tuesday, Feb. 13—Red Army forces, opening the second month of their Winter offensive, pushed sixteen miles across Silesia yesterday in an outflanking drive southeast of Berlin that carried to within seventy-four miles of Dresden. Marshal Ivan S. Koneff's First Ukrainian Army seized 100 Silesian communities as it advanced westward from its bridgehead on the west bank of the Oder and reached the Bober River on a fifteen-mile front. Berlin said the Russians already had forced the Bober at two points.

Far behind the main fighting front, the Russians all but crushed the last organized resistance in long-besieged Budapest, having

Continued on Page 10, Column 5

PACIFIC WAR ROLE FOR SOVIET HINTED

Date of United Nations Parley Follows 'Denouncing' Time of Russo-Japanese Treaty

By JAMES B. RESTON

Special to THE NEW YORK TIMES.

WASHINGTON, Feb. 12—The positive announcements in the Crimean communiqué produced general satisfaction in Washington tonight, but what really interested the capital were the things the Big Three statement did not even mention.

The first of these was Japan. The word does not appear in the longest communiqué ever issued after a meeting of the heads of state, but the date set for the opening of the United Nations Security Conference in San Francisco, April 25, is the day after the date on which Russia must denounce her five-year neutrality pact with Japan unless she wishes it to run for another five years.

There is naturally some reticence here about any hasty conclusions in regard to so decisive a factor in the Far Eastern war. But there has been a growing confidence

Continued on Page 6, Column 6

War News Summarized

TUESDAY, FEBRUARY 13, 1945

"Nazi Germany is doomed . . . Only when nazism and militarism have been extirpated will there be hope for a decent life for Germans, and a place for them in the comity of nations."

That was the message for the "common enemy" emanating from Yalta, in the Crimea, where President Roosevelt, Prime Minister Churchill and Premier Stalin, completing their historic conference, made clear the meaning of "unconditional surrender."

The combined military plans call for even more powerful blows from all directions, said their report made public yesterday. Germany will be divided into three separate occupation zones, coordinated through a commission of the three Supreme Army Commanders sitting in Berlin. France will be invited to take over a zone and join the commission.

Germany will be under strict control until all her armed forces have been disbanded, her General Staff broken up "for all time," her war industries eliminated, every vestige of the Nazi party and its doctrines eradicated and other measures taken "to insure that Germany will never again be able to disturb the peace of the world."

The Germans will have to pay in kind for all war damages, and a reparations commission will sit in Moscow to determine the extent and methods of payment.

The principles of the Atlantic Charter will govern the treatment of liberated Europe, it was agreed. A new Polish Government will be formed on a broad basis and universal secret elections will be held. The conference decided that the Curzon Line should be Poland's eastern boundary, with compensations from Germany in the west to be settled at the peace conference.

Yugoslavia was urged to put the Tito-Subasitch agreement into immediate effect and create a broad, provisional Parliament.

The Foreign Secretaries of the three nations will meet three or four times a year. The first time will be after a United Nations Conference to open in San Francisco April 25, which will prepare a charter along the lines of Dumbarton Oaks for the new international organization to maintain peace and security. [All the foregoing 1:8.]

While no mention was made of the Pacific war, it was pointed out that the period for denunciation of the Soviet-Japanese pact of neutrality would expire a day before the San Francisco meeting. [1:6.]

The Subasitch Cabinet will leave London shortly for Belgrade to set up a new Yugoslav Government. [3:4.] With Elas' agreement to disarm within two weeks and the Greek understanding that a plebiscite would be held within a year, difficulties in that country seemed about over. [6:1.]

On the fighting fronts Canadian and British troops captured Cleve, while Americans seized Pruem in two more important breaches of Germany's western defenses. [1:3; maps, P. 12.] The Red Army pressed its drive toward Danzig and also captured Bunzlau, seventy-four miles from Dresden. [1:5-6; map, P. 10.] Himmler ordered all German girls and women conscripted into the Volkssturm to meet the rising Allied threats. [9:1.]

American troops in south Manila joined forces when the First Cavalry made contact with the Thirty-seventh Infantry and also with the Eleventh Airborne Division. Bitter fighting was going on. The Sixth Division cut across Luzon by driving to Dingalan Bay. [1:4; map P. 16.]

Monday Meat Ban Flouted Again; Cafes Exhibit and Serve Steaks

By CHARLES GRUTZNER Jr.

Conservation Monday, which had got off to a false start last week when many restaurants served steaks, roasts and chops, tried the other foot yesterday and stumbled even more badly.

A restaurant opposite Radio City filled one show window with red, juicy steaks—and sold them, nicely broiled, at its dining tables. Less flaunting, perhaps, but equally open was the non-observance by eating places in all parts of the city of Mayor La Guardia's "little brother" to meatless Tuesday and meatless Friday.

More restaurants advertised major meat dishes among their daily specials yesterday than on last Monday. The non-observers included flashy Broadway dining places, chain restaurants, neighborhood eating rooms and lunch wagons.

The special at one of the food chains, with stool-and-counter shops scattered about the city, was sirloin steak with French fried potatoes for 50 cents. Some of the better-known Chinese restaurants in midtown made a feature of roast beef, lamb and pork chops, and roast ham. Even the five-and-dime stores played up veal cutlets (35 cents, with peas and potato) in their window displays.

A recheck of several scattered restaurants that had sold major meat dishes openly the previous Monday showed all selling them again yesterday. One place that had offered sirloin steak at 65 cents a week earlier, had as its special a hot roast beef sandwich at

Continued on Page 24, Column 3

ROOSEVELT PRESSES WORLD MONEY PLAN

He Asks Congress for Action on Monetary Fund and on Bank of Reconstruction

The President's message on world monetary unity, Page 17.

Special to THE NEW YORK TIMES.

WASHINGTON, Feb. 12—President Roosevelt urged Congress today to take immediate action on the Bretton Woods proposals for an international monetary fund and an international bank for reconstruction and development.

In a special message, the President said that the two projects, involving legislation for American participation in the $8,800,000,000 stabilization fund and the $9,100,000,000 bank, were essential "in our plans for a peaceful and prosperous world," which, he said, could be attained "only if solutions are found to the difficult economic problems we face today."

Mr. Roosevelt recognized the criticisms directed against the stabilization fund proposal, mostly by United States banking groups, by conceding that it was not perfect, but suggested that experience would permit necessary improvements to be made.

Wagner Plans Bill

He asked Congress to act with special promptness on the plan for the international bank, which would guarantee loans for important development and reconstruction projects in the member countries. But he added that "the monetary fund and the bank together comprise a

Continued on Page 17, Column 1

Elliott Roosevelt Made Brigadier By Senate, 53 to 11, on War Record

By JAY WALZ

Special to THE NEW YORK TIMES.

WASHINGTON, Feb. 12—The Senate voted 53 to 11 today to confirm the promotion of Col. Elliott Roosevelt to be brigadier general and then by voice vote confirmed seventy-seven other colonels for the higher rank.

Action was taken on the President's son after he was described both as "an amateur" and as an outstanding leader who had "proved his worth in combat."

Those voting against confirmation, all Republicans, were Senators Owen Brewster of Maine, Harlan J. Bushfield of South Dakota, Hugh Butler of Nebraska, Arthur Capper and Clyde M. Reed of Kansas, Bourke B. Hickenlooper of Iowa, Hiram W. Johnson of California, William Langer of North Dakota, E. H. Moore of Oklahoma, Charles W. Tobey of New Hampshire and Kenneth S. Wherry of Nebraska.

Following a request by Senator Alben W. Barkley, majority leader, that the Roosevelt nomination be considered separately, the two-hour debate centered on the 34-year-old Air Corps officer.

The only other name mentioned was that of Col. William H. Eaton, who was killed in a plane crash in France on Feb. 6. Chairman Elbert D. Thomas of the Military Affairs Committee read a letter from Secretary Stimson asking that the promotion be granted posthumously.

Senator Bushfield raised the question of Colonel Roosevelt's rise from a captaincy since 1940.

Continued on Page 13, Column 4

YALTA PARLEY ENDS

Unified Blows at Reich, Policing Spheres and Reparations Shaped

FRANCE TO GET ROLE

Broader Polish, Yugoslav Regimes Guaranteed—Curzon Line Adopted

The text of the report on the Big Three Conference, Page 4.

By LANSING WARREN

Special to THE NEW YORK TIMES.

WASHINGTON, Feb. 12—Allied decisions sealing the doom of Nazi Germany and German militarism, coordinating military plans for Germany's occupation and control and maintaining order and establishing popular Governments in liberated countries were signed yesterday by President Roosevelt, Marshal Stalin and Prime Minister Churchill near Yalta in the Crimea, the White House announced today.

The conference, held in the summer palace of former Czar Nicholas II on the Black Sea shore, also called for a United Nations security conference in San Francisco on April 25.

The parleys, hitherto shrouded in secrecy except for a brief outline of the agenda issued Feb. 7, were held day and night from Feb. 4 until the final signatures were affixed. The announcement did not refer to President Roosevelt's future movements except that he had left the Crimea.

Main Points of Accord

Major decisions of the conference include:

(1) Plans for new blows at the heart of Germany from the east, west, north and south.

(2) Agreement for occupation by the three Allies, each of a separate zone, as Germany is invaded, and an invitation to France to take over a zone and participate as a fourth member of the Control Commission.

(3) Reparations in kind to be paid by Germany for damages, to be set by an Allied commission. The reparations commission, which will establish the type and amount of payments by Germany, will have its headquarters in Moscow. [Secretary of State Stettinius and Ambassador Harriman arrived in Moscow Monday.]

(4) Settlement of questions left undecided at the conference at Dumbarton Oaks and decision to call a United Nations conference at San Francisco April 25 to prepare the charter for a general international organization to maintain peace and security.

(5) Specific agreements to widen the scope of the present Governments in Poland and Yugoslavia and an understanding to keep order and establish Governments in liberated countries conforming to the popular will and the principles of the Atlantic Charter.

(6) A general declaration of determination to maintain Allied unity for peace.

German People Apart

The statement announced common policies for enforcing unconditional surrender and imposing Nazi Germany's doom. The document draws a distinction between the Nazi system, laws and institutions, the German General Staff and its militarism, which will be relentlessly wiped out, and the German people.

"It is not our purpose," it declared, "to destroy the people of Germany, but only when nazism and militarism have been extirpated will there be hope for a decent life for Germans, and a place for them in the comity of nations."

Until this conference the Allies had laid down no iron-clad program for the control and complete reorganization of Germany. Military plans will be made known only

Continued on Page 4, Column 1

"All the News That's Fit to Print"

The New York Times.

LATE CITY EDITION
Clear and continued cold with moderate winds today.
Temperatures Yesterday—Max., 33; Min., 23
Sunrise today, 7:46 A. M.; Sunset, 6:35 P. M.

VOL. XCIV No. 31,803. Entered as Second-Class Matter, Postoffice, New York, N. Y. NEW YORK, MONDAY, FEBRUARY 19, 1945. THREE CENTS IN NEW YORK CITY

U. S. MARINES STORM ASHORE ON IWO ISLAND; 509 PLANES, 36 SHIPS SMASHED IN TOKYO BLOW; BRITISH AT EDGE OF GOCH; PATTON STRIKES AGAIN

STIMSON ASSAILS DELAY ON JOB BILL AS COSTLY IN LIVES

Using 'Plain' Words as 'Duty,' He Says Senate Committee Listens to 'Trivial' Pleas

'DEADLY SHORTAGES' LOOM

Secretary Calls It 'Failure' of Our Democracy Not to Compel Full War Output

Secretary Stimson's address is printed in full on Page 11.

Special to THE NEW YORK TIMES.

WASHINGTON, Feb. 18—Secretary of War Stimson denounced tonight Senate delay in acting on the National Service Bill and called absence of legislation to keep men at their wartime jobs a "failure of American democracy."

In a speech over the Blue Network, he addressed himself "to all Americans, but primarily to those who have sons or husbands or other dear ones at the front" and declared that it was his "duty to speak plainly."

He asserted that we had "reached a crisis in this war" and that "we dare not delay longer" in providing the legislation to give to our fighting men the full support of "our strength." Delay, he warned, meant prolonging of the war and waste of American lives.

He praised the House for having "risen to the occasion" and passed the National Service Bill, but said that the Senate Military Affairs Committee, listening to voices speaking for "special interests" and, by comparison with the national interest, "trivial interests," had kept the bill suffocated for nearly three weeks until "enemies of the measure are beginning to boast today in the streets of Washington that they have killed it."

Roosevelt Plea Possible

It was reported in Senate circles tonight that one of the first acts of President Roosevelt on his return from the Crimea Conference would be to call again for action on the bill.

Some Senators predicted tonight that "some sort of a bill" would be reported by the committee during the week. A group of conservative Republicans and several Democrats were reported to favor a substitute which would give statutory authority to the War Manpower Commission and order a survey of war plants to root out any hoarded labor. Other compromises were also being discussed.

Secretary Stimson was emphatic in his speech about the gravity of the situation. He declared that "ever since the beginning of the war" there had been "an alarming turnover of workers in war industries."

"Every responsible leader of the military and naval forces" from the President down, he said, agreed on the need for adoption of national service legislation to keep workers at their wartime tasks.

"The inevitable result of this failure of American democracy," he went on, "is now becoming apparent at this crisis of the war.

Warns of "Deadly Shortages"

"Shortages, deadly shortages, are now looming up before us at a moment when every ounce of power should be thrown into the combat. I mean both shortages of weapons and shortages of manpower caused by the misplacement of our men."

He pointed out that the United States alone among the Allies had no service law and that Britain and Russia had been working under such laws "since the very beginning of the war."

Our enemies, of course, he added, have been so organized from the start.

"We alone," he proceeded, "are depending upon voluntary and therefore ineffective methods of organization among the workers who

Continued on Page 11, Column 4

Battle in Skagerrak Reported by Swedes

By The United Press.

LONDON, Feb. 18—The Swedish radio said today that a "very large-scale" battle involving a southbound German convoy had been fought yesterday off the Swedish Skagerrak coast.

The battle was reported to have lasted four hours. The broadcast said that Allied naval and air units had probably participated. "Observers say they have never before heard anything like it and are of the opinion that direct hits must have been made on ships," the broadcast asserted.

ORDERS PRICE TAGS ON COTTON CLOTHES

OPA Demands Exact Ceiling Be Shown on Most Such Apparel to Avert Rises

Special to THE NEW YORK TIMES.

WASHINGTON, Feb. 18—Consumers, beginning on March 5, will find most cotton garments, from infants' rompers to women's dresses, tagged with a manufacturer's ticket showing the exact OPA ceiling price permitted on each separate article, Chester Bowles, OPA Administrator, said today in outlining the first step in a broad program to check clothing prices.

The action, the administrator said, would also have the effect of bringing back more of the essential articles of apparel to the low and medium price range. However, the benefits of this part of the program might not be noticeable before early summer, he warned.

Practically all infants' and children's cotton apparel and "a very large part" of the output of men's and women's cotton garments will carry the tags, according to Mr. Bowles.

Eventually from 65 to 90 per cent of all civilian woven cotton apparel will be subject to the program's controls, which, it was explained, would tie in with a recent War Production Board order channeling most of the cotton fabrics available for civilian use into popular and medium priced garments.

The Ticket for Each Garment

The plan, which Mr. Bowles described as one "easy" for both retailers and the buying public to understand, begins with the manufacturer pinning to each piece of clothing affected by the order a ticket which will read as follows:

"OPA Ceiling Price $0.00.

"Lot Number —— (or brand name).

"WPB 385 or WPB 328-B."

The WPB figures refer to War Production Orders through which the maker obtained the material in a piece of clothing.

The prices fixed by the manufacturer would be based on OPA regulations, which provided, Mr. Bowles said, for slight variations that had always been allowed in ceiling prices for similar garments in different retail stores. Such variations take into account differences in cost to the retailer, depending on whether he buys di-

Continued on Page 30, Column 5

NAZI BASE DOOMED

British Artillery Pounds Goch to Aid Infantry 1,000 Yards Away

CALCAR FIGHT RAGES

3d Army Enters Reich Above Vianden—7th Also Crosses Line

By CLIFTON DANIEL

By Wireless to THE NEW YORK TIMES.

SUPREME HEADQUARTERS, Allied Expeditionary Force, Feb. 18—From low hills overlooking Goch British gunners picked off targets inside the town today and under a canopy of artillery fire Gen. H. D. G. Crerar's infantrymen assaulted the anti-tank ditches on the eastern defense perimeter of the town, which now looks as if it were doomed.

At the same time the American Third Army again expanded its bridgehead over the Our and Sauer Rivers north of Echternach, spreading it out today to a width of almost five miles. [The United Press said that a new division, not yet identified, had invaded Germany at a new point north of Vianden, Luxembourg.]

[Press services also reported that the American Seventh Army had re-entered Germany in the Saarbruecken area.]

The Canadian First Army, with its Canadian and United Kingdom troops, still carried the burden of the Western Front fighting today, however. Goch, with its reinforced and fortified houses, was one of two strong bastions of the line that the Germans held when the Canadian First Army attacked the northern end of the Westwall ten days ago, but patrols prodding its outskirts today found that opposition was light, the town having been outflanked and all but surrounded.

German Defense Loose

The Germans began to lose coordination in their defense yesterday and it now looks as if they would give up another important stretch of ground, but meanwhile they are fighting fiercely to hold flanks of General Crerar's advance along the Meuse (Maas) on one side and the Rhine on the other. Having lost their firm grip on Goch, the Germans are struggling to retain Calcar, the second most important front-line supply center left to them in the battle area. On the opposite side of the front they are likewise trying to halt the United Kingdom forces creeping down along the Meuse beyond Afferden toward Venlo.

The suddenness of the break in the coordination of German defense was illustrated by the fact that in driving across the road from Goch to Calcar the British made a surprise move and captured more than 900 prisoners in one day. The total number of Germans now captured since the beginning of General Crerar's offensive is more than 8,000. In an effort to minimize the reinforcement and supply of the remnants

Continued on Page 6, Column 2

City-Wide Produce Tie-Up Looms As Drivers Halt Bronx Deliveries

A strike of truckmen affiliated with Local 202, International Brotherhood of Teamsters, was called early today at the Bronx Terminal Market, tying up all produce deliveries in that borough and was threatening to spread city-wide.

However, the full effects will not be felt in the other boroughs until the end of the week, as the contracts in Manhattan and Brooklyn do not expire until Friday.

Meanwhile, carloads of produce were piling up at piers and freight terminals, and Washington wholesale market was crowded with fruits and vegetables as union delegates warned their men not to handle any foodstuffs for sale or delivery to Bronx dealers. Then they added, "tonight the Bronx, next week Brooklyn and Manhattan."

At 1 A. M. when 300 trucks normally would start toward Washington Market to pick up produce for the Bronx Terminal for ultimate distribution through jobbers to retail outlets "not a wheel was turning." Two hundred platform men and 300 chauffeurs, meanwhile, were idling about with instructions from union delegates not to work as a contract that expired Friday had not been signed.

The proposed contract, union representatives said, called for a

Continued on Page 18, Column 3

AMERICAN TANK RUNNING A GANTLET OF STEEL IN MANILA

An amphibious vehicle crossing the Pasig River under Japanese machine gun fire while shells from a protecting barrage laid down by our artillery burst on the far shore.

Associated Press (U. S. Signal Corps)

FINAL ROUND IS ON, MONTGOMERY SAYS

Marshal Calls on His Soldiers to Help Strike Knockout Blow at German Army

By The Associated Press.

THE TWENTY-FIRST ARMY GROUP HEADQUARTERS, in Europe, Feb. 18—Field Marshal Sir Bernard L. Montgomery in a personal message to troops under his command declared today: "We now have come to the last and final round, and we want and will go for the knockout blow."

The text of his order follows:

The operations of the Allies on all fronts have now brought the German war to its final stage. There was a time some years ago when it did not seem possible that we could win this war. The present situation is that we can-

Continued on Page 6, Column 5

Americans Seize Hospital In Manila and Free 7,000

By LINDESAY PARROTT

By Wireless to THE NEW YORK TIMES.

ADVANCED HEADQUARTERS, on Luzon, Monday, Feb. 19—Seven thousand persons, including patients, internees and civilians, both American and Filipino, were freed as American troops seized the Philippine General Hospital on Taft Avenue in the Ermita section of Manila, where fanatically resisting Japanese fought back against an ever-tightening ring that was steadily pushing them into Manila Bay.

The hospital was captured after advancing Americans shelled the walls and north and east gates of the hospital grounds, adjoining the campus of the University of Philippines. Gen. Douglas MacArthur's communiqué stated that those released, including 100 Americans, had been evacuated to safety.

Last night the grounds of the hospital, extending to within four blocks of Dewey Boulevard and the

Continued on Page 3, Column 1

RED ARMY NEARING BORDER OF SAXONY

German Resistance Stiffens—Russians Capture Sagan and Break Into Grudziadz

By The United Press.

LONDON, Monday, Feb. 19—Red Army forces in German Silesia yesterday fought through stiff enemy resistance to within nineteen miles of the Saxon border and sixteen miles east of Goerlitz, key industrial city guarding the road to Dresden.

In its tenth major encirclement of the winter offensive the Red Army also surrounded and broke into the outskirts of the Vistula River fortress of Grudziadz in Poland, fifty-seven miles south of Danzig. Two additional pockets of enemy troops were wiped out in Pomerania and in Brandenburg.

In three other actions Russian troops hammered deeper into the streets of the Silesian capital of Breslau, virtually completed the mop-up of the Polish city of Posen, and tightened the ring around enemy troops in East Prussia, where Gen. Ivan D. Chernyakhovsky, 37, commander of the Third White Russian Army, was killed in action.

The new Soviet successes were carried out as six great battles

Continued on Page 8, Column 3

War News Summarized

MONDAY, FEBRUARY 19, 1945

United States Marines of the Fifth Amphibious Corps went ashore on Iwo Island in the Volcano group, establishing two beachheads. Tokyo reported bitter fighting on the island, 750 miles from the Japanese capital. The landings followed a fierce bombardment by naval craft, including battleships, and land-based planes. Other bombers hit Truk and targets in the Palaus, while carrier aircraft struck Chichi Island in the Bonins, nearer Japan than Iwo. [1:8; map P. 3.]

Five hundred and nine Japanese planes were destroyed, an escort carrier, three other warships and ten more ships were sunk, and heavy damage was done to airfields and factories in last week's 1,500-plane carrier attack on the Tokyo-Yokohama area, Admiral Nimitz announced today. An additional 150 enemy planes were probably destroyed. We lost forty-nine aircraft. [1:7.]

The blows now being struck at Japan were made possible by the heroic stand of the "Dead Army" of Bataan in 1942, General MacArthur said. He reported further gains on Corregidor and Bataan and in the Manila mop-up. [1:5-6.]

British troops in Burma crossed the Irrawaddy in captured Japanese boats thirty miles west of Mandalay, threatening to outflank that city. Another landing was made on the west coast at Ru-ywa, sixty-five miles southeast of Akyab, cutting the enemy's coastal escape road. [5:1.] In China the Japanese recaptured Pingshek and moved on Ichang in an effort to regain twenty-five miles of the Canton-Hankow railway. [3:1.]

Patrols of the Canadian First Army fought their way into the outskirts of Goch amid mounting signs of disintegration in the German defense. The United States Third Army crossed into the Reich near Vianden, and the Seventh reinvaded the Saar Basin southwest of Saarbruecken. [1:3; maps, P. 6.]

Field Marshal Montgomery told his troops they were in the "last and final round." It "may be long and difficult," he said, but a somewhat different "knockout blow" will be "delivered from more than one direction." [1:4.]

RAF planes hit Berlin and Mannheim last night after Wesel, sixteen miles from the Canadian First Army front, had been attacked. Allied bombers were reported over Germany later in the night. Americans from Italy blasted rail targets at Linz, Austria. [7:2.]

The Red Army advanced in most sectors, encircling and fighting into the outskirts of Grudziadz in the "Polish Corridor" and capturing the river strongholds of Sagan and Naumburg in Silesia. [1:6; map P 8.]

It was said in Paris that General de Gaulle had coupled his refusal to meet President Roosevelt in Algiers with an invitation to visit Paris. [9:2.]

Senator Bridges received from Geneva alleged Allied armistice terms to Italy that stripped that country of all military power and considerable territory and placed her economy under Anglo-Saxon control. Some 2,000,000 Italians would help reconstruct ravaged Europe. [7:5.]

Diplomats reaching Mexico City for the Inter-American Conference favored greater power for small nations in post-war plans and, while doubtful of Argentina's intentions, hoped for friendly relations. [1:6-7.]

AIR BLOW AT TOKYO 'DECISIVE VICTORY'

Nimitz Says Fifth Fleet Scored 'Complete Tactical Surprise' in Two-Day Attack

By The Associated Press.

ADVANCED HEADQUARTERS, Guam, Monday, Feb. 19—American carrier planes scored a "decisive" victory over the Japanese in the mighty 1,500-plane attacks on the Tokyo-Yokohama area of the Japanese homeland Friday and Saturday, Admiral Chester W. Nimitz announced today.

Admiral Nimitz announced the Americans, scoring a "complete tactical surprise," destroyed 332 Japanese aircraft in the air and 177 on the ground. At least 150 more Japanese planes were probably destroyed or damaged on the first day and an unknown number were damaged on the second day.

He said one Japanese escort carrier was bombed and set afire, nine coastal vessels were sunk, one destroyer was sunk, two escort destroyers sunk, one cargo ship sunk and twenty two enemy coastal ships damaged, besides various Japanese picket vessels destroyed.

Forty-nine American planes were lost in the two days of destructive raids, Admiral Nimitz said. Thirty to forty Yank fliers were lost.

"None of our ships suffered damage from enemy action," the special communiqué reported.

The Fifth Fleet force under Admiral R. A. Spruance, one of the greatest ever assembled, "achieved a decisive victory over the enemy in attacks on Tokyo, Feb. 16 and 17 (east longitude date)," Admiral Nimitz announced.

He said a "complete tactical surprise" was accomplished under a cover of weather so adverse it also hampered enemy operations.

Admiral Nimitz congratulated

Continued on Page 4, Column 6

Mexico Talks Designed to Link Hemisphere to Dumbarton Oaks

By JAMES B. RESTON

Special to THE NEW YORK TIMES.

MEXICO CITY, Feb. 18—The Inter-American Conference on Problems of War and Peace will not open until Wednesday but most of the delegates are here and many of the decisions that will be announced in the next few days are now being taken in a series of conferences in the capital.

In this respect the forthcoming conference is not unlike a political convention at home. Preparation is at least two-thirds of the battle and what important decisions have not already been made are likely to be made within the next few days.

The two main political questions before the conference, for example, are what policy the American nations are to take regarding the proposed Dumbarton Oaks international security organization and what they are to do about the Argentine Government whose undemocratic actions at home and defiance of the United States abroad have virtually isolated her from the American community of nations.

There will be many different opinions expressed here about these two questions in the next fortnight and Ezequiel Padilla, Mexican Foreign Secretary, will undoubtedly seize the opportunity to champion greater rights for the small na-

Continued on Page 4, Column 3

LANDING EFFECTED

Nimitz Reports Invasion of Volcano Isle 750 Miles From Tokyo

FIERCE FIGHTING IS ON

Japanese Report Battle at Futatsune Beach on Southwest Coast

By The Associated Press.

ADVANCED HEADQUARTERS, Guam, Monday, Feb. 19—American Marines, their path cleared by the most intensive neutralization campaign of the Pacific war, have landed on strategic little Iwo Island, one of the Volcano group, 750 statute miles south of Tokyo.

The landing was made this (Monday) morning. The Fourth and Fifth Marine Divisions made this first Marine operation since the Palaus were invaded last September. [Lieut. Gen. Holland M. Smith, victor over the Japanese on Saipan, was in command of the Marines, The United Press said.]

Admiral Chester W. Nimitz announced in a special communiqué today the momentous development in the fast-moving Pacific war which put American troops on the logical ocean stepping-stone to Tokyo.

Iwo is so close to Tokyo that it is administered by Tokyo prefecture.

American fighters and medium bombers based on Iwo's large airdrome would be within land-based striking range of Tokyo for the first time.

Japanese Tell of Invasion

American troops going ashore in 100 landing boats made a successful landing on Iwo at 8 A. M. Monday (Japanese time), the Tokyo radio announced late last night.

A broadcast, recorded by The United Press in San Francisco, said "part of the enemy forces have landed."

It was the first indication from the enemy radio that a successful landing had been made. Previously Tokyo had reported four "attempted landings" were made on the island Saturday but had been "repulsed."

The text of the enemy broadcast:

"Following a series of abortive landing attempts a part of the enemy forces have finally started landings on Iwo Jima since 8 o'clock this Monday morning.

Heavy Fighting Reported

"The landing is being made on the southeast coast of the island. The Japanese garrison immediately pushing the enemy invaders back to the shore is now engaged in fierce counter-attack against the enemy.

"The landing was preceded by persistent naval and air attacks since early last Wednesday morning."

The Japanese Domei agency reported that "heavy fighting" was in progress between the Japanese garrison and American forces that landed on the island with "about 100 landing vessels."

The Japanese Domei agency declared that the landing forces had hit Futatsune beach, on the southwestern sector of the island.

In an English-language dispatch recorded by the Federal Communications Commission, Domei

Continued on Page 3, Column 5

Fleet in Manila Bay, U. S. Radio Reports

The American Broadcasting Station in Europe declared last night that United States Seventh Fleet warships "have steamed into Manila Harbor without incident."

Quoting "a dispatch from Luzon," the broadcast said: "Manila Bay is described as now open to American naval vessels." The broadcast was recorded by the Columbia Broadcasting System.

1945

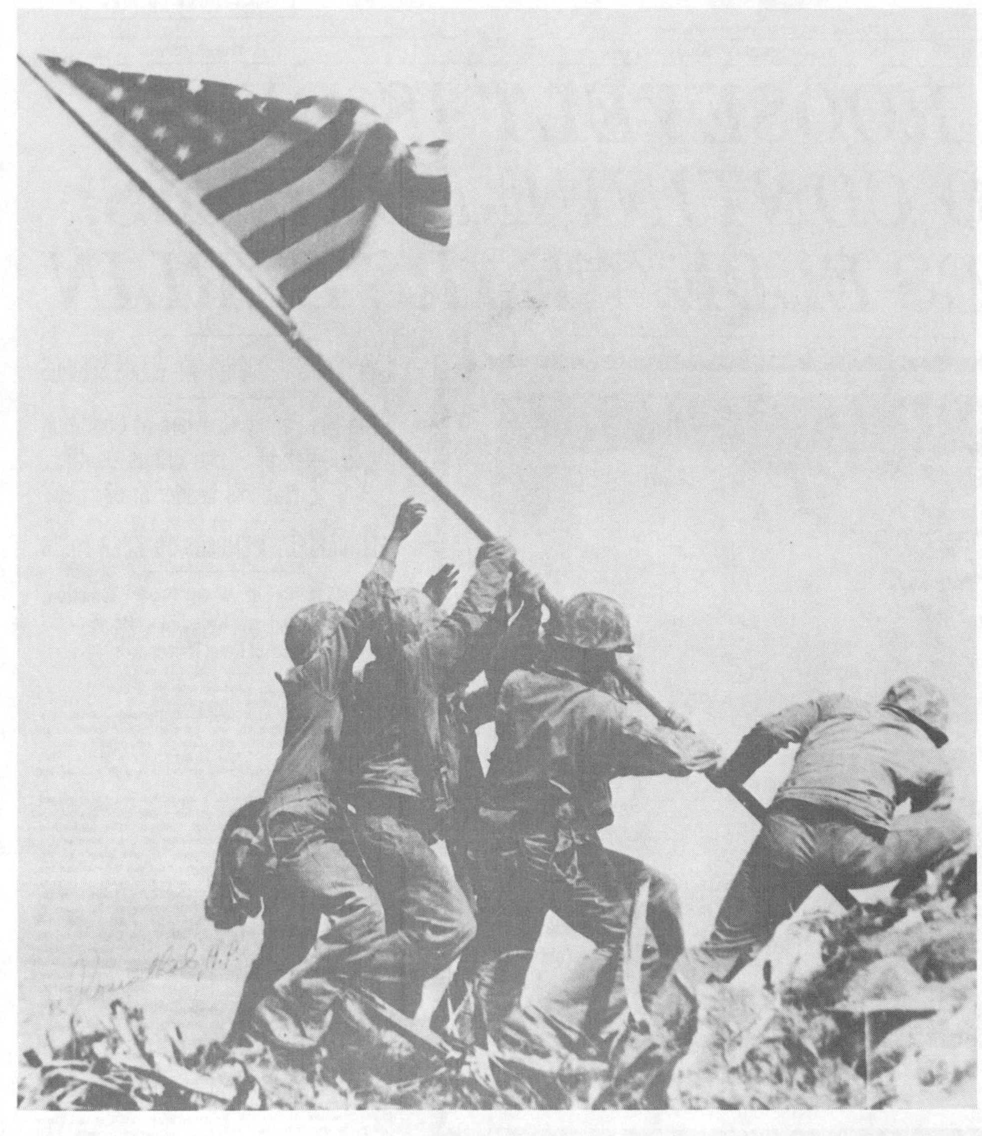

The American flag is raised on Mount Suribachi, on Iwo Jima.

An American flame-throwing tank goes into action as the battle for the possession of Iwo Jima rages on.

"All the News That's Fit to Print"

The New York Times.

LATE CITY EDITION
Clearing and warm today.
Fair, continued warm tomorrow.
Temperatures Yesterday—Max., 74; Min., 54
Sunrise today, 6:21 A. M.; Sunset, 7:31 P. M.

VOL. XCIV...No. 31,856. Entered as Second-Class Matter, Postoffice, New York, N. Y. NEW YORK, FRIDAY, APRIL 13, 1945. THREE CENTS IN NEW YORK CITY

PRESIDENT ROOSEVELT IS DEAD; TRUMAN TO CONTINUE POLICIES; 9TH CROSSES ELBE, NEARS BERLIN

U. S. AND RED ARMIES DRIVE TO MEET

Americans Across the Elbe in Strength Race Toward Russians Who Have Opened Offensive From Oder

WEIMAR TAKEN, RUHR POCKET SLASHED

Third Army Reported 19 Miles From Czechoslovak Border—British Drive Deeper in the North, Seizing Celle—Canadians Freeing Holland

By DREW MIDDLETON
By Wireless to THE NEW YORK TIMES.

PARIS, April 12—Thousands of tanks and a half million doughboys of the United States First, Third and Ninth Armies are racing through the heart of the Reich on a front of 150 miles, threatening Berlin, Leipzig and the last citadels of the Nazi power.

The Second Armored Division of the Ninth Army has crossed the Elbe River in force and is striking eastward toward Berlin, whose outskirts lie less than sixty miles to the east, according to reports from the front. [A report quoted by The United Press placed the Americans less than fifty miles from the capital.] Beyond Berlin the First White Russian Army has crossed the Oder on a wide front and a junction between the western and eastern Allies is not far off.

[The Moscow radio reported that heavy battles were raging west of the Oder before Berlin, indicating that Marshal Gregory K. Zhukoff had launched his drive toward the Reich's capital. The Soviet communiqué announced further progress by the Red Army forces in and around Vienna.]

Paris is wild with excitement tonight. A special edition of the newspaper France-Soir carries a report by the radio station "Voice of America" that places American forces fifteen and five-eighths miles from Berlin after an airborne landing that had linked up with Lieut. Gen. William H. Simpson's forces advancing eastward from the Elbe. This would put American forces only seventy-five miles from the Ninth Army vanguard.

No Confirmation at Headquarters

There was no confirmation of this report at Allied Supreme Headquarters, which by its own admission was thirty-six hours behind developments on some sectors of the front.

Resistance was continuing only on the northern and southern flanks. The center had burst wide open. Weimar fell to Lieut. Gen. George S. Patton's infantry, and reports from the front said Erfurt also had been cleared. Schweinfurt and Heilbronn, two German bastions on the south, had fallen to United States Seventh Army forces, who were driving on Bamberg, while farther north Third Army forces were about thirty-five miles from the Czechoslovak frontier in the area east of Coburg.

[The German radio reported American Third Army forces at Lichtenberg, nineteen miles from the Czechoslovak border, The United Press said.]

The offensives to liberate the Netherlands and reduce the Ruhr

Continued on Page 12, Column 2

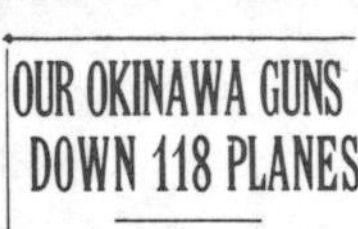

OUR OKINAWA GUNS DOWN 118 PLANES

Japanese Fliers Start 'Suicide' Attacks on Fleet, Sink a Destroyer, Hit Other Ships

By W. H. LAWRENCE
By Wireless to THE NEW YORK TIMES.

GUAM, Friday, April 13—Japanese attempting to halt the American march to Tokyo, have started "desperate, suicidal" aerial attacks upon our ships and men in the Okinawa area, losing 118 planes on Thursday alone, Fleet Admiral Chester W. Nimitz announced today.

The Japanese succeeded in sinking a destroyer and damaging several other surface units, the communiqué said. All of the damaged vessels remained in action.

It was the first time that the Navy had revealed the suicidal nature of the Japanese air missions against our ships and men. The Japanese radio has been saying that this type of assault was being carried on by a "special attack corps" known in Japanese as "kamikaze," which, translated literally, means "divine wind."

Attack at Low Levels

The Japanese fliers launched their attacks upon our ships and men at a high speed and from low levels, diving directly into a ship or troop concentration to explode their bombs as they crashed.

There was no official estimate of the total number of enemy aircraft engaged in the Okinawa area attack other than the report of the 118 enemy planes destroyed.

Admiral Nimitz reported that the attacks began early on April 12 (Eastern Longitude time) with seven enemy planes shot down during the morning in the vicinity of the Hagushi beaches.

The tempo of the attack was stepped up in the afternoon as the Japanese bore in on our ships in wave after wave. Admiral Nimitz said that ships' guns, carrier aircraft and shore-based anti-aircraft shot down 111 of the attackers.

The revelation of the suicidal Japanese air attacks was the highlight of Admiral Nimitz' regular morning communiqué, which also disclosed the identity of two Marine and two Army divisions that have gone into action on Okinawa. These included the Twenty-seventh Army Division, formed from New York National Guard units, which are seeing action for the first time since the Saipan campaign and previously had engaged in the Gilbert Islands assault. It is com-

Continued on Page 18, Column 3

Army Leaders See Reich End at Hand

By The Associated Press.

WASHINGTON, April 12—High Army officials told Senators today that the end of organized fighting in Germany probably would come within a few days.

Describing the pell-mell dash of American Armies across Germany, General Staff officers expressed the opinion to members of the Senate Military Committee that a collapse of German arms was imminent.

Those who attended said the army chiefs declared that they were so sure of the results that orders had been drawn for a drastic reduction in shipments of durable equipment to Europe.

Franklin Delano Roosevelt
1882-1945

© Perskie

SECURITY PARLEY WON'T BE DELAYED

State Department Urges That World Be Shown We Plan No Changes in Policy

By JAMES B. RESTON
Special to THE NEW YORK TIMES.

WASHINGTON, April 12—The United Nations Security Conference will open in San Francisco on April 25, despite the death of President Roosevelt, Secretary of State Edward R. Stettinius Jr. announced tonight.

Mr. Stettinius said that he had been authorized by President Harry Truman to make this announcement after a meeting of the Cabinet at the White House.

Most of the overseas delegations to the San Francisco conference have either arrived in this country or are now on their way, but while this was said to have been a factor in the decision to proceed with the conference, State Department officials urged that every attempt be made to give immediate evidence to the world that President Roosevelt's foreign policy would be sustained by the new Administration.

President Roosevelt had planned to address the San Francisco conference. His interest in an international organization of nations to maintain peace and security had gone back to his service in the Wilson Administration, when he sat in the gallery of the Senate and listened to the debate that resulted in the rejection of the League of Nations Covenant. He had expressed to friends his desire to participate in the San Francisco conference and to see the United States enter the new league during his term in office.

The sudden elevation of Presi-

Continued on Page 2, Column 1

War News Summarized

FRIDAY, APRIL 13, 1945

President Roosevelt died yesterday afternoon, suddenly and unexpectedly. He was stricken with a massive cerebral hemorrhage at Warm Springs, Ga., on the eve of his greatest military and diplomatic successes—the impending fall of Berlin and the opening of the San Francisco Conference to set up a World Security Organization that would make the world free from martial and economic strife [1:7-8.]

Mr. Roosevelt had been sitting in front of the fireplace of his Little White House, having gone to Warm Springs on March 30 for a three-week rest. About 2:15 Eastern war time he said, "I have a terrific headache," lost consciousness in a few moments and died at 4:35. He was 63 years old. [1:6.]

The tragic word spread quickly around the world. Expressions of sorrow poured in from all sections. [4:5.] American soldiers and sailors refused to believe the reports until there was no longer doubt that their Commander in Chief had gone. [4:2-3.]

Harry S. Truman was sworn in as President at 7:09 o'clock last night, and a few minutes later Mrs. Roosevelt left for Warm Springs. [1:7.] The new President immediately called a Cabinet meeting and declared that Mr. Roosevelt's policies would be continued, that the war would be carried on until Germany and Japan surrendered unconditionally and that the San Francisco Conference would open April 25 as scheduled. [1:3.]

Some 500,000 American soldiers of the Third and Ninth Armies, and thousands of tanks, sped along a 150-mile front toward Berlin and Leipzig. The Ninth, surging across the Elbe, according to delayed reports was less than fifty miles from the German capital and 115 from the Russians along the Oder. The Third Army captured Weimar, home of the late German Republic, and was twenty-three miles below Leipzig, with the First closing a pincers from the north. [1:1-2; map P. 2.]

The Moscow radio reported that the Red Army was waging fierce battles east of Berlin, indicating resumption of the drive on that city. Elsewhere Russian troops scored wide gains and cut the last escape railroad from Vienna. [13:1.]

Open cities were ruled out and every German was ordered by Himmler to fight to the death, although Goebbels said "the war cannot last much longer." [12:6-7.]

The Ninth Air Force destroyed at least 117 more German planes yesterday. [11:8.]

In Italy the Eighth Army advanced along a thirty-mile front toward Bologna and the Po Valley; the Fifth Army also made good gains and was eleven miles from La Spezia. [13:8, with map.]

Japanese planes resumed their suicide attacks on American ships off Okinawa, sinking a destroyer and damaging several other vessels. One hundred and eighteen enemy planes were shot down. [1:2.] The Americal Division invaded Bohol, last of the enemy-held central Philippines. [18:6.] The B-29 attack on Koriyama, 110 miles north of Tokyo, set a new Superfortress distance record. [18:2.]

Secretary of State Stettinius and Secretary of War Stimson, denouncing Germany's "steadily increasing" mistreatment of American prisoners, said those responsible would be brought to justice. [13:6-7.]

Clashes between Right and Left wing elements in Iran were reported from Moscow. [13:2.]

LAST WORDS: 'I HAVE TERRIFIC HEADACHE'

Roosevelt Was Posing for Artist When Hemorrhage Struck—He Died in Bedroom

By The Associated Press.

WARM SPRINGS, Ga., April 12—President Franklin D. Roosevelt's last words were:

"I have a terrific headache."

He spoke them to Comdr. Howard G. Bruenn, naval physician.

Mr. Roosevelt was sitting in front of a fireplace in the Little White House here atop Pine Mountain when what was described as a massive cerebral hemorrhage struck him.

The President's Negro valet, Arthur Prettyman, and a Filipino messboy carried him to his bedroom. He was unconscious at the end. It came without pain.

Dr. Bruenn said that he saw the President this morning and he was in excellent spirits at 9:30 A. M.

"At 1 o'clock," Dr. Bruenn added, "he was sitting in a chair while sketches were being made of him by an artist. He suddenly complained of a very severe occipital headache (back of the head).

"Within a very few minutes he lost consciousness. He was seen by me at 1:30 P. M., fifteen minutes after the episode had started.

"He did not regain consciousness, and he died at 3:35 P. M. (Georgia time)."

The artist sketching Mr. Roosevelt was N. Robbins of 520 West 139th Street, New York.

Only others present in the cottage were Comdr. George Fox, White House pharmacist and long an attendant on the President; William D. Hassett, Presidential secretary; Miss Grace Tully, con-

Continued on Page 4, Column 3

END COMES SUDDENLY AT WARM SPRINGS

Even His Family Unaware of Condition as Cerebral Stroke Brings Death to Nation's Leader at 63

ALL CABINET MEMBERS TO KEEP POSTS

Funeral to Be at White House Tomorrow, With Burial at Hyde Park Home—Impact of News Tremendous

By ARTHUR KROCK
Special to THE NEW YORK TIMES.

WASHINGTON, April 12—Franklin Delano Roosevelt, War President of the United States and the only Chief Executive in history who was chosen for more than two terms, died suddenly and unexpectedly at 4:35 P. M. today at Warm Springs, Ga., and the White House announced his death at 5:48 o'clock. He was 63.

The President, stricken by a cerebral hemorrhage, passed from unconsciousness to death on the eighty-third day of his fourth term and in an hour of high triumph. The armies and fleets under his direction as Commander in Chief were at the gates of Berlin and the shores of Japan's home islands as Mr. Roosevelt died, and the cause he represented and led was nearing the conclusive phase of success.

Less than two hours after the official announcement, Harry S. Truman of Missouri, the Vice President, took the oath as the thirty-second President. The oath was administered by the Chief Justice of the United States, Harlan F. Stone, in a one-minute ceremony at the White House. Mr. Truman immediately let it be known that Mr. Roosevelt's Cabinet is remaining in office at his request, and that he had authorized Secretary of State Edward R. Stettinius Jr. to proceed with plans for the United Nations Conference on international organization at San Francisco, scheduled to begin April 25. A report was circulated that he leans somewhat to the idea of a coalition Cabinet, but this is unsubstantiated.

Funeral Tomorrow Afternoon

It was disclosed by the White House that funeral services for Mr. Roosevelt would take place at 4 P. M. (E. W. T.) Saturday in the East Room of the Executive Mansion. The Rev. Angus Dun, Episcopal Bishop of Washington; the Rev. Howard S. Wilkinson of St. Thomas's Church in Washington and the Rev. John G. McGee of St. John's in Washington will conduct the services.

The body will be interred at Hyde Park, N. Y., Sunday, with the Rev. George W. Anthony of St. James Church officiating. The time has not yet been fixed.

Jonathan Daniels, White House secretary, said Mr. Roosevelt's body would not lie in state. He added that, in view of the limited size of the East Room, which holds only about 200 persons, the list of those attending the funeral services would be limited to high Government officials, representatives of the membership of both

Continued on Page 3, Column 3

TRUMAN IS SWORN IN THE WHITE HOUSE

Members of Cabinet on Hand as Chief Justice Stone Administers the Oath

By C. P. TRUSSELL
Special to THE NEW YORK TIMES.

WASHINGTON, April 12—Vice President Harry S. Truman of Missouri, standing erect, with his sharp features taut and looking straight ahead through his large, round glasses, became the thirty-second President of the United States in a ceremony lasting not more than a minute in the Cabinet Room of the White House at 7:09 o'clock tonight.

The oath was administered by Chief Justice Harlan F. Stone two hours and thirty-four minutes after the sudden death of President Roosevelt at Warm Springs. Mr. Truman had picked up a Bible from the end of the big Cabinet conference table, held it with his left hand and placed his right hand upon the upper cover. After repeating the oath, he bowed his head, lifted the Bible to his lips and kissed it.

Even before he had taken the oath Mr. Truman had asked President Roosevelt's Cabinet to continue in service. He also authorized Edward R. Stettinius Jr., Secretary of State, to announce that the United Nations Conference for International Organization would go on as scheduled.

To the newsmen at the White House he sent this word, through Stephen Early, press secretary:

"For the time being I prefer not to hold a press conference. It will be my effort to carry on as I believe the President would have done, and to that end I have asked the Cabinet to stay on with me."

Soon after he became President, Mr. Truman left the White House for the five-room Connecticut Avenue apartment where he has resided with Mrs. Truman and their 20-year-old daughter, Mary Margaret, for four years. He said he was "going home, to bed."

It was shortly after he had finished presiding over the Senate debate on the United States-Mexican Water Treaty late this afternoon that Mr. Truman received word from the White House of President Roosevelt's death. This was at about 5:15 P. M., a half hour before the news was made public. Reaching for his hat, he dashed out of the office, calling back to his staff that he was going to the White House.

Arriving at the White House, the

Continued on Page 3, Column 6

Byrnes May Take Post With Truman

Special to THE NEW YORK TIMES.

WASHINGTON, April 12—James F. Byrnes, recently resigned as Director of War Mobilization and Reconversion, known to be one of President Truman's warmest friends in official Washington, is expected to be called to the White House for consultation, and possibly to take an important post in the Cabinet, in the immediate future.

President Truman's admiration of former Justice Byrnes is well known here. He undoubtedly would have been Mr. Truman's choice as a successor to Cordell Hull as Secretary of State.

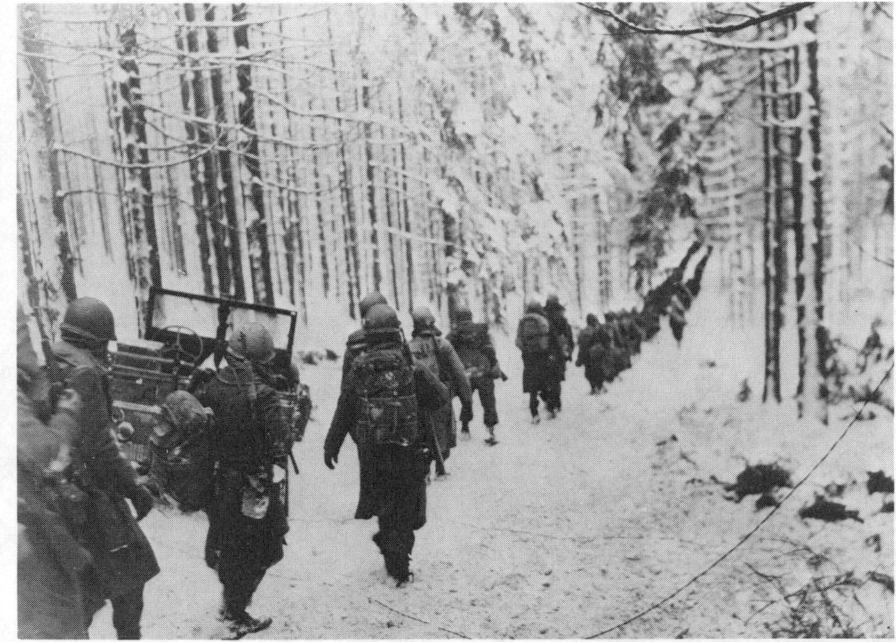

American foot soldiers advancing down a snow-covered Belgian road in early 1945.

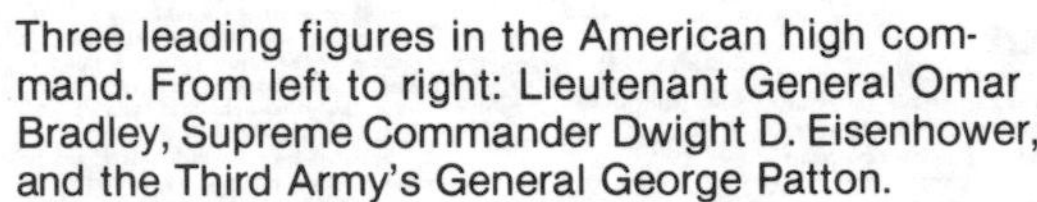

Three leading figures in the American high command. From left to right: Lieutenant General Omar Bradley, Supreme Commander Dwight D. Eisenhower, and the Third Army's General George Patton.

U.S. infantrymen keep their guns ready in case of a sniper attack as they trudge through devastated Zweibrucken, Germany.

"All the News That's Fit to Print"

The New York Times.

LATE CITY EDITION
Partly cloudy today. Mostly clear and warmer tomorrow.
Temperatures Yesterday—Max., 63; Min., 41
Sunrise today, 5:57 A. M.; Sunset, 7:58 P. M.

VOL. XCIV..No. 31,873. Entered as Second-Class Matter, Postoffice, New York, N. Y. NEW YORK, MONDAY, APRIL 30, 1945. THREE CENTS IN NEW YORK CITY

U. S. 7TH IN MUNICH, BRITISH PUSH ON BALTIC; RUSSIANS TIGHTEN RING ON BERLIN'S HEART; MILAN AND VENICE WON; MUSSOLINI KILLED

BIG POWERS SCAN 4 OAKS CHANGES PROPOSED BY U. S.

Revising of Charter by Later Parley and Wider Scope for Assembly Are Emphasized

LEAGUE FUNCTIONS KEPT

Soviet-Latin Trade on Bids to Argentina and Lublin Reported Sought

By JAMES B. RESTON
Special to The New York Times.

SAN FRANCISCO, April 29—Delegates of the big four nations at the San Francisco Conference began exchanging views on amending of the Dumbarton Oaks proposals this weekend, but the question of bringing Argentina and Poland into the United Nations Conference on International Organization continued to hamper progress on this important subject.

There were several private meetings among various members of the sponsor nations yesterday and today. In one of these it was apparently decided that White Russia and the Ukraine should be brought into the conference this week, but when the question of inviting Argentina was raised the Russian Foreign Commissar, Vyacheslaff M. Molotoff, again proposed inviting representatives of the Polish government in Warsaw.

This suggestion, which had been defeated in the steering committee, was again opposed in the firmest manner by the American Secretary of State and the British Foreign Secretary, and it now is likely that the Russians will not insist on forcing the Polish issue to a vote, although they are clearly not yet happy about inviting Argentina.

Four Changes Offered

The United States suggested to the other sponsor powers that four changes be made in the Dumbarton Oaks proposals. These changes would provide:

First, that the charter to be written at this conference be subject to revision in a United Nations constitutional convention at a future date. The principle of writing a temporary rather than a permanent charter has been accepted by all members of the American delegation and is supported by the British, but the amendment as it now stands does not stipulate when the constitutional convention would be held and some members of the delegation think that it should. This will be discussed when the conference commissions are set up this week and the subject will be followed up in the commissions by Comdr. Harold E. Stassen.

Second, that all members obligate themselves to settle disputes in accordance with justice and fundamental human rights, and specifically to adhere to the principles of the Atlantic Charter.

Third, that the assembly have the right to recommend the revision of treaties and the removal of conditions that might lead to a breach of international peace and security.

Fourth, that the charter make provision for taking over responsibility of the functions of the old League of Nations, including responsibilty for the League mandates, and also provide for a system of trusteeship over colonial areas.

Some Vandenberg Points Fail

In the final meetings here among members of the American delegation on the Dumbarton Oaks proposals, several specific proposals by various members of the delegation were rejected. Although Senator Arthur H. Vandenberg, Republican, of Michigan, put in several amendments that were accepted in the points listed above, two of his proposals dealing with the rights of the General Assembly were rejected.

One of these was that the General Assembly should—contrary to the Dumbarton Oaks proposals—be authorized to make recom-

Continued on Page 10, Column 4

Moscow Blackout Ends for May Day

By Wireless to The New York Times.

MOSCOW, April 29—Moscow's stifling blackout ends tomorrow after almost four years of war. For some weeks now, increasing numbers of street lamps have been turned on, but the obscuring of lights in homes remained rigidly enforced.

The removal of this confounded nuisance will add to the general festivities accompanying the May Day holiday and the imminent fall of Berlin and the end of the European conflict. Workmen on scaffolds have been putting light bulbs back into the huge stars on the Kremlin's towers.

CARRIER ROOSEVELT IS CHRISTENED HERE

Widow Speaks at Floating of $90,000,000 Ship—Forrestal Reveals Navy's Strength

As gray sea water lapped at her keel in building dock 5 of the New York Navy Yard in Brooklyn, a gigantic new aircraft carrier was christened the Franklin D. Roosevelt in impressive ceremonies yesterday morning. The 45,000-ton vessel, built at a cost of $90,000,000, is one of a class of three ships described by the Navy as the largest warships afloat and the biggest ships of any type ever built in this country.

At the ceremony Mrs. Franklin D. Roosevelt, clad in deepest mourning, made her first public appearance since her husband's funeral. In a brief, unscheduled address she expressed her gratitude that the Navy had given her husband's name to the new carrier, previously scheduled to be called the U. S. S. Coral Sea, and voiced a prayer that the ship would bring her officers and men home safe and victorious.

James V. Forrestal, Secretary of the Navy, who made the principal address, revealed some hitherto secret figures about the present size of the United States Fleet. He said that it now consists of twenty-three battleships, twenty-six combat aircraft carriers, sixty-five escort carriers, sixty-seven cruisers, 386 destroyers, 368 destroyer escorts, and 240 submarines.

For Strong Naval Force

Secretary Forrestal warned those at the ceremony that the United States must retain the military ability "for swift and effective application of force" if peace is to be maintained in future years. He said that the retention of force by the United States would not conflict with her aspirations at the San Francisco Conference, but was essential for realizing the aims sought there.

Unlike the previous 45,000-ton ships built at the New York Navy Yard, the battleships Iowa and Missouri, the Franklin D. Roosevelt was not launched in the traditional fashion down greased building ways into the East River.

Continued on Page 32, Column 2

SLAIN BY PARTISANS

Italy's Former Dictator Shot After Trial—Other Fascists Executed

SEIZED AS HE FLED

Onetime Premier Begged for Life—Bodies on Display in Milan

By MILTON BRACKER
By Wireless to The New York Times.

MILAN, April 29—Benito Mussolini came back last night to the city where his fascism was born. He came back on the floor of a closed moving van, his dead body flung on the bodies of his mistress and twelve men shot with him. All were executed yesterday by Italian Partisans. The story of his final downfall, his flight, his capture and his execution is not pretty, and its epilogue in the Piazza Loretto here this morning was its ugliest part. It will go down in history as a finish to tyranny as horrible as any ever visited on a tyrant.

At 9:30 A. M. today, Mussolini's body lay on the rim of the mass of corpses, while all around surged a growing mob wild with the desire to have a last look at the man who once was a Socialist editor in this same city. The throng pushed and yelled. Partisans strove to keep them back but largely in vain. Even a series of shots in the air did not dissuade them.

Bullet Hole in Head

Mussolini had changed in death, but not enough to be any one else. His closely shaved head and his bull neck were unmistakable. His body seemed small and a little shrunken, but he was never a tall man. At least one bullet had passed through his head. It had emerged some three inches behind his right ear. There was another small hole nearer his forehead where another bullet seemed to have gone in.

As if he were not dead or dishonored enough, at least two young men in the crowd broke through and aimed kicks at his skull. One glanced off. But the other landed full on his right jaw and there was a hideous crunch that wholly disfigured the once-proud face.

Mussolini wore the uniform of a squadrist militiaman. It comprised a gray-brown jacket and gray trousers with red and black stripes down the sides. He wore black boots, badly soiled, and the left one hung half off as if his foot were broken. His small eyes were open and it was perhaps a final irony that this man who had thrust his chin forward for so many official photographs had to have his yellowing face propped up with a rifle-butt to turn it into the sun for the only two Allied cameramen on the scene.

When the butt was removed the face flopped back over to the left. Meanwhile I crouched over the body to the left in order not to

Continued on Page 7, Column 1

THE INGLORIOUS END OF A DICTATOR

Benito Mussolini in Milan's Piazza Loretto after his execution by Italian Partisans. Also seen is the body of Clara Petacci
The New York Times Radiophoto

3 DIVISIONS ENTER

Americans Roll Into Nazi Birthplace Without Meeting Opposition

ITS FALL IS REPORTED

British Cross the Elbe and Drive Northeast to Cut Off Denmark

By DREW MIDDLETON
By Wireless to The New York Times.

PARIS, April 29—American and British Armies dealt shattering blows to waning German hopes of holding out in the southern and northern redoubts today.

Troops of the United States Seventh Army crashed into Munich, birthplace of the Nazi party and the principal enemy stronghold barring the roads to the redoubt in the Austrian Tyrol while Tommies of the British Second Army smashed over the Elbe southeast of Hamburg.

Elements of the Twelfth Armored and Forty-second Infantry Divisions entered Munich at 4 o'clock this afternoon, meeting only light resistance, according to reports from the front. Later the Twentieth Armored Division rolled in.

Beer Cellar Occupied

Reports from the front line tonight said that Munich had fallen. There was no confirmation of these reports, either at Supreme Headquarters or at any Army group, but in view of the slackening resistance all over Germany and the failure of the enemy to attack the first troops entering the city, it is entirely possible that Munich has been taken.

Munich was reached after a twenty-mile advance by Seventh Army columns. According to reports from the front the Americans hold the beer cellar where Hitler planned his premature putsch of 1923 and where he addressed Nazi leaders yearly. The cellar was partly destroyed by a bomb in the autumn of 1939.

The infamous concentration camp at Dachau is believed to have been overrun in the advance to the city.

Push on Redoubt Gains

The thrust into Munich was accompanied by a general advance to the south and southeast toward the northern face of the redoubt by the United States Third and Seventh Armies, while on the right flank of the Seventh Army infantry felt its way southeastward into the redoubt, pushing toward Innsbruck and the valley of the Inn River, the most important, indeed the only communications system within the redoubt.

The thrust over the Elbe by the Fifteenth Scottish Division and the British First Commando Brigade to the north followed a bombardment in typical Montgomery fashion in which more than 400 guns were employed. It was accompanied by heavy blows on the German line west and east of the Weser and the flattening of an enemy salient northeast of Bremen.

The Ninth Army front, long dormant, awoke today when Lieut. Gen. William H. Simpson's troops suddenly attacked out of their bridgehead over the Elbe, capturing the towns of Zerbst, Jutrichau and Bias and advancing northeast and southeast of the towns. This attack was described here as a "local attack."

Four divisions, the Twelfth and Twentieth Armored and the Third and Forty-second Infantry Divisions, moved on Munich this morning. The Twentieth is a new division, fed into the battle yesterday by Lieut. Gen. Alexander M. Patch.

Between Munich and the Austrian frontier around Fuessen, other armored, cavalry and infantry units of the Seventh Army drove on toward the southeast, crossing the Lech River in force.

The Forty-fourth Infantry Division, which is moving methodically

Continued on Page 3, Column 6

5TH SEIZES MILAN, FASCISM'S CRADLE

Americans Surge On to Como—8th Army Takes Venice and Cuts Adige Line

By VIRGINIA LEE WARREN
By Wireless to The New York Times.

ADVANCED ALLIED FIELD HEADQUARTERS, Italy, April 29—United States Fifth Army troops today entered Milan, Italy's largest, wealthiest and most politically conscious city, where the history of

Continued on Page 3, Column 4

Nazis in Berlin Compressed Into 18-Square-Mile Pocket

By C. L. SULZBERGER
By Wireless to The New York Times.

MOSCOW, Monday, April 30—Determined Russian troops drove deeper into the heart of Berlin's wreckage yesterday, nearing the hastily fortified Tiergarten from two sides and edging to within a mile of the Reichstag as division after division gave itself up to the Red Army. Within the past forty-eight hours the First White Russian Army and the First Ukrainian Army have captured more than 50,000 prisoners in and around the burning capital.

Southeast of the city, in the

Continued on Page 4, Column 5

AUSTRIA CREATES INTERIM REGIME

Moscow Announces Renner Is Premier—Britain and U. S. Not Consulted

By Wireless to The New York Times.

MOSCOW, April 29—An Austrian Provisional Government, the first independent authority in that German-speaking country since the Nazi annexation of more than seven years ago, has been created in Vienna under the leadership of Dr. Karl Renner, 74, a Social Democrat.

His Cabinet of thirteen men includes three non-party representatives, three Social Democrats, four Christian Socialists and three Communists. The Communists hold the key posts of the Interior and Education Ministries as well as one of the three seats on the political

Continued on Page 4, Column 7

NEW NAZI PROFFER ON PEACE AWAITED

Stalin Note to Truman and Churchill Said to Spurn Himmler's Proposals

By CLIFTON DANIEL
By Wireless to The New York Times.

LONDON, Monday, April 30—London took Saturday night's "peace scare" calmly and yesterday confidently marked time in anticipation of an actual capitulation by Germany and peace in Europe within a matter of days. Amid reports about negotiations with Heinrich Himmler and a variety of rumors of the death of Adolf Hitler, official quarters here quietly awaited a Nazi reply to the British and American Governments' statement that unconditional surrender could be accepted only by all three major Allies.

Opinion was strong that Himmler's offer of surrender would be extended to the Russians—an opinion based on the belief that the Gestapo chief, now evidently ruler of the Reich, would never have made his proposal if Germany's situation had not been so desperate as to preclude further resistance.

[Reuter reported that Premier Stalin in a note to President Truman and Prime Minister Churchill has urged rejection of Himmler's proposals. Mr. Church-

Continued on Page 3, Column 2

War News Summarized

MONDAY, APRIL 30, 1945

Munich, birthplace of nazism, and Milan, cradle of fascism, were entered by American troops yesterday while the world waited for further word on what Himmler was going to do about the Allied demand that Germany surrender unconditionally to Great Britain, the United States and the Soviet Union. Count Bernadotte, who carried the Nazi's proposal to give up to the western Allies only, was returning from seeing Himmler again, presumably with a reply to the Allied ultimatum. [1:7.]

It was the United States Seventh Army that smashed into Munich after a twenty-mile advance. Opposition was light, and the Americans were soon in occupation of that beer cellar from which Hitler launched his ill-fated revolt in 1923. Front reports said Munich had been captured. The Third Army was advancing on Berchtesgaden and Salzburg, while in the center the Ninth burst from its Elbe River bridgehead toward the Russians in the Wittenberg area. To the north the British Second Army crossed the Elbe southeast of Hamburg, and the Canadians progressed along the coast. The French First Army was twelve miles from Austria in the Alps. [1:8; map P. 3.]

Milan was taken by the United States Fifth Army, which also reached Como and the north end of Lake Garda. The British Eighth Army captured Venice and seized Mestre, eighty-five miles from Trieste. The Brazilian Expeditionary Force compelled a German division to surrender. The captured Marshal Graziani was arranging for the surrender of his Fascist Ligurian army. [1:4; map, P. 3.]

Mussolini's body was dumped from a moving van into a Milan square, where it received the scornful attention of the residents. He, his mistress and more than a dozen other Fascists had been executed by Partisans near Como. [1:3.]

Berlin's last-ditch defenders were squeezed into an eighteen square mile area in the center of the city, and Russian troops were within half a mile of Hitler's ruined chancellery. A German pocket southeast of the city was liquidated, while in the north two Soviet armies joined forces and swept toward Rostock and Swinemuende. [1:5-6, maps P. 4.] A wave of suicides was said to be sweeping Berlin. [4:1.]

Washington and London learned from Moscow that a provisional anti-fascist government had been set up in Austria headed by Dr. Karl Renner, former Chancellor and last president of the free Assembly. [1:6.]

A marked trend toward the Left was shown in early returns from France's first elections since 1937. Communists jumped into the lead in Paris. [1:6-7.]

A clearly marked Navy hospital ship was attacked off Okinawa by a Japanese plane, which killed twenty-nine and injured thirty-three; one man was missing. Some 200 other enemy planes kept the Pacific Fleet under prolonged attack, damaging some light units; 104 of the enemy aircraft were destroyed. On shore, troops captured the northern half of Machinato airfield in a general advance. [1:2-3.]

Americans on Mindanao seized the Padada airfield along Davao Gulf and advanced up to seventeen miles in the center. [8:5.] Japanese resistance slowed the British drive on Rangoon, in Burma. [8:7.]

Enemy Suicide Pilot Dives Plane On U. S. Hospital Ship Off Okinawa

By W. H. LAWRENCE
By Wireless to The New York Times.

ABOARD AMPHIBIOUS FLAGSHIP, off Okinawa, April 28 (Delayed)—A Japanese "suicide" pilot machine-gunned and then crashed his bomb-laden plane squarely into the well-lighted, unarmed United States naval hospital ship Comfort fully loaded with casualties from Okinawa in clear weather about sixty miles southeast of here at 8:58 o'clock tonight.

Twenty-nine were killed by the exploding airplane, which apparently struck the surgery section of the hospital ship as she was bearing wounded toward rear area hospitals.

Although first reports from the ship indicated that it would be necessary to abandon ship, it later was found that the damage was not as heavy as it seemed, and the vessel was able to continue under her own power.

Continued on Page 8, Column 3

Tempers ran high in naval circles at this premeditated and cold-blooded attack upon the hospital ship, which was proceeding alone with full illumination, including powerful searchlights that lighted up huge red crosses painted on the sides, superstructure and stack.

It was the first time that the Japanese had been known to attack an American hospital ship deliberately, although two other hospital ships were menaced during the Okinawa operation. Until tonight's incident, naval men had been inclined charitably to attribute these attacks to mistakes.

But there was no possibility of mistake about tonight's attack. There was a full moon and the sky was clear. The Japanese plane, one of several in the area, swept in

Communists Take Lead in Paris As France Holds First Elections

By The Associated Press.

PARIS, April 29—Communist candidates for municipal office in Paris held a commanding lead on the basis of almost complete returns today.

Election returns from other metropolitan centers indicated that their voters, too, had supported candidates of the leftist parties in contests for municipal offices, the only ones at stake in today's voting. Only a few returns had been received from traditionally conservative country districts.

In Paris and other principal cities the Communists' lead seemed to be safe, while Socialists and Radicals ran well ahead of center parties and rightists. Political observers speculated that eleventh-hour Communist demands for the quick trial and conviction of Marshal Henri-Philippe Pétain had drawn support to the party candidates, including many voters unaffiliated with any party.

André Mornet, Attorney General, who will conduct the case against Pétain, was returned to office with a heavy plurality. Edouard Herriot, former President of the Chamber of Deputies, who has just reached Switzerland from a German prison camp, was elected to the Municipal Council of Lyon by a 4-to-1 margin. Six members of the Cabinet who ran for city offices were also elected.

Joseph Paul-Boncour, a member of the French delegation to the San Francisco Conference, was also elected by a big margin.

Not only was this the first election that France had held since her fall to the Germans but it was the first time that women were al-

Continued on Page 5, Column 6

German Field Marshal Keitel surrenders to Allied troops. He was convicted at Nuremberg and hanged.

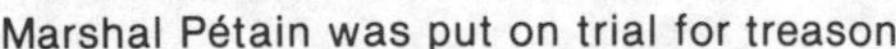

Marshal Pétain was put on trial for treason.

Benito Mussolini was executed by Italian patriots and then hanged by the heels on display in Milan.

1945

Hadamar, Germany,1945. Exhumed bodies of prisoners of the Nazis were found to have been poisoned.

German soldiers surrender to men of the 94th Infantry.

Men of the Third Army's 89th Infantry cross the Rhine at Oberwesel, Germany.

"All the News That's Fit to Print"

The New York Times.

LATE CITY EDITION
Clearing and warmer today. Cloudy with moderate winds tomorrow.
Temperatures Yesterday—Max., 51; Min., 44
Sunrise today, 5:54 A. M.; Sunset, 7:58 P. M.

VOL. XCIV..No. 31,875. Entered as Second-Class Matter, Postoffice, New York, N. Y. NEW YORK, WEDNESDAY, MAY 2, 1945. THREE CENTS IN NEW YORK CITY

HITLER DEAD IN CHANCELLERY, NAZIS SAY; DOENITZ, SUCCESSOR, ORDERS WAR TO GO ON; BERLIN ALMOST WON; U. S. ARMIES ADVANCE

MOLOTOFF EASES PARLEY TENSION; NEW MOVES BEGUN

Russian Says Country Will Cooperate in World Plan Despite Argentine Issue

4 COMMISSIONS SET UP

They Will Deal With Council, Assembly, Court and Some General Problems

By JAMES B. RESTON
Special to THE NEW YORK TIMES.

SAN FRANCISCO, May 1—The United Nations Conference on International Organization has survived its first basic crisis and after six days of political maneuvering on secondary issues, it began to move at rapid tempo today toward its primary task—the creation of a world organization which would stop what Field Marshal Jan Christiaan Smuts called "this pilgrimage of death."

The test came last night. Rebuffed by the conference on his attempts to keep Argentina out of the conference and bring the Warsaw Poles in, Soviet Foreign Commissar Vyacheslaff M. Molotoff went late last night to Secretary Stettinius' penthouse at the Fairmont Hotel. He immediately made his position clear.

He still disapproved the conference actions on the Poles and the Argentine, but he wanted the conference to succeed; he would cooperate in its labors, and while he was under urgent pressure by the events in Europe to return to Moscow, he would remain at least for a few days until the major issues on the charter were thrashed out among the four sponsor powers. Then, he said, he would have to leave, probably at the week-end or early next week.

"Friendly Meeting" Is Held

Immediately, in what the Foreign Ministers of the United States, Great Britain and China described to their colleagues as "the most friendly meeting of the conference," the big four approved the formation of the working commissions and committees of the conference, and other committees began discussing, not the personalities or procedures of the conference, but the basic questions of creating an organization which would win the support, with the power, of the great nations without violating the rights and principles of all nations.

The three main developments of the day were as follows:

First, the conference approved four commissions to deal with the security council of the proposed organization, the general assembly, the judicial agency and general problems, and established twelve committees to study specific problems under these four commissions.

The heads of the four commissions were: Trygve Lie of Norway, Security Council; Field Marshal Smuts, General Assembly; Carraciolo Parra Pez of Venezuela, judicial organization; and Paul Henri Spaak of Belgium, general provisions.

Second, Field Marshal Smuts called on the four major powers to accept the special responsibilities which flow from the special authority given them under the Dumbarton Oaks proposals and urged all the nations here to pay more attention to the spiritual and economic aspects of the new charter than they had in the past.

Third, the Russians began studying in some detail the sixteen amendments to the Dumbarton Oaks proposals which were submitted by the United States. The other delegations started circulating amendments and exchanging views on proposals already circulated.

The facts on the crisis among the Big Three over Poland, Argentina, White Russia and the Ukraine can now be put down with assur-

Continued on Page 18, Column 6

Allies Invade North Borneo; Fighting Fierce, Tokyo Says

Australia Informed of Landing by Treasury Minister—MacArthur Reports Only Air Attacks and New Gains on Luzon

By The United Press.

MANILA, Wednesday, May 2—An official Australian announcement said yesterday that Allied troops had invaded Borneo, the world's third largest island, but Gen. Douglas MacArthur's communiqué early today reported only that heavy bombers were neutralizing enemy bases and airdromes on the oil-rich island.

Tokyo also reported the landings and said they had been made on the ten-square-mile island of Tarakan on the northeast coast, a region rich in oil wells, which the Netherlanders destroyed before the Japanese captured them in 1942. The enemy broadcast said "fierce fighting" was in progress.

[A later Japanese broadcast, picked up in San Francisco, reported that Allied units had landed on Tarakan Island at 6:30 A. M., Tuesday, Tokyo time. The broadcast said "the enemy had been bombarding the island since April 27, and on Monday morning began approaching the island in their landing attempts." It reported the landing force consisted of "about 5,000 soldiers" and said Japanese forces on the island "are holding secure their positions, obstructing the enemy's advance."]

General MacArthur announced that heavy bombers in attacks on Borneo had struck Kuching, Macassar and Kendari, while medium units and fighters had attacked Japanese gun positions on Tarakan.

General MacArthur announced that on Mindano Island the Twenty-fourth Division, in another swift drive, had advanced eleven miles

Continued on Page 16, Column 2

NEW CIGARETTES FACE PRICE INQUIRY

OPA Calls on Manufacturers of 21-Cent Brands to Prove Quality Merits Charge

By JAMES E. POWERS

Manufacturers of hitherto unheard of brands of cigarettes that have appeared on the market in recent weeks and are being retailed at four or more cents a package higher than ceiling prices for scarce popular brands will be called upon by the Office of Price Administration to show that the new products are of a quality rating the prices charged, it became known yesterday.

Daniel P. Woolley, regional OPA administrator, said an investigation was in progress as a result of complaints by smokers who said they had paid 21 cents a package for cigarettes "they had previously never heard of."

The United Wholesale Tobacco and Cigarette Distributors Association, a sub-jobbers' group, in a telegram to Senator William Langer of North Dakota, who recently introduced a resolution to set up a committee to look into the "black market" in cigarettes, demanded an immediate investigation of the entire cigarette shortage.

Mr. Woolley declared that as a result of OPA prosecution of violators of price ceilings, the black-market condition largely had been corrected here. He said he was centering on the pricing of the new cigarette brands.

Mr. Woolley added that studies were being made to determine

Continued on Page 40, Column 4

HARD COAL 'HOLIDAY' BRINGS WLB BAN

New Order by Board Asserts Output Is Urgent—Seizure Action Is Postponed

By JOSEPH A. LOFTUS
Special to THE NEW YORK TIMES.

WASHINGTON, May 1—The War Labor Board issued a new order tonight to the United Mine Workers and the operators to resume the production of hard coal. To give the UMW leaders an opportunity to act on the order it decided to defer for twenty-four to forty-eight hours a recommendation to President Truman for Government seizure of the mines.

The miners went on a holiday today after expiration of their contract at midnight.

Dr. George W. Taylor, WLB chairman, in a telegram to both parties took cognizance of the miners' traditional "no contract, no work" policy.

"The board's order provides for a continuing contract," he said. "It is urgent that production should be immediately resumed."

As in acting on the soft coal dispute a month ago, the WLB provided in the new order that any legal wage adjustment agreed upon or finally ordered be retroactive to the expiration date of the old contract.

Union spokesmen told the WLB at a brief hearing that the Tri-District Scale Committee had voted to advise the miners to return to work when the operators accepted the settlement proposal made by Secretary of Labor Perkins.

Dr. Taylor, in questioning John Owens of the UMW, noted that

Continued on Page 40, Column 2

Eisenhower Halted Forces at Elbe; Ninth Had Hoped to Storm Berlin

By The Associated Press.

WITH THE UNITED STATES NINTH ARMY, in Germany, April 26 (Delayed by Censorship)—A direct order from Supreme Allied Headquarters halted the United States Ninth Army's drive to Berlin at the Elbe River at a time when the most pessimistic officers were predicting that Lieut. Gen. William H. Simpson's forces could reduce the German capital in ten days, "even if the Germans fought hard."

General Eisenhower's order said the Ninth would halt on the Elbe and await the arrival of Russian forces from the east, thereby leaving the capture of the capital to the Red Army. It also was understood that the American First and Third and British and Canadian armies received similar orders to halt at the Elbe.

It was not clear whether General Eisenhower's order was dictated by political policy agreed upon by the Great Powers or in a belief that it was a military necessity.

It was felt by high staff officers in the field, however, that the Ninth and other American forces could push on to the capital without great difficulty. While the order disappointed some staff officers, it was not altogether unexpected. It was known that the Ninth Army had pushed past the eventual British-American occupation area when it crossed the Weser River.

While the staff officers were disappointed, the American doughboys and tankmen who had to do the fighting and dying to get to Berlin expressed no regret. Almost to a man, they felt they could do with-

Continued on Page 4, Column 4

REDOUBTS ASSAILED

U. S. 3d, 7th and French 1st Armies Charging Into Alpine Hideout

NEAR BRENNER PASS

British in North Close About Hamburg—Poles Gain in Emden Area

Von Rundstedt Caught

By The Associated Press.

WITH UNITED STATES SEVENTH ARMY, Wednesday, May 2—Field Marshal Karl von Rundstedt has been captured by United States Seventh Army troops.

The Seventh Army caught the former German commander in the west in its drive into the Nazis' southeastern redoubt area.

By DREW MIDDLETON
By Wireless to THE NEW YORK TIMES.

PARIS, May 1—The last defenses of the Third Reich were crumbling as Allied tanks and infantry swept almost unopposed into the northern and southern redoubts.

Gen. George S. Patton's United States Third Army has resumed its offensive into Austria, crashing to within twenty miles of Linz, and is only fifty-four miles from Amstetten, where Marshal Fedor I. Tolbukhin's Third Ukrainian Army was last reported. According to reports from the front, radio contact has been established between tanks of the United States Eleventh Armored Division and the vanguard of the Soviet armies.

Other armored columns of the

Continued on Page 14, Column 1

NAZI CORE STORMED

Russians Drive Toward Chancellery Fortress, Narrowing Noose

BRANDENBURG TAKEN

Stralsund Port Swept Up in New Baltic Gains—Vah Valley Cleared

By C. L. SULZBERGER
By Wireless to THE NEW YORK TIMES.

MOSCOW, Wednesday, May 2—Street battles within smoldering Berlin today entered their twelfth day since the Russians first broke into the city, with Nazi die-hards still holding grimly to the central part of the town, whittled down by yesterday's fighting, in which Marshal Gregory K. Zhukoff's First White Russian Army group completely occupied Charlottenburg and Schoeneberg and more than 100 blocks in the capital's central region.

Some 14,000 prisoners were taken within the city on Monday, the Russians announced. At the same time, the remnants of a hold-out group south of Berlin, part of which had been annihilated at Wendisch Buchholtz, was split in two and the survivors are being ground to death by Marshal Zhukoff's men.

Curiously enough, the midnight communiqué does not mention Marshal Ivan S. Koneff's First Ukrainian Army group, which has been working from the southwestern sector of the city toward the desperately defended Tiergarten.

Marshal Zhukoff's forward spearheads meanwhile struck deep into Brandenburg Province, capturing the city of Brandenburg, halfway to Magdeburg from Berlin.

While Gen. Andrei I. Yeremenko proceeded apace in his lightning

Continued on Page 3, Column 3

War News Summarized

WEDNESDAY, MAY 2, 1945

Hitler is dead, according to the Hamburg radio, and on Monday, the day before he allegedly fell at his command post in the Chancellery in Berlin, he appointed Admiral Karl Doenitz to be the new Fuehrer. The head of the German Navy, who had made his mark directing the enemy's U-boats campaign, pledged continuance of the war. [1:8.]

Washington received the news, as did London, with some skepticism and a desire to see the body. Selection of Admiral Doenitz was considered logical in view of his strong Nazi feelings. [1:7.]

The new development was interpreted in London as a move to counteract Himmler's reported peace bids, but Prime Minister Churchill broadly intimated in the Commons that he might have "information of exceptional importance" to impart before Saturday. Peace will probably come before all enemy forces have surrendered, he said. [1:6-7.] Germany was reported to have begun evacuation of Denmark and to be ready to leave Norway. Count Bernadotte said in Sweden he had no new Himmler proposals, and the Nazis' Scandinavian withdrawals were related there to a prospective general capitulation. [11:1.]

Meanwhile, general Allied progress on the battlefields against slight resistance continued. The United States Third Army, on the day Hitler was declared to have died, captured Braunau, his birthplace. The drive into Austria was resumed and had reached to within twenty miles of Linz and fifty-four of the last known Russian position. The Seventh Army smashed through the Tyrol on a broad front and cleared Munich. The British Second Army, by-passing Hamburg, raced to within eighteen miles of the Baltic port of Luebeck. [1:4; map P. 14.]

General Eisenhower, it was revealed, personally ordered the halt of the Allied drive on Berlin from the west to permit the Russians to take the capital. [1:2-3.]

The Russians greatly cut down the German holding in Berlin, capturing the districts of Charlottenburg and Schoeneberg. West of the city they occupied Brandenburg and along the Baltic they seized Stralsund. [1:5; maps Pages 2 and 14.]

New Zealand troops in Italy made contact with Yugoslav Partisans at Monfalcone near Trieste and the British entered Udine. While the Eighth Army was closing a trap along the Swiss border, the Fifth neared France. [1:6-7; map P. 14.]

Mussolini and his mistress were buried in unmarked paupers' graves in Milan. [13:1.] Admiral Horthy, former Regent of Hungary, was captured. [4:3.]

Invasion of Borneo was officially disclosed in Australia, although no word of the break into the Japanese-held Netherlands East Indies had come from General MacArthur. On Mindanao in the Philippines, Americans were within six miles of the city of Davao. [1:2-3; map P. 16.]

Seventh Division troops on Okinawa resumed their southward advance, entering the village of Kuhazu. [15:1.] More than 400 starved, naked Allied prisoners of war were liberated by the British as they drove on Rangoon in Burma. [15:3.]

Good progress was made at the San Francisco Conference. Foreign Commissar Molotoff, after assuring Secretary of State Stettinius of his desire that the conference succeed, announced that pressure of events would compel his return to Moscow within a few days. [1:1.]

ADOLF HITLER The New York Times, 1936

Clark's Troops Meet Tito's In General Advance in Italy

By VIRGINIA LEE WARREN
By Wireless to THE NEW YORK TIMES.

AT ADVANCED ALLIED HEADQUARTERS, in Italy, May 1—After advancing fifty-five miles in less than a day along the coastal road rimming the Gulf of Venice, units of one division of the Fifteenth Army Group made contact this afternoon with Marshal Tito's forces at Monfalcone while other troops under Gen. Mark W. Clark continued to sweep German remnants from the valleys of north Italy and to seal off the few remaining escape routes through the Alps.

No details of the meeting at the small seaport northwest of Trieste between Marshal Tito's men, who had driven fourteen miles from Trieste, and leading elements of the Eighth Army's Second New Zealand Division were given in tonight's communiqué.

On the other side of Italy another historic meeting was imminent as Fifth Army troops, continuing their drive along the Gulf of Genoa, advanced on the Aurelian Way to within sixty miles of the French border, which has already been crossed by French troops headed this way.

General Clark announced yesterday that the military power of Germany had virtually collapsed, but there still are drives for his two armies to make and engagements still to be won. The Germans, trying to regroup for their flight across the Alps, were deprived of two key road junctions leading to mountain passes west of Brenner when Belluno and Udine were occupied this afternoon by units of the Eighth Army.

Udine, which was taken by the British Sixth Armored Division, is twenty-eight miles southwest of Caporetto, the scene of the Italian disaster in World War I. The forces that entered Belluno went on five miles to Ponte nell 'Alpi, guardian of the approach to Italy's

Continued on Page 13, Column 5

DOENITZ' ACCESSION VIEWED AS A BLIND

Capital Lays His Designation to General Ignorance of His Allegiance to Party

By The Associated Press.

WASHINGTON, May 1—If Adolf Hitler really designated Grand Admiral Karl Doenitz his successor, military men here believe, he did so for the following reasons:

1. Doenitz is a Nazi supporter who could be counted on to keep German resistance going if possible.

2. But he is not associated in the Allies' minds with German atrocities and the extreme policies of the Nazi party. Therefore, Hitler probably figured that he might be able to get better treatment from the Allies when the hour of surrender came.

3. He is immensely popular with the German people.

There was a disposition here tonight to look for continued organized resistance whose core would now be centered in the Baltic and North Sea port areas. Those places are the homes of the German Navy and especially of the U-boat fleet that Doenitz commanded from 1936 until he succeeded Grand Admiral Erich

Continued on Page 5, Column 5

Churchill Hints Peace This Week; 2-Day Celebration Is Authorized

By CLIFTON DANIEL
By Wireless to THE NEW YORK TIMES.

LONDON, May 1—The general belief that peace with Germany will be announced this week persisted in Britain today, encouraged by Prime Minister Churchill himself and by Grand Admiral Karl Doenitz's announcement of the death of Adolf Hitler.

The War Cabinet again held a session tonight but so far as was known did not have any concrete proposal to consider. The chances that Heinrich Himmler ultimately will deliver an acceptable peace are now held in some official quarters to be only "fifty-fifty."

Nevertheless the buoyant Prime Minister told the House of Commons today that he might have "information of importance" to announce before Saturday.

The public's hopes were raised still further by a long Home Office circular giving the Government's views on how Britain should observe V-E Day, which the British, it appears, will be expected to celebrate strictly according to form.

[Stockholm reported, with the return there of Count Bernadotte, the "imminent liberation" of Denmark and Norway—already taking effect locally in Denmark—as a phase of a prospective general German capitulation that must be acceptable to the Allies' military commands.]

The hurrahing will begin with the announcement of the cessation of hostilities by Mr. Churchill over a nation-wide radio network. The King will speak at 9 o'clock that evening. And throughout that day

Continued on Page 10, Column 4

ADMIRAL IN CHARGE

Proclaims Designation to Rule—Appeals to People and Army

RAISES 'RED MENACE'

Britain to Insist Germans Show Hitler's Body When War Ends

By SYDNEY GRUSON
By Cable to THE NEW YORK TIMES.

LONDON, May 1—Adolf Hitler died this afternoon, the Hamburg radio announced tonight, and Grand Admiral Karl Doenitz, proclaiming himself the new Fuehrer by Hitler's appointment, said that the war would continue.

Crowning days of rumors about Hitler's health and whereabouts, the Hamburg radio said that he had fallen in the battle of Berlin at his command post in the Chancellery just three days after Benito Mussolini, the first of the dictators, had been killed by Italian Partisans. Doenitz, a 53-year-old U-boat specialist, broadcast an address to the German people and the surviving armed forces immediately after the announcer had given the news of Hitler's death.

[The British Foreign Office said that it would demand the production of Hitler's body after the end of hostilities, The Associated Press reported.]

First addressing the German people, Doenitz said that they would continue to fight only to save themselves from the Russians but that they would oppose the western Allies as long as they helped the Russians. In an order of the day to the German forces he repeated his thinly veiled attempt to split the Allies.

Radio Prepares Germans

Early this evening the Germans were told that an important announcement would be broadcast tonight. There was no hint of what was coming. The stand-by announcement was repeated at 9:40 P. M., followed by the playing of excerpts from Wagner's "Goetterdaemmerung."

A few minutes later the announcer said: "Achtung! Achtung! In a few moments you will hear a

Continued on Page 5, Column 4

Copenhagen Writer Again Phones Story

By Cable to THE NEW YORK TIMES.

STOCKHOLM, Sweden, May 1—For the first time in more than five years THE NEW YORK TIMES correspondent in Copenhagen, Svend Carstensen, tonight telephoned a story from the Danish capital. The Nazi-imposed censorship there has been lifted. Mr. Carstensen said:

"The Danes are overjoyed at their imminent liberation, but it is not noticeable on the Copenhagen streets.

"Anxious to avoid trouble on May Day, Copenhageners have been staying indoors. The blackout is still enforced and it is pitch dark in Copenhagen tonight. All Copenhageners are glued to radios listening to broadcasts on Hitler's death.

"We expect King Christian will resume his functions and name a new Cabinet any day now. In the meantime the strictest discipline is being observed so as not to give the Germans any excuses for starting more trouble."

On April 9, 1940, Mr. Carstensen was the first to give the world the news of the German invasion of Denmark in a wireless dispatch to THE NEW YORK TIMES. His dispatch was cleared less than an hour before the Nazis seized the radio station and was the last to be sent.

"All the News That's Fit to Print"

The New York Times.

LATE CITY EDITION
Cloudy with showers today. Partly cloudy and cooler tomorrow.
Temperatures Yesterday—Max., 64; Min., 47
Sunrise today, 5:46 A. M.; Sunset, 7:59 P. M.

VOL. XCIV..No. 31,881. Entered as Second-Class Matter, Postoffice, New York, N. Y.

NEW YORK, TUESDAY, MAY 8, 1945. THREE CENTS IN NEW YORK CITY

THE WAR IN EUROPE IS ENDED! SURRENDER IS UNCONDITIONAL; V-E WILL BE PROCLAIMED TODAY; OUR TROOPS ON OKINAWA GAIN

ISLAND-WIDE DRIVE

Marines Reach Village a Mile From Naha and Army Lines Advance

7 MORE SHIPS SUNK

Search Planes Again Hit Japan's Life Line—Kyushu Bombed

By WARREN MOSCOW
By Wireless to THE NEW YORK TIMES

GUAM, Tuesday, May 8—In an island-wide American advance on Okinawa yesterday the First Marine Division drove south to the edge of Dakeshi Village, about a mile from Naha, the capital, straightening out the line on our right flank. In the center the Seventy-seventh Army Division used flame-throwing tanks for considerable advances, while the Seventh Army Division moved forward on the left flank.

[Airfields on Kyushu, southern Japan, were bombed Monday and Tuesday by Superfortresses, two of which were lost in heavy air opposition.

[Allied fliers started operating from the Tarakan airfield although fighting continued on that island off Borneo, and in the Philippines American troops made advances on Mindanao and Luzon.]

Japanese Dead at 36,535

As the United States forces on Okinawa resumed their drive, Fleet Admiral Chester W. Nimitz revealed that Japanese killed on the island had mounted to 36,535 on Monday, showing that the Americans were maintaining their rate of 1,000 a day.

The Americans have not yet taken the main Japanese artillery emplacements on Okinawa, which were the principal targets of the fleet off the island. The fleet's guns continued yesterday, along with carrier aircraft, to support the ground movements.

Meanwhile search bombers of Fleet Air Wing 1 continued to give an impressive demonstration of what the tightening air blockade of Japan will mean. Attacking at mast-head height with bombs and machine guns, these long-range aircraft, based in the Okinawa area, sank four more ships in waters off Korea and damaged five others.

The ships sunk were a large cargo ship, a medium cargo ship, a medium oiler and a large fleet tanker. Two small freighters were

Continued on Page 12, Column 2

Leopold Rescued By 7th Army Troops

By The Associated Press

WITH THE UNITED STATES SEVENTH ARMY, Tuesday, May 8—Léopold III, King of Belgium, and his wife, Princess Rethy, have been liberated by the Seventh Army, it was announced today.

They were found near Strobl, eight miles east of Salzburg. The Americans had been told of their whereabouts by civilians.

With the King and his wife were eighteen members of their staff and four children. All were in good health.

Elements of the American 106th Cavalry Group had to overpower German Elite Guards to make the rescue. Seventh Army troops are now closely guarding the royal party.

The Pulitzer Awards For 1944 Announced

The Pulitzer Prize awards announced yesterday by the trustees of Columbia University included: For a distinguished novel, to "A Bell for Adano," by John Hersey; for an original American play of the current season, to "Harvey," by Mary Chase.

Among the newspaper awards were those to Hal Boyle, Associated Press war reporter, for distinguished correspondence; to James B. Reston of THE NEW YORK TIMES for his reporting of the Dumbarton Oaks Security Conference; to Joe Rosenthal, Associated Press photographer, for his photograph of marines raising the American flag at Iwo and to The Detroit Free Press for "distinguished and meritorious public service" in its investigation of legislative corruption at Lansing, Mich.

Further details of the awards will be found on Page 16.

MOLOTOFF HAILS BASIC 'UNANIMITY'

He Stresses Five Points in World Charter, but His View on One Is Questioned

By JAMES B. RESTON
Special to THE NEW YORK TIMES

SAN FRANCISCO, May 7—The major allies who forced Germany's unconditional surrender have reached "unanimity" on the kind of world security organization which should be created at the United Nations conference to protect their newly won victory, Vyacheslaff M. Molotoff, Russian Foreign Commissar, said today.

While the delegates at the conference celebrated the end of the European war, and three Foreign Ministers, T. V. Soong of China, Paul Henri Spaak of Belgium and Trygve Lie of Norway left the conference to deal with urgent official business elsewhere, Mr. Molotoff told the press that the Soviet Union attached the "greatest importance" to five agreements reached by the heads of the Big Four delegations.

First, he said, these leaders agreed to support the principles of justice, international law, human rights and fundamental freedom for all.

Second, he added, the Big Four agreed not to make provision in the security charter for the revision of treaties.

His statement on this point was ambiguous and led to some speculation as to the unanimity of all four on the question.

Revision Power Called Danger

A reference in the United Nations charter to the necessity of revising treaties, Mr. Molotoff stated, "would play into the hands of enemy countries, which would certainly like to undermine and emasculate these treaties." Furthermore, he declared, to give the new League of Nations authority to consider revision of treaties would be a violation of national sovereign rights, which are guaranteed in the Dumbarton Oaks Charter.

For these reasons, he concluded, "the idea of revising treaties was rejected as untenable."

Third, Mr. Molotoff said, it was agreed among the Big Four that treaties directed against Germany, such as Russia's twenty-year alliances with Britain, France, Czechoslovakia, Yugoslavia and the Warsaw Poles, "should remain in force until such time as the Government concerned felt that the international security organization was really in a position to undertake the accomplishment of the tasks of

Continued on Page 15, Column 2

GERMANY SURRENDERS: NEW YORKERS MASSED UNDER SYMBOL OF LIBERTY

Thousands filling Times Square in spontaneous celebration yesterday. The New York Times

PRAGUE SAYS FOES ACCEPT SURRENDER

Czechoslovak Radio Reports All Fighting in Bohemia Will Be Ended Today

By The Associated Press

LONDON, Tuesday, May 8—The Czechoslovak-controlled Prague radio announced today that the Germans in Prague and throughout Bohemia, a last major holdout pocket of German resistance, had accepted unconditional surrender.

The announcement came as the United States Third Army was reported to have advanced to the outskirts of the Czechoslovak capital, and three Russian armies hammered toward the same goal from the east and north.

"The German military plenipotentiary is negotiating with the Czechoslovak National Council on the modalities of unconditional surrender," said the broadcast, detailing what purported to be the

Continued on Page 11, Column 2

Wild Crowds Greet News In City While Others Pray

By FRANK S. ADAMS

New York City's millions reacted in two sharply contrasting ways yesterday to the news of the unconditional surrender of the German armies. A large and noisy minority greeted it with the turbulent enthusiasm of New Year's Eve and Election Night rolled into one. However, the great bulk of the city's population responded with quiet thanksgiving that the war in Europe was won, tempered by the realization that a grim and bitter struggle still was ahead in the Pacific and the fact that the nation is still in mourning for its fallen President and Commander in Chief.

Times Square, the financial section and the garment district were thronged from mid-morning on with wildly jubilant celebrators who tooted horns, staged impromptu parades and filled the canyons between the skyscrapers with fluttering scraps of paper. Elsewhere in the metropolitan area, however, war plants continued to hum, schools, offices and factories carried on their normal activities, and residential areas were calmly joyful.

One factor that helped to dampen the celebration was the bewilderment of large segments of the population at the absence of an official proclamation to back up the news contained in flaring headlines and radio bulletins. With the premature rumor of ten days ago fresh in everyone's mind, and millions still mindful of the false armistice of 1918, there was widespread skepticism over the authenticity of the news.

By mid-afternoon loudspeakers were blaring into the ears of the exulting thousands in the amusement district the news that President Truman's proclamation was being held up by the necessity of coordinating it with the announcements from London and Moscow, and that the formal celebration of the long-awaited V-E Day would be delayed until today.

This sobering note gradually

Continued on Page 7, Column 6

SHAEF BAN ON AP LIFTED IN 6 HOURS

Action Comes After Protests From Newspapers and Public—Writer Still Barred

Suspension of filing facilities of The Associated Press in the European theatre was clamped on by Supreme Headquarters, Allied Expeditionary Forces (SHAEF), yesterday in an unprecedented action and was lifted six hours and twenty minutes later.

The ban was continued, however, on all copy submitted for clearance by Edward Kennedy, chief of the press association's staff on the Western Front, who sent the momentous story announcing Germany's final surrender in a dispatch from Reims, France, which was received in New York over the AP wires at 9:35 A. M. (EWT).

It was not until seven hours and fifty-five minutes had elapsed aft-

Continued on Page 4, Column 2

Summary of News of the War and German Surrender

TUESDAY, MAY 8, 1945

The war ended in Europe yesterday after five years, eight months and six days of the bloodiest conflict in history. Grand Admiral Karl Doenitz surrendered unconditonally to the Allies in a little red schoolhouse at Reims, France. At 8:41 P. M. Sunday, New York time, Col. Gen. Gustav Jodl signed for the enemy and Lieut. Gen. Walter Bedell Smith, General Eisenhower's Chief of Staff, for the Allies. In the absence of any official announcement there was some confusion as to the compliance with the surrender. Fighting had been going on in Czechoslovakia and nothing had been heard from German pockets along the French coast. [1:7-8.]

President Truman planned a broadcast from the White House at 9 o'clock this morning. Washington, gratified that the war in Europe was over, was confused by lack of confirmation. [2:2.]

Prime Minister Churchill will also broadcast at 9 A. M. from London and Premier Stalin is expected to make a simultaneous announcement in Moscow. King George will talk over the radio six hours later. [2:8.] London will celebrate V-E Day today, but, unable to restrain its joy, staged many impromptu celebrations yesterday. [2:7.]

Most New Yorkers took the news calmly and thankfully, sobered by realization that the war in the Pacific was far from over. There were, however, noisy outbursts in such centers as Times Square and Wall Street. Scrap paper showers fluttered from roofs and windows. [1:4-5.]

German Foreign Minister Lutz Schwerin von Krosigk broke the news to his people. The future will be difficult, he warned, and then added: "We must make right the basis of our nation. In our nation justice shall be the supreme law and the guiding principle. We must also recognize law as the basis of all relations between the nations." This sudden, complete reversal in German policy was received with skepticism by the Allies. [3:1.]

Perhaps one reason for this was the announcement from Moscow that 4,000,000 men, women and children had been done to death by gas, shooting, famine, poisoning and torture in the German extermination camp at Oswiecim, Poland. [12:5.]

The actual situation in Czechoslovakia was obscure. Late last night a Patriot broadcast said the Germans were negotiating with the Czechoslovak National Council details of surrender in Prague and Bohemia. Fighting had continued throughout yesterday and German planes had bombed public buildings and hospitals. [1:3; map P. 11.].

The United States Third Army continued its general advance into Czechoslovakia and the Fifth and Seventh Armies joined again in the Alps. The British Second Army moved to Denmark and Poles entered the shattered port of Wilhelmshaver [11:1.] Breslau fell to the Red Army after an eighty-four-day siege; 40,000 Germans were captured. [11:5.]

Japan accepted the surrender of her Axis partner with a statement that she never had expected German aid and would go on to victory without the Reich. [13:1.]

Infantry and marines on Okinawa scored another general advance after naval bombardment had pulverized Japanese strong points. Pacific Fleet planes sank or damaged thirteen more ships off Korea and Japan. [1:1; map, P. 12.] B-29's maintained their assault on Kyushu airfields. Two of the big planes were shot down. [14:3-4.]

On Tarakan Allied troops were within a mile and a half of the eastern shore. Americans gained on Mindanao and Luzon in the Philippines. [12:3-4.]

Foreign Commissar Molotoff said in San Francisco that unanimity on amendments to Dumbarton Oaks assured success of the conference. He declared that the Big Four consultations had ended. [1:2.]

GERMANS CAPITULATE ON ALL FRONTS

American, Russian and French Generals Accept Surrender in Eisenhower Headquarters, a Reims School

REICH CHIEF OF STAFF ASKS FOR MERCY

Doenitz Orders All Military Forces of Germany To Drop Arms—Troops in Norway Give Up—Churchill and Truman on Radio Today

By EDWARD KENNEDY
Associated Press Correspondent

REIMS, France, May 7—Germany surrendered unconditionally to the Western Allies and the Soviet Union at 2:41 A. M. French time today. [This was at 8:41 P. M., Eastern Wartime Sunday.]

The surrender took place at a little red schoolhouse that is the headquarters of Gen. Dwight D. Eisenhower.

The surrender, which brought the war in Europe to a formal end after five years, eight months and six days of bloodshed and destruction, was signed for Germany by Col. Gen. Gustav Jodl. General Jodl is the new Chief of Staff of the German Army.

The surrender was signed for the Supreme Allied Command by Lieut. Gen. Walter Bedell Smith, Chief of Staff for General Eisenhower.

It was also signed by Gen. Ivan Susloparoff for the Soviet Union and by Gen. Francois Sevez for France.

[The official Allied announcement will be made at 9 o'clock Tuesday morning when President Truman will broadcast a statement and Prime Minister Churchill will issue a V-E Day proclamation. Gen. Charles de Gaulle also will address the French at the same time.]

General Eisenhower was not present at the signing, but immediately afterward General Jodl and his fellow delegate, Gen. Admiral Hans Georg Friedeburg, were received by the Supreme Commander.

Germans Say They Understand Terms

They were asked sternly if they understood the surrender terms imposed upon Germany and if they would be carried out by Germany.

They answered Yes.

Germany, which began the war with a ruthless attack upon Poland, followed by successive aggressions and brutality in internment camps, surrendered with an appeal to the victors for mercy toward the German people and armed forces.

After having signed the full surrender, General Jodl said he wanted to speak and received leave to do so.

"With this signature," he said in soft-spoken German, "the German people and armed forces are for better or worse delivered into the victors' hands.

"In this war, which has lasted more than five years, both have achieved and suffered more than perhaps any other people in the world."

LONDON, May 7 (AP)—Complete victory in

Continued on Page 3, Columns 2 and 3

1945

People massed in New York City's Times Square to celebrate. There was not a frown to be found.

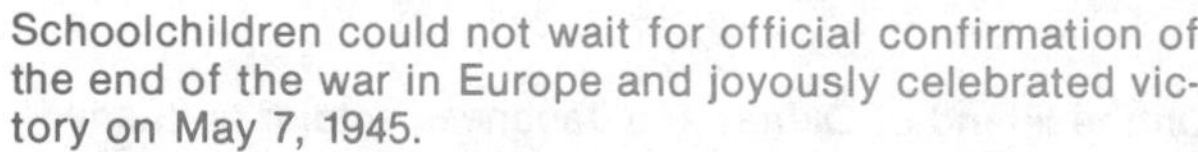

Schoolchildren could not wait for official confirmation of the end of the war in Europe and joyously celebrated victory on May 7, 1945.

Russian soldiers rushing to greet their American liberators.

U.S. Marines advance on Okinawa. Over 7,000 Americans died in battle on the island.

On the island of Okinawa, a Japanese soldier is flushed from a cave by a smoke grenade and surrenders to the Marines.

This church was used as a sniper's nest by the Japanese during fighting on Okinawa, the last real battle of the war.

"All the News That's Fit to Print"

The New York Times.

LATE CITY EDITION
Sunny and warm today. Tomorrow fair and warm.
Temperatures Yesterday—Max., 82; Min., 62
Sunrise today, 5:24 A. M.; Sunset, 8:31 P. M.

VOL. XCIV...No. 31,926. Entered as Second-Class Matter, Postoffice, New York, N. Y. NEW YORK, FRIDAY, JUNE 22, 1945. THREE CENTS IN NEW YORK CITY

OKINAWA IS OURS AFTER 82 DAYS; 45,029 U. S. CASUALTIES, FOE'S 94,401; GEN. STILWELL HEADS 10TH ARMY

HOUSE REPUBLICANS SEEK TO STRIP OPA OF FOOD CONTROLS

Leaders Act on Hoover Plan to Give Real Authority to the Secretary of Agriculture

'BUNGLING' IS CHARGED

Limitation to Six Months and Cost-Plus for Farms Are Expected to Fail

Special to THE NEW YORK TIMES.

WASHINGTON, June 21—Republican support for a reorganization of the price control structure along the lines suggested by former President Hoover developed today as the House ended two days of general debate on the Administration bill to extend the present price control act without change.

The Democratic and Republican leaders planned, with doubtful prospects of success, to seek a final vote tomorrow.

The "Hoover Plan," made public by the former President in a letter to Representative Jenkins of Ohio, was embodied by Mr. Jenkins in an amendment which would give the Secretary of Agriculture control over production, processing, distribution and pricing of food, and leaving to the Office of Price Administration only the routine mechanism of rationing.

There was a prospect that the Republicans in general would make their greatest effort to push through this amendment, hoping to recruit Democratic dissenters, particularly because the new Secretary of Agriculture, Representative Clinton P. Anderson of New Mexico, is an Administration Democrat popular with his colleagues.

Attacks Likely to Fail

It was indicated that the two other major attacks on continued price control as the Administration wants it would not succeed. These controls include the Wherry Senate amendment to guarantee farmers and stockmen a "cost-plus" price formula, and another amendment to limit the extension of the OPA to six months rather than a year.

The Democrats were especially anxious to reach a vote tomorrow. They fear that a postponement of the decision until Saturday might weaken their position by reducing their numbers on that customarily inactive day.

The day's debate found Administration speakers attacking the Wherry "cost-plus" amendment and the effort to limit OPA's extension to six months. Republican speakers, led by Representative Martin, the minority leader, attacked the administration of the Price Control Act.

Mr. Martin, asserting that "bungling and inefficiency" in OPA had been confirmed by the Democrats themselves, insisted that OPA, "right from the beginning has been run by crackpot theorists."

"And I am not referring," he added, "to the head man."

He continued:

"I will say," without publicly mentioning just what amendments he proposed to support, "that the situation has gone far enough. Congress has permitted this agency a free hand in the adoption of its regulations. We have given it every opportunity to order its affairs and to create a stable and sane method of operation which would guarantee to our people at least a minimum of the necessities of life."

Opposes Limited Extension

Representative Monroney of Oklahoma, a member of the House Banking Committee and a leader for the Administration in the fight over the bill, protested that an extension of OPA for only six months would "demoralize" the agency.

As to Republican claims of "unfairness" and poor administration in OPA, he declared the administration had in fact been "sensible" on the whole, adding:

"The umpire can't always call the plays in favor of your team."

Of the Wherry amendment, Mr. Monroney argued that it would be impossible to reach any agreed determination as to what was the legitimate "cost of production" of the farmers of the country, and that it would actually operate against the farmer's best interests by causing him to be blamed for "the devastating rise in prices" that would result.

He submitted a statement by Chester Bowles, head of OPA, declaring that the present act had ample provisions "to afford protection to farm producers."

Round-World Flight For Civilians Is Set

The round-the-world flight on commercial passenger planes of Pan American Airways in eighty-eight hours flying time on the resumption of post-war travel was announced yesterday by the Atlantic division of that organization, with headquarters at La Guardia Field. The cost of the flight was listed as $700, or less than the present round-trip rate to Europe.

Reservations have been made by eleven passengers, including several who have become nationally known as "pioneers" on first flights to new destinations.

The route from New York will cover Lisbon, Marseille, Rome, Athens, Cairo, Basra and Karachi to Calcutta of the Atlantic division, and then return via Bangkok, Canton, Tokyo, Paramushiru, Anchorage, Seattle and San Francisco to New York.

MEAT BETTERMENT PLEDGED BY TRUMAN

President Forecasts Single Control Over Prices, Food—Praises Trade Bill Passage

By The Associated Press.

OLYMPIA, Wash., June 21—President Truman promised improvement in the meat situation and forecast a single control over prices and food at a press conference today, his first outside the White House. After the conference he went on a salmon fishing trip.

The President wore a wool pull-over sweater borrowed from Gov. Mon C. Wallgren, who, with Senator Magnuson, Democrat, of Washington, sat in on the meeting. It was knitted by the Indians over on Vancouver Island, Mr. Truman explained.

The President also told reporters that he had expected the United Nations Conference to be a success; expressed confidence that Congress would pass the Bretton Woods monetary agreements as it had done with the reciprocal trade program, and called General Eisenhower a grand gentleman who is entitled to anything he wanted, adding that the President would see that he received it.

Mr. Truman spoke reassuringly of the food situation and added that the Administration was at work on a plan for single control over prices and food, but did not disclose how it would function.

Sees Meat Shortage Easing

He said that the meat shortage would automatically be straightened out as soon as Representative Anderson, Democrat, of New Mexico, took office as his new Secretary of Agriculture and War Food Administrator. The President asserted that it would have been straightened out under the contemplated program under Marvin Jones, retiring Food Administrator, as well.

He told a questioner he had not seen a statement of former President Hoover that food controls over meat distribution had broken down. He added that Mr. Hoover had been very helpful in his recent White House talk on the subject.

Saying that the San Francisco Conference seemed to have accomplished its purpose, the President pointed out that the delays were technical, involving translations into many languages which consumed time.

He said he would address the closing session Tuesday, leaving here Monday by plane, stopping over in Portland for a brief tour of the city, and flying on to San Francisco.

"The action of the Senate in ap-

Continued on Page 32, Column 5

7TH LOAN OVER TOP AT $15,982,000,000; E-BOND SALES LAG

On 39th Day of Drive Nation Passes Its Over-All Quota by Nearly 2 Billions

INDIVIDUAL GOAL IS NEAR

Both City and State Achieve Objectives in This Class—Further Effort Stressed

With the aid of heavy corporation investments, the Seventh War Loan drive surged yesterday past its $14,000,000,000 over-all national goal by almost $2,000,000,000, but the anti-inflationary E Bond Series scored up only two-thirds of quota, The Associated Press reported in Washington. Secretary of the Treasury Henry Morgenthau Jr. warned the nation that complete success would not be achieved until the total set for individuals had been reached.

Both New York State and City surpassed their quotas for individual sales, but local War Finance Committee officials feared they might fail to meet their separate goals in E Bonds by the campaign deadline June 30.

On the thirty-ninth day since the drive opened May 14, total sales throughout the country climbed to $15,982,000,000. Of that sum corporation sales accounted for $9,782,000,000 and individual sales for $6,200,000,000. Each category had a quota of $7,000,000,000.

In contrast to that, sales of E Bonds, the popular securities for small investors, had reached a total of only $2,779,000,000 of the $4,000,000,000 goal.

Morgenthau Hails Achievement

Commenting on the progress of the drive, Secretary Morgenthau said it was "most gratifying to the Treasury" but that it meant corporations had passed their quota. A large job remained to be done, he noted, before the final accounting period ends July 7.

"Reports reaching me give me every confidence that our $7,000,000,000 goal for individuals will be met by that date," he added.

Frederick W. Gehle, New York chairman of the War Finance Committee, announced that the State had exceeded its goal of $1,134,000,000 for sales to individuals. The total—$1,139,200,000—constituted a new record in war financing for New York, he said.

But, with E Bond sales continuing in a "slump," New Yorkers faced the possibility that their purchases of that series would be insufficient to meet the city and State drive quotas, he pointed out.

"This fact," he commented, "increasingly evident during the past week, means that unless subscribers put forth greater effort than at any time during the war, the current campaign, in so far as the vitally important, anti-inflationary E Bonds are concerned, will fall short of full success. The factor that counts most is represented in E Bonds and not enough people are buying them."

67.1 Per Cent of E Bonds Sold Here

To date $192,707,215 in E Bonds has been sold in the city, which is 67.1 per cent of the $287,300,000 quota. All sales to individuals amounted to $12,695,613 on Wednesday, bringing the drive total in this group to $892,986,250, or 105.4 per cent of the local goal of $847,430,000.

All investors purchases—including corporate and financial institutions—totaled cumulatively $2,535,049,837, or 74.2 per cent of the

Continued on Page 32, Column 7

Okinawa Costliest Of Pacific Battles

By The Associated Press.

GUAM, Friday, June 22—The conquest of Okinawa was the longest and costliest of all the campaigns in the central and western Pacific.

With casualty figures still incomplete, the toll of enemy and American killed, captured and wounded all but equals the grand total of casualties in six major campaigns which led up to Okinawa.

The eighty-two days it took to break all organized resistance dwarfs the twenty-six days of Iwo Island. The latter, however, is less than eight square miles in area, and Okinawa is roughly 485 square miles.

The figures for Okinawa, which include Japanese casualties through June 20 and American casualties only through June 19, compared with those of six other campaigns follow:

	Japanese Killed	Japanese Captured	American Killed	American Wounded
Okinawa	90,401	4,000	11,260	33,769
Iwo	23,244	1,038	4,630	15,308
Saipan	27,586	2,161	3,426	13,099
Guam	17,442	524	1,437	5,648
Palau	13,354	435	1,302	6,115
Tarawa	5,000	150	913	2,037
Tinian	6,939	523	314	1,515

Note: Figures for Americans killed include missing.

LONDON IS PICKED AS INTERIM SEAT

Connally and Vandenberg Will Speak in Senate Two Days After Conference Adjourns

By JOHN H. CRIDER

Special to THE NEW YORK TIMES.

SAN FRANCISCO, June 21—The United Nations Conference selected London, the "nursery" of the League of Nations, as the site for meetings of the committee which will do the planning to put life into the new world organization, as it became known today that the effort in the Senate for ratification of the new charter would start two days after the conference adjourns on Tuesday.

Senator Tom Connally of Texas, chairman of the Foreign Relations Committee, and Senator Arthur H. Vandenberg of Michigan, the two Senate representatives of the United States delegation, will make speeches Thursday, the day after they arrive by air in Washington from this conference.

Persons close to Senator Vandenberg said they were convinced

Continued on Page 8, Column 2

OKINAWA CONQUEST EXPANDS OUR ATTACKING RADIUS

JAPANESE HELD AREAS

June 22, 1945

With the end of the campaign on the chief island of the Ryukyu group (1), southern Japan is brought within reach of our fighter-bombers and virtually the entire enemy empire within reach of our long-range aircraft. Already apprehensive over the next American step, the enemy reported that planes had scouted Kyushu (2) and southern Honshu (3). B-29's attacked the latter island. On the Asiatic mainland the Chinese advanced thirty-one miles beyond Wenchow (4).

AUSTRALIANS SEIZE BORNEO OIL PLANT

Make New Surprise Landing in Lutong Area, 80 Miles South of Brunei Bay

By The United Press.

MANILA, Friday, June 22—Australian Ninth Division troops have landed unopposed in Borneo's Lutong oil refinery area, eighty miles down the west coast from Brunei Bay, and dispatches from the front today said that the Australians already had captured the important refinery there—potentially the most productive in the British Empire.

Gen. Douglas MacArthur announced the new amphibious operation—this one aimed at the heart of northern Borneo's rich oil industry. A dispatch from the front said the Australians sent pa-

Continued on Page 2, Column 6

'Vinegar Joe' in Command Of Okinawa's Conquerors

By The United Press.

MANILA, Friday, June 22—Gen. Joseph W. Stilwell has been named to lead the triumphant United States Tenth Army, conquerors of Okinawa, to new battles against the Japanese, it was announced today. The disclosure was made on the very day that Fleet Admiral Chester W. Nimitz announced the complete victory on Okinawa.

General Stilwell was appointed by Army Gen. Douglas MacArthur, acting in his capacity of commander of all United States Army forces in the Pacific. He succeeds the late Lieut. Gen. Simon Bolivar Buckner, who was killed last Monday on Okinawa by a Japanese shell. The new command lifts General Stilwell out of his post as Commander of Army Ground Forces in the United States and gives him an active combat command in the field, which virtually guarantees that he will be one of the leading figures in the final destruction of Japan.

General Stilwell already is in the Pacific and has been inspecting battle conditions on northern Luzon.

The Tenth Army comprises veteran units of the Pacific fighting, including the First, Second and Sixth Marine Divisions, and the Ninety-sixth, Seventy-seventh, Twenty-seventh and Seventh Infantry Divisions.

General Stilwell is a veteran of the Burma and China fighting. He speaks several Chinese dialects. Up until last Oct. 28 he was commander of United States forces in the China-Burma-India theatre, Chief of Staff to Generalissimo Chiang Kai-shek and deputy to British Ad-

Continued on Page 2, Column 2

450 B-29'S SMASH TARGETS IN HONSHU

Kure Arsenal Is Main Site of 3,000-Ton Explosive Blow—Foe Sees Invasion Move

By Wireless to THE NEW YORK TIMES.

GUAM, Friday, June 22—Six important industrial targets in Japan, headed by the Kure naval arsenal, one of the two most important naval arsenals in Japan, were hit today in a daylight strike by a large force of approximately 450 American "Superforts," operating from bases in the Marianas.

Earlier the Tokyo radio had linked recent air strikes to preliminary operations for an invasion of Japan.

The Kure arsenal, plus the Hiro arsenal, which was virtually destroyed in a B-29 strike on May 5, furnished the weapons and the powder for the Japanese.

There is not much of a Japanese fleet left, but what there is, we are out to deprive of supplies.

The "bombs away" signal over the six separate targets came in

Continued on Page 3, Column 3

ISLE DECLARED WON

1,700 Japanese Troops Surrender Last Day of Bitter Battle

OTHERS JUMP INTO SEA

Great Base That Opens All of Japan to U. S. Attack Already in Operation

By WARREN MOSCOW

By Wireless to THE NEW YORK TIMES.

GUAM, Friday, June 22—The battle of Okinawa is officially at an end. In a special communiqué issued at 10 o'clock last night, Fleet Admiral Chester W. Nimitz reported the end of organized resistance, and in a second one this morning he told of mopping-up operations.

Today's communiqué revealed how costly has been the price for the island for which we battled for eighty-two days. United States casualties so far disclosed amount to 45,029, and they are sufficiently far behind to indicate that the island bastion, four hundred statute miles from Japan, will have cost nearly 50,000 men in dead, missing and wounded from United States Army, Navy and Marine forces.

The cost of the Okinawa campaign was twice the toll of bloody Iwo, up to Okinawa the most costly of all our Pacific campaigns.

90,401 Japanese Killed

Through June 19 we had lost 6,990 men killed or missing in the land operations from the Army and marines and had 29,598 wounded for a total of 36,588.

The fleet losses, far higher than in any other campaign, have not been announced past May 23, almost a month ago. At that time 4,270 sailors had been killed or were missing and 4,171 wounded. This brings the Okinawa casualties to 45,029. It is likely that a month's fleet losses and the last two days of organized resistance plus what comes from mopping up will carry the total to the 50,000 mark.

The Okinawa campaign cost the Japanese around 94,401. Of these, 90,401 had been killed on Okinawa or in the Kerama Islands or on Ie Island, the three major battlegrounds of the Ryukyus campaign. About 4,000 Japanese had been captured up to last night, with the number growing rapidly. About 1,700 gave up yesterday alone.

The communiqué that announced the end of Okinawa resistance was brief and to the point. Issued at 10 P. M., Guam time, last night, it read:

"After eighty-two days of fighting, the battle of Okinawa has been won. Organized resistance ceased on June 21. Remnants of the enemy garrison in two small pockets in the southern portion of the island are being mopped up."

"Well Done," Says Nimitz

The communiqué was No. 400, issued from Pacific Fleet Headquarters. Ironically, the first communiqué, issued on June 4, 1942, told of the beginning of the Battle of Midway in the form of an announcement of a Japanese air attack on that island. Previously communiqués had been issued from Washington. That battle was the high watermark of the Japanese advance in the Pacific.

Shortly after telling of the end, Admiral Nimitz sent a "well done" to the officers and men under his command. It read as follows:

"To officers and men of all United States armed forces of the Pacific Ocean areas and of the British Pacific Fleet who have had their part in achieving this important victory, well done."

Communiqué No. 401, issued this morning at 10 o'clock, revealed that Japanese resistance ceased first in the Marine Corps sector of the island at 10:27 yesterday morning, Okinawa time. Two small pockets were still being cleaned up in the Army sector last night. All over the island's southern tip our troop movements were being hampered by the Okinawan civilians, who had been living underground

Continued on Page 3, Column 3

Queen Mary Never Saw a Torpedo As She Roamed Seven Seas Alone

By GEORGE HORNE

The role of the Atlantic liner Queen Mary at war is a story of high adventure—the tale of a ship with a charmed life.

It is one that should be spun from the rich memory of Sir James Gordon Partridge Bisset, K.B.E., commodore of the Cunard White Star Line, who stood on the bridge of the towering sea giant for more than three years, coursing the seven seas across the Atlantic, and from the Clyde to Sydney, from Halifax to the storm-wracked Cape, to Singapore, Bombay and Trincomalee.

And spun it was yesterday by Sir James himself, a stocky man with a bit of a roll to his gait and a rich mingling in his speech of the original Scottish burr with the salty sea jargon that knows no nationality.

"I was born in Liverpool of a Scot family," he said, stating first things first.

"I'm half Scotch and half soda," he went on, and then quickly corrected himself, "English, I mean."

Sir James loves the Queen Mary, and well he might. She has traveled 600,000 miles in the war, delivering 500,000 American soldiers where their generals wanted them to be, and another 100,000 British troops in addition. She has carried a heavy armament of fifty or sixty guns, some of them manned by

Continued on Page 6, Column 2

War News Summarized

FRIDAY, JUNE 22, 1945.

Okinawa has been conquered by infantrymen and marines of the United States Tenth Army, backed by the guns and planes of the Pacific Fleet. Fighting, except for two small pockets around Medeera and Mabuni, ended yesterday on the eighty-second day of the invasion. Through Wednesday 90,401 Japanese had been killed and 4,000 taken prisoner. Tenth Army casualties to the day before were 6,990 killed and missing, 29,598 wounded. Pacific Fleet casualties to May 24 were 4,270 killed and missing, 4,171 wounded. [1:8.]

There was no final "banzai" charge by fanatical Japanese; to the contrary, the enemy at the end surrendered in unprecedented numbers. The campaign, started on Easter Sunday, April 1, was the most bitterly fought and costliest in the Pacific war. Rapid progress has been made in converting the island into a major base for future operations. [3:1.]

General MacArthur has appointed General Stilwell to succeed the late Lieutenant General Buckner in command of the Tenth Army. General Stilwell, who was in the Pacific on an inspection tour as Commander of Ground Forces, may lead an invasion of China or head an Army group against Japan. [1:6-7.]

In China Japanese troops were chased thirty-one miles up the coast from Wenchow, with indications that the enemy was abandoning the entire coast between Canton and Ningpo. Three Chinese columns were closing in on Liuchow. [2:1.]

Australians hopped eighty miles down the Borneo coast to land unopposed at Lutong in the heart of the Seria-Miri oil refining center. [1:5; map P. 2.] Filipino guerrillas captured Tuguegarao, capital of Cagayan Province, fifty miles south of Aparri, thus splitting the enemy forces. [3:6-7.]

B-29's switched to heavy explosives yesterday; great numbers dropped heavy loads on military and industrial targets on Honshu, Japan's main island. Tokyo continued to forecast an early American invasion. [1:7.]

Senator Kilgore declared that secret documents had revealed detailed plans by German industrialists to rearm the Reich for another attempt at world conquest, and the intention to finance an underground Nazi movement. Field Marshal Montgomery, from his headquarters in Germany, said members of the German General Staff would be kept in isolated prisons outside the country until militarism was broken up and that SS troops would be imprisoned for twenty years. [1:6-7.]

Yugoslavia, submitting a detailed report on 10,000 Fascist crimes, asked for the surrender of General Mikhailovitch and protested against the lenient treatment of Italian war criminals. [4:4-5.] Crowds in Milan demonstrated for a severe purge of Fascists and demanded more food and jobs. [4:3.]

German Staff to Be Kept in Exile; Kilgore Reports Third War Plot

By The United Press.

TWENTY-FIRST ARMY GROUP HEADQUARTERS, Germany, June 21—The Allies plan to stamp out German militarism by imprisoning the German General Staff in isolated camps outside Germany and holding all SS troops in North German camps for the next twenty years, Field Marshal Sir Bernard L. Montgomery announced today.

He did not state how long the officers of the German General Staff would be held, but he left no doubt of the Allies' determination to make sure that there was an end to Germany's ceaseless planning of wars and world conquest. The General Staff, which remained

Continued on Page 6, Column 4

Special to THE NEW YORK TIMES.

WASHINGTON, June 21—Secret documents not presently identifiable as to source show that German industrialists last August laid plans for re-industrialization and rearming of Germany after the expected defeat, Senator Harley M. Kilgore of West Virginia asserted today.

Mr. Kilgore, who recently returned from a trip to Europe in his capacity as chairman of the war mobilization subcommittee of the Senate Military Affairs Committee, released an analysis of the documents to the press.

"Masquerading as 'neutral' business men without political allegiance," he asserted, "they [the Ger-

Continued on Page 6, Column 6

"All the News That's Fit to Print"

The New York Times.

LATE CITY EDITION
Sunny and warm today. Showers and warmer tomorrow.
Temperatures Yesterday—Max., 76; Min., 67
Sunrise today, 5:26 A. M.; Sunset, 8:32 P. M.

Copyright, 1945, by The New York Times Company.

VOL. XCIV..No. 31,931. Entered as Second-Class Matter, Postoffice, New York, N. Y. NEW YORK, WEDNESDAY, JUNE 27, 1945. THREE CENTS IN NEW YORK CITY

TRUMAN CLOSES UNITED NATIONS CONFERENCE WITH PLEA TO TRANSLATE CHARTER INTO DEEDS; B-29'S KEEP UP ASSAULT ON HONSHU PLANTS

TWO BLOWS IN DAY

50 'Superforts' Batter Oil Works Few Hours After Strike by 500

TOP REFINERY IS HIT

Five Bombers Lost, 70 Reach Iwo From the Earlier Japan Mission

By The Associated Press.

GUAM, Wednesday, June 27 — Nearly fifty B-29's struck the Utsube River oil refinery on Honshu, Japan's principal producer of aviation gasoline, in a precision demolition attack before midnight last night.

The attack followed by half a day the greatest Superfortress demolition assault to date, a pin-pointing of Honshu industries in which nearly 500 of the sky giants blasted ten enemy war factories with 3,000 tons of bombs.

[Twentieth Air Force headquarters in Washington reported five B-29's missing after the earlier Tuesday assault, which it said hit "the largest number of individual military and industrial targets yet attacked on a single Superfortress mission."

[Twenty-first Bomber Command crews reported "good to excellent" results in the multiple attack. They met slight Japanese fighter opposition and meager anti-aircraft fire.]

Refinery Damaged Previously

The Utsube refinery is located near Yokkaichi, eighteen miles southwest of Nagoya on Ise Bay. Since the destruction of Japanese fuel centers at Tokuyama and Otake by B-29's on May 10, the Utsube plant was the enemy's largest remaining producer of aviation gasoline.

The city of Yokkaichi was heavily damaged in an incendiary assault June 18. Some fire bombs fell into the Utsube refinery area in that attack, causing slight damage to the plant, but last night's strike was the first with the Utsube plant and storage area as the primary objective.

Ice-coated, as the result of soupy weather on their great demolition strike, more than seventy B-29's of the huge fleet in the early Tuesday attack made emergency landings on Iwo Island, the Twenty-first Bomber Command reported.

At one time Superfortresses were stacked in circles above our

Continued on Page 2, Column 6

Generalissimo Rank For Stalin Indicated

By The Associated Press.

LONDON, June 26—The Presidium of the Supreme Soviet conferred its four highest awards today on Premier Joseph Stalin and created a new rank of generalissimo to be given "for particularly outstanding services to the motherland in the task of commanding all armed forces of the state during war," Moscow said tonight.

The broadcast did not say who would be named generalissimo, but the requirement given for this highest possible military rank seemed to indicate that Marshal Stalin might receive it.

The principal decoration conferred upon the Russian leader was the Order of Victory "for exceptional services in the organization of all the armed forces of the Soviet Union and for skillful leadership of these forces in the great patriotic war, which ended in full victory over Hitlerite Germany."

He received the Hero of the Soviet Union medal as the Marshal "who headed the Red Army in defense of our motherland and its capital, Moscow, and with exceptional courage directed the struggle against Hitlerite Germany." He also received the Order of Lenin and the Gold Star.

New Invasion Attack Near South of Japan, Tokyo Says

Enemy Reports Our Convoys Moving North From Okinawa and Speculates That Upper Ryukyus May Be Goal

By The United Press.

WASHINGTON, June 26—Tokyo hinted tonight that a new United States invasion blow was impending against the northern Ryukyus, 180 miles south of Kyushu. An invasion fleet of some 200 transports, cruisers, destroyers and a battleship was moving northward along both coasts of Okinawa, Japanese broadcasts said, as recorded by the Federal Communications Commission.

[The Tokyo radio reported Tuesday night that Allied troops had landed on Kume Island, fifty miles west of Okinawa, according to The Associated Press. Later, a Japanese Domei agency broadcast said "the Japanese garrison intercepted the enemy and heavy fighting is now in progress." The broadcast, recorded by the Federal Communications Commission, referred to the Kume invasion as a "fresh landing."]

At the same time it was speculated that the Americans needed still more "stepping-stone" bases before carrying out their "certain" invasion of the home islands.

A Yomiuri Hochi newspaper dispatch quoted by Tokyo asserted that Amami and Kikai Islands, 180 miles south of Kyushu, had been chosen as the objectives of the next landing attempts. The two islands lie side by side 110 miles north of Okinawa, at the end of the Ryukyu chain.

"Apparently the enemy intends to make Okinawa the main base for the invasion of the Japanese homeland," the correspondent wrote. "Large amounts of war material are being poured into Okinawa from the Philippines and the Marianas."

However, he added, the Americans will need 500,000 to 1,000,000 men to carry out an invasion of the home islands and auxiliary bases will be needed to debark and quarter them, as well as to move

Continued on Page 3, Column 2

GOLDSTEIN, O'DWYER TO BE UNOPPOSED IN THE PRIMARIES

Surpless Withdraws Despite Having More Than Enough Backing to Enter Race

MANY DEMOCRATIC FIGHTS

Six Candidacies for Public Office and 10 Leaderships in Tammany Involved

General Sessions Judge Jonah J. Goldstein of Manhattan and District Attorney William O'Dwyer of Brooklyn were assured uncontested nominations for Mayor yesterday as the deadline for filing designations was reached at 5 P. M. without the appearance of any opposition petitions. There still remained a remote possibility that opposition petitions might be placed in the mails before midnight.

The last threat of primary opposition to Judge Goldstein was removed earlier in the day when George H. Ittleman announced that Magistrate Abner C. Surpless of Brooklyn would not make a contest for the Republican nomination despite the fact that more than enough signatures had been collected to enter him in the race. Mr. Ittleman had been serving as chairman of the Surpless campaign committee.

O'Dwyer's Mates in Clear

Mr. O'Dwyer was without opposition from the start for the Democratic and American Labor nominations, and there were no last minute surprises in this respect yesterday.

An appearance of opposition to Mr. O'Dwyer's running mates on the Democratic and Labor party tickets, Vincent R. Impellitteri for President of the Council and State Senator Lazarus Joseph for Controller, was created through the filing of the Queens Democratic designating petitions bearing the names of other candidates for these offices. But the Queens candidates have already signed declinations that will be filed before the Friday deadline and Mr. Im-

Continued on Page 8, Column 2

INDIANS IN ACCORD ON WAVELL BASIS

Viceroy's Plan for a Regime Almost Entirely Native Is Accepted by Conferees

By TILLMAN DURDIN

By Wireless to The New York Times.

SIMLA, India, June 26—Today's conference between the Viceroy, Field Marshal Viscount Wavell, and Indian political leaders is authoritatively understood to have agreed to the overall acceptance of the Wavell plan for the formation of a new central government for India almost entirely Indian in composition.

This acceptance of the main principle of the Wavell proposals represents a big stride toward a successful outcome for the "little round table" sessions here and hopes are high that full accord will be reached. Difficult problems remain to be settled, however, and these may still wreck the conference.

Probably the main unsolved problem is the allocation of posts in the new government among the various political and religious groups. In accepting the Wavell proposals, the conference members agreed on parity between caste Hindus and Moslems in the new government, but it is still to be decided whether all the Moslems will be members of Mohammed Ali Jinnah's Moslem League or whether all caste Hindus will be representatives of the Congress party.

Other Problems Canvassed

After assembling at 11 o'clock this morning, the conference adjourned at 12:30 and issued a brief statement saying provisional agreement had been reached on certain main principles and that the conference had adjourned to enable the delegates to consider the remaining problems in private discussions outside the conference chamber.

It was decided to meet again tomorrow morning. This afternoon the Congress party delegates conferred with Mohandas K. Gandhi and Moslem League leaders held separate talks. Later Pandit Govind Vallabh Pant, one of the Congress party delegates, visited Mr. Jinnah in the latter's hotel room, where it is assumed the problem of apportioning posts in the new government was discussed.

In addition to accepting the Wavell plan providing for equal numbers of caste Hindus and Moslems among the Ministers of the proposed new Government, it was learned, the conference agreed on other important points, all stated outright or implied in Viscount Wavell's recent broadcast of his proposals.

It was decided that the new Government's Cabinet or Executive Council, as it is called, would

Continued on Page 4, Column 4

2 JAPANESE CHIEFS OKINAWA SUICIDES

Generals Stabbed Themselves in Formal Ceremony on Cliff —Aides Hastened Deaths

By The United Press.

OKINAWA, June 26—The bodies of Lieut. Gen. Mitsuru Ushijima, Japanese commander in chief on Okinawa, and his chief of staff, Lieut. Gen. Isama Cho, were found yesterday in shallow graves on the southern sea cliff where they had been taken after a dramatic harakiri ceremony.

The two generals had decided to kill themselves June 21 when their last stronghold, an elaborate system of inter-connecting caves on Mabuni ridge, had been surrendered, according to a prisoner of war.

The prisoner, who had been

Continued on Page 4, Column 3

War News Summarized

WEDNESDAY, JUNE 27, 1945

The United Nations Conference in San Francisco ended its work at 8:39 last night, completing a historic nine weeks of deliberations designed to give nations security, peoples liberty and the world peace. Adjournment came at the close of President Truman's speech, which followed signing by the fifty nations present of the Charter of the United Nations. [1:6-7.]

"You have won a victory against war itself," Mr. Truman told the conferees, and have just created "a solid structure upon which we can build a better world." But this is only a first step, he emphasized, adding: "If we fail to use it we shall betray all those who have died in order that we might meet here in freedom and safety to create it."

No nation or group can expect special privileges and all must make sacrifices for the Charter to work, Mr. Truman said. He pointed out that powerful nations have "no right to dominate the world" but must "assume the responsibility for leadership toward a world of peace," resolved that "power and strength shall be used not to wage war, but to keep the world at peace and free from the fear of war."

Fascism did not die with Mussolini nor nazism with Hitler, the President declared, and the forces of tyranny are even now trying to undermine the Allied unity that made the Charter possible. [All the foregoing 1:8.]

President Truman will personally present the Charter to the Senate on Monday and urge prompt ratification. Opposition strength was estimated at twelve to fifteen votes [1:7.]

Allied forces in the Pacific stuck to their job of defeating Japan. B-29's hit the main enemy home island of Honshu again. The city of Yokkaichi, near Nagoya, was bombed during the night only a few hours after a massive attack upon ten key factories, the largest number of such targets hit on a single B-29 mission. [1:1; map, P. 2.]

Two American columns in Luzon's Cagayan Valley were less than twenty miles from closing a trap on the Japanese between Tuguegarao and the north. [2:6.] Capture of Miri by Australians completed the reconquest of west Borneo oilfields. Allied planes concentrated on Macassar Strait targets. [4:2, with map.] Chinese forces were within 165 miles of Shanghai. [2:8, with map.]

Tokyo, still fearing invasion, declared Allied landings were imminent on Amami and Kikai, between Okinawa and the home islands. Twelve Japanese planes were shot down in a futile attack on Okinawa. [1:2-3.]

In Europe it appeared that the American plan for mass trial of war criminals by an international military tribunal would be approved by the four-power conference. [6:4.] The Big Three may discuss Russia's proposal to ease restrictions on use of the Dardanelles. [7:3-6.] The London Poles will refuse to cede authority until a new Government is chosen at free elections. [6:1.]

All factions in India were reported to have accepted in principle the new British proposals for a revised central Government, including parity of caste Hindus and Moslems. [1:2.]

PRESIDENT WITNESSES SIGNING OF SECURITY PACT

Mr. Truman looking on as Secretary of State Stettinius affixes his name to the document

100,000 HOMES HERE FACE HIGHER RENTS

U. S. Court Order on Luxury Apartments Scored by Mayor —OPA Weighs Next Step

By LEE E. COOPER

One hundred thousand families in the New York area who pay $100 or more a month in rent are subject to higher charges under the decision handed down on Monday by the United States Emergency Court of Appeals, holding rent for the so-called luxury type of living quarters to be "inadequate" under present ceilings, a study of rental records showed last night. Nearly 50,000 of these higher-rent suites are in Manhattan, and about 8 per cent of the apartments there are affected by the order.

While officials of the Office of Price Administration were considering whether they should grant an increase without further ado or try a court appeal, it was reported in authoritative circles that if the former course of action were followed the OPA order probably would not call for much more than a 5 per cent rise in the higher-priced suites.

Rentals of $99 or less are not affected by the order, and even for the "luxury" apartments and hotel suites present rentals will apply until the OPA acts. The appeals court gave the rent officials thirty days, or until July 25, to comply with its decision.

Reactions to the Decision

Mixed reactions and some uncertainty followed announcement of the decision, which applies to all of New York City, Nassau and Suffolk Counties.

Mayor La Guardia, who had opposed the appeal by the Metropolitan Fair Rent Committee and other representatives of landlords for a blanket rise of 10 per cent on rent for housing here, expressed disappointment over the court's position.

"I don't like it," he commented. "From the facts submitted, I do not believe the finding is warranted. Here we broke our backs to reduce realty taxes, and immediately the rents are raised. The court is wrong!"

Spokesmen for several realty organizations expressed gratification, but contended that the decision did not go far enough and that increases were in order also for apartments renting for less than $100, on the ground that operating costs and other charges had risen for all types of buildings. OPA executives expressed the view that the ruling was a victory for rent control because present ceilings and the general purposes of control were upheld and the order for a rise affected "only a small per-

Continued on Page 36, Column 3

Nation After Nation Sees Era Of Peace in Signing Charter

By LAWRENCE E. DAVIES

Special to The New York Times.

SAN FRANCISCO, June 26—A Charter drawn to give the world a new start on the way to lasting peace was signed today by the men and women from fifty nations who had fashioned it during nine weeks of laborious effort. They sat, one at a time, at a huge round table, autographing their handiwork while newsreel and newspaper camera men recorded the event for millions, now and later, to see and hear. Great spotlights, focused on the signers and their surroundings, made the scene in the Veterans Building look like a Hollywood movie set.

To China, first of the United Nations to suffer attack by a member of the Axis, went the honor of signing first. Dr. V. K. Wellington Koo, Chungking's Ambassador to the Court of St. James, using his country's writing brush, inscribed his name at noon in two freshly printed and freshly bound volumes, one containing the text of the Charter and the statute of the New International Court of Justice and the other authority for a preparatory commission to begin at once the enormous task of getting the new league functioning.

Signing Schedule Changed

The Big Powers began the day's work, with the United States, as the host nation, listed in the official advance order as the last signer. As things worked out, however, Russia, led by Ambassador Andrei A. Gromyko, followed China, with the United Kingdom third and Argentina slipping in ahead of France.

And the delegates of the United States, instead of waiting for the

Continued on Page 11, Column 6

TRUMAN WILL HAND CHARTER TO SENATE

President Will Speak Before Chamber Monday — Plans for Ratification Pushed

By C. P. TRUSSELL

Special to The New York Times.

WASHINGTON, June 26—President Truman will personally present the Charter, signed today at the United Nations Conference, to the Senate on Monday in one of the rare appearances of a Chief Executive before a single chamber of Congress.

As he presents the pledge of international collaboration to secure the peace and block future aggressions, the President will make a statement to the Senate, whose function it will be to ratify its provisions.

These plans came to light at the Capitol today as the Senate and the House, while grappling with war and administrative appropriations, followed as closely as they could the concluding proceedings at San Francisco and looked to the first-hand reports which are to be made to the Senate by its own rep-

Continued on Page 10, Column 2

Storm Skirts City and Goes to Sea, Giving Relief From the Heat Wave

After two days of mild apprehension over a tropical storm that was swinging erratically northward along the Atlantic Coast, New York City unexpectedly enjoyed its most agreeable recent weather yesterday, as the storm veered out to sea. Only cooling winds and storm warnings for small craft marked its passing in this area.

Temperatures, as a result, touched a high of only 74 degrees in midafternoon, compared with 90 on Monday. The mean temperature was 72—one degree above the normal of 71 for the date—but the humidity was in the 80's most of the day.

Benjamin Parry, meteorologist in charge of the Weather Bureau here, announced in the forenoon that the storm would skirt the city. At that time it appeared likely, however, that New York would have stiff winds and rain most of the day.

Instead, the storm center plowed steadily northeastward at about twenty miles an hour, passing some seventy miles east of Nantucket last evening. The winds here did not reach their expected maximum velocity of thirty miles an hour until just before 6 P. M. The steady rain mentioned in earlier forecasts did not materialize.

Sunny, warm weather, with the highest temperature near 80 and with moderate northerly winds was the forecast for today. For tomorrow the Weather Bureau foresaw showers and warmer weather.

NEW WORLD HOPE

President Hails 'Great Instrument of Peace, Insists It Be Used

HISTORIC LANDMARK

Meeting Gives Standing Ovation as Executive Pictures Peace Gain

President's address, Page 10; other texts, Pages 12, 13 and 14.

By JOHN H. CRIDER

Special to The New York Times.

SAN FRANCISCO, June 26—The United Nations Conference ended at 5:28 this afternoon with a demand by President Truman to translate the lofty words of the new world Charter into worthy deeds ringing in the ears of the delegates from fifty nations.

The conference had presented to the world for the second time in three decades the outlines of machinery for the maintenance of world peace — better machinery, all of the speakers at the closing session agreed, than it had ever had before. But, as President Truman admonished in his address closing the conference, "the world must now use it."

"If we fail to use it," he declared to the solemn final meeting of the delegates, "we shall betray all those who have died in order that we might meet here in freedom and safety to create it.

"If we seek to use it selfishly—for the advantage of any one nation or any small group of nations—we shall be equally guilty of that betrayal."

Fervent Interpolation

The President, speaking in the auditorium of the War Memorial Opera House, built in memory of sons of the Golden Gate city who gave their lives in the first World War, in which he himself had served, seemed to give unconscious expression to the solemn feeling of the occasion when, at the outset of his speech, he interpolated the words, half a hope, half a prayer:

"Oh, what a great day this can be in history!"

Just before the plenary session the President accompanied the eight United States delegates to the auditorium of the Veterans' Memorial Building to witness their signing of the new world security Charter.

The signing had not been completed by the time of the closing session and, for the President to witness the United States signatures, the American delegates were permitted to sign out of turn, after Nicaragua, at about 3:15. The United States was the thirty-eighth nation to sign, leaving twelve to sign. Signing was completed at 7:20.

The plenary session began at 3:50 with three bangs of the gavel by Secretary Stettinius, presiding. The President, while waiting to make the closing speech, sat, tight-lipped, reading the English versions of speeches given in seven languages which preceded his in the two-hour final session.

The President's voice had been heard once before, when he opened the conference nine weeks ago with an address delivered by wire from Washington.

Points Stressed in Speech

Points he emphasized most strongly today were:

That this Charter is only a beginning—"our thinking and all our actions must be based on the realization that it is in fact only a first step."

That the Charter is no more perfect than was our own Constitution, it must be made to live.

That the fact there is a charter, in view of the diversity of interests, "is a great wonder" for which we should give "profound thanksgiving to Almighty God."

The differences which developed at this conference, he said, were resolved in the democratic way,

Continued on Page 11, Column 2

Ray Milland in the haunting film *The Lost Weekend.* Hollywood was becoming more realistic in its treatment of human faults.

Hurd Hatfield and George Sanders in *The Picture of Dorian Gray.*

Robert Walker and Judy Garland in *The Clock,* a film about a New York girl who meets and marries a soldier who is on a 48-hour leave.

Humphrey Bogart married Lauren Bacall . . .

Bess Myerson was crowned Miss America . . .

and Dizzy Gillespie characterized the new sound of 'be-bop'.

"All the News That's Fit to Print"

The New York Times.

LATE CITY EDITION
Fair, warm and less humid today and tomorrow.
Temperatures Yesterday—Max., 85; Min., 68
Sunrise today, 5:47 A. M.; Sunset, 8:17 P. M.

Copyright, 1945, by The New York Times Company.

VOL. XCIV..No. 31,961. Entered as Second-Class Matter, Postoffice, New York, N. Y. NEW YORK, FRIDAY, JULY 27, 1945. THREE CENTS NEW YORK CITY

CHURCHILL IS DEFEATED IN LABOR LANDSLIDE; ATTLEE PROMISES PROSECUTION OF PACIFIC WAR; ALLIES ORDER JAPAN TO QUIT OR BE DESTROYED

SUSPENDED OPA MAN ACCUSES WOOLLEY OF INTERFERENCE

Ross Alleges Chief Hampered Enforcement in the Milk and Cigarette Drives

DEMANDS PUBLIC HEARING

Makes His Counter-Charges at Last Minute in 25,000-Word Reply in Dismissal Action

By CHARLES GRUTZNER Jr.

The twice-deferred showdown over maladministration of price control in this five-State area was made public yesterday when Paul L. Ross, suspended regional enforcement executive of the Office of Price Administration, filed his defense and counter-allegations to the charges lodged against him last month by Daniel P. Woolley, regional OPA head.

Mr. Ross' reply, loaded with accusations of interference by Mr. Woolley with his own enforcement division in the carrying out of national policies, and mentioning companies said to have benefited by Mr. Woolley's action, was brought to regional OPA headquarters in the Empire State Building by a messenger from the office of [illegible] O'Dwyer, counsel to the suspended official, at 4:59 P. M., sixteen minutes before the deadline for making answer.

The 25,000-word reply was accompanied by a demand for a public hearing of Mr. Woolley's charges and the counter-charges by Mr. Ross before an impartial board.

Woolley Has No Comment

Mr. Woolley had left the office before the messenger arrived with the bulky document, which was accepted for Mr. Woolley by Charles Staff, regional personnel officer. A spokesman for Mr. Woolley said later that the Regional Administrator had "no comment to make at this time on the contents of the answer." He said the document had been turned over to the regional legal and civil service staffs for study and that Mr. Woolley's ouster action against Mr. Ross would be carried out in compliance with civil service procedure, which permits but does not require a public hearing in such a case.

Besides accusing Mr. Woolley of hampering the effectiveness of price control by going counter to national enforcement policy—in some cases to serve his own political ambitions, according to Mr. Ross—the reply defended Mr. Ross' record of enforcement. It said that in May court proceedings were brought in this region in some 975 price cases, 30 per cent of the national total, and that OPA "was successful in 99.4 per cent of the cases." This region covers New York, New Jersey, Delaware, Maryland, Virginia and the District of Columbia. The only region with a higher percentage of success was the New England region, with a perfect score, but that was based on only 130 cases, 4 per cent of the national total, Mr. Ross pointed out.

Charges Early Interference

The cases cited by Mr. Ross in support of his contention that Mr. Woolley had hampered enforcement ranged from one involving the Continental Food Company in December, 1943, less than a month after Mr. Woolley joined the OPA, to a cigarette drive last winter that Mr. Ross said had been engineered by Mr. Woolley, to the detriment of more important food price control work, because Mr. Woolley believed the resultant publicity would strengthen his political chances.

There were allegations also of "unwarranted interference" by the regional administrator in cases involving the Dairymen's League and the price of milk; Fan & Bill's, a well-known restaurant in Washington, and Dinty Moore's restaurant in this city. The roll of alleged interference extends to April

Continued on Page 10, Column 1

Truman Pledges Free World As He Reviews U. S. Troops

Tells Them They Fought So 'We Can Live, Think and Act as We Like'—He Says He Will Follow Roosevelt Ideas

By DREW MIDDLETON
By Wireless to THE NEW YORK TIMES.

FRANKFORT ON THE MAIN, Germany, July 26—The United States Commander in Chief saw his countrymen in arms today and they, lean young men who had fought halfway across the Continent of Europe, looked back and liked what they saw.

On a day so hot and so bright that it was like those "dog" days of the great Missouri region from which he comes, President Truman, accompanied by Secretary of State James F. Byrnes and Gen. Dwight D. Eisenhower, drove fifty miles through rigid lines of soldiers, saw the United States Army now settled into its job of occupation and told them simply how much he would have liked to have been in uniform and how soldierly they looked.

"You fought so the United States and the nations of the world can live and act and do as they like," he said. I want to implement that in following the footsteps of my predecessor, Franklin Delano Roosevelt.

At the end of the tour the President stood on an airfield outside Frankfort on the Main and pinned Distinguished Service Medals on the tunics of four officers, three British and one Canadian.

They were Gen. H. D. G. Crerar, Commander in Chief of the Canadian First Army; Maj. Gen. Sir Frederick W. De Guingand, chief of staff of the Twenty-first Army Group; Air Marshal Sir Arthur Conningham, commander of the British Second Tactical Air Force, and Air Marshal Sir James M. Robb, former Deputy Chief of Staff for Air at Supreme Allied Headquarters.

It was the first time that an American President had decorated the soldiers of an allied nation on

Continued on Page 5, Column 2

Supporters Set the Stage For Implementing Charter

By JAMES B. RESTON
Special to THE NEW YORK TIMES.

WASHINGTON, July 26—The Administration has not only assured during the present Senate debate the almost unanimous ratification of the United Nations Security Charter, according to general agreement, but has also greatly improved its chances of implementing the Charter effectively.

When the debate started on Monday there was some doubt about the way in which the Administration would assure that effective force could be put at the disposal of the League and used by it without reference in each case to Congress.

In the last four days, however, the supporters of the Charter, its opponents admit, have succeeded in establishing these two important points:

Once the treaty is ratified by the Senate on Saturday or early next week, the President, as Commander in Chief of the armed forces and particularly as the officer charged with carrying out treaty obligations, will be authorized to use the American quota of troops to "maintain international peace and security" through the World Security Council.

Cannot Bind Senate

Instead of being bound to decide on the size and type of the league forces by a treaty, as it seemed obligated to do at the beginning of the debate, the administration will be free to decide this question through the device of a joint resolution of both houses of Congress, which requires a majority of both houses of Congress.

There is, of course, no way in which the administration can bind a future Senate to agree to the record which has been established in the debate, but the record now emphasizes the following three things:

The treaty obligates this country

Continued on Page 9, Column 2

MEAT RISE OF 11% IS DUE IN AUGUST

Public Will Also Gain by Cuts in Point Values—Sugar for East Increased

Special to THE NEW YORK TIMES.

WASHINGTON, July 26—About 11 per cent more meat, a little more sugar for the East and fewer canned goods appeared today to be in prospect for civilians during August.

With more meat available to civilian consumers as a result of reductions in military demand, the Office of Price Administration lowered by one and two points a pound, and in one instance by three points, the ration values of nearly all cuts of beef, lamb and veal for the rationing period beginning Sunday, July 29.

As much as 80,000,000 more pounds of sugar will be directed into the East by September as a result of a reshuffling of sugar quotas throughout the country. This resulted from an amendment to War Food Order 131.1, which allocates sugar among various consumers and refiners for the period of April through September.

The ruling, while not increasing the total amount of sugar available to civilians, is understood to

Continued on Page 20, Column 5

Federal Jobs Up 126,130 in June; Byrd Asks Reduction of 300,000

Special to THE NEW YORK TIMES.

WASHINGTON, July 26—The number of Federal civilian employes increased by 126,130 in June, and of that total 110,049 were hired by the War Department outside the United States, Senator Byrd, chairman of the Joint Committee on Reduction of Non-Essential Federal Expenditures, said today. The number of Army employes within the United States was reduced by 3,378 in the same month.

Reporting that the civilian payroll of the Government in this country had passed the three-million mark without reference to the more than a half-million War Department employes abroad, Senator Byrd said that it was his firm conviction "that at least 300,000 Federal employes could be immediately eliminated without interference with the prosecution of the war."

After the war ended, he said, "we should return to a total Federal employment of certainly less than a million employes," adding that even this figure was in excess of the Federal employment of normal times.

The increase during June, Senator Byrd stated, meant that 100 civilian employes were added to

Continued on Page 11, Column 3

TERMS LAID DOWN

U. S., Britain and China Plan Disarmament and Occupation

DOOM THE WAR LORDS

Offer Japanese People Opportunity to Gain Democratic Rule

Text of Allies' ultimatum to Japan to end war, Page 4.

By RAYMOND DANIELL
By Wireless to THE NEW YORK TIMES.

BERLIN, July 26—Against the background of the Three-Power conference in the heart of shattered Germany, President Truman and retiring Prime Minister Churchill, with the concurrence of Generalissimo Chiang Kai-shek, called on the Japanese Government and people tonight to surrender unconditionally or face "prompt and utter destruction" at the hands of the Allied land, sea and air forces "poised to strike the final blows."

The joint declaration, it was said, was drawn by Messrs. Churchill and Truman after their arrival here. Its text was transmitted to Generalissimo Chiang and released here as soon as his concurrence had been received in a personal message to Mr. Truman. At 9:30 P. M., after the President's return from Frankfort, the text of the proclamation was issued here and orders were cabled to the Office of War Information in Washington to get the message to the Japanese people by every means possible.

The joint proclamation was in the nature of an ultimatum. While it reiterated the demands for unconditional surrender, it repeated the Cairo declaration that Japan's sovereignty would be limited to her home islands, stripped of the power to wage war. It promised that the Japanese people would be neither "enslaved as a race nor destroyed as a nation."

The Japanese militarists will have to go to make way for a

Continued on Page 4, Column 3

WINNER AND LOSER IN BRITISH ELECTIONS

Clement R. Attlee — Associated Press

Winston Churchill — © British Combine

3 JAPANESE CITIES FIRED BY 350 B-29'S

Omuta, Chemical Center, Is Hit in 2,200-Ton Triple Blow —Shanghai Ripped Again

By W. H. LAWRENCE
By Wireless to THE NEW YORK TIMES.

GUAM, Friday, July 27—More than 2,200 tons of petroleum jelly incendiary bombs were dumped early today by a Marianas-based force of more than 350 Superfortresses on the Japanese cities of Omuta, Matsuyama and Tokuyama.

The three urban targets had a combined population of 377,000, most of it engaged in war production.

[Meanwhile Gen. George C. Kenney's Far East Air Forces, returning to Shanghai in strength, blasted five major airdromes and

Continued on Page 6, Column 3

War News Summarized

FRIDAY, JULY 27, 1945

Great Britain swung to the left so completely in the recent elections that the Labor party and the Conservative party almost exactly changed their positions. Labor won 390 out of 640 seats in the Commons, compared with 163 in the outgoing Parliament, while Prime Minister Churchill's party, which had had 358, won only 195. Labor received nearly half of the popular vote. Mr. Churchill and his Foreign Secretary, Anthony Eden, were about the only survivors among Conservative Cabinet members. The Liberal and Communist parties also fared badly.

"I regret that I have not been permitted to finish the work against Japan," Mr. Churchill said after relinquishing the post he had held since May, 1940. "For this, however, all plans and preparations have been made and the results may come quicker than we have hitherto been entitled to expect." [All the foregoing 1:8.]

"We have first of all to finish the war with Japan," Clement Richard Attlee, who was advanced by the election from Deputy Prime Minister to Prime Minister, told a Labor meeting. "We want the fullest cooperation of all nations,' he added. "We want a security that will banish war forever. We want a widespread prosperity among all the peoples and nations of the world." [1:6-7.]

The Big-Three conference was in recess and President Truman visited American troops along the Rhine. He told them he wanted to follow in President Roosevelt's footsteps. [1:2-3.]

Japan was ordered to surrender unconditionally quickly or face "utter devastation." Mr. Truman, Mr. Churchill and Generalissimo Chiang Kai-shek gave their answer to the enemy's pleas for softer terms in a proclamation that reaffirmed the principles of the Cairo Declaration: the end of militarism, punishment of war criminals, establishment of democracy and limitation of Japanese territory to the home islands. [1:4.]

General Devers said United States troops were being trained in "radical" new methods of warfare for a single gigantic blow against Japan.'[1:6-7.]

Planes continued to carry the war to Japan and her occupied territory. B-29's set three industrial cities on Honshu, Shikoku and Kyushu afire; Iwo-based Privateers hit shipping in the Gulf of Sagami south of Tokyo; Okinawa-based planes struck Korean waters and airfields on Honshu, and 300 bombers smashed five airfields at Shanghai. [1:5; map P. 6.]

British and American carrier planes of the Third Fleet beat off the first enemy air attack since the warships went into action off Japan on July 10. Four out of ten enemy aircraft were shot down. [5:6.]

Chinese troops recaptured the seventh of eleven former American air bases lost to the Japanese when they seized Namyung, 150 miles northeast of Canton. Inconclusive fighting was raging on other fronts. [5:1, with map.]

A member of the de Gaulle Government sustained the legality of the Vichy regime in testifying against Marshal Pétain on trial for treason in Paris. The defendant was again accused of betraying France. [8:3-4.]

Attlee in First Talk Backs Harmony With U.S., Russia

By SYDNEY GRUSON
By Cable to THE NEW YORK TIMES.

LONDON, July 26—Maj. Clement R. Attlee, in his first speech as Britain's Prime Minister, pledged anew tonight this nation's determination "to finish the war with Japan" and expressed the belief that the result of the British election would give heart throughout the world to those "who believe in freedom, democracy and social justice."

Coming directly from Buckingham Palace after accepting King George VI's commission to form a new Government, Mr. Attlee addressed a wildly enthusiastic Labor party victory rally in Westminster Central Hall, not more than 100 yards from the House of Commons his party now dominates.

Seeming just the slightest bit dazed by the tumultuous day, Mr. Attlee outlined his new Government's job in a few sentences.

"We have, first of all, to finish the war against Japan," he declared. "We shall see to it that our men in the East get all the support they need.

"We want the fullest cooperation with all nations.

"We want a security that will banish war forever.

"We want a widespread prosperity among all the peoples and nations of the world.

The Tasks at Home

"Here at home we have our own great tasks. We have to bind up the wounds of war. We have to reconstruct our ruined homes—a great task in itself. We have to bring back in due course the workers who have been working on the war to be workers for peace. We have a job to build up in this country the highest standard of life that we can achieve for all."

Flanked by his chief lieutenants, Herbert Morrison and Ernest Bevin, and with the wives of all three beaming beside them, Mr. Attlee called on the crowd of 2,000

Continued on Page 3, Column 6

BRITISH BUSINESS IN GENERAL IS CALM

Coal, Power Industries Shaken by Nationalization Prospect, Rest Expect Little Change

By CHARLES E. EGAN
By Wireless to THE NEW YORK TIMES.

LONDON, July 26—Britain's business circles reacted calmly to Labor's election sweep today. Coal and power interests were shaken because the victorious party is deeply committed to nationalization in both those fields, but other industries, including cotton, iron and steel and manufacturing generally saw little immediate change in prospect.

"Leaders of the Labor party are all men with Cabinet experience accustomed to the responsibilities of government," a leading industrialist said today. "There is little danger of ill-considered radical policies sweeping the country.

"Members of my organization feel it is improbable that the party will vote to take over any of the enterprises mentioned except fuel and power. They are so deeply committed on the coal and electric power industries that it is impossible to see how they can avoid nationalizing them."

The Financial Times in its leading editorial tomorrow will say that both business and financial

Continued on Page 2, Column 4

7,000,000 Troops for Single Blow At Japan Planned, Says Devers

By SIDNEY SHALETT
Special to THE NEW YORK TIMES.

WASHINGTON, July 26—The United States Army will train and deploy its European veterans and its new troops so that, in conjunction with divisions already in the Pacific, it can hurl 7,000,000 men in a coordinated "single blow" against Japan, instead of attempting to do the job 'piecemeal,' Gen. Jacob L. Devers, new Commanding General of Army Ground Forces, declared today.

At his first news conference since he succeeded Gen. Joseph W. Stilwell, now in the Pacific, as head of the Ground Forces, General Devers, who commanded the Sixth Army Group in southern France, hinted at the plans for a massive blow against the enemy's homeland, and also asserted that our forces being prepared for the Pacific would be trained in "radical" new methods of warfare.

General Devers explained that he should not be taken "too literally" in his description of a 7,000,000-man blow against Japan. Obviously, he pointed out, an Army does not land that many men overnight on an enemy beachhead.

But the Army Ground Forces does intend, he asserted, to have the 7,000,000 men who will consti-

Continued on Page 7, Column 2

BRITISH TURN LEFT

War Regime Swept Out as Laborites Win 390 of 640 Seats

CHURCHILL BIDS ADIEU

Hints at Early Peace—He Stays in House, but Many Ex-Aides Lose

By HERBERT L. MATTHEWS
By Cable to THE NEW YORK TIMES.

LONDON, July 26—In one of the most stunning election surprises in the history of democracy, Great Britain swung to the Left today in a landslide that smothered the Conservatives and put Labor into power with a great majority.

Winston Churchill has resigned as Prime Minister and Clement R. Attlee has accepted the King's invitation to form a Laborite Government. The Liberals went down to an equally surprising defeat. The world, which looked to Britain for a guiding trend, has had its tremendous answer. Today and tomorrow and for months or years to come, the Left is the dominating power in global politics.

When the final result came in from the constituency of Hornchurch at 10:30 P. M., Labor had a staggering total of 390 seats out of a Parliament of 640, of which the holders of thirteen seats will not be known until early in August. In the last Parliament, Labor had only 163 and in its greatest previous triumph, in 1929, it had 288.

Conservatives Cut to 195 Seats

The Conservatives had fallen from 358 seats to 195. The Liberals, too, lost seven seats and now have only eleven members in Parliament.

Adding fourteen Liberal Nationals and one National, the former Government is down to 210 seats, whereas if the Liberals, Independent Labor with three seats, the Commonwealth with one, the Communists with two and the Independents with ten are added to Labor, one gets a total of 417.

Such a tremendous majority means that the Labor party can confidently count on a full five-year tenure of office, for it cannot be beaten on any vote of confidence. Out of nearly 25,000,000 votes, Labor alone won nearly 12,000,000. The Conservatives got a little more than 9,000,000 votes. The Labor party did not lose a single seat to the Conservatives, although it gained 130 from that party.

[The vote, according to the press services, was: Labor, 11,962,678; Conservative, 9,018,235; Liberal, 2,280,135; Independent, 545,862.]

The results were a personal, decisive repudiation of Mr. Churchill as a peacetime leader. He himself

Continued on Page 3, Column 2

Churchill Reported Ending Berlin Role

By Cable to THE NEW YORK TIMES.

LONDON, July 26—The News Chronicle will say tomorrow that Winston Churchill will not return to the Berlin conference, although the first thing Prime Minister Attlee did was to ask him to do so.

Anthony Eden, former Foreign Secretary, who has been re-elected to the Parliament, said today: "I am anxious still to do my best to help our nation hold its head high in the world as it has the right and pride to do."

Asked whether he would return to Berlin, Mr. Eden said that his services were at the country's disposal and, if he were asked to return tomorrow, as had been previously arranged, he would continue to do his best to help.

LONDON, July 26 (UP)—When Prime Minister Attlee was asked whether Mr. Churchill would return to Berlin with him, he smiled and remained silent.

"All the News That's Fit to Print"

NEWS INDEX, PAGE 41, THIS SECTION

The New York Times.

LATE CITY EDITION

Showers, thunder showers; warm and humid today and tomorrow.
Temperatures Yesterday—Max., 70; Min., 67
Sunrise today, 5:49 A. M.; Sunset, 8:15 P. M.

Section 1

VOL. XCIV..No. 31,963. Entered as Second-Class Matter, Postoffice, New York, N. Y. NEW YORK, SUNDAY, JULY 29, 1945. Including Magazine and Book Review. TEN CENTS New York City and Suburban Areas (15c Elsewhere)

SENATE RATIFIES CHARTER OF UNITED NATIONS 89 TO 2; TRUMAN HAILS AID TO PEACE

FOES ARE CRUSHED

With Hiram Johnson Ill, Only Shipstead and Langer Vote 'No'

WORLD OBLIGATION CITED

Leaders Say Today's Ratification Is 'Master Plan,' With Military Pacts Secondary

By JAMES B. RESTON
Special to THE NEW YORK TIMES.

WASHINGTON, July 28—The United States Senate paid a first installment on an old debt today. It ratified, 89 to 2, the United Nations Security Charter, successor to the League of Nations Covenant which it rejected twenty-six years ago, and thereby fulfilled Woodrow Wilson's prophecy that one day the upper chamber would reverse its decision.

The vote came 107 days after the death of Franklin D. Roosevelt, who helped guide the Charter past the pitfalls that defeated Wilson's Covenant, and at a moment when American statesmen were settling the fate of a defeated Germany and American warships were closing in on the heart of Japan.

The two Senators who voted against ratification were William Langer of North Dakota and Henrik Shipstead of Minnesota, both Republicans. Mr. Langer, who worked actively for Hiram Johnson and Robert M. La Follette when those two "irreconcilables" were candidates for President, said he was voting against the Charter because it would mean "perpetual war" and the "enslavement" of millions of poor people from Poland to India.

Hiram Johnson Sends Word

Senator Hiram Johnson, Republican, of California, sent word from the Naval Medical Center outside Washington that if he had been well enough to be present he would have joined Mr. Langer and Mr. Shipstead in opposition, but the four other members of the Senate who were with Mr. Johnson in the upper chamber during the League of Nations debate—Arthur Capper, Republican, of Kansas, and Peter G. Gerry of Rhode Island, Kenneth McKellar of Tennessee, and David I. Walsh of Massachusetts, Democrats, all voted for ratification.

As soon as the results were made known, President Truman and Cordell Hull, former Secretary of State, who started work on the Charter in the State Department in 1942, issued statements praising the Senate's action.

"It is deeply gratifying that the Senate has ratified the United Nations' Charter by a virtually unanimous vote," the President's message from Potsdam said. "The action of the Senate substantially advances the cause of world peace."

It was a grim-appearing Senate that rolled off the "ayes" on the final count this evening. Despite the long parliamentary debate in the chamber on the subject, and despite its overwhelming approval at the end, there was no sense of a job finished but merely of a difficult job just beginning.

Since a league to enforce peace had first been mentioned to members of this chamber by Woodrow Wilson in 1914, some 40,000,000 human beings, armed and unarmed, had been killed in two great wars. In the first German war total military casualties were estimated at 37,000,000 men; in the European phase of the second German war some 14,000,000 more had been killed, and our own casualties in this war, still unfinished, were over the million mark.

Chaplain Tells Senate's Hopes

Throughout the debate, the Senate seemed to realize this and to approach the problem more in hope than anything else.

"Under the old order of strife," the Senate's chaplain said in his prayer opening today's session, "we learned how to destroy ourselves. Under a new charter of mutual aid and tolerance of diversity, may we learn at last how to save ourselves."

Today's vote does not put the

Continued on Page 33, Column 4

Truman Deeply Gratified, He Says in Cable Message

President Promptly Recognizes Senate's Action as Advancing 'the Cause of World Peace'—Grew and Hull Applaud

Special to THE NEW YORK TIMES.

WASHINGTON, July 28—President Truman was swift to applaud the passage of the World Security Charter. In a message from Potsdam he said:

"It is deeply gratifying that the Senate has ratified the United Nations Charter by a virtually unanimous vote.

"The action of the Senate substantially advances the cause of world peace."

Joseph C. Grew, Acting Secretary of State, and Cordell Hull, former Secretary of State, also commended the Senate for its approval of the Charter.

Mr. Grew said:

"The passage of the United Nations Charter by the Senate today is a memorable event in the history of the United States and the world. By their action, the members of the Senate have taken a most important step toward establishing security and peace throughout the world.

"Millions of men, women and children have died because nations took to the naked sword instead of the conference table to settle their differences.

"The United Nations Charter, approved by such an overwhelming majority, represents the labor of citizens of fifty nations, united in their desire for a peaceful world. The Charter itself is the foundation and cornerstone on which the international organization to keep the peace will be built. This organization can survive only through the faith and labor of the citizens of all these nations.

"I congratulate the members of the Senate for their work today."

Continued on Page 38, Column 1

Poles, at Big 3 Meeting, Ask Stettin, Oder-Neisse Border

By RAYMOND DANIELL
By Wireless to THE NEW YORK TIMES.

BERLIN, July 28—A delegation of the Polish Government, including Vice Premier Stanislaw Mikolajczyk and, it is believed, Labor Minister Jan Stanczyk, has been here this last week to ask for a final delimitation of their country's western frontier to include Stettin and run from there southward along the east bank of the Oder-Neisse River line.

It was officially announced that Britain's new Prime Minister, Clement R. Attlee, and his Foreign Minister, Ernest Bevin, after formal calls on President Truman, Secretary of State James F. Byrnes, Premier Stalin and Foreign Commissar Vyacheslaff M. Molotoff, had participated today in a plenary session of the tripartite conference.

It is now believed, although there has been no inkling of their plans from official sources, that neither Winston Churchill nor former Foreign Secretary Anthony Eden will return. The new Prime Minister and his Foreign Secretary, who as Labor Minister in Mr. Churchill's coalition Government had access to all secrets of the War Cabinet, are the only new members of the British delegation. Inasmuch as Mr. Attlee sat in at all sessions of the Big Three before his election and saw all the official documents at the conference, it can hardly be said that he is a newcomer to the council table.

Parley Continuity Maintained

The downfall of the Churchill Government has caused little break in the continuity of the conference. Little more than forty-eight hours elapsed between Mr. Churchill's departure from Berlin and Mr. Attlee's return today.

In the absence of the head of the British delegation experts worked steadily to clear the decks

Continued on Page 5, Column 4

WOOLLEY DISMISSES ROSS IN OPA DISPUTE

Refuses to Grant the Public Hearing Demanded by Aide He Suspended June 22

Paul L. Ross, regional enforcement executive of the Office of Price Administration, who was suspended June 22 on charges of maladministration, was discharged yesterday by Daniel P. Woolley, regional OPA administrator, who refused to grant Mr. Ross the public hearing for which he had pleaded.

The discharge, effective at once, was contained in a registered letter mailed to Mr. Ross at noon, and followed by less than forty-eight hours the filing of Mr. Ross' reply to the administrator's charges.

In a brief statement, Mr. Woolley declared "utterly untrue and unfounded" serious counter-charges against him preferred by Mr. Ross in his answer. The enforcement officer had accused Mr. Woolley of hampering the enforcement of OPA regulations, interfering in behalf of certain alleged violators and obstructing the Federal enforcement policies.

Upon learning of his discharge,

Continued on Page 37, Column 5

Kweilin and Three Airfields Seized; Chinese Also Gain in Other Areas

By The Associated Press.

CHUNGKING, China, July 28—Chinese troops recaptured the airbase city of Kweilin yesterday and seized its three former American airfields from the Japanese, the Chinese High Command said tonight. The victory ended a six-week battle.

Kweilin, walled capital of Kwangsi Province, once was the biggest United States airbase in South-Central China. It had been occupied by the Japanese since last November. Its recapture was the most significant victory in the recent comeback of the Chinese armies.

Generalissimo Chiang Kai-shek's veterans smashed into the rubbled streets of Kweilin, 360 miles southeast of Chungking, at 4 P. M. yesterday after mowing down the defenders of the city's south and west gates. Most of the Japanese garrison had fled and enemy rear-guard remnants swiftly were routed from machine-gun nests in cellars and on roofs, a communiqué said.

The Japanese, headquarters added, withdrew to the northwest to escape annihilation. Their escape route northeastward to Hengyang was severed several days ago. The Chinese said: "Our troops are in hot pursuit."

Kweilin, abandoned by the United States Fourteenth Air Force eight months ago, was the third former American airbase recovered in three days by the Chinese, whose current drive is rapidly strengthening American air power on the Asiatic mainland. It was

Continued on Page 3, Column 5

CRIPPLED WARSHIPS OF JAPANESE NAVY SMASHED BY FLIERS

2 Battleships and 3 Cruisers Set Afire in Saturday Strike by the Third Fleet

HYUGA IS FOUND SUNK

Returning U. S. Pilots Report Waters Off Kure Strewn With Burning Vessels

By Wireless to THE NEW YORK TIMES.

GUAM, Sunday, July 29—Two Japanese battleships, the Haruna and Ise, and three cruisers were set afire and a third battleship, the Hyuga, which was heavily damaged on Tuesday, was found to be resting on the bottom at her anchorage as United States Third Fleet carrier planes struck heavily Saturday at crippled remnants of the Japanese Navy in the Inland Sea.

An aircraft carrier also was further damaged.

Fleet Admiral Chester W. Nimitz today announced the results of the strike, which were incomplete. No reports had yet been received from British carrier pilots, who also participated.

Enemy Air Opposition Sporadic

The enemy's air opposition was sporadic, with American fighters shooting down one Japanese plane near Task Force 38, another eighteen near the target areas and destroying seventy-five on the ground. Fifty-six other parked enemy aircraft were damaged.

[Pilots returning from the Saturday strike reported waters off the Kure naval base littered with burning ships, and fleet dispatches said every major Japanese warship was believed to have been put out of action for the duration of the war, The United Press stated.]

The Third Fleet assault was directed at Japanese shipping between the once great ports of Kobe and Kure.

Pilots reported that the Hyuga, a modernized battleship with carrier type runway aft permitting it to handle aircraft, was on the bottom, water lapping over her main deck amidships.

It was disclosed also that Saturday's aerial assault, resulted in the sinking of three submarines, presumably in dry dock, and damage to four destroyers, two destroyer escorts, two medium-size freighter transports, three small cargo ships and an unidentified vessel.

Five Warships Left Burning

Whether these ships were among those damaged in the Tuesday attack, which battered twenty-three warships, was not revealed. However, it is definite that yesterday's attack further damaged six warships hit on Tuesday, the battleships Haruna and Ise, the cruisers Tone, Aoba and Oyodo and the escort carrier Kaiyo. All of these ships except the carrier were left burning in the latest assault.

Thus it seems that Admiral Halsey is well along toward his objective—the neutralization of Japan's remaining naval warships in order to provide a thoroughly clear field for future amphibious

Continued on Page 3, Column 2

War News Summarized

SUNDAY, JULY 29, 1945

The United States Senate ratified, 89 to 2, the United Nations Security Charter. The two Senators who voted against ratification were William Langer of North Dakota and Henrik Shipstead of Minnesota, both Republicans. [1:1.]

Two battleships and three cruisers, all previously damaged, were hit again in the latest Third Fleet attack on the Inland Sea area, Admiral Nimitz disclosed, and it was found another battleship had been sunk. Returning pilots reported that the Japanese Navy probably was out of action for the rest of the war. [1:4.]

Between 550 and 600 Superfortresses set fire to six of the eleven Japanese cities warned previously of their coming destruction. [1:5; map P. 2.]

General Minami, chief of Tokyo's would-be totalitarian party, said Japan would be ready to discuss peace when East Asia was free from British-American "colonial exploitation." [9:1.]

Captain Zacharias, United States naval spokesman, broadcast to Japan a declaration that peace with Japan had now been made possible by the Potsdam proclamation. [4:5.]

Chinese forces took Kweilin and three former United States airfields. Other Chinese pressed toward Kukong, 120 miles north of Canton, gaining thirty miles in two days. [1:2-3; map P. 3.]

The British in Burma reported that the Japanese Twenty-eighth Army had been annihilated with more than 5,500 killed and the remnant fleeing toward Thailand. [3:1.]

Prime Minister Attlee and six new Ministers took the oath of office in London. [5-1.]

A Polish Government delegation was in Potsdam pleading for a western frontier running along the Oder and Niesse Rivers. Meanwhile, the conference was resumed with Mr. Attlee and Foreign Secretary Bevin in the places of Winston Churchill and Anthony Eden. [1:2-3; map P. 5.]

Michel Clemenceau accused Marshal Pétain at the latter's treason trial of having been indirectly responsible for handing over Georges Mandel, former Minister of Colonies, to the Germans who killed him. [12:1.]

BOMBER HITS EMPIRE STATE BUILDING, SETTING IT AFIRE AT THE 79TH FLOOR; 13 DEAD, 26 HURT; WIDE AREA ROCKED

WHERE BOMBER CRASHED INTO EMPIRE STATE BUILDING

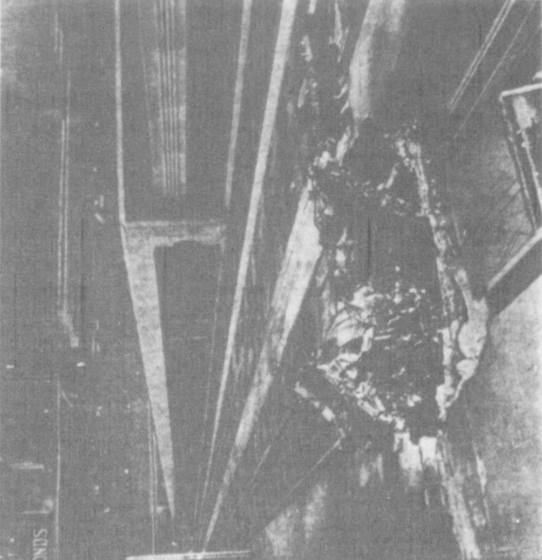

Hole torn between seventy-eighth and seventy-ninth floors The New York Times (by Sisto)

B-25 CRASHES IN FOG

Hole 18 by 20 Feet Torn Through North Wall by Terrific Impact

BLAZING 'GAS' SCATTERED

Flames Put Out in 40-Minute Fight—2 Women Survive Fall in Elevator

By FRANK ADAMS

A twin-engined B-25 Army bomber, lost in a blinding fog, crashed into the Empire State Building at a point 915 feet above the street level at 9:49 A. M. yesterday. Thirteen persons, including the three occupants of the plane and ten persons at work within the building, were killed in the catastrophe, and twenty-six were injured.

Although the crash and the fire that followed wrecked most of the seventy-eighth and seventy-ninth floors of the structure, causing damage estimated at $500,000, Lieut. Gen. Hugh A. Drum, president of the Empire State, Inc., Corporation, said last night that an inspection by the city's building department and by other engineers and architects showed that the structural soundness of the building had not been impaired.

Landing Advice Disregarded

The plane, en route from Bedford, Mass., to Newark on a cross-country mission, had flown over La Guardia Field a few minutes before the crash, and its pilot, Lieut. Col. William F. Smith Jr., deputy commander of the 457th Bomber Group and recently decorated for his service overseas, was advised by the control tower to land. Instead he asked for the weather at Newark Airport and headed in that direction.

Horror-stricken occupants of the building, alarmed by the roar of engines, ran to the windows just in time to see the plane loom out of the gray mists that swathed the upper floors of the world's tallest office building. The plane was banked at an angle of about fifteen degrees as Colonel Smith swung it in a curve out of the northeast.

It crashed with a terrifying impact midway along the north or Thirty-fourth Street wall of the building. Its wings were sheared off by the impact, but the motors and fuselage ripped a hole eighteen feet wide and twenty feet high in the outer wall of the seventy-eighth and seventy-ninth floors of the structure.

Brilliant orange flames shot as high as the observatory on the eighty-sixth floor of the building, 1,050 feet above Fifth Avenue, as the gasoline tanks of the plane exploded. For a moment watchers in the street below saw the tower clearly illumined by the glare. Then it disappeared again in gray murk and the smoke of the burning plane.

Motor Hits Another Building

One of the plane's two motors hurtled clear across the seventy-eighth floor, tore a hole in the south wall of the building, and plummeted to the roof of the twelve-story office building at 10 West Thirty-third Street, where it started a fire that demolished the penthouse of Henry Hering, noted sculptor, with resulting damage estimated at $75,000.

A propeller was imbedded in the wall of the Empire State Building; the other motor and part of the landing gear crashed into an elevator shaft, where they fell to the sub-cellar 1,000 feet below, and other sections of the fuselage were blown as high as the eighty-sixth floor observatory. The steel girder at the seventy-ninth floor level was bent inward eighteen inches by the shock.

Cascading torrents of flaming gasoline poured through the seventy-eighth and seventy-ninth floors, setting fire to everything that was combustible. The burning fuel ran down stair wells into hallways as far as the seventy-fifth floor, while choking fumes

Continued on Page 25, Column 1

B-29'S FIRE 6 CITIES IN PROMISED BLOWS

Oil Refinery Target on Honshu Added to List LeMay Gave Japanese in Advance

By Wireless to THE NEW YORK TIMES.

GUAM, Sunday, July 29—The Twentieth Air Force early today bombed six out of eleven Japanese cities that hardly twenty-four hours previously had been told that they were on a list of enemy communities marked for aerial destruction by Superfortresses.

Seven task forces of the B-29 bombers, totaling 550 to 600 planes, dropped more than 3,500 tons of incendiaries on the six industrial centers situated from Shikoku in the south to northern Honshu and demolition bombs on an oil refinery near Osaka.

[Gen. Douglas MacArthur reported Okinawa-based Army planes had sunk enemy shipping in Japan's Inland Sea area. He disclosed that our new B-32 super-bomber has been in action since May against the foe on Formosa and along the China coast.]

One of the B-29 task forces, sent

Continued on Page 4, Column 1

Catholic War Relief Office Is Chief Victim of Tragedy

By LARRY RESNER

An agency that has been in the vanguard of supplying aid and comfort to thousands of homeless and destitute persons in the war zones became yesterday, through one of those curious quirks of fate, the victim of the worst local tragedy of the war. The point of greatest impact of the low-flying bomber that crashed into the Empire State Building was at the seventy-ninth floor, where the principal tenant was the War Relief Services of the National Catholic Welfare Conference.

Throughout the war years, this agency has sent many field representatives into the lands laid waste by war to work with other relief and welfare agencies in helping war victims.

And only yesterday, as the bomber struck and destroyed their office, the reduced Saturday staff of workers was busily engaged in arranging the final details of a trip to Europe on Tuesday of two of their principal functionaries.

Only five of an estimated working staff of fifteen to twenty persons in the office, including men and women, were known to have escaped the flames that swept the skyscraper floor as the gasoline of the crashing plane exploded.

W. Paul Dearing, correspondent here for The Buffalo Courier-Express and publicity director of the War Relief Services for the last year, either jumped or was blown from his seventy-ninth-floor office to his death on a ledge on the sev-

Continued on Page 32, Column 3

SURVIVOR LIKENS CRASH TO A QUAKE

Building Moved Twice, Then Settled, Says Occupant Who Felt Shocks in China

By ALEXANDER FEINBERG

The towering Empire State Building that is a city of 102 stories, reaching 1,250 feet high, "moved" twice yesterday when struck by the bomber and then it "settled." That was a dread moment for one who had felt that double movement and the settling many times before.

Recently returned from China after twenty-seven years, the man who told of his sensations when the B-25 struck said the impact was precisely that of an earthquake, to which he is no stranger. Preferring not to give his name, he said he was in an office on the sixty-eighth floor of the building when he felt the double "move-

Continued on Page 28, Column 1

Red Cross and Hospital Groups Speed to Aid of Victims, Rescuers

The last fireman barely had leaped from his truck to the raging four-alarm blaze caused by the bomber crash in the Empire State Building when hospital disaster units and two Red Cross Service canteen wagons were on the scene to aid the victims and rescuers of the catastrophe.

While fifteen Red Cross aides set up shop and dispensed hot coffee and doughnuts to the toiling fire fighters and others helping them, two disaster units from Bellevue Hospital, replete with the latest equipment, were making their way into the upper reaches of the building to assist in the rescue work.

Only twelve minutes elapsed between the sounding of the first alarm at 9:49 A. M. and the fourth alarm and from the moment the Telegraph Bureau at Police Headquarters received the first report the city's fire-fighting equipment, a small army of police and squads of Army and Navy units, mostly military police and shore patrols, moved with clock-like precision through the fog-shrouded streets.

The fire sirens screeched constantly as apparatus sped to the scene. The second alarm hit at 9:57 A. M., the third at 10 A. M. and the last at 10:01 A. M. After that there were other calls but only for specialized equipment.

The four alarms brought to the scene forty-one pieces of fire-fighting apparatus, including "walkie-talkie" radio units. All were under the immediate command of Fire Commissioner Patrick Walsh. Almost simultaneously the Police Department's ranking officers dispatched more than 400 policemen.

Continued on Page 32, Column 6

"All the News That's Fit to Print"

The New York Times.

LATE CITY EDITION

Partly cloudy, less humid today. Cloudy and warm tomorrow.

Temperatures Yesterday—Max., 72; Min., 66

Sunrise today, 5:17 A. M.; Sunset, 8:06 P. M.

VOL. XCIV..No. 31,972. Entered as Second-Class Matter, Postoffice, New York, N. Y. NEW YORK, TUESDAY, AUGUST 7, 1945. THREE CENTS IN NEW YORK CITY

FIRST ATOMIC BOMB DROPPED ON JAPAN; MISSILE IS EQUAL TO 20,000 TONS OF TNT; TRUMAN WARNS FOE OF A 'RAIN OF RUIN'

HIRAM W. JOHNSON, REPUBLICAN DEAN IN THE SENATE, DIES

Isolationist Helped Prevent U. S. Entry Into League—Opposed World Charter

CALIFORNIA EX-GOVERNOR

Ran for Vice President With Theodore Roosevelt in '12 —In Washington Since '17

Special to THE NEW YORK TIMES.

WASHINGTON, Aug. 6—Senator Hiram Warren Johnson of California, lifelong isolationist who helped prevent this country's entry into the League of Nations and fought all "foreign entanglements" through a second World War, died in his sleep this morning at Bethesda Naval Hospital, nine days after, ill but consistent, he had paired his vote against ratification of the United Nations Charter. Death was caused by a thrombosis of a cerebral artery. Mrs. Johnson was with him when the end came.

When word reached the Capitol of the passing of the oldest member of the Senate in point of service, save Senator Kenneth McKellar, the President pro tempore, the mourning was deep. With great personal affection colleagues paid humble tribute to his integrity of character, his liberalism and his steadfastness to his ideals and convictions. They joined in declaring that the country had lost a great statesman.

Senator Johnson, who was serving the fourth year of his fifth term in the Senate, would have been 79 years old on Sept. 2. Although his health had been failing during the last two years and though the thundering voice which had conveyed his eloquence through innumerable stirring debates had become little more than a whisper, friends believed he planned to seek a sixth term in 1947.

He went to the hospital July 18. Five days before that he had cast the lone vote in the Foreign Relations Committee, of which he was the ranking minority member, against reporting the new World Charter to the Senate without change. He did not participate in the floor debate on this document, which won Senate approval by a vote of 82—2. However, he clashed spiritedly with colleagues while the hearings were in progress.

Funeral arrangements awaited the arrival of the Senator's son, Lieut. Col. Hiram W. Johnson Jr., who was flying here from California.

Capper Becomes the Dean

The death of Senator Johnson made Senator Arthur Capper of Kansas, who last month marked his eightieth birthday, the Republican dean of the Senate. It also elevated him to the ranking minority membership on the Foreign Relations Committee, with which Senator Johnson had been so conspicuously identified through the many years of his unshaken position on foreign policy. Mr. Capper, too, with Senators McKellar, Carter Glass of Virginia, David I. Walsh of Massachusetts and Peter G. Gerry, was in the League fight of 1919 and 1920. He supported it, with reservations.

The career of Senator Johnson from his entrance into the Senate from the Governorship of California in March of 1917, was one distinctly lacking in compromise or reservation. In 1912 he had bolted his party with Theodore Roosevelt and had become his running mate on the Bull Moose ticket. In 1932 he again bolted to support Franklin D. Roosevelt for the Presidency but broke bitterly with the President when he ran for his third term.

In 1919 Mr. Johnson joined with Senators Lodge, Borah, Reed,

Continued on Page 23, Column 4

Jet Plane Explosion Kills Major Bong, Top U. S. Ace

Flier Who Downed 40 Japanese Craft, Sent Home to Be 'Safe,' Was Flying New 'Shooting Star' as a Test Pilot

By The United Press.

BURBANK, Calif., Aug. 6—Maj. Richard Bong, America's greatest air ace, died today in the flaming wreckage of a jet propelled fighter plane which crashed while he was testing it.

Only 24 years old, he wore twenty-six decorations including the nation's highest award, the Congressional Medal of Honor. He had survived countless air battles and shot down forty Japanese planes without a scratch.

The knowledge he gained in those battles was too valuable to risk, so he was brought home to "safe" duty. He was on that "safe" duty today when his P-80, the Shooting Star, hurtled over a clump of trees and burst like a bomb in a field.

Witnesses did not agree on the cause of the crash. One Army flier said that Major Bong overshot the Lockheed airport. Another witness, John McKinney of North Hollywood reported that he saw something fall out of the plane's tail.

"The plane started to wobble up and down, then went into a left bank and hit the ground," he stated. "It exploded and burned and scattered wreckage over about a block square."

Major Bong was trying to get out of the ship when it crashed. He had released the escape hatch and was partly clear. He had pulled the ripcord to his parachute, and the silken folds lay about the body as the flames swept over it.

With a roaring sigh, the plane, like a giant blowtorch, shot over the airport just before 3 P. M. and then lurched over the trees and nosed down into the field, a mile away.

Smoke and flame surged up and crowds rushed from the airport. By the time anyone could reach the scene the ship had been almost consumed.

The crash scene was near the intersection of Cahuenga and Oxnard Boulevards and barely out-

Continued on Page 15, Column 2

MORRIS IS ACCUSED OF 'TAKING A WALK'

Fusion Official 'Sad to Part Company'—McGoldrick Sees Only Tammany Aided

The No Deal ticket, headed by Council President Newbold Morris, "can only serve the interests of Tammany Hall," Controller Joseph D. McGoldrick, candidate for reelection on the Republican-Liberal-Fusion party slate, declared yesterday in a fresh attack on the third-party ticket injected over the week-end into the city Mayoralty campaign.

A short while later Gabriel A. Wechsler, general secretary of the City Fusion party, which supported Mayor La Guardia and Mr. Morris in previous city campaigns, accused Mr. Morris of "taking a walk away from the good government forces."

To both charges Mr. Morris declared he would stand on his statement of Sunday that he was not interested in "just taking votes" away from Judge Jonah J. Goldstein, Republican-Liberal-Fusion candidate for Mayor, or from William O'Dwyer, his Democratic-American Labor party opponent.

"I have no comment," he said, "since I stand on my statement of Sunday. We are waging an affirmative campaign."

Informed that Hyman Blumberg,

Continued on Page 19, Column 6

Turks Talk War if Russia Presses; Prefer Vain Battle to Surrender

By SAM POPE BREWER

By Wireless to THE NEW YORK TIMES.

ANKARA, Turkey, Aug. 6—Russo-Turkish relations weigh heavily on Turkish minds these days. All leading editors commented today on various aspects of the Russian claims against Turkey.

The Potsdam conference leaves the situation virtually unchanged so far as the Turks can see, but they seem to agree that they would go to war, however hopeless such a war might be, rather than yield before the threat of force. Suggestions from London and Washington that the Russians have been asked to moderate their demands give little reassurance here.

The Potsdam communiqué created more confusion than confidence and the Turks are still trying to decide whether the fact that the conference did not deal with certain specific questions means that it was a failure.

Many point out that all the really thorny questions still are unsettled. The Turks probably do not see a relative importance among world problems of Russian demands on Turkey, but point out that the important question of principle is involved. The general and apparently official argument is that the status of the Straits cannot be modified by a bilateral agreement but must be discussed at a conference of the signatories of the Montreux Convention, with America replacing Japan. The signatories were Great Britain, France, Russia, Japan, Turkey, Greece, Rumania, Yugoslavia and Bulgaria.

The grounds for the Russian claims to Kars and Ardahan are not clear, but throughout the Near and Mideast in recent months

Continued on Page 13, Column 1

KYUSHU CITY RAZED

Kenney's Planes Blast Tarumizu in Record Blow From Okinawa

ROCKET SITE IS SEEN

125 B-29's Hit Japan's Toyokawa Naval Arsenal in Demolition Strike

By FRANK L. KLUCKHOHN

By Wireless to THE NEW YORK TIMES.

MANILA, Tuesday, Aug. 7—More than 400 fighters and bombers, speeding at chimney-top level for two hours Sunday over Tarumizu in southern Kyushu in the largest single attack launched by Gen. George C. Kenney's Far East Air Forces to date, leveled that city's munitions factories and aircraft and munitions storage depots and waterfront installations.

Rockets and demolition bombs were poured by waves of B-26 Invaders, B-25 Mitchells and Mustangs and Thunderbolts of the Fifth and Seventh Air Forces from Okinawa, supported by a few B-24 Liberators carrying big bombs.

[Tarumizu, about 350 miles from Okinawa, appeared to be a site at which the Japanese might be preparing a rocket campaign against the American base, said a United Press dispatch. FEAF pilots reported seeing in the area, which has extensive cave construction, what seemed to be Japanese robot planes and also a huge catapult-like machine, extending over the water, that might be a rocket launcher.

[About 125 B-29's hit the Toyokawa naval arsenal of Japan in a demolition bombing Tuesday noon, Strategic Air Forces headquarters at Guam reported.]

The planes over Tarumizu met scant resistance, as our fliers took their time to assure the highest

Continued on Page 11, Column 2

REPORT BY BRITAIN

'By God's Mercy' We Beat Nazis to Bomb, Churchill Says

ROOSEVELT AID CITED

Raiders Wrecked Norse Laboratory in Race for Key to Victory

The text of Mr. Churchill's statement is on Page 8.

By CLIFTON DANIEL

By Wireless to THE NEW YORK TIMES.

LONDON, Aug. 6—The hitherto secret details of the grisly race between Germany and the Allies to find a weapon so destructive that it would insure absolute victory—a race not only between scientists but also between under-cover agents—were recounted in London tonight after it had been disclosed that the first atomic bomb had been dropped on Japan.

"By God's mercy British and American science outpaced all German efforts," said a statement by former Prime Minister Churchill written before he left office and issued from 10 Downing Street by his successor, Clement R. Attlee.

"The possession of these powers by the Germans at any time might have altered the result of the war," Mr. Churchill said, "and profound anxiety was felt by those who were informed."

The British Isles, which endured the terrors of flying bombs and rockets, did hear repeated rumors that Adolf Hitler's V-3 weapon was to be an atomic bomb, but they never knew until tonight how close they came to being the first victims of its destructive power. Much less did they suspect what

Continued on Page 9, Column 1

CHINESE WIN MORE OF 'INVASION COAST'

Smash Into Port 121 Miles Southwest of Canton—Big Area Open for Landing

By The Associated Press.

CHUNGKING, China, Aug. 6—Chinese troops have broken into the South China port of Yeungkong and cleared a fifty-mile stretch of the Chinese "invasion coast" west of Hong Kong, Generalissimo Chiang Kai-shek's headquarters said today.

Swaying block-by-block street fighting is raging in the strategic coastal highway town, 121 miles southwest of Canton, a communiqué said.

By breaking into Yeungkong Chinese forces won control of a fifty-mile coastal stretch leading west to Tinpak, which lies east of Luichow Peninsula on the South China Sea. The coastal area now is open to a virtually unopposed landing should American forces choose it for a staging point for supplies to the armies of South China.

West of Luichow Peninsula another 145-mile coastal stretch extending to the Indo-China frontier is under Chinese control and observers believe the Chinese soon may launch a concerted drive from the west and east that would seal off the Japanese on the Luichow

Continued on Page 2, Column 7

War News Summarized

TUESDAY, AUGUST 7, 1945

One bomb hit Japan on Sunday night, but it struck with the force of 20,000 tons of TNT. Where it landed had been the city of Hiroshima; what is there now has not yet been learned.

The attack, dramatically announced by President Truman sixteen hours after the missile had struck, was with an atomic bomb, a "harnessing of the basic power of the universe," he said. "The force from which the sun draws its power has been loosed against those who brought war to the Far East. And the end is not yet."

Details of the missile are closely guarded, but the 125,000 workers who saw materials pour into their factories never saw anything go out. The bomb is the result of pooling British-American scientific knowledge begun in 1940. "We have spent two billion dollars on the greatest scientific gamble in history—and won," Mr. Truman said, and warned:

"We are now prepared to obliterate more rapidly and completely every productive enterprise the Japanese have above ground in any city. It was to spare the Japanese public from utter destruction that the ultimatum of July 26 was issued at Potsdam. If they do not now accept our terms they may expect a rain of ruin from the air."

Secretary of War Stimson detailed the story of research and production and forecast improvements to increase the effectiveness of the "atomic bomb" several times. Congress will be asked to establish a committee to control peacetime use.

Hiroshima was a major military target, a city of 318,000 persons thickly settled around a quartermaster's depot, an embarkation port, armament and airplane parts plants. [All the foregoing 1:8.]

All production was in the United States at two plants at Oak Ridge, near Knoxville, Tenn., and one at Richland, Wash. A scientific laboratory was maintained in Sante Fe, N. M. [1:6.]

Former Prime Minister Churchill told of Britain's part, including costly attacks on German "heavy water" plants and the race to outstrip the Nazis. He praised American scientific achievement and gave full credit to President Roosevelt and his advisers. [1:5.]

Tokyo made no mention of what had happened to Hiroshima but rail service in that area was canceled. [1:7.]

Okinawa sent out 400 planes that left Tarumizu, on Kyushu's Kagoshima Bay, in flaming wreckage. About 125 "Superforts" bombed Toyokawa naval arsenal by daylight. [1:4; map p. 11.]

Chinese troops have broken into the port of Yeungkong and have cleared a large stretch of the south China coast west of Hong Kong and east of the Luichow Peninsula. [1:3; map P. 2.]

Moscow, moving to implement Potsdam decisions, has resumed diplomatic relations with Finland and Rumania. [11:4.]

The Germans received an opportunity to develop democratic talents when the United States and Great Britain authorized local trade unions and political parties in their zones of occupation. [12:2.]

France is expected to ratify the United Nations Charter and then the Bretton Woods monetary plan in the near future. [13:6.] Marshal Pétain was accused of having asked Hitler for help in regaining France's colonies. [13:1.]

Argentina has lifted the state of siege in effect since Pearl Harbor. [14:6.]

Steel Tower 'Vaporized' In Trial of Mighty Bomb

Scientists Awe-Struck as Blinding Flash Lighted New Mexico Desert and Great Cloud Bore 40,000 Feet Into Sky

By LEWIS WOOD

Special to THE NEW YORK TIMES.

WASHINGTON, Aug. 6—A blinding flash many times as brilliant as the midday sun and a massive, multi-colored cloud boiling up 40,000 feet into the air accompanied the first test firing of an atomic bomb on July 16, three weeks ago today. Set in the remote desert-lands of New Mexico, the experiment was seen against a wild background where rain poured in torrents, and lightning pierced the sky up to the zero hour of the explosion at 5:30 A. M.

A steel tower from which the atomic weapon hung was vaporized. In its place was only a huge, sloping crater. At the moment of the explosion a mountain range three miles distant stood out sharply in brilliant light.

"Then," said the War Department in a description, "came a tremendous, sustained roar and a heavy pressure wave which knocked down two men outside the control tower (10,000 yards, or more than five miles, away.)"

Before the detonation scientists waited in tense expectancy. Minutes lengthened seemingly to hours. Lying face downward, with their feet toward the steel tower, the watchers waited, nearly breathless. They were "reaching into the unknown" and did not know what would happen.

On the instant that all was over these men leaped to their feet. The terrible tension ended, they shook hands, embraced each other and shouted in glee. Behind their triumph was sober consciousness of possessing the means to "insure the speedy conclusion of the war and save thousands of American lives."

The scene of the great drama was the Alamogordo Air Base, 120 miles southeast of Albuquerque. Here the scientists strove to unlock the secret upon which $2,000,000,000 had been spent.

Graphic word pictures of the

Continued on Page 5, Column 1

NEW AGE USHERED

Day of Atomic Energy Hailed by President, Revealing Weapon

HIROSHIMA IS TARGET

'Impenetrable' Cloud of Dust Hides City After Single Bomb Strikes

Truman, Stimson statements on atomic bomb, Page 4.

By SIDNEY SHALETT

Special to THE NEW YORK TIMES.

WASHINGTON, Aug. 6—The White House and War Department announced today that an atomic bomb, possessing more power than 20,000 tons of TNT, a destructive force equal to the load of 2,000 B-29's and more than 2,000 times the blast power of what previously was the world's most devastating bomb, had been dropped on Japan.

The announcement, first given to the world in utmost solemnity by President Truman, made it plain that one of the scientific landmarks of the century had been passed, and that the "age of atomic energy," which can be a tremendous force for the advancement of civilization as well as for destruction, was at hand.

At 10:45 o'clock this morning, a statement by the President was issued at the White House that sixteen hours earlier—about the time that citizens on the Eastern seaboard were sitting down to their Sunday suppers—an American plane had dropped the single atomic bomb on the Japanese city of Hiroshima, an important army center.

Japanese Solemnly Warned

What happened at Hiroshima is not yet known. The War Department said it "as yet was unable to make an accurate report" because "an impenetrable cloud of dust and smoke" masked the target area from reconnaissance planes. The Secretary of War will release the story "as soon as accurate details of the results of the bombing become available."

But in a statement vividly describing the results of the first test of the atomic bomb in New Mexico, the War Department told how an immense steel tower had been "vaporized" by the tremendous explosion, how a 40,000-foot cloud rushed into the sky, and two observers were knocked down at a point 10,000 yards away. And President Truman solemnly warned:

"It was to spare the Japanese people from utter destruction that the ultimatum of July 26 was issued at Potsdam. Their leaders promptly rejected that ultimatum. If they do not now accept our terms, they may expect a rain of ruin from the air the like of which has never been seen on this earth."

Most Closely Guarded Secret

The President referred to the joint statement issued by the heads of the American, British and Chinese Governments, in which terms of surrender were outlined to the Japanese and warning given that rejection would mean complete destruction of Japan's power to make war.

[The atomic bomb weighs about 400 pounds and is capable of utterly destroying a town, a representative of the British Ministry of Aircraft Production said in London, the United Press reported.]

What is this terrible new weapon, which the War Department also calls the "Cosmic Bomb"? It is the harnessing of the energy of the atom, which is the basic power of the universe. As President Truman said, "The force from which the sun draws its power has been loosed against those who brought war to the Far East."

"Atomic fission"—in other

Continued on Page 2, Column 2

ATOM BOMBS MADE IN 3 HIDDEN 'CITIES'

Secrecy on Weapon So Great That Not Even Workers Knew of Their Product

By JAY WALZ

Special to THE NEW YORK TIMES.

WASHINGTON, Aug. 6—The War Department revealed today how three "hidden cities" with a total population of 100,000 inhabitants sprang into being as a result of the $2,000,000,000 atomic bomb project, how they did their work without knowing what it was all about, and how they kept the biggest secret of the war.

One of these, Oak Ridge, situated where only oak and pine trees had dotted small farms before, is today the fifth largest city in Tennessee. Its population of 75,000 persons has thirteen supermarkets, nine drug stores and seven theatres.

A second town of 7,000 was built for reasons of isolation and security on a New Mexico mesa. The third, named Richland Village, houses 17,000 men, women and children on remote banks of the Columbia River in the State of Washington.

None of the people, who came to these developments from homes all the way from Maine to California, had the slightest idea of what they were making in the gigantic Gov-

Continued on Page 3, Column 2

TRAINS CANCELED IN STRICKEN AREA

Traffic Around Hiroshima Is Disrupted — Japanese Still Sift Havoc by Split Atoms

By The United Press.

WASHINGTON, Aug. 6—The Osaka radio, without referring to the atomic bomb dropped on Hiroshima, hinted tonight at the terrific damage it must have caused by announcing that train service in the Hiroshima and other areas had been canceled.

First mention of the bomb came in a Japanese Domei agency dispatch announcing that President Truman and Prime Minister Attlee had disclosed that the new missile had been dropped on Hiroshima.

The Office of War Information began telling the Japanese today what hit them. OWI branch transmitters in San Francisco, Hawaii and Saipan beamed President Truman's statement on the atomic bomb to Japan.

Edward Barrett, director of the OWI's overseas branch, said that the President's announcement and related information on the atomic bomb will dominate the OWI's normal Japanese transmissions for the next several days.

LONDON, Tuesday, Aug. 7 (U.P.)—The Japanese Domei news agency, in a dispatch recorded by the British radio, said today that

Continued on Page 7, Column 3

Reich Exile Emerges as Heroine In Denial to Nazis of Atom's Secret

Special to THE NEW YORK TIMES.

WASHINGTON, Aug. 6—How Germany twice narrowly missed the secret of harnessing atomic energy by splitting uranium atoms and releasing the most powerful destructive force on earth was recalled today in War Department reports on the atomic bomb.

Development of the bomb after more than ten years of experimentation and research marks the first time that Prof. Albert Einstein's theory of relativity has been put to practical use outside the laboratory: the equation by which he showed the existence of a definite relationship of matter, energy and the velocity of light.

That the new bomb may be far from its maximum devastating potential was indicated by the War Department's statement that said:

"The energy we are now able to utilize in the atomic bombs, at 100 per cent efficiency, constitutes only one-tenth of 1 per cent of the total energy present in the material. But even one-hundredth of 1 per cent is still the most destructive force by far on this earth."

The principal character in the dramatic story of the long search for a method of releasing atomic energy is Dr. Lise Meitner, a woman physicist whom the Nazis expelled from Germany as a "non-Aryan." With her associates, Dr. Otto Hahn and Dr. F. Strassmann, both chemists, she had been working in the Kaiser Wilhelm Institute in Berlin, bombarding uranium atoms with neutrons and then submitting the uranium to chemical analysis.

As the War Department tells the story:

To their amazement, they found the element barium in the debris of the smashed uranium atoms.

Continued on Page 7, Column 1

A cloud of radioactive material rose after the atomic bomb was dropped on Japan.

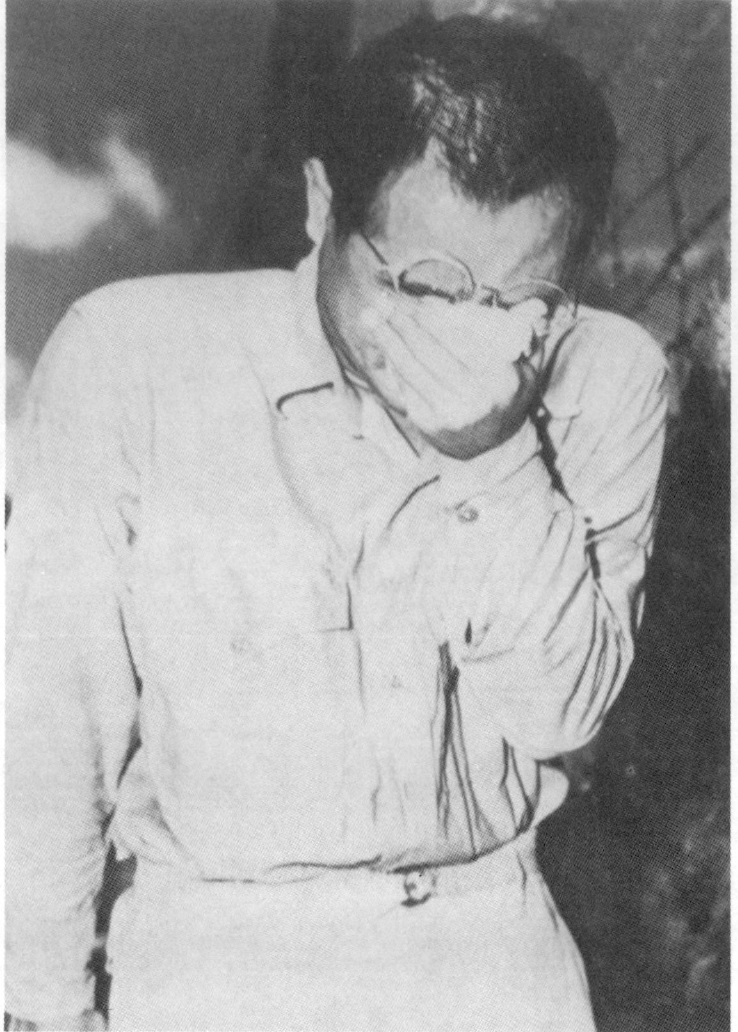

On Guam, a Japanese POW weeps as he listens to his country's surrender announcement.

The Clinton Engineering Works in Oak Ridge, Tennessee, where the first atomic bombs were produced. The headquarters for the United States Department of Energy is now located here.

"All the News That's Fit to Print"

The New York Times.

LATE CITY EDITION
Sunny with low humidity today. Partly cloudy, warmer tomorrow.
Temperatures Yesterday—Max., 77; Min., 66
Sunrise today, 5:58 A. M.; Sunset, 8:02 P. M.

VOL. XCIV..No. 31,974. Entered as Second-Class Matter, Postoffice, New York, N. Y. NEW YORK, THURSDAY, AUGUST 9, 1945. THREE CENTS NEW YORK CITY

SOVIET DECLARES WAR ON JAPAN; ATTACKS MANCHURIA, TOKYO SAYS; ATOM BOMB LOOSED ON NAGASAKI

TRUMAN TO REPORT TO PEOPLE TONIGHT ON BIG 3 AND WAR

Half-Hour Speech by Radio to Cover a Wide Range of Problems Facing the World

HE SIGNS PEACE CHARTER

And Thus Makes This Country the First to Complete All Ratification Requirements

By The Associated Press.

WASHINGTON, Aug. 8—President Truman will report to the country on the Potsdam conference over all radio networks at 10 P. M., Eastern war time, tomorrow in a thirty-minute speech.

The Presidential secretary, Charles G. Ross, said today that the speech, which probably would also be short-waved abroad, would go into greater detail than the communiqué issued by the Big Three at the close of the meeting July 26.

Mr. Truman worked on the speech today as well as on a mass of other paper work which accumulated during his month-long absence, and signed into full ratification the United Nations Charter.

He held his calling list to a minimum, including brief conferences with Senators Hatch of New Mexico and Kilgore of West Virginia, and Henry L. Stimson, Secretary of War.

The Stimson conference was devoted to further discussion of the atomic bomb.

Associates of the President indicated that his report on the Potsdam conference would probably mention the new and revolutionary bomb used for the first time against Japan.

Full Appraisal May Be Given

A full appraisal of revised conditions, including Russia's declaration of war against Japan, may come in Mr. Truman's broadcast.

Originally the speech was expected to be primarily a report on the Soviet-British-American agreements announced at the end of the Potsdam conference. These dealt mainly with Europe, keeping Germany under strict surveillance, and the writing of peace treaties.

It became known today that Mr. Truman had four or five names under consideration for the vacancy on the Supreme Court, and the decision appeared imminent.

One of the names is that of Senator Austin, Republican, of Vermont, who has been endorsed by his Democratic colleague, Senator Hatch. It was to renew his suggestion that Mr. Austin be appointed to succeed Justice Owen Roberts, who retired, that brought Mr. Hatch to the White House today.

"Of course the President made no commitments," Mr. Hatch told reporters later, "but he definitely is considering both the appointment of a Republican and Senator Austin. Of course that is only a possibility."

Justice Roberts, appointed by President Hoover in 1930, was one of two Republicans in the present makeup of the high court. Chief Justice Harlan F. Stone is the remaining member of that party.

Charter Goes to Archives

Special to The New York Times.

WASHINGTON, Aug. 8—When President Truman signed today the document by which he ratified the Charter of the United Nations, the United States thereby became the first country to complete its action for bringing the Charter into force.

Several other countries have ratified or taken action with a view to ratification, but no instrument of ratification has yet been received from any of them by the State Department, which is the

Continued on Page 3, Column 5

Foreigners Asked To Stay at Home

Special to The New York Times.

WASHINGTON, Aug. 8—Discouragement of unessential travel by foreigners to the United States was ordered by the Government today through the State Department.

"The Department of State has always traditionally done everything in its power to promote the travel of citizens of other countries of the Western Hemisphere to the United States," said the announcement. "However, the United States Government is now engaged in a gigantic military operation in deploying forces and supplies from the European theatre to the Pacific area. This tremendous task places an unprecedented burden on the transportation system."

The citizens of other countries should realize the situation, the statement said, and postpone trips to the United States unless they were directly connected with the war.

TAMMANY OUSTS LAST OF REBELS

County Committee Ratifies Executive Group's Action—Meeting Picketed

Without the slightest opposition, the New York County Democratic Committee, popularly known as Tammany, last night ratified the selection of an executive committee on which there remained no opposition to the leadership of Edward V. Loughlin or to the influence in the organization repeatedly exercised by Bert Stand, secretary, and Clarence H. Neal Jr., chairman of its elections committee.

In Brooklyn the Kings County Democratic Committee nominated United States Attorney Miles F. McDonald for District Attorney of Kings County to run for the vacancy caused by the resignation of William O'Dwyer, Democratic and American Labor party candidate for Mayor. Mr. McDonald, a graduate of Holy Cross College and Fordham Law School, in accepting the nomination, told the members of the committee that he would resign as United States Attorney.

Nearly 2,000 members, the largest number in recent years, attended the Tammany meeting in the Central Commercial High School, 214 East Forty-second Street. All resolutions presented were adopted unanimously by voice vote.

The committee ratified action taken by the executive committee in setting Robert B. Blaikie as leader of the Seventh Assembly District in place of Joseph H. Broderick and Assemblyman Patrick H. Sullivan, in spite of the claim of Mr. Broderick that he had elected a majority of county com-

Continued on Page 17, Column 2

2D BIG AERIAL BLOW

Japanese Port Is Target in Devastating New Midday Assault

RESULT CALLED GOOD

Foe Asserts Hiroshima Toll Is 'Uncountable' —Assails 'Atrocity'

By W. H. LAWRENCE

By Wireless to The New York Times.

GUAM, Thursday, Aug. 9—Gen. Carl A. Spaatz announced today that a second atomic bomb had been dropped, this time on the city of Nagasaki, and that crew members reported "good results."

The second use of the new and terrifying secret weapon which wiped out more than 60 per cent of the city of Hiroshima and, according to the Japanese radio, killed nearly every resident of that town, occurred at noon today, Japanese time. The target today was an important industrial and shipping area with a population of about 258,000.

The great bomb, which harnesses the power of the universe to destroy the enemy by concussion, blast and fire, was dropped on the second enemy city about seven hours after the Japanese had received a political "roundhouse punch" in the form of a declaration of war by the Soviet Union.

Vital Transshipment Point

GUAM, Thursday, Aug. 9 (AP)—Nagasaki is vitally important as a port for transshipment of military supplies and the embarkation of troops in support of Japan's operations in China, Formosa, Southeast Asia and the Southwest Pacific. It was highly important as a major shipbuilding and repair center for both naval and merchantmen.

The city also included industrial surburbs of Inase and Akunoura on the western side of the harbor, and Urakami. The combined area is nearly double Hiroshima's.

Nagasaki, although only two-thirds as large as Hiroshima in population, is considered more important industrially. With a population now estimated at 253,000, its twelve square miles are jam-packed with the eave-to-eave buildings that won it the name of "sea of roofs."

General Spaatz' communiqué reporting the bombing did not say whether one or more than one "mighty atom" was dropped.

Hiroshima a 'City of Dead'

The Tokyo radio yesterday described Hiroshima as a city of ruins and dead "too numerous to be counted," and put forth the claim that the use of the atomic

Continued on Page 6, Column 3

RED ARMY STRIKES

Foe Reports First Blow by Soviet Forces on Asian Frontier

KEY POINTS BOMBED

Action Believed Aimed to Free Vladivostok Area of Threat

By The United Press.

SAN FRANCISCO, Aug. 8—Russia's mighty Far Eastern Army began hostilities against Japan at 12:10 A. M. Thursday [Russian time], launching a sudden attack along the eastern Soviet-Manchuria border only nine minutes after Moscow's declaration of war became effective, the enemy reported today.

A Kwantung Army headquarters communiqué issued at Changchun [Hsinking] and recorded here reported the attack and also announced that the Red Air Force already was bombing strategic points in Manchurian territory behind Japanese lines.

No details of the attack were given, but presumably the Russians would drive west from the Vladivostok area into Japanese-held territory north of the tip of Korea. Vladivostok is only about twenty miles east of the border, separated from the Japanese by fortified positions along the rugged, mountainous terrain.

The communiqué made it clear that ground forces had opened the attack—part of the Soviet Union's Far Eastern Army of more than 1,000,000 well-equipped troops, who never were called into action against Germany, but remained along the border, a constant threat to Japan.

Although the communiqué did not locate the fighting, it was believed the Russians would strike out as quickly as possible from the Vladivostok region, which is highly

Continued on Page 4, Column 6

CIRCLE OF SPEARHEADS AROUND JAPAN IS COMPLETED

Aug. 9, 1945

With the entry of the Soviet Union into the war against Japan, the enemy is confronted with armed might from new directions—the north and northeast. Japan was already being battered by American power pressing in from the northeast and the south and by Chinese and British power from the west and southwest. The Russians are reported attacking Manchuria.

385 B-29'S SMASH 4 TARGETS IN JAPAN

Tokyo Arsenal and Aircraft Plant Are Seared—Fukuyama and Yawata Cities Ripped

By Wireless to The New York Times.

GUAM, Thursday, Aug. 9—Gen. Carl A. Spaatz, armed with the confirmed knowledge that his Strategic Air Force possesses in the atomic bomb the most powerful destructive agent devised by man since gunpowder was discovered, sent four separate forces

Continued on Page 2, Column 1

U. S. Third Fleet Attacking Targets in Northern Honshu

By ROBERT TRUMBULL

By Wireless to The New York Times.

GUAM, Thursday, Aug. 9—Admiral William F. Halsey's mighty Third Fleet, including British carriers, is now throwing strong air attacks at northern Honshu in the Japanese home islands, where the enemy has twenty to twenty-five airfields, Fleet Admiral Chester W. Nimitz announced this morning.

Although no specific targets were designated, the communiqué said shipping, air installations and "other military targets" were hit by strong air attacks beginning at dawn.

Today's communiqué broke nine days of silence by the Third Fleet after strikes in the Tokyo area July 30. It is possible that persistent fogs, caused by the warm Japanese Current at this time of year, forced Admiral Halsey to desist during that time from the sea-borne attacks carried out in conjunction with land-based air activity over the empire.

Northern Honshu, an area of 30,669 square miles, a little smaller than Maine and populated by 9,500,000 persons, has twenty to twenty-five airfields that are considered operational although some are small, poorly developed bases and probably are used only for the dispersal of the Japanese air force hiding out in that area.

While the northern Honshu district as geographically defined is outside the main military and industrial area of the island there is

Continued on Page 2, Column 8

TRUMAN REVEALS MOVE OF MOSCOW

Announces War Declaration Soon After Russian Action —Capital Is Startled

By FELIX BELAIR JR.

Special to The New York Times.

WASHINGTON, Aug. 8—President Truman announced a few minutes after 3 P. M. today that Russia had just declared war on Japan. The dramatic statement, issued with all the casualness of a routine proclamation, came during the shortest White House press conference on record.

Flanked by Secretary of State James M. Byrnes and Admiral William D. Leahy, his Chief of Staff, the President stood before hastily summoned reporters and in steady, matter-of-fact tones declared: "I have only a simple an-

Continued on Page 3, Column 1

RUSSIA AIDS ALLIES

Joins Pacific Struggle After Spurning Foe's Mediation Plea

SEEKS EARLY PEACE

Molotoff Reveals Move Three Months After Victory in Europe

By BROOKS ATKINSON

By Wireless to The New York Times.

MOSCOW, Aug. 8—Russia declared war on Japan tonight. In a dramatic press conference held at 8:30 P. M., Foreign Commissar Vyacheslaff M. Molotoff read the declaration, which was announced to the public at 10 P. M., Moscow time [3 P. M. New York time].

In view of Japan's refusal of the Allies' demand for unconditional surrender, Mr. Molotoff said, the Allies proposed that the Soviet Union "join the war against Japanese aggression and thus shorten the duration of the war, reduce the number of victims and facilitate the speedy restoration of universal peace.

"Loyal to its Allied duty," the Foreign Commissar continued, "the Soviet Government has accepted the proposal of the Allies and has joined in the declaration of the Allied Powers of July 26. The Soviet Government considers that this policy is the only means able to bring peace nearer, free the people from further sacrifice and suffering and give the Japanese people the possibility of avoiding the dangers and destruction suffered by Germany after her refusal to capitulate unconditionally."

Closing his concise statement, Mr. Molotoff declared:

"In view of the above, the Soviet Government declares that from tomorrow, that is Aug. 9, the Soviet Union will consider itself to be at war with Japan."

The Soviet Government's declaration comes three months after the victory over Germany, supporting rumors that some months ago the Soviet Government intimated it would join in the war against Japan three months after victory was won in Europe.

For the first time Mr. Molotoff revealed that the Japanese Government had asked the Soviet Union to mediate for a cessation of hostilities about the middle of June. Japanese Ambassador Naotaka Sato delivered the message, and also a special message from

Continued on Page 3, Column 2

Tokyo 'Flashes' News 3 Hours After Event

By The Associated Press.

SAN FRANCISCO, Aug. 8—Japan's first recorded wireless reaction to Russia's war declaration was a brief factual announcement of that action by the Domei agency in an English-language transmission to Europe.

The Domei account, broadcast five hours and fifty-five minutes after the Moscow announcement, reported:

"Flash! Flash! Tokyo, Aug. 9—Tass News Agency announced late last night that Foreign Commissar Vyacheslaff M. Molotoff communicated to Naotake Sato, Japanese Ambassador to Russia, that the Soviet Union will consider itself in a state of war with Japan from Thursday, Aug. 9, according to the Moscow radio recorded here this morning."

By the time the "flash" was read, the state of war already had existed for several hours.

Allies Cut Austria Into Four Zones With Vienna Under Joint Control

By LANSING WARREN

Special to The New York Times.

WASHINGTON, Aug. 8—A four-power control machinery, including France with the Big Three, has been established in Austria in accordance with an agreement between the Soviet Union, the United States, the United Kingdom and France, it was announced today.

The system resembles the military control arrangement for Germany. It divides Austria into four zones of occupation and provides that Vienna, the capital city, shall also be occupied by the forces of the four controlling powers. It creates an Allied Council, consisting of the four military commissioners, who will govern Austria as a whole. The commissioners will make the decisions for all Austria and will insure a uniformity of action in the different zones.

[The text of the statement on Austria is on Page 11.]

Under the direction of this combined Allied council each military commander will have full authority in his zone. The council will act through the commanders and through an executive committee, which will advise the council and carry out its decisions.

By this means the agreement seeks to prevent a situation that would separate too rigidly the

Continued on Page 11, Column 5

War News Summarized

THURSDAY, AUGUST 9, 1945

Russia has declared war against Japan because that country is the only great power standing in the way of peace. Foreign Commissar Molotoff so informed Ambassador Sato in Moscow yesterday. He said it was in the interests of shortening the war and bringing peace to the world that Moscow acceded to the Allied request to join the war in the Far East and subscribed to the Potsdam ultimatum of July 26. Mr. Molotoff revealed that Japan had asked the Soviet Union to mediate for peace, but that proposal "lost all foundation" when Tokyo rejected the Potsdam demands. [1:8.]

Hostilities were begun nine minutes after the war declaration went into effect at 12:01 this morning, according to Tokyo, when Soviet troops struck along Manchuria's eastern frontier with Siberia. Air attacks, it was said, quickly followed. [1:4.]

President Truman broke the news when he told a hastily called press conference: "Russia has declared war against Japan—that is all." [1:7.] Secretary of State Byrnes declared there was "still time—but little time—for the Japanese to save themselves from the destruction which threatens them." Mr. Byrnes said the President had convinced Premier Stalin that Russia must enter the war if she was to be responsible for peace. [4:2.]

Congress, jubilant and confident that Russia's aid and the atomic bomb would shorten the war materially, expected to be called back soon. [4:1.]

Japan received another blow when the second atomic bomb to fall struck Nagasaki on Kyushu. Crew members reported good results. "Practically all living things" in Hiroshima were destroyed beyond recognition by heat and pressure from the first atomic bomb, Tokyo reported. [1:3.] Fires leaped seven rivers. [6:3, with map.]

The Third Fleet, after nine days of silence, sent its carrier planes in a strong attack, still continuing at last reports, against northern Honshu and its score of airfields. [1:6-7.] B-29's hit four Japanese cities in twenty-four hours and mined home waters. [1:5; map P. 2.]

Wuhu Island, at the mouth of the Min River east of Foochow, was captured by the Chinese. [8:2, with map.]

Russia, Britain, France and the United States have signed an agreement for the occupation and administration of Austria similar to that in effect in Germany. Complete separation from Germany, restoration of the 1937 frontiers and return of democratic government were set as Allied goals. [1:2-3; maps P. 11.]

A new code of international law was adopted by the Big Four listing wars of aggression as a crime against peace. [1:6-7.]

General de Gaulle and his Cabinet, contrary to the wishes of the Consultative Assembly, will submit the questions of a new constitution and government responsibility to a referendum on Oct. 21. [13:5.]

President Truman signed the United Nations Charter yesterday. He will discuss the Potsdam Conference and the military situation in a broadcast at 10 o'clock tonight. [1:1.]

4 Powers Call Aggression Crime In Accord Covering War Trials

By CHARLES E. EGAN

By Wireless to The New York Times.

LONDON, Aug. 8—A new code of international law, defining aggressive warfare as a crime against the world and providing punishment for those who provoke such wars, was announced here today.

By agreement among representatives of the United States, Great Britain, the Soviet Union and France, the legal framework necessary for the trial of the key German and Italian leaders held by the Allies was promulgated this afternoon. The document sets precedents in international law and, in the words of United States Supreme Court Justice Robert H. Jackson, the American representative, "ought to make clear to the world that those who lead their nations into aggressive war face individual accountability for such acts."

"If we can cultivate in the world the idea that aggressive war making is the way to a prisoners' dock rather than the way to honors," he said "we will have accomplished something toward making peace more secure."

[The texts of the War Crimes Committee report and Mr. Jackson's statement are on Page 10.]

The agreement, upon which the international committee has been laboring since June 26, represents

Continued on Page 11, Column 6

Under Hitler's government, Nuremberg had been the site for Party Congresses; after the war, major Nazi war criminals were put on trial and hanged there. The old city, one of the finest examples of Gothic architecture in Germany, looked like this after the war.

Hiroshima was practically annihilated when the atomic bomb was dropped. Three days later, a second bomb destroyed Nagasaki. The destruction that took place is almost beyond comprehension.

"All the News That's Fit to Print"

The New York Times.

LATE CITY EDITION
Clearing early today; cooler. Clear and cool tomorrow.
Temperatures Yesterday—Max., 88; Min., 72
Sunrise today, 6:11 A. M.; Sunset, 7:18 P. M.

Section 1

NEWS INDEX, PAGE 33, THIS SECTION

Copyright, 1945, by The New York Times Company.

VOL. XCIV..No. 31,998. Entered as Second-Class Matter, Postoffice, New York, N. Y. NEW YORK, SUNDAY, SEPTEMBER 2, 1945. Including Magazine and Book Review. TEN CENTS New York City and Suburban Areas (15c Elsewhere)

JAPAN SURRENDERS TO ALLIES, SIGNS RIGID TERMS ON WARSHIP; TRUMAN SETS TODAY AS V-J DAY

HOLIDAY TRAFFIC NEAR 1941 LEVEL; 'GAS' IS PLENTIFUL

Exodus From City Is Greatest Since Pre-War Days but Congestion Is Avoided

GOOD WEATHER PROMISED

Near-by Resorts Do Capacity Business—3 Persons Die in Queens Accidents

America's millions, deprived since 1941 of the chance to cruise the highways of their nation, hit the road in traditional Labor Day week-end style yesterday.

There was a plentiful supply of gasoline, the sun shone warm out of blue skies, and everyone felt free from war worries. This combined to roll up traffic that continued heavy all day.

New York City's heat-ridden population took to car, train, bus and plane. The exodus to near-by mountain and seashore resorts was the greatest since that of 1941.

The weather formed a perfect lure. Not even the thunder showers predicted by the Weather Bureau for late afternoon took place. Today's prediction is for clearing weather early, followed by cooler, with the highest temperature around 80 degrees, and with fresh to strong northwest winds. A clear and cool Monday is forecast by the bureau. The temperature yesterday reached 88 degrees at 3:30 P. M. with the humidity at 52 per cent. The all-time high for the date was set in 1924 with 92.5 degrees and the low in 1872 with 51.

Many Cars Come Into City

Travel in the city was two-way. As cars streamed out of the city over bridges, on ferries and through tunnels, out-of-towners poured in. The main idea for Labor Day seemed to be change of scenery.

Thousands of automobiles, many of them looking as though they had just been taken off the jacks for the first time in years, formed a continuous procession along the main highways leading up-State, out on Long Island and to the South Jersey shore.

The Port of New York Authority reported that 69,400 automobiles had crossed the George Washington Bridge into New Jersey. Forty-five thousand cars passed through the Holland Tunnel during the sixteen hours preceding 6 o'clock last night. Lincoln Tunnel police said traffic was heavier than usual.

Few serious accidents were reported. "Maybe it's because the cars just don't have the pep," remarked a Westchester County parkway policeman.

Sights along the parkways bore out his contention. Many cars became pathetically silent as their drivers resignedly hauled them over to the side of the road to patch up tires or to fume over engine repairs.

Gasoline Supplies Abundant

Assured of as much gasoline as they wanted, motorists traveled leisurely and did not cause congestion. Filling station pumps received their heaviest workout in years. Station operators estimated that demands for gasoline ranged from 10 to 30 per cent over last week-end, but they reported there was no difficulty in obtaining supplies.

The Cities Service Oil Company said it was having difficulty in meeting orders for premium gasoline, ordinarily accounting for 25 per cent of sales, as the supply was limited, but no company reported shortages of non-premium gasoline. No motorist was forced to stay in town because of lack of fuel.

Trains, buses and airlines were crowded, as they have been all through the war. The airlines re-

Continued on Page 30, Column 2

Times Sq. Takes V-J News Quietly

Times Square throngs, which had greeted Japanese capitulation explosively last month, took the formal signing of terms in much calmer fashion last night.

Two hundred policemen, including twenty-five mounted patrolmen, who had been assigned to the area in case of another outburst of feeling, reported that the street crowds took the flashing of the bulletin from Times Tower at 10:04 P. M. with a few cheers and good-natured remarks, and did not attempt to start a celebration.

In numbers the crowd was no larger than an average Saturday night, and of the persons present perhaps half or more were out-of-town visitors here for the Labor Day week-end, the police estimated. Other parts of the city were similarly quiet.

Mayor La Guardia had said earlier that the people "have had their big time and are satisfied." He decided not to hold a celebration in Central Park today as had been planned.

PRESIDENT STRESSES LABOR DAY OF PEACE

But He Warns That After Six Holidays of Hostilities Great New Problems Lie Ahead

Special to The New York Times.

WASHINGTON, Sept. 1—President Truman hailed the first Labor Day of peace in six years today and declared a grateful world would always remember the workers of all free nations for their contribution to victory.

Secretary Forrestal and J. A. Krug, chairman of the War Production Board, also lauded the men and women of labor, and Philip Murray, chairman of the Congress of Industrial Organizations, told a radio audience that America's vast war plant must be put to work on peacetime products which would give prosperity unlimited to this country.

Mr. Truman's statement said that six years ago today the workers of the United States, and of the world, awoke to a Labor Day in a world at war, and added:

"We in the United States had two years of grace, but the issue was squarely joined at that hour, as we now know. There was to be no peace until tyranny had been outlawed.

"Today we stand on the threshold of a new world. We must do our part in making this world what it should be, a world in which the bigotries of race and class and creed shall not be permitted to warp the souls of men.

"We enter upon an era of great problems, but to live is to face problems. Our men and women did not falter in the task of saving freedom. They will not falter now in the task of making freedom

Continued on Page 24, Column 3

HAILS ERA OF PEACE

President Calls On U.S. to Stride On Toward a World of Good-Will

SALUTES HEROIC DEAD

Cautions Jubilant Nation Hard Jobs Ahead Need Same Zeal as War

Text of the President's address proclaiming V-J Day, P. 4.

By WILLIAM S. WHITE

Special to The New York Times.

WASHINGTON, Sept. 1—President Truman, in remembrance of all who have fallen and in an appeal to all Americans to go forward now in hope and fraternity toward "a new and better world of peace and international good-will," tonight solemnly proclaimed tomorrow to be V-J Day.

The moment that he began to speak was, in the official and historical sense, the first moment of peace this country had known since a December day nearly four years ago, when, at a sudden, a harsh and an incredible blow the whole of the Pacific world went into flames.

Into the human calendar of great American holidays, like the Fourth of July and the Eleventh of November, the President thus entered another date, the Second of September, although it does not technically signify the end of the "duration" and will have no basis as a legal end of the war. The termination of hostilities, for purposes of computing military service, for setting the limit to war agencies and for all other like formalities, will be set only by final decision of Congress.

Japanese Surrender Signaled

But Mr. Truman's speech was a speech to the heart of a country that had had the skill to make the atomic bomb and could now "use the same skill and energy and determination to overcome all the difficulties ahead," rather than to the keepers of its books of law.

It was notice from the White House, so long awaited, that nearly four years of war, a struggle of sacrificial grandeur such as the United States had never known, had at last come to an end, and that the terrible ledger opened at Pearl Harbor had now been balanced and closed.

The President spoke in this mood, a mood of valedictory and of dedication, as he proclaimed "this . . . victory of more than arms alone . . . this . . . victory of liberty over tyranny." He had just received the signal from across the world that the Japanese had signed, aboard the great battleship Missouri, the last, humiliat-

Continued on Page 4, Column 1

JAPANESE FOREIGN MINISTER SIGNING SURRENDER ARTICLES

Mamoru Shigemitsu (right, seated), on behalf of Emperor Hirohito, affixes his signature to document as Gen. Douglas MacArthur (left) and Lieut. Gen. Richard K. Sutherland (center) look on during ceremony aboard the Missouri in Tokyo Bay.

Associated Press Wirephoto (via Navy Radio from U. S. S. Iowa)

BYRNES FORESEES A PEACEFUL JAPAN

Says People Are Expected to Force Development—World Amity Vital, Hull Warns

Special to The New York Times.

WASHINGTON, Sept. 1—Secretary of State James F. Byrnes declared tonight that with Japan's surrender we have entered the second phase of our war—"what might be called the spiritual disarmament of that nation, to make them want peace instead of wanting war."

The intention of this Govern-

Continued on Page 5, Column 1

Japan's Surrender Ordered Over Militarist Opposition

By FRANK L. KLUCKHOHN

By Wireless to The New York Times.

TOKYO, Sept. 1—In the rubble of this once-proud imperial capital the story of how the Japanese Army opposed the surrender and how the Emperor made the final decision to capitulate after having heard the opinions of all his advisers, and how War Minister Korechika Anami had committed suicide was unfolded today by one of a handful of those in a position to know without bias what occurred.

It was also learned how the Japanese reacted step by step to wartime developments and how propaganda that Japan could win had been continued to the last moment, thus leaving the industrious long-

Continued on Page 7, Column 1

U. S. CHIEFS DIVIDED ON ITALY'S COLONIES

State Department Split Over Russia and Influence Zones Is Projected by Issue

By JAMES B. RESTON

Special to The New York Times.

WASHINGTON, Sept. 1—A fundamental issue has developed in the Department of State over the future of the Italian colonies, particularly Eritrea, Libya and Italian Somaliland.

The issue is whether these colonies should go back to Italy as part of her sovereign territory, be taken from her and administered by the United States, Britain, France and the Soviet Union under the United Nations Organization or be administered by a neutral international commission under the United Nations.

The major powers that defeated Germany are soon to start draft-

Continued on Page 15, Column 1

TOKYO AIDES WEEP AS GENERAL SIGNS

Imperial Staff Chief Hastily Scrawls His Signature—Shigemitsu Is Anxious

By The Associated Press.

ABOARD U. S. S. MISSOURI in Tokyo Bay, Sunday, Sept. 2—The solemn surrender ceremony, on this battleship today, marking the first defeat in Japan's 2,600-year-old semi-legendary history, required only a few minutes as twelve signatures were affixed to the articles.

Surrounded by the might of the United States Navy and Army, and under the eyes of the American and British commanders they so ruthlessly defeated in the Philippines and Malaya, the Japanese representatives quietly made the marks on paper that ended the bloody Pacific conflict.

The Japanese delegation came aboard at 8:55 A. M., 7:55 P. M. Saturday, E. W. T., as scheduled. They reached the Missouri in personnel speed boats flying the American flag.

Foreign Minister Mamoru Shigemitsu led the delegation. He climbed stiffly up the ladder and limped forward on his right leg, which is artificial. He was wounded by a bomb tossed by a Korean terrorist in Shanghai many years ago.

On behalf of Emperor Hirohito, Mr. Shigemitsu signed first for

Continued on Page 9, Column 1

World News Summarized

SUNDAY, SEPTEMBER 2, 1945

The rulers of Japan, who set the Pacific ablaze nearly four years ago with their surprise attack on Pearl Harbor and hoped to culminate that assault with a peace dictated in the White House, formally signed their unconditional surrender to the Allied powers in Tokyo Bay. Foreign Minister Shigemitsu signed the historic document for his country in the shadow of the sixteen-inch gun muzzles of the battleship Missouri. General MacArthur, who signed in behalf of the Allies, said mankind hoped a better world would result from the solemn occasion. [1:8; map P. 12.]

President Truman proclaimed today as V-J Day. He urged the nation to observe the day of victory over Japan in a spirit of dedication and as a symbol of "victory of liberty over tyranny." He also asked his countrymen to remember "our departed gallant leader, Franklin D. Roosevelt." [1:3.]

Japan's decision to surrender was dictated by Emperor Hirohito after he had overruled a strong faction within the Cabinet and the army that wanted to keep on with the war in the belief that the Japanese could defeat an invasion of the homeland, according to well-informed observers in Tokyo. [1:5-6.]

Medical "experiments" recalling medieval sadism were carried out on dying American prisoners of war by young Japanese Army doctors, two American physicians interned with their compatriots said aboard a United States hospital ship. [1:6-7.]

With the Foreign Ministers' Council scheduled to meet in London next week to begin consideration of peace terms, it was learned that a serious division of opinion over the disposition of the Italian colonies had developed in the State Department. [1:6.]

Former Secretary of State Stettinius said in London that the development of the atomic bomb emphasized the need for "the speedy creation of the United Nations Organization to keep the peace of the world" and predicted that as soon as the organization began functioning it would appoint a military staff to deal with the use of atomic bombs, as well as all other types of force in preserving peace. [18:2.]

"ALL THE NEWS THAT'S FIT TO PRINT"

In the first eight months of this year, The Times published 6,092 more columns of news than any other newspaper. With World Peace still to be won, and reconversion a topic of daily import, The New York Times continues to print the complete news.

Enemy Tortured Dying Americans With Sadist Medical 'Experiments'

By ROBERT TRUMBULL

By Wireless to The New York Times.

ABOARD THE HOSPITAL SHIP BENEVOLENCE, in Tokyo Bay, Sept. 1 — Seriously ailing American prisoners at Shinagawa, the only hospital serving 8,000 prisoners of war held in the Tokyo area, were guinea pigs for fantastic experiments recalling the sorcery and sadism of the middle ages, Drs. Mack L. Gottlieb and Harold W. Keschner, both of New York, told this correspondent today.

Both doctors are recuperating aboard this ship after their rescue from Shinagawa on Wednesday by a special Navy evacuation mission headed by Comdr. Harold A. Stassen, former Governor of Minnesota and now Assistant Chief of Staff and Flag Secretary to Admiral William F. Halsey, commander of the Third Fleet.

[In an interview in Tokyo the Japanese Army doctor to whom some of these practices were charged confirmed the cruel treatment of American prisoners.]

Dr. Gottlieb, who had his home and office at 307 East Forty-fourth Street, was a Naval officer captured at Guam. Dr. Keschner, of 451 West End Avenue, was taken with an Army force in the Philippines. Both are in good physical

Continued on Page 14, Column 1

Public Gets Big Army Food Stocks; Whipping Cream Is Freed of Bans

Special to The New York Times.

WASHINGTON, Sept. 1—The national food situation continued its steady improvement today as the Department of Agriculture, with four orders, increased the supplies of butter, canned salmon and ice cream and signalled the return of whipping cream.

This action was a direct consequence of the sharp reduction of military requirements of these foods. With the discontinuance of butter purchases by the armed forces, the Department explained, it is now possible to revoke the limitations on the sale of heavy cream and the use of butter fat in the production of all frozen desserts. Both these rulings will make whipping cream and ice cream of a higher butter fat content readily available.

In a simultaneous direction, the agency ordered released for civilian use all butter currently held by creameries and receivers for the armed forces and other Government buyers. Although as much as 20,000,000 pounds of butter may be returned to civilian consumers under this ruling, ration values will not be changed, it was indicated.

"At the time ration point values were established for September, the Office of Price Administration recognized the possibility of these

Continued on Page 33, Column 1

WAR COMES TO END

Articles of Capitulation Endorsed by Countries in Pacific Conflict

M'ARTHUR SEES PEACE

Emperor Orders Subjects to Obey All Commands Issued by General

The texts of the surrender documents and statements, P. 3.

By The Associated Press.

ABOARD THE U. S. S. MISSOURI in Tokyo Bay, Sunday, Sept. 2—Japan surrendered formally and unconditionally to the Allies today in a twenty-minute ceremony which ended just as the sun burst through low-hanging clouds as a shining symbol to a ravaged world now done with war.

[A United Press dispatch said the leading Japanese delegate signed the articles at 9:02 A. M. Sunday, Tokyo time, and that General MacArthur signed them at 9:07 A. M.]

Twelve signatures, requiring only a few minutes to inscribe on the articles of surrender, ended the bloody Pacific conflict.

On behalf of Emperor Hirohito, Foreign Minister Mamoru Shigemitsu signed for the Government and Gen. Yoshijiro Umezu for the Imperial General Staff.

MacArthur Voices Peace Hope

Gen. Douglas MacArthur then accepted in behalf of the United Nations, declaring:

"It is my earnest hope and indeed the hope of all mankind that from this solemn occasion a better world shall emerge out of the blood and carnage of the past."

One by one the Allied representatives stepped forward and signed the document that blighted Japan's dream of empire built on bloodshed and tyranny.

First was Admiral Chester W. Nimitz for the United States, then the representatives of China, the United Kingdom, the Soviet, Australia, Canada, France, the Netherlands and New Zealand.

The flags of the United States, Britain, the Soviet and China fluttered from the veranda deck of the famed superdreadnaught, polished and scrubbed as never before. More than 100 high-ranking military and naval officers watched.

Pledges Justice and Tolerance

"As Supreme Commander for the Allied powers," General MacArthur told the Japanese, "I announce it my firm purpose, in the tradition of the countries I represent, to proceed in the discharge of my responsibilities with justice and tolerance, while taking all necessary dispositions to insure that the terms of surrender are fully, promptly and faithfully complied with."

All through this dramatic half hour, only those aboard the battleship knew of what was taking place, because the Missouri has no broadcasting facilities.

But recordings were rushed to the near-by communications ship Ancon, and the solemn words of General MacArthur beginning the ceremony—"We are gathered here, representatives of the major warring powers"—were flashed around the world.

The Japanese representatives were present at the command of Emperor Hirohito contained in a proclamation issued by order of the Supreme Allied Commander.

The Emperor further commanded his officials "to issue general orders to the military and naval forces in accordance with the direction of the Supreme Commander

Continued on Page 2, Column 3

1945

Churchill, Truman and Stalin attended the Potsdam Conference in mid-1945.

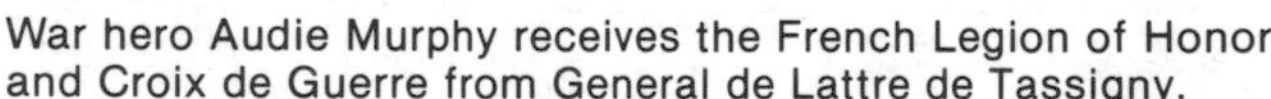

War hero Audie Murphy receives the French Legion of Honor and Croix de Guerre from General de Lattre de Tassigny.

The signing of the Japanese surrender document aboard the U.S.S. Missouri. General Douglas MacArthur is at the right-center of the picture.

"All the News That's Fit to Print"

The New York Times.

LATE CITY EDITION
Sunny, cold in the morning today.
Tomorrow partly cloudy.
Temperatures Yesterday—Max., 46; Min., 37
Sunrise today, 6:44 A. M.; Sunset, 4:38 P. M.

Copyright, 1945, by The New York Times Company.

VOL. XCV...No. 32,073. Entered as Second-Class Matter, Postoffice, New York, N. Y. NEW YORK, FRIDAY, NOVEMBER 16, 1945. THREE CENTS IN NEW YORK CITY

WE KNEW JAPANESE SECRETS 6 MONTHS BEFORE DEC. 7, 1941, PEARL HARBOR DATA SHOW

THE INQUIRY OPENS

Enemy's Code Broken by American Experts, Documents Reveal

FOE ALSO KNEW ABOUT US

Kimmel, Short Attend Hearing, Starting of Which Is Called Premature by Republicans

By WILLIAM S. WHITE
Special to The New York Times.

WASHINGTON, Nov. 15—A joint Congressional Committee opened today its investigation of the Pearl Harbor attack, over the protests of its senior Republican members that a premature beginning was being made, with disclosures that at least some part of official Washington had known six months before Dec. 7, 1941, some of the most intimate secrets of the Japanese intentions for war.

This revelation, the most significant on the first day of an inquiry unique in American history, was made in the introduction by the committee's chief counsel, William D. Mitchell, of two previously highly secret volumes giving in detail hundreds of messages, diplomatic and military, which the Japanese had transmitted around the world.

These volumes, totaling 379 pages, represented a compilation of such messages whose meaning was laid bare to this country through the success of our cryptographers in breaking the highest of Japanese secret codes.

Told of Indies Attack

The code fell into our hands certainly as early as December, 1940. Our knowledge of it, however, did not give us an insight of Japanese secret plans and objectives until July 19, 1941. Then there was translated a diplomatic message of July 14, in which the Japanese said baldly that they intended ("if possible with the backing of the Axis") to go on from French Indo-China to the Netherlands Indies and still onward to take Singapore and to break forever the power of the English-speaking world in the Orient.

How the sinister maze hiding such messages was resolved, by whom and under what circumstances, was not revealed by Mr. Mitchell, who dryly submitted his volumes as "exhibits 1 and 2."

One of the first results of this unmasked secret was a disclosure to reporters that counsel for Rear Admiral Husband E. Kimmel, who was in naval command at Pearl Harbor when the Japanese attacked, proposed to argue when their time came that some of the most significant of all the Japanese decoded military messages, as distinguished from diplomatic messages, or all military messages after July 1, were never received by the Admiral in Pearl Harbor.

They will assert that he had asked Admiral Harold Stark, then

Continued on Page 4, Column 2

Eisenhower Holds Training Essential to Safety of U. S.

General Says It Is Best Way to Avoid War, or if Sudden Blow Comes to Avert Disaster —Declares Russia Wants Amity

By W. H. LAWRENCE
Special to The New York Times.

WASHINGTON, Nov. 15—Gen. Dwight D. Eisenhower declared today that a militarily strong United States, including an adequate trained civilian reserve obtainable only through universal military training in peacetime, was the best protection against another war, and if war came such a reserve might well mean the difference between victory and defeat.

For two hours the House Military Affairs Committee listened to and questioned the former Allied Supreme Commander, who is slated to become Army Chief of Staff in the very near future, succeeding Gen. George C. Marshall. Even Representatives opposed to the military training measure conceded that the General was a very effective witness, and the crowd that jammed the House Ways and Means Committee room rose to its feet and greeted him with sustained applause as he entered and left the hearing room.

General Eisenhower said he would leap from his airplane in the mid-Atlantic if he thought another war inevitable, but that it would be equally suicidal for this nation not to train its youth and otherwise keep itself strong, on the assumption that there never would be another war. He expressed the conviction that "the greatest single motivating force for world peace today is the organized military potential of the United States—its resources, its technological advancement and its superbly trained manpower." He said it was essential to the success of the United Nations Organization that the military potential of the United States should be kept so organized that it could be vitalized "in time to meet any threat of aggression from any other power."

Representative J. Parnell Thomas, Republican, of New Jersey, vainly attempted to get General

Continued on Page 6, Column 1

General Eisenhower's statement on military training, Page 6.

Ford Joins in Big Line-Up Against Pay Rises of 30%

Company Goes Beyond GM and Chrysler by Demanding the Union Give Management as Much Security as It Receives

By WALTER W. RUCH
Special to The New York Times.

DETROIT, Nov. 15—The issue between big business and big labor was firmly joined tonight after the Ford Motor Company, in the most sensational of the developments of the day, dispelled any hopes still cherished by affiliates of the Congress of Industrial Organizations that they could, with a "divide-and-conquer" strategy, drive home swiftly a major victory in their campaign for large wage increases.

Going even further than the stand taken by the General Motors Corporation, the Chrysler Corporation and the United States Steel Corporation, Ford not only asked that the United Automobile Workers forego a discussion at present of a demand for a wage increase of 30 per cent, but that the union grant at once thirty-one modifications of the present contract to give to management as well as labor comparable security against one another.

The company, which described as an "unhappy experiment" its relations with the UAW since, in 1941, it terminated a riot-scarred strike by signing a contract regarded as one of the most liberal ever negotiated between management and labor, said today that the time had come for corporations to seek the same measure of "company security" as that sought by unions for themselves.

The announcement by Ford was indisputably a complete surprise, with union officials making no effort privately to hide their astonishment at what they said was a "reversal of position," but it was nearly matched by other developments showing that the "Big Three" of the automotive industry, along with "Big Steel," were locked in a battle of such economic importance as to permit of hardly any overstatement.

For, with the Ford situation approaching

Continued on Page 11, Column 1

Text of the Ford and union statements, Page 11.

3 NATIONS OFFER ATOM BOMB TO UNO ON RECIPROCAL BASIS, INSPECTIONS AS SAFEGUARDS

AAF Seeks a Leading Role In Testing Bomb on Fleets

Army Fliers, as Pioneers in Use of Atomic Missile, Want to Make Trials So Full as to Answer Every Question

By SIDNEY SHALETT
Special to The New York Times.

WASHINGTON, Nov. 15 — The Army Air Forces is aggressively seeking to take a leading role in carrying out the Navy's proposed tests of the atomic bomb against surface ships. The AAF, it was learned today, expects not only to fly the bombs but to propose conditions under which the tests should be conducted.

The AAF has made no official statement on the subject. In fact, it has refrained from doing so because its policy is to avoid any Air Force-Navy controversy in the hope that the tests can be arranged and executed in a spirit of complete cooperation and harmony.

However, it was learned, considerable study has been given to the matter by the top planners on the staff of Gen. H. H. Arnold, Commanding General of the AAF, and there have been informal discussions between the Air Forces and the Navy about the forthcoming tests.

Admiral Ernest J. King, Chief of Naval Operations, has disclosed that the Navy plans to use some eighty to one-hundred old ships, possibly including some from the German and Japanese navies, in two types of atomic bomb tests. In one, a bomb would be exploded above the water, and in the other detonation would be below the surface.

The Air Forces' position is that every conceivable type of test under every conceivable condition and against every type of ship should be conducted. Some of the questions the AAF wants answered —and, in private conversations some spokesmen declare that "the public is entitled to know all the answers"—include these:

(1) What happens to an assembled fleet if an atomic bomb scores a direct hit on a centrally located ship?

(2) What happens if a hit is scored within the center of an area

Continued on Page 2, Column 5

BAN ON WAR IS AIM

Truman, Attlee, King in the Proposals Declare Peace Surest Safety

UNO ATOM BODY PLANNED

It Would Take Over World's Basic Scientific Knowledge, Promote Use of Energy

The official statement on atomic power is on Page 3.

By FELIX BELAIR Jr.
Special to The New York Times.

WASHINGTON, Nov. 15—President Truman and Prime Ministers Attlee of Great Britain and W. L. Mackenzie King of Canada expressed their willingness in a joint statement today to share, on a reciprocal basis with other United Nations, detailed information on the practical application of atomic energy "just as soon as effective enforceable safeguards against its use for destructive purposes can be devised." Inspection of nations is one of the provisions.

To this end and for extension and consolidation of the authority of the United Nations Organization as an instrument for world peace they proposed the creation within the organization of a new commission to formulate recommendations to eliminate the use of atomic energy for destructive purposes and to promote its widest use for industrial and humanitarian purposes.

Meanwhile the three atomic-energy custodians said they were "not convinced that the spreading of the specialized information regarding the practical application of atomic energy, before it is possible to devise effective, reciprocal and enforceable safeguards acceptable to all nations, would contribute to a constructive solution of the problem of the atomic bomb."

"Opposite Effect" Possible

"On the contrary," they said in the joint communiqué, "we think it might have the opposite effect."

Thus after five days of continued conferences the three leaders combined a concrete program for sharing their knowledge of atomic force with a strong appeal to all nations to contribute toward strengthening of the United Nations Organization to the end of banishing the scourge of war from the earth forever.

"Faced with the terrible realities of the application of science to destruction, every nation will realize more urgently than before the overwhelming need to maintain the rule of law among nations and to banish the scourge of war from the earth," the communiqué concluded.

"This can only be brought about by giving wholehearted support to the United Nations Organization, and by consolidating and extending its authority, thus creating conditions of mutual trust in which all peoples will be free to devote themselves to the arts of peace. It is our firm resolve to work without reservation to achieve these ends."

As had been anticipated, the communiqué contained no direct reference to the Soviet Union or

Continued on Page 3, Column 2

SENATE IN REVOLT ADOPTS HOUSE PLAN ON REORGANIZATION

Overrides Judiciary Group to Vote Truman Freer Hand in Pruning Agencies

By C. P. TRUSSELL
Special to The New York Times.

WASHINGTON, Nov. 15—The Senate overrode its Judiciary Committee today to vote President Truman a freer hand in reorganizing and streamlining the war-swollen Federal establishment, but added another agency to its "touch-not" list, bringing the total tentatively exempted from Presidential action to fourteen.

Before the bill is passed, however, there may be attempts to strike all exemptions from it. This was indicated after Senator Tydings, Democrat of Maryland, had accused members who long had assailed bureaucracy, inefficiency and waste of "scuttling like a lot of rats" when opportunity came to make corrections.

Giving the President a victory after a succession of legislative setbacks, the Senate voted 35 to 24, almost wholly along party lines, to follow the House-approved

Continued on Page 13, Column 3

GM PAY RISE OFFER FOR ALL HOURLY MEN REJECTED BY UAW

10 Per Cent Increase Would Have Affected 350,000 Regardless of Job Qualification

Special to The New York Times.

DETROIT, Nov. 15—The General Motors Corporation offered today a wage increase of 10 per cent for hourly workers as its third counter-proposal to the demand of the United Automobile Workers-CIO for a blanket 30 per cent increase.

The offer, which would have matched increases for hourly workers with those granted voluntarily yesterday to 70,000 salaried employes earning less than $500 a month, was as quickly rejected by Walter P. Reuther, vice president of the UAW and director of its General Motors department.

Mr. Reuther's rejection had the effect of nullifying the proposal, since the company had stated that the suggestion would die with such a reception. The UAW leader did say that it was a better offer than was made last week, when the company suggested an increase of 8 to 10 per cent with the work week to

Continued on Page 12, Column 3

O'DWYER MAPS WAY TO RECRUIT POLICE

He Proposes to Lift Age Limit for Veterans and Hold Annual Examinations

Mayor-elect William O'Dwyer announced yesterday a program to relieve the shortage in Police Department personnel, with returning war veterans getting the preference in seeking positions as city patrolmen.

Mr. O'Dwyer, admitting the need for more policemen immediately, made public his plan after a half-hour's conference with Police Commissioner Arthur W. Wallander, who will continue as head of the department after Jan. 1.

Action by the Municipal Civil Service Commission will be needed in carrying out the plan. Mr. O'Dwyer suggested that the maximum age limit for patrolmen be raised from 29 years in the case of war veterans, and that Police Department examinations be held once a year instead of every four years until the emergency is over.

A former policeman himself, Mr. O'Dwyer went carefully over the figures showing the present depletion in the Police Department ranks. They had been prepared by Commissioner Wallander, who stood near him at the press conference in the Mayor-elect's suite in the Hotel Commodore.

Since Dec. 7, 1941, Mr. O'Dwyer explained, there had been a total of 4,556 vacancies in the Police Department—3,920 retirements, 434 deaths, 86 dismissals and 116 resig-

Continued on Page 20, Column 3

SPAATZ DECLARES FOR SERVICE UNITY

Asks Air Arm on Par With the Other Two—Says We May Be Attacked via Arctic

By ANTHONY LEVIERO
Special to The New York Times.

WASHINGTON, Nov. 15—The shortest invasion route to the United States in a future war is by air over the Arctic Polar Cap and air power is the only defense, Gen. Carl Spaatz said today in a double-barreled argument for an independent air force and a single Department of Armed Forces.

The commander of the Strategic Air Force in Europe and later in the Pacific and Gen. Omar N. Bradley, the highest field commander under General Eisenhower, testified before the Senate Military Affairs Committee.

General Bradley pointed to the successful unified command of his chief as an example of what should be done at the highest level of national defense organization.

General Spaatz presented three "imperatives": Unity of command, equality of the Air Forces with the other services and immediate action to arrest "disintegration" of the Air Forces under demobilization.

Showing photographs of destruction by fire, high-explosive and atom bombs, he pointed out that World War II started with an air attack on Pearl Harbor and ended with atomic attacks. Asserting that the next war would be predominantly an air war, he added: "The Pearl Harbor of a future

Continued on Page 5, Column 2

TEL AVIV RIOTERS CURBED BY TROOPS

One Killed and 27 Wounded as British Halt Burning and Looting of Buildings

By GENE CURRIVAN
By Cable to The New York Times.

TEL AVIV, Jerusalem, Nov. 15—This city was an armed camp tonight with one full British brigade in control in an attempt to curb the spread of a wave of violence that already has caused considerable bloodshed and damage. The casualty list today was one dead and twenty-seven injured.

[The disorders spread to Jaffa, where police and soldiers fired on and wounded a Jewish mob, wounding eleven rioters, The United Press reported. There were minor outbreaks in Jerusalem, also.

[At the Haifa naval base, though there was no rioting reported, several hundred Jewish sailors of the British Navy did not appear for their pay and also remained away from barracks at lunch time in protest against British Foreign Secretary Ernest Bevin's Palestine speech in the House of Commons Tuesday.]

Tonight the Palestine Administration issued a press statement declaring that the general officer commanding the troops, Gen. J. C. Darcy, and acting Chief Secretary Robert Scott had conferred with the commanding general of the Sixth Airborne Division, Maj. Gen. E. L. Bols, and had decided to maintain the curfew rigidly until

Continued on Page 8, Column 2

CHINA REDS CIRCLE MANCHURIA CAPITAL

Communists Said to Aim to Bar Chiang Men From Landing at Changchun Airport

By The United Press.

CHUNGKING, China, Nov. 15—Chinese Communist troops, spreading through southern Manchuria, are closing in on the Changchun airport to prevent Nationalist airborne landings at the capital, informed Nationalist circles said today.

These sources said that the Communists had moved so close to the airport that the landing of Nationalist soldiers from unarmed troop transports would be impossible within five days when Russian forces are scheduled to withdraw from Changchun and all Manchuria south of Harbin.

Communist forces, entering Manchuria by three passes in the Great Wall and by sea in a fleet of 500 junks from the Shantung Peninsula, have taken over nearly all strategic points, including airfields, evacuated by the Russians.

Neutral observers said that all Manchuria would be lost to the Central Government through Communist occupation if Nationalist forces were not landed in Changchun before the date of the Soviet evacuation.

Government sources indicated that the Communists had been able to halt the landing of a plane carrying Government officials to join the Nationalist military delegation in Changchun. This air transport was stopped Nov. 9 on

Continued on Page 5, Column 2

World News Summarized

FRIDAY, NOVEMBER 16, 1945

The United States, Great Britain and Canada are perfectly willing to share the secret of the atomic bomb with other United Nations, but not until all are ready to turn over their comparable military secrets reciprocally to a concession of the UNO. Spreading the information without safeguards would not solve the problem and might have the opposite effect, President Truman and Prime Ministers Attlee and King said in a joint statement summarizing their five-day conference. [1:8.]

General Eisenhower told the House Military Committee the same thing, going on to say that "nothing guides Russian policy so much as a desire for friendship with the United States," and that there never would be a war with Britain. The committee was visibly affected by his plea for post-war universal military training. [1:2-3.]

The Army Air Forces seek to fly the atomic bombs in tests upon ships and naval formations, wanting many questions of their own answered. [1:6-7.]

Byron Price, President Truman's special investigator, said French opposition was responsible for delays in establishing a central government for Germany. [1:2-3.]

The International Military Tribunal was considering the substitution of Alfried Krupp for his father Gustav in the war criminals trial after having decided not to try the latter in absentia. [9:1.] A former President, two former Premiers and five former Cabinet members went on trial in Helsinki as Finnish war criminals. [9:3-4.]

British troops rushed into Tel Aviv to halt the burning and looting of public buildings and British stores by young rioters. [1:6, map P. 8.]

Japan's resources are so depleted that they probably will supply "insignificant" reparations and not even cover occupation costs, Ambassador Pauley said in Tokyo. [1:6-7.]

Chinese Communists were reported closing in on Changchun to prevent Chungking's airborne troops from landing in the Manchurian capital. [1:7.] British forces occupied the Government buildings in Surabaya. [5:4.]

Six months before Pearl Harbor some Washington officials knew Japan's plans to sweep from Indo-China into the Netherland Indies and Singapore, it was disclosed at the opening session of the Congressional Committee hearing. [1:1.] The enemy's code had been cracked in December, 1940, and its intentions were revealed in intercepted messages. [4:5-6.]

The Senate overrode its Judiciary Committee and voted President Truman a freer hand in reorganizing the Executive Department but exempted more agencies from his action. [1:4.]

The automobile industry faced a general strike following the Ford Motor Company's demand that the United Automobile Workers Union agree to thirty-one modifications in its contract in order to grant industry, as well as labor, security. [1:4-5.] The General Motors offer to increase pay of hourly workers 10 per cent was immediately rejected by the union. [1:5.]

Management and the CIO combined at the labor-management conference to vote down the AFL-Mine Workers demand for a unit rule in voting on all recommendations. [12:2.]

Censorship Bureau Comes to an End

Special to The New York Times.

WASHINGTON, Nov. 15—After a life of one month and four days less than four years, the war-created Bureau of Censorship went out of existence tonight. Byron Price, the director, and the remaining seventy of the staff, turned over the keys of their desks, already tagged for delivery to other Federal agencies.

At its peak the bureau employed 14,500 persons, with 800 to 900 in Washington. Besides supervising a voluntary censorship by newspapers and radio, it inspected millions of tons of mail.

Begun Dec. 19, 1941, twelve days after Pearl Harbor, actual censorship ceased Aug. 15, three days after V-J Day. Since then the bureau has been liquidating itself.

Mr. Price, former executive news editor of The Associated Press, has made no plans beyond taking a rest.

France Blocks Central Reich Rule, Price Says on Return From Tour

By LEWIS WOOD
Special to The New York Times.

WASHINGTON, Nov. 15—Byron Price, who recently completed a personal investigation in Germany for President Truman, presented his report to the President today and said later that France was blocking the efforts to set up a central government in the defeated Reich. Until the Bureau of Censorship went automatically out of existence tonight Mr. Price was its director.

After an eight-week inquiry, Mr. Price found that the American military occupation forces had "done a good job under very difficult conditions" in a country where "all relation to civilization has gone, the clock has stopped; it's just kaput." Explaining that he had been chosen by the President, "I suppose because of complete former ignorance of the subject," Mr. Price said that his appearance as Mr. Truman's representative had given him an entree wherever he wished. He traveled all over the American occupation zone and went into some parts of Germany handled by the other nations.

"The four-power control is deadlocked on account of the French," Mr. Price said. "Unfortunately, the French decline to cooperate in any move to establish a central government in Germany. General de Gaulle has already taken the view that Germany is not ready for any sort of central government. Our Army has done a good job and the situation in Germany is not the Army's fault; it is the fault of the French."

The director emphasized that when discussing France or any other matter he was giving his personal view and not attempting

Continued on Page 9, Column 3

Pauley Says Japan Can Pay Little In Reparations or for Occupation

By LINDESAY PARROTT
By Wireless to The New York Times.

TOKYO, Nov. 15—The United States probably will receive only "insignificant" reparations from conquered Japan and it is doubtful if the shattered empire even will be able to pay a large part of the American occupation costs, Edwin S. Pauley, President Truman's special representative, said today at a press conference.

Mr. Pauley's statement was made after his two-day survey of Japanese resources and on the basis of mass statistics and other information furnished by the Supreme Allied command.

The picture Mr. Pauley drew of Japan was one of a nation stripped of virtually every valuable resource with the exception of "second-hand machinery," which the Presidential representative termed valueless to the United States, though much of it will be removed as soon as possible to the Philippines and China to restore their war-torn industries.

Though the special representative revealed that he had seen in the vaults of the Bank of Japan "great quantities" of gold and silver coins, jewels, platinum and foreign currencies, including United States dollars, he said that the total would be negligible in comparison with the war costs and the "staggering" expense of occupation.

At the same time Mr. Pauley revealed that the Japanese had given to Allied headquarters an estimate of the value of Emperor Hirohito's personal collection of jewels and curios, which the Emperor had said he was willing to sell to provide funds for vital imports, such as foodstuffs. This

Continued on Page 2, Column 2

Rumanian Leaders Reported Vanished

By The United Press.

LONDON, Nov. 15—The Bucharest radio said today that Juliu Maniu, the leader of the Rumanian National Peasant party, and the Liberal party's leader, Constantin Dinu Bratianu, both critics of the present Rumanian regime, had "disappeared."

The broadcast quoted the Communist Minister of the Interior, Tohari Georgescu, as its source. The reports of the "disappearance" came just a week after the riots on the King's birthday, in which at least eleven persons were killed. Government sources charged that Mr. Bratianu and Mr. Maniu were implicated in organizing a previously forbidden demonstration in front of the palace. The demonstrators clashed with Communists.

"All the News That's Fit to Print"

The New York Times.

LATE CITY EDITION
Cloudy and cold today. Tomorrow rain or snow.
Temperatures Yesterday—Max., 41; Min., 32
Sunrise today, 7:18 A. M.; Sunset, 4:36 P. M.

VOL. XCV...No. 32,115. Entered as Second-Class Matter, Postoffice, New York, N. Y. NEW YORK, FRIDAY, DECEMBER 28, 1945. THREE CENTS IN NEW YORK CITY

BIG THREE RE-ESTABLISH UNITY IN WIDE ACCORD; AGREE ON ATOM, TREATIES, JAPAN, CHINA, KOREA; 28 NATIONS SET UP THE BRETTON WOODS BANK

COUNCIL SLASHES BUDGET $55,000,000; MAYOR PROTESTS

Funds for Idlewild Hangars and Arcade and for New Market Are Eliminated

O'DWYER GIVES APPROVAL

La Guardia Pleads With Him to Change Action, Saying Projects Are 'Smashed'

The City Council, carrying out a policy laid down by Mayor-elect William O'Dwyer, struck from the 1946 capital budget yesterday the $45,000,000 earmarked for work on the hangars and arcade structure at the Idlewild Airport in Queens. It also eliminated the $10,000,000 allocated for work on the first stage of construction of the proposed $42,000,000 wholesale fruit and produce market on the lower West Side in Manhattan.

The action was by a vote of 12 to 0, with three Councilmen not voting. By thus cutting $55,000,000 of city funds from the capital budget of $298,521,086 adopted by the Board of Estimate on Nov. 30, the Council brought the total down to $243,521,086. Councilmen Genevieve B. Earle of Brooklyn, Gertrude W. Kline of the Bronx and Stanley M. Isaacs of Manhattan were those who refrained from voting.

La Guardia Appeals to O'Dwyer

Mayor La Guardia, in a radio broadcast from the Lotos Club, where he was the honor guest at a private dinner, appealed to Mayor-elect O'Dwyer to cooperate in restoring the deleted items to the capital budget, declaring that their elimination had "smashed to smithereens" his ten years of work and planning on the market project and his five years of hard labor on the Idlewild Airport. The Council's action, he declared, had threatened the city's air supremacy and jeopardized the contracts already made with major airlines.

"Now, I am going to make a public appeal to my successor," the Mayor exclaimed. "Don't do it, Bill, don't do it. I will call a meeting of the Board of Estimate for tomorrow if you will approve it, and we will call a special meeting of the City Council before Tuesday. We can amend the budget and put back those two items. The other item is the market. Bill, you don't want the market to go to New Jersey, do you? That's what's going to happen.

"I again appeal to you, Mayor-elect William O'Dwyer. I will call a meeting of the Board of Estimate tomorrow, if you will consent to have these items reinstated in the budget."

The Mayor said he had called Mr. O'Dwyer regarding the Council's action and also had asked Grover A. Whalen, chairman of his official reception committee, to telephone to the Mayor-elect and inform him that the deletion of the $45,000,000 item for hangars and arcade structure had placed the entire Idlewild project in jeopardy.

O'Dwyer Issues Statement

After a meeting between Mr. O'Dwyer and budget experts on city finances, the Mayor-elect issued the following statement:

I shall not be drawn into a last-minute controversy with the Mayor. His administration on the whole has been successful, but it has unfortunately been marked in recent months by an increasing tendency to denounce, ridicule and vilify those who do not happen to share all of his views and prejudices. So far as I am concerned, the era of denunciation and damnation from City Hall is over. I can stand honest differences of opinion.

In this instance, all the evidence obtained from his own commissioners and consultants points to certain irrefutable facts which no doubt guided the Council in its decisions. I endorse these decisions, support them and will not

Continued on Page 10, Column 1

Terrorists Raid Jerusalem; Police Post Blasted, 3 Dead

Chief and His Deputy Narrowly Escape—Explosions Also Rock Tel Aviv and Jaffa—Deaths Total 10; Curfew Imposed

By GENE CURRIVAN
By Cable to The New York Times.

JERUSALEM, Dec. 27—Terrorists struck tonight in the heart of Jerusalem, blowing up the Civil Investigation Department building in the Russian compound near the main postoffice.

At least three policemen are dead and six injured.

[The United Press, reporting a similar attack on the Jaffa police station and an attempt to storm the Royal Engineers Workshop at Tel Aviv, put the total dead at ten and the injured at twelve. The dispatch said eight were killed in Jerusalem and two in Tel Aviv, one of the latter being a British lance corporal.]

Inspector General Rymer Jones, head of Palestine police, and Deputy Inspector General Giles narrowly escaped with their lives.

They were sitting in Inspector Giles' second floor offices 500 feet from the corner of the building blown up when the explosion occurred, throwing them both from their chairs and covering them with debris.

Despite the shock both men ran to the blasted part of the building and as this is written they are helping to remove the dead and injured.

One of the first on the scene was the Rev. Eugene Hoade who administered last rites. Father Hoade said he believed that there were seven dead, including two small Arab boys.

One of the severely injured was Assistant Police Superintendent Dennis Flanagan who was machine-gunned near the spot where the police afterward found a suitcase full of anti-tank mines with detonators set. This was near a

Continued on Page 3, Column 3

LACK OF GM'S DATA WON'T HALT PANEL

Fact Finders Will Ask for SEC, OPA Records Should Company Withhold Information

By LOUIS STARK
Special to The New York Times.

WASHINGTON, Dec. 27 — The possibility that the General Motors Corporation will refuse to cooperate with President Truman's fact-finding board will not deter the panel from pressing its inquiry and making recommendations to the Chief Executive concerning wage adjustments.

The panel's decision became known today when doubts appeared that the General Motors executives, who will appear before the board tomorrow, would agree to furnish the relevant data requested by the panel.

The board, headed by Lloyd K. Garrison, it was stated, is determined to complete its task as expeditiously as possible regardless of the corporation's attitude.

Should the company withhold the requested information, the fact-finding board will obtain whatever data it can find available in government agencies, such as the Securities and Exchange Commission, the Office of Price Administration and the Labor Department. It will also accept data furnished by the CIO United Automobile Workers and check this with whatever other sources may be available.

Milton Eisenhower, a member of the board, was said to be flying here from Kansas, and Judge Walter P. Stacy of Raleigh, N. C., is coming by train. The hearing is scheduled for 10 A. M. tomorrow.

General Motors takes the posi-

Continued on Page 32, Column 6

PAY RISES GRANTED IN BUILDING TRADES

Adjustment Board Approves Increases Slightly Under 15% for 200,000 Here

Special to The New York Times.

WASHINGTON, Dec. 27 — The Wage Adjustment Board approved today wage increases averaging slightly under the 15 per cent Little Steel formula for approximately 200,000 building trades and heavy construction workers in New York City and vicinity.

The Building Trades Employers Association of New York and the Building and Construction Trades Council of Greater New York had requested the full 15 per cent for all employes up to a maximum of 25 cents an hour. While the adjustment board granted a maximum of 25 cents an hour to some trades it shaded the proposal somewhat under the Little Steel formula in averaging the increases. Most of the skilled trades will receive on Tuesday, when the new rates become effective, an hourly wage of $2.25, compared to the $2 an hour they had been receiving.

Some of the adjustments are on a basis of a seven-hour day, but whether any downward changes in hours were made was not apparent from the formal telegrams sent to the parties.

Forty-nine trades are affected by the wage adjustments that were sent out from the board's office in the Labor Department.

The majority of the workers affected are employes of construction concerns affiliated with the Building Trades Council of Greater New York and vicinity while

Continued on Page 32, Column 3

CPA Will Speed Low-Cost Suits To Veterans in New Program

Special to The New York Times.

WASHINGTON, Dec. 27—To meet the large demand for clothing from returning veterans and speed the return of apparel in the lower price ranges, the Civilian Production Administration is starting in the new year a low-cost clothing program designed to replenish the empty racks of men's and boys' low and medium-priced suits and overcoats, J. D. Small, administrator of the agency, stated today.

Under the program, Mr. Small estimated that 3,500,000 men's and boys' suits in the lower brackets would be produced in the first three months of 1946. He said he expected that the men's suits to be made under the plan would sell at retail at and below $33.

At this rate of production, the CPA chief hoped that the men's clothing industry would be able to make about 14,000,000 low and medium-priced suits for seniors and juniors out of an estimated total production in 1946 of 28 to 30 million suits.

With 23,000,000 yards of wool fabrics earmarked for use in the less expensive garments in the first quarter of 1946, Mr. Small contemplated, in addition to suits, the production of 7,000,000 pairs of men's and boys' trousers and 1,500,000 overcoats and topcoats in the first three months of next year.

The program includes, besides wool fabrics, provisions for "channeling" to apparel manufacturers in the first quarter of 1946 about 168,000,000 yards of cotton mate-

Continued on Page 7, Column 2

FUND ESTABLISHED

$8,800,000,000 Will Be Employed to Stabilize World Exchanges

BANK HAS 9 BILLION

Plans Rebuilding Loans —Russia Absent but May Sign Later

By JOHN H. CRIDER
Special to The New York Times.

WASHINGTON, Dec. 27—The International Monetary Fund and the Bank for Reconstruction and Development came into being this afternoon when representatives of twenty-eight nations signed documents confirming that their Governments had ratified the Bretton Woods Agreements and deposited the nominal initial payment toward expenses of the organizations.

Although representatives of the Soviet Union signed the first documents at Bretton Woods in July, 1944, Russia was not among the twenty-eight signers today. There was no official indication of what Soviet action would be, but most officials expected that the U.S.S.R. would qualify and sign by the Dec. 31 deadline.

The International Monetary Fund is a new kind of world currency pool to maintain stable conditions of exchange as an essential prerequisite for a high level of international trade.

The Bank is a medium for international sharing of risks in the making of loans for world reconstruction and development. The Fund will have $8,800,000,000 in gold and currencies at the start, and the Bank initial subscriptions of $9,100,000,000.

The agreements provide that the

Continued on Page 21, Column 3

BYRNES IS JUBILANT

Says 'Important Thing' Is That 'Cordial' Ties Make Unity Likely

NO 'DEALS' IN SECRET

Communique Tells All, He Insists—Bevin Happy but More Reserved

By The Associated Press.

MOSCOW, Dec. 27 — Secretary of State James F. Byrnes was flying home tonight from Moscow, jubilant over the accomplishments of the Big Three Foreign Ministers' Conference in reaching agreement on vital questions, including atomic energy control, and in creating a "friendly spirit" for meeting future world problems.

In excellent spirits just before he boarded his plane at the snow-covered Moscow airport, Mr. Byrnes declared that the "important thing" about the conference "is that closer relations have been established, so that the possibility of agreement has been greatly increased."

The British Foreign Secretary, Ernest Bevin, who has not yet left Moscow, jotted down a more somber postscript when he told newsmen tonight that the Foreign Ministers had discussed the problem of Iran at length, but had not reached any final agreement.

Mr. Byrnes declared that the Moscow Conference had been "very constructive," not only because of the settlement of many problems but because of the "cordial relations between the three countries represented."

He said: "There is great hope for the settlement of other problems in the same friendly spirit."

Mr. Byrnes gave assurance that

Continued on Page 5, Column 2

World News Summarized

FRIDAY, DECEMBER 28, 1945

Agreement has been reached at Moscow on a wide number of international problems by the same men who only a few months before in London had been unable to see eye to eye. A communiqué issued simultaneously from Washington, London and Moscow last night declared that Secretary of State Byrnes, Foreign Secretary Bevin and Foreign Commissar Molotoff had agreed:

1. On a formula for European peace treaties, details of which were announced earlier.

2. On Russia's participation in a reconstituted Far Eastern Advisory Commission with headquarters in Washington but able to meet anywhere and an Allied Control Council for Japan consisting of the United States, Britain, Russia and China to sit in Tokyo. General MacArthur's supremacy as Allied commander was reaffirmed.

3. On creation of a Provisional Korean Democratic Government operating under a trusteeship of the same Big Four for not more than five years until Korea could assume national independence and full self-government. In the meantime, the thorny problems resulting from the two zones of occupation will be handled by an American-Soviet commission to meet within two weeks.

4. That Russia and the United States will withdraw their troops from China at the earliest possible moment. The importance of a unified, democratic China was strongly emphasized.

5. That Rumania and Bulgaria must broaden their Governments and prove that freedom of speech, press and elections exist; then they will be recognized by the United States and Britain.

6. That permanent members of the United Nations Security Council and Canada will sponsor a resolution at the General Assembly next month creating a commission for the control of Atomic Energy. The commission will be responsible to the Security Council.

Throughout the lengthy communiqué it was clear that the big powers retained control, that the veto power remained unimpaired, that American primacy in the Pacific and Russian predominance in the Balkans were recognized. Germany and the Middle East were not mentioned. [All the foregoing 1:8; map P. 4.]

Mr. Byrnes, before boarding his plane to return to Washington, said the friendly atmosphere of the conference had greatly increased the possibility of future agreements. He added that no secret arrangements had been entered into. [1:5.]

Failure to discuss the Iranian situation was attributed in London to Mr. Molotoff's insistence that the Azerbaijan autonomy movement was an internal affair and that the Red Army had taken no part in it. [1:6-7.]

Palestine, also unmentioned in the Moscow communiqué, was the scene of widespread violent and fatal eruptions. [1:2-3.]

General MacArthur said that reforms already instituted had eliminated the "last evil roots" of the Emperor system and State Shinto from Japan. [6:4.]

Chinese Communists submitted in writing their proposals for a truce with the Nationalist forces. [1:6-7.] Heavy fighting broke out again in Java and the British took "more active measures" to end Indonesian resistance. [6:1.]

Twenty-eight nations signed in Washington documents bringing into existence the International Monetary Fund and Bank agreed upon at Bretton Woods. Russia was not among them. [1:4.]

Two hundred scientists, including Nobel Prize winners, offered to assist Congress in drafting atomic energy and scientific development legislation. [5:1.]

Further Government aid for veterans unable to buy civilian clothing was seen in a program to make 3,500,000 suits in the next three months. [1:2-3.]

End of Partition in Korea And 5-Year Trusteeship Set

Moscow Plan, Not Yet Revealed in Detail, Gives Veto Powers to Four-Nation Control Group—Country Aided Economically

By W. H. LAWRENCE
Special to The New York Times.

WASHINGTON, Dec. 27—Allied treatment of Korea as an economic and political unit in the immediate future, looking toward complete independence after a period of not more than five years of "trusteeship" rule by the Big Four powers in collaboration with a provisional national regime, was the promise read by Washington tonight into the Foreign Ministers' declaration at Moscow.

To American military men, charged with occupying and administering the southern half of Korea (below Lat. 38 N.), the most welcome section of the Korean pledge was the directive from the Soviet Union to its commanders in northern Korea to confer with American authorities within two weeks. That conference will be concerned with "urgent problems affecting both southern and northern Korea and for the elaboration of measures establishing permanent coordination in administrative-economic matters" between the two occupation zones.

Such Russian-American collaboration has been sought by American authorities almost since the very beginning of the occupation of Korea, but until now the Russians have not been receptive to our advances.

The division between the two occupation zones admittedly has jarred Korean unity and created grave problems relating to communications, trade and free passage of individuals between the two zones. In the Russian zone is concentrated almost all of the manufacturing capacity of Korea, most of the coal and iron, railroad rolling stock, railroad repair shops

Continued on Page 5, Column 3

Russians Blocked Any Plan On Iran and Barred Premier

By C. L. SULZBERGER
By Cable to The New York Times.

LONDON, Friday, Dec. 28—The most glaring negative fact that emerges from the communiqué on the Moscow talks is the complete failure of the United States, British and Soviet Governments to reach an agreement on the delicate Iranian situation, which the Soviet Union apparently insists on regarding as a fait accompli and which already is developing into what appears to be a ramified Middle Eastern crisis, shifting its dynamism toward Turkey.

Authoritative sources point out that as Secretary of State James F. Byrnes announced, "There is no agreement on any subject which is not covered in the communiqué," it is strikingly evident that there was no accord on Iran—one of the cardinal issues facing the Foreign Ministers and the most urgent one in terms of current events.

The feeling of letdown on this question is in nowise allayed by Foreign Secretary Ernest Bevin's Moscow press conference statement that "the matter continues to be dealt with through diplomatic channels," since, obviously, the best opportunity for a settlement was in these direct talks between the Foreign Ministers.

This, according to persons who have seen some of the confidential reports on the Moscow discussions, is more or less what happened:

When the subject of Iran arose for discussion on the agenda, Foreign Commissar Vyacheslaff M. Molotoff explained that the Soviet Government regarded the movement of Azerbaijan autonomists as entirely spontaneous and normal.

It is understood that the Foreign Commissar emphasized that the fact that Red Army troops were present in northern Iran under the

Continued on Page 3, Column 2

BRITISH TAKE HOPE FROM THE ACCORD

They Feel That Mere Fact of Agreement Is Gain, Though They See Omissions

By HERBERT L. MATTHEWS
By Cable to The New York Times.

LONDON, Friday, Dec. 28—The simple fact that the representatives of the United States, Britain and Russia have met and reached an agreement on certain important problems, including atomic energy, overshadows every other consideration in the minds of Britons. That is why today's press and the first unofficial comments express great satisfaction.

The feelings are not unmixed, however, and there is concern that the vital and immediate problems of Iran and Turkey and Germany have been ignored, that the Soviet Union appears to have come out best and that it all smacks too much of a return to power politics of the Big Three.

All these second thoughts undoubtedly are going to be voiced when Parliament reconvenes Jan. 22, but meanwhile the overwhelming consideration is that collaboration with the Soviet Union for the

Continued on Page 3, Column 6

China Truce Talks Are Resumed; Reds Put New Offer in Writing

By TILLMAN DURDIN
By Wireless to The New York Times.

CHUNGKING, Dec. 27—Kuomintang and Communist representatives met here today in a renewal of their efforts to halt civil strife in China and settle the differences between the two parties.

Details of the discussions were cloaked in secrecy, and, delegates of neither side were willing to talk afterward. Communist headquarters, however, revealed that General Chou En-lai, chief Communist delegate, had submitted a written proposal for what was described as a "nationwide immediate and unconditional truce."

General Chou declined to release the text of the proposal, but a Communist spokesman said it contained three main points:

(1) Both sides to cease fire immediately;

(2) All problems related to the civil war should be taken up after the cease fire order and solved by peaceful means;

(3) Investigation groups should be organized and sent to the scene of hostilities to observe the situation.

The spokesman declined to give the reason why General Chou was unwilling to reveal the text of his proposal, but said that the Kuomintang delegates had promised to submit the proposition to Generalissimo Chiang Kai-shek who might give his reply tomorrow or next day.

Today's meeting was not a session of the People's Consultative Council, which is made up of rep-

Continued on Page 6, Column 2

UNANIMITY TO RULE

Principle Is Extended to UNO Atom Body, Korea, Japan, Peace Pacts

ARMIES TO QUIT CHINA

Accord Agrees on Need for Democracy There—Reaction Is Divided

Text of the Foreign Ministers' communiqué is on Page 4.

By JAMES B. RESTON
Special to The New York Times.

WASHINGTON, Dec. 27 — The Foreign Ministers of the United States, the Soviet Union and Great Britain, meeting in Moscow, announced tonight that they had reached a wide area of agreement about the machinery to control the atomic bomb; how to supervise Japan, Korea, Rumania and Bulgaria, when to withdraw Russian and American troops from China, and how to draft peace treaties with the defeated European nations.

In a 4,500-word communiqué released "simultaneously" in Washington, London and Moscow at the end of their eleven-day conference, the Big Three made clear that they had broken the stalemate that developed at the London meeting of the Foreign Ministers' Council last September, and emphasized that they intended to protect their new agreement by voting unanimously before taking major future decisions about atomic bomb recommendations, the control of Japan and Korea, and the peace treaties with Rumania, Bulgaria, Italy, Hungary and Finland.

The Major Decisions

The communiqué confirmed advance reports about the agreement published in this newspaper today and listed the following major decisions of the conference:

(1) They agreed, with China's approval, to propose to the first meeting of the General Assembly of the United Nations, opening in London Jan. 10, a resolution turning over to the eleven nations on the Security Council of the UNO (plus Canada, which is virtually assured a place on the Council) the task of forming a commission to deal with the problems raised by the discovery of atomic energy.

It was emphasized that this commission was subject to the control of the Security Council (under the voting procedure of that body which gives the Big Five the power to veto its recommendations), particularly on all questions which touch on the security of member States. This is taken to mean on all matters dealing with the atomic bomb as distinguished from the industrial possibilities of atomic energy.

Council for Japan Ordered

(2) They revised and strengthened the authority of the Far Eastern Advisory Commission, dropping the word "advisory" from its title and giving it the power to define the major policy that the United States shall instruct Gen. Douglas MacArthur to carry out. The communiqué states that General MacArthur is "the sole executive authority for the Allied powers in Japan" and it gives him authority to take interim decisions on urgent matters on which the commission has not laid down policies, but it also states that neither he nor the United States Government can issue directives providing for fundamental changes in the control of Japan unless the Far Eastern Commission approves.

Moreover, the communiqué states that policy decisions of the Far Eastern Commission in Washington shall be taken by a majority vote, "including the representatives of the four following powers: United States, United Kingdom, U.S.S.R. and China."

The Foreign Ministers in Moscow also agreed to create a four-

Continued on Page 4, Column 2

1946

1946

Meet the Press made its debut. The show was started by Martha Rountree and Lawrence Spivak. In this photo, James Roosevelt (far right) is being quizzed by the panel.

Queen for a Day master of ceremonies Jack Bailey receives an award from Evelyn Bixby, editor of *Radio Life.*

Fred Allen — one of America's great funny men.

"All the News That's Fit to Print"

The New York Times.

LATE CITY EDITION
Mostly sunny today and cold.
Fair and warmer tomorrow.
Temperatures Yesterday—Max., 34; Min., 14
Sunrise today, 6:58 A. M.; Sunset, 5:31 P. M.
Full U. S. Weather Bureau Report Page 16

VOL. XCV..No. 32,165. Entered as Second-Class Matter, Postoffice, New York, N. Y. NEW YORK, SATURDAY, FEBRUARY 16, 1946. THREE CENTS IN NEW YORK CITY

STEEL STRIKE IS SETTLED WITH 18.5C PAY RISE; COMPANIES GET PRICE INCREASE OF $5 A TON; TRUMAN STRESSES BATTLE AGAINST INFLATION

COUNCIL IS DIVIDED ON UNO AUTHORITY IN LEVANT POLICING

All Agree British and French Troops Should Leave, but Date-Fixing Is Snarled

SOVEREIGNTY ISSUE JOINED

Majority Seeks to Avoid Direct Reply, Pressed by Vishinsky, Syrian and Lebanese

By JAMES B. RESTON
By Cable to THE NEW YORK TIMES.

LONDON, Feb. 15—The United Nations Security Council agreed today without a dissenting voice that British and French troops should be withdrawn from Syria and Lebanon, but the members—and particularly the Big Five—were divided sharply over when the troops should be withdrawn and who should set the date for their departure.

After five hours and fifty minutes of a debate that failed to reach a decision on the matter, the members of the Council gave these answers to the questions when the troops should go and who should tell them when to go:

Britain and France — The troops should go as soon as the Security Council lays down a plan to take over responsibility for security of the Near and Middle East.

Two States Make Accusation

Syria and Lebanon — They should get out as soon as practical arrangements for moving them can be made. Their presence is "a very serious violation" of sovereignty and neither Britain nor France nor the Security Council has any right to determine how Syria and Lebanon shall protect themselves.

United States and China — They should go as soon as the parties concerned can work out a mutually satisfactory agreement and the Security Council should be kept informed of the progress of these negotiations.

Soviet Union (Vice Foreign Commissar Andrei Y. Vishinsky)—"We must meet the demands put forward by the Governments of Syria and Lebanon. These demands are just and have the full support of the Soviet delegation. The Council must pronounce that there is no ground for the presence of these foreign troops on the soil of Syria and Lebanon and that these troops should be withdrawn within a time to be fixed by the Security Council."

Ruling May Define Sovereignty

These points of view raised a single question, which the Security Council is expected to decide tomorrow before winding up its proceedings until it meets in the United States probably in late March or early April.

The question is whether Britain and France have the right to insist on keeping troops in the Levant States until the Council has troops at its disposal to look after security in this region or whether such a demand by Paris and London is a violation of the sovereignty of Syria and Lebanon.

Most of the members of the Council were prepared to avoid a straight answer by letting the principals talk over the problem among themselves and report to the Council on the results, but Syria, Lebanon, the Soviet Union and Egypt insisted that the British-French demand was a basic violation of the sovereignty of the Levant States and a violation of the United Nations Charter as well.

"We must agree," Mahmoud Riaz, delegate of Egypt, said, "that every state is responsible for the maintenance of security and order within its own territory and that no other state is entitled to intervene by military or other means in the maintenance of order in the area of a sovereign state."

"If we allow a wedge to be driven into this principlae," he continued, "we shall have allowed a breach to be made in the United Nations itself. If such a clear principle is called into question I would suggest that the best thing would

Continued on Page 5, Column 2

Canada Seizes 22 as Spies; Atom Secrets Believed Aim

Leaks to 'Foreign Mission' in Ottawa Are Said to Involve Russia—Commission Is Named to Conduct Inquiry

By The Associated Press.

OTTAWA, Feb. 15—Royal Canadian Mounted Police, striking suddenly, detained at least twenty-two men today as the Government launched an investigation into the disclosure of "secret and confidential information," authoritatively reported to concern atomic energy, to members of a foreign mission here. Sources that cannot be named said the country involved was Russia.

Prime Minister W. L. Mackenzie King announced the appointment of two Royal Commissioners to head the investigation tonight hours after police made early morning raids on the homes of present or former employes of Canadian Government departments and agencies. Officials said they were certain that they could place serious charges against at least twelve of the men taken for questioning.

Some of them were known to have been employed by the National Research Council, the Government agency through which atomic energy information has been channeled. The atomic bomb was developed through the combined efforts of American, British and Canadian scientists.

Mr. King said that Justice Robert Taschereau and Justice R. L. Kellock of the Supreme Court of Canada had been placed in charge of the investigation which, it was learned, was first begun soon after the war ended last summer. The Prime Minister and President Truman were believed to have discussed the leak of the secret information in Washington last fall.

"Information of undoubted authenticity," Mr. King said in his announcement, "has reached the Canadian Government which establishes that there have been disclosures of secret and confidential information to unauthorized persons, including some members of the

Continued on Page 6, Column 6

CHINA'S REDS ASK ROLE IN MANCHURIA

Joint Control Is Demanded—Communist Army in the Area Said to Be Near 300,000

By TILLMAN DURDIN
By Wireless to THE NEW YORK TIMES.

CHUNGKING, Feb. 15 — The Chinese Communist party today demanded joint control of Manchuria with the Kuomintang and other "parties, groups and nonpartisans" and announced that it now commanded in Manchuria an army of nearly 300,000 men in addition to militia and police to back up its demands.

The Communists asked a limitation on the number of Kuomintang troops permitted to enter Manchuria and advocated the recognition and reorganization of "all anti-Japanese democratic forces" in China's northeast "so that they may jointly preserve local peace and order with the troops sent there by the National Government."

The Communist policy on Manchuria was laid down in a statement radioed here today from Yenan by the Communist New China News Agency. The statement was presented in the form of an interview with the spokesman of the Central Committee of the Communist party.

The demands open up the possibility of a Manchuria governed by an administration with a strong Communist influence and with considerable autonomy. Such an administration may be what Russia wants.

The new expression of policy on

Continued on Page 4, Column 6

RISE OF $153,029,812 IN BUDGET SOUGHT

Patterson, However, Says Full Requests Cannot Be Granted—Transit Deficit Rises

Thomas J. Patterson, Budget Director, announced yesterday that the budget estimates of 109 departments and agencies of the city government wanted a total increase of $153,029,812 for the 1946-47 fiscal year.

The modified 1945-46 budget provided $763,570,703 for the departments. After a series of hearings in the last five weeks, Mr. Patterson learned that the department chiefs needed $916,600,516. The increases represented $123,635,256 chargeable to tax levy and $29,374,555 chargeable to other than tax-levy funds.

Lazarus Joseph, Controller, submitted a financial report to the Board of Estimate and the City Council indicating that the general fund for the 1946-47 fiscal year would approximate $174,259,000. He said that with an anticipated surplus of $26,319,808 on July 1, the general fund total should reach $200,578,808.

Mr. Patterson, in a statement, made it plain that the departmental requests for 1946-47 could not be granted with the estimated general fund revenues and the 2 per cent constitutional tax limitations. He said the budget estimates would be studied carefully, but explained that he had instructions from Mayor O'Dwyer to reduce the figures to "a minimum consistent with the require-

Continued on Page 26, Column 4

'This Means War,' Said Roosevelt Of Japanese Note, Witness Avers

By WILLIAM S. WHITE
Special to THE NEW YORK TIMES.

WASHINGTON, Feb. 15—President Roosevelt, after reading an intercepted and incomplete text of the final Japanese reply to the United States on the eve of Pearl Harbor, expressed instant conviction that "this means war," but gravely declared that this "democracy of a peaceful people" could not strike out first to seize the advantage of initiative, the Congressional investigating committee was told today.

Comdr. Lester R. Schulz, a former assistant naval aide at the White House, who was returned from sea on the battleship Indiana, of which he is now executive officer, to testify, stated that Mr. Roosevelt tried almost at once to reach Admiral Harold R. Stark, Chief of Naval Operations, but was informed that the admiral was at the theatre and decided not to have him paged while the performance was on lest it cause "public alarm."

Neither the President nor Harry Hopkins, who was with him in the Presidential study on the second floor of the White House, mentioned Pearl Harbor as a point of Japanese attack, the commander recalled, nor was there "any suggestion that tomorrow would be the day."

The life of the committee, which would have terminated at midnight, was again extended by Congress today, this time to June 1, with the understanding that public hearings, so far as the present schedule of witnesses was concerned, would end on Wednesday night. After that, the taking of testimony may be resumed only by a majority vote upon the application of any member for what

Continued on Page 4, Column 2

TRUMAN CHAMPIONS PAULEY, SAYS ICKES ONCE PRAISED HIM

President Asserts Forrestal Proposed Appointment but Latter Avers Roosevelt Did

JULY, '45, TALK INVOLVED

Executive Says the Secretary Then Hailed His Nominee—New Testimony Awaited

By THOMAS J. HAMILTON
Special to THE NEW YORK TIMES.

WASHINGTON, Feb. 15—President Truman again reaffirmed today his confidence in Edwin W. Pauley, predicted that Mr. Pauley's nomination as Under-Secretary of the Navy would be confirmed by the Senate and declared that Harold L. Ickes, when Secretary of the Interior, praised Mr. Pauley on the one occasion on which they had discussed his qualifications.

The President's emphatic defense of Mr. Pauley, going beyond the remarks at his press conference on Feb. 7, which led to Mr. Ickes' resignation, also included the statement that Mr. Pauley's appointment had been recommended by James Forrestal, Secretary of the Navy, who told him last October or November Mr. Truman was not sure of the month—that Mr. Pauley had been selected for the position by President Roosevelt.

The President said that Mr. Forrestal had taken the initiative in proposing Mr. Pauley, but a statement issued later by Mr. Forrestal offered a different view.

Mr. Forrestal said he had informed Mr. Truman at the Potsdam Conference in August, 1945, that President Roosevelt had wanted Mr. Pauley as Assistant Secretary of the Navy, and added that he had told Mr. Truman: "I would be agreeable to Mr. Pauley's coming to the Navy following the

Continued on Page 3, Column 6

World News Summarized

SATURDAY, FEBRUARY 16, 1946

The United States Steel Corporation and the United Steel Workers, CIO, reached an agreement late last night calling for a wage increase of 18½ cents an hour. Earlier it was indicated that the industry would get a rise of $5 a ton in the price of steel. Company and union officials announced that the strike at the plants of the five operating steel-producing subsidiaries would end at midnight Sunday. [1:8.]

In Detroit James F. Dewey, special mediator appointed by Labor Secretary Schwellenbach, reported "much progress" after a conference of President Thomas of the UAW and President Wilson of General Motors. The conferees will get together again this morning. [1:6-7.]

President Truman described his new wage-price policy in the battle against inflation as "not a new line," but "a bulge." The Chief Executive emphasized that there would be no "break-through" if all cooperated until the bulge was eliminated. [1:5.]

After nearly six hours of debate, the UNO Security Council agreed unanimously that British and French troops should be withdrawn from Syria and Lebanon as demanded by those nations. However, four divergent views as to when and by whose orders the troops should leave were upheld by Britain and France, Syria and Lebanon, the United States and China and the Soviet Union. [1:1.]

A map, said to be the authentic original one, showing the frontier between Italy and Yugoslavia as envisaged by President Wilson has been found by the Italians, who will submit it to the deputies of the Council of Foreign Ministers. [4:8.]

Pope Pius conferred with Archbishops Spellman and Glennon as the arrival of three more Cardinals-designate raised to twenty-nine the number in Rome for next week's Consistory. [15:6.]

Following the sudden resignation of Egyptian Premier Nokrashy's Cabinet, King Farouk was reported to have asked Ismail Sedky Pasha to form a new Cabinet. A nonparty man, he is known as an advocate of greater speed and directness in negotiating for the end of the British occupation of Egypt. [6:2.]

Chinese Communists, declaring they command an army of nearly 300,000 men in Manchuria, in addition to militia and police, asked for joint control of that rich province with the Central Government and other "parties, groups and nonpartisans." They also demanded that the number of Central Government troops in Manchuria be limited. [1:2.]

At least twenty-two men, some of them employes of a Canadian Government agency, were arrested for disclosing data, reportedly on atomic energy, to a foreign mission. [1:2-3.]

President Truman and Secretary of State Byrnes said the State Department's Blue Book criticizing Argentina as a center of Nazi activity had been made public at their direction. [14:2.]

The Pearl Harbor inquiry was told that President Roosevelt, after reading an intercepted and incomplete text of the Japanese reply to Washington on the eve of the Pearl Harbor attack, had commented "this means war," but had emphasized that the "democracy of a peaceful people" could not seize the advantage of the initiative by striking first. [1:2-3.]

President Truman once again voiced confidence in Edwin W. Pauley, the center of the dispute that led to the resignation of Secretary Ickes, and predicted that the Senate would confirm his nomination to be Under-Secretary of the Navy. [1:4.]

PAY PLAN DEFENDED

President Calls the New Wage-Price Policy 'Bulge' in Old Line

'RETREAT' IS DENIED

Bowles Says He Is Satisfied With New Set-Up Under Snyder

By FELIX BELAIR Jr.
Special to THE NEW YORK TIMES.

WASHINGTON, Feb. 15—President Truman denied today that the Administration was retiring to a new "price line" and asserted that the wage-price policy announced last night was a "bulge" in the old line.

The Chief Executive, permitting direct quotations, told his news conference:

"This is not a new line. It is a bulge in the old line. You've heard of a bulge in the military sense. If everybody cooperates, there will be no break-through."

At the same time, Administration officials, from the President down, sought to dispel fears that the new policy might come to grief through the inability of John W. Snyder, reconversion director, and Chester Bowles, new director of economic stabilization, to compose their differences and work together as a team.

Any doubt that Mr. Snyder would remain as the man at the controls of the national economy was ended by Mr. Truman, who said that Mr. Bowles would continue to take his orders from the reconversion director. In case of any arguments between the two, Mr. Truman said that he would decide the issue.

The Chief Executive emphasized repeatedly that Messrs. Snyder and Bowles, along with other members of his economic high command,

Continued on Page 2, Column 2

Wage-Price Formula Poses Puzzle Over Its Operations

Supplementary Rulings Might Require U. S. Approval of All Rises—Employers Expected to Ask Price Relief First

Special to THE NEW YORK TIMES.

WASHINGTON, Feb. 15—The new wage-price policy provides a more liberal basis of computing cost-of-living wage increases but will expand the Government's administrative job of passing on these increases, according to the general view here.

These are some of the effects of President Truman's executive order. The full effect of the order in practice will not be clear until the supplementary regulations are issued. Chester Bowles, who will become Stabilization Director in a few days, could require approval of all wage or salary increases, but this is regarded as improbable, at least at the present time.

As matters stand, there is no direct Government restraint on wage and salary increases as such, except in the building and construction industry. The restraint is indirect, through price ceilings. If employers grant wage or salary increases without prior Government approval, they waive the right to ask price relief later.

The regulations to be issued later will make some exceptions to this rule, but the tendency will be for employers to get approval of increases and this will mean more work for the Wage Stabilization Board. Previously, employers could put wage increases into effect without approval and still have the right to ask for price review later.

The board has no authority to order wage or salary increases.

A significant change in the basis of computing approvable cost-of-living wage increases is in the use of the word "rates" instead of straight time hourly earnings.

Where there is no general industry wage pattern, or local labor market pattern for the wage stabilization board to follow, the board is required to approve increases

Continued on Page 2, Column 6

GM Peace Outlook Brightens As Wilson and Thomas Meet

By WALTER W. RUCH
Special to THE NEW YORK TIMES.

DETROIT, Feb. 15—New optimism prevailed in the General Motors Corporation strike situation tonight following the first meeting of the so-called "first teams" representing each side in the tie-up, now eighty-seven days old. James F. Dewey, special mediator appointed by the Secretary of Labor to attempt to settle the walkout, brought together Charles E. Wilson, president of the corporation, and R. J. Thomas, international president of the United Automobile Workers.

It was the first time since 1942 that Mr. Wilson had sat at a table with UAW negotiators. He was in a jovial mood, and his spirit of buoyancy was reflected later by Mr. Dewey in an announcement to reporters that "much progress" had been made during the three-and-one-half-hour session.

Mr. Dewey said that the conferees including Mr. Wilson and Mr. Thomas, would meet again at 10 o'clock tomorrow morning, marking the first time before or during the strike that negotiations have been set for a Saturday. The meeting today was the first held since Tuesday, when Walter P. Reuther, international vice president of the UAW and director of its General Motors department, walked out to break off negotiations.

At that time the company had offered an increase in wages of 18½ cents an hour, with all other points to be negotiated. The union is holding out for an increase of 19½ cents, as recommended by the fact-finding board named by President Truman to investigate the merits of the case.

The union delegation today also

Continued on Page 3, Column 2

TIMES SQ. LIGHTS UP AS BROWNOUT ENDS

Most Signs Go On 45 Minutes Early—Stebbins Lifts the 60-Degree Heat Rule

At dusk last night a million lights blazed again in Times Square and the city had officially recovered—at least outwardly—from the ten-day tugboat strike that ended late Wednesday.

The Great White Way blossomed and the fabulous "spectaculars" joined in signaling the return to normal conditions, but it was a bitterly cold White Way and few persons noticed the change as they hurried along, heads down, against the piercing wind.

The brownout lifting had been officially scheduled for 6 P. M., but Broadway beat the gun at 5:15, while on the East Side from Eighty-sixth to Forty-second Streets the signs went on at 5:30.

Word had gone to the lunar reaches, too, and as the night darkened a rivaling moon shone out of the pale sky.

Along the entire length of the theatre district there were only a few exceptions to the early dis-

Continued on Page 3, Column 3

First Big Cut in National Debt In 15 Years Is Due Next Month

By The Associated Press.

WASHINGTON, Feb. 15 — The first big reduction in the national debt in more than fifteen years was projected by the Treasury today as the debt rolled to a record high of $279,496,766,104.49, an average of $1,991.52 for each American.

The cut will amount to $2,779,720,600—about 1 per cent of the total—and will be accomplished in the next thirty days by redeeming Government securities with cash, the Treasury stated. Nothing like it has happened since the late Nineteen Twenties, officials said.

President Truman in his recent budget message announced plans to lower the debt about $7,000,000,000 by June 30, 1947, by dipping into the Treasury cash balance, which stood above $25,557,000,000 today.

The Administration gave no indication of any policy change on the question of interest rates. Along with the redemptions, the Treasury said that it would merely offer an identical exchange for $3,147,310,000 in low-rate one-year certificates.

The Treasury proposal conformed to some recent demands in Congress for cutting down the cash balance so as to reduce the interest which must be paid on the thumping "idle" sum.

It ran headlong into Federal Reserve Board criticism, however, of the President's proposal to use the Treasury cash in paying off Government obligations.

The Reserve Board's monthly publication said that this would be "more inflationary in its effect than increasing the public debt through the sale of additional securities to non-bank buyers."

Paying out cash from the national strong box to redeem obligations already outstanding would,

Continued on Page 3, Column 4

DECISION IS SUDDEN

U. S. Steel, Union End Retroactivity Issue by 'Splitting Difference'

WORKERS GET 9¼

Agreement Covers 125,000 Who Will Return to Job Monday

By JOSEPH A. LOFTUS
Special to THE NEW YORK TIMES.

WASHINGTON, Feb. 15—A four-week strike at the mills of the United States Steel Corporation will end at midnight Sunday, and the rest of the industry is expected to return to production soon thereafter on the basis of a wage increase of 18½ cents an hour and a price rise of $5 a ton on steel.

"Big Steel," whose five producing subsidiaries employ more than 125,000, and the United Steel Workers, CIO, reached an agreement tonight which the principals said assured a year of peace for the concern.

John W. Snyder, director of War Mobilization and Reconversion, announced the settlement to reporters in a hotel suite in the presence of Secretary Schwellenbach, John Steelman, special assistant to President Truman, Charles Ross, White House press secretary, and the conferees of the corporation and the union.

Truman Suggestion Is Accepted

The 18½ cents was the figure suggested by Mr. Truman several days before the strike began.

The retroactivity issue, which kept the parties apart for the last several days, was resolved by "splitting the difference." The President suggested the increase be made effective as of Jan. 1, three weeks before the strike began.

The company said that it could not accept the principle of retroactivity, but agreed to a clause whereby an increase of 9¼ cents would be paid for all work performed between Jan. 1 and Feb. 17 when the strike ends. Beginning Monday, the 18½-cent increase will go into effect.

Philip Murray, union president, said that work would not be resumed at the plants of other steel companies until contracts were agreed on, but he added that he expected that would be accomplished quickly. Now that the pattern has been set, negotiations for the most part will be handled by local or regional union committees.

High Production Pledged

John Stephens, vice president of the United States Steel Corporation in charge of industrial relations, who reached the agreement with Mr. Murray, said that the existing contract, which would have expired in October, was extended to Feb. 15, 1947, and that the union subscribed to a new clause providing for cooperation in maintaining high productivity. The contract also contains a non-strike clause.

Mr. Stephens said that all employes would be reinstated without discrimination, and that the union agreed not to discriminate against any employes who did not cooperate in the strike.

The corporation also said that this was the highest single wage rise in the history of the industry. Increases also will be given to many of the salaried employes. The concern estimated that all the increases would cost about $100,000,000 during the life of the contract in excess of the realization from the $5 a ton price rise.

The application of the price increase to all kinds of steel will be worked out by the Office of Price Administration in consultation with its industry advisory committee.

The increase of $5 a ton is estimated at 8 to 9 per cent. The wage increase, which figures about 17½ per cent, raises the basic labor rate from 78 cents to 96½ cents.

The corporation said that straight time hourly earnings in the industry previously averaged

Continued on Page 2, Column 4

"All the News That's Fit to Print"

The New York Times.

LATE CITY EDITION
Sunny, warm today. Sunny, with increasing cloudiness tomorrow
Temperatures Yesterday—Max., 70; Min., 49
Sunrise today, 5:48 A. M.; Sunset, 6:15 P. M.
Full U. S. Weather Bureau Report, Page 51

Copyright, 1946, by The New York Times Company.

VOL. XCV..No. 32,205. Entered as Second-Class Matter. Postoffice, New York, N. Y. NEW YORK, THURSDAY, MARCH 28, 1946. THREE CENTS IN NEW YORK CITY

RUSSIAN, DEFEATED ON IRAN, WALKS OUT OF UNO; TEHERAN'S ENVOY PUTS PLEA BEFORE COUNCIL; SAYS SOVIET ASKED OCCUPATION AND OIL RIGHTS

REUTHER ELECTED PRESIDENT OF UAW BY NARROW MARGIN

8-Year Reign of Thomas Is Ended in Balloting Marked by Fist Fights, Near-Riots

VICTOR MAKES UNITY PLEA

Plans Campaign Among Farm Equipment Makers, Pledges Assistance to Murray

By WALTER W. RUCH
Special to THE NEW YORK TIMES.

ATLANTIC CITY, N. J., March 27—The United Automobile Workers, CIO, crowned ten years of trade unionism for Walter P. Reuther today by electing the 38-year-old red-head to the union presidency that had been held for eight years by R. J. Thomas.

In an election in the Municipal Auditorium that was as close as it was bitter, the delegates at the tenth convention of the huge union elevated the fiery leader from his post of vice president to one of the most powerful positions in the labor movement by a majority of only 124.4 votes.

The final tabulation, under a system of fractional voting, gave Reuther 4,444.8 and Thomas 4,320.4.

Mr. Reuther's first gesture was one of friendliness toward the Left Wing element that had battled furiously to keep him from office, and his first promise was one that he would exercise every power at his command to bring unity into an organization that has, admittedly, been disintegrating at the top level.

Plans Membership Drive

As for the "common enemy," he immediately outlined plans to expand the membership through drives to organize the farm machinery workers, the white collar workers and the engineers and technicians of the automotive industry as part of the UAW.

In his first address as president, Mr. Reuther sought to scotch, once and for all, rumors of dissension between him and Philip Murray, president of the Congress of Industrial Organizations, by extending full cooperation and expressing an anxious desire to walk at Mr. Murray's side to help bear "his heavy burden."

In a word, Mr. Reuther stepped into the presidency with a plea for unity that he might bind up the factionalism that abounds in a union harboring virtually every breed of political faith in the nation.

The man he had defeated, who had lost in a seventh attempt at re-election, was on the verge of tears as he gave up the office he held since Homer Martin, the first president, was ousted in 1938. He accepted a hearty handshake from the winner, who was heard to say: "Well, Tommy, now we can work together for a better union."

Mr. Thomas was understood reliably to be slated for appointment by Mr. Murray to serve as representative of the CIO on the newly formed World Federation of Trade Unions.

A movement was under way late tonight, however, to draft Mr. Thomas as a candidate for one of the two vice-presidential posts, which will be filled tomorrow. Among those urging such action were a number of Reuther delegates, who called at the Thomas headquarters to express their personal good-will toward the defeated candid .e. Mr. Thomas promised an answer in the morning.

Fights Enliven Voting

Fist fights and near-riots enlivened the voting session, which began with nominations at noon and ended at 4:30 P. M., with the most tumultuous demonstration of the convention. So near exhaustion were the frenzied partisans as a result of the narrow margin separating the candidates throughout the day that an overnight recess was taken before proceeding with the election of a secretary-treasurer and two vice presidents.

His red locks flecked with red,

Continued on Page 31, Column 5

U. S. Tutor Sought For Hirohito's Son

By Wireless to THE NEW YORK TIMES.

TOKYO, March 27—Emperor Hirohito has asked the members of the American education mission at present here under the chairmanship of Dr. George D. Stoddard, New York State Commissioner of Education, to recommend an American tutor for the 12-year-old Crown Prince Akihito, it was learned in palace circles today.

The report came as members of the mission were received in audience this afternoon, later attended a tea party and witnessed court dances in the presence of the Emperor and his younger brother, Prince Nobuhito Takamatsu.

Prince Akihito now is enrolled in the Peers School, of which his father also is a graduate. He also has the tutorial services of R. H. Blythe, an Englishman long resident in Japan, who is teaching him English. It is understood that an American tutor is being sought to supplement Mr. Blythe's teachings.

DRASTIC PROGRAM ON FOOD ADOPTED

UNRRA Resolution Outlines Steps, Including Rationing, to Meet Famine Crisis

UNRRA resolution outlining world food policy, Page 14.

By BESS FURMAN
Special to THE NEW YORK TIMES.

ATLANTIC CITY, N. J., March 27—The eleven-nation special food committee, which has been hard at work here since Friday on ways of meeting the famine crisis, recommended today rigorous food-saving measures. It also called for a recess in this United Nations Relief and Rehabilitation Administration Council to permit assessing the scarce supply situation, with provision to reconvene in Washington as soon as the director general can report.

With a few slight word changes, the resolution of the food committee was adopted unanimously at a session of the committee of the whole on policy held tonight to close the two weeks debate here on world food.

The expectation here was that the Council would reconvene in Washington in two or three weeks. In the interim the UNRRA director general would be requested under the resolution of the food committee "to consult immediately and continuously with representatives of the supplying Governments and with the combined food board to consider the effectiveness of steps being taken and to report thereon to the Central Committee and the Council." This duty no doubt will devolve on Fiorello H. La Guardia, slated to succeed Director General Herbert H. Lehman, although Mr. Lehman earlier had agreed to serve through the Council, not anticipating a recess.

Dallas W. Dort, second alternate of the American delegation, who served as chairman of the eleven-

Continued on Page 14, Column 2

IRAN'S STORY TOLD

Ambassador Ala Says He Does Not Know of Any Agreement in Force

DISCLOSES DEMANDS

Byrnes Asks That Case Be Confined to Purely Procedural Issue

Iranian Ambassador's statement of his country's case, P. 9.

By WILL LISSNER

In relief at becoming a participant in the deliberations of the United Nations Security Council on Iran's case, Ambassador Hussein Ala of Iran took a place at the Council table at 5:50 o'clock yesterday afternoon and disclosed demands made by the Soviet Union upon his country in secret Moscow negotiations between Feb. 19 and March 3 of this year.

The Iranian Ambassador plunged almost at once to one of the most vigorously discussed points, the question of whether or not there was a Soviet-Iranian agreement, as both Marshal Stalin and the Soviet delegate had indicated, when he stated:

"May I say once and for all that I know of no agreement or understanding, secret or otherwise, having been entered into between my Government and the Soviet Union with respect to any of the matters involved in the dispute now referred to this Council."

Mr. Ala, a short, spare man of quiet dignity, moved on the invitation of the chairman, Dr. Quo Tai-chi, from the seat in the front row of the Council chamber, where for two days he had been a mute witness of the Council's proceedings, to a seat on the extreme right of the table next to Dr. Oskar Lange, Polish representative, after the Council had voted to hear him.

"It was a relief," he said at the close of the session. "Imagine being obliged to watch all this discussion and not being able to begin making a statement."

Keen Interest Shown

While the members of the Council listened with keen interest, Mr. Ala began his presentation of Iran's reasons for opposing delay in consideration of her case.

"The issue between Iran and the Soviet Union was that the latter was interfering in the internal affairs of Iran through the medium of Soviet officials and armed forces," he asserted.

When Prime Minister Ahmad Ghavam of Iran went to Moscow on Feb. 19 to negotiate, as directed by the Security Council in its resolution of last Jan. 30, Mr. Ala continued, the Soviet officials "would not agree to withdraw their troops from Iran or to refrain from interfering in the internal affairs of Iran."

Instead, he said, the Soviet officials made a series of proposals. Soviet troops were to continue to stay in some parts of Iran indefi-

Continued on Page 11, Column 2

SOVIET DELEGATE WALKS OUT OF UNO—IRAN'S ENVOY TAKES A SEAT

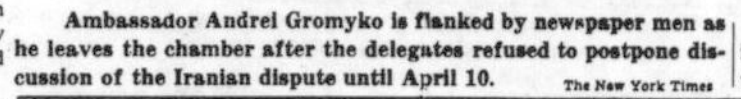

Ambassador Andrei Gromyko is flanked by newspaper men as he leaves the chamber after the delegates refused to postpone discussion of the Iranian dispute until April 10. The New York Times

Ambassador Hussein Ala addressing the delegates. At the left is an assistant to Dr. Oskar Lange, Poland's representative, and at the right is Akbar Daftari of the Iranian Embassy. Associated Press

IRAN AGAIN DENIES NEW SOVIET PACT

Premier Reiterates No Written or Oral Accord Was Reached in Talks in Moscow

By GENE CURRIVAN
By Wireless to THE NEW YORK TIMES.

TEHERAN, Iran, March 27—Official sources here reiterated today that there was no new agreement with the Soviet Union despite all the clamoring for details from other parts of the world. Premier Ahmad Ghavam has not altered his position one degree since he returned from his conference in Moscow.

He said then that he had failed

Continued on Page 11, Column 5

Gromyko Is Stern and Silent As He Leaves UNO Chamber

By W. H. LAWRENCE

With grim, stony-faced determination, young Andrei A. Gromyko took a fateful walk out of the United Nations Security Council at 5:19 P. M., yesterday. He went because the Kremlin had told him that under no circumstances would the Soviet Union present to the Council before April 10 a defense of its actions in Iran. The Council had just rejected, 9 to 2, his motion to postpone the case for two weeks.

He did not wait for his opponent to begin to speak. He did not wait even until the Council had decided the issue affirmatively by inviting his opponent, Hussein Ala, Iranian Ambassador to the United States, to join the Council table.

But Mr. Gromyko will be back.

Continued on Page 3, Column 5

BLUM PUTS NO TOP ON SIZE OF U. S. LOAN

Emissary Says France Needs $5,000,000,000 of Our Goods to Modernize Industry

By JOHN H. CRIDER
Special to THE NEW YORK TIMES.

WASHINGTON, March 27—Léon Blum, special French emissary to the United States, opened the current financial negotiations by painting a pitiable picture of France as "a nation twice ruined in thirty years," but citing the post-war accomplishments of her people as evidence of their courage and determination to recover.

The release today by the French Embassy of excerpts from M. Blum's lengthy presentation at the opening session on Monday was the first of a series of official releases under the rule of liberal public information adopted yesterday by the negotiators.

M. Blum opened on a note of "great solemnity" to stress the unity of all French political parties in supporting the "principles of democracy" and the "unconditional and unqualified" acceptance by France and all her constituent parties of the "principles of collec-

Continued on Page 17, Column 2

ALLIES WARN TITO ON VENEZIA GIULIA

Issue Blunt Statement Against Any Yugoslav Move to Invade Disputed Zone at Trieste

By SAM POPE BREWER
By Wireless to THE NEW YORK TIMES.

ROME, March 27—The Allied Governments issued a firm warning tonight to the Yugoslavs against any effort to stage a sudden invasion of the disputed Zone A of Venezia Giulia, now occupied by Anglo-American forces.

In the most blunt statement made on the subject in many months, Lieut. Gen. William D. Morgan, Supreme Allied Commander in the Mediterranean theatre, from his headquarters in Caserta, speaking in the names of the American and British Governments, said: "Public order will be enforced with justice, and in our zone we shall tolerate no attempt to prejudge in any way the final disposition of the territory.

"To this end, the American and British Governments have authorized me to declare that it is their firm intention to maintain their present position in Venezia Giulia until an agreed settlement of the territorial dispute has been reached and put into effect."

Allied Forces Reduced

This is the first time since the agreement was signed with Marshal Tito last June for the present division of Venezia Giulia into Zones A and B that such action has been necessary by the British and Americans.

[Zone A constitutes about a quarter of the area on the western side of the peninsula against the Italian frontier, and includes

Continued on Page 15. Column 2

COUNCIL PROCEEDS

Soviet Departure Fails to Swerve Body in Hearing of Issue

SOVIET COURSE HAZY

She Will Be Present at a Meeting Today—Poland Backs Her

Transcript of UNO proceedings on Iran question, Page 8.

By JAMES B. RESTON

The Soviet Union took a walk at the United Nations Security Council meeting yesterday, but it will be represented at the Council's Committee of Experts today, and it will come back to the Council when it feels like it, which will probably be on April 10.

This action, which broke, temporarily, the rule of Big Five unanimity, which the Russians have supported from the start, was not a break with the UNO. It was not to be compared, as some observers have been comparing it, with the German, Italian and Japanese departures from the League of Nations; nor was it an indication that the coalition that produced victory had been dissolved.

It is a decision by the Soviet Government, carried out by its Ambassador to Washington, Andrei A. Gromyko, to leave the Council for two weeks while the question of Red Army troops in Iran is being discussed. It is a parliamentary maneuver. It is an expression of protest against the Council. It is, admittedly, a psychological blow to the new organization and an illustration of the Soviet thesis that the great powers should direct, and even dictate, procedure as well as issues of substance in the Council.

Not a Break With Council

But it is not a break with the Council. In fact, not only do the Soviet representatives say they will be in the meeting of the Committee of Experts today, but in addition it is reported that if today's closed session of the Council deals only with the procedural aspects of the Iranian question, they may even attend that, though this is not at all certain.

At 5:04 yesterday afternoon, at the end of what began to look strangely like a filibuster by the Soviet Union, the Council defeated the Soviet Union's motion to postpone discussion of the Iranian case until April 10. Only the U.S.S.R. and Poland voted for it.

At 5:19, before the Council had voted to invite the Iranian Ambassador to sit at the Council table and tell why he thought the case of the Soviet troops in Iran was urgent, the youthful, pokerfaced Soviet delegate, Ambassador Gromyko, raised his hand and addressed the chair.

Soviet Statement on Withdrawal

As he was recognized, the spotlights in the chamber room went on slowly. The chamber was crowded. The delegates, weary of endless argument on legal points, frustrated by the lack of any rules of procedure and frankly out of patience with the Soviet Ambassador's repetitive argument, turned indulgently toward him and settled down for what looked like another long speech. But he was brief and to the point.

"For reasons which I explained clearly enough in our meeting of yesterday and in today's meeting, Mr. Chairman," he said in Russian, "I, as representative of the Soviet Union, am not able to participate further in the discussions of the Security Council because my proposal has not been accepted by the Council, nor am I able to be present at the meeting of the Council, and I therefore leave the meeting."

For a few minutes the audience did not understand the meaning of this, for when he finished speaking he waited expressionless in his chair until the translators had finished. The first indication the

Continued on Page 3, Column 1

World News Summarized

THURSDAY, MARCH 28, 1946

The Soviet Union walked out of the UNO Security Council session late yesterday afternoon after the Russian proposal to defer consideration of the Iranian question until April 10 had been defeated, 9 to 2. Only Russia and Poland voted for it. When it became evident that Iranian Ambassador Ala would be invited to the table to present his case, Ambassador Gromyko announced he was unable to participate further in the discussions or remain present, picked up his papers and departed. [1:8.]

Mr. Gromyko's withdrawal was in conformity with strict instructions from Moscow and he is expected to attend any sessions before April 10 at which the merits of the Iranian question are not discussed. [1:5-6.] Oskar Lange, Poland's delegate, defended Mr. Gromyko's action and declared that Poland would continue in attendance. [2:2.]

Russia, at the Moscow conferences with Premier Ghavam, instead of agreeing to withdraw from Iran, made counter-proposals that were unacceptable, Mr. Ala disclosed to the Council. The Russians wanted Soviet troops to remain in some parts of Iran "for an indefinite period"; they demanded recognition of Azerbaijan's autonomy and proposed a joint Soviet-Iranian oil company in which Russia would hold 51 per cent of the stock. There have been no further discussions or agreements, he said, and he had not been authorized to agree to a delay. The session adjourned before Mr. Ala finished. [1:3.]

Official sources in Teheran confirmed the lack of any agreement. [1:4.]

The day of debate was marked by frequent sharp exchanges. The Council will meet in executive session this afternoon. [4:2.]

The Military Staff Committee began work on the international police force to maintain world security and peace through the UNO. [10:2.]

Russian Naval Lieutenant Redin was held in $25,000 bail in Portland, Ore., on espionage charges that Soviet officials called a "frame-up" to damage Russian prestige. He was accused of having induced some unnamed person to obtain data about the destroyer-tender Yellowstone, described as a "floating shipyard." [6:3.]

The British Labor party attacked Communists and dissident left-wingers in a manifesto rejecting a proposal to affiliate with the Communist party, which was accused of harboring fifth columnists. [10:3-4.]

In this country, observers saw a rebuke to leftists in the labor movement [31:2] in the defeat of R. J. Thomas by Walter P. Reuther for president of the United Auto Workers Union, CIO. [1:1.]

All nations were urged to their greatest efforts to cut food consumption and increase production to meet the world famine crisis in an UNRRA resolution. [1:2.]

Yugoslavia was warned in a sharp Allied communiqué that American and British occupation troops would oppose any sudden attempt by Marshal Tito's men to seize part of the Venezia Giulia area. [1:7; map P. 15.] Russia presented new draft peace treaties for Bulgaria and Hungary designed to meet Anglo-American objections. [15:2.]

León Blum told American negotiators that France would have to spend at least $17,000,000,000 in five years to re-establish her economic position and to permit her to play her full part in collective security. [1:6.]

10c Fare Resolution Withdrawn; Defeat by Board Was Indicated

By PAUL CROWELL

Cornelius A. Hall, Borough President of Richmond, withdrew yesterday, "pending further conferences with Mayor O'Dwyer," the ten-cent subway fare resolution submitted by him to the Board of Estimate on March 14.

Mr. Hall's announcement came soon after the committee of the whole of the Board of Estimate ended a three-hour executive meeting at City Hall. Mayor O'Dwyer and the other Democratic members of the board declined to discuss Mr. Hall's announcement, but it was reliably reported that he decided to withdraw the higher-fare resolution after his colleagues had indicated that they would vote it down today and would not agree to lay it over for consideration at some future meeting.

The resolution called for a ten-cent fare on all transit lines owned and operated by the city, with free transfers for any single continuous trip. It also provided for a ten-cent fare on the Staten Island ferries, with free transfers to subways and certain bus lines. Another provision called for retention of a five-cent fare for school children traveling to and from school.

Mr. Hall declined to discuss details of the proceedings at the executive meeting, but did say that "it was a lengthy discussion."

"I am withdrawing my resolution pending further conferences with Mayor O'Dwyer," he declared.

Mayor O'Dwyer recently indi-

Continued on Page 29, Column 5

Braden Bars a Break With Peron; Says Europe Needs Argentine Aid

Spruille Braden, Assistant Secretary of State and leading exponent of a firm policy in dealing with Argentina, indicated yesterday that there was nothing we could do at the moment about the Perón regime, recently victorious in the election held there.

In a frank discussion here, Mr. Braden ruled out the breaking of diplomatic relations as "silly," and any attempt to impose sanctions as futile, because neither France nor Britain would back us, nor would we, in this country, want to assume the resposibility of depriving the starving of Europe of the food Argentina could supply.

Mr. Braden was the principal speaker at a seminar for women's clubs, arranged by THE NEW YORK TIMES in cooperation with the General Federation of Women's Clubs, held at Times Hall, 240 West Forty-fourth Street.

Other speakers on the program, the first of three scheduled, included Turner Catledge, assistant managing editor; Foster Hailey, editorial writer; James B. Reston, national correspondent; Anne O'Hare McCormick, editorial correspondent, all of THE TIMES; John J. McCloy, former Assistant Secretary of War, Mrs. William Dick Sporborg of the General Federation of Women's Clubs and Mrs. Arthur Hays Sulzberger, who welcomed the guests.

Mr. Braden's exposition of our present attitude toward Argentina came during the question and answer period. The question to which he addressed himself was:

"If the United States applies

Continued on Page 19, Column 1

Ernest Hemingway married his fourth wife, the former Mary Welsh, in Havana, Cuba, in 1946. Hemingway then settled down to write what would prove to be his greatest works.

The "Laff King of America" — Milton Berle. Berle proclaimed "National Laff Week" on April Fool's Day.

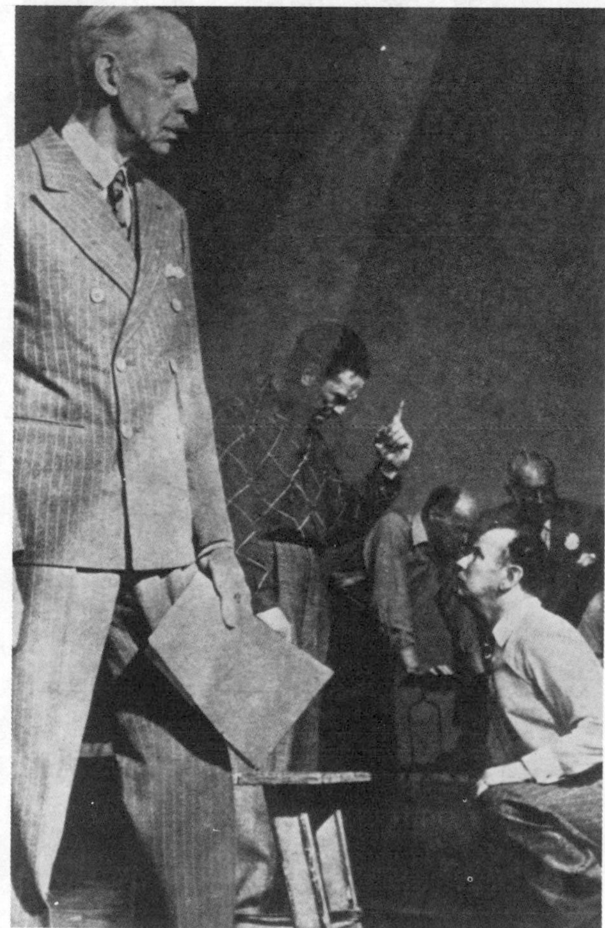

Eugene O'Neill at a rehearsal of the original Broadway production of *The Iceman Cometh* in 1946.

Ethel Merman as Annie Oakley in the musical *Annie Get Your Gun.* One of the first really big Broadway musicals, *Annie Get Your Gun* was to run for many years.

Harold Russell, Dana Andrews and Frederic March in *The Best Years of Our Lives.*

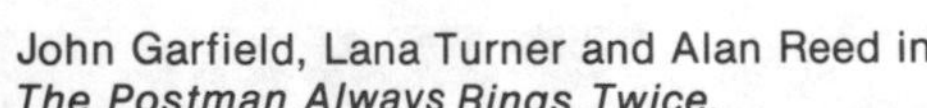

John Garfield, Lana Turner and Alan Reed in *The Postman Always Rings Twice.*

Lauren Bacall with Humphrey Bogart in *The Big Sleep.*

"All the News That's Fit to Print"

The New York Times.

LATE CITY EDITION
Partly cloudy and mild today. Occasional showers tomorrow.
Temperatures Yesterday—Max., 64; Min., 41
Sunrise today, 5:56 A. M.; Sunset, 7:51 P. M.
Full U. S. Weather Bureau Report, Page 51

VOL. XCV..No. 32,239. Entered as Second-Class Matter. Postoffice, New York, N. Y. NEW YORK, WEDNESDAY, MAY 1, 1946. THREE CENTS IN NEW YORK CITY

JOINT PALESTINE BODY BARS A JEWISH STATE, BUT URGES ENTRY OF 100,000 REFUGEES

Arabs 'Outraged' by Report; Jews Are Far From Satisfied

Rival Agencies Reiterate Their Arguments —U. S., British Talks Are Forecast on Easing Burden Too Big for London

By HERBERT L. MATTHEWS
By Wireless to THE NEW YORK TIMES.

LONDON, April 30—Now that the report of the Anglo-American Committee of Inquiry on Palestine has been published, one can safely predict tonight that the next step will be for the British to consult the United States Government about it. The British have reached the point at which they consider that Palestine is far too great a burden for them to be forced to handle alone.

No Government spokesman would say anything about the report tonight because the Cabinet and other officials have not had time to study it. One must keep in mind that the members of the committee had a mandate only to make recommendations, which do not in any sense involve Governmental responsibility.

The Arab Office in London has lost no time in issuing a scorching statement condemning the report lock, stock and barrel. The Jewish Agency for Palestine gave the report a mixed reception. It was happy about the proposal to allow 100,000 Jewish refugees to enter Palestine but asserted that without the formation of a Jewish state there could be no solution to the problem of homeless Jews.

On all sides one hears dubious comment about the fact that the committee's report makes no suggestion in terms of any sort of finality nor does it even offer any kind of long-term solution to the Palestinian problem. It is feared that even moderate elements among the Arabs will be more disturbed about that feature of the report than any other.

In their present mood of shocked disgust over the murder of seven British soldiers in Tel Aviv last Thursday the British are inclined to place the most prominence on that part of the report dealing with security and with making it clear that violence and terrorism will be resolutely repressed. The state-

Continued on Page 14, Column 5

TRUMAN FOR ACTION

Inquiry Upholds His Visa Proposal, Urges End of White Paper

WOULD GUARD ARAB RIGHTS

Report for Change in Holy Land Property Curbs—Demands a Firm Stand on Violence

The text of the report of the Anglo-American Committee of Inquiry on Palestine, Pages 15 to 21, inclusive.

FELIX BELAIR JR.
Special to THE NEW YORK TIMES.

WASHINGTON, April 30—The Anglo-American Committee of Inquiry on problems of Jews in Europe and Palestine, reporting to the two Governments today on its four-month investigation, urged the admission of 100,000 European Jews into the Holy Land as soon as possible, but flatly rejected the idea of a Jewish state, together with Arab claims for dominance. It asserted Christendom's own interest in the area.

Released simultaneously for publication in Washington and London, the report drew from President Truman an expression of satisfaction that his proposal for the admission of 100,000 Jews into Palestine had been recommended. He added that "the transference of these unfortunate people should now be accomplished with the greatest dispatch."

The President declared it significant that the report aimed at guarantees for Arab civil and religious rights and urged measures to improve Arab cultural, educational and economic position.

Land Changes Asked

"I am also pleased," he said, "that the committee recommends, in effect, the abrogation of the White Paper of 1939."

The report repudiated the 1939 White Paper principles, which made further Jewish immigration dependent on Arab consent and banned Jewish land purchases in a major part of Palestine.

Dependent for its final effect on adoption by both Governments, the report covered a wide range of controversial subjects on which President Truman gave no hint of his attitude except to say that he was taking them under advisement.

However, Mr. Truman seemed to have embraced the major policy statement rejecting "once and for all the exclusive claims of Jews and Arabs to Palestine," which the committee enunciated as follows:

"(I, That Jew shall not dominate Arab and Arab shall not dominate Jew in Palestine. (II) That Palestine shall be neither a Jewish state nor an Arab state. (III) That the form of government ultimately to be established shall, under international guarantees, fully protect and preserve the interests in the Holy Land of Christendom and of the Moslem and Jewish faiths."

Stress on Unique Status

With deliberate emphasis, the Committee of Inquiry declared that "Palestine is a Holy Land, sacred to Christian, to Jew and to Moslem alike; and because it is a holy land, Palestine is not, and can never become, a land which any race or religion can justly claim as its very own."

With equal emphasis, the committee said the same considerations set Palestine apart from other lands, and dedicated it to the precepts and practices of the brotherhood of man rather than to those of narrow nationalism.

The 42,000-word report was signed in Lausanne, Switzerland, by Judge Joseph C. Hutcheson, United States chairman, Sir John E. Singleton, British chairman, Frank Aydelotte, Frank W. Buxton, Bartley C. Crum, James G. McDonald and William Phillips, American members, and W. F. Crick, R. H. S. Crossman, Frederick Leggett, R. E. Manningham-Buller and M. Morrison for Britain.

For the immediate future the

Continued on Page 14, Column 2

Truman Said to Plan Start Of Jewish Entry 'Forthwith'

By LAWRENCE RESNER

Bartley C. Crum, one of the six United States members of the Joint Anglo-American Committee of Inquiry on Palestine, predicted here yesterday, on the basis of a discussion he had with President Truman at the White House on Monday, that the directives authorizing the admission of 100,000 European Jews into Palestine would "issue forthwith."

Mr. Crum, a San Francisco lawyer, also expressed the belief that most Jewish groups would endorse the affirmative aspects of the report, although reserving their right to continue a fight for the achievement of their ideological tenets, principally a Jewish state.

An immediate endorsement of the recommendation to obtain the admission of the 100,000 European Jews came from Joseph M. Proskauer, president of the American Jewish Committee, who said the provisions for immediate action were "obviously based on the highest considerations of statesmanship and humanity."

The World Zionist Emergency Council, which speaks for some of the largest and most active Zionist groups in the United States, said a statement outlining its position probably would be issued today, after the report had been studied.

The initial negative response by a Jewish group came from the Political Action Committee for Palestine, whose executive vice chairman, Dr. Baruch Korff, said that despite "the report's few fine points, the commission had proved

Continued on Page 13, Column 4

U. N.'S SPAIN INQUIRY COMMENCES TODAY

5-Man Subcommittee to Meet Here In Secret—No Outside Witnesses at First Session

By W. H. LAWRENCE

The Franco regime in Spain goes on trial today on charges that it is a cause of international friction and a threat to world peace.

Meeting privately at 3 P. M., representatives of Australia, China, France, Poland and Brazil will set in motion the first formal investigation by the United Nations, authorized Monday by a 10-to-0 vote of the Security Council, in which Russia did not participate but refrained from exercising an asserted right to veto the inquiry.

How, where and when the Council subcommittee will function presumably will be decided in the early part of today's meeting, and the members then will turn to analyzing the evidence now before them, listing the specific charges

Continued on Page 7, Column 5

MacArthur Plot Alarms Japanese; They See Possible Repercussions

By The Associated Press.

TOKYO, April 30—News of a frustrated assassination plot against General Douglas MacArthur tonight shocked the Japanese.

Their first reaction was twofold: A feeling that their country had lost face; fears that repercussions might be felt in every household.

The Government officially apologized. Katsuo Okazaki, representing Foreign Minister Shigeru Yoshida, visited General MacArthur's office two hours after Allied Headquarters had announced discovery of the plot. He did not see the general personally, but delivered a verbal message to aides.

Mr. Okazaki expressed "deep regret and concern" and said his Government was "greatly embarrassed." He asked if there was anything his Government could do.

Earlier, Premier Kijuro Shidehara, Mr. Yoshida and Home Minister Chuzo Mitsuchi conferred. Japanese reporters speculated that they discussed tighter precautions than previously were planned for the May Day demonstrations.

Many Japanese immediately asked, "Will this create more anti-Japanese feeling in America?" They linked this with fear that adverse American reaction might complicate efforts to obtain food and might mean a longer, harsher occupation.

They also expressed regret that the incident might mar the occupation and change the attitude of General MacArthur, whom the Japanese generally respect.

Allied headquarters had previously given some details of the plot. One conspirator was seized and a nation-wide hunt was launched for a die-hard Japanese militarist named as the arch plotter.

The accused and hunted plot leader was Hideo Tokayama, former member of the dread Kempeitai or "thought police." In the

Continued on Page 12, Column 6

WARSHIP BLOWS UP AT MUNITIONS PIER IN PORT, KILLING 5

60 on Escort Vessel Injured —Blasts Shake New Jersey Towns Near Big Depot

BOMBS ASHORE SET OFF

Sailor Is Only Slightly Hurt as Depth Charge Explodes as He Is Carrying It

By MEYER BERGER
Special to THE NEW YORK TIMES.

LEONARDO, N. J., April 30—One officer and four sailors of the destroyer escort Solar's complement of fourteen officers and 185 enlisted men vanished utterly before noon today in an ammunition explosion that tore away one-third of the 306-foot ship's forward structure.

About sixty of the ship's crew were injured, but only thirty-five were hospitalized, and of them only a handful remained tonight for further treatment. The Navy withheld the names of the five missing men and the names of the injured because not all their families had been officially notified.

The explosion happened as the Solar's crew was unloading her ammunition supply in preparation for an overhaul. Normally she carries about fifteen tons of assorted ammunition, including depth bombs and smaller charges, torpedoes and shells for her cannon. Only one-third of this amount was still aboard when the blast occurred.

Tons of Explosives Near By

Near by, when the detonation shook the New Jersey coast in and around the Raritan Bay district, were a number of other vessels preparing to unload ammunition. It was unofficially estimated here that these vessels held, all told, about 25,000 tons of explosives. Tugs dragged these craft out of the danger zone.

Burning fragments from the Solar, hurled at tremendous force against freight cars on the pier, started other explosions. One car in a freight string, filled chiefly with depth charges, blew up and all but vanished in dust and smoke, scattering its parts in all directions. Three strings of cars were hauled shoreward by their locomotive crews, at great risk.

No one seemed certain tonight what had caused the explosion, but what seemed like a possible explanation came from Jack Horne, fireman second class, of Charlotte, N. C. He thought a piece of ammunition carried by Joseph Stuchinski, seaman, of Baltimore, might have done it.

"Ski," the fireman said, "was carrying a 'hedgehog' from the forward magazine. While he was holding it, it just went off. He must have bumped it against something, because those things go off when anything touches them."

Seaman Stuchinski, oddly enough, was not seriously injured. He was deafened, a few minor scratches showed on his chest when he got to the first-aid station and his dungarees were split.

"It went off. The thing just went off," he said.

The "hedgehog" Stuchinski carried was an anti-submarine depth charge. Metal-cased, weighing about sixty pounds, it is generally cylindrical, about thirty inches long and between four and five inches in diameter.

Bow Like Elephant's Trunk

The Solar lay at the northern, or bay end, of the easternmost of the three great piers that jut out from the Navy's Earle Ammunition Depot, when she blew up. She was approximately one and one-half miles from the beach end of the depot. The blast curled her bow in much the same shape as an elephant's back-bent trunk.

The concussion was felt twenty to thirty miles around. The detonation rushed across Raritan Bay to shake homes in Tottenville, Richmond Valley, Pleasant Plains, Princes Bay, Great Kills, Oakwood and New Dorp, all on Staten Island, and shattered panes in some of those communities.

Ground tremors were felt to the west and to the southwest. There were some freakish effects. Residents in Middletown Township, including Rumson, Fair Haven, Red Bank and Little Silver, for example, seemed certain the explosion was local. Several frightened housewives called the police to say, "The boiler just blew up in my cellar."

Dogs raced away from the beach

Continued on Page 2, Column 3

AFTER EXPLOSIONS RIPPED DESTROYER ESCORT

The wrecked U. S. S. Solar at the Navy Ammunition Depot in Earle, N. J., yesterday
The New York Times (U. S. Navy)

BAN BY MUSICIANS BLOW TO TELEVISION

Petrillo Plans to Prolong the Refusal of Union Men to the Industry Indefinitely

By JACK GOULD

The American Federation of Musicians, headed by James C. Petrillo, plans to forbid its members to work in television until some indefinite date in the future when the union can determine the effects of video's advent on present-day radio, it was learned yesterday.

Television broadcasters were agreed that Mr. Petrillo's stand would retard the immediate development of video programs, since it could be a matter of months if not years before anyone could determine to what extent television would supplant or complement sound broadcasting.

Use of "live" musicians was first denied the television industry in February, 1945, by the international executive board of the federation, but yesterday was the first time that Mr. Petrillo explained the action and indicated that the ban would be of prolonged duration.

Musical Films Already Banned

Last week Mr. Petrillo's union and the Hollywood motion picture producers entered into an agreement not to permit films containing music to be used in television, a move leaving the telecasters with only records as a possible source of music. Beginning July 1, under a rule of the Federal Communications Commission, the television stations are scheduled to offer twenty-eight hours of programs a week, but under Mr. Petrillo's edicts they will be forced to rely primarily on talks, sporting events and other non-musical fare.

Coincidentally with stating the union's position on television, Mr. Petrillo also reiterated his stand against permitting standard radio programs containing music to be presented simultaneously on frequency modulation outlets. The union is insisting on double crews of musicians in the event of such duplication.

The re-statement of the union's views on FM were regarded with

Continued on Page 28, Column 2

Stalin Warns of War Plot By 'International Reaction'

By The Associated Press.

LONDON, April 30—Generalissimo Stalin promised tonight that the Soviet Union would be true to a policy of peace and security but charged that what he described as "international reaction" was "hatching plans of a new war." In an order of the day broadcast by the Moscow radio the Russian leader also declared that it was necessary to be constantly vigilant, "to protect as the apple of one's eye the armed forces and defensive power of our country."

TEXT OF STALIN ORDER

His broadcast order, issued in connection with the Soviet Union's May Day celebration, was heard in London by the Soviet monitor, who issued the following text:

Comrades, Red Army and Red Navy men, sergeants and petty officers, comrade officers, generals and admirals, working people of the Soviet Union:

Today, for the first time since the victorious termination of the Great Patriotic War we celebrate May 1—the international holiday of working people—in conditions of peaceful life, won in a hard struggle against the enemies at the cost of heavy sacrifices and privations.

One year ago the Red Army hoisted the banner of victory over Berlin and completed the defeat of fascist Germany. Within four months after the victorious termination of the war against Germany, imperialist Japan downed her arms. The Second World War, prepared by the forces of international reaction and unleashed by the chief fascist states, ended in a full victory of the freedom-loving nations. The smashup and liquidation of the main hotbeds of fascism and world aggression resulted in changes in the political life of the nations of the world, in a wide growth of the democratic movement of the nations.

Taught by the experience of war, the popular masses realized that the destinies of states cannot be entrusted to reactionary leaders, who pursue the narrow caste and selfish anti-popular aims. It is for this reason that nations, which no longer wish to live in the old way, take destinies of their states into their own hands, establish democratic order and actively fight against the forces of reaction, against instigators of a new war. The nations of the

Continued on Page 5, Column 4

INQUIRY FINDS 'PERIL' TO SECRETS OF WAR

Senators Hear Radar Makers on Russian Buying and Urge Law Tightening

By C. P. TRUSSELL
Special to THE NEW YORK TIMES.

WASHINGTON, April 30—Need for a tightening of the laws to provide protection for wartime secrets in the electronics and other fields was declared by Senate investigators today to be "very definite." The statement came after a closed-session inquiry into negotiations for sales of radar and similar equipment to Russia.

Members of a special Senate Judiciary subcommittee, conducting the investigation, said that there was no evidence that "classified,"

Continued on Page 3, Column 4

BIG FOUR RULE OUT AUSTRIA'S DEMAND FOR SOUTH TYROL

Paris Conference Rejects Any Major Frontier Revision in That Region of Italy

NO PROGRESS ON TRIESTE

Rome and Belgrade Are Asked to Send Delegates—Report of Experts Confusing

By C. L. SULZBERGER
By Cable to THE NEW YORK TIMES.

PARIS, April 30—Italy's retention of most of the Province of Bolzano [South Tyrol], which is claimed by Austria, was virtually assured tonight after the Council of Foreign Ministers had agreed that no requests for a major frontier change would be accepted in that area so valuable in hydro-electric power.

At the same time, after examining a verbose and confused report on Trieste and Venezia Giulia, submitted at long last by the special commission sent by the Foreign Ministers' deputies to investigate the Italian-Yugoslav border area, the Ministers agreed to invite the Yugoslav and Italian Governments to send delegates here on Friday to present once again their views on this hotly disputed and vitally important region.

The report showed a complete divergence in opinion between the Soviet investigator and the three other participants on the value of a census taken in 1945 by a Yugoslav, Professor Rodlich. The Soviet member of the commission said the census was fine and the three others said it was just the opposite. Since this census is of vital importance in deciding the ethnic basis for a decision, that leaves everything up in the air.

Suggested by Molotov

The move to widen the scope of the Foreign Ministers' meeting by inviting in the Italians and Yugoslavs was suggested by Vyacheslav M. Molotov. The Soviet Foreign Minister recalled that the Potsdam decisions, the "bible" under which the peace treaties are being drafted, provided that the interested parties should be included when necessary. Thus, the doors have been opened to permit entry of those delegations—Greek, Italian, Yugoslav, Hungarian and Bulgarian—now clamoring for a

Continued on Page 4, Column 2

Sharp Restrictions in Distilling Ordered in Food Conservation

By CHARLES E. EGAN
Special to THE NEW YORK TIMES.

WASHINGTON, April 30—World famine is more than a short term problem, and plans to meet its reappearance next winter should be drafted immediately, Chester C. Davis, chairman of the President's Special Famine Emergency Committee, asserted today.

Mr. Davis, who conferred with President Truman, later said that emergency measures, taken to insure larger relief shipment of grains and other foods to famine-stricken areas in the next few weeks, could not be considered as final, but were merely "the first sprint" in a continuing race to avert death for millions who otherwise would starve.

Meanwhile, Secretary Anderson issued an order restricting distilleries who operated for five days at full mashing capacity in April to three capacity days in May.

The order also limited the use of grain by the entire distilling industry to 2,500,000 bushels a month; banned use of wheat in the manufacture of spirits and restricted distillers to the use of corn which is unsuitable for human consumption.

In January, distillers were permitted ten capacity mashing days, but were cut to seven and one-half in February and to five days in March and April.

Brewers, operating on a 30 per cent reduction of grain, were not included in today's order.

"Every report coming before us makes it plain that the present famine is not a short run emergency that ends on July 1," Mr. Davis' statement said, adding:

"The present food shortages have been seriously aggravated by drought in many parts of the world, but even with good weather the wartime destruction of agricultural facilities will be felt for a long time.

"Farm animals and farm machinery have been destroyed. The strength of farm workers has

Continued on Page 22, Column 2

World News Summarized

WEDNESDAY, MAY 1, 1946

Palestine should become neither a Jewish state nor an Arab state, the Anglo-American Committee of Inquiry declared in its report made public simultaneously last night in Washington and London. Admission of 100,000 Jews this year and virtual abrogation of the 1939 British White Paper with its restrictions on land holdings were recommended. Other suggestions included continuation of the present mandate until establishment of a United Nations trusteeship and resolute suppression of violence and terrorism by Jews or Arabs. [1:8.]

Although President Truman expressed pleasure over certain parts of the report, it was felt in Washington that neither the Jews nor Arabs would be satisfied. [13:1.] In fact, Arab leaders threatened to combat any additional Jewish immigration [13:3] and Zionists expressed their opposition. Bartley C. Crum, a member of the committee, predicted that a directive authorizing the entry of 100,000 Jews into Palestine would "issue forthwith." [1:6-7.]

British reaction counted heavily upon American support in whatever was done, but regretted the absence of any long-term solution. [1:5.]

Italy will be permitted to retain most of southern Tyrol despite Austrian claims, the Foreign Ministers tentatively agreed at their conference in Paris, but they were as wide apart as ever on what to do about Trieste and the Venezia Giulia area. It was decided to invite Yugoslavia and Italy to present their cases anew. [1:5.]

Britain tried to meet French desires by suggesting internationalization of either the Ruhr or both the Ruhr and the left bank of the Rhine for fifty years. [3:1.] Secretary Byrnes' proposed four-power treaty to keep Germany disarmed was favorably received in the Senate Foreign Affairs Committee. [3:8.]

The United Nations Security Council subcommittee opens its investigation into Franco Spain this afternoon. [1:7.] Europe's ruined industries should be restored before attempts to eradicate world unemployment, the Economic and Employment Commission heard [8:5], while the Transport and Communications Commission debated the relative merits of free enterprise and government control of shipping. [7:1.] The Commission on Human Rights may seek a new international bill of rights and ask authority to supervise its implementation. [8:2.]

Tabriz, capital of Azerbaijan, has been formally evacuated by Russian troops, the Tabriz radio reported. [3:6.] Premier Stalin declared that, while the world must remain vigilant against reaction, it had "no reason to doubt" that Russia would remain steadfast in her devotion to international peace and security. [1:3-4.]

Japan was shocked at the plot to assassinate General MacArthur and the Government offered its apologies. No arrests have been announced. [1:6-7.]

Ammunition being unloaded from the destroyer-escort Solar in Raritan Bay exploded, killing an officer and four sailors. [1:1.]

John L. Lewis served notice that anthracite miners intended to strike on May 31 unless they obtained the same demands that led to the soft-coal strike. Negotiations will start in New York on May 10. No progress was made toward settling the bituminous dispute. [29:1.]

Further restrictions were placed on the use of grain by distillers in order to make more food available for world famine relief. [1:2-3.]

General Motors was authorized by the OPA to raise prices on its cars from $16 to $60 to cover wage increases. [27:6-7.] House members returned to Washington still opposed to extending price control without heavy restrictions. [30:5.]

"All the News That's Fit to Print"

The New York Times.

LATE CITY EDITION
Cloudy with rain today. Partly cloudy tomorrow.
Temperatures Yesterday—Max., 77; Min., 56

Copyright, 1946, by The New York Times Company.

VOL. XCV. No. 32,256. Entered as Second-Class Matter, Postoffice, New York, N. Y. NEW YORK, SATURDAY, MAY 18, 1946. THREE CENTS IN NEW YORK CITY

GOVERNMENT SEIZES THE NATION'S RAILROADS BUT UNIONS FAIL TO CANCEL STRIKE DUE TODAY; AFL PLEDGES AID TO LEWIS AS DEADLOCK HOLDS

BRITAIN-U. S. JOIN TO EXPORT CEREALS FOR HUNGRY WORLD

Agreement Fixes 10,000,000 Tons as Goal for Relief Purposes to September

RUSSIA OUT OF PROGRAM

Reported Rejection of Truman's Appeal for Aid Is Held to Increase 'Risk of Famine'

By The Associated Press.

WASHINGTON, May 17—An Anglo-American agreement for distributing 10,000,000 tons of cereals among nations requiring 13,400,000 tons from now to September was reported today by Herbert Morrison, president of the British Cabinet Council.

He also told a news conference that the United States and Britain had agreed to pursue "common rationing standards at the earliest possible date" in their zones in Germany.

"I think the French will follow," he added.

The common rationing program does not extend to the Russian zone, Mr. Morrison explained, because the Russians do not participate in the Combined Food Board, a British-Canadian-American agency which allocates food supplies to needy countries.

Mr. Morrison said that the agreement had been completed after his meetings here with President Truman and other officials.

Later the United States and Britain declared jointly that "a risk of famine remains" despite the best they could do for other countries and that "even more energetic measures are needed throughout the world" to cope with it.

Early May Grain Exports

Meanwhile the Agriculture Department reported grain exports of 105,000 tons during the first ten days of May, against a quota of 1,100,000 tons for the whole month. Its statement added that the figure did not reflect "the accelerated movement" of grain from inland points in recent weeks.

Mr. Morrison disclosed that Britain had agreed to relinquish another 200,000 tons of wheat for other nations during the May-September period and called this "a hard blow." Asked whether this would mean bread rationing for Britain, he replied that "is up to the Cabinet to decide."

Britain had previously given up 200,000 tons for immediate shipment to hungry countries with the understanding that it would be replaced later from the United States. The additional 200,000 tons relinquished now, however, would not be replaced, Mr. Morrison said.

The joint communiqué said that the United States and Britain reaffirmed "their belief that common measures should be taken in all zones of Germany with respect to the collection of indigenous foodstuffs, the setting of common ration standards and the adoption of a common basis for calculating import requirements."

The American and British commanders will be directed to confer toward this end in the American, British and French zones for which the Combined Food Board makes allocations.

Rationing in United Kingdom

"The United Kingdom representatives have reported fully on the measures of consumer rationing and other economies currently in effect in the United Kingdom," the communiqué said, and added:

"Consumer rationing has been continued, and in the case of fats, bacon, dried eggs, meat and preserves, rations have been reduced below the austere low wartime levels. Rations of the British forces in the United Kingdom have twice been cut since V-E Day."

In connection with Japan, the communiqué said the American Government had reviewed the import program to insure that "no

Continued on Page 10, Column 8

Unified Arctic Defense Plan Proposed by U. S. to Canada

Joint Bases, Weather Stations in Far North, Coordinated Training and Equipping of Forces in Scheme Put to Ottawa

By JAMES RESTON

Special to The New York Times.

WASHINGTON, May 17—The United States has proposed to Canada an unprecedented defense agreement under which the two countries would coordinate certain branches of their armed forces for the protection of North America, and particularly for the defense of the American Arctic frontier.

It is understood that the proposal, if accepted, would involve the standardization of many forms of equipment between the armed services of the two countries, the coordination of United States-Canadian training methods and military organization, and the joint erection and staffing of defense and weather stations in the continental Arctic zone.

The proposal for such a military understanding is believed to have developed out of a number of recommendations placed before the two Governments by the United States-Canadian Permanent Joint Board on Defense. These recommendations are understood to have been approved in principle by the United States, which has been discussing them with officials of the Ottawa Government.

It is emphasized in Washington that the proposed understanding would not be several things. It would not be a military alliance; it would not involve any political commitments from the United States to Canada or from Canada to the United States; it would not disturb Canada's relations with the British Commonwealth of Nations or involve the United States in any commitments Canada might take in the future to the British Commonwealth; and it would not take precedence over, or in any

Continued on Page 6, Column 1

U.N. BARES EVIDENCE OF GIRAL ON FRANCO

Spanish Republican, in Eight Indictments, Says Leader Is a Menace to World

By W. H. LAWRENCE

Documentary evidence from the Spanish Republicans in exile, the Soviet Union and Belgium, branding the Franco regime in Spain as a cause of international friction and a constant threat to world peace, was made public yesterday by the special United Nations subcommittee investigating the Spanish situation.

As expected, the bulkiest, most critical document was offered by Dr. José Giral y Pereira, Premier of the Government in exile, which made eight major points against Generalissimo Francisco Franco in an effort to persuade the United Nations Security Council that it should at least direct a collective break in diplomatic relations with the present Spanish Government.

Dr. Giral's lengthy brief pointed out that "a regime intimately bound up with the aggressor countries dominates one of the most important strategic zones in the world."

After having examined the Giral document, the subcommittee decided to summon Dr. Giral to attend a public meeting, which presumably will be held in the Security Council chamber in Hunter College. The subcommittee met at 4 P. M. and examined the analysis of the Giral memorandum prepared by the Secretariat, using as a basis

Continued on Page 8, Column 3

GANDHI SUPPORTS BRITISH PROPOSAL

Extols Sincerity of Offer—Wary Approval Is Heard in Two Main Indian Groups

By Reuter

NEW DELHI, India, May 17—Mohandas K. Gandhi tonight commended to the people of India the British Cabinet mission's proposals for a union of India, the formation of which Lord Pethick-Lawrence, chief of the mission and Secretary of State for India, said today would result in immediate withdrawal of British troops from the country if the Indians decided on complete independence.

Mr. Gandhi's approval of the plan was voiced tonight at a prayer meeting at which he said he regarded the scheme as "seed to convert this land of sorrow into one without sorrow and suffering."

"There are some who said the British were incapable of doing the right thing," he said. "I do not agree with them. The mission and the Viceroy are as God-fearing as we ourselves claim to be.

"Whatever the wrong done to India by British rule, if the statement of the mission is genuine, as I believe it is, it is in discharge of the obligation they have declared the British owed toward India, namely, to get off India's back."

Reaction Is Cautious

By GEORGE E. JONES

By Cable to The New York Times.

NEW DELHI, India, May 17 — India's political leaders continued to withhold authoritative comment today on the British Cabinet mis-

Continued on Page 4, Column 2

MINE OWNERS HIT

Federation Backs Welfare Fund—Offers Aid 'Until Victory'

PIT SEIZURE PLANNED

Dispute Is Discussed by Cabinet as Operators, UMW Mark Time

By LOUIS STARK

Special to The New York Times.

WASHINGTON, May 17—While President Truman "side-tracked" action in the coal controversy today pending the outcome of Government seizure of the railroads, his aides went forward with plans for taking over the soft-coal mines in a few days.

In the meantime, the executive council of the American Federation of Labor, after hearing John L. Lewis, a council member, make a comprehensive report on the coal negotiations, adopted a resolution pledging the Federation's 7,000,000 members to support the miners "to the limit until victory is won."

Mr. Truman will call in Mr. Lewis and Charles O'Neill, spokesman for the bituminous coal operators, before the Government seizes the mines.

He will ask them, it is understood, to carry on the production of coal pending the outcome of further joint negotiations or the efforts by a Federal Fuel Administrator to arrange a settlement of the controversy.

The President discussed the coal and railroad labor disputes at a Cabinet meeting today. Secretary Wallace, when he was asked on leaving the meeting what occurred, replied:

"Just the things you would expect."

Secretary Patterson told report-

Continued on Page 3, Column 4

CONFERRING ON PLANS TO OPERATE RAILROADS

Charles H. Buford (left) and J. Monroe Johnson in Washington following President Truman's seizure order yesterday.

Associated Press Wirephoto

SENATORS INSISTING ON NEW LABOR LAW

Determination of an Apparent Majority to Go Ahead Now Threatens Draft Measure

By C. P. TRUSSELL

Special to The New York Times.

WASHINGTON, May 17—Determination of an apparent majority of the Senate to go ahead with labor legislation, despite the seizure of the railroads, the coal-strike truce and other developments expected to have a "cooling-off" effect, threatened today to force postponement of action on a

Continued on Page 3, Column 8

World News Summarized

SATURDAY, MAY 18, 1946

With a strike of engineers and trainmen scheduled to begin at 5 P. M. today, President Truman ordered seizure of the nation's railroads and urged the workers to remain on duty. Union officials said that wage talks had failed and the strike order would stand. [1:8.]

After hearing John L. Lewis report on the coal-strike negotiations, the executive council of the American Federation of Labor pledged its support to the miners "to the limit until victory is won." Meanwhile, President Truman's aides went ahead on plans to seize the mines. [1:4.]

A Senate majority appeared determined to push the Case labor disputes bill despite the coal truce and seizure of the railroads, causing postponement of action on a new draft bill and other measures. [1:5.]

The United Steel Workers of America, CIO, urged President Truman to ask Civilian Production Administrator Small to resign and to repudiate his statement favoring anti-strike legislation. [1:7.]

Under an Anglo-American agreement, 10,000,000 tons of cereals will be sent to nations in need of 13,400,000 tons from now to September. [1:1.]

The special subcommittee of the United Nations investigating the charge that the Franco regime in Spain is a threat to peace made public supporting documentary evidence from three sources—the Spanish Government in Exile, the Soviet Union and Belgium. The committee invited Dr. José Giral, Premier of the Spanish Government in Exile, to attend a public meeting. [1:2.]

In Moscow Izvestia published a statement attributed to two captured Nazi officers alleging that Franco had dropped his plan to enter the war by seizing Gibraltar when Hitler chose to attack Russia instead of invading Britain. [8:8.]

A unanimous decision by the Security Council postponed until August consideration of applications for membership. Rules dealing with membership were approved. [8:2.]

Secretary Byrnes left Paris for Washington after expressing the conviction that the major differences between Russia and the Western Powers at the Foreign Ministers' meeting would be resolved at the next conference. [7:3.]

British and American "reactionaries" were blamed for friction between their countries and Russia by the Information Bulletin of the Soviet Embassy in Washington. It said "the Soviet Union's position in international affairs is dictated exclusively by the desire to insure peace for the constructive labors of the Soviet people." [7:1.]

Marshal Antonescu was sentenced to death by a Rumanian war crimes tribunal. [6:4.]

Washington denied it was seeking a military base in the eastern Mediterranean and reaffirmed its pledge to consult with both Arabs and Jews before acting on the Palestine issue. [9:5.]

Mohandas K. Gandhi gave his approval to the British plan for Indian independence. Unofficial sources in both main parties also appeared to be cautiously favorable. [1:3.]

A defense agreement has been offered to Canada by the United States calling for the coordination of certain branches of their armed forces for the defense of the Continent, particularly its Arctic frontier. [1:2-3.]

An attempt by Cuban rebels to seize Camp Columbia near Havana failed, Army leaders announced. [5:1.]

President Truman favored an increase of $1,250,000,000 for the Export-Import Bank. [1:6-7.]

Utilities, Commuters Face Hardships in Rail Strike

By LEO EGAN

If railroad engineers and trainmen strike today despite President Truman's seizure of the lines yesterday afternoon, it appeared that gas and electric utilities, their fuel stockpiles already depleted by the coal strike, would be the first to feel the effects of cutting off freight movements.

Railroad commuters, it appeared, would be forced to fall back on private cars and taxis to get to work on Monday if passenger service is cut off by a strike. Existing bus lines running into New York from suburban areas are near the limit of their capacity and will be unable to handle the additional traffic that cessation of rail service would involve, according to bus line officials.

What steps the Office of Defense Transportation has planned to meet the emergency if engineers and trainmen refuse to work for the Government were not disclosed last night. Operating officials of the railroads declined to speculate on the possibilities pending instructions from Washington.

Wallander in Conference

Police Commissioner Arthur W. Wallander conferred yesterday at police headquarters with representatives of the rail lines serving New York on arrangements for policing railroad property in the event of a walkout. He described the discussions afterward as "fact-finding."

Plans announced March 8 for dealing with a strike are being elaborated upon and a new announcement may be made today, the Commissioner said.

"In all probability," he added, "it will be necessary to broadcast

Continued on Page 2, Column 6

STEEL WORKERS ASK SMALL'S DISMISSAL

Truman Is Urged to Repudiate Appeal of CPA Head for a 6-Month Ban on Strikes

By LAWRENCE RESNER

Special to The New York Times.

ATLANTIC CITY, N. J., May 17—President Truman was asked today by the United Steel Workers of America, CIO, to request the immediate resignation of John D. Small, Civilian Production Administrator, and to repudiate promptly Mr. Small's statement urging Congress to pass legislation outlawing strikes for the next six months.

In its bitterest attack to date on a member of the Truman Administration, the Steel Workers' union accused Mr. Small of advocating "involuntary servitude" and of having failed in months past to take any decisive action against "price strikes," the deliberate creation of scarcities and other activities inimical to reconversion for which employers were responsible.

This action, voted unanimously by the 2,700 delegates to the

Continued on Page 3, Column 6

$1,250,000,000 More to Be Asked For Export-Import Bank Lending

By JOHN H. CRIDER

Special to The New York Times.

WASHINGTON, May 17—President Truman plans to ask Congress in the near future for $1,250,000,000 additional lending power for the Export-Import Bank, which will represent the official ceiling on foreign loans by the Government through June 30, 1947.

The White House plans were confirmed today by several high ranking officials. They said that had it not been for the preoccupation of the persons advising the President on these matters with urgent unexpected duties the Presidential request would have gone to Capitol Hill immediately following Senate approval of the $3,750,000,000 credit to Great Britain last week.

Increase of the Export-Import Bank's lending power has become a first order of Administration business owing to a recent decision that the French Government shall receive a $650,000,000 loan from the Bank.

Even this loan, the subject of long negotiations with a French mission now in this country, would have been impossible had not officials recently decided to eliminate any reservation of the Bank's funds for Soviet Russia.

As the French negotiations got under way the $3,500,000,000 lending power of the Bank shrunk below $1,500,000,000. Meanwhile, the State Department had resumed diplomatic correspondence with the Kremlin relative to a $1,000,000,000 credit from the Export-Import Bank.

Almost coincidentally, Gen. George C. Marshall urged a decision on a loan to China which seemed to be connected with his Presidential mission to help straighten up internal Chinese af-

Continued on Page 5, Column 1

Hoover Asks Food for 800,000,000 By Filling 'Gap' of 3,600,000 Tons

By The Associated Press.

CHICAGO, May 17—Herbert Hoover, reporting on his world survey of famine areas, called upon Americans tonight for greater self-denial to help save 800,000,000 persons from the "grimmest spectre of famine in all the history of the world."

Mr. Hoover departed from his prepared text to assert that "these spectres are only thirty days away in most of these famine areas, for that is the outside limit of their supplies in transit."

He warned that unless more food were shipped to hunger-ridden areas during the next several months, millions would be condemned to a diet like that of prisoners in the Nazi concentration camps at Buchenwald and Belsen.

[Text of Mr. Hoover's address, Page 10.]

His address, made at a meeting of the Chicago Famine Emergency Committee, was broadcast over the country.

The former President said that his 35,000-mile tour through twenty-five countries suffering from acute food shortages showed that "hunger hangs over the homes of more than 800,000,000 people—over one-third of the people of the earth."

"We can save these people from the worst, if we will," he added.

He offered two methods:

1. Still more intensive conservation of breadstuffs and fats in North America, and

2. The marketing of every grain of cereal on farms.

"If we can succeed in persuading every man and woman, every nation to do their utmost, we shall master this famine," he promised.

Mr. Hoover did not touch upon suggestions that this country return to food rationing to save more

Continued on Page 10, Column 5

RAILS FACE TIE-UP

Truman Asks Workers to Stay on Job After He Puts ODT in Charge

CHIEFS DEAF TO PLEA

Walkout Set for 4 P. M., Standard Time—Mails to Go by Plane, Truck

Texts of orders in seizure of railroads, Page 3.

By JOSEPH A. LOFTUS

Special to The New York Times.

WASHINGTON, May 17—President Truman seized the country's railroads today in the face of a strike of engineers and trainmen called for 4 P. M., standard time, tomorrow. He appealed to the workers to remain on duty and directed the Office of Defense Transportation to operate the carriers.

Mr. Truman signed the order at 2:50 P. M. in the presence of the chiefs of the two brotherhoods, Alvanley Johnston of the Brotherhood of Locomotive Engineers, and A. F. Whitney of the Brotherhood of Railroad Trainmen, after they had formally told him of the breakdown of wage negotiations with management. Seizure was effective at 4 o'clock.

J. Monroe Johnson, ODT Director, immediately appointed Charles H. Buford as Federal manager of the properties.

The union chiefs on leaving the White House said the strike order would stand. Chief executives of the organizations of firemen, conductors and switchmen stated that their members would continue to work as long as work was provided, but they would perform only their own duties.

Plans Made to Carry Mails

Postoffice officials said the mails would move by plane, truck or other conveyance. They said that legally there was no difference between a mail train and any other train.

Union officials said that freight in transit at the time the strike began would continue to the nearest terminal.

President Truman announced his action in a statement which stated that "in the strike thus confronting us, governmental seizure is imperative for the protection of the rights of our citizens."

"It is essential to the public health and to the public welfare generally," he continued, "that every possible step be taken by the Government to assure to the fullest possible extent continuous and uninterrupted transportation service.

"I call upon every employe of the railroads to cooperate with the Government to this end by remaining on duty."

His statement pointed out that only two of the twenty railroad labor organizations involved in wage disputes were threatening to strike and that these two had rejected the recommendation of an emergency board for an increase of $1.28 per day.

The President asked the parties to continue negotiations, but no preparations were made to do so. Mr. Whitney and Mr. Johnston left for Cleveland tonight.

War Labor Act Invoked

The Executive Order cited the War Labor Disputes Act, among other sources, as authority for the seizure. This meant that after 4 P. M. today it became illegal to encourage in any way an interruption of service.

It was learned that a telegram sent from Cleveland at 3:48 P. M. over the name of Mr. Whitney directed all general chairmen and lodges of the trainmen in the United States as follows:

"Regardless of who operates the railroads the only way the strike order can be recalled is by tele-

Continued on Page 2, Column 3

"All the News That's Fit to Print"

The New York Times.

LATE CITY EDITION
Partly cloudy and mild today. Fair and warmer tomorrow.
Temperatures Yesterday—Max., 72; Min., 56
Sunrise today, 5:24 A. M.; sunset, 8:12 P. M.
Full U. S. Weather Bureau Report, Page 43

Copyright, 1946, by The New York Times Company.

VOL. XCV..No. 32,260. Entered as Second-Class Matter, Postoffice, New York, N. Y. NEW YORK, WEDNESDAY, MAY 22, 1946. THREE CENTS IN NEW YORK CITY

GOVERNMENT SEIZES COAL MINES, UNIONS SILENT ON RESUMING WORK; RAIL PEACE COMPROMISE SNAGGED

RED ARMY QUIT IRAN BY MAY 6, ALA SAYS; ISSUE IN U. N. TODAY

Teheran Envoy Silent on Earlier Charge That Soviet Hand Is Still Felt in Country

POINT IS BEFORE COUNCIL

U. S. and British Delegates May Seek to Defer Action Until They Get Own Reports

By W. H. LAWRENCE

Iran officially notified the United Nations Security Council last night that Red Army troops had evacuated Iran, including Azerbaijan Province, by May 6.

The Security Council will convene at 11 A. M. today to discuss what, if anything, should be done about the Iranian question. The issue of continuing Soviet interference in Iranian affairs was not completely removed by the latest report.

The Iranian communication did not elaborate this point. It said that an Iranian mission sent to Azerbaijan Province to investigate had found, after a careful search, that there were no Red Army troops there. "According to trustworthy local people," the message said, Soviet troops had evacuated the province by May 6.

Official Inquiry Unlikely

It was impossible to forecast with accuracy the probable decision of the Council, but it seemed unlikely that any official investigation would be voted at this time. The United States and Britain have taken the leadership in Council discussion of the case and their delegates declined to predict the course they would adopt.

The official word that the Russians had left Iran as required by their latest agreement was communicated to the Council by Hussein Ala, Iranian Ambassador to the United States.

Less than twenty-four hours earlier Mr. Ala had told the Council that it was impossible to confirm whether the Red Army had left because "as a consequence of the interference previously complained of, the Iranian Government is still prevented from exercising any effective authority in the Province of Azerbaijan." His note had added: "Soviet interference in the internal affairs of Iran has not ceased."

Interference Not Mentioned

Yesterday, however, the Ambassador received from Premier Ahmad Ghavam the message reporting that a state investigating committee that had gone to Azerbaijan had confirmed the complete withdrawal of Russian forces.

Although Prince Mozaffar Firouz, Iranian Propaganda Minister, had criticized Mr. Ala for his renewed complaint about Soviet interference, Premier Ghavam's telegram to the Ambassador did not mention the interference question.

Mr. Ala did not withdraw his previous statement about continued efforts of Soviet intervention as demonstrated in the Azerbaijan army, which was mobilized and equipped while Red Army forces kept the Iranian Central Government from exercising its authority in Azerbaijan.

On the basis of Ambassador Ala's letter on Monday night, it had seemed not improbable that there would be a demand in the Council for an official investigation of the situation in Iran. This would have been put forward in the face of a Soviet boycott of Council meetings at which Iran is discussed. The boycott is expected to continue through today.

Showdown on Veto Unlikely

A demand for an investigation might have brought a showdown on the explosive veto question. Under the Charter, the concurring vote of the Soviet Union, as well as that of the United States, Britain, France and China, is required for the adoption of a substantive motion. Whether Andrei A. Gromyko, Soviet delegate, could exercise his veto by absenting himself from meetings was a question that neither the Council nor Mr. Gromyko had answered definitively.

On the basis of the latest Iranian letter, it seemed unlikely that the Council would want to authorize a full investigation.

Mr. Ala would not comment beyond his letter informing the Council of the new instructions from his Government to confirm the withdrawal of Red Army forces. It

Continued on Page 2, Column 5

Montgomery Plans Youth Peace Force

By Wireless to THE NEW YORK TIMES.

LONDON, May 21—Field Marshal Viscount Montgomery of Alamein, recently appointed Chief of the Imperial General Staff, spoke tonight of his plans "when the state will have no further use for my services." Britain's 58-year-old top-ranking soldier will spend "the evening of my life" training youngsters "so that they may become worthy citizens of our great and glorious empire."

Speaking at a dinner of the National Association of Boys' Clubs, Viscount Montgomery said the aim of youth clubs should be to make boys fit to take their proper place in the community so that they would be able to take over from "us older men" and lead the country in peace.

CHARGES ON FRANCO ARE REFUTED BY U. S.

Memorandum to U. N. Inquiry Discounts Atomic Production and Strength of Army

By C. BROOKS PETERS

Some of the most serious allegations made by the Polish Government in presenting its case before the United Nations Security Council charging that Generalissimo Francisco Franco's Spanish Government represented a threat to international peace have been refuted by the Government of the United States.

The refutations are contained in a memorandum submitted by the United States, in response to specific requests for information, to the Council's subcommittee investigating the Franco regime. The memorandum was released to the press yesterday.

Although the American memorandum, a voluminous document containing much information previously published, neither makes any recommendations nor draws any conclusions, there is nothing contained in it to suggest that Washington has altered its view with relation to the Franco regime. That frequently expressed view is that although the United States disapproves of the present Madrid Government, it does not consider that adequate evidence has yet been offered to warrant United Nations action under the Charter.

Reduction of Army Cited

The American memorandum refutes specific allegations made by the Polish delegate, Dr. Oscar Lange, before the Council on April 17 with relation to the Spanish military potential and deployment and Spanish preparations for research in atomic warfare.

Contrary to the Polish allegation, the United States memorandum declares that "the military potential of Spain has not changed significantly during the past few months" and "the armed forces have continued their over-all trend of gradual reduction in size."

With relation to "Secret Order No. 27," a document submitted in evidence by Dr. Lange, the American memorandum makes the following observation: "The authenticity of the paper * * * referred to here as 'Secret Order No. 27' has not yet been established, but preliminary information indicates that it may be the partial text of an order issued by the chief of staff of a regional command in Spain in September."

Continued on Page 3, Column 3

PLANE HAD CHANCE TO LAND IN NEWARK BEFORE CRASH HERE

Airport Clearance Given and at 8:08 P. M. Pilot Said He Was Approaching Field

ARMY INQUIRY IS STARTED

4 of 5 Victims Experienced Combat Airmen—Trip Made to Retain Flying Pay

By MEYER BERGER

Army Air Forces investigators collected wreckage, control tower transcripts and eyewitness accounts yesterday in attempts to figure out why an AAF C-45 plane, on routine navigational training flight, crashed into the Manhattan Company Building at 40 Wall Street on Monday night. The pilot and his four passengers died in the crash.

As the Army investigations started, Fire Commissioner Frank J. Quayle announced that he would confer with Mayor O'Dwyer on the advisability of seeking local legislation to prevent similar accidents. He pointed out that it was the second of its kind in ten months. In the other a bomber hit the Empire State Building.

"I think," Mr. Quayle said, "that there should be some regulation to make it incumbent on pilots to maintain sufficient altitude to avoid such accidents."

Aeronautic authorities, however, pointed out that such legislation already existed. Under regulations drawn up by the Civil Aeronautics Administration aircraft are not supposed to come lower than 1,500 feet while passing over populated areas. These regulations apply all over the United States.

Property Damage Small

Property damage caused by the C-45's collision with the fifty-eighth floor of 40 Wall Street was much less than at first reported, it developed. William Schiff of 99 John Street, an insurance agent, said insurance appraisers who viewed the damage said it probably would amount to $50,000. Damage that resulted when the bomber hit the Empire State Building last July 28 was estimated at $300,000 to $500,000.

Mr. Schiff said the owner of 40 Wall Street, the 40 Wall Street Building, Inc. (not the Bank of the Manhattan Company as erroneously reported yesterday), was covered for the loss by a policy for damage from aircraft taken out only three months ago. Mr. Schiff added that if Army appraisers approved the damage claims, the American Insurance Company, which issued the policy, would be reimbursed.

It was learned at Newark Airport yesterday that the C-45, bound in from the Army Air Base at Smyrna, Tenn., was over Newark Airport at 7:56 P. M. The pilot—whether it was Maj. Mansell R. Campbell of Pontiac, Mich., or Capt. Thomas L. Hall of Austin, Tex., both veteran fliers—reported by radio to the control tower at that time that their ship was at an altitude of approximately 2,000 feet.

Fog hid the field when that contact was established. The ceiling changed by the minute, from 100 feet to 400 feet. The tower reported all runways empty. The C-45 got clearance for landing.

Continued on Page 14, Column 3

House for a Gift But Not by Lottery

Special to THE NEW YORK TIMES.

WORCESTER, Mass., May 21—The housing shortage being what it is, Frank Dubinski has a $10,000 house he wants to give away, but he needs a "legal" method.

The house, at 474 Burncoat Street, was part of a builders' and home furnishers' project which included an exhibit at the Municipal Auditorium last week. Townspeople were invited to inspect the house and buy tickets at 35 cent apiece, the winner to be drawn on the final day of the show. Almost 70,000 persons took chances.

On the day set for the drawing, City Councilman George J. Abdella protested the use of the auditorium for a lottery and the police warned Mr. Dubinski. So the latter announced the house would be disposed of in some "legal" way and asked for suggestions.

COLLEGE FEES JUMP WITH ENROLLMENTS

Survey Shows Rise in Tuition or Living Costs, or Both, Laid to Increased Expenses

By BENJAMIN FINE

Coincident with the greatest enrollment in 300 years of higher education, colleges and universities in the United States are increasing their tuition and dormitory fees in both undergraduate and professional schools, according to a survey of forty representative institutions conducted by THE NEW YORK TIMES.

Located in all parts of the country, the colleges studied showed a substantial tuition increase ranging from 15 to 30 per cent, and in some instances going as high as 50 per cent. Many institutions reported that they had appointed committees to study the situation

Continued on Page 14, Column 6

DAY'S TALKS FAIL

White House Reports No 'Conclusive' Steps to Avert Rail Strike

NEW PARLEYS DUE TODAY

Steelman to Call Carriers—Truce Plan Went Beyond Pay Award of $1.28 a Day

By JOSEPH A. LOFTUS

Special to THE NEW YORK TIMES.

WASHINGTON, May 21—Failure of day-long efforts to reach a compromise in the railroad wage controversy left the capital without fresh hope tonight that a recurrence of the transportation crisis could be averted Thursday.

A White House statement, given out as separate conferences with representatives of the carriers and the railway brotherhoods broke up tonight, said:

"No conclusive results were achieved today toward averting a rail strike, now set for 4 P. M. Thursday."

Conferences first with representatives of the Brotherhood of Railroad Trainmen and the Brotherhood of Locomotive Engineers and then with the railroad representatives were conducted by John R. Steelman, special labor consultant to President Truman.

One source said tonight's meeting with the operators broke up with the understanding that Dr. Steelman would call the railroad representatives back for a renewal of conferences tomorrow. But no time was set.

Unions Issue Statement

Earlier today reports that a compromise settlement was under consideration gave rise to the possibility that the controversy would be settled before Thursday afternoon, when the five-day strike postponement obtained by President Truman expires.

In an afternoon statement A. F. Whitney and Alvanley Johnston,

Continued on Page 24, Column 3

'Wait and See,' Say Miners, Asking the Views of Lewis

First Thought of Workers Is of Meetings to Vote on Return—General Prospect Does Not Please Them

Special to THE NEW YORK TIMES.

PITTSBURGH, May 21—Western Pennsylvania's soft coal miners, the majority of whom have defied John L. Lewis' two-week strike truce, adopted a "wait and see" attitude today after President Truman ordered Federal seizure of the mines.

Around the pits, at their homes, in taprooms and on street corners they discussed the Presidential action, then decided to hold meetings between tomorrow and Saturday for voting on the return-to-work issue.

On the whole, the feeling was not one of pleasure. One Library, Pa., miner, who works in a mine closed since Friday by pickets, expressed it this way:

"Hell, man, no contract, no work. If I had my way we'd never go back until the contract was signed on the dotted line."

Twenty diggers, standing outside the Coverdale, Pa., mine of the Castle Shannon Coal Company, unanimously agreed that they would vote first, but added that the ballot would be guided by what the leaders said, principally the views of Mr. Lewis.

In Washington and Greene Counties in southwestern Pennsylvania, miners questioned whether they would get more pay under Government operation and whether they would like to work again under Federal control, as they did for a time during the war.

Steel and coal industry officials here leaned to the gloomy side, and one steel executive said:

"Let us wait and see what happens."

The reason is that nearly 50,000 miners in western Pennsylvania have refused to work under the truce, and whether they will work for the Government at Mr. Lewis' direction is something which time will answer.

Roving pickets, meanwhile, closed twenty more mines in this district today, reducing the day's output to about 63,000 tons against a potential capacity of 300,000.

Continued on Page 24, Column 2

Byrd and Pepper in Clash In Labor Curb Bill Debate

By C. P. TRUSSELL

Special to THE NEW YORK TIMES.

WASHINGTON, May 21—Tempers cracked in Senate debate on labor control legislation today with Senator Harry F. Byrd of Virginia flinging the word "skunk" at Senator Claude Pepper of Florida, leader of the group fighting to protect the modified Case Bill from toughening amendments.

Mr. Byrd was joined by other Senators in accusing the Floridian of having waged his oral battle with innuendoes, personal attacks on a colleague, threat and attempts to stir up class prejudices. Mr. Pepper, disclaiming an intent to do these things, apologized for words which had been so construed.

As the sixth full day of voteless controversy ended it appeared that the first tests would be made soon, possibly tomorrow.

Canvasses in expectation of early voting were reported to indicate that the seizure of the coal mines by the Government would prove to be little if any deterrent to Senators to proceed with labor control legislation. At one key point it was declared that not in ten years had there been so many members of the Senate professing an eagerness to apply legislative curbs.

The first action is due on a Pepper proposal. It is designed to make it an unfair labor practice under the Wagner Act for employers to refuse to bargain collectively for the establishment of health and welfare funds such as is demanded by John L. Lewis for the United Mine Workers. At key points it

Continued on Page 24, Column 5

CITY COUNCIL VOTES $865,212,820 BUDGET

Adoption of Record Total Is Unanimous—Basic Tax of 2.72 Indicated

By ROBERT W. POTTER

The City Council, working in an unwonted atmosphere of good-will, adopted unanimously yesterday a 1946-1947 budget totaling $865,212,820—the first of the O'Dwyer administration and the biggest in the city's history.

Not only was no attempt made to exercise the Council's authority to reduce the budget, as the Democratic majority always sought to do in the La Guardia administration, but members of the minority went so far as to praise Mayor O'Dwyer for his courage in increasing the budget to raise salaries and bring departments up to standard.

The new budget is expected to re-

Continued on Page 15, Column 1

KRUG TAKES OVER

Lewis Is Said to Put Decision to Work for U. S. Up to the Individuals

BUT HIS SUPPORT IS ASKED

Truman Empowers Secretary to Negotiate With Union on Pay, Other Concessions

Text of coal mine seizure order is printed on Page 24.

By LOUIS STARK

Special to THE NEW YORK TIMES.

WASHINGTON, May 21—President Truman ordered Secretary J. A. Krug today to seize the country's soft coal mines and to arrange with spokesmen for the United Mine Workers "appropriate changes in the terms and conditions of employment for the period of the operation of the mines by the Government."

Some Administration forces felt confident that mining operations would continue after the two-week truce ends Saturday, but union officials would not comment. The operators stated in a letter to Mr. Truman that they would cooperate with the Government.

Saying that he would take over the coal properties at 12:01 o'clock tonight, Mr. Krug named Vice Admiral Ben Moreell to be his operating chief.

Mr. Krug acted rapidly soon after the President's order was issued. He conferred with John L. Lewis, UMW chieftain, and John O'Leary, union vice president. The Secretary later talked with Charles O'Neill, operators' spokesman, and the latter's associates.

At a press conference tonight Mr. Krug was asked whether Mr. Lewis had agreed to his request that the miners remain at work when the truce expires.

Parley Set for Today

The Secretary replied that Mr. Lewis made it clear that under the Smith-Connally law the union officials had no alternative but to stay out of the affairs of the workers, and that it was up to the miners as individuals to act as they saw fit.

"We asked his support to keep the mine workers on the job," Mr. Krug said. "He has that matter under consideration and we will discuss it further tomorrow."

Asked whether Mr. Lewis indicated that the union policy committee would meet to consider the situation, Mr. Krug quoted the UMW president as saying that "there was some question as to whether the policy committee could operate in view of the Smith-Connally Act."

The Secretary asserted that Mr. Lewis made no promises and had not pledged to give his answer at tomorrow's conference.

The Smith-Connally law makes it a crime to induce or to aid a strike when a plant or mine is in Federal possession. Thus the policy committee could, if it met, legally have but one decision, which would be to order the miners to continue at work after Saturday.

Saying that he would keep the public informed of developments, the Secretary, as Coal Mines Administrator, told reporters that talks with operators and miners showed that neither side felt that direct conferences would result in an agreement.

Problem Is Called Unusual

Therefore, he said, the Government would have to work out the principles of a new contract. He referred to the unusual problem before the Federal officials by recalling that some new features, such as a health and welfare fund and safety provisions, furnished part of the controversy.

Meanwhile, from New York came a report that a health and welfare fund arrangement had been decided on, calling for a payroll assessment of between 1½ per cent and 3 per cent and tripartite administration by Government, miners and operators. The union asked for a 7 per cent fund to be administered solely by it.

Union and operator sources pro-

Continued on Page 24, Column 1

Vandenberg Hails Foreign Policy, Calling It Positive and Bipartisan

By HAROLD B. HINTON

Special to THE NEW YORK TIMES.

WASHINGTON, May 21—Outside of the uncertainties and disappointments of the Big Four's efforts to bring the world to peace has sprung a positive, constructive and bipartisan United States foreign policy, Senator Arthur H. Vandenberg, Republican, of Michigan, told the Senate today.

The Senator was reporting to his colleagues on his mission to the Paris meeting of the Council of Foreign Ministers as an adviser to Secretary of State James F. Byrnes.

Mr. Vandenberg described this new-born foreign policy as demanding just and immediate peace treaties with Italy, Rumania, Bulgaria, Hungary, Finland and Austria, and action on decisions for a unified Germany. The policy also demands, he said, maximum guarantees against the resurgence of any former Axis aggressors. Such a policy, Mr. Vandenberg said, he will support under any administration, and he looks for any administration, of whatever political complexion, to follow it.

In the House, Representatives Jerry Voorhis, Democrat, of California; John E. Rankin, Democrat, of Mississippi, and Karl E. Mundt, Republican, of South Dakota, took the floor to praise Secretary Byrnes' radio report of the Paris meeting, delivered last night.

Mr. Mundt urged an immediate conference between President Truman and Premier Stalin as the only means of breaking the existing deadlock over the peace settlements.

"The Secretary is to be praised for his candor," Mr. Mundt said, "but it is more and more clearly indicated that a conference is needed to be between the Big Two—the leaders of the United States and Russia. This constant bickering and long range is accomplishing nothing. They ought to get to-

Continued on Page 4, Column 3

World News Summarized

WEDNESDAY, MAY 22, 1946

The nation's soft-coal mines came under Government operation at midnight when Interior Secretary Krug, acting under orders of President Truman, seized the properties and placed Vice Admiral Moreell in charge. The operators pledged their cooperation, but John L. Lewis gave no hint of what the union's position will be when the truce expires Saturday. [1:8.]

Some indication of the miners' attitude was found in Pennsylvania. The men, who returned to the pits in scant numbers when the truce was declared, were not enthusiastic about working for the Government and will vote on what to do. [1:6-7.]

Early hopes that the rail stoppage would not be resumed when the truce ends tomorrow disappeared when union and carrier representatives failed to reach an agreement on wages after conferring all day. [1:5.]

Other Washington developments included a setback to proponents of a strong draft in the Senate, making doubtful the extension of Selective Service before it finally expires on July 1. [15:1.] A Senate committee rejected 10 to 6 flat removal of all price controls, but was inclined to favor gradual reduction as production rises. [14:2.]

UNRRA Director General La Guardia, taking issue with former President Hoover on famine relief, urged a permanent world trading corporation to distribute surplus food. [12:3.]

Iran officially announced the evacuation of all Russian troops from the country as of May 6. The "civil war" in Azerbaijan disappeared and martial law was lifted from the province. [3:1.]

This left the United Nations Security Council somewhat nonplussed over what to do when it meets today. Ambassador Ala transmitted the latest word to the Council last night, but did not retract his charges of the day before that Soviet interference continued. The United States and Britain may try to defer action until they hear from their own observers in Iran. [1:1.]

Franco Spain's military activities are defensive, the United States said in a memorandum submitted to the subcommittee investigating that regime's threat to peace. Everything Franco represents was held loathsome to this country, but the memorandum challenged major points raised by Poland in demanding international action. The subcommittee meets today. [1:2.]

Senator Vandenberg endorsed Secretary Byrnes' report on the Paris Foreign Ministers' Conference, adding that "eastern communism and western democracy were unable, for the time being, to see eye to eye" on most matters. "The more important news," he said, was the disclosure of "a positive, constructive, peace-seeking, bipartisan foreign policy for the United States." [1:2-3.]

General McNarney said conditions in Germany were approaching the "acute" stage because of the inability of the occupying powers to agree on economic matters. [5:1.] American constabulary, in a sudden raid to break up smuggling and an underground railway for SS fugitives, seized 372 vessels on the Danube along the Austro-German border. [1:6-7; map P. 5.]

Karl Hermann Frank, who ordered the destruction of Lidice, will die on the gallows. [4:5.]

German assets in Switzerland will not be used to finance a new war as the result of an agreement turning most of the funds over to the Allies. [13:4.]

Premier Yoshida completed his Cabinet in Japan after General MacArthur ordered the removal of a Mitsubishi official and a director of the jingoistic Imperial Rule Assistance Association originally named. [10:2.]

New York City's record budget of $865,212,820 was unanimously approved without change by the City Council. [1:7.]

U. S. Force Raids Danube 'Fleet'; Russian River Control Disputed

By DANA ADAMS SCHMIDT

By Wireless to THE NEW YORK TIMES.

VILSHOFEN, Germany, May 21—Four thousand members of the new constabulary of the United States zone, assisted by Counter-Intelligence Corps and Criminal Investigation Division agents and German river police boats, at dawn this morning seized 372 Danube River craft of a dozen nationalities. These included twelve gunboats and eighteen auxiliary craft of the Hungarian Navy that had been gathering moss for the last year tied up along a forty-five-mile stretch between Passau and Deggendorf.

Constabulary aircraft droned up and down over the formidable deployment of force, called "Operation Grab-Bag." Its officially designated purpose was to investigate and break a suspected far-flung smuggling ring and underground railroad for escaping SS [Elite Guard] men believed to be conducted by the 3,000 persons, including families, living aboard the boats.

The first check yielded five heavy machine guns in perfect working order, three radio transmitters, some gun sights, periscopes, ammunition and explosives and several holds crammed with leather, rugs, shoes, bolts of cloth, furs, candles, flour, beans, noodles, parts of motors and junk.

Some arrests were made, but no complete tally for the investigation, which will take several days, was available.

Gen. Joseph T. McNarney, commander of the United States forces in Europe, ordered the raid and directed that Hungarians, numbering several hundred, who fled to American-controlled waters after a disastrous engagement with the Russians at the end of the war, be either interned and processed for repatriation as prisoners of war or discharged as refugees.

It was the first large-scale operation for the constabulary, commanded by Maj. Gen. Ernest N.

Continued on Page 5, Column 4

The inimitable Groucho Marx was the star of *You Bet Your Life.* The show became a big radio hit in the mid-40s and remained one for years after the show made the jump to television.

Xavier Cugat was a regular on *Spotlight Bands.*

Perry Como's 1946 hit, *Prisoner of Love,* was one of the many songs that helped establish him as one of the most popular singers of all time.

"All the News That's Fit to Print"

The New York Times.

LATE CITY EDITION
Considerable cloudiness, cooler today. Fair and mild tomorrow.
Temperatures Yesterday—Max., 83; Min., 57
Sunrise today, 5:31 A. M.; Sunset, 8:15 P. M.
Full U. S. Weather Bureau Report, Page 32

Section 1

NEWS INDEX, PAGE 33, THIS SECTION

Copyright, 1946, by The New York Times Company.

VOL. XCV No. 32,264. Entered as Second-Class Matter, Postoffice, New York, N. Y. NEW YORK, SUNDAY, MAY 26, 1946. Including Magazine and Book Review. TEN CENTS New York City and Suburban Areas (15c Elsewhere)

RAIL STRIKE ENDS AS TRUMAN DEMANDS LAWS, INCLUDING DRAFT, TO STOP ACTION AGAINST U. S.; AMENDED CASE BILL ENACTED; TRAINS RUN AGAIN

TRUMAN SUMMONS U. N. ECONOMIC UNIT TO WIPE OUT WANT

His Message Opening Session Says Council Can Make Peace Reality for Common Man

PRESIDENT PLEDGES U.S. AID

Group Begins Task Tomorrow of Nursing World's Material and Social Well-Being

By W. H. LAWRENCE

The United Nations Economic and Social Council tackled yesterday the task of translating the slogan, "Freedom from Want," into a reality for peoples and nations all over the world.

It faced squarely the fact that human misery and insecurity for peoples and Governments are a fundamental cause of war and that prosperity and peace are indivisible.

Meeting at Hunter College in the Bronx in its first session in the United States the eighteen-member Council was welcomed by a special message from President Truman, who declared: "We did not struggle to prevent the domination of the world by the Axis Powers only to accept hunger, disease, poverty and insecurity in a world made free by brave men."

Truman Pledges U. S. Aid

The text of the President's address follows:

The opening of this second session of the Economic and Social Council stirs the hearts of the common people all over the world. You can make the peace a reality for them.

As you begin your deliberations, I extend to you the heartfelt welcome of this country and the sincere wishes of all the American people for your success.

While the Security Council stands guard against new threats to peace, the Economic and Social Council mobilizes the constructive forces of mankind for the victories of peace.

We did not struggle to prevent the domination of the world by the Axis Powers only to accept hunger, disease, poverty and insecurity in a world made free by brave men.

Your task is to achieve freedom from want, to encourage production, help to open up transport and clear communications, and to assure higher standards of living.

It is for you to promote a fuller recognition of the dignity and worth of the human person, and to advance fundamental rights of man through the world.

To this great task the United States pledges its full support.

Goal Is to Help Common Man

The magnitude of the job facing the Economic and Social Council and the high goals its subsidiary organs already have established tentatively, were made clear in opening speeches by Trygve Lie of Norway, United Nations Secretary General, and the Council's President, Sir Ramaswami Mudaliar of India.

Yesterday's one hour and forty-eight-minute meeting was devoted to formalities, with regular business sessions scheduled to begin at 10:30 A. M. tomorrow.

President Truman's message set the tone of yesterday's meeting as the first step toward realization of the goals that can make peace "a reality" for the common people of the world. Because the Chief Executive could not attend himself the statement was read by John G. Winant, United States delegate, recently retired Ambassador to Great Britain and a veteran of national and international efforts to lift the standard of living.

The response to the President was made by Brooke Claxton, Canadian Minister of National Health and Welfare, who declared that "prosperity, like peace, is indi-

Continued on Page 12, Column 1

House Votes Curbs, 303-13; Senate Passes Own Bill First

New 'Teeth' Put in Labor Disputes Act as President's Measure Waits After House Approves Its Wide Powers

By SAMUEL A. TOWER
Special to The New York Times.

WASHINGTON, May 25—In less than two hours after hearing President Truman's recommendations for strike control legislation the House, by a vote of 306 to 13, passed and sent to the Senate today a temporary emergency measure designed to curb strikes against the Government in industries essential to the national economy.

[Text of Truman strike control legislation, Page 26.]

Heeding the behest of the President that "We must work together and we must work fast," the House bill provided for the induction of strikers into the armed services and for the transfer of all profits of strike-bound plants under Government control to the Treasury Department.

These were the principal provi-

Continued on Page 26, Column 6

By C. P. TRUSSELL
Special to The New York Times.

WASHINGTON, May 25—The Senate sidetracked President Truman's emergency strike control bill today, but passed late tonight, by a vote of 49 to 29, the long-controverted Case labor disputes bill in a form perhaps tougher than that which was approved by the House in February.

The President's program ran into trouble in the Senate, even before its overwhelming approval by the House, with opposition developing from both labor and conservative elements, which appeared to be forming a coalition.

Bent on enacting long-range labor control legislation, the Senate blocked immediate action on the new, separate measure which the leadership sought to give the right of way.

But, when the final roll was

Continued on Page 26, Column 1

ON TRUMAN TERMS

Unions Accept 18½ Cents, Part in Lieu of New Work Rules

'IN PUBLIC INTEREST'

Whitney Admits Defeat, Calls President Unfair, Asks Caution on Laws

By JOSEPH A. LOFTUS
Special to The New York Times.

WASHINGTON, May 25—The railroad strike, which had paralyzed America's commerce, was settled today on President Truman's terms forty-eight hours after it had begun.

The chiefs of the two striking brotherhoods signed the memorandum of agreement in a hotel room as Mr. Truman was about to begin his address to a joint session of Congress. Dr. John R. Steelman, the President's consultant, witnessed the signing and telephoned the news to the Capitol in time for the President to make an extemporaneous announcement of the settlement to the legislators.

Within an hour after the announcement, strikers were "marking up" for duty. The Association of American Railroads forecast a restoration of normal operations by tomorrow afternoon.

18 Other Unions Accept

The basis of the settlement, which the two union chiefs had formally rejected the day the strike began, is an increase of 18½ cents an hour, of which 2½ cents is in lieu of changes in working rules for one year. The eighteen other railroad unions signed earlier in the day an agreement covering those terms.

A. F. Whitney, president of the Brotherhood of Railroad Trainmen, and Alvanley Johnston, chief of the Brotherhood of Locomotive Engineers, said they had ended

Continued on Page 24, Column 6

PRESIDENT LEARNS OF RAIL STRIKE SETTLEMENT

Leslie L. Biffle, Secretary of the Senate, hands a note to the Chief Executive during his address before the joint session of Congress. Associated Press Wirephoto

ASKS 6-MONTH ACT

President Wants This to Outlaw Leaders of Strikes on Government

SEEKS LABOR STUDY

Urges Congress to Use It in Long-Range Laws for Industrial Peace

President's address to joint session of Congress, Page 23.

By FELIX BELAIR JR.
Special to The New York Times.

WASHINGTON, May 25—President Truman asked Congress in a special message today to grant him temporary emergency powers to break strikes against the Federal Government in any specified industry, including authority to draft strikers into the armed services, and to formulate a comprehensive long-range labor policy calculated to reduce the number of work stoppages hurting the nation.

The joint session of the Senate and House of Representatives before which the President appeared at 4 P. M., Eastern Standard Time, gave Mr. Truman the most enthusiastic ovation he had received since entering the White House. He announced that the railroad strike had been settled on his original terms and pandemonium broke, with Republicans joining Democrats in the cheering.

Says Drastic Law Is Required

The emergency powers that President Truman requested and apparently will get easily would provide him weapons never before at the Chief Executive's disposal and were aimed at both John L. Lewis and the coal miners as well as the walkout of the National Maritime Union scheduled for June 15. He said the powers he asked might appear drastic, and were, but that the situation demanded them.

At the same time the President said he had no intention of injuring labor or depriving it as a group of any of the gains it had won during the past thirteen years. He sought to head off the Case bill and other pending measures to curb labor in its right to strike by proposing that a joint Congressional committee be appointed to study the whole problem and within six months to bring in recommendations.

He said the time had come when the whole subject of labor relations should be studied afresh, but that the right to strike against private employers must be preserved and that the recommendations of the joint committee appointed to study the problem should be "fair to labor and to industry and to the public at large."

Stressed Temporary Nature

In leading up to his request for the emergency legislation the President emphasized that the new authority was to last only for six months after a declaration of an official end of World War II and that it would be applicable only "to those few industries in which the President by proclamation declares that an emergency has arisen which affects the entire economy of the United States" and where the Government has taken over the industry.

But in such cases the President asked authority to do these things:

Authorize injunctive proceedings against union leaders, forbidding them to encourage or incite union members to leave their work or to refuse to return to work, and subjecting them to contempt proceedings by failure to obey an order of the court in such proceedings.

Deprive workers of seniority rights who, without good cause, persist in striking against the Government.

Provide criminal penalties against employers and union lead-

Continued on Page 23, Column 2

Gromyko Protests Welcome To Bor by Official of U. N.

Strongly backing a previous protest by Dr. Oscar Lange, Polish delegate to the United Nations Security Council, Andrei A. Gromyko, representing Soviet Russia, sharply attacked yesterday a welcome given Friday "on behalf of the United Nations" by J. B. Hutson, Assistant Secretary General of the United Nations, to Lieut. Gen. Tadeusz Komorowski (General Bor), leader of the abortive Warsaw uprising against the Germans in 1944.

Calling General Bor an "enemy of the Polish people," Mr. Gromyko charged that Mr. Hutson's welcome in the name of the United Nations compromised "not only the members of the staff of the organization but the name of the organization itself." The action, he said, "cannot be regarded as but an inadmissible one."

Dr. Lange chose far stronger words in phrasing his protest, which was in the form of a letter to Trygve Lie, Secretary General of the United Nations. The communication, which was delivered to Mr. Lie late Friday night, was made public for the first time yesterday afternoon. It read, in part:

"May I draw your attention to the fact that General Bor-Komorowski refuses to recognize the jurisdiction of the Government of the Republic of Poland, and that his appearances in the United States are part of a hostile campaign against the officially recognized Government of Poland.

"I would also like to remind you that the campaign of which General Bor-Komorowski is the spearhead openly advocates a third world war. Under the circumstances, an official greeting extended to General Bor-Komorow-

Continued on Page 13, Column 1

U. S. STILL WEIGHS 2 COURSES ON IRAN

Decision Due This Week-End on Inquiry in Azerbaijan or Rebuke to Soviet

By JAMES RESTON
Special to The New York Times.

WASHINGTON, May 25—The State Department is understood to be studying two plans for dealing with the Soviet Union's activities in the Azerbaijan Province of Iran.

The first is a proposal that the United States should ask the United Nations Security Council to carry out a thorough investigation of conditions in Azerbaijan, which has been taken over by pro-Soviet factions in defiance of the Teheran Government.

The second, proposed by other members of the Council, is to drop the Iranian case from the Security Council's agenda with a rebuke to the Soviet Union for its policy of interference in Iran and non-participation in the debates of the Council.

A resolution calling for an investigation by the Security Council is already prepared here, but it is less certain that it will be in-

Continued on Page 12, Column 5

IRKED TRAINMEN GO BACK TO WORK HERE

Service Is Resumed Slowly as Paralyzed Economy Revives —Word Received Quickly

By WILL LISSNER

Striking engineers and trainmen grudgingly returned to work in New York and the East last night under orders rushed to them by their union chiefs. The railroads in the area resumed service on a limited basis at first, but this was slowly being accelerated as the economy of the region, paralyzed for forty-eight hours, began to lumber toward normal.

Denounced twice within twenty-four hours by President Truman

Continued on Page 25, Column 1

Lewis, Krug Fail to Agree; Coal Strike Going On Again

Negotiations Will Be Resumed Today in Hopes of Peace by Tomorrow—Moreell Calls On the Miners to Return

By LOUIS STARK
Special to The New York Times.

WASHINGTON, May 25—The United Mine Workers of America were officially to resume their strike at the completion of a two-week truce at the end of this working day—actually at 12:01 A. M. Sunday—after John L. Lewis, head of the union, and his associates failed to agree with Secretary Krug of the Department of the Interior upon terms for a suitable contract during Government operation.

Despite this latest development, the negotiations will continue tomorrow, at which time, if an agreement should be reached, there would still be time for Mr. Lewis to order the men to resume work Monday. They do not work on Sunday.

In a last-minute effort to keep the men at work Admiral Ben Moreell, Deputy Mine Administrator for the Government, issued an appeal to the mine workers urging them to return to the pits on Monday. He reminded them that negotiations were continuing and that, whatever arrangements were made, the wage and other terms would be retroactive to May 22, when the mines were seized by the Government.

Mr. Lewis failed to respond to an appeal made several days ago by Mr. Krug to call on the miners to remain at work before the truce expires. His explanation was that he could not do so pending "clarification" of the Smith-Connally Law which bans aid to those striking while a facility is in the hands of the Government.

The union committee spent nearly six hours with Secretary Krug today at morning and afternoon sessions.

Between these two sessions labor history was written at the Capitol when President Truman appealed for drastic legislation aimed at curbing strikes which would cripple the country.

The afternoon session began at 5 P. M. instead of at 3:30 as had been arranged. Presumably the delay was due to the desire of Mr. Lewis to listen to the President's recommendations.

At that hour, 5 o'clock, looking grim and worn, Mr. Lewis returned to Mr. Krug's office accompanied by his negotiating committee.

"No comment," he said to reporters who requested his reaction on the President's recommendations. He looked neither to the right nor to the left, but kept on walking toward Mr. Krug's office, repeating to a barrage of questions, "Nothing, nothinng, nothing!"

His associates also appeared grave.

When he emerged from Mr. Krug's office nearly three hours

Continued on Page 19, Column 1

World News Summarized

SUNDAY, MAY 26, 1946

An agreement ending the nation-wide railroad strike was signed by the leaders of the striking unions at 3:57 P. M., Eastern standard time, and immediately thereafter the code words "Cahill" and "Division," signifying instructions to return to their jobs, were flashed to the strikers. All railroads quickly began moving toward resumption of complete service. [1:4.]

In New York and elsewhere in the East the railroads offered service only on a limited basis at first, but gradually stepped up schedules. [1:5.]

President Truman took heed of the paralysis of the nation's economy caused by strikes and appeared before Congress to ask for temporary emergency powers to break strikes against Government-operated industries. He received an enthusiastic reception from members of the Senate and House, meeting in joint session, as he appealed for wide authority to deal with strikers, including the power to draft them into the armed services. [1:8.]

The House approved the emergency labor legislation ninety minutes after it had been requested by the President. The vote was 306 to 13. [1:2.] Similar legislation was delayed in the Senate, which passed a Case bill with new "teeth." [1:3.]

In the other major labor dispute that has been hobbling the nation, John L. Lewis and his soft-coal union aides resumed negotiations with Secretary Krug shortly after Mr. Truman's address, but no agreement was reached. [1:6:7.]

The United Nations Economic and Social Council held its first meeting in this country to tackle the problem of eliminating the economic causes of war and heard a message from President Truman pledging this nation's help to eradicate poverty. [1:1.]

Andrei Gromyko, the Russian delegate to the Security Council, protested against the participation of a United Nations official in the welcome given to General Bor on Friday. [1:2-3.]

Two proposals were said to be under consideration by the State Department in dealing with the Iranian issue. Under the first the Security Council would be asked to investigate conditions in Azerbaijan Province; under the other, the case would be dropped from the Council's agenda with criticism of the Soviet Union's tactics. [1:2.]

Atomic energy is producing an international fear psychology, according to a committee of psychologists who urged that "our first objective must be to mobilize a healthy, action-goading fear for effective measures against the real danger—war." They warned of "escapist thinking" that might minimize the danger of the atom bomb or lead to war. [7:1.]

Czechoslovakia will hold her first election in eleven years today. It was generally expected that the Communists would receive the largest number of votes but that the conservatives would be the strongest group of parties. [2:2.]

Sixty-four-year-old Abdullah Ibn Ul-Hussein formally assumed rule over 300,000 subjects as he became King of Trans-Jordan. He appealed to the rest of the Arab world to join in a federation of Arab States. [1:2-3.]

The British Cabinet mission and the Viceroy stated in a reply to Indian political parties that the British proposal for Indian independence stood as a whole and that sovereignty would not be transferred until a Constitution was formed that safeguarded minorities and until a treaty was concluded with Britain. [15:1.]

Trans-Jordan Emir Becomes King In Setting of Arabian Pageantry

By GENE CURRIVAN
By Wireless to The New York Times.

AMMAN, Trans-Jordan, May 25—The emirate of Trans-Jordan became a kingdom today and Emir Abdullah became King Abdullah Ibn Ul-Hussein in spectacular ceremonies and amid a setting that in some respects resembled a frontier town in the Western United States when the first railroad came through.

Amman was jammed. Dignitaries from all the surrounding countries were on hand to pay their respects to the world's newest king. The narrow bazaar-lined streets were flag-bedecked and crowded with colorfully garbed Arabs.

Crowns decorated the festooned and illuminated archways and ever present were photographs of the 64-year-old monarch who some day hopes to rule a kingdom that will include Syria, Lebanon and Iraq.

During his acceptance speech at the palace, King Abdullah intimated as much when, after thanking God and his loyal subjects for his good fortune, he said:

"My hope is that soon there will be a federation, effective and powerful, of all Arab states. I offer my throne as a rallying point for that federation."

His remarks also were construed to mean a federation of Arab states to meet the threat of Jewish encroachment, because he later added that "Palestine is a special case and will be given special treatment."

His speech occupied a few minutes of the fourteen-minute ceremony in the throne room where the dignity of the setting received a bit of a setback as the klieg lights flooding the dais for the battery of cameramen gave the scene a Hollywood flavor.

The King, wearing a black flow-

Continued on Page 4, Column 2

President Scores Personal Triumph In His Grim Speech to Congress

Special to The New York Times.

WASHINGTON, May 25—President Truman's visit to Capitol Hill today to tell Congress about the railroad strike situation turned into a personal triumph for the Chief Executive when he interrupted the speech he had prepared to announce settlement of the strike "on the President's term.s"

For more than a minute the chamber of the House, where Senators and Representatives were gathered in joint session, rang with applause from Republicans and Democrats alike. The announcement brought all who heard to their feet. The crowded galleries quickly followed the example of the members of Congress, took up the cheering which started among a group of Representatives on the outer rim of the majority side of the House and spread to all parts of the floor.

Veteran observers of events at the capital said that while they had expected the Democratic side to show enthusiasm they were completely surprised by the warmth of the accord given Mr. Truman by Republican Senators and Representatives alike. Many said they had never seen a President elected by the Democratic party applauded as enthusiastically by the Republican side.

The President drew a standing tribute of two minutes when he was escorted into the chamber and another similar tribute from all sides when he rose to speak. He was interrupted frequently by outbursts of hand-clapping and his announcement that he would use the Army, if necessary, to run the railroads brought applause from both sides of the chamber, although there were a few, including the minority leader of the House, Jo-

Continued on Page 24, Column 2

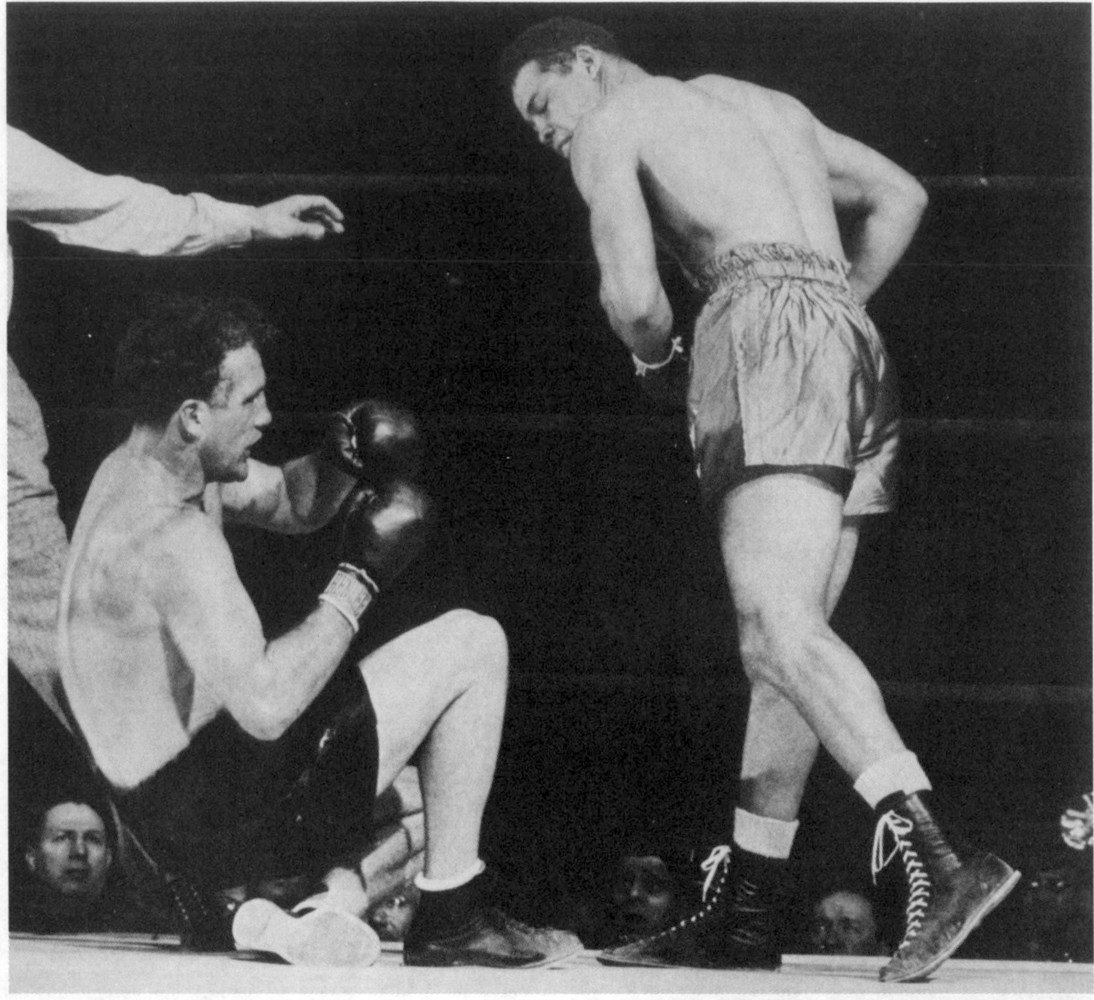

Joe Louis, World Heavyweight Champion for the entire decade, knocked out Billy Conn in the eighth round of their second fight.

The immortal Ted Williams knocked out three home-runs in baseball's all-star game.

"All the News That's Fit to Print"

The New York Times.

LATE CITY EDITION
Partly cloudy and mild today. Tomorrow partly cloudy, warmer.
Temperatures Yesterday—Max.,71; Min.,60
Sunrise today, 5:23 A. M.; Sunset, 8:29 P. M.
Full U. S. Weather Bureau Report, Page 35

VOL. XCV..No. 32,284. Entered as Second-Class Matter. Postoffice, New York, N. Y. NEW YORK, SATURDAY, JUNE 15, 1946. THREE CENTS IN NEW YORK CITY

U. S. WILL TELL ATOM SECRET, DESTROY BOMBS, IF U. N. ESTABLISHES CONTROLS WITHOUT A VETO; SHIP STRIKE BEGINS DESPITE MIDNIGHT ACCORD

NEW YORK HIT FIRST

2 to 3 Day Tie-Up Here Seen Despite Agreement Reached at Capital

500 SHIPS IN PORT

Boston, Philadelphia, Jacksonville Are Also Affected in East

By GEORGE HORNE

The long-threatened nation-wide maritime strike went into effect last midnight, hitting New York first, despite the fact that negotiators in Washington had reached a final agreement by the deadline.

Differences in time placed busy New York Harbor in the van of struck cities as strike leaders here interpreted the deadline to mean local time in all ports of the nation. That would have meant a settlement in Washington by 11 P. M standard time.

Strike headquarters at the National Maritime Union office building on West Seventeenth Street had issued a call for all members with trucks and cars to report to the hall immediately; and the union "contact and investigation squads" were also called in. It was evident that the strike call was soon to be issued.

Orders Set Throughout U. S.

Similar orders for striking were being prepared throughout the country and cities immediately reported affected were Boston, Philadelphia, Jacksonville, Fla., San Francisco and Seattle. In San Francisco, Committee for Maritime Unity headquarters said it had received no official notification or the terms of the agreement and that in any event the longshoremen would not work today.

In Seattle the Northwest Maritime Strike Strategy Committee said the "rank and file members of unions in the Northwest will strike and stay on strike pending acceptance or rejection of the National Committee for Maritime Unity's recommendations."

In Norfolk, Va., the men returned to their ships.

Regardless of the outcome in Washington it was apparent that national shipping faced a period of at least a day and perhaps forty-eight hours of confusion and strike action, for some ports, including San Francisco, had already received strike orders.

Union mass meetings had been waiting in all the ports for word of the agreement, but it required approval by a majority of the seamen attending the meetings, and regardless of the time the settlement announcement had come, the deadline would have passed before approval votes could have been relayed back to Washington.

The strike call in New York actually came at 11:33 P. M. when the following statement was issued at National Maritime Union headquarters by the New York Joint Maritime Committee:

"In line with national CMU (Committee for Maritime Unity) policy which calls for a strike at 12:01 A. M. local time, June 15, if all unions in CMU have not received satisfactory agreements, the New York Joint Maritime Committee is recommending to its members that they strike at midnight.

"All seamen are to secure the ships and walk off."

No Word From Washington

At the National Maritime Union hall, at 12:45 A. M., it was said no word has been received from Washington. A spokesman said officials of the union were not at the hall, and that they would have to decide later what to do about reversing the strike call when the CMU official committee in Washington sent out a settlement report.

In any case a membership meeting will have to be called to pass on the terms of the agreement, it was said.

The order affected more than 500 vessels on the active list in New York harbor. It was the first

Continued on Page 10, Column 3

Ship Settlement at Deadline Accepted to Defer the Strike

'Greatest Gains Ever Made,' Unions Assert—Operators Say 'Government-Imposed' Terms Mean 135% Rise Since 1941

By LOUIS STARK
Special to THE NEW YORK TIMES

WASHINGTON, Saturday, June 15—An agreement officially averting the threatened maritime strike of 200,000 workers was reported at the Department of Labor five minutes before the deadline expired at midnight, Eastern daylight time.

The announcement was made by Harry Bridges, co-chairman with Joseph Curran of the Committee for Maritime Unity. The last hurdle to the completion of the agreement was the form of signature to the agreement which had been drawn up earlier in the day.

"The International Longshoremen's Union has reached a tentative agreement subject to ratification of the rank and file," said Mr. Bridges. "I am recommending that the strike be postponed by our members on the basis of this agreement."

It was assumed that the other six members of the Committee for Maritime Unity would soon announce adherence to the agreement.

Approval of the agreement was announced promptly by the Wage Stabilization Board and the Director of Economic Stabilization, Chester Bowles.

Participating in the last-minute conference which began at 2 P. M. yesterday were Capt. Granville Conway, Administrator of the War Shipping Administration; John W. Gibson, Assistant Secretary of Labor; Philip Murray, president of the Congress of Industrial Organizations; Edgar L. Warren, chief of the Conciliation Service of the Department of Labor, and the heads of the Unions Negotiating Committee.

Mr. Curran, president of the National Maritime Union, told reporters that the fifty-six-hour

Continued on Page 10, Column 2

PETRILLO AT BAR IN LEA LAW FIGHT

Chicago Court Permits Him to Delay Plea Until Sept. 9—$1,000 Bond Is Posted

Special to THE NEW YORK TIMES.

CHICAGO, June 14—James Caesar Petrillo's battle to test the constitutionality of the Lea act began today when the president of the American Federation of Musicians was arraigned in Federal District Court on charges of violating the law by attempting to force radio station WAAF here to employ music librarians it did not want.

After brief proceedings, Judge Walter J. La Buy gave the "boss" of 180,000 AFM members until Sept. 9 to enter a plea. The court will then set the time for oral argument. Bond was fixed at $1,000.

Radiating confidence, Mr. Petrillo appeared in the courtroom soon before 10 A. M. He was flanked by Joseph A. Padway, general counsel for the American Federation of Labor, of which the AFM is an affiliate, and David Katz, attorney for the Chicago Federation of Musicians, which Mr. Petrillo also heads.

J. Albert Woll, Federal District Attorney, filed a criminal information yesterday based on the Lea act against the musicians' head.

Mr. Padway told the court that he wanted to file several written motions. Mr. Woll offered no objections, and Judge La Buy gave defense counsel until July 15 to file them.

Mr. Woll said that he under-

Continued on Page 12, Column 2

PRESIDENT ASKED JACKSON SILENCE

But Justice Failed to Delay Attack on Black Until Talk With Executive, Truman Says

By FELIX BELAIR JR.
Special to THE NEW YORK TIMES.

WASHINGTON, June 14—President Truman, without attempting to mask his displeasure over the incident, disclosed today that Supreme Court Justice Robert H. Jackson had ignored his suggestion that he hold up his attack on Justice Hugo L. Black, made at Nuremberg, until the Chief Executive had had a chance to talk to him about the matter.

Apparently disappointed in the man once mentioned for Chief Justice, the President unsmilingly explained his own part in the episode to a crowded White House news conference. He told how he tried to dissuade Justice Jackson from his course on being notified by him last Sunday of the statement he proposed to make and what in substance he would say. The opportunity for the requested telephone conversation never came.

Then the President sought to leave the impression that if Justice Black had "threatened" to resign from the Supreme Court bench in protest if Justice Jackson were named Chief Justice, the threat had not been made to him either directly by Justice Black or indirectly through a representative. The President's reply to a question on the point was oblique, but the intent was clear.

The way the President replied to

Continued on Page 12, Column 6

Horace Mann to Be Closed in '48; Parents, College Plan Court Test

Rejecting the vigorous pleas of the Parent-Teachers Association, the board of trustees of Teachers College, Columbia University, has voted to close Horace Mann-Lincoln School, one of the leading progressive institutions for elementary and secondary education in the country.

Approving the 119-page report of a special committee, the trustees, at a closed meeting on Thursday, continued the life of the school until June 30, 1948. After that the $3,000,000 grant made by the General Education Board, together with the building at 123d Street between Amsterdam and Morningside Avenues, will revert to Teachers College.

Although the parents have threatened court action over the transfer of the trust fund, the trustees have anticipated this move by directing the college to seek a declaratory judgment to determine whether it has the right to sell the building and appropriate the various funds for other purposes.

Expressing disappointment at the trustees' decision, the parents' group refused to accept the verdict as final. Mrs. Elinor S. Gimbel, president of the association, declared that "this action is exactly what we had expected." She said that the parents would immediately join with the trustees in asking for a declaratory judgment to restrain Teachers College from abolishing Horace Mann-Lincoln School.

"The parents are convinced that the school must continue," Mrs. Gimbel asserted. "It may be necessary to operate it under a separate board of trustees. We are willing to take over the school and put in a board of trustees consisting of prominent educators and laymen who are interested in progressive education. The parents

Continued on Page 12, Column 3

PRESIDENT DECIDES TO CONTINUE OWMR UNDER STEELMAN

He Bows to Appeals of Cabinet Not to Let Agency Lapse, as Previously Announced

ARBITER ROLE STRESSED

New Appointee Will Stay On as White House Labor Adviser, Truman Says

Special to THE NEW YORK TIMES.

WASHINGTON, June 14—President Truman, bowing to the wishes of his Cabinet and other Federal agency heads, decided today to continue the Office of War Mobilization and Reconversion, and appointed John R. Steelman, White House labor adviser, as its fourth director.

In elevating John W. Snyder from the head of OWMR to the Treasury Secretaryship being vacated by Fred M. Vinson, the President had announced that he would allow the agency and its functions to lapse, except for some unfinished business which was to be taken over by the Stabilization Director, Chester Bowles.

As he opened his news conference today, however, the President surprised reporters with the statement that all Cabinet officers, many agency heads and the OWMR Civilian Advisory Committee had appealed for continuance of the office with or without Mr. Snyder at its head. Mr. Truman said that he was, therefore, appointing Mr. Steelman as OWMR Director, and he would continue as White House labor adviser at the request of Secretary Schwellenbach.

Mr. Truman did not disclose the Cabinet arguments for the continuation of OWMR, the existence of which ends officially with the Second War Powers Act June 30, 1947, but they were believed to have re-

Continued on Page 10, Column 6

STRONG DRAFT PLAN SUFFERS REVERSAL IN CONFEREE VOTING

House Delegates Stand 4 to 3 Against Restoring Power to Take 18-Year-Old Class

BUT A BALLOT MAY SHIFT

Compromise to Put Teen-Agers at End of List Fails—Maximum Age of 45 Favored

By WILLIAM S. WHITE
Special to THE NEW YORK TIMES.

WASHINGTON, June 14—Leaders of the movement for a strong draft suffered a reverse, although by no means a final one, today in the Senate-House conference committee, the House delegation in the first provisional vote standing 4 to 3 against restoring the power to conscript the 18-year-old class.

By agreement, this ballot was exploratory rather than binding, and those supporting the administration hoped to restore the position at another meeting on Monday. Representative Brooks, Democrat, of Louisiana, became by circumstance the key to the issue.

Mr. Brooks had been regarded by his colleagues as likely to agree to a dual compromise by which the Army would be empowered to resume taking 18-year-old men provided they were called up only after all other eligibles had been inducted and provided they were not sent overseas before reaching 19.

He cast a tentative vote, however, against this plan, but with the understanding that he was not foreclosing a reversal if he became convinced that drafting of the 18-year-old group would offer the sole assurance that the Army could obtain the men required.

Before the day was out, it was learned, the War Department had arranged to send an officer to Mr.

Continued on Page 6, Column 3

World News Summarized

SATURDAY, JUNE 15, 1946

Destruction of its store of atomic bombs and the offer of its atomic secrets to an international Atomic Development Authority in which no nation could exercise a veto power were proposed by the United States yesterday before the first meeting of the United Nations Atomic Energy Commission. Bernard M. Baruch, who outlined this country's program, warned that the choice was "world peace or world destruction." [1:8.]

The Senate overrode two members' opposition to the atomic bomb tests at Bikini Atoll and passed a bill authorizing the use of thirty-three naval combat ships as targets. [4:1.]

The Foreign Ministers of the Big Four will meet in Paris today to resume their deadlocked negotiations for European peace treaties. Russia made a contribution by agreeing to accept her 1940 Rumanian border. [1:6-7.]

Settlement of the south Tyrol issue by negotiation between Austria and Italy was considered possible if the United States were to act in favor of such action. [7:1.]

General Mikhailovitch admitted at his trial for treason in Belgrade that he had personally collaborated with the enemy. [3:1.]

Britain has not rejected the proposals of the Anglo-American Committee and is "most anxious" to go ahead with efforts to solve the problem of Palestine, the British Government declared in an apparent attempt to mitigate the effect of Foreign Secretary Bevin's Bournemouth statement. [8:1.] President Truman said he would press for action on his demand for the admission of 100,000 Jews into Palestine. [8:4.]

Azerbaijan Premier Pishevari offered to resign as Tabriz and Teheran jointly announced a ten-point agreement under which the northern Iranian province will return to the authority of the central Government. He was asked to remain in office until elections are held. [2:2.]

Afghanistan renounced all claim to the Russian border district of Kushka, in the corner where Iran, Afghanistan and Russia meet, under the new Soviet-Afghan agreement. [2:5.]

The proposals for Indian independence advanced by the British mission were rejected in their present form by the Congress party. [1:6-7.]

The threat of an attack by Chinese Communists on Tsingtao, where about 9,000 United States marines and naval personnel are based, appeared to be diminishing. [9:1.]

An agreement to avert the threatened maritime strike was reached five minutes before the midnight deadline. Harry Bridges, co-chairman of the Committee for Maritime Unity, announced the agreement under which the 200,000 workers will remain on their jobs. [1:2-3.] Despite this the strike got under way in New York and other ports. [1:1.]

President Truman, acting at the behest of his Cabinet and other Federal agency heads, decided to maintain the Office of War Mobilization and Reconversion and named John Steelman as its director. [1:4.]

The Chief Executive also disclosed that Supreme Court Justice Robert H. Jackson had disregarded his suggestion that he make no attack on Justice Black before discussing it at the White House. [1:3.] Myron C. Taylor will remain as his personal representative at the Vatican until completion of the peace treaties, Mr. Truman said. [1:7.]

The House delegation to the conference committee on the draft voted 4 to 3 against restoration of the power to take 18-year-old youths. [1:5].

Soviet Accepts 1940 Border Of Rumania on Parley Eve

Shows Western Ministers Map of Proposed Frontier—Delegates Express Restrained Optimism for Accord on Major Issues

By C. L. SULZBERGER
By Wireless to THE NEW YORK TIMES.

PARIS, June 14—The Foreign Ministers of the four big Allied powers, all of whom were in Paris today, will resume their deadlocked peace discussions here tomorrow in a mood that at best can be described as forced optimism.

That mood is dominated by a will to believe that obstacles hitherto preventing harmony can be overcome and that the one-world scheme of alliance that brought a wartime victory can be held together despite the increasing strains upon its fabric.

There have been no diplomatic exchanges between the four Governments during the interim period since the Council adjourned here in a stalemate a month ago and thus there is no information available to the Ministers regarding possible shifts in their respective viewpoints on the basic issues involved.

However, one extremely important development has been registered quietly. The Soviet Government has submitted to the three other powers a map of Rumania's frontier with the Soviet Union that is considered entirely satisfactory by the United States, Britain and France and clears up considerable worry about possible Russian efforts to penetrate down across the main Danubian outlets to control all egress from that river.

In the past Moscow has been strangely reluctant to clarify this issue. This led to Anglo-American suspicions that the Soviet Union was planning to consider Sulina at the mouth of the Danube as Soviet territory.

Inquiries were made to Soviet Ambassador Fedor T. Gusev in London by James C. Dunn, United States Assistant Secretary of State, and Gladwyn Jebb of Britain

Continued on Page 5, Column 2

'Angel' of U. S. Reds Goes To Russia to See Browder

By ALEXANDER FEINBERG

Confirmation of the departure for Moscow on June 7 of A. A. Heller, long-time "angel" for Communist undertakings here, intensified speculation yesterday over the real purpose and meaning of Earl Browder's visit to the Soviet capital. The reputedly wealthy Mr. Heller, purchasing agent more than a quarter-century ago for the Russian Bolshevist regime, has been a stanch supporter of Mr. Browder. When the latter was deposed as head of the American Communist movement, Mr. Heller abruptly cut off his "contributions" to The Daily Worker and other Communist projects. This has been a heavy blow financially, it was learned, to the present leadership headed by William Z. Foster.

In the past the leadership counted on Mr. Heller and several other "angels" to make up publication deficits that were said to run a quarter of a million dollars a year.

Now Mr. Heller is supposed to be bound for Moscow to meet Mr. Browder and that is given as the reason for a week's delay on Mr. Browder's part in returning to this country. He was due back last Sunday or Monday on an American Overseas Airline plane. It is known that he had booking from Stockholm, the European terminal for the airline, and that he failed to pick up his reservation.

Mr. Heller left La Guardia Field on a Pan-American clipper on a United States passport and made out under the name of Abraham Heller, executive, with a home address at 104 East Thirty-seventh Street, according to the manifest.

Continued on Page 3, Column 2

TAYLOR'S JOB PEACE ONLY, SAYS TRUMAN

When His Helping to Put World Back on Feet Is Done Vatican Post Will End, He Asserts

Special to THE NEW YORK TIMES.

WASHINGTON, June 14—President Truman announced his intention today to terminate the post of Personal Representative of the President to the Pope, but said that Myron C. Taylor, presently accredited to the Vatican, would remain on the job until completion of his mission, which he defined as aiding in re-establishing the peace of the world.

The President denied to his news conference ever having consented to the "recall" of Mr. Taylor during a recent White House conference on the subject with Protestant churchmen, or fixing a termination date for his mission.

He explained that he had sent Mr. Taylor to Rome to help in making the peace, just as President Roosevelt had sent him to aid in keeping the peace, and that when his current mission was completed there would be no official

Continued on Page 6, Column 3

India's Congress Party Rejects British Plan in Its Present Form

By Reuter.

NEW DELHI, India, June 14—After a day of intense negotiations, the Congress party—numerically the largest in India—tonight finally rejected, in their present form, the British Cabinet mission's plans for an interim Indian Government and its long-term proposals for India's constitutional future.

In a letter to Viscount Wavell, the Viceroy, Dr. Maulana Abul Kalam Azad, Congress president, is understood to have based his rejection of the interim arrangements on the ground that the Viceroy introduced into all discussions equality of representation either between the Congress and the Moslem League or between caste Hindus and Moslems.

Dr. Maulana Azad added that the Congress would also reject the long-term proposals unless European members of the Bengal and Assam Legislative Assemblies were excluded from taking part in elections for the Constituent Assembly.

He indicated that this was the Congress Working Committee's last word on the mission's proposals, and that any new move must come from the mission.

Dr. Maulana Azad's letter came as a climax to a series of sudden developments.

Yesterday the Congress informed the Viceroy that it unequivocally rejected the principle of equal Congress-Moslem League representation on the interim Government.

The three members of the British mission thereupon held a two-and-a-half-hour talk with the Viceroy this morning.

Viscount Wavell immediately afterward received Dr. Maulana Azad and Pandit Jawaharlal Nehru, talked with them for seventy-five minutes and submitted new proposals that were then dis-

Continued on Page 8, Column 6

BARUCH URGES PACT

Favors Rule by a Treaty to Outlaw New Missile, Bar Atomic Race

ASKS DIRE PENALTIES

Speech at First Sitting of U. N. Board Sees the World at Crossroads

The text of Mr. Baruch's speech will be found on Page 4.

By W. H. LAWRENCE

The United States formally offered yesterday to give up its store of atomic bombs and turn over all the secrets of harnessing atomic energy for peaceful means to an international Atomic Development Authority in which no nation could wield a veto power.

Bernard M. Baruch, elder statesman and a key figure in two World Wars, outlined the program in a forceful and eloquent speech in which the world was warned that its choice was a simple one, "world peace or world destruction."

The American offer highlighted the first meeting of the United Nations Atomic Energy Commission at Hunter College in the Bronx. The Commission consists of representatives of the United States, the United Kingdom, the Soviet Union, Canada, France, China, Poland, Australia, the Netherlands, Egypt, Mexico and Brazil.

Under U. N. Auspices

Mr. Baruch's plan was a bold bid to outlaw atomic energy as a means of mass destruction and thus avert a mad armament race among the nations of the world.

The United States representative on the commission proposed instead that an authority to be established by treaty under auspices of the United Nations and ratified by all peaceful nations should receive exclusive control over raw materials and the production of atomic energy under a system by which nations would be speedily punished for any violation of the international pact. This treaty would renounce the use of the atom bomb in war and limit the development of atomic energy to peaceful means.

Stressing the paramount importance of the problem, Mr. Baruch said:

"There is a famine throughout the world today. It starves men's bodies. But there is a greater famine—the hunger of men's spirit. That starvation can be cured by the conquest of fear and the substitution of hope, from which springs faith—faith in each other; faith that we want to work together toward salvation, and determination that those who threaten the peace and safety shall be punished."

Essential Rules Enumerated

The white-haired Mr. Baruch, whom President Wilson called "Dr. Facts," went directly to the heart of a great political issue, the veto power, in outlining the safeguards that this country regards as essential to set up before it gives up its monopoly, the possession of atomic bombs and the knowledge how such weapons are made.

It is essential to world security, Mr. Baruch said, that there should be immediate, certain and serious penalties for any nation that committed any of the following violations of international atomic control:

(1) Illegal possession or use of an atomic bomb.

(2) Illegal possession, or separation, of atomic material suitable for use in an atomic bomb.

(3) Seizure of any plant or other property belonging to or licensed by the authority.

(4) Willful interference with the activities of the authority.

(5) Creation or operation of dangerous projects in a manner contrary to, or in the absence of, a license granted by the international control body.

"It would be a deception, to which I am unwilling to lend myself, were I not to say to you and to our people that the matter of

Continued on Page 4, Column 3

"All the News That's Fit to Print"

NEWS INDEX, PAGE 39, THIS SECTION

The New York Times.

LATE CITY EDITION
Hot today and tomorrow; showers this afternoon or evening.
Temperatures Yesterday—Max., 84; Min., 69
Sunrise today, 5:27 A. M.; Sunset, 8:31 P. M.
Full U. S. Weather Bureau Report, Page 39

Section 1

VOL. XCV..No. 32,299.
Entered as Second-Class Matter. Postoffice, New York, N. Y.
Copyright, 1946, by The New York Times Company.
NEW YORK, SUNDAY, JUNE 30, 1946.
Including Magazine and Book Review.
TEN CENTS
New York City and Suburban Areas (15c Elsewhere)

OPA PRICE CONTROLS END AT MIDNIGHT TONIGHT AS HOUSE 173 TO 142 SUSTAINS TRUMAN VETO; PRESIDENT ASKS NATION NOT TO RAISE PRICES

BRITAIN LAUNCHES ARMY DRIVE TO END PALESTINE TERROR

At Least 3 Are Slain and 1,000 Held in Nation-Wide Raids to Get Hagana Leaders

JEWISH AGENCY IS SEIZED

4 High Officials Are Placed in Custody on Suspicion of Abetting Resistance

By CLIFTON DANIEL

By Wireless to The New York Times.

JERUSALEM, June 29—Palestine's Jewish population remained under virtual military siege tonight while thousands of troops and police pursued a country-wide campaign to root out the leadership of Hagana, the Jewish community's underground army, which, so far, has resulted in the arrest of about 1,000 persons for questioning and the deaths of two Jews and one British soldier.

[A London dispatch said that the United States Embassy had been informed of the drive only after it was under way.]

The operations, which began with the first military occupation of the Jewish Agency for Palestine and the arrest of four of its senior officials, are still continuing without any indication of when they will be completed. So far twenty rifles and 30,000 rounds of ammunition have been found in the searches of Jewish settlements.

Passive resistance to the military operations increased as the day wore on, but no major clashes were reported by Palestine Government authorities and there was practically no use of firearms. There is no indication that Hagana appeared as an organized force.

Meanwhile Dr. Chaim Weizmann, president of the Jewish Agency, was received by the British High Commissioner, Lieut. Gen. Sir Alan G. Cunningham, and discussed the situation.

Drive Opens at Dawn

With full knowledge of the London Government the operations began before dawn and continued through the day with a series of raids, arrests and searches in Jerusalem, Haifa, Tel Aviv and at least eleven Jewish communal settlements. Large portions of the country are in a virtual state of military siege by troops in war kit.

Although official reports accounted for only three dead, late today unofficial accounts mentioned six, including five Jews.

A report circulated in Zionist circles that Hagana leaders had learned of the raids in advance and gone into hiding. Hagana, with a membership sometimes estimated as high as 80,000 active and reserve members, is distinct from the smaller extremist groups of Irgun Zvai Leumi and the so-called Stern gang.

The Jewish Agency's building in Jerusalem was occupied without opposition and throughout the

Continued on Page 19, Column 3

Bikini Atom Blast On Today; Epic Naval Test Is Set Up

Blandy Decision Sends Men Scurrying From Target Ships—Thousands of Gauges in Place to Record Cosmic Burst

By The Associated Press.

ABOARD THE U. S. S. APPALACHIAN, Bikini Atoll, Sunday, June 30—Vice Admiral William H. P. Blandy today designated 8:30 A. M. tomorrow [5:30 P. M. Sunday, Eastern daylight time] as zero hour for the detonation of the world's fourth atomic bomb on a guinea-pig fleet of old warships in Bikini Lagoon.

The decision was made after weather experts had informed the commander of Joint Task Force 1 that the cloud cover would be about 20 to 30 per cent and visibility about twelve miles.

Admiral Blandy can change his plans up to 10 P. M. tonight Bikini time [7 A. M., Sunday, Eastern daylight time] without serious disruption in the complex machinery of ships, planes and men. If plans for the test are changed by that time it would be possible to make adjustments for another try on Wednesday, assuming that meteorological conditions were satisfactory that day.

Promptly on receipt of Admiral Blandy's order, skippers of more than 100 support ships began making their vessels ready for the sea, there to take their assigned stations for the test.

A few minutes after the announcement had come from the staff conference room of the U. S. S. Mount McKinley, the flagship's hoarse whistle roared out a series of long blasts.

Skies at the time were clearer than they had been in several days and all hands crossed their fingers in the hope the bomb would be dropped on time.

Weather men estimated that winds in the extreme upper levels would be from the northeast and that therefore radiological safety was assured.

The time for the test set by Ad-

Continued on Page 3, Column 4

MOLOTOV INDICATES READINESS TO JOIN PEACE PARLEY CALL

Declares He Thinks Decision on July 20 Conference Can Be Made in a Few Days

BYRNES INSISTS ON ACTION

Bidault Offers Seven-Point Plan to Internationalize Trieste to End Deadlock

By C. L. SULZBERGER

By Wireless to The New York Times.

PARIS, June 29—The Council of Foreign Ministers moved closer today than at any other time to the convocation of a European peace conference when, after United States Secretary of State James F. Byrnes had insisted that invitations to such a meeting on July 20 be issued immediately, Soviet Foreign Minister Vyacheslav M. Molotov hesitated and then replied that he thought within two or three days the Ministers could agree to take this momentous step.

Thus, although the Secretary of State was unable to get that definite yes or no answer that he already had announced he would seek at this afternoon's session, the log jam appeared to be slowly breaking up.

At the same time French Foreign Minister Georges Bidault finally submitted to his colleagues in writing a seven-point proposal to solve the Trieste stumbling block by internationalizing the city and placing it under a combined Four-Power, Yugoslav and Italian administration for ten years, with the United Nations Security Council responsible for final decisions.

Although M. Bidault offered this suggestion in his capacity as Council host and said that French desires still were based on the French line in Istria and Venezia

Continued on Page 12, Column 2

CONGRESS REVOLTS

Moves to Obtain Brief Extension Fail in Both Houses

RULES AID OPPONENTS

Leaders Told Truman Measure Was Best They Could Get

By JOHN D. MORRIS

Special to The New York Times.

WASHINGTON, June 29—The House sustained President Truman's veto of the price control extension bill today, and Congress adjourned later until Monday without enacting a substitute measure, thus letting all price and rent control expire with the present law at midnight tomorrow.

Attempts in both House and Senate to obtain consideration of a resolution continuing the Office of Price Administration in its present form for twenty days were blocked by opponents who successfully invoked parliamentary technicalities.

After a hectic day of maneuvering to save something out of the parliamentary confusion caused by the last minute veto, Administration leaders gave up their attempts to put through a continuing resolution to replace the vetoed measure.

The resolution was then scheduled for consideration in the House Monday. There was still doubt whether it could be brought up in the Senate before the middle of the week if opponents continued their obstructive tactics.

Whether the President would be able to find some authority to continue price control without the price control act, if he so desired, was considered doubtful. Congress recently sent to the White House

Continued on Page 26, Column 4

Truman Appeals to People To Carry Fight to Congress

In Radio Address He Asks That Public Back Him and Make Views Known to the Nation's Lawmakers

Special to The New York Times.

WASHINGTON, June 29—President Truman, in a radio speech broadcast over all national networks, appealed to the American people tonight to support and make known to Congress their determination "to retain price controls and so prevent inflation."

Speaking only a few hours after the House had upheld his veto of the OPA bill and with price and rent controls ending at midnight tomorrow, Mr. Truman declared that "the fight is not over."

Having in mind the effort that is to be made in Congress to pass stop-gap legislation for continuance of existing controls until a permanent bill can be passed that will have his approval, the Chief Executive invoked "the patriotism and good sense" of citizens.

He called upon "every business man, every producer and every landlord to adhere to existing regulations even though for a short period they may not have the effect of law."

He requested every employe of the Office of Price Administration to "stay at his battle station."

Finally, he told the American people that they could themselves make the post-war period the greatest in opportunity and prosperity in our history, but warned that "if partisanship and greed are allowed to triumph over the efforts to maintain economic stability, this grand opportunity will have been sacrificed."

To give concrete effect to his appeal, Mr. Truman urged the people to make known to Congress their determination to "retain price controls and so prevent price inflation."

In commenting on the withhold-

Continued on Page 29, Column 6

PRESIDENT IS SHARP

Rejecting OPA Bill, He Tells House It Would Legalize Inflation

ASKS STOP-GAP LAW

Maps 'Effective' Plan for Year of Stabilization to Be Voted Later

Texts of President's veto message and radio talk on Page 28.

By BERTRAM D. HULEN

Special to The New York Times.

WASHINGTON, June 29—President Truman vetoed the OPA bill today in a strong message of 4,000 words to the House, declaring that it presented "a choice between inflation with a statute and inflation without one."

At the same time he put forward in detail recommendations for what he considered a sound law on the subject. With such a measure, he contended, "we can win the war against inflation just as decisively as we won the war against the Axis." Pending passage of such a measure, which he wants now, he requested temporary extension of present controls by resolution.

The vetoed measure, he said in his message to Congress, is one that "continues the Government's responsibility to stabilize the economy and at the same time it destroys the Government's power to do so." It was only fair, he maintained, to tell the American people "now" that it would not protect them.

Points to Inflation Abroad

"In the end this bill would lead to disaster," he emphasized, adding, "inflation and collapse in this country would shake the entire world."

"I cannot bring myself to believe," he said, "that the representatives of the American people will permit the great calamity which will befall this country if price and rent control end at midnight Sunday."

The fact that inflation has already "gutted the economy of country after country all over the world should shake our comfortable assurance that such a catastrophe cannot happen here," he said.

Much of his fire was directed at amendments to the bill, especially one by Senator Robert A. Taft, Republican, of Ohio, which he rated as most inflationary.

"With all the earnestness at my command," he told Congress, he urged it "to reconsider the whole problem of stabilization."

Calls for Early Action

What he desired, he explained, was a bill "now" which would give the nation adequate assurance of completing a successful transition to a sound peacetime economy. His outline of what such a bill should contain included:

1. "Extension of the stabilization laws for a full year."

2. Continuance of stabilization subsidies "on a scale sufficient to avoid serious increases during the next six months and to permit the orderly termination of subsidies during the first half of 1947," at a minimum cost of perhaps $1,250,000,000.

3. A declaration of Congressional policy "with respect to the

Continued on Page 29, Column 2

NEGOTIATIONS LAG IN EXPRESS TIE-UP

All Parleys Off Until Tomorrow—Volume of Packaged Mail Shows Marked Increase

By LAWRENCE RESNER

An increase in the volume of packaged mail was reported yesterday at the postoffice as all possibility of a settlement of the three-day-old Railway Express Agency tie-up in New York City was precluded until tomorrow afternoon at the earliest.

What may happen then was said to hinge on a meeting scheduled for 10 A. M. tomorrow between J. F. Ross, general superintendent of the company in the New York area; Adolph J. Mazanec, district chairman of the Brotherhood of Railway Clerks, AFL, and the actual depot superintendents and chairman of the brotherhood's six New York lodges.

This meeting will get down to a consideration of the twenty-three grievances that prompted the walkout at midnight Wednesday of 10,000 express company employes, but any decision, union officials said, would be referred to a membership meeting scheduled for 2 P. M. tomorrow at Manhattan Center.

Tomorrow's session at Manhattan Center will amount to a resumption of the "continuous mass meeting" the union called at midnight Wednesday to enforce its demands for a settlement of the twenty-three grievances. The principal demands are that Sunday workers start work at midnight so they can get overtime pay and the

Continued on Page 31, Column 5

POLES TERRORIZED ON EVE OF VOTING

Armed Bands Clash With Secret Police—Balloting to Settle Western Border Issue

By The Associated Press.

WARSAW, June 29—Roving armed bands clashed with units of Polish security police and the Army today in rising unrest on the eve of tomorrow's national referendum on legislative reform and the nationalization of basic industries.

A spokesman for the Foreign Ministry declared that outlaw gangs were wounding and killing hundreds of persons, "and probably thousands," in pre-election disturbances. He said many polling officials had been attacked. Recently officials said 8,000 persons had been killed in ten months.

The two major opposing factions in the referendum are the four-party coalition including the Communist-backed Polish Workers' party, supporting the Provisional Government, and the Polish Peasant party of Vice Premier Stanislaw Mikolajczyk.

M. Mikolajczyk charged that security police were making mass arrests of party members, and were confiscating all his party literature demanding a negative vote on the first question in the referendum—whether voters want a one-House Parliament.

The two other questions are: Do you approve of the actions of the Provisional Regime nationalizing basic industries and agrarian reform? and Do you approve establishment of Poland's western

Continued on Page 5, Column 7

World News Summarized

SUNDAY, JUNE 30, 1946

The OPA extension bill was vetoed by President Truman and cessation of all price controls at midnight tonight appeared certain as the House sustained the veto and the Senate adjourned until Monday without action.

President Truman in a strong veto message said the bill presented "a choice between inflation with a statute and inflation without one." He outlined a desirable law that would enable the nation to "win the war against inflation just as decisively as we won the war against the Axis." He urged temporary extension of OPA controls by resolution. [1:8.] Consideration of such a resolution was blocked both in the House and Senate. [1:5.]

President Truman, in a radio address to the nation, urged the public to let Congress know their desire "to retain price controls and so prevent inflation" and emphasized "the fight is not over." [1:6-7.]

A considerable rise in prices as a result of the lifting of price controls was forecast in Washington. The end of wage controls, the strangling of black markets and depreciation of the value of the dollar were also predicted. [1:6-7.] Governor Dewey was prepared to name a State Housing Rent Commission with sweeping powers to maintain present rent ceilings. [1:6-7.]

Vice Admiral Blandy announced that the atom bomb test at Bikini Atoll would be held late this afternoon, New York time. Everything was made ready for the great experiment to gauge the effect of the new weapon on naval craft and the crews of the seventy-three ships that will form the "guinea pig" target fleet were being evacuated. [1:2-3.]

The atomic bombs dropped on Hiroshima and Nagasaki caused complete physical and moral devastation, according to the official report of the United States Strategic Bombing Survey. Survey officials said the destruction of the Japanese cities was the most "forceful argument for peace and the international machinery for peace." [3:1.]

Without mentioning Russia or Andrei Gromyko's frequent use of the veto power recently in Security Council sessions, the Council delegates of the United States and China condemned "irresponsible" exercise of the veto. [7:3.]

The prospect for a twenty-one-nation peace conference in July brightened when Foreign Minister Molotov told the Council of Foreign Ministers that he believed an agreement to issue invitations for such a meeting could be reached within two or three days. [1:4.]

Poland prepared to go to the polls today in a referendum on government reform and nationalization of basic industries amid mounting tension and pre-election disturbances. [1:3.]

At least two persons were killed as British troops and police swooped down on Jerusalem, Tel Aviv and other settlements in Palestine. About a thousand Jews, including leaders of the Jewish Agency, were arrested during the widespread raids, which the British said were intended to root out terrorist leadership. [1:1.]

A "caretaker" Executive Council for India, composed of six Britons and two Indians, was announced by Viscount Wavell. [14:1.]

Premier Sjahrir of the unrecognized Indonesian Republic and five members of his Cabinet were kidnapped in an apparent coup. "President" Soekarno announced that he had assumed dictatorial powers. [1:2-3.]

In China a new peace proposal offered by the Communists, including a plan for the evacuation of Harbin in northern Manchuria, was submitted to Generalissimo Chiang Kai-shek by General Marshall. [15:1.]

What Limits on Prices Now, Is Big Unanswered Question

By JOHN H. CRIDER

Special to The New York Times.

WASHINGTON, June 29—The consensus of Washington economic opinion is that the absence of price controls after tomorrow midnight will mean a considerable rise in prices. But the big unanswered question is how much will prices rise? Beyond price increases, other economic consequences of the price control death-knell were deemed to be these:

1. The end of wage controls. Since existing wage controls were related to the price level by the Wage Stabilization Board, the effect of ending price control is to end wage control. Employers may now grant wage increases, and employes demand them, wherever the situation seems to warrant such action.

2. A gradual end of black markets and a return of goods to normal distributive channels.

3. The value of the United States dollar, in terms of its purchasing power, for everything but gold and silver, the prices of which for a monetary purpose are fixed by statute, becomes a matter of speculation around the world. A dollar more inflated than at present will create great difficulties for the International Monetary Fund in its task of setting initial exchange rates for world currencies, a task which it expected to have well under way by the fall.

4. A highly inflated dollar would be of tremendous competitive advantage to Great Britain and other countries seeking to rebuild their world trade, with the possibility that, with a sustained high-cost level in the United States, our country could price itself out of world markets for some commodities and manufactured goods.

5. The problem of greater in-

Continued on Page 25, Column 4

PRICE RISES HERE LIKELY TOMORROW

But Survey Indicates Business Will Avoid Sharp Advances Until Trend Is Evident

By WILL LISSNER

An upward adjustment tomorrow of prices on items where ceiling prices do not cover costs and a normal profit is expected by business men as a result of the deadlock in the Government over continuing price control, a canvass of business leaders and trade association executives showed yesterday.

But none would predict how high the average level of prices might go, for there are too many uncertain factors that would affect it. Most anticipated that, outside of foodstuffs, there would be no sharp rise immediately except in a few spectacular lines.

"We have to feel our way," they say. "There's no profit in increasing the value of your inventory unless you move it."

As far as goods en route or yet to be shipped are concerned, business men here did not know what the prices would be. It had be-

Continued on Page 28, Column 1

U. S. Sailors Join In Trieste Fighting

By The United Press.

TRIESTE, June 29—Rioting pro-Yugoslav and pro-Italian mobs battled on Trieste streets tonight and American sailors from the cruiser Fargo pitched into one mêlée that police broke up with tear-gas bombs.

Police cruised the streets in jeeps and weapon carriers. They reported fighting in all sections of the city.

Sailors from the Fargo broke into one mob that was beating a civilian and fought until M. P.'s and shore patrols dragged them away.

Other sailors and soldiers were involved in a riot in front of the United States 88th Division officers' hotel, when police tossed tear-gas bombs into their midst.

'Premier' of Java Is Kidnapped; All Power Assumed by 'President'

By The United Press.

BATAVIA, Java, June 29—The unrecognized Indonesian "Government" announced today that its Premier, five members of his Cabinet and a member of the Indonesian Army's general staff had been kidnapped by an armed band in an apparent coup d'état.

Radio Jogjakarta, voice of the Government, said that "President" Soekarno, recently reduced to relative impotence in the independence movement, had assumed dictatorial powers, taken over all governmental functions and declared a "state of emergency" throughout the Netherlands East Indies.

"Premier" Sutan Sjahrir, Major General Sudipyo, a member of the general staff; Dr. Santoso, Minister of Social Affairs, and four other Cabinet Ministers were kidnapped from a hotel at Surakarta Thursday night, the radio report said.

The reported kidnappings bore all the aspects of a coup d'état by "President" Soekarno. He recently was ousted as Premier, a position which Mr. Sjahrir assumed, in addition to the Foreign and Home Affairs portfolios.

Mr. Soekarno became "President" of the Indonesian Government and a mere figurehead in the independence movement.

Premier Sjahrir is 36. Netherlands authorities exiled him to Digul, New Guinea, in 1935 and later transferred him to the Banda Islands. After the Japanese occupation he returned to Batavia. He is described as a moderate, far-

Continued on Page 15, Column 3

Dewey Acts to Freeze Rentals In State at Present OPA Levels

Special to The New York Times.

ALBANY, June 29—Governor Dewey acted today to prevent residential rents in New York State from skyrocketing if and when Congress permits the OPA to expire at midnight tomorrow. The Governor, moving under a State rent-control law signed by him on March 30, is prepared to appoint within twenty-four hours a one-man State Housing Rent Commission clothed with sweeping powers to maintain existing residential rent "ceilings." The law carries an appropriation of $1,000,000 for administration.

In one major respect the State law differs from present OPA rent orders. It exempts new construction, or buildings under construction at the time the State orders take effect.

Charles D. Breitel, counsel to the Governor, said today that there would be no hiatus between any relinquishing of Federal jurisdiction and the beginning of State jurisdiction in the residential rent field.

"The State law is effective now," he said. "Its applicability awaits only certain ministrial acts. Anyone who disregards it would be acting at his own peril, at least economically. It would not pay for anyone to try to beat the gun."

The State statute contains sharp enforcement "teeth." Landlords violating the rent orders of the State Commissioner would be subject to a year in jail or a $5,000 fine or both.

Provision is made for appeals to the courts, but in such cases it would be necessary for the peti-

Continued on Page 24, Column 3

On the last leg of his U.S. tour, Winston Churchill flashes the "V" sign as he arrives in New York.

John F. Kennedy poses with a group of Boston women during his successful 1946 campaign for the House of Representatives.

Post-war inflation was still out of control, prompting one merchant to display this message in his window.

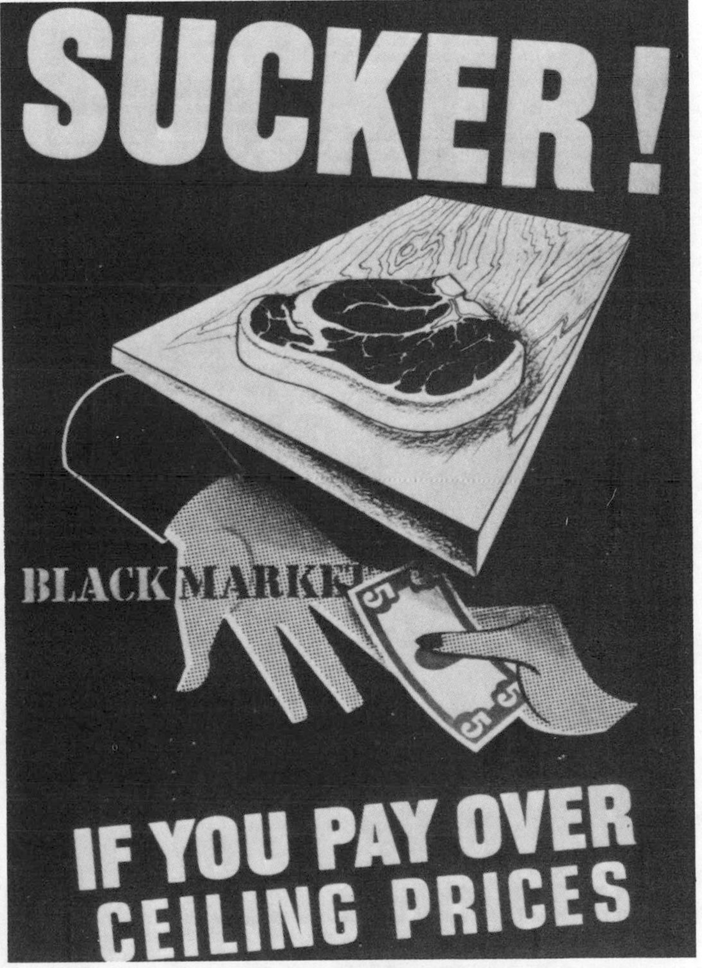

The black market still flourished after the war ended. This Office of Price Administration poster blatantly warned against "under-the-counter" food purchases.

These servicemen seem rather happy as they wave their discharge papers in the air.

The full-skirted look of the post-war era was already in full bloom as these models' garments attest.

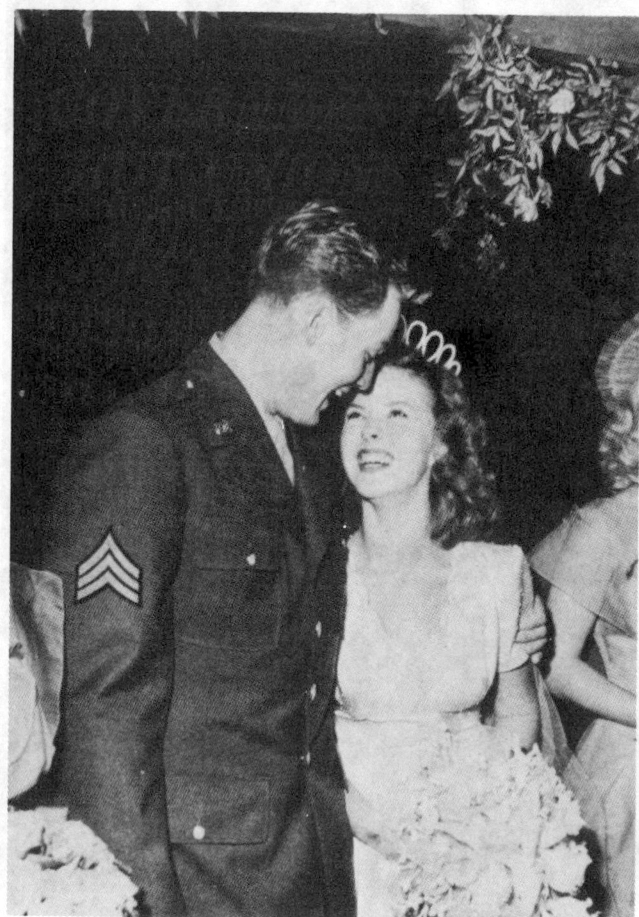

Shirley Temple married actor and Air Force Sergeant John Agar, and thousands of Hollywood fans tried to storm the church.

One feature of the post-war years was "un-rationed," cheap and plentiful gasoline; these men seem oblivious to the wastefulness of their ways.

"All the News That's Fit to Print"

The New York Times.

LATE CITY EDITION

Showers and thunder showers today; clearing late tomorrow.
Temperatures Yesterday—Max., 80; Min., 69
Sunrise today, 5:43 A. M.; Sunset, 8:21 P. M.
Full U. S. Weather Bureau Report, Page 45

VOL. XCV...No. 32,322. Entered as Second-Class Matter. Postoffice, New York, N. Y. NEW YORK, TUESDAY, JULY 23, 1946. THREE CENTS IN NEW YORK CITY

EXTENSION OF OPA FOR YEAR IS VOTED BY CONFEREES, 11-3

HOUSE ACTS TODAY

Leaders Are Confident of Congress Passage and Truman's Approval

BILL DECLARED IMPROVED

Porter Calls It Better 'in Many Important Respects' Than One President Vetoed

Text of conferees' measure to revive OPA, Pages 18 and 19.

By C. P. TRUSSELL

Special to The New York Times.

WASHINGTON, July 22—An eleven-to-three vote of Senate and House conferees sent to both houses today for final ratification the much-mauled bill to extend the life of OPA for another year but to prevent any renewal of controls on the prices of meat, milk, dairy products, grains and other key commodities before Aug. 20, at the earliest.

Yet, the measure over which Congress has battled bitterly since President Truman vetoed its last restrictive program for bringing OPA back, was viewed by Paul A. Porter, Price Administrator, as being "better in many important and material respects" than that first effort.

He told the President, Mr. Porter said, after a mid-afternoon conference, but, he added, he made no recommendations as to whether the Chief Executive should approve or veto the new draft. Recommendations may be made, the Price Administrator said, after Congress has completed its action.

Leaders Consult President

Congressional leaders, after a conference of their own with the President earlier in the day, returned to the Capitol and prepared with apparent confidence to press the conference agreement to ratification and a Presidential signature. They said that they had not asked the President whether he would approve or disapprove; nor, they added, did he tell them.

Senator Alben W. Barkley, the Majority Leader, indicated, however, that Mr. Truman had let it be understood that he would act promptly on the appointment of the three-member price decontrol board which, created by the bill, would have authority in many situations and instances exceeding that of the OPA itself. This was taken as a signal that the President, now at least, was inclined to sign, rather than veto the bill.

It has been for many days a foregone conclusion at key Capitol points that a veto this time would mean the absolute end of OPA, with little if any effort being made to save any controls but those on rents.

House Passage Due Today

The bill which the House is scheduled to vote upon tomorrow, and approve by a comfortable margin according to tonight's outlook, with the Senate acting next, would put the OPA back in business in much the same manner it would have been had it been extended on June 30.

Except in the cases of the specifically exempted market-basket and other items, the OPA could largely pick up where it left off, handling ceilings and regulations, perhaps in the light of the things that have happened to prices since the curbs lapsed, until the decontrol board was a functioning concern.

Rent controls would be re-established immediately the new law became effective. Although floods of notices of rent rises have de-

Continued on Page 19, Column 1

The New York Times now broadcasts its **NEWS BULLETINS** *over its own radio stations every hour on the hour*
WQXR (1560 on the dial) 7 A. M. to Midnight
WQXQ (FM-45.9 megacycles) 5 P. M. to Midnight

Half of U.S. Incomes Under $2,000 a Year

By The Associated Press.

WASHINGTON, July 22—Almost half of America's families have incomes of less than $2,000 a year, and two out of three take in less than $3,000, a joint survey by the Federal Reserve Board and the Bureau of Agricultural Economics stated today.

The survey counted 1945 income before taxes and the figures represented the combined income of all members of each family.

Since 1945 set a record for individual income, the current average "take" is likely to be less.

About one in ten families had pooled incomes of $4,000 to $7,500, and only one in each thirty-three or thirty-four had joint income totaling more than $7,500.

MEAT BLACK MART FEARED UNDER OPA

Spokesmen for Restaurants, Hotels and Clubs Forecast Illegitimate Deals Again

Restaurant and hotel men of the city and representatives of the meat industry forecast yesterday an immediate return of the black market if Federal controls again were put on meat through revival of Office of Price Administration regulations.

Spokesmen for leading restaurant, chains, cafeterias, Broadway night clubs and hotels were agreed that in the open and competitive market beef and other meat cuts were becoming plentiful at prices far below those that prevailed in the black market.

Although prices are higher than former OPA ceilings, these spokesmen contend those ceilings were "fictional" and meant nothing because it was virtually impossible to buy meat legitimately at OPA prices. S. Ernest, assistant to the president of the Hotel Commodore, said that under OPA no hotels were able to obtain more than 5 per cent of the meat they needed through legitimate channels.

Black Market Seen on Way

"If meat controls are restored conditions will be the same as they were before with the black market back and black market operators doing business at the same old stand," Mr. Ernest said. "At the present time we can buy all the meat we want legitimately."

Robert K. Christenberry, president of the Hotel Astor, said that with the end of OPA controls his hotel was able to serve a variety of meat cuts, something that was impossible under price regulations "because we can't and won't compete by paying black market prices." He also forecast a "reblossoming" of the "lush black market" if meat controls were restored.

Butter took another drop of 2½ cents a pound wholesale on the New York Mercantile Exchange yesterday with Grade AA selling for 68¼ cents a pound, compared

Continued on Page 15, Column 5

Oil Tideland Rights for States Voted After Fight in the Senate

By The Associated Press.

WASHINGTON, July 22—The Senate voted, 44 to 34, today to give the States clear title to the oil-rich tidelands extending three miles or more into the oceans.

The vote was taken after a wild parliamentary battle in which the anti-poll tax bill was offered as a rider and finally shelved.

By a margin of ten votes the Senate approved and sent back to the House the measure renouncing Federal claim to ownership not only of the tidelands but of lands beneath navigable waters within the boundaries of the States.

Democratic Leader Alben W. Barkley of Kentucky told his colleagues in a futile battle against a proposal that if the Senate and House agree on a final version he hopes President Truman will veto it "in the interest of national defense."

All set to vote on the measure at 3 P. M., Eastern standard time, the Senate ran into a threat of a Southern filibuster when Senator Wayne Morse, Republican, of Oregon, took advantage of a parliamentary situation to offer the anti-poll tax measure as an amendment.

This bill, previously passed by the House, would outlaw the payment of State poll taxes as a prerequisite to voting in Federal elections. Southern Democrats have always greeted with a filibuster any effort to bring it up.

When Senator Morse stood his ground and demanded a vote on the politically explosive proposal Senator Richard B. Russell, Democrat, of Georgia, began a debate that had all the earmarks of a filibuster.

After a careful count of noses Senator Barkley finally broke this

Continued on Page 23, Column 3

DRASTIC REDUCTION IN IDLEWILD COSTS SOUGHT BY MAYOR

Decisions on Airport's Size and Financing to Precede Renegotiation of Contracts

2-HOUR CONFERENCE HELD

Board of Estimate Gets Data—Reidel Assigned to Study Changes in Program

By WILLIAM R. CONKLIN

Mayor O'Dwyer laid down a three-step procedure yesterday for the completion of Idlewild Airport in Queens.

The size of the airport is the first question to be settled, he declared; its financing by the city or the New York City Airport Authority comes second; and the third step will be renegotiation of city contracts with air and oil companies to obtain more city revenue from the field.

The policy laid down by the Mayor dispelled confusion that had surrounded the airport controversy and served to refute published reports that he was ready to scrap the Airport Authority and to take the revised program into his own hands. As the Mayor outlined the situation, the Airport Authority is still in the foreground and is likely to continue there until a final decision is made on which agency will finance the improvement. Unofficial sources said this decision might not be made for as long as two months.

The Mayor's statement followed a two-hour executive session of the Board of Estimate at City Hall. He disclosed that the session was held primarily to put the board in possession of all the facts relating to the airport and to determine how much money would be required to put the field into usable condition for operation. He made clear that the choice of an agency to finance its completion could not be made until the primary question of size had been settled.

Mayor Explains Problem

Summing up the results of the executive session, the Mayor said:

"I was anxious to have the Board of Estimate brought up to date on all the facts relating to the building of Idlewild Airport.

"After discussion, it was agreed that the Board should first have before it the minimum requirements to meet present traffic needs. When I came into City Hall at the first of the year, we were supposed to spend $189,000,000 of the city's capital funds on this project. Present-day costs have increased that figure to at least $230,000,000. Obviously, the city is in no financial position to spend that much money if we are going ahead with a program of schools and hospitals. The project can be made usable to meet present needs by reducing the construction program considerably.

"It was agreed that the Board's chief engineer, Mr. John Reidel, should be appointed to study the proposed reduced program, and to make recommendations to the Board.

"The second point discussed, on which no action was taken at this time, was a consideration of the existing air company and oil company leases for the purpose of obtaining more revenue for the city than has been provided in the existing leases."

Asked whether Mr. Reidel had received a time limit for completion of his study, the Mayor said no deadline had been set because

Continued on Page 23, Column 2

May Says He Is Too Busy To Testify on War Profits

An Appearance Later Is Under Discussion, He Reveals in Answer to a Subpoena—Coffee Charges Are Investigated

By WILLIAM S. WHITE

Special to The New York Times.

WASHINGTON, July 22—Representative Andrew J. May refused today to appear tomorrow under subpoena before the Senate War Investigating Committee, where his name has been mentioned in the war profits inquiry, by pleading "press of constant legislative activities."

In a statement prepared after long consultation with his counsel, however, Mr. May, the chairman of the House Military Affairs Committee, observed that arrangements for a later appearance were "under discussion."

He recalled his previous offer to testify before the committee on conditions of his own, a proposal at once rejected as one that would put him in a category different from other witnesses, but left the investigators uncertain as to whether he intended still to stand on this demand.

In an unrelated matter before the committee, Senator James M. Mead, Democrat, of New York, its chairman, announced that a preliminary investigation was in progress into accusations that Representative John M. Coffee, Democrat, of Washington, in May of 1941 had received $2,500 from Eivind Anderson, a war contractor, of Tacoma.

"This payment," Mr. Mead added, "is stated to have been made in connection with a contract between Mr. Anderson and the Government involving approximately $1,000,000."

He recalled that the matter had first been raised by a committee member, Senator Owen Brewster, Republican, of Maine, and said:

"In referring these charges to the committee, Senator Brewster submitted clippings from The Tacoma News Tribune dated Tues-

Continued on Page 21, Column 1

RUPTURE WITH ALP DENIED BY MAYOR

Leaders Are Assured Parley With Rose of Liberal Party Did Not Mean Break

Leaders of the American Labor party received assurance yesterday from Mayor O'Dwyer that his conference Saturday night with Alex Rose, one of the leaders of the rival Liberal party, did not mean that the Mayor was breaking away from the ALP, which supported him in the 1945 election.

The assurance was given by the Mayor as soon as reports of the O'Dwyer-Rose conference were published yesterday, and the ALP leadership therefore remained relatively unconcerned during the day, which saw the Mayor confer with two more Liberal party leaders at City Hall.

It is expected that leaders of the ALP and the Mayor will confer at City Hall today as a public demonstration that the Mayor has not swung from one group to the other.

The Mayor's message to the ALP was to the effect that the conference with Mr. Rose was to make sure that the coalition of "liberal" forces in the city was broadened

Continued on Page 15, Column 2

MME. SUN ASKS BAN ON OUR AID TO CHINA

Widow of Republic's Founder Sees Plot for War Between Us and Soviet Union

By The United Press

SHANGHAI, July 22—Mme. Sun Yat-sen, widow of the man who founded the Chinese republic, said today that American and Chinese "reactionaries" were fanning the flames of civil war in China, hoping to bring the United States and Russia into armed conflict.

Mme. Sun, who is the sister-in-law of Generalissimo Chiang Kai-shek, President of the Chinese Republic, broke a two-year political silence to ask the United States to withdraw its forces from China and to make no loans to a Government that is not reorganized and truly representative.

Her statement evidently was designed to stress a plea to the American people by fifty-six Chinese educators, liberals, industrialists and professional leaders that no more aid be given to the Central Government, which, they said, was "permeated with the forces of reaction."

This plea was addressed to the

Continued on Page 5, Column 3

World News Summarized

TUESDAY, JULY 23, 1946

At least forty-one persons were killed yesterday when a bomb, believed planted by Zionist terrorists, wrecked one wing of the King David Hotel in Jerusalem, headquarters of the British Army and of the Palestine Government secretariat. The bombers pinned down a British major who intercepted them while they were about to plant the explosives. Jerusalem was placed under virtual martial law. [1:8, map P 3.]

Secretary Byrnes has asked the other members of the Foreign Ministers' Council to make available for immediate publication the texts of the draft treaties to go before the Peace Conference next week. [2:2.]

Any treaty that fails to give Trieste to Yugoslavia will be rejected by Belgrade, but will not be used as a pretext for war, Ambassador Kosanovich, the new Yugoslav envoy, said in Washington. [2:6.]

General Koenig, French Military Governor in Germany, has incorporated more than 600 square miles of the Rhineland into the Saar territory. Some observers interpreted this as a preliminary move to acceptance of the United States plan to treat occupied areas as an economic entity. [3:1.]

Russia was reported to have reached a final decision that the veto power in the Security Council should remain unaltered regardless of any stand the United Nations Assembly, which will meet Sept. 23, might take. [1:7.]

The British Labor party won a narrow victory in electing its candidate at Bexley by a greatly reduced majority. [14:1.] Bread rationing, a major issue in the by-election, got off to a smooth start. [31:6.]

Incomplete and unofficial returns from Turkey's first free election showed that, while the Government Republican party would have a large majority, the new Democratic party had scored notable successes, especially in the large cities. [10:2.]

Free elections, liberation of political prisoners and restoration of democratic processes have been promised in Bolivia by Nestor Guillen, acting president of the revolutionary provisional government. [1:6.]

Chinese Nationalists, reporting a series of victories, declared they had driven back the Communist Fourth Army threatening Nanking. [4:3, with map.]

Mme. Sun Yat-sen, widow of the founder of the Chinese Republic and sister-in-law of Generalissimo Chiang Kai-shek, accused American and Kuomintang "reactionaries" of fomenting civil conflict in China to embroil Russia and the United States in a war that would crush Chinese communism. She asked for the withdrawal of American forces and the end of financial aid except to a "reorganized and truly representative" regime. [1:5.]

India's mounting labor unrest, highlighted by strikes that have paralyzed Bombay, may have serious political consequences. The Congress party, it was said, has shown little interest in the workers, leaving the field open for Communists to agitate. [5:1.]

Both houses of Congress will begin discussion today on the compromise OPA bill, which Price Administrator Porter reported to President Truman was "better in many important and material respects" than the vetoed measure. [1:1.] Congressional leaders, after conferring with the President, reached a tentative agreement to adjourn the middle of next week. [15:4.]

Representative May of Kentucky has declined to appear before the Mead Investigating Committee today because of "constant legislative activities," but may do so later. [1:4-5.]

BOLIVIANS INSTALL A LIBERAL REGIME; PLEDGE FREE VOTE

Head of La Paz Supreme Court Directs Interim Junta of Workers, Intelligentsia

FREE PRESS IS RESTORED

Call Issued to Exiles to Return—Early Recognition in Latin America Is Foreseen

By The United Press.

LA PAZ, Bolivia, July 22—Nestor Guillen, provisional President installed by student and worker rebels after Sunday's successful uprising, announced today that the revolution had won a nation-wide victory.

Dr. Guillen said that declarations of "warm support" had come from all Bolivia for the rebels who assassinated President Gualberto Villarroel, swept away his dictatorship, and formed a Leftist provisional government.

Rebel leaders estimated the casualties in the week-long revolt at 260 dead and 520 wounded. Hospitals, dispensaries and private homes were still jammed with casualties from yesterday's fighting.

Unofficial estimates of casualties ran as high as 2,000 dead and wounded.

Inside the bullet-pocked palace where Major Villarroel had ruled for two years and seven months after his own violent seizure of power by a military coup, workers, students and university professors worked today to form a democratic government.

Civil Liberties Promised

Dr. Guillen, dean of the Supreme Court of the La Paz District, promised free democratic elections, the restoration of civil liberties to the people, freedom of the press, the release of all political prisoners and an invitation to political exiles to return to participate in the Government.

With Dr. Guillen on the provisional junta or governing board were: Luis Gonsalvez Indaburo, University of La Paz professor, as students' representative; Dr. Aniceto Solares, president of the University of Sucre, teachers' representative, and Aurelio Alcoba, workers' representative.

In its first communiqué, issued at midday, the Provisional Government declared:

"The people of La Paz, Bolivia, in five days of heroic action in which hundreds of victims fell, have culminated their fight with the complete triumph of the revolution, thereby restoring popular liberties.

Junta Recalls Political Exiles

"The Supreme Court of Justice of this [La Paz] district, with its president, have taken charge of a National Government by the mandate of the people who rose in arms. President Gualberto Villarroel is dead.

"It is decreed that political prisoners in the national territory and all exiles, without exception of political shades, may return with the object of collaborating in the restoration of liberties and democratic guarantees.

"From all the confines of the Republic have come messages of warm support for the restoration movement."

Worker groups demanded that the new Government promptly bring to trial on charges of "assassination" all Villarroel officials implicated in the firing-squad executions of Government opponents on Nov. 11, 1944, and June 6, 1946. They also asked for the removal of

Continued on Page 12, Column 2

Writer Uncurbed by 'Iron Curtain' Finds Poles Avoid Soviet Rigidity

By W. H. LAWRENCE

By Wireless to The New York Times.

BERLIN, July 22—I have just come back from behind "the iron curtain" and for me it was neither a barrier nor a screen.

After three weeks inside Poland I found, frankly, that conditions from a political and economic point of view were much better than I had expected.

I was free to go where I would and see whom I would—both friends and foes of the present Government. There was no censorship of anything I wrote and, unlike other correspondents who have been there, I encountered no hostility from Government quarters, which knew that the views I held were not the same as theirs.

Every facility for which I asked I obtained and I held interviews with all top governmental political figures. I thought they talked frankly with me on many subjects on which their opinions will not win friends for them in America.

The best example was the frank admission of nearly all Left-Wing leaders that the November Parliamentary elections will not in any sense be free, as the Western democracies understand that word. They will be more like the Soviet elections, with the Government attempting to control the result in advance through a single slate.

If Deputy Premier Stanislaw Mikolajczyk holds out, and it is apparent that he is going to try, then there will be a campaign of abuse and calumny, accompanied by Trojan horse tactics inside the Polish Peasant party designed to divide and conquer. If that fails, there is still the fact that the Government controls the vote-counting

Continued on Page 12, Column 3

Paraguayan Leader Seen Ready to Quit

By The Associated Press.

BUENOS AIRES, July 22—Advices tonight from Asunción reaching the town of Formosa on the Argentine-Paraguayan border said President Higinio Moriñigo of Paraguay had asked permission from the armed forces to resign and leave the country.

The advices added that President Moriñigo's entire Cabinet had presented its resignation and that the President then had told the Army chief that he wanted to resign and leave for Brazil some time this week.

The reason for the resignations was reported to be the outcome of yesterday's successful civilian revolution in neighboring Bolivia.

Gen. Vicente Machuca, Commander in Chief of the armed forces, was expected to be named acting President. The task of forming a new Cabinet was said to have been offered to the Febrerista and Colorado political groups.

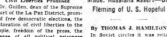

SOVIET SAYS ITS 'NO' ABOUT VETO IS FINAL

No Change in Stand Will Be Made, Russians Assert—Dr. Fleming of U. S. Hopeful

By THOMAS J. HAMILTON

In Soviet circles it was reiterated yesterday that the veto in the United Nations Security Council must remain unchanged. This, it was said, is the definite and final view of the Soviet Government, and it was declared that there would be no alteration no matter how many speeches were made in the General Assembly, where Dr. Herbert V. Evatt of Australia plans to raise the issue.

Mainly as a result of the disagreements at the meeting of the Big Four Foreign Ministers in Paris, which are expected to become still plainer when the other powers appear at the peace conference on July 29, hopes have been diminishing in recent weeks over the possibility of obtaining Russia's consent to abolition of the veto on atomic matters or to the establishment of an effective system of inspection.

American sources have expressed a belief recently that the Soviet Union ultimately would accept the establishment of an international atomic authority, with control over raw materials, but the veto and inspection are something else again.

Steps to Offset Soviet Plan

For this reason it is known that several delegations supporting the American plan have already begun study of possible steps to be taken in the event the Soviet Union remains obdurate. Presumably an effort would be made to have all the other members of the United Nations sign it, though, of course, if Russia remained outside the international control system much of the security to be gained from outlawing atomic weapons would be lost. Thus far, however, the American delegation in the United Nations Atomic Energy Commis-

Continued on Page 6, Column 4

JERUSALEM BOMB KILLS 41 IN ATTACK ON BRITISH OFFICES

52 BURIED IN DEBRIS

Zionist Terror Raiders Accused of Blast in King David Hotel

SHOOT BRITISH OFFICER

Strict Curfew Imposed in Hunt for Killers—Jewish Groups Urge End of Violence

By JULIAN LOUIS MELTZER

By Wireless to The New York Times.

JERUSALEM, July 22—An entire six-story corner and basement at the southwestern wing of the King David Hotel were destroyed and at least forty-one British, Jewish and Arab Government officials were killed and fifty-three were injured soon after midday when terrorists, believed to belong to either Irgun Zvai Leumi or the Stern gang, blew up a large part of the offices of the chief secretary of the Palestine Government.

Prominent Britons, including British Jews, are among the casualties. The dead include eight unidentified bodies, according to the latest semi-official figures, and fifty-two missing persons are buried under a huge pile of debris. They include twelve senior British civil servants and four senior Palestinian civil servants.

I was on the scene, outside the fashionable hotel—a Jerusalem landmark overlooking the Old City—just after the heavy explosions shattered the southwestern corner. Rescue operations had already been begun by British troops and police sweating under the hot July sun. They were bringing out bodies on stretchers, leaving a trail of blood over the rubble.

Postmaster General Killed

People standing outside or just entering or leaving the building were among the casualties. Postmaster General Gerald Donald Kennedy was killed outside the southern wing. The Superintendent of Police, Kenneth Page Hadingham, was badly injured. Richard Mowrer, correspondent of The New York Post, suffered a leg fracture.

The corner was destroyed by a heavy charge of gelignite planted in the basement by four or five armed gunmen. The six floors included a well-known basement cafe called La Regence and consisted of thirty or thirty-five rooms, mostly occupied by the chief secretary's offices. British Army headquarters had the entire top floor of the hotel and only a small section is situated at the southwestern corner. This explains the comparatively small casualties among the British military.

The first detonation occurred at about 12:10 P. M., when a small smoke-bomb exploded near a parked automobile on Julian's Way about fifty yards south of the hotel. It was intended to hold up all cars. Then came several shots from automatic guns.

Grenade Is Thrown

The second explosion came almost immediately as a man dressed in Arab clothing alighted from a blue limousine and threw a small grenade along a lane on the northern end of the hotel. A military sentry fired at him and the man threw away a submachine gun and limped to the car, which sped off toward the Jaffa Gate—one of the main gates of the walled Old City. The car was found abandoned later at the foot of the Tower of David, not far from district police headquarters.

Five minutes later came a third, shattering explosion. It was preceded by a mysterious telephone warning to the hotel's switchboard operator by a woman caller who said: "Tell everyone to leave the hotel. It is going to be blown up in a few minutes."

A few minutes before this third detonation a truck drove down the sunken driveway at the northern end of the hotel and four or five men jumped out at the service entrance to the kitchens. They assembled all the hotel staff—cooks, waiters and kitchen boys—below stairs at gunpoint as one man laid several milk cans full of explosives with fuses, wires and detonators. Then the men dashed off and the

Continued on Page 3, Column 2

"All the News That's Fit to Print"

The New York Times.

LATE CITY EDITION
Mostly sunny, less humid today. Partly cloudy, warm tomorrow.
Temperatures Yesterday—Max., 80; Min., 71
Sunrise today, 5:46 A. M.; Sunset, 8:18 P. M.
Full U. S. Weather Bureau Report, Page 25

VOL. XCV..No. 32,325. Entered as Second-Class Matter, Postoffice, New York, N. Y. NEW YORK, FRIDAY, JULY 26, 1946. THREE CENTS IN NEW YORK CITY

TRUMAN SIGNS THE OPA BILL; IF INEFFECTIVE HE INTENDS TO CALL A SPECIAL SESSION

CONGRESS WARNED

President in a Message Says It Must Act if Inflation Threatens

BILL 'FAR SHORT' OF HOPES

But It Is Worth a Trial, Executive Holds—Promises a Fair Decontrol Board

Text of Truman's Message to Congress on OPA, page 10.

By JOHN D. MORRIS
Special to THE NEW YORK TIMES.

WASHINGTON, July 25—President Truman signed the Price Control Bill shortly after it reached his desk today—"reluctantly," he said in a message to Congress, because it fails to assure the maintenance of stable prices.

The President stated in his message that if the combined efforts of the Government and the people under the new law failed to block inflation, "I shall have no alternative but to call the Congress back into special session to strengthen the price-control laws and to enact such fiscal and monetary legislation as we need to save us from the threat of economic disaster."

In signing the bill Mr. Truman ended a twenty-five-day hiatus in Federal price and rent controls, revalidating Office of Price Administration regulations and price schedules, with specified exceptions, that existed when the agency expired June 30. The legislation revives the OPA, with drastic restrictions on its powers, until next June 30.

Board to Be Named Soon

The President announced at a news conference that he would name members of a Decontrol Board, created by the bill, within a day or two. He said he had made up his mind on the selection of two members and was now trying to get the third one to accept.

The board, which will have power to order price controls removed from any commodity and to restore ceilings on exempted items after Aug. 20, will be an unpacked jury, Mr. Truman told reporters in reply to a question. He said no body connected with the OPA or the Office of Economic Stabilization would be appointed.

He announced further that he had put the OES under the Office of War Mobilization and Reconversion, with Dr. John R. Steelman in charge of both for the time being, and that he was considering a request of labor leaders to call a conference to discuss wage adjustments to compensate for price increases resulting from the expiration of price control.

Measure Held Improved

The President told Congress that its bill to revive price control fell "far short" of his hope for a measure under which the Government could assure the people with full confidence that prices would remain generally stable "in these last few months of the transition to a free economy."

He said he was advised, however, that it was the best bill that Congress would now pass and "it is clear, moreover, that it is a better bill than the one I was forced to veto on June 29."

"If that bill had become law," he stated, "inflation would have been inevitable. While the present measure by no means guarantees that inflation can be avoided, it offers a sufficient prospect of success to warrant the making of a whole-hearted effort to keep our economy on an even keel until a

Continued on Page 10, Column 6

OPA Rents Are Restored, New Price Rules Drafted

Proclamation Revives June 30 Ceilings and Voids Pay-Period Changes—Agency Completing 142 Other Decrees

By CHARLES E. EGAN
Special to THE NEW YORK TIMES.

WASHINGTON, July 25—A proclamation re-establishing all rent regulations of the Office of Price Administration which were in effect on June 30, when price controls lapsed, was issued within an hour after President Truman signed the compromise measure that Congress sent to him today.

The decree, putting rent controls back in effect in 520 rental areas and adding eight areas to the list, was the first of more than a hundred regulations and statements which will be coming from the OPA in the coming twenty-four hours. At a late hour tonight, officials at the price agency were at work putting the finishing touches on some 142 regulations granting higher ceilings on some items and removing other commodities from price controls entirely. The orders are scheduled to begin pouring from OPA headquarters at the opening of business tomorrow morning.

Although OPA officials made little secret of their feeling that a stronger measure should have been enacted by Congress, they evidenced gratitude that some measure of price control had been restored.

The attitude of the officials was perhaps summed up best in a brief statement authorized by Paul A. Porter, Price Administrator, after he had been conferring with President Truman for most of the afternoon.

"OPA will do its best to make this bill work and we think that it will work," Mr. Porter said. He added that "decisions on specific problems will be announced as rapidly as possible."

In announcing the restoration of rent controls, Ivan D. Carson, Deputy Administrator of OPA for Rent, said the new Federal law superseded all State and local rent controls which went into effect since July 1. He summarized the

Continued on Page 9, Column 1

House Votes $12,500 Pay And Expenses of $2,500

By C. P. TRUSSELL
Special to THE NEW YORK TIMES.

WASHINGTON, July 25—The House passed tonight its own Congressional reorganization bill, a measure designed to modernize the legislative branch so it might meet more effectively the impacts of the present-day load—and in doing it rejected a pay increase for each member from $10,000 a year to $15,000, such as the Senate recently approved.

Instead, the House voted, by voice, that the salary rise be to $12,500 a year, but added to this an expense account of $2,500 a year, payable in monthly installments, which would not have to be accounted for to anyone.

"Let's do it the honest way," shouted Representative Clarence J. Brown, Republican, of Ohio, sponsor of the change.

Many figured that the arrangement would mean more than the $15,000 salary as the Brown amendment specified that the $2,500 expense account would not be subject to income taxation.

Just before taking the passage vote, the House concurred with the Senate in approving a plan under which members of Congress could qualify for entry into the Federal retirement and pension system.

The final passage vote was 229 to 61.

The House measure now goes to conference for the adjustment of numerous differences between its program and that of the Senate.

It was predicted freely that these differences would be ironed out and that the first efforts of Congress since 1921 to reorganize its physical set-up and operational procedures would be sent to the White House for President Tru-

Continued on Page 5, Column 2

BUSINESS PLEDGES OPA COOPERATION

Industry Spokesmen Believe New Legislation Will Fail Without Price Increases

The "rebirth" of the Office of Price Administration found business and industry spokesmen eager yesterday to cooperate but unanimous in their belief that the new legislation would fail unless price increases were allowed and OPA officials adopted a "realistic attitude" that acknowledged the profit incentive and the competitive spirit.

It was generally agreed that business interests should recognize that the future of price control depended in part on the extent to which prices range in the next few weeks on meat, dairy products and other items now exempt but facing re-controls on Aug. 20.

A rush of applications by manufacturing companies for pricing adjustments was predicted. It was said also that much of the confusion bound to arise may be averted if the OPA will urge industry to

Continued on Page 11, Column 2

5th Avenue Bus Service Curtailed As 1,100 Employes Refuse Overtime

A "no overtime" strike by 1,100 members of the Transport Workers Union, CIO, curtailed service yesterday on bus lines of the Fifth Avenue Coach Company.

A company spokesman estimated that between twenty-five and thirty buses had been kept off the street by the decision of the union members not to work overtime and not to work on their days off. The union said its members would continue to refuse extra work until the company agreed to hire between seventy and one hundred war veterans as additional drivers.

The dispute seemed likely to force the discontinuance tonight of special bus service to the Lewisohn Stadium concerts. The union had originally planned to withdraw its members from this service Tuesday, but agreed to a two-day extension at the request of Mayor O'Dwyer. Edmund C. Collins, vice president of the company, said it would be impossible to run special buses to the concerts unless the union cancelled its ban on overtime work.

Slower service and increased congestion on regular bus runs were the immediate result of the controversy, with Mr. Collins predicting further disruption of service if the impasse over extra work continued. He said 15 to 20 per cent of the normal service was represented by the buses idle yesterday.

Austin Hogan, president of Local 100 of the CIO union, maintained that the responsibility for the situation rested with the company because of its refusal to take on more drivers. Mr. Collins said that the company had hired fifty veterans two months ago and was reluctant to take on more because it wanted to hold jobs open for con-

Continued on Page 19, Column 2

HEART ATTACK BARS MAY'S APPEARANCE TO TESTIFY TODAY

Committee Hears He Appealed to Eisenhower Over Army's Trial of Young Garsson

SERVICE PLANS AN INQUIRY

Report Finds Mortar Deaths Were Not Linked to Part Which Subjects Made

By JOSEPH A. LOFTUS
Special to THE NEW YORK TIMES.

WASHINGTON, July 25—The Senate War Investigating Committee was advised late today that Representative Andrew J. May, chairman of the House Military Affairs Committee, had suffered a heart attack and would not be able to appear as a witness tomorrow in the committee's inquiry into the munitions business of Dr. Henry M. Garsson and associates.

[Dr. Garsson told The United Press in Chicago that Joseph Freeman, his lawyer, had telephoned from Washington that Mr. May was "not expected to live through the night."

[The Associated Press reported from Washington that Mr. Freeman, in a telegram addressed to newspapers, had denied making such a telephone call. He said all he knew of Mr. May's illness was what he had heard on the radio.]

Among the disclosures today was a document showing that Representative May appealed to General Eisenhower in the spring of 1945 in behalf of Capt. Joseph H. Garsson, son of Murray Garsson, when the captain faced disciplinary action in France for disobeying a superior officer. The document showed that Gen. Alden H. Waitt, present chief of the Chemical Warfare Service, carried a letter from Mr. May to General Eisenhower's headquarters.

Army Plans Own Inquiry

The War Department stated, meanwhile, it would conduct its own inquiry into the matters which the Mead committee brought out in relation to the Army. The Department said, however, that the two letters from Mr. May were handled in "the normal routine manner" and had "no influence whatever in the disposition of the case."

An additional report, still incomplete, to the Mead committee on

Continued on Page 4, Column 5

ALL-CIVILIAN RULE OF ATOM IS VOTED IN CONFERENCE BILL

Completed Measure Gives Post Just Under the Commission to Military Director

ARMY CAN ASSEMBLE BOMB

House Yields on Licensing and Patents—Fight on Changes Seen in Lower Chamber

By WILLIAM S. WHITE
Special to THE NEW YORK TIMES.

WASHINGTON, July 25—The creation of an all-civilian commission to control atomic energy and to exercise Government monopoly over the terrible new force, under the greatest grant of administrative power in the history of this country, was approved today by Senate and House conferees.

This was the central feature of a compromise reached at the end of two days of negotiations to reconcile the sharply differing bills passed previously in both houses. At the two most vital points, it represented a victory for the Senate plan.

The House delegation receded from its demand for military representation on the control commission, and yielded as well to the more stringent patent and licensing controls insisted upon by the Senate.

Two Provisions on the Military

In turn, the Senate conferees deferred to their colleagues, accepting two provisions to keep the military close to, although not on, the councils of ultimate power and decision.

One of these was that the director of military application of atomic energy, to serve just under the control commission, must be a military man.

The other was that, if the President so directed, the Army and Navy could assemble their own atomic weapons, using the essential force to be supplied by the commission itself.

Military participation at a high point already had been assured by the acceptance earlier of a provision for a military liaison committee that would be abreast of every step taken or contemplated by the commission. It would have the right to appeal to the President, through the Secretaries of War and Navy, against any contemplated action deemed injurious to military or national security.

Continued on Page 3, Column 6

World News Summarized

FRIDAY, JULY 26, 1946

Federalization of Palestine, with major authority vested in a British-controlled central government over separate Arab and Zionist provinces enjoying limited autonomy, has been urged upon Washington and London by the Anglo-American Cabinet Committee, it was learned last night. The existing mandate would be transferred to a trusteeship status under the plan, which recommends delaying the admission of 100,000 Jews to the Holy Land until the "federalist constitution" has been approved. The Arab League has been invited to conferences in London and Zionist reaction will also be sought. [1:8.]

Zionist leaders in Jerusalem discussed but reached no decision on what steps to take to prevent further terrorist activities. The Jewish Agency for Palestine denied the authenticity of telegrams quoted in the British White Paper linking that body with disorders. [4:4.]

The British Cabinet delayed action on the American proposal to unify the two powers' zones in Germany until Russia had positively stated her position on treating the country as an economic whole. [6:7.]

Premier de Gasperi's Government won an overwhelming vote of confidence from the Italian Assembly and was instructed to "fight for a just and honorable peace." [5:1.]

Yugoslavia, while admitting that some priests had been executed as war criminals, denied the existence of an anti-Catholic persecution plan. [6:2-3.]

Reports from Bikini indicated that eleven ships had been sunk and six damaged in the underwater atomic bomb test. [1:6-7.]

Domestic atomic energy control was restored to an all-civilian commission but with closer liaison with military departments in the bill reported by conferees to the Senate and the House. [1:5.]

In China's civil war Nanking claimed and the Communists conceded further gains by Government forces in the Kiangsu-Anhwei area. [1:7; map P. 2.]

At least 750,000 tons of wheat should be rushed from this country to India, the American Famine Mission reported on its return to Washington. [18:7.]

President Truman "reluctantly" signed the compromise OPA bill into law, holding that while it "by no means guarantees that inflation can be avoided" it was sufficiently better than the measure he vetoed to justify giving it a trial. [1:1.] The OPA immediately re-established all rent controls [1:2-3] and Governor Dewey declared the State rent control law ended. [8:3-4.]

Business and industrial leaders in New York predicted a rush of applications for price adjustments and asked OPA officials to administer the new law with a "realistic attitude." [1:2.]

The House passed its own version of a Congressional reorganization, including raising its members' salaries to $12,500 a year plus $2,500 expenses. [1:2-3.] The President urged House leaders to speed action on the long-range housing program "so essential to the welfare of veterans" as "time is of the essence." [8:2.]

The President returned the functions of the Office of Economic Stabilization to the Office of War Mobilization and Reconversion under Director Steelman. [9:1.] He also nominated James E. Webb to be Director of the Budget. Treasury Secretary Snyder indicated that he would seek no new tax legislation this year. [1:6-7.]

Representative May of Kentucky, who was to testify today on his connections with the Garsson munitions combine, has suffered a heart attack and will not be able to appear, the Senate War Investigating Committee was informed. [1:4.]

DIVIDED PALESTINE IS URGED BY ANGLO-U. S. CABINET BODY, DELAYING ENTRY OF 100,000

NEW DEAL IN HOLY LAND PROPOSED

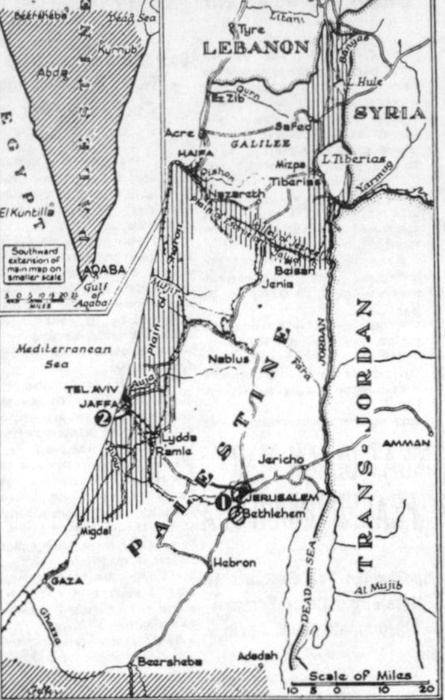

Under the plan for federalization suggested by the Anglo-American Cabinet Committee, Government areas would be those shown on the map by diagonal shading, plus Jerusalem and Bethlehem and their environs (1). Zionist areas would be those indicated by vertical shading, with the exception of Jaffa (2), which would remain Arab. The rest of Palestine would be Arab areas.

PARTITION SOUGHT

Zionists Would Get 1,500 Square Miles Under Tight Federal Rule

GRADY FAVORS PROPOSAL

Both Sides Will Be Consulted —Immigration May Depend on Approval of Plan

By MICHAEL L. HOFFMAN
By Wireless to THE NEW YORK TIMES.

LONDON, July 25—A so-called federalist constitution for Palestine is recommended to the American and British Governments in the report of the Anglo-American Cabinet Committee studying the problem, it was learned today.

The proposed constitution would vest strong powers in a British-controlled central government, leaving very little autonomy to the separate Arab and Zionist provinces. The report also proposes that the admission of 100,000 homeless European Jews to Palestine, urged ten months ago by President Truman and recommended as an immediate step by the Anglo-American Committee of Inquiry on Palestine, be made conditional on the adoption of the federalization proposal.

The exact wording of the recommendation presented to Mr. Truman on the admittance of the 100,000 new immigrants is that the plan is "to be initiated immediately it is decided to put the constitutional proposals into effect." This is the real meaning of the statements of the British early in the London discussion to the effect that they agreed on the admission of the recommended number of new immigrants.

Arab States to Confer

It will not be decided whether to put the proposals into effect until after the conference of the Arab League States in London, for which the British Government issued invitations today. The date will be sometime before Sept. 23, the tentative date of the next meeting of the United Nations' General Assembly. Though it is fairly obvious in advance what the Arabs' reaction will be, their views will be sought on the whole plan, including the entry of the 100,000 Jews.

The plan calls for dividing Palestine into Zionist, Arab and central-government districts. The central government would directly control Jerusalem, Bethlehem and their environs, and the region known as Negev, south of Beersheba.

The Zionist district would include about two-thirds of the southern coastal Plain of Sharon, except Jaffa, the Plain of Esdraelon, the Valley of Jezreel and eastern Galilee north of Beisan. The rest of Palestine would be Arab.

1,500 Square Miles for Jews

The Zionist district would include 1,500 square miles, compared with the 2,600 recommended by the Peel report proposing partition in 1936 and the 45,000 in the area constituting Palestine when it was originally promised as a Jewish "national home."

The most striking aspect of the proposals is the degree of power to be left in the hands of the central government, which, contrary to advanced reports, is far greater than the British have proposed in the case of India. Under the plan the British would control defense, foreign relations, the police, prisons, the courts, railway and port facilities in Haifa, the postoffice, the telephone and telegraph systems, customs, excise taxes, civil aviation, broadcasting and antiquities. They would also retain final authority over immigration, but the provincial governments would have the right of appeal to the United Nations' Trusteeship Council.

The provinces would have their own assemblies but the central government would appoint speakers without whose approval no bill could become law. The executive authority in the provinces would be vested in councils of ministers appointed by the British High Commissioner. He would have emergency power to supercede a provincial government in whole or in part. Under such a constitution, Palestine's provinces would have

Continued on Page 4, Column 3

11 Ships Sunk, 6 Damaged In Maelstrom of Atom Test

By HANSON W. BALDWIN
By Wireless to THE NEW YORK TIMES.

ABOARD U. S. S. APPALACHIAN, in Bikini Lagoon, Friday, July 26—Gone—but not forgotten—are the "Sara" and the "Ark." These two proud ships of the Navy, veterans of years of service, today lay deep in the blue-green waters from which no ships return as the toll of vessels sunk and damaged in yesterday's atomic blast slowly mounted.

Thirty fathoms down, on the bottom of Bikini Lagoon, the mighty carrier Saratoga and the doughty old battleship Arkansas lay wrecked and riven—their war records still painted on their bulkheads, their traditions forever alive in the minds of men. Beside them, canted on their beams' ends or deep in the muck, were the five battered victims of the first atomic test on July 1 and at least four other craft sunk in yesterday's subsurface burst—the first underwater explosion of an atomic bomb in history.

[Press-service and other reports indicated that eleven ships had been sunk, although this total included five submerged submarines, whose condition apparently had not been fully established. At least six other ships appeared to be damaged.]

The official toll—at an early

Continued on Page 3, Column 2

SIX CHIANG DRIVES ROUT CHINESE REDS

Communists Tell of Losses in Fighting North of Nanking—New Peace Talks Likely

By HENRY R. LIEBERMAN
By Wireless to THE NEW YORK TIMES.

NANKING, July 25—Gen Tang En-po's Nationalist troops have captured Lingpi, fifty-five miles southeast of the rail junction of Suchow, and have penetrated fifty miles from the south into the Kiangsu-Anhwei border region, Communist sources said today.

The farthest advance on the southern front was said to be in the area of Pantachi, forty-five miles north of Nanking, which had already been captured by the Cen-

Continued on Page 2, Column 3

Webb Is Named for Budget Chief; Republicans Asks 20% Tax Cut

By JOHN H. CRIDER
Special to THE NEW YORK TIMES.

WASHINGTON, July 25—President Truman today nominated James E. Webb, 39-year-old former vice president of the Sperry Gyroscope Company, to be Director of the Budget, succeeding Harold D. Smith, who resigned to become vice president of the World Bank.

Announcement of the appointment was made as the House Republican Tax Study Committee called for a 20 per cent reduction in taxes next year and denounced "reckless spending of the people's money" by the Administration.

On the other hand, John W. Snyder, Secretary of the Treasury, when asked at his news conference what he was going to do now about balancing the budget this year when estimates of expenditures were constantly mounting, replied that he must "work diligently to curtail Federal expenditures and encourage economy in Government."

Another Treasury official, commenting on the statement of the House Republicans, observed that about 50 per cent of Federal spending in the current year was for the Army, the Navy and veterans. He asked if the Republicans would care to reduce those items.

Secretary Snyder said there would be no tax recommendations from the Treasury until Congress returned, which would probably not be until after the first of the year.

Meanwhile, O. Max Gardner, Under-Secretary of the Treasury, met with the Treasury's tax staff to prepare extensive studies of the Federal tax system for Congress in connection with tax legislation

Continued on Page 10, Column 2

Rita Hayworth, the flamboyant movie star of the 1940s, in *Gilda.*

Larry Parks as Al Jolson in *The Jolson Story.*

Sig Ruman and Harpo Marx in *A Night in Casablanca.*

Italian soldiers move up in Rome to control a demonstration protesting the internationalization of Trieste.

Among other Nazis at the final session of the Nuremberg trials were (front row, left to right) Field Marshal Hermann Göring, Rudolf Hess, Foreign Minister Joachim von Ribbentrop and Field Marshal Wilhelm Keitel.

The first stirrings of the Cold War took place at the bombed-out Potsdamer Platz in Berlin, when U.S. and Russian troops engaged in conflict.

"All the News That's Fit to Print"

The New York Times.

LATE CITY EDITION
Partly cloudy and cool today.
Fair and cool tomorrow.
Temperatures Yesterday—Max., 68; Min., 54
Sunrise today, 5:51 A. M.; Sunset, 5:40 P. M.
Full U. S. Weather Bureau Report, Page 47

VOL. XCVI—No. 32,392. Entered as Second-Class Matter, Postoffice, New York, N. Y. NEW YORK, TUESDAY, OCTOBER 1, 1946. THREE CENTS NEW YORK CITY

ALL EXCEPT 3 OF NAZI WAR CHIEFS GUILTY; GOERING, HESS, VON RIBBENTROP CONVICTED; SCHACHT, VON PAPEN, FRITZSCHE ACQUITTED

PORT TIE-UP BEGINS AS SEA UNIONS CALL STRIKE OF OFFICERS

Government Efforts to Stave Off Second Walkout in a Month Prove Unavailing

TOTAL PARALYSIS FEARED

Stoppage Comes Only 11 Days After Previous Settlement—Picketing Starts Today

By JACK SHANLEY

The nation faced its second critical maritime strike in a month today as union members of the Marine Engineers Beneficial Association, CIO, and the Masters, Mates and Pilots, AFL, went on strike after ineffective Government efforts to defer the walkout had extended past a midnight deadline.

Word of the MEBA decision to strike came from Washington shortly before 12:30 A. M. There had been previous indications that all-day-and-night sessions in the capital might bring about a postponement of the walkout, and they were strengthened when the hour for the strike passed and no announcement was made.

The engineers' decision to strike will bring about a repetition of the virtually complete immobilization of deep-water commerce that affected every major port on the Atlantic, Gulf and Pacific Coasts during the sixteen-day walkout involving AFL and CIO workers that was settled only eleven days ago.

Either Can Cripple Commerce

Either the MEBA or the MMP can effectively cripple merchant marine activities on the three coasts since each represents about 90 per cent of the total officer personnel of its respective department (engine and deck) on American dry cargo and passenger vessels.

Word of the MEBA decision to strike was received here by members of Local 33 at a mass meeting that began at 8 P. M. at Manhattan Plaza, 66 East Fourth Street.

They were told to proceed immediately after the strike announcement to MEBA strike headquarters at Irving Plaza, Irving Place at Fifteenth Street, to register for strike duty.

Picketing was scheduled to begin at 7 A. M. today.

All MEBA contract ships are to be picketed except tankers, colliers, "bona fide" troop ships and Army and Navy supply vessels, according to the instructions.

MEBA members in San Francisco were told to walk out at 9 A. M. today. All vessels except foreign-flag, Army and Navy ships and tankers will be affected. Twenty-four hours' grace will be given for unloading refrigerated cargo vessels.

On the West Coast, a spokesman for the militant 25,000-man International Longshoremen's and Warehousemen's Union, CIO, headed by Harry Bridges, announced at 12:05 A. M. that "we are officially on strike but are remaining in negotiations." He did not amplify this statement.

Conciliators Are Cheered

Labor Department conciliators in Washington had been cheered early last night by reports that the ILWU had deferred strike action until 8 A. M. today.

It had been reported early last night that refusal of West Coast operators to budge on union demands for security was the chief stumbling block in the Washington negotiations.

The MMP, which had operated on a "no contract, no work" basis, and had not taken a strike vote is expected to do so in the next few days. Meanwhile, its members will not cross picket lines.

The estimated membership of the MMP is 12,000; the MEBA, 15,000.

Paul Palazzi, New York port agent for the National Maritime Union, CIO, said that trustees of the New York Port Committee for Maritime Unity, in a meeting yes-

Continued on Page 5, Column 3

Moving Day Finds City Staying Put

Five years ago this morning, traditional moving date, trucking outfits in this city expected to move "about 1,000,000 people," from apartment to apartment. They expected "the worst moving jam in history."

New Yorkers were described as "nomadic," and it was estimated that the average New York City family moved to new quarters every eighteen months.

Yesterday Louis Schramm Jr. of the Movers and Warehousemen's Association of Greater New York laughed and commented:

"Sorry, there's no story on Moving Day. You see, there's no moving."

He added, however, that moving companies were doing a lot of business in transferring furniture and similar articles from storage houses to the docks for shipment abroad, where large business concerns were expanding post-war operations, chiefly in South America.

PLANE OVER COAST IN RECORD FLIGHT

Truculent Turtle Spans Pacific From Australia in 44 Hours —Heads On to the East

By The Associated Press.

SEATTLE, Tuesday, Oct. 1—The Navy announced at 12:45 A. M., Eastern standard time Tuesday, that the Navy patrol bomber Truculent Turtle was over the United States mainland and definitely had broken the world long distance non-stop flight record. The record was 7,916 miles and the distance covered by the plane to the Coast was approximately 9,243 miles.

[A Salt Lake City dispatch said the Truculent Turtle was reported over Humboldt, Nev., about 2:35 A. M., New York time, by the Elko Tower.]

They said the plane, making landfall after a flight from Perth, Australia, in less than forty-four hours, was in voice communication with several Civil Aeronautics Administration wireless stations and that the pilot would shortly decide his future course. The Navy said he was checking weather conditions, his plane's fuel supply and other data before making a decision as to continuing his flight.

One message from the plane, intercepted here, asked weather reports to Scotts Bluff, Neb.

Another said: "We are climbing to 12,000 feet. Have you any reports of icing. I am unequipped with de-icing equipment."

Apparently the plane was in the Red Bluff, Calif., area at the time.

The Thirteenth Naval District headquarters here said weather conditions from Red Bluff eastward included an eight-mile-an-hour tail wind, with excellent visibility and a high-pressure area east of the mountains virtually to the

Continued on Page 6, Column 3

PRICE AID TO BRING MORE MEAT BARRED BY ANDERSON RULING

He Keeps Product on Short Supply List While Admitting Range Cattle Abundance

ASKS LIVESTOCK RELEASE

Plea to Growers Cites Public —Thompson Suggests Two Meatless Days a Week

By BESS FURMAN
Special to THE NEW YORK TIMES.

WASHINGTON, Sept. 30—Secretary of Agriculture Anderson retained meat today on his list of commodities which are in short supply. The action apparently ended any possibility of early price decontrol in the meat field.

Announcement of the new short supply list followed a speech by Mr. Anderson at his home town of Albuquerque, N. M., where he is on vacation. In the speech he declared that in the list he could not mention "range cattle" because the supply of range cattle was adequate, even on some ranges more than adequate.

"I must deal with pork and mutton and beef," he added. "Beef, to look at receipts in Chicago and Kansas City, is in short supply. Hogs are also short, to look at receipts. Cattle receipts at twelve markets for the week up to last Thursday totaled 160,000, whereas a year ago they totaled 305,000. Hogs were 26,200, against 95,200.

"That, to a nation that already has 80,000,000 cattle—52,000,000 of them beef cattle—may have some serious implications."

His speech was to a meeting of cattle men of his home State and he asked cooperation of the live stock industry in "trying to bring meat back to the American public in lawful trade at legitimate prices."

He called on growers to "sit down" with him and "see if, working within the framework of what the Congress has given us and the Decontrol Board has decreed, we cannot preserve in legitimate channels the great meat industry of the United States."

Roy L. Thompson, chairman of the Price Decontrol Board, indicated that the board planned no action pending possible receipt on appeal of a petition for decontrol from the OPA's Meat Industry Advisory Committee. Such a petition is scheduled to be filed with Secretary Anderson Oct. 8 or 9.

Mr. Thompson expressed astonishment at the number of members of Congress, Republicans and Democrats, who have been sending the board telegrams calling it "bullheaded" for not taking off the meat controls immediately.

"We did expect them to know what they placed in our lap to handle, but they overlooked it," he commented.

His plea on the whole length and

Continued on Page 4, Column 2

JUDGMENT DAY: NAZI LEADERS WHO HAVE LEARNED THEIR FATE

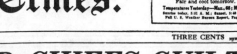

The defendants in the prisoners' box in Nuremberg yesterday. Front row, left to right: Hermann Goering, Rudolf Hess, Joachim von Ribbentrop, Wilhelm Keitel, Ernst Kaltenbrunner, Alfred Rosenberg, Hans Frank, Wilhelm Frick, Julius Streicher, Walther Funk and Hjalmar Schacht. Rear row, left to right: Karl Doenitz, Erich Raeder, Baldur von Schirach, Fritz Sauckel, Alfred Jodl, Franz von Papen, Arthur Seyss-Inquart, Albert Speer, Constantin von Neurath and Hans Fritzsche. At the lower right are unidentified court attachés. Associated Press Radiophoto

TITO'S 'PROPAGANDA' STIRS U. S. PROTEST

Note Charges Yugoslavs Make 'Mischievous' Statements and Ignore AMG Rules in Trieste

The State Department's note to Yugoslavia is on Page 15.

By WALTER H. WAGGONER
Special to THE NEW YORK TIMES.

WASHINGTON, Sept. 30—The United States, in a strong and impatient note, today accused the Yugoslav Government of ignoring Allied military regulations in Trieste and issuing "mischievous

Continued on Page 15, Column 1

U. S. to Support Turks Again In Straits Row With Russia

Special to THE NEW YORK TIMES.

WASHINGTON, Sept. 30—The State Department tonight indicated a probability that the United States again would intervene diplomatically in the dispute between Soviet Russia and Turkey over control over the Dardanelles and Bosporus, linking the Black Sea with the Mediterranean.

In response to questions, a department spokesman issued a statement that, while it denied any special request from Turkey for this country's views, hinted strongly that the United States Government might follow its previous course and give its views to the Russians, Turks and British.

The statement further declared that if such a course were followed

Continued on Page 15, Column 5

World News Summarized

TUESDAY, OCTOBER 1, 1946

All but three of the twenty-two Nazi war leaders were convicted in verdicts delivered by the International Military Tribunal this morning. Those cleared were Hjalmar Schacht, Franz von Papen and Hans Fritzsche. Hermann Goering, Wilhelm Keitel, Alfred Rosenberg, Constantin von Neurath, Alfred Jodl and Joachim von Ribbentrop were convicted on all four counts against them and Rudolf Hess was convicted on two. Sentences were to be pronounced later today. [1:8.]

Two major issues probably will remain unsolved at the Conference of Paris and be handed to the Council of Foreign Ministers. Although the United States and Britain accepted a French proposal establishing the principle that the Danube shall be free to the commerce of all nations, it was not carried by a two-thirds vote. The Slav bloc opposed the compromise. [1:6.]

American warships will remain in the Mediterranean and eastern Atlantic to support United States foreign policy and protect United States interests, Secretary Forrestal declared. This country has no intention of acquiring any European shore bases, he added. [1:7.]

The State Department intimated that it might intervene again in the Dardanelles dispute between Russia and Turkey after consultations with the War and Navy Departments. [1:5-6.]

Ranking Navy officers disclosed that United States plans in the Pacific included conversion of Guam into a powerful base linked by a chain of airfields and natural anchorages with Pearl Harbor, development of Truk and establishment of other bases. [5:5.]

Washington rejected Belgrade's protest against the arrest of six Yugoslav UNRRA guards and expressed resentment at "mischievous propaganda without any foundation in fact" in the Belgrade note. [1:4.]

An Arab "shadow government" for Palestine, headed by the exiled Mufti of Jerusalem, was reported by Arab sources. [11:1.]

General Eisenhower declared that there was "too much pessimism in the world about international relations." [17:5.]

The World Bank is now ready to consider applications for reconstruction loans and the International Monetary Fund will soon start currency evaluation for world trade stabilization, the Governors of the two institutions were informed. [33:2.]

Fleet Admiral King demanded what amounted to a public apology from the Senate War Investigating Committee for having singled him out as "the villain of the piece," in its Canol project report. [1:6-7.]

Massachusetts investigators discovered 6,000,000 pounds of dressed meat during the first day of a search for hidden supplies [4:6], and in this city Mayor O'Dwyer, saying that the meat shortage "smacks of a conspiracy against the public," ordered a similar search. [1:4.] Secretary Anderson declared meats to be in short supply and not subject to lifting of price ceilings. [1 3.]

There was no indication, as the midnight deadline passed, that a new maritime strike could be averted. [1:1.] Federal conciliators pressed their efforts toward some settlement. [3:3-4.]

Labor Department mediators trying to end the Pittsburgh power strike planned to bring both sides together again. [2:5.]

The Navy patrol bomber Truculent Turtle, after a forty-four-hour silence, reached the United States early today, establishing a new non-stop distance record on its flight from Australia. [1:2.]

U. S. DROPS DEMAND FOR DANUBE PLEDGE

Joins With Britain at Paris in French Plan for a Big Four Parley With River States

By MICHAEL L. HOFFMAN
Special to THE NEW YORK TIMES.

PARIS, Sept. 30—The United States and Britain withdrew today a demand for the incorporation in the Rumanian peace treaty of clauses specifying measures Rumania should take to insure nondiscriminatory administration of the Danube.

On behalf of the United States and Britain, Senator Arthur H. Vandenberg accepted a French proposal put forward at the conference of Paris as a "compromise." It retained a statement of the principle that the Danube should be free to the commerce of all nations and provided that the international conference consider a new international regime for the river.

United States sources denied that acceptance of the French proposal constituted a retreat from the United States' position in favor

Continued on Page 14, Column 3

NAVY PUT IN EUROPE AS POLICY BULWARK

Forrestal Says Warships Arm Our Foreign Views—Denies We Seek Shore Bases

Special to THE NEW YORK TIMES.

WASHINGTON, Sept. 30—Secretary of the Navy James Forrestal, in a firm and clear statement of naval policy, declared today that United States naval forces were in the Mediterranean and eastern Atlantic to support American foreign policy and that they would remain there. He also asserted that we had no intention of acquiring European shore bases.

There is nothing new in the use of United States naval vessels in European waters, the Cabinet officer declared. His statement, in effect, said the Navy was engaged in a useful and legitimate mission and intended to continue with this mission.

Policy Criticized by Russia

The statement was temperately worded. It did not mention the observations of any foreign powers. There was no reference to the criticisms that Russia and some of her satellite states had been pouring on the United States for having sent carriers, battleships, cruisers and destroyers to the troubled Mediterranean area.

Mr. Forrestal asserted that the Navy was "continuing to maintain forces" in the eastern Atlantic and Mediterranean to support the Allied occupation forces and the Military Government and "to protect United States interests and to support United States policies."

He stated that overseas opera-

Continued on Page 14, Column 4

Admiral King Accuses Senators Of Unfairness in Report on Canol

By WILLIAM S. WHITE

WASHINGTON, Sept. 30—Admiral Ernest J. King accused the Senate War Investigating Committee today of treating him unfairly and demanded the equivalent of a public apology.

In two and a half hours in the witness chair, the former chief of naval operations stood on his assertion that a committee report condemning him in connection with the $133,000,000 wartime Canol oil project was "a willful distortion of the facts."

Although Chairman Harley M. Kilgore of West Virginia told him that his accusation was tantamount to calling the committee "a liar," Admiral King made no use of several opportunities to soften his statement.

He made it plain, however, that the basis of his protest was that he was "singled out" for the committee's rebuke when he believed that the other members of the Joint Chiefs of Staff should have shared it with him.

In its recently issued fifth annual report the committee denounced the Canol Project, designed to obtain petroleum from the Norman wells in Canada, as a "flaring waste which had been persisted in by the Joint Chiefs of Staff," after the Secretary of the Navy, the Petroleum Administrator and the Budget Director had opposed it, and after the committee had urged its abandonment.

For this, the report largely put the blame on Admiral King and Gen. Brehon B. Somervell, wartime chief of the Army Service Forces, and it asserted:

"This action constitutes a blot upon the records of two otherwise able officers."

To answer this and other accusa-

Continued on Page 8, Column 5

VERDICTS ARE IN

Nuremberg Court Gives Findings That Point to Death for Many

4 COUNTS INVOLVED

Goering Is Among Six Guilty on All—Fate to Be Heard Today

By The United Press.

NUREMBERG, Tuesday, Oct. 1—Hermann Goering, Rudolf Hess, Joachim von Ribbentrop and sixteen other arch-conspirators of the Nazi regime were found guilty of war crimes by the International Military Tribunal today, and it was virtually certain that all or most of them would hang or be shot.

Three of the twenty-two defendants, Hjalmar Schacht, Franz von Papen and Hans Fritzsche, were acquitted on all four counts of the indictment—the common plan or conspiracy to wage aggressive war, crimes against the peace, crimes violating the laws of war and crimes against humanity.

Six of the defendants were found guilty of all four counts—Goering, von Ribbentrop, Field Marshal Wilhelm Keitel, Alfred Rosenberg, Col. Gen. Alfred Jodl and Constantin von Neurath.

Sentences This Afternoon

Sentences will be pronounced by the court at the afternoon session which begins at 12:30 P. M. (5:30 A. M., EST).

It was expected the judges representing the four great powers, the United States, Russia, Britain and France, would mete out the supreme penalty against most of those convicted and that it would be carried out within two weeks.

Goering, the man who was subordinate only to Adolf Hitler in Nazi Germany, was the first on whom sentence was passed. The tribunal denounced him bitterly in rendering its verdict.

"There is nothing to be said in mitigation," the tribunal said. "Goering often, indeed almost always, was the moving force second only to his leader.

"He was a leading war aggressor, both as a political and as a military leader. He was a director of the slave-labor program and a creator of the oppressive program against the Jews and other races at home. All these crimes he frankly admitted. His guilt is unique in its enormity—the record discloses no excuses for this man."

Unrelenting Toward Hess

The court was equally unrelenting toward Hess, Hitler's close friend, the man who made the fabulous "peace" flight mission to Britain and who, feigned or actual, has acted like an insane man since his capture and during the trial.

Guilty of the worst crimes man can commit, too, was Joachim von Ribbentrop, the champagne salesman turned master diplomat—the Hitler henchman who put the clamps on Austria and Czechoslovakia and tried the same tactics on Poland, advising war when that country, backed by France and Britain, stood firm.

Brief findings read out by the Tribunal were:

Ernest Kaltenbrunner, head

Continued on Page 13, Column 1

The text of the French draft constitution, which was passed by the Assembly in Paris on Sunday and will be voted on in a referendum on Oct. 13, appears on Page 16.

Sarnoff Predicts Weather Control And Delivery of the Mail by Radio

Control of the weather by man is a scientific possibility of the future, Brig. Gen. David Sarnoff, president of the Radio Corporation of America, said last night in a speech at a testimonial dinner in the Waldorf-Astoria Hotel commemorating his forty years of service to radio.

Other possibilities, General Sarnoff asserted, include delivery of mail by radio, portable communication sets that will enable one individual to communicate with another anywhere, transformation of deserts into gardens through diversion of ocean currents and nuclear energy, world-wide television and use of atomic energy to combat disease.

These developments, he said, are the alternative to devastation and destruction from atomic bombs and rocket-propagated disease germs if peace becomes the chosen course of man.

War, with the new weapons that scientific ingenuity can devise, he declared, would bring an abrupt end to all progress. Discussing the matter with noted men of science at home and abroad, he asserted, he had shown scant hope that an adequate defense can be provided against new weapons capable of mass destruction on a world-wide scale.

Besides General Sarnoff, speakers at the dinner included Owen D. Young, retired chairman of the board of General Electric, and Dr. Karl T. Compton, president of Massachusetts Institute of Technology. Lieut. Gen. James G. Harbord, chairman of the RCA board, was toastmaster.

General Sarnoff, who started his career as an office boy in the New York headquarters of the Marconi Wireless Telegraph Company of America, told an audience of industrialists, educators and scientists that the world has seen only

Continued on Page 48, Column 3

"All the News That's Fit to Print"

The New York Times.

LATE CITY EDITION
Sunny and mild today. Fair and warmer tomorrow.
Temperatures Yesterday—Max., 69; Min., 52
Sunrise today, 6:07 A. M.; Sunset, 5:15 P. M.
Full U. S. Weather Bureau Report, Page 55

VOL. XCVI. No. 32,407. Entered as Second-Class Matter, Postoffice, New York, N. Y. NEW YORK, WEDNESDAY, OCTOBER 16, 1946. THREE CENTS IN NEW YORK CITY

GOERING ENDS LIFE BY POISON, 10 OTHERS HANGED IN NUREMBERG PRISON FOR NAZI WAR CRIMES; DOOMED MEN ON GALLOWS PRAY FOR GERMANY

RETAILERS OFFER $1 A POUND MEAT; SUPPLY UNCERTAIN

Wholesale Prices Rise Far Above Former OPA Ceiling Rates for the City

POULTRY SHOWS DECLINE

Consumer Council Promises to Retaliate With Plan for 'Political Action'

By DORIS GREENBERG

Meat reappeared yesterday in many retailers' showcases. The asking prices ranged from former ceilings to a flat "dollar-a-pound for anything you see." Some consumers just looked, but others lined up to wait their turn.

The overnight change from near-famine to comparative plenty—evident in most areas of the city, but not in Nassau or Westchester—was explained thus by Joseph Eschelbacher, secretary of the New York State Association of Retail Meat Dealers:

"Some butchers had meat that they planned to stretch out over a week or so. Others went out and bought some in the morning. They wouldn't buy black, but black is white now."

Replenishments to Be Available

President Truman's radio address, in which he announced abandonment of meat controls, meant to butchers that replenishments will be available in a few days, Mr. Eschelbacher said.

Not only will supplies move quickly through regular channels, but retailers will again be able to compete against buyers for hotel and restaurant supply houses that could legally offer higher bids under Office of Price Administration rulings, Mr. Eschelbacher asserted.

Whether cuts of meat will still be on view later this week was a big question in trade circles. Another unanswered query was the probable price of meat next week.

Clyde F. House, United States Department of Agriculture market analyst here, offered without comment the facts that little meat was sold "openly" by wholesalers yesterday. Transactions that were observed were completed at prices far in excess of former ceilings.

Sample Prices Provided

Cautioning that unsettled conditions prevented assessing any trend, he provided these sample prices:

Cow beef, $50 a hundredweight, compared with the former ceiling of $20.05; good and choice steer beef, $55 to $60, compared with $25.50 to $26.80; commercial veal, $30 to $36, compared with $20.05; good and choice veal, $32 to $50, compared with $25.50 to $26.80; and good and choice lamb, $40 to $60, compared with $34.

As predicted by opponents of meat control, poultry prices began to show a slight downward trend. The decline of two to five cents at wholesale was reflected in many retail shops.

City Commissioner of Markets Eugene G. Schulz, confirming the weakening of poultry prices, promised a full-scale survey this morning. Inspectors were out all day yesterday, he said, but their reports took longer than usual to prepare, for they were instructed to compare the meat prices they discovered with the former ceilings of the same cuts.

Mrs. Jeanette Turner, executive secretary of the New York City Consumer Council, which has steadily fought against relaxation of controls, disclosed that plans for "political action" are afoot.

Plan Retaliation at Polls

Phones in the council's Long Island City, Queens, office rang all day as members called to voice their indignation, Mrs. Turner said. While details have not been worked out, the group will swing its weight in the coming election against candidates who have voted to weaken the Administration's stabilization program, she said.

Consumers who had been represented as desperate for meat showed some disinclination yester-

Continued on Page 2, Column 5

'Politics' Laid to Truman By Reece in Meat Action

GOP Chairman's Radio Reply to President Charges 'Familiar Pattern' Is Followed in Lifting of Curbs 'Before Election'

By LEWIS WOOD
Special to THE NEW YORK TIMES.

WASHINGTON, Oct. 15—President Truman has furnished another powerful argument for the election of a Republican Congress Nov. 5, Carroll Reece, chairman of the Republican National Committee, asserted tonight.

In a radio reply to the President's networks' speech of last night, announcing the lifting of price controls on meat, Mr. Reece said Mr. Truman's denunciation of "a few men in Congress" had provided this argument.

[Text of Mr. Reece's address will be found on Page 4.]

The Republican national chairman ascribed a political motive to the abandoning of price controls. The veto of the original OPA bill in June made the President responsible for lapse of controls, he said. Then, Mr. Reece continued, a Government agency restored controls after the second bill was enacted. Now the executive branch of the Government removes controls once more, he went on.

"This is a familiar pattern, before election, whether it's meat or anything else in the field of Government control," said the National Chairman.

The Reece speech was made after the Republicans demanded equal time on the air to that afforded President Truman last night. The National Chairman spoke over the Columbia Broadcasting Company network just twenty-four hours later.

Mr. Reece gave the President credit for taking a step in the "right direction," but said this was done only "finally and belatedly." And, Mr. Reece declared, the tragedy of the situation was that Mr. Truman waited until "very substantial damage" had been done.

It was unfortunate that the meat shortage should ever have become a political issue, he declared. This came about, he asserted, when Mr. Truman refused the advice of his Congressional leaders, and listened

Continued on Page 4, Column 2

Ending of Pay-Rise Curbs Urged by OWMR Advisers

By JOSEPH A. LOFTUS
Special to THE NEW YORK TIMES.

WASHINGTON, Oct. 15—The advisory board of the Office of War Mobilization and Reconversion recommended unanimously today that President Truman terminate speedily controls over wage increases. Members conferred with Mr. Truman at the White House, after which the expectation was unofficially expressed that Presidential action probably would be taken within a few days.

Termination of control over wage increases would mean, for all practical purposes, the abolition of the Wage Stabilization Board even more quickly than the elimination of price controls.

An administrative shell probably would be necessary for a few months to liquidate the agency and to carry out secondary obligations imposed by law. These include:

Approval or disapproval of requests for wage decreases, of which there have been a few; enforcement of these decisions as well as the decisions on increases already made, and action on requests for changes in wages and working conditions in plants and properties seized by the Government under the War Labor Disputes Act.

The board also endorsed Mr. Truman's removal of price controls on meat. Some of the board members foresaw the need for strong disputes machinery, regardless of what happened to price and wage controls.

The principal function of the

Continued on Page 5, Column 3

ONLY 15% OF FOODS NOW UNDER CONTROL

Early End to These Ceilings Likely as OPA Aides Indicate 'Clear the Deck' Policy

By SAMUEL A. TOWER
Special to THE NEW YORK TIMES.

WASHINGTON, Oct. 15 — Only 15 per cent of the family food budget remained under controls after all regulations on livestock, meat and food and feed products made from them were ended today.

The decontrol of meat freed 25 per cent of the food budget, the Office of Price Administration estimated. Dairy products make up 20 per cent, fruits and vegetables 20 per cent, and fresh fish, poultry, eggs and most grains constitute about another 20 per cent. All of these have been decontrolled.

Carrying out President Truman's order, Paul A. Porter, Price Administrator, drew up revocations of

Continued on Page 3, Column 2

Cattle, Hog and Sheep Prices Make Biggest One-Day Gains in History

By GEORGE ECKEL
Special to THE NEW YORK TIMES.

CHICAGO, Oct. 15—Cattle, hog and sheep prices staged the greatest one-day advances in the meat industry's history today at Chicago, but receipts were below those of a week ago, both locally and nationally.

Industry spokesmen stated that prices would settle as soon as the flow of livestock to market increased in reaction to the President's action last night.

Top grade hogs sold at $27.50 a hundred pounds here, an all-time record, up $11.25 from yesterday's ceiling price of $16.25. Cattle prices reached $28.75 a hundred pounds, short of the all-time record of $30.25 set last August, but $8.50 over the former ceiling of $20.25. Lambs went up $4 to $25, also an all-time high.

Even higher prices were reported at some other markets. Top hog prices at Indianapolis and St. Louis were $30 today.

Receipts at the twelve leading markets today were 29,000 cattle, compared with 41,100 last Tuesday. Today's total hog run at these markets was 7,500, as against 9,500 a week ago. The sheep run was 53,000 today, 48,100 a week ago.

The markets used in this count are Chicago, Cincinnati, Denver, Fort Worth, Indianapolis, Kansas City, St. Louis National Stockyards, Omaha, Oklahoma City, Sioux City, South St. Joseph and South St. Paul.

In Chicago the big packers—Swift, Armour, Wilson and Cudahy, and others of moderately large size—bought very little. All of the local receipts of 800 hogs and 2,500 sheep were sold to local packing plants and to shippers, who bought for out-of-town packers and for feed lots.

The big packers bought only a few of the cattle. This was explained by the disinclination of the big packers to enter the bidding competition during the morning hours, until it had been learned

Continued on Page 2, Column 3

CARDS TAKE SERIES AS BRECHEEN BEATS RED SOX 3D TIME, 4-3

Relieving Dickson in Eighth, Left-Hander Wins on Daring Dash Home by Slaughter

WALKER'S DOUBLE DECIDES

36,143 See 2-Run Fifth Rout Ferriss, but Boston Ties With Pair in Eighth

By JOHN DREBINGER
Special to THE NEW YORK TIMES.

ST. LOUIS, Oct. 15—Eddie Dyer's Cardinals, an amazing club that simply refused to accept defeat, hurtled to the top of the baseball universe today. Underdogs from the beginning of the world series, they defeated the heavily favored Red Sox in the seventh and deciding game, 4 to 3.

The decisive moment, which threw a wildly cheering crowd of 36,143 into a frenzy of excitement, came in the eighth inning.

With the score deadlocked at 3-all, Enos Slaughter fired a single into center field. Patiently he waited on first while Bob Klinger, veteran relief hurler who had just then entered the battle for Boston, retired the next two.

But Harry Walker followed with a line drive double into left center and for the next few seconds the gathering was to witness an electrifying spurt that doubtless will linger for many years with those who saw it.

Country Goes to Town

At first it didn't seem possible that Slaughter could score on the hit, but the Carolinian they call Country ran as perhaps he never had run before. He rounded second, third and then sped for home while a bewildered Boston shortstop, handling the relay from the outfield, spun around to make a futile throw to the plate.

On the wings of that amazing

Continued on Page 37, Column 2

MEAD SAYS DEWEY MAKES 'HENCHMEN' OF STATE OFFICIALS

Senator, in Jamestown Speech, Declares Rival Shifts Men to Own Political Benefit

GOVERNOR DEFENDS FUND

Tells Rochester Rally Surplus Will Be Spent on Things Democrats Neglected

By CLAYTON KNOWLES
Special to THE NEW YORK TIMES.

JAMESTOWN, N. Y., Oct. 15—Senator James M. Mead, candidate of the Democratic, American Labor and Liberal parties for Governor, singled out tonight the State Tax Commission as an agency of State government that Governor Dewey had put to use for his "personal political advantage."

He recalled that the Governor had appointed both Alger B. Chapman, now chairman of the Dewey campaign, and Glen R. Bedenkapp, now Republican State chairman, to the Tax Commission "with its control of the adjustments of income and corporation taxes and other tax collections."

"In other words," Mr. Mead declared, "two successive members of this vital agency of State government were graduated with honors by Governor Dewey to political positions wherein they could utilize whatever advantages had accrued to them by reason of their former official connections.

"We do not have to look very far therefore to know from what sources the immense campaign funds of Mr. Dewey are derived."

[Governor Dewey, at Rochester, said his administration had proved that government could serve the people without becoming their master. He defended his plans for spending the State's $517,000,000 surplus with an indictment of neglect of mental hospitals, other institutions and

Continued on Page 31, Column 1

World News Summarized

WEDNESDAY, OCTOBER 16, 1946

Hermann Goering took his life by poison two hours before he was scheduled to be executed, but ten other leading Nazis paid on the gallows for their crimes. They were hanged in the Nuremberg prison gymnasium. [1:8.] Seven others, sentenced to imprisonment, will serve their terms in Spandau, in the British sector of Berlin. [19:1.] Justice Jackson, submitting his final report and his resignation as American prosecutor to President Truman, declared "large numbers" of Germans equally guilty remained to be punished. [1:6-7.]

Democracy's frontier is in Germany, according to the chairman of an educational committee sent to that country by the State and War Departments. The committee in its report drew a virtual blueprint for reorganizing German life to enable the people to assimilate democracy. [17:1.]

The lack of harmony that characterized the Conference of Paris during its eleven weeks and two days of existence marked the final session. Yugoslavia, because of her disapproval of the Italian draft treaty, refused to attend or share in transmitting recommendations to the Big Four. [1:7.]

A special UNRRA commission found that Yugoslavia had "effectively distributed" relief supplies and discovered no evidence of large-scale diversion. [13:2.]

An ordinance creating an interim legislative assembly for southern Korea was approved by the American military governor. [8:6.]

Moslem League participation in India's interim Government was announced by Viceroy Wavell, who named five League members to the Cabinet. [8:3.]

"If any discourtesy was shown" to Soviet Ambassador Novikov when he landed at La Guardia Field, the United States "deeply regrets" it, the State Department said in a note. An investigation disclosed only that the envoy had not been permitted to use a telephone. [10:5.]

A Polish resolution to bar Franco Spain from access to the International Court of Justice was defeated in the United Nations Security Council. [13:4.]

Absolute security against illegal production of the atomic bomb is impossible, technical advisers to Bernard M. Baruch said in a report submitted to the Atomic Energy Commission. Effective international control must prevent the manufacture of even one bomb a year. [16:1.]

Liberal and progressive groups, forming a nation-wide movement here, continued the attack on the Baruch plan by renewing a demand that the United States stop making the bombs. [1:6-7.]

Meat appeared in New York butcher shops on the first day of decontrol at prices ranging from former ceiling levels to a flat $1-a-pound for all cuts. Poultry dropped slightly. [1:1.] The greatest single-day advances on record were made in livestock trading, most prices touching new highs. [1:2-3.]

Only 15 per cent of the nation's food budget remained under price control after the OPA implemented President Truman's order lifting ceilings off livestock, meat and allied products. [1:2.] The Advisory Board of the Office of War Mobilization endorsed the decontrol of meat and recommended to the President that wage controls be terminated speedily. This would mean the end of the Wage Stabilization Board. [1:2-3.]

Republican National Chairman Reece, having won his demand for radio time to reply to the President, blamed the Administration for the meat shortage and price confusion. [1:2-3.]

11 Nazis Calm on Last Day; Some Read Escapist Books

Devote Themselves to Novels and Poetry—Most Also Turn to the Bible—Eat Usual Suppers and Write Final Letters

Special to THE NEW YORK TIMES.

NUREMBERG, Germany, Oct. 15—As the final hours before their execution passed swiftly today, Hermann Goering and ten others of Adolf Hitler's innermost clique immersed themselves in an assortment of escapist literature.

Prison officials reported that the condemned men were calm and unemotional, and that almost all at one time or another read the Bible. [Only Alfred Rosenberg did not turn to the Bible, press services said.]

The eleven at their last meals tonight ate their usual supper of potato salad, sausage, cold cuts, black bread and tea. They also wrote letters until the lights were dimmed at 9 o'clock.

Goering, as on several previous occasions, refused to take a morning or evening walk and spent the day on his cot reading Theodor Fontane's novel, "Effie Briest." He wrote one letter and received one, but was not allowed to see fifteen crank letters addressed to him.

Joachim von Ribbentrop complained of insomnia and a headache, kept his cell in a mess as usual, read a historical novel by Gustav Freytag, wrote one letter and received five.

Rosenberg complained of the regulation requiring that prisoners keep their hands above the blanket when sleeping. [He said his hands became cold, press services reported.] He read a novelette called "The Violin" and received three personal letters, but wrote none.

Julius Streicher inquired again: "How are the others taking it?", read a novel by Jeluich called "The Soldier," received one letter and sent six. Col. Gen. Alfred Jodl, still icily reserved, read Knut Hamsun's "Traveler" and selections from a book of ballads, received seven letters and wrote one.

Field Marshal Gen. Wilhelm Keitel asked to be notified of the executions in time to set his cell in order before leaving. He read short stories and a book of anecdotes by

Continued on Page 20, Column 3

Jackson Urges More Trials Of Germans by Each Power

By WALTER H. WAGGONER
Special to THE NEW YORK TIMES.

WASHINGTON, Oct. 15—Justice Robert H. Jackson, chief United States prosecutor at the trial of the German war criminals, has informed President Truman that "large numbers" of Germans remain unpunished although their crimes and their guilt are no different from those of the men who have been convicted.

Mr. Jackson's letter, dated Oct. 7, was released by the White House tonight at 7:30, less than an hour and a half after the first of the doomed Germans was due to be hanged in Nuremberg for crimes against peace and peoples. Formally resigning as chief of counsel of the International Military Tribunal, which conducted the trials, Mr. Jackson described the demonstration of four-power unity in Nuremberg as "the world's first post-mortem examination of a totalitarian regime."

[The text of Mr. Jackson's letter appears on page 23.]

The trial "has put the handwriting on the wall for the oppressor as well as the oppressed to see," he wrote. For the prosecution of the many "industralists, militarists, politicians, diplomats and police officials whose guilt does not differ from those who have been convicted except that their parts were at lower levels and have been less conspicuous," Mr. Jackson proposed separate trials by the four occupying countries.

This would be the speediest and least expensive way of continuing the efforts to punish the guilty,

Continued on Page 23, Column 2

PARIS PARLEY ENDS; BOYCOTTED BY TITO

His Delegation Is Absent From Last Session—Assails Vote Method, Italian Treaty

The text of the Yugoslav letter is on Page 15.

By HAROLD CALLENDER
Special to THE NEW YORK TIMES.

PARIS, Oct. 15—"I declare the Conference of Paris closed," said Premier-President Georges Bidault of France at 5:26 o'clock this afternoon. After a scattering of applause, the weary delegates then filed out of Luxembourg Palace without the slightest illusion regarding the modesty of their achievement in the eleven weeks and two days that had passed since M. Bidault had opened their sessions.

A reflection of the unsolved

Continued on Page 15, Column 5

Liberals Form Political Group For United, National Campaigns

Organization of a nation-wide movement to set a common policy for liberal and progressive groups was announced yesterday by Philip Murray, president of the Congress of Industrial Organizations. The announcement was made after a meeting here of seventeen sponsors of the recent Chicago Conference of Progressives.

"Will the movement engage in political activities?" Mr. Murray was asked.

"Unquestionably so," he replied, but added that there had been no discussion of a third party.

In their first statement of policy, the leaders of the new group continued criticism of the American plan for atomic power control as proposed by Bernard M. Baruch. The criticism was begun by former Secretary of Commerce Henry A. Wallace. Mr. Wallace, however, is not listed as one of the organizers of the new movement.

While proclaiming that they and Mr. Baruch were now in full accord on the "single package" proposal for international [illegible] agreement in "easy stages," the group repeated the demand that the United States should "cease at once the manufacture of the bomb" and charged that Mr. Baruch had not clarified his stand on this proposal.

Mr. Baruch, who earlier had blamed "either misinformation or complete distortion" for the Chicago criticism of the American plan, said last night: "No comment."

Mr. Murray announced the formation of the new group and its renewed criticism of Mr. Baruch at the Hotel Commodore, following a three-hour closed meeting. Among those who attended were Jack Kroll, director of the CIO-PAC; Henry Morgenthau Jr., Dr. Frank Kingdon, chairman of the National Citizens Political Action Committee; Robert Kenny, president of the National Lawyers Guild; and Clark Foreman, president of the Southern Conference for Human Welfare.

Senator Claude Pepper of

Continued on Page 14, Column 4

GUILT IS PUNISHED

No. 2 Nazi a Suicide Two Hours Before the Execution Time

OTHERS GO GRIMLY

Shout Praise of Their Country as They Mount Scaffold

By DANA ADAMS SCHMIDT
Special to THE NEW YORK TIMES.

NUREMBERG, Germany, Wednesday, Oct. 16—Ten Nazi war criminals were hanged in the prison here early today, but the eleventh, Hermann Wilhelm Goering, committed suicide by swallowing poison in his cell some two hours before he was to have gone to the gallows.

Goering, former No. 2 Nazi and chief of the Luftwaffe, took cyanide of potassium, which he somehow had succeeded in secreting, Col. Burton C. Andrus, commandant of the prison security detail, announced.

A guard saw Goering twitching on his cot at 10:45 o'clock last night and summoned aid, but Adolf Hitler's erstwhile heir-apparent could not be revived. Colonel Andrus said glass from a capsule containing the poison was found in Goering's mouth.

Intervention Too Late

The guard did not see Goering put his hand under his blanket, and intervened the instant he saw the prisoner twitch, but it was too late.

[An envelope containing penciled notes and a small brass cartridge case that apparently had contained the poison vial were found on Goering's body, press services reported.]

Except for Goering, the executions then took place in the order of the indictment and in which the condemned men had sat in the prisoners' dock during the ten-month trial before the International Military Tribunal.

The Nazis walked to the gallows in this order:

Joachim von Ribbentrop, former Foreign Minister; Field Marshal Gen. Wilhelm Keitel, chief of the German High Command; Ernst Kaltenbrunner, head of the Gestapo; Alfred Rosenberg, Minister for Occupied Territories; Hans Frank, who led in the killing of thousands of Poles; Wilhelm Frick, former Minister of the Interior; Julius Streicher, leader of Nazi anti-Semitism; Fritz Sauckel, director of forced labor; Col. Gen. Alfred Jodl, head of the German General Staff, and Arthur Seyss-Inquart, who sold out Austria.

The condemned men were notified on two occasions of the date of the executions, authoritative sources said, but the ten who were hanged did not know the time until an hour before they began.

Repeated shouts as of the conclusion of frenzied speeches, followed by a thudding like the springing of a heavy trap door, were heard from a building at the rear of the prison courtyard between 2 and 3:15 A. M., according to the German News Agency.

Defiant to the Last

NUREMBERG, Wednesday, Oct. 16 (UP)—While officials started an investigation into Goering's suicide, his ten fellow-criminals paraded to the gallows and were hanged. Goering was to have led the procession. The prison gymnasium was used as the execution chamber. Three gallows had been erected there under electric lights. Two of them were used.

Witnesses said the first execution took four minutes and that the hangings continued from 1:01 A. M. (7:01 P. M. Tuesday Eastern Standard Time) to 2:45 A. M.

Von Ribbentrop entered the execution chamber first.

"God save Germany! My last wish is that Germany rediscover her unity and that an alliance be made between East and West and that peace reign on earth," he shouted a moment before he died. The hangman's trap dropped him into space at 1:14 A. M. Seyss-

Continued on Page 19, Column 2

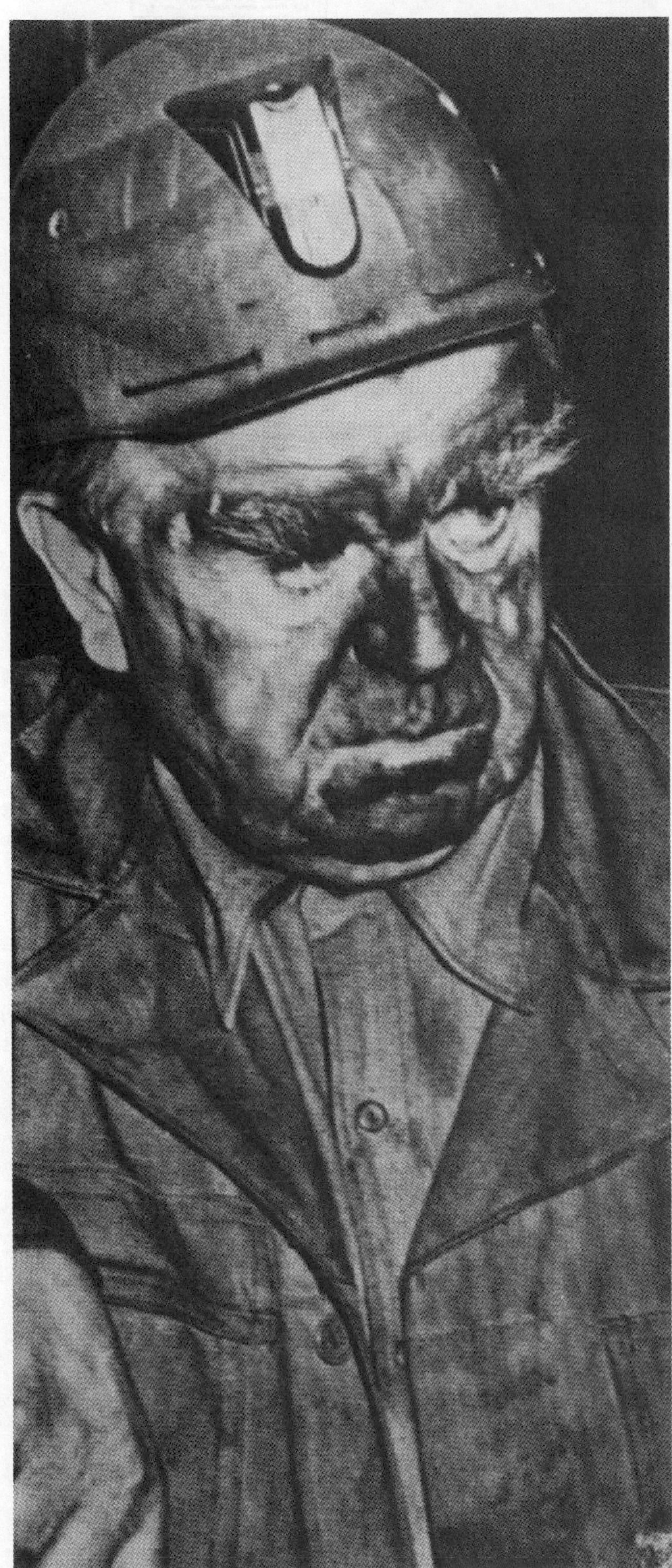

Head of the United Mine Workers, John L. Lewis. Coal miners engaged in a 44-day work stoppage over wages and welfare funds.

The coal miners' work stoppage ended when President Truman seized the mines, and met most of the union's demands. Truman is shown here with Eleanor Roosevelt during a visit to the Roosevelt home at Hyde Park, New York.

"All the News That's Fit to Print"

The New York Times.

LATE CITY EDITION
Fair and mild today and tomorrow.
Temperatures Yesterday—Max., 54; Min., 37
Sunrise today, 7:01 A. M.; Sunset, 4:29 P. M.
U. S. Weather Bureau Report, Page 7, Sect. 1

Section 1

NEWS INDEX, PAGE 79, THIS SECTION

Copyright, 1946, by The New York Times Company.

VOL. XCVI..No. 32,460. Entered as Second-Class Matter, Postoffice, New York, N. Y. NEW YORK, SUNDAY, DECEMBER 8, 1946. Including Magazine and Book Review. TEN CENTS New York City and Suburban Areas (15c Elsewhere)

LEWIS ENDS STRIKE, MINES OPEN TOMORROW; SURRENDERS AFTER LAWYERS SEE VINSON; RAIL EMBARGO, MAIL CURBS, DIMOUT HALT

127 KILLED BY FIRE IN ATLANTA HOTEL; MANY DIE IN LEAPS

Worst Such Disaster in U. S. Traps 280 in Their Rooms and Scores Are Injured

15-STORY BUILDING RUINED

Thousands of Spectators See Flames Engulf Victims—Bedsheets Aid Many Escapes

Special to THE NEW YORK TIMES.

ATLANTA, Ga., Dec. 7—In one of the most tragic fire disasters in the country's history, the fifteen-story Winecoff Hotel on Peachtree Street in the heart of downtown Atlanta was destroyed early this morning with a toll estimated at 127 dead. Many scores were injured.

The deaths were fifty-six more than the previous record number of seventy-one hotel fire deaths in the burning of Newhall House in Milwaukee in 1883. Of the dead 114 had been identified.

At least twenty-five or thirty persons lost their lives by leaping from windows of the flaming building. Police Chief M. A. Hornsby said. Many other guests were carried to safety down firemen's ladders or jumped into fire nets.

Some of those who perished were burned beyond recognition, and it appeared that several days might be required before their identities were established.

About 280 guests were registered in the hotel's 194 rooms, it was said.

City Investigation Started

City authorities immediately began an investigation to determine the origin of the fire, which was believed to have started on the fourth or fifth floor of the structure and spread rapidly.

They expressed amazement when they learned that the hotel, regarded as one of the city's major establishments, had no fire escapes or other emergency means of safety.

The fire was first discovered by a Negro girl elevator operator at 3:15 A. M. Comer L. Rowan, the hotel's night manager, said he instructed the girl and a bellboy to awaken as many guests as they could and that he began phoning the rooms. The flames, however, apparently had made great headway before the alarm was given.

Persons on the upper floors could be seen at their windows pleading vainly for help. Several guests crawled out on ledges waiting for firemen to rescue them.

Some were observed lowering themselves from one floor to another on tied-up bed clothing. Several were seen to die when their grips gave way or the knotted sheets broke under their weight or were burned by flames.

Two Girls Jump Ten Floors

Two girls jumped from the tenth floor into a fireman's safety net and were saved.

One man was observed trying to reach a firemen's ladder. He swung down from a rope and hung between the building and the ladder. Two other persons jumped or fell from above and hit him and all three fell to their deaths.

Thousands of spectators jammed the area and occasional shrieks from the crowd in the streets could be heard amid scenes of heroism, tragedy and horror.

A woman yet unidentified was seen to jump from one of the upper floors and her body struck a steel cable and hung there over the street.

Another woman was said to have thrown two small children to their deaths in the street and then to have jumped to her own death. One man died when he missed a life net by inches, ripping the coat of one of the net holders in a last effort to save himself.

Three persons were seen in win-

Continued on Page 28, Column 1

New York Skyscraper Home Now Possible as U. N. Center

Mayor O'Dwyer Says City Offers New Bid for the World Capital—Rockefeller Site Considered a Likely Prototype

By GEORGE BARRETT

Special to THE NEW YORK TIMES.

LAKE SUCCESS, N. Y., Dec. 7—The world capital of the United Nations may be established as a huge "international skyscraper" center in New York City, it was disclosed here today.

The construction in Manhattan of a separate international zone containing tall buildings and its own Assembly chambers was presented as a strong possibility tonight shortly after Mayor O'Dwyer had confirmed to reporters at City Hall that New York, in effect, was making another dramatic bid for the world capital.

The Mayor, questioned about reports that New York was going to increase its former offer of 350 acres of free land at Flushing Meadow to match the more pretentious offers made by Philadelphia, Boston and San Francisco, disclosed that he had only this morning attended "informal discussions with various members of the United Nations Site Committee and members of the United Nations." He added that he had "presented several possible sites inside the city, in addition to Flushing Meadow."

It had been reported here with increasing frequency during the last twenty-four hours that the United Nations was contemplating a permanent home within the limits of New York City if it would be possible to get enough land for the project. Mayor O'Dwyer elabo-

Continued on Page 11, Column 2

Byrnes Urges Troop Cuts As Big 4 Discuss Germany

By C. BROOKS PETERS

A drastic reduction of United States, British, Soviet and French forces of occupation in Germany, Austria, Poland and the Balkans was recommended to the Council of Foreign Ministers by Secretary of State Byrnes when the Council met yesterday morning to begin discussion of the peace treaty with Germany.

In an unanticipated move, Mr. Byrnes recommended two slashes in the number of occupying troops, both of which would affect most severely the Soviet armies deployed over Eastern Europe.

The United States proposal was contained in one of three memoranda submitted to the Council by Mr. Byrnes concerning the work the Council should do before completing its present session. Soviet Foreign Secretary Molotov also submitted a memorandum.

[The texts of the Byrnes and Molotov proposals appear on Page 20.]

Two Reductions Urged

The first cut would reduce to 620,000 men, including only 240,000 Russians, the forces of occupation in Germany, Poland, Austria, Hungary and Rumania on April 1, 1947.

The second reduction would reduce occupation forces proportionately in these countries another 25 to 33 1-3 per cent by April 1, 1948, "subject to such earlier withdrawal from Austria, Hungary and Rumania as may be required by the Austrian treaty."

The Ministers did not get round to discussing this issue yesterday. The basic question that confronted them in their two-hour meeting in the Waldorf-Astoria Hotel was what preparatory decisions they should make now to assure that the Council at its next session

Continued on Page 20, Column 1

U. S. WILL EXPEDITE GRAIN TO GERMANY

17 Ships to Sail From Albany This Month—Clay Says Food Is Vital to Occupation

Special to THE NEW YORK TIMES.

WASHINGTON, Dec. 7—Asserting his determination to get enough food to Germany to prevent a collapse of our occupation program, Robert P. Patterson, the Secretary of War, estimated today that 300,000 tons of grains would be needed monthly.

To cope with the crisis afflicting the United States and British zones, Mr. Patterson added that a fleet of seventeen food-bearing ships would leave from Albany, N. Y., during December.

He said that food stocks in the United States zone were at "ware-house-bottom," and the British zone could survive only if United States food shipments reached it.

His summary of the situation was prompted by a warning from Lieut. Gen. Lucius D. Clay, Deputy Military Governor of the United States zone, that democracy would not win in Germany if the people were unable to obtain sufficient food.

"Food is the key to our entire

Continued on Page 23, Column 4

Atlanta Crowds View Hotel Ruin, Talk at Scene Is for More Safety

By BENJAMIN FINE

Special to THE NEW YORK TIMES.

ATLANTA, Ga., Dec. 7—Pitiful sobbing women and tight-lipped men, with faces drawn and eyes reddened, swamped the hospitals and morgues of this proud city, seeking to identify relatives or friends who were trapped in the Winecoff Hotel fire early this morning.

Shocked and horrified, Atlanta residents by the thousand jammed the midtown section to view the gutted hotel structure. Until early afternoon the sheets and curtains that had been used by guests in their desperate efforts to get to safety still hung from the windows and fluttered in the breeze.

Unequalled heroism, together with miraculous escapes from death, marked the course of the country's most disastrous hotel fire. Praise was heard on all sides for a Negro girl elevator operator, identified only as Rosita, who was credited with being the first person to report the blaze. Comer L. Rowan, the hotel's night manager, said that the girl had reported the fire to him.

"I sent her to find the bellboy, who was making a routine floor check," he said, "and asked her to aid him in arousing the guests."

Wherever people were assembled today they talked about the fire.

"Something must be done to make hotels safer," a number said. Ironically enough, the Winecoff

Continued on Page 27, Column 1

RULES END QUICKLY

Federal Officials Rush to Restore the Normal Flow of Commerce

FREIGHT BANS OFF

Limits on Packages Are Removed, Restrictions on Coal Use Cease

By WALTER H. WAGGONER

Special to THE NEW YORK TIMES.

WASHINGTON, Dec. 7—The Government moved swiftly this afternoon and evening to lift restrictive coal-conservation measures and to restore transportation, commerce and industry as quickly as possible to pre-strike normalcy.

John L. Lewis' sudden back-to-work order to his miners brought about prompt cancellation, or a promise of it in the immediate future, of the following emergency rulings:

The "brownout" of ornamental and non-essential lighting.

The Postoffice limitations on weight and size of parcel-post and mail shipments.

The general embargo on all rail freight and express transport imposed by the Interstate Commerce Commission.

The railroads' own ban on all freight shipments, except food and fuel, bound for export.

The 50 per cent cut in passenger service by coal-burning railroads, to have become effective Monday.

Most restrictions on use and movement of coal by commercial, industrial and utility users.

Officials Taken by Surprise

The suddenness of the Lewis announcement appeared to have caught Washington and the Federal Government completely off guard and unprepared. In view of the fact that Saturday is a normal Government holiday, many officials who otherwise would have

Continued on Page 5, Column 3

RUSH TO PITS DUE

Miners, Eager for Yule Cash, Expected Back on the Job Promptly

LAYOFFS WILL END

Eaton, Linked to Lewis Decision, Hails Him as 'Brilliant Leader'

By A. H. RASKIN

Special to THE NEW YORK TIMES.

PITTSBURGH, Dec. 7—The first reaction of the nation's soft coal miners to John L. Lewis' back-to-work order was a mixture of puzzlement, disbelief and joy. Many, feeling the whole thing might be a hoax, said that they would wait for official instructions from the United Mine Workers before going back to their jobs.

Unworried over the prospect that there would be any resistance to ending the seventeen-day-old strike, jubilant operators and Government officials were making rush preparations tonight to reopen virtually all mines on Monday. Operators predicted that the full pre-strike production of 2,000,000 tons a day would be restored by Wednesday.

Union officials were equally confident that the 400,000 men would flock back to the mines as soon as official word was received.

"Boss Has Said It, That's All"

There was no rejoicing among the miners over the terms under which they were resuming work, but there was no disposition to question Mr. Lewis' authority to send them back as abruptly as he called them out.

"The boss has said it, and that's all," was the way William Blizzard, president of UMW District 17 in Charleston, W. Va., summed it up.

Most miners said that they were glad the strike was over, even though they could not understand

Continued on Page 4, Column 1

World News Summarized

SUNDAY, DECEMBER 8, 1946

John L. Lewis unexpectedly called off the soft coal strike yesterday afternoon. It was indicated that there would be no further interruption of production between now and April 1, 1947. [1:8.]

Miners were puzzled, incredulous and joyful, wondering what purpose had been served by their walkout, but it seemed likely that they would be back in the pits tomorrow. [1:5.]

The Government moved swiftly to cancel its various restrictions and conservation orders. [1:4.] In New York the dimout was lifted at 6 o'clock yesterday evening and the White Way blazed again as the city moved back toward normal. [1:6-7.]

In the broad struggle over labor's powers, the Ninth Circuit Court gave a decision that was held to place some statutory regulation on the interpretation of closed-shop contracts. [1:7.]

When the Council of Foreign Ministers met yesterday, Secretary Byrnes proposed a drastic reduction of United States, British, Russian and French occupation forces in Europe. Russia opposed some of the opening moves in discussing a treaty for Germany. [1:2-3.]

In the General Assembly White Russia was elected to one of the two remaining vacancies on the Social and Economic Council. [16:1.] The controversy between India and South Africa was sharply debated: the Assembly adjourned until today. [19:1.]

In the moot case of Spain, the United States announced that it would not be bound to any United Nations decision to break relationships. [13:1.] Madrid reacted in worried fashion to United Nations condemnation, the Cabinet denouncing "interference" in Spanish internal affairs. [14:1.]

In an exchange of letters with General Clay, Secretary of War Patterson asserted his determination to get enough food into Germany to prevent the collapse of the occupation program. [1:2.]

General Eisenhower, meanwhile, quoted the Secretary of War as having said that no atomic bombs and no fissionable material had been sent from the United States to any other country. [60:2.]

In United Nations circles there was further discussion of the problem of a site for the permanent headquarters. New York City suggested the possibility of erecting a "skyscraper city," within the metropolitan area itself. [1:2-3.]

There was temporary easement in the critical case of Iran when the Government refrained from issuing its expected order to troops to enter Azerbaijan to police elections. [21:1.]

The Palestinian situation was further vexed. An Arab spokesman said that Arab leaders would refuse to attend any more conferences on Palestine that considered partition. [41:2.]

The Indian stalemate continued. Pandit Nehru left London for New Delhi. The Congress party was cool to the British declaration that some accord was essential prerequisite to a Constitution. The Moslems, on the other hand, found some satisfaction in the British position. [46:2.]

City's Lights Go On Again; Thousands Recalled to Jobs

Mayor Quickly Proclaims Suspension of Brownout—Transport Agencies Act to Speed Return to Normal

By LAWRENCE RESNER

Few moments were wasted yesterday, after news of the calling off of the coal strike had been received from Washington, in starting New York City on the road back to normal business activity.

Mayor O'Dwyer issued a proclamation suspending the brown-out, thousands of furloughed railroad workers were recalled to work, and the business community generally heaved a deep sigh of relief.

Many of the theatres and amusements and business establishments on Broadway and in other parts of the city that had given almost perfect compliance to lighting restrictions were ablaze more than an hour in advance of the 6 o'clock deadline set by the Mayor in ending the brown-out.

The New York Central, the Pennsylvania Railroad, the Long Island Rail Road and the New York, New Haven & Hartford Railroad announced in swift succession that they had canceled the additional 25 per cent reduction of steam locomotive passenger service that was to have taken effect tonight. Other railroads were expected to follow the same program.

The New York Central, which was believed a typical case, said, however, that the first 25 per cent reduction in passenger service would remain unchanged until it started receiving new coal.

At the offices of the Railway Express, clerks who had been busy throughout the day notifying 6,500 of the agency's employes that they

Continued on Page 2, Column 2

Labor Law Revision Pushed To Prevent a Similar Crisis

Special to THE NEW YORK TIMES.

TOLEDO, Ohio, Dec. 7—The end of the coal strike will not divert the Republican party's determination to prevent a recurrence of such a situation, Carroll Reece, Republican National Chairman, said today on his arrival in Toledo to address the executive committee of the Young Republican National Federation.

He reiterated his party's conviction that labor legislation was still the first and foremost problem facing the new Congress next month.

"Regardless of the Court action against John L. Lewis and the subsequent end of the coal strike, the basic problem involved in such a situation must be removed to prevent a recurrence," Mr. Reece said.

Congress Hails End of Strike

WASHINGTON, Dec. 7 (AP)—Members of Congress hailed the ending of the soft coal strike but some insisted that new labor legislation was still needed.

"Thank God, and I mean it with all due reverence," was the comment of Senator Edwin C. Johnson of Colorado.

Senator Scott W. Lucas of Illinois said: "As one United States Senator, I am happy that Mr. Lewis has seen fit to capitulate."

"I am glad the miners are going back," said Senator Bourke B. Hickenlooper of Iowa. "That meets the thing of immediate importance, the production of coal. But other vital issues must be met and settled, the threat of recurring situations hanging over the head of the American public. That issue and its solution must be one of the first problems of the new Congress.

Continued on Page 5, Column 1

CLOSED SHOP CURB IS UPHELD BY COURT

Worker Cannot Be Dropped for Preferring Another Union, It Is Held

Special to THE NEW YORK TIMES.

WASHINGTON, Dec. 7—An important doctrine of the National Labor Relations Board, extending statutory limitations on the use of the closed shop, has been upheld in the courts for the first time.

The crux of the board's interpretation is that a union's right under its contract to expel a member and obtain his dismissal from employment cannot be invoked merely because the member exhibited a preference for another union at a collective bargaining election.

The decision enforcing the NLRB order was issued by the Ninth Circuit Court of Appeals. The principals were the Portland (Ore.) Lumber Mills, the Lumber and Sawmill Workers Union of the Brotherhood of Carpenters, AFL, the International Woodworkers Association, Congress of Industrial Organizations, and Ward Wilmarth, a member of the AFL union.

The AFL union had a closed shop contract with the company,

Continued on Page 3, Column 5

2 Held on Complaints by 32 GI's Of Swindle on Homes in Suffolk

Special to THE NEW YORK TIMES.

LINDENHURST, L. I., Dec. 7—Acting on complaints of thirty-two ex-service men, the Suffolk County District Attorney's office caused the arrests last night and today of Benjamin Embinder, 45 years old, sales manager for "Lindenhurst Shores, Inc.," and Lawrence Calvert, a salesman, on charges of second-degree grand larceny.

According to the complaints the real estate concern sold lots to former GI's for $1,500 to $2,000 in the southern part of West Babylon. Complainants told the authorities that they got the impression that $10,000 homes would be built upon the lots within three to four months after the land had been bought. When the homes failed to materialize, the veterans scrutinized their contracts closely and found they had contracted only for the purchase of the lots.

Embinder, who gave his address as 656 West 204th Street, Manhattan, and Calvert, who lives at Lake Ronkonkoma, L. I., posted $500 bail each. They will have a hearing Wednesday in Lindenhurst Police Court before Justice William F. Wolters.

Investigation of the operations of Lindenhurst Shores, Inc., began several weeks ago when complaints began coming into various veterans' agencies. Former service men said they had bought lots in the development for prices ranging from $1,500 to $2,000, with

Continued on Page 60, Column 4

CAPITAL SURPRISED

UMW Head Bows in Face of Court Action and Agrees to Negotiate

TRUMAN DROPS TALK

Mine Operation Ordered Till April 1—Contempt Case Still Pending

By JOSEPH A. LOFTUS

Special to THE NEW YORK TIMES.

WASHINGTON, Dec. 7—John L. Lewis, president of the United Mine Workers of America, AFL, unexpectedly called off the country-wide soft coal strike today and directed all members to return to their jobs immediately.

He ordered the miners to continue working until April 1 at the wages and under the conditions existing before the stoppage.

With a bow to the United States Supreme Court and an acknowledgment of an economic crisis, the leader of nearly all the men who mine coal in the United States read to reporters at a suddenly called conference his letter of capitulation, directed to all UMW members and local unions in the bituminous districts.

He gave a virtual warranty of uninterrupted production at least until April 1, at the same time serving notice that the union would enforce the existing terms of employment at each mine.

Truman Cancels Address

The surprising announcement, on the fifth anniversary of the Pearl Harbor disaster and the seventeenth day of the strike, caught most of official Washington unprepared.

Within an hour President Truman canceled a radio address he was writing for tomorrow night. Revocation of the restrictions on transportation and coal consumption came later. Indeed, the Government at the time of Mr. Lewis' announcement was working on even more rigorous coal-conservation measures.

Mr. Lewis called his news conference for 2 P. M., a few hours after his lawyers and Government counsel conferred with Chief Justice Fred M. Vinson on the Government petition to the Supreme Court to take immediate jurisdiction of the contempt conviction and $3,510,000 fines levied against the union and its president.

It was learned that the United Mine Workers joined in the Government's petition to by-pass argument in the intermediate court of appeals. Lawyers left the Chief Justice with the impression that the court would accept the case immediately.

Court Argument May Be Delayed

The subsequent termination of the strike may alter that, however, perhaps to the extent of delaying argument for a few weeks. The national hardship factor has been eliminated by the strike termination, it was pointed out, even though the legal importance of the case remains.

Mr. Lewis' letter referred to the Administration's injunction as a "yellow dog" writ, which he said had "reached the Supreme Court." He called the Court "the protector of American liberties" and said the issues before it were "fateful for our republic."

"These weighty considerations," the letter continued, "and the fitting respect due the dignity of this high tribunal imperatively required that, during its period of deliberation, the Court be free from public pressure superinduced by the hysteria and frenzy of an economic crisis. In addition, public necessity requires the quantitative production of coal during such period."

Mr. Lewis said that in the meantime he would be willing to negotiate a new wage agreement

Continued on Page 3, Column 1

1947

1947

Gregory Peck and Jennifer Jones starred in David O. Selznick's *Duel in the Sun.*

Clark Gable, Ava Gardner and Edward Arnold in *The Hucksters.*

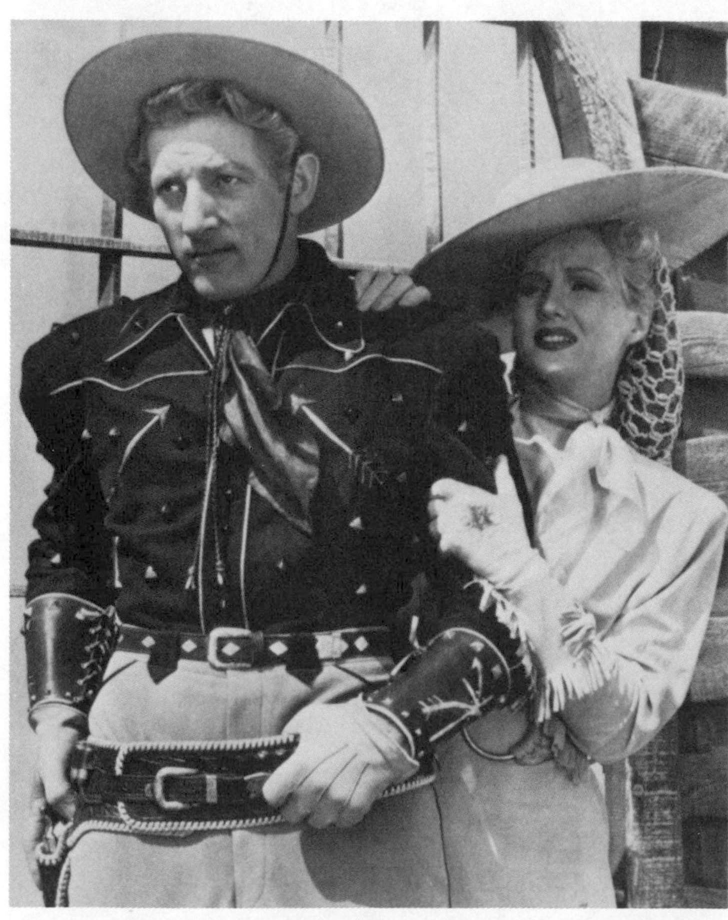

Danny Kaye and Virginia Mayo in *The Secret Life of Walter Mitty.*

Groucho Marx and Carmen Miranda in *Copacabana.*

"All the News That's Fit to Print"

The New York Times.

LATE CITY EDITION
Cloudy, mild today; showers this evening. Much colder tomorrow.
Temperatures Yesterday—Max., 50; Min., 40
Sunrise today, 7:18 A. M.; Sunset, 5:18 P. M.
Full U. S. Weather Bureau Report, Page 46

VOL. XCVI...No. 32,513. Entered as Second-Class Matter, Postoffice, New York, N. Y. NEW YORK, THURSDAY, JANUARY 30, 1947. THREE CENTS IN NEW YORK CITY

U. S. ENDS MEDIATION IN CHINA; TROOPS WILL BE WITHDRAWN; FIERCER CIVIL WAR FORESEEN

TAXES ON LUXURIES EXTENDED IN HOUSE BY VOTE OF 373-35

NO DEADLINE IS SET

Knutson Pledges Review of Excise Rate List, but Not This Year

NEW YORKERS FIGHT BILL

Assert Levies Stagnate Sales—Parties Clash Over GOP Income Tax Cut Proposal

By JOHN D. MORRIS
Special to The New York Times.

WASHINGTON, Jan. 29—By a vote of 373 to 35, the House passed today a bill to peg excise taxes on furs, jewelry, liquor and a number of other "luxuries" at their present wartime rates.

While the opposition vote to the bi-partisan measure was unexpectedly large, the House's first full-dress debate of the new Republican Congress was devoted largely to inter-party recriminations on a variety of indirectly-related subjects.

Arguments frequently progressed to the shouting stage as Republicans and Democrats clashed over such issues as responsibility for the country's past and present financial condition and Republican campaign pledges to reduce taxes.

When the showdown came on the excise tax bill in the House's first roll-call vote of the session, 149 Democrats joined 224 Republicans to pass the measure and send it to the Senate, where Chairman Eugene D. Millikin of the Finance Committee promised prompt consideration.

Voting against the bill were 8 Republicans, 26 Democrats and Representative Vito Marcantonio, American Labor party.

Would Save U. S. 1.1 Billion

The bill is designed to save the Treasury an estimated $1,131,000,000 in the fiscal year beginning July 1 by preventing the excise rates from reverting to pre-1943 levels on that date. In the absence of Congressional action, the reduction would automatically occur six months after the formal end of war hostilities, proclaimed Dec. 31 by President Truman.

In addition to the liquor, fur and jewelry taxes, the measure would freeze for an indefinite period the present levies on admittances, leases on boxes and seats, ticket sales outside of box offices, cabarets, dues, membership and initiation fees, toilet preparations, billiard and pool tables and bowling alleys.

Also electric light bulbs and tubes, long distance telephone charges, domestic telegraph, cable or radio dispatches, leased wires, wire and equipment service, transportation of persons, seats and berths, on conveyances and luggage.

Opposition, principally by Democratic members of the New York City delegation, was based chiefly on the argument that many of the taxes should be adjusted immediately to prevent stagnation in sales of many of the taxed articles.

Amendment Ban Protested

It was asserted that many of the goods and services covered were not luxuries. Frequent protests were made against a "gag rule" prohibiting amendments from the floor to revise specific rates.

Representative Harold Knutson of Minnesota, chairman of the Ways and Means Committee, suggested to the protestants that they take their proposals up with the Senate Finance Committee.

"If we open up this Pandora box on the floor of the House," he said, "then we don't know where it would end."

The excises, he asserted, "are all New Deal children foisted on the people." He expressed regret that it was necessary to continue them to provide revenues required by President Truman's proposed $37,500,000,000 in expenditures in the next fiscal year.

The committee will "go over the whole excise tax list before long and see if we can't make something of it," he said, but he gave no indication as to when this would be. Not this year, he earlier told reporters.

Representative Thomas A. Jen-

Continued on Page 16, Column 4

House Acts to Extend GI Insurance Right

By The Associated Press.

WASHINGTON, Jan. 29—The first veterans' bill of the Eightieth Congress, one which would give former service men more time to reinstate their Government life insurance policies, was passed by the House today without opposition.

The Veterans Committee approved it only yesterday on recommendation of the Veterans Administration and veterans' organizations.

Unless the Senate votes promptly the reinstatement privilege for the World War II veterans will expire Saturday. Under the House bill the Veterans Administration would determine how long they might have to put their policies back in force.

Without waiting to hear all scheduled testimony the Veterans Committee approved another insurance bill today. It would permit some 37,000 veterans of World War I to keep on carrying Government term life insurance policies.

UNION 'MONOPOLIES,' WAGNER ACT SCORED

Senators Told Latter Is Root of Bad Labor Relations—Electrical Union Held Dictator

By LOUIS STARK
Special to The New York Times.

WASHINGTON, Jan. 29—Witnesses before the Senate Committee on Labor and Public Welfare attacked today the "monopoly" aspects of unions and called the National Labor Relations (Wagner) Act the "root of unsatisfactory labor relations in the United States." They approved a group of bills that would restrict union powers.

R. Stafford Edwards, president of the National Electrical Manufacturers Association, said that the American Federation of Labor's International Brotherhood of Electrical Workers was a union that, by boycotts, had established monopoly control of such a nature that for the last twelve years many electrical manufacturers had been excluded from the most important markets in the nation Or, he added, they were admitted only on terms imposed by the IBEW locals.

While Mr. Edwards confined himself to approval of the proposal to ban secondary boycotts, Theodore R. Iserman, a member of the New York law firm of Rathbone Perry, Kelley and Drye ranged over the entire field of labor relations.

Mr. Iserman said he was a representative of companies whose workers were numbered "in tens and tens of thousands."

He declared that Senator Joseph H. Ball's bills to end industry-wide bargaining and the closed shop were sound measures that would take the nation a long way toward industrial peace.

In the meantime the United States Chamber of Commerce announced its stand on some of the

Continued on Page 12, Column 3

O'DWYER PROPOSES COMPROMISE PLAN ON CITY AIRPORTS

Offers City Maintenance and Operation if Airlines Build Hangars at Idlewild

ALL-DAY HEARING IS HELD

Mayor Outlines City Policy to Complete New Field Soon Without Financial Strain

By WILLIAM R. CONKLIN

Moving suddenly last night for a compromise arrangement on city operation of the three city airports, Mayor O'Dwyer said the city would maintain and operate the fields if the major airlines financed and built their own hangars at the new Idlewild Airport in Queens.

The Mayor's offer came at 8:30 o'clock, after an all-day public hearing before the Board of Estimate in City Hall. During the nine-hour session the board examined the merits of the $80,000,000 operating plan of the New York City Airport Authority and of the $191,000,000 plan of the Port Authority.

Before a half-hour recess at 5:30 the Mayor indicated that neither plan was wholly satisfactory to the board, and hinted that a compromise would be the best solution. He put the idea into specific form when Juan T. Trippe, president of the Pan American Airways System, was speaking for seventeen major airlines.

Blue Pencil on Plan

"I'll show you how the airlines can help the city and it won't cost a dime," the Mayor said. "Take the $191,000,000 Port Authority plan and take your blue pencil and take out the things you can get along without.

"If you build your own hangars, to that extent it might be possible to build Idlewild ourselves."

Siding with the Mayor, Lazarus Joseph, Controller, urged Mr. Trippe to induce the major lines to help finance Idlewild. In reply to the Mayor's suggestion, Mr. Trippe said:

"The airlines are gambling on the future. It's a great business, but all the airlines have loans outstanding against them. However, we are looking to the future. We think we are going to bail out."

"We can't afford to gamble," Mr. Joseph cut in. "We have $90,000,000 already invested in Idlewild."

"The city should plan to handle future air commerce," Mr. Trippe returned.

"But the kids of today are more interested in whether new schools will be built, new hospitals, housing, libraries and subways, than they are in the commerce of the future," Mr. Joseph objected.

Earlier, the Mayor charged that the airlines had refused to play fair with the city and said they had put pressure on the city "to get exactly what they want."

Attitude of Board Outlined

Expressing the Board of Estimate's attitude, the Mayor said:

"The Board of Estimate considers that its members are impartial, and are acting for the best interests of the city. The question before the board is whether it can get either the Airport Authority or the Port Authority to improve the plans submitted to us.

"We want Idlewild Airport built without delay, we want it adequate, and we want it constructed without undue financial strain on

Continued on Page 4, Column 5

British Defer Cuts In Scotch for U. S.

By The United Press.

LONDON, Jan. 29—Food Minister John Strachey told the House of Commons today that distillers had promised to postpone their proposed cuts in Scotch whisky exports to the United States and other countries as a result of the Food Ministry's allocation of 50,000 tons of barley for distilling this year.

Winston Churchill, minority leader, intimated he believed Scotch whisky was being sold too cheaply in the United States but Mr. Strachey said "this is a question for the exporters and surely they will look after their own interests and charge what they consider is the best price."

NEW STATE TAXES COUPLED TO BONUS

Republicans Favor Levies on Cigarettes, Gasoline, Liquor to Meet Proposed Expense

By LEO EGAN
Special to The New York Times.

ALBANY, Jan. 29—Strong sentiment for coupling the proposed $400,000,000 State veterans bonus with the imposition of special taxes to finance it developed today among Republican legislative leaders as a sequel to Governor Dewey's speech at an American Legion dinner.

One proposal receiving serious consideration calls for the enactment of a law imposing an additional 2-cent-a-package cigarette tax, an additional 1-cent-a-gallon gasoline tax or some additional tax on liquor with the proviso that the additional levies would not become operative unless or until the bonus is approved.

Republican legislators who have discussed the subject with the Governor believe he had some such idea in mind when he told the Legion that consideration should be given at the present session to means of raising the revenue to retire bonus bonds.

New Taxes Involved

Enactment of such a contingent tax law, Republicans observed, would transfer the onus for increasing taxes next year from the Legislature to the voters.

Because it involves an amendment to the State Constitution, the bonus cannot be authorized without a referendum on the subject next fall. By making the levying of additional taxes contingent upon approval of the bonus, the Legislature and Governor, in effect, would be serving notice on the voters that a vote for payment of the bonus would also be a vote for additional taxes.

There is no thought in the minds

Continued on Page 11, Column 5

U. S. RECONVERTING MILITARY STATIONS TO PACIFIC AIRWAYS

Radio and Landing Aids Are Considered the Chief Problems of Civil Planes

NEGOTIATIONS ARE TENSE

Incidents Show Radio of Army Is No Longer Reliable Because of Demobilization

By ANTHONY LEVIERO
Special to The New York Times.

WASHINGTON, Jan. 29—Top Government officials, it was learned today, are engaged in negotiations of a most complex nature to open the overdue Western Pacific airways by rehabilitating military air bases and stations.

For more than a month the War, Navy and Commerce Departments and the Civil Aeronautics Board have been struggling with what amounts to the creation of a commercial airways system west of Honolulu and along points in the Aleutians.

What they have to work with are the skeletons of the demobilized Air Transport Command and the Naval Air Transport Service.

American, British, Canadian, Dutch and Australian scheduled and non-scheduled airlines are waiting impatiently to launch their airliners across the vast Pacific wastes.

Two major problems must be overcome: 1, maintenance at a high level of efficiency of the low-frequency, high-powered all-direction transoceanic radio ranges, without which airliners cannot operate; 2, the building of hotels, rebuilding of rundown facilities and provision of food for itinerants.

Latest reports state that many of the smaller bases are in sad shape, the jungle having moved in when the GI's moved out.

A Month for Program

It will take a month, according to the most optimistic estimate, to work out a new program for the communications facilities.

With Gen. Douglas MacArthur's occupation forces at the end of a long line of communications, the War Department was reported to be most reluctant to yield any of the radio facilities. The alternative was to try to keep the wartime system of the ATC in operation with reduced staffs, lacking many of the skilled wartime men.

The fate of Army budget requests was also involved. Any sizable cut would make the issue simple—the Civil Aeronautics Administration or a private contractor

Continued on Page 4, Column 3

World News Summarized

THURSDAY, JANUARY 30, 1947

The United States yesterday wrote off General Marshall's unsuccessful efforts to end China's civil war. The State Department announced withdrawal from the two agencies through which peace was to be brought about and the early removal of all but a few of the 12,000 military personnel in China. [1:8.]

Chinese observers were inclined to the opinion that the only result could be intensified warfare between Nationalists and Communists. [1:6-7.]

Underground forces in Palestine released the former British major kidnapped from his home in Jerusalem. He was dazed and weak from rough handling. [5:5.] The British Cabinet, it was learned, has decided that partition is the only solution of the Palestine problem. [1:6-7.]

A Russian proposal to permit Albania to take part in discussing the German peace treaty was rejected by the Foreign Ministers' deputies. [6:1.]

Senator Vandenberg demanded a Big Three conference to fix responsibility for the "rigged" Polish election. He also suggested that the United Nations launch an inquiry. [1:7.]

This country's moral responsibility to the world in preventing another war was outlined by United Nations Delegate Austin to a joint session of the Senate and House military committees. Although he stressed the need of universal military training, it was said such a bill had only an even chance of passage and Selective Service would not be extended. [9:1.]

Developments in the United Nations included proposals by the United States for an international bill of rights and guarantees of freedom of press and information [10:3], the protest of a French representative against the reluctance of some Latin-American countries "to hurt" Franco Spain [10:6], and Britain's decision to join the International Refugee Organization. [8:4-5.] A special committee reported that six European countries would need help totaling $583,000,000 this year after the end of UNRRA. [8:3.]

Wartime excise and luxury taxes were continued at their current rates by the House, 373 to 35. The bill now goes to the Senate. [1:1.]

The White House, maintaining that action on rent controls rested with Congress, denied a report that the OPA was about to grant a 10 per cent increase in ceilings. [1:2-3.] The report brought the warning from labor leaders that any cost-of-living increase would upset peaceful wage negotiations. [12:2.]

"Monopoly" aspects of union activities, the Wagner Act and secondary boycotts were attacked by witnesses before the Senate Labor and Welfare Committee. [1:2.] The House committee will open hearings Wednesday with the aim of presenting a single omnibus labor reform bill by March 15. [12:5.]

An arbitrator fined a New York teamsters union because its members went on an outlaw strike. [15:1.]

Albany Republicans suggested coupling the proposed veterans' bonus with the imposition of special taxes to finance it. [1:4.] A Staten Island Senator called for a legislative investigation of New York City's finances. [17:1.]

White House Disavows Any Plan To Increase Rent Ceilings by 10%

By SAMUEL A. TOWER
Special to The New York Times.

WASHINGTON, Jan. 29—The White House denied late this afternoon a reported Administration move to authorize a general increase of 10 per cent in rent ceilings.

The denial came after reporters had been informed in Administration sources that an announcement of a 10 per cent increase had been prepared and would probably be made public during the day. In a statement to reporters, Senator J. William Fulbright, Democrat, of Arkansas, had also said that an order increasing rents was in preparation.

Charles G. Ross, White House press secretary, taking cognizance of spreading reports that the President had approved an increase, denied the reports and declared that it was the President's position that a decision on modification of the rent-control structure rested with Congress.

He told reporters that he had just checked with the President and that the President's views were unchanged from those he expressed at a news conference Thursday.

Three times during that news conference, Mr. Ross recalled, the question of rent control was brought up and the President had indicated clearly that he did not regard an increase at this time as a wise move.

Mr. Ross quoted the President as saying that he thought the line ought to be held on rent control but that, of course, Congress would have to act on that.

At that time the President pointed out that the policy on rent control was to permit increase on an

Continued on Page 12, Column 2

Deterrent to Strife in China Removed by American Step

Nationalists Blame Communists for Failure to Make Peace—Red Leaders Expect New Government Military Measures

By TILLMAN DURDIN
Special to The New York Times.

NANKING, Jan. 29—The United States announcement that it had ended peace efforts in China removed another barrier, however slight, to all-out combat in the civil war.

Intensification of warfare can be expected, particularly in the light of reports that the Government has decided to attempt to open the Tientsin-Pukow railway by pushing a corridor through Communist-held Shantung.

Formal notification of today's American action was conveyed this afternoon by Ambassador John Leighton Stuart to Generalissimo Chiang Kai-shek and to the chief local Communist representative, Wang Ping-nan. Dr. Stuart advised them that American personnel connected with the Peiping Executive Headquarters would be withdrawn as soon as possible.

The Ambassador indicated that American air transport facilities would be available for a reasonable period to carry Nationalist and Communist Chinese in Headquarters units to points where they desire to go.

The job of shifting Communists from Government-controlled cities, where they are stationed in connection with Headquarters work, into Communist territory will be a particular responsibility of American planes.

The Government issued a statement of its reaction to the American announcement soon after the news had been formally conveyed to the Generalissimo. The statement stressed the Government's past readiness to make peace with the Communists and take them into the Government and blamed the Communists for the continued civil war.

The Government statement cited the Government cease-fire order of

Continued on Page 3, Column 2

Britain Decides in Principle On Partitioning of Palestine

By CHARLES E. EGAN
Special to The New York Times.

LONDON, Jan. 29—The British Cabinet has finally decided on the partitioning of Palestine and now seeks definite suggestions for the lines along which such a program can be carried out, it was learned authoritatively today.

The quest for a basis on which an autonomous Zionist state can be created alongside its Arab counterpart accounts for the fact that Foreign and Colonial Office executives are holding alternate conferences this week with Zionist and Arab elements. The decision for partition was made after considerable discussion in a Cabinet meeting late last week, it is now learned.

The details of the partition, as well as the decision whether to approach the United Nations' General Assembly and ask its blessing, is still hanging fire. The Cabinet is gathering reactions now from the Arab League and the Jewish Agency for Palestine and proposes to leave the final decision on the details of the plan open for Cabinet decision within a few months.

[H. A. I. Collins, kidnapped on Sunday by Zionist terrorists, reached a Jerusalem clinic on Wednesday and said he had fought his way to freedom after having been badly treated. Physicians said his condition was "dangerous."]

Foreign Secretary Bevin and Colonial Secretary Arthur Creech Jones spent more than two hours today with David Ben-Gurion and other Jewish Agency leaders. Their talk, the Colonial Office announced, dealt with long-term policies.

The delegates of the Arab League states and the Palestinian Arabs were notified that the con-

Continued on Page 5, Column 3

VANDENBERG URGES BIG 3 POLISH TALK

He Also Suggests U. N. Inquiry on 'Rigged' Voting—Calls Issue No Longer Internal

By C. P. TRUSSELL
Special to The New York Times.

WASHINGTON, Jan. 29—Immediate consultations between the United States, Great Britain and Russia, to determine "exactly who's who and what's what" in responsibility for the "rigged and terrorized" elections in Poland Jan. 19, were called for today by Senator Arthur H. Vandenberg.

Mr. Vandenberg indicated later that he would suggest a United Nations inquiry, as the charges concerning the Polish elections appeared to involve violations of its Charter.

The president pro tempore of the Senate and chairman of its Foreign Relations Committee left his presiding officer's chair to address the Senate in support of the State Department charges yesterday that the Provisional Government of Poland had violated its pledges for free and unfettered polling. The Michigan Republican acted, he said, "to register America's unity behind" the allegations.

"We must establish the total

Continued on Page 6, Column 2

YEAR'S WORK HALTS

U. S. Cuts Its Ties With Committee of Three and Truce Body

MOST OF 12,000 MEN TO GO

Admission of Failure of Our Efforts Seen—$500,000,000 Loan Still in Abeyance

By BERTRAM D. HULEN

WASHINGTON, Jan. 29—The way was paved today for withdrawal of virtually all American forces from China as the State Department announced abandonment of the American effort to mediate between the Chinese Nationalist and Communist forces.

This country, it was announced, will end its connection with the Committee of Three. The committee, representing the United States, Chinese Nationalists and Chinese Communists, was set up at the instance of Secretary of State Marshall when he was President Truman's special envoy to China. It was the agency through which efforts were made during the past year to promote domestic peace and national unity.

The decision also involves ending United States connection with Executive Headquarters in Peiping, the organization representing the three groups that was designed to oversee the carrying out of the agreement of the Chinese factions for a truce and national unity.

Many Marines Likely to Go

Of 12,000 American Army, Navy and Marine Corps personnel in China, more than 9,000 are Marines, most of them occupied in supporting Executive Headquarters. The termination of that organization, therefore, is expected to result in the withdrawal of those Marines.

There will then remain in China 1,000 to 2,000 Marines at the training base at Tsingtao, the American Military Group of 750 officers and men at Nanking, which is engaged in training Chinese personnel at military schools in the use of latest weapons, and Army units stationed at various places to dispose of surplus property.

China is now expected to lose interest in the Committee of Three and Executive Headquarters and dissolve them.

Whether the United States decision will lead to an intensification of civil war or give impetus to the establishment of a coalition Government on liberal lines can only be surmised here for the present. It is regarded as a virtual admission of the inability of General Marshall to bring about peace in China. It was foreshadowed by his return to the United States and his personal statement on China of Jan. 7.

Action Not Punitive

The decision, it was emphasized in informed quarters, was in no sense punitive. Dr. John Leighton Stuart will remain as American Ambassador to China. If he resigns, a new Ambassador will be appointed, it was said. Dr. Stuart is accredited to the Government of Generalissimo Chiang Kai-shek, from which it was stressed the United States was not withdrawing recognition.

Ambassador Stuart is expected to facilitate the effort for unification and peace in China as opportunities arise but it was predicted that his role would not be as important as General Marshall's was.

The tendency appears to be to await the full Chinese reaction to General Marshall's statement of Jan. 7, in which he denounced the extremists in the Nationalist and Communist parties and called for the establishment of a Government that would utilize the services of liberals.

Officials insisted that the cessation of the organized peace effort did not end the American interest in promoting unity in China. They said the objective remained the same, the creation of a unified, strong China, friendly to the United States and a bulwark of peace and security in Asia.

"We are hopeful but not particularly optimistic regarding the

Continued on Page 3, Column 3

Five GI's Flee Governors Island After Sawing Bars; 3 Recaptured

By JOHN N. POPHAM

Five Army privates, all of whom were being held in Governors Island's historic fortress-prison, Castle Williams, as a safeguard against their pronounced disposition to escape military confinement, hacksawed their way to freedom early yesterday.

Eight hours later three of them were captured without a struggle by Jersey State police in the woods near Browns Mills, N. J., five miles east of the Fort Dix Army post. They admitted to authorities that they had left Governors Island by "hitching" a ride on a Government ferryboat that during the early morning leaves every hour for Battery Park at the lower tip of Manhattan.

Last night the three captured men were being detained in the Post Fire House at Fort Dix, a thick, brick building with several barred cells, rather than at the post stockade. For it was in the stockade that they, and seven others, had tunneled forty feet last New Year's Day in an unsuccessful escape attempt.

Agents of the Federal Bureau of Investigation and the Army's Criminal Investigation Division, as well as the police, continued to search under a thirteen-State alarm for the two other escaped prisoners, whose means of leaving Governors Island was still unknown to authorities. The three captured men indicated under questioning that they and the other two men still at large had parted company soon after dropping from the ground floor window of the formidable old fortress that has walls forty feet high and eight feet thick.

The three men captured in New

Continued on Page 17, Column 3

"All the News That's Fit to Print"

The New York Times.

LATE CITY EDITION
Mostly sunny and mild today.
Occasional rain and mild tomorrow.
Temperatures Yesterday—Max., 47; Min., 32
Sunrise today, 6:13 A. M.; Sunset 6:06 P. M.
Full U. S. Weather Bureau Report, Page 55

VOL. XCVI...No. 32,555. Entered as Second-Class Matter, Postoffice, New York, N. Y. NEW YORK, THURSDAY, MARCH 13, 1947. THREE CENTS IN NEW YORK CITY

TRUMAN ACTS TO SAVE NATIONS FROM RED RULE; ASKS 400 MILLION TO AID GREECE AND TURKEY; CONGRESS FIGHT LIKELY BUT APPROVAL IS SEEN

DEWEY TO REQUEST $135,000,000 MORE TO AID CITY HOUSING

O'Dwyer, by Agreement, Drops Further Bid for Money in '47, Insures Planned Projects

REALTY TAX TO GO TO $2.97

Due, Says Mayor, to Jump in Budget—City Wins Albany Accord on Finance Bills

By LEO EGAN
Special to The New York Times.

ALBANY, March 12—Governor Dewey and Mayor O'Dwyer agreed today at a conference in the Governor's office that the state housing loan fund should be increased by $135,000,000 and that New York City could get along without any further financial help from the state this year.

The additional housing loan fund, which must be approved by the Legislature and then by the voters at a referendum in the fall, will insure that projects already planned can be completed. It will not permit the undertaking of any new projects beyond those already under contemplation.

Construction costs on public housing are running so far ahead of estimates made in pre-war years that the whole state program, particularly New York City projects, faces drastic curtailment unless additional funds are provided. Mayor O'Dwyer said after today's conference that six New York City projects might have to be dropped and two reduced in size to keep within available funds unless additional state money was forthcoming.

Resentment in Both Parties

In arriving at the agreement, Governor Dewey retreated from the contention he had previously made that no further funds were needed for public housing at this time and that additional funds could not be translated into additional housing, while Mayor O'Dwyer abandoned his claim that New York City was in urgent need of $102,000,000 in additional financial grants from the state.

Senator Arthur H. Wicks, chairman of the Senate Finance Committee, and Assemblyman D. Mallory Stephens, chairman of the Assembly Ways and Means Committee, participated in the conference that led to today's agreement. Senator Elmer F. Quinn and Assemblyman Irwin Steingut, leaders of the Democratic minority in the Senate and Assembly, were informed of it later by the Mayor.

Rank-and-file Republican and Democratic members of the Legislature were irritated and resentful of the agreement when they heard of it.

Republicans' irritation was caused by the fact that they had been called upon earlier in the session to vote down various proposals for increasing the housing loan fund and now were put in the light of surrendering to Democratic demands.

Realty Tax Rise Set at $2.97

Democrats' resentment was caused by the Mayor's concession that the additional state aid they have been fighting for since the session began was not needed.

Meeting with reporters after his talks with the Governor, Mayor O'Dwyer confirmed a statement by Mr. Dewey that the city's revenues for next year, under existing taxing powers, would be $111,000,000 higher than this year's.

He said that the city's expense budget for next year would probably reach $825,000,000, an increase of $114,000,000 over this year's, and that this would make necessary a rise in the real estate tax rate to $2.97 per $100, an increase of 25 points. It will bring the rate to within 3 points of the maximum permitted by the State Constitution, he said.

Asked if the city contemplated using any of the additional taxing powers that would be granted under legislation proposed by Governor Dewey and now pending, he said

Continued on page 30, Column 3

Bridges Says Plan to Slash Budget 'Is Knocked Askew'

He Indicates Revisions Must Be Made to Fit Truman's Plea for Aid to Greece, Turkey—Proposal to Reduce Income Tax Upset

By JOHN D. MORRIS
Special to The New York Times.

WASHINGTON, March 12—Republican fiscal leaders in Congress gave serious attention today to the effect on proposed tax and budget reductions of the new foreign policy line as enunciated by President Truman.

"It knocks budget plans askew," said Senator Styles Bridges of New Hampshire, chairman of the Senate Appropriations Committee. Mr. Bridges is a member of the Joint Conference Committee named to settle differences between House and Senate resolutions to limit Federal spending in the next fiscal year.

The impact, if any, on Republican plans to reduce personal income taxes 20 per cent was unsettled as the House Ways and Means Committee planned to go ahead with hearings on the question tomorrow.

Senator Bridges said the President's request for $400,000,000 to strengthen Greece and Turkey was something that had not been taken into consideration in the Congressional economy drive.

Other Republican budget conferees, however, either were not prepared to assess the effect on their plans or disagreed with Mr. Bridges' conclusions.

Representative Everett M. Dirksen, Republican, of Illinois, who indicated his opposition to the recommended outlays, said that if Congress should approve them they still would be charged against the present fiscal year instead of the year beginning next July 1.

Mr. Bridges maintained, on the other hand, that the funds were requested for expenditure in the coming fiscal year and consequently would have to be taken into ac-

Continued on Page 3, Column 8

SCHOOL PAY VOTED BY STATE SENATE

Republicans Also Pass Taxes for Bonus, Barring Minority Changes in Both Bills

By CLAYTON KNOWLES
Special to The New York Times.

ALBANY, March 12—Overriding a series of Democratic amendments, the Republican-controlled Senate approved today the teacher pay and bonus bills, two major items in Governor Dewey's program. Both still require Assembly action.

The final vote on the teacher pay bill, establishing single schedule minimums running to $5,325 in New York City, was unanimous, but the bonus taxes, featuring a 20 per cent increase in the income tax, were passed exclusively with Republican votes.

Noting that the Democrats and the sole American Labor member were all in the negative in the 39 to 15 vote, Senator Benjamin F. Feinberg, leader of the majority, said:

"I want to place it on the record indelibly that the Democrats have gone on record not to pay for the veterans' bonus."

Tax Proposals by Democrats

This brought a rejoinder from Senator Samuel L. Greenberg, Brooklyn Democrat, who said:

"I was a member of the bipartisan committee on the veterans' bonus. We are all for the bonus, Republicans and Democrats alike, but men have the right to disagree on the means of paying for the bonus. We don't think adding an extra cent to the cigarette tax and

Continued on Page 22, Column 1

PRESIDENT STARTS KEY WEST VACATION

Makes Air Trip in Five Hours for Four Days of Sunshine and Swimming in Florida

By HAROLD B. HINTON
Special to The New York Times.

KEY WEST, Fla., March 12—President Truman arrived here tonight on a vacation which he hopes will last four days. He came by air in a five-hour trip begun after delivery of his message to Congress in the early afternoon.

He looked rested as he stepped from his plane at the Boca Chica Naval Air Station.

As he entered his car a newspaper reporter asked him what impression he thought his message to Congress was producing in Moscow.

"I haven't the slightest idea," he replied.

Some members of the Presidential party felt that some newspaper accounts of the President's vacation, which he deferred from Saturday to prepare and deliver his message to Congress, created the impression that he was ill. They insist that he is in excellent condition, considering the demands of his trip to Mexico and his office activities after his return.

Before the departure from Washington today Brig. Gen. Wallace Graham, his personal physician, said that all the President needed was a little "sunshine, swimming and relaxation."

"I am not prescribing long vacations for the boss," he declared, "but only brief rests which put him at the top of his physical en-

Continued on Page 3, Column 3

Two-Term Presidency Limit Set By Senate in Voting Tenure Plan

Special to The New York Times.

WASHINGTON, March 12—A resolution to submit to the states a Constitutional amendment limiting the tenure of the Presidency to two terms was adopted tonight by the Senate by a vote of 59 to 23.

In the event that a Vice President or another successor serve less than two years in succession to the Presidency, the Senate provided that he serve two full elective terms, or a maximum of ten years. A Vice President succeeding to a term of more than two years would be limited to one elective term, or a maximum of six years.

Eleven Democrats, virtually all from the South, joined the solid Republican forces in support of the measure. Opposition came entirely from other Democrats.

The measure now goes to conference with the House, which approved over a month ago a bill limiting Presidential tenure to two terms without any extenuating provisions and counting a partially served term as a regular term.

When differences are reconciled, the measure upon final enactment will have to be submitted to the Legislatures of the states for approval by three-fourths of them within seven years.

The limitation of the tenure of those succeeding to the Presidency, excepting President Truman, was adopted by the Senate by a voice vote on an amendment offered by Senator Robert A. Taft, Republican, of Ohio, which read:

"No person shall be elected to the office of the President more than twice and no person who has held the office of President or has acted as President for more than two years of a term to which some

Continued on Page 21, Column 2

BEVIN SHARP IN BIG 4

Cites Report That Soviet Is Enlisting Germans in Armed Forces

MOLOTOV IS SET BACK

He Admits Delay in Ship Demolition, Agrees to Prisoner Census

Excerpts from Bevin statement at Big 4 parley, Page 12.

By DREW MIDDLETON
Special to The New York Times.

MOSCOW, March 12—Ernest Bevin, Britain's chunky, gravel-voiced Foreign Secretary, demanded of the Russians today an explanation of reports that they were enlisting German war veterans in the Soviet armed forces.

Interrupting a Soviet recital of alleged United States and British failings in demilitarization in Germany, Mr. Bevin also demanded in the Council of Foreign Ministers that Foreign Minister Molotov of Russia explain what the Briton described as the transfer of a "vast number" of old and unfit Germans from the Soviet zone of occupation.

Mr. Bevin called for categorical assurance that German prisoners of war were not being "induced to join" the Soviet Army, Navy and Air Force, and asked for details on the number of prisoners still in Soviet prisoner-of-war camps.

There is no assurance, the Foreign Secretary also declared, that the Russians are moving ahead on the destruction of capital ships of the German Navy, as well as on aircraft carriers and submarines, that were turned over to them at the war's end by the tripartite naval commission.

Mr. Molotov was slightly ruffled by Mr. Bevin's speech, which covered seventeen points defending

Continued on Page 12, Column 3

CONGRESS IS SOLEMN

Prepares to Consider Bills After Hearing the President Gravely

SOVIET CALLED ISSUE

Some Hold Truman Plan Is Blow to U. N.—All but Marcantonio Applaud

By C. P. TRUSSELL
Special to The New York Times.

WASHINGTON, March 12 — A much-shaken Congress squared off today to meet, concededly, one of the toughest deadlines in modern history. This deadline was the providing of the financial and technical aid to Greece and Turkey that President Truman urged at the Congressional Joint Session before British commitments are withdrawn from those countries on March 31.

Congress stepped into its new task somewhat bewildered. Members, as they listened to the Chief Executive, saw their country's foreign policy undergo radical change in the space of twenty-one minutes.

They reacted sharply. At points they were in violent conflict. At the same time there was evident constantly an agreement that decisive action under the bold recommendations of the President must be taken. Key men of Congress predicted that the action would be taken, and on time.

There was evidence, too, that a Congressional storm of great dimensions was in the making. Some members saw "a new, world-wide Monroe Doctrine" going into force. Some saw in the President's words a "declaration of war" upon Russia. What the President had proposed was viewed in some quarters as "intervention" in the Mediterranean; in others it was concluded that a new lend-lease had come into supposed peacetime being.

There were expressions of ap-

Continued on Page 4, Column 2

World News Summarized

THURSDAY, MARCH 13, 1947

President Truman enunciated a new foreign policy when he asked a joint session of Congress yesterday to authorize $400,000,000 in financial, technical and material aid to help Greece and Turkey repel "totalitarian aggression" threatening their national integrity.

"I believe," he said, "that it must be the policy of the United States to support free people who are resisting attempted subjugation by armed minorities or by outside pressure." He also declared that "we must take immediate and resolute action" and "must not falter in our leadership."

At the outset Mr. Truman told Congress that the "gravity of the situation which confronts the world today" involves "the foreign policy and the national security of this country." The alternative to granting aid, he said, "is much more serious."

The President blamed the Communists for Greece's internal difficulties, but did not give the Greek Government a clean bill of health. Although not mentioning Russia by name, he left no doubt that he considered the Soviet Union the source of "totalitarian aggression." [All the foregoing 1:8; map P. 2.]

Mr. Truman departed immediately after speaking for a four-day rest in Florida. [1:3.]

While majority opinion in Congress supported the President's objectives, there was some criticism [1:5] of what London observers considered a bold, direct challenge to Russia. [3:5.] Diplomats in Paris saw an extension of the Monroe Doctrine bound to force a show-down with Moscow [3:1], and in Athens only the Communists protested [6:3.] Republican fiscal leaders in Washington considered the effect of the speech on their plans to reduce the President's budget and to cut income taxes. [1:2-3.]

Secretary Marshall was said to be determined to retain the diplomatic offensive at the Foreign Ministers' Conference in Moscow, anxious for Russian cooperation but resolved to push ahead without it if necessary. [1:6-7.] Foreign Secretary Bevin denied Foreign Minister Molotov's charge that German demilitarization in the British and American zones had been slow, and asked what Russia had done with millions of war prisoners and why captured naval craft had not been destroyed. [1:4.]

Moscow has suddenly recalled its Ambassadors from Washington and London, presumably in connection with the Big Four meeting. [8:2-3.]

Entry into Yugoslavia was barred to a United Nations commission because it sought to visit Dragos, said to be a supply center in Yugoslavia for Greek guerrillas. [1:6-7.]

Government troops in Paraguay surrounded Concepción, center of a Leftist revolt. [20:4-5, with map.]

Britain's Labor Government, withstanding a three-day debate on economic policies, won a 371-204 vote of confidence. [1:7.]

Southern Democratic Senators helped Republicans place a ten-year limit on Presidential tenure. [1:2-3.]

The State Senate passed bills increasing teachers' pay and for taxes with which to pay the proposed veterans' bonus. [1:2.]

Governor Dewey agreed to push an increase of $135,000,000 in State housing aid to this city and Mayor O'Dwyer withdrew his request for additional fiscal help. The Mayor later said the local realty tax would jump twenty-five points to $2.97. [1:1.]

AFL employes of Wall Street houses will vote today on a strike that may tie up the Stock Exchange. [23:4.]

ASKING AID FOR GREECE AND TURKEY

President Truman addressing Congress yesterday
Associated Press Wirephoto

Yugoslavs Block U. N. Entry To Reported Guerrilla Base

By W. H. LAWRENCE
Special to The New York Times.

ON THE GREEK-YUGOSLAV FRONTIER, March 12—Yugoslav authorities barred a United Nations Investigating Commission team from entering Dragos, Yugoslavia, today. This town has been named as a supply center and station on the underground railway for Yugoslav-trained Greek guerrillas reentering Greece to resume the civil war.

The Yugoslav action brought into sharp focus the United States' insistence on full, free international inspection without any veto before the atomic bomb secret is shared with other countries, especially in Russian-dominated eastern Europe.

The Yugoslav commander of the sector said he would permit the team to proceed to Bitolj, Yugoslavia, but his orders did not include a visit to Dragos.

The flat refusal to permit the commission to visit Dragos was communication to J. D. L. Hood of Australia, chairman of the United Nations commission's team No. 1, which left Salonika Monday by automobile for a study of frontier incidents in Greece, Yugoslavia and Albania.

Mr. Hood protested without avail. He declared that the Yugoslav military or secret police was assuming enormous responsibility in impeding the work of the United Nations, of which Yugoslavia is a member.

The commission team halted at a Yugoslav frontier post between the Greek village of Aghia Paraskevi and Dragos at about noon. The group waited nearly two hours while the Yugoslav liaison officer, Lale Ivanovitch, confirmed by telephone that authorities in Bitolj

Continued on Page 6, Column 4

ATTLEE IS UPHELD IN CONFIDENCE VOTE

Regime's Prestige Drops, but It Wins, 374-198—Churchill Sees 'Crime Against Britain'

By MALLORY BROWNE
Special to The New York Times.

LONDON, March 12—Great Britain's Labor Government emerged tonight, battered but victorious, from three days of the hardest hitting political battle it had yet experienced.

The House of Commons, by a vote of 371 to 204, approved the Government's economic policy and its plans for getting out of the present grave production crisis.

An Opposition amendment of "no confidence" moved by Winston Churchill today in his fiercest attack yet on Socialist planning was defeated, 374 to 198.

In both cases the votes against the Government were significantly high. They were regarded by British political observers as confirming the general impression that the Labor Government came out of the highly critical debate on its economic policy with its prestige definitely lowered.

In fact, there was a feeling in

Continued on Page 15, Column 4

Marshall Ready to By-Pass Soviet If It Rejects 4-Power Cooperation

By C. L. SULZBERGER
Special to The New York Times.

MOSCOW, March 12—A thoroughly prepared United States delegation to the Council of Foreign Ministers' meeting is ready to take the offensive wherever the diplomatic chess game permits. It is resolved not to be outmaneuvered into tactical positions where the United States would lose prestige, and is determined to press for four-power cooperation on a realistic basis.

If such cooperation is not forthcoming at this meeting, Secretary of State Marshall intends to go ahead with plans tantamount to the exclusion of the Soviet Union from participation in basic areas.

For example, he is already prepared—if Foreign Minister Molotov continues to oppose Western ideas for German reconstruction, and Premier Stalin eventually comes out against them—to strive to integrate the United States, British and French zones on a basis sufficently workable that the Soviet zone not only would compare unfavorably but would in the end be technically unworkable.

The Big Four Council is still in the initial, feinting stage. Things have not gone badly from anybody's viewpoint. Each delegate is eagerly talking for the record, knowing that his remarks will be eagerly reported with the national emphasis given by his spokesman at the press briefings. The more discreet aspects of diplomatic horse-trading will certainly develop later.

General Marshall is evidently resolved to maintain the diplomatic

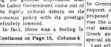

Continued on Page 10, Column 2

NEW POLICY SET UP

President Blunt in Plea to Combat 'Coercion' as World Peril

PLANS TO SEND MEN

Goods and Skills Needed as Well as Money, He Tells Congress

Truman's message to Congress on Mid-East crisis, Page 2.

By FELIX BELAIR Jr.
Special to The New York Times.

WASHINGTON, March 12 — President Truman outlined a new foreign policy for the United States today. In a historic message to Congress, he proposed that this country intervene wherever necessary throughout the world to prevent the subjection of free peoples to Communist-inspired totalitarian regimes at the expense of their national integrity and importance.

In a request for $400,000,000 to bolster the hard-pressed Greek and Turkish Governments against Communist pressure, the President said the constant coercion and intimidation of free peoples by political infiltration amid poverty and strife undermined the foundations of world peace and threatened the security of the United States.

Although the President refrained from mentioning the Soviet Union by name, there could be no mistaking his identification of the Communist state as the source of much of the unrest throughout the world. He said that, in violation of the Yalta Agreement, the people of Poland, Rumania and Bulgaria had been subjected to totalitarian regimes against their will and that there had been similar developments in other countries.

Cardinal Points of Departure

As the Senate and House of Representatives sat grim-faced but apparently determined on the course recommended by the Chief Executive, Mr. Truman made these cardinal points of departure from traditional American foreign policy:

"I believe that it must be the policy of the United States to support free peoples who are resisting attempted subjugation by armed minorities or by outside pressures.

"I believe that we must assist free peoples to work out their own destinies in their own way.

"I believe that our help should be primarily through economic and financial aid which is essential to economic stability and orderly political processes."

In addition to the $400,000,000, to be expended before June 30, 1948, the President asked Congress to authorize the detail of American civilian and military personnel to Greece and Turkey, upon the request of those countries. The proposed personnel would supervise the use of material and financial assistance and would train Greek and Turkish personnel in special skills.

Lest efforts be made to cast him in the role of champion of things as they are, the President recognized that the world was not static and that the status quo was not sacred. But he warned that if we allowed changes in the status quo in violation of the United Nations Charter through such subterfuges as political infiltration, we would be helping to destroy the Charter itself.

Aware of Broad Implications

President Truman said he was fully aware of the "broad implications involved" if the United States went to the assistance of Greece and Turkey. He said that, while our aid to free peoples striving to maintain their independence should be primarily financial and economic, he reminded Congress that the fundamental issues involved were no different from those for which we fought a war with Germany and Japan.

The standing ovation that marked the close of the President's address was echoing through the Capitol

Continued on Page 2, Column 3

1947

Cars with wood side-paneling were very popular all through the decade. This post-war Plymouth Special DeLuxe wagon sold for approximately $1,500.

Tommy Dorsey and his band.

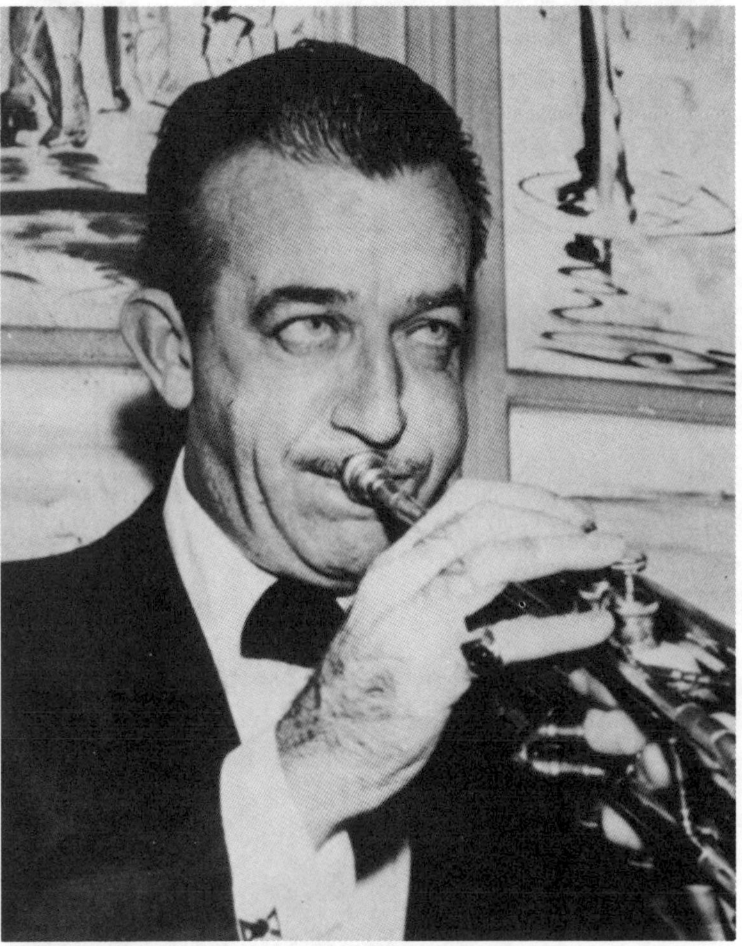

Harry James is still one of the great trumpet players and band leaders of all time.

Singer Nat "King" Cole's *Christmas Song* was a big hit in 1947, and is now considered a classic.

Comedian Jack Benny's radio show was one of the most popular of all time.

Tennessee Williams, one of the great American playwrights of our day, had a big hit in 1947 with *A Streetcar Named Desire.*

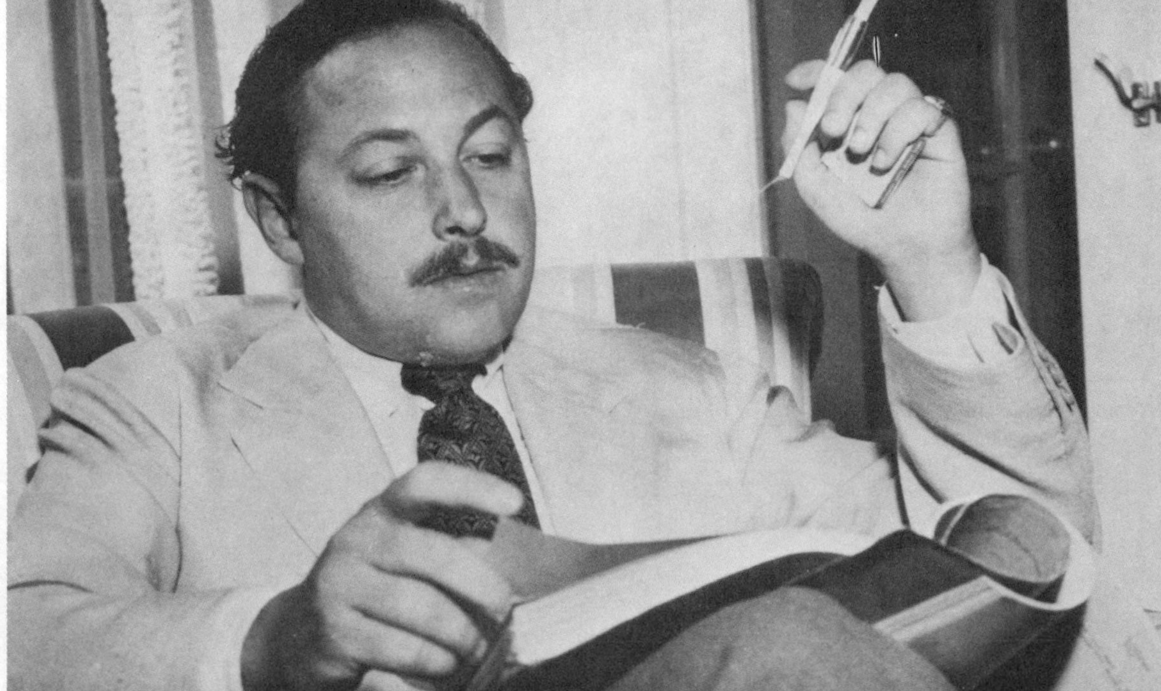

"All the News That's Fit to Print"

The New York Times.

LATE CITY EDITION
Mostly sunny and warmer today and tomorrow.
Temperatures Yesterday—Max., 42; Min., 37
Sunrise today, 5:57 A. M.; Sunset, 6:10 P. M.
U. S. Weather Bureau Report, Page 10, Sect. 5

Section 1

NEWS INDEX, PAGE 63, THIS SECTION

VOL. XCVI. No. 32,565. Entered as Second-Class Matter, Postoffice, New York, N. Y.

NEW YORK, SUNDAY, MARCH 23, 1947.

Including Magazine and Book Review.

TEN CENTS New York City and Suburban Areas (15c Elsewhere)

PRESIDENT ORDERS INQUIRY ON DISLOYAL JOBHOLDERS; COMMUNISTS FIRST TARGET

Special Board Insists Posts Go Only to Loyal Citizens

Report, Released by President, Declares This Must Be a Governing Factor in Determining an Employe's Fitness

Special to The New York Times.

WASHINGTON, March 22—The report by the President's Temporary Commission on Employe Loyalty, released by President Truman today, provides for the first time a systematic program for weighing loyalty to the United States Government with other qualifications in determining a person's eligibility for a Federal job.

Before 1939, the report states, qualifications for Federal employment were "assayed" independently of the attribute of loyalty.

Acting upon the commission's recommendations, Mr. Truman issued his Executive Order immediately putting into effect a comprehensive plan for eliminating disloyal persons from the employ of the Government.

The report represents the combined efforts of top-ranking officials of six Government agencies which are concerned most acutely in the problem of employe loyalty. Chairman of the group was A. Devitt Vanech, Assistant Attorney General and formerly special assistant to the Attorney General.

Other members were John E. Peurifoy, Acting Assistant Secretary of State for Administration; Edward H. Foley Jr., Assistant Secretary of the Treasury; Kenneth G. Royall, Under-Secretary of War; John L. Sullivan, Under-Secretary of the Navy, and Harry B. Mitchell, president of the Civil Service Commission.

The group was named by the President in an Executive Order of Nov. 25, 1946, and held its first meeting on Dec. 5.

It was specifically established to inquire into:

"(A) The standards, procedures and organizational provisions for the investigation of persons who are employed by the United States Government, or who are applicants for such employment,

"(B) The removal or disqualification from employment of any

Continued on Page 48, Column 1

FBI WILL AID STUDY

In Unprecedented Step Heads of Departments Must Back 'Purge'

REVIEW BOARD IS CREATED

It Will Hear Final Appeals of All Workers or Applicants Marked For Job Elimination

The text of the President's order appears on Page 49.

By WALTER H. WAGGONER
Special to The New York Times.

WASHINGTON, March 22 — President Truman, by executive decree, ordered into effect today an elaborate and unprecedented program of security and precautions against Federal employment of any person who, on "reasonable grounds," can be judged disloyal.

The Presidential Order called for an immediate investigation of the loyalty and intentions of every person entering civilian employment in any department or agency of the Executive Branch of the Government.

Present job holders who have not already been checked for loyalty will be scrutinized by the Federal Bureau of Investigation, and their fate will rest on the decision of department heads held "personally responsible" for the character of their subordinates.

Although they were not singled out in the order, Communists and Communist sympathizers would be the first targets of the President's prescribed loyalty standards, it was indicated.

There have been repeated allegations in Congress that Communists held Federal posts, and many attacks have been made on the Administration for not ridding itself of them.

Charges Made By House Group

The House Civil Service Committee charged this week that only nine persons had been discharged from Government jobs as Communists since July 1, and promised a "full-scale investigation" of additional suspected employes.

Mr. Truman called for this sweeping program on the recommendation of his six-agency Temporary Commission on Employe Loyalty, which he named by Executive Order on last Nov. 25.

The President received the Commission's thirty-eight-page report on Feb. 20. Its publication had been held up, according to Charles G. Ross, White House press secretary, so that Mr. Truman could "study it and give time for the preparation of an Executive Order which carries out and implements the recommendations of the Commission."

Introducing his order, the President stated that every Government employe "is endowed with a measure of trusteeship over the democratic processes which are the heart and sinew of the United States."

It was of vital importance that all Federal employes be of "complete and unswerving loyalty" to this country, he continued, adding that the presence of any disloyal or subversive persons "constitutes a threat to our democratic processes."

Major Provisions of Order

Other major provisions of the ruling, in summary form, are as follows:

1. A "central master index" will be compiled of the records of all persons who have undergone loyalty checks by any agency or department since Sept. 1, 1939.

2. An over-all "Loyalty Review Board" will be set up in the Civil Service Commission, consisting of three "impartial" officers or employes of the commission. The board will review cases as an authority of final appeal for employes recommended for dismissal on grounds of disloyalty.

3. One or more three-member loyalty boards will be named by the head of each department or

Continued on Page 48, Column 3

MARSHALL URGES NATIONAL COUNCIL TO RULE GERMANY

Limited Central Authority and Ban on Special Rights for Any Party Proposed

SOVIET ALSO OFFERS PLAN

Molotov Suggests Big Four Use Weimar Constitution as Model for Future

The Marshall and Molotov proposals, Page 12.

By DREW MIDDLETON
Special to The New York Times.

MOSCOW, March 22—The establishment of a German national council as the provisional government at an early date was advocated by United States Secretary of State Marshall in the Council of Foreign Ministers' meeting tonight.

The decisions of this government would be carried out through a German federal state composed of not less than ten nor more than eighteen Laender, according to Secretary Marshall's plan on the form and scope of the provisional political organization in Germany.

The United States plan would strictly limit the powers of the central government over the police, include a bill of rights and prevent any political party from enjoying a privileged status.

Seeks to Guard Freedoms

These provisions are the guarantees the United States seeks in its efforts to provide true political freedom in Germany and to prevent the rise of another totalitarian government.

This historic document, which was the most concrete plan ever presented by a United States representative for the Government of a conquered nation, followed the presentation of two other plans for Germany's future political organization.

The creation of a provisional German government without further delay was proposed by Soviet Foreign Minister Molotov. The Soviet plan was coupled with a denunciation by Mr. Molotov of plans for federalizing Germany.

Mr. Molotov's introductory remarks and his plan taken together forecast a German regime considerably more centralized and stronger than that envisaged by Secretary Marshall. British Foreign Secretary Bevin or French Foreign Minister Bidault.

Main Provisions in Proposal

The plan submitted by Secretary Marshall asked for the prompt election of governments in all German states. Once this had been done the Allied Control Council would be instructed to:

(1) Establish at an early date a German national council as a provisional government "to be composed of the heads of present Laender governments."

(2) Refrain from "direct operation or detailed supervision" of provisional government activities.

(3) Instruct the provisional government to prepare a democratic constitution and call a constitutional convention elected by the people. This would submit a draft constitution to the convention for debate, revision and adoption.

(4) Direct the provisional government to submit to the Allied Control Council any modifications in the territorial composition of the provisional Laender "necessary to form a German federal state composed of not less than ten or more than eighteen Laender."

Under the United States proposal the German provisional government also would be told by the Allies that approval of the constitution by them would depend on the fulfillment of two basic conditions.

One of these is that Germany is to be "a democratic state" and the other is that "the German Government is to be one of limited powers."

The Marshall proposal insisted that Germany was to be a democratic state in the respect that all political power originate with the people "and is subject to their control."

Elections would be held at frequent intervals and would be conducted under conditions in which political parties "competing freely" would submit their programs.

Secretary Marshall then inserted

Continued on Page 13, Column 1

U. S. Seeks Palestine Move By British Before U. N. Acts

Presentation of Final Proposal to Arabs and Zionists Reported Pressed—Attitude of Jewish Agency Held Vital

Special to The New York Times.

LAKE SUCCESS, N. Y., March 22—The British Government has been asked by the United States to consider making one last try at solving the Palestine problem by presenting a final proposal to the Arabs and Zionists before handing the case to the United Nations, it was reported today.

Five weeks after Foreign Secretary Bevin first announced that he would submit the Palestine question to the United Nations, high level talks are still going on among Foreign Office and State Department officials.

The conferences were begun to work out a way of starting United Nations action on Palestine but they also have dealt with the American suggestion that the British might make still another attempt at working out an agreement between the two Palestine factions.

For their part, British spokesmen are reported to be echoing Mr. Bevin's statements to the effect that London has made every effort to bring the Jews and the Arabs together and that repeated failures left recourse to the United Nations as the only remaining step.

Meanwhile, the problem of just how to put Palestine before the United Nations, if there is no other settlement, is being handled gingerly by the American and British delegations.

The chief possibility being discussed is Secretary General Trygve Lie's suggestion of a United Nations commission to do some investigational spadework in the next few months and prepare a report for the General Assembly meeting in September. Mr. Lie put forward the idea with the clear understanding that it would be dropped if any of the Big Five had objections.

The American answer came two weeks ago and it was a flat statement that the United States would

Continued on Page 27, Column 4

REPLIES ON GREECE SPED FOR CONGRESS

Dewey Backs Truman Program for Aid—Barkley Doubts Deadline Will Be Met

By ANTHONY LEVIERO
Special to The New York Times.

WASHINGTON, March 22—The State Department was busy today preparing answers to more than 100 "very intelligent, fair and useful questions" from Congress on President Truman's Greek-Turkish aid program. The queries were assembled by Senator Arthur H. Vandenberg, president pro tempore of the Senate.

[Governor Dewey in a statement endorsed President Truman's project to aid Greece in her resistance to "armed and ideological aggression."]

[Greece now has an area of martial law in southern Peloponnesus, where Rightists on Friday broke into a jail and killed Leftist prisoners, while fighting throughout Macedonia between Greek Army and guerrilla forces is increasing, Athens reported.]

Answers Due Tomorrow

The answers to Congress' questions will be made public Monday morning, when the Congressional inquiry on the plan designed to bolster Greece and Turkey against feared totalitarian engulfment goes into a double-barreled phase.

Dean Acheson, Acting Secretary of State, who has completed his testimony on the issue in the House Foreign Affairs Committee, will face the Senate Foreign Relations Committee as its first witness Monday. Mr. Vandenberg, who collected the questions on a bipartisan basis, will receive the answers then. He heads the committee.

On the House side the inquiry will continue. William L. Clayton, Under-Secretary of State for Economic Affairs, will be a witness. He will be followed by Robert P. Patterson, Secretary of War, and James Forrestal, Secretary of the Navy.

The description of the questions as intelligent, fair and useful was made by an official who had stud-

Continued on Page 3, Column 6

REDS' DEAL SAVES CABINET IN FRANCE

Communists Abstain From Vote on Credits but Allow Their Ministers to Approve

By HAROLD CALLENDER
Special to The New York Times.

PARIS, March 22—The Government crisis was surmounted today by agreement that the Communists in the Assembly might abstain from voting on military credits for the forces in Indo-China so long as their Ministers voted for those credits and remained in the Cabinet.

As a result of this compromise, proposed by the Communists, the Assembly's vote of confidence by 411 to 0 was accepted by Premier Paul Ramadier although the Communist Deputies withheld their ballots while the Communist Ministers voted with the Government.

Jacques Duclos, Communist floor leader, made a conciliatory appeal, saying his party differed with the Cabinet only on Indo-China and did not intend to destroy the Cabinet's solidarity during the Moscow conference. Premier Ramadier, who had indicated Thursday that he would not accept this "equivocal situation," accepted it today on the theory that he had gained both a vote of confidence and Cabinet solidarity.

Radicals Shift Stand

The Radical group first decided by a margin of two votes to withdraw its Ministers, which would have created a new crisis, then changed its mind and rescinded this decision.

The result is that the Cabinet will continue unchanged for the present, but by virtue of accepting a novel principle in parliamentary government, the principle that a party may repudiate the policy of the Government and of its own Ministers without withdrawing those Ministers from the Cabinet.

Today's precedent seems to mean that whenever they choose, and on any issue, the Communists may be both technically for and against the Government, that they may vehemently oppose a Govern-

Continued on Page 5, Column 3

CONGRESS PARLEY ENDS IN DEADLOCK ON CUTS IN BUDGET

Conference Committee Splits as House Group Insists on Reduction of Six Billion

$5,250,000,000 IS REJECTED

Democrats Charge Republicans Plan to Shelve Problem Till Foreign Situation Clears Up

By JOHN D. MORRIS
Special to The New York Times.

WASHINGTON, March 22—Republicans presented the issue of how much President Truman's budget should be cut to a Senate-House conference committee today, and a deadlock promptly resulted.

The development served to emphasize a disagreement between Senate and House Republican members of the committee, who had been holding private meetings for more than two weeks in an effort to settle the question among themselves before submitting it to the full committee.

The conference committee was appointed March 4 to adjust differences between House and Senate resolutions to limit Federal spending in the fiscal year beginning next July 1. The House voted Feb. 20 for a $6,000,000,000 reduction in the President's $37,500,000,000 budget.

The Senate approved on March 3 a revised resolution reducing the proposed cut to $4,500,000,000 and advocating the application to the public debt of $2,600,000,000 plus $1,100,000,000 of anticipated receipts from surplus war property sales.

Debt Reduction Discussed

At today's first meeting of the full joint conference committee, the House delegation unanimously rejected a proposal to compromise on a cut of $5,250,000,000, as moved by Senator Kenneth D. McKellar, Democrat, of Tennessee, and supported by the Senate conferees, 7 to 2.

It was explained that the House Republicans were holding out for the full $6,000,000,000 slash, while their Democratic colleagues and the two dissenting Senators, Alben W. Barkley, Democrat, of Kentucky, and Chan Gurney, Republican, of South Dakota, felt that even $5,250,000,000 was too drastic a cut.

The conferees discussed the Sen-

Continued on Page 33, Column 2

SENATE GOP SPLIT ON EFFORT TO KEEP RENT, SUGAR CURBS

Neither Question Is Put to Vote Despite Truman Pressure as Deadline Nears

FACTIONS ARE FAR APART

President Signs a Bill to End OTC but Orders Controls Stay on Effective Basis

Special to The New York Times.

WASHINGTON, March 22—Senate Republicans failed today in an attempt to agree on a policy with respect to extension of controls over rents and sugar. President Truman said prompt Congressional action was "urgently needed."

The Senate majority conference, comprising the upper chamber's fifty-one Republican members, was divided to such an extent that neither question was put to a vote, members reported after a closed meeting.

In recognition of the urgency of the situation, with rationing authority slated to expire March 31 and price and rent control powers to end on June 30, Senator Alexander D. Wiley of Wisconsin proposed a three-month extension beyond March 31 of the Second War Powers Act, from which the Administration draws its rationing authority. However, the proposal received no support.

New Talks Are Planned

Senator Milton R. Young of North Dakota, conference secretary, reported that further efforts would be made to settle differences over sugar between a group headed by Senator Joseph R. McCarthy of Wisconsin, who advocates removal of all controls, and another led by Senators Charles W. Tobey of New Hampshire and Ralph E. Flanders of Vermont, who want them retained.

The House has passed a bill to extend sugar control authority until Oct. 31. The Senate Banking and Currency Committee has reported out a bill to continue the powers until March 31, 1948.

Failure of Senators to settle differences over rent control increased prospects that the issue would go to the floor with Republicans still seriously divided.

A rent subcommittee of the Senate Banking Committee has approved extension of controls until Feb. 29, 1948, without a gen-

Continued on Page 33, Column 3

World News Summarized

SUNDAY, MARCH 23, 1947

An executive decree by President Truman put into effect a program calling for an investigation of the loyalty of all persons about to be employed in any department or agency of the executive branch of the Federal Government. The order also asked a check on present employes who have not already been investigated by the Federal Bureau of Investigation. Communists, it was indicated, will be the first to come under scrutiny. [1:8.]

This sweeping program was adopted by Mr. Truman after his six-agency Temporary Commission on Employe Loyalty had made its report. This report provides a systematic plan for assessing loyalty to the United States Government and judging other qualifications. [1:6-7.]

The Senate-House conference committee was deadlocked over the issue of how much to slash from President Truman's proposed budget. [1:4.] Senate Republicans also were divided on a policy for extension of controls over rents and sugar. [1:5.]

Secretary of State Marshall urged the Council of Foreign Ministers to approve the early creation of a German national council as the provisional government of Germany. This government, under Secretary Marshall's plan, would function as a German federal state consisting of no fewer than ten and no more than eighteen Laender. Earlier, Foreign Minister Molotov had opposed any federalization of Germany and had urged that the constitution of the Weimar Republic be taken as the basis for the fundamental laws of the new Germany. [1:1.]

Foreign Secretary Bevin issued a detailed proposal for augmenting German industry and fixing by Aug. 15 the total quantity of plant and equipment to be removed from Germany. [12:3.]

The Foreign Ministers ended their second week of discussions in an atmosphere of harmony that encouraged observers to feel that the Council was ready to tackle the thorny problems of real negotiation and might conclude its meeting more quickly than had been hoped. [1:2-3.]

The State Department will make public tomorrow its answers to more than 100 "very intelligent, fair and useful questions" from members of Congress on President Truman's proposal to aid Greece and Turkey. [1:2.] Some of the documents that had been given to the House Foreign Affairs Committee to support Mr. Truman's plan were made public. These stressed that only substantial aid could avert a paralysis of Greek economy. [4:1.]

Governor Dewey, in a proclamation naming March 25 as Greek War Relief Day, backed the Truman proposal to extend a political loan to aid Greece to resist "armed and ideological aggression." [3:5.]

In London, authoritative sources declared that the British Government opposed at this time ceding Cyprus to Greece. [3:3-4.]

The Greek Government imposed martial law in the Laconia district of southern Greece, where leftist political prisoners were killed Friday in an attack on a jail in the town of Gythium. [2:2, with map.]

Washington was reported to have asked London to consider making a final attempt to solve the problem of Palestine before submitting it to the United Nations. [1:2-3.]

A compromise plan under which the Communists in the French Assembly abstained from voting on military credits for the campaign in Indo-China while their representatives in the Cabinet supported the credits averted the crisis that had threatened the Government. [1:3.]

HUNT FOR COLLYER SET FOR TOMORROW

Police to Enter Home Again if Surviving Brother Fails to Make an Appearance

The whereabouts of Langley Collyer, now sole heir to more than $100,000 since the death on Friday of his blind brother Homer, remained unknown yesterday.

Four relatives of the eccentric Harlem recluses, who lived for thirty-nine years in their once-fashionable mansion at 2078 Fifth Avenue, came forward with some details of the early life of the two brothers. But none of them had any idea of where Langley could be. Neither did the police.

John R. McMullen, lawyer for the Collyers for fifteen years, thought that Langley might still be in the decaying house.

"Your guess is as good as mine," he said, "but I think he is in the house, myself."

Mr. McMullen added that he believed Langley still was alive. The police agreed, but their theory was that he was not in the house, which has been boarded up since Friday afternoon.

Detectives of the West 123d Street station argued that the younger Collyer brother frequently took shopping trips for more than twenty-four hours, sometimes walking as far as the Williamsburg section of Brooklyn for whole wheat bread. He might be on one of those trips at present, they said.

If he does not appear by 1 P. M. tomorrow, Deputy Inspector Christopher Salsieder said, a missing person's alarm would be sent

Continued on Page 28, Column 2

SENATORS RULE OUT HIGH COURT INQUIRY

Judiciary Group Says Congress Lacks Power of Removal Except by Impeachment

Special to The New York Times.

WASHINGTON, March 22—An echo of last summer's outburst in the bitter feud between Supreme Court Justices Robert H. Jackson and Hugo L. Black rumbled out of the Senate Judiciary Committee today. The justices will not have to face a Congressional inquiry after all.

The committee produced a printed document with the imposing title of "Memorandum on Removal Power of Congress With Respect to the Supreme Court."

Some interesting conjectures began to grow around this paper. Speculation got really fanciful over the statement accompanying the "memorandum." It was signed by Senator Alexander Wiley of Wisconsin, committee chairman. Some observers thought the statement was cryptic, as if implying that an inquiry, strongly rumored last June, was impending. They could just see the nine justices awaiting their turn in the witness chair.

Congress' Power Discussed

Puzzlement on Capitol Hill grew out of a misunderstanding of the objective of the study, in spite of this carefully phrased passage in Senator Wiley's statement:

"I firmly believe in the Constitutional system of three independent and co-equal branches—legislative, executive, and judicial—and I have felt that Congress should approach this matter only on the

Continued on Page 39, Column 3

Optimism of Big Four Increases; Committee Named to Speed Work

By C. L. SULZBERGER
Special to The New York Times.

MOSCOW, March 22—The Council of Foreign Ministers completed the initial stage of its Moscow meeting this evening—that of the individual presentation of national views on Germany's future. This phase was concluded in record time and in an atmosphere of broad generalized harmony, which exceeded some preliminary hopes.

Statements for the record by each Minister would appear to have been concluded. None of them during the past twelve days gave the impression of stalling for time to avoid eventual decisions.

The period of vague debate and rebuttal would seem to be over and next week the Council should commence a phase of real negotiation. This will have two basic purposes:

(1) To achieve general agreement on principles of a provisional German Government and economic unification. This does not mean the structure of the eventual permanent German Government, although obviously it would have influence upon that.

(2) To accelerate the process of drafting an Austrian treaty.

Austrian Foreign Minister Dr. Karl Gruber and his delegation are expected here next week and after having heard his views the Council can begin real bargaining. If the question of German assets in Austria can be compromised, there should be nothing to prevent a really swift completion of the Austrian draft.

United States Secretary of State

Continued on Page 11, Column 2

Wage Truce Averts Rubber Strike; Union Gets 11½-Cent Increase

By WALTER W. RUCH
Special to The New York Times.

CLEVELAND, March 22—A strike against the "Big Four" of the rubber industry was averted at the eleventh hour tonight when union representatives agreed to accept a wage increase of about 11½ cents an hour, or less than half of the 26 cents which comprised their original demand.

The importance in labor-management relations of the agreement between the companies, which make about 90 per cent of the automobile tires in the nation, and the United Rubber Workers, CIO, could hardly be overestimated.

Telegrams were sent immediately to all locals in thirty-five cities from coast to coast. They had been standing ready to post picket lines around factories Monday morning.

The agreement was announced by L. S. Buckmaster, international president of the union, following a long meeting of the steering committee of the union, a meeting of company representatives with the smaller negotiating committee, and finally discussion over coffee by an even smaller group.

The companies involved in the dispute are Goodyear, Goodrich, Firestone and United States Rubber.

Representatives of the union met with reporters late tonight to announce the agreement which ended the threat of a strike of 110,000 workers. Such a strike would have forced the automotive industry to a standstill within three weeks.

Mr. Buckmaster had insisted from the start that the union

Continued on Page 44, Column 4

"All the News That's Fit to Print"

The New York Times.

LATE CITY EDITION
Fair and warmer today and tomorrow.
Temperatures Yesterday—Max., 65; Min., 54
Sunrise today, 5:24 A.M.; Sunset, 8:23 P.M.
Full U. S. Weather Bureau Report, Page 46.

VOL. XCVI...No. 32,640. Entered as Second-Class Matter, Postoffice, New York, N. Y. NEW YORK, FRIDAY, JUNE 6, 1947. THREE CENTS IN NEW YORK CITY

TRUMAN CALLS HUNGARY COUP OUTRAGE, DEMANDS RUSSIANS AGREE TO INQUIRY; MARSHALL PLEADS FOR EUROPEAN UNITY

PRESIDENT HOLDS TAFT'S ECONOMICS FALSE, DANGEROUS

BOOM-BUST IDEA HIT

Truman Attacks a View That Demand Justifies Keeping Prices High

INSISTS THEY CAN BE CUT

Decline From April Peak Noted in Formal Reply to Charge High Levels Are Wanted

Truman's statement criticizing Taft's economic views, Page 18.

By HAROLD B. HINTON
Special to THE NEW YORK TIMES.

WASHINGTON, June 5—President Truman, in a highly unusual step, denounced today as "fallacious and dangerous" certain economic views he attributed to Senator Robert A. Taft, Republican, of Ohio, one of the leaders of the majority party in Congress. A year ago he condemned Mr. Taft's economics in his message vetoing the first bill for the extension of price control.

In a long prepared statement which he read at his news conference today Mr. Truman took the position that the Ohio Senator stood for the theory that "high demand justifies or necessitates high prices." The President said that this view could only rely on "the old idea of boom and bust."

The Chief Executive included in his statement a table, prepared by the Bureau of Labor Statistics, which showed that prices of all commodities, taken together, had declined by two points by May 31 from the peak reached on April 30. The figure was 147.4 for the end of May, as compared with 149.4 for the end of April. These figures are based on 1926 levels as equaling 100.

Calls Again for Price Cuts

Still showing resentment at the virtual abandonment of price controls last summer, the President repeated his belief that the danger of collapse in the national economy could be averted by voluntary price reductions, now that price controls no longer existed. This has been his principal suggestion throughout his price-reduction campaign of the past few months.

The Presidential statement was a reply to a remark Senator Taft was said to have made to the effect that "the President and the Administration are abandoning talk of keeping prices down in favor of heavy spending abroad that will keep them up." Mr. Truman took this as an allusion to the Greek-Turkish aid program, which he considered the foundation of the Truman Doctrine.

He conceded that all foreign aid programs would put a strain on the American economy, but he said their abandonment would be as unintelligent as would have been the renunciation of the war effort because it created national economic problems.

The President took the position that these added burdens should stimulate the thinking of business and industrial leaders to exercise voluntary price restraint, "in their own interests as well as the interest of the American economy and the world situation."

Taft Delays His Reply

Senator Taft was busy all day on the Senate floor, piloting the labor bill. At the end of the session he said he would have no statement to make tonight, preferring to prepare at a later time what he will consider to be an adequate reply to the Presidential statement.

The President said that the administration's program to "aid starving millions and restore their economies was designed to promote world prosperity, and to enable them to resist totalitarian aggression until such time as they could stand on their own feet. The fact that this program entailed economic problems in the United States, he added, "makes it all the more important that we handle these domestic problems with vigor and common sense."

He accused Senator Taft of advocating reduction in demand as the only way of lowering prices.

Continued on Page 18, Column 3

'Death to Perón' Cry Interrupts His Talk

By The Associated Press.

BUENOS AIRES, June 5—A mysterious voice, shouting "Death to Perón!" interrupted a broadcast by President Juan D. Perón tonight. An Argentine Nationalist is believed to have been responsible.

President Perón was broadcasting over a national hook-up at a public farewell for his wife, Eva Duarte Perón, who is to leave tomorrow on a European tour.

The Argentine News Agency said authorities were examining the theory that a clandestine radio transmitter had broken into the Presidential broadcast.

When the President's speech was broken off, the unidentified broadcaster made a short speech denouncing "those who proclaim themselves supporters of a false social justice" and ending, 'Death to Perón!'

VETO TACTIC DELAYS SENATE LABOR VOTE

Foes Assail Bill to Set Case for Rejection—Tell Truman Signing Means '48 Defeats

By WILLIAM S. WHITE
Special to THE NEW YORK TIMES.

WASHINGTON, June 5—President Truman was put under powerful pressure today direct and oblique, to veto the Hartley-Taft labor bill as the Senate opened its last grand detailed debate on that measure.

Senate action on the bill was hoped for by tomorrow by its principal author, Senator Robert A. Taft, Republican, of Ohio.

The minority opposition plainly was not in the mood for any rapid decision and began a running attack on the bill almost from the moment Mr. Taft had taken the floor in the afternoon to open the debate. It was still possible that tomorrow might not bring the end.

The Taft forces had believed it possible to get a vote today, but this prospect vanished quickly.

The strategy of the opposition, in its efforts to bring about a veto, was in dual movements.

One of these was a direct personal appeal to Mr. Truman, made during the day by three Democratic callers from the House, who suggested to the President in effect that unless he disapproved the legislation the Democratic party would lose in 1948 some of the great metropolitan areas, and specifically New York City.

Representative Arthur G. Klein, Democrat, of New York, asserted to Mr. Truman flatly that the city was lost without a veto, and submitted to the President the photographs of a Madison Square Garden veto rally published in this morning's NEW YORK TIMES.

Representative John Lesinski, Democrat, of Michigan, was understood to have exhibited similar pictures of a recent unionist demonstration in Detroit.

Representative Ray J. Madden.

Continued on Page 18, Column 7

SUBWAY SHUT-DOWN AS SAFETY MEASURE ENVISAGED BY QUILL

Union Leader Charges Laxity of Car Inspection on City-Operated System

EMERGENCY ACTS SCORED

Transit Board Denies Neglect of Safety—Sees Slow-Down Virtually Overcome

By CHARLES GRUTZNER

The possibility of a shut-down of the subway system, today or Monday, on the ground that operation is unsafe under present conditions, was raised yesterday by City Councilman Michael J. Quill, international president of the Transport Workers Union, CIO.

Mr. Quill said at City Hall that the union would "stand by the workers in their refusal to operate any subway cars which are not fully inspected." He added that the union was compiling a list of Board of Transportation supervisors who were "trying to force motormen to take out cars without brake inspection."

The allegedly unsafe conditions, according to TWU officials, are the result in part of emergency operational measures taken by the board to counteract effects of the "book of rules" slowdowns in subway service during the last week. They are due also, according to the union, to a relaxation of safety requirements over a longer period.

"Unsafe" Cars Listed

Austin Hogan, president of TWU Local 100, and Barney Heslin, TWU official assigned to shops of the IND subway, made public a list of allegedly unsafe conditions. Mr. Hogan charged that safeguards against overheating of armature bearings had been removed last week upon order of the shop superintendent. Mr. Heslin said a squad of road car inspectors, whose job was to check on proper application of hand brakes, had been whittled down gradually. The union officials also listed many cars that they said had run beyond the required time without safety checkups.

The union announced that 150 car inspectors from IRT yards in Manhattan, Brooklyn the Bronx and Queens had sent to Mayor O'Dwyer a telegram complaining of allegedly inadequate inspection practices adopted by the board in the last few days.

A denial of the union's charges of neglect of safety requirements was made by a board spokesman who said:

"The New York City transit system is still the safest railroad in the world. It is as safe today as it was last month or last year, unless some of these people who are talking know about some things that haven't been reported to us."

Inspection in Barns

The board spokesman added that the road car inspection squad had been discontinued last fall because it was found more efficient to make the same inspections in the car barns. He insisted that there had been no lessening of inspections.

A reward of $500 was authorized by the board for information leading to the arrest and conviction "of the person or persons found guilty of violating Section 1991 of the Penal Law." The section covers

Continued on Page 17, Column 1

SENATE APPROVES 4 PEACE TREATIES, REJECTING DELAY

Ratifies Italian Pact, 79 to 10, and Then Accepts Others Without Recorded Vote

FEAR FOR ITALY IS VOICED

Connally and McMahon Warn of Communist Dangers After U. S. Leaves Area

By C. P. TRUSSELL
Special to THE NEW YORK TIMES.

WASHINGTON, June 5 — The Senate ratified the long-disputed peace treaty with Italy today by a nearly 8-to-1 vote of 79—10. A two-thirds majority was all that was required for formal approval.

This test made, the Senate abandoned roll calling and in rapid succession shouted virtually unanimous ratification of the accompanying treaties with the three former Axis satellite states, Hungary, Rumania and Bulgaria, generally agreed to be now under Soviet domination.

Senate action was thus completed on the first treaties with former enemy nations of World War II. Great Britain already has ratified them. The Soviet Union and France still are to act on the Italian instrument, though France is in technical process of ratification now. France is not an enacting power concerning the treaties with Hungary, Rumania and Bulgaria.

Motion for Delay Defeated

The way for the Senate's fast and decisive action was cleared by a record vote which defeated, 67—22, a motion by Senator J. William Fulbright, Democrat, of Arkansas, that further consideration of all four treaties be postponed until next Jan. 25. Mr. Fulbright, as a member of the House, sponsored in 1943 the first resolution to express Congressional favor for the creation of international machinery, such as developed into the United Nations, for the maintenance of peace.

Voting for the ratification of the Italian treaty were forty-two Republicans and thirty-two Democrats.

Opposing ratification were three Democrats—Senators James O. Eastland of Mississippi, Pat McCarran of Nevada and W. Lee O'Daniel of Texas—and seven Republicans—Senators Styles Bridges of New Hampshire, C. Wayland

Continued on Page 3, Column 3

AS 'CURE' FOR ILLS

Only Then Can Our Aid Be Integrated, Says the Secretary

HITS 'PIECEMEAL' BASIS

He Tells Harvard Alumni Our Policy Is Not Set Against 'Any Country or Doctrine'

Marshall's speech calling for European unity, Page 2.

By FRANK L. KLUCKHOHN
Special to THE NEW YORK TIMES.

CAMBRIDGE, Mass., June 5—The countries of Europe were called upon today by the Secretary of State, George C. Marshall, to get together and decide upon their needs for economic rehabilitation so that further United States aid could be provided upon an integrated instead of a "piecemeal" basis. This was important to make possible a real "cure" of Europe's critical economic difficulties, he asserted in an address to Harvard alumni this afternoon after he had received the honorary degree of Doctor of Laws at this morning's commencement exercises.

General Marshall supported President Truman's statements in Washington earlier today that United States aid abroad was necessary. He declared that Europe "must have substantial additional help or face economic, social and political deterioration of a very grave character."

"There must be some agreement among the countries of Europe as to the requirements of the situation," he warned, adding that no American aid would be given to "any government which maneuvers to block the recovery of other countries." The Secretary emphasized that governments or parties or groups, seeking to make political capital by perpetuating human misery, would encounter "the opposition of the United States."

General Marshall was the recip-

Continued on Page 2, Column 3

U. S. Called Enemy by Reds In Rallies All Over Hungary

Socialists, Now Working With Communists, Believed Next Target of Latter—Soviet-Controlled Banks Not Nationalized

By ALBION ROSS
Special to THE NEW YORK TIMES.

BUDAPEST, June 5—Hundreds of speakers daily at hundreds of meetings throughout Hungary are engaged in agitating against Western nations and in particular against the United States. Communists and Socialists are speaking in the propaganda campaign, which began last Monday and is to last until a week from Sunday. It is now based on the clear-cut theme that the enemy is the United States and the West.

The so-called conspiracy is now presented as essentially a Western "conspiracy" and the victory over former Premier Ferenc Nagy as a victory over the United States. Every effort is being made to convince the Hungarian people that America is the root of evil, representing belligerent imperialism, reaction, Fascist tendencies, monopoly and every other severe epithet that can be found.

Joseph Revai, editor of the Communist organ Nepszava, has announced that Mr. Nagy arranged when he went to the United States to set up a counter-government in America to "betray the Hungarian democracy." The same speaker said:

"America wanted to eliminate Communists merely to save the rich classes [of Hungary] from the capital levy and to prevent nationalization of the banks.

"The reactionaries want to intimidate Hungary by saying she will not receive the $15,000,000. The $15,000,000 would mean eighteen forints for each Hungarian. I am sure there is not a worker who will sell the salvation of his soul to the stockjobbers of Wall Street for eighteen forints."

Communist speakers also are beginning to interpret more openly the purpose of the overthrow of

Continued on Page 3, Column 6

Halt in Palestine Agitation Here Requested by Truman

Special to THE NEW YORK TIMES.

WASHINGTON, June 5—By proclamation today, President Truman called on citizens and residents of the United States to refrain from undermining law and order in Palestine and from promoting violence there. The proclamation was blanket in form and named no organizations or individuals as having engaged in such activities.

The British Government has repeatedly protested the activities of organizations in the United States raising funds to facilitate the entry of Jewish immigrants, styled "illegal" by the British, into Palestine. One such note expressed inability to understand how such organizations could advertise that contributions to such funds may be deducted from personal income for taxation purposes in the same manner as gifts to charitable institutions.

Further complaints have charged that some of the most vigorous instigations of Jewish immigration into Palestine, despite British regulations, have been carried on by non-citizens of the United States who are here on visitors' visas.

TEXT OF STATEMENT

Mr. Truman's statement said:

The General Assembly of the United Nations in special session on May 15, 1947, unanimously adopted the following resolution:

"The General Assembly calls upon all Governments and peoples, and particularly on the inhabitants of Palestine, to refrain, pending action by the General Assembly on the report of the special committee on Palestine, from the threat or use of force or any other action which might create an atmosphere prejudicial

Continued on Page 5, Column 2

TAFT HEALTH BILL REPORTED TO FLOOR

Aiken Group Backs Creation of New Cabinet Post, 9 to 1—Enactment Held Likely

By BESS FURMAN
Special to THE NEW YORK TIMES.

WASHINGTON, June 5—A compromise bill on a Cabinet post for health, education and security was reported favorably today by a 9 to 1 vote of the Senate Committee on Expenditures in the Executive Departments.

Chairman George D. Aiken of Vermont said that this vote, which had surprised him in its expression of strong favorable sentiment, indicated that the bill would become law.

"What it really does is to raise the human being to the level of dignity already enjoyed by the Holstein cow through the Department of Agriculture," he said.

The bill as reported would set up an executive department of health, education and security, with a secretary of Cabinet rank and a $15,000 annual salary.

It would provide for three undersecretaries, one for each field, as

Continued on Page 12, Column 6

YALTA BREACH SEEN

U. S. Note Prods Russia—A Terrible Situation, the President Says

U. N. APPEAL IN RESERVE

State Department Cites Terms of Occupation Pact—Vague Reports Accuse Nagy

By JAMES RESTON
Special to THE NEW YORK TIMES.

WASHINGTON, June 5—President Truman denounced the Communist coup in Hungary today as an outrage and approved the dispatch of a sharp note of protest to the Soviet commander in Budapest.

Nothing was said officially in the capital about the note, but responsible officials at the State Department confirmed that it did these things:

(1) Implicated the Soviet authorities in Hungary in the exile and resignation of the Hungarian Premier, Ferenc Nagy, and characterized this as a serious intervention in the internal affairs of Hungary.

(2) Called on the Russians to agree to a United States-Soviet-British investigation of the situation in Hungary.

(3) Charged the Soviet officials in Hungary with breaking the terms of the Yalta agreement, and

(4) Suggested that unless a satisfactory reply was obtained to this communication, the United States might submit the case to the appropriate division of the United Nations.

The President Speaks Out

Without waiting for either the investigation or the reply, however, President Truman spoke out in brisk and general terms in his news conference this morning about the charges that the Communist minority in Hungary, with the aid of Russian Army officials, had forced changes in the Hungarian Government.

Asked for comment on the Hungarian situation, the President replied that it was an outrage. It was a terrible situation, he added, and the United States did not intend to stand idly by under the circumstances. The State Department, he concluded, was making a full investigation.

The direct judgment of the President on the Hungarian situation was the subject of some speculation in diplomatic quarters this evening, in view of certain vague reports that have been reaching here from embassies in the Hungarian capital. These reports do not make any direct charges against former Hungarian Premier Nagy and the former President of the Hungarian Assembly, Bela Varga, but they do suggest that there is reason for believing that the Russians have some concrete evidence that both these officials were engaged in unconstitutional activities.

These reports do not suggest what these "unconstitutional activities" were, but they counsel caution in jumping to conclusions about the internal situation in Hungary until more details are obtained.

State Department Is Milder

Whether or not President Truman was aware of these vague words of caution from Budapest when he commented on the Hungarian situation this morning is not known, but the State Department has seen them, and the official note to Hungary, drafted at the State Department, evidently took them into account.

This note is written in milder terms than the President used. It does speak of the aggressive measures of the Communist minority; and it charges the Russians with interfering in Hungary's internal affairs; but it does not speak about the outrages.

Indeed, it states that the United States does not want to engage in recrimination in this matter, but it points out that the Soviet officials in Hungary have certain obligations to the American and British members of the Allied Control Commission in Hungary, and it

Continued on Page 3, Column 2

City Seeks 'Authority' to Finance $25,000,000 Parking Program

The use of some form of "authority" to finance, construct and operate the thirty-three municipal parking lots and nine parking garages recommended on Wednesday by Mayor O'Dwyer's Special Traffic Committee will be considered by the Board of Estimate in executive session next week, it was indicated last night.

Direct city financing of the $25,000,000 program or any substantial part of it now seems unlikely because of the limitations of the capital budget, some of the projects of which already face curtailment because of increased costs of labor and materials.

It has been suggested that either the Triborough Bridge and Tunnel Authority or the World Trade Corporation undertake the $25,000,000 traffic relief program.

The former organization already has declared that it does not care to tackle the problem. It prefers to confine its activities in the parking garage field to the structure now planned at the Manhattan approach to the Battery-Brooklyn Tunnel and the proposed 2,000-car parking garage proposed in connection with the new Madison Square Garden project in the Columbus Circle area.

It has been suggested at City Hall, however, that the authority might be induced to alter its stand.

The charter granted by the state to the World Trade Corporation is broad enough to empower that agency to handle the proposed parking lot and garage program, but its entry into that field is doubted.

The corporation is about to start a $150,000 survey of the city's waterfront properties, both public and private, as a preliminary to presentation to the Board

Continued on Page 21, Column 7

World News Summarized

FRIDAY, JUNE 6, 1947

President Truman yesterday denounced the Communist coup in Hungary as an outrage and said the United States did not intend to stand idly by. He approved a sharp note to the Soviet commander in Budapest charging the Russians with implication in the ousting of Premier Nagy in violation of the Yalta Agreement. The note asked for a tripartite investigation and suggested an appeal to the United Nations if no satisfactory reply was received. [1:8.] Leftists in Hungary were busily trying to convince the people that the United States was responsible for Hungary's troubles. [1:6-7.]

Although many Senators were fearful of Italy's fate when American troops were withdrawn, the Senate ratified the Italian peace treaty, 79 to 10, and by voice vote approved the pacts with Hungary, Rumania and Bulgaria. [1:4.]

Dwight Griswold, former Republican Governor of Nebraska, was named to direct the Greek aid program and Richard F. Allen to be Field Administrator of the $350,000,000 post-UNRRA foreign relief fund. [4:1.]

Europe's economic ills can be cured only by an integrated Continental program and not by "piecemeal" palliatives, Secretary Marshall declared in accepting an honorary degree from Harvard. The United States will help, he said, but the European countries themselves must adopt a joint program. Aid, however, will be withheld from "any government which maneuvers to block the recovery of other countries" or, directly or indirectly, seeks "to perpetuate human misery to benefit therefrom." [1:5.]

In reaction to the Marshall address, British opinion held that the United States must relieve the world dollar shortage if Europe is to be revived [3:1] and the French also were uncertain how to reach unified action. [3:8.]

Senator Taft's economic views were characterized by President Truman as "fallacious and dangerous" and "the old idea of boom and bust." [1:1.] Within the Democratic ranks, Henry A. Wallace said he could not support Mr. Truman for another term. [15:1.]

A determined minority prevented the Senate from voting on the Taft-Hartley labor bill. Veto pressure on the President increased. [1:2.] Mr. Truman said he would act on the Republican income-tax reduction measure as soon as it reached him. [12:4-5.]

The House passed and sent to the Senate an Army military fund bill after restoring $40,000,000 for aircraft eliminated in committee. [9:4.] A Senate committee favorably reported, 9 to 1, a compromise bill to create a Cabinet post of Health, Education and Security. [1:7.]

Friendly relations with Argentina have been restored, President Truman announced. Ambassador Messersmith has completed his mission and resigned. [8:4-5.] The United States is not "disposed" to deal with the Nicaragua regime set up by the Somoza coup pending further developments. [8:4.]

President Truman, in a proclamation, asked citizens and residents to avoid action that might "tend to inflame the passions" of Palestine inhabitants during the United Nations inquiry. [1:6-7.] More British officials received "explosive letters," believed sent from Italy by Zionist sympathizers. [1:6-7.]

Chinese Communists were reported closing in on Mukden, in Manchuria. [11:2.]

In this city, Councilman Quill accused the Board of Transportation of permitting unsafe subway operation and intimated that his men might refuse to run the trains. [1:3.]

Bevin and Eden Get 'Letter Bombs'; Stern Gang Asserts It Sent Them

By MALLORY BROWNE
Special to THE NEW YORK TIMES.

LONDON, June 5—More explosive letters from Italy were handed over to Scotland Yard today, including one addressed to Foreign Secretary Bevin.

At least two other postal bombs arrived today but the police refused to identify their recipients. One is reported to have been Colonial Secretary Arthur Creech Jones but this is unconfirmed.

[The Stern gang claimed the responsibility for the explosive letters, according to a Jerusalem dispatch to THE NEW YORK TIMES. It said they had been sent by its "branch in Europe." Similar envelopes have been found in Palestine in the past. The gang's spokesman said recently that some of its major figures "may have left the country," but he did not say why.]

Former Foreign Secretary Anthony Eden carried a letter bomb in his briefcase for more than twenty-four hours. It was addressed to him at the London offices of The Yorkshire Post and forwarded to the House of Commons on Tuesday. He put it in his briefcase with other letters. "It looked very dull, just like a circular; otherwise I might have opened it on the way home," he said.

Yesterday he went to Eton College for the June celebrations, and when he got home received a warning from Scotland Yard. Even then, however, he did not look, but his secretary pounced on the letter bomb today.

The police have now exploded

Continued on Page 5, Column 4

Idiosyncratic, but a veritable genius, Henry Ford passed away at his home in Dearborn, Michigan.

Howard Hughes is surrounded by reporters as he emerges from Senate War Investigating Committee hearings.

Leaving Westminster Abbey in London, are Princess Elizabeth and Prince Philip, Duke of Edinburgh, following their marriage.

Outspoken baseball manager Leo Durocher (with Burt Shotton, left) was suspended for a season due to "conduct unbecoming." He was replaced by Shotton, and never returned to the Brooklyn Dodgers.

Celeste Holm and Gregory Peck starred in *Gentleman's Agreement.*

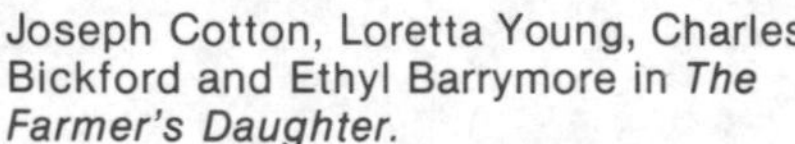

Joseph Cotton, Loretta Young, Charles Bickford and Ethyl Barrymore in *The Farmer's Daughter.*

Edmund Gwenn (as Santa Claus), Maureen O'Hara and John Payne in the classic *Miracle on 34th Street.*

"All the News That's Fit to Print"

The New York Times.

Copyright, 1947, by The New York Times Company.

LATE CITY EDITION
Fair and warm today. Increasing cloudiness, warmer tomorrow.
Temperature Range Today—Max.,80; Min.,61
Temperatures Yesterday—Max., 74; Min., 62
Full U. S. Weather Bureau Report, Page 47

VOL. XCVI..No. 32,658. Entered as Second-Class Matter, Postoffice, New York, N. Y. NEW YORK, TUESDAY, JUNE 24, 1947. THREE CENTS IN NEW YORK CITY

BILL CURBING LABOR BECOMES LAW AS SENATE OVERRIDES VETO, 68-25; UNIONS TO FIGHT FOR QUICK REPEAL

TENEMENT CRASHES AS BOYS' WARNING SAVES OCCUPANTS

Children See Crack Widening in Second Ave. Structure, Hail Policemen Near By

RESCUERS BARELY ESCAPE

Building Recently Condemned, With Evacuation Notices to Families in Mail

By JOSEPH C. INGRAHAM

A four-story tenement house at 636 Second Avenue collapsed at 3:55 P. M. yesterday only a few minutes after the police had evacuated safely the occupants of that building and three others of the same height that adjoin it.

The rescuers barely had gotten out themselves, without even time to shut off the inside gas main, when the eighty-year-old brick structure crashed with a roar that aroused the neighborhood and sent clouds of dust through the area.

A week ago the building, one door south of Thirty-fifth Street, had been damaged when a water pipe burst and water poured down from the roof through the cold-water flats on the upper three floors, residents said.

Dr. Armando Ferraro of 180 Cabrini Boulevard, owner of the collapsed building, said that only yesterday he had mailed a notice to the tenants advising that he had agreed to a condemnation order issued five days ago by the Department of Housing and Buildings. They were told to vacate by July 1, as he was required to start demolition by that time. He said he had been advised that there was "no immediate danger," but that he had told the occupants that they remained "at their own peril."

Tenant Told of Crack

The Housing and Building Department acted after one of the tenants had notified the landlord of the crack in the wall, then about one-half inch wide, Dr. Ferraro said.

The store floor was occupied by Nelson's Folly, an antique shop. Nelson Cowell and Virginia Mouradoff, the co-owners, estimated their loss at $160,000, partly covered by insurance.

Excited but clear-thinking boys at play in the rear of the building sounded the warning that probably saved the lives of the three families in 636. At 3:30 P. M. they saw a widening crack in the rear wall and notified a policeman.

Plainclothes patrolmen Michael Ward and John Foley, passing the block on routine duty, also heard the warning and dashed into the building to arouse the tenants. They carried out Mrs. Esther Menendoz, who a few hours before had returned to her fourth floor quarters after a stay in Bellevue Hospital involving an operation. Her four children and her husband, Robert, walked out unaided.

Meanwhile Lieut. Frank Seibert, supervisor of the plain clothes detail, sped to the building at the corner, 638 Second Avenue. He ordered out the patrons of a bar and grill owned by William Graham, and then went to the second floor to awaken the sleeping caretaker. The third and fourth floors were used for storage.

Man, Woman Carried Out

By that time reenforcements from the East Thirty-fifth Street Station and the crew of Emergency Squad 3 had arrived at the scene. They concentrated on the two buildings south of the buckling structure and carried out Mrs. Agnes Graham, a former nurse at Bellevue Hospital now crippled by arthritis, and her nephew, Philip Phillips, 67 years old, a lawyer, who retired recently after an illness. They live at 630 Second Avenue. Last night that building was pronounced safe and the families housed there returned to their rooms.

However, the red-brick corner building was condemned immediately by William A. Faiella, Acting Borough Superintendent of Buildings, and laborers were set at work preparing to raze it.

Mr. Faiella also barred the five families residing in 632 from that building for the night, but said he would have a detailed inspection made today to determine if it was to be demolished.

The Department of Welfare also moved at a brisk pace and sent five investigators to help the eight families dispossessed. Temporary shelter was found for all of them.

The crash brought many pieces of city apparatus and attracted a

Continued on Page 25, Column 3

U. S. Is Encouraged Over Paris Meeting

Special to The New York Times.

WASHINGTON, June 23—A United States "hands-off" policy in the forthcoming three-power talks in Paris was indicated today by a State Department spokesman.

The spokesman said the department had no official comment on Russia's acceptance of the British-French invitation to participate in the talks and added that "any indication of implementation of what Secretary Marshall has proposed is encouraging."

Asked if there was any official reaction to the Russian decision, the spokesman replied:

"Our position in this has been repeatedly stated. The whole department is waiting for Europe to take the initiative. We don't want to react every five minutes. There is indication that they are getting together. Now let's let them get together and not confuse them."

ASCAP SUED BY U. S. AS A WORLD TRUST

Society Quits International Unit in London as Membership Is Under Attack Here

The American Society of Composers, Authors and Publishers (ASCAP) was accused of illegally engaging in a world-wide cartel and conspiracy to monopolize music-performing rights in a suit filed in Federal court here yesterday by the Anti-trust Division of the Department of Justice.

Simultaneously there opened in London the convention of the International Confederation of Authors and Composers Societies, with which ASCAP is accused of having conspired to maintain world monopoly of performing rights in violation of the Sherman Anti-Trust Act.

ASCAP Quits World Body

In a surprise move at the convention ASCAP resigned its membership. This was described in a London dispatch as a legal maneuver to help ASCAP fight the anti-trust charges. One of the principal purposes of the Government's suit, according to John F. Sonnett, chief of the Anti-trust Division, is to obtain "a directive from the court requiring ASCAP to withdraw from membership in illegal foreign societies like the confederation."

ASCAP, which was formed in 1911 to collect royalties and protect the copyrights of its members, is described in the complaint as the world's largest music-performing rights society and the organization that controls virtually all performing rights in the United States.

The Government alleges that ASCAP has joined with similar organizations in principal foreign countries to cross-license each other exclusively, thus barring other groups or individuals from access to the musical compositions controlled. The cross-licensing has been done, the complaint charges, through the International Confederation of Authors and Composers Societies, which has headquarters in Paris and is composed of ASCAP and twenty-five foreign societies.

Attorney General Tom Clark said the Justice Department had found that thousands of businesses, such as radio stations, theatres, hotels, dance halls and restaurants, had been prevented from getting music

Continued on Page 21, Column 2

SOVIET WELCOMED TO PARLEY ON AID BY FRANCE, BRITAIN

But Fears That Russians May Block Progress Are Noted in Paris and London

BASIC DIVISIONS INVOLVED

French Hope That Conference, Beginning Friday, Will End Its Work Within Week

By HAROLD CALLENDER

Special to The New York Times.

PARIS, June 23—France accepted today with "lively satisfaction" the Soviet Union's agreement to join Friday with Britain and France in a Foreign Ministers' conference on Secretary of State Marshall's proposal of United States aid for Europe.

Russia's agreement was contained in a note replying to a French-British suggestion for such a meeting this week.

[In London, British Foreign Secretary Bevin also welcomed the Soviet acceptance. British hopes for a successful conference were reported to be tempered by fears that the Russians might again adopt stalling tactics.]

The three-power meeting probably will be held in the historic Salle de l'Horloge in the French Foreign Office, where the Foreign Ministers of the Big Four powers discussed and argued for nearly two months last spring and summer over the peace treaties with Italy and the former Axis satellites.

Short Conference Desired

French officials hope that this conference will prove to be less disputatious and will finish within a week, at the most. But they said today that this was merely a guess since they had no indication as to how far Soviet Foreign Minister Molotov might insist upon carrying the discussion beyond the question of machinery for assessing European assets and needs. The French want to confine the discussion to that question.

The issue this year appears to be much simpler than those presented last year by the peace treaties with five countries lying either within the Soviet sphere of influence in Europe or on the borders of the Russian and Western spheres. It seems to involve merely the method of applying United States aid, which the prospective recipients agree is desirable.

Yet the present problem closely touches political as well as economic questions and might easily reopen the basic disputes that have dragged on vainly for nearly two years between the Soviet bloc and the Western world. If this happened, hopes for the three-power conference would dwindle rapidly, in the opinion of the best-informed observers here, who were not at all sure it would not happen.

"Good Work" Expected

"The conference will begin in four days; I will say no more," said Foreign Minister Bidault in the National Assembly today. He thus hinted that France, as a candidate for United States economic aid, should get her house in order, at least to the extent of quick adoption of emergency financial measures, before the conference began in her capital. The whole Assembly applauded, even the Communists, who opposed those measures, but welcomed

Continued on Page 9, Column 5

Marshall and Patterson Appeal For Speedy Arms Aid to Americas

By C. P. TRUSSELL

Special to The New York Times.

WASHINGTON, June 23—Prompt Congressional authorization for military aid to Latin-American countries by the United States, to prevent them from seeking weapons and training "elsewhere," was urged jointly today by Secretary of State Marshall and Robert P. Patterson, Secretary of War.

"I believe firmly," Mr. Marshall told the House Foreign Affairs Committee, "that the opportunity presented to us to give material assistance to the foreign policy of our country at so little cost should not now be lost. I urgently recommend early and favorable action."

"I believe," Mr. Patterson added, "that the [pending] Inter-American Military Cooperation Act will provide sound and practicable means of translating into actuality our planned system of collective action to safeguard the peace and security of the Continent. Indeed, I feel that without the assistance which it authorizes the inter-American regional arrangement can never function with full effectiveness. I most earnestly recommend to you favorable consideration of this measure."

Although the program was before a committee apparently overwhelmingly for it, it soon ran into difficulties, and questions were raised. It was disclosed that even since Mr. Marshall had been Secretary of State an interdepartmental communication of the State Department to the War and Navy Departments had entered sharp objections to the program.

It developed that Secretary Marshall, stanch advocate of the inter-American military coopera-

Continued on Page 11, Column 2

MINERS WALK OUT

Other Strikes and Court Battling Threatened in Wide Reprisal

GREEN URGES A REVERSAL

He Warns of Danger to Nation —Murray Summons Union Heads to Take Action

By CHARLES GRUTZNER

More than 18,000 of the nation's 400,000 soft coal miners stopped work yesterday within a few hours after the Taft-Hartley labor measure became law over the President's veto.

About 8,600 men quit the pits in Pennsylvania, more than 6,000 in Alabama, 2,600 in West Virginia and 1,500 in Ohio, according to The Associated Press.

Leaders of the American Federation of Labor, the Congress of Industrial Organizations and independent unions all over the country announced their intention to test the new law on picket lines and in the courts. A prediction that 90 per cent of all organized labor would go on a protest strike within a week was made in Birmingham, Ala., by R. E. Farr, district president of the United Steelworkers of America, CIO.

National Stoppage Urged

A nation-wide work stoppage for twenty-four hours in protest against what was termed the "slave law" was urged by the San Francisco CIO Council in a telegram to Philip Murray, president of the CIO. Earlier, Mr. Murray had called a meeting for Friday in Washington of the CIO executive board. Lee Pressman, general counsel, summoned legal representatives of every CIO union to the nation's capital.

William Green, president of the AFL, announced the start of a campaign to induce members of Congress to repeal the act, which he warned would produce "chaotic conditions," reduce industrial production and "endanger our national economy."

In New York, Detroit, Pittsburgh and other centers of industry and trade the constitutionality of the new law was challenged at once by the leaders of shipyard,

Continued on Page 4, Column 2

WATCHING FINAL ACTION ON LABOR BILL

Representative Fred A. Hartley Jr. (left) and Senator Robert A. Taft, co-authors of the measure, looking on as Carl A. Loeffler, secretary of the Senate, certifies its passage. The New York Times (by Tames)

20,000 HALT WORK IN SHIPYARDS HERE

Members of Six Union Locals Attend Mass Meeting Held Over Pay, Work Demands

Almost 20,000 members of six union locals from shipyards in the Port of New York halted work yesterday afternoon as a port-wide mass meeting was held here in connection with union demands for higher pay and improved working conditions.

Six thousand members of the Industrial Union of Marine and Ship Building Workers of America, CIO, attended the meeting at Manhattan Center, 311 West Thirty-fourth Street.

The union contract with more than fifty shipyards throughout

Continued on Page 2, Column 3

World News Summarized

TUESDAY, JUNE 24, 1947

The Taft-Hartley labor bill became law yesterday afternoon when the Senate overrode President Truman's veto, 68 to 25, six votes more than the two-thirds majority needed. Just before the vote, the President made a last appeal to Democrats to sustain his veto. [1:8.] Most of the new act's provisions went into effect immediately. [1:6-7.]

Industry spokesmen praised Congress and predicted that industrial harmony would be encouraged by the new law. [1:6-7.] Labor leaders denounced the legislation and plans were laid to test its constitutionality. More than 18,000 miners walked out in three states and there was talk of a nation-wide protest strike. [1:4.]

Nearly 20,000 workers quit in six shipyards in the Port of New York to attend a meeting on their new contract demands, and one leader said this might provide the first legal test of the law. [1:5.] On the other hand, AFL unions and contractors in New York and New Jersey signed an agreement freezing wages and working conditions on heavy industrial construction for two and a half years. [2:2.]

The Supreme Court, before adjourning for the term, upheld, 5 to 3, the constitutionality of the Lea "anti-Petrillo" Act [1:7] and sustained, 5 to 4, the conviction by a "blue ribbon" jury here of labor leaders Joseph S. Fay and James Bove. [4:1.] It also sustained the Government's claim to oil-bearing land under the coastal waters of California. [18:2.]

The American Society of Composers, Authors and Publishers was accused in a suit filed by the Government, of participating in a world-wide cartel and conspiracy to monopolize musical performing rights. [1:2.]

Robert Moses, it was disclosed, will leave for Berlin tomorrow to be special economic adviser to General Clay. [12:2.]

Congress was urged by Secretary Marshall and Secretary Patterson to authorize prompt military aid to Latin-American countries to prevent them from seeking weapons and training "elsewhere." [1:2-3.]

Negotiations for settlement of China's war accounts and talks on possible future aid were opened by Ambassador Koo in Washington. [16:2.]

France accepted with "lively satisfaction" Russia's suggestion for a three-power meeting in Paris on Friday to discuss a plan for Europe's economic rehabilitation to which the United States could lend financial support. Some Frenchmen feared that Foreign Minister Molotov might attach conditions that would make agreement impossible. [1:3], a consideration that served to temper Britain's optimism. [8:3.]

The French Assembly debated the Government's new financial plan while Paris police held in check massed workers demonstrating outside. [9:2.]

A gigantic swindle involving Government property in Germany has been uncovered. A senior Army officer, civilian employes of the AMG in Bavaria and Germans were said to be implicated. [12:3-4.]

The Punjab's Legislative Assembly voted for partition of the Province into Moslem and Hindu states. [15:2.]

NAM Asks Industry to Help Labor Law Work Smoothly

Special to The New York Times.

WASHINGTON, June 23—The following statement was issued today by Earl Bunting, president of the National Association of Manufacturers, on overriding by the Congress of President Truman's veto of the Labor-Management Relations Act of 1947 (the Taft-Hartley Act):

"Congress, in enacting the Labor-Management Relations Act of 1947, and passing this measure over the President's veto, has carried out the clear mandate of the American people, expressed at the last election, that steps be taken to end labor strife in this country.

"Beyond that, the American people also served notice upon both labor and management to see that there is industrial peace, once the rules have been established by the adoption of a new and more equitable national labor policy.

Good-Will Approach Urged

"No law, in itself, will guarantee industrial harmony. Everyone knows that. A fair law such as we now have will provide fertile soil, but industrial peace will flourish only if it is nourished by complete sincerity and good-will on the part of both management and labor.

"The National Association of Manufacturers calls upon management to take the initiative in demonstrating this sincerity and good-will.

"When its employes desire to bargain collectively, management must do so in complete good faith. It must seek no unintended advantage from technicalities in the new law, and even beyond its legal obligation to bargain, management

Continued on Page 3, Column 7

HIGH COURT CURBS PETRILLO POWERS

Rules, 5 to 3, That Musicians' Union Head Cannot Force Extra Hiring on Radio

By JAY WALZ

Special to The New York Times.

WASHINGTON, June 23—The Supreme Court sustained today the law preventing James Caesar Petrillo, president of the American Federation of Musicians, AFL, from forcing broadcasters to hire more workers than were actually needed to perform radio station services.

In its decision the court held constitutional the Lea "Anti-Petrillo" Act passed by Congress in 1946, and left to the United States Attorney at Chicago the decision whether Mr. Petrillo should be prosecuted under the law.

Justice Hugo L. Black said for the 5-3 majority that the case involving the number of musicians employed at a Chicago radio studio did not show Congress to have stepped beyond its powers.

The decision reversed the ruling of Judge Walter J. La Buy of the

Continued on Page 5, Column 5

Analysis of the Labor Act Shows Changed Era at Hand for Industry

By LOUIS STARK

Special to The New York Times.

WASHINGTON, June 23—The "Labor Management Relations Act, 1947," is the first amendment to the National Labor Relations (Wagner) Act of 1935. It adds a new story and a new façade to the earlier law in an effort to "equalize the relations between employers and employes."

By removing most of the administrative work of the National Labor Relations Board and vesting it in a new statutory general counsel, the act turns the board into a labor court.

In order to cope with the backlog of cases which continue to mount, the act increases the NLRB from three to five members. Their salaries are increased from $10,000 to $12,000 a year.

The provisions applying to the NLRB, the general counsel and unfair labor practices by employes become effective within sixty days. Also deferred for that period are the provisions outlawing the closed shop, regulating the union shop, requiring registration of data by unions, depriving unions with Communist officers of their rights under the law and forbidding foremen a recognition by law.

The other sections become effective at once. They include the following subjects:

Creation of a new statutory Federal mediation service to replace the present Conciliation Service in the Department of Labor; emergency machinery for handling "national-paralysis" disputes or strikes which "imperil the national health or safety"; stability of unions; regulation of welfare funds and check-off; banning of strikes by government workers; appointment

Continued on Page 4, Column 5

TRUMAN PLEA FAILS

Barkley Reads His Letter Opposing Bill, but 20 Democrats Desert Him

FIRST CURBS IN 12 YEARS

Republican Sponsored Measure Is Enacted by Six More Votes Than Needed

By WILLIAM S. WHITE

Special to The New York Times.

WASHINGTON, June 23—The Senate by 68 to 25, or six votes more than the necessary two-thirds, overrode President Truman's veto of the Taft-Hartley Labor Bill today, and at 3:17 P. M., Eastern daylight time, made it the law of this country.

It automatically went on the statute books at that moment as the Senate's presiding officer announced the result of the ballot because the House had voted to override last Friday by 331 to 83.

The Senate cast aside one brief and final appeal from Mr. Truman as, in a warm, hushed and crowded chamber, it took the last decision to turn away from much of the labor policy of the Roosevelt and Truman Administrations. The measure it approved represented the first peacetime Federal restraint on the power of labor unions in half a generation.

Truman Writes to Barkley

In a letter to Senator Alben W. Barkley of Kentucky, minority leader, Mr. Truman made his third and final effort to sustain his veto, but it caused little change in Senate sentiment as it had been established in previous tests on the bill.

However, two Democrats who had not heretofore been with him voted today to uphold him. They were Senator Scott W. Lucas of Illinois, the party whip, and John J. Sparkman of Alabama, who had for some days been counted with the anti-veto forces.

Twenty Democrats joined forty-eight Republicans in voting to override. Twenty-two Democrats voting to sustain the head of their party were aided by three Republicans, who were Senators William Langer of North Dakota, George W. Malone of Nevada and Wayne Morse of Oregon.

Where Mr. Truman had been unsparing in his denunciation of the bill in his veto message last Friday and his speech to the country that night, he was more restrained today in his letter to Mr. Barkley, who read it to the Senate just before the vote was taken.

The text of the President's letter was as follows:

"Dear Senator Barkley:

"I feel so strongly about the labor bill which the Senate will vote on this afternoon that I wish to reaffirm my sincere belief that it will do serious harm to our country.

"This is a critical period in our

Continued on Page 3, Column 2

Senate Vote Voiding Veto of Labor Bill

By The Associated Press.

WASHINGTON, June 23—The vote by which the Senate today overrode President Truman's veto of the Taft-Hartley labor bill (two-thirds majority being required to override):

FOR OVERRIDING—68

Republicans—48

Aiken	Dworshak	Reed
Baldwin	Ecton	Revercomb
Ball	Ferguson	Robertson (Wyo)
Brewster	Flanders	Saltonstall
Bricker	Gurney	Smith
Bridges	Hawkes	Taft
Brooks	Hickenlooper	Thye
Buck	Ives	Tobey
Bushfield	Jenner	Vandenberg
Butler	Kem	Watkins
Cain	Knowland	Wherry
Capehart	Lodge	White
Capper	McCarthy	Wiley
Cooper	Martin	Williams
Cordon	Millikin	Wilson
Donnell	Moore	Young

Democrats—20

Byrd	Hoey	Overton
Connally	Holland	Robertson (Va.)
Eastland	Maybank	Russell
Ellender	McClellan	Stewart
Fulbright	McKellar	Tydings
George	O'Conor	Umstead
Hatch	O'Daniel	

AGAINST OVERRIDING—25

Republicans—3

Langer	Malone	Morse

Democrats—22

Barkley	Kilgore	Myers
Chavez	Lucas	O'Mahoney
Downey	Magnuson	Pepper
Green	McCarran	Sparkman
Hayden	McFarland	Taylor
Hill	McGrath	Thomas (Okla.)
Johnson (Col.)	McMahon	
Johnston (S.C.)	Murray	

Not voting but announced against overriding: Thomas (Utah) and Wagner, both Democrats.

"All the News That's Fit to Print"

The New York Times.

LATE CITY EDITION
Not and humid with scattered showers today. Cooler tomorrow.
Temperature Range Today-Max., 90; Min., 73
Temperatures Yesterday-Max., 91.6; Min., 73
Full U. S. Weather Bureau Report, Page 35

Copyright, 1947, by The New York Times Company.

VOL. XCVI. No. 32,710. Entered as Second-Class Matter, Postoffice, New York, N. Y. NEW YORK, FRIDAY, AUGUST 15, 1947. THREE CENTS NEW YORK CITY

LAWS ON GAMBLING BREED CORRUPTION, O'DWYER DECLARES

Mayor Says, However, He Will Enforce Them and Keep the Police Department Clean

ASKS INQUIRIES BY JURIES

Praises Wallander for the Job He Is Doing—Inspector Kennedy Raids Dice Game

By MEYER BERGER

Existing gambling laws, Mayor O'Dwyer said at City Hall yesterday, tend to breed corruption. He said he would, as long as his administration lasts, like to see a grand jury in each county in the city inquire into gambling and its attendant evils.

"The Police Department," the Mayor said, "has a responsibility for enforcing a law which applies outside the fence of a racetrack, but not inside—a law for which a considerable portion of the public has shown very little respect.

"There is a danger of corruption in this picture. One investigation after another during my thirty-seven years in this city has publicly charged corruption in the enforcement of these laws. It is something with which every honest administration of the city's business is deeply concerned. This administration is no exception. We need and will need all the help we can get from law agencies to prevent corruption."

Praises Queens Jury

Mr. O'Dwyer praised the Queens County grand jury inquiring into alleged police grafting on bookmakers, which on Wednesday advocated that the state legalize off-the-track betting because existing laws are unenforceable and breed rackets.

Mr. O'Dwyer was asked what he intends to do about the current situation.

"I am going to enforce the law as best I can and keep the Police Department as clean as I can," he said. "That is why I am so happy to have the aid of grand juries—to do both, enforce the law and prevent corruption."

Someone wanted to know if Police Commissioner Arthur W. Wallander, who has shaken up his force in an anti-gambling crusade, is "fighting for his job."

"The city," the Mayor said warmly, "could stand 100 Wallanders. That's based not only on his record since he became Commissioner but on the thirty-one years I have known him intimately. He can be Commissioner as long as I am Mayor, if he wants it. A man who works as long and as intelligently as he does deserves the job."

Inspector James R. Kennedy, in charge of the Eighth Uniformed Division, Manhattan East, led a raid last night on a four-story vacant building at 203 East 101st Street. The police arrested nineteen men, whom they said were playing dice in a room on the ground floor.

Seventeen of the men were booked at the East 104th Street station for disorderly conduct and two for violation of Section 970 of the Penal Code. The two were Ralph M. Osca, 37 years old, of 1954 Second Avenue, accused of being the "cutter" in the game, and Joseph Benfari, 22, of 219 East 101st Street, charged with being the "steerer."

Inspector Kennedy, who was accompanied by Lieut. George Oest and six plainclothes men, was the only one of twenty-three inspectors who was not transferred in the recent shake-up.

3 Booked for Perjury

Three witnesses who had appeared before the Queens grand jury and who were named by that body on Wednesday in perjury informations, surrendered yesterday in District Attorney Charles P. Sullivan's office in Long Island City. Each was booked on a perjury charge ar. held for hearing on Nov. 10.

The three are Eugene Conklin, 43 years old, of 41-28 Seventy-seventh Street in Jackson Heights; William (Willie The Ice) Perillo, 42, of 21-12 Tw..nty-eighth Street, Astoria, and William (Willie Shephard) Mosca, 44, of 32-42 Thirty-third Street, Astoria, all of Queens. They were accused, among other alleged perjurious statements before the grand jury, of denying they are, or were, bookmakers.

The charges against Perillo said he testified that he had quit bookmaking ten months before he appeared as witness and had returned to the ice business, "when

Continued on Page 36, Column 6

Truman Backs Price Inquiry As Possibly Showing Gouge

He Says Clark's Investigation May Reveal Who Is Causing High Cost Levels—Plea for Labor-Farm-Industry Talk Is Rejected

By LOUIS STARK
Special to The New York Times.

WASHINGTON, Aug. 14—President Truman expressed approval today of Attorney General Tom C. Clark's investigation to determine who might be responsible for conspiring to increase prices of food, clothing and housing.

Reporters asked whether the President felt that the Federal inquiry would check the rise in prices or indicate those who had profited beyond normal margins.

While Mr. Truman believed that the latter result would be the outcome of Mr. Clark's efforts, he said that as to a possible check on prices the newsmen would have to wait and see.

In giving his endorsement to the Attorney General's investigation, the President indicated that he held high hopes for the inquiry.

The President was asked about the corn crop which has been affected by great flood damage. He said that a Cabinet food committee was looking into the entire food picture, including corn as well as other crops.

The Chief Executive indicated that he had no plan for calling together spokesmen for labor, industry and agriculture to consider the problem of prices, as suggested several days ago by Emil Rieve, administrative chairman of the Full Employment Committee of the Congress of Industrial Organizations.

Recalling that he had convened a labor-management conference in November, 1945, and that it had not been successful, the President turned down Mr. Rieve's proposal.

The question on crops addressed to the President was intended to ascertain if he had been considering some possible limitation on exports in view of the reduced crop outlook in some commodities. He felt, he said, that the Cabinet committee would determine whatever steps might be necessary on the

Continued on Page 14, Column 7

U. S. CANCELS DEBTS OF BILLION BY ITALY IN FINANCIAL PACTS

Frees $60,000,000 in Blocked Properties—Will Return 28 Freight Ships to Rome

WOULD RELIEVE BURDENS

Lovett Expresses Hope Accords Will Reduce the Weight of Peace Treaty Clauses

By WALTER H. WAGGONER
Special to The New York Times.

WASHINGTON, Aug. 14—The United States today crossed off about $1,000,000,000 in debts owed by Italy and, in addition, liberalized its interpretation of the terms of the financial section of the Italian peace treaty to aid that country's frail economy.

The State Department, in making the agreement public, said the action would relieve Italy of many "burdensome" financial and economic clauses in the peace pact and aid "substantially" in her recovery.

Terms of the debt relief were contained in one of three "memoranda of understanding" with which the two Governments concluded three months of negotiations. The other documents provided for protection of private American property in Italy and the disposal of German assets there. France and Great Britain joined in the negotiations on the last point.

Hopes It Will Help Italy

Robert A. Lovett, Acting Secretary of State, said upon signing the documents relating to American claims that he hoped the agreement would ease Italy's "difficult financial situation."

"These understandings, furthermore," he went on, "reflect the recognition given to the fact that the Italians themselves overthrew the Fascist Government, and beginning September, 1943, your people joined the Allies as a co-belligerent against the Nazis.

"The questions which have been settled in these negotiations constitute an additional substantial step in the establishment of good economic and political relations between our two countries."

On behalf of his government, Ivan Matteo Lombardo, chief of the Italian economic and financial delegation and signer of the agreement, declared that the prosperity of Italy "is highly beneficial to the greater prosperity of this country, which in turn reverberates upon

Continued on Page 4, Column 1

TWO INDIAN NATIONS EMERGE ON WORLD SCENE

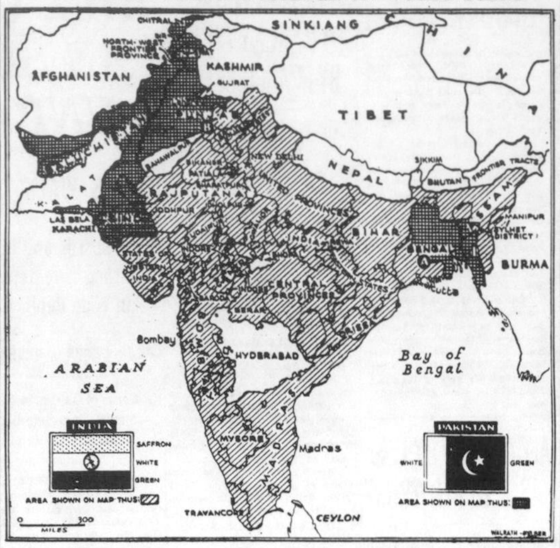

The New York Times Aug. 15, 1947

Princely states that have not yet adhered to either India or Pakistan are shown without shading. Pakistan has recognized the independence of Kalat, on the Arabian Sea. The boundaries running through Bengal (A) and the Punjab (B) are to be announced by a commission.

INDIA AND PAKISTAN BECOME NATIONS; CLASHES CONTINUE

Ceremonies at New Delhi and Karachi Mark Independence for 400,000,000 Persons

NEHRU ACCLAIMS GANDHI

But He Warns of Trials Ahead—Death Toll in Communal Fighting Reaches 153

By ROBERT TRUMBULL
Special to The New York Times.

NEW DELHI, Friday, Aug. 15—India achieved her long-sought independence today through the transfer of British power to the two dominions into which that land of 400,000,000 persons has been divided, India and Pakistan.

While the ceremonies marking this major historic event were taking place communal strife continued to cast a grim shadow over the future.

[Communal clashes, fires and looting continued in Lahore, Punjab, with the rising death toll estimated at 153, The Associated Press reported. In London King George conferred an earldom on Viscount Mountbatten for his role in solving the Indian problem and the Government made available to the Indian Government £35,000,000 of India's sterling balance.]

The Dominion of India reached the goal of freedom here at midnight with minimum celebration and a few speeches that stressed the gravity of the tasks ahead of the new nation.

In Karachi, capital of Pakistan, Mohammed Ali Jinnah will take the oath this morning as Governor General of the Moslem dominion which he was the primary figure in creating against the demand for a united India.

Viceroy at Both Ceremonies

This ceremony at the Sind Provincial Government House, which is now Mr. Jinnah's official residence, will be the only event marking the transfer of power from British to Indian hands in that dominion.

The Viceroy, Viscount Mountbatten, addressed the Pakistan Constituent Assembly yesterday—his last official act as Viceroy—and then flew back to New Delhi to attend the formal transfer here. No special events were scheduled in Karachi, as they were in New Delhi, to mark the actual moment when the rule of the King-Emperor came to an end at midnight except in so far as both dominions continued to owe formal allegiance to the British crown.

Mohandas K. Gandhi, the real hero of the New Delhi ceremony, was absent from the capital of his country in its triumphant hour. At the moment his great dream came true—though not precisely in the form he wished—Mr. Gandhi was in humble surroundings of his own choosing among the Moslems of Calcutta, where he felt he was needed more. But his name was publicly praised by others who remained here to carry on the work to which he has devoted his life.

Climax at Midnight

The Constituent Assembly of the Government of India assumed its sovereign power solemnly in a special session that began at 11 P. M. last night and reached its climax at twelve o'clock. As the hands of the clock in the stately assembly hall of the State Council building met at midnight India's Cabinet Ministers and Members of the Assembly listened in silence to the chimes of the hour.

As the last note died an unidentified member blew a conch shell of the kind used in Hindu temples to summon the gods to witness a great event. Instantly a great cheer arose. India at that moment had become a free member of the British Commonwealth of Nations — free even to leave the commonwealth if she chooses.

The members then stood and repeated after the Assembly President, Dr. Rajendra Prasad, this oath in Hindi and then in English:

"At this solemn moment when the people of India, through suffering and sacrifice, have secured freedom, I, a member of the Constituent Assembly of India, do dedicate myself in all humility to the service of India and her people to the end that this ancient land attain her rightful place in the world and make her full and willing contribution to the promotion of world peace and the welfare of mankind."

Then in accordance with a formal motion made by President

Continued on Page 2, Column 4

RELIEF FROM HEAT LIKELY TOMORROW

Continued High Temperatures Today Expected to Be Ended by Thunder Showers

Relief from the heat wave here was forecast for tomorrow by the Weather Bureau last night. The forecast followed a high temperature of 91.6 degrees at 4:15 P. M. yesterday, the second successive day when the mercury touched 91.

Collars, shirts and dresses are expected to wilt again today as a spokesman for the bureau said it would be hot and humid with the highest thermometer reading near 90. Afternoon or evening thunder showers probably will precede the cool air mass pushing in from the West that, it is hoped, will end the hot spell on the Eastern seaboard.

Meanwhile, in the Midwest, according to The Associated Press, scattered showers cooled that area after a two-week heat wave had reduced harvest prospects, especially for corn.

Locally, the lowest temperature for the twenty-four-hour period yesterday was 73, registered at 6 A. M. The mercury mounted steadily during the early morning, generally recording a point or two higher each hour than for a corresponding hour Wednesday.

By noon the thermometer registered 85, two degrees below the listing at noon Wednesday, but the humidity stood at 72 per cent, 5 higher than at the same time the preceding day.

After that hour the mercury rose and the humidity decreased, the humidity standing at 60 per cent when the high temperature for the day was reached. The highest humidity of the day was 95 per cent at 8 A. M.

[*A table of yesterday's temperatures will be found on Page 35.*]

Although many persons felt as if they were perspiring more because of accumulated heat, the temperature dropped steadily during the early evening. Thermometer readings for 5, 6 and 7

Continued on Page 34, Column 6

U. S. RENT CURB HERE IS BADLY SNARLED

Many Tenants Tell of Futile Attempts to Get Relief—ORC Soon to Cut Staff

By CHARLES GRUTZNER

A bad snarl in the administration of Federal rent controls in New York came to light yesterday, with the backlog of tenant complaints increasing in area rent offices.

At the same time, the Office of Rent Control announced it would drop "about 150" employes in this city on Sept. 15 in line with a 30 per cent nation-wide reduction in staff. The Federal agency will also close its area offices at St. George, S. I., and Mineola, L. I. The Brooklyn office will take over Staten Island cases, and the Queens office is to absorb the Nassau and Suffolk work loads.

Tenants, attorneys and representatives of veterans and civic organizations told yesterday of repeated and futile attempts to obtain action on cases where excess rents allegedly have been charged for several months and in some cases for a full year. Their descriptions of local rent offices ranged from "overloaded with work" to "completely demoralized."

Not Covered By City Law

Tenants have been coming to the City Rent Commission at 500 Park Avenue with cases involving apartment house rentals and evictions, although the city law covers only hotels and rooming houses. The apartment dwellers have said they went first to the Federal rent offices and were advised to seek advice from the municipal agency.

The expected passage by the City Council of three bills sponsored by Vice Chairman Joseph T. Sharkey will give the City Rent Commission power to prosecute violations of Federal and City rent laws covering apartments and small houses as well as hotels and rooming houses Although this will take some of the local burden from

Continued on Page 15, Column 2

WORLD PEACE TIED TO AMERICAS TALKS

Marshall, at Rio de Janeiro, Says Hemisphere Defense Aim Is Within Framework of U.N.

By C. P. TRUSSELL
Special to The New York Times.

RIO DE JANEIRO, Aug. 14—Secretary of State George C. Marshall, landing amid applauding crowds of Brazilians at this city's Santos Dumont Airport today, said the United States delegation to the inter-American defense conference had come "for the purpose of helping to consolidate the peace of the world."

In thus going beyond the strictly hemispheric implications of the twenty-nation conference that is to open in the summer capital of Petropolis tomorrow, Secretary Marshall put upon the American republics the obligation of setting an example for all nations.

To the Brazilian and other diplo-

Continued on Page 7, Column 2

'Crudest' U. S. Interference In Greece Charged by Soviet

By THOMAS J. HAMILTON
Special to The New York Times.

LAKE SUCCESS, N. Y., Aug. 14—Andrei A. Gromyko, Soviet Deputy Foreign Minister, launched a determined attack today on the new United States resolution under which the United Nations Security Council would order Yugoslavia, Albania and Bulgaria to "cease and desist from rendering any further assistance or support in any form to the guerrillas fighting against the Greek Government."

Mr. Gromyko's statement was interpreted as giving unmistakable notice that he would veto both the United States resolution and an Australian proposal, which, without attributing responsibility to either side, orders all four nations to stop the fighting. Both resolutions invoke Chapter VII of the Charter, applying to threats to the peace, breaches of the peace, or acts of aggression, under which the Council can order enforcement measures, going as far as a collective declaration of war by the fifty-five member nations.

The Soviet representative said that the United States resolution constituted "the crudest interference" in the internal affairs of Greece. He added that the Australian resolution was worse than an earlier and milder United States resolution, which he vetoed two weeks ago, and "competes successfully with the second American resolution."

"One cannot solve the Greek question as proposed in the American and in the Australian resolutions," said Mr. Gromyko. "They are missing their mark. They may correspond to the interests of one or two countries but not to the interests of the development of good neighborly relations between states and, consequently not to the interests of the United Nations as a whole."

Mr. Gromyko was silent, how-

Continued on Page 4, Column 4

TASS SAYS GREEKS MOLEST RUSSIANS

Charges Workers in Embassy Are Seized and 'Tortured'—Sees Threat to Relations

By The Associated Press.

LONDON, Friday, Aug. 15—The Soviet news agency Tass said today in a dispatch from Athens that Greek authorities had "been arresting and even subjecting to torture persons at work in the Soviet Embassy" in the Greek capital.

The dispatch said the Soviet Chargé d'Affaires in Athens had protested to the Greek Government that such actions were "incompatible with the maintenance of diplomatic relations between Greece and the Soviet Union."

A summarized version of the dispatch was distributed in London by the Soviet Monitor.

The arrests and torture, the dispatch said, extended to members of "other Soviet institutions in Greece" besides the Embassy.

"Persons who have commercial ties with the trade delegation of the U.S.S.R. are subjected to repressions," it added.

The dispatch failed to make clear, however, whether the persons affected by the alleged maltreatment were Soviet citizens, Greeks working for the Moscow

Continued on Page 3, Column 7

Actors Win an Anti-Bias Contract In Fight on Negro Ban in Capital

The League of New York Theatres, an organization of theatre owners, operators and producers, agreed yesterday to sign a new contract with Actors' Equity Association embodying a clause whereby actors shall not be required to play in Washington unless Negroes are admitted to the audiences.

James F. Reilly, executive director of the league, said the disputed clause would be in the next agreement, becoming effective on Aug. 1, 1948, at which time the nation's capital would face a virtual ban that would keep all actors and stage attractions out of its theatres unless the rule against Negroes was revoked. The present two-year contract between Equity and the League expires on Aug. 31.

Mr. Reilly asserted that the time element in the controversial clause was included to permit theatres in Washington to effect a change in policy. He said other factors remained to be cleared up before the agreement is accepted by both sides, but that it was his belief that a complete agreement may be reached "by early next week."

The league's action was taken at a closed meeting yesterday afternoon at the Astor Hotel. While the league made no detailed statement on its capitulation to Equity's contractual demand, it was reported that forty-six members attended, with twenty-nine voting in favor of the Equity condition, seven against and ten abstaining. Attendance by forty-two members constitutes a quorum.

Even as the league acceded to Equity's demand, Marcus Heiman, president of the operating company for the National Theatre in Washington, declared last night that he would not lift the ban on Negroes as patrons.

When informed of the league's vote, Mr. Heiman referred to an announcement he made on Tuesday regarding the situation. He reiterated that the National would drop its whites-only rule only if: 1. The

Continued on Page 10, Column 4

World News Summarized

FRIDAY, AUGUST 15, 1947

Today is Independence Day in India. British rule over the vast land, with its population of 400,000,000, ended at midnight and the territory was divided into two independent nations, the dominions of Pakistan and India. Viscount Mountbatten gave up his role of Viceroy and became Governor General of India. [1:8.] Earlier, he addressed the Pakistan Constituent Assembly and rode to the Government House in a state procession with Mohammed Ali Jinnah, who is the new Governor General of Pakistan. [2:2.]

Britain abolished the India office and named Arthur Henderson as Minister of State for Commonwealth Relations. Lord Mountbatten was rewarded with an Earldom. [3:6-7.]

India's new chapter opened amid more outbreaks of violence. In Lahore, capital of Punjab Province, which is to be divided between Pakistan and India, 153 persons had been reported killed in two days. [2:6.]

In Palestine, fighting between Arabs and Jews in the Tel Aviv region continued for the fifth day. Jewish underground forces went to the rescue of areas attacked by Arab mobs. [1:6-7.]

In Java, fire swept the Netherlands Indies Petroleum Board's main dump at the port of Tanjungpriok. Saboteurs were believed to have set the blaze. [3:1.]

The Indonesian Republic, appearing for the first time before the United Nations Security Council, urged the Council to order the Netherlands to evacuate all of her troops from Java, Sumatra and Madura. [3:5.]

Andrei A. Gromyko declared that a United States resolution before the Security Council, asking it to order Yugoslavia, Albania and Bulgaria to stop aiding Greek guerrillas, was "the crudest interference" in the internal affairs of Greece. His attack was taken to foreshadow a Soviet veto. [1:6-7.]

Moscow may sever relations with Athens, it was feared, following charges that Russians had been tortured by Greeks in Athens. [1:7.]

About $1,000,000,000 of debts owed by Italy were canceled by the United States in an effort to help Italy's difficult economic position. Rome also was relieved of several other "burdensome" clauses of the peace treaty in recognition of Italian help to the Allied cause in the latter part of the war. [1:4.]

The United States has offered to rehabilitate the Ruhr coal mines with 600,000 tons of American steel ingots. [4:4.]

In Nuremberg, twenty-one former officials of the I. G. Farben chemical trust pleaded not guilty when arraigned before the war crimes court on charges of having plotted the war for profit. [5:4.]

President Truman marked the second anniversary of V-J Day by expressing disappointment that world peace, whose attainment had seemed so certain two years ago, had yet to be achieved. [8:6-7.] He said he could see no justification for calling a special session of Congress before January. [4:1.]

Secretary of State Marshall and his party of delegates arrived in Rio de Janeiro for the Inter-American Conference, which opens today. He told a cheering crowd of Brazilians at the airport that the United States delegation would work "to consolidate the peace of the world." [1:5.]

The inquiry undertaken by Attorney General Clark into the high prices of food, clothing and housing was approved by President Truman. He said the investigation might show who was profiteering. [1:2-3.]

Jews, Arabs Battle Amid Fires; Armed Zionist Troops Aid Police

Special to The New York Times.

JERUSALEM, Aug. 14—For the first time Jewish underground defense forces came today to the rescue of Jewish districts menaced by Arab mobs in the embattled borderland between Tel Aviv and Jaffa.

Three more Jews and one Arab were slain. A fourth Jew died of stab wounds received yesterday. More than fifty Arabs and Jews were wounded today.

The three murdered Jews were all truck men whose vehicles were stoned and shot at by Arab gangs. One of them, Aharon Hanovici, 27, was an American. He was discharged last year from the United States Army, in which he served as a truck driver in North Africa with the 404th Quartermaster Company.

The fourth day of the rioting, which appeared to be intensifying rather than diminishing despite appeals from Arab and Jewish leaders, brought wholesale destruction of property. Three great fires lighted the sky tonight over the silent and deserted no man's land between the twin Arab and Jewish cities, whose border areas have been placed under a dawn-to-dusk house curfew. The curfew area was extended eastward today after clashes between Arabs and Jews began to spread.

While counseling Jews to avoid provocation, Haganah, the Zionist secret militia, came into the open with its arms today to reinforce the Palestine police in repelling depredations of roving Arab crowds.

When a small band of Arabs invaded the highly inflammable Maccabi slum quarter of Tel Aviv, Haganah units formed to defend the district. Meantime Arab constables on the roof of a police building opened fire. Someone threw a grenade at the invaders who fled.

Arab gangs were dispersed in

Continued on Page 3, Column 2

"All the News That's Fit to Print"

The New York Times.

LATE CITY EDITION
Increasingly cloudy today. Cool with showers tomorrow.
Temperature Range Today—Max.,78; Min.,65
Temperatures Yesterday—Max.,83; Min.,65
Full U. S. Weather Bureau Report, Page 27

VOL. XCVI..No. 32,725. Entered as Second-Class Matter, Postoffice, New York, N. Y. NEW YORK, SATURDAY, AUGUST 30, 1947. THREE CENTS NEW YORK CITY

NEW ATOMIC POWER PLANT PRESAGES PEACETIME USES; IT UTILIZES FAST NEUTRONS

RATE IS REGULATED

Vast Possibilities Opened by Controlled Release of Plutonium Force

SIZE OF POWER UNIT CUT

Adaptation for Propulsion of Ships and Locomotives Now Held Feasible

By WILLIAM L. LAURENCE

Successful operation of an atomic power plant of revolutionary design, using for the first time fast, instead of slow, neutrons for liberating nuclear energy from plutonium at a controlled rate, was announced yesterday by Dr. Norris E. Bradbury, director of the Los Alamos Scientific Laboratory at Los Alamos, N. M., where the atomic bomb was developed.

The announcement, regarded as the most important of its kind since President Truman revealed the existence of the atomic bomb, was released by the United States Atomic Energy Commission in Washington.

The new plant, it is revealed, "has been operated successfully at low power since November, 1946." The initial proposals for its construction were made in December, 1945, shortly after completion of the Los Alamos laboratory's wartime job.

The new plant, the announcement states, is unique in two respects: It is the first to employ the fission of the man-made element, plutonium, instead of normal, unseparated uranium. It is also the first to use fast neutrons, thus eliminating the need for a moderator to slow the neutrons down.

Energy Liberated Slowly

These two unique features open up new vistas in the use of atomic energy for power, of enormous potentialities for peacetime as well as military uses. In the words of the announcement, the new plant is "in a sense a controlled version of the atomic bomb" which also utilizes a fast neutron chain-reaction, the principal difference being that in the bomb the reaction is allowed to go uncontrolled, whereas in the new power unit the fast neutrons are kept in check by a system of controls, so that the energy is liberated at a steady, instead of an explosive rate.

It is also revealed that the "heart of the new atomic power plant, known as a 'fast reactor,' is a small vessel containing a critical mass of the nuclear explosive, plutonium, which emits neutrons of high energy." Since a "critical mass" of plutonium is the amount used in the atomic bomb, which, with all its auxiliaries, could be carried in a B-29, it becomes obvious that the active material in

Continued on Page 2, Column 2

Ex-GI Seized Here In Atom Photo Theft

Special to THE NEW YORK TIMES.

WASHINGTON, Aug. 29—The arrest of Arnold Frederick Kivi, 27 years old, a former soldier, for the theft of "highly confidential photographs" from the Los Alamos, N. M., atomic installations was announced tonight by the Federal Bureau of Investigation.

The FBI said its agents in a raid tonight at Kivi's home, 341 Seventeenth Street, Brooklyn, N. Y., had seized thirty-seven photographs and ten negatives.

J. Edgar Hoover, director of the FBI, said that Kivi had at first denied being in possession of any highly confidential pictures. Later, however, he had admitted removing certain classified photographs, Mr. Hoover said.

He added that the pictures found in Kivi's possession showed various phases of atomic research equipment used in connection with the bomb and several pictures of visitors. Kivi worked as a photographer in the Army.

Kivi served in the Army from Sept. 1, 1942, to Feb. 6, 1946.

Soviet Says U. N. Atom Plan Fosters Monopoly of U. S.

Gromyko Rejects Control Blueprint Favored by Majority—Leans to Proposed Fixing of Production Quota in Treaty

By A. M. ROSENTHAL

Special to THE NEW YORK TIMES.

LAKE SUCCESS, N. Y., Aug. 29—Andrei A. Gromyko, Soviet Deputy Foreign Minister, turned down today a blueprint for the operation of an international atomic agency. He said it was based on principles that would give the United States a virtual monopoly in the atomic field.

The specific proposals for the agency were written into six working papers that had the approval of a majority of the twelve members of the United Nations Atomic Energy Commission. The feeling among delegates after Mr. Gromyko's speech was that it would be futile to try to reach unanimous agreement by Sept. 15, the deadline for their report to the Security Council.

Speaking before the commission's Committee on Controls, Mr. Gromyko coupled his rejection of the working papers with a restatement of the Soviet Union's stand opposing the United States' original plan for a vetoless set-up for atomic control. His main objections, he said, were based on the fact that the papers were founded on the American plan. Then he listed his three major charges against the United States' principles for atomic control and everything that stemmed from them:

(1) That they would delegate to the background the prohibition of atomic weapons and other instruments of mass destruction;

(2) That they would protect the interests of "one country," giving it a monopoly, and ignore the interests of the others;

(3) That they were incompatible with the fundamental principles of the United Nations Charter and with the sovereignty of nations.

The six papers marked the first intensive effort to set down just what the proposed agency would be allowed to do and would be forbidden to do. They cover research,

Continued on Page 2, Column 3

Ruhr Output Will Be Raised To 1936 Production Level

By JACK RAYMOND

Special to THE NEW YORK TIMES.

BERLIN, Aug 29—The United States and British Military Governments in Germany announced today their detailed plan to raise the industrial output of their economically merged zones to virtually the 1936 standard. In addition, the plan called for a 15 per cent increase in exports from that area over the 1936 figure and an increase in the German standard of living to approximately 75 per cent of that prevailing in 1936.

[The statement on production in Germany is on page 5.]

The new plan set aside the Allied Control Council's agreement of March, 1946, based on the Potsdam Declaration. That provided for reparations from Germany's war and other industries and designated specific minimum capacities for the peaceful reconstruction of the defeated country.

The announcement of the new plan explained that the upward revision of German industrial levels in the bi-zonal area was necessary because some of the basic provisions of the 1946 plan had not been fulfilled.

The most important of these was that Germany would be treated as an economic unit. Another was the admitted miscalculation of the ability of the Western zones to sustain themselves.

The decision to raise the bi-zonal industrial level to the 1936 figure represented a sharp increase over the 70 to 75 per cent capacity level set in the 1946 plan.

United States officials said the

Continued on Page 5, Column 4

TSALDARIS SWORN AS GREEK PREMIER

10 Populists, 1 Independent in Cabinet—Coalition Fails—Early Broadening Pledged

By DANA ADAMS SCHMIDT

Special to THE NEW YORK TIMES.

ATHENS, Aug. 29—King Paul swore Constantin Tsaldaris into office tonight as Premier with a Cabinet of ten Populists, including himself as Foreign Minister, and one independent.

This surprise ending to the seven-day governmental crisis—one precisely contrary to the emphatically expressed United States desire for a broad Government—came at 11 o'clock after Mr. Tsaldaris had announced the failure of all attempts to form a coalition government under Demetrios Maximos similar to the Government that fell last Saturday.

Upon leaving the palace, Premier Tsaldaris declared that his small Cabinet would be broadened by the

Continued on Page 7, Column 2

Quick End to Palestine Mandate Urged by U. N. Inquiry Committee

By The Associated Press.

GENEVA, Switzerland, Aug. 29—Members of the United Nations Special Committee of Inquiry on Palestine said tonight that the committee's report to the United Nations General Assembly would call for the termination of the British mandate in the Holy Land at the earliest possible moment.

The informants said that the report, now nearing completion, would imply no criticism of the mandatory power but would leave no doubt that the present situation in Palestine can not be permitted to continue.

The committee also will stress the need for a transition period for Palestine, beginning immediately, under the administration of an authority responsible to the United Nations.

However, committee members failed to designate the administrative power or to lay down the conditions under which the responsibilities of the United Nations should be exercised, informed sources said.

The committee members were pictured as feeling that such decisions must be taken by the General Assembly itself when the Assembly meets in New York on Sept. 16.

The committee's agreed draft report, due for signature within a few days, would place before the Assembly the choice of establishing a joint Arab-Jewish federal state or two separate states bound by economic cooperation, the informants said. The informants added that a majority of the committee favored the second alternative—the setting up of independent Jewish and Arab states by September, 1949.

While the committee was split on the question of a federalized Palestine or a division of the Holy Land into two separate states, there were a number of points on which unanimous or nearly unanimous agreement was reached.

Regarding the problem of Jewish displaced persons as one for

Continued on Page 16, Column 3

4-POWER MEETING ON KOREA IS URGED ON SOVIET BY U. S.

State Department Emphasizes Disappointment Over Failure of Parleys With Russia

TALK SET FOR WASHINGTON

Four Pacific Powers Would Get Together Sept. 8 to Study Independence

U. S. note to Russia calling for Korea conference, page 6.

By WALTER H. WAGGONER

Special to THE NEW YORK TIMES.

WASHINGTON, Aug. 29—The State Department, out of patience with the breakdown of negotiations between the United States and the Soviet Union, today proposed a four-power conference for setting up a united independent Korea.

In a note delivered yesterday to Vyacheslav M. Molotov, Soviet Foreign Minister, Robert A. Lovett, Acting Secretary of State, declared that this Government had tried its "utmost" for nearly two years to reach agreement with Moscow on the future of Korea. It is now "abundantly clear," he continued, that bilateral action will not work.

"The United States Government cannot in good conscience be a party to any such delay in the fulfillment of its commitment to Korean independence and proposes that the four powers adhering to the Moscow agreement meet to consider how that agreement may be speedily carried out," he added.

It was specifically suggested that the four powers, the United States, the Soviet Union, Britain and China, begin conversations on this matter in Washington on Sept. 8.

To improve the possibility of success at the proposed conference, Mr. Lovett said that the United States would try to reach some accord with Moscow on a joint report on the status of deliberations of the Joint Commission for Korea. It was suggested that this preliminary report be submitted by Sept. 5.

Accompanying Mr. Lovett's letter to Mr. Molotov was a list of seven proposals outlining procedure for the establishment of a provisional government of Korea. The proposals are expected to encounter opposition from Russia, which has already rejected the first one, which calls for a general election of Legislatures for each zone.

The six other points of the program are:

The provisional "zone" Legisla-

Continued on Page 6, Column 2

World News Summarized

SATURDAY, AUGUST 30, 1947

General Eisenhower told the American Legion convention here yesterday that he saw no immediate threat of another war, but warned that in a world divided into two great camps of dictatorships and democracies the friends of freedom must rally to its support or see it driven from the earth by its foes. General Eisenhower, who is soon to assume the presidency of Columbia University, received a tremendous ovation. Admiral Nimitz and General Spaatz joined him in urging that the country be strong to meet any eventuality. [1:8.]

An atomic power plant of revolutionary design, which for the first time uses fast instead of slow neutrons to obtain nuclear energy from plutonium at a controlled rate, has been developed, opening new vistas of vast peacetime and military uses. [1:1.]

At Lake Success, Soviet delegate Gromyko rejected proposals for the creation of an international atomic agency approved by the majority of the twelve members of the United Nations Atomic Energy Commission. He said the plan would give the United States a monopoly. [1:2-3.]

The State Department declared two years of "utmost" effort to achieve agreement with Moscow on the future of Korea had failed and proposed a four-power conference to consider the organization of a united, independent Korea. [1:4.]

Moscow announced ratification of the peace treaties with Italy, Hungary, Rumania, Bulgaria and Finland. [1:5.]

The Indonesian Republic was barred from exercising authority in the most important economic areas of Java, Sumatra and Madura by the Government of the Netherlands East Indies, which listed the areas where it declared itself pledged to maintain law and order after having occupied them by "police action." [8:5.] The Hague declared it would accept "the general tendency" of the resolutions by the United Nations Security Council. [8:1.]

Members of the United Nations Committee on Palestine said it was preparing a report to the General Assembly calling for the end of the British mandate in the Holy Land. [1:2-3.] Meanwhile, the Security Council, deadlocked over the Egyptian issue went on a ten-day holiday. [16:4.]

A British-American plan to raise the level of German industry in the United States-British zone to that of 1936 was made public. [1:2-3.]

Against a background of spreading coal strikes, the Archbishop of York urged the British Labor Government to convene a round-table conference of all political parties "to save the country from ruin." [7:8.]

An all-Populist party Cabinet headed by Premier Tsaldaris took office in Athens despite the wishes of Washington for a broader Government. [1:2.] London, determined to withdraw all British troops from Greece by the end of the year, refused Washington pleas to alter its decision. [7:1.]

At the Inter-American Conference in Brazil a dispute between Argentina and the United States over an Argentine proposal to limit the hemispheric defense treaty to areas under the "effective jurisdiction" of the members of the conference was resolved amicably. [1:6-7.]

EISENHOWER, CHEERED BY LEGION, WARNS U. S. TO STAY STRONG IN A DIVIDED WORLD; NIMITZ AND SPAATZ SUPPORT HIS APPEAL

SERVICE CHIEFS ADDRESSING LEGIONNAIRES YESTERDAY

Gen. Dwight D. Eisenhower | Admiral Chester W. Nimitz | Gen. Carl A. Spaatz

The New York Times (by Falk)

UNITY EMPHASIZED

Chief of Staff Declares Alternative Is Work 'Under the Whip'

SEES NO GLOBAL WAR NOW

Griffith Bans a Political Rally as the Kansas Delegation Attempts to March

Addresses by Eisenhower, Nimitz and Spaatz, on Page 4.

By FRANK S. ADAMS

Warning that the world has divided into two great camps of dictatorships and democracies, Gen. Dwight D. Eisenhower told the American Legion yesterday that the friends of freedom everywhere must stand staunchly in its support, or its foes would eliminate freedom from the earth.

Shouts of approval greeted the Army Chief of Staff as he told 5,000 Legion delegates at a meeting in the Seventy-first Regiment Armory, Park Avenue and Thirty-fourth Street, that as long as aggression threatens free governments, this country must be prepared for whatever may come.

Perhaps the most vociferous of the cheers came when he warned that "all must work together—or eventually we will all work under the whip." The Legion also shouted its approval when he said that we must gird ourselves so strongly that a predatory aggressor would realize that the war he provoked would be fought over his own territory.

However, he said, he did not foresee a "global war as an immediate threat." No great nation was in a position today deliberately to provoke a world-wide conflict, he added.

Reception Greater Than Dewey's

Observers mindful of the increasing frequency with which General Eisenhower has been mentioned recently as a possible Republican nominee for the Presidency next year noted that his reception was far more enthusiastic than that of two other possibilities who have appeared at the convention, Governor Dewey and former Gov. Harold E. Stassen of Minnesota.

The volume of cheers, whistles and handclapping evoked by General Eisenhower yesterday was vastly greater than that accorded Governor Dewey when he spoke at the opening session of the convention on Thursday. Mr. Stassen has not addressed the convention, but he went almost unnoticed when he appeared on the convention floor as a delegate yesterday.

An attempt, however, to convert yesterday's meeting into a major demonstration for General Eisenhower was blocked by the swift intervention of National Commander Paul E. Griffith of Uniontown, Pa. When General Eisenhower appeared, the delegation from his home state of Kansas raised its standard and started a march about the floor.

Commander Griffith promptly announced from the rostrum that

Continued on Page 4, Column 1

RUSSIA RATIFIES 5 PEACE TREATIES

Proposes an Early Formalizing of Pacts With Italy, Finland, Hungary, Rumania, Bulgaria

Special to THE NEW YORK TIMES.

LONDON, Aug. 29—The Soviet Union has ratified the peace treaties with Italy, Hungary, Rumania, Bulgaria and Finland, the Moscow radio announced tonight. The Presidium of the Supreme Soviet has issued the ratifying decrees, according to the broadcast announcement.

In a note from Deputy Foreign Minister Andrei Y. Vishinsky to Frank Roberts, British Minister in Moscow, the Soviet Government has informed Britain that it is prepared to agree to an early date

Continued on Page 6, Column 6

Argentine Hitch in Rio Pact Eased by Night Compromise

By MILTON BRACKER

PETROPOLIS, Brazil, Aug. 29—The Argentine delegation threw a hitch in the projected Treaty of Rio de Janeiro today with a restrictive amendment. But after the hottest debate of the Inter-American Defense Conference here, with the United States and Argentina squarely lined up against each other, a compromise was reached tonight. It ended the possibility that agreement on the treaty would not be absolute by Tuesday, when President Truman is to address the conference before the signing of the pact.

Argentina sought to limit the scope of the treaty by an amendment that would have prevented applying it in case of an attack on American forces abroad.

Senator Arthur H. Vandenberg, the United States member of commission No. 2, where the Argentine plan was offered at a morning session, fought it vigorously.

The compromise—proposed by Mexico and amounting in effect to an Argentine withdrawal—was unanimously accepted at 10:15 P. M.

It was followed by a demonstration of handshaking and expressions of good-will. Argentine Delegate Pascual La Rosa crossed the floor of the conference chamber and gave Senator Vandenberg the traditional abrazo or embrace.

Mr. Vandenberg drew applause by beginning his speech accepting the compromise with four words

Continued on Page 7, Column 3

TRUMAN NAMES SIX AS DEFENSE CHIEFS

Generals Draper, Gruenther, Civilians are Chosen to Fill Out New Military Set-Up

By FELIX BELAIR Jr.

Special to THE NEW YORK TIMES.

WASHINGTON, Aug. 29—President Truman virtually completed today the organization of the new national military establishment with the filling of six key posts in the unified defense system, including those involving the National Security Council, National Security Resources Board and the Munitions Board.

He appointed Maj. Gen. William H. Draper Jr., economic adviser to the Commanding General of the European Theatre, as Under-Secretary of the Army, a post left vacant by the promotion of Secretary of the Army Kenneth C. Royall. This was a recess appointment and General Draper took the oath of office this afternoon.

The White House also announced

Continued on Page 5, Column 2

Hirshberg Gets 10 Months in Prison; Dishonorable Discharge Ordered

Placing his stamp of legality on the proceedings and giving approval to the findings of the court-martial, Rear Admiral Monroe Kelly, Commandant of the Third Naval District, announced yesterday that Chief Signalman Harold E. Hirshberg had been sentenced to serve ten months in a Naval prison, after which time he is to be dishonorably discharged from the service.

The Brooklyn petty officer had been tried and convicted on Aug. 12 on two of nine specifications that charged he had maltreated two men under his command in Japanese prisoner-of-war camps in the Philippines. He was acquitted by a court-martial of seven officers on seven additional counts of assaulting other American fellow prisoners and informing the enemy of escape plans.

While the sentence called for penal service in the Naval Retraining Command at Norfolk, Va., Admiral Kelly ordered that Hirshberg continue to be confined at the Naval Receiving Station in Brooklyn until determination of a writ of habeas corpus proceeding now pending in the United States District Court.

Hirshberg's conviction on the two minor specifications came after a three-week trial at the New York Naval Shipyard, Brooklyn. The sentence was read to him yesterday in the Receiving Station across the street, where he has since been confined, by Capt. James G. Petrie of the Marine Corps. His reaction was not reported.

In making the announcement Admiral Kelly pointed out that "no recommendation of clemency was made by the court." As convening authority Admiral Kelly held the court-martial proceedings to be legal. They had been challenged on the ground that the offenses were committed while in enemy hands, that Hirshberg had received an honorable discharge subsequent to the offenses and that he had then re-enlisted. Admiral

Continued on Page 2, Column 6

Legion to Parade Up 5th Ave. Today

A twelve-and-a-half-hour parade up Fifth Avenue by 65,000 Legionnaires, augmented by Army, Navy, West Point and Coast Guard detachments, will be the feature of today's convention program.

The parade will begin at 9:30 A. M. at Thirty-fourth Street, swing up the avenue and disband on streets leading east, between Seventy-third and Seventy-eighth Streets. The official reviewing stand for Comdr. Paul H. Griffith and his party will be in front of the Public Library at Forty-first Street.

First-aid tents, manned by physicians and policemen, will be located at Madison Square Park, the Fortieth Street entrance to the Public Library's inside courtyard, St. Nicholas Church on Forty-eighth Street and in Central Park at Sixtieth, Seventy-second and Seventy-ninth Streets.

1947

My Friend Irma was a popular situation comedy starring Marie Wilson and Alan Reed. The show later became a TV hit.

Hopalong Cassidy, portrayed by actor Bill Boyd, had a firm place in the hearts of millions of children.

Probably the most famous puppet of all time, Howdy Doody remained popular with millions of children for well over a decade.

The *First Nighter* dramas were very popular in 1947. They starred Olan Soule and Barbara Luddy.

"All the News That's Fit to Print"

The New York Times.

LATE CITY EDITION
Mostly sunny and warm today.
Fair and warm tomorrow.
Temperature Range Today—Max.,80; Min.,65
Temperatures Yesterday—Max.,78; Min.,65
Full U. S. Weather Bureau Report, Page 47

VOL. XCVII..No. 32,745. Entered as Second-Class Matter. Postoffice, New York, N. Y. NEW YORK, FRIDAY, SEPTEMBER 19, 1947. THREE CENTS NEW YORK CITY

VISHINSKY ACCUSES AMERICANS OF SEEKING WAR, CONDEMNS ENTIRE RANGE OF U.S. FOREIGN POLICY; OTHER NATIONS RALLY TO OUR STAND ON VETO

HURRICANE RAGES OVER GULF TO HIT LOUISIANA COAST

Residents Flee Inland as Fury Nears—New Orleans Ready for Battering Winds

DAMAGE PUT IN MILLIONS

At Least Four Die and Florida Citrus Crop Is Beaten Down After 12-Hour Lashing

By The Associated Press.

NEW ORLEANS, Friday, Sept. 19—Storm winds of seventy-five miles an hour or more threatened this city early today as a vicious, unpredictable hurricane swept toward Louisiana from the Gulf of Mexico with widespread distress and multimillion dollar damage in its wake.

The Weather Bureau reported last night that the center of the hurricane was expected to strike by mid-morning near the mouth of the Mississippi River, about fifty miles south of the city. Blasts of hurricane force were predicted for that area by daylight and for New Orleans a few hours later.

Velocities up to 100 miles an hour prevailed at the storm's core, located at midnight, Eastern daylight time, 140 miles east southeast of Burwood, La., east of New Orleans. Its lateral movement at that time was about fifteen miles an hour.

Panicky refugees were fleeing from coastal danger spots or were waiting in boarded-up buildings for the blow.

Winds at Gale Force

Extreme caution was urged by the Weather Bureau against devastating winds and tides from northwest Florida to Louisiana. Winds of gale force blew over that sector last night. Hurricane warnings were posted from Cedar Keys, Fla., to Morgan City, La.

The great storm's path has been erratic since it rose up out of the Caribbean eight days ago. After pointing northward, it veered westward into the south Florida "gold coast" and lashed the heavily populated peninsula for twelve hours. Winds rose to 120 miles an hour and higher.

Florida property damage was estimated at $12,000,000, with the figure still mounting. Only four persons were known to have lost their lives but hundreds received minor injuries and thousands were driven from their homes and suffered hunger and other hardships.

The winds left Florida at Fort Myers on the west coast at midnight and began weaving offshore up the Gulf Coast. At first they threatened to center their fury on the Pensacola-Apalachicola sector of the Florida coast.

New Orleans, huge port city and center of Southern culture, is no stranger itself to storm disaster. A 120-mile-an-hour blow struck it in 1915 and left 350 persons dead in the city and in neighboring Louisiana and Mississippi gulf areas. The Cheniere Caminada storm of 1893 snuffed out 3,000 lives in coastal Louisiana, although the city itself did not suffer heavily.

With these disasters still remembered, Gulf Coast residents took every precaution against the latest threat.

Schools Are Closed

Along the Mississippi and East Louisiana coasts, boats put into harbors, aircraft were stored or flown out of the area, schools were ordered closed and a general alarm was spread. Some sixty ships tied up or anchored in the Mississippi River at New Orleans.

At Mobile City buses evacuated 3,500 persons from a wartime housing project on Blakely Island. Acting Mayor Charles Baumhauer said the Bankhead vehicular tunnel under the Mobile River would be closed if waters inundated the approaches.

A two-masted schooner, the Valkyrie, her decks awash, was

Continued on Page 3, Column 2

Retail Butter Prices Drop; Meats Are Generally Steady

Little Relief Seen in Wholesale Decline of Latter—Dairymen Called to Inquiry—Mayor's Committee Takes No Action

By WILL LISSNER

The embattled housewife won a small victory yesterday against rising food prices. Butter sold for 2 cents less in retail stores in New York and other cities, with a few reporting declines up to 4 cents, reflecting previous declines on the wholesale market.

Meat prices dropped again in the wholesale markets, where buyers and sellers were at a stalemate, but at retail the prices generally held, pork cuts moving higher. Egg prices were unchanged at wholesale and retail. In the day-by-day struggle with the high cost of living, there was little to give the consumer satisfaction.

In the nation's grain and cattle markets, however, the upward trend of prices was definitely checked, at least temporarily. Although the Chicago Board of Trade deferred action on the Government's request for an increase in trading margins, prices responded to the announcement of a 35 per cent cut in November grain export allocations.

Prices of all corn futures dropped the full 8-cent limit permitted in a day's trading. Wheat dropped the permitted 10 cents, but regained some of the loss. Oats closed 2½ to 3½ cents lower, after dipping to 4 and 5 cents lower.

Cattle prices also weakened in the Midwest livestock markets. At Chicago some grades of cattle dropped as much as $2 a hundred pounds. Steers generally were $1 to $1.50 lower, with the top prices down from $35.75 to $34.

Dealers attributed the situations of the wholesale and the primary markets to consumer resistance and Government pressure and said these must continue if the retail price level were to be brought down significantly.

From the grain trade in New York came a proposal that the Government control grain trading. Charles Schaefer, president of Charles Schaefer & Son, Inc., grain distributors of Brooklyn, wrote President Truman urging that the

Continued on Page 4, Column 2

Extra Session Not Needed, Speaker Martin Declares

By LEWIS WOOD

Special to The New York Times.

WASHINGTON, Sept. 18—Joseph W. Martin Jr. said today that he had "pretty good information" that Europe was not in immediate danger from hunger. The House Speaker criticized the Truman Administration for not furnishing Congress with details of the European situation which might necessitate a special session of Congress.

Mr. Martin said that he had heard that crops were coming along in all the European countries, and that he had no reason to believe that relief would be needed before Congress met regularly in January. He also said that he had no information to the contrary, and stated that he "had not been honored" by the Administration with details of the Marshall Plan.

"Nothing more has been presented to my attention," he said at a news conference, "more than when Congress went out of here in August. If the Administration wants a special session it has been very negligent."

Returning to Washington for the first time since Congressional adjournment, the Republican Speaker faced a large number of reporters. A newsman humorously asked Mr. Martin, who is next in line for the Presidency, about the state of President Truman's health.

"It's very good, and I am happy that it is," he replied with a roaring laugh.

Later, he said he was not a candidate for the Republican Presiden-

Continued on Page 15, Column 6

LA GUARDIA FAILS TO SHAKE OFF COMA

Receives Liquid Nourishment but His Trend Is Downward With No Hope of Recovery

Former Mayor Fiorello H. La Guardia lay dying yesterday in his Riverdale home at 5020 Goodridge Avenue. The 64-year-old "Little Flower" had been almost continuously in a coma since Tuesday evening and no hope was held out for his recovery.

Dr. George Baehr, the former Mayor's personal physician, in his first bulletin of the day declared that the "general trend" of Mr. La Guardia's condition was downward, that he never became fully conscious, though he was sufficiently alert at one period early yesterday morning to take some liquid nourishment.

The news of Mr. La Guardia's illness permeated the consciousness of the citizens of the city during the day, and newspapers and radio stations received many calls of in-

Continued on Page 3, Column 7

TWU Counsel and Witness Battle As Latter Links Santo to Eisler

By ALEXANDER FEINBERG

Gerhard Eisler was pictured yesterday at the John Santo deportation hearing as the Communist who spurred the party's drive that resulted in the organization of the Transport Workers Union in 1934.

Testimony also was given to show that Eisler ranked so high in the international Communist set-up that he was able to "tell off" with impunity leaders of the Communist party in the United States.

Occupying the witness stand for the second day, Manning Johnson, former Negro organizer who quit the party in 1939, placed Mr. Santo at a meeting of the national committee of the party as a representative of the "borers" who were to take over the existing transit unions. Eisler, he said, urged the party to put all its resources into a drive to organize the transportation industry, which he regarded as vital to the revolutionary cause.

The injection into the proceedings of the name of the man who has been called the No. 1 Communist in the United States and the secret agent of the Kremlin came in the course of a day replete with name-calling between Mr. Johnson and Harry Sacher, counsel for Mr. Santo and the TWU.

Goaded by Mr. Sacher's taunts on his failure to remember specific wage demands by the union in the formation of which he had testified he had a hand, Mr. Johnson said he had every reason to remember the Eisler-Santo meeting.

"Who else," he demanded, "would dare excoriate American Commu-

Continued on Page 2, Column 3

DEFENSE COMMAND FILLED AS 2 MORE TAKE SERVICE OATH

Sullivan Made Navy Secretary, Symington Chief of Air as Aides to Forrestal

ARMY-AIR PACT IS REACHED

This Covers a Wide Unification but Some Fliers Protest at Lack of Own Medical Arm

By ANTHONY LEVIERO

Special to The New York Times.

WASHINGTON, Sept. 18—The top ranks in the new national military establishment were filled today when oaths were taken by John L. Sullivan as Secretary of the Navy and by W. Stuart Symington as the Secretary of the now independent Air Force.

Immediately after assuming his new office, Mr. Sullivan announced that tomorrow W. John Kenney, Assistant Secretary of the Navy, would be sworn in to succeed him as Under-Secretary.

Another development on the first day of the unification of the armed forces was the announcement by Kenneth C. Royall, Secretary of the Army, and by Secretary Symington of a separation agreement by the Army department and the new Air Force department embracing more than 200 specific points.

This agreement was reached amicably at the highest level by the two secretaries and by Gen. Dwight D. Eisenhower, Army Chief of Staff, and Gen. Carl Spaatz, commanding general of the old Army Air Forces.

It was learned on high authority, however, that the air staff was dissatisfied with an agreement which disallowed a separate medical corps and a chaplain's corps for the Air Force and would leave under Army control thousands of

Continued on Page 7, Column 1

U. S. POLICY BACKED

Latins, Europeans and Asiatics Voice Their Support in U. N.

EVATT NOTES CHANGE

He Finds Satisfaction in Our Stand—Romulo Stresses Crisis

By A. M. ROSENTHAL

Representative countries from almost every part of the world formed a swiftly growing line-up yesterday behind United States foreign policy, as voiced by Secretary of State Marshall Wednesday, in the United Nations General Assembly.

From morning to evening speaker after speaker—from the Pacific, from Latin America, from Europe—walked to the rostrum to announce support of the United States stand on the veto, on the atom and on Secretary of State Marshall's plan for a year-round "Little Assembly."

The big issue of the day—before Deputy Foreign Minister Andrei Y. Vishinsky's "warmongering" sensation—was the veto. Secretary Marshall, in his speech Wednesday, called for elimination of the veto on cases involving peaceful settlements, and it set the stage for yesterday's developments. In swift succession these countries gave Mr. Marshall notice of their backing: Chile, Australia, China, the Philippines, Canada, El Salvador, Venezuela and Peru.

The tenor of a good part of the one-sided debate was set by Brig. Gen. Carlos P. Romulo, chief of the Philippine delegation.

"Quite calmly and deliberately, we say that the world must choose between the United Nations and

Continued on Page 17, Column 2

MR. VISHINSKY DENOUNCING THE U. S.

The Russian Deputy Foreign Minister addressing the General Assembly yesterday. The New York Times

Fury of Vishinsky's Attack On U. S. Stuns Many in U. N.

By GEORGE BARRETT

Delegates to the United Nations General Assembly session at Flushing Meadow yesterday expressed shock and dismay at the fury of the attack that Russia's Deputy Foreign Minister, Andrei Y. Vishinsky, made against the United States.

Many of them ignored the usual courtesy of waiting to hear the speaker who followed Mr. Vishinsky, and the moment he was finished, poured out of the great hall. There they exchanged excited comments and compared reactions openly on the long, impassioned charge Mr. Vishinsky raised against what he bitterly described as this country's "war psychosis" concerning the Soviet Union.

One of the first to protest Mr. Vishinsky's accusations was John Foster Dulles, one of the five principal United States delegates, who emphatically denied that he had made the anti-Soviet statement attributed to him by the chief Moscow representative.

Mr. Vishinsky told the representatives of the fifty-five nations that Mr. Dulles had urged a "tough foreign policy toward the Soviet Union" in a speech delivered on Feb. 10 in Chicago.

Mr. Dulles quickly issued a categorical denial. "I did not make the statement which Mr. Vishinsky attributed to me," he declared. "I have repeatedly said, and I again say, that another war need not and must not be. And I have directed myself to that end."

"I am confident," he added, "that the Assembly will quickly forget

Continued on Page 20, Column 1

ALLIES VOICE AIM TO DEFEND TRIESTE

British Commander Declares Troops Are Ready to Meet Any 'Eventuality' There

By CAMILLE M. CIANFARRA

Special to The New York Times

TRIESTE, Sept. 18—British General Terence S. Airey, supreme commander of the United States and British forces in the Free Territory of Trieste authorized today a statement saying that "British and United States troops and the Allied Military Government are prepared quickly to meet any eventualities."

Allied officers stressed that the statement was General Airey's way of saying that any attempt by Yugoslavia against the territorial integrity of Trieste would be opposed with all the Allies' available resources.

"Internal conditions in Trieste and throughout the British and the United States zone of the Free Territory approximately are back to

Continued on Page 12, Column 2

RUSSIAN URGES GAG

Asks Assembly to Seek a Ban on War Talk as Felonious

SCORES 'CRAZY IDEA'

He Sees Plan in U. S. to Dominate World—Nine Americans Accused

Vishinsky, Wang addresses; other excerpts, pages 18, 19, 20.

By FRANK S. ADAMS

Andrei Y. Vishinsky, Deputy Foreign Minister of the Soviet Union, excoriated every phase of United States foreign policy in an amazing address that occupied an hour and thirty-two minutes before the United Nations General Assembly in Flushing Meadow yesterday. His vehemence left many of his listeners stunned and heartsick.

Accusing influential American "reactionary circles" of building up a war psychosis against the Soviet Union in the minds of the American people to further a "crazy" plan for world domination, Mr. Vishinsky offered a resolution calling upon the Assembly to urge all member Governments of the United Nations to forbid war propaganda within their borders, on pain of criminal punishment.

In language of a violence never heard before from the rostrum of an international organization, Mr. Vishinsky named a large number of prominent American persons and organizations as "war mongers." He lumped together such diverse personalities as John Foster Dulles, who sat listening in the ranks of the United States delegation, and Senators Brien McMahon of Connecticut and C. Wayland Brooks of Illinois. He included the Morgan, Rockefeller and Ford interests, Yale University, the "notorious" American Legion and many others.

Says They Fear Economic Crisis

Mr. Vishinsky charged that these "war propagandists" were afraid of an approaching economic crisis. He said they were instigating a new war to prevent "the approaching menace and collapse of their profits." He charged that American corporations had made net profits of $52,000,000,000 during World War II.

The Soviet spokesman branded the Truman Doctrine and the Marshall plan as attempts to subjugate European countries to United States economic monopolies, and he charged that the British and French Governments were assisting in this attempt. He said the United States was seeking to divide Europe into two groups and to use western Germany, including the Ruhr, as a base for United States expansion in Europe.

As for the proposal advanced on Wednesday by Secretary of State Marshall for the creation of an "Interim Committee on Peace and Security" by the General Assembly, Mr. Vishinsky said it was an attempt to by-pass the Security Council. He said it could only undermine the very basis of the United Nations. He branded Secretary Marshall's action in bringing the independence of Korea before the Assembly as a violation of the Moscow Declaration of December, 1945.

Denies Threats to Greece

Mr. Vishinsky said Secretary Marshall's action in placing alleged threats to Greece on the agenda of the General Assembly was "devoid of any foundation." He declared the charges made by the United States delegation against Yugoslavia, Bulgaria and Albania were "utterly arbitrary and without any proof" and that he would deal with them in detail later in the Assembly.

Mr. Vishinsky declared the principle of the unanimity of the great powers—the language by which

Continued on Page 20, Column 7

World News Summarized

FRIDAY, SEPTEMBER 19, 1947

Deputy Foreign Minister Vishinsky yesterday gave Russia's reply to Secretary Marshall's speech suggesting means by which the United Nations General Assembly might restore the prestige of the world organization. The Russian accused the United States of "expansionist plans, the keystone of which is a crazy idea of world domination." Reactionary circles, he told the Assembly, are fanning a war psychosis, and he named as figures in those circles John Foster Dulles, a member of the United States delegation; two Senators, the Morgan, Rockefeller and Ford interests, the American Legion and Yale University.

In his ninety-two minute speech Mr. Vishinsky attacked the entire range of American foreign policy. He denounced the Truman Doctrine and the Marshall plan, asserted the United States stand on control of atomic energy, blamed this country for the Korean impasse and denied that there was any need to regulate the use of the veto in the Security Council. Secretary Marshall's proposal for a "Little Assembly" was called an attempt to by-pass the Council. Mr. Vishinsky introduced a resolution urging all member nations to forbid war propaganda on pain of criminal punishment. [All the foregoing 1:8.]

Delegates expressed shock and dismay at the violence of Mr. Vishinsky's speech, some describing it as a "bombshell" and "vitriolic." Mr. Dulles immediately denied having made "the statement which Mr. Vishinsky attributed to me." [1:6-7.]

Before the Russian official took the platform Australia, China, the Philippines, Canada and four Latin-American countries endorsed Secretary Marshall's proposal for restrictions on the veto. His suggestion for a "Little Assembly" and America's position on atomic energy control also were praised. [1:5.]

It was announced that the United States, Belgium and Australia would constitute the Security Council's Indonesian mediation committee. [17:4.]

Differences between Russia and the United States were emphasized overseas, too. In Korea the Russians accused the Americans of deliberately thwarting a decision on Korean independence. [9:4.] In Vienna, Russia was accused by the United States of blocking progress on an Austrian peace treaty. [12:2.]

United States and British troops in Trieste were prepared to meet any Yugoslav attempt to seize territory there, the Allied commander said. [1:7.]

Moscow sent a new note to Iran demanding an end to the "delaying tactics" that have halted action on oil concessions to the Soviet Union. [15:4.]

Britain's "limited direction" of labor, which becomes effective Oct. 6, provides for fines and jail sentences for workers refusing to take jobs to which the Government has directed them. [1:6-7.]

Speaker Martin saw no need for a special session of Congress. "Good sources," he said, had told him Europe was in no immediate danger of hunger. [1:2-3.]

Butter alone of the major food items dropped in retail price, although there was further weakening in wholesale and exchange prices. [1:2-3.] Distributors denied before a Congressional subcommittee that meat, butter and eggs had been hoarded to "rig" prices. [4:1.]

All pending eviction cases here except for non-payment of rent were stayed by the City Rent Commission. [25:8.]

The five operating railroad brotherhoods demanded a 30 per cent wage rise on Nov. 1. [2:6.]

Former Mayor La Guardia continued to fail; hope for his recovery was given up. [1:2.]

The hurricane that swept across Florida was headed for the Louisiana coast. [1:1.]

British Labor Direction Law Sets Fines and Jail for Defaulters

By MALLORY BROWNE

Special to The New York Times.

LONDON, Sept. 18—The British Government announced today the details of an emergency order instituting the "limited direction" of labor in an effort to increase production in essential industries.

Explaining the plan at a press conference, George Isaacs, Minister of Labor and National Service, emphasized that the workers would receive as wide a choice as possible of essential jobs and that "direction" would be used only as a last resort.

He warned, however, that defaulters faced penalties in the form of fines or jail terms, or both.

The first reaction to the plan in London is that it is likely to prove too tentative and limited to succeed in solving the problem of getting more manpower into essential exporting industries while at the same time it will be disliked by labor and employers as a serious infringement of individual liberty.

Mr. Isaacs was pointedly reminded at the press conference of the Labor Government's statement in the White Paper on the economic crisis issued in February. Referring to the "essential difference between totalitarian and democratic planning," this document said that in normal times the people of a democratic country will not give up their freedom of choice to their government.

Asked if, in view of this statement, the present measure was part of a democratic or totalitarian plan, Mr. Isaacs replied:

"This is not a part of democratic planning, but it is a measure intro-

Continued on Page 13, Column 6

1947

The 1947 World Series, between the New York Yankees and the Brooklyn Dodgers, was the first to be televised. In this photo, the Dodgers are celebrating their last inning victory in the first game of the classic.

Baseball standout Jackie Robinson became the first black major-leaguer when he signed with the Brooklyn Dodgers.

"Babe" Zaharias earned the distinction of being the first American to win the British Women's Amateur Championship.

"All the News That's Fit to Print"

The New York Times.

LATE CITY EDITION
Sunny and mild today. Increasing cloudiness tomorrow.
Temperature Range Today—Max.,75; Min.,56
Temperatures Yesterday—Max.,72; Min.,55
Full U. S. Weather Bureau Report, Page 45

VOL. XCVII..No. 32,762. Entered as Second-Class Matter. Postoffice, New York, N. Y. NEW YORK, MONDAY, OCTOBER 6, 1947. THREE CENTS IN NEW YORK CITY

TRUMAN CALLS ON NATION TO FOREGO MEAT TUESDAYS, POULTRY, EGGS THURSDAYS

ALL TO AID EUROPE

Anderson, Harriman, Luckman and Marshall Join in Radio Plea

LESS BREAD A DAY URGED

'Gambling' in Grain Is Ordered Curbed—60-Day Closing for Distilleries Is Advised

Texts of broadcasts on the food crisis are on Page 5.

By SAMUEL A. TOWER
Special to The New York Times.

WASHINGTON, Oct. 5—President Truman asked the American people tonight to observe meatless Tuesdays and use no poultry or eggs on Thursdays and to save a slice of bread a day.

He urged adoption of other food conservation measures to provide the necessary shipments needed to prevent starvation and suffering in Europe this winter.

Among other steps, he suggested a sixty-day shutdown by distillers, saying that "this action alone will feed millions of hungry people."

Mr. Truman also said that he was moving against "gambling" in grain. He said he had directed the Commodity Exchange Commission to require the grain exchanges to raise their margin requirements to at least 33 1/3 per cent. He served notice that refusal might mean action by the Government to limit the amount of trading.

Examples Set for Nation

In a half-hour broadcast from the White House to further the Government's campaign for voluntary food conservation to meet European relief needs, the Chief Executive gave his whole-hearted approval and endorsement to an immediate food-saving program mapped out by a preceding speaker, Charles Luckman, chairman of the President's Citizens Food Committee.

In addition to aiding the survival of European peoples crushed by the misfortunes of nature and the aftermath of war, adherence to the food conservation program, the President pointed out, would contribute to the struggle against inflation and foster lower prices.

He told his audience that Mrs. Truman had directed the White House to follow the food-saving program and that he in his capacity as Commander in Chief, had ordered the military services to comply.

Grain Saving by Industries

Mr. Luckman, in advancing a plan of action for the preservation of food by all segments of the economy, announced that the distilling industry, at a meeting here this week, would be asked to declare a sixty-day emergency suspension of operations.

At a meeting last week more than half of the industry had pledged a 50 per cent reduction in the use of grain.

This proposal was disclosed by Mr. Luckman in the course of outlining a three-way program for all consumers, for industry and for agriculture.

On the industrial side, he announced that the baking industry was undertaking important conservation steps that would result

Continued on Page 5, Column 3

4 Steps to Save Food Offered by President

Special to The New York Times.

WASHINGTON, Oct. 5—President Truman's guide for the nation's food consumers during the crisis in Europe:

1. Use no meat on Tuesdays.
2. Use no poultry or eggs on Thursdays.
3. Save a slice of bread every day.
4. Public eating places will serve bread and butter only on request.

"It is simple and straight forward," said the President. "It can be understood by all. Learn it—memorize it—keep it always in mind."

Meat Industry Council Asks Price Ceilings on Livestock

Requisitioning of Animals if Growers Refuse to Sell Also Urged—Two 'Meatless Days' a Week Opposed as No Economy

Price ceilings on livestock, and Government requisitioning of cattle if growers refused to sell at maximum legal prices, were recommended yesterday by the National Meat Industry Council.

The executive board of the council, after a series of week-end conferences, went on record as opposed to two "meatless days" a week on the ground that it might lead to heavier rather than lighter consumption of meat.

Jack Kranis, council president, said that many families, through the use of fish, poultry and vegetable dinners, were eating meat on fewer than five days a week. He said that general observance of two "meatless days" would tend to standardize five days of meat-eating, thus increasing the meat consumption of many families.

"If every family will reduce voluntarily its consumption of meat, whether it now has meat on the table three, four, five, or six days a week, the nation will achieve a maximum saving of meat and reduce the demand for grain to feed cattle and hogs," said Mr. Kranis. "This will also produce a downward pressure on meat prices, and help curb living costs."

Mr. Kranis suggested also that housewives buy the cheaper cuts and grades of meat, rather than choice steaks and chops, to bring down prices and reduce waste. He said that 75 per cent of the cheaper meats were not being used on the average American dinner table.

"If the housewife will make greater use of the cheaper cuts," said Mr. Kranis, "we will have about 25 per cent more use of the entire animal. This will help feed starving Europe and cut our meat bills at home. All that is needed is for the housewife to learn how to cook the cheaper cuts. They are fully as nutritious as the choice cuts if properly prepared. Unskillful cooking will, of course, produce unpalatable dishes. It is time the American housewife learned how to cook the cheaper cuts."

The Meat Industry Council's board decided that price controls

Continued on Page 5, Column 2

CITY TRANSIT LOSES $18,000,000 IN YEAR

Operating Deficit for 1946-47 Compares with $8,095,980 Surplus in 1945-46 Period

By PAUL CROWELL

The Board of Transportation announced yesterday that it had submitted to the Board of Estimate a report showing an operating deficit of $18,000,000 for the city's unified transit system for the fiscal year ended June 30. Operating revenues fell $16,711,927 below operating expenses, and it was necessary to set aside an accident claim reserve of $1,288,073 for the surface lines, making a total deficit of $18,000,000.

The report took on special significance in the light of Mayor O'Dwyer's recent announcement that he would appoint Deputy Transportation Commissioner William Reid, an avowed higher fare man, as chairman of the Board of Transportation when Charles P. Gross retires at midnight on Oct. 21.

Mr. Gross predicted last spring that the operating deficit on a five-cent fare would reach $27,000,000 by June 30, 1948, and soar to $31,500,000 by June 30, 1949. The city's expense budget would have to bear the burden of such deficits in addition to $6,200,000 in 1947-48 and 1948-49 for redemption of budget notes issued to meet the cost of $18,000,000 in pay rises granted last year to the 29,000

Continued on Page 16, Column 4

AFL WAITS ON NLRB IN AFFIDAVIT ISSUE

Council, on Eve of Convention, Decides to Postpone Action in Hope Denham Is Vetoed

By LAWRENCE E. DAVIES
Special to The New York Times.

SAN FRANCISCO, Oct. 5—The fifteen-member executive council of the American Federation of Labor, at a session lasting almost three hours this afternoon, failed to iron out its differences and take a convention-eve stand on the lively issue involving non-Communist affidavits.

President William Green announced after the meeting that the council "has finally decided to postpone action till Thursday." He said that "in view of the probability or the possibility" that the National Labor Relations Board would pass tomorrow on an appeal made to modify a ruling by Robert N. Denham, general counsel of the board, on the affidavit matter, council members "felt that we could well wait till the said ruling was made."

Under Mr. Denham's ruling, every member of the AFL executive council must sign a non-Communist affidavit before any AFL union may bring cases before the NLRB. John L. Lewis, eleventh vice president of the AFL and president of the United Mine Workers, has refused to do so.

The position of the UMW on this matter "remains unchanged,"

Continued on Page 17, Column 5

Manchurian Reds List Wide Gains In Offensive Along Vital Rail Line

By HENRY R. LIEBERMAN
Special to The New York Times.

NANKING, Oct. 5—The strategic railway hub of Szepingkai has been cut off on all sides by the capture of Kaiyuan, sixty miles northeast of Mukden, according to the Communist radio. A broadcast tonight said Gen. Lin Piao's Red forces in Manchuria controlled almost two-thirds of the Changchun-Mukden Railway.

The broadcast said the Communists held 120 miles of track from "immediately south" of Changchun down to the suburbs of Tiehling, on the railway forty miles north of Mukden. Although it reported the capture of Kaiyuan, the broadcast said the Kaiyuan railway station west of the city was still in Government hands.

This was the first mention of the Manchurian offensive by the Communist radio, which said the drive began with a vast pincers movement "on each side of the Chinese Changchun Railway." Kaiyuan was seized by a western column, driving down from northwest of Changchun in a sweep that also took Kungchuling, forty miles southwest of the Manchurian capital, and the towns of Lishu, Pamiencheng and Changtu west of the tracks, according to the broadcast.

An eastern column, the broadcast continued, captured Itung, thirty-eight miles south of Changchun, and Sifeng, thirty miles southeast of Szepingkai. The new gains claimed by the Communists isolated Szepingkai, which is midway between Changchun and Mukden.

The broadcast indicated an attempted squeeze on Szepingkai from Lishu, nine miles to the north, from Pamiencheng, fifteen miles to the west; from Changtu, thirty miles to the southwest, from Kaiyuan forty miles to the south and from Sifeng, thirty miles to the southeast.

The Nationalists acknowledged

Continued on Page 13, Column 5

DODGERS SET BACK YANKEES BY 8 TO 6 FOR 3-3 SERIES TIE

Rout Page With Four in Sixth to Win Before 74,065, New Crowd Mark for Classic

38 PLAYERS IN THE GAME

Gionfriddo's Great Catch of DiMaggio's Drive Prevents Losers From Tying Score

By JOHN DREBINGER

Incredible as it may seem to a bewildered world at large, the 1947 world series is still with us, and so are the Dodgers.

For in one of the most extraordinary games ever played, one that left a record series crowd of 74,065 limp and exhausted, Burt Shotton's unpredictable Flock fought the Yankees in a last-ditch stand at the Stadium yesterday and defeated them, 8 to 6.

As a consequence, the classic, which in this same park last Tuesday had started as a soft touch for Bucky Harris' American League champions, now stands tied at three victories apiece. The seventh and deciding game will be played at the Stadium today.

It was a conflict that lasted three hours and nineteen minutes, the longest on record for nine innings in a world series. Had it gone into an extra inning, another series precedent would have been set, as permission had been obtained to turn on the floodlights.

As for the gathering, which had shelled out record gross receipts of $393,210, it was to thrill to a show that scarcely left a moment's breathing spell. The Yanks tossed twenty-one players into the fray, six of them hurlers, while the battling Bums countered with seventeen, four of them flingers, the last of all being the astounding Hugh Casey.

The game also was marked by one of the greatest catches in series history—Al Gionfriddo's collaring of Joe DiMaggio's 415-foot drive in the sixth inning.

The fans saw the aroused Dodgers fighting to keep the series alive, rout Allie Reynolds inside of three rounds, getting two runs in the first and two in the third. It saw the Bombers roar back in the lower half of the third to blast Vic Lombardi from the mound with a four-run demonstration.

The Yanks added one more tally off Ralph Branca in the fourth to take a 5-4 lead, while the Bums screamed to the high heavens that the umpires were blind in calling

Continued on Page 28, Column 2

REDS OF 9 NATIONS REVIVE COMINTERN TO FIGHT U. S. 'IMPERIALIST HEGEMONY'; 2 STALIN AIDES ATTEND SECRET MEETING

CAPITAL STUDY DUE

Sources in Washington Expect Deterioration in Soviet Relations

THREAT TO U. N. IS SEEN

British Spokesman Suggests That Attack on Attlee May Strengthen His Position

Special to The New York Times.

WASHINGTON, Oct. 5—Neither White House nor State Department spokesmen would comment tonight on the news from Moscow of the formation of a Communist international organization to fight "United States imperialism."

But while official reaction was withheld, it was evident that this latest development in the contest between the United States and the Soviet Union would receive serious and immediate attention by the Government.

It cannot be said that officials here were surprised by the announcement. This is not intended to indicate that such a Communist program for Europe was definitely anticipated in Washington, but simply that the general expectation here is that Russian relations will grow worse rather than better and that a new development in the first direction is not surprising.

In other quarters, not official, it was speculated that there might be more behind the move than an attempt to knit the Communists of Europe more closely together. Here, it was recalled that in 1943, when the Soviet Union, the United States and Britain were most closely bound as allies, the old Comintern, whose purpose was propagation of the Red ideology throughout the world, was dissolved.

Then followed the first steps in the formation of the United Nations, victory in Europe and in the Pacific, and then the United Nations in full operation but no re-establishment of the Comintern. This suggests, some observers think, that the Kremlin may now be preparing in advance against the possibility that the Soviet

Continued on Page 4, Column 4

De Gaulle Backs U.S. Policy As That of Freedom Lovers

Calls Upon the French to Resist Penetration of Communists, Whom He Describes as 'Separatists' at Huge Rally

By LANSING WARREN
Special to The New York Times.

PARIS, Oct. 5—Communism and the resistance to it under the leadership of Charles de Gaulle came into open conflict in the French political arena here today. France's alliance with the United States and Great Britain is the stake.

While M. de Gaulle at the Vincennes racetrack in an election address called upon the French to rally against what he said was the Soviet menace, the Communists, through their official organ l'Humanité, announced a coalition of their parties in nine European countries to combat the influence of the United States and Britain.

M. de Gaulle retorted in his speech that "There is no freedom-loving man who does not hold the American policy to be salutary."

In the immense concourse an estimated half a million persons, assembled in the huge park at Vincennes, heard M. de Gaulle, resuming and concluding a long campaign in all parts of the country, call upon the French to unite again, as they did in the resistance, against the threat of communism.

"Today we are in peril," he declared. "We are tottering on the brink of an abyss, which is financial, economic and social. We are a country that is menaced."

This threat, he told his auditors, comes from the Soviet dictatorship, whose servitors in the Communist party in France he repeatedly described as "Separatists." France will unite against them, he predicted, but he prayed that this would not be too late.

De Gaulle's call upon the French to meet this challenge was his first address to an open air public meeting in Paris since the days of the liberation and the demonstration was organized by his followers to attract the largest possible throng.

The speech was preceded by folkdances and entertainments resembling the attractions of a coun-

Continued on Page 3, Column 6

Vandenberg Says U.S. Moves To Pacts to Circumvent Veto

By THOMAS J. HAMILTON
Special to The New York Times.

LAKE SUCCESS, N. Y., Oct. 5—Senator Arthur H. Vandenberg, chairman of the Senate Foreign Relations Committee, says that United States policy already is starting to move "in the general direction" of the use of Article 51, the self-defense article of the United Nations Charter, to make possible "protective actions" that would not be subject to the veto.

Mr. Vandenberg said he would not pass final judgment on detailed proposals to this effect by Hamilton Fish Armstrong, editor of Foreign Affairs Quarterly magazine, but emphasized that it never was intended at the San Francisco conference at which the Charter was written that the veto "should become a tool to frustrate all efforts to lay a firm basis of world peace and security."

Mr. Armstrong, in an article published in THE NEW YORK TIMES Magazine on Sept. 14, strongly criticized the Soviet use of the veto and proposed that members of the United Nations sign treaties of mutual defense.

Article 51 confirms the right of collective or individual defense against armed attack, pending action by the Security Council, and the "Armstrong plan" proposed that the decision to provide help should be taken by a two-thirds vote of the signatory countries.

The Charter also authorizes regional arrangements to maintain peace and security, and the recent Inter-American Conference in Rio

Continued on Page 6, Column 3

AUSTRIANS EXPECT PRO-RUSSIAN PLOT

Gruber Says Communists Plan Incident to Seize Control With Aid of Soviet Army

By JOHN MacCORMAC
Special to The New York Times.

VIENNA, Oct. 5—Two Austrian Cabinet Ministers charged today that Austrian Communists, with the help of the Soviet Army of occupation, were planning to use here the "plot" technique already employed with such success in Hungary and now being tried out in Czechoslovakia.

They were Dr. Karl Gruber, Foreign Minister, and Ferdinand Graf, Under-Secretary of the Interior in charge of the police.

Dr. Gruber predicted flatly that the London conference of Foreign Ministers in November would not produce an Austrian peace treaty. He and Herr Graf then told an audience of 50,000 members of the People's party that the Russians were planning to stay in Austria

Continued on Page 2, Column 3

BELGRADE IS SEAT

New Information Bureau Will Seek to Unify Strategy of Reds

SOCIALIST RIGHT WING HIT

Attlee, Ramadier, Renner and Others Are Accused as 'Traitors' to Workers

Texts of statements by European Communists are on Page 3.

By SYDNEY GRUSON
Special to The New York Times.

WARSAW, Poland, Oct. 5—The leaders of world communism proclaimed today what amounted to the re-establishment of the Communist International [Comintern] to combat what they called United States "dollar imperialism."

A manifesto issued after a secret meeting in Poland declared that the world was split in two and called on Europe to align itself on the side of the "Soviet Union and other democratic countries," against "the camp of imperialism and anti-democratic forces whose chief aim is the establishment of a world-wide American imperialist hegemony."

The wording of the manifesto also indicated that the establishment of the "Information Bureau" was a measure directed against the Marshall plan in western Europe.

Nine Nations Represented

A communiqué on the meeting said that party chieftains of nine European countries had decided to establish an "Information Bureau" in Belgrade, Yugoslavia, charged with "organizing the exchange of experience and in case of necessity coordinating the activities of Communist parties on the basis of common agreement."

The communiqué was accompanied by a long manifesto charging the United States with attempting to enslave the world through dollar imperialism and warmongering. It also bitterly attacked the "Right-ist Socialists" who it said were leading their countries to "vassal-like dependence on the United States."

The manifesto recorded as "traitors" to the working class Prime Minister Attlee and Foreign Secretary Bevin of Britain, Léon Blum and Premier Paul Ramadier of France, Dr. Kurt Schumacher, Socialist leader in Germany, President Karl Renner and Adolf Schaerf of Austria, and Giuseppe Saragat, Socialist leader in Italy.

Stalin's Advisers Present

The eighteen delegates to the conference were led by Col. Gen. Andrei A. Zhdanov and Georgi M. Malenkov of the Soviet Union, two of Prime Minister Stalin's closest advisors. Other delegates were Edward Kardelj and Milovan Djilas of Yugoslavia, Vulko Chervenkov and V. Poptomov of Bulgaria, Anna Pauker and George Gheorgiu-Dej of Rumania, M. Farkasz and Joseph Revai of Hungary, Vice Premier Wladislaw Gomulka and H. Minc of Poland, Jacques Duclos and Etienne Fajon of France, R. Slansky and S. Basztovanski of Czechoslovakia and Luigi Longo and Eugenio Reale of Italy.

The communiqué gave no details of the conference itself but it is believed to have taken place in a Silesian resort town from Sept. 21 to Sept. 28.

No word of the presence in Poland of General Zhdanov and Mr. Malenkov has been allowed to leak out, although the press reported at various times in the last two weeks that one or another of the others were paying a short visit to Warsaw.

M. Duclos, in fact, made a fairly widely publicized trip around western Poland at the Polish Communist party's invitation ostensibly to review the industrialization of that territory.

The "Information Bureau" will be composed of two delegates from the Central Committees of the Communist parties in the nine countries. According to the communiqué, the bureau will issue a bi-monthly

Continued on Page 3, Column 5

World News Summarized

MONDAY, OCTOBER 6, 1947

Communist leaders from nine European nations met secretly in Poland last month and adopted a program that amounted to the re-establishment of the Comintern which, until dissolved in 1943, planned and directed the international Communist fight. A manifesto, made public yesterday, assailed the United States, Britain and right-wing Socialists everywhere. It proclaimed that the "Soviet Union and other democratic countries" were leading the fight against "dollar imperialism" and "a world-wide American imperialist hegemony." The new organization will have headquarters in Belgrade, Yugoslavia. [1:8.]

There was no official comment in Washington, but some observers saw in this development a reversal of the 1943 dissolution of the Comintern and a first step toward Russia's withdrawal from the United Nations. The British were unworried and felt that the only effect would be to strengthen the Labor Government, which had been attacked in the manifesto. [1:5.] Former President de Gaulle told a crowd of 500,000 in France that "we are in peril" and called on the French to resist communism. [1:6-7.]

Italian Communists branded Right-Wing Socialist leader Saragat a traitor bribed by American dollars. [2:2.] Czech Communists said American and British bombers had destroyed factories to eliminate them from post-war competition. [5:1.] Austria's Foreign Minister declared that the Communists would produce a "reactionary plot" to justify Russia in opposing a peace treaty. [1:7.]

Voters in Germany's Saar Basin overwhelmingly elected candidates pledged to economic union with France. [1:6-7.]

Premier Ghavam won by 93 to 27 in a test of confidence in the Iranian Parliament. [10:2.]

Americans were asked by President Truman to use no meat on Tuesdays and no poultry or eggs on Thursdays, and to save a slice of bread daily for the double purpose of aiding starving Europe and bringing down domestic prices. He asked restaurants to serve bread and butter only on request and said that he was moving to end "gambling" in grains. He concluded a half-hour save-food radio program in which Chairman Luckman of the Citizens Food Committee outlined the program for the nation and Secretary Marshall said: "Our foreign policy has entered the American home and taken a seat at the family table." [1:1.]

The meat industry, questioning the value of meatless days, urged the Government to restore price ceilings on livestock and to seize cattle if ranchers refused to sell. [1:2-3.]

Palestine, the Balkans and a successor to Poland in the Security Council are major items on the United Nations calendar this week [8:1.] Senator Vandenberg said that the United States was already moving "in the general direction" of using the "self-defense" Article 51 of the United Nations Charter, which permits protective action not subject to the veto. [1:6-7.]

Chinese Communists reported important gains in their Manchurian drive. [1:2-3; map P. 12.]

Floods in eastern India have made 1,000,000 homeless and famine is spreading. [11:2.]

The Board of Transportation reported an $18,000,000 operating deficit last year on this city's transit lines. [1:2.]

Saar Votes for Economic Fusion With France, Reversing '35 Stand

By KATHLEEN McLAUGHLIN
Special to The New York Times.

SAARBRUECKEN, Germany, Monday, Oct. 6—Proponents of economic fusion of the coal-rich Saar with France scored an overwhelming victory in the election yesterday that decided the issue by indirect ballot. The voting reversed the result of the plebiscite of Jan. 13, 1935, that turned the Saar over to Adolf Hitler's Germany.

Candidates of two of the three parties committed to ratification of the proposed Constitution, which provides for such an economic union, held long leads for seats in the Landtag [State Parliament]. The Communists, who opposed the plan, ran third, with the Democratic party, which favored fusion, a close fourth.

In all, 449,504 ballots were cast out of 520,860 eligible votes. Unofficial figures released shortly after midnight indicated that 96 per cent of the votes cast favored the Constitution, which was drafted by a committee representing all parties.

The Democratic party showed the greatest increase, its total rising from 9,025 in 1946 to 34,253; the party will hold three seats.

The Christian People's party led in the vote with 230,062, giving it twenty-eight seats. The Social Democrats, in second place, received 147,255 votes and will have seventeen seats.

The Communist party, which will receive two seats in the new Parliament, registered the single decrease in popular support, in comparison with the totals for the communal elections last year.

Actually, the populace had no opportunity to express an opinion directly on the matter of economic fusion and autonomous political status. Those who disliked the proposal had the alternative of staying away from the polls or voting for Communist candidates as a gesture of disapproval. The second course was hardly likely to

Continued on Page 9, Column 5

"All the News That's Fit to Print"

The New York Times.

LATE CITY EDITION
Fair and continued cold today and tomorrow
Temperature Range Today—Max.,38; Min.,26
Temperatures Yesterday—Max.,45; Min.,30
U.S. Weather Bureau Report, Page 19; Sect. 1

Section 1

NEWS INDEX, PAGE 79, THIS SECTION

VOL. XCVII..No. 32,817. Entered as Second-Class Matter, Postoffice, New York, N. Y. NEW YORK, SUNDAY, NOVEMBER 30, 1947. Including Magazine and Book Review. FIFTEEN CENTS.

ASSEMBLY VOTES PALESTINE PARTITION; MARGIN IS 33 TO 13; ARABS WALK OUT; ARANHA HAILS WORK AS SESSION ENDS

U. N. REJECTS DELAY

Proposal Driven Through by U. S. and Soviet Will Set Up Two States

COMMISSION IS APPOINTED

Britain Holds Out Hand to It—Arabs Fail in Last-Minute Resort to Federal Plan

By THOMAS J. HAMILTON

The United Nations General Assembly approved yesterday a proposal to partition Palestine into two states, one Arab and the other Jewish, that are to become fully independent by Oct. 1. The vote was 33 to 13 with ten abstentions and one delegation, the Siamese, absent.

The decision was primarily a result of the fact that the delegations of the United States and the Soviet Union, which were at loggerheads on every other important issue before the Assembly, stood together on partition. Andrei A. Gromyko and Herschel V. Johnson both urged the Assembly yesterday not to agree to further delay but to vote for partition at once.

The Assembly disregarded last-minute Arab efforts to effect a compromise. Although the votes of a dozen or more delegations seesawed to the last, supporters of partition had two votes more than the required two-thirds majority, or a margin of three.

How Members Voted

The roll-call vote was as follows:

For (33)—Australia, Belgium, Bolivia, Brazil, Canada, Costa Rica, Czechoslovakia, Denmark, Dominican Republic, Ecuador, France, Guatemala, Haiti, Iceland, Liberia, Luxembourg, the Netherlands, New Zealand, Nicaragua, Norway, Panama, Paraguay, Peru, Philippines, Poland, Sweden, the Ukraine, South Africa, Uruguay, the Soviet Union, the United States, Venezuela, White Russia.

Against (13)—Afghanistan, Cuba, Egypt, Greece, India, Iran, Iraq, Lebanon, Pakistan, Saudi Arabia, Syria, Turkey, Yemen.

Abstentions (10) — Argentina, Chile, China, Colombia, El Salvador, Ethiopia, Honduras, Mexico, United Kingdom, Yugoslavia.

Absent (1)—Siam.

All other questions before the Assembly were disposed of a week ago, and it ended its second regular session at 6:57 P. M. after farewell speeches by Dr. Oswaldo Aranha, its President, and Trygve Lie, the Secretary General. The Assembly's third regular session is to open in a European capital on Sept. 21.

The vote on partition was taken at 5:35 P. M. Representatives of Iraq, Saudi Arabia, Syria and Yemen, four of the six Arab member states, announced that they would not be bound by the Assembly's decision and walked determinedly out of the Assembly Hall at Flushing Meadow. The Egyptian and Lebanese delegates were silent but walked out, too.

Briton Seeks Contact

Sir Alexander Cadogan, representative of Britain, which is to terminate the League of Nations mandate over Palestine and withdraw all British troops by Aug. 1, made a brief statement after the vote. He requested the United Nations Palestine Commission to establish contact with the British Government about the date of its arrival in Palestine and the coordination of its plans with the withdrawal of British troops.

The United Nations commission, which will be responsible to the Security Council in the event that the Arabs carry out their threats to fight rather than agree to partition, will be composed of representatives of Bolivia, Czechoslovakia, Denmark, Panama and the Philippines.

This slate, which is understood to have the backing of the United States, was proposed by Dr. Aranha and approved without opposition after the Arab delegates had walked out.

The commission, as proposed by the partition subcommittee of the

Continued on Page 62, Column 2

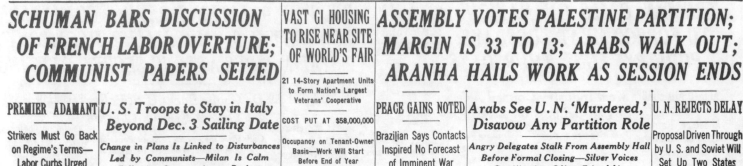

Arabs See U. N. 'Murdered,' Disavow Any Partition Role

Angry Delegates Stalk From Assembly Hall Before Formal Closing—Silver Voices Gratification, Offers Friendship

By A. M. ROSENTHAL

Bitter Arab delegates walked out of the General Assembly hall at Flushing Meadow last night after the vote for the partition of Palestine and solemnly announced that in their eyes the United Nations had died.

"No, not died," said Faris el-Khouri of Syria. "Murdered."

The representatives of the Arab states swept out of the building without waiting for the formal end of the Assembly and the farewell speeches. But before they entered their limousines they announced that they would have absolutely nothing to do with the United Nations Commission for Palestine, nothing to do with the transitional period after the end of the mandate and nothing to do with partition.

There was an open thread of warning running through all the Arab delegates' comments on the Assembly's action. They spoke of bloodshed to come and said the responsibility would not be theirs, but would be on the shoulders of the countries that had pressed for partition.

On the other side of the quarter-century Arab-Zionist dispute there was jubilance and hope for the future. Dr. Abba Hillel Silver, chairman of the American section of the Jewish Agency for Palestine, expressed his gratitude to the Assembly and especially to the United States and the Soviet Union.

Dr. Silver's statement follows:

"We are deeply gratified with the action of the General Assembly of the United Nations. It marks a turning point in Jewish history. It is an impressive reaffirmation of the just claim of the Jewish people to rebuild its national life in its ancestral home.

"This noble decision to re-establish the Jewish state and restore

Continued on Page 60, Column 1

PEACE GAINS NOTED

Brazilian Says Contacts Inspired No Forecast of Imminent War

CITES ROLE OF MINORITY

Lie Regrets That Economic Issues Were Sidetracked—Others Hail Aranha

By MARSHALL E. NEWTON

It is the mission of the United Nations to achieve world peace and the General Assembly made a memorable contribution in that direction, Dr. Oswaldo Aranha of Brazil, president of the Assembly, told the delegates of the fifty-seven member nations yesterday in his speech closing the second regular session in Flushing Meadows.

When he finished his address the delegates rose and applauded Dr. Aranha, whose talents and statesmanlike handling of the difficult task of presiding at the international assembly had been lauded by several preceding speakers.

Dr. Aranha pointed out that the present post-war period had not been marked by the armed conflicts that had followed the Peace of Versailles and he said that we lived today in a different era, in which our minds must turn to the future and not the past.

Calls for Foresight

"But close contact with international political life leads to no forecast of world war in the near future," he said. "The world seeks, however, new forms of political, economic and social integration in which the contest of ideas will supersede the clash of arms. The status quo is no longer possible. A new reality is rising in our days, to which we must impart the spirit of the United Nations, the only conception capable of insuring peace, solidarity, dignity and equality for all peoples.

"Our action should not be pure factum. Our task is one of foresight and of organized prevention to eliminate the elements and factors capable of disturbing world

Continued on Page 67, Column 3

SCHUMAN BARS DISCUSSION OF FRENCH LABOR OVERTURE; COMMUNIST PAPERS SEIZED

PREMIER ADAMANT

Strikers Must Go Back on Regime's Terms—Labor Curbs Urged

ASSEMBLY SPLIT ON CODE

324 Saboteurs Are Arrested—Paris to Expel Aliens Who Help Ruin Economy

By HAROLD CALLENDER

Special to The New York Times.

PARIS, Sunday, Nov. 30—Premier Robert Schuman refused early today to meet the leaders of the Confederation of Labor to discuss a strike settlement different from that offered by the French Government.

Meanwhile, the Premier pressed hard for immediate passage by the Assembly of a law to strengthen the Government's hand by enlarging its police force and enabling it to imprison those who sought to force men to strike or who committed or urged sabotage.

As intense activity continued throughout the night inside and outside the Assembly, it became clear that the labor leaders who had encouraged the strikes had at last taken the initiative in seeking to end them, and that the Cabinet was divided regarding the policy the Government should adopt.

Early last evening Paris police surrounded the plants of the two Communist newspapers, l'Humanité and Ce Soir, entered the buildings and seized the plates of special editions whose publication had been forbidden. No papers were allowed to leave the plants. Later the police vacated the premises.

The special edition of l'Humanité, in large headlines printed in red ink, proclaimed: "They wish to assassinate the Republic!"

Minister Begins Parley

Shortly after M. Schuman had placed his proposed law before the Assembly early yesterday, Pierre Lebrun, a Communist secretary of the labor confederation, issued a statement urging renewed negotiations and mentioning that the striking workers would have a hard time when the Dec. 1 pay day came on Monday without pay envelopes.

At the same time, Daniel Mayer, Socialist Minister of Labor, who is understood to have opposed the law that M. Schuman sought, opened negotiations with the executive committee of the confederation, which sat most of the night in his office while the Cabinet met in the Palais Bourbon. Through M. Mayer the committee asked to see M. Schuman, but the Premier refused its request and denied that the Government was negotiating with the strike leaders.

A sharp divergence of view be-

Continued on Page 46, Column 3

U. S. Troops to Stay in Italy Beyond Dec. 3 Sailing Date

Change in Plans Is Linked to Disturbances Led by Communists—Milan Is Calm Following Compromise on Prefect

By ARNALDO CORTESI

Special to The New York Times.

ROME, Nov. 29—The United States Army Department today ordered Maj. Gen. Lawrence Jaynes, commanding the Mediterranean Theatre of Operations, and his entire staff to postpone their departure from Italy. With them will remain about 2,500 officers and men who are leading specialists of the United States Army in Italy.

The order is believed to reflect the anxiety with which the Government in Washington views the Communist-fomented disturbances in Italy.

General Jaynes and his officers and men had planned to leave from Leghorn on Dec. 3 aboard the Admiral Sims. Washington ordered a postponement of departure until Dec. 14, the deadline set by the Italian peace treaty. No explanation was given for the change of plans and this strengthened the impression that it was dictated by preoccupation over Italy's political outlook.

The officers and men with General Jaynes form the skeleton organization for a large army. They include highly trained specialists, familiar with conditions in Italy. They belong to the Engineer, Signal, Ordnance, Secretariat, Quartermaster, Medical and Military Police Corps and other auxiliary services.

Washington's change of plans came after General Jaynes had said farewell to Pope Pius and President Enrico de Nicola. Ambassador James C. Dunn called on Premier Alcide de Gasperi two days ago, and it is presumed that he informed the Italian Government then of the postponement of the American troops' departure.

Though the American troops should, under present plans, leave

Continued on Page 45, Column 1

VAST GI HOUSING TO RISE NEAR SITE OF WORLD'S FAIR

21 14-Story Apartment Units to Form Nation's Largest Veterans' Cooperative

COST PUT AT $58,000,000

Occupancy on Tenant-Owner Basis—Work Will Start Before End of Year

By LEE E. COOPER

On a fifty-five-acre tract overlooking the site of the World's Fair of 1939, the country's largest veterans' cooperative apartment community soon will begin to take form, it became known last night.

After nearly a year of negotiations, and with the official blessing of the city and of the Veterans Administration, plans for the $58,000,000 project were revealed by Frederick Briggs, chairman of the board of the Communities Redevelopment Corporation, which is sponsoring the enterprise.

The new Queens housing center, which will occupy a large part of the former Arrowbrook Golf Club grounds, will be for occupancy exclusively by veterans of World War II and their families on a tenant-ownership basis.

Plans call for the erection of twenty-one fourteen-story apartment houses of the fireproof type, to accommodate 5,699 families. Each building will have its own garage facilities, to be rented separately, for tenants' automobiles.

Shopping Centers Will Rise

In furtherance of the plan to create a self-contained community, the builders will erect shopping centers at the edges of the property, which is bounded by Main Street, Jewel Avenue and Park Drive East, within the boundaries of Forest Hills. A promenade, with stores beneath it, will be constructed on the hillside overlooking Flushing Meadow Park. The residential buildings will be set amid winding tree-lined walks and landscaped park spaces.

The Board of Estimate gave its unanimous sanction to the over-all plan for the project at a special closed session last Wednesday, after receiving a favorable report on it from Robert Moses, City Construction Coordinator who had been in consultation with the sponsors.

The city's cooperation will be limited to street changes and zoning aids permitting stores and the erection of fourteen-story houses on the site. No municipal financial

Continued on Page 12, Column 2

No-Parking Area Is Created From City Hall to Canal St.

After a two-hour conference with Mayor O'Dwyer at Police Headquarters, Police Commissioner Arthur W. Wallander announced yesterday two further moves in the department's efforts to ease traffic congestion in the city.

Commissioner Wallander added the section of Manhattan north of City Hall as far as Canal Street and west to but not including West Street to the restricted parking areas already established in a large part of the borough below Fifty-ninth Street.

He also said that a survey was being made throughout the city in an effort to discover additional sites for municipal parking lots like the one established at the old World's Fair parking lot in Flushing, Queens. The lot set up experimentally there "looks promising," he said, reporting that 766 motorists had used it on Friday.

Mayor Explains Needs

The Commissioner announced the moves at a press conference at the end of his talk with the Mayor. Mr. O'Dwyer sat in on the press conference and added some comments of his own after his aide had made the announcement.

About forty traffic policemen will be needed to enforce the parking restrictions in the new areas, the Mayor said. Commissioner Wallander has asked for 2,000 additional men for the Police Department to take care of this and other needs, which would add $6,000,000 to the department's budget, he continued.

Together with $4,000,000 for the men added to the force last July, this would amount to a total of $10,000,000 that would have to be appropriated for the Police Department next year in addition to

Continued on Page 78, Column 3

WAR PAY 'RACKET' HUNTED BY TRUMAN

Gen. Vaughan Says President Wants Army, Navy, Air House-Cleaning on Disability Cases

Special to The New York Times.

WASHINGTON, Nov. 29—The armed services are preparing to turn over to President Truman at his request the records of 28,000 wartime Army officers who have been retired for disability on tax-free pay normally amounting to three-fourths of their active service remuneration.

This became known as an aftermath of the case against Maj. Gen. Bennett E. Meyers and was confirmed today by Maj. Gen. Harry H. Vaughan, the President's military aide, who said at Philadelphia that Mr. Truman was determined to "wipe out any possible racket" in tax-free disability retirement pay.

The President has already spoken about the matter to James Forrestal, Secretary of Defense, and it is expected that a formal directive will be received soon.

Presumably the order will apply also to naval officers retired for disability so that once the President has the records in hand he

Continued on Page 27, Column 1

Molotov Insists on Regime Before Treaty on Germany

By DREW MIDDLETON

Special to The New York Times.

LONDON, Nov. 29—Soviet Foreign Minister Molotov urged with new fervor in the Council of Foreign Ministers today the early establishment of a central German government as a precondition of the peace treaty.

Mr. Molotov's argument was based on the futility of completing a German peace treaty with no German government to sign it or assist in its preparation. But it was obvious that the Soviet delegate was moved by fears that the Western Allies, if this Council meeting failed, would make their own arrangements for a German government and treaty.

With a stridency that disrupted an otherwise decorous meeting, Mr. Molotov declared the Soviet Union would never recognize a peace signed by Western Germany and the Western powers. No government set up in Frankfort on the Main in the United States zone as an "ersatz government for Bizonia" will be an adequate substitute for the Soviet proposal, he asserted.

Secretary of State Marshall and French Foreign Minister Bidault both flatly opposed any tendency to make the establishment of a German government a precondition of signing the German peace treaty.

A compromise proposal presented by British Foreign Secretary Bevin was as abruptly turned down by Mr. Molotov, who said it did not go far enough. Then he proceeded to add a clause that made the British proposal an echo of the Soviet suggestion.

This brisk exchange of German participation in the peace making followed an encouraging agreement by the Big Four on the ad-

Continued on Page 54, Column 3

ZIONIST AUDIENCE JOYFUL AFTER VOTE

Tears, Excited Laughter Mark Tension—Aranha Commends Public's Good Behavior

By WALTER S. SULLIVAN

The attention of the entire Arab and Jewish worlds focused on Flushing Meadow yesterday to hear the verdict of the United Nations General Assembly on the future of Palestine.

The reaction in the packed hall to the decision for partition typified that of listeners far and near. While members of the Arab delegations walked out, Zionists in the audience rejoiced.

It was a rejoicing that started with silence and grew as the meeting neared its end. In the public lobby there were kisses and tears and excited laughter. In the delegates' lounge a rabbi cried, "This is the day the Lord hath made! Let us rejoice in it and be glad!"

The initial silence resulted from a call to order by the Assembly's president, Dr. Oswaldo Aranha. A burst of applause had greeted the surprise vote of France in favor of partition, and it was this that had

Continued on Page 67, Column 2

Major Sports Results

FOOTBALL

With Rip Rowan passing for the first touchdown and dashing ninety-two yards for the second, Army beat Navy yesterday for the fourth straight year. N.Y.U. rallied to tie Fordham. Scores of leading games:

Alabama	21	Miami, Fla.	6
Army	21	Navy	0
Florida	25	Kansas State	7
Fordham	13	N. Y. U.	13
Ga. Tech	7	Georgia	0
Holy Cross	20	Boston Coll.	6
Maryland	0	N. C. State	0
Mich. State	58	Hawaii	19
Mississippi	33	Miss. State	14
N. Carolina	40	Virginia	7
Oklahoma	21	Okla. A.&M.	13
Oregon Sta.	27	Nebraska	6
Rice	34	Baylor	6
S. M. U.	19	T. C. U.	19
Tennessee	13	Vanderbilt	7
Texas Tech	14	Hardin-Sim.	6
West Va.	17	Pittsburgh	2

CROSS COUNTRY

Curtis Stone of Philadelphia won the National A.A.U. championship at Van Cortlandt Park, but the New York A. C. took the team title for the third successive time.

HORSE RACING

Incline outran Galiorette to capture the Bryan and O'Hara Memorial Handicap at Bowie on the last day of the major Eastern season.

(Full details in Section 5.)

Congress Action Lags on Aid Bill Despite Warnings Need Is Urgent

By JOHN D. MORRIS

Special to The New York Times.

WASHINGTON, Nov. 29—Congress set aside the troublesome problems of European aid and domestic inflation today and attended the Army-Navy game practically en masse, while pressures for accelerated action on the legislative problems awaited members' return to work Monday.

Despite repeated representations of urgency in both fields, the Congressional machinery faced a slowdown in production of the authorization for winter relief to France, Italy and Austria.

Formulation of anti-inflation legislation still had hardly begun, and completion of the task was far out of sight.

The Senate was prepared to resume consideration Monday of the foreign relief bill, but earlier expectations of passage on that day had been diminished by failure yesterday to dispose of four amendments proposed by Senator James P. Kem, Republican, of Missouri.

While some of them are acceptable to the bill's managers, at least one is expected to cause considerable discussion and possible delay of a vote on the bill until Tuesday.

This would require detailed, written acknowledgement by every recipient of relief supplies that the goods were gifts of the United States.

Senator Kem successfully opposed action on the amendments yesterday, asserting that he wanted Thanksgiving holiday absentees to be present when the votes were taken. He thus disrupted leaders' plans for clearing the slate of all proposed amendments so that the bill itself could be disposed of Monday.

Hope for a final vote Monday

Continued on Page 26, Column 1

World News Summarized

SUNDAY, NOVEMBER 30, 1947

The General Assembly of the United Nations yesterday approved the plan for the partition of Palestine by a vote of 33 to 13 with ten abstentions and one absence. After the vote there were repeated statements of bitterness and disillusion from the Arab representatives. One after another they asserted that the Charter had been violated and that their nations would not be bound by the action and would reserve "freedom of action." The Arabs then walked out of the Assembly. [1:8.]

The Arabs subsequently pronounced the United Nations "dead," and disavowed any intention of playing a part under the partition plan. They went on to say, however, that this did not mean their retirement from the United Nations. Zionist leaders were jubilant over the outcome. [1:6-7.]

Zionists attending the Assembly expressed their joy with tears and excited laughter. Dr. Oswaldo Aranha praised the public for its good behavior. [1:7.]

The Palestine debate concluded the business of the current session of the General Assembly, and Dr. Aranha of Brazil gave his closing address. He declared that this second meeting had made a notable contribution to world peace, and after the delegates had risen to applaud him the session adjourned. [1:5.]

In London, Soviet Foreign Minister Molotov demanded the early establishment of a German government to accept the peace treaty. The other Ministers, seeing this as a move to commit them against any possible partition of Germany, opposed him. [1:6-7.] Secretary Marshall plans to ask the Council of Foreign Ministers next week to achieve the economic unification of Germany through the removal of all sonal barriers in what is expected to be the most important United States proposal at the conference. [50:3.]

In the deputies' meeting the Soviet delegation continued to study the French proposals on Austria and refused to agree on principle at any point. Action was delayed, but it was felt the Russians might accept. [51:1.]

In Paris, Premier Schuman declined to discuss with leaders of the Confederation of Labor any strike settlement on terms other than the Government's. He asked for police powers to suppress Communist agitators and moved against Communist papers. They had charged that a "revolutionary coup" was planned for midnight and that "assassination of the Republic" was its objective. The editions were suppressed. [1:1.]

In Italy, the United States commander and 2,500 American troops were ordered by Washington to postpone departure, presumably because of the troubled situation. The general strike in Milan, however, was ended. [1:2-3.]

The Ronne Expedition in the Antarctic reported the exploration and mapping of a total of about 100,000 square miles of territory in the name of the United States. [56:3.]

A scientific advance that may be of importance in insect pest control was announced by the United States Army. Ultrasonic waves have been developed that are lethal to mice and small insects. [14:1.]

Defense Secretary Forrestal has been instructed by President Truman to turn over the records of 28,000 wartime Army officers who have been retired for disability on tax-free pay, in determination to wipe out any possible "racket." [1:2.]

Company Asks Rise in Gas Rate From $1.15 to $2 Sliding Scale

The Consolidated Edison Company of New York, Inc., announced yesterday it had applied to the State Public Service Commission for permission to increase the maximum charge for gas from $1.15 a thousand cubic feet to $2 with declining rates after the first thousand.

The petition said that neither Consolidated Edison nor any of its predecessor companies had increased its rates since Oct. 1, 1922, and that existing rates were confiscatory of the company's property. It was estimated that the company would lose $1,498,500 in 1947 through its gas operations.

According to the company, 57 per cent of the gas it supplies is sold at the maximum rate of $1.15 a thousand cubic feet. The company's service area includes 1,100,000 customers in Manhattan, the Bronx and the first and third wards of Queens—Astoria, Long Island City, Flushing, College Point, Whitestone, Douglaston, Bayside, Little Neck and Bellerose.

The company proposed an immediate schedule of temporary rates, which it estimated would increase its annual revenues approximately $8,239,700 on the basis of estimated gas sales for 1947.

If this increase had been in effect through 1947, the company said, it would have provided the company with a net return after taxes of $4,200,000 in connection with its gas operations.

If approved by the Public Service Commission, the new classifications would provide a minimum charge of $2 for the first thousand cubic feet or less of gas consumed in any bi-monthly billing period.

For the first 4,000 cubic feet consumed bi-monthly after the initial 1,000-foot block, residential customers would be charged 12 cents a hundred; 10 cents a hun-

Continued on Page 13, Column 1

"All the News That's Fit to Print"

The New York Times.

Copyright, 1947, by The New York Times Company.

LATE CITY EDITION
Considerable cloudiness and mild today and tomorrow.
Temperature Range Today—Max.,53; Min.,36
Temperatures Yesterday—Max.,50; Min.,30
Full U. S. Weather Bureau Report, Page 50

VOL. XCVII..No. 32,820. Entered as Second-Class Matter. Postoffice, New York, N. Y. NEW YORK, WEDNESDAY, DECEMBER 3, 1947. THREE CENTS NEW YORK CITY

JERUSALEM TORN BY RIOTING; ARABS USE KNIVES, SET FIRES; JEWS REPLY, HAGANAH IN OPEN

Moslem Sages Ask Holy War As Duty to Bar Palestine Split

Egyptian Army Chief Checks on Border Troops—Mid-East Hostility Fanned—U. S. Couple Assaulted in Baghdad

By The United Press.

CAIRO, Egypt, Dec. 2—The holy men of al-Azhar University, fountainhead of Moslem learning, called today on the Moslem world to proclaim a holy war as Suleiman did against the Crusaders 800 years ago. They acted in protest against the proposed partition of Palestine.

The call to arms was sounded by the Council of Ulemas, ruling body of the 1,000-year-old university. The council has no official standing and is not connected with the Arab League or government groups, but its opinion is highly respected by Moslems.

"The Council of Ulemas calls on all Moslems throughout the world for jihad [holy war]," a statement announced. "Jihad is an unconditional obligation, and whoever neglects it is a sinner."

An Arab League spokesman in Cairo said that a meeting of league states would probably be held Dec. 10. At the session the Premiers of Egypt, Syria, Lebanon, Saudi Arabia, Yemen, Iraq and Trans-Jordan will plot in Cairo the Arab strategy against partition. The spokesman said that no Arab state recognized any part of Palestine as a non-Arab area.

Official sources confirmed a report that Gen. Ibrahim Attallah Pasha, Chief of Staff of the Egyptian Army, had visited el Arish, twenty-five miles southwest of the Palestine border, to inspect his troops. He said the border troops were supplied adequately for any eventuality that might develop as the result of the United Nations' decision to partition Palestine.

An unofficial informant asserted that army units in other parts of Egypt had been alerted because of the tension. All officers' leaves have been canceled, he said.

The Arab Palestine News Center said that numbers of Libyans, who fought the Italians, had volunteered to fight for Palestine and that their applications had been turned over to the Palestine Arab Higher Committee's bureau here.

The call for a holy war con-

Continued on Page 6, Column 3

14 ARE SLAIN IN DAY

8 Jews Reported Killed in Palestine Clashes —Mob Loots Shops

ZIONIST MILITIA ARRESTED

Members Try to Calm Crowd—British Warn U. N. Mission—Troops Told Not to Act

By SAM POPE BREWER

Special to The New York Times.

JERUSALEM, Dec. 2—Arab threats of violence in protest against the Palestine partition plan materialized today in stoning and stabbing attacks against Jews and in the burning and looting of their shops. In reprisal, Jews burned an Arab-owned movie theatre and an Arab-owned garage.

[Eight Jews and six Arabs were killed in the Palestine clashes, according to an unofficial casualty list cited by The Associated Press. The same compilation placed the number of wounded at thirty-two Jews and six Arabs.]

Sporadic firing continued at night on the Jaffa-Tel Aviv boundary, always a danger point.

Almost miraculously, no death was reported in Jerusalem up to 5 P. M., when a curfew was clamped on Arab quarters. Four Jews were gravely wounded and some less seriously hurt and many thousands of dollars of damage was done in the outbursts, which went on all day. The police smothered them as well as they could. British troops, under orders not to interfere, stood by and watched.

Haganah Grenades Found

Among those arrested were six members of Haganah, the Zionist defense organization. They were found with grenades and recently fired pistols. The organization as a whole operated openly for the first time in this strife in efforts to keep the peace.

Haganah called all its members to battle stations. Through loudspeakers mounted on a truck, the organization urged Jewish crowds to disperse and await orders.

At that time the Jews were an unruly, belligerent mob and it seemed certain that blood would have run in Jerusalem's streets if they had had their way. However, before they could have reached the Arabs, who were in the lower part of town, in the direction of the Old City, the Jews would have had to penetrate Haganah defense lines, composed of scores of men stretched across a street, their arms linked, and beyond that, roadblocks of police and the military.

[According to other sources, Jews gathered in Zion Square and moved toward the scene of the rioting but were stopped by police at Princess Mary Avenue.]

The mob finally dispersed, but not before it smashed Arab shops and set fire to the Rex Theatre.

Jewish Agency Aide Slain

Among those killed was Max Pinn, 40, head of the Department of Trade and Transfer in the Jewish Agency for Palestine. He was struck in the head by a stone as his auto passed through the Arab town of Ramleh, and died in a hospital. His companion was slightly injured.

Two Jews were killed and one was wounded when an army truck in which they were riding was fired upon near Jaffa. Two other army trucks were attacked near Gaza, in southern Palestine, and the Arab driver of one was wounded by a bullet. A Mauritian driver of the other was injured by a stone.

Other attacks were reported from Jaffa, Ramleh, Lydda and Safad.

A senior police official said that the incidents so far had undoubtedly not been organized but were acts of individuals or groups, possibly influenced by agitators but acting without direction.

Of a report that the United Nations implementation commission would make its headquarters in Jerusalem, he said "impossible," because the British could not un-

Continued on Page 4, Column 3

BANK RESERVE IDEA OF ECCLES UNSOUND, HIS ADVISERS HOLD

Councilmen of Federal Board Say It Would Hit Production Loans, Might Spur Inflation

OPPOSE TIME BUYING CURB

Bankers Testify Effect of Installments Since Control Ended Is Not Yet Known

By WILLIAM S. WHITE

Special to The New York Times.

WASHINGTON, Dec. 2—The most important of the anti-inflation controls on credit proposed by the Federal Reserve Board, a requirement that the commercial banks set aside big new "special reserves" of untouched money, came under powerful attack today before Congress.

The effect was to leave the sponsor of the program, Marriner S. Eccles, chairman of the Federal Reserve Board, isolated from all twelve members of his advisory Federal Reserve Council, and still lacking the support of John W Snyder, the Secretary of the Treasury.

Before the Senate Banking Committee, three members of the advisory council testified that its opposition to the Eccles plan was unanimous. They declared also that the council of twelve stood as one against a companion Eccles proposal for renewing restrictions on installment buying, the first item on the agenda against inflation presented to Congress by President Truman.

Secretary Snyder for his part appeared before the committee in closed session. Its chairman, Senator Charles W. Tobey, Republican, of New Hampshire, reported afterward that Mr. Snyder had not come up primarily to talk about his disagreement with Mr. Eccles.

Payroll Bond Drive Planned

It was learned, however, that in passing the Secretary made it plain that he still was not prepared to go along on the proposed special reserve requirement, a position he had taken publicly last week, but intended to try to make some sort of compromise with the Federal Reserve chairman.

As to the question of curbs on installment buying, which Secretary Snyder is wholly supporting, it developed that he plans to meet with the country's leading industrialists on Dec. 10 to lay out a national plan for greatly stimulating the payroll deduction method of selling Government bonds to salaried people.

This was disclosed parenthetically and without elaboration by Robert V. Fleming, president of the Riggs National Bank of Washington, the first of the three members of the Federal Reserve Advisory Council who testified before the committee.

Mr. Fleming declared that bank credits and bank operations in general were not responsible for the present inflationary movement. He contended that the Eccles plan for new bank reserves, running to a maximum of 25 per cent on demand deposits and 10 per cent on time deposits, "might well" operate as an inflationary, rather than a deflationary, influence.

Cashing in of Bonds Pictured

If some of the smaller banks were confronted with the necessity of setting aside such reserves, apart from those maintained, he said, the result probably would be that they would feel compelled to restrict loans even for productive enterprises.

Moreover, Mr. Fleming argued, a parallel result might be a compulsion upon such banks to cash in their long-term Government bonds, in order to have at hand more liquid money to meet the necessities of the new reserves.

His testimony and that of his colleagues on the advisory council raised the strong impression that on the point of requiring new bank reserves the Federal Reserve Board and the council had arrived at a disagreement so fundamental and deeply felt as to be most extraordinary.

Mr. Fleming told the committee that the Advisory Council had "most strongly objected" to a process of reasoning "singling out" bank loans as the cause of inflation, and that in the "unanimous" view of the Council the trouble lay almost altogether in Government policies.

Of these he mentioned half a dozen, apart from "Government

Continued on Page 24, Column 3

CIO Maps Pay-Rise Policy; Schwellenbach Asks Curbs

Union Chiefs Aim at Third Round of Increases Since End of the War

By LOUIS STARK

Special to The New York Times.

WASHINGTON, Dec. 2—The Congress of Industrial Organizations decided today to lead labor's fight for a third round of wage increases since the end of the war. This policy was adopted at a meeting of the group's vice presidents presided over by Philip Murray, president.

At a press conference Mr. Murray gave out a statement declaring that it had been determined to seek "substantial" wage increases through collective bargaining.

This decision ignored President Truman's proposals to Congress on Nov. 17 asking for authority to impose price controls, consumer rationing and wage control in limited areas of the national economy. It also ignored Secretary Lewis B. Schwellenbach's suggestion that labor go slow in seeking wage adjustments at this time.

Mr. Murray was asked whether today's meeting had been called

Continued on Page 18, Column 5

He Warns House Group Alternative to Controls Is Giving More Pay

By HAROLD B. HINTON

Special to The New York Times.

WASHINGTON, Dec. 2—Profits, far more than increased wages, are responsible for the cost of living being at the highest level the United States has ever known, Secretary of Labor Lewis B. Schwellenbach told the House Banking Committee today. He was testifying in favor of the Administration's request for inflation controls.

"There is no major segment of the price structure in which we can confidently expect declines in the near future," he said.

Under these conditions, he continued, the only way to prevent a third round of wage demands, which he considered would be an inflationary factor, was to give labor "some real assurance that price rises will be checked." He said that "the success of the President's program is indispensable to labor's welfare."

"During the war and post-war periods," he told the committee,

Continued on Page 22, Column 1

Lilienthal Calls for Doubling Our Atomic Energy Outlays

Special to The New York Times.

ATLANTIC CITY, N. J., Dec. 2—Plants for producing fissionable uranium and plutonium are going through a large-scale improvement and expansion program that in the "next several years" may double the expenditures made up to now on atomic energy, David Lilienthal, chairman of the Atomic Energy Commission, said here today.

At Hanford, Wash., and Oak Ridge, Tenn., as well as other atomic centers, the present expansion of facilities and improvement of plants was described by Mr. Lilienthal as a "major effort, even for this country." In this, he added, the commission must obtain the active cooperation of American industry to design, develop and produce quickly the materials needed.

Mr. Lilienthal spoke at the sixty-eighth annual conference of the American Society of Mechanical Engineers. Today is the fifth anniversary of the first self-sustaining nuclear chain reaction, operated by a group of scientists under Dr. Enrico Fermi at the University of Chicago on Dec. 2, 1942.

All the atom bombs set off thus far were the very first products of nuclear research, Mr. Lilienthal said, adding that at Los Alamos, N. M., the Atomic Energy Commission was now carrying out its responsibilities for "redesign and improvement of atomic weapons."

"The nation has now expended "in the order of two and a half billions of dollars" on atomic energy, he said, and "if this country really means business, then within the next several years this total expenditure will increase to approximately five billions."

The use of atomic energy for the commercial production of power will not come for some time, he said.

"In an industrial sense nuclear power's ultimate importance can hardly be exaggerated," he said, "but I want to underline the word ultimate, for the use of atomic energy for power production is not just around the corner or anywhere near the corner."

Both uranium and the man-made

Continued on Page 24, Column 5

JOBLESS AID RISES FAVORED BY DEWEY

Corsi Presents Program for 1948 Which Opposes Laws Repressive to Labor

Special to The New York Times.

ALBANY, Dec. 2—Edward Corsi, State Industrial Commissioner, told the legislative conference of the State Federation of Labor today that the Dewey state administration favors an increase in unemployment insurance benefits and is opposed to any "repressive" labor legislation.

While he did not specify the amount of unemployment insurance increase that will be proposed to the next Legislature, Mr. Corsi indicated that it might be $5 or $6 a week to bring the maximum benefits to $26 or $27 a week. The Industrial Commissioner also indicated that the administration favors a straight increase rather than the introduction of a system of dependency benefits, as the Congress of Industrial Organizations is requesting.

Mr. Corsi's references to the administration's opposition to "repressive labor legislation" was taken by his listeners as an assurance that it will fight any attempt to write a counterpart of the Taft-Hartley law into the labor laws of the state.

The Industrial Commissioner also told the conference, which consists of representatives of American Federation of Labor unions from all parts of the state, that the Dewey administration is not yet ready to enact any sickness com-

Continued on Page 21, Column 5

4,000 Jam Office for City Jobs As Laborers; 1,000 Will Be Hired

For the first time in ten years the city accepted applications for laboring jobs yesterday and more than 4,000 men stormed West Fifty-ninth Street from dawn to dusk to put in their bids for the openings.

The line, which at its longest covered three sides of the block bounded by Tenth and Eleventh Avenues and West Fifty-eighth and West Fifty-ninth Streets, included at its head several hundred men who had formed outside the Department of Parks Recreation House, 535 West Fifty-ninth Street, late Monday night.

They escaped a night of frigid waiting on the sidewalk when the American Legion arranged for sheltering them in Haaren High School until 6 A. M. Soon afterward they were out on the street, huddling over curb fires and can stoves and sending relays of messengers for hot coffee and sandwiches. The office was opened at 9 and within an hour the first-comers had been processed.

A staff of thirty-eight, including examiners, notaries and fingerprinters from the Municipal Civil Service Commission aided by a large contingent of police, herded the applicants through an Army-type maze at the rate of 450 an hour. By 5 P. M., when the last man straggled through, the team had processed 3,500 men.

The line swelled to mass proportions shortly after 7 A. M. and as applicants continued to pour into the area on foot and by bus, many became discouraged and left. They will have an opportunity to apply today and tomorrow between 9 and 4.

There are an estimated 1,000 positions open, according to an official of the commission. They are in various departments of the city and pay $41.54 a week. Yesterday the commission merely took applications for the openings, fingerprinted the job-seekers, accepted $1.12 from each to cover costs and told them they would be notified to return at a later date for a physical examination.

Under the civil service law pref-

Continued on Page 31, Column 3

RHATIGAN ASSERTS REDS WERE FACTOR IN RELIEF ACTIVITIES

Ex-Welfare Head Tells State Inquiry He Tried in Vain to Get Abuses Corrected

MAYOR DEFENDS COURSE

Says Party Membership Is Not Basis for Dismissal, Denies Knowing of Such List

By WILLIAM R. CONKLIN

Communist party membership is not a sufficient ground for dismissal from the city payroll, Mayor O'Dwyer said yesterday, following testimony that there was strong Communist influence in New York's $142,000,000 relief set-up.

The testimony came from Edward E. Rhatigan, the Mayor's former Welfare Commissioner, who resigned at the Mayor's request on Oct. 24. Mr. Rhatigan was an all-day witness before the relief inquiry committee of the State Board of Social Welfare, which held a public hearing in the State Office Building at 80 Centre Street. Mr. Rhatigan told the committee that the United Public Workers, CIO, was a powerful union in the Welfare Department and that it had followed the Communist party line for the last ten years.

Mayor O'Dwyer's statement came after the hearing ended, when City Hall reporters asked for his reaction to Mr. Rhatigan's testimony. Benjamin Fielding, the city's new Welfare Commissioner, and Deputy Mayor John J. Bennett were present at the interview. When the Mayor was asked about Mr. Rhatigan's statement that the United Public Workers Union followed the Communist party line, he said:

"The workers in the Welfare Department, as in all city departments, are civil service employes, protected by civil service law in their positions as long as they perform faithful service to the department. Removal can only be on charges that the employes' activities are detrimental to the efficiency of the department. I do not recall the former commissioner dismissing anyone for this reason."

When Mr. Fielding pointed out that 2,065 of the Welfare Department's employes were provisionals, the Mayor said:

"On that point, I think Mr. Rhatigan appointed the provisionals himself. If there are Commu-

Continued on Page 25, Column 1

COMMUNISTS RENEW FILIBUSTER IN PARIS; 7 DIE IN RAIL WRECK

Assembly, 402 to 183, Adopts First Article of Schuman Bill, Bars Curb on Strike Right

LABOR STRIFE DWINDLES

Subway Normal, Electricity Up —But Sabotage Is Indicated in Fatal Train Derailment

By HAROLD CALLENDER

Special to The New York Times.

PARIS, Wednesday, Dec. 3—The National Assembly was still in a weary battle at 7 A. M. today as the Communists continued their delaying attacks against Premier Robert Schuman's emergency strike bill.

The Assembly had got no further than the first article, which it had approved at 2 A. M., 402 to 183. The article suspends for three months certain provisions of the Penal Code in favor of harsher penalties for sabotage, incitement to strike and interference with the right to work. A Communist amendment to the effect that the proposed law would not be interpreted as a limitation of the right to strike was passed unanimously.

The bitterness of the debate reached a climax at 6 A. M. when Rene Mayer, Minister of Finance, announced that seven persons had died in a derailment, a short time before, of a mail train from Paris to Arras. The locomotive had hit a torn-up track, M. Mayer said:

[A railway official said at least twelve were killed and forty injured in the derailment, according to The Associated Press.]

The Communists answered M. Mayer's statement on the condition of the track with a shower of insults. Charles Tildon, a former Minister, called M. Mayer "the despicable Minister of Rothschild" and declared he was "looking for blood."

With the aid of naval crews, officials restarted electric power stations in the Paris region that the police had seized from sit-down strikers Monday night. The Paris subway service was normal, while electric current approached its pre-strike status. Railway service generally improved and postal deliveries became general in Paris for the first time since the strike began.

However, railway service and in-

Continued on Page 3, Column 2

World News Summarized

WEDNESDAY, DECEMBER 3, 1947

Rioting swept over Palestine yesterday as Arabs took to stoning, stabbing, arson and looting in resentment over the United Nations decision to partition the Holy Land. Jews opened reprisal attacks. The Zionist military organization, Haganah, operating openly for the first time, helped to restore peace. Several deaths resulted from the clashes. [1:8; maps P. 4.] Arab protests continued throughout the Middle East. Theological leaders called for a Holy War as "an unconditional obligation," adding, "whoever neglects it is a sinner." [1:6-7.]

The United Nations named Australia, China, France, Mexico, Britain and the United States to draft a constitution for the proposed international zone of Jerusalem. [7:1.]

Argentina unleashed a bitter attack in the United Nations Conference on Trade and Employment against what was called the attempt by the United States to force capitalism on a world wanting socialism. [8:3.]

An AFL proposal that the United Nations investigate charges of slave labor, particularly in Soviet-dominated areas, will be taken up by the Social and Economic Council. [10:2.] A Berlin newspaper said Russia maintained political concentration camps as nefarious as any run by the Nazis. [14:4-5.]

Differences among the Big Four, especially the United States and Russia, widened during yesterday's discussion on a German treaty. [1:6-7.]

France and Italy seemed to be gaining the upper hand in the fight against Communist-led strikes. Naval crews restored electric power to Paris, but a Communist filibuster delayed adoption by the French Assembly of the proposed strike-control law. One restricting section was approved. [1:5.]

Unconfirmed reports in Italy said that the United States had offered the de Gasperi Government military "assistance and advice." [2:2.]

Stop-gap aid to France, Italy and Austria was overwhelmingly endorsed by a conference of House Republicans, but there was strong sentiment for further cuts in appropriations. The committee bill for $590,000,000, including $60,000,000 for China, was introduced. [1:7.] Nanking imposed "economic martial law" on four major commercial cities to halt inflation. [16:3.]

In Washington the Treasury was drawing an order to unfreeze the $400,000,000 balance of the British loan to tide that country over until the Marshall plan became operative. [3:1.]

The entire advisory Federal Reserve Council opposed Chairman Eccles' plan for "special reserves" by banks as an anti-inflation measure. The members also opposed controls in installment buying. [1:1.]

Only "some real assurance that price rises will be checked" can prevent a third round of wage demands, Secretary Schwellenbach told a Congress committee considering the President's anti-inflation program. Almost simultaneously, the CIO announced it would seek a third round of pay rises to meet increased living costs. [1:2-3.]

Chairman Lilienthal of the Atomic Energy Commission, disclosing progress of work on atomic fission, called for doubling present expenditures to a total of $5,000,000,000. [1:2-3.]

Communist influence in the Welfare Department is strong, former Commissioner Rhatigan told a state inquiry. He said City Hall had failed to help him meet the problem. Mayor O'Dwyer declared membership in the Communist party was not grounds for dismissal. [1:4.]

Marshall, Rebuking Molotov, Cites Small Allies' War Role

By DREW MIDDLETON

Special to The New York Times.

LONDON, Dec. 2—The split between the United States' policy of wide representation at a German peace conference and Soviet proposals for a restricted parley widened today in the Council of Foreign Ministers.

Secretary of State Marshall chided Soviet Foreign Minister Molotov for disregarding the contribution that Canada and other powers that Russia wished to exclude had made not only to victory but also to the Russian war effort.

A warm tribute to Canada's war effort was paid by the Secretary of State, who also sharply criticized Mr. Molotov for the disparaging terms he had applied to the contributions of the smaller powers.

Today's debate centered on participation in the peace conference. In the course of a long afternoon of argument the Foreign Ministers did manage to agree on two clauses in the document on preparation of the German peace treaty, but neither of these affects the fundamental argument between the United States and the Soviet Union.

Secretary Marshall, who presided today, was drawn out of his habitual calm by Mr. Molotov's insinuation that the United States delegation had changed its mind, now that there was a new Secretary of State, on a "decision" taken at the Council's New York meeting last year.

Secretary Marshall replied that

Continued on Page 14, Column 3

HOUSE GOP FAVORS PROMPT AID ACTION

Some Members Talk of Cuts—$590,000,000 Bill Is Offered, Set for Passage by Tuesday

By C. P. TRUSSELL

Special to The New York Times.

WASHINGTON, Dec. 2—House Republicans, in a long party conference, indicated almost universal support today for the authorization without undue delay of an emergency winter relief program for France, Italy and Austria. What they would seek to do to the program recommended by the Foreign Affairs Committee, however, was left open to widespread speculation.

Leaders declined to predict the outcome of floor consideration, which was scheduled to begin Thursday.

The committee's relief bill was introduced in the House at noon. It recommended an authorization

Continued on Page 16, Column 4

Jubilant Zionists Hold Rally Here; Mayor Sees Turn in World History

A jubilant and excited crowd overflowed the Manhattan Center last night to celebrate the United Nations vote for a Jewish state in Palestine. The meeting was under the auspices of the Zionist Organization of America.

Speakers were Mayor O'Dwyer, Dr. Emanuel Neumann, president of the Zionist Organization, and Dr. Abba Hillel Silver, chairman of the American Section of the Jewish Agency for Palestine.

Long before the meeting began 5,000 persons packed the block on Thirty-fourth Street between Eighth and Ninth Avenues and the parallel one on Thirty-fifth Street, where a loudspeaker on a flood lighted truck brought the speeches from the auditorium.

The police had to clear a path through the throng for special guests to be admitted. After the meeting started the crowds on Thirty-fourth Street were asked to go to Thirty-fifth Street, where they could hear the speeches and also make way for Thirty-fourth Street crosstown traffic.

The police estimated that 20,000 persons tried to get into a hall seating a quarter of that number. It became necessary to close the doors long before the program started because of the pushing, shoving crowd outside, producing the anomalous situation of vacant seats inside while persons outside struggled vainly to enter. Later, when Thirty-fourth Street had been cleared, enough ticket holders to fill all vacant seats were admitted.

Dr. Silver told his audience that the decision of the United Nations was traceable to the everlasting will and determination of the Jewish people. He recounted the history of the Jews' struggle to regain the Holy Land and asserted that "this generation of Jews drove an empire behind barbed wire in Palestine and forced a decision from the United Nations."

The speaker expressed regret

Continued on Page 5 Column 2

1947

Popular for three decades, Jim and Marian Jordan's *Fibber McGee and Molly* became the most popular radio show in America.

One of the top figures of the "big band" era—Benny Goodman. Goodman, shown here on a radio show, also composed and performed in the classical music field.

Burl Ives was very popular all through the mid-40s. His *Burl Ives Show* always was high in the ratings.

"All the News That's Fit to Print"

The New York Times.

LATE CITY EDITION
Partly cloudy and cold today and tomorrow.
Temperature Range Today-Max., 30; Min., 24
Temperatures Yesterday—Max., 30; Min., 23
Full U. S. Weather Bureau Report, Page 27

VOL. XCVII..No. 32,844. Entered as Second-Class Matter, Postoffice, New York, N. Y. NEW YORK, SATURDAY, DECEMBER 27, 1947. THREE CENTS IN NEW YORK CITY

RECORD 25-INCH SNOW CRIPPLES CITY AND EAST; ALL TRAFFIC SLOWED, LONG ISLAND IS DISRUPTED; THOUSANDS MAROONED; FOOD AMPLE, FUEL SHORT

REBELS' OFFENSIVE IN EPIRUS IS HELD BY GREECE'S ARMY

Thrust From Albanian Border at Konitsa May Be Aimed to Put Markos Capital There

TOWN SAFE; FIGHT GOES ON

Guerrillas Defeated in Strike at Road Center to South—Athens Curbs Red Backers

By A. C. SEDGWICK
Special to THE NEW YORK TIMES.

ATHENS, Dec. 26—About 2,000 heavily armed rebels were trying today to capture the Epirus town of Konitsa, ten miles from the Albanian border. They were engaged by Greek regular army forces.

A first wave of attackers, according to military sources here, was repulsed with considerable losses. The battle continues. On its outcome a great deal depends.

[Near Agrinion, 100 miles south of Konitsa, 1,500 guerrillas who had tried to take the city had been beaten off, said an Associated Press dispatch. Agrinion controls the main communications road for the Greek army to Konitsa. The army was also battling a "strong" rebel force at Philiates, near the Albanian border forty miles southwest of Konitsa.

[An Athens edict outlawing the Communist party, the EAM and other Leftist groups was to be put in effect Saturday, the Associated Press quoted informants as saying.]

Some observers here voiced the opinion that the taking of Konitsa would mean the acquisition of a seat for the new Communist Government of "Gen." Markos Vafiades and the prestige involved therein. They think the rebels have launched an offensive expressly for that purpose.

Key to Grammos Mountain Zone

Konitsa is on the only accessible route from central Greece and also from most of Albania to the Grammos Mountain region. One group of observers in Athens believe this factor, rather than the placing of a Markos capital at Konitsa, motivates the rebel attack there.

The rugged Grammos upland is an inland Gibraltar. It could well serve as a rebel state. From east and south it is practically unassailable. On the north it abuts on Albania.

If the rebels sealed off the southwestern approach to the Grammos Mountains at Konitsa, then the Markos Government could take up its abode in any of the many fastnesses and later, after gaining in strength, could push out for the acquisition of a town possibly more suitable to its purposes as a capital.

The attack on Konitsa was launched simultaneously from the north and northeast, according to Greek military sources. Greek army officers say the Communist-led attack originated on Albanian territory and that it was preceded by a bombardment in which some 200 shells fell in Konitsa on Christmas afternoon before the first rebel infantry went in. Many townspeople were killed and fires were started.

The guerrilla force suffered heavily, military sources stated, and the Government troops, too, had casualties. Brigadier Dovas, commander of the Konitsa garrison, was among several officers known to have been seriously wounded.

Before flying from Athens for the front this afternoon, Minister of War George Stratos indicated the battle was turning in favor of the Government forces. He said army reinforcements were speeding to Konitsa.

At the same time, none in authority was optimistic enough to believe that the rebels could be beaten decisively at this point, because their retreat into Albania is easily effected.

Meanwhile, in Athens, arrests of persons believed to be in active sympathy with the Communist-led

Continued on Page 6, Column 4

U. S. Near '44 Peak In Soft Coal Output

By The Associated Press.

WASHINGTON, Dec. 26—Soft coal production in the United States this year has exceeded 600,000,000 tons for the second time in history and is near the 1944 record of 620,000,000 tons, the Bureau of Mines reported today.

As of Dec. 20, production of bituminous coal and lignite totaled 603,671,000 tons, 16.6 per cent more than the 1946 figure on the same date.

T. W. Hunter, chief of the bureau's Coal Economics Division, said the increase was due to a reduction in the number of strikes and an increase in the number of railroad cars available for coal transportation.

AID PLAN DIRECTION GIVEN TO MARSHALL

Truman Transfers Authorized $522,000,000 for European Relief to Secretary

By ANTHONY LEVIERO
Special to THE NEW YORK TIMES.

WASHINGTON, Dec. 26—President Truman formally started the interim European aid program today, delegating all his authority over it to the Secretary of State George C. Marshall, and transferring the $522,000,000 authorized for winter relief to the State Department.

Implementing the plan by an Executive order, Mr. Truman specified, however, the points of coordination and clearance in other Federal departments which Mr. Marshall would be required to observe in purchasing relief commodities and in otherwise carrying out the program.

The order also put the overseas field administrator of the program, who has not been appointed, under the direction of the Secretary of State.

The administrative machinery spelled out in the order follows the general outline of the larger, long-range European Recovery Program which Mr. Truman sent to Congress for action a week ago today. Thus the interim program appeared to take shape as a little Marshall plan.

Role of Field Administrator

The field administrator called for in the interim program is also cast in Administration plans for a similar role in the European Recovery Program, a roving director with ambassadorial status. Thus the early period of operation of the winter relief program was expected to provide some experience which Congress could study in considering ERP.

The proposed administrative structure for that program has been criticized in Congress and elsewhere as unwieldy and as providing for great responsibility without commensurate authority.

The President's order followed the requirements of the interim aid bill, the Foreign Aid Act of 1947,

Continued on Page 8, Column 4

ALL FOOD BROKERS ORDERED TO BARE DEALS BY U. S. MEN

Anderson Also Demands Data on Any Trades by State or Local Government Workers

SECOND ROSTER PUBLISHED

1,240 Persons Dealing in Grain Futures Named, Without Any Attempt at Analysis

New list of grain traders is printed on page 2.

By WILLIAM S. WHITE
Special to THE NEW YORK TIMES.

WASHINGTON, Dec. 26—The Administration, making public a second list of traders in commodities futures, simultaneously opened today a sworn census to bring forth the names of those venturing on the markets who had any connection with Government, Federal, state or local.

The new and second roster which it issued was simply a roll of 1,240 names of persons who were in wheat futures in Chicago as of April 30, 1946. It was without visible political significance, since the Department of Agriculture attempted in it no analysis of the traders either as to occupation or as to whether each was a speculator or a mere normal "hedger."

Clinton P. Anderson, the Secretary of Agriculture, accompanied this disclosure, however, with the announcement that he had directed the Commodity Exchange Authority to demand of all registered brokerage firms a statement "under oath" as follows:

"Whether or not, during the period Jan. 1, 1946, to Dec. 15, 1947, they carried any account on their books with transactions in commodity futures for any person employed by or connected with the United States Government, its agencies or commissions, or by any state or subdivision thereof, or for any member of the immediate family of such person."

Crux of Bitter Fight

The information would go to the heart of the present bitter political controversy in which some Republican leaders, and particularly Harold E. Stassen, a Presidential aspirant, have been asserting that "Administration insiders" had found it possible to profit improperly in grain and other markets.

Two imminent Republican-controlled investigations in Congress, one in the Senate and one in the House, are to be directed toward this issue, rather than to the subject of speculation as such.

Secretary Anderson, in a formal statement issued through his department, pointedly stressed the observation that he was now going out, on his own motion, for information which would be "in addition to that requested of him" by one of these investigating groups, the

Continued on Page 2, Column 2

THE HEART OF THE CITY DURING YESTERDAY'S SNOWSTORM

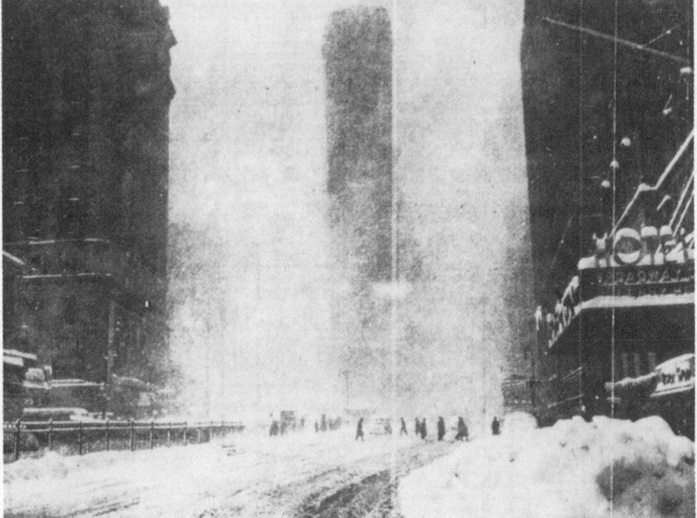

Times Square looking south from Forty-sixth Street — The New York Times

ARABS KILL AIDE OF JEWISH AGENCY

Immigration Official Is Among 13 Slain in Day in Palestine —Haganah Besieges Village

By SAM POPE BREWER
Special to THE NEW YORK TIMES.

JERUSALEM, Saturday, Dec. 27—An immigration official of the Jewish Agency for Palestine was shot dead yesterday by Arabs in an attack on a convoy in which Mrs. Golda Meyerson, acting head of the Agency's Political Department, was traveling. Mrs. Meyerson was unhurt.

Thirteen persons were killed in incidents during the day.

Heavy gunfire broke out about 10 P. M. on the edge of Jerusalem and was continuing toward mid-

Continued on Page 8, Column 7

Nightfall Brings Paralysis To Surface Transportation

New York City's transportation systems suffered a creeping paralysis that became more and more acute yesterday as the snowfall piled higher and higher.

Air traffic was completely blanked out by the snow. Railroads ran more and more behind time as the hours passed and the Long Island Rail Road finally announced over the loudspeaker system in the Pennsylvania Station at 6:09 P. M. that service was suspended indefinitely.

Surface lines, both bus and trolley, maintained service of a sort throughout the day but by evening more buses were stalled and collecting snow than were operating and collecting passengers. The subway and elevated lines continued to operate but on much slower headways, which created additional jams at stations when the homeward rush started. Subur-

Continued on Page 4, Column 2

World News Summarized

SATURDAY, DECEMBER 27, 1947

The greatest snowfall in the city's recorded history gripped this area yesterday, disrupting transportation to and from as well as within the city. Beginning at 5:25 A. M., the storm dropped more snow on the city in a little over twelve hours than fell during the thirty hours of the famous blizzard of 1888. At times the rate of fall exceeded three inches an hour. Up to 9:10 P. M., when the storm officially ended, the fall measured 25.4 inches.

While the New York area was heaviest hit, the storm extended from lower New England and southeastern New York State to just below Washington, D. C. By mid-afternoon highways leading to this city had become impassable. Hospitals were deluged with calls for aid. Many places of business closed early to allow their staffs to get home but thousands of commuters were unable to do so. [All the foregoing, 1:8.]

The storm caused suspension of air traffic. Railroads suffered from a progressive paralysis as the snowfall continued. In many parts of the city and suburbs buses became hopelessly snarled in drifts. Subways continued to operate, but often at a slow pace, with passengers unable to enter some stations because of the congestion. [1:5-6.]

Every available worker was pressed into service by the city's Department of Sanitation to clear the streets sufficiently to permit resumption of traffic over the week-end. [1:7.]

Athens reported that attacks by rebel forces in Epirus had been held by Greek Army forces. The main thrust of the Leftists from the Albanian border was aimed at Konitsa, possibly with the objective of setting up a rebel capital there. [1:1.]

Thirteen Jews, including an official of the Jewish Agency for Palestine, were killed in new outbreaks in the Holy Land. [1:4.]

In China, as the Communists pressed their drive on Mukden the Government imposed a rigid military censorship on all press dispatches from that besieged Manchurian stronghold. [1:2-3.]

Japanese newspapers are featuring the trial of Japan's wartime leader, former Premier Tojo, on the charge of being a war criminal, as the biggest news event of the year. [7:2-3.]

President Truman issued an executive order formally starting the $522,000,000 European emergency relief program and delegating full authority over it to Secretary of State Marshall [1:2.]

A second list of traders in the commodity markets was made public by the Administration. At the same time Secretary of Agriculture Anderson announced a survey designed to reveal the names of traders who had any connection with the Government. [1:3.]

Mukden Placed Under Censorship; Many Starve in Communists' Siege

By HENRY R. LIEBERMAN
Special to THE NEW YORK TIMES.

NANKING, Dec. 26—Rigid military censorship was clamped today on all press dispatches from Mukden, Manchuria's leading city whose 1,000,000 population is undergoing extreme winter hardship as a result of the Communist blockade.

The Government Information Office said the step had been taken on a "temporary" basis to "prevent military secrets reaching the enemy."

The censorship, which was personally ordered by Generalissimo Chiang Kai-shek, applies to foreign as well as Chinese correspondents. This is the first time that a press curb has been officially imposed on foreign journalists since the abolition of wartime censorship in 1945.

"Thus far censorship has been applied to Mukden only," the information statement said. "The extension of censorship to other points in the northeast will be considered should the need arise."

Actually the censorship action is more embracing than is indicated by the official announcement. Most news transmitted from Manchuria is routed through Mukden, which is the headquarters of the Nationalist armies trying to cling to their tenuous hold on the northeast provinces.

Large Communist forces are now attacking Mukden's outer defenses within a fifty-mile radius of the city. On the basis of consistent Communist strategy in the past, however, foreign military observers here do not expect the Reds to try and take the heavily fortified city by direct assault.

The new Communist attacks are interpreted as an intensified attempt to wear down the population, already suffering in a bitter win-

Continued on Page 7, Column 5

CITY WELL STOCKED WITH FOODSTUFFS

Shipments Before Holidays, Christmas Leftovers Help Avert Shortage in Storm

The city is "well-stocked" with food, so no serious hardship is likely to result from the storm, Commissioner of Markets Eugene G. Schulz said yesterday afternoon.

As he spoke, the Weather Bureau was predicting an early end to the snowfall, which then had reached about sixteen inches. Later in the day, food officials still preserved a guarded optimism about supply prospects.

The one exception was in the matter of milk. Dealers reported that deliveries had been made more or less on schedule yesterday morning, and they said that ample milk would be in the city to meet today's demand. But they could not promise that trucks would be

Continued on Page 4, Column 8

STREET CLEANERS FIGHT AGAINST ODDS

Lack of Warnings on Holiday, Stalled Cars and Record Fall Handicap Work

William J. Powell, commissioner of sanitation, directed an army of workers last night in the enormous job of getting enough snow off city streets to enable operation of traffic over the week-end.

The commissioner was getting the help of all municipal departments, but he admitted at 9 P. M. that his department never before had faced such a problem in keeping traffic lines open.

The Sanitation Department was handling the snow-moving equipment in all five boroughs, aided by the Police and Fire Departments and temporary help that had been hired during the day. Their operations, however, were impeded by automobiles stalled not only in the outlying areas, but even in Times Square by the heavy downfall.

As last midnight approached, Commissioner Powell said a night crew of 4,850 permanent and temporary employes was on duty, but that the department had no easy job on its hands for the next forty-eight hours.

The Commissioner indicated that it would require additional funds from the city treasury to complete the snow removal job. He said

Continued on Page 4, Column 7

More Heatless Homes Predicted As Snow Impedes Fuel Deliveries

A temporary spurt in the number of heatless homes in and around the city was predicted yesterday.

Fuel companies said the record snowfall might seriously aggravate an already bad situation. Deliveries of coal and oil on hand here were cut to a fraction of normal because of blocked streets—and it was said that new supplies might be held back by continued bad weather.

By 3 P. M., the Department of Health had received 605 complaints from tenants who said there was no heat in their apartments. This was a record for the year and a high number for any year. Borough offices will be open today and tomorrow from 8 A. M. to 10 P. M. to receive calls and investigate them.

The department reported it also had heard from eighty-five landlords who said they had been unable to buy fuel oil.

The latter callers were referred to the Mayor's Emergency Fuel Committee at Police Headquarters, where three men from the Health Department's bureau of sanitary engineering had been stationed.

At headquarters, it was said that every effort was being made to arrange for deliveries of fuel oil to hardship cases.

However, oil companies throughout the metropolitan area reported overwhelming difficulties in their attempts to deliver available stocks. One large dealer in Brooklyn said he had fourteen trucks stuck in drifts by the middle of the afternoon.

Several fuel dealers were critical of the city officials in charge of snow removal operations. They said that even where streets were passable, it was virtually impossible for a truck to park near

Continued on Page 5, Column 2

FAST RATE OF FALL

1888 Mark Topped in 12 Hours as City Gets Brunt of the Storm

MAYOR ON WAY HERE

Flying From California—Storm Resumes After Ending Officially

New York City and its environs wore last night a snow mantle 25.8 inches deep, dropped on the area by the greatest snowfall in the city's recorded history. The storm started at 5:25 A. M. The 25.8 inches was measured at midnight, with light snow flurries continuing.

Earlier, at 9:10 P. M. the Weather Bureau had officially declared the storm ended, but forty minutes later snow began falling again. The forecast at midnight was for "some light snow flurries, or blowing snow, with strong northwest winds" today. The Weather Bureau said it did not expect these to add any appreciable depth through the night.

1888 Mark Eclipsed

More snow fell on the metropolis yesterday than fell during the thirty hours of the Blizzard of 1888, which set the previous snowfall record of 20.9 inches.

The rate of yesterday's snowfall was extraordinary. It ranged from three-fourths of an inch an hour when the storm first swept in, to more than three inches per hour between 3 P. M. and 4 P. M.

The city's towers wore tremendous tufts and beards of snow. Avenues and side streets were blocked by stalled and abandoned motor cars, trucks and trailers to the dismay of the Fire and Sanitation Departments. Snowplows and bulldozers were held up by the derelicts. The Fire Department, uneasy over the congestion, appealed to the city's millions to guard against fire more sharply than ever.

Because the storm swept in from the Atlantic at a point where there are no weather observers, the city was utterly unprepared for it. Mayor O'Dwyer, apprised of the emergency in El Centro, Calif., where he was on vacation, announced that he would try to fly home at once—get in possibly tonight—and ordered a meeting of the Emergency Board set up to meet city crises.

Board Meets This Morning

This board, composed of the city department heads and the Borough Presidents, is to meet at 9 o'clock this morning at Police Headquarters to decide on what measures shall be taken, particularly with regard to clearing main arteries for fire apparatus and for assuring an adequate flow of foods and fuel for New York's millions. Whether a state of emergency shall be declared is up to the men at this session.

Police Commissioner Arthur W. Wallander, who stayed up all night, as did Acting Mayor Vincent Impellitteri and Deputy Mayor John Bennett and most of the city commissioners, appealed to veterans' organizations and to the former units of the Civilian Volunteer Defense Office to help clear "fire runs"—main streets used by fire apparatus—before they turn into side streets, and to clear space around fire hydrants.

The Police Commissioner ordered all precinct commanders to instruct their men on patrol and in radio cars to watch for persons wandering the streets in distress for lack of shelter for the night. Precinct commanders were told to prepare beds in the shelters for men, accommodations in welfare shelters, or hospitals, for women.

An unofficial survey indicated that at least sixteen persons died in the storm in northeastern towns and cities, nine in Greater New York, four in northern New Jersey, two in Rhode Island, one in Connecticut. Most of these were middle-aged persons who succumbed to heart attacks trying to struggle

Continued on Page 3, Column 4

"All the News That's Fit to Print"

The New York Times.

LATE CITY EDITION
Possibly snow or sleet tonight changing to rain tomorrow.
Temperature Range Today—Max., 32; Min., 16
Temperature Yesterday—Max., 28; Min., 20
Full U. S. Weather Bureau Report, Page 47

VOL. XCVII..No. 32,847. Entered as Second-Class Matter, Postoffice, New York, N. Y. NEW YORK, TUESDAY, DECEMBER 30, 1947. THREE CENTS IN NEW YORK CITY

MORE SNOW IS DUE FOR CITY AS IT DIGS BACK TO USUAL LIFE

BUSINESS RESUMED

Subways Handle Record Crowds With Surface Traffic Still Slow

WALK CLEARANCE ORDERED

Block Parties to Be Formed for Task—Service on Long Island Lines Disrupted

The city appeared to have achieved a partial victory in the battle against the snow yesterday, the first full business day since Friday's record fall, when it received with a foreboding shudder the weather forecast for today and tomorrow.

More snow or sleet was said to be on the way. It is expected by tonight but in any event should strike the city not later than tomorrow. Accompanying it will be freezing temperatures, which will usher in the New Year with bitter cold. If the snow materializes it will be a fall of one to two inches, the weather bureau predicted.

There was no sign of an impending change in the weather yesterday as an army of more than 30,000 worked with tractor, snow plow, ice breaker and pick and shovel to dig the city out. They labored under benign skies, the rays of a winter sun aiding materially in melting the packed snow and the stubborn ice. At no time did the temperature rise above freezing.

Subways Carry Record Crowds

In the main the city met well its first real test in trying to resume its normal life.

Expanded rush hours helped subway riders to reach their places of employment and to return to their homes in the evening without too much delay. The subways carried the heaviest loads in their history but they were the most reliable form of transportation.

Commuter trains were running late, but running. The Long Island Rail Road experienced the greatest difficulty in maintaining schedules.

Suburban and interstate buses got to the city over treacherous roads but their arrival times were uncertain.

Through railroad operations were near-normal, but many trains were late.

Surface transportation, both bus and trolley, was only 50 per cent of normal.

Food and other essentials flowed into the city in surprisingly good fashion, aided by an embargo on incoming non-essential commodities. And even more surprising, considering the condition of the snow and ice-encrusted streets, was the fact that retail deliveries came through in ample supply to meet householders' immediate needs.

Traffic Tie-ups Are Serious

As was to be expected the greatest difficulty lay in surface transportation of passengers and commodities. Most of Manhattan's broad avenues had been cleared in readiness for early morning traffic although the six lanes on most of them had been narrowed to two. Through these narrowed lanes buses and trucks rumbled for the first time since the city became snowbound, and a sprinkling of private cars also was in evidence. It was not long, however, before tie-ups resulted on most avenues.

Typical of the slow progress made was the ene at 2 P. M. below Fourteenth Street on Eighth and Hudson Avenues, which usually carry heavy truck and trailer traffic. Looking south as far as the eye could see was a long line of stalled trucks and buses. In the space of a block or two could be counted several Eighth and Amsterdam Avenue buses, sandwiched in between trucks carrying food, milk and produce.

Traffic policemen stood helplessly by, guiding those who needed aid across the treacherous streets, as truck wheels whirred furiously in efforts to get loose and break the chain of stalled vehicles.

Stalled taxis and private cars added to the confusion. Many cabs that ventured forth had to be dug out of the snow. The drivers

Continued on Page 3, Column 3

May Ask Oil Users To Convert to Coal

Special to THE NEW YORK TIMES.

WASHINGTON, Dec. 29—Plans to b discussed tomorrow at a meeting of Government agencies are expected to propose, among other things, that those using fuel oil for heat convert to coal or consider other ways to aid in overcoming the oil shortage, it was disclosed today.

The meeting was called by Maj. Gen. Philip B. Fleming, Federal Works Administrator. Representatives of the agencies will discuss conservation measures applicable to buildings housing their units.

After the meeting the representatives will decide which of the measures are particularly adaptable to their agencies. A second meeting will be held within a few weeks at which a definite program is expected to be adopted.

FUEL CRISIS GROWS AS DELIVERIES LAG

Hundreds of Homes Without Oil—Supplies Are Here, but Snow Keeps Trucks Away

Hundreds of homes and apartment houses in New York were without fuel yesterday and thousands more were nearing the exhaustion of their supplies. Widespread suffering was threatened as snow-choked streets continued to hamper deliveries.

The Health Department orted that it had received 1,397 complaints of lack of heat yesterday, compared with 995 on Sunday and 776 on Saturday. It also received 1,136 requests for assistance in obtaining fuel, more than double the 435 requests made on Sunday.

Complaints by Boroughs

The breakdown by boroughs was as follows: Manhattan, 567 complaints of lack of heat and 218 requests for assistance in getting fuel; the Bronx, 321 complaints and 135 requests; Brooklyn, 115 complaints and 404 requests; Queens, 386 complaints and 254 requests, and Richmond, eight complaints and 126 requests.

Typical of many sections of the city was the situation in the Rockaways, where George Wolpert, executive secretary of the Chamber of Commerce of the Rockaways, reported that his office had received more than 200 telephone appeals for help from householders with little or no oil. Most of them reported that delivery trucks were unable to traverse blocked side streets.

Fuel oil deliveries in the city yesterday were estimated at 40 per cent of normal by Brice P. Disque, president of the Coal Consumers Protective Association. This organization of sixty coal and fuel oil dealers normally supplies 60 per cent of the city's heating fuel.

Mr. Disque said he did not regard the situation as serious yet, but that it might become so within two or three days if the streets were not cleared sufficiently to

Continued on Page 4, Column 3

SCHOOLS OF NATION SHOW GAIN IN YEAR AS STAFFS EXPAND

But Survey Reveals Shortage of Teachers Is Still Acute, With 110,000 Needed

SALARY AVERAGE UP 3400

But This Is More Than Offset by Price Rises—Extra Funds Sought for Pay, Buildings

By BENJAMIN FINE

Despite a slight improvement in the past year, the nation's schools are confronted with a serious teacher shortage on both the elementary and high school levels. At present 110,000 teachers, or just about one of every eight in the country, are serving on substandard or emergency certificates, with the result that 3,000,000 children are being deprived of an adequate education.

A survey of the forty-eight states and the District of Columbia conducted by THE NEW YORK TIMES indicates that every section of the land is troubled by a teacher shortage. School systems report that it is impossible to get competent teachers to meet the classroom needs. The growth in school population, which is expected to continue for at least six more years, has further complicated an already difficult situation.

But there is a brighter side to the picture. In 1947-48 the teachers of this country will receive nearly $.00 more on the average than in 1946-47. The average annual salary for teachers has reached the record high of $2,424, or $47 a week for a fifty-two week year. A year ago teachers received an average of $2,026 yearly, or $39 a week.

Costs Rise Faster Than Pay

Many of the educators consulted in the survey were quick to point out, however, that the increase in teacher pay had been more than offset by the increased cost of living. They estimated that the present salary was worth less in purchasing value than the average of $35 a week which teachers received before the war. As a result, students are reluctant to prepare for the teaching profession, holding that they can earn more in the other professions or in industry.

A comparison with 1946-47 shows that the number of emergency teachers has dropped from 130,000 to 110,000. A drop is noted in virtually every state, although in some communities the decrease is so slight as to be meaningless. School authorities are dismayed at the way the teacher shortage is continuing and are worried at the harm substandard teachers are doing to their educational systems.

The greatest number of emergency instructors are found in rural schools, although a number of the large cities are unable to obtain all the adequately trained teachers they need. Among the states reporting the largest proportion of substandard teachers are Alabama, with 9,636; California, 14,000; Georgia, 4,500; Kentucky, 5,000; Michigan, 4,800; Ohio, 4,200; Washington, 4,388, and Wisconsin, 3,652.

Every state except New Mexico reports that it cannot get all the elementary school teachers it needs. Only Maryland, Massachusetts and New Mexico can get a sufficient number of high school teachers. Many of the states indicated that it was more difficult to get teachers this fall than it was a year earlier.

Even the more favored regions,

Continued on Page 20, Column 2

Moscow Suffering Food Shortage; British Embassy Rustles Rations

Special to THE NEW YORK TIMES.

LONDON, Dec. 29—British Government sources have been receiving accounts of grave disorganization and shortages in the Soviet Union following the end of rationing and the devaluation of the ruble on Dec. 16, it was learned today.

Evidently the sudden strain on Russian economy and especially on consumer goods, including basic foods, was too great to be handled smoothly.

The British Embassy in Moscow, for instance, has a staff of about sixty. On Dec. 16 the special "diplomatic" food shops were closed, which meant that food for the embassy staff has had to be bought in the ordinary shops.

However, there has not been enough food to buy. Moreover, each shop—under orders—severely restricted the amount of bread, butter, meat, sugar, cheese and similar products that could be sold to any one person.

British Ambassador Sir Maurice Peterson's reports to the Foreign Office tell of having to send many servants and many members of the staff out every day, each to different shops or sometimes to three or four shops, to queue up and buy the maximum amounts allotted. Since these amounts are small, enough can be bought only to keep going from day to day.

Undoubtedly the United States Embassy and the rest of the diplomatic corps are having similar troubles, although in the long run they will be able to straighten themselves out by getting shipments from abroad. For the Russian people it is a far more serious matter.

In the first place, the Russians are going short. In the second

Continued on Page 8, Column 4

Quick Build-Up of Air Force Despite Atom Respite Urged

Finletter Committee Declares Plane Power Nation's Best Shield—Old Conception of Relying on Navy Found No Longer Safe

By JAMES RESTON
Special to THE NEW YORK TIMES.

WASHINGTON, Dec. 29—President Truman's Air Policy Commission has completed and will send to the White House this week one of the most solemn reports on the defense of the United States ever prepared in time of peace.

It is understood that this commission, under the chairmanship of Thomas K. Finletter, has reached the conclusion that the United States is in little danger of an atomic war within the next few years, but for the purposes of defense planning, cannot assume that such an attack cannot take place within a decade.

According to officials who have seen the Finletter report, it makes the following points and recommendations:

1. The best defense of the United States in the modern world is a good air offense. The certain ability to mount from well dispersed bases in various parts of the world an overwhelming retaliatory attack on any aggressor is the greatest deterrent against aggression and therefore a fundamental necessity for world peace.

2. The old conception of the Navy as our defense in being will no longer do. Even the World War II tactics of radar warnings and defensive aircraft and home guards are out of date. The United States Air Force, starting immediately, with the calendar year 1948, must be conceived as our primary military arm; it must be conceived as a striking force; and since every war is fought to a conclusion with weapons planned before that war broke out, the long-range bomber program should begin even before the next fiscal year in July of 1948.

3. Along with an immediate effort to build up our world retaliatory force in the air, a sustained diplomatic effort should be made to give the United Nations the

Continued on Page 13, Column 3

IRGUN BOMB KILLS 11 ARABS, 2 BRITONS

Missile Thrown From a Taxi in Jerusalem—Rift in the Jewish Agency Growing

By SAM POPE BREWER
Special to THE NEW YORK TIMES.

JERUSALEM, Dec. 29—A bomb thrown by the Jewish terrorist organization Irgun Zvai Leumi from a speeding taxi today killed eleven Arabs and two British policemen and wounded at least thirty-two Arabs by the Jerusalem Damascus Gate, the same place where a similar bombing took place sixteen days ago.

The day's casualties were twelve Arabs, three British policemen, one Jew, one British soldier and one Trans-Jordan frontier force trooper killed—a total of eighteen. Thirty-four Arabs, three Jews, two British soldiers and one Trans-Jordan trooper were wounded.

[Warships of the British Mediterranean Fleet were preparing to intercept the two Panamian vessels, Pan York and Pan Crescent, bearing 14,000 Jewish

Continued on Page 7, Column 1

GREEK GUERRILLAS SEAL KONITSA GAP

Smash Into Outskirts After Athens Unit Relieves Garrison—Block Road From Yanina

By The Associated Press.

ATHENS, Dec. 29—Fresh guerrilla battalions fought their way into the outskirts of Konitsa tonight and re-established their siege, Government sources said, after Greek Army troops had broken open the rebel lines long enough to rush a brigade of reinforcements into the battered city.

That brigade and the tired and outnumbered Konitsa garrison were fighting to beat off desperate guerrilla efforts to seize the town for a capital of the newly proclaimed Greek rebel Communist state.

[The Athens Government, in the initial reaction in the United Nations since the proclamation of the "First Provisional Democratic Government of Free Greece," formally charged Yugoslavia on Monday with violations of the General Assembly's

Continued on Page 5, Column 2

World News Summarized

TUESDAY, DECEMBER 30, 1947

Henry A. Wallace formally announced last night that he would head a third party and be its 1948 candidate for President. Denouncing Democrats and Republicans with equal vigor, Mr. Wallace pledged his new party to "a positive peace program of abundance and security, not scarcity and war." [1:8.] In Washington, where the announcement created considerable comment, Senator Taylor of Idaho said he had been asked to be Mr. Wallace's running mate. [14:2.]

President Truman's Air Policy Commission, it was learned, is about to report that by 1953 some other nation may have perfected atomic weapons and planes to carry them for an attack on this country. The United States must start immediately, the report is said to urge, to build around the Army Air Force a defense to discourage a would-be aggressor. [1:4-5.]

The President's personal physician, Brig. Gen. Wallace H. Graham, was listed with the Democratic Governor of Utah among ninety-nine public employes who had speculated in wheat futures last September. The White House said General Graham "will remain." He explained that he had left all trading to his broker. [1:6.]

Another potential political issue was unveiled by Senator Langer of North Dakota, who asked the Attorney General to investigate alleged pressure for campaign contributions on Federal employes in Kansas. [15:7.]

The Republican anti-inflation bill President Truman had intended to sign "reluctantly" was not signed because it had mysteriously disappeared. A copy was rushed by air to Speaker Martin in Massachusetts for signature and return to Washington in time for Presidential approval before midnight tonight. [1:7.] Senator Taft accused the President of "playing all the politics he can with high prices." [4:4.]

Governor Dewey is expected to oppose any increase in State taxes in 1948. Observers saw in this a blow to increased local aid by the state. [1:6-7.]

Just as New York was effectively pulling itself out of last Friday's snowfall, the Weather Bureau held out the threat of more snow or sleet tonight, probably changing to rain tomorrow. [1:1.] Hundreds of homes and apartment houses were without heat as clogged streets cut fuel deliveries to 40 per cent of normal. [1:2.] Police handed out 800 "snow summonses" to owners of some of the 10,000 snowbound motor vehicles. [2:2.] Railroads clamped a partial embargo on freight, exempting only food, fuel, medicine and other emergency items. [2:5.]

A nation-wide survey by THE NEW YORK TIMES disclosed only a slight improvement in the country's schools during the last year. [1:3.]

Greek guerrilla forces broke into the outskirts of Konitsa. [1:5; map P. 5.] American authorities expressed confidence that the "Free Greek" junta would be overthrown [6:3-4], but London sources felt that at least a token United States force should be sent to Greece. [5:1.] Greece charged Yugoslavia in the United Nations with having violated resolutions prohibiting warmongering and aid to guerrillas. [5:6.]

London heard reports that Russia was suffering serious shortages in foods and that prices had soared since devaluation of the ruble and the end of rationing. [1:2-3.] THE NEW YORK TIMES received a protest from a Russian engineer on its recent comparison of living costs in Russia and here. [8:3.]

This Is Meatless Tuesday

TRUMAN'S DOCTOR AMONG 99 LISTED AS SPECULATORS

Gen. Graham Says Dealing Was Done by Broker Who Had Full Charge of Account

KEEPS WHITE HOUSE POST

Governor Maw of Utah, Three Minor Agriculture Department Aides Also Are Named

By WILLIAM S. WHITE
Special to THE NEW YORK TIMES.

WASHINGTON, Dec. 29—Brig. Gen. Wallace H. Graham, President Truman's personal physician, was speculating in wheat to the extent of 50,000 bushels on Sept. 17, seventeen days before the President denounced "the greed of speculators" in grain.

That was disclosed today by the Department of Agriculture, and General Graham later said that his participation in wheat futures was unwitting, since he had left the entire conduct of his account to the judgment of his broker.

Five days ago Harold E. Stassen, Republican Presidential aspirant, who was the first of his party to raise the issue of "Administration" insiders in the commodities markets, suggested that they included personages in "the Executive Department of the White House."

It was made clear tonight through Charles G. Ross, Presidential press secretary, that General Graham would stay on in his White House post. "He will remain," Mr. Ross responded to a question.

Truman Told on Dec. 18

Mr. Ross also told reporters that Mr. Truman had first learned on Dec. 18 from the General himself of his speculations and had known "absolutely nothing" of the matter beforehand.

The President, thus knowing that one of his associates was involved, later on this same day issued a statement, Mr. Ross recalled, authorizing the direct quotation that the complete list of all speculators "should be made public."

In the third list of traders issued by the Department for the use of Republican controlled investigating committees which are preparing election-year inquiries, General Graham was among ninety-nine persons connected with Federal, state or local governments who were speculating in Chicago wheat futures last Sept. 17 to 20.

Governor Maw on List

The most prominent of the ninety-nine, apart from General Graham, was the Democratic Governor of Utah, Herbert B. Maw. There also were three minor field officials of the Department of Agriculture, as well as a resigned official.

The hundredth name on the roster of those politically connected, E. F. Springer, Postmaster at Matador, Tex., was that of a non-speculative trader, or "hedger."

In his statement issued from the White House soon after these disclosures, General Graham asserted:

"I have had a very small savings of money in a few common stocks since approximately 1929.

"A portion of my savings was lost in one stock; so, when transferring my account to Washington in the spring of 1547, I asked the broker to handle the account the best way he knew how and to use his own judgment. I also told him

Continued on Page 21, Column 1

Dewey Will Oppose Any Tax Rise; To Ask That State Limit Spending

By LEO EGAN
Special to THE NEW YORK TIMES.

ALBANY, Dec. 29—Gov. Thomas E. Dewey has decided to oppose any increases in state taxes this year in the belief that they would stimulate inflationary pressures by cutting production. He also believes additional imposts would impair New York's competitive position.

A substantial part of the Governor's annual message to the Legislature, it was learned today, will be devoted to a discussion of the state's fiscal policy and the need for keeping expenditures for the new fiscal year within the yield of existing taxes.

By implication, the message is likely to give strong support to Republican efforts in Congress to cut Federal taxes if this can be done without requiring resort to deficit financing to meet the costs of the European Recovery Program.

Such a stand in favor of Federal tax cuts can be counted upon to enhance Mr. Dewey's position as a leading but undeclared candidate for the Republican Presidential nomination.

In his message the Governor is expected to base his stand against any increase in state taxes on two main grounds: it would discourage production at a time when maximum output of labor, industry and agriculture is needed vitally to sop up excess purchasing power, and it would discourage the establishment of new businesses in New York.

The converse of the argument that increased taxes would curb production is that a cut in taxes would stimulate it. Aware of the national political implications of this reasoning, Mr. Dewey is ex-

Continued on Page 2, Column 7

WALLACE TO RUN; PLEDGES 3D PARTY TO BAR WAR POLICY

Wallace Resigns New Republic Post

The resignation of Henry A. Wallace as editor of The New Republic was announced yesterday by that magazine, a weekly publication which Mr. Wallace has edited for more than a year. Michael Straight, the publisher, said Mr. Wallace would become a contributing editor and would continue to write a weekly page.

The arrangement, made last week by Mr. Straight, caused the resignation of William Harlan Hale, one of the editors, in protest, but no reference to this was contained in the announcement. Mr. Straight will take over the editorship held by Mr. Wallace, and Daniel Mebane, now treasurer, will become publisher.

A letter of resignation from Mr. Wallace, made public at the same time, expressed his satisfaction with the magazine and the publisher, and his hope that "The New Republic will continue to be a much needed voice for a better world."

INFLATION BILL LOST IN THE WHITE HOUSE

Copy Signed by Vandenberg Is Flown to Speaker Martin —Action Due by Tomorrow

By ANTHONY LEVIERO
Special to THE NEW YORK TIMES.

WASHINGTON, Dec. 29—The Republican anti-inflation bill, product of dispute and compromise, and roundly denounced by President Truman yesterday, has vanished in mystery-book fashion from the White House.

Tonight, while the Secret Service was sleuthing for the original document, the Air Force was flying a duplicate of the measure in a dramatic round-trip flight to Massachusetts. In Dedham, at 11:01 P. M., Speaker Joseph W. Martin of the House signed it.

The copy of the lost engrossed bill is expected to be flown back to the White House by morning for the signature which Mr. Truman had pledged for today.

If the President does not sign the bill by Wednesday night, the deadline for action, the measure will succumb to an involuntary pocket veto.

Machinery Can't Start

The business of getting the signatures which would give the force of law to the measure might have been even more complicated if Senator Arthur H. Vandenberg had been in his home state. Instead of going to Grand Rapids for the holidays, however, he was in the capital and promptly signed the duplicate document.

The mystery, amid an atmosphere of exacerbated partisan tempers, had some humorous angles. But the loss of the unsigned paper had the effect of preventing the start, for a day at least, of the anti-inflation machinery.

For instance, Clinton P. Anderson, Secretary of Agriculture, was

Continued on Page 26, Column 7

DEMOCRATS SCORED

He Calls Insurgents to Fight 'Bipartisan' Plan for 'Armed Camps'

CONFERS WITH LIBERALS

Candidate Tells Leaders of 18 States 'Coalition Dry Rot' Makes Step Necessary

The text of Mr. Wallace's address is on Page 15.

By LOUTHER S. HORNE
Special to THE NEW YORK TIMES.

CHICAGO, Dec. 29—Henry Agard Wallace, backed by the Progressive Citizens of America and other liberal groups throughout the country, announced tonight that he would be a candidate for President in 1948 on a third-party ticket, pledged to "a positive peace program of abundance and security, not scarcity and war."

The 59-year-old former Vice President and former Secretary of Commerce denounced the Democratic party as a party of "war and depression" and asserted that the time had come for "a new party to fight these war-makers."

At the same time, he summoned Democratic party insurgents to take up the third-party banner to show the world that "the United States is not behind the bipartisan reactionary war policy which is dividing the world into two armed camps and making inevitable the day when American soldiers will be lying in their Arctic suits in the Russian snow."

"To that end," he said, "I announce tonight that I shall run as an independent candidate for President of the United States in 1948."

In a press conference at the end of his address Mr. Wallace stated that if either of the major parties became "a peace party" he would withdraw his name as a Presidential aspirant.

He expected that a preliminary third party organizing meeting would be held early in January and that a national convention would be assembled in the spring. He asserted that he would ask that his name be withdrawn if it were entered in Democratic primaries.

Announces Candidacy on Radio

The Iowan made his announcement over the coast-to-coast network of the Mutual Broadcasting Company, of which Col. Robert R. McCormick, editor and publisher of The Chicago Tribune, is a large stockholder.

The address was offered to more than 450 of the network's outlets. How many stations made use of it could not be learned. WGN, Mutual's Chicago station, where Mr. Wallace delivered his address, did not make it available to its listeners, however.

Ralph E. Shikes, a spokesman for the Progressive Citizens of America, charged prior to the broadcast that the advertiser holding the fifteen-minute time spot had agreed to relinquish his time, but that WGN officials had refused the offer.

In reply to this accusation, Frank P. Schreiber, manager of WGN, said that the Chicago outlet would not carry the Wallace broadcast "because the political nature of his address is in conflict with the station's policy governing broadcasting political speeches."

"For several years," he added, "WGN has maintained the policy of accepting political broadcasts by recognized candidates for national and major state offices only during political campaigns in election years.

Cites Controversial Issue

"Like most American radio stations, WGN has a well-established policy of granting time to both sides of controversial questions. If we were to broadcast Mr. Wallace's controversial political talk, we would be obliged to grant time to persons desiring to answer Mr. Wallace, which would be further violation of our policies on political broadcasts."

Mr. Schreiber added that "naturally, if anything that Mr. Wallace says tonight is of newsworthy character, it will be covered by

Continued on Page 15, Column 2

1948

The Israeli flag was flown as the Jewish state of Israel was proclaimed at Tel Aviv.

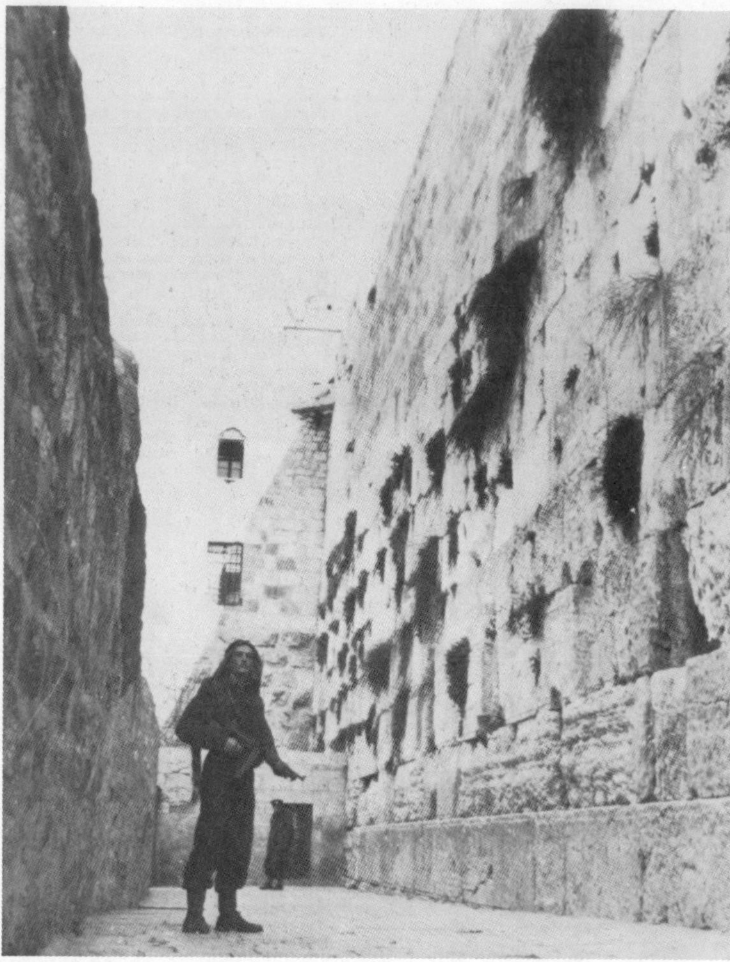

In Jerusalem, an Arab soldier guards the Wailing Wall in the Old City. Jews had previously been barred from the holy place.

Former Japanese Prime Minister Tojo took the stand during war crimes trials at Tokyo. Tojo accepted full responsibility for the attack on Pearl Harbor, but admitted no personal guilt. He was found guilty and hanged.

Indian spiritual and political leader Mohandas K. Gandhi was assassinated by a Hindu nationalist; news of the assassination set off riots in Bombay and Calcutta.

"All the News That's Fit to Print"

The New York Times.

Copyright, 1948, by The New York Times Company.

LATE CITY EDITION
Increasing cloudiness, cold today. Snow, not so cold tomorrow.
Temperature Range Today—Max., 18; Min., 0
Temperatures Yesterday—Max., 24; Min., 5.5
Full U. S. Weather Bureau Report, Page 31

VOL. XCVII No. 32,879. Entered as Second-Class Matter. Postoffice, New York, N. Y. NEW YORK, SATURDAY, JANUARY 31, 1948. THREE CENTS NEW YORK CITY

MANY HOMES WITHOUT HEAT AS ZERO COLD IS DUE HERE; U. S. CUTS OIL EXPORTS 18½%

FUEL CRISIS GROWS

Hundreds of Families Reported Suffering in City Area

BAY STATE SEIZES PLANT

Bradford Acts When Walkout Threatens Boston Gas—Oil Diversion Denied Here

By WILL LISSNER

Hundreds of families in the city were reported by their landlords to be in cold homes for lack of fuel oil last night as temperatures dropped toward zero in Manhattan and toward subzero levels in the suburbs.

At 3 A. M. today the temperature dropped to 2.2 degrees, establishing a new low record for the season. The previous record was 5 degrees, registered last Saturday.

The winter's coldest weather gripped not only New York but the whole Northwest. The Midwest and South, however, got some relief yesterday from the protracted cold spell. The fuel situation was reported acute in many cities throughout the East.

Temperatures, after falling to points between zero and 5 degrees above in Manhattan and zero and 10 degrees below in the suburbs, are expected to rise today to 20 degrees. The cold is due to continue, according to the United States Weather Bureau, but whereas yesterday was sunny, increasing cloudiness was expected today. More snow is threatened tomorrow. The lowest temperature yesterday was 5.5 degrees at 9:50 A. M.

Yesterday's hourly temperatures were:

1 A. M.	23	2 P. M.	12
2 A. M.	23	3 P. M.	15
3 A. M.	22	4 P. M.	14
4 A. M.	18	5 P. M.	13
5 A. M.	13	6 P. M.	12
6 A. M.	9	7 P. M.	11
7 A. M.	7	8 P. M.	9
8 A. M.	6	9 P. M.	8
9 A. M.	6	10 P. M.	7
9:50 A. M.	5.5	11 P. M.	7
10 A. M.	6	12 M.	6
11 A. M.	7	1 A. M.	5
Noon	9	2 A. M.	4
1 P. M.	10	3 A. M.	2.2

Petroleum Exports Cut

As the fuel shortage produced critical conditions for many apartment and home owners in this and other cities, officials took steps to relieve the situation.

The Commerce Department announced in Washington that it had ordered exports of petroleum products cut 18½ per cent from 11,850,000 to 9,650,000 barrels during the first quarter of the year. Oil exports to Japan and the Ryukyus were cut from 1,600,000 barrels to 100,000. Exports will be allowed only from areas where fuel can be spared best, the department said.

In Massachusetts Gov. Robert F. Bradford ordered the seizure of a gas plant in Everett where a walkout of 900 workers was threatened that would have affected service to sixty-four hospitals and 1,500,000 residents of Greater Boston. After seizure and issuance of a temporary injunction, union leaders ordered their followers to remain at work.

In Tennessee, Governor James McCord proclaimed a state of emergency and announced a voluntary fuel conservation program.

In Rochester, Sheriff's deputies and city policemen were organized to make emergency deliveries of fuel oil in extreme cases.

In Endicott, Mayor E. Raymond Lee declared an emergency due to the gas shortage and urged residents to conserve fuel. Many homes there and in Binghamton and Johnson City were without heat and residents sought emergency shelter.

Philadelphians Warned

Residents of Philadelphia were warned of a gas shortage caused by the oil shortage and were urged to restrict use of gas to the absolute minimum.

Police Commissioner Arthur W. Wallander of this city, regional fuel coordinator, sent telegrams asking eighty-six terminal dealers here to remain open today and tomorrow, because of the expected severe cold, to supply fuel oil to hardship cases.

Mayor O'Dwyer declared during the afternoon that it was not necessary at this time to proclaim a state of emergency and to divert

Continued on Page 12, Column 5

Petroleum Shipment Abroad Is Curbed to Ease Shortage

Department of Commerce Orders Quotas Reduce ' From 11,850,000 to 9,650,000 Barrels for Quarter—Slashes Japan

Special to THE NEW YORK TIMES.

WASHINGTON, Jan. 30—The Department of Commerce announced today that "in view of the serious shortage of fuel oils," in this country it had ordered an 18½ per cent cut in exports of petroleum products during the first quarter of this year. Its action will reduce from 11,850,000 to 9,650,000 the barrels of petroleum designated for overseas.

The Department also announced that it would limit licenses for export of petroleum products to shipments for those areas of the United States where the fuel can best be spared during the emergency.

In addition, it was disclosed that a separate quota of gas oil and distillate fuel oil had been established for the first quarter for shipments to Japan and the Ryukyus, drastically cutting their supply from 1,600,000 barrels to 100,000. The Department said that the difference would be met from oil producing areas outside the United States.

Proposals had been made in Congress to stop all shipments abroad except those going to American military forces. Bills designed to accomplish this end have been introduced in the House and the Senate.

Walter S. Hallanan, chairman of the National Petroleum Council, said today that the petroleum industry had taken "prompt and forthright action to alleviate the shortages of some petroleum products which have been rendered acute in certain sections by the severe cold weather." The industry "takes pride in the fact that it was the first to develop a voluntary agreement under the recent authorization of Congress," he added.

Canada Is Not Affected

WASHINGTON, Jan. 30 (AP)—The action today of the Depart-

Continued on Page 11, Column 4

Hope Wanes in Sea Search For 28 Aboard Lost Airliner

By FREDERICK GRAHAM

The Atlantic area northeast of Bermuda was being searched last night for survivors of a British South American Airways plane that disappeared in the area early yesterday morning with a crew of six and at least twenty-two passengers, but hope had almost been abandoned.

The thirty-two-passenger plane, which listed among those aboard Air Marshal Sir Arthur Coningham, Royal Air Force, who commanded the Second Tactical Air Force of the Allies at the invasion of Normandy, was out of London and on the Azores-to-Bermuda leg of the flight when last heard from about 1 A. M. (EST) yesterday.

At least fifteen United States Air Force, Navy and Coast Guard planes plus three Coast Guard cutters, two commercial steamers and a British South American Airways plane worked over a large area, about 400 miles northeast of Bermuda without success. More aircraft are scheduled to continue the search today.

The plane, a converted Lancaster bomber of the type used by the RAF for saturation bombing of Germany, had stopped in Santa Maria in the Azores to refuel. An Associated Press dispatch from Bermuda said the plane, believed to have been commanded by Capt. David Colby, radioed to Bermuda that it would arrive there at midnight Thursday, an hour and a half late. One hour later it reported to Bermuda again, saying it was 440 miles northeast of Bermuda, that there was a moderate sea swell and that it was bucking strong headwinds. Nothing more has been heard from the plane.

The only other report that might

Continued on Page 10, Column 2

ORVILLE WRIGHT, 76, IS DEAD IN DAYTON

Co-Inventor With His Brother, Wilbur, of the Airplane Was Pilot in First Flight

Special to THE NEW YORK TIMES.

DAYTON, Ohio, Jan. 30—Orville Wright, who with his brother, the late Wilbur Wright, invented the airplane, died here tonight at 10:40 in Miami Valley Hospital. He was 76 years old.

Mr. Wright, who had been confined to a hospital in October, collapsed in his office on Tuesday. He was suffering from lung congestion and coronary arteriosclerosis.

At the bedside when Mr. Wright died were Horace A. Wright, a nephew; Mrs. H. S. Miller, a niece, and Delyle Myers, a nurse.

The announcement of his death was made by Dr. A. B. Brower, family physician.

Engrossing Amusement

In the early fall of 1900 fishermen and Coast Guardsmen dwelling on that lonely and desolated spot of sand dividing Albemarle Sound from the Atlantic Ocean on the coast of North Carolina called

Continued on Page 12, Column 2

Arms Get Atomic Energy Priority In Policy Set by Congress Group

By WILLIAM S. WHITE

Special to THE NEW YORK TIMES.

WASHINGTON, Jan. 30—The Joint Committee on Atomic Energy laid down today a firm policy that the production of atomic weapons, rather than work on peacetime applications of atomic energy, must be the "vital business" of the United States for the foreseeable future.

It declared also that "uninterrupted operation" of the "critical," or military, facilities of the Atomic Energy Commission was so essential to national security that an investigation was in motion to find a formula to assure "continuity of work" under all labor eventualities.

In its first report to Congress, the committee indicated some dissatisfaction "in a number of cases" with certain aspects of the handling of internal security within the personnel of the Atomic Energy Commission.

"In certain of these cases," the report went on, "the committee has requested that the commission outline in detail its security policy as applied to these specific instances."

"In the majority of these cases," it was added, "the men in question had been employed while atomic energy still was under Army control."

As to the essential policy to be followed in atomic development, the committee declared:

"Until such time as an effective, enforceable and reliable program for the international control of atomic energy is in successful operation, the most vital business of the Atomic Energy Commission must be the meeting of the atomic requirements of national defense.

"The joint committee has been assured that those charged with these responsibilities are keenly aware thereof. This phase of the atomic energy program is of para-

Continued on Page 4, Column 5

Record 799-Million Budget Is Asked by Dewey for State

He Estimates Actual Outlay at 753 Millions for Next Fiscal Year, but Says No Rise in Taxes Is Needed—Warns on Inflation

By LEO EGAN

Special to THE NEW YORK TIMES.

ALBANY, Jan. 30—Governor Dewey submitted another record-breaking budget to the Legislature tonight, calling for appropriations of $799,600,000, including deficiencies for the current year, but estimating expenditures in the new budget year at a figure of $753,500,000. The Governor regards the lower figure as his "budget" total.

Appropriations recommended are $128,200,000 higher than those carried in last year's budget message but, because of supplemental grants for teacher pay, veterans' housing, college housing, central schools and rent control, only $53,400,000 higher than actual appropriations, which were $746,200,000.

The expenditures of $753,500,000 contemplated in Mr. Dewey's message compare with an actual total of $707,500,000 in the current year, according to revised estimates. The revised figure reflects increased relief contributions and higher food prices for inmates of state institutions which are being provided for in deficiency appropriations.

Allowing for continuance of the reductions made in 1946, which he recommended, the Governor estimated that existing regular taxes would produce $758,600,000 in the new budget year, enough to balance expenditures and leave a $5,000,000 surplus.

The regular tax structure does not include the additional one-cent-a-package levy on cigarettes or the 20 per cent increase in existing income tax rates which were voted to finance the $400,000,000 veterans' bonus. If the present return from these special levies continued, Mr. Dewey said, the bonus bonds might be retired in eight or

Continued on Page 9, Column 1

Text of Gov. Dewey's budget message will be found on pages 8 and 9.

REALTY VALUATIONS RISE $745,775,468 IN CITY FOR 1948-49

Higher Accrued Value Is Chief Factor in $17,684,240,921 Total, Biggest Since '33

By LEE E. COOPER

New York's land and buildings, regarded as the richest segment of real estate in the world, have risen in value to $17,684,240,921 on the city's tax books for the coming fiscal year.

Municipal assessors have chalked up a tentative increase of $745,775,468 over current figures on taxable properties for the year beginning July 1, 1948, to carry the aggregate valuations to the highest level since 1933.

A report submitted to Mayor O'Dwyer yesterday by Harry B. Chambers, president of the Tax Commission, showed an average rise of about 4½ per cent for the five boroughs, accounted for largely by an upswing in "accrued value" rather than by addition of new construction to the assessment rolls.

The report set the following ten-

Continued on Page 11, Column 3

GOP GROUP SHAPES SHARP ERP REVISION WITH FUND REDUCED

A Proposal to Sell U. S. Goods to Latin America for Food for Europe Wins Favor

By FELIX BELAIR Jr.

Special to THE NEW YORK TIMES.

WASHINGTON, Jan. 30—A fighting nucleus of eighteen Senate Republicans agreed late tonight to press for important changes in the Administration's European Recovery Program as the party's legislative leaders brushed aside President Truman's demand for approval of the full $6,800,000,000 asked for the first fifteen months of operations.

The group of eighteen Senators, in which Westerners predominated, called for a complete shift in emphasis of the Marshall Plan "from the underwriting of trade deficits to the support of specific production programs" in which financial aid would be contingent on increased output of food, coal, steel and transportation facilities.

Senator Joseph H. Ball of Minnesota said the principles agreed

Continued on Page 6, Column 2

World News Summarized

SATURDAY, JANUARY 31, 1948

Mohandas K. Gandhi, 78-year-old spiritual leader of hundreds of millions of Indians, was shot in New Delhi yesterday as he walked toward a pergola to lead 1,000 of his followers in evening prayer. He died twenty-five minutes later. His assassin, a Hindu, was seized after he had fired three quick shots into the frail leader, who only recently had ended a hunger strike in protest against communal strife. [1:8.]

News of the tragedy shocked the world. In Bombay, it ignited a new outburst of rioting. [2:3.] United Nations officials at Lake Success feared this might be the beginning of a new wave of violence throughout India. [2:4-5.] President Truman said the whole world would mourn and expressed hope that the assassination would "not retard the peace of India and the world." [2:1.] Similar expressions of regret were voiced in London, where the King and the Queen and Prime Minister Attlee were among the many leaders to pay tribute to Mr. Gandhi. [1:6-7.]

The French National Assembly approved, 308 to 242, the Government's program to establish a free gold market and to allow Frenchmen to repatriate foreign assets by paying a tax. The Socialists reversed their previous stand and voted for the program. [1:6-7.]

Two recent Russian notes protesting the reopening for American use of an airfield in Tripolitania and the presence of American naval craft in Italian ports will be rejected by the State Department. [6:5.] The Navy announced that another 1,000 marines would go to the Mediterranean soon to replace an equal number now serving in that area. [6:4-5.]

The United States consulate in Jerusalem declared American citizens participating in the fighting would lose their passports and right to protection. [1:7.] Britain announced at Lake Success before the Palestine Commission that she could not allow the formation of any armed militia in Palestine before her mandate ends. [4:3.]

In Washington a group of eighteen Senate Republicans urged a change in the European Recovery Program to support specific production goals and brushed aside the Administration's request for approval of the full initial fund of $6,800,000,000. [1:5.]

An 18½ per cent reduction in exports of petroleum products was ordered by the Commerce Department "in view of the serious shortage" of oil in this country. [1:2-3.]

Also in Washington, the Joint Committee on Atomic Energy declared this nation must concentrate for the foreseeable future on the "uninterrupted" production of atomic weapons in preference to the peaceful utilization of atomic energy. [1:2-3.]

Governor Dewey asked the Legislature to appropriate $799,600,000 as he submitted another record-breaking budget. Appropriations last year totaled $746,200,000. [1:4-5.]

Winter's coldest weather hit the metropolitan area, with the thermometer hovering near zero in the city. In the suburbs the temperature was expected to fall to sub-zero levels during the night. Some homes suffered from a shortage of fuel oil. [1:1.]

A thirty-two passenger British plane was feared lost on its way to Bermuda. [1:2-3.]

Orville Wright, air pioneer, died in Dayton, Ohio, at 76. [1:2.]

GANDHI IS KILLED BY A HINDU; INDIA SHAKEN, WORLD MOURNS; 15 DIE IN RIOTING IN BOMBAY

MOHANDAS K. GANDHI

The New York Times

THREE SHOTS FIRED

Slayer Is Seized, Beaten After Felling Victim on Way to Prayer

DOMINION IS BEWILDERED

Nehru Appeals to the Nation to Keep Peace—U. S. Consul Assisted in Capture

By ROBERT TRUMBULL

Special to THE NEW YORK TIMES.

NEW DELHI, India, Jan. 30—Mohandas K. Gandhi was killed by an assassin's bullet today. The assassin was a Hindu who fired three shots from a pistol at a range of three feet.

The 78-year-old Gandhi, who was the one person who held discordant elements together and kept some sort of unity in this turbulent land, was shot down at 5:15 P. M. as he was proceeding through the Birla House gardens to the pergola from which he was to deliver his daily prayer meeting message.

The assassin was immediately seized.

He later identified himself as Nathuran Vinayak Godse, 36, a Hindu of the Mahratta tribes in Poona. This has been a center of resistance to Gandhi's ideology.

Mr. Gandhi died twenty-five minutes later. His death left all India stunned and bewildered as to the direction that this newly independent nation would take without its "Mahatma" (Great Teacher).

The loss of Mr. Gandhi brings this country of 300,000,000 abruptly to a crossroads. Mingled with the sadness in this capital tonight was an undercurrent of fear and uncertainty, for now the strongest influence for peace in India that this generation has known is gone.

[Communal riots quickly swept Bombay when news of Mr. Gandhi's death was received. The Associated Press reported that fifteen persons were killed and more than fifty injured before an uneasy peace was established.]

Appeal Made By Nehru

Prime Minister Pandit Jawaharlal Nehru, in a voice choked with emotion, appealed in a radio address tonight for a sane approach to the future. He asked that India's path be turned away from violence in memory of the great peacemaker who had departed.

Mr. Gandhi's body will be cremated in the orthodox Hindu fashion according to his often expressed wishes. His body will be carried from his New Delhi residence on a simple wooden cot covered with a sheet at 11:30 tomorrow morning. The funeral procession will wind through every principal street of the two cities of New and Old Delhi and reach the burning ghats on the bank of the sacred Jumna River at about 4 P. M. There the remains of the greatest Indian since Gautama Buddha will be wrapped in a sheet, laid on a pyre of wood and burned. His ashes will be scattered on the Jumna's waters, eventually to mingle with the Ganges where the two holy rivers meet at the temple city of Allahabad.

These simple ceremonies were announced tonight by Pandit Nehru in respect to Mr. Gandhi's wishes, although many of the leaders desired that his body be embalmed and exhibited in state. India will see the last of Mr. Gandhi as it saw him when he lived—a humble and unassuming Hindu.

News Spreads Quickly

News of the assassination of Mr. Gandhi—only a few days after he had finished a five-day fast to bring about communal friendship—spread quickly through New Delhi. Immediately there was spontaneous movement of thousands to Birla House, home of G. D. Birla, the millionaire industrialist, where Mr. Gandhi and his six secretaries had been guests since he came to New Delhi in the midst of the disturbances in India's capital.

While walking through the gardens to this evening's prayer meeting Mr. Gandhi had just reached the top of a short flight of brick steps, his slender brown arms

Continued on Page 2, Column 6

All Britain Honors Gandhi; Truman Deplores Tragedy

By HERBERT L. MATTHEWS

Special to THE NEW YORK TIMES.

LONDON, Jan. 30—Mohandas K. Gandhi, in death, has won the unanimous tribute of Britons—something he never hoped for or expected during his life. Nowhere outside of India has the shock of his assassination contained the feelings and emotions evident here today because Britain and Mr. Gandhi have been linked for good or evil over the last forty years.

In a special broadcast to the British people tonight the Prime Minister said:

"The voice which pleaded for peace and brotherhood has been silenced, but I am certain that his spirit will continue to animate his fellow countrymen and will plead for peace and concord."

[President Truman and Secretary Marshall expressed their grief and condolences in messages to India. Members of Congress were apprehensive. Leaders of many other lands joined in paying tribute and in deploring the manner of Mr. Gandhi's death.]

The sincerity of today's expressions of regret, which came from the King and Queen, the Prime Minister, the political parties—even the Communist—and from many humble Londoners who filed silently into India House this afternoon to pay tribute, cannot be doubted.

Those many quarrels when Mr. Gandhi fought with his passive resistance against the imperial power of Britain are truly things of the past. Mr. Gandhi himself paid high tribute to Britain for her policy of freeing India and of trying to help to keep the two dominions at peace with each other.

The British, on their side, have

Continued on Page 2, Column 2

U. S. WARNS CITIZENS IN PALESTINE FIGHT

Consulate General Says They Face Loss of Passports and All Protective Rights

By SAM POPE BREWER

Special to THE NEW YORK TIMES.

JERUSALEM, Jan. 30—United States citizens fighting in the armed services of the Jews or the Arabs will lose their passports and their right to protection, the United States Consulate General warned Americans in Palestine tonight. Furthermore, naturalized citizens, it was said, would lose their American nationality if they fought for a foreign power.

[Zionist hopes for getting United Nations help in arming a Jewish militia in Palestine were dimmed by the statement of Sir Alexander Cadogan, chief British representative, that the British Government would not allow formation of such forces before the end of the mandate.]

The consular warning is being twisted by Arab sources into a promise that those fighting for the Jews may have their passports back when the fighting ends. The relevant passage reads: "American passports valid only for direct

Continued on Page 4, Column 4

France Votes Free Gold Market, Legalizes Hidden Assets by a Tax

By HAROLD CALLENDER

Special to THE NEW YORK TIMES.

PARIS, Jan. 30—Parliamentary sanction was given today for the Government's devaluation of the franc and its accompanying monetary policy.

By a vote of 308 to 242, the National Assembly passed the Government's bill to create a free gold market and to legalize the hitherto illegal possession of foreign securities held by Frenchmen, if those assets were repatriated and the owners paid a special tax of 25 per cent of the assets' value.

As a comparatively free market in dollars had already been established by decree—although its opening was delayed by the freezing of bank notes of 5,000 francs—today's vote by the Assembly completed the series of measures framed by the Government to derive maximum benefit from devaluation by getting possession of privately owned foreign securities and hoarded gold.

Estimates of the total of these illegal securities have been in the neighborhood of $300,000,000 in the United States alone, while official guesses have placed the value of the hidden gold in France at $2,000,000,000.

Apparently placated by the freezing of the bank notes, the Socialists once again switched their position and voted today for the gold market bill, which they had opposed bitterly Wednesday, although their Ministers had apparently accepted it in the Cabinet meeting last Saturday. They were not reluctant to switch, for they did not desire to upset the Government and wreck the "Third Force," hostile though they were to the Government's departure from a planned economy.

The freezing measure, taken when the Socialists had precipitated a Cabinet crisis by balking at the gold market, was considered mainly a political move. But René Mayer, Finance Minister, told the

Continued on Page 5, Column 2

"All the News That's Fit to Print"

The New York Times.

LATE CITY EDITION
Mild, light rain today. Little change in temperature tomorrow.
Temperature Range Today—Max.,44; Min.,38
Temperatures Yesterday—Max., 47; Min., 29
Full U. S. Weather Bureau Report, Page 45

VOL. XCVII..No. 32,905. Entered as Second-Class Matter, Postoffice, New York, N. Y. NEW YORK, THURSDAY, FEBRUARY 26, 1948. Times Square, New York 18, N. Y. Telephone LAckawanna 4-1000 THREE CENTS IN NEW YORK CITY

BENES BOWS TO COMMUNISTS, GOTTWALD FORMS CABINET; ONE SLAIN IN PRAGUE PROTEST

London and Paris Shocked By Coup in Czechoslovakia

British Bitter Over Lack of Resistance by Leaders—Bidault Warns of Extreme Danger for France and Europe Soon

By DREW MIDDLETON
Special to The New York Times.

LONDON, Feb. 25—The fall of democratic Czechoslovakia, easternmost bastion of parliamentary democracy in Central Europe, has produced anxiety, bitterness and surprise in British Governmental and diplomatic circles.

It is necessary to go back a decade to find a situation in what is nominally peacetime that has produced such profound shock. The installation of Dr. Alexej Cepicka as Minister of Justice in the new Czechoslovak Cabinet completes the melancholy process of Communist domination, in the eyes of many.

"They already had a Communist Minister of the Interior [Vaclaw Nosek] to arrest people; now they have a Communist Minister of Justice to execute them," was the way one diplomatic source put it.

Thus far the British Government has refrained from commenting on the changes in Prague. This probably will come in the House of Commons when fuller details of the events there have arrived from the newly appointed Ambassador, J. Pierson Dixon.

The surprise over the swiftness with which the Czechoslovak Communists moved reflected the faith of many members of the Labor Government in the strength and political ability of the Czechoslovak Social Democrats and Socialists. The bitterness obviously was directed at the Czecholovak politicians and diplomats, well known and well liked in London, whose part in the present crisis had not been a dynamic one, to say the least.

This group did not include President Eduard Benes, for whom there was warm regard, mixed with sorrow and anxiety for his eventual personal safety.

Once more today the British referred to the presence in Prague of Valerian A. Zorin, Deputy Russian Foreign Min'ster, and the reference was sharp enough to disturb

Continued on Page 3, Column 2

REDS FORCE ISSUE

Thousands of Workers Threaten to Walk Out if President Resists

POLICE CURB OPPOSITION

Beat Back Group of Students Attempting to Gain Palace to Protest New Cabinet

Texts of Benes letter and the Communists' reply, Page 2.

By ALBION ROSS
Special to The New York Times.

PRAGUE, Feb. 25 — President Eduard Benes gave Communist Premier Klement Gottwald permission this afternoon to install a Communist dominated Czechoslovak Government of the type found in other Eastern European countries now considered satellites of the Soviet Union.

The President accepted the program after an exchange of letters between him and the presidium of the Communist party. In his letter M. Benes insisted upon a parliamentary government representative of all parties in the National Front. The Communists replied that the government would be representative but they barred the leaders of the three parties whose ministers had resigned from the Government last week.

Today the chiefs of the Communist-controlled Genera l Confederation of Labor ordered a general strike if the President refused to bow to the demands of the Communist party. Factory and office workers councils ordered out into the main square of Prague 50,000 to 100,000 members to demonstrate for a strike or to express support for the President if he accepted the Communist program.

Police Kill One Student

At least one person was killed and several were wounded when the police fired on a procession of 1,500 students marching to ask President Benes not to install the new government. The police beat the students with rifle butts and blocked off every route to the Hradcany castle toward which they were marching.

After a long discussion with the President at the castle on the Communist victory, the Premier told the workers they must "be faithful to the President" and that the President had decided for the will of the people on something that was certainly not entirely in accord with his own wish.

The presidency agreed to a perfectly constitutional solution of the Government crisis. The new Cabinet installed by Premier Gottwald will have a parliamentary majority made up of Communists, at least part of the Social Democrats and a group of men from the parties whose ministers resigned Friday in a protest against what they described as efforts to set up a police state.

Communists Rule Courts Now

In the new cabinet both the Ministry of the Interior, controlling the police, and the Ministry of Justice, controlling the courts, will be held by Communists.

The Cabinet will have thirteen Communists, four Social Democrats, two men who split off from the Czech National Socialist party, two who split off from the People's party and one who left the Slovak Democratic party.

Two members of the Cabinet, Jan Masaryk, remaining as Minister of Foreign Affairs, and Gen. Ludwig Svoboda, remaining as Minister of War, are without party affiliations.

In the former Cabinet were nine Communists, four Czech National Socialists, three Social Democrats, four People's party members, four Slovak Democrats and two nonpartisan members. In the new Cabinet five ministers have no official party connection.

Two Social Democrat Ministers, Vaclav Majer, Minister of Food, and Frantisek Thymes, Deputy Premier, resigned before the new Government was formed. The former president of the Social Democratic party, Bohumil Lausmann, made his peace with the victors after having signed a pro-

Continued on Page 2, Column 2

CITY BILLS LINKED TO PAY REDUCTIONS IN O'DWYER LETTER

He Says Cost-of-Living Rises May Be Voided Unless State Provides Requested Aid

'PACKAGE' FORMALLY FILED

Higher Fare and Increase in Business Taxes Likely, but Some Items Face Axe

By LEO EGAN
Special to The New York Times.

ALBANY, Feb. 25—Mayor William O'Dwyer's "legislative package" for New York City was submitted formally in full to the Legislature today despite reports that it would be cut to less than half its size before it is approved.

In a letter to legislative leaders transmitting his proposals, Mayor O'Dwyer declared that the program was the minimum for the city's essential requirements and that the entire package was vital to the proper running of the city.

As submitted the program calls for legislation permitting the city to raise an additional $81,200,000 locally next year as follows:

By increasing subway fares	$51,200,000
By doubling business taxes	30,000,000

It also calls for a $129,000,000 increase in state aid for the city as follows:

State aid for medical indigents and neglected children	$40,000,000
Increase in state aid for schools	50,000,000
Increase in per capita grants to the city	24,000,000
State reimbursement to the city for half United Nations headquarters	15,000,000

Unless the requested state funds were made available, the Mayor's letter declared, the city's employes would receive no additional cost-of-living pay rises and might suffer recision of those already granted. Rejection of the program, the letter said, would prevent adequate staffing of hospitals and health stations and bar enlargement of the city's police and sanitation forces.

Amendments Proposed

The program offered by the Mayor also calls for the initiation of constitutional amendments increasing the city's real estate taxing powers by an initial $82,000,000, starting in 1950, and increasing its debt-incurring power by $500,000,000, also starting in 1950.

Since no new legislation is required for these steps, the Mayor's letter made no reference to his reported intention of raising an additional $17,800,000 through an increase in real estate taxes within the existing constitutional limits nor his plan to raise $5,600,000 through a $5 and $10 use tax on automobiles, the amount dependent on weight.

All that the Mayor is likely to get, in the private opinion of Republican and Democratic members of the Legislature, is:

1. The bill authorizing, without a referendum, a subway fare increase to raise $51,200,000.

2. Power to double the city's gross receipts tax on ordinary businesses, making it one-fifth of 1 per cent, and double the tax on financial businesses, making it two-fifths of 1 per cent, the increases to yield $30,000,000.

3. The increase in state aid to education involved in the Feinberg Bill, already passed, which will amount to from $6,600,000 to $8,500,000 dependent upon average daily public school attendance.

4. A state grant of $3,000,000 for operation of teacher training courses in the four municipal colleges as recommended by the Young Commission and approved by Governor Dewey.

Taxing Power Rise Likely

5. Initiation of the constitutional amendment increasing the city's real estate taxing power.

6. Initiation of an amendment broadening debt incurring power to a lesser extent than the Mayor has asked.

In introducing the bills in the Assembly today, Irwin Steingut, Democratic leader, said:

"We're for this package. This is no idle gesture. I will try to demonstrate that to the best of my ability."

Asked if it was being submitted on an "all or nothing" basis, Mr. Steingut replied that it was as far as "we are concerned." When asked about a possible compromise, he stated, "We'll cross that bridge when we come to it."

Mr. Steingut flew down to New

Continued on Page 19, Column 3

Republicans Win $170,000 To Scan Truman's Regime

Override Democrats in Senate to Set Wide Inquiry With Attorney General as a Target—Lucas Charges 'Fishing'

By WILLIAM S. WHITE
Special to The New York Times.

WASHINGTON, Feb. 25—The Senate's Republican majority forced today a grant of $170,000, the largest such sum ever given at one time, to a powerful committee with almost limitless jurisdiction to investigate the Truman Administration.

The action was taken by storm over strong Democratic opposition led by Senator Scott W. Lucas of Illinois. He and his protesting colleagues accused the Republicans of setting off upon "a fishing expedition" in declining to indicate against what and whom their inquiries were being poised.

Unmentioned during the debate was a clear, though unacknowledged, understanding that the designated principal investigative agent for the Republicans, Senator Homer Ferguson of Michigan, intends to use the new powers and funds to seek to investigate Attorney General Tom C. Clark.

Specifically, the Senate's action was one of refusing, by a voice vote in which Republican "nays" overwhelmed the "ayes" of the Democrats, to reconsider a routine and little noticed decision by which the $170,000 appropriation had been provisionally approved. The effect was finally to approve the allotment.

Apart from $125,000 thus awarded to the Committee on Expenditures in the executive departments, it was authorized to take over $45,000 remaining in the till of a now inactive group which investigated war surplus matters.

Along with this the committee, which is headed by Senator George D. Aiken, Republican, of Vermont, was authorized not only to carry out the functions laid down by the Reorganization Act and the Senate rules, but also "any other duties imposed upon it."

Senator Lucas attacked this phrase, asserting that this meant that the Republicans were empowered to "go out fishing some-

Continued on Page 15, Column 2

President Flies to Key West After Rough Voyage to Cuba

By ANTHONY LEVIERO
Special to The New York Times.

KEY WEST, Fla., Feb. 25—President Truman fought that familiar inward fight against seasickness today and won out by staying in his bed while the yacht Williamsburg made a rough trip across the Windward Passage. His face lobster red and his nose peeling, the Chief Executive arrived here tonight after winding up his Caribbean tour with an inspection of the big United States naval base at Guantanamo, Cuba.

The President flew to Key West from Cuba in the "Sacred Cow," landing at Boca Chica airport here.

He will remain here resting until his return to Washington on March 5, but will attend to state business. He is receiving official documents by courier service, and by this means he is expected to get the measure for stop-gap extension of the rent control law in time to act on it before the Sunday midnight deadline.

The President was steady on his legs and smiling when the Presidential yacht and its escorting seaplane tender, the Greenwich Bay, dropped anchor in the green waters of Guantanamo Bay. He stepped ashore at 2 P. M. Members of his official party acted less chipper than he.

Accompanied by Capt. C. E. Battle Jr., commander of the base, Mr. Truman inspected the Marine Corps guard of honor like the old soldier that he is. As the men came to "inspection arms," Mr. Truman grabbed the rifles from the hands of two of them and peeked into the barrels. He also talked to some about their campaign ribbons.

In a big turnout at the naval base nearly 200 school children sang "America" for the President. One of them, Bill Barrett, son of a chief pharmacist's mate, stepped forward to present Mr. Truman with an album showing school activities. The boy began to read the presentation, became overawed and stopped.

"Never mind," said the President

Continued on Page 20, Column 3

INJUNCTION RIGHTS OF TAFT ACT UPHELD

Constitutionality Is Sustained in Action of NLRB Against Typographical Union

Special to The New York Times.

INDIANAPOLIS, Ind., Feb. 25—Federal Judge Luther M. Swygert, in a Circuit Court decision handed down here today, upheld the constitutionality of the Taft-Hartley law's provision that the National Labor Relations Board may seek injunctions while labor-management dispute hearings are in progress before the board. He also set aside a motion of the International Typographical Union, American Federation of Labor affiliate, that the injunction sought against it be dismissed. He set next Wednesday for hearing on the injunction itself.

[NLRB officials in Washington said it was the first court decision which ruled specifically on the constitutionality of the Taft-Hartley law's injunction processes.]

The injunction was instituted against the typographical union by Robert N. Denham, general counsel for the labor board, to restrain the ITU from continuing any of twenty-three acts alleged to constitute unfair labor practices, most important of which is the union's efforts to continue in effect closed shop conditions despite their ban by the Taft-Hartley law.

The injunctive relief sought is based on charges filed against the printers' union by the American Newspaper Publishers Association.

Continued on Page 16, Column 4

House Subcommittee Backs Bill To Make Lynching a Federal Crime

Special to The New York Times.

WASHINGTON, Feb. 25—A House Judiciary subcommittee approved today a bill to make lynching a Federal crime. The vote was 4 to 2. The measure was sponsored by Representative Clifford P. Case of New Jersey. It contains some provisions of a similar bill by Representative Kenneth B. Keating, Republican, of New York.

With Speaker Joseph W. Martin Jr. publicly committed to House action this session, the main question is whether after the full committee reports scheduling will be postponed until final action on the tax reduction bill to avoid the risk of angering Southerners whose votes are desired to help override a possible veto of tax cuts.

House passage of the anti-lynching bill is believed certain, but a filibuster is likely in the Senate. Policy makers there have already decided to defer action on the anti-lynch proposal and others contained in President Truman's civil rights message until disposal of the tax bill and the European Recovery Program.

Coincident with the House subcommittee's action, Congressional leaders of the Southern revolt announced that seventy-four House Democrats had signed a pledge to "oppose to the finish" the President's recommendations on lynching, poll taxes and racial segregation.

Representative Tom Murray, Democrat, of Tennessee, made a speech today in which he condemned the report of President Truman's civil rights committee and said:

"I now call upon the chairman of this committee, Mr. Charles E. Wilson, to tell the public who prepared or drafted this report. I know that he did not prepare the report, and I do not believe that

Continued on Page 20, Column 4

RENT BILL VOTED BY SENATE; GOING BY AIR TO TRUMAN

Chamber Quickly Passes the House's Month Extension—Signing Due in South

YIELDS ON 1949 MEASURE

Barkley Deplores Need to Act Twice Due to Proximity of End of Control Sunday

By SAMUEL A. TOWER
Special to The New York Times.

WASHINGTON, Feb. 25—The Senate whisked through a one month extension of the existing rent control law today, following up swiftly yesterday's enactment of the measure by the House.

Passage was by a voice vote, with less than five minutes' deliberation, after the Senate had suspended its rules to make it unnecessary for its Banking and Currency Committee to consider the bill.

The stop gap extension of rent control to April 1, one month beyond its scheduled expiration this Sunday, will be flown to President Truman, now in Key West. The President is expected to sign the measure.

Although the Senate approved yesterday a fourteen-months' continuance of controls, with some changes, it was obliged to act today on the interim measure in view of the belief of House leaders that the legislative position there and the wish to evaluate current economic trends precluded any chance of House action on a long range rent bill before the deadline.

Following suspension of the rules, Senator Alben W. Barkley of Kentucky, the minority leader, deplored the need for the Senate's acting twice, asserting:

"I think it is extremely unfortunate that we are not prepared to enact legislation for the full period for which Congress is willing to extend rent control. I do not assess any blame at any particular point; but we have been in cession for two months, and we have known all the time that there had to be an extension of rent control.

"Yesterday the Senate passed a bill extending rent control for fourteen months. It is unfortunate that the Congress will not be able to complete action on that legislation this week, so as to avoid taking two or three bites at the cherry before we are through."

Senator Robert A. Taft of Ohio,

Continued on Page 15, Column 4

U.S. MOVES BIG FIVE REPORT ON OUTLOOK IN PALESTINE STRIFE

Austin Asks Security Council Name Body to Inquire if Peace Is Threatened

ADVERSE VOTE POSSIBLE

Britain and China Expected to Abstain—Egypt Says Arabs Would Fight U. N. Force

By MALLORY BROWNE
Special to The New York Times.

LAKE SUCCESS, N. Y., Feb. 25—The United States presented a formal resolution to the Security Council today calling for a committee of the Big Five to decide whether the Palestine situation constituted a threat to peace, and, if so, what to do about it.

Warren R. Austin, in submitting the United States resolution, made it clear that his move was timed as a deliberate step to oppose at once the Colombian proposal to call a special session of the General Assembly for reconsideration of the whole partition plan.

Egypt, whose delegate was the only other speaker at today's short meeting, warned the Security Council that the Arab states would "rush to the rescue" of Palestine if the United Nations sent armed forces there to implement partition.

Because it calls for consultations with the Palestine commission, the mandatory power and representatives of Arabs and Jews on the "implementation" of the partition plan, the United States resolution has no chance of being accepted by Britain in its present form, an authoritative British source said.

Even if amended to make allowances for Britain's rigid refusal to do anything that could be called taking part in the implementation of partition, however, the outlook tonight was that the United States resolution would not easily rally the necessary seven votes, including the "concurrent votes" of all five permanent members, out of the total of eleven.

Both Britain and China are likely to abstain, and while there are precedents for considering that abstention by a Big Five power does not constitute a veto, the impression at Lake Success was that neither an adverse vote nor a veto could be ruled out.

A report from an authoritative

Continued on Page 5, Column 4

World News Summarized

THURSDAY, FEBRUARY 26, 1948

Communists took over the Government of Czechoslovakia yesterday after President Benes bowed to demands that Premier Gottwald receive permission to install a Cabinet of his own choosing. Workers mobilized by the Communists demonstrated freely for the change, but the police killed one person and wounded several others when they fired on students trying to reach the President's residence to urge him not to yield. [1:8.]

The "bloodless revolution" caused anxiety in Britain and French Foreign Minister Bidault saw in the change dangers for his country and Europe. [1:6-7.] There was talk in Washington of releasing official documents revealing why United States troops stopped after entering Czechoslovakia in 1945 and permitted the Russians to occupy most of the country. [1:6-7.]

Zionists raided a British military court building in Jerusalem and the Irgun Zvai Leumi threatened to drive all Britons from the city. [1:7.] The United States formally asked the United Nations Security Council to name the Big Five to a committee to decide whether the Palestine situation constituted a threat to peace and to advise how to act. [1:5.]

Support grew in the Little Assembly for the American proposal to hold elections for a national assembly in South Korea despite Russia's boycott. A Norwegian suggestion to reconvene the General Assembly found no support. [8:3.]

An economic commission for Latin America was approved by the Economic and Social Council, 14 to 0. [8:6.] In Washington, the Pan American Union made public the draft of a proposed hemisphere economic agreement for consideration by the twenty-one American Republics at the coming Bogota Conference. [9:4.]

What is now the Dominion of India would become the Indian Union, a "sovereign democratic republic," under a proposed constitution. Such long-established customs as untouchability and child marriage would be abolished. India's relation to Britain would be fixed later. [11:1.]

The Senate passed the House bill extending federal rent controls through March 31. The measure will be sent by plane for signing to President Truman [1:4], who landed at Key West after his Caribbean trip [1:2-3]. Over strong Democratic opposition, Senate Republicans pushed through a $170,000 grant to a committee with almost unlimited power to investigate the Truman Administration. [1:2-3.]

A Republican bill to make lynching a Federal crime and to punish state and local officials not "diligent" in trying to stop mob action was approved by a House committee. [1:2-3].

The provision of the Taft-Hartley Act giving the NLRB the right to seek injunctions while hearing disputes was upheld by a Federal court in Indianapolis. The International Typographical Union had challenged its constitutionality. [1:2.]

There will be no strike in midtown office buildings here under a new three-year contract with a $5 wage rise. [1:6-7.]

Mayor O'Dwyer's bills to relieve the city's financial strain were introduced in the Legislature with the prospect that less than half the desired aid would be approved. [1:1.] Governor Dewey signed the bill raising legislators' pay. [38:2.]

Elementary schools would be open six days a week, throughout the year, and teachers would be employed on a twelve-month basis under a modernization plan presented to the American Association of School Administrators. The estimated annual cost would be $4,000,000,000. [25:1.]

Czech Crisis May Impel U. S. To Publish Secret Documents

By The Associated Press.

WASHINGTON, Feb. 25—The political upheaval in Czechoslovakia may blow the lid off secret documents explaining Soviet-American wartime arrangements for liberating that nation. These papers would supply Washington's official answers to such questions as why American forces did not aid in the liberation of the Czech capital, Prague, from the Germans and why the United States troops stopped short just inside the Czech western border.

Apparently they also would add another chapter to the story of how the Soviets were able to get the upper hand in Eastern European countries from the very end of the war.

From wholly authoritative informants, it was learned that these documents would show:

(1) That a Soviet high command request from Moscow to Gen. Dwight D. Eisenhower was the immediate reason why American troops did not help free Prague in May, 1945;

(2) That the simultaneous withdrawal of Russian and American armies from Czechoslovakia in late 1945 came after President Truman made a personal request to Generalissimo Stalin to approve such a step;

(3) That the United States "leaned over backward," as one official said today, to prove to the Russians that American troops would not rush into areas that the Russians wanted to occupy.

The secrecy about the wartime

Continued on Page 2, Column 5

JEWS STORM COURT IN PALESTINE RAID

Building Saved as Fire Bombs Prove Duds—Day's Fighting Takes Toll of 12 Lives

By SAM POPE BREWER
Special to The New York Times.

JERUSALEM, Feb. 25—Jews raided the British military court building here today and killed one Arab auxiliary policeman, wounded another and escaped. An effort to destroy the building failed because the home-made incendiary bombs did not ignite.

The court was not in session and only two Arabs were on guard when four men made their attack at 2:15 P. M.

Two men ignited two cans of kerosene in the road outside to distract the attention of the guards. Two others ran up and shot one guard dead and then went to the back of the building and seriously wounded the other guard and placed two bombs in the hallway and left. The bombs were

Continued on Page 7, Column 4

Elevator Men Sign New Contract Under First Peaceful Agreement

By A. H. RASKIN

For the first time since Manhattan elevator operators and other classes of building service employes became organized fourteen years ago, a union contract covering service workers in midtown skyscrapers was signed yesterday without a strike or the threat of a strike.

Representatives of the Midtown Realty Owners Association and Local 32-B of the Building Service Employes International Union, AFL, made no secret of their jubilation at the signing of the three-year pact, which provides a general wage increase of $5 a week and guarantees that there will be no interruption in the vertical transportation on which hundreds of thousands of office and factory workers depend.

The agreement directly affects 2,000 starters, operators, porters and handymen in 200 buildings, most of them in the garment, fur and millinery districts. Forty-five hundred other workers in 600 midtown commercial buildings operated by members of the Realty Advisory Board or by independent owners are expected to receive identical benefits under separate agreements between their owners and the union.

David Sullivan, president of Local 32-B, expressed the hope that a similar peace pattern would be adopted to cover an additional 20,000 workers in 1,000 office and loft buildings and 2,000 apartment houses outside the scope of the midtown contract. These buildings are covered by a master agreement with the Realty Advisory Board that expires April 20.

The union head said Local 32-B would insist that all the commercial buildings accept the standards established under the midtown pact, but indicated that some con-

Continued on Page 17, Column 4

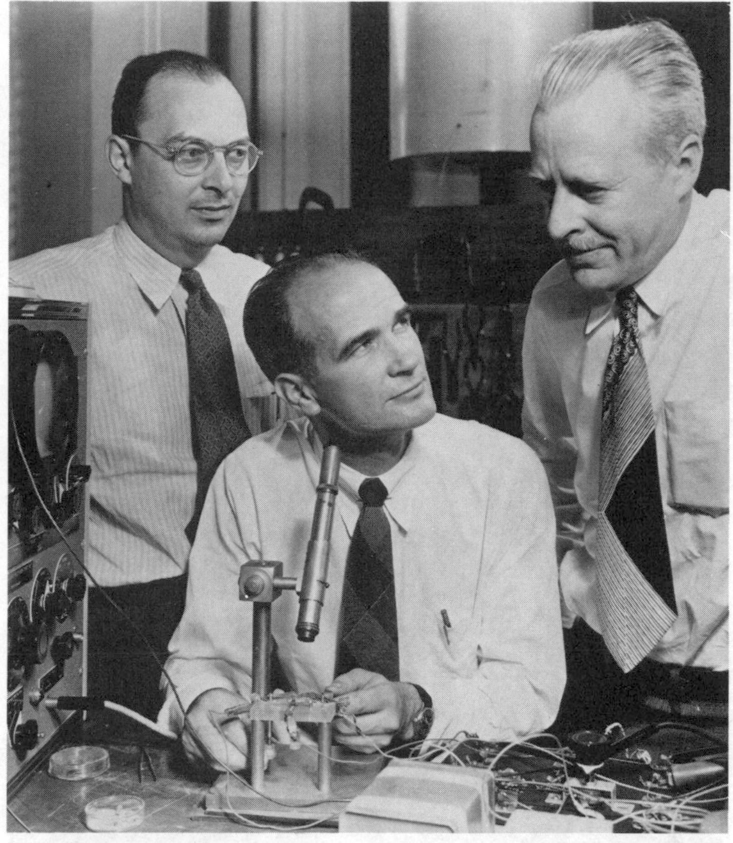

Reproduced with permission by A.T.&T. Co.

The invention of the transistor was announced by Bell Laboratories. The three Nobel Prize-winning scientists are Drs. John Bardeen, William Shockley and Walter H. Brattain. The apparatus on the table was used in the development of the first transistor.

Also introduced in 1948 was the xerographic printer. Chester F. Carlson (center), founder of the process, is shown here at the first public demonstration of the revolutionary machine.

Long-playing and 45 rpm records were introduced. Dr. Peter Goldmark, inventor of the LP, holds a pile of 33 rpm records containing all the music in the eight-foot stack of 78s.

1948

Citation, ridden by Eddie Arcaro, won the triple crown and became the first thoroughbred to win over a million dollars.

American Bob Mathias won the coveted decathlon in the 1948 Olympic Games, in London.

Barbara Ann Scott won the women's singles figure skating title at the Winter Olympics at St. Moritz.

The immortal Babe Ruth addresses a huge throng at Yankee Stadium on Babe Ruth Day, shortly before his death.

"All the News That's Fit to Print"

The New York Times.

LATE CITY EDITION
Snow and colder today. Clearing and colder tomorrow.
Temperature Range Today—Max., 36; Min., 25
Temperature Yesterday—Max., 51; Min., 30
Full U. S. Weather Bureau Report, Page 48

VOL. XCVII..No. 32,919 Entered as Second-Class Matter, Postoffice, New York, N. Y. NEW YORK, THURSDAY, MARCH 11, 1948. Times Square, New York 18, N. Y. Telephone Lackawanna 4-1000 THREE CENTS NEW YORK CITY

MASARYK KILLED, A SUICIDE, REDS SAY; U. N. SHELVES CZECH PLEA FOR INQUIRY; MARSHALL IS STIRRED BY WORLD CRISIS

FARE BILL PASSAGE IS PROMISED TODAY BY GOP AT ALBANY

Majority's Version of Measure in Mayor's 'Package' of 15 Is Not Acceptable to Him

TWO MORE SET FOR ACTION

Doubling of Gross Receipts Tax Rates, Amendment to Push Hospital Building Backed

By LEO EGAN
Special to The New York Times.

ALBANY, March 10—Passage of a thoroughly revised and deflated version of Mayor William O'Dwyer's "package" for New York City was promised tonight by Republican legislative leaders following a long conference with Governor Dewey and state administration officials.

In place of the fifteen measures requested by the Mayor, Senator Benjamin F. Feinberg, majority leader, and Speaker Oswald D. Heck, Republican Assembly spokesman, said the city would get these measures:

The Republican transit fare bill, which is reported to be highly objectionable to Mayor O'Dwyer and which he has said he will not use.

Power to double the gross receipts tax rates, now one-tenth of one per cent on ordinary business and two-tenths of one per cent on financial business.

First action on a constitutional amendment to exempt $150,000,000 for new hospital construction from the city's debt limit.

More State Aid Voted Down

All three measures were scheduled for passage in both Senate and Assembly tomorrow. The Republican majority in the Assembly had voted down three Democratic proposals to take up for final passage measures that would have increased state aid to New York City by $84,000,000.

It was the Republican refusal to make any concessions with respect to increased state aid that led Mayor O'Dwyer and Democratic leaders to abandon their own fare bill and the rest of the "package" earlier in the week.

Irwin Steingut, minority leader, told the Assembly tonight that the Republican refusal of more state aid would be made a issue in the legislative election campaigns in the fall.

"Our case does not end here," he declared as the Democratic proposals were rejected. "We have another forum and we shall appeal to it after we leave here. I am sure there will be keen resentment in New York City at the treatment of its proposals here."

Increased School Aid Loses

One of the proposals defeated called for state payment of half the city's education costs, representing an increase in state aid of $32,000,000. It was rejected 100 to 45 with only two Republicans, Samuel Roman of Manhattan and Lewis W. Olliffe of Brooklyn voting with the minority.

The second Democratic move called for state reimbursement of 50 per cent of the city's expenditures for the medically indigent and for neglected and dependent children. Mr. Roman was the only Republican to vote for it. It would have cost $32,000,000.

The third motion proposed to take up for passage a bill increasing per capita payments to the city from $6.75 to $10, representing an additional cost to the state of $22,000,000. Again Mr. Roman was the only Republican to vote in favor.

Democratic members of the Legislature were highly elated at the turn of events with respect to the O'Dwyer transit bill and the rest of the "package." Most of their high spirits stemmed from the fact that they were released from commitments to vote for the transit measure, which they regarded as politically dangerous. The Mayor is assured of a fare bill that he can use if he wants to and which puts only himself on a political spot.

Mr. Steingut said tonight that the Democrats would vote for the increase in gross receipts tax, which was part of the original "package," and also for the exemption of hospital debt, which Mayor O'Dwyer wants. The latter had been part of a much larger debt-exemption proposal.

The Republican program for meeting New York City's needs was announced officially by Senator Feinberg and Speaker Heck after the conference in the Gov-

Continued on Page 20, Column 4

Senate Group Is Set to Trim Tax Cut to $4,600,000,000

As Hearings End, House Exemptions Rise and Income Split Seem Likely to Be Kept —Schram Pleads for Risk Capital

By JOHN D. MORRIS
Special to The New York Times.

WASHINGTON, March 10—The Senate Finance Committee concluded tax-reduction hearings today with a majority apparently determined to trim the $6,500,000,000 of annual relief voted by the House to about $4,600,000,000.

One of the final-day witnesses, Emil Schram, president of the New York Stock Exchange, called for wider action to alleviate what he called an "alarming shortage" of risk capital. Besides the individual income tax reductions under consideration, he proposed a 50 per cent cut in the capital gains levy and modification of the so-called double tax on corporate profits.

It was virtually certain, however, that the Finance Committee would not go beyond the scope of the House-approved bill and accept these or any other miscellaneous recommendations made during the seven days of hearings.

Prospects were that two of the House measure's three main provisions would be accepted without change. They call for an increase to $600 in the present $500 personal exemption and extension to all states of income-splitting benefits now available to married couples in states having community property laws.

The cost of the bill in losses of revenue is expected to be trimmed by modification of the third major clause, providing percentage cuts in addition to the reductions entailed by the other proposals. These range from 30 per cent in the lowest bracket to 10 per cent in the highest.

One plan is to substitute a scale of reductions ranging from 20 per cent to 5 per cent. In any event, it was reported, the committee probably will retain the House bill's distribution of relief, with 70 per cent going to persons with incomes of less than $5,000. The cuts are expected to be retro-

Continued on Page 21, Column 1

Airliner Crashes in Chicago, Killing 12 of the 13 Aboard

Special to The New York Times.

CHICAGO, Thursday, March 11—A Delta Air Lines plane carrying nine passengers and a crew of four crashed into a field northwest of the Chicago Airport late last night and burst into flames. Only one person was believed to have survived.

The survivor was identified as Mrs. Tripolina Mio of Chicago. She was in critical condition at Holy Cross Hospital. Badly burned, she was screaming for her son, Alfred, 9, who was listed as a passenger on the plane.

Other passengers aboard the plane, according to the airline, were:

Harold L. Levy, 47, Chicago lawyer; his brother, Ralph R. Levy, Chicago insurance broker; Albert F. Kahle, Cincinnati; Mrs. C. R. Richards, Cincinnati; Dr. G. E. Garven, San Francisco; Fred Wilkins, Oak Lawn, Ill.; Dan J. Courtney, Appleton, Wis.

The crew members, all of Miami, were: Capt. Lee Holloway; Sue Young, stewardess; J. S. Disosway, first officer, and Glen Hairston, purser.

Mrs. Harold Levy said her husband and his brother were flying to Miami to the bedside of their father, Robert R. Levy, who is critically ill. Harold Levy was an assistant state's attorney from 1923 to 1929 and a master in chancery from 1929 to 1933.

Wreckage and bodies were strewn over a wide area by the impact of the fast plane, which dived into the earth less than a minute after it cleared the airport.

The wreckage burst into flames, which hampered rescue efforts of the crash trucks and fire ambulances which rushed to the scene. The work was further complicated by the deep snow on the field.

Witnesses at the airport said that the plane took off into a north wind and had a clear field ahead. There was an explosion when it hit the earth.

The plane was bound for Miami via Cincinnati.

The DC-4 is the commercial version of the wartime C-54 Skymaster, dubbed the "Flying Boxcar" by troops in both theaters

Continued on Page 40, Column 6

FORRESTAL CALLS DEFENSE PARLEY

Army, Air, Navy Chiefs Will Confer With Him on Their War Roles and Missions

By HAROLD B. HINTON
Special to The New York Times.

WASHINGTON, March 10—The roles and missions of the Army, the Navy and the Air Force in future wars will be decided over the next week-end, Secretary of Defense James Forrestal said today. Exact dilineation of their responsibilities has been in abeyance since their unification last September.

The Joint Chiefs of Staff, to whom was confided this task, have been unable to reach complete agreement, and for failure to do so were criticized in the report of the President's Air Policy Commission and in the report of the Joint Congressional Aviation Policy Commission.

Mr. Forrestal said he intended to sit down with Gen. Omar N. Bradley, Gen. Carl Spaatz and Admiral Louis E. Denfeld, and if they were still unable to agree, he himself would make the decision for them.

He will ask them to outline their disagreements and then attempt to obtain an accommodation of their views. The time the Joint Staff has spent in discussion thus far has been profitably expended, he said, adding that he considers the persistence of disagreement thus far as a healthy state of affairs.

"I don't want people 'yessing'

Continued on Page 16, Column 4

Newspapers Here Accuse Printers Of Violating the Taft Labor Act

By A. H. RASKIN

Warning of the possibility of a printers' strike April 1 on fourteen major daily newspapers in this city, the Publishers Association of New York City filed unfair labor practice charges yesterday against New York Typographical Union No. 6 and its parent organization, the International Typographical Union, AFL.

The publishers accompanied their National Labor Relations Board action with assurance that New York newspapers would continue to publish in the event of a strike. Asserting that the sole obstacle to a new wage agreement was the "no contract" policy adopted by the ITU to fight the Taft-Hartley law, the association said the newspapers planned to utilize the same engraving process that has proved effective in Chicago to maintain publication if the 2,500 union printers walked out after the present contract expires at midnight March 31.

Under the substitute process, the operations normally performed in newspaper composing rooms are eliminated and newspaper pages are printed through the use of engravings made up from specially prepared typewritten copy.

The filing of the NLRB action brought from the New York local a statement accusing the publishers of having refused to bargain in good faith. The union asserted that the harmonious relations between the association and the printers would "unquestionably be severely shattered" as a result of the publishers' action.

The publishers declared that they were "interested only in a firm and lawful contract." They said the charges had been filed because the employers were convinced that the international union had forbidden the local to bargain

Continued on Page 32, Column 5

U. S. HINTS ASSENT TO FEDERAL REGIME IF JEWS CONCURRED

Spokesman Says the Palestine Plan Is Acceptable if Others Involved Are for It

HELD AGREEABLE TO ARABS

Project Is Being Presented to Higher Committee—Zionists' Position Thought Precarious

By THOMAS J. HAMILTON
Special to The New York Times.

LAKE SUCCESS, N. Y., March 10—A spokesman for the United States delegation hinted today that the United States would agree to the establishment of a federal regime in Palestine, instead of the proposed Jewish and Arab states, if the change was accepted by the Jewish Agency for Palestine.

"Why shouldn't we be for it if everybody supports it?" the spokesman asked.

Since several representatives of Arab states are already proposing such a solution, it is believed that they would agree to a federal regime. According to some sources, in fact, they have already indicated that they might agree to a token Jewish state, corresponding to the status of Vatican City in Italy, in order to win adherents to the change.

Jewish Agency View on Partition

No difficulties are expected with the British, who have made no secret of their dislike of partition. However, spokesmen for the Jewish Agency emphasized during the United Nations General Assembly debate last fall that they accepted partition with reluctance, and that this was as far as they would go.

Since the establishment of an international military force to carry out partition depends primarily upon the attitude of the United States, it was agreed that pressure by the United States conceivably could change the position of the Jewish Agency.

Throughout the Assembly the Agency was quick to accept proposals by the United States for the revision of the partition plan, but Zionists insisted today that partition represented their minimum program.

In any event, the hint from the United States spokesman appeared to be in agreement with a statement last night by Warren R. Austin, United States representative.

Continued on Page 17, Column 2

Masaryk Talked Last With Benes

By The Associated Press.

PRAGUE, March 10—The conversation between Czechoslovak President Edward Benes and Foreign Minister Jan Masaryk yesterday may hold the key to M. Masaryk's death, in the opinion of some who knew him well.

M. Masaryk remained behind to talk with the President after a state visit by the Polish Ambassador yesterday. It was their first conversation since the Government crisis in which Dr. Benes yielded against his will to Premier Klement Gottwald's demands for Communist control of the country.

It is doubtful that even during the crisis M. Masaryk saw much of the President.

Thus, in the quiet little village of Sezimovo Usti, on the winding Luznice River, Masaryk and the man who stood with his father in building the nation sat and talked.

AUSTRIANS THWART COMMUNIST MOVE

Government Outlaws Action Committees—Factories' Guards Now Are Armed

By JOHN MacCORMAC
Special to The New York Times.

VIENNA, March 10—The first attempt by the Austrian Communist party and its ally—the Soviet Army of occupation—to panic Austria into concessions on the heels of the Czechoslovak coup appears to have failed.

The Socialist and People's parties have declared their solidarity with each other in a Government coalition.

"Action committees," which the Communists have attempted to form in the trade unions on the Czechoslovak model, were declared illegal by the Socialist Minister of the Interior. Today the Communists themselves attempted to deny they had ever tried to create them.

The Socialist organ Arbeiter

Continued on Page 10, Column 5

RUSSIA IS ACCUSED

Czech in U. N. Charges That Moscow Installed Regime in Prague

CALLS STALIN INSINCERE

But Lie Rejects Petition by Papanek on the Ground It Is 'Non-Governmental'

Appeal of U.N. Czech delegate to Security Council, Page 2.

By A. M. ROSENTHAL
Special to The New York Times.

LAKE SUCCESS, N. Y., March 10—The Czechoslovak crisis exploded in the United Nations today when Prague's chief delegate charged that the Soviet Union had installed a Communist dictatorship in his country by threat of arms and he demanded an investigation by the Security Council.

In a direct appeal to the Council Dr. Jan Papanek, head of the Czechoslovak mission, asked for a judgment against Russia for violating Czechoslovak independence and putting the peace of the world in jeopardy.

Dr. Papanek's defiance of the Prague regime sent Secretary General Trygve Lie into all-day conferences with his advisers, and at 6 P. M. his answer was that the complaint would not be presented by him to the Security Council. The decision was said to have been supported by the departments of Security Council affairs and legal affairs and Dr. T. F. Tsiang of China, chairman of the Security Council.

The chief of the Security Council department is Assistant Secretary General Arkady Sobolev, a Russian, and the head of the legal department is Assistant Secretary General Ivan Kerno, a Czechoslovak.

Mr. Lie ruled that Dr. Papanek's official letter of accusation came under the heading of "non-governmental" communications. Mr. Lie apparently followed the theory that the Czechoslovak delegate had himself severed connections with Prague and was not handing on the views of the Czechoslovak Government.

Specifically refusing to resign his post, Dr. Papanek said he represented the only legal government of Czechoslovakia, the regime of President Benes before the Communists took over control of the Cabinet. And he put it up to the Security Council to rule whether today's Czechoslovakia had a right to a seat in the world organization.

Observers here said that Mr. Lie had been put in a tight spot and chose the "common sense" way out since there was no doubt that the delegate would be dismissed by the Prague Government, but there was some talk that Mr. Lie had acted too quickly and had in effect confirmed Dr. Papanek's dismissal before it had even been announced in Prague.

As things stand, Dr. Papanek's letter will be filed in the cabinets

Continued on Page 2, Column 2

Jan Masaryk
The New York Times Studio

'REIGN OF TERROR' SEEN BY MARSHALL

He Says Masaryk Case Shows 'Plainly What Is Going on'—Warns Against Passion

By BERTRAM D. HULEN
Special to The New York Times.

WASHINGTON, March 10—Secretary of State Marshall declared today that Czechoslovakia was under a "reign of terror," and warned that the world situation was "very, very serious."

The tragic death of Jan Masaryk, the Czechoslovak Foreign Minister, he emphasized, "indicates very plainly what is going on."

Replying to questions at a news conference, Secretary Marshall, in an unusual statement that he permitted to be quoted, voiced concern over both developments abroad and passions that have been aroused in this country with demands for action.

The Secretary was asked for an expression of views on the world situation. The reporter pointed out that fears had been aroused over the Czechoslovak crisis and remarked that the concern ranged from that to apprehension that the Communists might win the elections in Italy on April 18.

Secretary Marshall replied informally and then permitted direct quotation after carefully and slowly examining in the stenographic record what he had said.

"I think you correctly described the situation in your question—that there are great fears as to the developments," he said.

"There is also a very strong feeling regarding these developments and a considerable passion of view

Continued on Page 6, Column 4

NEWS IS DELAYED

Czech Cabinet Holds Up Reports on the Foreign Minister Six Hours

BLAMES CRITICS ABROAD

State Funeral Is Ordered—His London Friends Doubt Masaryk Took Own Life

By ALBION ROSS
Special to The New York Times.

PRAGUE, March 10—Jan Masaryk, veteran non-party Foreign Minister of the new Communist-dominated Czechoslovak Cabinet, jumped to his death at 6 o'clock this morning, the Prague Government announced at noon today.

The statement said the 61-year-old son of the first President and liberator of the country, Dr. Thomas G. Masaryk, had leaped from the bathroom window of his third-floor apartment in the Foreign Ministry. It added that his body had been found about 6:25 A. M. on the stone courtyard below.

Announcement of his death was said to have been delayed all morning while officials of the new Cabinet debated the reaction, though international press services had spread the news. M. Masaryk was to have made his first appearance before Parliament as a member of the new Cabinet of Communist Premier Klement Gottwald and the Communists were reported to be disturbed by the prospect of his empty chair.

Blames Criticism Abroad

Finally, just before noon Communist Minister of the Interior Vaclav Nosek said that M. Masaryk had committed suicide and attributed his action to criticism from abroad for his remaining in the Cabinet after the Communist coup.

[Czechoslovak citizens and a close friend of M. Masaryk in London expressed doubt that he had committed suicide. Dr. Jan Papanek, head of the Czechoslovak mission to the United Nations, in a press conference at Lake Success, also said he could not believe the suicide report.]

In his announcement of M. Masaryk's death, M. Nosek told Parliament:

"That good man and patriot and friend of our people, that man who just a few days ago said he was going on by the side of the people, has voluntarily put an end to his life."

State Funeral Planned

A great state funeral was announced immediately for Saturday afternoon. The Minister of Interior ordered public buildings to fly black streamers in a sign of mourning and ordered the national flag flown everywhere at half staff.

Premier Gottwald will deliver the funeral oration and Communist Deputy Foreign Minister Vladimir Clementis will deliver an address at the grave.

In his statement to Parliament, M. Nosek said that "during the night M. Masaryk must have read a number of letters and telegrams from his former friends in England and America full of reproaches about their disappointment over his uncompromising attitude during the recent crisis."

The Government radio announcer said: "M. Masaryk was a sensitive man who suffered under the attacks of the foreign press. He had become the object of invectives and attacks and reproaches and accusations. The more painful and sorrowful is his loss to all of us."

The official description of the reported suicide emphasized that it could have been only a deliberate act of self-destruction. Describing the bathroom from which M. Masaryk was said to have jumped, it stated that in front of the window was a couch. To get out it would be necessary to climb up onto this couch to open the window and to climb over the edge, the Government announcement declared.

M. Masaryk had instructed two servants, Vaclav Topenka, who had been with the Masaryk family for many years, and Bohumil Pricho-

Continued on Page 3, Column 5

World News Summarized

THURSDAY, MARCH 11, 1948

Jan Masaryk, non-party Foreign Minister of Czechoslovakia and son of that country's liberator, met death in Prague yesterday. A delayed announcement by the Communist-dominated Cabinet asserted that he had jumped to his death from his apartment. Friends of the Czech leader and observers were skeptical of the report that he had taken his own life. [1:8.]

Shortly after news was received of M. Masaryk's death, Dr. Jan Papanek, head of the Czechoslovak mission to the United Nations, formally accused Russia of having forced a Communist dictatorship on his country by direct order and by the threat of troops massed along the border. He demanded an investigation by the Security Council. His letter was held to be a "non-governmental" communication that would not be placed on the Council's agenda or circulated until called up by some member. [1:6.]

The death of M. Masaryk, taken together with other events in Czechoslovakia, "indicates very plainly what is going on," Secretary Marshall said, and he added: "It is a reign of terror." Events abroad and the passions aroused here, he said, have created a "very, very serious situation." [1:7.]

The Socialist and People's parties in Austria proclaimed their solidarity in an anti-Communist front against a repetition in their country of the Czechoslovak coup. [1:5.]

It is time to decide "who does what with what weapons," Defense Secretary Forrestal said in announcing that he had called Army, Navy and Air Force chiefs to a week-end conference. [1:2.] In Paris, French Foreign Minister Bidault reported virtual agreement by the five nations of Western Europe on an all-inclusive union. [15:1.]

Maj. Gen. Chennault, urging billions in economic and military aid to China, told a House committee that China's fight against the Communists was preventing Russia from starting an aggressive war in Europe. [16:6.]

The Senate will go into night sessions in an effort to pass the European Recovery Program this week. A 74-to-3 vote buried Senator Taylor's third-party proposal to turn the whole program over to the United Nations. Senator Taft said that, while he favored a cut in funds, he would not go below $4,000,000,000. [1:6-7.] Union labor leaders from the Marshall Plan countries set up a permanent body to work for complete success before ending their London meeting. [16:3.]

At the United Nations, where the big powers were still trying to solve the Palestine problem, an American spokesman hinted that the United States might agree to an Arab-favored federalized regime instead of partition, the minimum Zionist demand. [1:4.]

Republican leaders in Albany decided to pass a transit and city tax bill unacceptable to Mayor O'Dwyer. [1:1.] The Senate approved bills for a state university [29:8] and the Legislature prepared for final adjournment on Saturday. [28:2.]

Newspaper publishers in this city, warning of a possible strike April 1, filed with the NLRB unfair labor practice charges against the printers' union. [1:2-3.] Mayor O'Dwyer intervened to avert a threatened stoppage in commercial printing plants. [32:2.]

A plane with nine passengers and four crew members crashed and burned in a field in Chicago immediately after taking off; only one person was believed to have survived the crash. [1:2-3.]

Senate Votes, 74-3, to Repudiate Wallace's Substitute for the ERP

By FELIX BELAIR Jr.
Special to The New York Times.

WASHINGTON, March 10—In a repudiation of the foreign policy views of Henry A. Wallace and his third party running-mate, Senator Glen Taylor of Idaho, the Senate voted, 74 to 3, today against turning the European Recovery Program over to the United Nations with a $25,000,000,000 United States contribution.

The unexpected showdown came after Senator Taylor held the floor for five and a half hours. It was dramatically staged by Senator Arthur H. Vandenberg, Republican, of Michigan, to emphasize the overwhelming sentiment of the Senate. The Idaho Senator coupled an attack on the bi-partisan foreign policy with a defense of Russia.

Shortly before the vote, Chairman Robert A. Taft of the Senate Republican Policy Committee let it be known that he would support a reduction in the first year's authorization for ERP to $4,000,000,000, but would fight any effort to cut below that amount.

The Foreign Relations Committee recommended $5,300,000,000 for the first year and Senator Vandenberg hopes to have enough votes to sustain it. Senator Taft is expected to support the measure with or without the committee figure and to make no strong fight for the lower amount after telling the Senate of his views.

Senate leaders, meanwhile, revived hope of bringing the bill to a final vote by Saturday night by ordering night sessions tomorrow and Friday. It is hoped in this way to facilitate adoption of the Senate bill by the House Foreign Affairs Committee, which will be-

Continued on Page 15, Column 4

"All the News That's Fit to Print"

The New York Times.

LATE CITY EDITION
Showers ending this afternoon; cooler tonight. Cloudy tomorrow.
Temperature Range Today—Max.,60; Min.,44
Temperature Yesterday—Max.,61; Min.,49
Full U. S. Weather Bureau Report, Page 51

Copyright, 1948, by The New York Times Company.

VOL. XCVII..No. 32,940. Entered as Second-Class Matter, Postoffice, New York, N. Y. NEW YORK, THURSDAY, APRIL 1, 1948. Times Square, New York 18, N. Y. Telephone Lackawanna 4-1000 THREE CENTS IN NEW YORK CITY

AMERICAN, BRITISH TRAINS HELD IN SOVIET BERLIN ZONE FOR INSPECTION BY RUSSIANS

MAIN LINE TIED UP

Soviet Blockade Halts Traffic on Railway From Western Zones

ALLIES RESIST RUSSIANS

Dispute Comes After Moscow Attempts to Control All Travel Around Berlin

By The Associated Press.

BERLIN, Thursday, April 1—The Russians refused today to let United States and British military trains go through their occupation zone without inspection.

Two Berlin-bound United States trains, one from Bremerhaven and one from Frankfort on the Main, and two British trains, one eastbound and the other westbound, were stopped at Marienborn, a check point five miles inside the Soviet zone. [The United Press said the Soviet action had held up the only line leading from Berlin to the western zone.]

Both United States trains later returned to Helmstedt, west of Marienborn in the British zone. Soviet authorities refused to let the trains proceed because they were barred from carrying out a new Russia order—announced only yesterday and effective last midnight—for inspection of all military trains and freight entering and leaving Berlin.

Berlin, under four-power control, is an island in the midst of the Soviet zone. Trains must pass through the Soviet jurisdiction to and from the Western zones.

Demand Rejected By U. S.

The United States rejected early today a Soviet demand that Russian troops be allowed to inspect United States military trains and freight entering and leaving Berlin. Train guards were instructed to bar Soviet troops entry to the train.

The British also ordered their train guards to refuse to allow Soviet inspection.

An earlier United States train from Berlin to Bremerhaven passed through the Soviet zone. The train commander said when it reached Helmstedt that he had let the Russian commander in Marienborn come aboard and inspect passengers' papers. Asked why, he said, "you will have to ask Berlin." [The United Press said passengers had been awakened for the examination of their travel cards.]

A United States major in charge in Berlin said he could not understand why the train commander had allowed the Russian on the train. He said the orders were for train commanders to hand the usual travel orders and papers to the Russians, but not let them on trains.

Authoritative French sources in Berlin said French officials had told the Russians their demand was "too vague" and had asked further explanation.

Outgoing Trains Guarded

By EDWARD A. MORROW

Special to The New York Times.

BERLIN, Thursday, April 1—The United States Military Government rejected last night Soviet proposals presented Tuesday night to put traffic to and from Berlin under virtually complete Russian control.

The United States officials' statement said they were prepared "for train commanders to give proper documentation, but we cannot permit entry into our trains as a new procedure."

Last night the "Berliner," regular United States military train to Frankfort on the Main left with a military guard of thirty men, double the usual number. Before the train left the lieutenant in charge told the military policemen, armed with tommy guns and carbines, that there was to be "no shooting tonight."

Early yesterday afternoon Gen. Lucius D. Clay said that "the procedures outlined in the Soviet requests are not in accord with our agreement and we are preparing an answer." General Clay's statement appeared to make the United States position more adamant

Continued on Page 14, Column 3

Action to Halt Coal Strike Is Postponed by President

Truman Wants to Study Board's Report, Which Is Said to Blame Lewis for Walkout —Backstage 'Deal' Reported in Making

By LOUIS STARK

Special to The New York Times.

WASHINGTON, March 31—In a surprise move today, President Truman withheld from publication the report of his board of inquiry, which is understood to have blamed John L. Lewis for the coal strike. The report also criticized the bituminous coal operators.

Instead of immediately directing the Attorney General, Tom C. Clark, to open injunction proceedings against the United Mine Workers and its officers, as had been generally expected, the President decided to study the report.

Charles G. Ross, White House secretary, said that its contents would not be disclosed until Saturday at the earliest.

The President's action followed the board's delivery of the report to him. The panel consisted of Judge Sherman Minton, chairman; Mark F. Ethridge, publisher of the Louisville Courier-Journal, and Dr. George W. Taylor of the University of Pennsylvania.

Mr. Truman's delay in ordering action toward a Federal Court crackdown on Mr. Lewis and the miners' union was attributed in informed circles to the following two possibilities:

A "deal" is in the making for a meeting between bituminous coal operators and miners to settle the controversy over miner pensions.

Some White House advisers are dubious over the obtaining of an injunction because of the difficulty of proving that it was Mr. Lewis and his officers who ordered the strike which began on March 15.

The latter view is not shared by Justice Department officials close to the situation. They believe they have a strong case against Mr. Lewis and the union.

The first possibility arose when it was learned that George M. Humphrey, president of the M. A. Hanna Company, and George Allen, former Reconstruction Finance Corporation chairman, have

Continued on Page 20, Column 4

Ban on Sectarian School Aid Rejected by Senate, 80 to 5

By WILLIAM S. WHITE

Special to The New York Times.

WASHINGTON, March 31—The Senate beat down today by 80 to 5 an attempt to deny to private and parochial schools any benefit under the Taft aid-to-education bill. The measure's principal sponsor, Senator Robert A. Taft of Ohio, then quickly accepted a Southern amendment which would lay a barrier against any future attempt by way of appropriations riders, to withhold such Federal help from states which segregate white and Negro school children.

The result of all this was to bring the bill close to final passage. This was expected to come tomorrow.

Mr. Taft agreed to the Southern proposal, which was put in by Senator Tom Connally of Texas, with the observation that it was entirely "consistent" with one of the principal declared objectives of the measure.

This objective was to guard against any sort of Federal interference with the administration and local control of the country's local school systems.

The effort to exclude private and parochial schools from either "support or benefit" of Federal funds was made by Senator Forrest C. Donnell, Republican, of Missouri.

Its effect would have been to lay it down, in what Senator Donnell termed "unmistakable" language, that Federal money could not be used directly in aid of parochial or private schools or indirectly in such ways as helping

Continued on Page 22, Column 6

ITU STAYS ON JOB AS NEWS PACT DIES

Union Says It Will Comply With Injunction and Withdraws All Contract Proposals

By A. H. RASKIN

Printers on New York daily newspapers remained at work last night, despite expiration of their union contract with the Publishers Association of New York City.

Laurence H. Victory, president of New York Typographical Union No. 6, AFL, promised that there would be no strike of the union's 2,500 members in newspaper composing rooms as long as negotiations for a new agreement continued.

The next negotiating session between the union, an affiliate of the International Typographical Union, and the association will be held at 2:30 P. M. tomorrow in the association offices, 1475 Broadway. The date was fixed at a two-hour conference yesterday, at which the union gave the publishers formal notice of its intention to comply

Continued on Page 21, Column 3

Congress Told UMT Racial Bars Would Unleash Civil Disobedience

By C. P. TRUSSELL

Special to The New York Times.

WASHINGTON, March 31—Congress was warned bluntly today that unless all forms of racial discrimination were prohibited in the proposed Universal Military Training and stop-gap selective draft programs, white and Negro youths throughout the country would be urged to resist induction by "civil disobedience."

A pledge to organize such a movement was made before the Senate Armed Services Committee by A. Philip Randolph, president of the Brotherhood of Sleeping Car Porters, American Federation of Labor. He was backed up, "shoulder-to-shoulder," by Grant Reynolds, national chairman of the Committee Against Jimcrow in Military Service and Training and New York State Commissioner of Correction.

"I reported last week to President Truman," Mr. Randolph told the Senators, "that Negroes are in no mood to shoulder a gun for democracy abroad so long as they are denied democracy here at home. In particular, they resent the idea of fighting or being drafted into another Jim Crow army.

"Today I should like to make clear to this committee and through you to Congress and the American people that passage now of a Jimcrow draft may only result in a mass civil disobedience movement along the lines of the magnificent struggles of the people of India against British imperialism."

Committee members indicated anxiety as Mr. Randolph, who is also national treasurer of the committee headed by Mr. Reynolds, continued:

"I personally pledge myself to openly counsel, aid and abet youth,

Continued on Page 10, Column 6

CHILE URGES FIGHT ON REDS' IDEOLOGY AT BOGOTA PARLEY

Her Delegate Asks Americas to Line Up on the Side of Democracy and Liberty

MARSHALL SPEAKS TODAY

Credentials of Nicaraguans Accepted—Mexico Pleads for U. S. Aid to Latins

By MILTON BRACKER

Special to The New York Times.

BOGOTA, Colombia, March 31—Chile today renounced her neutrality in the undeclared war of ideologies and exhorted the nations of the Americas to line up with her on the side of "democracy and liberty."

Coming after the United States move yesterday to assure discussion of the Communist threat to this hemisphere, and on the eve of Secretary of State Marshall's speech tomorrow, the address by Dr. Juvenal Hernández, chief of the Chilean delegation, re-emphasized that the basic division in the world today would tend to subordinate purely regional matters in the ninth conference of the American states.

[Dr. Hernán Santa Cruz of Chile, urging the United Nations Security Council to examine the Communist coup in Czechoslovakia, said it was another link in a Soviet chain to enslave the world. His plea won new backing.]

By the "spontaneous" reaction of her people, according to Dr. Hernández, Chile had chosen an exact stand. "She is neither indifferent nor neutral," he declared. "She is with the countries who defend democracy and liberty."

Reply to Argentina Seen

"And this should be, in my opinion, the attitude of all the countries of America," he added.

To many here, his remarks sounded like a reply to Foreign Minister Juan Bramuglia's assertion Monday that Argentina would not undertake to war against communism on ideological grounds.

Dr. Hernández justified his frank appeal for an ideological break with a declaration that the problem must be met face to face. It must be recognized, he declared, that daily more countries are losing the liberties for which millions

Continued on Page 13, Column 4

STRIKERS THREATEN GENERAL WALKOUT IN FINANCIAL AREA

Pickets, Abetted by Seamen, Spread From the Exchanges to Two Office Buildings

MASSED LINES CONTINUE

Little Hope Seen for Speedy Settlement—Stock Trading Reported Above Normal

By FRANK S. ADAMS

Local 205 of the United Financial Employes, AFL, moved yesterday to extend its strike against the New York Stock and Curb Exchanges to some of their member firms. Strike leaders voiced the threat that eventually they would bring about a general strike throughout the financial district.

Pickets from the local, strongly reinforced by white-capped members of two American Federation of Labor seamen's unions that are backing the strike, surrounded the buildings at 61 Broadway and 60 Wall Tower, which house many leading brokerage houses. They passed out leaflets that read:

"Brokerage employes in this building, be ready for a general strike of all Wall Street and the entire financial district. Watch for further notice. Be ready."

Union Says Others Have Quit

A spokesman for the union at its strike headquarters, 51 Beaver Street, said some employes of member firms already had quit work in response to the union's call, and that the strike would be extended eventually to many other firms. He declined, however, to name any firms affected or to estimate the number who had struck.

Representatives of firms in the two picketed buildings denied that any of their employes had left and belittled the union's threats of a general stoppage. Merrill Lynch, Pierce, Fenner & Beane, the largest Stock Exchange firm in point of business transacted, said that all its employes, including the one known union member, were at work in their offices in the 60 Wall Tower Building.

Mass picketing of the Stock and Curb Exchanges continued meanwhile, but under extremely heavy police guard, which prevented any recurrence of the violence that developed Tuesday morning. A detail of 500 policemen under Assistant

Continued on Page 22, Column 1

World News Summarized

THURSDAY, APRIL 1, 1948

The House last night passed its $6,205,000,000 omnibus foreign aid bill by a vote of 329 to 74. The measure, which authorizes $5,300,000,000 for the first year of the European Recovery Program and lesser amounts for economic and military aid to China, Turkey and Greece, differs from the Senate bill and will now go to conference with the Senate for adjustment of differences. The House also reaffirmed its move to include Spain among aid beneficiaries. [1:8.]

The president of the Brotherhood of Sleeping Car Porters warned the Senate Armed Services Committee that the nation's youth would be urged to refuse induction into the armed services by "civil disobedience" if Congress did not bar all forms of racial discrimination in the proposed draft and universal military training programs. [1:2-3.]

The report of President Truman's board of inquiry on the soft coal walkout was said to blame John L. Lewis for the strike and also to criticize the conduct of the coal operators. Mr. Truman withheld publication of the report for more detailed study instead of moving promptly to open injunction proceedings against the miners. [1:2-3.]

Leaders of the United Financial Employes, who are striking against the New York Stock Exchange and the Curb Exchange, threatened a general strike in the financial district. [1:5.]

The Chilean delegate to the United Nations told the Security Council that the recent change of government in Czechoslovakia was another move in the Soviet "imperialist, totalitarian expansion" to enslave the world. He asked that a subcommittee be set up to hear six Czechoslovak leaders who escaped before the coup in Prague. [4:2.]

In Bogota the Chilean delegate to the twenty-one-nation Inter-American conference described the world as divided into two fronts and pleaded with the other nations to align themselves on the side of "democracy and liberty." [1:4.]

The United Nations Palestine Commission agreed to the creation of special police for Jerusalem to maintain order after the British withdrawal on May 15. It also moved to perfect detailed plans for a provisional council of government for the proposed Jewish state. [1:7.]

Near the Palestine seaport of Haifa, a train from Cairo was wrecked by three mines. Forty Arabs were killed and sixty injured. [7:1.]

American and British trains were halted in Berlin by the Russians in pursuance of a plan to put all traffic to and from the city under Soviet control. Passengers were awakened and their documents inspected. The United States Military Government had previously rejected the Russian decision. [1:1.]

Two Russian concessions surprised the deputies of the Council of Foreign Ministers who are discussing the Austrian peace treaty in London. The Soviet Union proposed to reduce its claims on Austria by $25,000,000 to $150,000,000 and offered to extend from two to six years the time allowed for the payments. [1:6-7.]

A Russian proposal that under the planned mutual assistance treaty with Finland Moscow should decide when Russian troops might enter Finland was reported to have been rejected by Helsinki. [1:6-7.]

Cries of "Long Live the United States!" disrupted a Communist rally in southern Italy at which the Italian Communist leader, Palmiro Togliatti, was making a pre-election appeal in which he criticized American aid to Italy. [1:6-7.]

The Chinese Nationalists announced the evacuation of three key ports on the Shantung peninsula that they had captured from the Communists in last fall's offensive. [2:2, with map.]

$6,205,000,000 FOREIGN AID IS PASSED BY HOUSE, 329-74; INCLUSION OF SPAIN UPHELD

Communist Rally in Italy Ends in 'Viva U. S.' Cries

Crowd Boos Togliatti, the Reds' Chief—Unions Plan General Strike—Leftists Protest Letters From Americans

By The United Press

ROME, March 31—A Communist rally turned into a pro-American demonstration today when Palmiro Togliatti, Italy's Communist chieftain, was booed and shouted down by cries of "Long Live the United States."

[Communists and left-wing Socialists protested against letters from the United States urging Italians to vote against extreme Leftists as an unwarranted interference in Italian affairs.]

Signor Togliatti was addressing 20,000 persons at a Communist-Left-Wing Socialist election rally at Lecce, in the heel of the Italian boot. He denounced American aid to Italy and stressed the possibility that Russia might send wheat to Italy.

Boos and catcalls forced him to be silent for five minutes, during which anti-Communists shouted praise of the United States. Then the anti-Communists marched off in a body, continuing their cries of "Long Live the United States," leaving Signor Togliatti to finish his speech to only a few remaining Communists and Leftist Socialists.

ROME, March 31 (P)—The Communists threatened tonight to order a nation-wide strike to paralyze Italy for ten days before the April 18 national elections.

Giuseppe di Vittorio, Communist president of Italy's 6,000,000-member General Labor Confederation, announced in Palermo, Sicily, that the organization's executive committee would call the strike if the police failed to find a missing Sicilian labor leader by April 8.

If the strike is called April 8, Signor di Vittorio said, it will be one hour long that day and will be increased by one hour each day until the labor leader's disappearance is solved. Thus workers throughout the nation would be on strike for ten hours on April 17, the day before the election.

One exception was made, however,

Continued on Page 3, Column 2

Soviet Cuts Austrian Claim And Extends Payment Time

By BENJAMIN WELLES

Special to The New York Times.

LONDON, March 31—In a surprise move, the Soviet Union agreed here today to reduce its claims on Austria by $25,000,000, thus limiting the indemnity demands as payment for part of the German assets in the country to $150,000,000. Originally the Russians had requested $200,000,000.

At the same time Soviet Delegate Nikolai P. Koktomov startled the meeting of Big Four Foreign Ministers deputies by offering to extend the time limit of the Austrian payments to six years. Heretofore Moscow had insisted that Austria's payments be completed within two years.

The latest Soviet moves left the Western deputies cautiously optimistic about the possibility of eventual agreement on an Austrian treaty. While conceding that the new Soviet proposals had raised hopes for a four-power pact, one Western deputy said that these proposals would be subject to "very careful scrutiny and fullest consultation."

Declaring that a Soviet diplomat connected with the Austrian talks had flown to Moscow for consultations over the Easter recess, this delegate added:

"It looks as if our policy of standing firm and refusing to make any further concessions during the past six weeks and a half is now beginning to have its effect."

While the Western deputies had anticipated further Soviet reductions in monetary claims against Austria it is known that the pro-

Continued on Page 12, Column 6

U. N. UNIT TO SET UP JERUSALEM FORCE

Commission Will Act After Plea From Advance Party—40 Arabs Die in Rail Blast

By MALLORY BROWNE

Special to The New York Times.

LAKE SUCCESS, N. Y., March 31—The Palestine Commission decided today to take immediate steps to set up a special police force for Jerusalem.

Acting on a cabled warning from Dr. Pablo Azcarate, head of the United Nations advance party now in the Holy Land, the commission agreed to go ahead with preliminary arrangements for the selection of a specialist to go to Jerusalem at once to recruit and organize an interim force of 1,000 non-Palestinian police to preserve order in the holy city when the British withdraw on May 15.

[In Palestine forty Arabs were killed and sixty injured when mines derailed a train near Haifa.]

The commission also decided at

Continued on Page 7, Column 1

Finns Refuse to Let Russia Decide When Soviet Troops Should Enter

By GEORGE AXELSSON

Special to The New York Times.

HELSINKI, Finland, March 31—Finland has rejected a Soviet proposal that the Soviet Union should decide when Russian troops might enter Finland under the projected mutual assistance and friendship pact now being negotiated in Moscow. This was learned tonight from exceptionally well-informed sources.

A Finnish courier flew to Moscow this morning to communicate the text of this important Finnish reservation to Soviet Foreign Minister Molotov through the delegation in Moscow. For some days the Finnish Government has been studying the Soviet wish to include a paragraph in the military clauses reserving the right to decide when mutual aid stipulations became operative. Helsinki's reply has been to decline military cooperation save in an actual state of war.

To forestall local Communists from staging disturbances to force the issue, on orders from their leaders who know of the Finnish Government's reservations, Army units guarding the Presidential palace, strategic public buildings, foreign legations and the Army's munitions and stores have received an issue of weapons.

The Finnish Diet's keen desire for information on the status of pact negotiations was partly met this afternoon when a group of chairmen of the parties represented in the Diet received confidential and rough outlines of what had taken place. But the Finnish Government's reply to the Russian pact views had left many hours before, thwarting the Diet's purpose of influencing that answer.

The Finnish reply insisted on reserving the right to invite the Soviet Army across the border in the event of war and that the Finns alone must decide when the Russians should take charge of Finnish defenses. This point embraces the main objection to the pact and

Continued on Page 14, Column 5

ALL CURBS BEATEN

Omnibus Bill Carries $5,300,000,000 ERP and Funds for East

$425,000,000 IN ARMS AID

To Go to China, Greece and Turkey—Conferees Are Due to Meet This Morning

By FELIX BELAIR Jr.

Special to The New York Times.

WASHINGTON, March 31—The House passed the $6,205,000,000 foreign aid bill tonight by a vote of 329 to 74 and sent the omnibus measure to conference with the Senate for adjustment of differences.

Authorizing $5,300,000,000 for the first twelve months of a four-year European Recovery Program and lesser amounts for economic and military aid to China, Greece and Turkey, the legislation was identified in the last hours of debate as "a measure short of war" for halting the spread of communism.

In addition to the European Recovery Program already passed by the Senate, the omnibus measure provided $425,000,000 of outright military aid to China, Greece and Turkey to bolster their front against totalitarian aggression. It carried $420,000,000 of added economic aid to China and a $60,000,000 contribution toward the International Children's Emergency Fund.

Appeals Made by Leaders

In the vote on final passage, 158 Democrats joined with 171 Republicans to pass the measure. Appeals had been made by leaders on both sides for a sufficiently substantial majority to produce a favorable psychological effect on the forthcoming elections in Italy.

Against the bill were sixty-one Republicans and eleven Democrats, with two American Labor party members from New York.

Just before the showdown the House divided along party lines in turning back a Democratic effort to reverse its action of yesterday in designating Spain as eligible to participate in the European Recovery Program. By a standing vote of 188 to 104 the House reaffirmed its step and then swamped a substitute proposal by Representative Vito Marcantonio, American Labor of New York, to turn the entire program over to the United Nations. This standing division was 270 to 6.

As the dinner hour approached and members began clamoring for a vote, the House turned back suc-

Continued on Page 3, Column 1

Votes Cast in House Against the Aid Bill

By The Associated Press.

WASHINGTON, March 31—Sixty-one Republicans, eleven Democrats and two members of the American Labor party voted today against the Europe-China aid bill. They were:

Republicans—Allen of Ill., Arnold, Banta, Bennett of Mich., Bennett of Mo., Bishop, Buffett, Case of S. D., Chenoweth, Chiperfield, Church, Clevenger, Clippinger, Cole of Mo., Crawford, Curtis, Dondero, Ellis, Gillie, Griffiths, Gwinn of N. Y., Gwynne of Iowa, Hagen, Hand, Harness, Hoffman, Hull, Jenison, Johnson of Ill., Johnson of Ind., Knutson, Landis, Lemke, Lewis, Love, McCowen McGregor, Martin of Iowa, Miller of Neb., O'Hara, Owens, Phillips of Calif., Reed of Ill., Reed of N. Y., Rich, Sanborn, Schwabe of Mo., Schwabe of Okla., Scrivner, Shafer, Short, Smith of Ohio, Smith of Kan., Smith of Wis., Stefan, Twyman, Vail, Vursell, Wilson of Ind., Woodruff, Youngblood.

Democrats — Barden, Dorn, Doughton, Harrison, Johnson of Okla., Larcade, Morris, Powell, Rankin, Sadowski, Wood.

American Labor — Isacson, Marcantonio.

Paired against the bill were—Mason, Busbey and Rizley, Republicans, and Passman, Democrat, voting present was Macy, Republican.

A crowd of 250,000 gathers in Prague to hear Premier Klement Gottwald announce the cabinet changes that ensured Communist domination of the government.

The Berlin airlift began soon after the Russians blockaded Berlin.

Due in part to Marshall Aid, all kinds of goods reapppeared in West German shops.

The Marshall Plan was America's answer to Europe's post-war plight. In this photo, Congressional leaders witness the birth of the plan as President Truman signs the authorization.

1948

Laurence Olivier in his Oscar-winning portrayal of *Hamlet.* With him is Basil Sydney as the king.

Bogart and Bacall in *Key Largo.*

Humphrey Bogart and Walter Huston in a scene from *The Treasure of Sierra Madre,* written and directed by John Huston.

"All the News That's Fit to Print"

The New York Times.

LATE CITY EDITION
Showers followed by partly cloudy today. Sunny tomorrow.
Temperature Range Today—Max.,58; Min.,48
Temperatures Yesterday—Max.,62; Min.,48
Full U. S. Weather Bureau Report, Page 45

Copyright, 1948, by The New York Times Company.

VOL. XCVII No. 32,941. Entered as Second-Class Matter. Postoffice, New York, N. Y. NEW YORK, FRIDAY, APRIL 2, 1948. Times Square, New York 18, N. Y. Telephone Lackawanna 4-1000 THREE CENTS IN NEW YORK CITY

U. N. SETS SPECIAL ASSEMBLY ON PALESTINE FOR APRIL 16 TO RECONSIDER PARTITION

COUNCIL VOTE 9 TO 0

Soviet, Ukraine Abstain as Body Approves the U. S. Proposal

TRUCE MOVE ALSO BACKED

Arab Higher Committee and Jewish Agency Invited to Confer on Peace

Excerpts from addresses in the Palestine debate, Page 10.

By THOMAS J. HAMILTON
Special to THE NEW YORK TIMES.

LAKE SUCCESS, N. Y., April 1—The United Nations Security Council decided today to call a special session of the United Nations General Assembly to reconsider the partition of Palestine. The vote was 9 to 0, with the Soviet Union and the Ukraine abstaining. Trygve Lie, Secretary General, announced immediately afterward that the special session would be convened at Flushing Meadow Friday, April 16.

Immediately before it approved the United States proposal the Security Council accepted another United States resolution urging a truce in the Holy Land. The resolution invited both the Arab Higher Committee, spokesman for the Palestinian Arabs, and the Jewish Agency for Palestine to confer with the Council, and the vote was unanimous.

[In Palestine a Jewish food convoy from Tel Aviv to Jerusalem failed in a second attempt to breach Arab obstacles. As a result, food conditions in the Holy City were said to be critical.]

"Blank Check" for U. S. Seen

As one authoritative source interpreted today's action, the United States, which was primarily responsible for the adoption of the partition resolution, obtained a "blank check" from the Security Council today.

The question of supplying a military force to carry out the recommendations of the General Assembly was not mentioned at the Council session. American reluctance to have Russian troops sent to Palestine, together with fear of jeopardizing supplies of oil in the Near East, was the primary reason for the reversal of the American position.

Although representatives of France and Canada insisted last week that it was necessary to know in advance what the United States proposed to do to carry out its proposal for a "temporary" trusteeship, they joined with the majority today. As had been expected, Andrei A. Gromyko, Soviet Deputy Foreign Minister, did not use his power to veto the decision for a special session.

Austin to Press Trusteeship

Warren R. Austin, United States representative, invited the members of the Council to a secret meeting in his office at 2 Park Avenue on Monday afternoon to discuss the terms of the proposed temporary trusteeship. These, it is acknowledged, will be of vital importance in determining whether the General Assembly will give the required two-thirds majority.

Whether the trusteeship is assigned to an individual country or to the United Nations collectively, the General Assembly will have to decide whether to continue the restrictions Great Britain imposed in 1939 on Jewish immigration and the purchase of land by Jews.

The resolutions adopted today give effect to only two of the four points proposed by Mr. Austin on March 19. At the same time, he said that he would introduce later resolutions under which the Security Council would recommend both a temporary trusteeship and the suspension of measures by the United Nations Palestine Commission to carry out partition.

Faris el-Khouri, Syrian representative, argued today that Mr. Austin's proposal for a "standstill" agreement in Palestine, together with his statement to the Security Council last week proposing a suspension in "political activities," gave the Council's decisions today

Continued on Page 11, Column 2

Conferees Bar Spain in ERP, Complete Bill to Pass Today

Action on Madrid Follows White House Demand—Final Aid Measure Provides $6,098,000,000 for Europe and East

By FELIX BELAIR Jr.
Special to THE NEW YORK TIMES.

WASHINGTON, Friday, April 2—House and Senate conferees a few minutes before midnight completed action on a $6,098,000,000 compromise foreign aid bill and placed the measure in position for final passage and Presidential signature today.

Working continuously from 10 A. M. yesterday, the conferees first struck Spain from the list of countries named to participate in the European Recovery Program, for which $5,300,000,000 was authorized for the first twelve months.

Before reaching the end of the aid bill Chairman Arthur H. Vandenberg of the Senate Foreign Relations Committee succeeded in restoring the Senate's original "moral commitment" to a four-year program ending in 1952 by providing a continuing authorization and leaving it to future sessions of Congress to fill in the amount to be appropriated.

In addition to the authorization for the first twelve months of the four-year European Recovery Program, the compromise measure authorized $463,000,000 of economic and military aid to China, $275,000,000 of military aid to Greece and Turkey and a $60,000,000 contribution to the international children's emergency fund.

It authorized $20,000,000 for rehabilitation in Trieste but stipulated the amount should come either from ERP funds or the unappropriated balance of the interim authorization.

Reasoning that acceptance of the Government of Generalissimo Francisco Franco was up to the Marshall Plan nations which would share in the program, Senate and House managers of the legislation nullified House votes by which Spain was named as an eligible participant.

The action of the joint conference committee came on the heels

Continued on Page 19, Column 5

EDUCATION AID BILL PASSED BY SENATE

Cost of the First Year Is Put at $300,000,000 With Parochial Aid Left to States' Policy

By WILLIAM S. WHITE
Special to THE NEW YORK TIMES.

WASHINGTON, April 1—The Senate passed tonight, 58 to 22, the Taft Aid-to-Education Bill authorizing Federal grants intended to make certain that no state should spend less than $50 per pupil per year in any of its schools.

It was left to the states individually to determine, by way of their own constitutions, laws and policies, whether any of this Federal help could be extended, even indirectly, to private and parochial schools.

A similar measure lies inert in the House Labor Committee.

The estimated cost of the program to the Federal Government for the first year of its operation would be $300,000,000. Aid would be given primarily on the basis of need, so that the rich states would receive very little and the poor states a great deal.

The minimum received from the Government per school child would be $5 a year, as specified in an amendment by Senator Irving M. Ives, Republican, of New York. The maximum would go to $25 a year, or perhaps more.

New York, the wealthiest and most populous state, would have an allotment of about $12,010,000

Continued on Page 2, Column 4

CITY WELFARE HEAD DEMANDS LOYALTY

Hilliard, First Day in Office, Warns Communists Anyone Who 'Gets in Way' Will Go

On his first day in office as the city's new Welfare Commissioner, Raymond M. Hilliard served notice yesterday on Communists in his department that he would not tolerate disloyalty or interference from them.

"Communism is contrary to everything I believe in personally," he told reporters at his offices, 902 Broadway. "As far as the department is concerned, I am going to look for loyalty from the employes and devotion to its principles. I will insist on it. Any swerving from that loyalty to other causes—if such causes deflect from the discharge of duties—will have to be dealt with."

The 40-year-old former executive secretary of the Illinois Public Aid Commission, who was called to his new job by Mayor O'Dwyer after a state inquiry into the administration of the department, added:

"I'm not worried too much about Communists. If they get in the way, they better get out of the way. If their affiliation with other causes conflicts with their duties here, the sooner they are former employes of this administration, the better."

Mr. Hilliard, who will administer a department that expects to get

Continued on Page 18, Column 5

Red Row Stirred in Melish's Church By Son's Outside Leftist Activities

The "outside activities" of the Rev. William Howard Melish, associate rector of Holy Trinity Episcopal Church, Clinton and Montague Streets, Brooklyn, have been condemned by the church's lay governing body in a letter sent to the parishioners March 15 last, it was disclosed yesterday.

Specific objection was voiced to Mr. Melish's chairmanship of the National Council of American-Soviet Friendship and his sponsorship or active support of organizations with similar leanings. In a unanimous expression of opinion the two wardens and nine vestrymen characterized these activities as being "most detrimental to the interests of Holy Trinity Church."

Disclosure of the letter and the revolt within the church was made by Mrs. Bruce Bromley of 104 Willow Street, Brooklyn, a member of the Municipal Civil Service Commission and active in the affairs of the Brooklyn Heights church for thirty-eight years.

Mrs. Bromley said that Mr. Melish and his father, the Rev. Dr. John Howard Melish, rector of Holy Trinity for forty-four years, had walked out of a meeting of the vestry on Jan. 19 last. The vestry, denied access to membership records, obtained through other means the names and addresses of 381 members of the congregation to whom they later addressed their letter, she said. It asked for an expression of opinion on the part of the parishioners with a view to determining a future course of action.

In the letter the vestry said that "a considerable number of active members of the church have stated strong objections to these activities (the activities condemned by the vestry); some families have already withdrawn from the church; others have expressed their intention of doing so; and it is the belief of the vestry that the situation threatens the continued successful progress of the church."

Mrs. Bromley said she has already written her own reply to the vestrymen's letter. In this she said that she was tired of hearing about

Continued on Page 18, Column 7

Marshall Urges Latins to Put Need of Our Help After ERP

Secretary Pledges Greater, but Limited, Aid While Europe Is in Crisis—Wins Ovation by Recalling Two 'Bolivars'

By BERTRAM D. HULEN
Special to THE NEW YORK TIMES.

BOGOTA, Colombia, April 1—Secretary of State Marshall won prolonged applause today from the ninth Inter-American Conference here when he made an extemporaneous personal appeal to the Latin republics. He asked those nations to recognize the heavy burdens that the United States, because of the clouded world situation, had been compelled to assume.

The Secretary made his personal plea after he had delivered his formal address. The conferees had listened attentively, but without much demonstration.

After his main talk, he looked up from the manuscript he had finished reading, placed his hands on either side of his stand, and became changed in manner.

"My friends," he said. The Secretary spoke easily and informally for five minutes, asking for a greater awareness of the position confronting the United States, and, indirectly, the position faced by all the Western Hemisphere.

A burst of applause followed his plea. "How wonderful!" many in his audience exclaimed.

At a dramatic moment, when emphasizing what the United States armed contribution to security had meant in the war, he turned and pointed to a large mural painting of Simón Bolívar behind the rostrum. It depicts Bolivar, the Liberator, with his associates at the Congress of 1821, which wrote the Constitution for Great Colombia [New Granada and Venezuela]. He recalled to him directly, he said, the capture of

Continued on Page 12, Column 2

Secretary Marshall's addresses are on Page 12.

RISE IN CITY BUDGET PUT AT $105,029,625; 3,864 JOBS ADDED

$1,137,306,741 Total Is New High—Use Tax for Autos Planned—5-Cent Fare Kept

The text of the city budget is on Pages 16, 17, 18.

By PAUL CROWELL

An executive budget of $1,137,306,741 for the fiscal year beginning July 1 was submitted to the Board of Estimate yesterday by Acting Mayor Vincent R. Impellitteri as agent for Mayor O'Dwyer. It was the largest in the city's history, exceeding by $105,029,625 the record 1947-48 budget as modified to March 15.

Prepared on the assumption that the 5-cent fare would be retained on the municipal transit lines, the new budget contemplates enactment of local laws imposing a use tax on automobiles and doubling the existing taxes on gross re-

Continued on Page 18, Column 2

3 BILLION TO REARM ASKED BY TRUMAN; TAX CUT VETO SET

President Writes Martin of the Defense Need—Tax Message and Overriding Due Today

By JOHN D. MORRIS
Special to THE NEW YORK TIMES.

WASHINGTON, April 1—President Truman made it known today that he would veto the Republican tax-reduction bill tomorrow. He coupled the disclosure with formal notification to Speaker Joseph W. Martin Jr. that a minimum of $3,000,000,000 in new rearmament outlays would be required in the next fiscal year to insure peace.

With both houses set to override the tax veto within hours of its receipt, Mr. Truman sent a letter to the Speaker of the House outlining the $3,000,000,000 defense program and in addition asking authority to make long-term contracts for procurement of $375,000,000 of strategic and critical materials.

The President revealed moreover

Continued on Page 19, Column 3

World News Summarized

FRIDAY, APRIL 2, 1948

In defiance of Russian moves to halt United States, British and French trains and automobile transportation to and from Berlin, the United States Army began to transport food into the German capital by air yesterday to frustrate the apparent Russian aim of forcing the Western Powers out of the city. Soviet troops who had set up a traffic control station in the British sector of Berlin withdrew after they had been almost surrounded by 400 British troops. [1:8; map P. 4.]

United States officials in Washington declared the Russians were legally and morally bound to allow United States trains into Berlin, although available legal documents covering the situation were subject to contradictory definitions. [1:6-7.] In London, the British Foreign Office was angered by the Russian action, but baffled on how to meet it. [1:7.]

The Palestine problem will be considered anew by a special session of the United Nations General Assembly starting April 16. The Security Council, by a vote of 9 to 0, approved a United States resolution to call the Assembly together. The Soviet Union and the Ukraine abstained from voting. The Council unanimously approved a resolution calling for a truce in Palestine and urging Jewish and Arab leaders to confer on measures to effect the truce. [1:1.]

The call for the special session raised the possibility that the regular session of the Assembly next September might be held here, instead of Paris, to save expenses. [9:2-3.]

Strife and bloodshed again marked the day's developments in Palestine. A Jewish food convoy from Tel Aviv tried to penetrate an Arab cordon on the road to Jerusalem, where the Jewish quarter faced an increasingly critical situation, but failed to get through. Nine Jews were killed and seventeen wounded in the battle. [11:1.]

Secretary of State Marshall told the twenty-one-nation Inter-American Conference in Bogota that while the United States was ready to increase its economic aid to Latin America it must continue to give top priority to Europe in view of the grave world situation. He appealed for a fuller understanding of the burden this nation has assumed in defense of world freedom. [1:4-5.]

The conference committee of Senate and House members, swiftly reconciling the differences between the programs for foreign aid approved by the two branches of Congress, eliminated Spain from the list of nations to receive aid despite two House votes favoring Madrid. [1:2-3.]

Several veterans' organizations, including the American Legion and the Veterans of Foreign Wars, supported President Truman's program for a temporary draft and universal military training. [1:6.]

President Truman notified Congress he would ask for at least $3,000,000,000 in new rearmament appropriations as he made known that he would veto the Republican-sponsored tax-reduction measure today. [1:5.]

The Taft bill to aid education was approved by the Senate, 58 to 22. The bill authorized the states to decide for themselves whether any of the Federal help, estimated to cost $300,000,000 in the first year of operation, should be extended to private and parochial schools. [1:2.]

Governor Dewey, opening his campaign to win Wisconsin's support in the Republican National Convention, said the Truman Administration's foreign and domestic policies were dominated by military men "who by instinct and training think only in terms of war." [1:6-7.]

The Board of Estimate received an executive budget for the fiscal year beginning July 1 that called for expenditures of $1,137,306,741, the largest in this city's history. [1:4.]

U. S. FLIES FOOD INTO BERLIN AS RUSSIANS BLOCK TRAFFIC; BRITISH FOIL SOVIET SALLY

Experts Say U. S. Has Right To Operate Trains to Berlin

Base Opinion on Four-Power Agreements—Vague Wording Causes Confusion on Course—Americans to Stay

By JAMES RESTON
Special to THE NEW YORK TIMES.

WASHINGTON, April 1—The United States has a legal basis for running its supply trains through the Soviet zone into Berlin, but, as usual, the Big Four documents covering the case are vague and open to various contradictory interpretations.

That's the unhappy tentative conclusion the legal experts here have reached after a quick survey of all the Allied documents available on the regulations governing the four-power occupation of the former German capital.

The United States case, according to officials at the State Department, is as follows:

(1) On Nov. 14, 1944, the European Advisory Commission, composed of representatives of the United States, the Soviet Union and Great Britain, agreed that an inter-Allied governing authority should be established in Berlin. This agreement did not say anything about the right of transport through the Soviet zone of Eastern Germany into the United States, British and French sectors of Berlin, but the official view here is that it assumed the right of passage.

(2) On June 5, 1945, the United States, the Soviet Union, Britain and France issued a declaration that included the general instrument of Germany's surrender, and the arrangements for administering that country under an Allied Control Council.

This agreement stated that "the administration of the 'greater Berlin' area will be directed by an inter-Allied governing authority, which will operate under the general authority of the Control Council * * *"

Again this document did not make specific provision for the Western powers to have free access into their sectors of Berlin. However, the official view here is

Continued on Page 5, Column 5

DRAFT, UMT BACKED BY LEGION AND VFW

Other Service Groups Join in Support at Senate Hearing—AVC Opposed—Labor Split

By C. P. TRUSSELL
Special to THE NEW YORK TIMES.

WASHINGTON, April 1—The country's two largest veterans' organizations—the American Legion and the Veterans of Foreign Wars of the United States—threw their strength today behind the proposed Universal Military Training and stop-gap peacetime draft.

In rapid succession other service groups joined them in support of the measures under hearing before the Senate Armed Services Committee. These were the Reserve Officers Association of the United States, the Blinded Veterans Association and the National Guard Association.

The American Veterans Committee (AVC) disagreed with the larger service groups. It opposed both UMT and the draft.

Organized labor, as represented by some of its largest unions, was indicated, so far as today's hearing was concerned, to be heavily if not solidly opposed to UMT.

The American Federation of Labor, through its president, William Green, spoke "reluctantly" for the draft to build the armed forces to a strength designed to back up American determination to halt Communist expansion.

The Brotherhood of Railroad

Continued on Page 3, Column 6

LONDON INDIGNANT OVER RUSSIAN BAN

Foreign Office in Dilemma Over Procedure to Break Blockade on Berlin

By HERBERT L. MATTHEWS
Special to THE NEW YORK TIMES.

LONDON, Arpil 1—British Foreign Office officials were indignant today about the developments in Berlin and prepared to be very firm, but as yet they do not know what to do about it.

The situation as seen from here is a real dilemma. On one hand there is no desire or intention on the part of the British to shoot their way in and out of Berlin. On the other hand Britain, like the United States, is determined to stay in Berlin.

Chief concern here centers on the inability to find any legal ground on which to attack the Russians. Experts in the German office of the Foreign Office have feverishly searched all documents available without being able to find any precise agreement about conditions under which the three Western powers would proceed from their zones to Berlin.

There is what one official called a "gentleman's agreement" and another "a tacit agreement" on the subject. But written agreements cover only the Four-Power occupation and control of Berlin.

No one doubts that the Soviet Union has violated the spirit of the Four-Power understanding but it is realized that such an ap-

Continued on Page 5, Column 2

Dewey Assails Use of Military Men In Foreign, Domestic Policy Making

By LEO EGAN
Special to THE NEW YORK TIMES.

MILWAUKEE, Wis., April 1—Gov. Thomas E. Dewey of New York attacked tonight the "domination" of American foreign and domestic policies by military men "who by instinct and training think only in terms of war."

The obvious targets of Mr. Dewey, who is making a personal bid for Wisconsin's twenty-seven delegates to the Republican National Convention, were Secretary of State George C. Marshall, former Army Chief of Staff, and other officials of the Truman Administration. His criticism of the military influence was broad enough, however, to include Gen. Douglas MacArthur within its terms.

The general is an avowed rival of Mr. Dewey for the Republican Presidential nomination and is credited by most local observers with a good chance of winning a majority of this state's convention delegates who will be chosen at Tuesday's primary. Harold E. Stassen, former Governor of Minnesota, also has a slate of convention delegates entered in the primary.

Mr. Dewey's speech, which was broadcast over a coast-to-coast radio network, was interrupted several times by outbursts of applause. A capacity audience of 1,600 was in the theatre where he spoke and another 500 listened over loudspeakers in the street.

Mr. Dewey described as "ominous" the news from Germany that Russian forces had cut off land traffic to the American sector of Berlin "in violation of an agreement."

"The purpose is obviously to make harder work for American occupation forces and to give a further demonstration of apparent American weakness," the Governor said. "The Soviet intention is to warn the people of Germany, of the Scandinavian countries and the rest of Europe and the world not to cooperate with the United

Continued on Page 3, Column 2

CLAY HALTS TRAINS

Gives Up Ground Links Temporarily—Soviet Increases Barriers

CANAL BARGES STOPPED

Britons Force the Russians Out of a Road Blockade Set Up in Their Sector

By The Associated Press

BERLIN, April 1—The United States began flying food into Berlin today to thwart a Soviet squeeze aimed at forcing its wartime Western Allies out of this former German capital.

[A Berlin dispatch to THE NEW YORK TIMES said that Soviet fighter planes had "buzzed" every United States military passenger craft flying in and out of Berlin but otherwise had not molested them.]

The Russians put swiftly into effect a calculated program of travel and transport restrictions to this isolated Allied outpost deep in the Soviet zone. The restrictions were:

(1) Halting of all military trains between Berlin and the Western zones, cutting off normal military supply channels.

(2) Stopping British barge traffic to the four-power capital.

(3) Instituting rigorous examinations of traffic on the Autobahn, only highway linking the city with the West.

(4) Turning back one rail coach occupied by civilians of several nationalities.

For several hours the Russians maintained a traffic-snarling inspection along the edges of their Berlin sector but later they removed the barriers.

Clay Cancels U. S. Train

But the air was free, and Gen. Lucius D. Clay, the United States commander, announced he would use it to supply the 8,575 United States military personnel and civilians in the city. He canceled military train service to Berlin which could not be pushed through the Soviet cordon without inviting a clash, and called on air power to win the political battle for Berlin.

[The British reported that 400 soldiers had forced the Russians to retire from a roadblock they had established illegally in the British sector by having set up counter blocks, another dispatch to THE NEW YORK TIMES said.]

At stake in the dispute was the question of prestige in the cold war between the East and the West. If the Russians succeeded in dislodging the Western Allies from the former German capital, their stock would rise, and the hopes of the supporters of the Western powers in all Germany and Europe would sag.

Tonight a United States official said United States planes had flown 15,000 pounds of food into Berlin in the first few hours after the Clay order.

The four-power agreement laying out air corridors over the Soviet zone to Berlin does not restrict the number of flights.

No Restrictions on Planes

The United States Air Force based in Wiesbaden will be able to fly in any number of planes with supplies, and the only apparent way the Russians can interfere is to attempt to force or shoot them down. It seemed apparent any such attempt would bring serious international incidents.

The Tempelhof Airdrome in Berlin is in the United States sector and the Russians could interfere with it only by sending armed forces across United States occupied territory in the city.

The British also announced two extra flights into Berlin as a temporary measure.

Dispatches from Hamburg said the tense situation had given Germans living along the 400 miles of frontier in the British zone a case of jitters.

The British verified reports that Russian border posts had been strengthened by the addition of ten or a dozen men at each place, presumably to bolster the guard against border crossers. Persons crossing from the Soviet zone said

Continued on Page 4, Column 5

Dr. Alfred C. Kinsey's *Sexual Behavior in the Human Male* created quite a stir. He interviewed over 5,000 American males in the process of compiling his data. His report was denounced by many religious groups as an insult.

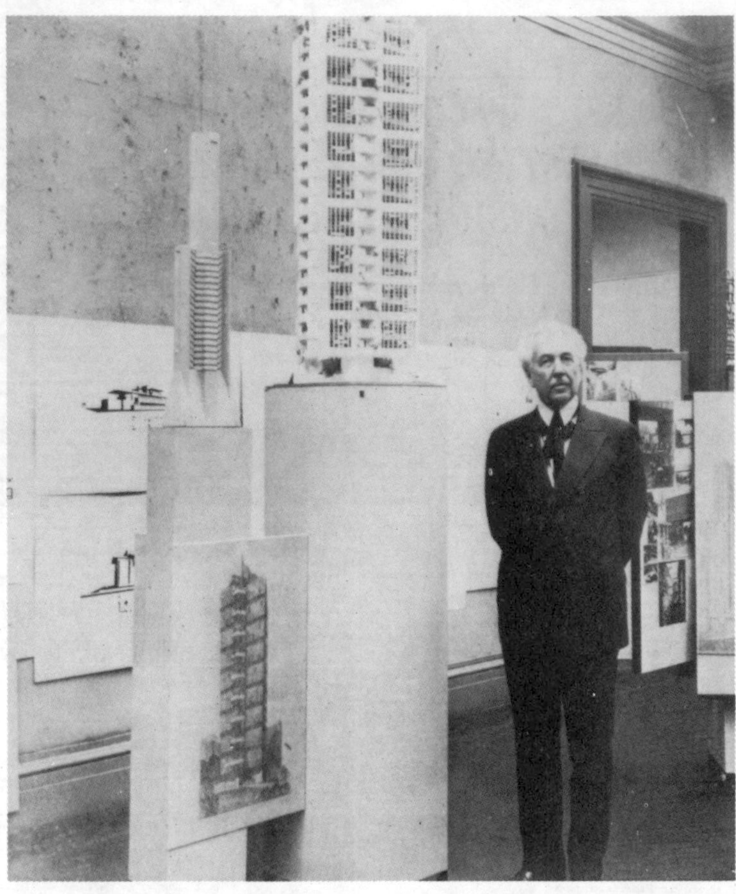

Architect Frank Lloyd Wright, shown with an early model of a glass and concrete building he designed, was awarded the American Institute of Architects Gold Medal.

Entertainer Dinah Shore made the Hit Parade with *Buttons and Bows.*

William Faulkner's *Intruder in the Dust* was published. He went on to win the Nobel Prize for Literature the next year.

"All the News That's Fit to Print"

The New York Times.

LATE CITY EDITION
Fair and warmer today and tomorrow.
Temperature Range Today—Max., 65; Min., 46
Temperature Yesterday—Max., 53; Min., 46
Full U. S. Weather Bureau Report, Page 31

Copyright, 1948, by The New York Times Company.

VOL. XCVII..No. 32,984. Entered as Second-Class Matter, Postoffice, New York, N. Y. NEW YORK, SATURDAY, MAY 15, 1948. Times Square, New York 18, N. Y. Telephone Lackawanna 4-1000 THREE CENTS IN NEW YORK CITY

ZIONISTS PROCLAIM NEW STATE OF ISRAEL; TRUMAN RECOGNIZES IT AND HOPES FOR PEACE; TEL AVIV IS BOMBED, EGYPT ORDERS INVASION

NAVY PUSHES PLAN FOR CONSTRUCTION OF MISSILE VESSELS

Sullivan Asks House Committee to Approve Halting Work on Battleship, Destroyer Types

WANTS 65,000-TON CARRIER

Floating 'Submarine Killers' Are Also Stressed in Plea for Diverting $300,000,000 Fund

By C. P. TRUSSELL
Special to The New York Times.

WASHINGTON, May 14—The Navy asked Congress today for authority to shift sharply its construction of fighting craft from battleship, cruiser and destroyer types to guided missile vessels, a 65,000-ton carrier able to base, far at sea, planes with an operating radius of 1,700 miles, better submarines and floating "enemy submarine killers."

Such new ships, John L. Sullivan, Secretary of the Navy, told the House Armed Services Committee, must have a higher priority "because of the more immediate need for them in the event of an emergency." The immediate reaction of the committee appeared to favor prompt action.

For such a shift in construction, Secretary Sullivan brought out, the Navy wanted to halt the building of thirteen naval vessels, including the battleship Kentucky, the large cruiser Hawaii, seven destroyers, two destroyer escorts and two submarines. To date about $197,000,000 has been spent on them.

However, this money was not to be abandoned, Mr. Sullivan emphasized. These craft could be converted now to the new program, he explained, or be put aside for a fitting-out later as new weapons were developed.

New Aims for $300,000,000 Fund

What the Navy wanted, Secretary Sullivan asserted, was Congressional permission to divert some $300,000,000 remaining in the present ship construction account to these purposes:

Starting the 65,000-ton aircraft carrier (the biggest ones now are the two of the Midway class, at 45,000 tons), which might cost around $124,000,000.

Building, for reproduction later, of a "submarine killer." (Hearings on the defense program have indicated that Russia has made great progress in the submarine field.) A "killer" machine, it is indicated, is developing in new work on the cruiser type of seacraft.

The construction of four submarines of types advanced beyond those now building.

In addition, there was under plan a conversion in an unidentified way of a carrier and two submarines.

Secretary Sullivan told the committee that the Kentucky and the Hawaii would not have to stand by for the development of new weapons. It is planned, he disclosed, that they be converted into guided missile ships. Apparently to allay fears in Congress that larger aircraft carriers make easier targets for enemy bombers, Mr. Sullivan drew upon experience in the second World War and the results of atom-bomb tests at Bikini.

Speed Held Bomb Defense

"The experiments at Bikini," Mr. Sullivan said, "have proved that a fast-moving fleet is an unprofitable target for an atomic bomb."

Members of the committee interpreted this as a Navy Department conclusion that even though a potential enemy might acquire the atomic bomb, the revised construction program proposed today promised a maximum of safety. Mr. Sullivan recalled that the Navy lost three large and two light carriers in the Pacific, but none was sunk by aircraft landbased. He indicated that mobility of a fleet, equipped to latest model, would discourage the spending of atomic bombs, even if an enemy had some.

Today, the Senate Republican

Continued on Page 7, Column 4

Heaviest Trading in 8 Years Marks Stock Market Spurt

3,840,000 Shares Change Hands as Wave of Bullish Enthusiasm Increases Securities 1 to 7 Points

The hectic days of the Nineteen Twenties were re-enacted yesterday on the floor of the New York Stock Exchange when the most turbulent session in recent years produced increases of 1 to 7 points in the share list. Accompanied by a burst of bullish enthusiasm not witnessed in almost a decade, the deluge of buying orders so taxed the facilities of the Exchange that the reporting ticker tape lagged behind floor transactions by five minutes.

The cracking of the 1947 high level at the approach of mid-day served as the signal for a buying rush. Public participation suddenly enlarged and buying orders pressed floor traders to the utmost. This condition existed for forty-five minutes in the final hour when 1,350,000 shares were traded.

Accompanied by the broadest market on record with a total of 1,151 issues dealt in, volume on the Stock Exchange spiraled to 3,840,000 shares, the largest since May 21, 1940, in contrast to the Thursday turnover of 2,030,000 shares.

Brokers termed it the "wildest" bull market in twenty years on the premise that at no time in the interval had the industrials and rails advanced with such a unity of force.

While the ground had been well laid for a movement of such scope earlier this week, it was the piercing of the 1947 resistance point that confirmed the presence of a bull market to those who act by the charts, or averages. Early in the day, telegrams were sent by several advisory services to their clients urging the purchase of securities. The response to this advice showed primarily in the late

Continued on Page 23, Column 4

Truman Sees His Election; Calls GOP 'Obstructionist'

By ANTHONY LEVIERO
Special to The New York Times.

WASHINGTON, May 14—President Truman asserted tonight that there would be a Democrat in the White House during the next four years and that he would be the man. He made the statement to a cheering audience of 1,000 young Democrats at their meeting here.

The President's speech was a fighting one in the new Truman manner. He spoke extemporaneously, resorting to whimsy and irony and using forceful gestures of his arms to underscore his points.

Mr. Truman accused the Republican party of stealing Democratic platform planks. "You know," he said, "it has been their habit since 1936 of taking a few planks out of the old Democratic platforms and building a platform and then saying, 'Me, too.'"

[The text of President Truman's speech is on Page 7.]

"What have the Republicans done in the last fifteen and a half years?" Mr. Truman asked, then said:

"They have been obstructionists. They have spent most of their time while I was in the Senate—and I was there for ten years—in obstructing progressive legislation that was for the welfare of the common man, and throwing bricks and mud at the greatest President that ever sat in the White House."

Mr. Truman was interrupted by applause at this obvious allusion to President Roosevelt.

"That has been their record," he continued, "and they haven't changed a bit. They were against Social Security. They were against TVA. They were against wages

Continued on Page 7, Column 2

MINNESOTA'S GUARD OUT IN MEAT STRIKE

Governor Acts After 200 Raid Cudahy Newport Plant, Attack 60 Workers and Abduct 25

Special to The New York Times.

ST. PAUL, Minn., May 14—National Guard troops were ordered to South St. Paul and Newport, towns on opposite banks of the Mississippi River near here, by Governor Luther Youngdahl today following violent disorders at strike-bound packing plants in the area and the statement of the local sheriffs that their forces could not maintain law and order.

The Governor did not proclaim martial law but said the troops would take their orders from the civil authorities.

The Governor's action followed a serious outbreak at the Cudahy packing plant in Newport shortly before last midnight in which a group of about 200 men raided the plant with clubs, knives and hammers. In South St. Paul on Thursday strikers forced back police who tried to open a way through picket lines at the Swift & Co. plant in

Continued on Page 16, Column 3

Princess Elizabeth, in Paris Talk, Asks Common Effort of 2 Nations

By LANSING WARREN
Special to The New York Times.

PARIS, May 14—Speaking in faultless French with just the touch of a British accent to delight French ears, Princess Elizabeth today asked France and Britain to make a common effort to lead Europe to moral and intellectual as well as economic reconstruction.

Her well-worded and discerning speech was cheered, but she went straight to the hearts of the Parisian throng when, with disarming frankness, she avowed her joy that her first foreign trip since her marriage had brought her here to Paris.

"For a long time," she said, "I have wanted to come to France. More fortunate than I, my husband already knew your admirable capital and he is all the happier to return. This trip is all the more important and agreeable for the warmth of your welcome which has touched us both."

From the time they stepped down from the train at the Gare du Nord early today, Princess Elizabeth and Prince Philip, Duke of Edinburgh, were the center of admiring attention from the throngs that lined the streets and from all the French officials who received them throughout the day.

President Vincent Auriol voiced the general feeling when in a statement issued tonight he said:

"I have been personally struck by her grace, her charm, her modesty and her nobility. I feel sure that the sentiments that she has expressed went straight to the hearts of all the French."

Elizabeth's address, broadcast to the French nation, was delivered from the top of the monumental entry to the Galliera Museum, where she came to open the British Government's exhibition of relics and souvenirs of famous Brit-

Continued on Page 6, Column 3

AIR ATTACK OPENS

Planes Cause Fires at Port—Defense Fliers Go Into Action

BORDER IS BREACHED

Cairo Vanguard Takes Colony—Trans-Jordan Reports a Movement

By The Associated Press.

TEL AVIV, Palestine, Saturday, May 15—Air raiders bombed this all-Jewish city at about dawn today.

First reports said there were "some casualties' 'near the power and light station.

[Cairo reported that Egyptian armed forces had been ordered to enter Palestine. Arab armies moved from Trans-Jordan at 12:01 A. M. Saturday to "liberate the Holy Land from Zionism," said a Trans-Jordan communiqué reported by The United Press from Amman.]

Tel Aviv was under complete blackout all night but no sirens were sounded during the raid. Civil guards were alerted and fifteen to twenty ships in the port area moved out to sea.

The planes swooped over Tel Aviv little more than twelve hours after Jewish leaders proclaimed the existence of a new Hebrew state of Israel.

Some bombs fell in the vicinity of the power station along the Yarkum River near Tel Aviv.

Persons at the scene said there was one hit on or near the power station, causing "some casualties."

TEL AVIV, Saturday, May 15 (UP) — Some ten bombs were dropped on Tel Aviv by two aircraft described as bombers and accompanied by two small fighters. One Jew was killed and three were hospitalized. Jewish Army aircraft took to the skies a few minutes after the enemy planes whizzed over rooftops at an estimated altitude of 300 feet.

Several fires could be seen north

Continued on Page 2, Column 3

U. S. MOVES QUICKLY

President Acknowledges de Facto Authority of Israel Immediately

TRUCE AIM STRESSED

Soviet Gesture to New Nation Anticipated—Others Due to Act

By BERTRAM D. HULEN
Special to The New York Times.

WASHINGTON, May 14—President Truman announced early tonight recognition by the United States of the new Jewish State of Israel. The President acted instantly upon being informed that the new nation had been proclaimed.

"This Government," he announced, "has been informed that a Jewish state has been proclaimed in Palestine and recognition has been requested by the provisional government thereof.

"The United States recognizes the provisional government as the de facto authority of the new State of Israel."

These two paragraphs constituted the text of the President's statement.

Coupled with the announcement was an expression of hope for peace in Palestine. This was made known through a separate White House statement issued by Charles G. Ross, Presidential press secretary.

"The desire of the United States to obtain a truce in Palestine," this said, "will in no way be lessened by the proclamation of a Jewish state.

"We hope that the new Jewish state will join with the Security Council Truce Commission in redoubled efforts to bring an end to the fighting—which has been throughout the United Nations' consideration of Palestine a principal objective of this Government."

[Pending stabilization of the Palestine situation and indications that the State of Israel

Continued on Page 3, Column 2

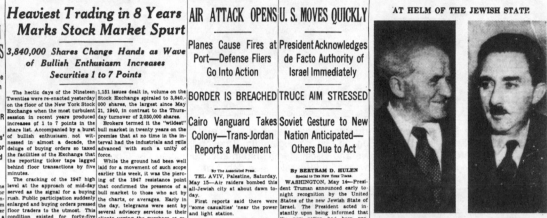

AT HELM OF THE JEWISH STATE

David Ben-Gurion
Premier

Moshe Shertok
Foreign Minister

The New York Times

U. N. Votes for a Mediator; Special Assembly Is Ended

By THOMAS J. HAMILTON

After hearing both the Soviet Union and the Arab delegates denounce the United States for its sudden recognition of the new Jewish state in Palestine, the United Nations General Assembly decided last night to send a Mediator to the Holy Land to do what he could to arrange a truce and carry on public services.

The vote was 31 to 7, with sixteen abstentions and four delegates absent, and the General Assembly, which was called into special session at Flushing Meadow on April 16 at the request of the United States, adjourned for good at 8:32 P. M.

The failure of the General Assembly either to repeal the partition resolution of last November or to provide military force to keep the peace means that the fate of Palestine will be decided by the impending war between Jews and Arabs, not by any United Nations action.

The mediation resolution conforms substantially with a United States proposal announced last Wednesday, after it had become obvious that the General Assembly would not accept the original United States plan for a temporary trusteeship.

However, the General Assembly refused to accept a United States plan for a temporary trusteeship over Jerusalem, which was rejected earlier in the evening by a vote of 20 to 15, less than the necessary two-thirds majority.

Two other proposals regarding Jerusalem were rejected, but presumably the provisions of the partition resolution on Jerusalem, which was to have been established as an international enclave under the administration of the Trusteeship Council, still stand.

In addition, the Assembly de-

Continued on Page 4, Column 4

CUNNINGHAM GOES AS MANDATE ENDS

British Commissioner Boards Cruiser Off Haifa—Jews Take Down Union Jack

By The Associated Press.

HAIFA, Palestine, Saturday, May 15—Britain ended her mandate over the Holy Land last midnight. Lieut. Gen. Sir Alan Cunningham, the last British High Commissioner, sailed from Haifa port, finishing British mandate guidance.

Sir Alan's departure from Palestine's richest port caused little excitement among the Jews, who control most of the city.

The British fired a few rockets and searchlights spotlighted the cruiser as it steamed from the harbor.

Wearing the uniform of a British Army general, Sir Alan walked down a few steps of dock into a launch that took him to the cruiser Euryalus.

Upon getting into the launch, he turned and looked soberly up across the docks. There stood an honor guard of the King's Company of Grenadier Guards and Royal Marine commandos

The launch pulled away amid the

Continued on Page 2, Column 7

THE JEWS REJOICE

Some Weep as Quest for Statehood Ends—White Paper Dies

HELP OF U. N. ASKED

New Regime Holds Out Hand to Arabs—U. S. Gesture Acclaimed

Text of declaration setting up new Jewish state, Page 2.

By GENE CURRIVAN
Special to The New York Times.

TEL AVIV, Palestine, Saturday, May 15—The Jewish state, the world's newest sovereignty, to be known as the State of Israel, came into being in Palestine at midnight upon termination of the British mandate.

Recognition of the state by the United States, which had opposed its establishment at this time, came as a complete surprise to the people, who were tense and ready for the threatened invasion by Arab forces and appealed for help by the United Nations.

In one of the most hopeful periods of their troubled history the Jewish people here gave a sigh of relief and took a new hold on life when they learned that the greatest national power had accepted them into the international fraternity.

Ceremony Simple and Solemn

The declaration of the new state by David Ben-Gurion, chairman of the National Council and the first Premier of reborn Israel, was delivered during a simple and solemn ceremony at 4 P. M., and new life was instilled into his people, but from without there was the rumbling of guns, a flashback to other declarations of independence that had not been easily achieved.

The first action of the new Government was to revoke the Palestine White Paper of 1939, which restricted Jewish immigration and land purchase.

In the proclamation of the new state the Government appealed to the United Nations "to assist the Jewish people in the building of its state and to admit Israel into the family of nations."

The proclamation added:

"We offer peace and amity to all neighboring states and their peoples, and invite them to cooperate with the independent Jewish nation for the common good of all. The State of Israel is ready to contribute its full share to the peaceful progress and reconstitution of the Middle East."

World Jews Asked to Aid

The statement appealed to Jews throughout the world to assist in the task of immigration and development and in the "struggle for the fulfillment of the dream of generations — the redemption of Israel."

Plans for the ceremony had been laid with great secrecy. None but the hundred or more invited guests and journalists was aware of the meeting until it started, and even the guests learned of the site only ten minutes before. It was held in the Tel Aviv Museum of Art, a white, modern-design two-story building. Above it flew the Star of David, which is the state's flag, and below, on the sidewalk, was a guard of honor of the Haganah, the army of the Jewish Agency for Palestine.

As photographers' bulbs flashed and movie cameras ground out reels of the scene, great crowds gathered and cheered the Ministers and other members of the Government as they entered the building. The security arrangements were perfect. Sten guns were brandished in every direction and even the roofs bristled with them.

The setting for the reading of the proclamation was a dropped gallery whose hall held paintings by prominent Jewish artists. Many of them depicted the sufferings and joys of the people of the Diaspora, the dispersal of the Jews.

The thirteen Ministers of the

Continued on Page 2, Column 6

World News Summarized

SATURDAY, MAY 15, 1948

Several hours after the state of Israel, the first Hebrew nation in 2,000 years, had been proclaimed in a Zionist declaration of independence in Tel Aviv, [1:8.]. President Truman announced that the United States recognized the "provisional government" of Israel as "the de facto authority of the new state." A second White House statement expressed the hope that the new regime would cooperate with United Nations efforts to bring about peace in Palestine. [1:5.] The British High Commissioner departed from Palestine and boarded a cruiser at Haifa as Britain's rule over the Holy Land formally ended. [1:7.]

The special session of the United Nations General Assembly ended last night after it had agreed to send a mediator to Palestine to try to arrange a truce. [1:6-7.] The trusteeship plan for Jerusalem sponsored by the United States was rejected by the Assembly, with the Arab states and the Soviet opposed to the measure. [1:6-7.]

Tel Aviv was bombed at dawn. Egypt ordered her troops to invade Palestine. Trans-Jordan reported her army on the move also. [1:4.] Haganah claimed that its forces captured Acre in the north. [2:8.]

In Moscow the newspaper Pravda, in the first editorial comment on the recent exchange between Washington and Moscow, accused the United States of double-dealing. [4:8.]

Paris crowds gave an enthusiastic welcome to Princess Elizabeth and the Duke of Edinburgh when they arrived for a visit. [1:2-3.]

Congress received a request from the Navy for authority to shift the emphasis in its construction of fighting craft to guided-missile vessels. [1:1.]

President Truman predicted that he would be re-elected next November. [1:2-3.]

Minnesota National Guard troops were rushed to South St. Paul and Newport after 200 persons had raided the Cudahy meat packing plant at Newport, where a strike is in progress, attacking about sixty workers and abducting twenty-five of them. [1:2.]

The New York Stock Exchange enjoyed one of its biggest days in recent years as an avalanche of buying orders sent stocks up from 1 to 7 points. Trading reached a total of 3,840,000 shares, the largest since May 21, 1940. [1:2-3.]

Winston Churchill's War Memoirs

See Page 17 for today's installment, in which Mr. Churchill describes the invasion of Norway and the clash of the British and German fleets.

U. N. Bars Jerusalem Trusteeship; Vote Follows Mandate Deadline

By MALLORY BROWNE

The United Nations General Assembly rejected yesterday the United States plan for a temporary trusteeship regime in Jerusalem.

Solidly opposed by the Arab States and the Russian bloc, the plan to set up a United Nations Commissioner authorized to protect the Holy City and its holy places failed to obtain the necessary two-thirds majority at the closing session at Flushing Meadow.

The vote, which came just after the bombshell of the United States recognition of the new Jewish State had burst in the Assembly, was 20 in favor, 15 against and 19 abstentions. The balance was turned by the hostility of Britain and most of the Dominions.

The United States fought hard all day, first in the Political and Security Committee of the Assembly, sitting at Lake Success, and then in the evening session of the Assembly, to get the trusteeship plan adopted before the end of the mandate at 6:01 P. M., New York time.

An Arab filibuster, aided by the Soviet bloc, defeated this effort. It was well past the zero hour when a roll-call vote showed that the Assembly preferred to leave Harold Evans, newly appointed Jerusalem municipal Commissioner, in sole charge of the Holy City and its treasures.

As one Arab after another filed up to the tribune and took up the maximum five-minute period allowed in repeating the arguments against a trusteeship plan, 6:01 o'clock went by.

At once Awni Khalidy of Iraq, who had led the Arab fight against the trusteeship plan, rushed up to the tribune and exultantly proclaimed that the time had passed; that the mandate was at an end, and that, since, as Francis B. Sayre of the United States had said, the measure must

Continued on Page 3, Column 5

The premiere telecast of Ed Sullivan's *Toast of the Town* featured a panorama of stars and personalities from all fields. Included in the show were singing fireman John Kokoman; pianist Eugene List; comedian Jim Kirkwood; Jerry Lewis and Dean Martin; dancer Kathryn Lee; fight referee Ruby Goldstein; Richard Rodgers and Oscar Hammerstein 2nd; comedian Lee Goodman; and the original "Toastettes," the dancing girls flanking the cast. The show marked the television debut of the Lewis-Martin duo.

Bob Hope and Bing Crosby walked, danced, sang and laughed their way into the hearts of millions of fans all around the world.

The remarkable Milton Berle became the first big TV star with his weekly show. "Uncle Miltie" is shown here in a typically outrageous costume.

"All the News That's Fit to Print"

The New York Times.

LATE CITY EDITION
Cloudy, warm with evening showers today. Fair, cooler tomorrow.
Temperature Range Today—Max.,85; Min.,68
Temperature Yesterday—Max.,89; Min.,60
Full U. S. Weather Bureau Report, Page 47

VOL. XCVII..No. 33,025. Entered as Second-Class Matter, Postoffice, New York, N. Y. NEW YORK, FRIDAY, JUNE 25, 1948. Times Square, New York 18, N. Y. Telephone LAckawanna 4-1000 THREE CENTS in NEW YORK CITY

DEWEY UNANIMOUS REPUBLICAN CHOICE FOR PRESIDENT ON THE THIRD BALLOT; RUNNING MATE WILL BE NAMED TODAY

CLAY DECLARES U. S. WON'T QUIT BERLIN SHORT OF WARFARE

But Military Sources Imply West May Go if Germans Suffer Under Soviet Curb

TENSION IN CITY MOUNTS

British Stop Ruhr Shipments to Russians as Latter Cut Electricity and Milk Supply

By JACK RAYMOND
Special to THE NEW YORK TIMES

HEIDELBERG, Germany, June 24—In a serious appraisal of the Berlin situation and the attendant policy in Germany, Gen. Lucius D. Clay, United States Military Governor, concluded today that the Russians were exerting their "final pressure to drive us out of Berlin."

He added, however, that the Western Allies would consider nothing short of war as a reason for withdrawal, and that the Russian tactics would not delay the program to create a German government in the Western zones.

There was an impression here, however, as General Clay met with United States military commanders and Military Government officials in a regularly scheduled meeting, that the Western Allies would consider leaving the former German capital if the suffering of the populace became too great.

Supply By Air Impossible

Should the Russians maintain transport restriction, the city, which requires 2,000 tons of supplies daily, could not be fed by air. In that case a Western Allies' decision to leave could be explained as a diplomatic sacrifice in the interests of Germans.

[The Soviet Military Administration increased its pressure against the Western sectors Thursday, Berlin dispatches reported. It cut off electricity from the United States sector, announced that further power cuts would be made and stopped the delivery of fresh milk from the Soviet zone into the United States area.

[The British, in return, halted the shipment of the monthly allotment of coal and steel from the Ruhr to the Soviet zone over railway lines other than the Soviet-blocked Helmstedt-Berlin route. Infantry and armored cars moved through the United States and British sectors, causing considerable alarm among Western Berliners.]

In an interview at newly established European Command headquarters General Clay declared: "They can't drive us out by any action short of war as far as we are concerned."

Says Germans Are Sufferers

The real sufferers in the former capital, he emphasized, are the Germans. The Russian acts against the Western Allies hurt not only the Germans in the Western sectors but those of the Soviet sector as well, he added. "It would be hard for the Russians to maintain the squeeze without hurting their sector unless they built an iron gate through the city," he said.

"The Germans of Berlin apparently are prepared to take considerable suffering," the general declared.

General Clay declared that the families of United States personnel would be ordered out of the city "only if war were around the corner."

Another impression gained here is that the United States Military Government feels the Berlin situation has long since passed into the governmental level. There appears to be no way to retaliate against the Russians in Germany without making a possibly regrettable error.

Yet, it is felt that the Republican convention appears to have engrossed Washington. In contrast with the April crisis, military sources said, Washington authorities who then seemed "over-

Continued on Page 18, Column 4

Draft Bill Signed by Truman; Youths Register in Six Weeks

President Acts Without Comment—Rush Into Guard Units for Exemption Is Halted —Big Defense Funds Also Approved

By ANTHONY LEVIERO
Special to THE NEW YORK TIMES.

WASHINGTON, June 24—The draft act requiring military service of men from 19 through 25 years of age became law at 5:40 P. M. today when President Truman signed the measure without comment.

Registration of youths was expected to begin within six weeks, but under the law no one could be drafted until ninety days from today.

In the first year 200,000 to 225,000 men would be called. A provision of the law also permitted 161,000 youths of 18 to volunteer for one year in any of the regular services.

The signing of the bill cut off an unparalleled recruiting stimulus which had more than filled the post-war strength of the National Guard and swelled the ranks of other reserve components. Under the terms of the measure, youths who joined the civilian components were exempt from the draft.

President Truman signed the measure, cornerstone of the Administration rearmament program, within twenty-four hours after it had reached him, squelching reports that he would delay as long as possible in order to fill the ranks of the reserve units.

Members of the National Guard and other part-time units need drill only once a week and go to camp for only about two weeks in a year for three years, whereas drafted men must serve full time for twenty-one months.

The draft bill was the second major measure of the 263 passed in the closing days of the Congressional session to reach the President's desk. Earlier in the day he signed a bill appropriating $3,749,-059,250 for the Navy and Marine Corps in fiscal 1949.

The Navy funds included construction of a mammoth carrier of

Continued on Page 7, Column 2

Louis Fight Off to Tonight When Rain Drenches City

By JAMES P. DAWSON

A near-cloudburst which deluged the Yankee Stadium commencing at 7:40 o'clock last night forced a second postponement of the scheduled fifteen-round heavyweight championship bout between Joe Louis, the titleholder, and Jersey Joe Walcott, Camden, N. J., challenger. The bout was postponed until tonight.

In the meantime, Louis has returned to his training quarters at Pompton Lakes, N. J. Walcott will spend the time at the Capitol Hotel, where he has been staying since weighing in at Madison Square Garden on Wednesday, the original date of the battle.

If there's more rain today—and the forecast is for late-afternoon or evening thunder showers—the contest will be postponed to tomorrow night. Monday night also may be available if inclement weather continues.

Neither champion nor challenger plans any extra training work of a strenuous nature. Louis' manager, Marshall Miles, said the titleholder would engage in a brief road workout this morning. Walcott's trainer, Dan Florio, satisfied that the challenger will be unaffected by the double postponement, said Walcott would probably confine his exercise to a walk in Central Park this morning.

Louis and Walcott were at the Stadium prepared to don ring togs when the postponement announcement was made at 8:15. It had been held off until the last minute while officials of the Twentieth

Continued on Page 29, Column 1

BEN-GURION UPHELD BY ISRAELI COUNCIL

2 Rejoin Cabinet on Amnesty Pledge — Unified Army Is Mapped, 400 'Rebels' Held

By GENE CURRIVAN
Special to THE NEW YORK TIMES

TEL AVIV, Israel, June 24—The Provisional Government of Israel passed its first important political crisis tonight when it received a vote of confidence from the State Council. The possibility that dissident groups might overthrow the Government as an aftermath of Tuesday's rebellion was thus averted.

[Heavy explosions were heard Thursday night and early Friday south of Tel Aviv, The Associated Press said. Reports circulated in Tel Aviv that the Israeli Army was attacking Irgun Zvai Leumi strongholds in the vicinity of Abu Kebir.]

The vote was 24 against 7, with 5 abstaining.

At the same time the two Cab-

Continued on Page 12, Column 3

Soviet Bloc Urges 4-Power Accord On German Rule, Occupation End

Special to THE NEW YORK TIMES.

LONDON, June 24—In a five-point program for the unification of Germany issued tonight through the Moscow radio, the eight Eastern European Foreign Ministers proposed the formulation of a German peace treaty providing for the withdrawal of occupation troops within one year of signature.

The points that the Moscow radio said the conference had agreed upon in the Warsaw parley presided over by Soviet Foreign Minister Molotov were:

(1) That Great Britain, the United States, France and the Soviet Union implement agreements for the completion of Germany's demilitarization.

(2) That the Ruhr's heavy industry be placed under four-power control for a definite period.

(3) That a provisional government for all Germany be established, consisting of representatives of the democratic parties and organizations of Germany, with the objective of creating guarantees against a repetition of German aggression.

(4) That a peace treaty be concluded in accordance with the Potsdam decisions and that occupation forces be withdrawn.

(5) That arrangements be made for Germany to fulfill her reparations obligations to the countries that suffered from German aggression.

The Warsaw conference was called to consider the six-power Western proposals for the setting up of a provisional government in Western Germany and internationalization of the Ruhr.

The broadcast, which was received here by the Soviet monitor, said that the proposals had been adopted today at the conference of the Foreign Ministers of the Soviet Union, Albania, Bulgaria, Czechoslovakia, Yugoslavia, Poland, Rumania and Hungary.

It said the Ministers considered "the solution of the following

Continued on Page 16, Column 1

COAL OWNERS YIELD ON PAY AND RELIEF TO PREVENT STRIKE

$1-a-Day More in Wages With Relief Fund of 100 Million a Year Won in Lewis Victory

AGREEMENT BEING DRAWN

'Onerous' Clauses Retained by Union—Steel Company Plants Go Along 'Reluctantly'

By LOUIS STARK
Special to THE NEW YORK TIMES.

WASHINGTON, June 24—John L. Lewis and the United Mine Workers of America today won a smashing victory in forcing bituminous coal operators to agree on a wage increase of $1 a day for 400,000 mine workers and a doubling of their payments into the welfare fund.

The union's price for averting a nation-wide coal strike when the present agreements expire on June 30 came high. The concession on the welfare fund alone means that the operators will pay 20 cents a ton into the fund instead of 10 cents. This will increase the fund from $50,000,000 to $100,000,000 annually.

President Truman's Board of Inquiry, which was to have turned in its report to the White House tonight, deferred action for another day after being advised that operators and miners had reported "progress toward a complete agreement."

In the hope of completing their agreement tonight operators and miners resumed conferences after dinner.

However, at 10 P. M., operators who left the conference room for a few minutes declared that they were "disgusted" with Mr. Lewis' methods at this evening's session.

They asserted that despite their major concessions, the union chief-

Continued on Page 6, Column 4

World News Summarized

FRIDAY, JUNE 25, 1948

Gov. Thomas E. Dewey of New York was unanimously nominated as the Republican candidate for President on the third ballot of the party's national convention in Philadelphia last night. [1:8.] The "stop Dewey" coalition fell apart even before the roll could be called, leading contenders publicly releasing their delegates. [2:6.]

On the first ballot Mr. Dewey took a commanding lead, with 434 votes to 224 for Senator Taft, 157 for Harold E. Stassen and others far behind. On the second ballot the Dewey vote reached 515, thirty-three less than the required majority. [2:2.] Mr. Dewey would have been nominated on that ballot if the opposing group had not forced a recess and Senator Baldwin had not delayed switching Connecticut's vote for him to Dewey. [1:7.]

Governor Dewey went immediately to the convention hall to accept the nomination. He told the delegates he had made not a single pledge to anyone to obtain the nomination. In a move to erase battle scars, he paid tribute to his six rivals by name. [1:5.]

The convention will select a candidate for Vice President today. House Majority Leader Halleck, who had been looked upon as the almost certain nominee, was said to be strongly challenged by advocates of Mr. Stassen and Senator Knowland of California. [1:6-7.]

In Washington, President Truman signed the Selective Service Act. Although the draft will not become effective for ninety days, registration of men from 19 through 25 is expected to start within six weeks. The President also signed a $3,749,059,250 Navy and Marine Corps appropriation bill. [1:2-3.]

Soft-coal operators and miners agreed on a new contract, lessening the danger of a strike next month. The pact, a sweeping victory for John L. Lewis, provides a $1-a-day pay increase and doubles industry payments into the welfare fund. [1:4.]

A Federal statutory court here reserved decision in the first action directly challenging the constitutionality of the non-Communist affidavit section of the Taft-Hartley Act. [6:1.]

The City Planning Commission made public plans for an integrated Manhattan civic center, with parks, tunnels, public buildings and the elimination of slums in the Brooklyn Bridge-Manhattan Bridge area. [1:6.7.]

The Russians "can't drive us out" of Berlin "by any action short of war," General Clay declared. It was indicated that the Western powers might consider leaving the city if Russian action imposed too great suffering on the Germans. [1:1.] American and British forces patrolled the streets of their sectors and the British placed an economic sanction on the entire Soviet zone of occupation in Germany. [19:1.] A French Foreign Office spokesman said the real issue was not that of currency but of Russia's desire to rule all of Berlin. [17:2.]

A German peace treaty calling for the withdrawal of occupation troops within a year after the signing of the pact and agreement on a provisional government of all Germany, with the Ruhr under four-power control, was demanded by the Foreign Ministers of Russia and her seven satellites at their Warsaw conference. [1:2-3.]

The Provisional Government of Israel, threatened by dissident forces, won a 24-to-7 vote of confidence in the State Council. There were seven abstentions. Plans were laid for a single Israeli army. [1:2.] Britain was reported urging the Arabs to prolong the truce. [12:1.]

DEWEY GIVES CALL

Accepting Nomination, He Bids People Seek Unity in New Faith

UNFETTERED, HE SAYS

Praises All Opponents and Avoids Partisan Attack on Truman

Text of Governor Dewey's address to convention, Page 2.

Special to THE NEW YORK TIMES.

PHILADELPHIA, June 24—Gov. Thomas E. Dewey accepted the nomination tonight and immediately appealed to the party and the country for unity on the basis of a new spiritual faith.

The unity America sought, the nominee told a cheering audience, was more than material. Spiritually, he said, the people had yet to find the means to put together the world's broken pieces.

Mr. Dewey, who was accompanied to the platform by his wife and a big group of supporters, told the delegates that he had accepted the nomination and that he came to the convention hall and the nomination "unfettered by a single obligation or promise to any living person, free to join with you in selecting to serve our nation the finest men and women in the nation."

Mr. Dewey was generous in victory to his opponents for the nomination. He praised them all—and called them out by name. When he came to that of Harold E. Stassen, the galleries burst into one of the loudest tributes of the night, and loud, though somewhat less responsive shouts, greeted the names of Senators Robert A. Taft and Arthur H. Vandenberg.

The Governor avoided any partisan attack on the Truman Ad-

Continued on Page 4, Column 5

NOMINATED FOR PRESIDENT

Thomas E. Dewey The New York Times (by Tames)

Stassen-for-Vice-President Urged, Challenging Halleck

By C. P. TRUSSELL
Special to THE NEW YORK TIMES.

PHILADELPHIA, Friday, June 25—Harold E. Stassen was represented by a spokesman early today as being willing to submit to "a real draft" by the Republican National Convention for nomination for Vice President. This spokesman added, however, that Mr. Stassen did not expect such a draft as he believed Gov. Thomas E. Dewey had another nominee in mind.

Mr. Dewey consulted by telephone with Senator Robert A. Taft and Mr. Stassen before calling a conference on the Vice Presidential nomination in his room at the Bellevue-Stratford early today.

In the course of this communication, it was reported authoritatively that Senator Taft had said that if Senator John W. Bricker of Ohio should be nominated he, Mr. Taft, would fight for his election. Mr. Bricker was Governor Dewey's running mate on the Presidential ticket of 1944.

The commanding lead of Charles A. Halleck of Indiana, majority leader of the House, had been challenged at high party levels. There remained signs that Mr. Halleck might still win, however, unless he faced Mr. Stassen. Mr. Bricker also might make the vote nip and tuck.

Opposition to the Indiana Representative, largely because of his record on foreign policy, spurred a Stassen-for-Vice-President drive. Early today there gathered in the Dewey suite a widely representa-

Continued on Page 4, Column 2

CONNECTICUT LOST CHANCE TO BE KEY

Would Have Gone to Dewey on Second Test, Taking Others, Except for Baldwin Word

By FELIX BELAIR Jr.
Special to THE NEW YORK TIMES.

PHILADELPHIA, June 24—Connecticut's delegation to the Republican National Convention almost, but not quite, achieved the role here today that the key California and Texas delegations held in the nomination of Franklin D. Roosevelt by the Democrats in 1932.

Connecticut would have switched to Governor Dewey before the result of the second ballot was announced but for one thing—a promise made by Senator Raymond E. Baldwin. But it still was clear that Harold E. Mitchell, Connecticut's national committeeman and boss, had taken the decisive step and the recess between the second

Continued on Page 3, Column 6

Downtown Manhattan Face-Lifting Proposed by City Planning Board

A blueprint for changing the face of the entire downtown Manhattan area surrounding the Civic Center was made public yesterday by the City Planning Commission.

The long-range plan calls for an integrated Manhattan Civic Center combined with sweeping street, building and park improvements designed to rehabilitate an area that has endured without plan or alteration for almost a century, except for the comparatively new public and private buildings in Foley Square. The area encompasses the approaches to Brooklyn Bridge and City Hall Park on the south and extends north between Broadway and the East River to Canal and Pike Streets.

Salient features of the plan include tunnel approaches and improvements to Brooklyn Bridge; the marking out of proposed sites for a Municipal Courts Building, an office building to house the city's engineering and building staffs, a new Police Headquarters, and other public buildings; the widening of Park Row and other streets and the closing of some; construction of a bus terminal and public parking garage, and the transformation of Foley Square into a single large park area as the heart of the integrated Civic Center.

It envisages also the demolition of the old Tweed Court House and consequent improvement of City Hall Park, the rehabilitation of squalid slum areas for residential purposes, the reconstruction of the projecting decks of the Brooklyn Bridge and the razing of its honeycomb of warehouses at arch openings and in streets under the bridge.

The plan, prepared by the Commission in collaboration with the office of Manhattan Borough President Hugo E. Rogers and other city agencies, will be the subject of discussion at a "preview luncheon" today at the Downtown Ath-

Continued on Page 2?, Column 3

OPPOSITION FALLS

Taft and Stassen Join in Urging Selection of New Yorker

GOP PRECEDENT SET

Dewey Is First Defeated Candidate to Be Chosen Again

By WILLIAM S. WHITE
Special to THE NEW YORK TIMES.

PHILADELPHIA, June 24—Thomas E. Dewey was nominated tonight by the Republicans for the Presidency of the United States.

His selection, on the third ballot of the twenty-fourth Republican National Convention, was unanimous after his forces had smashed an opposing coalition.

When two ballots had shown that the Governor of New York was not to be stopped, his erstwhile antagonists renounced their rivalries with him and pledged all their power to his success in November.

Mr. Dewey came at once to the convention hall and, before the hot and shouting delegates, accepted his nomination in a placating spirit toward his former opponents.

"In all humility," he said, "I pray God that I may deserve this opportunity to serve our country."

"Lasting Peace" Put First

Above all its efforts, he declared, the Republican party and the country must seek for the world "a just and lasting peace."

The convention will select tomorrow a Vice Presidential nominee in what is described in the most authoritative quarters as a "wide open field."

Mr. Dewey said pointedly that he was "unfettered by a single obligation or promise to any living person." It was understood that the Dewey group wanted to consider overnight the available men for second place on the ticket.

Governor Dewey is the only Republican in the party's history to be nominated for President after having been once defeated. He lost in 1944 to Franklin D. Roosevelt.

On the first ballot today the Governor got 434 votes to 224 for Senator Robert A. Taft of Ohio, his strongest opponent.

On the second ballot, he climbed to 515 votes, as compared with 274 for Mr. Taft.

The results of the three ballots for the major leaders were as follows:

First—Dewey, 434; Taft, 224; Harld E. Stassen, 157; Senator Arthur H. Vandenberg of Michigan, 62.

Second—Dewey, 515; Taft, 274; Stassen, 149; Vandenberg, 62.

Third—Dewey, all 1,094 votes.

When the second roll-call ended associates of Senator Taft, Mr.

Continued on Page 3, Column 2

Hottest Day of Year Cooled by Showers

New York got its warmest weather of the year yesterday as the temperature rose to 89 degrees at 6 P. M., five notches above the previous high mark of 84 on May 12.

The heat and high humidity combined to give the city a sweltering atmosphere, but some relief came in the early evening with heavy showers. The mercury dropped from 89 at 6 P. M. to 69 degrees at 9 P. M. The humidity, 48 at 8 P. M., rose to 96 at 9 P. M. The humidity had reached the saturation point, 100, in the late morning.

The downpour caused short-circuits in signals on the Independent Subway Division at Thiry-sixth Street and Northern Boulevard in Queens, halting Jamaica and Brooklyn Crosstown trains for ten minutes after 8:39.

Steaming weather also is in prospect for today.

"All the News That's Fit to Print"

The New York Times.

LATE CITY EDITION
Afternoon or evening thundershowers today and tomorrow.
Temperature Range Today—Max.,89; Min.,71
Temperatures Yesterday—Max.,87; Min.,67
Full U. S. Weather Bureau Report, Page 47

Copyright, 1948, by The New York Times Company.

VOL. XCVII...No. 33,029. Entered as Second-Class Matter, Postoffice, New York, N. Y. NEW YORK, TUESDAY, JUNE 29, 1948. Times Square, New York 18, N. Y. Telephone LAckawanna 4-1000 THREE CENTS IN NEW YORK CITY

ROYALL SETS DRAFT AT 225,000 IN CALLS OF 30,000 A MONTH

Says Enlistments and Other Factors Will Limit the Need for Using the System

TRAINING ULTRA-MODERN

Methods and Equipment Will Embody Advances Made In and Since World War II

Questions and answers on draft procedure on Page 18.

Special to THE NEW YORK TIMES.

WASHINGTON, June 28—Secretary of the Army Kenneth C. Royall, in a detailed outline today of plans for the draft, said that calls would probably go to 225,000 to 250,000 men, with the rate of inductions reaching about 30,000 a month.

He declared that through the new Selective Service Law the Army would be able to organize for the first time since the end of hostilities in World War II "a really effective mobile striking force," to be composed of twelve Regular Army divisions and six National Guard divisions.

The estimate of a need for 225,000 to 250,000 inductees, he said, was based on plans for reaching full strength by July 1, 1949. Strength permitted by appropriations is 790,000, he added, although Congress has authorized an ultimate strength of 837,000.

The estimated inductee need, Mr. Royall declared, took into consideration discharges, enlistments, re-enlistments and normal attrition. Inductions cannot start under the law before Sept. 22.

First Calls in October

The Army now stood at 542,000, he said, and the first inductions would probably be on a small scale in October.

Mr. Royall issued his detailed statement on the Army plans and discussed them at a news conference at the request of Secretary of Defense James Forrestal.

In a statement telling of the request, Mr. Forrestal declared that "for the next few months at least practically all of the selectees will be assigned to the Army, since the immediate personnel requirements of the Navy and Air Force probably will be met by voluntary recruitment under existing procedures."

Mr. Royall noted that the inductees, ranging from 19 to 25 years of age, would serve for 21 months. In addition, he stated, the Army would train up to 110,000 18-year-old volunteers for one year, receiving the same basic training and as much specialized training as is possible. They will be known as "enlistees." Regular volunteers will be accepted.

The inductees are to be trained by eight training divisions, four of which are now in operation. The enlistees will be trained, until other provisions can be made, by combat organizations with which it is intended that they spend their entire year of service.

Scope of the Training

In discussing training Mr. Royall said:

"Principles learned in World War II and developed at the Universal Military Training Experimental Center at Fort Knox, Ky., have been incorporated into basic and advanced training.

"These principles lie in the field of leadership and discipline. Leadership in our Army is based upon better understanding of basic human relations, a development of mutual respect and trust between the leader and the soldier who performs the many and varied tasks of the Army. Our concept of discipline is based upon the willing obedience of the informed soldier who, after with his comrades, accomplishes his tasks because of his intelligent understanding of their necessity rather than through external compulsion or fear.

"The objective of the training will be to produce a well-coordinated, physically conditioned, mentally alert, thoroughly trained soldier, capable of efficiently performing any task to which he may be assigned.

"In order to develop the individual as a soldier and as a citizen it is essential that he be given the maximum amount of personal liberty consistent with the proper performance of his duty. His training will seek to promote his individual initiative and resourcefulness, and it is our intention that these qualities not be handicapped or restricted by harsh or unnecessary discipline.

"The military equipment for

Continued on Page 19, Column 2

City Calls for the Dismissal Of All Communist Teachers

Brief Supports Ouster of Dr. F. J. Thompson and Asks State Revise Ruling in Case—Discharged Instructor Is Defended

Special to THE NEW YORK TIMES.

ALBANY, June 28—Members of the Communist party as well as "fellow travelers" should be dismissed from the public school teaching staff, the New York City Board of Education contended today in a brief filed here with Dr. Francis T. Spaulding, State Commissioner of Education.

The brief was submitted by Nicholas Bucci, law secretary of the education board, supporting the New York Board of Higher Education's appeal in the case of Dr. Francis J. Thompson, former City College instructor. Dr. Thompson was dismissed from his job in December, 1946, on charges that he concealed membership in the Communist party and that he obstructed the Rapp-Coudert investigation.

An appeal by Dr. Thompson denying membership in the Communist party was upheld last January by Dr. Lewis A. Wilson, Acting Commissioner of Education, who held that the Board of Higher Education had failed to prove Dr. Thompson's alleged membership in the party.

Dr. Wilson also ruled that membership in the Communist party could not be made the ground for dismissal by the educational authorities unless the State Legislature outlawed the party. Commissioner Spaulding, it was reported here today, is expected to render a decision in the case "early in July."

In a brief filed in behalf of Dr. Thompson, Dr. Ernest E. Cole, former Acting State Commissioner of Education, declared that the former City College instructor "is not and never was a member of the Communist party or guilty of conduct unbecoming a member of the (City College) staff."

After asserting that Dr. Thompson had "fought both fascism and communism," Dr. Cole said that "it is sheer nonsense" that an avowed Communist could be elected to official office and be permitted to serve while a teacher accused of

Continued on Page 21, Column 2

TRUMAN SIGNS BILL FOR AID AS PLEDGE U.S. BACKS FREEDOM

$6,030,710,228 Fund Token That We Work Side by Side With Sharers, He Says

FIRST PACTS COMPLETED

France, Italy, Ireland Accept Terms—Peace Aim Stressed in President's Statement

By WALTER H. WAGGONER

Special to THE NEW YORK TIMES.

WASHINGTON, June 28—President Truman signed the foreign-aid appropriation bill today and, with more than $6,000,000,000 at its disposal, the United States formally embarked on the greatest economic rehabilitation project the world has ever known.

With the President clearing the way, the State Department and the Governments of France, Italy and Ireland promptly signed the first bilateral aid agreements under the Economic Cooperation Act of 1948, made possible by the foreign aid funds. Secretary of State George C. Marshall described the pacts as "one more step" toward European recovery.

The $6,030,710,228 made available in the foreign-aid appropriation act will meet the costs, for not less than twelve months nor more than fifteen, of the European Recovery Program, aid to Greece, Turkey and China, "occupation responsibilities" in both Europe and the Far East, and participation in the International Children's Fund and the International Refugee Organization.

Act Hailed as Nonpartisan

Mr. Truman said he signed the bill with "a deep sense of satisfaction," which, he added, he knew the American people shared with him. This was a marked change from the attitude, usually either regret or reluctance, the President has shown in signing into law other bills that had come to him recently from a Republican Congress.

This law, the President said, represented the "combined judgment and will of the Executive and Congress," having been born "in the spirit of cooperation and not of partisan conflict."

"It furnishes concrete evidence and assurance to the free peoples of the world that we stand ready to work side by side with them to

Continued on Page 14, Column 3

EARTHQUAKE, FIRES TAKE SEVERE TOLL IN WESTERN JAPAN

Fukui, City of 85,000, Badly Hurt—Total of Casualties Cannot Be Estimated

UNIT OF AMERICANS SAFE

Theatre and Railway Station Destroyed—Honolulu Has Sharp but Minor Shock

By The Associated Press.

TOKYO, Tuesday, June 29—A violent earthquake and fire wiped out 70 per cent of the western Honshu city of Fukui and leveled surrounding towns, a United States Military Government team reported today.

The team said that the remaining part of the city—which was nearly destroyed by American Superfortress raids in July, 1945—was "partly damaged" by the tremors late yesterday.

There were plenty of rough guesses, but no reliable casualty figures were available before noon today. All indications were that the toll would be heavy.

The earthquake, its heaviest tremor lasting a minute, jolted an area twenty by ten miles 200 miles west of Tokyo along the coast of the Sea of Japan. The earth shocks began at 5:14 P. M., Japanese Daylight Time (2:14 A. M., Monday, EST) and continued intermittently for nearly twelve hours.

The Maizuru Military Government team said that all United States military installations at Fukui, except four houses for dependents, had been destroyed in the fire that followed the quake.

Trains Rolled Over

Capt. F. M. Shipley of Warsaw, Ind., and S/Sgt. William Hutley of Wilkesboro, N. C., returned from a flight over the city to report two trains at Fukui were lying on their sides. Rail and highway bridges north of the city were out, they said, but one bridge on the southern outskirts seemed intact.

A report from another Military Government team at Takefu, about fifteen miles south of Fukui, said that large cracks opened in the earth in that area. In some places concrete pavement buckled like a ribbon, with folds up to two feet high, the team added.

In Fukui, a city of 85,000, the first shock was followed immediately by fire which destroyed a

Continued on Page 6, Column 3

COMINFORM DENOUNCES TITO, CHARGING HE LEANS TO WEST; HIS EXPULSION THREATENED

Marshall Plan Cracks Bloc In East, Washington Holds

But Observers Appear Doubtful of Full Moscow-Belgrade Break—Rift Found Likely to Stiffen West on Berlin

By JAMES RESTON

Special to THE NEW YORK TIMES.

WASHINGTON, June 28—The general reaction in Washington today to the Communist Information Bureau's split with Marshal Tito of Yugoslavia was much like the reaction of Winston Churchill to the sudden arrival of Rudolf Hess in Scotland during the war.

"It would appear," said Mr. Churchill, "that there is a maggot in the apple."

[Leaders in London hailed the Cominform's denunciation of the Yugoslav Communist party as a gain for the Western democracies.]

Officially, the Truman Administration said nothing, but informed persons made these observations:

1. It is unlikely that there will be any complete break between Belgrade and Moscow. Marshal Tito will either satisfy the will of the Kremlin or be replaced, these sources suggested.

2. The Marshall Plan has been more of a thunderbolt in Eastern Europe than the United States realized. It has cracked the smooth facade of the Communist world by demonstrating that the interests of the Soviet satellites are not necessarily identical to the interests of the Soviet Union.

3. These circles said that the Yugoslav crack would undoubtedly be smoothed over but that meanwhile it had confirmed an important fact: that even in Eastern Europe the foundation of communism is not secure and that nationalism is still a force capable of challenging communism.

4. The cleavage has come at a critical time in the relations between East and West and will stiffen the opposition to the Soviet efforts to drive the United States, Britain and France out of Berlin.

5. Finally, reliable official reports suggest that the action by the Cominform may be Moscow's reaction to the recent purge by

Continued on Page 11, Column 5

SOVIET RIFT BARED

Yugoslav Leaders' Acts Termed 'Hateful' and 'Slanderous' of Russia

VIEWS HELD TROTSKYIST

Belgrade Accused of Retreat From Leninism and Straying From Cominform Fold

Text of Communist charges against Tito is on Page 10.

By The Associated Press.

PRAGUE, June 28—The Communist Information Bureau denounced today Marshal Tito's leadership of Yugoslav Communists. The international Communist organization declared that Belgrade's Premier and other top members of the party must hew to the Moscow line or get out.

The Yugoslav leaders were accused by the Moscow-blessed bureau of pursuing a hateful and slanderous policy toward Russia and of leaning toward Western methods.

The blast came in a 3,000-word statement adopted at a meeting in Rumania this month of the Cominform, a meeting at which Yugoslav Communists, among the Cominform's founders, were not represented. The statement was published here today. According to the statement, the Yugoslav Communist leaders had placed themselves outside the Cominform ranks.

Marshal Tito and his top aides were accused of retreating from Marxism-Leninism by "undertaking an entirely wrong policy on the principal question of foreign and internal politics."

Confidence in Party Expressed

The statement called for "either a true return to Marxist policy or a change of Communist leaders in Yugoslavia."

One section of the declaration indicated that Marshal Tito and his chiefs might get a chance to change their ways before final action was taken. It said:

"The aim of * * * sound elements of the Communist party of Yugoslavia is to force their present leaders to confess openly and honestly their faults and correct them; to part from nationalism, to return to internationalism and in every way to fix the united Socialist front against imperialism; or, if the present leaders of the Communist party of Yugoslavia prove unable to do this task, to change them and to raise from below a new internationalistic leadership of the Communist party of Yugoslavia. The Information Bureau does not doubt that the Communist party can fulfill this task."

Kardelj Among Four Named

Singled out for criticism were Marshal Tito, Vice Premier Edvard Kardelj, a founder of the Cominform; Milovan Djilas, Minister for Montenegro, a Yugoslav state, and Col. Gen. Alexander Rankovitch, who as Minister of the Interior has bossed Yugoslavia's police force.

There was speculation that such a blast would have been issued only after specific action had been taken against Marshal Tito, but there was no confirmation of this. Dispatches from Belgrade said Marshal Tito was believed to be at his summer home in Bled.

Col. Gen. Andrei A. Zhdanov, a member of the Soviet Union Communist Politburo and often rated one of the three most powerful men in Russia, attended the Cominform meeting and signed its official statement. As published in Rude Pravo, official newspaper of the Czechoslovak Communist party, the statement said that the Yugoslav Communist leaders had "created a hateful policy in relation to the Soviet Union and to the All-Communist Union of Bolsheviks."

An "undignified policy of underestimating Soviet military specialists was allowed" by the Yugoslavs and members of the Russian Army were discredited by them, it said.

Russian "private specialists" in Yugoslavia were put under guard of the organs of state security and were watched, the statement added. It said that the Soviet Union's delegate to the Cominform in Bel-

Continued on Page 11, Column 2

FIND THE ITU GUILTY, DENHAM PROPOSES

NLRB Counsel Recommends Trial Examiner Declare Taft-Hartley Act Violated

By LOUIS STARK

Special to THE NEW YORK TIMES.

WASHINGTON, June 28—Attorneys of the National Labor Relations Board, acting under orders of General Counsel Robert N. Denham, recommended today that an NLRB trial examiner find officers of the International Typographical Union guilty of unfair labor practices in violation of the Taft-Hartley Act.

Allen Sinsheimer Jr. and Caroll L. Martin of Mr. Denham's regional office in Cincinnati, also urged, in a proposed order directed to Arthur Leff, NLRB trial examiner, that the ITU's operations be drastically limited.

The case in which the action was taken was originally brought by the American Newspaper Publishers Association but was linked also with that brought by the Chicago Newspaper Publishers Association against Local 16, ITU, of Chicago.

The proposed order which the trial examiner was asked to approve bars the international union from refusing to bargain in good faith, and would prevent it from demanding that the rules of the international union be adopted as a condition of employment, and from permitting the union to veto employment of an applicant, or from requiring employers to pay for reproduction of advertisements already set.

Mr. Leff began hearings in the cases on Dec. 9 in Indianapolis and ended them on May 19 in Washington. In those five months hearings were held also in Chicago, Detroit, Buffalo and Albany.

On March 27 an injunction was issued against the international union by District Court Judge Luther Swygert of Indianapolis,

Continued on Page 17, Column 2

DEWEY, WARREN MAP PLANS TODAY

Strategy Meeting at Pawling Will Cover Roles of Each and Weigh Big Drive in West

By LEO EGAN

Special to THE NEW YORK TIMES.

PAWLING, N. Y., June 28—Gov. Thomas E. Dewey and Gov. Earl Warren of California, Republican candidates for President and Vice President, respectively, are to hold a strategy conference at Mr. Dewey's 300-acre dairy farm here tomorrow. Mr. Dewey has been resting at the farm since his return last Saturday from Philadelphia, where he was nominated.

It is understood that the main subjects for discussion will be the roles each will play in the fall campaign and the establishment of arrangements for exchanging views and information during the campaign.

Both candidates are expected to devote most of the summer to writing speeches and developing a joint interpretation of the platform adopted by the Republican Convention last week.

In the mapping of Republican campaign plans, it is likely that Governor Warren will be asked to campaign intensively in western areas where reclamation and irrigation are key issues.

The California Governor has long been a champion of Federal appropriations for irrigation and reclamation and, in the view of Republican strategists should be particularly useful in combating Democratic criticism of the Republican-controlled Eightieth Congress for failing to make more funds available for these projects.

Mr. Warren may be asked also to seek the support of organized labor for the Republican Presidential ticket. He is reputed to stand well with labor unions because of his support of state sickness-compensation payments in California.

Under California law, enacted at

Continued on Page 26, Column 6

'Juggling' of Posted Garage Rates Brings Warnings to Ten Operators

By JOSEPH C. INGRAHAM

Ten garage operators adjudged guilty of increasing rates to customers without proper notification to the Department of Licenses have been warned that repetition of the offense would bring a drastic fine or possible revocation of license, it was learned yesterday.

The cases stemmed from complaints by the Automobile Club of New York that garages were evading the recently enacted city licensing law and were gouging customers by billing them at rates varying from those filed with the department. While the law does not control prices, it provides that rates cannot be changed without sixty days' notice.

Confirming that only warnings had been issued, Acting License Commissioner Patrick J. Meehan added that all the guilty operators were first offenders and in addition had not raised rates above the maxima filed with the department.

Mr. Meehan said he had told the violators that they must not "juggle" posted rates, that the charges for storage space must accurately reflect "going conditions" and that his department was determined to protect the public.

All the garages involved are in the area bounded by Seventy-second and Ninety-sixth Streets, the Hudson River and Second Avenue, where demand far exceeds the space. Other complaints of illegal price alteration made through the auto club were proved unfounded or had been corrected by the time inspectors checked, it was reported.

However, the inspectors making spot checks independent of club sources found that some parking lot operators were flouting the licensing laws. Eight were summoned to court and fined a total of $1,300. Forty-seven more cases are pending.

The proposed local law to hold garage and parking lot rentals and service charges at levels not more than 15 per cent above prices on

Continued on Page 46, Column 1

World News Summarized

TUESDAY, JUNE 29, 1948

Marshal Tito of Yugoslavia was denounced by the Communist Information Bureau and warned to hew to the Moscow line or get out. A statement issued yesterday accused the Yugoslav Communists of "anti-party, anti-Soviet opinions incompatible with Marxism-Leninism," of "secession from the united socialist front against imperialism," of abandoning internationalism for nationalism and of seeking favor with "imperialist" states through a "series of concessions" that would plant capitalism firmly in the country. Marshal Tito and his fellow-leaders were called upon to admit their mistakes or give way to a new leadership. [1:8.]

The people of Yugoslavia heard nothing about the action of the Cominform, but word from Belgrade indicated that Marshal Tito and his Politburo were in complete control. [1:6-7.] Communist officials in Poland made no attempt to disguise their surprise and dismay. [9:6.]

Informed sources in Washington attributed the break in part to the impact of the Marshall Plan on Eastern Europe. A complete rupture between Belgrade and Moscow was not looked for, but it was felt that this evidence of Communist disunity would stiffen the Western powers in the current "battle of Berlin" with Russia. [1:6-7.]

London observers saw a victory for Yugoslav nationalism over international communism and a weakening in the Soviet circle. [9:2.] French officials welcomed the disclosure of disunity behind the "iron curtain," linking developments in Yugoslavia with events in Germany. France has proposed that the three Western powers consult at Cabinet level on the Berlin crisis. [4:3.]

General Clay conferred with Marshal Sokolovsky in Berlin. The Russians eased some travel restrictions on Germans, but maintained the rail blockade of Berlin. [1:7.] British officials were confident that the Russians eventually would yield. [3:1.] Some Berlin observers felt that the main Soviet purpose was to bring about a resumption of the Council of Foreign Ministers, in which Russia would be able to push her desire for a share in controlling the Ruhr. [2:2.] Secretary General Lie was studying how to place the Berlin dispute before the United Nations Security Council. [4:4-5.]

King George, at the request of Prime Minister Attlee, proclaimed a "state of emergency" to enable the British Government to counter the spreading strike of dock workers. [1:6-7.]

President Truman signed the bill appropriating funds for the European Recovery Program. [1:4.] Ireland, Italy and France signed the pacts qualifying them for participation. [14:5.]

The Army will call up 225,000 to 250,000 men under the new draft, Army Secretary Royall said. [1:1.] An explanation of the application of the draft to selectees was issued by the Army. [18:2-7.] Representative Ploesser sought to quiet industry's fears that one part of the law might bring back wartime production controls. [33:3.]

The three railroad unions that were enjoined from striking after having rejected a 15½-cent hourly pay rise recommended by a Presidential board demanded a 16-cent hourly increase above the original order. [46:1.]

City mediators continued efforts to avert a strike on six Queens bus lines. The Public Service Commission approved 12-cent transfer exchanges between municipal rapid transit lines and private bus lines in Queens and the Bronx. [25:8.]

Earthquake and fire wrecked the Japanese city of Fukui and vicinity. A different tremor shook Honolulu. [1:5; map P. 6.]

Tito's Grip on Nation Is Firm; Reply to Charges Due Today

By M. S. HANDLER

Special to THE NEW YORK TIMES.

BELGRADE, Yugoslavia, June 28—Marshal Tito and his deputies in the Politburo and Central Committee of the Yugoslav Communist party were in complete control of the situation tonight. Judging by the calm prevailing at party headquarters and government offices, they are likely to retain this hold against the powers of the Communist Information Bureau.

There were no special military or police precautions at any of the party or Government buildings to reinforce normal security measures. Means of entry and exit to these buildings were no more complicated than they had been before the Cominform's action [denouncing the Yugoslav leaders]. The calm aspect of Belgrade indicated that Marshal Tito and his deputies had no fears that the Cominform had the backing of a Yugoslav group to challenge their power or was likely to find one.

The secretariat of Milovan Djilas, propaganda and agitation chief of the Central Committee of the Communist party, said that a statement would be issued tomorrow afternoon.

The rift between the Yugoslav Communist party and the Cominform and between Yugoslavia and the Soviet Union is not interpreted here to mean a complete reversal of the Yugoslav position on essential domestic and foreign policies but rather as a split of historic

Continued on Page 9, Column 3

SOVIET EASES CURB ON GERMAN TRAVEL

Move Follows Clay-Sokolovsky Talk—But Rail Blockade of Berlin's Food Remains

By DREW MIDDLETON

Special to THE NEW YORK TIMES.

BERLIN, Tuesday, June 29—The Russians announced the first break in their iron curtain around the Soviet zone occupation early this morning, a few hours after Gen. Lucius D. Clay and Marshal Vassily D. Sokolovsky, the United States and Soviet commanders in chief, had conferred at the latter's Berlin headquarters.

The break is not a big one, but it marks a definite change in the hitherto adamant Russian attitude toward the blockade. The Russians announced that Germans carrying passes issued before June 19, when the currency reform began in the Western zones, would be allowed to move from the Western

Continued on Page 3, Column 2

Emergency Declared in Britain To Cope With Strike of Dockers

By BENJAMIN WELLES

Special to THE NEW YORK TIMES.

LONDON, June 28.—As the London dock strike passed its fifteenth day with signs that sympathy strikes were beginning to spread to Liverpool, the Merseyside and other vital port areas, King George VI, on the advice of the British Government proclaimed a "state of emergency" throughout the United Kingdom tonight.

The proclamation, which was signed at a hastily gathered meeting of the Privy Council at Holyrood Palace in Edinburgh, where the King is vacationing, is the first of this type since the general strike of 1926.

This action is regarded here primarily as a psychological move by the Government, designed to bring home to the workers and the country alike the increasing gravity of the situation. The proclamation sets in motion the Emergency Powers Act of 1920, which gives the Government the power to take virtually any action it deems necessary to maintain order in strike-bound areas and to keep running freely the communications facilities for the distribution of foods and other vital commodities.

While it is not expected that these full powers will immediately be used, the Government may now assume complete control of all port areas, utilize troops to handle port operations and generally assure that needed supplies are landed and distributed within the country while exports are loaded and dispatched abroad.

The latest strike figures released by the Government tonight showed that 19,040 dock workers in the London area were still out, with only 5,977 at work. In Liverpool reports indicated that fully 50 per cent of the dockers had stopped work in sympathy with the London strike while other reports

Continued on Page 46, Column 2

Irene Dunne, Rudy Vallee and Oscar Homolka in *I Remember Mama.*

Bing Crosby and Bob Hope in *The Road to Rio.*

John Wayne and Walter Brennan in *Red River.*

"All the News That's Fit to Print"

The New York Times.

Copyright, 1948, by The New York Times Company.

LATE CITY EDITION
Partly cloudy and mild today. Increasing cloudiness tomorrow.
Temperature Range Today—Max.,82; Min.,67
Temperature Yesterday—Max.,81; Min.,69
Full U. S. Weather Bureau Report, Page 47

VOL. XCVII..No. 33,045. Entered as Second-Class Matter, Postoffice, New York, N. Y. NEW YORK, THURSDAY, JULY 15, 1948. Times Square, New York 18, N. Y. Telephone LAckawanna 4-1000 THREE CENTS IN NEW YORK CITY

TRUMAN, BARKLEY NAMED BY DEMOCRATS; SOUTH LOSES ON CIVIL RIGHTS, 35 WALK OUT; PRESIDENT WILL RECALL CONGRESS JULY 26

MOSCOW REJECTS PARLEY ON BERLIN TO BREAK IMPASSE

Reply to Protests on Blockade Asserts Any Talks Must Embrace All of Germany

BLAMES WEST FOR SPLIT

Soviet Says Currency Reform and Proposed New State Made Its Action Necessary

Text of Soviet reply to protest on Berlin is on page 16.

By HERBERT L. MATTHEWS
Special to The New York Times.

LONDON, July 14—The Soviet Union rejected the Western powers' demand for the lifting of the blockade of Berlin in notes to Washington, London and Paris delivered today by Soviet Ambassadors in those capitals.

The text of the reply to the United States, as broadcast by the Moscow radio and translated here by the Soviet monitor, said the Soviet Union would conduct four-power negotiations on the "general question of quadripartite control in relation to Germany" but not only on Berlin as the Western powers had proposed. The Moscow broadcast said the replies to Great Britain and France were similar. The note to the United States repeated the Russian contention that "Berlin is in the center of the Soviet zone and is part of that zone."

Deny Pressure Is Intended

In reply to one crucial passage in the Western Allies' notes it had this to say:

"As regards the declaration of the Government of the United States [similar passages appeared in the British and French notes] that it will not be induced by threats of pressure or other actions to abandon its right to participate in the occupation of Berlin, the Soviet Government does not intend to enter into a discussion of this declaration for it has no need of a policy of pressure since by violation of the agreed decisions on the administration of Berlin the above mentioned Governments are themselves rendering null and void their right to participation in the occupation of Berlin."

There were a few good features in the note from the Western Allies' viewpoint, such as a reference to the blockade moves as "temporary measures" and the fact that they had been necessitated by the Western currency reform. There also was an offer to feed all of Berlin with Soviet supplies.

However the Soviet reply was basically a refusal to meet any of the Western Allies' demands and therefore it brought the United States, Britain and France face to face with further serious decisions.

[Washington sources said the Soviet reply left the Berlin situation unchanged and indicated that new Western power talks would be held.]

Discussions between these three powers began almost immediately today and will continue on a more intense basis tomorrow because many hours were lost today in translations, comparisons and preliminary soundings.

The British Foreign Office unaccountably gave out during the afternoon that there were "no major sensations" in the Soviet note and that was the official attitude up to the time the Foreign Office closed late tonight. However, the text of the note was the clearest possible demonstration that the Russians had replied with a firm categorical "no."

This was the vital passage replying to the Western Allies' demand that the blockade of Berlin be lifted preliminary to the holding of four-power talks on Berlin—not Germany as a whole—recognized as the crucial issue:

"While not objecting to negotiations, the Soviet Government, however, deems it necessary to declare that it cannot link the start of these

Continued on Page 16, Column 3

Stalin Is 'Outraged' By Togliatti Attack

By The United Press.

LONDON, July 14—The Moscow radio declared tonight that Premier Stalin and the Soviet Communist party were "outraged" by the attempt to slay Palmiro Togliatti in Italy.

The broadcast said the following telegram was signed by Premier Stalin and sent by Russian Communists to the Italian Communist party:

"The Central Committee of the Communist party of the Soviet Union is outraged by the villainous attempt of an outcast of humanity on the life of the teacher of the working class and all the laboring people of Italy, our well-loved Comrade Togliatti.

"The Central Committee of the Communist party of the Soviet Union is grieved that Comrade Togliatti's friends were not able to protect him from the foul underhand attack."

SOVIET BACKS U. S. ON PALESTINE EDICT

Four Other Countries Support U. N. Threat of Sanctions to Halt War in Holy Land

By THOMAS J. HAMILTON
Special to The New York Times.

LAKE SUCCESS, N. Y., July 14—The Soviet Union and four other countries gave their support today to a United States proposal that the United Nations Security Council invoke Chapter VII of the Charter and order both sides to stop the fighting in Palestine. These announcements apparently guaranteed the passage of this part of the resolution introduced by the United States yesterday, but left in doubt the fate of the sections to which the Soviet Union objected.

It was expected that Andrei A. Gromyko, Soviet representative, or Dmitri Z. Manuilsky, Ukrainian Foreign Minister, who is this month's chairman of the Council, would demand tomorrow that it vote paragraph by paragraph on the United States resolution. Apart from these two countries, the United States can count on six votes—one short of the needed majority—for most of its resolution.

[An offensive by Israeli forces in Galilee resulted in the capture of three towns in the vicinity of Nazareth. At the same time Israeli units pressed their attack from the coastal plain in an effort to dislodge the Arabs from Latrun, key point on the Tel Aviv-Jerusalem supply road. On the Jerusalem front, the Arabs opened an attack on Israeli-held Mount Zion.]

The United States resolution would determine that the situation in Palestine constitutes a "threat to the peace" and would bind the

Continued on Page 15, Column 1

RIOTS SWEEP ITALY AFTER AN ASSASSIN WOUNDS TOGLIATTI

Six Dead, Scores Hurt as Reds Battle Police, Who Are Said to Be in Control

GENERAL STRIKE IS BEGUN

Communist Chief Improves After 3 Bullets Are Removed —Assailant Captured

By ARNALDO CORTESI
Special to The New York Times.

ROME, Thursday, July 15—Palmiro Togliatti, Italy's Communist chief, was shot three times yesterday morning outside the Chamber of Deputies by a university student who fired four revolver bullets at him at point-blank range. One bullet entered his left lung. The other wounds were not serious.

At 10 o'clock last night a bulletin issued at Polyclinic Hospital, where he was fighting for his life, said Signor Togliatti's condition was slightly improved. He was said to have a good chance of recovery from his wounds, but fear was expressed that his heart, which has been weak for some years, might not hold out.

The assassin was arrested running from the scene.

Nearly all Italian cities were swept by rioting as soon as the news of the shooting was broadcast. [Six policemen and demonstrators were killed and scores wounded, according to news agencies.]

General Strike Called

The Communists started a powerful campaign to force the resignation of the Government. The General Confederation of Labor, which they control, called a general strike on a national scale. It began at midnight and was to continue for an indefinite time. The strike order applies to every form of activity except a very few of the most essential public services. It applies even to the railroads and the postal and telegraph services, which have hitherto always been excluded.

In Milan generally and especially in the "red citadel" of Sesto San Giovanni, a suburb of Milan, the workers last night had begun to occupy factories and were preparing to stand a siege in them.

This is without question the most serious challenge that Communists have yet hurled at the Government. They evidently reckon that they can tie up the whole country and keep it tied up till the Government has no option but to resign.

The Government, however, has met the challenge squarely. It addressed a proclamation to the

Continued on Page 18, Column 6

West Replies to Russians' Rebuff With Another Air Tonnage Record

By DREW MIDDLETON
Special to The New York Times.

BERLIN, Thursday, July 15—The Western Powers met the Soviet refusal to raise the siege of Berlin with a record number of air supply flights carrying a record tonnage and solid determination, generally expressed this morning, to keep the Western flags flying in the city.

News of the Soviet reply to the United States, British and French notes of protest circulated slowly through the Western sectors of the city, already darkened by electricity restrictions and facing perhaps more stringent rationing in the future.

Everywhere reaction to the wording of the Soviet note was the same: resolution in the face of the Soviet blockade of the city and hope that the Russian answer would lead to an expansion of the air lifeline into the city.

"Perhaps the tone of the Russian note will impress on the people of the United States just what we are up against here," said one senior member of Gen. Lucius D. Clay's staff. "I hope we can look forward to an early increase in the airlift as a result."

Another United States official declared he hoped that the Russian emphasis on such things as currency reform would not blind Americans to "the far larger issues at stake" in the Berlin crisis.

The tone of the Soviet note was not a surprise to United States and British military government officials who forecast the temper of the Russian reply on the basis of an editorial in the Taegliche Rundschau, Soviet Army newspaper, Wednesday morning.

The editorial called the Western proposal to negotiate a solution of the Berlin crisis "ridiculous" and demanded that any conference between the East and the West embrace the entire German question

Continued on Page 17, Column 6

IN A FIGHTING MOOD

'Will Win the Election and Make the Republicans Like It'

SCORNFUL OF RIVALS

Housing, Education and Civil Rights Issues for Special Session

Text of President Truman's acceptance speech, Page 4.

By JAMES RESTON
Special to The New York Times.

PHILADELPHIA, Thursday, July 15—President Truman accepted the Democratic Presidential nomination in a fighting mood this morning, predicted victory in November and announced that he would call Congress back into session on July 26 to deal with housing, education, civil rights and other controversial measures.

The President was in turn scornful and bitter about the Republicans. They had made a lot of proud statements in their campaign platform, he said, and now he would give them a chance to prove that they meant what they said.

The Congress would have every chance later this month to deal with most of the questions that needed to be settled. These questions could be debated in a hurry, in fifteen days, he said, if the Republicans really meant what they were saying. But the real test the people would make, he emphasized, would be action not words.

The immediate reaction at Convention Hall was that the President's summons to Congress would create even more bitterness than now exists between the Republican-controlled branch and the Democratic executive. In midsummer, the inhabitants of the steaming capital are never precisely in a deliberative mood, and with an election campaign going on simultaneously the temperature is not likely to be reduced.

Housing and high prices, Mr.

Continued on Page 3, Column 5

THE DEMOCRATIC NATIONAL TICKET

Harry S. Truman
President

Alben W. Barkley
Vice President

The New York Times

TRUMAN IS SHUNNED IN VOTES OF SOUTH

Eleven States Give Him 13 of Their 278—Mississippi and Half of Alabama Bolt

By WILLIAM S. WHITE
Special to The New York Times.

PHILADELPHIA, Thursday, July 15—The eleven states of the old Confederate South gave today to the nomination of President Truman only thirteen of their 278 votes in the Democratic national convention.

The entire Mississippi delegation of twenty-two and thirteen of the Alabama delegation bolted the con-

Continued on Page 9. Column 1

South Beaten on Race Issue As Rights Plank Is Widened

By C. P. TRUSSELL
Special to The New York Times.

PHILADELPHIA, July 14—The Democratic National Convention, by a roaring voice vote, committed its party today to what was called a straightaway Roosevelt-Truman platform for 1948. In scenes of emotional demonstration, with Southern Democrats pleading rather than demanding as Northern liberals were firmly in the saddle, the document was changed at only one point. That was where a majority of the convention, in effect, accused its platform committee of hedging on the civil rights program which had precipitated the South into bitter revolt against President Truman.

[*Text of the platform as adopted by the convention is on page 8.*]

By a roll call of 651½ to 582½, the convention demanded that four objectives of that program be spelled out: abolition of poll taxes in Federal elections, a national law against lynching, creation of a permanent fair employment practices system and non-segregation of the races in the armed services.

In another cracking-down action, the convention refused bluntly and decisively, in the face of Southern argument that the upholding or throwing down of the Constitution itself was at stake, to put a states'

Continued on Page 8, Column 7

BARKLEY IS CHOSEN AFTER BRIEF FLURRY

Only Rival, Senator Russell, Quits the Race—Truman Hails Kentuckian

Text of Senator Barkley's acceptance speech, Page 7.

By FELIX BELAIR Jr.
Special to The New York Times.

PHILADELPHIA, Thursday, July 15—Senator Alben W. Barkley of Kentucky was nominated by acclamation early today as the Democratic Vice Presidential candidate, leading even President Truman as the overwhelming choice of the delegates to the party's thirtieth national convention.

A few minutes later the man whose choice was dictated by an

Continued on Page 7. Column 2

World News Summarized

THURSDAY, JULY 15, 1948

President Truman was nominated by the Democratic National Convention this morning as the party's Presidential candidate against Governor Dewey and Henry A. Wallace. He received 947½ votes against 263 for Senator Richard B. Russell of Georgia, named by the Southern states' rights bloc as a gesture of defiance to Mr. Truman, and ½ vote for Paul V. McNutt. Senator Barkley was nominated for Vice President by acclamation after Senator Russell, again named by the Southerners, had withdrawn as the only opposing candidate. [1:8.]

In an acceptance speech that ripped into the Republicans the President told the convention he would call Congress back into session on July 26 to act on housing, high prices and other vital measures to show "if there is any reality" behind Republican platform pledges. [1:4.]

The Southern revolt reached its climax at the night session, when the entire Mississippi delegation of twenty-two and half of Alabama's twenty-six delegates walked out of the convention hall at the start of the roll-call for Presidential nominations. Then the name of Senator Russell was presented after Governor Laney of Arkansas, around whom the opposition first rallied, had withdrawn. [1:5.]

During the afternoon a series of Southern attempts to soften the civil rights plank of the platform and to incorporate a State's rights plank went down to overwhelming defeat. The Southerners' crowning disappointment came unexpectedly when Northern liberals, rejecting Administration pleas to do nothing to upset party unity, put over by a vote of 651½ to 582½ a strengthened civil rights plank that lauded President Truman's program and called for its enactment. The platform was then adopted by voice vote. [1:6-7.]

In this city Governor Dewey criticized the Democratic plank on foreign relations as containing "extremely partisan and provocative assertions." [8:1.]

Russia rejected the protest of the Western powers on the Berlin blockade. She told Washington, London and Paris in notes that they had lost all legal status in Berlin by having broken the Yalta and Potsdam pacts for four-power rule in Germany. The Soviet Union again urged four-power talks on all of Germany, but refused to accept settlement of the Berlin dispute as a precondition. [1:1.] A record number of 500 United States and British planes flew 2,500 tons of food and supplies into Berlin. [1:2-3.]

Palmiro Togliatti, Communist leader in Italy, was shot and seriously wounded by a student. The Communists blamed the Government and demanded its resignation. Strikes, attended by fatal riots, broke out all over the country. [1:3; map P. 18.]

The United States proposal to order both sides in Palestine to cease fighting won the support of Russia and four other countries in the United Nations Security Council. [1:2.] Israeli forces captured several towns near Nazareth. [14:3.]

Truman, in a Gay Mood, Receives Acclaim of Big Convention Crowd

Special to The New York Times.

PHILADELPHIA, Thursday, July 15—Democratic delegates and galleries filled with guests paid dignified tribute at 1:30 A. M. to President Truman and Senator Alben W. Barkley as they came to Convention Hall platform to accept their nominations.

The President, dressed in white, moved to the rostrum to "Hail to the Chief," and Mrs. Truman and his daughter, Margaret, walked with him, all smiling. The entire audience of some thirteen to fifteen thousand delegates and visitors stood to cheer them. Confetti and streamers flew.

Then the band played "The Missouri Waltz" for the President and "My Old Kentucky Home" for the grizzled Kentucky Senator, as the two shook hands. Chairman Sam Rayburn had asked for "a short demonstration" but his attempts to choke off the band's version of "My Old Kentucky Home" went unheard. The President shook with laughter.

Mrs. C. E. Miller of Philadelphia gave the President a floral replica of the Liberty Bell, and with the statement that through him the nation expected "peace in out time, and peace for all time," released forty-eight white doves from a basket on the platform. The birds zoomed toward the brilliantly-lighted dome, some ninety feet from the floor.

They were bewildered and frightened, at first. They flew against the rafters, against the bunting and swooped and dived at the President on the platform. Most were caught within a few minutes but others flew on silent wings, circling in the harsh light, all through th eacceptance speeches of Senator Barkley and the President.

The great throng in the hall listened attentively to the speeches.

The President had a friendly reception from the moment he entered the hall until he left it, at 2:20 A. M., with the cheers and "Hail to the Chief" resounding behind him.

VICTORY SWEEPING

President Wins, 947½ to 263, Over Russell on the First Ballot

BARKLEY ACCLAIMED

Nominees Go Before Convention to Make Acceptance Talks

Text of the Donnelly speech nominating Truman, Page 5.

By W. H. LAWRENCE
Special to The New York Times.

PHILADELPHIA, Thursday, July 15—President Harry S. Truman won nomination for a full term in the Democratic National Convention early today and promptly made the Republican record in Congress the 1948 key issue by calling a special session of Congress to meet July 26 to challenge the GOP to keep its platform pledges.

The President, selected by well over two-thirds of the Democratic delegates, although the Solid South dissented and thirty-five delegates from Mississippi and Alabama walked out, was in a fighting mood as he went before the convention with his running mate, Senator Alben W. Barkley, who was chosen by acclamation.

Confidently predicting his and Senator Barkley's election because "the country cannot afford another Republican Congress," the President said that the special session would be asked to act on legislation of various types.

Cites Republican Platform

He would call on it, he declared, to act to halt rising prices, meet the housing crisis, provide aid to education, enact a national health program, approve civil rights legislation, raise minimum wages, increase social security benefits, finance expanded public power projects and revise the present "anti-Semitic, anti-Catholic" displaced persons law.

The Republicans said they were for all these things in their 1948 platform, the President stated, and, if they really meant it, all could be enacted into law in a fifteen-day session.

President Truman set the convention on fire with his acceptance speech, which came at the end of a long, tiring, tumultuous session in which the north-south party split was deepened appreciably, although only a handful of southern delegates bolted.

The Southerners who remained were almost as angry as those in the "walk" about the convention's strong civil rights pledge and its overwhelming refusal to include a state's rights plank in the platform.

Senator Barkley promised to follow the President's leadership, agreed to carry out the platform and pledged himself to carry the story of Democratic accomplishments to every precinct to insure victory in November.

The acceptance speeches completed, the convention adjourned at 2:30 A. M.

Truman Margin of Victory

President Truman's margin over his chief rival, Senator Richard B. Russell of Georgia, was 947½ to 263, while Paul V. McNutt received half a vote in the final tabulation.

Senator Russell got almost the solid Southern vote remaining in the convention after the bolt by delegates from Alabama and Mississippi.

As soon as Mr. Truman was nominated, at 12:42 A. M., the convention moved ahead to the nomination of his Vice-Presidential running mate.

There was an attempt to present Senator Russell again for the Vice Presidency, but he stopped it and

Continued on Page 3, Column 1

"All the News That's Fit to Print"

The New York Times.

Copyright, 1948, by The New York Times Company.

LATE CITY EDITION

Hot, humid with evening thunder showers today. Showers tomorrow.

Temperature Range Today—Max.,90; Min.,70
Temperature Yesterday—Max.,83; Min.,69
Full U. S. Weather Bureau Report, Page 47

VOL. XCVII..No. 33,051. Entered as Second-Class Matter, Postoffice, New York, N. Y. NEW YORK, WEDNESDAY, JULY 21, 1948. Times Square, New York 18, N. Y. Telephone LAckawanna 4-1000 THREE CENTS IN NEW YORK CITY

MEN 25 TO REGISTER AUG. 30 FOR DRAFT BY TRUMAN EDICT; OTHERS TO ENROLL BY SEPT. 18

9,500,000 INVOLVED

Proclamation Does Not Set Date for Starting Induction of Men

THIS COULD BE ON SEPT. 22

Army Is Expected to Get Bulk of Draftees, With Air Force, Navy Drawing Volunteers

The text of the President's draft proclamation, Page 18.

By ANTHONY LEVIERO
Special to THE NEW YORK TIMES.

WASHINGTON, July 20—President Truman started the draft today with a proclamation requiring 9,500,000 youths to register during seventeen designated days of August and September.

From those millions of men, volunteer draft boards throughout the nation will select the manpower to match the material build-up of air, land and sea forces under the rearmament program.

All youths 18 years of age and under 26 years of age will be required to register, with the oldest group leading on Aug. 30. Thereafter enrollment will be continuous for the eight other age groups right through Sept. 18, with Sundays and Labor Day excluded.

The Presidential proclamation did not, however, specify when inductions would begin, although the earliest possible date is Sept. 22. Nor did the document designate the order in which the age groups would be called into service.

Order of Call Undetermined

Selective Service headquarters said that the draftees might be called one age group at a time or selections might be made in all groups simultaneously. A spokesman said a decision on method had not yet been made.

The primary objective of the draft is to build up the Army, which now stands at 542,000 men, to 790,000 by next July 1 for the avowed purpose of rebuilding the national security structure in a time of increasing international tension.

Kenneth C. Royall, Secretary of the Army, said recently that the Army would need an average of about 30,000 men a month, but the proportion of this figure who would be drafted would depend on the number of volunteers. He also expected the first call to be "relatively small."

Thus the Army's goal in the draft was about 248,000 men. The proclamation, however, was expected to draw many volunteers, a factor which would leave Maj. Gen. Lewis B. Hershey, Director of Selective Service, the task of inducting the difference between the number of volunteers and the required strength.

Registration Dates Specified

The Navy and Air Force, as glamour services attracting sea-yearning and air-minded young men, probably will get volunteers to meet all their needs so that the role of the revived Selective Service was expected to be largely one of producing manpower for the post-war Army.

Registration dates specified by Mr. Truman for each age follow:

The oldest group, meaning men born in 1922 after Aug. 30, will be registered on Monday, Aug. 30.

Men born in 1923, Aug. 31 and Sept. 1.

Men born in 1924, Sept. 2 and 3.

Men born in 1925, Sept. 4 and Sept. 7.

Men born in 1926, Sept. 8 and Sept 9.

Men born in 1927, Sept. 10 and Sept. 11.

Men born in 1928, Sept. 13 and Sept. 14.

Men born in 1929, Sept. 15 and Sept. 16.

Men born in 1930 before Sept. 19, Sept. 17 and Sept. 18.

The proclamation stated that youth born after Sept. 19, 1930, will register on their eighteenth birthday, or within five days thereafter. About 1,200,000 youth come into this category yearly.

The act provides for inductions during the next two years. Each

Continued on Page 18, Column 3

President to Bid Rivals Hold To Bipartisan Foreign Policy

Message to Congress Will Request Adoption of Wheat Pact and U. N. Building Loan as Linked to Aim of World Peace

Special to THE NEW YORK TIMES.

WASHINGTON, July 20 — The omnibus message loaded with controversial issues which President Truman has promised to send to the session of Congress next week will plead also for continued Republican support of the bipartisan foreign policy, the White House disclosed today.

This was made evident in the announcement that President Truman would ask Congress to ratify the international wheat agreement and to supply the $65,000,000 which this country had planned to lend to the United Nations for its permanent home in New York. These were items of unfinished business when Congress adjourned.

Charles G. Ross, White House press secretary, related both the wheat agreement and the loan to President Truman's general aim of achieving world peace.

It was learned also that advisers of the President were urging him to stress the need of continuing the bipartisan alliance in foreign affairs when he requests action on these two measures.

The addition of the two foreign-affairs measures brought to a total of eleven the issues which President Truman has suggested for action in the extraordinary session. At the Democratic convention last week he named nine domestic issues and declared that Congress could "do this job in fifteen days, if they want to do it."

Mr. Truman, it was learned, will most likely face in person "this last, worst Eightieth Congress," as he called it, to deliver his message. This was not finally decided, however. Mr. Ross left open the possibility that the message would be sent up for reading by a clerk.

The inclusion of the United Nations loan in the President's broad-scale message was regarded as Mr. Truman's strongest point in his effort to prevent the Republican

Continued on Page 15, Column 4

Brownell Says 'Rump' Session Cannot Enact GOP Platform

By CLAYTON KNOWLES
Special to THE NEW YORK TIMES.

WASHINGTON, July 20—Herbert Brownell, manager of Thomas E. Dewey's Presidential campaign, declared today it would be impossible for a "rump session of Congress, convened in an atmosphere of politics, to enact the Republican platform, drafted for adoption under a Republican President.

The statement by Mr. Brownell, limited to forty-five terse words and just two sentences, was the first official Republican pronouncement on the session which is to open Monday. It was taken as an indication that the Republicans feel under no compulsion to perform now on 1948 campaign pledges.

"The Republican platform," said Mr. Brownell, "calls for the enactment of a program by a Republican Congress under the leadership of a Republican President. Obviously this cannot be done at a rump session called at a political convention for political purposes in the heat of a political campaign."

That was the full text of the statement, carefully read from copy by the campaign chairman to a news conference that had been summoned to receive it.

Mr. Brownell spent the next half-hour parrying questions by reporters who sought amplification of the statement. About all that was gleaned from the questioning was the knowledge that Mr. Dewey had been consulted on the statement.

Continued on Page 16, Column 4

VALENTE BARS PACT OF MAYOR, ROGERS

They Agree on a Compromise Choice for Surrogate but He Refuses to Quit

By WARREN MOSCOW

The internal fight within Tammany Hall over the nomination of a Surrogate was deadlocked last night after a rapid series of dramatic developments which included the following:

Mayor O'Dwyer in conference with Hugo E. Rogers, Borough President of Manhattan and new leader of Tammany Hall, agreed to "go along" with the now dominant bloc in Tammany provided that it produced a candidate for Surrogate selected from a list that included District Attorney Frank S. Hogan, Supreme Court Justice James B. M. McNally and General Sessions Judge John A. Mullen in place of General Sessions Judge Francis L. Valente or Vincent R.

Continued on Page 14, Column 3

Palestine Truce Breaches Go On; Israeli Units Close Latrun Trap

By GENE CURRIVAN
Special to THE NEW YORK TIMES.

TEL AVIV, Israel, July 20—There were continued violations of the truce today, with Israeli forces and the Syrians still tangling in the northern area, the Arabs under Fawzi el Kawukji shelling points around Jenin and Tulkarm and the Egyptians launching an armored column attack near Hatta in the Negeb area.

While these engagements were going on today it was disclosed tonight that Latrun, crucial point on the Tel Aviv-Jerusalem highway, was completely surrounded and its Arab Legion battalions cut off from their outside bases. The only road still open is the one to Ramallah but this is within range of Israeli guns and can be used only with Israeli condescension.

In the north the Israeli forces and the Syrians were having it out around Azaziyat in Syria, where the Syrians recaptured the town after the truce, according to the Israeli commanders. Israeli authorities insist they will take back anything captured after the truce deadline, so the fight continues with both sides violating the cease-fire.

At Mishmar hay Yarden, just below, there is another battle going on as though Count Folke Bernadotte, the United Nations Mediator, had never been heard of.

And at the top of Lake Galilee, near biblical Capernaum, the Arabs attempted to cross the Jordan River but were repulsed with "very heavy losses."

At Geulim, southeast of Tulkarm, and at Kfar Saba, directly north of Petah Tiqva, Fawzi el Kawukji's Arab forces shelled both places but did not otherwise attack.

In the south an Egyptian lieutenant colonel approached Israeli commanders and asked permission to remove the dead from the battlefield east of Gaza where there were heavy losses just before the truce period. He received permission and

Continued on Page 10, Column 4

Clay, Murphy Called Home To Confer on Berlin Crisis

Will Consult With Truman and Marshall on Policy, Start of West German State—Russians Offer to Feed Entire City

By DREW MIDDLETON
Special to THE NEW YORK TIMES.

BERLIN, July 20—Gen. Lucius D. Clay, United States Military Governor in Germany, and Ambassador Robert D. Murphy, his political adviser, are flying to Washington tonight for important conferences with President Truman, Secretary of State Marshall and Secretary of the Army Kenneth C. Royall on the Berlin crisis. [They started home from Frankfort on the Main after attending the conference of Western Military Governors.]

The situation here is moving toward a climax, with the Russians today offering to feed the city and with some doubt about the French attitude toward United States-British policy as a result of the overthrow of the Schuman Cabinet.

In besieged Berlin, both the United States and British Military Governments issued new restrictions to cut gasoline consumption by private cars.

At Helmstedt, on the border of the Soviet zone, Russian soldiers turned back at least nine United States automobiles because their drivers had not obtained Russian exit permits from the Soviet military administration.

A steady procession of United States and British planes flew through clear skies to deliver an estimated 2,509 tons of food to this blockaded city in the twenty-four hours ending at 4 o'clock this afternoon.

The visit of General Clay and Ambassador Murphy, decided upon early this morning, came at an opportune moment. General Clay, who is believed to favor a "strong" policy in the current crisis, probably will have to explain in Washington his views on Berlin and, indeed, on the entire German problem, including immediate implementation of the London decision.

Continued on Page 4, Column 3

WEST EUROPE UNION FINDS SOLIDARITY ON GERMAN COURSE

5 Nations Agree at The Hague —U. S. and Canada to Join Them in Military Talks

By DAVID ANDERSON
Special to THE NEW YORK TIMES.

THE HAGUE, the Netherlands, July 20—Complete identity of views exists among the five partners of the Western European Union in their attitude toward Germany, according to a communiqué issued today at the end of a two-day conference of Britain, France, Belgium, the Netherlands and Luxembourg.

[The United States and Canada will participate in joint military planning with the five members of the Western European Union, the British Foreign Office announced Tuesday.]

It declared that the five nations "were completely at one" on "a number of international problems of direct interest to the five countries, including that of Germany." This indicates that French fears about the consequences of a possible three-power action about Berlin

Continued on Page 8, Column 3

1C INCREASE ENOUGH ON PRIVATE BUSES, CONTROLLER HOLDS

Making No Recommendation, His Reports Imply Pleas for 3c Rise Are Excessive

By ALEXANDER FEINBERG

City Controller Lazarus Joseph submitted yesterday to the Board of Estimate without recommendations exhaustive reports on the applications of thirteen private bus lines for higher fares. These clearly reflected his belief that the companies could show a profit if they received a one-cent increase.

In a prepared statement that he read at a brief special session of the board, the Controller went further, declaring that a three-cent fare increase would produce revenues about five times the amount required to meet the 24-cents-an-hour wage rise promised to their employes.

While the companies' petitions, filed with the board on May 12 did not specify the amount of the increase, their figures sought to justify an increase to 8 cents a ride on the five-cent-fare lines and to 13 cents, or two rides for a

Continued on Page 19, Column 4

World News Summarized

WEDNESDAY, JULY 21, 1948

William Z. Foster, Eugene Dennis, City Councilman Davis and four other leaders of the Communist party in this country were arrested by FBI agents yesterday on indictments charging them with conspiracy to overthrow the United States Government. Five more top Communists were also indicted by a special Federal grand jury that handed up findings, sealed at the time, to Judge Leibell. The arrested men were held under bail for hearings. [1:8.]

Several hundred foreign agents have used the United Nations to cover subversive activities here, State Department representatives told a Senate committee. United Nations officials expressed surprise at the charge. [1:6-7.]

Registration for this country's first peacetime draft will start on Aug. 30 and continue through Sept. 18. President Truman set no date for induction in a proclamation. [1:1.] Sixty-eight local boards and one appeals board will be organized in this city. [Follows the foregoing.]

President Truman will ask the special session of Congress to ratify the international wheat agreement and approve the $65,000,000 loan to the United Nations for its East River home. It was indicated that he would appeal for a continuation of bipartisan foreign policy. [1:2-3.] It will be impossible for a "rump session" of Congress to translate the Republican 1948 platform pledges into law, said Herbert Brownell, manager of the Dewey Presidential campaign. [1:2-3.]

General Clay and his political adviser, Ambassador Murphy, left Germany for Washington to lay the latest facts on the Berlin situation before the President and his aides. Russia offered to feed the Western sectors of Berlin, a proposal generally accepted as a propaganda device. [1:4-5.] The views of General Clay and Mr. Murphy are expected to be reflected in the next note to Moscow on the Berlin blockade. [4:2.]

The five nations in the Western European Union proclaimed complete identity of views on Germany and other issues in a communiqué at the close of the Hague conference. London disclosed that the United States and Canada had agreed to participate in joint military planning with the five nations. [1:4.] Ireland, in a future conflict, would no longer be isolationist but would side with Western Europe, Foreign Minister MacBride told the Dail. [8:6.]

In an effort to restore the unity of action among the Western Allies broken by the fall of the Schuman Cabinet, President Auriol strove to create a new French Government. [9:1.]

Fighting continued despite the new truce in Palestine, particularly between Israeli and Syrian forces. [1:2-3.] Egypt promised the United States to punish those responsible for stoning an American citizen to death in Cairo. [10:2.]

The United States Steel Corporation restored the $1.25-a-ton cut made in April and added 9.6 per cent to the price of finished steel products. [1:6-7.]

In this city Controller Joseph declared that a 3-cent fare increase on private bus lines would be unwarranted. He presented figures at a Board of Estimate hearing to show that the three largest systems could make a profit on a ½-cent rise. [1:5.]

12 U. S. COMMUNISTS INDICTED IN ANTI-GOVERNMENT PLOT; FOSTER, DAVIS, OTHERS SEIZED

BAIL SET AT $5,000

Special Federal Grand Jury's Action Follows Year's Investigation

PARTY CONDEMNS TRUMAN

Calls Charges the 'American Version' of Reichstag Fire —Hearing Due Aug. 23

By MEYER BERGER

Six of twelve high-ranking Communists indicted yesterday by a special Federal grand jury that has investigated Communist activity for more than a year were arrested here last night on charges of conspiring to overthrow the United States Government.

Of the six others, some of whom live in cities elsewhere, one was arrested last night in Detroit. He is Carl Winter, chairman of the Communist party in Michigan. He was held in $10,000 bail for hearing in a fortnight.

The six arrested in New York were held in $5,000 bail each for hearing Aug. 23; but they were released at 10 P. M. in custody of their attorney, Abraham Unger, on the promise that they would reappear at 10 A. M. today before Federal Judge Vincent L. Leibell with the bond.

Held On 2 Indictments Each

The six taken in New York included William Z. Foster, party chairman and several times Communist candidate for President of the United States; Benjamin Davis, New York City Councilman; and several members of the Communist National Board. Each of the six was held on two indictments. Hearing date was set for Aug. 23.

The men named in the indictments in addition to Foster, Davis and Winter, were:

John Williamson, member of the Communist national board.

Eugene Dennis, general secretary of the Communist party.

Henry Winston, member of the national board.

Jack Stachel, member of the national board.

Robert Thompson, member of the national board and chairman of the New York State Communist party.

John Gates, editor of the Communist Daily Worker since 1947.

Irving Potash, manager of the Furriers' Joint Council of New York, CIO, member of the Communist national board.

Gilbert Green, Chicago Communist district chairman.

Gus Hall, chairman of the Communist party in Ohio.

Several Are Aliens

Several of these men are aliens, among them Williamson, Stachel and Potash.

United States Attorney John F. X. McGohey described the twelve men as "the Communist party's governing board." "They run the party," he said. "They make the policy and decide what it will do."

The indictments, which had been sealed when they were handed up before noon, in Judge Leibell's court, were opened at the arraignment here. A blanket indictment accused all twelve of the men named of conspiracy to violate the so-called Smith Act, a defense measure passed in June, 1940. Each of the men was indicted individually for specific violation of the act.

The general indictment set forth:

"That from on or about April 1, 1945, and continuously thereafter up to and including the date of the filing of this indictment the defendants unlawfully, wilfully and knowingly did conspire with each other, and with divers other persons to the Grand Jurors unknown, to organize as the Communist party of the United States a society, group and assembly of persons who teach and advocate the overthrow and destruction of the Government of the United States by force and violence, and knowingly and wilfully to advocate and teach the duty and necessity of overthrowing and destroying the Government of the United States by force and violence, which said

Continued on Page 3, Column 1

Subversive Agents Believed In U. S. Under Wing of U. N.

Officials of State Department Say Several Hundred Are Here and Protected by Pacts—Lake Success Dubious

By JOSEPH A. LOFTUS
Special to THE NEW YORK TIMES

WASHINGTON, July 20—Officials of the State Department believe that several hundred subversive foreign agents have used the United Nations as a cover for their activities in this country.

Department representatives have been testifying before staff members of a Senate Judiciary Subcommittee that is studying immigration.

Robert C. Alexander, assistant chief of the State Department's Visa Commission, said that some of the agents were employes of the United Nations, or came here in some way related to the U. N. Such persons are covered by the International Immunities Act which was passed in 1945.

Mr. Alexander, who testified last Thursday and Friday, said that "they are not subject to exclusion under our laws, even though we know that their coming here would not be in our best interests. The question has arisen as to whether we are not going to build up in this country, within the next few years, a large number of people who have no sympathy with us, or for our form of government, and whom we can't get rid of because no country will take them back."

He declared that the UNRRA (United Nations Relief and Rehabilitation Administration) "was the greatest offender," and that "there are people still here who came in under the UNRRA and you can't send them anywhere."

Further, Mr. Alexander said, some of the foreigners who came here under U. N. auspices have been trained as "terrorists" and in undercover activities "contrary to the peace and good order of this country." He did not believe, however, the U. N. was responsible for bringing subversive agents here, but that the U. N. or its affiliates should assume responsibility for getting such persons out of this country when their employment terminates.

He told the committee how the

Continued on Page 4, Column 2

Price Rise of $9.34 a Ton Is Announced by U. S. Steel

A 9.6 per cent increase in the price of finished steel products was announced yesterday by the United States Steel Corporation. The new levels, effective today at all subsidiaries of the corporation, include an average increase of $8.09 a ton in the base price for major steel products. In addition, the new prices at mills or shipping points embrace a restoration of the average price reduction of $1.25 a ton made last April.

In his announcement of the price rise last night, Benjamin F. Fairless, president of United States Steel, pointed to the 9 per cent wage increase granted last Friday to the company's steel workers. He recalled that, when the wage rise had been announced earlier last week, the company had said that "constantly rising costs compel its steel-producing subsidiaries to increase their prices for steel products."

Mr. Fairless declared that the prices of many steel competitors were "substantially higher" than those of United States Steel subsidiaries, adding that the company's price reductions made last April were part of an "unsuccessful effort" to aid in retarding further rises in the cost of living.

The increases are being made to compensate United States Steel for rising costs of operation due to conditions beyond its control, the president of America's largest steel producing company said.

The text of his announcement follows:

"Last week United States Steel.

Continued on Page 17, Column 4

ASCAP HELD GUILTY IN MOVIE TRUST SUIT

Court to Bar Exacting of Fees From Houses Showing Films Containing Society's Music

Federal Judge Vincent L. Leibell ruled yesterday that the American Society of Composers, Authors and Publishers had violated the anti-trust laws by exacting fees from theatres exhibiting motion pictures containing ASCAP music.

His decision was the result of a suit filed in April, 1942, by 164 owners of 200 theatres in the metropolitan area but tried only last March. The owners asserted that since they already had to pay the motion picture producers for the right to show the films, they were being subjected to a double charge when ASCAP demanded fees in connection with the presentation of its music.

Referring to an attempt by ASCAP in August, 1947, to increase substantially the license fees for exhibitors, Judge Leibell

Continued on Page 28, Column 1

Nation's Entertainment Industry In Decline Toward Pre-War Level

By MURRAY SCHUMACH

Trapped between rising costs and shrinking attendance, the nation's entertainment industry has been squeezed steadily until it is now well on the way down to its pre-war status. The present decline, a survey indicates, is beyond that of last summer's lull and may be the most serious manifestation to date of a trend that set in eighteen months ago.

Domestic box-office volume of movies is reported to have fallen between 7 and 12 per cent this year from the same period in 1947. The number of legitimate shows on Broadway is already less than for this time last year and several current productions are in precarious financial condition.

Many radio stars are fighting salary cuts, and among the numerous night clubs that have closed are some that never before shut down in warm weather. Decreases in the sale of records, estimated between 10 and 35 per cent from last year, have compelled closing of some plant facilities. Sheet music is off almost 40 per cent.

Television has thus become virtually the only major entertainment field—with the possible exception of some concert programs—to show continued growth. Yet, despite the accelerated pace of video's progress it has not yet begun operating at a profit.

The customary autumn spurt in entertainment, already in preparation, has spurred the hope that the upsurge might exceed that of last fall and put an end to the downward trend that has already brought employment lay-offs and salary cuts. However, industrial leaders are agreed that this prospect is not too bright. Their opinions, combined with financial statements and trade paper reports, indicate the causes of the entertainment drop are too fundamental to be wiped out by an occasional stage, screen, night club or Tin Pan Alley smash-hit.

In agreement on the existence

Continued on Page 26, Column 1

"All the News That's Fit to Print"

The New York Times.

LATE CITY EDITION

Showers this morning; partly cloudy later. Sunny, mild tomorrow.

Temperature Range Today—Max.,83; Min.,71

Temperatures Yesterday—Max.,83; Min.,66

Full U. S. Weather Bureau Report, Page 43

Copyright, 1948, by The New York Times Company.

VOL. XCVII..No. 33,057. Entered as Second-Class Matter, Postoffice, New York, N. Y. NEW YORK, TUESDAY, JULY 27, 1948. Times Square, New York 18, N. Y. Telephone LAckawanna 4-1000 THREE CENTS IN NEW YORK CITY

U.S., BRITAIN BAR RAIL TRAFFIC WITH RUSSIAN GERMAN ZONE; SOVIET'S POLICE CHIEF OUSTED

OTHER NATIONS HIT

Retaliation for Blockade of Berlin Denied by Western Allies

ACTION CALLED TECHNICAL

Suspension of Police Head by Berlin Council Reversed by Russian Commandant

By EDWARD A. MORROW

Special to THE NEW YORK TIMES.

BERLIN, July 26—All international railway traffic to and from the Soviet zone through the Western zones of Germany was halted today by order of the United States and British Military Governments.

Col. Hans Holmer, chief of the United States Military Government's Transport Group, explained that the order had been issued because of "technical difficulties." He estimated that approximately 300,000 tons of material was being moved annually over the tracks of the Western zones into the Soviet zone.

While some observers considered this move to be the first step in a counter-blockade, United States and British spokesmen asserted emphatically that it was in no way to be considered a retaliatory move to the Russian blockade of the Western sectors of the city. To prove their point, they cited a list of technical difficulties in allowing such traffic to continue.

This move against the Soviet administration by the United States and British Military Governments was matched by one taken by the City Council. Dr. Ferdinand Friedensburg, Deputy Mayor, announced the suspension of Paul Markgraf, Communist police chief, and the appointment of the Socialist Johannes Stumm in his place.

Soviet Commandant Takes Action

Late tonight the Russians announced that Maj. Gen. Alexander G. Kotikov, the Soviet Commandant in Berlin, had sent specific instructions to the Acting Lord Mayor that Herr Stumm be dismissed from the police force and not be made police chief. Herr Stumm, he charged, has been active in a move to split the force.

[An official British statement said that General Kotikov had gone "entirely beyond his powers" in ordering the dismissal of Herr Stumm, press services reported.]

In a sternly worded letter, he ordered that Herr Markgraf be instructed to carry on an investigation of all those engaged in such activity "regardless of the positions and offices they hold."

At a press conference, Dr. Friedensburg pointed out that the Council on several occasions had asked the Kommandatura to dismiss Herr Markgraf because of the allegedly unsatisfactory management of the police force, stating that the force had given protection only to Communists. Recently Herr Markgraf was said to have dismissed illegally more than 100 non-Communist men on the police force and to have permitted Communists to attempt to break up a meeting of the City Assembly.

Other Nations Affected

The ban on railway traffic, which will cut off Switzerland, Italy, France, the Low Countries and the Scandinavian nations from trade with the Soviet zone, is the first large-scale action in the East-West struggle over Berlin that affects countries other than the four occupying powers. The Governments of the countries affected were informed a few days ago that the Western zones would no longer accept such transit traffic, a British spokesman said. International transit traffic for Poland and Czechoslovakia will continue to be routed through the Western zones.

It is expected that Switzerland will be the greatest loser in traffic. Military government transport officials said that the Soviet zone had exported approximately 15,000 tons of brown coal and timber to that country.

Transport officials were unable

Continued on Page 6, Column 3

Molotov to Be Approached For Parley on Berlin Crisis

Allied Envoys to Make Proposal Orally in Hope of Ending Impasse—Truman Has No Bid for Talk With Stalin

By HERBERT L. MATTHEWS

Special to THE NEW YORK TIMES.

LONDON, July 26—The next approach to Moscow on the Berlin situation will most likely be an oral one by envoys of the United States, Britain and France directly to Foreign Minister Molotov, it was learned from an authoritative source here today.

It is hoped that by making their demarche in this way instead of by formal notes it will be possible to break down the barriers that have prevented any real diplomacy on an issue that involves war or peace. Foreign Minister Molotov might be in a position to say something or react in some way and in that case the envoys would be able to talk things over with him and perhaps make progress.

[President Truman has received no official proposal for a conference with Premier Stalin on Germany, according to the White House. The President would be glad to see the Soviet leader in Washington, it was said.]

Each of the envoys, according to present plans, will receive a written aide memoire that will be the formal basis of what the Western Allies want to say about Berlin.

The idea for this form of approach is American, it is understood, but the State Department originally felt that the envoys should seek to deliver their messages to Premier Stalin. This was put up to the British and French by United States Ambassador Lewis W. Douglas on Saturday when the Standing Committee consisting of himself, Rene Massigli, French Ambassador to Britain, and Sir William Strang, British

Continued on Page 6, Column 5

Western German Leaders Agree to Launch New State

By JACK RAYMOND

Special to THE NEW YORK TIMES.

FRANKFORT ON THE MAIN, Germany, July 26—The Minister-Presidents of Western Germany formally accepted today the responsibility of initiating a Government for the eleven states of non-Soviet Germany, and agreed with the United States, British and French Military Governors to begin their task at once.

Certain observations of the German leaders are to be forwarded to the Governments of the three occupying powers, but no reservations or conditions were placed on German acceptance.

The significance of today's action was regarded as two-fold:

First, although the Western Allies in the last few days had emphasized their willingness to negotiate with the Russians on the German problem, they are not countenancing any delay in carrying out the London agreement on Western Germany that precipitated the Berlin crisis.

Second, although the Germans had attempted to modify the impact of their participation in a "splitting" of Germany, they are accepting in full the authorization to proceed with the central regime that they have sought all along.

After a conference of more than three hours, the following communiqué, drafted by the participants, was issued:

"As a result of the final meeting between the Military Governors and the Minister-Presidents of the three Western zones, held under the chairmanship of General Koenig [Lieut. Gen. Joseph-Pierre Koenig, French Military Governor], an agreement was reached that the organization of the three

Continued on Page 6, Column 2

U.S. TO HELP BRITAIN IMPROVE INDUSTRY

Cripps, Hoffman Agree on a Joint Employer-Union Council—Chancellor Denies Rifts

By HAROLD CALLENDER

Special to THE NEW YORK TIMES.

PARIS, July 26—After a three-hour talk today with Paul G. Hoffman, United States Economic Cooperation Administrator, Sir Stafford Cripps, Britain's Chancellor of the Exchequer, announced that they had agreed upon a joint undertaking to improve British methods of industrial production by utilizing United States technical advice.

Sir Stafford said that as a result there soon would be established a joint council composed of representatives of British and United States employers and trade unions to advise the London Government how the efficiency of British industry might be increased. He suggested that British engineers might be sent to the United States to study methods there.

Referring to a recent statement by Mr. Hoffman that the United

Continued on Page 9, Column 1

Israel Claims Rule in Jerusalem; Will Name Governor of New City

By GENE CURRIVAN

Special to THE NEW YORK TIMES.

TEL AVIV, Israel, July 26—The New City in Jerusalem, with a population of 100,000 Jews, has been declared Israeli-occupied territory.

In an announcement to this effect a spokesman for the Provisional Government of Israel declared tonight that the Israeli Administration would take into account the "special Jewish character of the city" and that a military governor would be appointed for the city.

This move is in conformity with a previously announced principle that any territory occupied by Israeli forces would come under the jurisdiction of the state.

Jerusalem is outside the Israeli boundaries defined by the United Nations General Assembly and, along with the metropolitan area, which includes the Old City and Bethlehem, was proclaimed an international zone.

The decision was disclosed a few hours after Count Folke Bernadotte, United Nations Mediator for Palestine, had left for Rhodes. He had conferred with Foreign Minister Moshe Shertok on the proposed demilitarization of Jerusalem. United Nations observers and officials have been gathering in Jerusalem to supervise the truce and prepare the ground for the city's demilitarization.

It is believed the Israeli decision on Jerusalem was influenced by the presence in the city of the dissident Irgun Zvai Leumi and Stern Group, which defied the command of the Israeli Army because they were functioning in an area outside the jurisdiction of the Provisional Government.

The Israeli maneuver may set up a barrier to the proposal to demilitarize Jerusalem, a recommendation put forth by Count Bernadotte. With Jerusalem under

Continued on Page 11, Column 2

Housing Shortage to Ease In Year, Survey Indicates

Moses Calls on Savings Banks and Congress to Aid—Ross Urges Public Projects, Real Estate Group Backs Private Industry

By WILLIAM M. FARRELL

The housing shortage here will ease appreciably in the next year, but earnest efforts on the part of Government, financiers and builders are necessary if the improvement is to continue. This is the consensus of experts, including Robert Moses, who see the situation from a variety of viewpoints.

The bright aspects of the picture, Mr. Moses pointed out, are apparent to anyone who travels about the city and neighboring Long Island, Westchester and New Jersey. Rows of tiny bungalows are going up, and larger one-family homes are under construction everywhere, while big apartment houses and garden-apartment communities are being erected in the city and in suburban communities where once they were rare or unknown.

The brightness dims noticeably when rentals and prices are considered, but nevertheless the new construction will provide for thousands of families.

With available sources of materials and labor it would be hard to speed the present rate of housing construction, the City Construction Coordinator said. But he pointed to large-scale moves that are necessary to improve the city's ability to win the constant battle against obsolescence and to meet the needs of the growing population.

Savings banks, Mr. Moses said, have failed badly to contribute to the construction of new housing. Excepting the Bowery Savings Bank, he asserted, they have refused to meet an obligation to help in the development of the community they serve.

"They are public institutions," Mr. Moses said, "and of course they ought to protect the dimes and dollars of the poor who are their depositors, but they ought to invest locally. I believe it is almost time to have public representation on their boards of directors—by the State Banking Commissioner, perhaps."

The Veterans Administration also should devote more of its re-

Continued on Page 44, Column 4

U. N. BODY PUTS END TO TALKS ON ARMS; SOVIET VOTED DOWN

Better International Feeling Awaited—Issue Goes Back to Assembly Session

By A. M. ROSENTHAL

Special to THE NEW YORK TIMES.

LAKE SUCCESS, N. Y., July 26—**The last phase of United Nations disarmament work—the negotiations in the Commission on Conventional Armaments — was abandoned today and the whole arms reduction controversy made ready for full debate in the General Assembly.**

Meeting in closed session, the commission's working committee voted, 9 to 2, against the Soviet Union and the Ukraine, to adopt a British resolution stating that arms reduction could be accomplished only in an atmosphere of international confidence and security.

Technically, the committee must meet once more to approve its report to the Assembly and the parent commission will have to hold another session before the end becomes formal. But delegates agreed

Continued on Page 10, Column 4

CITY RELIEF ROLLS CUT 1,064 IN MONTH TO TOTAL OF 139,521

June Drop Is First Substantial Post-War Decline—Stress on Job-Finding Credited

By DORIS GREENBERG

The first substantial post-war decrease in the city's relief rolls was reported yesterday by Commissioner of Welfare Raymond M. Hilliard.

At the end of June, the number of recipients of some form of public assistance had dropped 1,064 under the total at the beginning of the month, Mr. Hilliard said.

He also noted that preliminary figures pointed toward a July decline of possibly 2,000 more.

This reversal of a trend that started in September, 1945, and continued virtually unchecked, has resulted largely from new stress on the finding of jobs for relief applicants who are capable of working, the Commissioner said.

In a resume of Welfare Department operations during June—the initial report of a monthly series planned by Mr. Hilliard—the financial saving accompanying the

Continued on Page 17, Column 2

World News Summarized

TUESDAY, JULY 27, 1948

President Truman ordered the armed forces to put an end to discrimination "as rapidly as possible," and decreed a fair employment practices policy throughout the civil branches of the Government in which "merit and fitness" would be the only qualifications for a job. He put the double-barreled policy into effect by executive orders issued yesterday. [1:8.] Southern Democrats were further angered by the President's action, but had little hope of defeating civil rights bills in the special session of Congress. [4:2.]

When the President delivers his message to Congress at 12:30 today, he will ask the special session to act on eleven matters, among them anti-inflation legislation, the Taft-Ellender-Wagner Housing Bill, Federal aid to education, a 75-cent minimum legal wage, extended Social Security, reform of Federal pay schedules and the civil rights program. Congress met briefly yesterday and party leaders mapped their strategy. [1:6-7.] Republicans and Democrats blamed each other for living costs. [1:7.]

While retail meat prices continued high and milk was scheduled to rise one cent a quart in this city on Sunday and another cent on Oct. 1, industry leaders remained divided over renewed rationing and price controls. [1:6-7.] Experts predicted easing of the housing shortage here if the Government, industry and finance cooperated. [1:4-5.]

This city's relief rolls showed the first substantial post-war drop last month; the trend continued in July. [1:5.]

Right-wing candidates swept all Communist sympathizers out of office in the National Maritime Union, CIO, council. [45:1.]

International rail traffic through the Western zones of Germany into the Soviet zone was halted by United States and British occupation chiefs. This action was taken, it was explained, because of "technical difficulties" and was not in retaliation for the Russian blockade of Berlin. [1:1; map, P. 6.] It was learned in London that the Western powers probably would make their next approach to Moscow orally to Foreign Minister Molotov. The White House said no official proposal had been received for a Truman-Stalin meeting. [1:2-3.]

The Minister-Presidents of the eleven German states in the Western zones agreed to assume responsibility for a Western German government. [1:2-3.]

Sir Stafford Cripps announced that a joint United States-British council representing labor and industry would be established soon to help increase the efficiency of British industry. [1:2.]

A new French Cabinet was formed by Premier Marie after he had surmounted a left-wing Socialist rebellion. [5:1.]

A United Nations committee voted to suspend activities on conventional disarmament until international confidence and security had returned. [1:4.] The Little Assembly approved a program to facilitate the peaceful settlement of disputes. [13:1.]

Indonesia's economic revival has been prevented by the Netherlands' blockade, a United Nations group reported. [14:2.]

The New City of Jerusalem was declared Israeli-occupied territory by the Israeli Government, which said a military governor would be named. [1:2-3.]

TRUMAN ORDERS END OF BIAS IN FORCES AND FEDERAL JOBS; ADDRESSES CONGRESS TODAY

CONGRESSIONAL LEADERS CONFER

Joseph W. Martin Jr., Speaker of House, and Arthur H. Vandenberg, President pro tempore of Senate. The New York Times (by Tames)

PRESSES FOR RIGHTS

President Acts Despite Split in His Party Over the Chief Issue

LITTLE 'FEPC' IS CREATED

'Merit, Fitness' Set as U. S. Employment Guides—Military Equality Is Demanded

Texts of the President's two executive orders are on Page 4.

By ANTHONY LEVIERO

Special to THE NEW YORK TIMES.

WASHINGTON, July 26—President Truman ordered today the end of discrimination in the armed forces "as rapidly as possible" and instituted a fair employment practices policy throughout the civil branch of the Federal Government.

On the eve of his appearance before Congress, the President issued two executive orders to carry out his sweeping aims. He said that men in uniform should have "equality of treatment and opportunity" without regard to race, color, religion or national origin.

Similarly, he decreed that "merit and fitness" should be the only application for a Government job, and that the head of each department "shall be personally responsible for an effective program to insure that fair employment policies are fully observed in all personnel actions within his department."

The two orders were expected to have a thunderbolt effect on the already highly charged political situation in the Deep South, a situation which is expected to be aggravated further tomorrow when Mr. Truman makes his omnibus call on Congress for action. The message, in one of its eleven major elements, is expected to go down the line for his ten-point civil rights program, which last February started the deep fissures in the Democratic party.

Enforcement Machinery Set Up

The Presidential orders, which require no Congressional sanction, specified in detail the machinery that would be employed to monitor both anti-discrimination programs.

In the National Military Establishment, Mr. Truman created an advisory panel, called the President's Committee on Equality of Treatment and Opportunity in the Armed Services. It will consist of seven members, none of whom was named today.

It was said, however, that one man who probably would be recommended for membership is Dr. Frank Graham, president of the University of North Carolina. It was believed he would be acceptable to North and South, Negro and white.

The civilian employe order directed that a Fair Employment Board be formed from among members and employes of the Civil Service Commission. This, too, is to be a seven-member board, as yet unnamed.

The committee of the armed forces received the mission of determining how present practices might be altered to carry out the Presidential order. In stipulating rapid application of the policy, Mr. Truman said that it should be done with due regard to "the time required to effectuate any necessary changes without impairing efficiency or morale."

Hearings, Appeals Provided

In the civil departments, the head of each was directed to designate an official as "Fair Employment Officer," who was charged with full operating responsibility for the non-discrimination program. Provision was made for hearings of complaints, appeals and disciplinary action.

As the top agency in this program, the Fair Employment Board in the Civil Service Commission received a six-point program providing for review of decisions, drafting of regulations, advice on problems to all departments, publication of information relating to the program, coordination of the policy in the departments and re-

Continued on Page 4, Column 3

Republican Chiefs Cautious, Awaiting President's Word

By C. P. TRUSSELL

Special to THE NEW YORK TIMES.

WASHINGTON, July 26—The Eightieth Congress returned to work today in response to the July 15 call of President Truman. It did not come back happily. The first flashes of smiling greetings on reassembly soon wore off.

The Senate sat for twelve minutes, just long enough for the opening prayer, a quorum call to which sixty-five members answered "present" and for the naming of a committee to notify the White House formally that Congress was back in business.

In the House, 310 members answered to their names. Many of them immediately set out to give oral previews of the extra session and the campaigns. It appeared that the nearly two hours of debate on many subjects covered about the whole eleven-point program which Mr. Truman will deliver in person to a joint Senate-House session at 12:30 P. M. (EDT) tomorrow.

Late today, while Republican leaders were in a huddle over prospective programs and the question of just where the GOP stood as the extra session opened, Democratic leaders paid a call at the White House. Mr. Truman read to them lengthy passages from the speech he will make to the whole Congress tomorrow. There were suggestions for change, it was reported later. The President made notes and indicated, it was said, that the suggestions would be followed.

A "score card," made public later by Charles G. Ross, Presidential secretary, disclosed that Mr.

Continued on Page 3, Column 2

HOUSE SKIRMISHES ON LIVING COSTS

Opposing Parties Shunt Blame for Inflation — Selective Curbs Held Truman Aim

By SAMUEL A. TOWER

Special to THE NEW YORK TIMES.

WASHINGTON, July 26—Congressional skirmishing over the blame for the high cost of living and the housing shortage broke out between the Republicans and the Democrats today, virtually immediately after the opening prayers had marked the convening of the recalled Congress.

While many legislators remained silent, awaiting tomorrow's message from President Truman, a number of Representatives were unable to withhold their fire and exchanged oratorical salvos across the aisle in attempts to pin the onus for the situations on the opposition.

The White House listed anti-inflation legislation and enactment of the long-range Taft-Ellender-Wagner Housing Bill among the points that would be covered in

Continued on Page 3, Column 5

Meat Men Here Split on Controls As Prices Stay High; Milk Going Up

As retail meat prices continued high yesterday, with little promise of any marked reductions in the next six to eight months, sharp differences over renewing rationing and price controls arose in the industry. Meanwhile, milk price advances of 1 cent a quart, scheduled here for Aug. 1, and a similar increase on Oct. 1, received official sanction of the Department of Agriculture in Washington.

Only the American Meat Institute held forth the hope that a seasonal increase in meat production by fall and winter "should tend to modify prices in some degree, unless offset by further increased consumer income." Joining with the institute in opposing controls was the New York State Association of Retail Meat Dealers.

Favoring controls, with a ceiling price on livestock at the source, was the National Industry Meat Council, representing 25,000 shops in eight Eastern states. In a complete reversal of its 1946 stand, the New York Retail Appetizers Association, representing 250 grocery and delicatessen shops, requested President Truman to reinstate the Office of Price Administration.

Milk prices to consumers here will advance as the result of the minimum fluid milk prices established for the New York area by the Department of Agriculture. The alternate formulae for minimum prices set by the department were identical with those recommended on July 6, the department specifying as follows:

"Minimum prices per hundredweight for milk of 3.5 per cent butterfat content are: (1) $5.68 for August and September, and $6.12 for October through December; or (2) a New York price for the August-December, 1948 period comparable to that established under the Boston Federal milk order for Class 1 milk of 3.7 per cent butterfat content. The higher of the alternate minimums will be the effective price."

Department officials said that

Continued on Page 3, Column 7

Ventriloquist Jimmy Nelson and his dummy, Danny O'Day, were permanent cast members on Milton Berle's *Texaco Star Theater*.

DeForest Kelley, playing an unidentified "good guy," shakes the hand of the masked-man—The Lone Ranger. Clayton Moore played the Ranger, and the late Jay Silverheels was his faithful Indian companion, Tonto.

Lucky Pup was the name of the popular children's show that featured puppeteers Hope and Morey Bunin. The puppets were named Pinhead and Foodini, and the show was a kids' favorite for years.

William Boyd earned a fortune from his portrayal of Hopalong Cassidy. The shows, which made their debut in 1948, have since become children's classics.

Tokyo Rose, who "entertained" GIs in the Pacific during the war, re-enacts the way she broadcast to U.S. troops.

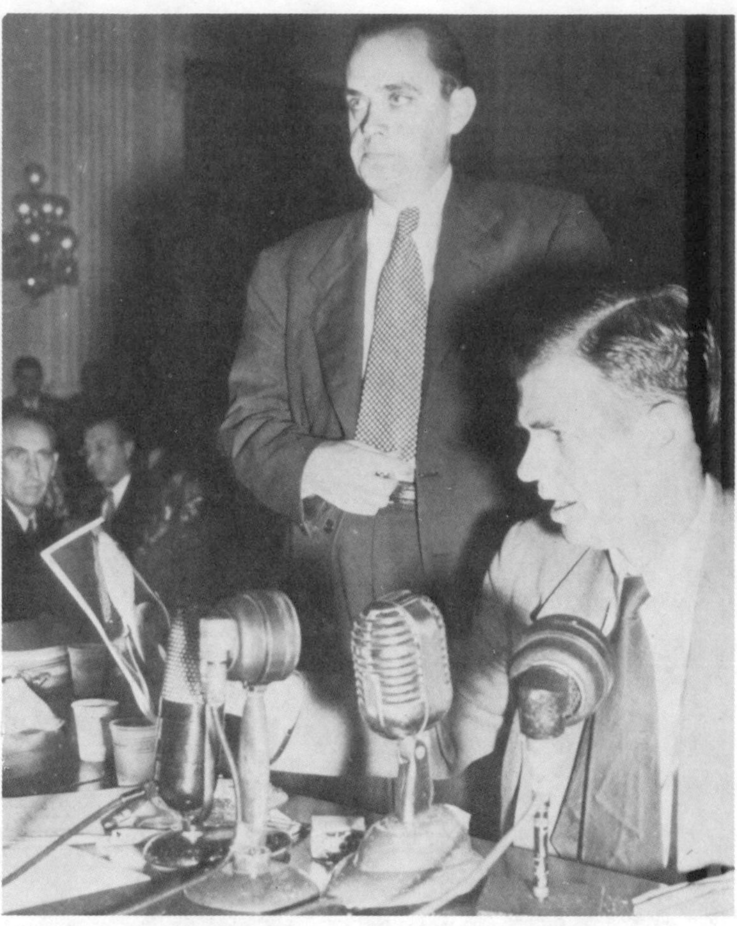

Alger Hiss studies a photograph of Whittaker Chambers while giving testimony before the House Un-American Activities Committee. Committee investigator Robert Stripling stands over him.

A young Congressman named Richard Nixon was present at the Alger Hiss hearings. Nixon was co-sponsor of a bill that would have denied Communists passports or access to Federal jobs.

Republican Senator Robert Taft of Ohio led the conservative bloc which dominated the 80th Congress. He nearly became the Republican candidate for president.

"All the News That's Fit to Print"

The New York Times.

LATE CITY EDITION
Occasional showers today and ending tomorrow; warmer tomorrow.
Temperature Range Today—Max.,77; Min.,66
Temperature Yesterday—Max.,75; Min.,65
Full U. S. Weather Bureau Report, Page 37

VOL. XCVII...No. 33,065. Entered as Second-Class Matter, Postoffice, New York, N. Y. NEW YORK, WEDNESDAY, AUGUST 4, 1948. Times Square, New York 18, N. Y. Telephone LAckawanna 4-1000 THREE CENTS IN NEW YORK CITY

RED 'UNDERGROUND' IN FEDERAL POSTS ALLEGED BY EDITOR

IN NEW DEAL ERA

Ex-Communist Names Alger Hiss, Then in State Department

WALLACE AIDES ON LIST

Chambers Also Includes Former Treasury Official, White—Tells of Fears for His Life

By C. P. TRUSSELL
Special to THE NEW YORK TIMES.

WASHINGTON, Aug. 3 — An "underground" Communist organization, led by men at key posts of government and operating to infiltrate the whole establishment with its party members, was described to the House Committee on Un-American Activities today by an admitted former Communist, Whittaker Chambers, who said he served as a courier for the group.

Mr. Chambers, now a senior editor of Time magazine, swore that this organization, which he viewed as a forerunner of the Soviet spy rings testimony of which has shaken Washington recently, had these leaders:

Alger Hiss, former director of special political affairs in the State Department, executive secretary of the Dumbarton Oaks conversations and secretary general of the San Francisco Conference at which the United Nations charter was written. Mr. Hiss accompanied President Franklin D. Roosevelt to Malta and the Yalta conference in 1945 and the following year was a principal adviser to the American delegation at the first session of the United Nations General Assembly at London. He is now president of the Carnegie Endowment for International Peace, in New York.

Donald Hiss, a younger brother of Alger Hiss, who held posts in the State and Agriculture Departments.

Former NLRB Secretary Named

Nathan Witt, former general secretary of the National Labor Relations Board, who resigned in 1941 after eight years of service. He is now practicing law in New York.

Lee Pressman, who held posts as assistant general counsel in the Agricultural Adjustment Administration under appointment by former Secretary Henry A. Wallace; general counsel for the Works Progress Administration by appointment of the late Harry L. Hopkins, and general counsel of the Resettlement Administration under Rexford G. Tugwell. Later Mr. Pressman was general counsel for the Congress of Industrial Organizations and the CIO's Steelworkers' Organizing Committee. He is now associated with Mr. Wallace's Progressive party.

John J. Abt, who from 1933 to 1935 was chief of litigation for the AAA, an assistant general counsel for the WPA in 1935, chief counsel for the Senate (La Follette) Civil Liberties Investigating Committee in 1936 and 1937 and special assistant to the Attorney General in 1937 and 1938. Mr. Abt was accused last Saturday by Miss Elizabeth T. Bentley, confessed courier for the alleged Soviet spy ring, as being a member of the "Perlo group" of that organization.

War Production Board Aide

Victor Perlo, formerly with the War Production Board, the alleged head of one of several espionage groups about which Miss Bentley testified.

Charles Kramer, also described as Charles Kravitzky, who was identified as counsel to special Senate labor problems committees under the chairmanships of Senators Claude Pepper of Florida and Harley M. Kilgore of West Virginia. Mr. Kramer was said by committee attachés to be now associated with the Progressive party.

Henry Collins, formerly in the Agriculture Department, at whose apartment the meetings of the organization described by Mr. Chambers were said to have been held.

Meanwhile William W. Remington, formerly with the War Production Board and now in the Department of Commerce, told a Sen-

Continued on Page 3, Column 2

Communism Hunted In Three Inquiries

Special to THE NEW YORK TIMES.

WASHINGTON, Aug. 3—Congressional committees conducted three simultaneous hearings today on the same subject, communism.

The Committee on Un-American Activities, a standing House group, inquired further into espionage among Government employes.

A subcommittee of the Senate committee on expenditures in the executive departments covered some of the same ground to determine the effectiveness of the loyalty test for Government employes.

A third group, a House Labor and Education subcommittee, resumed hearings on Communist influence in unions of New York City department store employes.

COMMUNISTS SEEK MAJOR ROLE BY '52

Convention Talks Hint Plan Is to Use 3d Party—Platform Seen Waiting on Kremlin

By WARREN MOSCOW

In the midst of the nation's most vigorous anti-Communist drive, the American Communist high command affirmed yesterday the intention of the party to move into a major political contending role. While party statements only hinted at it, they indicated that the Communists intended to achieve this by working through the Wallace Progressive party with the 1952 elections in mind.

Meanwhile, another possibly significant development of the Communist national convention being held here was an extension of the convention's duration to Friday, and a postponing of adoption of the party's platform for 1948 until tomorrow, instead of today and tomorrow, as originally scheduled.

Nothing on the party's agenda, as announced, explained the delay. It was thought possible that the American Communists decided to await further news from the Moscow conference between Premier Stalin and the Ambassadors of the Western powers before committing themselves irrevocably for the remainder of the Presidential year.

The Communist convention, the first held since Earl Browder was "purged" in 1945, was held with the press barred from its sessions, in a small ballroom on the sixth floor of the Hotel Riverside Plaza, on West Seventy-third Street. Reporters were confined to a press room at the rear end of the floor, as one entered from the elevators, and photographers were again barred from picture-taking.

The rules were applied in all strictness not only to the press. William Z. Foster, national chairman of the party, was stopped as he entered for the afternoon session, and required to produce his card. This was not rehearsed, or announced, and was spotted only by a reporter who happened to be looking the right way at the right

Continued on Page 2, Column 3

STALIN REPORTED LEAVING DOOR OPEN TO 4-POWER TALKS

High Sources Believe Russian Would Place on the Agenda More Subjects Than Berlin

BUT ARE STILL SKEPTICAL

Think East-West Solution Is Not Imminent—Lifting of Blockade Held Likely

By HAROLD CALLENDER
Special to THE NEW YORK TIMES.

PARIS, Aug. 3—Diplomats here who have been informed of the nature of the talk yesterday between Premier Stalin and the three Western envoys, said today that the head of the Soviet Union had not proposed or promised a four-power conference on Germany, but had left the door open for one.

These officials agreed in predicting that a four-power discussion of the whole German problem, either at such a conference or otherwise, would result from the Western powers' messages to Mr. Stalin. They also predicted that no solution of the problem, and no important agreement between the Soviet Union and the West would result.

Their theory was that the Soviet Union wanted to talk at length with the Western powers rather than to carry the test of strength in Berlin to a conclusion, and added that the reason for this Russian desire was to avoid further trouble with the West just when new difficulties in Iran, China and the Balkans were coming to a boil.

Berlin Blockade Still an Issue

These diplomats said that this inclination of Moscow would suit the Western governments, which also sought to ease the tension over Germany and to resort to all possible diplomatic means of achieving a modus vivendi.

The question arose whether the desire for negotiations would cause the Russians to lift the Berlin blockade. It was said here that no clear answer had been given but that there was hope of such a concession because the Western powers considered it indispensable to further talks.

[A Berlin dispatch indicated that restrained optimism existed there that the Russians would soon lift the blockade of the city by announcing that "technical" obstacles to the transit of goods had been overcome.]

One reason that the observers predicted the negotiations would prove futile was, they said, that Russia undoubtedly would want to place the Ruhr on the agenda and would seek to share control of the Ruhr, or at least a right to be present there and watch what the Western powers were doing. To this the West would not agree, these observers contended.

Pressure on Iran Increases

In connection with the present visit of the Shah of Iran in Paris, it became known today that the Russians had taken advantage of his absence to bring new pressure upon his Government to ratify an oil agreement and to resist United States military aid. Reports reaching Paris are that Moscow has already begun to remove the Russian colony from Teheran. Iranian authorities were reported to be greatly disturbed and to have suggested that the Shah cut short his European tour.

Meanwhile it is said here in diplomatic circles that the Russians

Continued on Page 5, Column 1

Szakasits Is Hungary's President; Pro-Communist Socialist Sworn In

By The Associated Press.

BUDAPEST, Hungary, Aug. 3—Arpad Szakasits, pro-Communist Socialist, succeeded to the Presidency of Hungary today. He was sworn in immediately, taking the place of Zoltan Tildy, a member of the Small Landholders party, who resigned Friday when his son-in-law was accused of spying and treason.

President Szakasits, a former bricklayer and Socialist newspaper editor, was declared elected unanimously by the Parliament after about thirty members of the Democratic Peoples party and the Christian Women's Camp walked out. The two Opposition groups returned after the unanimous ballot was cast.

His election had been forecast since Saturday when the dominant United Workers party, a merger of Communists and Socialists headed by Mr. Szakasits, had declared for him and other parties followed suit. His was the only candidacy presented to the 241-member Parliament by the Speaker, Imre Nagy.

President Szakasits, at a formal swearing-in ceremony, promised to deal with "satellites of imperialists at home" with an iron fist and to cooperate closely with neighboring "people's democracies"—the countries of the Soviet bloc.

Mr. Szakasits was Vice Premier in the Cabinet and for many years was Socialist deputy in Parliament.

Many prominent politicians were called home for his inauguration today. These included Foreign Minister Erik Molnar, who was attending the Danubian conference in Belgrade, the Hungarian Ministers to Paris and Berne, and Minister Zoltan Vas and Sandor Ronai, who were in Moscow negotiating a trade agreement.

British Offer Soviet $140,000,000 Trade

Special to THE NEW YORK TIMES.

LONDON, Aug. 3—A new trade agreement to supply Britain with £35,000,000 (about $140,000,000) worth of grain, lumber and other materials from Russia will be sought when negotiations with the Soviet Union open here within ten days. The present agreement provides for £23,000,000 worth of Russian raw materials in exchange for steel rails, machine tools, locomotives and portable saw mill equipment.

According to information here, a group of trade specialists will leave Moscow this week-end for London to assist Soviet Ambassador Georgi N. Zarubin in his discussions with the British.

Russia is insistent that the British Government guarantee delivery dates for all capital equipment purchased. The British are equally determined not to agree to such a provision.

VISHINSKY IS TOLD TO CEASE BULLYING

Briton at the Danube Parley Scores Russian's Tactics—Soviet Marshals Data

By M. S. HANDLER
Special to THE NEW YORK TIMES.

BELGRADE, Yugoslavia, Aug. 3—Sir Charles Peake, British Ambassador to Belgrade and chief British delegate to the Danubian conference, protested vehemently at today's session against tactics of Andrei Y. Vishinsky, Soviet Deputy Foreign Minister. Sir Charles said that the United Kingdom delegation could not be "bullied and intimidated."

He charged that Mr. Vishinsky had a tendency to treat anyone who disagreed with his point of view as if he were a prisoner in the dock and that he (Sir Charles) must remind Mr. Vishinsky that he would not permit the Soviet Deputy Minister to treat him in such a manner. The British delegate concluded with the remark that all delegations present could judge for themselves as to who were the potatoes in the conference and who was the cook. Sir Charles made his statement in reply to what he termed a misrepresentation of his remarks last Saturday by Mr. Vishinsky.

Mr. Vishinsky ignored Sir Charles' sallies and proceeded with a detailed legal and historical analysis of the Danubian problem in an effort to demolish the British

Continued on Page 4, Column 7

World News Summarized

WEDNESDAY, AUGUST 4, 1948

Republican leaders indicated in Washington yesterday that next Wednesday had been set as the date of adjournment for the special session of Congress. Credit control and housing measures presumably will receive attention. The Senate was still immobilized by the poll tax filibuster. [1:8.]

The President proposed that Congress pass an excess profits tax designed to bring in $4,300,000,000. Such an act was assailed in the House Banking and Currency Committee by Marriner S. Eccles, former chairman of the Federal Reserve Board. [1:6.]

It seemed likely that Congress would approve a loan of $65,000,000 to the United Nations for headquarters construction. A Senate-House compromise was reached. [1:7.]

President Truman returned to the capital from his visit to Missouri and was immediately immersed in work. [13:3.]

Testimony about alleged espionage for Russia continued to take the spotlight in Washington. Whittaker Chambers, a senior editor of Time magazine and admitted former Communist, accused Alger Hiss, formerly of the State Department; Nathan Witt, formerly of the NLRB, and six other former Federal officials of having been leaders in an "underground" Communist movement. [1:1.]

Mr. Hiss denied charges made against him, as did Louis Adamic. Lee Pressman, CIO counsel, had "no comment." [3:1.]

William Remington of the Department of Commerce testified before the Senate committee that allegations against him were false. He was confronted with an application for a Navy commission in which he had indicated familiarity with the Manhattan Project. [3:6.]

The Communist party, in its national convention in New York, indicated its intention of moving into a major role in American politics through control of the Wallace party. The Communist meetings were secret and there was evidence that the schedule had been slowed down to await developments in Moscow. [1:2.]

In respect to those developments, diplomatic sources in Paris stated that Premier Stalin had not proposed or promised four-power talks, but that there was reason to believe that conversations would go on. The Russians were believed to be eager to avoid a genuine crisis in relations with the West because of difficulties elsewhere. President Truman was obviously informed of the details of the Kremlin meeting, but he was silent. So were Foreign Office circles in London. [1:3.]

There was cautious optimism in Berlin over the prospects for lifting the Soviet blockade soon. It was believed there that important four-power talks would take place shortly. [4:2.]

In Hungary, Arpad Szakasits was sworn in as President. Thirty members of the Opposition groups walked out of Parliament before the vote that confirmed him. [1:2-3.]

At the Danube conference in Belgrade, the British representative declared that the United Kingdom did not propose to be bullied or intimidated by Andrei Y. Vishinsky, Russian Deputy Foreign Minister. The protest was ignored. [1:4.]

The United Nations Mediator, Count Bernadotte, began conferences in Cairo on problems of the demilitarization of Jerusalem and the handling of Arab refugees. [8:3.] At Lake Success it was disclosed that officials of the Arab Higher Committee were proceeding with plans to proclaim an Arab Government for all Palestine. [9:1.]

3D AVE. STRIKE SEEN AS COMPANY SCORNS CITY 7C FARE PLAN

Union Is Told 24c Pay Rise Cannot Be Paid After Estimate Board Bars 8c Demand

ISSUE IS SHARPLY DEBATED

Mayor Refuses to 'Put Money Into Stockholders' Pockets at Public's Expense'

By WILLIAM R. CONKLIN

The threat of a strike on lines of the Third Avenue Transit Company and two affiliates became imminent last night, when the company repudiated a wage increase arrangement after its failure to win a permanent eight-cent fare from the city.

John M. MacDonald, president of Third Avenue, announced last night that the company would not meet the demands of its 3,800 employes for a wage increase of 24 cents an hour.

His action followed by a few hours the decision of the Board of Estimate to restrict the lines to a temporary seven-cent fare for twelve months. Company officials told the board this plan would bankrupt them and argued in vain for a permanent eight-cent fare.

Mayor O'Dwyer said he would not "put money into stockholders' pockets at the expense of the riding public," and charged that $59,000,000 of the company's capital investment was "water."

Incensed over the Board of Estimate's attitude, Mr. MacDonald said:

"I think this is still America, but I may be wrong. I hold bonds in this company, and if it's any crime to hold a bond or make a profit, I don't know what it is."

"Did you tell the Mayor about that $59,000,000," Controller Lazarus Joseph began.

"Don't holler!" Mr. MacDonald shouted.

"I'll treat you fairly on the money that's actually there," Mayor O'Dwyer said, "but I'm not going to follow you around Wall Street to see what the juggling is. Now, what do you consider a fair return on your investment?"

"We're entitled to an 8 per cent return, and we're entitled to as much of a fare as we can get," the company president replied. "We want an eight-cent fare."

"I think he'd trade on less," said

Continued on Page 42, Column 2

CREDIT CONTROL AND HOUSING NOW SET AS CONGRESS GOALS; EXCESS PROFITS TAX RESISTED

LEVY BILL DRAFTED

$4,300,000,000 Impost Urged by President to Be Asked Today

ECCLES AGAINST MEASURE

Former Chairman of Federal Reserve Scores Piecemeal Attack on Inflation

By H. WALTON CLOKE
Special to THE NEW YORK TIMES.

WASHINGTON, Aug. 3—A $4,300,000,000 excess-profits tax, designed to aid in the fight on inflation, was proposed to Congress today by President Truman. Simultaneously, Marriner S. Eccles, former chairman of the Federal Reserve Board, told a House Banking and Currency Committee that he was opposed to re-enactment of any such measure.

Mr. Eccles, who has fought every aspect of the President's anti-inflation program with the exception of controls on bank and consumer credit, said that to enact a new excess-profits tax would take time and "involve an entire new program." The principal question relative to an excess-profits tax at this time, he said, was "on what basis would it be re-enacted?"

"Our whole tax structure needs to be overhauled, but it shouldn't be done piecemeal," he told the committee. "The big mistake," he contended, "was made back in 1945 and early 1946, when the entire harness of controls was prematurely removed."

"That included the excess-profits tax," he said, "which was the biggest mistake of all. That opened the door for justifiable wage demands."

Enabling Bill Ready

Representative John D. Dingell, Democrat, of Michigan, and a member of the House Ways and Means Committee, said that he would introduce the enabling bill tomorrow. He told reporters that "with corporate profits after taxes nearly 100 per cent above the level of the peak war year 1943," the bill would protect the public against "peacetime profiteers."

The measure would be aimed at the larger corporations, he added, and would be patterned after the wartime excess-profits tax. Exemptions, however, would be broader and the graduated tax less stringent than the 85.5 per cent of the old excess-profits levy. Further, it would apply to less than 25,000 of the 360,000 corporations that now file tax returns with the Treasury.

If enacted, Representative Dingell said, the bill would have these four points of attack on inflation:

1. Large corporations would lose $4,300,000,000 of purchasing power.

2. It would aid the Government in maintaining an excess of receipts over expenditures, which "should be one of the Government's principal weapons against inflation."

3. Limited to the larger corporations, the tax would be "an induce-

Continued on Page 11, Column 4

New Mexico Indians Get Right to Vote

By The United Press.

SANTA FE, N. M., Aug. 3—A special three-judge Federal court ruled today that a New Mexico constitutional provision denying the right to vote to Indians was contrary to the United States Constitution.

The decision, in effect, gives the voting privilege in New Mexico to Indians.

The court ruled that New Mexico's law providing that "Indians not taxed" may not vote contravenes the Fifteenth Amendment of the Unitd States Constitution, which assures a ballot for everyone of voting age regardless of race, creed or color.

The far-reaching decision was made in a suit that had been filed in behalf of Miguel H. Trujillo, an Isleta Indian, living at the Laguna Pueblo. It charged that Eloy Garley, the clerk of Valencia County, had refused to register Trujillo before the New Mexico primary election on June 8.

HOUSE SOON TO VOTE U. N. BUILDING LOAN

$65,000,000 Fund Approved by Committee—Measure Has Already Passed Senate

Special to THE NEW YORK TIMES.

WASHINGTON, Aug. 3—Congressional approval of a $65,000,000 building loan to the United Nations in the present session was virtually assured today.

A resolution already adopted by the Senate will be called up in the House, perhaps on Thursday, under a compromise reached by the House leadership and the House Foreign Affairs Committee.

The compromise excludes consideration of United Nations policies until early in the next session of Congress. The resolution merely authorizes the loan, $25,000,000 of which the Reconstruction Finance Corporation would advance immediately. This will permit an early start on the United Nations Secretariat building.

The Foreign Affairs Committee had urged the enactment of a bill that included a comprehensive statement of policy and provisions for enlarging and strengthening American representation and assistance to the United Nations.

"Members of the committee believe," a statement by the group said today, "that the most important part of the bill (H. R. 6802) is the statement of policy with respect to improvements in the practices, procedures and structure of the United Nations which we should strive for if it is to be made capable of functioning as intended.

"However, because of the fact that this special session was called by the President to consider only certain limited matters, including the headquarters' loan; and because the consideration of H. R. 6802, which in large part is outside the designated scope of the session, would make it difficult for the leadership to refuse considera-

Continued on Page 6, Column 4

AGENDA RESTRICTED

Proposed Credit Curbs Would Affect Banks and Consumers

SENATE MEETS INTO NIGHT

Southern Poll-Tax Filibuster Drones On—Closing Day of Session in Doubt

Special to THE NEW YORK TIMES.

WASHINGTON, Aug. 3—Republican leaders in Congress agreed tonight to take action on three points of President Truman's anti-inflation program. Their limited legislative list would include bank and consumer credit controls and housing.

Senator Robert A. Taft of Ohio, chairman of the Senate Republican policy committee, and Representative Jesse P. Wolcott of Michigan, chairman of the House Banking and Currency Committee, announced the Republican plan.

Previously the Republican leaders had indicated that they considered that adjournment on Saturday, as planned, would be impossible and that they would point instead for Wednesday of next week as the final day.

The Senate, meanwhile, went into a night session as the Southern filibuster on the anti-poll-tax bill continued, but adjourned at 10:16 P. M. until noon tomorrow.

Bill Drafting Slated Today

Agreement on the Republican agenda was reached at a two-hour meeting which was attended also by Senator Charles W. Tobey of New Hampshire, chairman of the Senate Banking and Currency Committee, and the following committee members: Senator Harry P. Cain of Washington, Senator Ralph E. Flanders of Vermont, Senator Joseph R. McCarthy of Wisconsin and Senator John W. Bricker of Ohio.

Representative Wolcott told reporters that his committee would make an effort to agree on a bill tomorrow and place it before the House on Thursday. He said the group would give immediate consideration to a Senate-approved bill to re-establish consumer credit controls.

Using this as a base, he said that he would offer amendments in committee to restore the gold reserve requirements for the Federal Reserve Banks to the 1945 level. In addition, he said that he probably would offer an amendment to increase the reserve requirements of the Federal Reserve Banks. The increase would be 3 per cent on demand deposits and 1 per cent on time deposits.

Representative Wolcott's amendment to increase the reserve requirements would apply only to members of the Federal Reserve System. This particular phase has drawn some caustic comment from Marriner S. Eccles, former chairman of the Federal Reserve Board, who contends that non-member banks should be included.

Predicts Fast House Action

The Administration's proposal, as outlined before the House and Senate Banking Committees last week by Thomas B. McCabe, chairman of the Federal Reserve Board, called for an increase of ten percentage points on demand deposits and four percentage points on time deposits.

Representative Wolcott predicted that the House would pass the bill drawn up by his committee and send it to the Senate the same day. Senator Taft said that it would be sent directly to the Senate Banking and Currency Committee. There it is expected to run into an amendment or two.

Senator Tobey has indicated that he favors Mr. Eccles' proposal to include all banks in the new reserve requirements and he apparently favors the Administration's proposal to increase the reserves by 10 and 4 per cent. In addition, he made it known that he considered the gold provision unnecessary.

"The public should not get the idea," the Senator said, "that this credit stuff is going to be translated into lower prices for them." He conceded that it might have

Continued on Page 12, Column 4

Two Men Battle in Crowded Plane; Held Here for 'Crime on High Seas'

How two men, both Puerto Ricans, battled savagely in a sixty-passenger plane, filled with men, women and children, and clawed the pilot and the steward, while flying over the ocean off the Florida Coast Monday evening, was revealed here yesterday when the plane landed at La Guardia Field.

In response to messages sent by wireless beforehand from the plane, owned by the Flying Tigers, Inc., and bound here from San Juan, Federal agents were on hand at the field and arrested the bruised and blood-stained combatants as soon as the plane landed. The prisoners were Diego Cordova, 28 years old, an automobile mechanic, of 44 Nassau Street, Brooklyn, and Benito Santano, 31, a merchant seaman, of 69 Columbia Street, Brooklyn. In addition to pummeling each other in a quarrel over a bottle of rum, they were accused of clawing the plane's pilot and steward for interfering in their fight.

Accused of "unlawfully interfering with the navigation of an airplane and committing a Federal crime on the high seas in violation of the United States Admiralty Laws," the two men were later held by United States Commissioner Martin C. Epstein in Brooklyn, in $1,000 bail each for the action of the Federal Grand Jury.

The uproar began about 8 P. M. Monday, when the plane, with twenty men, twenty-six women and fourteen children aboard, was 600 miles north of Puerto Rico. Cordova went to the men's room at the rear. Upon returning to his seat he shouted indignantly because a bottle of rum he had left there was missing. He accused Santano of taking it.

Volatile tempers flared and soon

Continued on Page 42, Column 8

1948

Newscaster John Cameron Swayze moved from radio to television to telecast the summer's presidential conventions.

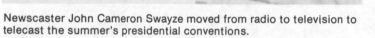

The *Quiz Kids* program featured brilliant youngsters who answered difficult questions that usually stumped the adult audience.

Shirley Booth, who was soon to become a great star of stage and screen, starred along with Ed Gardner in *Duffy's Tavern.*

Let's Pretend — the prize-winning fantasy series — was still going strong.

"All the News That's Fit to Print"

The New York Times.

LATE CITY EDITION
Mostly sunny and warmer today and tomorrow.
Temperature Range Today—Max.,86; Min.,62
Temperature Yesterday—Max.,73; Min.,57
Full U. S. Weather Bureau Report, Page 31

Copyright, 1948, by The New York Times Company.

VOL. XCVIII..No. 33,110. Entered as Second-Class Matter, Postoffice, New York, N. Y. NEW YORK, SATURDAY, SEPTEMBER 18, 1948. Times Square, New York 18, N. Y. Telephone LAckawanna 4-1000 THREE CENTS IN NEW YORK CITY

BERNADOTTE IS SLAIN IN JERUSALEM; KILLERS CALLED 'JEWISH IRREGULARS'; SECURITY COUNCIL WILL ACT TODAY

HOUSE BODY PLANS TO EXPOSE DETAILS OF ATOMIC SPYING

'Shocking Chapter' to Be Told in Next Few Days 'in Spite' of the President, It Says

CONDON DATA ASKED AGAIN

Ferguson Urges Clark to Seek Espionage Indictments in and Out of Government

By C. P. TRUSSELL
Special to THE NEW YORK TIMES.

WASHINGTON, Sept. 17 — A House subcommittee on Un-American Activities served notice today that "in spite of" President Truman, David E. Lilienthal, chairman of the Atomic Energy Commission, and "a few misguided scientists," it would reveal "within the next few days * * * a shocking chapter in Communist espionage in the atomic field."

At the same time the subcommittee, headed by Representative J. Parnell Thomas of New Jersey, chairman of the full House group, declared it to be "obligatory" on President Truman to let Congress have a Federal Bureau of Investigation report concerning Dr. Edward U. Condon, head of the National Bureau of Standards.

The subcommittee asserted that this report, which it said was "locked in President Truman's desk," related in detail "his [Dr. Condon's] association with alleged Soviet espionage agents, including Nathan Gregory Silvermaster, who was recently described before this committee as heading an espionage ring of Government employes."

President Stands Fast

The President has declined to surrender this report. The House subcommittee held that on the basis of its contents, Dr. Condon was "cleared for access to atomic information" by the AEC. It emphasized, in its statement today, that the AEC had not reviewed before taking this action "the evidence before this committee."

Senator Homer Ferguson, Republican, of Michigan, head of a Senate group looking into espionage, today urged Tom C. Clark, Attorney General, to assemble grand juries in six cities with a view to indictments in and outside the Government. Mr. Clark replied sharply that the Senator was seeking "headlines" and asked him to "keep your political activity out of the field of serious prosecution of offenses under Federal statutes."

A recent finding by an Un-American Activities subcommittee that Dr. Condon was "one of the weakest links" in the nation's atomic security set off a storm in Administration and scientific circles.

Last Monday the President, as he addressed the centennial meeting of the American Association for the Advancement of Science here, greeted Dr. Condon cordially on the stage before a vast audience.

The President charged, in the talk preceding this greeting, that scientific work "indispensable" for national security "may be made impossible by the creation of an atmosphere in which no man feels safe against the public airing of unfounded rumors, gossip and vilification."

It was conceded generally in Washington that he was shooting at the House committee.

Lilienthal Backs Truman

Yesterday, before the same scientific body, Mr. Lilienthal declared that the success of the atomic energy program was facing "a dangerous situation." Scientists, he said, were becoming increasingly unwilling to participate in atomic advancement for fear of having suspicion cast upon them by Congressional investigation.

As a result, he held, key scientists were walking away from Government experimentation to go into more secure and quieter fields to avoid risks of "public humiliation and smears on their character and patriotism."

The House subcommittee rejected these views unanimously today. Its report was signed by Representatives John McDowell, Republican, of Pennsylvania, and Richard B. Vail, Republican, of Illinois, as well as by Mr. Thomas.

"It has long been the custom of the House Committee on Un-American Activities to refrain from comment regarding criticisms of its operations, preferring to let results speak for themselves and to permit the public to draw its conclusions from the cold facts obtained through careful investiga-

Continued on Page 5, Column 2

Dewey Backs Farm Aid Bill Passed by 80th Congress

Approval of Price Support Follows Talks With Authors, Aiken and Hope, and Promises Rounded Program

By LEO EGAN
Special to THE NEW YORK TIMES.

ALBANY, Sept. 17—Gov. Thomas E. Dewey, in a statement issued here tonight, declared that he subscribed firmly to the principals of the farm price support program approved by the Eightieth Congress, "both for the present and the future." One of the main features of this legislation, which does not become fully effective until 1950, is a provision for flexible Government support of agricultural prices ranging from 60 to 90 per cent of "parity."

The Republican presidential candidate's statement was distributed following several hours of conferences with Senator George D. Aiken of Vermont and Representative Clifford R. Hope of Kansas, co-authors of the measure. Mr. Aiken is the prospective new chairman of the Senate Agricultural Committee. Representative Hope heads the House committee and has been mentioned as a possible Secretary of Agriculture in the Dewey cabinet if the Governor is elected.

Mr. Dewey told reporters at a press conference that the statement represented the views of all three participants in the conference.

Asked to comment on a Democratic charge that the Republicans planned to remove farm price supports, Mr. Dewey told reporters:

"That charge was created out of thin air. It was an intentional fabrication designed to deceive the producers of America's food."

To another question as to whether he referred specifically to a statement made by the Secretary of Agriculture, Charles A. Brannan, following a visit with President Truman at the White House, Mr. Dewey's reply was:

"The whole Administration is making it and they are making it up."

Today's formal statement, Mr. Dewey added, had been planned

Continued on Page 9, Column 3

Truman Off on Western Trip Promising He'll 'Fight Hard'

By W. H. LAWRENCE
Special to THE NEW YORK TIMES.

ON BOARD PRESIDENT TRUMAN'S CAMPAIGN TRAIN, Sept. 17—An exuberant, confident President Truman headed west on his first major extended campaign tour today, declaring his intention to "fight hard" and "give 'em hell" in a back-breaking, no-quarter contest for the Presidency between now and Nov. 2.

Moving swiftly through Maryland, Pennsylvania, Ohio and Indiana, Mr. Truman headed toward speaking engagements tomorrow in Illinois and Iowa.

His running mate, Senator Alben W. Barkley of Kentucky, who returned from Europe only yesterday, had a final conference with the President on the rear platform just before the train left the capital and exhorted him to "mow 'em down."

"It's a victorious trip," said the Kentucky Senator.

Mr. Truman, who, as President, had proclaimed "V-E Day" to mark victory over the Germans and "V-J Day" to celebrate the Japanese surrender, added another alphabetical designation to the American vocabulary—this time it was "V-T" to signalize his agreement with the Kentucky Senator's description of this tour through eighteen states with 240 electoral votes as a victorious trip.

The President was in no mood to accept Republican victory claims or public opinion polls pointing to his defeat as he left Washington. He told reporters at the train that he would like to reserve his own forecast until this trip ended, Oct. 2, one month before the election.

"I'm going to fight hard," he said. "And I'm going to give 'em hell."

The schedule mapped out for this tour, and the train-side conferences added to it, made it clear that Mr. Truman did not intend to pass up any opportunity to show himself to American voters in an effort to convince them that the national interest demanded the retention of the Democratic party in

Continued on Page 9, Column 4

JONES URGES TEXAS TO SUPPORT DEWEY

Member of Roosevelt Cabinet Calls for Democrats' Defeat in His Houston Newspaper

Special to THE NEW YORK TIMES.

WASHINGTON, Sept. 17—The Houston Chronicle, published by Jesse H. Jones, a member of the late President Franklin D. Roosevelt's Cabinet, recommended today the election of Thomas E. Dewey and Earl Warren.

An editorial, distributed to the press here by the Washington Bureau of The Chronicle, said: "It should be obvious to all thinking people that we need a change in our National Administration. To deny this would be to close our eyes to conditions both at home and abroad, and generally to the news we are in."

The declaration of the prominent Texas publisher, financier and Democrat added a new twist to the tangled state political affairs. A close fight for the Democratic nomination for Senator has landed in the courts, with former Governor Coke Stevenson refusing to accept the finding of the party's state convention that Representative Lyndon Johnson won the nomination by eighty-seven votes. The same convention promised the state's twenty-three electoral votes to President Truman and ejected four anti-Truman delegations.

Mr. Jones had been Secretary of Commerce, a post that then included administration of the Gov-

Continued on Page 9, Column 6

Murder and Suicide in Airplane Prior to Crash Bared by Autopsy

With the recovery yesterday of the bodies of a young man and woman who had crashed in a marsh near the New York International Airport at Idlewild Thursday night there came to light an air tragedy that may never be explained completely.

An autopsy disclosed that the woman, Hannah Laufer, 28 years old, of 84-12 Thirty-fifth Avenue, Jackson Heights, Queens, had been shot three times. The physical evidence indicated that the shooting had been done at close range as she sat beside and to the right of the pilot in the single-engined Bellanca.

Her companion on the ill-fated journey, a short, half-hour flight from Philadelphia, was Jesus Meneu Monleon, reputedly of noble Spanish birth, who was an air fighter for the Spanish Loyalists and during the recent war a member of the merchant marine of both Britain and the United States.

The autopsy in the case of the 31-year-old pilot disclosed that death apparently was due to a deep wound in the chest that might have been self-inflicted. There were no plane fragments in the wound, which penetrated to the heart.

Last night a knife with an eight-inch blade was found in the water-immersed wreckage of the plane. It was recovered by two patrolmen of the Harbor Squad who made their search in a small boat. In the wreckage, earlier, was found a letter written by Monleon, who was called Roberto by his friends, to Miss Laufer, which began on a brooding note of murder and suicide and ended with an endearing farewell. The note was in English and French. It was written at 2 o'clock Thursday morning, placed in a sealed envelope, but never mailed.

The known facts of the tragedy were pieced together by the police throughout the day.

At 1 P. M. on Thursday Monleon

Continued on Page 22, Column 4

NIZAM SURRENDERS TO INDIAN INVASION; ORDERS CEASE-FIRE

Hyderabad's Ruler to Disband Moslem Volunteers, Admit New Delhi's Garrisons

U.N. CHARGE IS CALLED OFF

State's Cabinet Resigns With Plea to End Bloodshed—Fate of Monarch Uncertain

By ROBERT TRUMBULL
Special to THE NEW YORK TIMES.

NEW DELHI, India, Sept. 17—Hyderabad surrendered today to Indian troops that had entered the independent Princely State at dawn on Monday "to restore order."

The Nizam [ruler], who took over the Government as an Indian armored column approached within fifty miles of his capital, ordered his representatives at the United Nations Security Council in Paris not to press their protest against India's actions.

"I am opening a new chapter of friendliness with India," the Nizam declared in a radio broadcast.

After his Cabinet had resigned this morning, the Nizam immediately ordered his troops to cease fire at 5 P. M. In his broadcast he invited Indian troops to occupy Secunderabad, adjacent to Hyderabad City, the capital, and Bolarum, twelve miles north, without opposition. He also banned the Razakars, military Moslem Volunteer Corps who had been fighting in the front lines against the Indian troops.

Thus the immediate demands made upon Hyderabad by India in recent weeks were obtained, but the terms of the surrender and the political status of the Nizam and his State were left undecided.

It was presumed that Lieut. Gen. Maharaj Sri Rajendrasinhji, commander of the Indian troops in Hyderabad, to whom this news was transmitted, had ordered a simultaneous cease-fire, but the decision was left to him. A spokesman for the Indian States Ministry said that it was not known late tonight what action the general had taken.

A communiqué issued by the Indian Southern Command Headquarters in Poona at 9 o'clock tonight said that although the cease-fire ordered by the Nizam was being carried out by the Hyderabad Army, no formal reply to an earlier ultimatum to the Hyderabad commander had been received "owing to bad communication"

Continued on Page 5, Column 2

U. N. MOVE IS SWIFT

Cadogan Calls Session, Lie Is Flying to Paris—Delegates Shocked

AMERICAN IS PUT IN POST

Dr. Ralph Bunche Is Ordered to Take Over Count's Work—Washington, London Stirred

By THOMAS J. HAMILTON
Special to THE NEW YORK TIMES.

PARIS, Sept. 17 — A special meeting of the United Nations Security Council will be held at 3 P. M. tomorrow in the Palais de Chaillot to consider what action should be taken regarding the assassination of Count Folke Bernadotte, United Nations Mediator, in Palestine.

The meeting was called by Sir Alexander Cadogan, this month's president of the Council, a few hours after officials here had received confirmation of the death of Count Bernadotte from his headquarters in Rhodes. Trygve Lie, United Nations Secretary General, who had sent word to Count Bernadotte yesterday to meet him in Paris Sunday afternoon made arrangements to return here from Oslo, Norway, tonight by special plane.

A statement issued by Arkady A. Sobolev, Acting Secretary General, announced the death "with profound shock and regret," adding that "on the basis of direct communication with the Mediator's headquarters on Rhodes it has been established that Count Bernadotte was shot and killed today at 2 P. M. in the New City of Jerusalem."

Mr. Sobolev directed Dr. Ralph Bunche, an American, who was head of the civilian staff under Count Bernadotte, to take over the Mediator's duties.

Count Bernadotte's headquarters had no information on the reported death of Colonel Serot, French officer who was accompanying Count Bernadotte, but a French Foreign Ministry spokesman said

Continued on Page 2, Column 3

U. N. MEDIATOR KILLED IN PALESTINE

Count Folke Bernadotte
The New York Times (by Neal Bo...)

Administration Helps Dulles To Cable U.N. Data to Dewey

John Foster Dulles, Governor Dewey's adviser on foreign affairs, announced yesterday that he was going to the United Nations Assembly meeting, which opens in Paris next Tuesday, not only in his official capacity as American representative but also as a Republican "with the approval and support" of Mr. Dewey.

He said the Government had arranged separate communications facilities whereby he could inform Mr. Dewey quickly of important developments and "get the guidance of his views."

It was the first time in history that an administration had made such facilities available to a rival candidate for the Presidency. Regarded as another step in the bipartisan approach to the nation's foreign problems, the setup will enable Mr. Dulles to send direct and secret messages to Mr. Dewey. Code machines will be used for transmission from Paris to New York and the messages then will be relayed to the Governor, probably by teletype.

In a statement issued at the Roosevelt Hotel on the eve of his departure for Paris, Mr. Dulles emphasized the "great importance" of the Assembly meeting.

He said that its chief contribution to peace and justice could be "its over-all impact on world opinion." But he warned that the Soviet delegation might use it "to launch another big propaganda offensive" picturing Russian leaders as peace-loving and those who disagreed with them as imperialistic and war-seeking.

"It is to be hoped that they will not do this, but that they will calmly discuss differences on their

Continued on Page 4, Column 7

FLIERS VOW RECORD IN BERLIN COAL LIFT

U. S. Planes Begin Project to Carry 5,000 Tons of Fuel in a 24-Hour Period

By DREW MIDDLETON
Special to THE NEW YORK TIMES.

BERLIN, Sept. 17—The United States Air Force in Europe pledged itself today to fly a record 5,000 tons of coal into Berlin in twenty-four hours in an expansive, politically shrewd salute celebrating Air Force Day.

Lieut. Gen. Curtis E. LeMay announced that in the twenty-four hours ending at noon tomorrow his flying freight cars would carry an estimated 8,000,000 to 10,000,000 pounds of coal into Berlin.

The coal delivered to the city will be distributed immediately at the rate of 100 pounds to all families of the Western sectors with two or more children under 10 years of age.

This sweeping promise of the United States airmen answers mounting Russian propaganda that what the Germans call the "air bridge" is the basis for all Berlin's economic difficulties. The problems are, in fact, caused by the Soviet blockade.

This morning Soviet propagan-

Continued on Page 6, Column 1

World News Summarized

SATURDAY, SEPTEMBER 18, 1948

Count Folke Bernadotte of Sweden, United Nations Mediator in the Palestine strife, was assassinated with his French aide as they drove through an Israeli-controlled sector of Jerusalem. They were shot dead by four men in an Israeli Army-type jeep that blocked Count Bernadotte's car. Col. Frank Begley, United Nations security chief, was wounded while fighting the assailants. The killings were ascribed by a United Nations truce staff announcement to "Jewish irregulars." The slayings were expected to lead to renewed violence in the Holy Land. [1:8.]

A few hours after United Nations officials in Paris learned of the assassinations, the President of the Security Council said that that group would meet today to consider measures in the case. Secretary General Trygve Lie, who had expected to meet Count Bernadotte in Paris tomorrow, prepared to fly to the French capital. Ralph Bunche, an American, who headed the civilian staff under Count Bernadotte, was directed to take control of the truce body. [1:5.]

News of the slaying shocked the world. Secretary of State Marshall said that it was "tragic" and that the mediation should be continued. There were suggestions that the mediator's job be taken over by several persons so no single assassination in the future could interrupt the work. [2:5.]

John Foster Dulles said he would attend the United Nations Assembly meetings not only as an official United States delegate but also as the personal representative of Governor Dewey. He added he would use the Government's code service to send messages to the Republican Presidential candidate. This step, a continuation of bipartisan unity on foreign policy, was believed to be unprecedented. [1:6-7.]

Lieut. Gen. Curtis LeMay said that the United States Air Force would fly 5,000 tons of coal into Berlin in twenty-four hours ending at noon today. This pledge for a record airlift operation was the general's Air Force Day comment. [1:7.]

The Princely State of Hyderabad surrendered to India. The Nizam, the ruler, accepted the resignation of his Cabinet and announced he would form a new regime. He stated that Hyderabad would drop its case against India in the United Nations, permit Indian troops to garrison strategic points, abolish the Moslem volunteers, and provide for release of imprisoned Indian Congress party leaders. [1:4.]

A House subcommittee on un-American activities promised to reveal in a few days a "shocking chapter in Communist espionage in the atomic field." The group said that scientists were not immune to investigation, but added that most of them had nothing to fear from it. Senator Ferguson, head of a Senate investigating group, called for indictment of Communists. [1:1.]

Governor Dewey said he "subscribed firmly" to the farm-price support program enacted by the Eightieth Congress. At a press conference the Republican Presidential candidate termed "deliberate fabrication" Democratic charges that the Republicans favored removing Government price supports. [1:2-3.]

President Truman, in a confident mood, left Washington on an eighteen-state tour. He said he would "fight hard" for re-election and refused to accept Republican forecasts of victory in November. Senator Barkley saw him off. [1:2-3.]

Stern Group Threatened Slaying; It Boasts a Record of Terrorism

By C. L. SULZBERGER
Special to THE NEW YORK TIMES.

PARIS, Sept. 17—Consul General John J. Macdonald's first report on the murder of Count Folke Bernadotte stated that the assassination had been presumably the work of the "Stern Gang" or, as it calls itself, the "Fighters for the Freedom of Israel."

Naturally this cannot yet be confirmed. Usually the Sternist group publicly announces the fact when it has accomplished an act of terrorism.

On July 24 this correspondent spent the morning in a hotel room at Tel Aviv with two young men who said they were members of the Stern group. One was a South African by birth. The origin of the other was not certain.

They stated, quite calmly but positively, "We intend to kill Bernadotte and any other uniformed United Nations observers who come to Jerusalem."

Both young men had just come to Tel Aviv from Jerusalem, where they had been fighting in a special Sternist unit.

Asked why they wished to assassinate Count Bernadotte or any other United Nations representative, they replied that their organization was determined to seize all of Jerusalem for the state of Israel and would brook no interference by any national or international body.

Furthermore, while emphasizing that they would not fight against regular officials or forces of the state of Israel as long as the war with the Arabs lasted, they said that their organization could not commit itself as to future acts involving fellow Israeli citizens when peace came. Asked whether they intended to murder any non-uniformed United Nations personnel, they said they did not. This conversation was reported to United

Continued on Page 4, Column 4

HIS CAR AMBUSHED

Mediator Was Defying Warnings by Tour—French Aide Dies

STERN GROUP IS BLAMED

U. S. Consul Calls Terrorists 'Presumably' Responsible—Palestine Is Tense

By JULIAN LOUIS MELTZER
Special to THE NEW YORK TIMES.

TEL AVIV, Israel, Sept. 17—Count Folke Bernadotte, United Nations Mediator for Palestine, and another United Nations official, detached from the French Air Force, were assassinated this afternoon within the Israeli-held area of Jerusalem.

Count Bernadotte was on his way from the former British High Commissioner's residence in southern Jerusalem and was passing through the Katamon suburb when "Jewish irregulars" held up the Mediator's car.

[John J. MacDonald, United States Consul General in Jerusalem, reported to the State Department that Count Bernadotte and Col. Andre Pierre Serot had been ambushed, "presumably by the Stern Gang."

[Reuters quoted a Stern Group spokesman in Tel Aviv as having said: "I am satisfied that it has happened," but added that the spokesman was unaware whether members of the group were responsible for the killing.

[A Jerusalem dispatch quoted Dr. Bernard Joseph, Military Governor for the Israeli part of Jerusalem, as saying that all possible measures had been taken to apprehend the assassins.]

Truce Staff Announcement

A United Nations truce staff announcement here said:

"Count Bernadotte killed by two Jewish irregulars in hold-up 1700 hours today on way to New City of Jerusalem. In same hold-up United Nations senior observer Col. Andre Serot of French Air Force killed.

"Mediator was on tour of Middle Eastern capitals to bring security and peace to Palestine.

"Arrangements made bring bodies in Red Cross ambulance from Jerusalem to Haifa."

Dr. Paul Mohn, acting chief of staff and legal adviser to the central truce supervision board at Haifa, ordered that all United Nations flags over the buildings that it occupies be lowered to half staff.

The Israeli-controlled "Voice of Jerusalem" radio gave the following account of the assassination of Count Bernadotte:

He was traveling in a car from Government House to Katamon. A jeep with three armed men approached the vehicle and automatic fire opened at the Mediator's car. Count Bernadotte was seriously injured and the French colonel was killed outright. The Count died shortly afterward.

Colonel Lundstroem Unhurt

The radio statement added that Gen. Aage Lundstroem, Count Bernadotte's chief of staff, in the same car, was unhurt. Col. Frank Begley of the United Nations Secretariat was slightly injured.

Numerous wall placards appeared recently in Jerusalem and Tel Aviv over the imprint of Fighters for the Freedom of Israel (Stern Group), declaring that Count Bernadotte should "get out" of Israel as he had failed properly to enforce the truce. One cartoon showed a huge boot kicking the Count.

When he held a news conference recently in the Belgian Consulate General at Jerusalem, two jeeps carrying young men and women of the Stern Group picketed the entrance with large signs. One said: "Stockholm is yours. Jerusalem is ours." The other advised him to clear out. If it is proved that the Fighters for Freedom group had any connection with the slaying, it undoubtedly will provoke rapid action by the Israeli military administration in Jerusalem.

Under the indeterminate position of Jerusalem, pending the solution of its future constitutional status, the Stern Group operates freely in the Israeli areas and, like the Irgun Zvai Leumi, maintains

Continued on Page 3, Column 1

1948

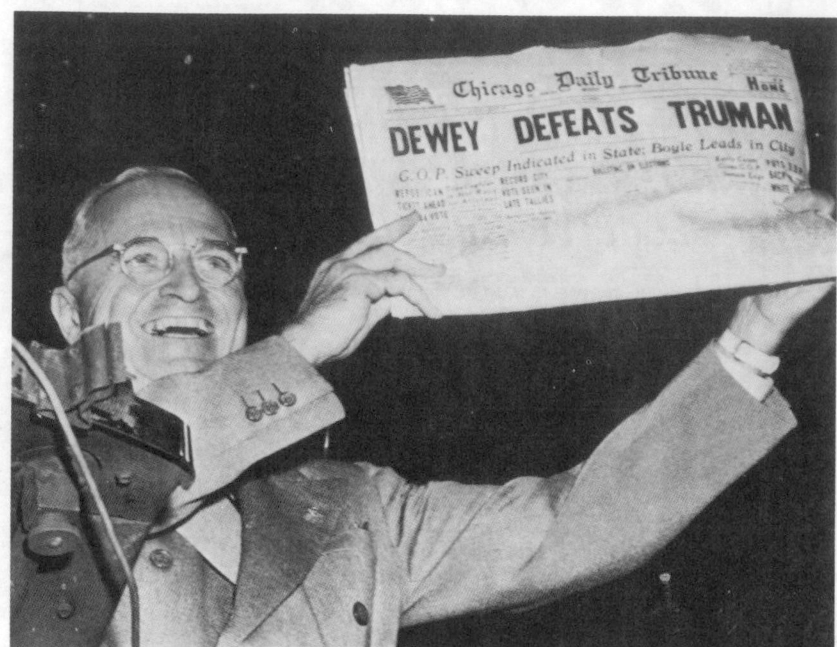

Harry S. Truman, one of America's most dynamic and candid Presidents, holds aloft the copy of the *Chicago Daily Tribune* with the errant headline.

Defeat at the polls is conceded by Thomas E. Dewey.

Early in the year, Truman "gave 'em hell," when he accepted the Democratic presidential nomination. He attacked the Republican-dominated Congress, and announced that a special session of Congress would be called.

"All the News That's Fit to Print"

The New York Times.

LATE CITY EDITION
Rain ending tonight. Partly cloudy and mild tomorrow.
Temperature Range Today—Max.,64; Min.,58
Temperatures Yesterday—Max.,61; Min.,46
Full U. S. Weather Bureau Report, Page 39

VOL. XCVIII..No. 33,157. Entered as Second-Class Matter, Postoffice, New York, N. Y. NEW YORK, THURSDAY, NOVEMBER 4, 1948. Times Square, New York 18, N. Y. Telephone LAckawanna 4-1000 THREE CENTS NEW YORK CITY

TRUMAN WINS WITH 304 ELECTORAL VOTES; DEMOCRATS CONTROL SENATE AND HOUSE; EUROPE SEES FOREIGN POLICY CONTINUING

NATIONS ARE UNITED IN ASSEMBLY VOTE FOR PEACE PACTS

Marshall and Vishinsky Back Mexican Resolution in U. N. to Bring About Treaties

ATOMIC DEBATE FOLLOWS

Austin Expresses Hope Russia Will Accept the Majority View to Effect Control

By A. M. ROSENTHAL

Special to The New York Times.

PARIS, Nov. 3—The United Nations General Assembly unanimously asked the Big Five today to start a new era of cooperation and a few hours later heard the United States invite Russia to "high level" atomic control negotiations.

Without debate the plenary session of the Assembly gave quick approval to the Mexican resolution calling on the major powers to try again to settle their quarrels and come to agreement on the terms of peace treaties with Germany and Japan.

Mexico's resolution was introduced to leaven the atmosphere of tension and animosity caused by the thrashing out of all major Soviet-West disputes in the full Assembly and in committee rooms. From the beginning it had the support of every member of the Big Five and all small and middle sized powers.

Marshall, Vishinsky Vote Yes

When Dr. Herbert Evatt of Australia, Assembly President, asked for a vote the delegates saw something they had not seen at a plenary session of this Assembly on any important issue. Secretary of State Marshall and Andrei Y. Vishinsky of Russia both raised their hands to vote yes.

But that about ended agreement for the day. The next major item on the agenda was the atomic control controversy, and the Assembly settled down to hear a rehashing of the arguments from the majority and the minority.

The two main documents are before the committee—the Canadian resolution adopted by the Political and Security Committee, and the rejected Soviet motion.

Canada's proposal approves the majority control plan, continues the life of the Atomic Energy Commission and suggests that the sponsors of the United Nations' atomic control idea—Canada and the Big Five—get together to try to break the deadlock.

On the other hand, the Russian resolution would ignore the majority control reports, but would instruct the Atomic Commission to continue. The Russian motion also contains a controversial proposal for simultaneous signing of conventions outlawing the atomic bomb and establishing atomic control.

Austin Accents Talks

The first and only speaker today was Warren R. Austin of the United States. He gave full support to the Canadian resolution, but put the accent on the paragraph dealing with private Big Five Canada talks.

"It is the desire of the United States that these consultations should be at a high level and principally concerned with the causes of the Soviet Union's finding itself at present unwilling or unable to take a cooperative part with other nations in the necessary measures for the maintenance of peace," he said.

Mr. Austin made it clear that he did not expect differences to disappear at the first consultation. But the United States, he said, believes the time is ripe for "quiet and mature discussion in an atmosphere of intelligent deliberation."

"We believe that the terrible problem of atomic energy would provide the framework which would keep constantly before the consulting powers the urgent necessity for agreements on measures which would resolve the present difficulties and which would lift from the hearts of nations the overshadowing fear of atomic warfare," said the United States delegate.

The tenor of the former Vermont Senator's speech was probably the most moderate of any made on the high-powered atomic dispute. He told the delegates that the United States felt that some day Russia would come to believe that it was in her interests to accept foolproof atomic control.

Mr. Austin acknowledged that the United States had gone into the session "just about" convinced that a continuation of the Atomic Commission would be futile. But many other delegates announced

Continued on Page 35, Column 7

10 U. S. Fliers Crash In B-29 in Britain

Special to The New York Times.

LONDON, Nov. 3—A United States B-29 Superfortress, on a routine flight between Scampton airfield in Lincolnshire and the Burtonwood air depot in Lancashire, crashed today with its crew of three officers and seven enlisted men.

Seven bodies had been recovered by nightfall. It was presumed that all aboard had been killed. The crash occurred in one of the lonliest regions of the British Midlands — atop Kinder Scout, a 2,000-foot mountain near Glossop in Derbyshire.

United States Air Force headquarters said tonight that no identification of crew members could be made until the next of kin had been notified. The plane, however, was revealed to be part of the 301st Bomb Group in the United Kingdom.

JAPAN HELD GUILTY OF AGGRESSIVE WAR

Court Cites Attack on China and Designs on Allies in Prelude to Tojo Verdict

By The Associated Press.

TOKYO, Thursday, Nov. 4—The International Military Tribunal held today that Japan was guilty of waging wars of aggression against China and planning similar hostilities against the United States, Britain, Russia and other allied powers.

The ruling came in the first day's reading of the voluminous judgment in the war crimes trial of former Premier Hideki Tojo and twenty-four co-defendants. It covered the period from 1928 to 1938.

The eleven-nation court narrowed the issues down to the simplest terms:

Was Japan guilty of waging aggressive war in violation of international treaties?

Were the twenty-five defendants responsible for making and carrying out those policies?

Were the defendants responsible for crimes against humanity and violations of the laws of war?

Thus far in its reading, the tribunal has declared that "militarists and their supporters" seized control of Japan's Government. This in effect means that any who joined in the seventeen Cabinets since 1928 adopted the militarists' policy as their own.

The court ruled that the Manchurian conquest of 1931 and the full-scale war against China, which opened July 7, 1937, were instigated by militarists and deliberately provoked on the part of Japan.

Earlier, the tribunal cleared the twenty-five defendants of thirty-eight of the fifty-five counts in their war crimes indictment.

It held that in the early 1930's the Japanese Government began preparations for war not only against China but against Russia, Britain, the United States and other Western powers.

The court has not reached the individual verdicts against the prisoners, however.

The tribunal blamed the Japanese Army for fomenting the Sept. 18, 1931, Mukden incident which gave Japan the excuse to seize Manchuria. And the war with China in 1937, it said, was a direct result of the foreign policy adopted

Continued on Page 32, Column 3

WEST IS HOPEFUL

Sees Marshall Plan Aid and Truman Doctrine Being Carried Out

END OF SNARLS FORECAST

Observers on Continent Say Berlin and Other Issues Will Be Discussed Soon

By C. L. SULZBERGER

Special to The New York Times.

MADRID, Nov. 3—As an immediate result of President Truman's astonishing electoral victory, many major foreign political developments that had been halted until after the voting in the United States almost certainly will be activated now more swiftly than had been expected.

Not only has Mr. Truman's reelection established his position in a fashion relatively more impressive to foreign eyes than it was in the past, but the shift in the Congressional picture is bound to convince other nations of the solidity of the United States administration and the permanence of the programs and attitudes adopted by the White House during the last two years.

[Astonishment and relief were expressed in London. Paris sources saw the continuance of the Truman Doctrine and the Marshall Plan. At the United Nations session John Foster Dulles said he believed President Truman would continue the "bipartisan foreign policies that have proved their worth." Dr. Herbert V. Evatt of Australia said the world owed Mr. Truman a tribute for his battles for mankind.]

It is obvious from the views foreign sources expressed before the vote that both the extreme Left and the extreme Right in Europe are disappointed. Likewise the center and non-Communist Left—the so-called "Third Force"—is bound to be delighted because it has derived considerable support from United States diplomacy.

It was generally considered that Moscow would have preferred a Republican victory. One Communist tactic used whenever possible was to attempt to disrupt the center forces and group the anti-Communist opposition as much as possible into coalitions that Kremlin propaganda could label the Right Wing.

One may assume that such would have been the Communist strategy in attacking a Dewey Administration as Rightist, even though it represented a scant change.

The Soviet Union obviously also must have been severely disappointed at the wretched showing of Henry A. Wallace.

Mr. Truman's moral position with "Third Force" elements must certainly now be high, because there was considerable interest abroad in his attitude on civil rights, even though this question

Continued on Page 24, Column 4

SWEEP IN CONGRESS

Democrats Obtain 54-42 Margin in Senate by Winning 9 GOP Seats

CERTAIN OF 258 IN HOUSE

Republicans Have 167, With 9 Still in Doubt—Shifts in Chairmanships Slated

By WILLIAM S. WHITE

The Democrats swept all of Congress yesterday, recapturing the supposedly impregnable Republican House by a landslide and seizing firm control of the Senate in one of the great political revolutions of American history.

As the story of Tuesday's elections yet unfolded in the late counts from the voting places, the first Republican Congress since 1932 looked out upon a scene of catastrophe as it prepared to relinquish its brief two-year tenure of leadership.

Broken were the great bastions of Republican Congressional strength; vanished was the almost universal presumption that no matter what happened to the Senate, the House would stay in Republican hands.

The labor vote, implacably angry over the Taft-Hartley Act and resentful over Republican tax reductions, had moved with strength and determination against the Republican incumbents.

Farm Vote Disappoints GOP

The farm vote had bitterly disappointed the Republicans. Where it did not turn upon them outright, the Democrats made sharp inroads in the grain belts.

President Truman's long campaign against the Eightieth Republican Congress, which he had called either "the worst" or "the second worst" of all time, apparently had a strong appeal at the ballot boxes.

Thus, last night, with all the votes not yet counted, the Democrats had taken in overflowing measure their revenge for their own Congressional rout of 1946.

The clear prospect was that in the Eighty-first Congress of next January the House would be overwhelmingly Democratic with as

Continued on Page 6, Column 3

A VICTORY SMILE AND SALUTE GIVEN BY THE PRESIDENT

Mr. Truman acknowledging plaudits of a crowd outside his hotel in Kansas City. He had just received Governor Dewey's message of congratulations. Associated Press Wirephoto

OHIO POLL DECIDES

It Clinches for President in Race Called Miracle of Electioneering

NO RECORD BALLOT IS SEEN

Dedicating Himself to Peace, Prosperity, Truman Says He Wants to Deserve Honor

By ARTHUR KROCK

The State of Ohio, "mother of Republican Presidents," furnished the electoral bloc early yesterday forenoon which assured to President Harry S. Truman a four-year term in his own right as Chief Executive of the United States. Until this late accounting of votes cast in Tuesday's general election put Ohio firmly in Mr. Truman's column, after it had fluctuated throughout the night, he was certain of but 254 electoral votes, which were twelve less than the 266 required.

The historic role played by Ohio was only one of the dramatic and extraordinary phases of the election of 1948. The President, opposed by the extreme right and left wings of the Democratic party, won a minimum of 304 electoral votes as against 189 acquired by his Republican opponent, Gov. Thomas E. Dewey of New York; carried a Democratic majority in Congress along with him after the Republicans had held this for two years; and gained victory through a multi-sectional combination of states that did not include New York, New Jersey, Pennsylvania and four of the Southern states in normal Democratic territory.

Miracle of Electioneering Seen

In the political history of the United States this achievement by Mr. Truman will be set down as a miracle of electioneering for which there are few if any parallels. His victory made him the undisputed national leader of the Democratic party, which, though bitterly divided for the past few years, has acknowledged none since the death of Franklin D. Roosevelt, whom Mr. Truman succeeded from the office of Vice President.

When it was assured that he would have Ohio's electors and hence the majority he needed, and Governor Dewey had wired his congratulations and publicly conceded defeat, the President dedicated his official future to world peace and domestic prosperity and said to his brother, J. Vivian Truman, simply: "I just want to deserve the honor."

No Record Vote Indicated

In the result, unexpected by nearly everyone who qualified as a judge of elections except the President himself, there were these other attendant circumstances:

1. The popular vote, expected to reach 51,000,000 or 52,000,000 and thus break the record of 49,548,000 in the Presidential contest of 1940, will probably be far short of the 1940 total.

2. It is possible that Mr. Truman's plurality over Mr. Dewey will not exceed 2,000,000 and may be less than that, which is smaller than the electoral division of 304 to 189 would ordinarily indicate. But this can be partly attributed to the fact that two splinter Democratic tickets were in the field—the States' Rights Democrats headed by Gov. J. Strom Thurmond of South Carolina, and the Progressives headed by Henry A. Wallace, which will poll almost 2,000,000 votes more than probably would have gone in large measure to the national Democratic ticket in normal circumstances.

3. To the vote cast for Mr. Wallace can be traced definitely the failure of the President to carry only one state, New York, with forty-seven electors.

4. California, after see-sawing all Tuesday night and yesterday morning as in 1916, and as Ohio did this year, ended in the Truman column as it did in Woodrow Wilson's contest with Charles E. Hughes thirty-two years ago. But then California made the drama of victory for Wilson; this year Ohio

Continued on Page 3, Column 4

DEWEY 'SURPRISED'; WILL NOT TRY AGAIN

Congratulates Truman, Asks Support for Him to Aid National Unity, Peace

By RUSSELL PORTER

After conceding defeat and sending congratulations to President Truman yesterday, Governor Dewey announced he did not intend to seek a third Presidential nomination. He said he had "no plans" about a third term as Governor and denied a reported intention of resigning. His term has two years to run.

In his telegram and in a press conference the Governor urged public support of the President for the sake of national unity and world peace. At the press conference he emphasized "most earnest-

Continued on Page 3, Column 1

Truman Humble in Pledging Service to American People

By ANTHONY LEVIERO

Special to The New York Times.

INDEPENDENCE, Mo., Nov. 3—President Truman accepted this day of supreme triumph in a spirit of humility and with a simple pledge to serve the American people for prosperity and peace. The fire-breathing campaigner, who "passed a miracle" unsurpassed in American political history, today was more like the man who appeared so overawed when he assumed the succession to the late Franklin D. Roosevelt.

Correspondents who have been recording his words in many weeks of hard campaigning gave him an opportunity to have an "I-told-you-so" fling at Thomas E. Dewey and the poll-takers. He had said that today they would be the red-dest-faced people in the United States. Mr. Truman did not take the opportunity.

To the American people he rededicated himself to four years of the Presidency with these words:

"I feel very deeply the responsibility which has fallen to my lot as the result of the election. I shall continue to serve the American people to the best of my ability. All my efforts will be devoted to the cause of peace in the world and the prosperity and happiness of our people here at home."

In fewer words, but as feelingly expressed, was his message to Mr. Dewey, who until yesterday was the almost universally acknowledged winner.

"I thank you sincerely for your congratulations and good wishes. Your fine sportsmanship is deeply appreciated. We jointly ow- con-

Continued on Page 7, Column 3

CHIEF RACE DELAYS REFERENDA COUNT

But Some States Decide Such Issues as War Bonus, Old-Age Aid, Labor Controls

By The Associated Press.

WASHINGTON, Nov. 3—In the general election voters of several states were called upon to decide upon bonuses for veterans of World War II, increased old-age pensions, labor issues and various tax and bond proposals.

The closeness of the Presidential race was delaying today reports on most of the results.

Twelve states posed veterans' benefit questions to their electorates. Reports from six show that Indiana, South Dakota and Louisiana approved bonuses; Nebraska and Wisconsin did not. The Indiana action is not binding on the 1949 Legislature. North Dakota defeated a proposal for a levy for a veterans' rehabilitation fund.

Eight states, in addition to Kansas, had the perennial wet vs. dry issue on the ballot in one form

Continued on Page 18, Column 4

World News Summarized

THURSDAY, NOVEMBER 4, 1948

President Truman's victory in Tuesday's election was assured yesterday when Ohio's final figures gave him that state. He was then certain of at least 304 electoral votes, with 189 for Governor Dewey and 38 for Governor Thurmond on the States' Rights ticket. [1:8.]

The President accepted his victory with humility. Thanking Governor Dewey for his congratulations, Mr. Truman said they both were indebted to the American people, who had shown the world once again "the vitality of our free institutions." [1:6-7.] Mr. Dewey, conceding defeat, urged national unity behind the President "to keep our nation strong and free and establish peace in the world." [1:5.]

Henry A. Wallace did not congratulate the President, but called on him to fulfill his campaign promises. [20:1.]

The Democrats' sweep of Congress in all sections gives them control of the House, with a majority that may reach 100. [1:4], and of the Senate, where the majority reached twelve. [2:2.]

Few immediate changes were seen in the Cabinet. Secretary Marshall wishes to retire to his farm and Secretary Forrestal may resign upon unifying the armed forces. [15:3.]

Labor support and general dissatisfaction with high prices were held responsible for cutting Governor Dewey's plurality in New York to 42,777. [18:3.] The Democrats gained nineteen seats in the Assembly and ten in the Senate. [12:4.]

In the eyes of foreign diplomats, the Truman victory assured a steadier and more vigorous American foreign policy than was possible with a Democratic President and a Republican Congress. [1:3.] A form of lend-lease arms assistance for Western Europe, it was said in Washington, will be started even before the new Congress takes office. [33:2-3.]

Britain saw the Marshall Plan undisturbed as a result of Mr. Truman's election [22:2] and the British people admired his fight. [22:4.] The French felt that their Third Force had been strengthened. [23:2-3.] Germans were encouraged [20:3], as were the Italians. [19:4.] South America felt there would be no important change in the diplomatic corps. [23:4.] The Chinese, however, were disappointed, having looked for more liberal help from Governor Dewey. [1:2-3.] Arab states saw Israel strengthened. [33:6.]

John Foster Dulles and Warren R. Austin, both Republicans, declared in Paris that the bipartisan policy would not be disturbed. [21:1.]

The United Nations General Assembly unanimously approved a Mexican resolution urging the big powers to settle their differences and to speed peace treaties. [1:1.]

The uncoordinated state of internal security controls is a grave threat to the nation's security, Secretary Forrestal told the President and the National Security Council. [33:1.]

The International Military Tribunal for the Far East, reconvening to pass judgment on Tojo, found Japan guilty of waging aggressive war. [1:2.]

Truman Vote Disappoints Nanking; Hope of Full Aid From Dewey Gone

By HENRY R. LIEBERMAN

Special to The New York Times.

NANKING, Thursday, Nov. 4—Manifestly hoping for a Republican victory in the United States elections, high Chinese officials were unable to conceal their disappointment today as the balloting returns, broadcast by American shortwave radio, showed President Truman's re-election.

The surprising vote figures were being carefully tallied in the Government Information Office yesterday afternoon, while Generalissimo Chiang Kai-shek conferred with Premier Wong Wen-hao and tried to persuade the latter not to resign in the midst of the present military, economic and psychological crisis in China.

Other Nanking officials telephoned American correspondents for the last word on the returns that the correspondents themselves were getting by shortwave radio.

Dr. Wong has submitted his resignation three times, but it has not been accepted by the Generalissimo. Before he conferred with Generalissimo Chiang, the harassed Premier asserted his determination to resign at a full meeting of the Cabinet yesterday morning. He was authorized by the Cabinet, as a matter of formal constitutional procedure, to report its resignation to the Generalissimo orally. However, each member was reportedly left free to carry on at his own discretion.

Encouraged by the Republican party platform and Gov. Thomas E. Dewey's campaign statements asserting Democratic neglect of China, the Government had been anticipating fuller American aid under a new administration after it took office in January. But with the time factor made critical by a series of morale-shattering, civil war defeats the Government seemed to be counting even more on the immediate magic

Continued on Page 26, Column 5

Kansas Votes Prohibition Repeal After 68 Years of Dry Experience

By The Associated Press.

TOPEKA, Kan., Nov. 3—Kansas voted repeal of its sixty-eight-year-old constitutional prohibition amendment. Wet forces piled up an apparent 46,000-vote majority in yesterday's voting.

Repeal of the amendment, however, was just the beginning of the fight for legalized liquor in Kansas. The issue now goes to the Legislature where some seats were upset as a result of the repeal vote. Many observers said the vote, which trailed the balloting for national and state offices in this Republican stronghold, was merely a division of wets and drys.

Kansas still has a "bone dry" law on the books which bans transportation and possession of liquor. The Constitution prohibited only manufacture and sale. Repeal means that the Legislature can decide what needs to be done but offers no solution for eliminating the "bone dry" law.

Prohibition leaders, apparently expecting repeal, were working on state legislators before the election. The city voting put repeal across but western dry counties control the State House.

The vote on repeal pulled with it another state matter of major interest to the legislators. They now will get a pay increase.

The end of prohibition as a political issue was predicted yesterday by leaders of the liquor industry when the repeal victory in Kansas was made known. Dest of prohibition measures in California, Washington and Colorado acted to strengthen this belief.

Vice Admiral F. E. M. Whiting, president of the Licensed Beverage Industries, an association representing all major liquor producers, made this comment:

"Kansas can now be added to the list of seventeen countries and provinces which have tried prohibi-

Continued on Page 18, Column 3

News Index, Page 39, this section

"All the News That's Fit to Print"

NEWS INDEX, PAGE 79, THIS SECTION

The New York Times.

LATE CITY EDITION
Partly cloudy and warmer today. Rain and mild tomorrow.
Temperature Range Today—Max.,50; Min.,35
Temperatures Yesterday—Max.,43; Min.,31
Full U. S. Weather Bureau Report, Page 86

Section 1

VOL. XCVIII No. 33,195. Entered as Second-Class Matter. Postoffice, New York, N. Y. NEW YORK, SUNDAY, DECEMBER 12, 1948. Including Magazine and Book Review. FIFTEEN CENTS

12 'SPY' PAPERS DISCLOSED, ONE HELD WRITTEN BY HISS; INQUIRY HERE TO GET FILMS

GIVEN BY CHAMBERS

House Group Releases State Department Data He Reported Filched

EXPERT LINKS ALGER HISS

Man Who Reproduced Papers on Microfilm Found, Say Committee Investigators

The documents made public by the House Committee, page 66.

By JOHN D. MORRIS
Special to THE NEW YORK TIMES.

WASHINGTON, Dec. 11—Twelve documents produced by Whittaker Chambers to substantiate his charges that Government officials passed secret data to him while he was a Communist spy in the Nineteen Thirties were made public today by the House Committee on Un-American Activities.

Along with copies of the papers, the committee gave out a Government handwriting expert's report that one of them, a digest of a 1938 diplomatic message from Herschel V. Johnson, then Chargé d'Affaires of the United States Embassy at London, was in the penmanship of Alger Hiss.

Its text was given as follows:

"March 3 Johnson U S charge at London cabled that Lord Chatfield had told the Naval Attache that whether escalation was eventually decided on or not he would not change his plans for cruisers this year and in any case new battleships would not be laid down before the end of the current year."

Papers Produced by Chambers

This and ten of the other papers had been produced by Mr. Chambers during a secret pre-trial hearing of the $75,000 damage suit filed against him for alleging that Mr. Hiss was a member of a Communist underground "apparatus" while a State Department official in 1938.

At the pre-trial session, Mr. Chambers for the first time described the objective of the alleged set-up as espionage and named Mr. Hiss, now president of the Carnegie Foundation for International Peace, and two others as the sources of secret information of state.

The committee released a copy of only one of the microfilms that Mr. Chambers later had produced for its investigators from a pumpkin shell cache at his Maryland farm.

This was an apparently verbatim copy of a 1938 dispatch to the War Department via the State Department from Samuel Sokobin, then consul at Tsingtao, North China, describing a Japanese troop movement.

Two "Strictly Confidential"

Of the other papers released today, six appeared to be verbatim transcripts in full of dispatches to the State Department from diplomats stationed abroad. One, from William C. Bullitt, then Ambassador to France, was marked "STRICTLY CONFIDENTIAL FOR THE SECRETARY." Another, from Joseph C. Grew, then Ambassador to Japan, was labeled "STRICTLY CONFIDENTIAL."

There were also nine typewritten digests of diplomatic dispatches, prepared in the same form as the handwritten paper, and five notations under various dates giving direct quotations from diplomatic dispatches.

While the excerpted and paraphrased entries gave only the date of the month, committee investigators believed they were from 1938 dispatches, since the other documents were all dated that year.

The twelve papers were among sixty that the State Department had cleared for release at the committee's request. While their publication ten years ago might have been dangerous to security and extremely embarrassing to the United States, Assistant Secretary John E. Peurifoy informed the committee that the department

Continued on Page 66, Column 2

DOCUMENT RELEASED IN SPY CASE

March 3 Johnson U S charge at London cabled that Lord Chatfield had told the Naval attache that whether escalation was eventually decided on or not he would not change his plans for cruisers this year and in any case new battleships would not be laid down before the end of the current year.

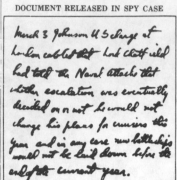

A memorandum that is identified in the records of the House Un-American Activities Committee as being in the handwriting of Alger Hiss.

The New York Times

GRAND JURY TO GET SECRET MICROFILMS

Member of House Committee Promises to Bring Material Chambers Hid in Pumpkin

By ALEXANDER FEINBERG

Assurances were given yesterday that the House Committee on Un-American Activities would accede to the demand of Federal officials and permit the special spy grand jury to view tomorrow the original microfilms secreted by Whittaker Chambers in a hollowed-out pumpkin on his Maryland farm.

The films, chief "documentary prop" to support Mr. Chambers' charges of the existence of a Washington "apparatus" for the supplying of pre-war top-secret documents to Russia, have passed through many hands since he turned them over to the committee early on the morning of Dec. 3.

Although the grand jury has been reconvened for a week, its members thus far have seen only enlarged photographs of some of the films. How much of the entire footage of the films these enlargements constitute, the Department of Justice and officials presenting the case to the grand jury have had no way of ascertaining.

Following up an earlier telephone conversation, United States Attorney John F. X. McGohey shortly after noon yesterday sent a formal request by telegram for the original films to Representative Richard M. Nixon, a committee member.

"Grand jury this [Southern New York] district requires production Monday, Dec. 13, 10 A. M. at United States Court House, Foley Square, New York, of original microfilms testified as produced by Whittaker Chambers on his farm," Mr. McGohey's telegram informed Mr. Nixon.

The Federal Attorney, noting

Continued on Page 65, Column 1

LEWIS MAY ORDER COAL OUTPUT HALT

Stocks Piling Up With Demand Slack—Operations Upset, Mines on Part Time

By JOSEPH A. LOFTUS
Special to THE NEW YORK TIMES.

WASHINGTON, Dec. 11—Soft coal production has so far outstripped demand and cut some working schedules that the industry would not be surprised, and most of it would not be disturbed, if John L. Lewis called an extended holiday for his miners.

The president of the United Mine Workers was noncommittal today, however, about the warning he gave two months ago that the union would spread the working time evenly among the country's miners if the industry itself did not do it. If any of the miners are going to starve, 'we will just all starve together," Mr. Lewis told the UMW convention. In the Pennsylvania anthracite area, a share-the-work plan has been in effect for several years.

There is no starvation problem, but here is what is happening in the bituminous industry:

The six-day week has been dropped in virtually all except the few mines producing special-purpose coals (for steel mills, gas plants, etc.).

Many mines in Eastern Kentucky and the adjoining field in Southern West Virginia are working only three or four days a week.

Surface diggings producing lower-grade coal in those two areas, as well as in Pennsylvania and Northern West Virginia, have been closed for thirty to sixty days.

Stockpiles are highest since pre-war days. They were reported as 69,000,000 tons on Nov. 1, and probably are higher now because of the continuing mild weather.

Continued on Page 51, Column 1

Doctors, Lawyers Unite on Bill To Treat Alcoholism as Disease

Proposed legislation for the rehabilitation of alcoholics, recognizing alcoholism as a disease rather than as a crime, has been drafted jointly by committees of the Association of the Bar of the City of New York and the New York Academy of Medicine for introduction into the State Legislature, it became known yesterday.

The recommended amendment of the state's present mental hygiene law was prepared by a subcommittee of the Association's committee on medical jurisprudence and a subcommittee of the Academy's committee on public health relations after a joint study of the problem.

Provision for treatment of chronic alcoholics or compulsive drinkers on a basis that views alcoholism as a medical problem, the legal committee reported, would in effect take the problem out of the corrective or penal category in which it has generally been regarded.

The proposed legislation makes provision for the establishment of hospitals, clinics and farms by the state authorities and for the certification of chronic alcoholics in such institutions or in approved private institutions for treatment. It also provides for the establishment of a bureau of alcoholic rehabilitation in the State Department of Mental Hygiene under a director to be appointed by the commissioner.

The creation of an advisory board, consisting of the director and eight members to make rules, regulations and determinations supplementing the provisions of the bill, is also recommended. The advisory board would include representatives of the State Medical

Continued on Page 76, Column 3

Costa Rican Invasion-Revolt Strikes at Figueres' Regime

Nicaragua Is Attack Base—Envoy Here Invokes Rio Defense Pact

By The United Press.

SAN JOSE, Costa Rica, Dec. 11—An invasion of Costa Rica was launched today from Nicaragua by opponents of Provisional President José Figueres, who immediately mobilized the country.

Charging that the Nicaraguan National Guard was the actual force behind the invasion, Colonel Figueres said it meant "real war" with Nicaragua. He said only a few Costa Rican exiles were involved as a "front" for the Nicaraguan National Guard.

[In Washington, Costa Rican Ambassador Mario A. Esquivel invoked the Rio de Janeiro defense treaty, calling upon the American signatory states to protect his country. The Council of the Organization of American States will meet at 3 P. M. today.]

The head of the invasion-revolt, former President Rafael Angel Calderon Guardia, was reported at the Nicaraguan border awaiting word to proceed to Liberia, about

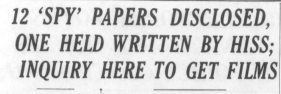

The New York Times Dec. 12, 1948

The Government announced that rebels from Nicaragua had taken La Cruz (1) and reached Liberia (2). Invasion barges were reported at San Juan del Sur, Nicaragua, northwest of La Cruz, and at Bluefields (3).

forty miles inside Costa Rica, to set up his headquarters there. Invasion troops were said to have reached Liberia after a successful landing on the Pacific coast, and to have taken La Cruz, on the coast nearer the border.

At Managua, the Nicaraguan

Continued on Page 13, Column 1

RUMANIA AND U. S. EACH ASK RECALL OF TWO DIPLOMATS

Washington's Action Follows Note by Bucharest Linking Americans to Plot

By BERTRAM D. HULEN
Special to THE NEW YORK TIMES.

WASHINGTON, Dec. 11—The United States and Rumania each demanded today the recall of two ranking diplomats in the legation of the other country. The demands are being complied with.

In addition, Rumania asked the recall of two officials of the British Legation in Bucharest.

Rumania in a note to Rudolf E. Schoenfeld, the United States Minister in Bucharest, asked for the recall, "to be effected in the shortest possible time," of Col. John R. Lovell, Military Attaché, and Henry P. Leverich, Counselor of the United States Legation.

The United States followed by demanding of the Rumanian Legation here the recall of Grigore Preoteasa, Minister Counselor and until recently Chargé d'Affaires, and Alexandru Lazareanu, Counselor of Legation.

The Rumanian demand was

Continued on Page 41, Column 3

DUTCH PUT AN END TO TALKS ON INDIES; CHARGE JAVA SHIFT

Republic Held to Be Incapable of Carrying Out Pledges Made by Premier Hatta

By DAVID ANDERSON
Special to THE NEW YORK TIMES.

THE HAGUE, the Netherlands, Dec. 11—The Netherlands Government announced today that negotiations for a settlement with the Indonesian Republic had broken down irretrievably.

In a note to the United Nations Good Offices Committee in Batavia it declared that no useful purpose could be served by further talks with the Republic of Indonesia conducted under the committee's auspices.

The note stated that the Netherlands had been faced with the choice of withdrawing from Indonesia or of accepting the Republic's challenge to fight it out. The latter course has been accepted, with an unwritten prayer that the forthcoming action may be confined to the political arena.

The Dutch Cabinet made its decision after two days of heart-searching debate. It is fully aware that the implications may be of

Continued on Page 5, Column 3

World News Summarized

SUNDAY, DECEMBER 12, 1948

The United Nations General Assembly approved last night, by a vote of 35 to 15, a compromise resolution for the establishment of a three-nation Conciliation Commission for Palestine. References to the Bernadotte plan and to the Assembly partition plan were deleted from the resolution. The United States, France and Turkey were named to the commission. [1:8.]

The Assembly, which had planned to close last night, delayed adjournment until today because of a Soviet bloc filibuster on the Korean issue. [10:1.]

Other major subjects acted on by the General Assembly since September have included the Balkans disarmament, atomic control, genocide and human rights. [Page 35.]

King Farouk of Egypt has informed the heads of all Arab states except Trans-Jordan that the proposals for the merging of Trans-Jordan and Arab Palestine under King Abdullah "do not represent the decision of the Palestinian people." [1:6-7.]

Rumania asked the recall of two United States and two British diplomats from Bucharest on the ground that the four officials had plotted to overthrow the Rumanian Government. Washington branded the charge "ridiculous" and asked that two Rumanians be recalled from their legation in the capital. [1:4.]

An agreement making Newfoundland a Canadian province was signed in Ottawa. [1:7.]

Costa Rica was invaded by rebels entering from Nicaragua. In Washington, Costa Rica's envoy invoked the Rio de Janeiro treaty to aid his country. [1:4-5.]

General MacArthur was described as of the opinion that the United States position in Japan had been weakened by the recent Communist successes in China. [1:6.]

A new success for the Chinese Communists was reported as air reconnaissance revealed that the remnants of the encircled Sixteenth Nationalist Army Group southwest of Suchow apparently had yielded. [3:1.] Economic Coordination Administrator Hoffman arrived in Shanghai. [5:1.]

The Netherlands said that negotiations with the Indonesian Republic had broken down irretrievably and that an interim government for a federated Indonesia would be proclaimed. [1:5.]

The special grand jury investigating espionage was assured yesterday by the House Committee on Un-American Activities that the microfilms of secret Government documents found in a pumpkin shell on the Maryland farm of Whittaker Chambers would be made available for its examination tomorrow. [1:2.]

Copies of twelve of the documents secreted by Mr. Chambers were made public by the House committee [1:1.] The papers contained confidential reports by high-ranking officials on questions that were of great international import in 1938. [67:3.]

The nation's soft-coal production was declared to be far above demand. The possibility was seen that John L. Lewis might call an extended miners' holiday. [1:3.]

Personal income reached an annual rate of $215,600,000,000 in October, a new high. [1:6-7.]

U. N. CREATES COMMISSION ON PALESTINE CONCILIATION; U. S., FRANCE, TURKEY NAMED

Farouk Scores Fusion Plan For Palestine, Trans-Jordan

Egyptian Ruler Says Jericho Resolution for Merger Under King Abdullah Does Not Represent Will of the People

By DANA ADAMS SCHMIDT
Special to THE NEW YORK TIMES.

CAIRO, Egypt, Dec. 11—The royal Cabinet disclosed today that King Farouk had transmitted a message to the Chiefs of State of all the Arab countries except Trans-Jordan declaring that the Jericho conference resolutions calling for a Palestine-Trans-Jordan merger under King Abdullah "do not represent the decision of the Palestinian people."

Meanwhile Abdul Rahman Azzam Pasha, secretary general of the Arab League, told correspondents that "we must continue fighting to liberate Palestine because the Jews do not respect the promises they give."

Challenging the validity of the Jericho resolutions, he added:

"I don't believe that Abdullah can take such resolutions as a basis for action. * * * I don't believe he is willing to separate himself from the Arab League and the other Arab States."

The newspaper Al Zaman forecast "serious action" by the Arab League if Abdullah went ahead with the merger, implying that Trans-Jordan might be expelled from the League.

It was also stated that Imam Ahmed, King of Yemen, had sent Abdullah a telegram exhorting him not to upset Arab unity.

It was rumored in Cairo that as a result of the pressure being brought to bear, Abdullah would postpone bringing the issue before the Trans-Jordanian Parliament.

Information reaching foreign diplomatic quarters, however, was that Abdullah was determined to go ahead with his acceptance of the crown of the United Hashimite kingdom of Palestine and Trans-Jordan regardless of consequences. It indicated also that he would accept an armistice in Palestine and that he had, in fact, reached an advanced stage in the negotiation of details.

The question in the mind of for-

Continued on Page 30, Column 1

PLAN WINS, 35 TO 15

Arab and Soviet Groups Vote Against Board in the Assembly

ADJOURNMENT IS BLOCKED

Filibuster by the Eastern Bloc on Korean Issue Forces Another Session Today

Text of Palestine resolution adopted by U.N. Assembly, P. 33.

By THOMAS J. HAMILTON
Special to THE NEW YORK TIMES.

PARIS, Sunday, Dec. 12—The United Nations General Assembly, which had set up late yesterday a Conciliation Commission to attempt to work out a permanent settlement in Palestine, early today named the United States, France and Turkey to the Commission.

After the Assembly had acted on the Palestine question, Dr. Herbert V. Evatt, the President, cut short a Soviet-bloc filibuster on Korea at 2 A. M. and adjourned the meeting until 3 o'clock this afternoon.

This decision dashed the hope that this night meeting would wind up the Paris session of the Assembly. Now, the weary delegates must meet once more today, to attempt to reach a decision on Korea.

The vote on the resolution to establish the Commission, which received no instructions whatever regarding boundaries, was 35 to 15, with 8 abstentions, as follows:

Vote on the Resolution

For (35)—Argentina, Australia, Belgium, Brazil, Canada, China, Colombia, Denmark, Dominican Republic, Ecuador, El Salvador, Ethiopia, France, Great Britain, Greece, Haiti, Honduras, Iceland, Liberia, Luxembourg, the Netherlands, New Zealand, Nicaragua, Norway, Panama, Paraguay, Peru, the Philippines, Siam, Sweden, Turkey, South Africa, the United States, Uruguay and Venezuela.

Against (15)—Afghanistan, Byelorussia, Czechoslovakia, Cuba, Egypt, Iraq, Lebanon, Pakistan, Poland, Saudi Arabia, Syria, the Ukraine, the Soviet Union, Yemen and Yugoslavia.

Abstentions (8)—Bolivia, Burma, Chile, Costa Rica, Guatemala, India, Iran and Mexico.

Under the provisions of the resolution, adopted a year and thirteen days after the passage of the original partition resolution at Flushing Meadow, the Conciliation Commission is instructed "to take steps to assist Governments and authorities concerned to achieve a final settlement of all questions outstanding between them." It calls upon them to seek agreement "by negotiations conducted either with the Conciliation Commission or directly."

An International Regime

An international regime is to be established eventually for the Jerusalem area, including Bethlehem and other outlying towns. Proposals for such an international regime are to be submitted to the session of the General Assembly, to be held in September, 1949. Meanwhile the Commission is authorized to appoint a representative to cooperate with local authorities regarding an interim administration.

Safeguarding of holy places, including those in Nazareth, together with freedom of access to them, was placed under supervision of the Conciliation Commission.

The Commission also was instructed to facilitate the "repatriation, resettlement and economic and social rehabilitation of the refugees" and payment of compensation for destroyed property. Although it did not specify what refugees, this referred mainly to the estimated 500,000 Palestinian Arabs and possibly 10,000 Jews

Continued on Page 32, Column 3

This section consists of 100 pages divided into three parts. The Index will be found on Page 79. Society news begins on Page 81 and Obituaries begin on Page 92.

M'ARTHUR WARNS U. S. ON CHINA TREND

Washington Studies Analysis of Effect of Reds' Gains on Our Security in Orient

By HANSON W. BALDWIN
Special to THE NEW YORK TIMES.

WASHINGTON, Dec. 11—The Communist victories in China will necessitate a reappraisal of the United States military position in the Far East, in the opinion of military observers. Some of the first major strategic repercussions of those victories already have made themselves felt in Washington; others will follow.

Gen. Douglas MacArthur, Supreme Commander, Allied Powers, in Japan, already has dispatched his estimate of the effects of the Communist victories upon his position—a document that was being studied in Washington this week. In essence, General MacArthur views the United States position in Japan as weakened materially by the flanking Communist positions in the north on the Kuriles and Kamchatka and Sakhalin, and in the south in China. Additional troops, ships and planes are needed if our position in Japan and the Ryukyus to the south is to be secure, his analysis states.

Apparently General MacArthur does not feel that much, if anything, can now be done to arrest the sweep of communism in China; his report is concerned primarily with strengthening the insular

Continued on Page 4, Column 1

NEWFOUNDLAND TIE TO CANADA SIGNED

Union Needs Only Ratification by Governments—One Aide of Island Rejects Terms

By P. J. PHILIP
Special to THE NEW YORK TIMES.

OTTAWA, Dec. 11—Canada and Newfoundland today signed the terms of union by which the ancient British colony will become a province of Canada.

The agreement signed by the representatives of the Canadian Government and the official delegation from Newfoundland must be submitted for approval to the Canadian Parliament and the Government of Newfoundland and for confirmation by the Parliament of the United Kingdom, but it is hoped that the formal act of union will be completed by March 31, 1949.

One member of the Newfoundland delegation, Chesley Crosbie, did not sign. Two days ago he declared himself dissatisfied with the financial terms of the agreement, which, he said, fell short by $8,000,000 of the amount of assistance that Newfoundland would need during the first years of the union. He left this morning before the ceremony to make a business trip to the United States and on his return to Newfoundland he will present a minority report to the present Governor, Sir Gordon MacDonald.

The ceremony of signing, which followed two months of close and careful negotiation, took place in

Continued on Page 39, Column 3

Personal Income at a New Peak But a Leveling-Off Is Apparent

Special to THE NEW YORK TIMES.

WASHINGTON, Dec. 11—Personal income rose to a new high in October, reaching an annual rate of $215,600,000,000, the Department of Commerce reported today.

The annual rate for October compared with the previous record of $214,900,000,000 for September, and $200,000,000,000 for October, 1947, according to the department's Office of Business Economics.

The increase has been evident since last year, with the first ten months of 1948 showing an annual rate of personal income at $210,800,000,000, substantially above the $193,200,000,000 for the same period in 1947.

The department reported, however, that the three months ended in October have shown a leveling off of personal income. Substantial increases were recorded earlier in the year as a result of wage-rate advances and expansion of employment.

A report by the Bureau of the Census fixed employment during November at an all-time high of 59,893,000 for that month, higher by 1,298,000 than the corresponding month of 1947.

In percentages, farmers and others receiving income from agriculture fared slightly better in the rise from September to October than those receiving non-agricultural income. Total farm income advanced from $22,400,000,000 to $22,800,000,000 in that period, while non-agricultural income eased forward only from $192,500,000,000 to $192,800,000,000. The slight increase in farm income was the result, the department said, of

Continued on Page 48, Column 5

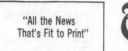

1949

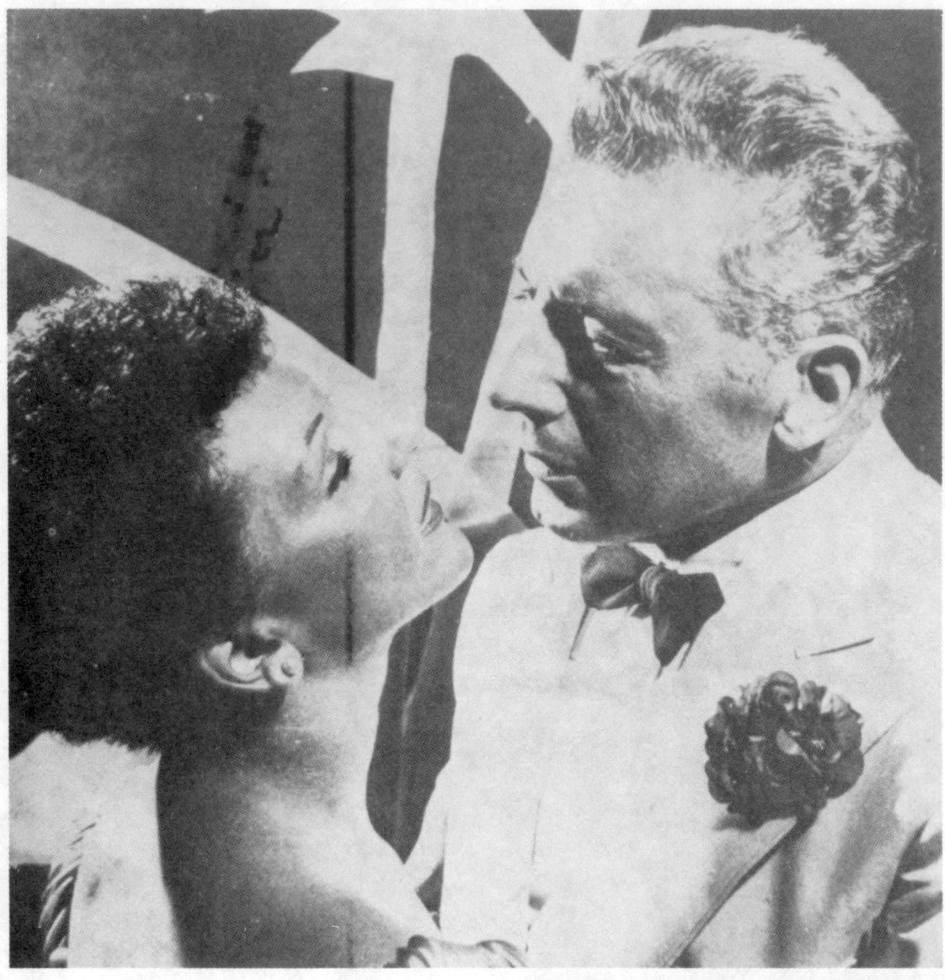

Mary Martin and Ezio Pinza starred in the Rodgers and Hammerstein musical *South Pacific* when the show began its run on Broadway.

Child actress Margaret O'Brien has a light-hearted talk with President Truman. Among other films, Margaret appeared in *Babes on Broadway* (with Judy Garland and Mickey Rooney), *Meet Me in St. Louis; Our Vines Have Tender Grapes;* and, in 1949, *Little Women.*

"All the News That's Fit to Print"

The New York Times.

LATE CITY EDITION
Cloudy today; rain tonight and tomorrow morning.
Temperature Range Today—Max.,42; Min.,32
Temperatures Yesterday—Max.,49; Min.,35
U. S. Weather Bureau Report, Page 8; Sect. 1

Section 1

NEWS INDEX, PAGE 71, THIS SECTION

Copyright, 1949, by The New York Times Company.

VOL. XCVIII No. 33,237. Entered as Second-Class Matter, Postoffice, New York, N. Y. NEW YORK, SUNDAY, JANUARY 23, 1949. Including Magazine and Book Review. FIFTEEN CENTS

PEIPING SURRENDERS TO REDS AS NANKING REGIME OFFERS TO CONFER ON FOES' TERMS

WAR IN NORTH ENDS

Transitional Coalition Is Arranged—Safety Assured Foreigners

NANKING PRESSES PEACE

Accepts Communist Formula as Basis, Names Mission to Talk With Reds

By JEAN LYON
Special to THE NEW YORK TIMES.

PEIPING, Jan. 22—Peiping fell to Communists today—quietly, politely and in accordance with her traditions—a feat possible only in China. The Nationalists are bowing their way out while the Communists bow their way in under a complicated and somewhat unfathomable agreement.

The agreement, which was formally announced to the press tonight by Gen. Fu Tso-yi's official spokesman Gen. Yen Yu-wen who has reportedly been one of the main peace negotiators, in effect, establishes a separate peace for North China.

[The Associated Press said that the surrender terms included the removal of General Fu's name from the Communists' "war criminal" list.]

Broader Compact to Follow

The agreement provides for a transitional coalition committee, made up of both Nationalists and Communists, to effect the takeover. Credit, thereby, goes to General Fu for negotiating the peace that the people of the city and North China have long been demanding. Credit goes at the same time to the Communists for the setting up of the long-promised coalition. What comes after the transition is not stated but reference is made to an "overall agreement" that will be drawn up by the coalition group.

The cease-fire order went into effect at 10 o'clock this morning and Nationalist troops were to begin moving out of the city at once for "reorganization" at designated points and the coalition committee was to be formed to take over all military and political affairs of the city at an unspecified time.

There are thirteen points in the agreement, all applicable only to the transition period. The safety of the lives and property of foreigners is assured, continued functioning of telegraphic and postal communications is promised, the freedom of worship and the protection of religious property is agreed upon, and all the present Government and private organizations, including the Provincial Government, are to continue without change for the present.

Nanking Speeds Talks

By HENRY R. LIEBERMAN
Special to THE NEW YORK TIMES

NANKING, Jan. 22—A separate peace settlement for the Communist-besieged city of Peiping was concluded today as Premier Sun Fo's Cabinet prepared to negotiate for a general peace on the basis of the Communists' terms.

The arrangement under which Peiping is being yielded was made with the Communists by Gen. Fu Tso-yi, Nationalist commander in North China. Peiping has been encircled for more than a month.

Here, five delegates were named by the Cabinet to negotiate for peace as acting President Li Tsung-jen announced that his caretaker Government was ready to talk terms on the basis of the eight conditions laid down by the Communist leader Mao Tse-tung.

Mr. Mao's conditions, which were broadcast by the North Shensi radio on Jan. 14 called for the virtual surrender of the Kuomintang [Government party] and the punishment of "war criminals."

"The five Government delegates are ready to start negotiations with the delegates of the Chinese Communist party at a suitable place to be agreed upon by both sides," an official Cabinet statement said.

The Kuomintang representatives named to talk peace are:

Shao Li-tze, a long time peace advocate, chairman. Mr. Shao, 67,

Continued on Page 5, Column 1

Asian Parley Votes U.N. Plea; Dutch Resist U. S. Proposals

New Delhi Draft Demands Transfer of Sovereignty in East Indies by 1950

By ROBERT TRUMBULL
Special to THE NEW YORK TIMES

NEW DELHI, India, Jan. 22—Representatives of nineteen Asian and African nations in closed session here today unanimously adopted a draft resolution calling upon the United Nations Security Council to order the Netherlands Government to effect a complete transfer of sovereignty over all its rich East Indies colonies to the United States of Indonesia by 1950.

The resolution includes recommendations to the Security Council for the following further demands upon the Netherlands Government:

(1) That Dutch forces be withdrawn immediately from the Jogjakarta Residency and progressively from the rest of the Indonesian Republic territory seized by the Dutch in the action that began on Dec. 19, the withdrawal to be completed not later than March 15, 1949.

(2) That all Republican officials, leaders and political prisoners be

Continued on Page 4, Column 1

Stikker Says Netherlands Has Already Pledged Steps Now Urged Upon Her

By DAVID ANDERSON
Special to THE NEW YORK TIMES

THE HAGUE, The Netherlands, Jan. 22—Strong indications were given in the Netherlands today that this country would fight to the bitter end against the latest United States resolution proposing a solution to the Indonesian question. Speaking before the Foreign Press Association in The Hague, the Foreign Minister, Dr. Dirk U. Stikker, said:

"I can foresee only chaos if the resolution is allowed to stand as it is now before the Security Council—chaos in Indonesia and subsequently chaos in The Netherlands—and all this because of a lack of confidence, a lack of faith in the spiritual forces and values of the West, a basic mistrust of our proclaimed intentions, of our most formal pledges."

Dr. Stikker said that there was "a basic mistrust also of the peoples of the areas outside the Republic—two-thirds of the popula-

Continued on Page 4, Column 4

ERP AIDE SEES ITALY IN FAST RECOVERY

Zellerbach, Here, Describes Vast Improvements Made Since End of War

Italy, once on the brink of collapse and revolt, is well and firmly started on the road to recovery, James D. Zellerbach, European Recovery Program Administrator in Italy, declared yesterday.

Mr. Zellerbach, who arrived from Rome last Thursday and is on his way to Washington to testify before Congressional committees on the renewal of the ERP appropriation for Italy, was interviewed at the Sherry-Netherland Hotel.

The average Italian's eagerness to work and the Italian Government's economic stabilization measures combined with United States aid have brought about measurable material improvement in Italy's economy in the last nine months, he said.

Marshall Plan benefits have caused communism to lose ground in Italy, even though the Communist party there was second in size only to the one in the Soviet Union, but the democratic nations must not relax their vigilance, he warned.

"We can't afford to quit now," he said. "The price is vigilance."

The Center and moderate Left parties, which got only 32 per cent of the seats in the regional and communal elections in 1947, won 54 per cent of the seats between April and November last year, he said. The extreme Left composed of Communist and Left Socialists who work with them won 26 per cent

Continued on Page 13, Column 1

SCANDINAVIAN RIFT DELAYS ARMS PACT

Sweden and Norway Disagree on Atlantic Defense Link At Copenhagen Session

By GEORGE AXELSSON
Special to THE NEW YORK TIMES.

COPENHAGEN, Denmark, Jan. 22—An eleventh-hour proposal to break the Swedish-Norwegian stalemate on a Nordic defense alliance was made today at the opening of the conference of the premiers and foreign and defense ministers of Norway, Denmark and Sweden, according to reliable sources.

The proposal sought to reconcile the firm Norwegian determination to join the North Atlantic pact with Sweden's decision to stick to her traditional policy of neutrality.

The Danes were said to have been most eager to keep the discussion alive, thus postponing the final decision. They nevertheless appeared to share the Swedish attitude that the present United States decision to refuse arms to non-members of the Atlantic alliance should not be taken at its face value and that it would be reconsidered in an emergency.

[Reports in London said that Sweden was trying to persuade Denmark not to join the Atlantic pact. Norway was reported to have decided to join.]

The only official comment on the conference was made by Danish Premier Hans Hedtoft, who told reporters as he left the conference room in the Danish Parliament building "You can see from our faces that everything is going

Continued on Page 37, Column 3

Builders Must Scrap Old Methods To Get Recovery, U. N. Body Says

By GEORGE BARRETT
Special to THE NEW YORK TIMES.

LAKE SUCCESS, Jan. 22—An international program to reorganize the building industry—specifically to scrap "backward handicraft" methods for quick, mass production by prefabrication—was urged here today as the surest way to ease the world's acute housing crisis.

The call for a cooperative attack by all countries to end the housing dilemma came from the United Nations Bulletin on Housing and Town and Country Planning, issued today for the first time by the world organization's Social Affairs Department. The inaugural copy of the bulletin, to be followed by other issues from time to time, is the latest product of a two-year-old General Assembly resolution urging nations to exchange views on how best to solve the world's housing shortage.

The 74-page broadside contains a number of articles on housing developments in the various regions of the globe, but the sharpest criticism of present-day methods as well as the most positive program for the future are presented by Ernest Weissmann, director of the Industry and Materials Divisions of the United Nations Economic Commission for Europe.

Mr. Weissmann draws a dismal picture of both American and European efforts to cure the housing problem. He contends, for example, that the present deficit of 14,000,000 dwellings in sixteen European countries may never be completely erased under present building techniques.

The United Nations expert goes on to say that even if the sixteen nations could today build at double the pre-war rate, even if they

Continued on Page 27, Column 1

IDLENESS IS RISING OVER THE NATION; OFFSET EXPECTED

Recipients of Insurance Go Up 10 to 100% as Varied Factors Cause Industrial Lay-Offs

THIS STATE'S ROLL HEAVY

But New Jobs Are Forecast to Restore Business Activity to Near High Level of '48

By A. H. RASKIN

Unemployment rolls have risen in many parts of the country, but business leaders and Government officials see few signs that the falling off in employment foreshadows any substantial drop from last year's high levels of industrial activity.

A survey made for THE NEW YORK TIMES by its correspondents in cities from coast to coast shows that a combination of seasonal factors, heavy inventories and consumer resistance to high prices has caused increases of 10 to 100 per cent in the number of workers drawing idleness insurance in many areas.

The rise in unemployment has been most marked in New York, New Jersey, New England and parts of the Midwest. On the other hand, such major centers as Pittsburgh, Birmingham and New Orleans report employment on the upgrade, with strong prospects for a continued advance.

The beneficial effects of the rearmament program on employment in aircraft, shipbuilding and other industries are just beginning to be felt in most areas, and officials are confident that defense orders and the European Recovery Program will create tens of thousands of new jobs by spring.

Uncertainty over the fiscal policies of President Truman and the Eighty-first Congress was cited as a factor in the decision of some industrialists to lay off workers and reduce inventories. Others said that a lack of orders had prompted them to return to the pre-war practice of closing their plants for periods ranging from a week to a month at the beginning of the year for inventory and plant repair.

Labor's Outlook Dimmed

Labor economists take a somewhat gloomier view of the dip in employment than that of most industrialists. Union officials contend that many items of apparel, household equipment and automobiles are being "priced out of the market."

They estimate that about 750,000 workers have lost their jobs in the last three months and that the total unemployed may reach 3,300,000 by spring, as against 1,900,000 last fall.

But most union leaders see no likelihood of a real recession so long as armament and ERP purchases remain high. They advocate Government planning for stimulating industry and construction in the event that the need for military expenditures dwindles.

In Los Angeles and some other large cities a sharp rise in the industrial population since 1940 produced the seeming paradox of near-record employment and mounting unemployment. In all regions unemployment insurance administrators said that the number of workers covered by the insurance systems had gone up substantially, making it difficult to obtain a valid comparison of present unemployment totals with those before the war.

New York Idleness Rises

The New York State unemployment insurance and veterans' readjustment rolls, which increased 86,000 during the week ended Jan. 7, dropped 6,600 in the following week. That left the total at 461,380, a rise of 42 per cent over the figure for the same week last year and 67 per cent above the total for the week ended Oct. 8, 1948. The significance of the 6,600 decline was further clouded by the fact that 10,000 workers exhausted their right to benefits during the week and were removed from the rolls, even though they had not found new employment.

In this city the number of jobless workers decreased from 293,-[illegible] to 289,588. A year ago the city's total was 209,490. Unemployment insurance recipients upstate numbered 171,692 for the week ended Jan. 14, as against 114,950 twelve months earlier.

Edward Corsi, State Industrial Commissioner, said that a preliminary analysis by his department of the situation in the metropolitan area and upstate had convinced him that there was "nothing to

Continued on Page 20, Column 1

A GEYSER OF STEAM ENSHROUDS MIDTOWN

A view of Broadway and Thirty-eighth Street yesterday as cloud of vapor hung over the area when water from broken main came in contact with steam pipes.

The New York Times (by John Sneddon)

BURST WATER MAIN TIES UP BROADWAY

All Traffic Diverted Between 35th and 40th Streets as Steam, Spray Fill Area

A burst water main yesterday gave three blocks of midtown Broadway the appearance of a volcano about to erupt. For more than two hours it was feared that an explosion might rip up huge sections of the street between Thirty-seventh and Thirty-ninth Streets. Broadway traffic in the area was shut off until tomorrow, and even pedestrians were barred for several hours.

From 12:40 P. M., when the first trickle of water and the first wisp of steam were detected, until nearly 3 o'clock, virtually every type of emergency apparatus in the city was in the vicinity of Broadway and Thirty-eighth Street, where the three-foot break occurred in a twenty-inch water main.

By drilling and pumping operations the danger of a break in steam pipes was averted. However, the frantic operations left a fifteen-foot hole at Broadway and Thirty-eighth Street. Along Broadway in that vicinity the asphalt had sunk several inches at some points and bulged a few inches at others.

Vehicular traffic was quickly diverted from Broadway between Thirty-fifth and Fortieth Street. During the danger period pedestrians were not permitted between Thirty-seventh and Fortieth Streets.

After sundown, municipal and utility repair crews were able to reduce the restricted traffic zone to an area between Thirty-sixth and Thirty-ninth Street. At the same time, pedestrians were permitted to use the east sidewalk on Broadway. The police said, however, that damage was so extensive that vehicular traffic would be detoured through today. Broadway buses were diverted to the Avenue of the Americas and Seventh Avenue.

Through the night, men fixed a

Continued on Page 42, Column 3

MAYOR CHALLENGES PSC ON FARES HERE

Threatens to Ask Legislative Aid—Hints the Commission Seeks to Force City Rise

By PAUL CROWELL

Mayor O'Dwyer threatened yesterday to ask for state legislation to keep the Public Service Commission from interfering with joint fare agreements between the city and private bus companies operating under city franchises.

The Mayor's threat was prompted by the order issued by the commission on Friday, directing six private bus companies to begin negotiations with the city for an "equitable" apportionment of the 12-cent fare now charged for a combined ride on their lines and the city's rapid transit lines. The city now collects 7 cents and the companies 5 cents under an agreement branded by the commission as "unlawful and discriminatory."

Hinting that the commission's order might be a move to force the city to increase the fare on its own lines, the Mayor declared that such a move would be resisted with every resource at his command.

"There will be fireworks," he promised.

The Mayor's challenge to the commission was issued at the end of a long conference with Chairman William Reid of the Board of Transportation, Transportation Commissioners Frank X. Sullivan and Sidney H. Bingham and first assistant Corporation Counsel Charles Preusse. Mr. Reid was summoned from Albany to attend the meeting.

"I am amazed," the Mayor said, "that the Public Service Commission would go so far to confuse a simple plan that we adopted last July to give a uniform fare on our combined rides, from subway to bus and from bus to subways.

"If this is an attempt by the Public Service Commission to compel the city to raise the fare further the commission will find out

Continued on Page 44, Column 3

Strike Threat Ends on Long Island; Union Will Test Repaired Engines

A week-old threat of a strike by 300 engineers of the Long Island Rail Road was lifted yesterday after three days of negotiation between the company and the Brotherhood of Locomotive Engineers.

M. E. McMahon, general chairman of Division 269 of the brotherhood, had announced last Saturday that a strike vote would be taken among the members in protest against the "unsafe" condition of the line's steam locomotives and multiple unit electric cars. He also accused the company of repairing this equipment badly and inspecting it superficially.

To this the railroad replied that the locomotives and cars were inspected regularly by Government men as well as the road's own staff.

The strike vote was started last Monday. With two-thirds of the ballots in, the pro-strike sentiment was 98 per cent, according to Mr. McMahon, but with the members empowering their leaders to make a settlement.

Technicalities of the National Railway Labor Act had made a speedy walkout uncertain. Alvanley Johnston, international president of the union, had disavowed the strike vote and said that he had not authorized it.

Talks between the company and the union began Thursday morning and continued three days. Both sides reported that they were nearing a settlement on basic issues. That agreement came yesterday at 5:43 P. M. when a joint statement outlined the truce.

Regarding the union's complaint that locomotives were "unsafe," the company agreed to appoint a

Continued on Page 54, Column 6

GOP CLASHES RISE AS SCOTT CHOOSES EXECUTIVE BOARD

Brown, Taft Leader, Weeks of Massachusetts, R. H. Cake Among Leaders Dropped

FIGHT AT OMAHA LOOMING

Chairman's Drive for National Policy Conference Also Stirs Further Controversies

By W. H. LAWRENCE
Special to THE NEW YORK TIMES.

WASHINGTON, Jan. 22 — New controversies among Republican leaders developed tonight as Representative Hugh D. Scott Jr. of Pennsylvania, chairman of the Republican National Committee, appointed a GOP Executive Committee of fifteen members—eight men and seven women.

As Republicans began to head for Omaha, where their Finance and National Committees will be in session Tuesday, Wednesday and Thursday, Representative Scott announced his selections. They were criticized immediately by some Republicans, who said the list was as notable for those who were left off as it was for those who were named.

On and off-the-record comments of Republican leaders here made it clear that there is no agreement among them as to why the party has now lost five successive Presidential elections or as to how it might win another one.

Mr. Scott made himself chairman of the Executive Committee to which he named the following other members of the National Committee: Harold E. Mitchell, Connecticut; James F. Dewey, Vermont; J. Russel Sprague, New York; Mrs. Worthington Scranton, Pennsylvania; Walter S. Hallanan, West Virgnia; Mrs. Cecil M. Harden, Indiana; Jouett Ross Todd, Kentucky; Mrs. Edna Basten Donald, Nebraska; Harry Darby, Kansas; Mrs. Daniel J. Schneider, Colorado; Mrs. Roy F. Priest, Utah; McIntyre Faries, California; Mrs. William Preston Few, North Carolina; R. B. Creager, Texas; and Mrs. Marshall E. Cornett, Oregon.

Such party stalwarts as Sinclair Weeks of Massachusetts, Representative Clarence Brown of Ohio, and Ralph H. Cake of Oregon, who had been members of the previous Executive Committee, were not reappointed by Representative Scott. Mr. Brown, the Taft campaign

Continued on Page 34, Column 1

ISRAEL AND EGYPT HELD NEAR CLIMAX IN ARMISTICE TALK

Source Predicts That Next 36 Hours Will See the End of Parley on Rhodes

DEADLOCK IS IN THIRD DAY

Tel Aviv's Refusal to Withdraw From Captured Territory Is Reportedly Its Cause

By The Associated Press.

RHODES, Jan. 22—The next thirty-six hours will see the end of the Israeli-Egyptian armistice talks, either in success or failure, an authoritative source said tonight.

As the deadlock that has hamstrung the meetings dragged into its third day, a source close to the Israeli delegation said that his country might modify its position "because Israel wants this conference to succeed so she can deal with the other Arab states." Apparently this is known to the Egyptians.

The deadlock has hinged, conference circles said, on an Israeli refusal to evacuate territory taken in two recent offensives.

The strain of the almost uninterrupted conferences of the last three days is beginning to tell on Dr. Ralph J. Bunche, acting United Nations Mediator for Palestine, who spent the afternoon "writing." A spokesman refused to say what he was writing, but he indicated that it was a revision of drafts of compromises offered to break the stalemate over boundaries, particularly in the Negeb, desert area in the south.

The Israelis have kept insisting that these talks were for "armistice," not "peace." Some sources said that the Israelis might make concessions with the reservation that they would be reconsidered at a peace table. This might be a long way off, and the long-range solution for peace still seems remote.

Both Sides Are Worried

By SAM POPE BREWER
Special to THE NEW YORK TIMES.

RHODES, Jan. 22—Egyptian representatives negotiating here for the armistice with Israel appear to be in terror of the effect that will be caused on the Egyptian public when it is known that they have dealt with the Israelis. The Egyptians' stand has been that the negotiations were purely

Continued on Page 9, Column 1

World News Summarized

SUNDAY, JANUARY 23, 1949

Peiping, the cultural capital of China, agreed yesterday to surrender to the Communists after a forty-day siege. The terms provide for transitional joint control of the city and protection of foreign persons and property. In Nanking, Acting President Li announced that the Chinese Government was ready to negotiate on the basis of the terms broadcast by the Reds on Jan. 14. These terms amounted to a virtual demand for unconditional surrender. [1:8.]

In New Delhi the conference of nineteen nations of Asia and Africa adopted without a dissenting vote a resolution that urged the United Nations Security Council to order the Netherlands Government to transfer sovereignty over its East Indies colonies to the United States of Indonesia by 1950. The resolution also asked the Security Council to order the withdrawal of Dutch forces from recently occupied areas and the liberation of all Republican leaders and political prisoners. [1:6.]

Foreign Minister Stikker of the Netherlands criticized as a "dangerous" intervention the United States resolution before the Security Council offering a solution of the Indonesian problem and declared he could foresee only chaos in both Indonesia and the Netherlands if the resolution were adopted. [1:7]

Marcel Cachin, French Communist leader, said in Rome that "it would be an excellent idea for President Truman to send one of his friends to Moscow to talk things over with Premier Stalin." The "peace offensive" recently launched by various European Communist leaders also received support in an editorial in the Italian Communist journal Unita that called for a policy of "international collaboration based on the premise that Socialist and capitalist regimes can coexist." [12:3.]

Italy, aided by United States help, has made rapid progress on the road to recovery, James D. Zellerbach, European Recovery Program Administrator in Italy, reported. [1:6.]

The conference of Premiers and Foreign and Defense Ministers of Norway, Denmark and Sweden in Copenhagen reportedly was attempting to reconcile a Norwegian intention to join the North Atlantic security treaty and a Swedish determination to adhere to strict neutrality. [1:7.]

The discussions on the island of Rhodes with the Israeli and Egyptian delegations looking to an armistice in Palestine were meeting rough going. The talks were expected to end in thirty-six hours in success or failure, according to authoritative sources. [1:5.]

A survey by THE NEW YORK TIMES indicated that, while there had been increases of 10 to 100 per cent in unemployment in many parts of the country, business and Government leaders believed that industrial activity would substantially retain its high levels of the past year. The rise in unemployment has been most noticeable in New York, New Jersey, New England and parts of the Midwest and was attributed to seasonal factors, heavy inventories and consumer resistance to high prices. [1:1.]

Representative Hugh Scott of Pennsylvania, Republican National Committee chairman, named eight men and seven women to the Republican Executive Committee and drew prompt criticisms from some Republicans for his selections. Against a background of controversy Republican leaders prepared to meet in Omaha for several days starting Tuesday to consider plan the party's future activities. [1:4.]

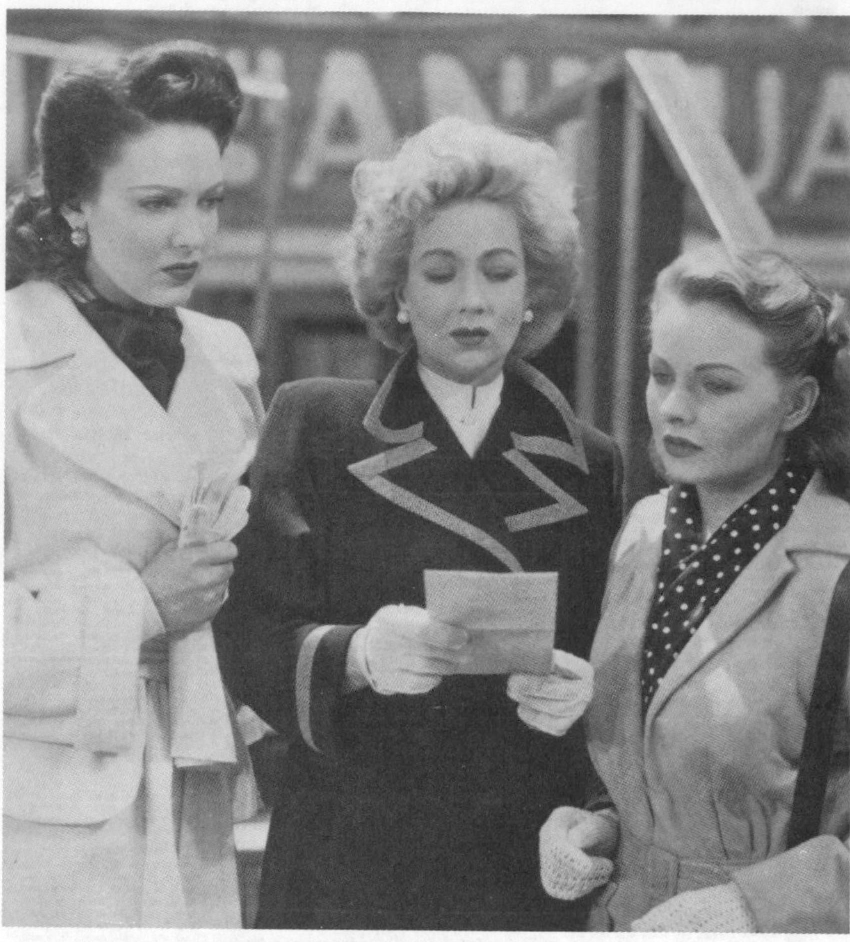

Linda Darnell, Ann Sothern and Jeanne Crain in *A Letter to Three Wives.*

Enzo Staiola in *The Bicycle Thief,* the Italian film which was voted among the world's ten best in an international poll conducted in the sixties.

Mario Lanza made his film debut opposite Kathryn Grayson in *That Midnight Kiss.*

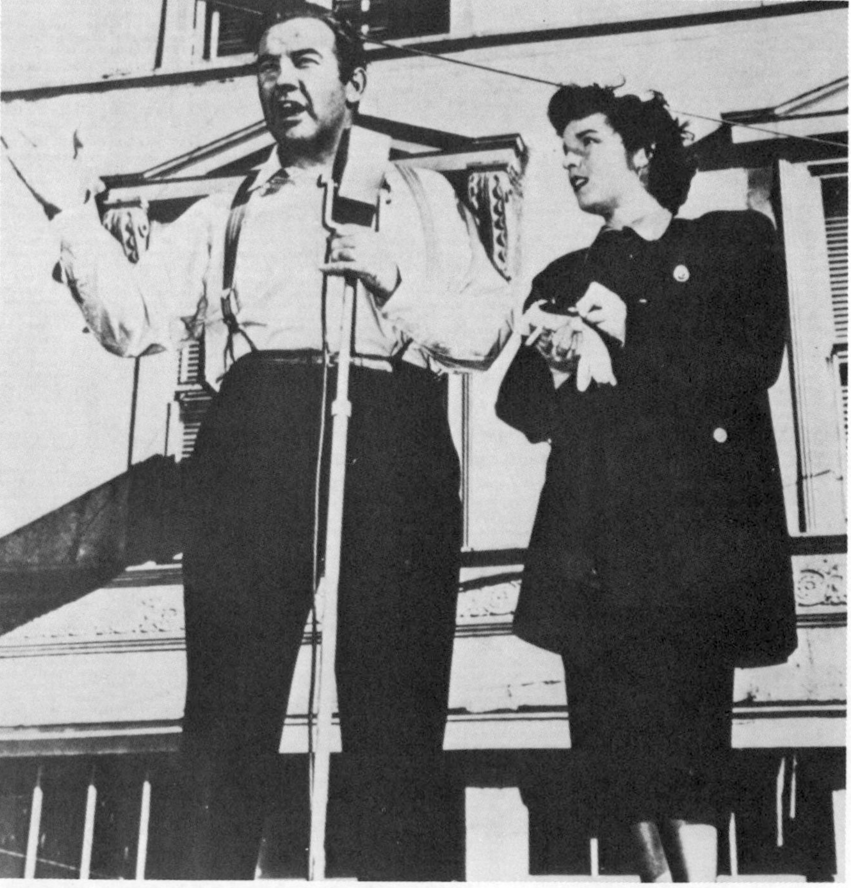

Broderick Crawford and Mercedes McCambridge in *All the King's Men.*

"All the News That's Fit to Print"

The New York Times.

LATE CITY EDITION
Sunny today, Rain tomorrow morning, clearing in afternoon.
Temperature Range Today-Max.,41; Min.,32
Temperatures Yesterday—Max.,50; Min.,35
Full U. S. Weather Bureau Report, Page 31

VOL. XCVIII..No. 33,253. Entered as Second-Class Matter, Postoffice, New York, N. Y. NEW YORK, TUESDAY, FEBRUARY 8, 1949. Times Square, New York 18, N. Y. Telephone LAckawanna 4-1000 THREE CENTS IN NEW YORK CITY

REORGANIZATION BILL VOTED IN HOUSE AS HOOVER REPORT ASKS CUT IN EXECUTIVE UNITS

NEW POWERS WIDE

Plan Allows President to Initiate Big Changes in Federal Set-Up

CONGRESS VETO PROVIDED

Approval Overwhelming, 356-9 —'Preferential' Consideration Allowed Seven Groups

Text of report of the Hoover Commission, Pages 18 and 19.

By CLAYTON KNOWLES
Special to THE NEW YORK TIMES.

WASHINGTON, Feb. 7—By a vote of 356 to 9, the House approved and sent to the Senate today a bill vesting in the President broad and permanent authority to initiate administrative reforms for greater efficiency and economy in the Federal Government.

The House acted as the Hoover Commission, formally known as the Commission on Organization of the Executive Branch of the Government, sent to Congress the first of fifteen formal reports pointing the way to reforms.

Under the measure endorsed by the House, any reorganization plan submitted by the President would become operative sixty days after it was offered if both Houses of Congress did not join in vetoing it.

Former President Herbert Hoover's group had recommended this authority for the President as a necessary preliminary to the implementation of a good part of its recommendations.

"Clear Line of Command" Aim

Mr. Hoover said that, armed with the powers his group proposed, the President would be able to "clear away a lot of the underbrush" that stood in the way of overhauling the Government effectively.

There were twenty-seven specific recommendations for the improvement of the general management of the executive branch of Government in the report submitted by the Hoover Commission a few hours before the House vote.

In general terms, the recommendations seek the establishment of a "clear line of command from the top to the bottom and a return line of responsibility and accountability from the bottom to the top."

The introduction to the report stated flatly that this clear line of authority did not exist, with the result that accountability and responsibility were impaired.

"The critical state of world affairs," it said, "requires the Government of the United States to speak and act with unity of purpose, firmness and restraint in dealing with other nations. It must act decisively to preserve its human and material resources.

Freedom to Build Peace Urged

"It must develop strong machinery for the national defense, while seeking to construct an enduring world peace. It cannot perform these tasks if its organization for development and execution of policy is confused and disorderly, or if the Chief Executive is handicapped in providing firm direction to the departments and agencies."

Standing out among the commission's specific recommendations was the proposal that the sixty-five departments, administrations, agencies, boards and commissions that now report directly to the President be reduced to about one-third of that number.

The commission said such a step was "the first necessity for the establishment of efficient and economical functioning of the Government" and would "relieve the President of onerous administrative detail which arises from lack of unification.

This and other recommendations, some of them of almost equal importance, were framed on the basis of the exhaustive research undertaken by a special task force headed by E. Struve Hensel, New York lawyer and former Assistant Secretary of the Navy, and Prof.

Continued on Page 19, Column 3

Senate Democrats Balk GOP On Move to Rush 'Gag' Vote

Knowland Motion to Force Filibuster Curb to Floor for Immediate Showdown Is Beaten, 56 to 31, in Partisan Battle

By WILLIAM S. WHITE
Special to THE NEW YORK TIMES.

WASHINGTON, Feb. 7 — The Democratically-controlled Senate broke late today a Republican effort to force at once to the floor a preliminary aspect of President Truman's harshly disputed civil-rights program.

By a vote of 56 to 31 the Democratic leadership defeated a motion by Senator William F. Knowland, Republican, of California, which would have forced the Senate to proceed at once toward hardening the closure, or "gag," rule against filibusters.

With the weapon of the filibuster—prolonged discussion intended to prevent or greatly to delay a vote upon a measure—the Southerners have always beaten off bills, such as those to repeal the poll tax and establish Federal sanctions against lynching.

In this first partisan floor struggle of the new Congress on an issue of high policy, every voting Democrat—including the most vehement advocates of Mr. Truman's civil-rights plan—stayed in line behind Senator Scott W. Lucas of Illinois, the Democratic leader. It was a show of solidarity rare in recent years.

Seven Republican rank-and-filers left their party to vote with the Democrats, but the entire Republican hierarchy, from Senator Robert A. Taft of Ohio down, stood with Mr. Knowland.

His resolution would have meant a repudiation of Senator Carl Hayden of Arizona, the Democratic chairman of the committee in control of the closure question, that on Rules and Administration.

The committee, which had put off action last Wednesday over the objections of the Republicans, intends to meet again this Wednesday under circumstances strongly suggesting that this time it might well recommend amendments to stiffen closure.

With this in mind, Senator Ken-

Continued on Page 21, Column 2

W. H. DAVIS FAVORS PLANT SEIZURE LAW

Ex-War Labor Board Head Asks Strike Powers for President—Denham Hits Truman Bill

By LOUIS STARK
Special to THE NEW YORK TIMES.

WASHINGTON, Feb. 7 — William H. Davis, former chairman of the War Labor Board, advocated today a four-point program to deal with critical strike emergencies and included in it Presidential authority to seize plants, which he said should be provided.

The New York patent attorney based his proposal on the argument that if the nation's health and safety were really threatened such as by a railroad strike, the President would act regardless of whether a law specifically directed him to do so or not.

Mr. Davis' proposal was as follows:

(1) Once a sixty-day cooling off period ends the President would take whatever action he could under his Constitutional powers to maintain essential services and then report the emergency to Congress.

(2) The President would take over the properties, call on management and employers to continue operations and if necessary call on every citizen to serve in the enterprise.

(3) Working conditions should remain unchanged for possibly thirty days after Government seizure.

(4) If the situation still remained

Continued on Page 28, Column 3

$5,430,000,000 ASKED FOR ECA TO JUNE, '50

House and Senate Measures to Aid Europe Set Less Than the 19 Nations Sought

By W. H. LAWRENCE
Special to THE NEW YORK TIMES.

WASHINGTON, Feb. 7—Administration bills to authorize outlays of $5,430,000,000 for the European Recovery Program during the next fifteen months were introduced in Congress today.

Hearings before a joint session of the House Foreign Affairs Committee and the Senate Foreign Relations Committee will begin tomorrow morning. Paul G. Hoffman, Economic Cooperation Administrator, and W. Averell Harriman, the "roving" ECA Ambassador to Europe, will lead off with testimony for the Administration.

The sums requested, embodied in bills offered by Representative Sol Bloom, Democrat, of New York, and Senator Tom Connally, Democrat, of Texas, were less than the estimates submitted by the European nations of their needs for 1949-50. The figure also is less than the amount spent in the first year of the Marshall Plan.

No breakdown of the funds by countries was immediately available. It was announced, however, that none of the new funds will go to China and Korea, since separate appropriation requests will be submitted for them later.

The over-all amount requested to-

Continued on Page 15, Column 5

Long Island Road Nearly Bankrupt, Vice President Says at Fare Inquiry

The Long Island Rail Road is on the verge of bankruptcy, having a total indebtedness of $53,100,000 and a cash balance of only $60,059 on hand as of last Jan. 31, a top executive of the road testified yesterday before the Public Service Commission.

Walter S. Franklin, executive vice president, sketched a dreary picture of the road's financial future from the witness stand as the commission heard final testimony in the line's petition for a 25 per cent increase in commuter rates. Even if the commission saw fit to grant the increase, he said, the road still would face an estimated deficit of $8,000,000 for 1949.

The Long Island, carrying 300,000 passengers in and out of New York daily, operated at a deficit of $1,250,000 last month, the witness reported. He added that it also failed to pay $2,900,000 to the Pennsylvania Railroad for interline settlements owed to other roads and would owe the Pennsylvania another $3,000,000 for similar settlements this month.

Before the noon recess Commissioner George A. Arkwright, who has been presiding at the hearings, took over the examination. Cutting through a maze of figures that the witness had been explaining, the commissioner questioned him on the road's confessedly shaky financial structure. Mr. Franklin indicated that the line had "no credit."

"Then you have a bankrupt railroad here?" Mr. Arkwright asked.

"Pretty close to it," the witness replied.

"How long can this situation exist?" the commissioner queried.

"That depends on how long the Pennsylvania Railroad wants to continue doing what it has been doing for the last twenty years or more," Mr. Franklin declared.

The Pennsylvania, he had testified previously, had bought the stock of the Long Island in 1900

Continued on Page 28, Column 6

'SOAK-POOR' POLICY IS LAID TO DEWEY BY TAX-RISE FOES

Democrats Declare 66⅔% Increase Would Cut Buying Power, Injure Economy

BUSINESS HELD FAVORED

Quinn, Steingut Note Slashes, Rebates—Feinberg of GOP Cites High Franchise Levy

By LEO EGAN
Special to THE NEW YORK TIMES.

ALBANY, Feb. 7—The 66 2/3 per cent state increase in personal income tax rates recommended by Governor Dewey was assailed tonight by the Democratic legislative leadership as inequitable, dangerous to the nation's economy and a potential cause of unemployment and depression.

In a joint statement, Senator Elmer F. Quinn, minority leader of the Senate, and Assemblyman Irwin Steingut, minority leader of the Assembly, charged that the Republican pattern of taxation was one of "soak the poor and middle income groups and reward the rich."

Senator Quinn and Mr. Steingut made their charge in opening an attack on both the revenue and spending phases of Governor Dewey's budget that they hope to sustain during the balance of the legislative session.

"Under the Republican State Administration, personal income taxes have increased 33 1/3 per cent, cigarette taxes have soared 50 per cent and motor fuel taxes have gone up 25 per cent from the last year of the Democratic Administration," the two Democrats said.

"Contrasted against these increases in consumer taxes are reductions of 10 per cent in the corporation franchise tax and 25 per cent in the unincorporated business tax even after taking into account the 168 million dollars in new tax bills proposed in the new budget by the Republican Administration.

"These reductions in favor of business are in addition to 300 million dollars in rebates paid to employers under the revision of the Unemployment Compensation Law engineered by Governor Dewey and the Republican-controlled Legislature in the past three years.

"In consequence, the state's unemployment compensation reserve

Continued on Page 16, Column 2

NORWAY WANTS U.S. TO DEFINE LIMITS OF PACT SECURITY

Asks What Protection Would Be Given to Oslo During Period of Negotiations

ARMS PRIORITY IS RAISED

Lange Meets for Half Hour With Acheson—Hopes to End Talks This Week

Special to THE NEW YORK TIMES.

WASHINGTON, Feb. 7—Halvard M. Lange, Norwegian Foreign Minister, conferred with Secretary of State Dean Acheson for half an hour today about the political and military implications of the proposed North Atlantic security pact.

Mr. Lange, who first discussed this subject with former Secretary of State George C. Marshall during the United Nations meetings in Paris last autumn, is understood to have raised with Mr. Acheson and John D. Hickerson, director of the State Department's Office of European Affairs, a number of fundamental questions, including the following:

(1) During the period when the North Atlantic pact is being negotiated by the various governments, and during the subsequent period when it is being debated by the several legislative bodies, what protection, if any, would Norway be able to get from the United States?

(2) If Norway should join in the discussions on the pact and eventually join it, would she, as the only signatory having a common frontier with the Soviet Union, have any assurance of priority in the shipment of military equipment?

(3) Realizing that the United States has limited quantities of military supplies for herself and the other nations negotiating the pact, what kind of military supplies would be available and roughly when could these be expected?

(4) In view of various statements that have been made in Washington about American military assistance to other nations, could Mr. Acheson clarify the United States Government's position on supplying arms to nations that do and do not join mutual defense treaties with the United States?

The nature of the questions asked emphasized that the Nor-

Continued on Page 6, Column 5

World News Summarized

TUESDAY, FEBRUARY 8, 1949

Cardinal Mindszenty, Primate of Hungary, was sentenced yesterday to life imprisonment after a three-day trial. [1:8.]

World-wide protests rose against the trial of Cardinal Mindszenty. Mayor O'Dwyer asked Secretary Acheson to prevent the "lynching" of the Hungarian primate; resolutions to the same effect were introduced in Albany and Washington; clergy and laymen of many faiths joined their voices and there were numerous protest meetings. [2:2.] In Britain, where there were many demonstrations, Foreign Secretary Bevin denounced the accusations. [3:5.] The Vatican reaffirmed the innocence of the Cardinal. [3:1.]

The capital of China was officially established at Canton, where Premier Sun Fo threatened a Nationalist offensive if the Communists insisted on unconditional surrender. [1:8.]

United States policy in Japan is centered on restoring that country's economic health to help re-establish world peace. Army Secretary Royall said. [12:2.]

Norway's Foreign Minister, Halvard Lange, discussed with Secretary Acheson and other State Department officials the extent of United States protection and security aid Norway could expect if she joined the North Atlantic defense alliance, over objections of Russia. [1:5.]

General Eisenhower will be away from Columbia University for nearly two months while serving as a consultant to the Army in Washington. [23:1.]

Presidential authority to seize plants involved in strikes creating a national emergency was recommended by William H. Davis in presenting to a Senate committee a four-point program for dealing with such walkouts. The former War Labor Board head said that injunctions were no safeguard against critical strikes and Congress should provide broad Presidential powers for use in emergencies. [1:2.]

The House, by a vote of 365 to 9, approved and sent to the Senate a bill granting the President permanent broad powers to initiate administrative reforms, subject to Congressional veto. The Hoover Commission, reporting to Congress, said such reorganization would greatly increase efficiency and result in large savings. [1:1.]

Housing Expediter Woods warned a House committee that unless Federal controls were extended and strengthened, rents would rise 50 to 60 per cent. [32:6.] Democratic leaders kept their forces in the Senate in line and defeated, 56 to 31, a Republican demand for immediate action on moves to prevent filibustering. [1:2-3.]

Administration bills were introduced in Congress to authorize the ECA to spend $5,430,000,000 in the fifteen months from April 3. This is less than the estimates by European countries of their needs. [1:3.]

In Albany, Republican plans to unseat Susan Brandeis, Democratic member of the Board of Regents, were threatened by party defections. [16:4.] A move was made to defer until next year action on consolidating the courts of this city. [16:1.]

The Long Island Rail Road is on the verge of bankruptcy, an executive testified at a hearing on rate increases. [1:2-3.]

"Operation Dynamo," or "The Deliverance of Dunkirk," is described by Winston Churchill in today's installment of his World War II memoirs. A total of 861 vessels evacuated 338,226 men, 98,780 by the "Mosquito Armada" of small boats from the beaches and 239,446 in larger craft from Dunkirk Harbor. Through the nine days the RAF scored a great victory. [1:6-7.]

Index to other news appears on Page 26.

MINDSZENTY IS FOUND GUILTY; COURT GIVES LIFE SENTENCE; FLOOD OF PROTESTS RISING

By Winston Churchill: *The Second World War*

Volume II—Their Finest Hour

Book I—The Fall of France

INSTALLMENT 4: THE DELIVERANCE OF DUNKIRK

ACCURATE and excellent accounts have been written of the evacuation of the British and French Armies from Dunkirk. Ever since the 20th [of May, 1940] the gathering of shipping and small craft had been proceeding under the control of Admiral Ramsay who commanded at Dover. On the evening of the 26th (6.57 p. m.) an Admiralty signal put "Operation Dynamo" into play, and the first troops were brought home that night. After the loss of Boulogne and Calais only the remains of the port of Dunkirk and the open beaches next to the Belgian frontier were in our hands. At this time it was thought that the most we could rescue was about 45,000 men in two days. Early the next morning, May 27, emergency measures were taken to find additional small craft "for a special requirement". This was no less than the full evacuation of the British Expeditionary Force. It was plain that large numbers of such craft would be required for work on the beaches, in addition to bigger ships which could load in Dunkirk harbour. On the suggestion of Mr. H. C. Riggs, of the Ministry of Shipping, the various boatyards, from Teddington to Brightlingsea, were searched by Admiralty officers, and yielded upwards of forty serviceable motor-boats or launches, which were assembled at Sheerness on the following day. At the same time lifeboats from liners in the London docks, tugs from the Thames, yachts, fishing craft, lighters, barges and pleasure-boats—anything that could be of use along the beaches—were called into service. By the night of the 27th a great tide of small vessels began to flow towards the sea, first to our Channel ports, and thence to the beaches of Dunkirk and the beloved Army.

The Admiralty did not hesitate to give full rein to the spontaneous movement which swept the seafaring population of our south and south-eastern shores. Everyone who had a boat of any kind, steam or sail, put out for Dunkirk, and the preparations, fortunately begun a week earlier, were now aided by the brilliant improvisation of volunteers on an amazing scale. The numbers arriving on the 29th were small, but they were the forerunners of nearly 400 small craft which from the 31st were destined to play a vital part by ferrying from the beaches to the off-lying ships almost a hundred thousand men. In these days I missed the head of my Admiralty Map-room, Captain Pim, and one or two other familiar faces. They had got hold of a Dutch schuit which in four days brought off eight hundred soldiers. Altogether there came to the rescue of the Army under the ceaseless air bombardment of the enemy about 850 vessels, of which nearly 700 were British and the rest Allied.

Here is the official list:

BRITISH SHIPS

	Total engaged	Sunk	Damaged
A.A. Cruiser	1	—	1
Destroyers	39	6	19
Sloops, Corvettes and Gunboats	9	1	1
Minesweepers	36	5	7
Trawlers and Drifters	113	17	2
Special Service Vessels	3	1	—
Armed Boarding Vessels	3	1	1
Motor Torpedo Boats and Motor Anti-Submarine Boats	13	—	—
Ex-Dutch Schuits (Naval Crews)	40	4	(Not recorded)
Yachts (Naval Crews)	26	3	(Not recorded)
Personnel Ships	45	8	8
Hospital Carriers	8	1	5
Naval Motor Boats	12	6	(Not recorded)
Tugs	34	3	(Not recorded)
Other Small Craft	311	170	(Not recorded)
Total	693	226	

ALLIED SHIPS

	Total engaged	Sunk	Damaged
Warships (All types)	49	8	(Not recorded)
Other ships and craft	119	9	(Not recorded)
Total	168	17	
Grand Total	861	243	

*Omitting ships' lifeboats and some other privately owned small craft of which no record is available.

* * *

Meanwhile ashore around Dunkirk the occupation of the perimeter was effected with precision. The troops arrived out of chaos and were formed in order along the defences, which even in two days had grown. Those men who were in best shape turned about to form the line. The enemy had closely followed the withdrawal, and hard fighting was incessant, especially on the flanks near Nieuport and Bergues. As the evacuation went on the steady decrease in the number of troops, both British and French, was accompanied by a corresponding contraction of the defence. On the beaches among the sand dunes, for three, four or five days scores of thousands of men dwelt under unrelenting air attack. Hitler's belief that the German Air Force would render escape impossible, and that therefore he should keep his armoured formations for the final stroke of the campaign, was a mistaken but not unreasonable view.

Three factors falsified his expectations. First, the incessant air-bombing of the masses of troops along the seashore did them very little harm. The bombs plunged into the soft sand, which muffled their explosions. In the early stages, after a crashing air

Continued on Page 27

U. S. URGED TO ACT

Cardinal and Six Others Are Convicted After Three-Day Trial

APPEALS HELD POSSIBLE

O'Dwyer Calls On Acheson to Prevent the 'Lynching' of Primate of Hungary

By The Associated Press.

BUDAPEST, Hungary, Tuesday, Feb. 8—Joseph Cardinal Mindszenty was sentenced today to life imprisonment.

He was convicted of treason, trying to overthrow the republic and foreign currency speculation.

The Communist People's Court also decreed the confiscation of his money.

Prof. Justin Baranyai was convicted of trying to overthrow the republic.

The Rev. Andras Zakar, the Cardinal's secretary, was convicted of the same charge and of treason.

Prince Paul Esterhazy was convicted of trying to overthrow the republic and of foreign currency speculation.

The Rev. Miklos Nagy, secretary of Catholic Action, was convicted of foreign currency speculation and of failing to do his duty to the Government in not exposing the other cases.

The Rev. Bela Ispanyi, another priest, was convicted of treason and of foreign currency speculation.

Laszlo Toth, a journalist, was convicted of treason.

Sentences of the Others

Professor Baranyai was sentenced to fifteen years and to loss of his fortune and political rights and loss of his job for ten years.

Father Zakar was sentenced to six years, loss of his job and fortune and suspension of his political rights.

Prince Paul was sentenced to fifteen years, loss of his job, political rights and fortune. He was once the richest man in Hungary.

Father Nagy was sentenced to three years plus suspension of his political rights and loss of his job for five years.

Father Ispanyi got life imprisonment and was deprived of his job, political rights and his fortune.

Mr. Toth, a Catholic editor, was sentenced to ten years plus ten years' suspension of his job, political rights and confiscation of his property.

[The United Press quoted the court as having said that there were extenuating circumstances in the case of the Cardinal.]

[Before the verdict was announced protests against the Cardinal's trial spread in the United States and Western Europe. In New York, Mayor O'Dwyer called on Secretary of State Acheson to do all he could to prevent the "lynching" of the

Continued on Page 3, Column 2

Canton Established As Chinese Capital

By The United Press.

CANTON, China, Feb. 7—Premier Sun Fo formally established Canton as China's temporary capital today. Thus he returned to this city the National regime that had its beginning here more than twenty years ago.

Before holding a meeting of his Cabinet, which act formally established Canton as the capital, Premier Sun made a fighting speech in which he threatened the Communists with a Government offensive if they persisted in their demands for unconditional surrender.

Premier Sun spoke at the weekly memorial services for his father, Dr. Sun Yat-sen, who came to Canton in the early 1920's and organized the Kuomintang (Government party) which has ruled China for twenty-one years.

From Canton in 1926, Chiang Kai-shek, taking over party leadership with the death of Dr. Sun,

Continued on Page 14, Column 3

"All the News That's Fit to Print"

The New York Times.

Copyright, 1949, by The New York Times Company.

LATE CITY EDITION
Partly cloudy today; fair and colder tonight. Fair tomorrow.
Temperature Range Today-Max.,41; Min.,27
Temperatures Yesterday—Max.,38; Min.,21
Full U. S. Weather Bureau Report, Page 51

VOL. XCVIII..No. 33,276. Entered as Second-Class Matter, Postoffice, New York, N. Y. NEW YORK, THURSDAY, MARCH 3, 1949. Times Square, New York 18, N. Y. Telephone LAckawanna 4-1000 THREE CENTS IN NEW YORK CITY

B-50 CIRCLES GLOBE NON-STOP IN 94 HOURS; REFUELED IN AIR AT 4 BASES BY B-29 TANKERS

L. I. RAIL ROAD FILES BANKRUPTCY PLEA DESPITE FARE RISE

Court Orders Present Officials to Continue Operation Until Trustees Are Named

DEBTS PUT AT $56,000,000

Assets Given as $11,000,000 —Legislature Gets Bill to Set Up Authority to Run Line

By CHARLES GRUTZNER

The Long Island Rail Road, which carries the world's largest commuter load daily, filed a bankruptcy petition yesterday in Federal Court, Brooklyn.

The plea for reorganization was made less than twenty-four hours after the Public Service Commission had authorized increases in commutation rates up to 33 1-3 per cent as an emergency measure to avert the 115-year-old railroad's threatened financial collapse.

A statement issued by the railroad said the newest fare rise, which is expected to add $3,280,000 to its annual income, was, like other increases allowed by the PSC in the last two years, "too little and too late" to overcome a deficit said to be $8,000,000 a year.

Commuters Disagree

This view was not shared generally by commuters, some of whom had urged at the rate rise hearings that the state take over and operate the Long Island Rail Road, which is owned by the Pennsylvania Railroad.

The rate rise, which has not yet been put into effect by the company, brought more than the usual amount of grumbling in the ranks of the 200,000 commuters who make up two-thirds of the Long Island's daily passenger load. Many commuters sought to beat the increase, for this month anyway, by buying monthly commutation tickets in advance of the expiration of their old ones. Ticket sellers enforced strictly a long-standing rule against sale of commutation tickets more than three days in advance of their starting date.

Richard R. Bongartz, general attorney for the road, filed with the Federal Court clerk at 9:58 A. M. a petition for reorganization under Section 77 of the Bankruptcy Law. The railroad was pictured as owing in excess of $56,000,000, and with assets of little more than $11,000,000, including only $80,000 in cash.

Judge Harold M. Kennedy directed the company's present officials to continue operating its lines, pending a hearing before him on March 11. The court will then, if the company establishes its insolvency, appoint one or more trustees to manage its affairs.

A bill for the creation of a Long Island Transit Authority, to take over and operate the railroad, was offered at Albany yesterday by two Republican legislators from Queens. Senator Seymour Halpern and Assemblyman Fred W. Preller, both of Kew Gardens, submitted their bill before word reached Albany of the bankruptcy proceedings. On hearing of the move in Brooklyn Federal Court they urged quick passage of the measure.

Road's Move No Surprise

The railroad's bankruptcy plea came as no surprise to the Public Service Commission. At a PSC hearing on Feb. 7 Walter S. Franklin, executive vice president of the road, drew a pessimistic picture of the railroad's financial future, using the same figures of huge indebtedness and comparatively meager assets on which yesterday's petition was based. In answer to a question by Commissioner George A. Arkwright whether he had "a bankrupt railroad," Mr. Franklin had replied: "Pretty close to it."

The bankruptcy move was decided upon by the railroad's directors at a meeting on Monday. The last straw, it was learned, was the imminent maturity of approximately $40,000,000 in bonds for the retirement of which there was no money on hand nor credit for floating a new loan.

The bonds fell due on Tuesday. The Pennsylvania Railroad, which had guaranteed the loan, had bought up to yesterday $38,747,000 of the $39,936,000 worth of bonds that had been in the hands of the public.

Missing from yesterday's developments were the lamentations of stockholders that often attend the failing of a corporation into a bankruptcy action. That was because there were no stockholders

Continued on Page 37, Column 5

Installment Buying Is Eased In Cash Down, Time to Pay

Federal Reserve Board Acts as Credit Sales Show Sharp Drop—First Payments 15%, Except Cars, Which Stay at 33 1-3%

By ANTHONY LEVIERO
Special to The New York Times.

WASHINGTON, March 2—While Presidential advisers renewed today their assurances of a "bright and promising" business outlook, a sharp decline in installment buying caused the Federal Reserve Board to loosen credit controls on such things as automobiles, furniture and appliances, beginning Monday.

The board decided to stretch out all installment payments to a uniform maximum of twenty-one months, instead of fifteen to eighteen months. It also reduced the required down payments on all goods from 20 per cent to 15 per cent, automobiles excepted.

The buyer of a car will still have to pay 33 1/3 per cent down, but he will have twenty-one months in which to finish payments. The present maximum is eighteen months.

President Truman was told "that business conditions are still very good," with the future outlook "bright and promising," when he received his customary monthly visit from his economic advisers.

This view was expressed to White House correspondents afterward by Leon H. Keyserling, vice chairman of the Council of Economic Advisers.

Mr. Keyserling was accompanied to the White House by John D. Clark, member of the council. They substituted for Dr. Edwin G. Nourse, chairman, who is on the West Coast.

Mr. Keyserling said he told the President there had been little change in business conditions in the last month. He noted the favorable factor of a decline in claims for unemployment compensation.

Retail sales in January and February were up to the levels of the same months last year and business investment plans continued to look good, Mr. Keyserling stated.

In reply to a question, he declared that the stand-by controls which Mr. Truman requested in his State of the Union Message were still needed. He asserted that latest statistics showed the prices of

Continued on Page 22, Column 3

Bishop Removes Dr. Melish; Rector's Son Loses His Post

By GEORGE DUGAN

Bishop James P. De Wolfe of the Protestant Episcopal Diocese of Long Island officially removed the Rev. Dr. John Howard Melish yesterday from the rectorship of Holy Trinity Church, Brooklyn, a post the 74-year-old clergyman has held for forty-five years. The removal order is effective April 4.

By terminating Dr. Melish's pastorate, the Bishop automatically ends the tenure of the Rev. William Howard Melish, the rector's son and assistant. The younger Melish, who is chairman of the National Council of American-Soviet Friendship, an organization listed as subversive by Attorney General Tom Clark, has been at odds with the vestry of Holy Trinity for nearly a year.

[Text of Bishop De Wolfe's statements on Page 11.]

On Jan. 21 the church's lay governing body, by a vote of 9 to 1, formally petitioned Bishop De Wolfe to terminate Dr. Melish's pastorate because of his avowed approval of the "outside activities" of his son. At the same time the vestry held that because of his age Dr. Melish could no longer keep abreast of parish duties.

The Bishop's decision, released by his public relations representative, Robert Lee, requires the vestry to pay Dr. Melish, in quarterly installments, a sum equal to the pension he is regularly entitled to receive from the Church Pension Fund. This will, in effect, amount to a "double pension."

A supplementary statement issued by Bishop De Wolfe in conjunction with his decision stated his belief that the assistant rector was "most mistaken in what he supposes to be the pastoral application of his ministry."

Asserting that he had twice asked both of the Melishes to resign voluntarily, the Bishop emphasized that the issues in the case were "essentially pastoral."

Dissension within Holy Trinity parish, said the Bishop's statement,

Continued on Page 10, Column 3

INSURANCE AGENCY ASKED FOR VETERAN

Hoover Commission Finds VA's Set-Up Inefficient, Proposes Separate U. S. Corporation

By CLAYTON KNOWLES
Special to The New York Times.

WASHINGTON, March 2—The Commission on Organization of the Executive Branch of the Government recommended today that the Veterans Administration's insurance operations, which it criticized severely, be put under a separate Government corporation.

Reporting to Congress on the work of the Veterans Administration, which spends more than one-tenth of the national budget, the commission, headed by former President Herbert Hoover, said the insurance reform would effect considerable savings. But it warned this step could "accomplish no miracles overnight in improving the operation of insurance programs."

"It would provide an opportunity for a fresh start," the report said. "It would make possible a whole new emphasis upon the economical and efficient performance of the insurance program."

In discharging its insurance functions, the Veterans Administration dealt with nearly seven million life insurance policies with a face value of almost $40,000,000,000 as of June 30, 1948. The commission found fault with the operation of eight specific counts.

Continued on Page 21, Column 3

Cardinal to Help Bury Dead Today As Seminarians Replace Strikers

Led by Cardinal Spellman, who said last night he would "do anything the foreman tells me to do," one hundred seminarians will take over burying of the dead today at the strike-bound Calvary Cemetery in Queens, largest Roman Catholic burial ground in the New York area. A smaller group of religious students will take over grave-digging and other cemetery duties at Gate of Heaven Cemetery in Hawthorne, N. Y.

The Cardinal announced this move at 6:30 last night after a breakdown in negotiations with a committee of Local 293 of the United Cemetery Workers, CIO, which on Jan. 13 called a strike of 240 employes at Calvary Cemetery in Queens and followed it by calling out on Feb. 10 the forty-nine workers at the Gate of Heaven Cemetery in Hawthorne, N. Y.

After his announcement the prelate went last night to St. Joseph's Seminary near Yonkers, where he recruited the students for the priesthood in the "work of mercy."

The students will leave for Calvary today in buses and cars.

The strike of cemetery employes, who include gravediggers, gardeners, foundation workers and chauffeurs, left unburied as of yesterday morning 1,020 bodies at Calvary alone. About sixty bodies arrive at the cemetery daily. These coffins have been placed in a temporary burial area and covered with tarpaulins. At least another hundred burials have been deferred at the Gate of Heaven Cemetery.

A deputy commissioner of the Department of Health, Matthew A. Byrne, yesterday urged Msgr. George C. Ehardt, managing director of Calvary, to take action on a situation that, if permitted to continue, might become a violation of the Sanitary Code. City law requires that the dead be buried within ten days except when special permission for a delay has been asked and granted. Such special permission has been granted

Continued on Page 26, Column 2

COMMUNISTS HERE WOULD OPPOSE U. S. IN WAR WITH SOVIET

Top Leaders of Party Follow Line of the Reds in Other Nations on Aid to Russia

'WALL STREET' IS ACCUSED

Foster and Dennis Statement Says Followers Would Act to Defeat 'Imperialists'

By WILL LISSNER

The top leaders of the American Communist party served notice yesterday that they would pursue a policy intended to defeat United States aims if this nation were involved in a war they considered "unjust, aggressive, imperialist."

Declaring that United States military preparedness and the North Atlantic defense pact raised a real threat of war embroiling France and Italy in military operations against the Soviet Union, the American Communist leaders said they would oppose such a war and cooperate to defeat its aims and bring it to a speedy conclusion.

The statement setting out this policy was signed by William Z. Foster, national chairman of the party, and Eugene Dennis, general secretary. It followed similar declarations by the top Communist leaders of France, Italy, Germany and Great Britain.

Mr. Foster and Mr. Dennis said: "If, despite the efforts of peace forces of America and the world, Wall Street should succeed in plunging the world into war, we would oppose it as an unjust, aggressive, imperialist war, as an undemocratic and an anti-Socialist war, destructive of the deepest interests of the American people and all humanity.

"Even as Lincoln, while a Congressman, opposed the unjust, annexationist Mexican War and demanded its termination, so would we Communists cooperate with all democratic forces to defeat the predatory war aims of American imperialism and bring such a war to a speedy conclusion on the basis of a democratic peace."

The flurry of declarations from the heads of the Communist parties began with that of Maurice Thorez of France in an address on Feb. 22 before a meeting of his party. He said:

"If the common efforts of the freedom-loving French do not succeed in bringing our country back into the camp of democracy and peace, if later our country should

Continued on Page 3, Column 6

FORRESTAL TO QUIT CABINET ON APRIL 1, WASHINGTON HEARS

L. A. Johnson, Former Assistant Secretary of War, Expected to Be Named Successor

BUILT UP PRE-WAR ARMY

Loyal Truman Man, He Is Said to Have Refused Anything Less Than Defense Chief

Special to The New York Times.

WASHINGTON, March 2—James Forrestal, Secretary of Defense, will resign about April 1, it was reliably reported tonight in a recurrence of speculation on changes in President Truman's Cabinet.

Louis A. Johnson of Clarksburg, W. Va., a former Assistant Secretary of War and now a lawyer here, is expected to succeed Mr. Forrestal, thus precipitating several other changes in key positions of the National Defense Establishment.

A former commander of the American Legion and an active Democratic party worker, Mr. Johnson served as chairman of the Democratic National Committee's finance committee. In this difficult job at a time when Mr. Truman was conceded no chance of winning the election, Mr. Johnson rendered yeoman service to the party. In consequence he was earmarked for a high reward right after election day and the Secretary of Defense was the only position associated with his name. It was reported he would consider nothing less.

There were reports current tonight that Mr. Truman might announce the prospective resignation at his news conference tomorrow, but no confirmation of this or of the resignation itself was given by White House sources.

Both Mr. Truman and Mr. Forrestal have sought in recent months to discourage speculation about the Secretary's plans. Reports that Mr. Forrestal would leave the Cabinet began right after election day.

In mid-January, however, Mr. Forrestal said after a conference with Mr. Truman that he expected to stay in the Cabinet. A few days later, in a news conference, Mr. Truman said that Mr. Forrestal had spoken correctly. Nevertheless, news reports were heard that Mr. Forrestal would stay in only long enough to get the defense budget

Continued on Page 2, Column 5

World News Summarized

THURSDAY, MARCH 3, 1949

Lucky Lady II, an Air Force B-50, completed the first non-stop, round-the-world flight when she returned to the Carswell Air Force Base, Fort Worth, Tex., yesterday. The medium bomber, refueled in the air over the Azores, Saudi Arabia, the Philippines and Hawaii, covered 23,452 miles in 94 hours 1 minute. [1:8.] The military significance of the flight and the need for a bigger Air Force were emphasized. [1:6-7.]

Defense Secretary Forrestal will resign about April 1, it was said, to be succeeded by Louis A. Johnson, former Assistant Secretary of War. [1:5.]

Communists in this country will adopt obstructionist tactics in any war they consider "unjust, aggressive, imperialist," party leaders declared. In a policy statement they assailed the proposed North Atlantic security pact and aligned the party with French, Italian and other European Communists who have pledged their support to Russia in event of war. [1:4.] Maurice Thorez declared at a Paris meeting that the Communists would "carry on the battle of France against the imperialist war" as exemplified, he said, in the North Atlantic grouping and the Marshall Plan. [5:1.]

The Rev. Dr. John Howard Melish was removed by Bishop James P. De Wolfe as rector of Holy Trinity Church in Brooklyn. Dr. Melish lost the post he had filled for forty-five years because of protests against his support of the pro-Soviet activities of his son and assistant, the Rev. William Howard Melish. [1:2-3.]

Russia will sharply cut her exports of manganese and chrome to the United States, apparently either to force this country to sell capital goods and machine tools or to cut the stock-piling of the essential ores by the United States. [4:1.]

Full support for Yugoslavia's new demands against Austria was voiced by Russia at the London talks on an Austrian treaty. The Western powers opposed the demands. [15:1.]

United States troops blockaded the house occupied by the Soviet repatriation mission that refused to quit the American zone of Germany. Gas, water, electricity and telephone lines were cut off. [6:5.] Western Berlin representatives will be permitted to attend sessions of the parliament of the proposed Western German state, but will not be admitted to membership. [8:3.]

President Truman's economic advisers told him the business outlook was "bright and promising," but the Federal Reserve Board, to meet a sharp drop in installment buying, eased consumer credit curbs. [1:2-3.]

Attempts to halt the battle by Southern Democrats in the Senate against a curb on filibustering were put off by Administration leaders, who failed to win a pledge from the Republicans to support closure. [1:7.]

The Hoover Commission urged that a separate Government corporation take over the insurance operations of the Veterans Administration. [1:2.]

A petition in bankruptcy was filed by the Long Island Rail Road less than twenty-four hours after the Public Service Commission had granted an emergency rise in commutation fares to avert such action. [1:1.]

A proposal that breweries in this city pay a guaranteed annual wage for guaranteed annual production was submitted to employers and union locals by an arbitrator. [28:5.]

Index to other news appears on Page 26.

FIRST NON-STOP FLIGHT AROUND WORLD

LEFT FT. WORTH	12.21 P. M. SAT. FEB. 26	ARR. MANILA	8.00 P. M. MON. FEB. 28
ARR. AZORES	3.55 A. M. SUN. FEB. 27	ARR. HAWAII	7.15 P. M. TUES. MAR. 1
ARR. DHAHRAN	11.30 P. M. SUN. FEB. 27	ARR. FT. WORTH	10.22 A. M. WED. MAR. 2

Total mileage . . 23,452 miles
Miles per hour . . 239 miles
Elapsed time . . 94 hrs. 1 min.
UNOFFICIAL
Eastern Standard Time

The New York Times March 3, 1949

In its 23,452-mile hop, which began at Fort Worth, Tex., the Lucky Lady II was refueled in the air over the Azores, Dhahran in Saudi Arabia, the Philippines and Hawaii. Table shows time at various points of flight.

Flight Spurs Congress Drive For a Strengthened Air Force

By The Associated Press.

WASHINGTON, March 2—Spurred by the Air Force's spectacular feat in circling the globe non-stop, Congressional air power advocates called anew today for a bigger and better air force to bolster the nation's defenses.

Senator Millard E. Tydings, Democrat, of Maryland, chairman of the Senate Armed Services Committee, said the flight "offers some measure of what another World War would mean to all peoples of the earth."

He told a reporter the successful test of long-range refueling operations shows the "increasing importance of air power in national defense."

Other committee members agreed with Senator Tydings that the flight of the B-50 Lady Luck II, greatly bolstered the Air Force's chances of getting Congressional approval for more money and more planes.

Perhaps significantly, the flight was staged at a time when Congress faces a decision on how much to spend on the Air Force, the Army and Navy.

Senator Tydings already has introduced a bill to expand the Air Force to seventy combat groups. The Eightieth Congress approved funds to start such a build-up, but President Truman's new budget calls for only forty-eight groups in the next fiscal year starting July 1.

Senator Burnet R. Maybank, Democrat, of South Carolina, a member of Senator Tydings' committee, said the flight "absolutely demonstrates the need for maxi-

Continued on Page 3, Column 5

FOES OF FILIBUSTER DELAY SHOWDOWN

Fear Hasty 'Gag' Rule Action Might Aid Southerners in Their Closure Fight

By WILLIAM S. WHITE
Special to The New York Times.

WASHINGTON, March 2—The Northern Democratic-Republican Senate coalition put off today, in fear that action now might harm its cause, its first scheduled sortie in force against the Southerners in the filibuster fight.

Leaders of the Republican side of the alliance formally abstained from offering any assurance that their party colleagues generally could be counted on to stand solid with Administration Democrats even when the showdown comes with the Southerners. It is slated for next week.

The Southerners, who have the advantage of being deeply allied on a single program of opposition, went forward quietly on the floor with their movement of resistance

Continued on Page 22, Column 5

21 Are Indicted as Rent Gougers; 3-State Alarm Out for Landlady

Twenty-one alleged rent gougers, a record number, were named yesterday in New York County grand jury criminal informations.

The defendants—landlords, rental agents and building superintendents, including two women—were accused of extorting $36,870 in illegal rental fees.

The gouges, said District Attorney Frank S. Hogan, ranged from $40 exacted by a janitor to permit a family to occupy an East Harlem cold-water flat to one instance in which $4,750 changed hands. The latter sum, he said, was paid for furniture later appraised at one-eighth of that value, as a condition for the leasing of a duplex apartment at 412 East Eighty-fourth Street.

Seventeen of the accused pleaded not guilty in Special Sessions. Justice William B. Northrop set the cases for trial April 4.

The four other defendants, who did not appear in court, included a 47-year-old landlady who is the object of a three-state police alarm; a married couple contesting extradition here from Connecticut, and an elderly realty operator confined to his home by illness.

The married couple, the prosecutor asserted, is accused of obtaining the $4,750 from Mr. and Mrs. Frank O. Behrens, who live at the East Eighty-fourth Street address. Mr. Hogan identified them as Udo Lindeman, a pianist, and his wife, Viola, and gave their address as Route 2, Terryville, Conn.

He charged they had informed their landlord, while living in the Manhattan duplex, that they wished to rent it to friends. Instead, he said, they advertised, the Behrens responded and paid an exorbitant amount for the furniture in order to get the lease.

Mr. Hogan said the woman sought is Mrs. Betty Weiss. He described her as the former rental agent and caretaker of the Sherman Square Studios, an apartment house catering to musicians and

Continued on Page 20, Column 3

FIRST IN HISTORY

High Officials Greet the Plane as It Ends Hop at Fort Worth

SPEED 239 MILES AN HOUR

LeMay Says Feat Shows U. S. Could Drop an Atom Bomb Anywhere in the World

By WALTER H. WAGGONER
Special to The New York Times.

CARSWELL AIR FORCE BASE, Fort Worth, Tex., March 2—A B-50 bomber, Lucky Lady II, returned here this morning from the first non-stop, round-the-world trip ever flown.

Taking on fuel in mid-air from B-29 Superfortresses converted to aerial tankers, the big plane, a modified B-29 itself, completed the globe-circling 23,452 miles in ninety-four hours and one minute—two hours under four days—and two minutes ahead of the time of arrival planned at the take-off.

Refuelings, at an undisclosed altitude and at a speed still a military secret, were made easily and without incident at four bases. The B-29 tankers rose and met the Lucky Lady at Air Force bases in the Azores, Dhahran in Saudi Arabia, the Philippines and Hawaii.

The Lucky Lady II left Fort Worth at 12:21 P. M. Eastern standard time, Saturday, Feb. 26. It reached Lagens Air Force Base in the Azores at 3:55 A. M. Sunday; Dhahran at 11:30 P. M. Sunday; Clark Air Base, Manila, at 8 P. M. Monday, and Hickam Air Force Base, Hawaii, at 7:15 P. M. Tuesday. The plane crossed the air base tower at 10:22 A. M. today and again touched earth at 10:31.

Officially, It's Just Routine

The trip, as significant in the matter of distance as the recent three hours and forty-six minute transcontinental flight by the jet bomber XB-47 was for speed, was officially described as "routine," which meant it proceeded according to plan.

But to the top-level officials here to greet the fourteen tired crewmen, the flight was of considerably more than "routine" importance. They were inclined to regard it as historic, a giant step in the direction of an American air power second to none.

It means, said Lieut. Gen. Curtis E. LeMay, commanding general of the Strategic Air Command, that the United States Air Force could drop an atomic bomb, taking off from this country, "any place in the world that required the atomic bomb."

He was asked whether a similar method of mid-air refueling could not also be adapted to the fighter escorts.

"Well," he answered, "I don't see why it couldn't be done."

During the war American forces had to take Iwo Jima before they were close enough to Japan to give fighter protection to B-29's attacking the enemy home islands from Guam.

"An Inevitable Step"

The relative importance that the Air Force attaches to the flight was made apparent also by the rank of the officials here to see the plane land. In addition to General LeMay were W. Stuart Symington, Secretary of the Air Force, who flew here from Boston; Gen. Hoyt S. Vandenberg, Air Force Chief of Staff, and Maj. Gen. Roger Ramey, commanding general of the Eighth Air Force.

Secretary Symington, a champion of the giant B-36, the world's biggest bomber and the Air Force's chief weapon of strategic warfare, stated without apparent reluctance today that the new mid-air fueling techniques "turn medium bombers into inter-continental bombers." This was a category to which the B-36 heretofore had exclusive rights.

"In our opinion," said the Secretary, "it was an inevitable step in the development of air power."

The crew of fourteen who took the Lady around the world seemed thoroughly satisfied with the trip. Capt. James Gallagher, of Melrose, Minn., commander of the plane,

Continued on Page 3, Column 2

Victims of the recession, thousands received unemployment compensation checks.

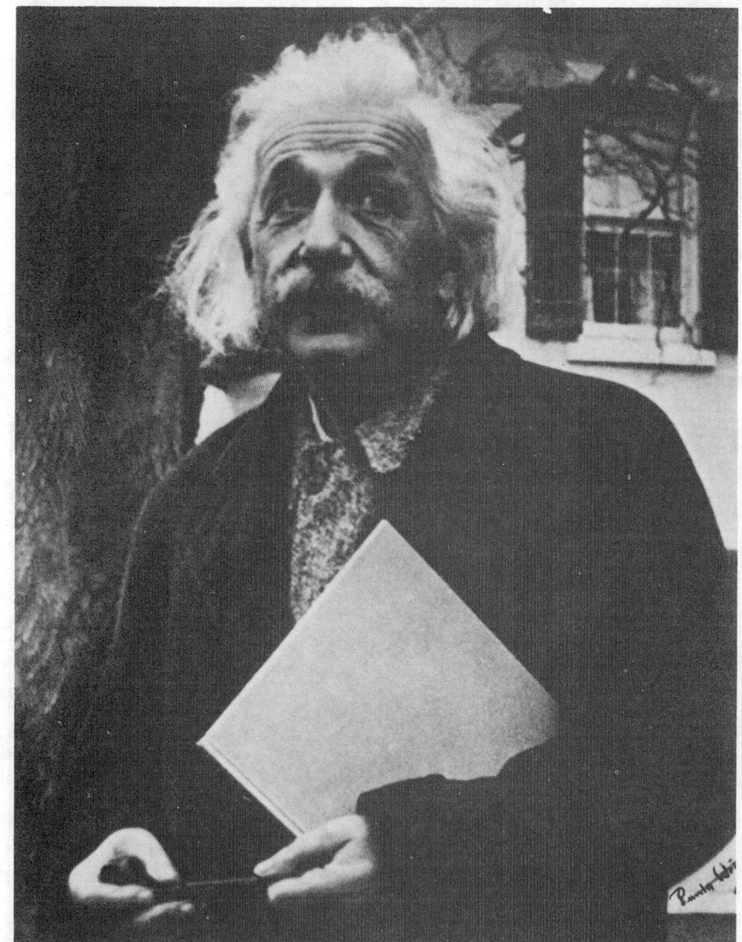

Dr. Albert Einstein propounded his "theory of gravitation" which reduced the basic physical laws of the Universe to four equations.

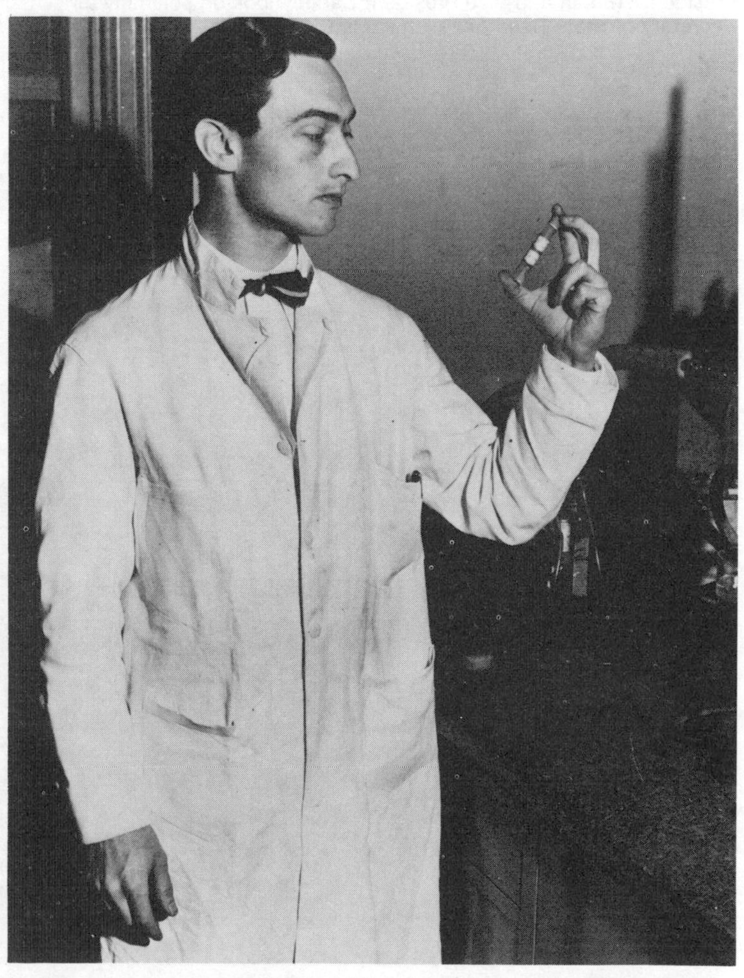

Cortisone came into use. Dr. Lewis H. Sarrett is shown holding the original synthetic sample of the substance; he accomplished the final stages of the synthesizing of the drug.

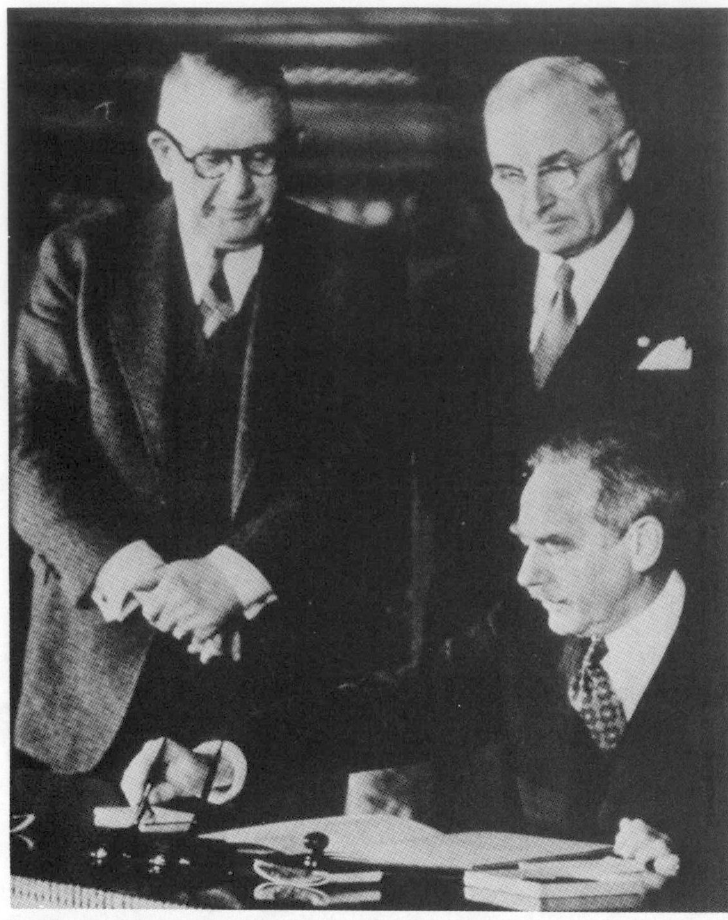

President Truman and Vice President Barkley look on solemnly as Secretary of State Dean Acheson signs the North Atlantic Treaty.

In Shanghai, Nationalist Chinese troops retreat from advancing Communist Chinese armies. By the end of the year, Chiang Kai-shek had moved the Nationalist government to Taiwan (Formosa).

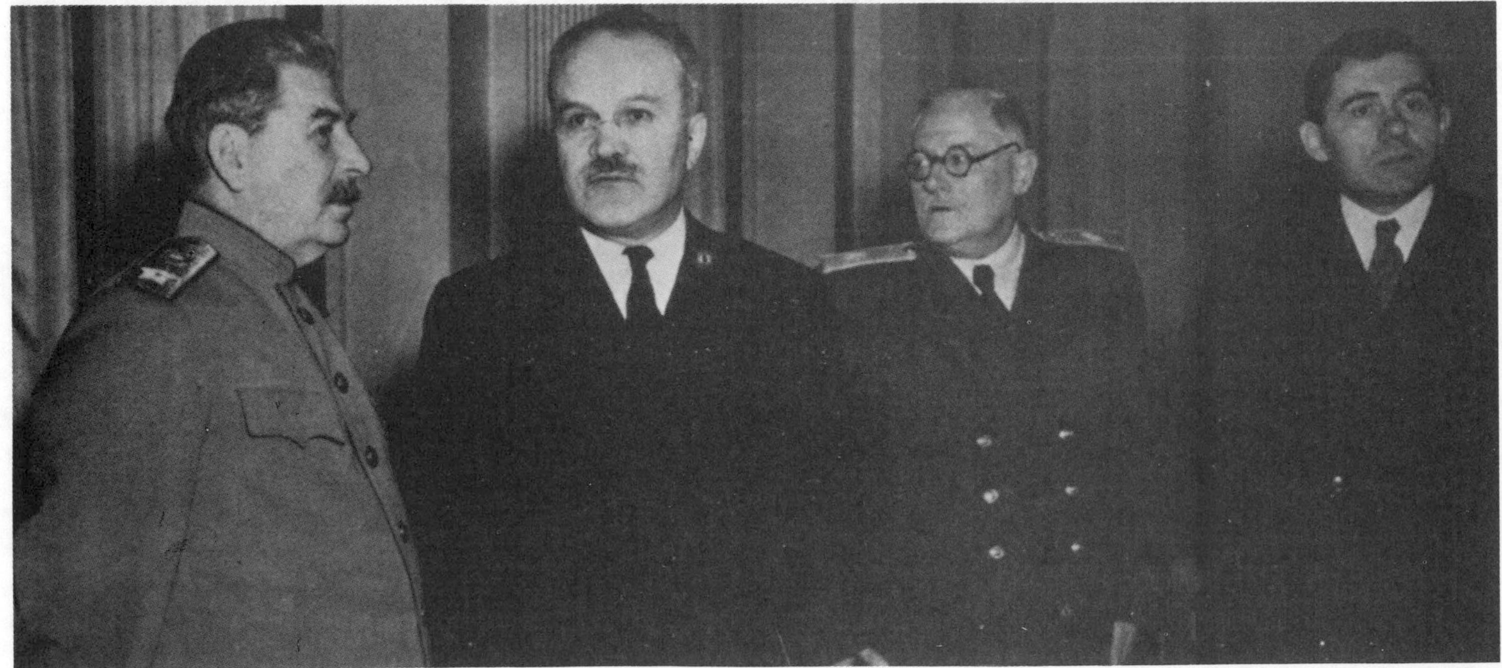

Four framers of the Soviet policy that demonstrated that Russia had no intention of accepting the *status quo* after World War II. Stalin, Molotov, Vishinsky, and Gromyko were largely responsible for Russia's violation of the Yalta agreement; the formation of the "Molotov Plan" (the Soviet answer to the Marshall Plan); and the U.N. policy adopted by Russia.

"All the News That's Fit to Print"

The New York Times.

Copyright, 1949, by The New York Times Company.

LATE CITY EDITION
Partly cloudy, cold today; fair tonight and tomorrow.
Temperature Range Today—Max.,36; Min.,24
Temperatures Yesterday—Max.,40; Min.,24
Full U. S. Weather Bureau Report, Page 29

VOL. XCVIII..No. 33,292. Entered as Second-Class Matter, Postoffice, New York, N. Y. NEW YORK, SATURDAY, MARCH 19, 1949. Times Square, New York 18, N. Y. Telephone LAckawanna 4-1000 THREE CENTS NEW YORK CITY

20-YEAR ATLANTIC TREATY BINDS SIGNERS TO ACT AGAINST ATTACK; ARMS AID FACES SENATE TROUBLE

TRUMAN IS HOPING TO SAVE 'FAIR DEAL' DESPITE REBUFFS

In Conference at Key West He Says Congress Is New and Behind Its Schedule

'DIXIECRATS' ARE SCORED

But President Bars Comment on Coalition as the Senate Heads to a New Fight

By ANTHONY LEVIERO
Special to The New York Times.

KEY WEST, Fla., March 18—Despite the rebuffs he has received in Congress this week, President Truman declared today that he was determined as well as hopeful that his "Fair Deal" program would be enacted.

In a news conference that was noteworthy for its conciliatory tone toward the Eighty-first Congress, the Chief Executive said its session had been set back a month by the Inauguration Week ceremonies.

He said he felt that Congress should have more time to act, and consequently held his fire against the opposition that has formed on Capitol Hill to destroy or cripple major Administration proposals. More than once he reiterated his confidence in ultimate success.

[In Washington, the Senate, halted by the civil rights filibuster since Feb. 28, got down to work, but it appeared to be heading toward a new controversy on other aspects of the Truman "Fair Deal" program.]

Mr. Truman dubbed the Southern States' Rights group as Democrats who were not good, and he asserted that they had imposed a third-party system on the country. This was the only suggestion of criticism that came from him, apart from an acid comment on newspaper speculation on what he might be thinking or planning to do.

Specific Questions Rejected

The States-Righters and other Southerners constituted the shock troops in the Democratic-Republican coalition that wrecked Administration plans to toughen the Senate rule against prolonged debate, as in the filibuster. Mr. Truman declined to comment on this defeat and on all other measures in which Administration forces have fought losing battles on Capitol Hill.

The substantial modification of his rent control bill and the refusal of the Senate Armed Services Committee to confirm his friend, Mon C. Wallgren, as chairman of the National Security Resources Board, failed to tempt Mr. Truman into some of the sharp language he used during his political campaign.

All questions on specific topics such as these were turned aside with "no comment" answers. Mr. Truman left open the possibility that he might tour the country again to rally the people behind his program. Even in this, however, he would not go beyond the bare statement to this effect which he made in his address at the Jefferson-Jackson Day dinner on Feb. 24.

The news conference was held on the lawn of the cottage which serves as a winter White House at the naval station here. White House correspondents and local newsmen sat in a circle around the President.

Mr. Truman started by saying he was having the usual vacation press conference and that there was no significance whatever in it, although he had seen all the questions and all the answers in the Miami newspapers and the local paper (The Key West Citizen).

Train Tour Still Planned

The President said he had not read Washington papers much since he came here but he thought that because most of the questions had already been asked and were now carefully answered in the newspapers, maybe there would not be many questions from the reporters this morning.

Mr. Truman also remarked that any prognostications might be of the same quality as those that were being made last September and October, when his defeat was being freely predicted.

When Mr. Truman ended these prefatory remarks, a reporter for a Miami newspaper asked, "You wouldn't say those answers are correct then?"

The answers would answer themselves at a later date, Mr. Truman replied. You have to depend on those because you made them yourself, he added.

The next question was whether he had given any more thought

Continued on Page 8, Column 5

Union to Halt Trucks In Check on Drivers

More than 6,600,000 commercial trucks operating in the United States are to be subjected to an intense check-up beginning April 1 to make sure that their drivers are members in good standing in the International Brotherhood of Teamsters, AFL. Orders for this were given by Dave Beck of Seattle, executive vice president of the union, it was learned last night.

Mr. Beck's orders are that union spotters be placed at all strategic points such as fueling stops, highway crossroads, roadside diners, tunnels, bridges, produce markets, waterfronts, docks, warehouses, etc. In accordance with a program for a check-up approved last month by the Chicago Trade Division of the union, a letter has been sent to employers.

SNOW CUTS TRAVEL ON ROADS, AIR, SEA

3,000 Men Work to Clear City as Slippery Highways Cause Accidents

Only two days before the arrival of spring, March was still roaring like a lion yesterday.

A storm area that developed over Virginia in the morning swept northeastward at 40 miles an hour, shedding two to four inches of snow from the Ohio Valley to southern New England during the day. The disturbance moved off the Nova Scotia coast, where it was fizzling out last night.

The snowstorm disrupted commercial air travel at the big ports in Boston and the New York area. Poor visibility and slippery roads from northern Pennsylvania to Rhode Island caused a few serious accidents and many minor collisions. In the thick weather a freighter seeking the entrance to New York Harbor ran up on the New Jersey beach. Harbor and coastal shipping was slowed.

The snow struck this city about 6:30 A. M. Northeast winds, up to 30 miles an hour in gusts, drove temperatures down to the mid-twenties, compared to the average of 38 degrees for March 18. At 3:45 P. M., the sun peeped through the overcast, and soon afterward the snow ceased.

3,000 Sanitation Men at Work

By that time, the Weather Bureau had measured 2.6 inches of snow at the Battery, with unofficial reports of 3 inches in further sections of Queens and Staten Island. The Weather Bureau saw nothing unusual in the storm, not even with the Vernal Equinox scheduled for 5:49 P. M. tomorrow.

Sanitation Commissioner William J. Powell put 3,000 of his men on snow work. The snow was cleared by 129 crosswalk and fifty truck plows, twenty of the latter being assigned to Richmond alone, and three mechanical snowbrooms. Ninety-one sand-spreaders were sent to the most slippery streets, while sixty-two other trucks were used to spread cinders on bridges, tunnel approaches, and inclined highway ramps.

In the suburbs motorists were using chains and snow tires for the last time this season—they hoped. Four inches of snow reported from many spots in southern New York, northern New Jersey and on Long Island slowed vehicular traffic. Many fenders were dented by skidding on slippery roads. Conditions

Continued on Page 9, Column 4

RYAN ADVOCATES INDICTING O'DWYER IN WIRETAP 'MESS'

He Says Grand Jurors Grinned as They Heard Him Charge Mayor With Fraud

TELLS OF SEEING SEABURY

But La Guardia Sponsor Won't Be Drawn Into the 'Plots'—Police Officials Testify

By ALEXANDER FEINBERG

Clendenin J. Ryan created a furor yesterday when after a brief appearance before the grand jury he told reporters that he had "recommended" to an Assistant District Attorney, in the presence of the jurors, that Mayor O'Dwyer be indicted as a way out of the wiretapping "mess" for the prosecutor.

The basis for his suggestion, the millionaire critic of the present city administration declared, were the Mayor's "actions" last Friday night and Saturday morning. It was early last Saturday at City Hall that the Mayor disclosed the alleged wiretapping plot against him and seventy-five municipal officials.

Mr. Ryan asserted that these actions constituted an indictable "fraud."

Several hours later Mr. Ryan repeated the statement he said he had made before the grand jury, altering the wordage slightly but not their meaning and omitting mention of the Mayor by name.

Written in His Own Hand

The first version, written in his own hand and read to reporters in the lobby of the District Attorney's office at 155 Leonard Street, said:

"I have just suggested to the District Attorney that he could get himself out of this mess by recommending that Mayor O'Dwyer be indicted for fraud perpetrated last Friday night and Saturday morning."

This was at 3:30 P. M. Reached at his office by telephone at 5:20 P. M. Mr. Ryan gave the following version of what had taken place:

"I just suggested to the District Attorney that he consider whether the actions that took place in the City Hall last Friday night and Saturday morning constitute the basis upon which the participants should be indicted for perpetrating a fraud. I include all the participants and I raise the question as a serious matter."

The second version was given out after Mr. Ryan had consulted with Edmund L. Palmieri, legal secretary to the late Mayor Fiorello H. La Guardia at a time when Mr. Ryan was one of Mr. La Guardia's secretaries, and later a Magistrate and Judge of the Domestic Relations Court.

Mr. Ryan's new "sensation" after several days of unwonted "no comments," overshadowed the fact that the Mayor was not called upon to go through with his scheduled appearance before the grand jury. Instead, he remained in his "budget" retreat in the Municipal Building ready for an instant summons. He is not expected to testify now before next Tuesday. Yesterday was "police day" at the grand jury with a number of police testifying and many police officials exhibiting to the jurors the instruments allegedly used in the wiretapping.

Developments yesterday also witnessed an attempt to inject the

Continued on Page 30, Column 1

PACT ITSELF HAILED

Administration Leaders in Congress Predict a Preponderant Vote

PUBLIC HEARINGS PLANNED

Legislators Air Reservations About Parallel Program to Help Western Europe

By W. H. LAWRENCE
Special to The New York Times.

WASHINGTON, March 18—The North Atlantic treaty text received a generally friendly reception in the Senate today, but storm signals were flying for the parallel program for United States aid to rearm Western European nations.

While Administration spokesmen predicted an overwhelming Senate vote to ratify the pact, one highly-placed Republican, who requested anonymity, said that it might be difficult to obtain a two-thirds majority for the agreement unless the Administration leadership could demonstrate clearly that the pact and the arms program were separate issues, not only legislatively but in fact.

Copies of the treaty text were distributed in the Senate when it convened today, but members of the Senate Foreign Relations Committee had been kept informed as the negotiations progressed, and already had given informal and tentative approval.

There was no clear indication as to how soon the Senate would debate and vote on the agreement. It will not be placed before the Senate committee until it has been signed on April 4.

Senator Tom Connally, committee chairman, said that the public hearings of undetermined length would be held because "we want the country to know all about the treaty and to understand it."

Senator Scott Lucas, Democrat, of Illinois, the majority leader and traffic regulator on the Senate floor, said it was his view that several issues affecting the national economy would have priority before the treaty could be considered. He listed rent controls, the second-year authorization for the European Recovery Program, repeal of the Taft-Hartley labor law and extension of the reciprocal trade agreement authority as matters that the Senate would wish to take up first. The Taft-Hartley

Continued on Page 4, Column 7

AREA EMBRACED IN NORTH ATLANTIC SECURITY PLAN

ORIGINAL MEMBER NATIONS
INVITED NATIONS

The New York Times March 19, 1949

An armed attack against any signatory in Europe or North America will be considered an attack against all. This includes attacks on the islands, vessels or planes of any party in the Atlantic north of the Tropic of Cancer (1), on the occupation forces in Germany (2) and Austria (3) and on the Algerian departments of France (cross-hatched area of Algeria).

PURPOSE IS PEACE

But Plan Is for Swift Help in the Event of Aggression

ACHESON CLARIFIES POINTS

Declares a Rebellion Directed From Abroad Might Bring Pact Into Operation

Atlantic Pact text, Page 2; Mr. Acheson's broadcast Page 4.

By JAMES RESTON
Special to The New York Times.

WASHINGTON, March 18—The official text of the North Atlantic Treaty was published today. The pact proposed a defensive twenty-year alliance between North America and Western Europe, designed to prevent war from starting and to meet it with all due constitutional haste if it comes.

The text, which will be signed in Washington on April 4 and submitted as a treaty to the United States Senate thereafter, said that the parties agreed "that an armed attack against one or more of them in Europe or North America shall be considered an attack against them all."

In defense of this principle, it obligated the signatories to take immediate action to restore and maintain the security of the North Atlantic area, but in defense of American political tradition, it authorized each nation to decide what action it should take.

Vast New Frontiers for U. S.

If the Senate consents to the ratification of the treaty, the security frontier of the United States will encompass the entire Western Hemisphere (under the Rio Pact), the whole of the Atlantic Ocean, north of the Tropic of Cancer, the west coast of Europe from the North Cape to the Bay of Biscay, Italy and Algeria in the Mediterranean, and all overseas areas where American forces are stationed, including the blockaded garrison in Berlin.

Article 6 of the text stated that an "armed attack" under the pact, would be one (A) on the territory of any of the parties in Europe or North America; (B) on the Algerian departments of France; (C) on the occupation forces of any party in Europe; (D) on the islands under the jurisdiction of any party in the North Atlantic area north of the Tropic of Cancer; or (E) on the vessels or aircraft in this area of any of the parties.

This was officially said to mean that if an American, British or French aircraft flying into Berlin were shot down by the blockading forces of the Soviet Union it could be interpreted as an "armed attack" under the North Atlantic Treaty.

Text Bears Out Predictions

The text followed advanced predictions in detail. It reaffirmed the obligations of the signatories under the United Nations. It proposed the creation of a North Atlantic Council and a Military Staff Committee to plan the defenses of the whole North Atlantic area. And Secretary of State Dean Acheson said tonight in a radio address that only "malicious misrepresentation" or "fantastic misunderstanding" could see any aggressive designs behind it.

"This country," he said, "is not planning to make war against anyone. It is not seeking war. It abhors war. It does not hold war to be inevitable. Its policies are devised with the specific aim of bridging by peaceful means the tremendous differences which beset international society at the present time."

The Foreign Secretaries of twelve nations are expected to sign the treaty here on the eve of the United Nations General Assembly meeting early next month.

They will represent the United States, Canada, Britain, France, the Netherlands, Belgium, Norway and Luxembourg — the original negotiating powers and Italy, Denmark, Iceland and Portugal, who have requested invitations to adhere to the alliance.

The text of the treaty suggests that the signatories undertake four specific commitments:

1. To strengthen their free institu-

Continued on Page 2, Column 3

GREAT PEACE STEP, BEVIN TELLS HOUSE

Treaty Only Defense Against Soviet, With U. N. Failing to 'Fulfill Purposes,' He Says

By HERBERT L. MATTHEWS
Special to The New York Times.

LONDON, March 18—The Atlantic pact was hailed here today with more fervor and hope than any agreement in the memory of living men. From Foreign Secretary Bevin, who spoke in Parliament and in a broadcast to the nation, to the humblest British citizen it seemed to bring the first genuine promise of peace in our time.

Mr. Bevin brought out much more clearly in his simple broadcast tonight than in his statement to Parliament that the Atlantic pact is primarily a defense against Soviet communism. He provided a catalogue, into which tones of bit-

Continued on Page 2, Column 6

De Gasperi Backed, 342-170, On Joining the Atlantic Pact

By ARNALDO CORTESI
Special to The New York Times

ROME, March 18—The Chamber of Deputies confirmed its confidence in Premier Alcide de Gasperi's government and authorized it to negotiate Italy's adherence to the Atlantic pact by 342 votes to 170, with 19 abstentions, at 5:15 o'clock this afternoon after having sat continuously for forty-nine hours except for two intermissions of a few minutes.

The vote led to the worst fist-fight on the floor of the Chamber in Italian parliamentary history.

After sitting fifty-one hours the Chamber, by 317 votes to 175, with one abstention, defeated a resolution presented by Communist Leader Palmiro Togliatti forbidding the Government to cede any bases on Italian territory to foreign powers.

With today's vote the Government overcame the first hurdle on the road to Italy's acceptance in principle of the Atlantic pact. The extreme left-wing parties, however, made it plain that they had by no means abandoned the struggle and that they would leave nothing unattempted to block Italy's effective participation.

In fact, Signor Togliatti, whose veiled threat began to find practical application only a few hours later when Communist "Activists" again provoked riots in the streets of Rome, told the Government in the chamber early this afternoon, "You will have to reckon with the Italian people."

Left-wing Socialist Leader Pietro Nenni was even more explicit. He said: "The fight against the Atlantic pact doesn't end but be-

Continued on Page 2, Column 8

WEST GERMANS GET RED UNITY APPEAL

Invitation to an Anti-Partition Parley Is Timed to Coincide With Atlantic Treaty

By DREW MIDDLETON
Special to The New York Times

BERLIN, March 18—Eastern Germany's Communist-dominated People's Council today invited the principal political and economic leaders of Western Germany to meet April 8 in Brunswick in the British zone and plan German unity.

This shrewd political stroke, timed to coincide with publication of the North Atlantic pact, is a bold attempt to disrupt Western plans for a West German state, which eventually would be an integral part of any European union.

Although initial reaction to the Eastern invitation on the part of Western leaders was cold, there is no doubt that some of them had been aware of this Communist move for some time and had kept silent.

Dr. Herman Puender, chairman of the bizonal administrative coun-

Continued on Page 3, Column 2

World News Summarized

SATURDAY, MARCH 19, 1949

A defensive alliance for a twenty-year period during which an attack on any signatory shall be considered an attack on all is set forth in the North Atlantic Treaty, the text of which was made public yesterday. The proposed treaty permits each signatory nation to decide the form of action it shall take to meet aggression. The treaty will be signed in Washington on April 4 and then will go to the Senate for ratification. [1:8.]

Administration spokesmen in the Senate foresaw an overwhelming vote of approval, but a high Republican predicted it would be difficult to get a two-thirds majority unless it was clearly demonstrated that the treaty and the program to supply arms to Western Europe were distinct issues. [1:4.]

The reaction in London was one of unqualified satisfaction. Foreign Secretary Bevin said the pact was a great step toward peace and security. [1:5.]

Foreign Minister Schuman declared that France had obtained what she wished. He said the Western nations had been provoked by Moscow into making the pact. [3:1.] Dutch officials felt that the pact provided a safeguard in the event of an internal uprising that might spread into an international conflict. [5:1.]

In Italy the Chamber of Deputies gave Premier de Gasperi's Government a 342-170 vote of confidence and authorized it to negotiate for Italian adherence to the pact. The Chamber also defeated a Communist resolution that would have denied Italian bases to foreign powers. Communists provoked street riots in protest against the Government's stand on the treaty. [1:6-7.]

The Communist-dominated People's Council in the Soviet zone of occupation invited German leaders in the Western zones to meet April 8 to plan German unity. [1:7.]

The immediate recall of a United States official was asked by Poland after a news bulletin published in Warsaw by this country had referred to Poland as a "Soviet satellite." [1:6-7.]

The Chinese Communists accused the United States of trying, through the Atlantic pact, to start another world war. They hailed Premier Stalin as "the great leader of mankind fighting for peace." [4:2.]

President Truman, vacationing at Key West, said that, despite the defeats for the Administration in Congress, he was confident of the ultimate success of his program. [1:1.] Senate business, virtually at a standstill since Feb. 28 because of the Southern filibuster, began to move forward. Debate on continuation of Federal rent controls will start Monday. [8:6.]

The wiretapping investigation in this city took a new turn. Clendenin J. Ryan asked that Mayor O'Dwyer be indicted because of his "actions" during the investigation. [1:3.]

Index to other news appears on Page 16.

Express Agency Seeks $5,000,000 In Suit Against Union in Slowdown

By STANLEY LEVEY

The Railway Express Agency filed yesterday a $5,000,000 damage suit against the Brotherhood of Railway and Steamship Clerks, AFL, charging that the union's slowdown strike had cost at least that much in lost business.

Even as the official papers in the suit were being presented in Federal Court, the union was widening its picketing of company installations in the East. Agency operations in Paterson and Bayonne, N. J., were halted by picket lines, and in Newark, where 300 workers left their jobs on Thursday, the company placed an embargo on air and rail freight.

Union "flying squads" were surveying the situation in Philadelphia and Trenton, with a view to setting up picket lines in those cities. Other crews were active in Westchester along similar lines, and the union said it had won from brotherhood members at the Yonkers terminal a promise not to handle freight trucked in from New York by manufacturers trying to circumvent the embargo.

The dispute between the company and the union began on the overnight shift of March 8-9, when thousands of workers engaged in a work stoppage that tapered off to a slowdown. The next day the company countered by embargoing all less-than-carload freight into and out of New York and abolished 9,000 jobs, effective on March 12. This week the union retaliated with picket lines.

In its complaint, the company asserted that the slowdown had interrupted and stopped its normal business in the metropolitan area. It contended that the union "caused and induced certain employes to suspend work." As a result, the papers added, the agency suffered damages in excess of $5,-

Continued on Page 9, Column 6

Poland Asks Recall of U. S. Aide; Bulletin Termed Her a 'Satellite'

By EDWARD A. MORROW
Special to The New York Times

WARSAW, March 18—The Polish Government has demanded the immediate recall of a United States State Department official because Poland was described as a "Soviet satellite" in a news bulletin published by the United States Information Service. It was the first such official action taken by the post-war Polish Government against the United States.

The demand was made orally yesterday to United States Ambassador Waldemar J. Gallman by Foreign Minister Zygmunt Modzelewski on the ground that the Polish Government considered Chester H. Opal, press attaché and acting public affairs officer, as persona non grata. The Ambassador is understood to have assured the Minister that the Polish Government's views would be immediately transmitted to Washington.

Asked to specify what feature of the Information Service was found objectionable to the Polish Government, the Minister cited one paragraph from last week's news bulletin.

Datelined Lake Success, it said: "President Truman's proposal of United States aid to underdeveloped countries has been welcomed by every nation speaking to date in the [United Nations] Economic and Social Council except Poland. The Soviet satellite alleges that it is a scheme to expand exploitation by American big business."

Mr. Opal has been directly in charge of the publication and distribution of the bulletin in both the Polish and English languages. A former Chicago newspaper man, he speaks fluent Polish and has been in Poland for twenty-six months. There is little doubt that his forced departure will put a strain, at

Continued on Page 3, Column 5

1949

New patterns in suburban housing emerged as a result of the proliferation of the automobile.

The traffic jam became a feature of downtown areas of many cities as automobile sales went up and up, a result of lower prices.

"All the News That's Fit to Print"

The New York Times.

LATE CITY EDITION
Partly cloudy and mild today; fair tonight and tomorrow.
Temperature Range Today-Max., 65; Min., 47
Temperature Yesterday-Max., 60; Min., 48
Full U. S. Weather Bureau Report, Page 51

VOL. XCVIII..No. 33,346. Entered as Second-Class Matter, Postoffice, New York, N. Y. NEW YORK, THURSDAY, MAY 12, 1949. Times Square, New York 18, N. Y. Telephone LAckawanna 4-1000 THREE CENTS IN NEW YORK CITY

BERLIN LAND BLOCKADE IS LIFTED; FIRST TRAIN, AUTOS REACH CITY; ZONE TROOP RETIREMENT STUDIED

ISRAEL WINS A SEAT IN U. N. BY 37-12 VOTE

ARABS INDIGNANT

Quit the Assembly Hall After Poll—9 Nations Abstain in Ballot

59TH COUNTRY IN BODY

Israel's Foreign Chief Sharett Pledges Peace Effort—Debate Brings Polish Attack

By THOMAS J. HAMILTON

Special to THE NEW YORK TIMES.

LAKE SUCCESS, May 11—

The General Assembly admitted Israel to membership in the United Nations at 7:28 last night by a vote of 37 to 12, with nine abstentions.

The delegations of the six Arab states—Egypt, Iraq, Lebanon, Saudi Arabia, Syria and Yemen—walked out of the Assembly Hall at Flushing Meadow in protest before the applause over the election of Israel as the fifty-ninth member of the United Nations had died away. They indignantly refused to make any statement to correspondents regarding their intentions, but drove away to New York.

The Arab delegates, who also walked out when the General Assembly adopted the resolution recommending the partition of Palestine on Nov. 29, 1947, gave no hint of their impending action in their speeches in the General Assembly in the afternoon.

Charge Israeli Violation

They protested bitterly, however, that Israel had refused to comply with the provisions of a General Assembly resolution adopted on Dec. 11, 1948, calling for an international regime in Jerusalem and the repatriation of Arab refugees. Also, they challenged the validity of a Security Council recommendation for the admission of Israel, since Britain, a permanent member of the Council, had abstained.

The Charter requires the concurring votes of the Big Five on all except procedural questions, and the Arab delegates insisted that the Assembly should first get a ruling from the International Court of Justice. This procedure was contained in a resolution presented by Iraq yesterday afternoon, but Dr. Evatt ruled it out of order on the ground that the General Assembly could not examine the decision of another United Nations body.

The Yemen delegation returned shortly after 10 o'clock for the night session of the Assembly, and an Egyptian delegate came back a few minutes later, but the other desks remained vacant.

Immediately after the vote Dr. Evatt summoned to the platform Moshe Sharett, Israeli Foreign Minister, who had arrived by plane from Tel Aviv early yesterday to hear the final speeches.

"We enter this Assembly, which represents the collective statesmanship of the world, in a spirit of humility, anxious for guidance and enlightenment," said Mr. Sharett, who re-stated the Israeli policy of "loyalty to the fundamental principles of the United Nations' Charter and friendship with all peace-loving states, especially with the United States of America and the Union of Soviet Socialist Republics."

Now a Working Member

Mr. Sharett took his seat at the desk that had previously been prepared for the Israeli delegation in the back of the Assembly hall, between the Iraqi and Lebanese delegations. United Nations officials said no additional formalities were required, and that Israel would have the right to participate in all further proceedings of the General Assembly on the same basis as the fifty-eight other members.

The vote came too late to permit the Israeli flag to be raised in the area in front of the main delegates' entrance. A flag pole, however, had been prepared in advance, and there will be a ceremony at Lake Success at 10:30 A. M. today.

The General Assembly took up the application at its afternoon session and the debate concluded at 7:30 as a result of the fact that the protests of the Arab delegates,

Continued on Page 15, Column 1

Protesters in Tripoli Tear U.S. Flag to Bits

By The United Press.

TRIPOLI, LIBYA, May 11—Demonstrators tore to shreds a United States flag in front of the United States Consulate in Tripoli today and set fire to a number of Italian establishments.

The demonstrators, demanding full independence for this former Italian colony, shouted "Long live Russia! Down with America and the United Nations!"

Special to THE NEW YORK TIMES.

LAKE SUCCESS, May 11—A United Kingdom proposal that Eritrea, except for the western province, be incorporated into Ethiopia was approved in a subcommittee of the Political Committee this morning by a vote of ten to three with two abstentions.

A second United Kingdom proposal that the western province be incorporated in the adjacent Sudan also was approved by a vote of seven to two with six abstentions.

WAR PENSION BILL IS SHARPLY LIMITED

House Group Confines Benefit to Unemployable and Reports Measure as Rankin Protests

By JOHN D. MORRIS

Special to THE NEW YORK TIMES.

WASHINGTON, May 11 — The new veterans pension bill was further watered down in committee today—to such an extent that its author, Representative John E. Rankin, Democrat, of Mississippi, voted, though in vain, against reporting it to the House.

The action was taken by the House Veterans Affairs Committee at a closed meeting that had been scheduled merely to formalize its action yesterday in approving pensions on a more liberal basis.

The committee voted, 14 to 8, to confine the $72-a-month payments to unemployable veterans. By a voice vote, it then cleared the measure formally to the House.

Approval of the limitation was prompted by Veterans Administration estimates, drawn up overnight, that without it the bill would add $65,000,000,000 to the cost of veterans' benefits over the next fifty years. Yesterday's action had been based on a $12,000,000,000 estimate.

As finally approved, the measure's fifty-year cost was estimated at $8,693,000,000 by Guy H. Birdsall, assistant veterans administrator.

Mr. Rankin was joined by Representative A. Leonard Allen, Democrat, of Louisiana, in voting against reporting the bill. Shortly afterward the Mississippi legislator arose in the House to protest the action of the commitee, of which he is chairman.

The employability clause, he asserted, would bar pensions from

Continued on Page 32, Column 4

KENNY TO ASK COURT FOR ORDER TO SEIZE JERSEY CITY BOOKS

Mayor-Elect Seeks to Prevent Any Alterations of Records to Shield Old Regime

FULL INQUIRY IS PLANNED

'It's All Right With Me,' Says Hague of Defeat—Fight for State Rule Likely

By LEO EGAN

The political coalition that dethroned Frank Hague as boss of Jersey City has decided to seek a court order barring the outgoing city administration from destroying or altering official records before it leaves office next Tuesday.

John V. Kenny, who headed the coalition and who will become Mayor in the new administration, said a formal application for an order impounding city books and records would be submitted tomorrow to Judge William Brennan in Hudson County Superior Court.

One of the first acts of the new regime, Mr. Kenny added, will be to order a full-scale audit of the records and accounts of the outgoing administration, headed by Mayor Frank Hague Eggers, nephew of the 73-year-old former Mayor, who was one of the last of the old-time bosses in the United States to yield up his political power.

Drive to End State Rule Seen

While the new regime was making its plans for sifting city records for evidence of illegal acts and misuse of public funds on behalf of the Hague machine, Democrats in other parts of New Jersey were contemplating a drive to strip Mr. Hague of his control of the Democratic party in the state.

Many Democrats fear that unless Mr. Hague's connections with the state organizations are severed the fall elections will result in an overwhelming victory for the Republican State ticket, headed by Gov. Alfred E. Driscoll.

In any reorganization of the Democratic State Committee, Mr. Kenny, who was leader of the Second Ward in Jersey City for the Hague organization for many years, is expected to play a leading role. So are former Mayor Meyer C. Ellenstein of Newark, who topped all candidates for City Commissioner there in Tuesday's election, and Mayor George Brunner of Camden.

David Wilentz, who prosecuted Bruno Richard Hauptmann for the Lindbergh kidnapping, and Mayor Michael De Vito of Paterson are also expected to play important parts in any reorganization movement.

In the interview yesterday afternoon in which he told of his plans for investigating the outgoing Administration, Mr. Kenny announced also that he would support State Senator Elmer Wene for Governor on the Democratic ticket this fall. Senator Wene won the Democratic nomination with the backing of Mr. Hague in a recent primary.

The interview was sandwiched in between posing for newsreels and making an appearance on a television program. Although he looked tired and his voice was hoarse, the Mayor-elect said he felt "fine."

With respect to his plans on taking over, Mr. Kenny said that

Continued on Page 25, Column 2

Johnson Approves Air Force Plan To Distribute Negroes Among Units

Special to THE NEW YORK TIMES.

WASHINGTON, May 11—Latest proposals by the Air Force to conform to armed service policy on racial equality were approved today by Louis Johnson, Secretary of Defense.

W. Stuart Symington, Secretary of the Air Force, wrote to Secretary Johnson on April 30 and assured the defense chief that his directive of April 6 asking equality of treatment and opportunity "without regard to race, color, religion, or national origin" would be put into effect.

One of the principal moves in this direction is an Air Force order disbanding the all-Negro 332nd Fighter Wing at Lockbourne Air Force base at Columbus, Ohio. Its 2,000 officers and men will be distributed throughout the service in non-segregated units, it was stated.

Another assurance given to Mr. Johnson, it was learned, was that "key" positions would be open to Negroes who are individually qualified to hold them.

Letters from Kenneth C. Royall, Secretary of the Army at that time, and Dan A. Kimball, Assistant Secretary of the Navy, answering the same April 6 directive, were in effect rejected by Mr. Johnson on the ground that they were too general. The Secretary of Defense asked the two officials to "clarify" the information contained in their responses. Both letters, it was learned, told Mr. Johnson that his policy was already in effect, and did not indicate that additional changes would be made.

In his reply to the Army and Navy, Mr. Johnson fixed a deadline of May 25 by which the two services are to provide more details of their plans to conform to the equality policy. The services were instructed to make their replies through Thomas R. Reid, chairman of the National Military Establishment's Personnel Policy Board.

Mr. Johnson made his April 6 directive to the armed service secretaries public on April 20, at which time he stated that he in-

Continued on Page 54, Column 1

U. S. PLAN WEIGHED

Big 3 Would Withdraw to Ports in the North Under Proposal

FRENCH WOULD GO HOME

Presentation of Suggestion Will Depend on Soviet Stand in Paris Talks

By JAMES RESTON

Special to THE NEW YORK TIMES.

WASHINGTON, May 11—The United States was reported today to have under consideration a plan under which all occupation troops in Germany would be withdrawn into restricted areas at the North German ports.

Under this plan, which is being discussed with Britain and France, Soviet troops would be situated on the West Bank of the Oder in Stettin, British troops would be restricted to the area of Hamburg, and United States troops would be concentrated in Bremen.

[Stettin was included in the Soviet zone in the Potsdam pact, but under a separate agreement reached Sept. 20, 1947, the Russians turned over control of the former German port to Poland. Bremen is a United States enclave in the British zone.]

These troops, it is understood, would be obliged, under this plan, to use only sea communications, and France, which has a common frontier with Germany, would withdraw her occupation troops into her own territory.

An understanding apparently already has been reached among the Western powers to reject any Soviet proposal at the forthcoming meeting of the Council of Foreign Ministers in Paris for the complete evacuation of all occupation troops from all of Germany.

It is felt here that total withdrawal of these troops would be detrimental to the economic recovery and sense of security of Western Europe.

However, if Soviet Foreign Minister Andrei Y. Vishinsky should demonstrate in Paris that his Government was now prepared to establish a central government in Germany along the lines laid down by the Western powers for the

Continued on Page 3, Column 2

IT'S A REAL HOLIDAY FOR THESE BERLIN YOUNGSTERS

Joyous children hold their lunch boxes over their heads as they get news that there will be no school in celebration of the end of the blockade. The sign reads "blockade free."

Associated Press Radiophoto

ACHESON STILL BARS FRANCO AS FASCIST

Says Spanish Regime Denies Basic Rights in the Pattern of Hitler and Mussolini

Secretary Acheson's remarks on Spanish regime, Page 10.

By BERTRAM D. HULEN

Special to THE NEW YORK TIMES.

WASHINGTON, May 11—Secretary of State Dean Acheson declared today that the question of restoring full diplomatic relations with Spain turned primarily upon the attitude of Western European countries that were still opposed to bringing her back into their international family for military and economic cooperation.

This attitude, the Secretary told his weekly news conference, was conditioned by the absence of fundamental freedoms under the Franco regime which, he said, originally and still was patterned on Nazi Germany and Fascist Italy. At an-

Continued on Page 10, Column 1

Eisler Reported Stowaway; Seizure in Britain Is Asked

By WILL LISSNER

A man who has identified himself as Gerhart Eisler, native of Germany, is fleeing from the United States aboard the Gdynia-America liner Batory, it became known yesterday. The fugitive is believed to be the former Comintern agent named by the House Un-American Activities Committee as America's No. 1 Communist, jumping $23,500 bail to escape serving a year in jail and other penalties, but his identity has not yet been definitely established.

The Federal Bureau of Investigation and the Immigration and Naturalization Service of the Department of Justice moved yesterday to fix the identity of the fugitive. If the man aboard the Batory is the German-born Communist leader Eisler, he will be placed in custody for eventual return.

The fugitive is bound for Gdynia, but the ship, which sailed last Saturday, will put into Southampton Saturday. To make sure that Polish Communists aboard the ship do not balk a return, the State Department, at the request of the Department of Justice, notified Scotland Yard of the incident and asked that top investigators meet the ship on her arrival in the English port. Scotland Yard was asked to hold the suspect.

If Eisler, the convicted Communist agent, has fled the jurisdiction of the Federal District Court, his bail would be forfeited even though the English authorities return him, it was said at the Federal Building.

The forfeiture of the $23,500 bail would be a blow to the Civil Rights Congress and the American Committee for the Protection of the Foreign Born. For a good part of

Continued on Page 4, Column 3

FIRST BERLIN TRAIN FROM WEST SEALED

Officials Lock Doors and Draw Shades to Keep Russians Out and Reporters In

By The United Press.

BERLIN, Thursday, May 12—The first western passenger train since last year arrived in Berlin at 5:11 A. M. today (11:11 P. M. Wednesday, Eastern Daylight Time)—hauled by a Soviet zone locomotive.

A combined British-American train of twelve cars, it carried approximately 140 Western nationals, including seventy-three British troops and at least a score of reporters.

Anglo-American officials ordered the doors locked and the shades drawn soon after the train left Helmstedt at 1:23 A. M., the first train to make the West-East run on the Helmstedt-Berlin road since last year.

The train officials said that the "sealing" of the cars was necessary "to keep the Russians out and to keep you newsmen in." The reporters peeked anyway but saw only a moonlit empty landscape during the eventless three hours

Continued on Page 2, Column 2

World News Summarized

THURSDAY, MAY 12, 1949

The 328-day Soviet blockade of Berlin ended on schedule at 12:01 o'clock this morning. Berlin time, and approximately an hour and one-half later the first vehicles from the Western zones of Germany entered the city followed by the first train. [1:8; maps P. 2.]

The first Western passenger train to Berlin was sealed; a jeep led the road convoy [1:7.] Russian guards at Berlin ignored automobiles going to Helmstedt; people watched on the Autobahn. [3:1.]

Secretary of State Acheson warned that the end of the blockade did not, in itself, solve the German problem. He said Russia's willingness at the forthcoming Big Four meeting in Paris to consider proposals that would not erase the progress made in Germany by the Western powers would determine the outcome. He praised the draft constitution for a West German state. [4:2.] The United States was said to be considering a plan for withdrawal of all occupation troops to North German ports, except for French forces, which would return to France. [1:4.]

Guarded optimism was expressed by Moscow's New Times in an editorial on the Big Four meeting. The editorial said the talks could be a "turning point" in East-West relations. [4:6.]

Communists, urging at a Senate hearing in Washington that ratification of the North Atlantic treaty be deferred until after the Paris meeting, likened the pact to "Hitler's Axis." [1:6-7.]

The United States will abstain from a United Nations vote to lift the curbs on full diplomatic relations with Spain, Secretary Acheson said, because of the opposition in Western Europe to any change. Explaining this country's position, he denounced the Franco regime as still functioning along Nazi and Fascist lines. [1:5.]

Israel became the fifty-ninth member of the United Nations when the General Assembly voted, 37 to 12, to admit her. The six Arab states left the hall in protest. [1:1.] Foreign Minister Sharett, the first Israeli delegate to the United Nations, pledged his country to work for peace with its Arab neighbors and to remain friendly with both the United States and Russia. [12:3.]

Japan is not what she was ten years ago, Premier Yoshida said in appealing for proper understanding by the world. He asked access to materials and markets to enable Japan to become self-supporting. [19:1.]

Representative Rankin disowned his veterans' pension bill when a "watered-down" version was reported by a House committee. [1:2.]

Labor leaders and President Truman were said to have agreed on pressing passage of the Administration's labor bill with some amendments. [24:2.]

A man who identified himself as Gerhart Eisler, called this country's No. 1 Communist, sailed secretly on a Polish liner now at sea. [1:6-7.]

Victorious anti-Hague forces in Jersey City will seek a court order impounding all public records until an audit can be made. [1:3.]

Index to other news appears on Page 32.

U.S. Reds Liken Pact to Hitler Axis; Norman Thomas Urges Ratification

By WILLIAM S. WHITE

Special to THE NEW YORK TIMES.

WASHINGTON, May 11 — The Communist party of the United States, through a statement filed by its general secretary, Eugene Dennis, likened the North Atlantic treaty today to "Hitler's Axis," and demanded that the Senate withhold any action toward its ratification until after the Big Four Foreign Ministers' conference.

However, Norman Thomas, Socialist leader, supported ratification of the treaty before the Senate Foreign Relations Committee, but stressed that he did so with much anxiety because of the "dangers" that might lie in it.

He expressed belief that the pact should not be ratified unless the Senate made it "absolutely plain" that Spain would not be included in it, and equally plain that proposed American military aid should not be used against colonial peoples.

Senator Tom Connally, Democrat, of Texas, committee chairman, said that Spain's inclusion was "highly improbable" since it could be done only by unanimous consent of the twelve countries that signed the treaty.

Above all, Mr. Thomas recommended that before ratification this country issue "a mighty appeal for an end of the armament race under effective international controls which would make the pact unnecessary."

The Communist party proposal that the pact be held back, first advanced last week by Henry A. Wallace, was offered also by representatives of the National Council of American-Soviet Friendship and the National Council of the Arts, Sciences and Professions.

Witnesses for the three organizations appeared before the committee and further urged Soviet-United States conferences looking toward resolving differences between the two countries.

Their recommendations for de-

Continued on Page 7, Column 2

SIEGE ON 328 DAYS

Leading Car Speeds 102 Miles From the British Zone in 1½ Hours

AIRLIFT PLANES CONTINUE

West Concerned as Russians Turn Back Some Trucks—City's Lights Turned On

By DREW MIDDLETON

Special to THE NEW YORK TIMES.

BERLIN, Thursday, May 12—Just as the morning sun rose over the jagged skyline of this broken but defiant city a Soviet zone locomotive chugged wearily into the Charlottenburg Station in the British sector hauling the first train to reach Berlin from the West in 328 days.

Arrival of the train completed the relief of the city from the iron vise of the Soviet blockade.

At one minute after midnight [6:01 P. M. Wednesday, Eastern daylight time] two jeeps and a convoy of cars, buses and trucks roared out of the city from the Western zones. An hour and three quarters later the first cars of a flotilla that simultaneously had left Helmstedt, in the British zone at the border of the Soviet zone, swept into Berlin to re-establish the land link with the West broken since the Soviet Military administration established a complete blockade of the city last June.

By morning it was evident that the Russians had observed the letter if not the spirit of the East-West agreement reached in New York. Traffic was flowing freely along the Autobahn.

Although there had been some difficulty over locomotives, the Russians had promised to send sixteen freight trains and one passenger train into Berlin each day. Pending settlement of the dispute the trains will be pulled by Soviet zone locomotives.

Western Officials Disturbed

To Berliners who awoke in the night to find lights burning in the streets and in their homes and intersector barriers dismantled, the blockade for the moment seemed over. Americans and British in Military Government offices, however, were distinctly disturbed by the turning back at Soviet checkpoints of trucks bound for the Western zones with Western sector exports.

This refusal to permit trucks to pass stems from a Soviet order of January, 1948. Hence it is not affected by the New York agreement on ending the blockade. But the Western Powers felt that the action indicated that the Russians would not give an inch more than called for by that agreement.

The first railroad train since June of 1948 passed through the checkpoint at Helmstedt, in the British zone at the border of the Soviet zone, at 1:23 A. M., bound for Berlin.

The first car from Helmstedt, driven by Walter G. Rundle, United Press manager for Germany, arrived at the American checkpoint outside Berlin at 1:44. Mr. Rundle had driven the distance, which the British declare is 102 miles, in an hour and thirty-seven minutes. He said that the bridge across the Elbe at Magdeburg was in good condition.

Aide's Wife Enters City

The first woman to enter Berlin after lifting of the blockade was Adelaide de Neufville, wife of Lawrence de Neufville, consultant to the civil affairs division of the United States Military Government.

The first two railroad trains to start across the Soviet zone for Berlin since June 17, 1948, left the Russian control point at Marienborn early this morning. The first of these was a passenger train carrying correspondents. It moved into the moonlit landscape of the Russian zone at 1:55 after an eleven-minute wait at the checkpoint.

Eight minutes later a freight train of forty-two cars carrying coal from the Ruhr for Berlin passed through the checkpoint en route to Berlin, symbolizing the end not only of the Russian block-

Continued on Page 2, Column 3

"All the News That's Fit to Print"

The New York Times.

LATE CITY EDITION
Fair and quite cool today and tomorrow.
Temperature Range Today—Max.,62; Min.,49
Temperatures Yesterday—Max.,66; Min.,59
Full U. S. Weather Bureau Report, Page 27

VOL. XCIX..No. 33,481. Entered as Second-Class Matter, Postoffice, New York, N. Y. NEW YORK, SATURDAY, SEPTEMBER 24, 1949. Times Square, New York 18, N. Y. Telephone Lackawanna 4-1000 THREE CENTS IN NEW YORK CITY

ATOM BLAST IN RUSSIA DISCLOSED; TRUMAN AGAIN ASKS U.N. CONTROL; VISHINSKY PROPOSES A PEACE PACT

SMALL STEEL MILL SETS PENSION PLAN, A POSSIBLE PATTERN

Proposal by Employer of 1,200, With Workers Sharing Costs, Is Held Poser for Union

LIMITS CAUSE FOR STRIKE

Murray Is Firm for 'Package' Urged by Panel — Wildcat Walkout Hits Another Plant

By A. H. RASKIN
Special to The New York Times.

PITTSBURGH, Sept. 23—The first hint at the strategy the steel industry may employ to head off a threatened strike of 500,000 steel workers Oct. 1 came today from one of the smallest companies in the industry.

While the United States Steel Corporation and other big companies marked time on the first day of their renewed negotiations with the United Steel Workers of America, CIO, the Follansbee Steel Corporation made a proposal to the union that was widely regarded here as the forerunner of similar offers to be made by the rest of the industry.

The company, which has 1,200 employes at plants in Follansbee, W. Va., and Toronto, Ohio, informed the union that it was prepared to commit itself to pay 6 cents an hour for pensions, provided its workers put up an additional 3 cents an hour.

Employes Pay for Insurance

The company already has a contributory program of social insurance, to which it gives about 4 cents an hour and the workers 2 cents.

The proposal would bring the company's outlay for pensions and welfare into line with the 10-cent "package" recommended by President Truman's fact-finding board. At the same time it would make an end run around the union's insistence that employers pay the whole cost of industrial social security.

The Truman panel endorsed the idea that employers should meet the bill for pensions and social insurance, but opened the door for supplementary payments by workers to increase the amount of protection that could be provided. The board said such arrangements could be effected through collective bargaining.

If other steel companies subscribe to the 6-cent figure for pensions and 4 cents for health, hospital and other forms of social insurance, on condition that their workers also contribute, the union would be maneuvered into the position of having to decide whether or not to strike solely for establishment of the non-contributory principle.

Philip Murray, president of the union, has stressed the union's belief that the most important element in the Truman board's report was its recommendation that care for the "human machine" should be as much a charge on industry as care of plant equipment. The union has barred any compromise on that issue.

Murray Again Threatening Strike

At a two-hour conference with representatives of United States Steel this afternoon, Mr. Murray reiterated the union's determination to strike unless the company agreed to shoulder the full cost of pensions and welfare on the 6-cent and 4-cent basis suggested by the fact-finders.

The company made no immediate reply. Subcommittees were set up by both sides to continue negotiations Monday, five days before the strike deadline.

There was nothing to indicate that "Big Steel" had abandoned the opposition it expressed in public statements last week to exemption of workers from any direct share of financial responsibility for their own pensions and insurance.

The company has committed itself to give 4 cents an hour for welfare, provided workers made an additional payment on their own, but it has declined to set any specific figure for pensions until a joint study of retirement benefits is completed next March 31.

Negotiations between the union and other large steel companies took place today in a dozen cities, but none of the companies gave any new indication of its position. In virtually all cases the talks were recessed until Monday without any sign of a break in the deadlock that has existed since the first negotiations got under way in June.

Union negotiators warned that the patience of the men in the steel mills was wearing thin at the lack of progress toward employer-

Continued on Page 28, Column 1

Cancer Patient Slain; Daughter Detained

Special to The New York Times.

STAMFORD, Conn., Sept. 23—Carol Paight, 20 years old, was placed under police guard in Stamford Hospital tonight pending investigation of whether she shot her police-sergeant father in pity after learning that he had an inoperable cancer.

The father, Carl Paight, 52, died seven hours after he was shot with his own service pistol at 5:45 P. M. He had been in the hospital since Sept. 15, suffering from the effects of an operation that showed he had cancer.

The daughter, who had been alone with him, became hysterical. Sedatives were administered before she could be questioned by the police and a psychiatrist.

Father and daughter had been deeply attached, friends said. Police who knew both because of Sergeant Paight's twenty-eight years of service here, said that she had declared upon being told of the cancer that she did not want her father to suffer.

RED DEFENSE RESTS; REBUTTAL WAIVED

Jury in 9-Month Trial Excused Till Summaries Begin Oct. 4, May Get Case Week Later

By RUSSELL PORTER

The defense rested in the nine-month Communist trial yesterday, and the Government waived its right of rebuttal. Federal Judge Harold R. Medina gave counsel until 2 o'clock Tuesday afternoon to submit requests for instructions to be included in his charge to the jury and announced that arguments on closing motions would be heard at 10:30 o'clock Wednesday morning.

Judge Medina excused the jury until Tuesday morning, Oct. 4, when, if he denies the usual defense motions to throw out the case, summaries will begin. In the absence of unexpected developments, the case should go to the jury by the week beginning Monday, Oct. 10.

Eleven members of the Communist party's American Politburo or national board have been on trial since January 17, for criminal conspiracy to teach and advocate overthrow of the Government and destruction of American democracy by force and violence. Government witnesses have testified that the defendants reorganized the party for this purpose in 1945 on orders from Moscow.

The defense took roughly six months to present its case, including a two-month preliminary challenge to the Federal jury system. The Government introduced its evidence in two months.

The defense called thirty-five witnesses and the Government fifteen. The defense offered 429 exhibits, the Government 332.

Of the 158 trial days, the defense used 109—eighty-two in the trial proper and twenty-seven in the jury challenge. The Government spent thirty-seven days in the presentation of evidence. Ten days were devoted to picking the jury and two days to opening statements by opposing counsel.

The Government called its first witness on March 23 and rested on May 19. The defense began to present evidence on May 23, four months ago yesterday.

Nearly 20,000 pages of testimony

Continued on Page 7, Column 2

CIO SEES LEFTISTS QUITTING TO FORM OWN ORGANIZATION

High Officers Say Such Action Is Called for by New Line of Communist Party

FIGHT AT CONVENTION DUE

National Body Plans to Set Up Rival Right-Wing Unions if Pro-Red Groups Depart

By LOUIS STARK
Special to The New York Times.

WASHINGTON, Sept. 23—High officers of the Congress of Industrial Organizations expressed the view today that the new Communist party line was to split all pro-Communist unions from the CIO and to form a new labor federation. This belief is supported by the following developments:

1. A factional struggle within the CIO Teachers Union in New York, in which the pro-Communists are demanding that the union leave the CIO, though their opponents proclaim loyalty to the parent body.
2. The decision of pro-Communist unions to carry the fight on autonomy and wage policies to the right wing, led by Philip Murray, president of the CIO.
3. The "impossible" demands decided on several days ago by the convention of the United Electrical Radio and Machine Workers that will be served on Mr. Murray.
4. Refusal of the Farm Equipment Workers Union to obey the CIO mandate to merge with the United Automobile Workers.

The Murray forces are prepared for a possible split. If it occurs, they will charter right-wing groups to form the nucleus of new organizations supplanting the dissidents.

Eleven Affiliates Involved

Eleven CIO affiliates may be affected by the possible schism. While they have been generally credited with a membership of 1,000,000 members, informed officials say that their total is more nearly 600,000.

The largest of the dissidents is the UE, which says it bargains for 600,000 members. This union, however, is reported by right-wing officers to be paying to the CIO on about 350,000 members. Some of the leftist-led unions have been in arrears in payments to the national organization for some months.

The largest nut that the CIO has to crack is the UE, its third largest affiliate. This union, well entrenched in General Electric, Westinghouse and other large radio and electrical manufacturing companies, is a strong, well-disciplined organization.

Despite its strength, CIO officials indicated that they would meet any challenge of the UE's re-elected officers. If the union should decide to leave the CIO, the latter's officers feel confident of winning adherence of the workers in the big General Electric and Westinghouse plants as the nucleus of a new electrical union.

Mr. Murray's associates are impatient for the battle because daily evidences of leftist dissidence convinces them that the latter have made up their minds to split the CIO and to put the blame on the right wing.

The latest aspect of the leftist attack on the CIO leadership is

Continued on Page 28, Column 7

ADDRESSING U. N.

Andrei Y. Vishinsky
The New York Times

VISHINSKY SAYS U.S. PLOTS ATOMIC WAR

Calls for Great Power Treaty to Strengthen World Peace in Assembly Speech

Text of Vishinsky address to U. N. Assembly is on Page 4.

By THOMAS J. HAMILTON

Andrei Y. Vishinsky, the Soviet Foreign Minister, accused the United States and Britain yesterday of planning an atomic war, and introduced a resolution at Flushing Meadow proposing that the United Nations General Assembly request the five Great Powers to conclude "a pact for the strengthening of peace."

The resolution also would call on all nations to settle their disputes without resorting to the use or threat of force, and would take note "of the unbending will and determination of peoples to ward

Continued on Page 4, Column 1

CAPITOL FOR ACCORD

Lucas Says 'Future of Civilization' May Rest on Atom Control

AIRING OF VIEWS URGED

McMahon Holds U. S. Should 'Demand Right' to Put Case Before Russians Via Radio

By WILLIAM S. WHITE
Special to The New York Times.

WASHINGTON, Sept. 23—In a great anxiety that passed soon into a positive response—demands for fresh tries at international control of the atomic bomb—Congress heard today the news that an atomic explosion had occurred in the Soviet Union.

The atmosphere at the Capitol almost everywhere was consciously quiet and restrained. Some of the most responsible members of Congress issued statements saying that the American people could have confidence, in any possible crisis, in the military leadership and the military power of this country.

Beyond this, Administration Congressional spokesmen said in substance that the implications of the President's disclosure of what had happened in Russia were beyond the scope of any Congressional action. They looked toward the United Nations as the forum for this matter.

Senator Scott W. Lucas of Illinois, the Democratic leader of the Senate, and Senator Brien McMahon, Democrat, of Connecticut, the principal Congressional authority on atomic energy, came out almost at once for another attempt at bringing the bomb under the world's seal.

"I believe," said Senator Lucas, "that nothing could give the world greater confidence in survival than for the delegates at the United Nations to reconsider the question of atomic energy control, and arrive at an agreement acceptable to all.

"The world knows that our rep-

Continued on Page 3, Column 5

Truman Statement on Atom

By The United Press.

WASHINGTON, Sept. 23—The text of President Truman's statement today announcing a recent atomic explosion in the Soviet Union:

I believe the American people to the fullest extent consistent with the national security are entitled to be informed of all developments in the field of atomic energy. That is my reason for making public the following information.

We have evidence that within recent weeks an atomic explosion occurred in the U.S.S.R.

Ever since atomic energy was first released by man, the eventual development of this new force by other nations was to be expected. This probability has always been taken into account by us.

Nearly four years ago I pointed out that "scientific opinion appears to be practically unanimous that the essential theoretical knowledge upon which the discovery is based is already widely known. There is also substantial agreement that foreign research can come abreast of our present theoretical knowledge in time." And, in the three-nation declaration of the President of the United States and the Prime Ministers of the United Kingdom and of Canada, dated Nov. 15, 1945, it was emphasized that no single nation could, in fact, have a monopoly of atomic weapons.

This recent development emphasizes once again, if indeed such emphasis were needed, the necessity for that truly effective and enforceable international control of atomic energy which this Government and the large majority of the members of the United Nations support.

Soviet Achievement Ahead Of Predictions by 3 Years

By WILLIAM L. LAURENCE

President Truman's announcement that we have evidence of the occurrence of an "atomic explosion" in the Soviet Union within recent weeks ranks only next to his original announcement of the explosion of the first atomic bomb over Hiroshima on Aug. 6, 1945. It marks the end of the first period of the atomic age and the beginning of the second.

The momentous event is bound to have profound repercussions the world over. Though the scientists have predicted its coming, it came at least three years sooner than was expected. This was largely the result of an erroneous assumption that Russian scientists did nothing about developing an atomic bomb until after we informed them about it following Hiroshima. The fact of the matter is that scientists everywhere recognized the tremendous potentialities of atomic energy for war and peace as soon as the discovery of uranium fission was announced to the world in January, 1939.

While it is likely that Soviet scientists tested the first and only bomb they had, it would be dangerous to assume that they are four years behind us and that it would take them that long to catch up with us. It would be much more reasonable to assume that they have geared their plants to produce at the rate of one bomb a week, so that they will have a stockpile of at least fifty bombs a year from now, enough to destroy fifty of our cities with 40,000,000 of our population.

On the other hand, it is also likely that the latest event will make possible a better understanding between us and Russia, leading toward an agreement for the international control of atomic energy. Bargaining between equals is more likely to produce desirable results than bargaining between two principals, one of which holds

Continued on Page 2, Column 6

ACHESON RULES OUT SHIFT IN U. S. PLANS

Western Diplomats and Atomic Experts at U. N. Agree to Uphold Control Program

Text of Secretary Acheson's statement is printed on Page 2.

By A. M. ROSENTHAL

Secretary of State Dean Acheson said yesterday that he assumed the explosion in Russia reported by President Truman had been caused by an actual atomic weapon. He insisted, however, that the news had come as no shock and would not change the United States-sponsored plan for international control of atomic energy.

Other Western diplomats and atomic control specialists at the United Nations Assembly at Flushing Meadow took the same line. Unanimously, they said that the majority of the members of the United Nations would stick to the plan that had been fought by the Soviet Union for more than three years.

United Nations officials took it for granted that the President's announcement had pushed the world organization back into the center of the atomic picture despite the long deadlock on control negotiations. Secretary General Trygve Lie summed up the Secretariat attitude by saying that the

Continued on Page 2, Column 5

U. S. REACTION FIRM

President Does Not Say Soviet Union Has an Atomic Bomb

PICKS WORDS CAREFULLY

But He Implies Our Absolute Dominance in New Weapons Has Virtually Ended

By ANTHONY LEVIERO
Special to The New York Times.

WASHINGTON, Sept. 23—President Truman announced this morning that an atomic explosion had occurred in Russia within recent weeks. This statement implied that the absolute dominance of the United States in atomic weapons had virtually ended.

"We have evidence that within recent weeks an atomic explosion occurred in the U.S.S.R.," President Truman said.

These words stood out in red-letter vividness in a brief undramatic statement in which the Chief Executive said that the United States always had taken into account the probability that other nations would develop "this new force."

He pleaded once again for adoption of the system of international control of atomic energy promulgated by the United States and supported by the large majority of countries now assembled in the United Nations General Assembly at Flushing Meadow.

McMahon Reveals News

Mr. Truman announced the discovery to the Cabinet, assembled in the White House at 11 A. M. for the usual Friday meeting. Simultaneously on Capitol Hill Senator Brien McMahon, Democrat, of Connecticut, stood before the members of the Joint Congressional Atomic Energy Committee and gave them the news, which Mr. Truman had passed on to him at 3:15 P. M. yesterday.

White House correspondents had their usual conference with Charles G. Ross, the President's secretary, at 10:30 A. M. It was routine, but as they filed out his secretary, Miss Myrtle Bergheim, advised them not to go away. A moment before 11 A. M. Miss Bergheim entered the press room and said: "Press!"

The news men filed into Mr. Ross' office. He said he wished the door closed, and a secret service man took his post there. Then Mr. Ross said that he would pass out an announcement and that nobody was to leave the room until everyone present had a copy. Then he began passing around the President's mimeographed statement.

Tass Correspondent Attends

One of the first reporters to scan his copy exclaimed, "Russia has the atomic bomb!" There was a wild rush through the door and to the telephones in the near-by press room. One of the news men who sprinted out was the correspondent of Tass, the official Soviet news agency.

"The President has just given it to the Cabinet," said Mr. Ross as they went.

Thus the President did not personally appear, and there was no opportunity then or later to put questions to him.

Secretary of Defense Louis Johnson came out of the Cabinet meeting soon afterward. He began shaking his head as the questions came. Reporters literally clutched his arms as he headed for his limousine.

"Have we made any change in the disposition of our forces since this happened?" This question was asked twice.

"No," Mr. Johnson finally said.

"Does the Cabinet know any more about this than is contained in the President's statement?"

"The Cabinet knows all about it," Mr. Johnson replied to this. "It was fully informed."

"Do you have reason to believe this was the first atomic explosion in Russia?" asked another reporter.

This time Mr. Johnson smilingly shook his head, negatively.

"Don't overplay it," remarked Mr. Johnson, departing. In the cir-

Continued on Page 2, Column 3

Auto Crash Kills Publisher's Wife As He Reaches for Spilling Cup

Special to The New York Times.

HARRISON, N. Y., Sept. 23—Marvin Pierce, president of the McCall Corporation, magazine and fashion publishers, at 230 Park Avenue, New York, was driving to the Rye railroad station this morning when he tried to prevent a cup of coffee from spilling on his wife's clothes. In an accident that followed, his wife, Mrs. Pauline Robinson Pierce, 53 years old, was killed and Mr. Pierce was injured.

The couple left their Purchase Street home, adjoining the Westchester Country Club, soon after 8 A. M. Mr. Pierce, who is 56, was at the wheel and his wife was beside him, ready to drive home from the station after her husband had boarded a commuters' train for New York.

Mrs. Pierce held in her hands a cup of coffee that she had carried from the breakfast table. After sipping the fluid, she placed the cup for a moment on the seat between her husband and herself. From a corner of his eye Mr. Pierce saw the cup tipping toward his wife.

As Mr. Pierce reached for the cup, the auto swerved to the left side of the road, hit a soft shoulder, plunged 100 feet down a moderate embankment, slid between a pole and a tree and crashed into a tree and a stone wall. Striking the windshield, Mrs. Pierce died of a fractured skull. The accident occurred on Highland Road near Purchase Street.

Taken to the United Hospital in Port Chester, Mr. Pierce told his story to the police. Detectives found the coffee cup, bone China of English manufacture, unbroken in the wreckage of the car and took it to police headquarters. Physicians listed Mr. Pierce's injuries as a cerebral concussion, fractured nose, four broken ribs and several bruises. His condition tonight was improving.

Besides her husband, Mrs. Pierce leaves two sons, James R. and Scott Pierce of Rye, and two daughters, Mrs. Walter G. Rafferty of West Hartford, Conn., and Mrs. G. H. W. Bush of Bakersfield, Calif.

World News Summarized

SATURDAY, SEPTEMBER 24, 1949

President Truman issued yesterday a terse statement containing this dramatic disclosure: "We have evidence that within recent weeks an atomic explosion occurred in the U. S. S. R." His announcement, indicating that United States monopoly in atomic weapons had ended, added that "ever since atomic energy was first released by man, the eventual development of this new force by other nations was to be expected." He said this "probability" had always been "taken into account" by this nation, and he renewed his plea "for that truly effective and enforceable international control of atomic energy which the Government and the large majority of the members of the United Nations support." [1:8.]

Secretary of State Acheson said he assumed that it was an atomic weapon that had been exploded in the Soviet Union. He said the news would not lead to any shift in the United States position on international atomic control. [1:7.]

New efforts to achieve an acceptable plan for international control of atomic weapons were urged in Congress, where Mr. Truman's announcement was received with restrained anxiety. [1:5.] Reassuring statements were made by General Eisenhower and Maj. Gen. Leslie R. Groves, wartime chief of the atomic bomb project. General Eisenhower said he saw no reason why "a development that was anticipated years ago should cause any revolutionary change in our thinking or in our actions." [2:2.] One result expected by Washington observers was a spur to the North Atlantic defense program. Closer cooperation among the United States, Britain and Canada in atomic development was also seen. [2:3-4.]

Scientists who had generally predicted that the Russians would eventually succeed in discovering the secret of setting off an atomic explosion saw the Russian development as having come at least three years earlier than had been expected. [1:6-7.]

Soviet Foreign Minister Vishinsky said nothing about Russian possession of an atomic bomb in his eagerly awaited address to the United Nations General Assembly. He accused the United States and Britain of planning an atomic war. Mr. Vishinsky introduced a resolution calling for "the unconditional prohibition of atomic weapons" and another asking the five major powers to make "a pact for the strengthening of peace." [1:4.]

Renewed negotiations by the Big Four Foreign Ministers' deputies on an Austrian state treaty got off to a bad start. Russian refusal to reconsider the controversial issues forced an indefinite adjournment. [6:2.]

The British Labor Government will ask for a vote of confidence after Parliament convenes next week to debate the Government's devaluation of the pound. [6:3.]

In China the battle for the important seaport of Amoy reached new intensity. [5:1; with map.]

In a move that might set the pattern for the big companies in the steel industry to stave off a threatened strike by 500,000 steelworkers, the Follansbee Steel Corporation offered a pension plan under which the company would pay 6 cents an hour and its employes an additional 3 cents an hour. [1:1.]

High CIO officials were reported to believe that the new Communist party line was to try to split all pro-Communist unions from the CIO to organize a new labor federation. [1:2.]

Index to other news appears on Page 14.

Couple Held in Quebec Air Crash; Woman Said to Have Planted Bomb

By The Associated Press.

QUEBEC, Sept. 23—Police reported tonight that a drug-dazed woman confessed to carrying a package, believed to have contained dynamite, which was placed aboard an ill-fated Quebec Airways plane that blew up Sept. 9, killing all twenty-three persons aboard.

Police said the woman, identified as Mrs. Arthur Pitre, admitted taking the package to the Quebec Airport where it was placed aboard the plane, but she insisted that she did not know the contents of the package.

Royal Canadian Mounted Police said the woman was recovering from sleeping pills she took at the suggestion of her lover, whose wife was aboard the plane.

Provincial police detained as a material witness J. A. Guay, a young Quebec jeweler, whose 28-year-old wife was one of the passengers who lost their lives when the plane was ripped open by a blast in its luggage compartment. The plane smashed into a mountain near Sault au Cochon, forty miles northeast of Quebec.

Mrs. Pitre was also being held as a material witness.

Police also are reported to have questioned a third person in connection with the case.

Police described the third person as a 26-year-old "pretty waitress." They said she was a close acquaintance of Guay.

The crash took the lives of three New York executives of the Kennecott Copper Corporation. They were President E. T. Stannard, President-designate Arthur D. Storke and Vice President R. J. Parker.

Quebec Provincial police detained Mrs. Pitre at her home in Quebec. Persons living near by saw police enter the woman's Gauvreau Street home, an apartment. Crowds gathered outside and police were called to keep the curious on the move.

Police Inspector René Belec told newsmen:

"We have definite proof that explosives were aboard the plane to

Continued on Page 26, Column 2

1949

Eve Arden, Dick Crenna, and Gloria McMillan performing on the *Our Miss Brooks* program.

America's Town Meeting of the Air brought provocative discussions to the radio audience. John Temple Graves, George V. Denny, Jr., director of the program, Langston Hughes and Carey Williams are shown here in a program entitled "Let's Face the Race Question."

Mystery programs like *Inner Sanctum* were still very popular. Vera Allen, Arlene Blackburn and Frank Mellow are shown on an *Inner Sanctum* broadcast.

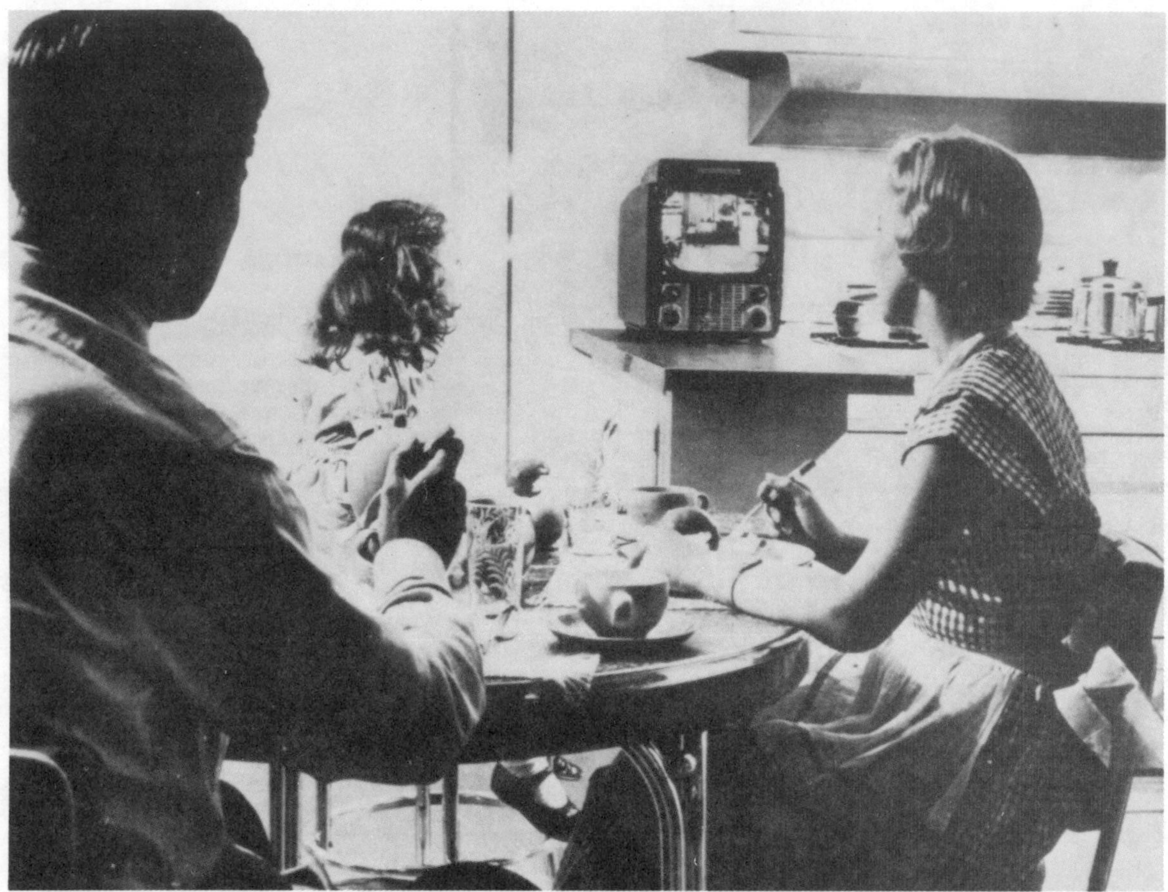

Either the food is not very good, or the TV show is. Television invaded millions of American homes with the advent of cheaper sets, and became a feature of modern life.

The nipped waist, lower hemline and higher heels were characteristic of the 1949 Paris look.

Ingrid Bergman was ostracized by the American film industry because of her affair with Italian film director, Robert Rossellini.

"All the News That's Fit to Print"

The New York Times.

LATE CITY EDITION
Sunny and mild today, cool tonight. Fair tomorrow.
Temperature Range Today—Max.,72; Min.,51
Temperature Yesterday—Max.,60; Min.,54
Full U. S. Weather Bureau Report, Page 19

Copyright, 1949, by The New York Times Company.

VOL. XCIX...No. 33,488. Entered as Second-Class Matter. Postoffice, New York, N. Y. NEW YORK, SATURDAY, OCTOBER 1, 1949. Times Square, New York 18, N. Y. Telephone Lackawanna 4-1000 THREE CENTS IN NEW YORK CITY

STEEL STRIKE STARTS AS 500,000 QUIT; TRUMAN PLANS NO NEW INTERVENTION; LEWIS RECALLS 102,000 MINERS TO PITS

SOVIET IN U. N. ASKS INDEPENDENT LIBYA, BRITISH EVACUATION

Proposes Military Withdrawal Within Three Months as Colonies Debate Opens

DELEGATES ARE SURPRISED

U. S. Suggests Independence Within 3 to 4 Years, Britain Would Set Like Limit

By THOMAS J. HAMILTON
Special to THE NEW YORK TIMES.

LAKE SUCCESS, Sept. 30—In a surprise move the Soviet Union proposed today that the United Nations General Assembly grant Libya immediate independence, and that "within three months all foreign troops and all military personnel shall be withdrawn from Libyan territory."

The proposal was aimed directly at the Western powers, since Britain maintains air bases in Cyrenaica, which, it is generally understood, would be available to the United States in the event of war.

The Soviet proposal, made public just as the Assembly's Political and Security Committee began its debate on disposition of the former Italian colonies in Africa, was timed to anticipate the speeches later in the afternoon announcing United States and British support of independence for Libya.

Dr. Philip C. Jessup, United States Ambassador at Large, said the United States would favor independence for Libya within three to four years.

McNeil Seeks 3-Year Limit

Hector McNeil, British Minister of State, suggested a time limit of three to five years, but he confined his statement to Cyrenaica and Tripolitania, which are being administered by Britain pending a decision by the Assembly. Mr. McNeil said he would leave it to France to say what should be done with the Fezzan, which is under French administration. It is understood that France will propose that she continue to administer the area.

The Soviet resolution was introduced by Georgi N. Zarubin, after Mr. McNeil had spoken, with the comment that the Soviet delegation would explain at a later meeting of the committee the reasons that motivated its proposal.

Mr. McNeil, who was the first speaker, had been shown a copy of the Soviet resolution while he was speaking. He said it looked "distressingly familiar" and that he hoped no attempt would be made to make "propaganda warfare" of the situation.

Until a year ago, the Soviet Union had been trying to persuade the other members of the Big Four that Libya, together with the two other former Italian colonies, Italian Somaliland and Eritrea, should be administered by Italy under a United Nations trusteeship.

Soviet Switches Stand

In Paris, however, before the Big Four handed the question to the General Assembly, the Soviet Union proposed a collective or direct United Nations trusteeship, and it fought unsuccessfully for this solution at the continuation of the General Assembly session here last spring.

The new Soviet proposal still provides for a direct United Nations trusteeship over Eritrea and Italian Somaliland. At the end of five years they would become independent.

In each case, the Trusteeship Council (of which the five great powers are permanent members) would appoint an administrator, who would be assisted by an advisory council consisting of the Big Five, Italy, Ethiopia, and one European and two native residents, to be appointed by the other members. The resolution also provides that at an unspecified time a part of Eritrea needed to give Ethiopia "access to the sea through the port of Assab" would be ceded to Ethiopia.

U. S. Stand Unchanged

Dr. Jessup and Mr. McNeil advocated the same solutions for the two other colonies that they supported at the Assembly's spring session: Italian administration of Italian Somaliland, cession of the western province of Eritrea to the Anglo-Egyptian Sudan, and cession of the remainder to Ethiopia.

The only other speaker today was Abte-Wold Aklilou, the Ethiopian representative, who insisted that Eritrea was an integral part of Ethiopia, and urged the Assembly to allot all of Eritrea, except the western provinces, to Ethiopia. He made no recommendation regarding the western prov-

Continued on Page 4, Column 8

Mao Heads Peiping Regime; Program Supports Moscow

Red Government Launched —Chou's Name Is Linked to Office of Premier

By WALTER SULLIVAN
Special to THE NEW YORK TIMES.

SHANGHAI, Sept. 30—Mao Tze-tung, chairman of the Central Committee of the Chinese Communist party, was elected chairman of the new Central Government of the People's Republic of China today as the Chinese People's Political Consultative Council completed its job of launching the new government of Communist China.

Three other leading Communists and three non-Communists were named vice chairmen. The Communists are Gen. Chu Teh, Commander in Chief; Liu Shao-chi, a member of the Political Bureau and usually rated the highest ranking member of the party under Mr. Mao, and Kao Kang, chairman of the Northeast People's Government.

The three non-Communist vice chairmen are Mme. Sun Yat-sen, widow of the founder of the Chinese Republic; Chang Lan, aged chairman of the Democratic League, and Li Chi-shen, chairman of the Kuomintang Revolutionary Committee.

The organ headed by Mr. Mao

Continued on Page 4, Column 3

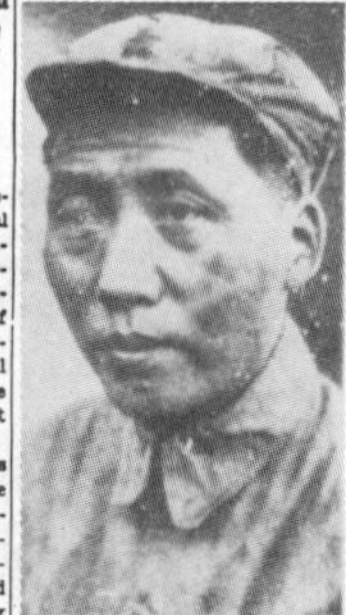

Mao Tze-tung
The New York Times

Yanks Lose, Trail Red Sox By One Game; Cards Beaten

As the major league pennant races enter upon their final two strides to the wire, Brooklyn's dauntless Dodgers today seemed to be sitting right handsomely in the National League scramble with a full game lead over the second place Cardinals and only two more encounters to play before the curtain rings down on the struggle tomorrow night. Though idle yesterday, they gained their advantage when the St. Louis Redbirds lost to the Cubs in Chicago, 6 to 5.

But not so the Yankees. The battered Bombers, season-long pace-setters in the American League until last Monday, fell out of their brief first place tie with the Red Sox yesterday by losing to the Athletics at the Stadium, 4 to 1, while Boston's Bosox downed the tail-end Senators, 11 to 9.

Thus, as the Yanks and Red Sox move into their final two games at the Stadium today and tomorrow, Joe McCarthy's Bosox, again leading by a full game, need only one victory to clinch the pennant. They could end the struggle by winning today. The Yanks, on the other hand, must win both games to capture the flag, with no chance left for even finishing the race in a deadlock, unless some circumstance, such as weather interference, should prevent one of the games from going to a decision.

At the moment the standing of the two American League contenders reads:

	Won	Lost	P.C.	G.B.	To Play
Boston	96	56	.632	..	2
New York	95	57	.625	1	2

Therefore, should the Red Sox win today, it would settle the race, for even were the Yankees to win the final game of the season tomorrow, the final standing would be:

	Won	Lost	P.C.
Boston	97	57	.630
New York	96	58	.623

Oddly, and perhaps for the first time in major league history, the National League goes into its final two days with the same figures prevailing as in the rival circuit.

However, there is a slight difference. For though the Dodgers lead the Cards by a full game and each club has two more games to play, they do not meet each other.

Continued on Page 17, Column 6

PAY RISE TO 1,355,000 CLEARED BY SENATE

Civil Service and Postal Bills Total $211,000,000—Fourth Spending Authority Ends

By C. P. TRUSSELL
Special to THE NEW YORK TIMES.

WASHINGTON, Sept. 30—The Senate today approved in rapid succession two bills to authorize an estimated $211,000,000 in annual pay increases for 1,355,000 classified and postal employes of the Government. About half a million of those slated for rises are in the Post Office Department.

This action raised the total of prospective increases voted by the Senate this week to more than $500,000,000 and affects 3,000,000 on the civilian and military payrolls. The House, in measures previously adopted, had approved rises of at least $120,000,000 more than the Senate's total.

The average increase for classified Civil Service workers is $121 a year. The increase for the post-office employes is $100. The House bill provides $150.

After the adjustment of differences in conference, appropriations must be authorized to cover the increases.

The pay rises are contained in four measures, these applying to the classified, or Civil Service, employes; to postmasters and postal workers; to top officials in the Executive Branch of the Government, and to military personnel in almost every rank or grade.

As the Senate acted today on the last of the major pay bills, Congress, as a whole, found itself under obligation to authorize, for a fifth time, the continued spending of funds by Federal establishments, even though formal appro-

Continued on Page 23, Column 4

Mrs. Patenotre Pays $2,000,000 In Tax Case; Fine, Term Suspended

By PAUL P. KENNEDY

Mrs. Eleanor Louise Patenotre, 80-year-old former owner of The Philadelphia Inquirer and widow of Jules Patenotre, one-time French Ambassador to the United States, pleaded guilty in Federal court yesterday to a charge of tax evasion and handed over a check for $2,000,000 in civil liability settlement.

The maximum penalty of $10,000 fine and a five-year jail sentence was suspended by Federal Judge Alfred C. Coxe, who placed the defendant on a one-day probation.

The Government has a lien on about $3,400,000 of the defendant's cash and securities in J. P. Morgan & Co., Inc., to satisfy additional tax claims amounting to about $3,000,000, it was announced after yesterday's hearing.

The Government's suit arose over the sale in 1930 of Mrs. Patenotre's 51 per cent interest in The Inquirer to the Curtis-Martin interests for $10,500,000. A few days before the sale, according to Thomas F. Murphy, assistant United States attorney, the stock had been transferred to her son, Raymond, a French citizen living in Montreal, where the sale was consummated.

The Government immediately began an inquiry with a view to recovering taxes, at that time slightly less than $200,000 and which this year amounted to about $2,184,000. When it was learned, however, that the sale had been made by a French citizen outside the United States, the investigation was dropped.

In 1945, however, through a treaty with Canada, some bank

Continued on Page 28, Column 7

POLAND, HUNGARY RENOUNCE PACTS WITH YUGOSLAVIA

Two Countries Move Day After Similar Action by Russia—Warsaw Expels Diplomats

TITO HITS BACK AT SOVIET

Moscow Considers Agreements 'Scraps of Paper,' States Belgrade News Agency

By EDWARD A. MORROW
Special to THE NEW YORK TIMES.

WARSAW, Sept. 30—Poland joined Hungary today in formally denouncing a treaty of mutual aid and friendship with Marshal Tito's Yugoslavia. The two countries acted a day after the Soviet Union had similarly voided its treaty of friendship with Yugoslavia.

Following Hungary's lead of last week, Poland also ordered the expulsion of eight Yugoslav diplomats because of alleged spying and diversionary activities.

The friendship treaty was denounced on the ground that Yugoslav agents were sowing confusion in Poland.

[Hungary declared that she had denounced the treaty because Yugoslavia had "defamed" it by plotting to overthrow her Government. Tanyug, official Yugoslav news agency, said that the Soviet Union, in renouncing its treaty with Yugoslavia, had shown that it considered its solemn agreements as "scraps of paper."]

In a note delivered to the Yugoslav Ambassador today, the Polish Government used language in the strongest possible terms the position it had taken earlier this month when on Sept. 8 it intimated that the friendship treaty was null and void.

Reminding Marshal Tito of that note, the Polish Government said "incontrovertible facts" had proved that the embassy had been engaged in spying and abetting a political diversion within this country. Such activities, the note continued, link Yugoslavia with the "Fascist underground and testify to its complete annexation with the imperialist camp."

Consequently, the note said, the immediate departure of eight Yugoslav officials was ordered. These included Ante Rukavina, counselor (who was mentioned in the recent Budapest spy trials as a diversionist planted in Poland); Lieut. Col. Janko Susnjar, the military attaché; Major Bogic Vlahovitch, his

Continued on Page 6, Column 3

World News Summarized

SATURDAY, OCTOBER 1, 1949

The 500,000 members of the United Steelworkers of America, CIO, were ordered out on strike by their leaders last night. An eleventh-hour conference of union and company representatives called by Federal mediators in a desperate effort to avert a nation-wide steel strike collapsed. Union and company representatives blamed each other for the strike. [1:8.] The White House said President Truman did not plan further intervention in the dispute. [1:6-7.]

About 102,000 of the 480,000 coal miners now on strike were ordered back to work Monday by union officials. The orders will affect 80,000 miners in the anthracite fields and 22,000 in bituminous fields west of the Mississippi River. However, no break in the deadlocked negotiations with soft-coal producers over pension and welfare funds was indicated. [1:5.]

The news of the steel strike broke as the nation's economy appeared to be taking a more hopeful turn with unemployment falling. The Census Bureau reported that unemployment dropped from 3,689,000 in August to 3,351,000 in September for the second successive monthly decline. [1:6-7.]

The Senate approved two bills that authorize an estimated $150,000,000 in annual pay increases to 855,000 classified Federal employes and an additional $61,000,000 to 500,000 postal employes. [1:2.]

The House Un-American Activities Committee named a faculty member of the University of Minnesota as the "Scientist X" who allegedly had given atomic secrets to a man described as a Communist spy. The accused denied the charge. [1:7.]

The Joint Congressional Committee on Atomic Energy was stirred to controversy when it received a confidential draft of a proposed report to clear Chairman David E. Lilienthal of the United States Atomic Energy Commission of charges of "incredible mismanagement." [1:6-7.]

Immediate independence for Libya was urged in a resolution introduced by the Soviet Union before the Political and Security Committee of the United Nations General Assembly, which opened debate on disposition of the former Italian colonies. The Russian proposal also called for the evacuation from Libya within three months of all military personnel and equipment. The United States and Britain also favored Libyan independence, but not for at least three years. [1:1.]

Nationalist China's request for an early hearing on her charges that the Soviet Union had been aiding the Chinese Communists was also considered by the Political and Security Committee. The committee decided to defer the request to fifth place on its agenda. [4:1.]

In China, the Communists at the final session of the Political Consultative Conference in Peiping elected their leader, Mao Tze-tung, chairman of their new Central Government. [1:2-3.]

Washington rejected proposals for use of naval aid to free three United States freighters being detained off Shanghai by the Chinese Nationalists. [4:4.]

Quickly following Russia's example, Hungary and Poland denounced their treaties of friendship and mutual assistance with Yugoslavia. Poland ordered eight Yugoslav diplomats to leave Warsaw. [1:4.]

The historic airlift operations that began June 26, 1948, to supply blockaded Berlin ended with their 277,264th flight. [7:7.]

Index to other news appears on Page 14.

COAL TIE-UP BREAKS

80,000 Anthracite Men and 22,000 Workers in West Return Monday

MAJOR WALKOUT PERSISTS

Big Shafts East of Mississippi Are Not Affected—UMW Calls Order Aid to Homes

Special to THE NEW YORK TIMES.

PITTSBURGH, Sept. 30—Orders for the 80,000 miners in the anthracite fields and for 22,000 in bituminous fields west of the Mississippi River to return to work Monday were issued by officials of the United Mine Workers today, but there was no indication of a break in the deadlocked negotiations with the major soft-coal producers of the country.

The UMW orders, which will return 102,000 of the union's estimated 480,000 members, or almost one-fifth of them, to the pits, were designed primarily to ease the fuel situation for domestic and public users, leaders indicated.

Unaffected will be the big bituminous fields in Pennsylvania, Kentucky, Alabama and other states east of the Mississippi from which heavy industry draws the bulk of its fuel.

Negotiations with the Northern and Southern groups of operators, employing about 378,000 miners in those fields, are stalemated at White Sulphur Springs and Bluefield, W. Va., where the groups have been meeting. The Western operators have been negotiating in conjunction with the Northerners.

In those two bituminous areas about 15,000 miners continued today to work in nonunion pits and strip operations in the face of continuing violence and mass picketing, which, however, was on a much smaller scale than in the preceding eleven days of the full work stoppage.

Another outburst of gunfire, in which a coal trucker's home and parked truck were "shot up," was reported in Pennsylvania but no

Continued on Page 3, Column 8

President 'Through' in Strike; Peace Hope Lies With Ching

Mediation Director Is Expected to Map Talks First With Major Operators Then With Union in Moves to Ease Deadlock

By FELIX BELAIR Jr.
Special to THE NEW YORK TIMES

WASHINGTON, Sept. 30—President Truman will make no further attempt to intervene in the steel strike, the White House announced late today after the Chief Executive's return from Kansas City. A close associate of Mr. Truman, who would not be identified by name, said:

"The President is through—from now on they are on their own."

With the shutdown in steel at hand, one economist whose opinions go regularly to the White House compared the seriousness of the situation to the first hundred days of the New Deal. Federal agencies prepared to revise all forecasts of business conditions and employment to take account of a steel strike that would be felt throughout the industrial fabric.

The Presidential press secretary, Charles G. Ross, said the Government's effort to bring about a settlement of the pension dispute among 500,000 steel workers was in the hands of Cyrus S. Ching, director of the Federal Mediation and Conciliation Service.

When Mr. Ching left his office at 5 P. M. today he had just hung up the telephone after a conversation with the assistant mediation director, William N. Margolis, in Pittsburgh. He reported that Mr. Margolis had advised that there was no change in the situation as a result of all-day conferences. He received similar advices all day from his mediators in other steel centers.

Assuming that the strike is still under way early next week, Mr. Ching is reported to be determined to seek a way out of the continued deadlock by further conferences.

Continued on Page 3, Column 5

McMahon Clears Lilienthal; Proposed Report Stirs Row

By JOHN D. MORRIS
Special to THE NEW YORK TIMES.

WASHINGTON, Sept. 30—Circulation of a proposed report clearing David E. Lilienthal of accusations of "incredible mismanagement" as chairman of the Atomic Energy Commission stirred a harsh controversy today in the Joint Congressional Committee on Atomic Energy.

The confidential draft, distributed among committee members by the chairman, Senator Brien McMahon, Democrat, of Connecticut, stated that the country's atomic program was in good hands and in excellent shape despite some mistakes in administration. The importance of security by achievement, distinguished from security by concealment, was emphasized.

The proposed report was drawn up by the staff of the joint committee under the direction of Senator McMahon in consultation with Representative Carl T. Durham, Democrat, of North Carolina, the committee's vice chairman.

Its distribution, in printed galley-proof form, was immediately protested by Senator William F. Knowland, Republican, of California, in a letter to Mr. McMahon. The Californian said that it should have been first discussed with other committee members.

"It is my first experience in six years of service in the State Legislature and four years in the United States Senate when a report of this nature has been prepared and put into type without any prior consultation or discussion with the committee membership," he wrote. "The members of the joint committee and not the staff must make the decisions."

Mr. McMahon stated in reply that the proposed report was printed "not with any idea of finalizing it or to put it beyond your crit-

Continued on Page 4, Column 5

NAMED 'SCIENTIST X,' HE DENIES CHARGE

Dr. J. W. Weinberg of University of Minnesota Is Accused by House Committee

By The Associated Press.

WASHINGTON, Sept. 30—Ending a year-old mystery, the House Un-American Activities Committee today named a young Midwest university professor as the "Scientist X" it accused of giving wartime atomic secrets to a man it called a Communist spy.

The committee said that "Scientist X" was Dr. Joseph W. Weinberg of the University of Minnesota and formally recommended that the Justice Department prosecute him on perjury charges.

Dr. Weinberg promptly denied the accusation, saying it was a case of "mistaken identity."

The Justice Department said the Federal Bureau of Investigation had been investigating Dr. Weinberg "for a long period of time."

In Minneapolis, Dr. Weinberg, 32-year-old Assistant Professor of Physics, said:

"I am innocent. At no time have I participated in any way in disclosure of any secret or classified information or formula to any unauthorized person."

The young scientist also took a

Continued on Page 4, Column 6

Unemployment Cut Second Month; Sawyer Hails Sign of Trade Gains

Special to THE NEW YORK TIMES.

WASHINGTON, Sept. 30—Unemployment declined from 3,689,000 in August to 3,351,000 in September, according to the latest Census Bureau figures released today. This was the second successive decline in monthly unemployment figures.

Total civilian employment also dropped in the week ended Sept. 10, it was stated. The latest employment figure was placed at 59,411,000, about half a million lower than that in August.

The simultaneous decline in employment and unemployment was attributed chiefly to the return to school of many summer workers and was smaller than that seasonally expected, said Charles Sawyer, the Secretary of Commerce.

Secretary Sawyer said that the September labor force report was gratifying as "it further bolsters accumulating evidence that general business conditions are improving."

While unemployment figures dropped appreciably in August they still remained nearly double the 1,899,000 reported in September, 1948.

The number of workers in civilian jobs in August was estimated at 59,947,000, against 60,312,000 in September, 1948.

Agricultural employment fell to 8,158,000 in the week ended Sept. 10 from 8,507,000 in the week ended Aug. 13. According to reports the cotton and tobacco crops were slow in maturing this year. As a result the usual heavy demand for workers for the harvest season had not as yet developed to the customary extent by the September survey week.

PARLEYS COLLAPSE

Murray Orders Men Out in Nation-Wide Tie-Up on Pensions Issue

SIDES ACCUSE EACH OTHER

CIO Chieftain Holds Industry 'Forced' Walkout—Fairless Blames Union Insistence

By A. H. RASKIN
Special to THE NEW YORK TIMES.

PITTSBURGH, Saturday, Oct. 1—The national steel strike began at 12:01 A. M. today. Telegraphic orders from Philip Murray, president of the United Steelworkers of America, CIO, ordered 500,000 workers from their jobs after Federal mediation efforts had collapsed.

All signs pointed to a long stoppage as President Truman, who had won three postponements of the walkout since last July 15, let it be known that he had no thought of again stepping into the dispute.

The bitterness of the conflict over whether employers should assume the full cost of pensions and social insurance for their workers was reflected in statements issued a few hours before the midnight strike deadline by leaders on both sides. Each blamed the other for a tie-up that meant the slow choking of the manufacturing industry.

The shutdown affected 401,216 workers in the plants of thirty-seven basic steel producers and their subsidiaries. It also halted mining of iron ore by 12,117 miners in the Mesabi range of northern Minnesota. The other workers involved were scattered over a score of allied industries.

No Hope for Week-End

Hope for bringing the strike to an end over the week-end vanished when Federal conciliators, who spent all day yesterday in conference with negotiators for Mr. Murray's union and the United States Steel Corporation, decided to return to Washington while both sides did "some soul-searching."

William N. Margolis, assistant director of the Federal Mediation and Conciliation Service, and Peter Seitz, its general counsel, reported that they had never encountered a situation in which the parties were "so adamant and yet so affable." They expressed the hope that the company and the union would seek to work out their differences "in their own interest and in the interest of the nation."

Before the mediators withdrew, Cyrus S. Ching, director of the service, talked by long-distance telephone with union and management representatives. He instructed members of his staff assigned to major steel companies to return to the capital for discussion of the Government's next moves.

The strike cut off virtually all the country's output of steel. Only a handful of plants—some nonunion and some having continuing contracts with the union—remained in production. The daily wage loss to the workers will run to $6,500,000 a day. No accurate estimate of the potential loss to industry was obtainable.

Each Accuses the Other

The gulf between the union and the companies was reflected in the telegrams sent by Mr. Murray and in a comment issued immediately afterward by Benjamin F. Fairless, president of United States Steel.

Mr. Murray charged that the steel industry had "forced" the strike upon the union and the American people by "stubbornly and obstinately" refusing to accept the recommendations of President Truman's Steel Fact-Finding Board for employer-financed pensions and social insurance. He accused the companies of proceeding in "complete disregard of the national interest."

Mr. Fairless retorted that the strike call was attributable solely to the union's insistence that the recommendations of the Truman panel be considered "equivalent to those of a compulsory arbitration tribunal," despite the President's advance assurance that neither side would be bound by the board's findings. He accused the union of demanding that the company

Continued on Page 3, Column 1

"All the News That's Fit to Print"

The New York Times.

LATE CITY EDITION
Fair and pleasant today. Partly cloudy, mild tomorrow.
Temperature Range Today—Max., 66; Min., 56
Temperature Yesterday—Max., 67; Min., 54
Full U. S. Weather Bureau Report, Page 31

Copyright, 1949, by The New York Times Company.

VOL. XCIX..No. 33,490. Entered as Second-Class Matter, Postoffice, New York, N. Y. NEW YORK, MONDAY, OCTOBER 3, 1949. Times Square, New York 18, N. Y. Telephone Lackawanna 4-1000 THREE CENTS IN NEW YORK CITY

SOVIET RECOGNIZES CHINA RED REGIME; DROPS CHIANG LINK

'EVENTS' ARE CITED

Note Says That Russia Is 'Confident' Republic Represents Majority

CANTON HELD 'PROVINCIAL'

Moscow Asserts Nationalists Have 'Ceased to Exercise Power in the Country'

By The Associated Press.

MOSCOW, Oct. 2—Russia today recognized the Central People's [Communist] Government of China.

The recognition was announced in a note to the Minister of Foreign Affairs of the new Chinese Communist Government from Soviet Deputy Foreign Minister Andrei A. Gromyko.

Russia also served formal notice that diplomatic relations had ceased to exist between Russia and the Chinese Government in Canton.

The Chinese Chargé d'Affaires said he had transmitted Mr. Gromyko's statement to Canton. "In the meantime," he said, "we are staying on here awaiting instructions."

The Chargé d'Affaires said he had been asked earlier in the day to come to the Soviet Foreign Ministry, where he received the Soviet declaration.

Diplomatic Colony Gets News

News of the recognition reached Moscow's diplomatic colony when most of its members were assembled at Spasso House, the home of United States Ambassador Alan G. Kirk, attending a movie. The picture was forgotten in the face of the news.

The next formal step in recognition by the Soviet Union is the exchange of ambassadors between the Central People's Government and the U. S. S. R. Each country must submit the name of an ambassador-designate to the other before the envoys are accepted.

Other countries may recognize the Central People's Government. It is assumed in diplomatic circles here that when this has been done, the Communist Government will ask the United Nations to recognize it as the Government of China and receive its representatives.

The Soviet Union is expected to press for the recognition of the new Chinese Government by the United Nations.

Soviet Press Hails Regime

By HARRISON E. SALISBURY
Special to The New York Times.

MOSCOW, Oct. 2—The Soviet press today editorially greeted the formation of the new Central Chinese Government.

Almost half of the Soviet press was dedicated to the news of the establishment of the new Chinese Republic, which was hailed by Soviet Historian Eugene Tarle in Izvestia as one of the two "stupendous events" of the year—the other being the "world failure of United States calculations upon atomic monopoly."

The first page of Soviet central newspapers usually is confined largely to domestic news. Today, however, the Soviet press published on its first page the text of the declaration by Mao Tze-tung, in which he said the Central People's Government was the only legitimate government representing all of the Chinese people and asserted that "this government is ready to establish diplomatic relations with any foreign government which is prepared to observe the principles of equality, mutual benefit and mutual respect of territorial integrity and sovereignty."

To Mr. Mao's declaration was appended the text of a brief note from Foreign Minister Chou En-lai to Soviet Consul General S. Tikvinsky at Peiping, forwarding Mr. Mao's declaration.

"American Bosses" Hit

The leading Tadjik poet, Mirzo Tursunzade, wrote in Izvestia: "Now in the East there is not a single country where the banner of struggle will not gleam red, where toilers will not be inspired by the example of the peoples of the Soviet Union. The struggle for independence and national sov-

Continued on Page 3, Column 3

Congressman Says Pole Shadowed Him

Special to The New York Times.

PRAGUE, Czechoslovakia, Oct. 2—Reporting that they had received cool treatment from the Polish Government and that one member had been shadowed by an attractive blonde while in Warsaw last week, a group of eight Congressmen arrived here tonight by plane from Vienna.

Seven of the eight Congressmen are members of a subcommittee of the House Committee on Expenditures in the Executive Department.

The eighth Congressman in the party, but not a committee member, is Wayne L. Hays, Democrat, of Ohio, who reported having been shadowed by a well-dressed woman. The woman, Mr. Hays said, had a room across from his in Warsaw's Hotel Bristol and left her quarters whenever he did his.

To determine that the woman's presence was not coincidental, Mr. Hays reported, he once walked down the hotel stairs, followed by the woman, and then stepped into an elevator going up. The woman quickly entered the elevator behind him, Mr. Hays declared.

NEW U. N. RIFT SEEN ON RED CHINA ISSUE

Soviet to Try to Get Communist Regime Accepted by World, Lake Success Believes

By SAM POPE BREWER
Special to The New York Times.

LAKE SUCCESS, Oct. 2—A new East-West struggle in the United Nations is expected to develop from the Soviet Union's recognition of Communist China and its break with the Nationalists, announced today by the Moscow radio.

The next step, it is believed, will be an application by the Chinese Communist regime, supported by the Soviet Union, for recognition as the legitimate representative of China in the United Nations.

This would undoubtedly produce a bitter conflict, with Russia and her satellites probably standing alone against the rest of the members. Russia has already tried unsuccessfully to have an observer from the Government of North Korea admitted to this session of the General Assembly.

There is apparently no specific provision in United Nations procedure for dealing with a case such as would arise if Communist China applied for United Nations membership. A legal expert of the United Nations Secretariat said tonight:

"No case remotely approaching it has arisen."

When the Communists took control of Czechoslovakia, it was a case of a revolution within the country, not of two rival governments, and though there was "an exile government," the right of the new regime to represent Czecho-

Continued on Page 3, Column 2

RUSSIANS PROTEST TO WESTERN ALLIES ON BONN REPUBLIC

Call Formation of West German State a Violation of Potsdam and of Big-Four Decisions

NOTES HANDED TO ENVOYS

They Hold That Establishment of Regime Leads to Delay in Concluding Peace Pact

Text of Soviet Union's note on Germany appears on Page 4.

Special to The New York Times.

LONDON, Oct. 2—The Soviet Government, in notes handed today to the United States, British and French envoys in Moscow, said it considered the formation of the West German state a violation of the Potsdam agreement and of the decisions of last June's meeting of the Council of Foreign Ministers.

The notes, broadcast tonight by Moscow radio, said that Western Germany had been changed into a "puppet state, into an obedient instrument of Western occupation authorities in carrying out their aggressive plans in Europe."

The step of the three Governments, the notes said, represents not only a violation of obligations for preserving the unity of Germany but also of obligations for the conclusion of a peace treaty with Germany as the formation of a separate West German state leads to a delay in the conclusion of a peace treaty.

Declaring that the Soviet Government considered as "completely unfounded" the attempt of the Western powers to justify their activities as being in the interest of the German population, the notes said that at last June's meeting of the Foreign Ministers, the Soviet Union and the three Western powers "undertook to continue their efforts to obtain restoration of the economic and political unity of Germany."

Gromyko Delivers Notes

The notes, the Moscow broadcast said, were delivered by Deputy Foreign Minister Andrei A. Gromyko to the ambassadors of the United States and Britain and to the French Chargé d'Affaires.

The notes accused the Western powers of having used reactionary German politicians to form the West German state and the "so-called Bonn Constitution."

They said that the Bonn Constitution had been worked out under pressure of the occupation authorities, who practically "dictated" the elementary articles of document. The federal system, the notes added, had not been agreed upon by a majority of the German people but had been imposed on them.

The notes declared that the attempt of the Western powers to show that the Occupation Statute aimed at allowing the German people to realize full democratic autonomy was a complete contradiction of the elementary rulings of the statute.

"The Soviet Government considers it necessary to state that inasmuch as there has been formed at Bonn the separate government indicated, a new situation has been created in Germany at the present time which renders of particularly great importance the fulfilment of tasks for the restoration of unity of Germany as a democratic and peace-loving state, and for the ensuring fulfilment by Germany of

Continued on Page 4, Column 6

JUSTICE HURT

William O. Douglas
The New York Times Studio

DOUGLAS INJURED IN FALL OFF HORSE

Justice Has 13 Ribs Broken When Mount Rolls Over Him in Washington Mountains

Special to The New York Times.

YAKIMA, Wash., Oct. 2—Justice William O. Douglas of the United States Supreme Court was thrown from a horse and injured seriously today while riding on the mile-high Pacific Coast Trail, in a rugged part of the Cascade Mountains, seventy-five miles west of Yakima.

Complaining of severe back pains, he was brought by stretcher, State Highway Patrol wagon and ambulance to St. Elizabeth's Hospital in this city.

Drs. Joseph H. Lowe and W. Schuler Ginn, both of Yakima, examined him, and tonight Dr. Ginn issued this statement:

"Justice Douglas' chest was crushed and we have counted thirteen broken ribs so far. As far as we can tell, his back is all right. He is resting easy at the present time."

Dr. Lowe said Justice Douglas' right lung had been punctured, but he denied a report that there was loss of blood and that a transfusion would be necessary.

Although any estimates of the length of hospitalization asserted-ly would be premature, Dr. Ginn voiced the belief that the justice would be in the hospital "for several weeks, at least."

Justice Douglas on the final day of his summer vacation had flown in from Seattle this morning to join his old friend, Elon J. Gilbert, of Yakima High School and Whit-

Continued on Page 32, Column 6

U. S. SEEKS TO SOLVE STEEL, COAL TIE-UPS AS DOUBLE MENACE

Economy of Nation Will Suffer in Prolonged Twin Strikes, Federal Officials Fear

PINCH IS DUE THIS MONTH

Ching Confers With His Aides —100,000 Miners Go Back Today on Lewis Order

By A. H. RASKIN
Special to The New York Times.

PITTSBURGH, Oct. 2—High Federal officials, convinced that a long strike in either steel or coal would be enough to send the national economy into a tailspin, were reported today considering a double-barreled "peace offensive" to restore production in both fields.

With nothing happening to encourage optimism that either major strike would be settled soon through direct agreement by the parties, top Government mediators reached the conclusion that they would have a pyrrhic victory if they won a settlement in steel without having found a basis for getting the soft-coal miners back to work.

It was understood that the mediators still were undecided on the specific methods to be employed in seeking a two-pronged settlement, but they were agreed that it would be futile for the Government to make its "big push" in either situation for at least two weeks.

This belief was based on the knowledge that the country would not begin to feel any acute shortage of steel or coal until some time after the middle of this month. President Truman has made it plain that he had no desire to inject himself into either of the big strikes unless a crisis were at hand.

Strikers Rely on "Friend"

Steel strikers in a Pennsylvania mill town, however, say that they are counting on "their friend" Harry S. Truman, for a quick settlement of the tie-up. Many of them are not well informed on what the union is demanding, but assert that they will stay out until it calls them back.

Cyrus S. Ching, Director of the Federal Mediation and Conciliation Service, is expected to make a statement on the situation tomorrow, but it is believed unlikely that he will go much beyond announcing plans for keeping members of his staff in close touch with strike developments.

Mr. Ching spent most of the week-end conferring in Washington with William N. Margolis, as-

Continued on Page 10, Column 4

YANKEES AND DODGERS WIN PENNANTS IN FINAL GAMES; 68,055 CHEER IN STADIUM

MANAGERS OF THE CHAMPIONS

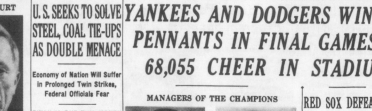

Casey Stengel, Yankees

Burt Shotton, Dodgers
The New York Times

RED SOX DEFEATED

Raschi Pitches Yanks to American League Flag With 5-3 Triumph

BROOKLYN VICTOR BY 9-7

Conquers Phillies in 10th for National Loop Title—World Series Opens Wednesday

By WILLIAM J. BRIORDY

It will be the New York Yankees against the Brooklyn Dodgers in the 1949 edition of the world series starting Wednesday at Yankee Stadium.

In pulse-quickening finishes to the keenest major-league races in forty-one years, the battered Yanks staved off a last-inning rally to beat the Boston Red Sox, 5—3, to win the American League pennant before 68,055 Yankee Stadium onlookers, while the Dodgers collared the National League flag by halting the Phillies, 9—7, in ten innings at Philadelphia's Shibe Park yesterday.

When the Yanks and Dodgers come to grips Wednesday, it will mark the third world series meeting of the interborough rivals and the second in three years. The Yanks won both previous series—in 1941 and 1947. The triumph was the sixteenth in the American League for the Yanks. Starting with 1890, the Dodgers have annexed the National League championship eight times. The Yanks' margin over the Dodgers in 1941 was 4—1 and in 1947 it was 4—3.

The Yanks and Red Sox were in a flat-footed tie when the teams took the field at the Stadium yesterday. The Dodgers entered the final day with a one-game lead over the St. Louis Cardinals, who snapped out of a four-game losing streak to beat the Chicago Cubs, 13—5.

Belated Card Victory

The Cards pulled out of their tailspin too late to catch the Brooks. The Yanks and Dodgers annexed their respective league titles by one game and, interestingly enough, the winners and runners-up in each circuit finished with identical records, 97 and 57 for the champions and 96 and 58 for the second-place clubs.

The Dodgers will be at Yankee Stadium Wednesday and Thursday and then the Brooks will be hosts to the Bombers Friday, Saturday and Sunday, at Ebbets Field, barring a sweep. In the event the series lasts that long, the final two games are listed for the Stadium on Monday and Tuesday, Oct. 10 and 11.

Stout-hearted hurling by their big righthander, Vic Raschi, enabled the gallant Yanks to defeat Joe McCarthy's Red Sox. It was a bitter pill, too, for the 62-year-old McCarthy, who saw his pennant hopes smashed in the same stadium where he led the Bombers to eight American League pennants and seven world championships. Moreover, itt was the second straight season the Bosox were beaten out in the last stage of the campaign. Last year the Red Sox lost in a play-off with Cleveland.

Raschi held Boston in check for eight innings behind a one-run lead which a triple by Phil Rizzuto had given him in the first inning. The Bomber hurler, up to the ninth, had the Bosox blanked on two hits in a tense mound battle with Ellis Kinder, who was trying for his twenty-fourth decision of the year.

Game Decided in Eighth

In the last of the eighth the Yanks put on the rally that won the flag. With Kinder going out for a pinch-hitter, the desperate McCarthy nominated Mel Parnell, his 25-game winning southpaw, to hold the Bombers until his own power hitters could have one last fling at Raschi.

Old Reliable Tommy Henrich greeted Parnell with a home run into the right field stands. Yogi Berra singled and Tex Hughson was called on to relieve Parnell. Joe DiMaggio hit into a double play but the Yanks proceeded to fill the bases. Then Jerry Coleman, rookie second baseman, cleared them with a pop fly two-bagger to short right field. That four-run outbreak carried the day, for the

Continued on Page 31, Column

Fewer Hours With Same Pay Urged on AFL Convention

By JOSEPH A. LOFTUS
Special to The New York Times

ST. PAUL, Minn., Oct. 2—The time has arrived to campaign for a shorter standard work day and work week, American Federation of Labor leaders suggested today. The suggestion was made in the Executive Council report that will be ready tomorrow at the opening session of the annual AFL convention.

A cut in working time "may very well be desirable" as an alternative to higher income now, unless both are obtainable through collective bargaining, the council said. Greater leisure for workers and a spread of job opportunities would result, it was asserted.

A cut in hours without a reduction in take-home pay would raise unit labor costs, but the council said it was aiming for a share in the rising productivity rate and did not want to cause higher prices.

The report said that "since the first half of 1948, productivity has been rising again at the rate of 2.3 per cent a year, a figure which is close to normal." The source of the productivity data was not given.

The council said workers fared better in the past year than in any year since the war, even though wage increases were smaller.

"Wage increases won by affiliated unions in 1949,'" the report said, "have for the most part been between 5 cents and 15 cents per hour, but even if these increases have been smaller than in previous post-war years, they have brought more benefit to our members because they have been real and not canceled by price rises."

A reduction in the hours of work will be necessary over the coming years to keep our national productivity in line with our national income, the report said. The council's reasoning was this:

"The long-term tendency, from the beginning of the century until the boom in World War II—a tend-

Continued on Page 10, Column 2

GENERAL IS OUSTED IN NATIONAL GUARD

Finch Is Expelled as Air Chief by Cramer, Then Reinstated as High Officials Intervene

By The United Press.

WASHINGTON, Oct. 2—A quarrel between the chief of the National Guard Bureau and his air branch chief burst into the open today when the Army confirmed that the air officer had been discharged and quickly reinstated.

It was reported that Louis Johnson, Secretary of Defense, might have to settle the dispute. It involves the issue of state versus federal control of the guard and the question whether ground officers should shape air guard policy.

The Army refused to elaborate on the incident except to say that an account first published by The Washington Post was "substantially correct." It added that Maj. Gen. George G. Finch, the air branch chief, had been restored to duty pending a study of the case.

According to the Post, the row came to a head last week when Maj. Gen. Kenneth F. Cramer, National Guard commander, expelled General Finch from his post and warned him to "get out and stay out" of his office in the Pentagon.

However, General Finch, backed by W. Stuart Symington, Secretary of the Air Force, refused to quit.

Continued on Page 6, Column 4

World News Summarized

MONDAY, OCTOBER 3, 1949

Russia has decided to recognize the Communist regime in China, the Moscow radio announced yesterday. The Kremlin ended relations with the Nationalist Government as "a provincial regime." [1:1.] This prompt diplomatic reaction to the formation of the Communist People's Republic of China raised diplomatic issues for the other powers, whose envoys have received formal requests for recognition, and for the United Nations. [2:2.]

In both Washington and London the Soviet action was seen as making some move urgent. It may hasten formulation of a new United States policy for the Far East. It was felt in London that neither the United States nor Britain would act precipitately. [3:1.]

The Russians are expected to demand that the United Nations supplant the Nationalist delegates with those from the new regime to represent China. Nationalist China's charges against Russia will soon be heard by the General Assembly and Soviet activities in Korea are scheduled for a committee debate today on resolutions by the United States and Russia. [1:2.]

Yugoslavia, whose amity pact with Russia was voided by the Kremlin last week, has no idea what the Kremlin's next move will be in the struggle between the two nations, but it is "hard to believe" there will be a direct attack, Foreign Minister Kardelj said. [5:4.] Diplomatic observers felt that Czechoslovakia would receive this month a leading role in the Cominform's fight against Yugoslavia. [6:1.]

The Soviet Government has made protests, in notes to the United States, Britain and France, against the creation of the West German state. Establishment of the state, Moscow said, is a violation of the Potsdam agreement and of the accord reached by the Big Four in Paris, keeps Germany divided and deprives her of a peace treaty. Moscow called the new Government a "puppet state" and "obedient instrument" in the "aggressive plans" of the Western occupying powers. [1:3.]

Supreme Court Justice Douglas was thrown from a horse on a Pacific coast mountain trail; thirteen of his ribs were broken and one lung was punctured. [1:4.] He will be absent from the opening today of the new term of the Supreme Court. [9:4.]

There were no new moves to end the steel and soft-coal strikes, but Federal officials, fearing the effect of prolonged walkouts on the nation's economy, were reported considering a double-barreled "peace offensive." [1:5.] Steel strikers seemed confident President Truman would find a quick solution. Some favored union contributions to pension funds. [11:6.]

AFL leaders suggested that unions should concentrate on winning a shorter work-day and work-week rather than on more pay. This, they said, would spread jobs. [1:6-7.]

The New York Yankees won the American League pennant, defeating the Boston Red Sox, 5 to 3. The Brooklyn Dodgers became the National League champions by beating Philadelphia, 9 to 7, in ten innings. [1:8.]

Index to other news appears on Page 18.

Pulaski Marchers Herald Hope Of Polish Freedom From Soviet

By RICHARD H. PARKE

Thousands of Polish Americans marched up Fifth Avenue yesterday under a bright autumn sun and into deepening twilight in the city's thirteenth annual Pulaski Day parade.

The procession, which took four hours to pass the reviewing stand in front of the New York Public Library, marked the 201st anniversary of the birth of Gen. Casimir Pulaski, who died in defense of American freedom in the Battle of Savannah in 1779.

It was on the whole a gay parade, for there were countless blaring bugle corps, cavorting drum majorettes and brightly bedecked floats. The sc ober note was struck in the banners that some of the marchers carried, banners that proclaimed Poland's wish to free herself from Russian domination.

Somber, too, was a delegation of 500 former Polish displaced persons. Deeply tanned men wearing dark uniforms, the group marched behind a huge sign that read: "Former Polish DPs Now Employed on Suffolk County Farms." They carried another placard reading: "The Hitler-Stalin Partnership Deprived Us of Our Country and Our Freedom."

In the reviewing stand were Gov. Dewey of New York, Gov. Alfred E. Driscoll of New Jersey, Senator John Foster Dulles, former Gov. Herbert H. Lehman, Mayor O'Dwyer, Mayor John J. Kenny of Jersey City and Gen. Casimir Sosnkowski, wartime commander in chief of the Polish Army.

It was the first appearance in this country of General Sosnkowski, who was deposed under Soviet pressure.

The parade also was reviewed from the steps of St. Patrick's Cathedral by Auxiliary Bishop Joseph F. Flannelly, administrator of the

Continued on Page 3, Column 4

O Frabjous Day! Dodgers Hailed By 25,000 Fans at Station Here

By MURRAY SCHUMACH

Pennsylvania Station sounded last night like Ebbets Field during a sustained Brooklyn rally. Nearly 25,000 Dodger fans milled through the vast station screaming a welcome to the Brooklyn ballplayers on their homecoming.

On hand for the team that had clinched the National League pennant just a few hours earlier were the cowbells, the five-piece band and that coterie of wildest Brooklyn rooters, the Section 8 Club.

More than an hour before the players returned from Philadelphia, at 7:50 P. M., Brooklyn rooters had begun swarming across the station trying to ferret out the track on which their team's train would arrive.

Then for fifteen minutes after the last of the Brooklyn players had either run the gantlet of screaming admirers or sneaked out a back staircase, the rooters were still pummeling one another along Seventh Avenue and staging celebrations.

The climax of the triumphal march was the quick passage of Jackie Robinson past thousands of men and women pressed against wooden horses. At one point they burst past the barricade and forced back the police. But the Brooklyn star was rushed out of the station and the crowd pushed back.

The fans not only pressed against the police lines, but swarmed along lower level stairways and even braced themselves along a ledge that was at least thirty feet above the Thirty-first Street driveway to the station.

The frenzied reception began in confusion and for a time it looked as though the players might be smuggled out without too much notice.

The first batches of Brooklyn fans gathered along the lower level where the time and track numbers

Continued on Page 22, Column 3

1949

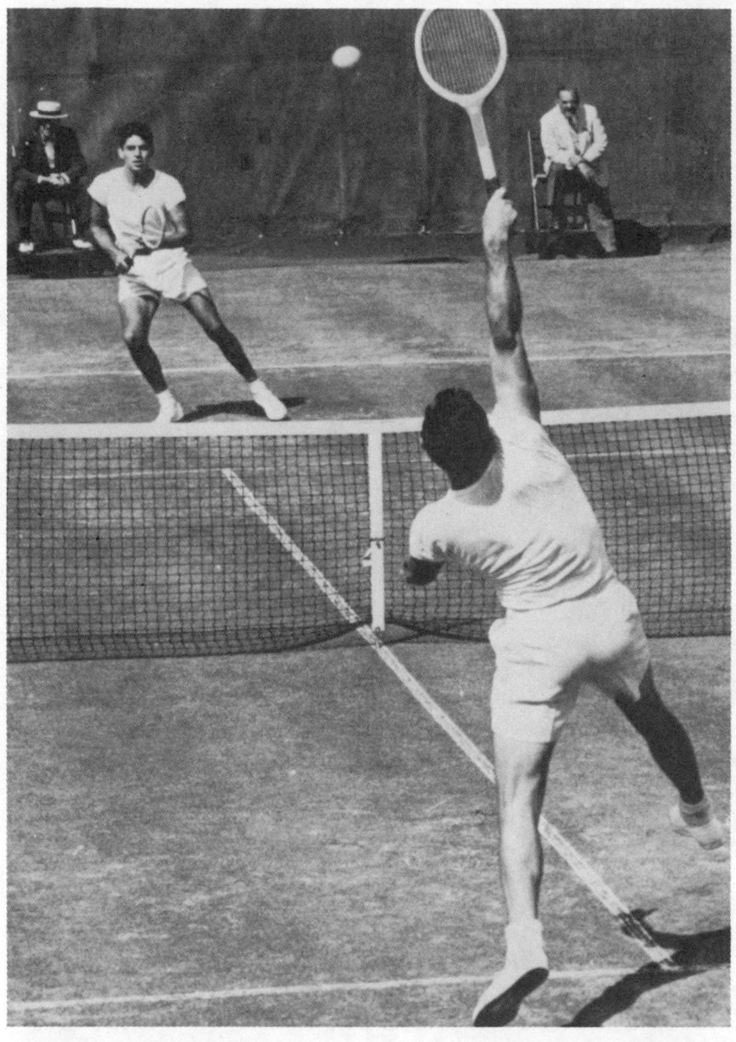

Tennis great Ted Schroeder (foreground) and defending champion Pancho Gonzales meet for the 1949 U.S. Men's Singles Championship at Forest Hills, New York.

Sugar Ray Robinson defeated Kid Gavalin in a brutal 15-round bout.

Casey Stengel, manager of the World Champion New York Yankees, with the Duke of Windsor.

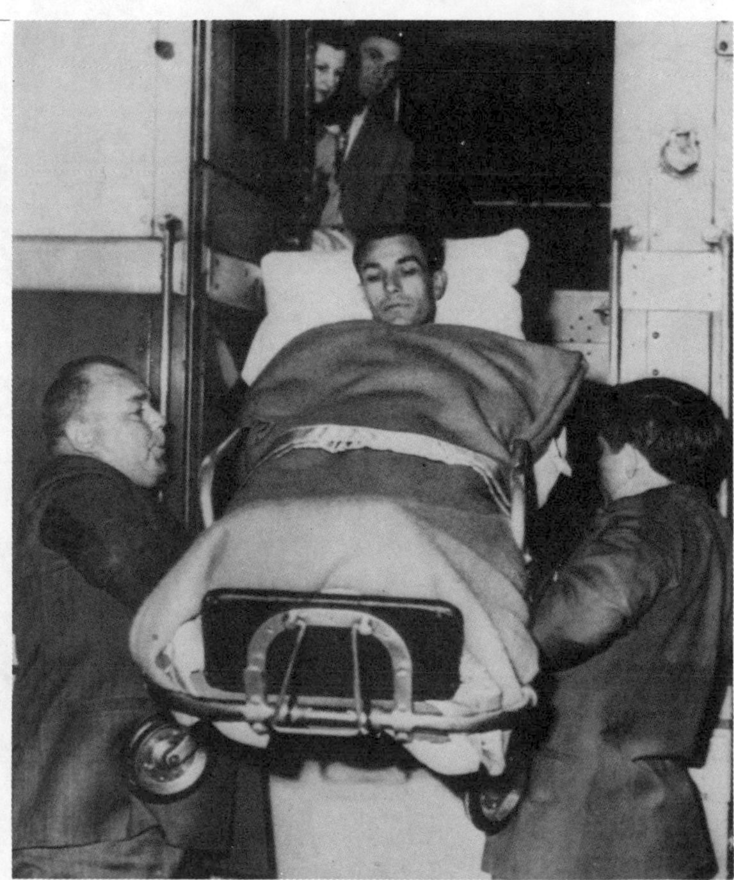

Ben Hogan, the golfer, was involved in an automobile accident that nearly killed him. The story of his amazing comeback served as inspiration to many.

Al Hodge as *Captain Video,* which was one of TV's first "space shows."

Your Show of Shows made its debut. The show was hosted by Sid Caesar, who is shown here with his partner, the great Imogene Coca.

Another 1949 arrival was *Kukla, Fran and Ollie.* Featured on the show were such notables as Madame Ooglepuss, Colonel Crackie and Buelah Witch. Fran Allison was the human member of the troupe of Kuklapolitans.

Al Jolson visits Bing Crosby on the *Bing Crosby Show.*

Ed Wynn, who portrayed the *Perfect Fool* and the *Fire Chief,* transferred to TV, but was not as successful as he had been on radio; he lasted only two seasons.

The late Chester A. Lauck (left) played the character of Lum, and Norris Gaff was Abner on the *Lum and Abner* series. The series, very popular in 1949, ran for 24 years and can still be heard on about 100 radio stations.

"All the News That's Fit to Print"

The New York Times.

LATE CITY EDITION
Occasional rain through today and ending early tomorrow.
Temperature Range Today—Max.,67; Min.,56
Temperatures Yesterday—Max.,69; Min.,56
Full U. S. Weather Bureau Report, Page 34

VOL. XCIX..No. 33,502. Entered as Second-Class Matter. Postoffice, New York, N. Y. NEW YORK, SATURDAY, OCTOBER 15, 1949. Times Square, New York 18, N. Y. Telephone Lackawanna 4-1000 THREE CENTS IN NEW YORK CITY

11 COMMUNISTS CONVICTED OF PLOT; MEDINA TO SENTENCE THEM FRIDAY; 6 OF COUNSEL JAILED IN CONTEMPT

LEWIS ASKS GREEN TO JOIN IN A FUND TO AID STEEL STRIKE

Mine Chief Urges $2,500,000 Weekly Go Into War Chest to Help Murray Win

HE BIDS FOR LABOR UNITY

Nine AFL Unions Would Give $250,000 Each, With Other Tenth From Diggers

Text of Mr. Lewis' letter to Mr. Green appears on Page 10.

By JOSEPH A. LOFTUS

Special to THE NEW YORK TIMES.

WHITE SULPHUR SPRINGS, W. Va., Oct. 14—John L. Lewis made a spectacular appeal today for labor unity. He suggested that nine American Federation of Labor unions and the United Mine Workers pour $2,500,000 a week into a war chest to win the steel strike sponsored by the United Steelworkers of America, a CIO union.

With the startling suddenness of which he is fond, Mr. Lewis advanced the idea in a letter to William Green, president of the AFL. Mr. Lewis has appraised Mr. Green in contrasting adjectives over the years, as he has Philip Murray, president of the CIO and of the steel union.

[Efforts to prevent an enlargement of the steel strike by the addition of 16,000 aluminum workers broke down in Pittsburgh Friday night.]

Mr. Lewis told Mr. Green that a "vast and barbaric attack" had been started against the steel workers.

"Formidable allies are out to crush the power and destroy the structure of the steel workers' union," he charged "This must not happen. It need not happen."

His letter raised at once the question whether his action was a bid for the leadership of a united labor movement, an ambition Mr. Lewis has long nurtured.

Coal Talks Recessed

The effect here was to overshadow for the moment the bogged-down negotiations for a wage contract to halt his own strike in the soft coal mines. Coal operators had just issued a statement answering Mr. Lewis' announcement of yesterday that he wanted contract improvements costing 30 to 35 cents a ton. They called his demands "fantastic." Just then Mr. Lewis made public his letter to Mr. Green. The coal negotiations then recessed until Tuesday.

Mr. Lewis declined to add a word to the text of the letter he distributed, although it left many questions unanswered. Not the least of these was, "What about the miners' strike?" Another was, "What will his miners think of this largesse toward another union?" One answer some observers inferred from the comment he made yesterday was that he believed the steel strike had to be won by the CIO union before the miners' demands would be met.

What Mr. Lewis proposed, in effect, was an economic cooperation administration for labor. The last sentence of his letter made clear that he was not obligating the miners' union to the proposed $250,000 weekly contribution unless the other unions joined him.

AFL Resources Surveyed

He told Mr. Green there were at least nine international AFL unions with substantial cash resources, that each could give $250,000 a week "for an indefinite period without strain, inconvenience or burden to their membership," and he added that "the United Mine Workers of America is similarly situated." Then he wrote:

"I propose:

"That each of these ten unions, through your office, create a financial credit for usage by the United Steelworkers of one-quarter of a million dollars to enable this great union to win beyond peradventure."

If the AFL unions go along, said Mr. Lewis, the steel strike could be made "the uncompromising fight of all American labor." He told Mr. Green that if he followed through successfully with this undertaking "you will crown yourself with distinction; you will safeguard the future of the labor movement of our country, and you will bulwark for posterity those freedoms and privileges cherished and revered by thoughtful citizenship of our land."

The United Mine Workers'

Continued on Page 10, Column 3

Forrestal Home Set As U. S. Guest House

Special to THE NEW YORK TIMES.

WASHINGTON, Oct. 14—The Government has leased the residence of the late James Forrestal as a guest house for distinguished foreign visitors, the State Department said today.

The department signed the lease on Oct. 12 with the widow of the former Secretary of Defense for a period ending June 30, 1950, with the right of renewal.

Situated at 3508 Prospect Avenue, N. W., in the old Georgetown area of this city, the big Georgian brick house sets high on a bluff overlooking the Potomac River.

The house was leased fully furnished, and the State Department said that it should be in operation as an official guest house by Nov. 1. The first occupant is expected to be His Imperial Majesty, the Shah of Iran.

CANTON TURNOVER TO REDS ARRANGED

First Troops Enter the City—Nationalists Wreck Biggest Bridge Before Leaving

By TILLMAN DURDIN

Special to THE NEW YORK TIMES.

HONG KONG, Saturday, Oct. 15—The big Pearl River bridge in Canton was blown up late yesterday by Nationalist demolition squads just before the last Nationalist troops cleared out of city and left it to the Communists.

Canton was plunged into darkness after the bridge explosion, leading to reports that the nearby power station had also been blasted. Windows were shattered for a distance of half a mile by the bridge demolition and it is believed that there may have been many casualties.

The destruction of the Pearl River span, the blasting of the runways and the burning of buildings on the city's two airfields were the parting Nationalist gestures to Canton.

The last Central Government troops in the city were reported in telephone messages here to have left around 8 o'clock last night. Thereafter, Canton became a military vacuum, with the Communist columns on its outskirts.

[Chinese Communist troops entered Canton peacefully Friday night, an official Nationalist source said in Hong Kong, according to a Reuters dispatch. The Communists have cut all communications between Canton and Hong Kong, the report added.]

With Canton abandoned by the Nationalist Army almost without a fight, what is hoped will be a peaceful turnover of the South China metropolis to the Communists has been arranged by local negotiators. Contact has been made with the Communist commanders outside the city and details of the Communist entry worked out.

Despite the virtual disappearance of Nationalist military power in Canton since yesterday, the city has been relatively calm.

Mysterious injunctions, assertedly originating from the Communist underground and gossiped throughout the populace, urged everyone to carry on as usual and warned against disturbances.

The Nationalist armies yester-

Continued on Page 9, Column 4

CONFEREES AGREED ON 75C BASIC PAY; CONGRESS ACTS SOON

Compromise on All Disputed Items Increases Minimum From 40 Cents an Hour

COST PUT AT $300,000,000

Compromise Clarifies Provision for Back-Wage Suits, Reduces Proposed Cut in Coverage

By LOUIS STARK

Special to THE NEW YORK TIMES.

WASHINGTON, Oct. 14—House and Senate conferees agreed today on all items in dispute over a minimum wage bill increasing the present 40 cents an hour to 75 cents. Representative John Lesinski, Democrat, of Michigan, chairman of the House Education and Labor Committee, said the House would act on the compromise first, but probably not before Tuesday.

Senator Claude Pepper, Democrat, of Florida, who piloted the Senate version through the Senate and the conference committee, said that 1,000,000 to 1,500,000 workers would gain pay increases under the new version of the bill.

The higher minimum wage, according to the Florida Senator, may cost employers about $300,000,000 a year. He added, however, that this represented only one-half of 1 per cent of the nation's total wage bill, "so that the law will not be burdensome to any industry."

The present Fair Labor Standards Act, enacted in 1938, covered about 22,600,000 workers. The House bill would have reduced this coverage by 1,005,000. The Senate would have excluded only 200,000. The new compromise version leans toward the Senate proposal.

Tobin Hails Agreement

The Secretary of Labor, Maurice J. Tobin, expressed his pleasure over the conference agreement.

"I am confident this will help to stablize our economy," he said. "The provision for a 75-cent minimum wage and the improved child labor provision embody notable advances over the 1938 law.

"I am disappointed that the President's proposals to extend coverage were not embodied in the bill. It is regrettable that so many special interests were served by exemption. The effect of many of the changes made will not be known until the bill has been thoroughly analyzed."

The main changes in the law proposed by the conference, according to Senator Elbert D. Thomas, Democrat, of Utah, chairman of the conference committee, deal with new enforcement authority granted to the administrator of the Wage-Hour Law, the child labor section, the sawmill and logging provision and the section dealing with retail establishments which also engage in manufacture.

Coverage of the law was reduced by insistence of House conferees who attacked the present section covering workers "necessary to" production by changing it to workers "indispensable to" production. The Senate conferees wished to retain the present language but yielded finally to a compromise which stated that workers "directly essential" to production were covered.

Senator Thomas said frankly that this compromise would be an invitation to break down collective

Continued on Page 10, Column 5

CONVICTED COMMUNISTS HANDCUFFED AND ON THEIR WAY TO JAIL

Defendants line up before leaving the Federal Courthouse for House of Detention. They are (left to right) Henry Winston, Eugene Dennis, Jacob Stachel, Gilbert Green, Benjamin J. Davis Jr., John B. Williamson, Robert G. Thompson, Gus Hall, Irving Potash, Carl Winter and John Gates.

The New York Times (by Ernest Sisto)

VERDICT IN 7 HOURS

Judge Approves It and Thanks Jurors at Tense Close of 9-Month Trial

TEN-YEAR TERMS FACED

Defendants and Advocates to Appeal—Latter Get One to Six Months as 'Example'

Text of Judge's statement in sentencing counsel, Page 3.

By RUSSELL PORTER

Eleven top leaders of the Communist party of the United States were found guilty yesterday of criminal conspiracy. They were convicted of secretly teaching and advocating, on secret orders from Moscow, overthrow of the United States Government and destruction of American democracy by force and violence.

The verdict was returned in the Federal Court House on Foley Square by a jury of four men and eight women, including two Negroes. They spent seven hours in actual deliberations.

Federal Judge Harold R. Medina approved the verdict as "amply supported" by the evidence. He remanded the defendants to jail pending imposition of sentence at 10:30 o'clock next Friday morning.

He also adjudged six members of defense counsel, including Eugene Dennis, the party's general secretary, acting as his own counsel, guilty of forty different criminal contempts during the trial. The judge sentenced counsel to terms varying between thirty days and six months in jail, beginning Nov. 15.

Arguments of Verdict Set

The maximum penalty for each defendant in the conspiracy case is ten years in prison and $10,000 fine.

Defense counsel announced they would appeal both the conspiracy verdict and the contempt sentences. They can appeal both cases to the United States Circuit Court of Appeals and finally to the United States Supreme Court. Judge Medina fixed Friday, Oct. 28, for arguments before himself on defense motions attacking the verdict.

The defendants in the conspiracy trial are members of the party's American Politburo or national board. Their trial, which began on Jan. 17, was one of the longest criminal trials on record, lasting just two days under nine months.

Judge Medina submitted the case to the jury at 3:53 o'clock Thursday afternoon. Unable to reach an immediate verdict, the jury was locked up for the night at 10:20 P. M., under the protection of deputy Federal marshals.

Yesterday morning the jury was taken by bus from the Knickerbocker Hotel, 120 West Forty-fifth Street, where it spent the night, to the court house. It returned to the jury room, behind the first-floor court room, and resumed its deliberations at 9:30 A. M.

Note From Jury to Judge

Judge Medina mounted the bench at 10:09 A. M., opened court, and immediately took a recess. At 11:10 A. M. Mrs. Thelma Dial, Negro foreman of the jury, sent a note from the jury room to Judge Medina in his chambers.

At that moment a few lawyers, newspaper men and spectators were lounging in the court room, reading newspapers, drinking coffee, or talking aimlessly. They knew nothing of the note to the judge.

This calm was broken by a sudden stir in the court room and a rise in tension. Strange faces began to appear as deputy marshals, summoned from other parts of the court house, hurried in. United States Attorney John F. X. McGohey, who headed the prosecution, arrived with his staff of young lawyers.

Defense lawyers and eight of the defendants, who had been pacing in the corridor, smoking one cigarette after another, came in. They were followed by their wives, rela-

Continued on Page 3, Column 6

CHURCH-RULE LAWS ADOPTED IN PRAGUE

Assembly Unanimously Backs Acts Giving Czech Regime Control Over Clergy

By DANA ADAMS SCHMIDT

Special to THE NEW YORK TIMES.

PRAGUE, Czechoslovakia, Oct. 14—In the presence of 150 applauding pro-Government priests of all denominations, the National Assembly unanimously approved today two laws superseding all other church legislation and making the churches administratively and financially entirely dependent on the state in Czechoslovakia.

Meanwhile, as arrests among "the bourgeoisie" continued, the official news agency published a denunciation of Western "pirates of the pen," which was understood to be the Government's answer to the Western press reports of the arrests.

Referring to the West in general, the agency wrote: "Like a shot goose, they cry out when we destroy their agents whom the Rajk

Continued on Page 9, Column 2

U.N. Unit Unanimously Votes 2 Plans for Backward Lands

By WILL LISSNER

Special to THE NEW YORK TIMES.

LAKE SUCCESS, Oct. 14—The United Nations General Assembly's Economic and Financial Committee adopted unanimously and without any substantial amendment today two programs devised by the Economic and Social Council for technical assistance, through the United Nations, to underdeveloped countries.

The action demonstrated the determination of the more developed countries to take a great new step forward immediately to help raise the living conditions of the great bulk of the world's population by improving the productivity of the economies of the retarded countries in which they live through self-help spurred by international cooperation.

So speedily did the committee act, with its leading members determined to impress the world with their unanimity on this non political issue, that it surprised some delegates from underdeveloped countries.

This surprise was voiced by Dr. Joza Vilfan of Yugoslavia, one of

Continued on Page 7, Column 3

EAST GERMANS PUSH TIES WITH SOVIET

Cabinet Signs Trade Accord With Hungary — Leaders Pledge Loyalty to Stalin

By DREW MIDDLETON

Special to THE NEW YORK TIMES.

BERLIN, Oct. 14—The Communist-dominated Eastern German Democratic Republic moved fast and far toward full membership in the new Soviet empire today.

Its cabinet, meeting for the first time, approved loyal greetings to Moscow by President Wilhelm Pieck and Premier Otto Grotewohl in a reply to Premier Stalin's letter of benign approval of the new Communist state.

The Cabinet then authorized the swift conclusion of a trade agreement between the Eastern German state and Hungary a step toward the inclusion of Eastern Germany in the economic structure of the Soviet satellite system.

The spirit of Soviet-German collaboration invoked by Mr. Stalin in his letter to the two Communist

Continued on Page 8, Column 6

HISS LOSES MOTION FOR VERMONT TRIAL

Judge Coxe Finds That Nothing Exists Here to Indicate a 'Great Prejudice'

The bid of Alger Hiss for removal of his second trial on perjury charges from New York to Vermont was lost yesterday when Federal Judge Alfred C. Coxe in a brief opinion, said that evidence submitted did not justify a change of venue.

Judge Coxe referred to Rule 21 (a) of the Federal Rules of Criminal Procedure and said that before a change could be granted the court must be satisfied that there exists "so great a prejudice against the defendant that he cannot obtain a fair and impartial trial" in the district in which the prosecution is pending.

"I find nothing in the papers submitted on the present motion to indicate that there exists in this district any such prejudice," the judge said. "The motion of the defendant to transfer the proceeding to the district of Vermont is accordingly denied."

A spokesman for the office of Edward C. McLean, attorney of record for Mr. Hiss, when told of the decision said, "The decision speaks for itself. There is no further comment."

Mr. Hiss is scheduled to go on trial for the second time Nov. 1. His first trial ended July 8 in a jury disagreement, eight for conviction and four for acquittal.

The former Assistant Secretary of State is accused of lying when he testified to a Federal grand

Continued on Page 2, Column 6

City Faces Acute Water Shortage; Reservoirs at Lowest in History

By CHARLES G. BENNETT

Disclosing that the city's reservoirs were down to about 50 per cent of capacity, Mayor O'Dwyer termed the situation yesterday as "most serious," appealed to the public for a reduction in water consumption and issued a series of orders designed to enforce strict conservation by several city departments.

The Mayor said this summer's small rainfall, coupled with increased consumption of water and depletion of reserves had made him "apprehensive about the immediate future."

The alternative to public cooperation and strict economy in the use of water for the next few weeks, the Mayor indicated, would be more restrictive measures, including the lowering of water pressures throughout the city.

The nub of the problem, the Mayor said, was Kensico, the reservoir through which two-thirds of the city's supply must pass. The limited aqueduct capacity from upstate was described as making it impossible to deliver water to Kensico Reservoir at the rate at which it is being withdrawn. About 125,000,000 gallons a day more are taken out of Kensico than are coming in.

Since June 1, when Kensico was full, 16,500,000,000 more gallons of water have been drawn out than the aqueducts could deliver, resulting in lowering the water level of the reservoir by twenty-seven feet.

"This represents the lowest level experienced since the reservoir was first placed in service in 1916," the Mayor said. "On Oct. 14, 1949, the water surface was at elevation 330 with contents of 13,800,000,000 gallons. When full, the reservoir holds 30,573,000,000 gallons with a water surface of 357. There is thus a depletion of 16,773,000,000 gallons, or 53 per cent of capacity."

After early morning conferences with department heads at Gracie

Continued on Page 30, Column 3

World News Summarized

SATURDAY, OCTOBER 15, 1949

The nine-month trial of eleven leaders of the Communist party on a charge of criminal conspiracy to teach and advocate overthrow of the United States Government ended yesterday with a verdict of guilty. Federal Judge Medina, who held the verdict justified by the evidence, said he would sentence the defendants next Friday morning. He also found six members of defense counsel guilty of forty acts of contempt and sentenced them to imprisonment of thirty days to six months. The defense announced it would appeal the conspiracy verdict and the contempt sentences. [1:8.]

Official Washington was deeply gratified by the verdict [3:1], the story of which was broadcast to many parts of the world by the Voice of America. [4:8.] The ouster of one of the defendants, Benjamin J. Davis Jr., from the New York City Council will be sought. [3:5.]

Federal Judge Alfred C. Coxe denied a motion in behalf of Alger Hiss asking that Mr. Hiss' second perjury trial, starting Nov. 1, be transferred to Vermont. [1:7.]

Agreement on a bill increasing minimum wages from 40 to 75 cents an hour was reached by House and Senate conferees. [1:3.]

The suggestion that nine AFL unions join with his United Mine Workers to contribute $2,500,000 a week to help the CIO steel unions in their strike was made by John L. Lewis in a letter to AFL President William Green. [1:1.]

In China, Communist vanguards entered Canton after its peaceful transfer had been arranged. The city was abandoned by the last Nationalist forces after they had blown up the Pearl River bridge. [1:2.]

A meeting of the Cabinet of the Communist-dominated German Democratic Republic sent greetings to Premier Stalin and authorized a trade treaty between the new state and Hungary in a move toward making eastern Germany part of the Soviet economic structure in Eastern Europe. [1:6.]

The Czechoslovak National Assembly unanimously enacted two laws making all churches in Czechoslovakia dependent on the state, administratively as well as financially. [1:4.]

Two programs to provide technical assistance through the United Nations to the retarded countries of the world were adopted unanimously by the United Nations General Assembly's Economic and Financial Committee. [1:5-6.] The Trusteeship Committee, overriding United States and British objections, voted that colonial authorities in areas under the international trusteeship system must submit within one year blueprints showing how those regions might become self-governing or independent. [8:1.]

Index to other news appears on Page 16.

2 Firemen Missing, 4 Are Saved As Floors Fall in W. 17th St. Blaze

Two firemen were trapped early today in a burning loft building at 21 West Seventeenth Street by the collapse of the roof and three floors. Four others were rescued. The missing men were identified by Fire Department officials as Fred Lehman and Daniel Shea, both of Fire Patrol Company No. 3.

Attempts to save the men, believed to have been pinned on the ground floor, about twenty feet from the entrance, were hampered by the danger that the front wall of the building might collapse. Unable to go through the main entrance, rescuers began to tunnel in from 23 West Seventeenth Street.

The fire in the five-story building was not considered serious by officials of the Fire Department until the upper floors and the roof crashed in, probably under the weight of water.

The missing firemen were believed to have been on the ground floor trying to protect property by spreading canvases. The collapse came without warning.

Peter Loftus, Chief of the Fire Department, said that shortly before 1 A. M. smoke puffed up from the roof of the building. This was followed by a loud rumble as the floors and roof fell through.

Those rescued were Acting Battalion Chief Charles William of Battalion 6, Firemen Henry Wahl and William Hack, both of Fire Patrol 3; and William Dworsak of Engine Company 14.

A physician at the scene said Fireman Hack was suffering from chest injuries, which might be serious. He was taken to St. Vincent's Hospital.

Second Deputy Fire Commissioner Harry Archer, Fire Department surgeon, was with one of the squads attempting to reach the trapped men. Absolution was given to the missing men by two Catholic priests from near-by St. Francis Xavier Church.

The first alarm was sounded at midnight, and a second went in fifty minutes later.

One of Ethel Waters' most memorable roles was as Jeanne Crain's grand-mother in *Pinky.*

Gloria Swanson as the fading silent screen star and William Holden as the penniless script writer in *Sunset Boulevard.*

Van Heflin and Jennifer Jones in *Madame Bovary.*

"All the News That's Fit to Print"

The New York Times.

LATE CITY EDITION
Sunny and cold today. Cloudy and continued cold tomorrow.
Temperature Range Today—Max.,37; Min.,26
Temperature Yesterday—Max.,38; Min.,26
Full U. S. Weather Bureau Report, Page 36

Copyright, 1949, by The New York Times Company.

VOL. XCIX.. No. 33,557. Entered as Second-Class Matter. Postoffice, New York, N. Y. NEW YORK, FRIDAY, DECEMBER 9, 1949. Times Square, New York 18, N. Y. Telephone LAckawanna 4-1000 THREE CENTS IN NEW YORK CITY | FIVE CENTS ELSEWHERE

BOARD OF ESTIMATE IGNORES PROTESTS, RAISES 24 SALARIES

'Political Grab' Charged as Civic Bodies Lead Fight on $73,100 Increases

OTHER RISES AWAIT VOTE

Action Affects Heads of City Departments, Agencies and the Mayor's Staff

By PAUL CROWELL

Unmoved by the protests of spokesmen for four civic organizations, the Board of Estimate voted unanimously yesterday to increase, by $1,000 to $10,000, the annual salaries of twenty-four heads of city departments and agencies and members of Mayor O'Dwyer's City Hall staff.

The salary increases, with one exception, become effective Jan. 1 and will be met by transferring $73,100 within the 1949-50 budget. The increase for Sanitation Commissioner William J. Powell becomes effective Dec. 16, fourteen days before his retirement.

A bill to raise the salaries of members of the Board of Estimate and the City Council is pending in the latter body, with a vote slated for Dec. 16. The measure would fix the salary of the Mayor at $40,000, that of the Controller at $30,000, and of the Council President and the five Borough Presidents at $25,000 each. An annual salary of $7,000 for Council members also is proposed.

Four Agencies Head Fight

The opposition to the increases was registered by spokesmen for the Citizens Union, the Commerce and Industry Association of New York, the Citizens Budget Commission and the Taxpayers Union.

In exchanging remarks with spokesmen for the objecting organizations, Borough President James J. Lyons of the Bronx suggested that some of the objections were politically motivated. It was possible, he said, that Newbold Morris, Oren Root and Joseph D. McGoldrick, who sat with a committee of Citizens Union officials that formulated a protest, had the recent city campaign in mind.

Myron D. Miller, speaking for the Commerce and Industry Association, declared that the proposed increases constituted a "political grab." He conceded their legality but contended that they should be subject to a referendum. He predicted that adoption would lead to a general demand for more pay by rank and file city workers. The same point was made by Miss Eleanor Tanzer of the Citizens Union.

Richard W. Thompson, research director of the Citizens Budget Commission, asked that action be deferred in order to insure proper consideration of the proposed salary rises for elected city officials.

How Increases Were Voted

The salary rises voted by the Board of Estimate were:

Deputy Mayor, from $17,500 to $25,000, paving the way for William Reid, chairman of the Board of Transportation, to succeed Deputy Mayor John J. Bennett on Jan. 1; Corporation Counsel John P. McGrath, from $17,500 to $25,000; Park Commissioner Robert Moses, from $15,000 to $25,000; Chief Justice of Special Sessions, from $16,000 to $18,000; William J. Donoghue, executive secretary to the Mayor, from $15,000 to $17,500; Louis Cohen, assistant to the Mayor, from $14,000 to $15,000; Miss Caryl Holley, secretary to the Mayor, from $6,900 to $8,000; Mrs. Hilda Schwartz, secretary of Board of Estimate, from $10,000 to $12,500.

Also Ralph L. Van Name, secretary of the New York City Retirement System, from $11,000 to $12,500; William Boyland, president of the Tax Commission, from $13,500 to $15,000; First Assistant Corporation Counsel Charles F. Preusse, from $14,000 to $17,500.

The following officials had their salaries of $12,500 each increased to $15,000: William M. Ellard, director of the Bureau of Real Estate; City Treasurer Spencer C. Young; License Commissioner Edward T. McCaffery; Purchase Commissioner John Spain; Housing and Buildings Commissioner Bernard J. Gilroy; Correction Commissioner Albert Williams; Commissioner Stephen J. Carney of the Department of Water Supply, Gas and Electricity.

Also raised by $2,500 to the $15,000 mark were the salaries of Market Commissioner Anthony Masciarelli, Sanitation Commissioner Powell and the Borough Works Commissioners of Manhattan, Brooklyn, Queens and the Bronx.

U. S. Fiscal Policies Depicted To N. A. M. as Sapping Nation

Welfare Programs and High Taxes, Deficits Held to Drain Venture Capital

By LEO EGAN

Rising taxes, Federal deficits and costly new Federal welfare programs are drying up venture capital and threatening the continuance of the American economic system, 3,000 business leaders were told yesterday at sessions of the fifty-fourth Congress of American Industry.

The warnings came from such speakers as Dr. Harold G. Moulton, president of Brookings Institute; Senator John W. Bricker of Ohio, the 1944 Republican candidate for Vice President, and several past presidents of the National Association of Manufacturers, which is sponsoring the Congress. The sessions are held at the Waldorf-Astoria Hotel.

Claude Adams Putnam, a machinery manufacturer of Keene, N. H., was chosen last night as president of the NAM to succeed Wallace F. Bennett of Salt Lake City, who becomes chairman of the board of directors. Mr. Putnam, whose first job was as apprentice in a machine shop in Torrington, Conn., boasts that his concern, which employs 200 men, has never laid off an employe. It has been in existence since 1911.

Dr. Moulton coupled his admonition yesterday with the prediction that the future of American industry lies in filling the needs of

Continued on Page 36, Column 1

NEW HEAD OF N.A.M.

Claude Adams Putnam
The New York Times (by Neal Boenzi)

MARSHALL PLAN CUT URGED BY SENATORS BACK FROM EUROPE

Democrats on Inspection Tour Will Support Congress Move to Slash Recovery Funds

SUGGEST LOAN TO SPAIN

Three in Group Propose Aid to Permit Buying Machinery, Cotton and Wheat Here

By WILLIAM S. WHITE
Special to THE NEW YORK TIMES.

WASHINGTON, Dec. 8—Formidable Congressional efforts for heavy reductions in the amount of money to be provided next year for the European Recovery Program were forecast today by Senators returning from inspection trips to the Continent.

Three of those just back from Europe, Senators A. Willis Robertson of Virginia, Burnet R. Maybank of South Carolina and John C. Stennis of Mississippi, came out also for a loan to Spain through the Export-Import Bank to permit her to buy cotton, wheat and machinery in this country.

Mr. Maybank suggested a specific figure for such a loan. He spoke of $100,000,000. None of the three directly mentioned diplomatic recognition for Spain.

As to the Marshall Plan, some reduction in funds for it had been expected by the Economic Cooperation Administration. The question raised was whether the ultimate cut might not be deeper than the Administration was willing to contemplate.

Even one of the stanchest of the friends of the program, Senator Robertson, proposed that the appropriation for the fiscal year 1951, which begins June 30, be held to about $2,500,000,000. The allocation for the fiscal year 1950, with which it is intended to end the program, ought to be about $1,000,000,000, he suggested.

Coincidentally, Neil Dalton, retiring information director of the Economic Cooperation Administration, had predicted that Paul G. Hoffman, administrator, would ask for about $3,000,000,000 for the coming fiscal year. This year's appropriation was $3,778,000,000.

Senator Maybank said that if all continued to go well in Europe "we could do with an appropriation of less than $2,500,000,000.

Senator Stennis, offering no specific figure, declared for a "very

Continued on Page 10, Column 4

REVISION IS PUSHED IN FOREIGN SERVICE ALONG HOOVER LINE

Committee to Advise Acheson on Joining High-Level Staff and 'Career' Personnel

PLAN STIRS SHARP FIGHT

Two of Three in Group Named and Study Is to Begin Soon After Holiday Season

By WALTER H. WAGGONER
Special to THE NEW YORK TIMES.

WASHINGTON, Dec. 8—A three-man committee of experts to advise Secretary of State Dean Acheson on one of the knottiest reorganization recommendations before the State Department—amalgamation of high-level department personnel with the Foreign Service "career" groups—will be named soon and will begin its study of the problem soon after the Christmas holidays.

Two members of the committee, it was learned today, already have been chosen by John E. Peurifoy, Deputy Under-Secretary of State for Administration. They are Robert Ramspeck, former Democratic Representative in Congress and a Civil Service expert, and James H. Rowe Jr., a lawyer with considerable Government experience and a member of the [Hoover] Commission on Organization of the Executive Branch of the Government.

A third member of the committee would be an outstanding Foreign Service officer. Two distinguished diplomats have declined committee membership for reasons of health. They were Ambassadors Edwin C. Wilson and Cavendish W. Cannon, both career diplomats of long and distinguished service.

State Department-Foreign Service amalgamation was one of the most precedent-shattering recommendations of the Hoover Commission's report on foreign affairs. Other proposals of the commission have been put in effect.

Amalgamation, although a dormant possibility since the days of Secretary of State James F. Byrnes, continues to be only a recommendation as a result of the sharp controversy it provokes within the Government's foreign affairs department.

Because of the intense feelings of advocates and opponents of amalgamation, comparable in State Department and Foreign Service quarters to the unification and Air Force-Navy friction in defense,

Continued on Page 21, Column 4

Water Crisis Is Proclaimed By Driscoll in North Jersey

By CHARLES G. BENNETT

The spotlight in the critical water shortage shifted yesterday to New Jersey where, in Trenton, Gov. Alfred E. Driscoll issued a proclamation declaring a state of emergency in the drought-stricken northern half of the state.

The Mayors of all municipalities in the area were requested to issue proclamations declaring the emergency and urging citizens to conserve water. Cities were called upon to impose "appropriate penalties" on persons found wasting water.

Water companies were asked by the State Water Policy Division to issue statements to newspapers giving detailed information on how to save water. The Governor said rationing of water through pressure reduction and "complete stoppages" was being considered, but "only as a last step."

State engineers informed Mr. Driscoll that available storage water in northern New Jersey's largest reservoirs that could be safely delivered would last only about forty-five days if there were no additional rainfall.

Situation in This City

In New York the Jamaica Water Supply Company, which regularly supplies about 33,000,000 gallons a day to 350,000 persons in its section of Queens, came to the aid of the city with an offer of 10,000,000 gallons daily for the duration of the emergency.

Stephen J. Carney, Commissioner of Water Supply, Gas and Electricity, announced that the offer had been "gratefully accepted." The Jamaica water will begin flowing through existing connections this morning. For many years the company and the city have been exchanging water whenever necessary.

At present the company owes the city a little less than 5,000,000 gallons. Ultimately the city hopes to pay back its debt in water. The

Continued on Page 54, Column 6

TRANSIT UNION ASKS CITY FOR A HEARING

Request for Immediate Talks Is Seen as Move for Public Backing of Slowdown

By WARREN MOSCOW

The Transport Workers Union, whose demand for a forty-hour week and a 21-cent-an-hour wage boost was rejected summarily Wednesday night by William Reid, chairman of the Board of Transportation, talked "tough" publicly yesterday. Privately, however, it was believed to be committed to a policy of exhausting all other possible procedures before embarking on its threatened slowdown of city bus, trolley and subway operations.

The TWU sent a letter to Mr. Reid denouncing the language of his letter of rejection, but containing a key demand that the grievances of the city's transit workers be heard at a collective-bargaining conference to be held "immediately." A similar request for a collective bargaining conference was made by the executive board of the city-wide CIO Council, as it announced support of the TWU in the controversy.

The union leaders also were said to be seeking intervention by Mayor O'Dwyer, before he leaves on a recuperative vacation in the South, to order such a hearing. At such a hearing the union would hope to obtain full publicity for its

Continued on Page 18, Column 5

President Turns Tables on Press; His Queries Are on Personal Side

By ANTHONY LEVIERO
Special to THE NEW YORK TIMES.

KEY WEST, Fla., Dec. 8—A mere cub reporter intruded himself among veteran White House correspondents here today during a news conference. This cub, a contributor to that obscure daily, The Federal Register, was trying to look like a journalist. He carried a cane and he wore a white pith helmet, and his name was Harry S. Truman.

This was as complicated and embarrassing a news conference as a reporter cared to cover. It was being held by Charles G. Ross, secretary to the cub reporter, and it concerned the activities of that cub. The cub took down everything his secretary was saying.

Then this cub asked the reporters a lot of questions. They were rather impertinent questions about things that the reporters were not eager to have their editors and wives read about.

President Truman turned reporter on his way to his daily swim. It was 10 A. M. when his car drew up at the bachelor officers' quarters. That's where the press room is. Evidently the Chief Executive thought he was taking the reporters by surprise. For when the extraordinary interview was over he remarked that "everybody was too surprised to ask any impertinent questions." Everybody but himself.

This cub reporter gets up early in the morning—usually at 6:30—but he will have to get up a lot earlier to outwit the professionals. The truth of the matter is that the grapevine was at work and the full complement of reporters and photographers, about a score of them, was on hand.

There was surprise in what Mr. Truman did, however. He walked to the end of the long press room. It looked as if he might have an

Continued on Page 23, Column 1

World News Summarized

FRIDAY, DECEMBER 9, 1949

China's Nationalist Government abandoned the Chinese mainland yesterday to establish itself on the island of Formosa. A temporary capital was set up at Taipei. In western China, military headquarters for continued activity against the Communists was placed at Sichang. [1:8.] Consul General Ward arrived in Tientsin after his release from prison by the Communists. [3:1.]

The United Nations General Assembly, 45 to 5, called on all members to respect China's territorial integrity, to forego special privileges in that country and to abide by the terms of their treaties and the United Nations Charter. By a smaller majority the Assembly directed the Little Assembly to keep Nationalist charges against the Soviet Union "under continuous examination" and to report next year. [1:6-7.]

A $54,900,000 public works and relief program to aid Arab refugees from Palestine was approved by the Assembly, 47 to 0. [4:2.] The Assembly will open debate today on the proposed internationalization of Jerusalem. Israel warned a committee that approved an $8,150,000 budget for administration that the Jews in Jerusalem would oppose any international rule. [3:5.]

Adrian Pelt of the Netherlands was unanimously nominated to administer the United Nations trusteeship over Libya until the country attains independence Jan. 1, 1952. [2:2.]

France, Italy and the Low Countries are expected to announce today agreement on broad easing of trade barriers. [11:3.] Britain is doing better since devaluation but not well enough, two Cabinet members reported. [8:3.] The French Cabinet was rebuffed in the Assembly on budget issues. [5:4.] Several Senators back from inspection trips to Europe, called for substantial cuts in next year's ERP funds. [1:4.]

Premier Grotewohl of the East German regime is in a hospital and is expected to be confined four weeks. [10:4-5.]

Six more defendants in Bulgaria's treason trial pleaded guilty. [6:3.]

Secretary Acheson is naming a committee to advise on reorganizing the State Department in line with the Hoover Commission's recommendations. [1:5.] President Truman has asked Byron Price to become Assistant Secretary of State for Public Affairs. [20:5.]

Republican members of the House committee that held the inquiry into charges that atomic and other secret data had been expedited to the Soviet Union in 1943 protested the hearings as a "whitewash." [1:7.] Washington was reported asking Britain, for reasons of economy, to halt manufacturing atomic weapons. [17:1.]

Federal deficits, welfare programs and rising taxes are threatening this country's economic system, speakers at the Congress of American Industry declared. Claude A. Putnam was chosen president of the National Association of Manufacturers. [1:2-3.] Washington estimated this year's total capital outlays for new plant and equipment at $17,900,000,000 [43.5.]

Northern New Jersey, with only a forty-five-day water supply left, was declared in a state of emergency by Governor Driscoll. In this city a private company in Jamaica offered 10,000,000 gallons a day to supplement the municipal supply. [1:2-3.]

The Board of Estimate, ignoring protests by civic groups, voted to increase salaries of twenty-four top appointive officials $1,000 to $10,000. [1:1.]

Index to other news appears on Page 32.

CHINESE NATIONALISTS MOVE THEIR CAPITAL TO FORMOSA; NOW PLAN A GUERRILLA WAR

DISPERSAL OF CHINESE NATIONALISTS

The New York Times Dec. 9, 1949

The Nationalist Government shifted its capital to Taipei on Formosa (1) after evacuating Chengtu (2). The military command transferred its headquarters to Sichang (3). The defection of Yunnan Province (4) to the Communists was believed under way. Communist forces have reached the Indo-China border at Tunghing (5). The Reds' radio said they had sealed all Kwangtung ports except Paksha (6) against further Nationalist evacuations from the mainland to Hainan Island.

YUNNAN TOTTERING

Turn-Over to Reds Seen—Effective Opposition on Mainland Ceases

RESISTANCE HEADS NAMED

Headquarters Are Set Up in Sichang for 'Land, Sea, Air' Raids on Communists

By TILLMAN DURDIN
Special to THE NEW YORK TIMES

HONG KONG, Dec. 8—The capital of the depleted Nationalist Government of China shifted for the fourth time today, this time to the island of Formosa, 110 miles off the mainland.

Premier Gen. Yen Hsi-shan arrived at the new capital city of Taipei this afternoon and announced his Cabinet would begin functioning there tomorrow.

The Nationalist move, signalising virtual termination of effective resistance to Communists on the mainland, it is believed here, will clear the way to early recognition of the Peiping Government as the Government of China by many foreign powers.

An extraordinary session of the Executive Yuan in Chengtu last night decided to evacuate the Government to Formosa and proclaimed that Sichang, in Sikang Province bordering Tibet, would be the military headquarters for continued "land, sea and air" activities on the China mainland. Appointments of leaders to carry on guerrilla warfare were made.

Reds Nearing Chengtu

Generalissimo Chiang Kai-shek was due in Tapei late today or tomorrow. Planes are in the process of shifting from Chengtu to Taipei roughly one hundred persons of the thousand-odd staff members of the Government still remaining together from the Chungking evacuation.

The Communists today were driving rapidly on toward Chengtu and were last reported only fifty miles away. Nationalist troops under Gen. Hu Tsung-nan were falling back southwestward in an effort to get into Sikang.

Premier Yen revealed in Taipei that he did not land at Kunming en route to Formosa because he had been warned of danger there. The turnover of Yunnan Province to the Communists was believed in process. Gen. Lung Yun, one-time warlord Governor of the province who has joined the Communists, is now in Hong Kong and has sent agents to Kunming to see his half-brother Gov. Lu Han.

Governor Lu is understood to advocate that Yunnan merely proclaim independence from the Chiang regime at this stage, whereas General Lung is urging the announcement of full allegiance to the Communists. Most of the Yunnan Provincial Government has moved to Tali but Governor Lu still is in Kunming. Communist guerrilla units are increasingly active around Kunming.

New Leaders Named

Before it left Chengtu the Nationalist Government accepted the resignation of Gen. Chang Chun as director of the Southwest Command Headquarters. General Chang, one-time Premier and Foreign Minister, presumably will remain in his native province of Szechwan for the coming of the Communists.

Gen. Ku Chu-tung was named to General Chang's post. Generals Hu Tsung-nan and Yang Sen were appointed General Ku's deputies. General Wang Tsang-hsu and Tang Shih-tsun, Szechwanese who are both closely linked with Szechwan's powerful, secret Elder Brother Society (Ko Lao Hui), were appointed to lead the guerrilla armies. Gen. Huo Kuo-kuang was named to head the Sichang garrison headquarters.

A Taipei report quoted Premier Yen as having said Generalissimo Chiang was not resuming the Presidency for the time being, but that he would concentrate on military affairs. It is reported the Generalissimo's advisers have counseled him to hold off at least a month before taking back his old post in order to see what Acting President Li Tsung-jen accomplishes on

Continued on Page 3, Column 4

U. N. Assembly Asks Nations To Respect China's Integrity

By THOMAS J. HAMILTON

A five-power resolution calling on all nations to respect the territorial integrity of China was approved yesterday morning by an overwhelming majority of the United Nations General Assembly.

The Assembly, by a considerably reduced majority, and with Britain and sixteen other countries abstaining, then directed its Interim Committee, the Little Assembly, to keep the Nationalist Government's charges against the Soviet Union "under continuous examination and study in the light of the resolution mentioned above."

The Little Assembly was directed to report its recommendations to the 1950 session of the General Assembly, and also was authorized to appeal to the Security Council if it decided this was necessary.

Neither Side Mentioned

The five-power resolution, which was introduced by the United States, Australia, Mexico, Pakistan and the Philippines, does not mention either the Nationalist or Communist regimes, but points out that the Charter called on all members of the United Nations "to refrain from the threat or use of force against the territorial integrity or political independence of any state." Its operative section is as follows:

THE GENERAL ASSEMBLY,

Desiring to promote the stability of international relations in the Far East,

CALLS UPON all states:

1. *To respect* the political independence of China and *to be guided* by the principles of the United Nations in their relations with China;

2. *To respect* the right of the people of China now and in the future to choose freely their political institutions and to maintain a Government independent of foreign control;

3. *To respect* existing treaties relating to China; and

4. *To refrain* from (a) seeking to acquire spheres of influence or to create foreign con-

Continued on Page 3, Column 2

HOUSE GROUP ROWS ON JORDAN INQUIRY

Three G. O. P. Members Assert 'Quickie' Hearings Open Body to Charges of 'Whitewash'

By C. P. TRUSSELL
Special to THE NEW YORK TIMES.

WASHINGTON, Dec. 8—The testimony of George Racey Jordan, a former Army Air Forces major, concerning shipments of atomic materials to Russia in 1943-44 led the House Committee on Un-American Activities into an intra-mural dispute today.

Three Republican members, Representatives Richard M. Nixon of California, Francis Case of South Dakota and Harold H. Velde of Illinois, jointly entered a "protest in the strongest terms" that majority members had conducted the investigation in such a way as to expose the committee to charges of "whitewash."

[The Associated Press reported that Lieut. Gen. Leslie R. Groves said that he had withheld secret atomic reports from former Vice President Henry A. Wallace. The United Press said General Groves asserted that his testimony in Washington should not be construed as completely refuting the story of Mr. Jordan.]

In another atomic development, the United States is known to be disposed to oppose manufacture of atomic weapons in the British Isles for reasons of economy. Should London agree to this, it would receive a guarantee of access to the United States stockpile of

Continued on Page 17, Column 3

Arnold Calls B-36 Air 'Keystone' In Face of Iron-Curtain Situation

Following is the fourth of a series of articles by the former Commanding General, United States Army Air Forces.

By GEN. H. H. ARNOLD

In the early fall of this year, when I heard the criticisms of the B-36, and of the methods of its operation, it brought a thought to my mind: What would the experts in their lines say were I to criticize battleships, destroyers, carriers and their operations? Or, perhaps, take a whack or two at the Golden Gate Bridge. Or pass judgment upon modern methods of producing automobiles or radios?

Man cannot and will not stand still in the aeronautical field of endeavor any more than he has remained or will remain static in other scientific fields.

The B-36 is an evolution. It came as the result of changes in modern warfare; the change in the mission of strategic bombers. It was made possible because of the improved technique of construction of modern planes, and the knowledge possessed by aeronautical engineers. It was just as logical a product of the aeronautical engineering phase of advancement as was the modern automobile of progress in the automotive industry.

If we had not produced the B-36, someone else would have, and the headaches for dealing with the problems and the possibilities it presents would now be ours instead of theirs.

In 1941 we were sorely pressed to find ways and means of reaching into the heart of Germany with our bombers. In our preliminary plans we counted on using bases in England, but the German submarines were about to chase our cargo ships and tankers from the

Continued on Page 12, Column 2